PENGUIN REFERENCE

Penguin Pocket German Dictionary

Peter Lewis read German at St Edmund Hall, Oxford, and Albert-Ludwigs-Universität, Freiburg, before taking his doctorate and teaching at St Anne's College, Oxford, from 1985 to 1990. He lives in Oxford and works as a freelance editor, translator, writer and publishing project manager.

PENGUIN POCKET GERMAN DICTIONARY
ENGLISH–DEUTSCH
GERMAN–ENGLISCH

Peter Lewis

PENGUIN BOOKS

PENGUIN BOOKS

Published by the Penguin Group
Penguin Books Ltd, 80 Strand, London WC2R 0RL, England
Penguin Group (USA) Inc., 375 Hudson Street, New York, New York 10014, USA
Penguin Group (Canada), 90 Eglinton Avenue East, Suite 700, Toronto, Ontario, Canada M4P 2Y3
 (a division of Pearson Penguin Canada Inc.)
Penguin Ireland, 25 St Stephen's Green, Dublin 2, Ireland
(a division of Penguin Books Ltd)
Penguin Group (Australia), 250 Camberwell Road, Camberwell, Victoria 3124, Australia
(a division of Pearson Australia Group Pty Ltd)
Penguin Books India Pvt Ltd, 11 Community Centre,
Panchsheel Park, New Delhi – 110 017, India
Penguin Group (NZ), cnr Airborne and Rosedale Roads, Albany,
Auckland 1310, New Zealand (a division of Pearson New Zealand Ltd)
Penguin Books (South Africa) (Pty) Ltd, 24 Sturdee Avenue,
Rosebank 2196, Johannesburg, South Africa

Penguin Books Ltd, Registered Offices: 80 Strand, London WC2R 0RL, England

www.penguin.com

First published 2006
1

Copyright © Market House Books Ltd, 2006

Set in Stone Sans and ITC Stone Serif
Printed in England by Clays Ltd, St Ives plc

ISBN-13: 978-0-141-02720-3
ISBN-10: 0-141-02720-7

Abbreviations/Abkürzungen

acc accusative, Akkusativ
adj adjective, Adjektiv
adv adverb, Adverb
anat anatomy, Anatomie
arch architecture, Architektur
art article, Artikel
astrol astrology, Astrologie
astron astronomy, Astronomie
biol biology, Biologie
bot botany, Botanik
chem chemistry, Chemie
coll colloquial, umgangssprachlich
comm commerce, Kommerz
comp computing, Computer-
  Technologie
dat dative, Dativ
derog derogatory, geringschätzig
elec electricity, Elektrizität
f feminine, Femininum
fig figurative, figürlich
gen genitive, Genitiv
geog geography, Erdkunde
gramm grammar, Grammatik
impol impolite, unhöflich
interj interjection, Ausruf
Jur Jura, Rechtswesen, law
Komm Kommerz, commerce
m masculine, Maskulinum
math mathematics, Mathematik
mech mechanics, machine,
  Mechanik

med medicine, Medizin
mil military, militärisch
mot motoring, Autofahren
n noun, Hauptwort, Substantiv
naut nautical, Schiffahrt
neut neuter, Neutrum
phone telephone, Telefon
phot photography, Photographie
pl plural, Plural
pol politics, Politik
poss possessive, possessiv
prep preposition, Präposition
pron pronoun, Pronomen, Fürwort
psychol psychology, Psychologie
rail railways, Eisenbahn
rel religion, Religion
Schiff Schiffahrt, nautical
sing singular, Singular, Einzahl
tech technical, Technik
Telef Telefon, telephone
TV television, Fernsehen
umg. umgangssprachlich, colloquial
univ university, Universität
unz. unzählbar, mass noun
US American, Amerikanisch
v verb, Verbum, Zeitwort
V vide (see, siehe)
vulg vulgar, gemein
Wissensch Naturwissenschaft,
  science
zool zoology, Zoologie

German pronunciation

a bald [balt]
a: sagen ['za:gən]
e Telefon [tele'fo:n]
e: nehmen ['ne:mən]
ɛ Geld [gɛlt]
ɛ: Bär [bɛːr]
i Idee [i'de:]
i: bieten ['i:tən]
ɔ Holz [hɔlts]
o Rosette [ro'zɛtə]
o: mohn [mo:n]
u bunt [bunt]
u: Schnur [ʃnu:r]
y fünf [fynf]
y: kühl [ky:l]
ə Butter ['butər]
œ böse ['bœ zə]
œ : Möbel ['mœ bəl]
ai bei [bai]
au Haus [haus]
ɔy Freund [frɔynt]
ã Chance ['ʃã:sə]
ɛ̃ Terrain [tɛ'rɛ̃:]
5 Champignon ['ʃam pin5]

b Bad [ba:t]
d Dank [daŋk]
f Frau [frau]
g gut [gu:t]
h halb [halp]
j ja [ja:]
k Kind [kint]
l Lied [li:t]
m Mensch [mɛnʃ]
n neu [nɔy]
p Person [pɛr'zo:n]
r Rad [ra:t]
s falls [fals]
t Gerät [gə'rɛ:t]
v Wein [vain]
z Reise ['raizə]
ç ich [iç]
x Buch [bu:x]
ʃ Schuh [ʃu:]
ʒ Garage [ga'ra:ʒə]
ŋ lang [laŋ]

The sign ' precedes a syllable having primary stress.

Aussprache auf Englisch

a hat [hat]
e bell [bel]
i big [big]
o dot [dot]
ʌ bun [bʌn]
u book [buk]
ə alone [ə'loun]
a: card [ka:d]
ə: word [wə:d]
i: team [ti:m]
o: torn [to:n]
u: spoon [spu:n]
ai die [dai]
ei ray [rei]
oi toy [toi]
au how [hau]
ou road [roud]
eə lair [leə]
iə fear [fiə]
uə poor [puə]
b back [bak]
d dull [dʌl]
f find [faind]
g gaze [geiz]

h hop [hop]
j yell [jel]
k cat [kat]
l life [laif]
m mouse [maus]
n night [nait]
p pick [pik]
r rose [rouz]
s sit [sit]
t toe [tou]
v vest [vest]
w week [wi:k]
z zoo [zu:]
θ think [θiŋk]
ð those [ðouz]
ʃ shoe [ʃu:]
ʒ treasure ['treʒə]
tʃ chalk [tʃo:k]
dʒ jump [dʒʌmp]
ŋ sing [siŋ]

Das Zeichen ' steht vor einer Silbe
  mit Hauptbetonung.
Das Zeichen , steht vor einer Silbe
  mit Nebenbetonung.

Guide to the dictionary

English irregular plural forms are shown at the headword and in the text. The following categories of plurals forms are considered regular:

cat	cat**s**
glass	glass**es**
fly	fl**ies**
half	hal**ves**
wi**fe**	wi**ves**

German plurals are shown for most words (for example, **Gemälde**) but not for many compounds (for example, **Wandgemälde**). The label *pl*-indicates that the plural does not vary.

Where no gender is shown for a German noun, it may be masculine or feminine, for example **Abgeordnete(r)**. Adjectival nouns are shown by -(**r**) or -(**s**), the final letter being used according to the article, for example: **der Abgeordnete, ein Abgeordneter, die Abgeordnete, eine Abgeordnete, Abgeordnete** (*pl*).

Under a German headword, a sub-entry may be shown preceded by a dash. The full form may be obtained by adding the sub-entry to the nearest preceding full word, less that part after the vertical strokes, if any. Thus, **außerhalb** is shown as follows:

außer||dem *adv* besides. -**halb** *adv, prep* outside.

Irregular verbs listed in the verb tables are marked with an asterisk in the body of the dictionary.

Leitfaden für das Wörterbuch

Englische unregelmäßige Plurale sind bei dem Stichwort und im Text gezeigt.
Die folgenden Kategorien von Pluralformen sind als regelmäßig anzusehen:

cat	cat**s**
glass	glass**es**
fl**y**	fl**ies**
hal**f**	hal**ves**
wi**fe**	wi**ves**

Deutsche Plurale sind für die meisten Wörter angeführt (z. B. **Gemälde**), aber
nicht für viele zusammengesetzte Wörter (z. B. **Wandgemälde**). Das Zeichen
pl -deutet an, daß der Plural mit dem Singular identisch ist.

Wo kein Geschlecht für ein deutsches Hauptwort angegeben ist, kann es
sowohl männlich als auch weiblich sein, z. B. **Abgeordnete(r)**. Hauptworte,
die aus Adjektiven gebildet sind, sind folgendermaßen gekennzeichnet -(**r**)
oder -(**s**), wobei der letzte Buchstabe von dem Artikel abhängt, z. B. **der
Abgeordnete, ein Abgeordneter, die Abgeordnete, eine Abgeordnete,
Abgeordnete** (*pl*).

Hinter einem deutschen Stichwort, findet man öfter eine weitere Eintragung
hinter einem Strich. Das komplette Wort erhält man durch Hinzufügen dieses
Wortes an das vorherige Wort ohne den Teil hinter die Vertikalen, wenn
nötig. So ist z. B. **außerhalb** wie folgt gezeigt:

außer||dem *adv* besides. **-halb** *adv, prep* outside.

Unregelmäßige Verben, die in der separaten Liste aufgeführt sind, sind mit
einem Sternchen (*) bei den Stichwörtern angezeigt.

Viele englische Adverbien sind in dem Wörterbuch nicht aufgeführt, wenn sie
aus den Adjektiven regelmäßig durch die Nachsilbe -*(al) ly* gebildet sind.

German irregular verbs

Infinitive	Preterite	Past Participle
backen	backte (buk)	gebacken
bedingen	bedang (bedingte)	bedungen
befehlen	befahl	befohlen
beginnen	begann	begonnen
beißen	biß	gebissen
bergen	barg	geborgen
bersten	barst	geborsten
bewegen	bewog	bewogen
biegen	bog	gebogen
bieten	bot	geboten
binden	band	gebunden
bitten	bat	gebeten
blasen	blies	geblasen
bleiben	blieb	geblieben
bleichen	blich	geblichen
braten	briet	gebraten
brauchen	brauchte	gebraucht (brauchen)
brechen	brach	gebrochen
brennen	brannte	gebrannt
bringen	brachte	gebracht
denken	dachte	gedacht
dreschen	drosch	gedroschen
dringen	drang	gedrungen
dürfen	durfte	gedurft
empfehlen	empfahl	empfohlen
erkiesen	erkor	erkoren
erlöschen	erlosch	erloschen
erschrecken	erschrak	erschrocken
essen	aß	gegessen
fahren	fuhr	gefahren
fallen	fiel	gefallen
fangen	fing	gefangen
fechten	focht	gefochten
finden	fand	gefunden
flechten	flocht	geflochten
fliegen	flog	geflogen
fliehen	floh	geflohen
fließen	floß	geflossen

Infinitive	Preterite	Past Participle
fressen	fraß	gefressen
frieren	fror	gefroren
gären	gor	gegoren
gebären	gebar	geboren
geben	gab	gegeben
gedeihen	gedieh	gediehen
gehen	ging	gegangen
gelingen	gelang	gelungen
gelten	galt	gegolten
genesen	genas	genesen
genießen	genoß	genossen
geschehen	geschah	geschehen
gewinnen	gewann	gewonnen
gießen	goß	gegossen
gleichen	glich	geglichen
gleiten	glitt	geglitten
glimmen	glomm	geglommen
graben	grub	gegraben
greifen	griff	gegriffen
haben	hatte	gehabt
halten	hielt	gehalten
hängen	hing	gehangen
hauen	haute (hieb)	gehauen
heben	hob	gehoben
heißen	hieß	geheißen
helfen	half	geholfen
kennen	kannte	gekannt
klimmen	klomm	geklommen
klingen	klang	geklungen
kneifen	kniff	gekniffen
kommen	kam	gekommen
können	konnte	gekonnt
kriechen	kroch	gekrochen
laden	lud	geladen
lassen	ließ	gelassen (lassen)
laufen	lief	gelaufen
leiden	litt	gelitten
leihen	lieh	geliehen
lesen	las	gelesen
liegen	lag	gelegen
lügen	log	gelogen

Infinitive	Preterite	Past Participle
mahlen	mahlte	gemahlen
meiden	mied	gemieden
melken	melkte (molk)	gemolken (gemelkt)
messen	maß	gemessen
mißlingen	mißlang	mißlungen
mögen	mochte	gemocht
müssen	mußte	gemußt
nehmen	nahm	genommen
nennen	nannte	genannt
pfeifen	pfiff	gepfiffen
preisen	pries	gepriesen
quellen	quoll	gequollen
raten	riet	geraten
reiben	rieb	gerieben
reißen	riß	gerissen
reiten	ritt	geritten
rennen	rannte	gerannt
riechen	roch	gerochen
ringen	rang	gerungen
rinnen	rann	geronnen
rufen	rief	gerufen
salzen	salzte	gesalzen (gesalzt)
saufen	soff	gesoffen
saugen	sog	gesogen
schaffen	schuf	geschaffen
schallen	schallte (scholl)	geschallt
scheiden	schied	geschieden
scheinen	schien	geschienen
scheißen	schiß	geschissen
schelten	schalt	gescholten
scheren	schor	geschoren
schieben	schob	geschoben
schießen	schoß	geschossen
schinden	schund	geschunden
schlafen	schlief	geschlafen
schlagen	schlug	geschlagen
schleichen	schlich	geschlichen
schleifen	schliff	geschliffen
schleißen	schliß	geschlissen
schließen	schloß	geschlossen
schlingen	schlang	geschlungen

Infinitive	Preterite	Past Participle
schmeißen	schmiß	geschmissen
schmelzen	schmolz	geschmolzen
schnauben	schnob	geschnoben
schneiden	schnitt	geschnitten
schreiben	schrieb	geschrieben
schreien	schrie	geschrie(e)n
schreiten	schritt	geschritten
schweigen	schwieg	geschwiegen
schwellen	schwoll	geschwollen
schwimmen	schwamm	geschwommen
schwinden	schwand	geschwunden
schwingen	schwang	geschwungen
schwören	schwor	geschworen
sehen	sah	gesehen
sein	war	gewesen
senden	sandte	gesandt
sieden	sott	gesotten
singen	sang	gesungen
sinken	sank	gesunken
sinnen	sann	gesonnen
sitzen	saß	gesessen
sollen	sollte	gesollt (sollen)
spalten	spaltete	gespalten (gespaltet)
speien	spie	gespie(e)n
spinnen	spann	gesponnen
sprechen	sprach	gesprochen
spreißen	sproß	gesprossen
springen	sprang	gesprungen
stechen	stach	gestochen
stecken	steckte (stak)	gesteckt
stehen	stand	gestanden
stehlen	stahl	gestohlen
steigen	stieg	gestiegen
sterben	starb	gestorben
stieben	stob	gestoben
stinken	stank	gestunken
stoßen	stieß	gestoßen
streichen	strich	gestrichen
streiten	stritt	gestritten
tragen	trug	getragen
treffen	traf	getroffen

Infinitive	Preterite	Past Participle
treiben	trieb	getrieben
treten	trat	getreten
triefen	triefte (troff)	getrieft
trinken	trank	getrunken
trügen	trog	getrogen
tun	tat	getan
verderben	verdarb	verdorben
verdrießen	verdroß	verdrossen
vergessen	vergaß	vergessen
verlieren	verlor	verloren
verschleißen	verschliß	verschlissen
verzeihen	verzieh	verziehen
wachsen	wuchs	gewachsen
wägen	wog (wägte)	gewogen (gewägt)
waschen	wusch	gewaschen
weben	wob	gewoben
weichen	wich	gewichen
weisen	wies	gewiesen
wenden	wandte	gewandt
werben	warb	geworben
werden	wurde	geworden (worden)
werfen	warf	geworfen
wiegen	wog	gewogen
winden	wand	gewunden
wissen	wußte	gewußt
wollen	wollte	gewollt (wollen)
wringen	wrang	gewrungen
zeihen	zieh	geziehen
ziehen	zog	gezogen
zwingen	zwang	gezwungen

Unregelmäßige Englische Verben

Infinitive	Präteritum	Partizip Perfekt
abide	abode	abode
arise	arose	arisen
awake	awoke	awoke
be	was	been
bear	bore	borne *or* born
beat	beat	beaten
become	became	become
begin	began	begun
bend	bent	bent
bet	bet	bet
beware		
bid	bid	bidden *or* bid
bind	bound	bound
bite	bit	bitten
bleed	bled	bled
blow	blew	blown
break	broke	broken
breed	bred	bred
bring	brought	brought
build	built	built
burn	burnt *or* burned	burnt *or* burned
burst	burst	burst
buy	bought	bought
can	could	
cast	cast	cast
catch	caught	caught
choose	chose	chosen
cling	clung	clung
come	came	come
cost	cost	cost
creep	crept	crept
cut	cut	cut
deal	dealt	dealt
dig	dug	dug
do	did	done
draw	drew	drawn
dream	dreamed *or* dreamt	dreamed *or* dreamt
drink	drank	drunk
drive	drove	driven
dwell	dwelt	dwelt
eat	ate	eaten
fall	fell	fallen
feed	fed	fed

Infinitive	Präteritum	Partizip Perfekt
feel	felt	felt
fight	fought	fought
find	found	found
flee	fled	fled
fling	flung	flung
fly	flew	flown
forbid	forbade	forbidden
forget	forgot	forgotten
forgive	forgave	forgiven
forsake	forsook	forsaken
freeze	froze	frozen
get	got	got
give	gave	given
go	went	gone
grind	ground	ground
grow	grew	grown
hang	hung *or* hanged	hung *or* hanged
have	had	had
hear	heard	heard
hide	hid	hidden
hit	hit	hit
hold	held	held
hurt	hurt	hurt
keep	kept	kept
kneel	knelt	knelt
knit	knitted *or* knit	knitted *or* knit
know	knew	known
lay	laid	laid
lead	led	led
lean	leant *or* leaned	leant *or* leaned
leap	leapt *or* leaped	leapt *or* leaped
learn	learnt *or* learned	learnt *or* learned
leave	left	left
lend	lent	lent
let	let	let
lie	lay	lain
light	lit *or* lighted	lit *or* lighted
lose	lost	lost
make	made	made
may	might	
mean	meant	meant
meet	met	met
mow	mowed	mown
must		
ought		
pay	paid	paid

Infinitive	Präteritum	Partizip Perfekt
put	put	put
quit	quitted *or* quit	quitted *or* quit
read	read	read
rid	rid	rid
ride	rode	ridden
ring	rang	rung
rise	rose	risen
run	ran	run
saw	sawed	sawn *or* sawed
say	said	said
see	saw	seen
seek	sought	sought
sell	sold	sold
send	sent	sent
set	set	set
sew	sewed	sewn *or* sewed
shake	shook	shaken
shear	sheared	sheared *or* shorn
shed	shed	shed
shine	shone	shone
shoe	shod	shod
shoot	shot	shot
show	showed	shown
shrink	shrank	shrunk
shut	shut	shut
sing	sang	sung
sink	sank	sunk
sit	sat	sat
sleep	slept	slept
slide	slid	slid
sling	slung	slung
slink	slunk	slunk
slit	slit	slit
smell	smelt *or* smelled	smelt *or* smelled
sow	sowed	sown *or* sowed
speak	spoke	spoken
speed	sped *or* speeded	sped *or* speeded
spell	spelt *or* spelled	spelt *or* spelled
spend	spent	spent
spill	spilt *or* spilled	spilt *or* spilled
spin	spun	spun
spit	spat	spat
split	split	split
spread	spread	spread
spring	sprang	sprung
stand	stood	stood

Infinitive	Präteritum	Partizip Perfekt
steal	stole	stolen
stick	stuck	stuck
sting	stung	stung
stink	stank *or* stunk	stunk
stride	strode	stridden
strike	struck	struck
string	strung	strung
strive	strove	striven
swear	swore	sworn
sweep	swept	swept
swell	swelled	swollen *or* swelled
swim	swam	swum
swing	swung	swung
take	took	taken
teach	taught	taught
tear	tore	torn
tell	told	told
think	thought	thought
throw	threw	thrown
thrust	thrust	thrust
tread	trod	trodden
wake	woke	woken
wear	wore	worn
weave	wove	woven
weep	wept	wept
win	won	won
wind	wound	wound
wring	wrung	wrung
write	wrote	written

English – Deutsch

A

a, an [ə, ən] *art* ein *m*, eine *f*, ein *neut*. *once a year* einmal im Jahr. *50 kilometres an hour* 50 Kilometer pro Stunde.

aback [ə'bak] *adv* *taken aback* verblüfft, überrascht.

abandon [ə'bandən] *v* (*leave*) verlassen; (*give up*) aufgeben. *n* **with abandon** ungezwungen. **abandoned** *adj* verfallen.

abashed [ə'baʃt] *adj* verlegen.

abate [ə'beit] *v* abnehmen.

abattoir ['abətwɑː] *n* Schlachthaus *neut*.

abbey ['abi] *n* Abtei *f*. **abbess** *n* Äbtissin *f*. **abbot** *n* Abt *m*.

abbreviate [ə'briːvieit] *v* (ab) kürzen. **abbreviation** *n* Abkürzung *f*.

abdicate ['abdikeit] *v* abdanken. **abdication** *n* Abdankung *f*.

abdomen ['abdəmən] *n* Bauch *m*, Unterleib *m*. **abdominal** *adj* Leib-, abdominal.

abduct [əb'dʌkt] *v* entführen. **abduction** *n* Entführung *f*.

aberration [abə'reiʃən] *n* Abweichung *f*; (*optics, astron*) Aberration *f*. **mental aberration** Geistesverirrung *f*.

abet [ə'bet] *v* begünstigen, Vorschub leisten (+ *dat*).

abeyance [ə'beiəns] *n* **in abeyance** in der Schwebe.

abhor [əb'hoː] *v* hassen, verabscheuen. **abhorrence** *n* Abscheu (vor) *m*. **abhor-**

rent *adj* abscheulich.

***abide** [ə'baid] *v* bleiben, verweilen; (*tolerate*) ausstehen. **abide by** festhalten an.

ability [ə'biləti] *n* Fähigkeit *f*; (*skill*) Geschicklichkeit *f*. **to the best of one's ability** nach besten Kräften.

abject [abdʒekt] *adj* (*wretched*) elend; (*contemptible*) verächtlich, gemein.

ablaze [ə'bleiz] *adj, adv* brennend, in Flammen. **set ablaze** entflammen.

able ['eibl] *adj* fähig; (*talented*) geschickt, begabt. **be able** können, fähig sein; (*be in a position to*) in der Lage sein. **ably** *adv* geschickt.

abnormal [ab'noːml] *adj* anormal, abnorm; (*unusual*) ungewöhnlich; (*malformed*) mißgestaltet. **abnormality** *n* Abnormität *f*; Mißbildung *f*.

aboard [ə'boːd] *adj, adv* (*ship*) an Bord. **go aboard** an Bord gehen, einsteigen.

abode [ə'boud] *V* **abide**. *n* Wohnsitz *m*.

abolish [ə'boliʃ] *v* abschaffen, beseitigen.

abominable [ə'bominəbl] *adj* scheußlich. **abominate** *v* verabscheuen. **abomination** *n* Abscheu *m*.

aborigine [abə'ridʒini] *n* Ureinwohner *m*. **aboriginal** *adj* Ur-, ursprünglich.

abortion [ə'boːʃən] *n* (*miscarriage*) Fehlgeburt *f*; (*termination of pregnancy*) Abtreibung *f*. **abortive** *adj* mißlungen.

abound [ə'baund] *v* im Überfluß vorhanden sein. **abound in** reich sein an.

about [ə'baut] *adv* (*approximately*) ungefähr, etwa; (*nearby*) in der Nähe. *prep* (*concerning*) über; (*around*) um … herum. **be**

about to do something eben etwas tun wollen. **walk about** hin- und herlaufen.

above [ə'bʌv] *prep* über. *adv* oben. **above-mentioned** oben erwähnt, obig. **above board** offen, ehrlich.

abrasion [ə'breɪʒən] *n* Abschleifen *neut*, Abrieb *m*; (*wound*) Abschürfung *f*. **abrasive** *adj* abschleifend.

abreast [ə'brest] *adv* **keep abreast of** Schritt halten mit.

abridge [ə'brɪdʒ] *v* (ab) kürzen. **abridgement** *n* Abkürzung *f*.

abroad [ə'brɔːd] *adv* (*go*) ins Ausland; (*be*) im Ausland.

abrupt [ə'brʌpt] *adj* (*sudden*) plötzlich; (*brusque*) kurz, unhöflich.

abscess ['absɛs] *n* Abszeß *m*.

abscond [əb'skɒnd] *v* flüchten.

abseil ['abseɪl] *v* abseilen.

absent ['absənt] *adj* abwesend. **absent-minded** *adj* geistesabwesend. **absence** *n* Abwesende(r), Abwesenheit *f*; (*lack*) Mangel *m*.

absolute ['absəluːt] *adj* völlig, vollkommen, absolut; (*unconditional*) bedingungslos; (*pure*) rein. **absolutely** *adv* völlig; (*interj*) gewiß! **absolutism** *n* Absolutismus *m*.

absolve [əb'zɒlv] *v* entbinden, freisprechen.

absorb [əb'zɔːb] *v* aufsaugen, absorbieren. **absorbed in thought** in Gedanken vertieft. **absorbent** *adj* absorbierend. **absorbent cotton** Watte *f*. **absorbing** *adj* fesselnd.

abstain [əb'steɪn] *v* (*voting*) seine Stimme enthalten. **abstain from** verzichten auf. **abstinence** *n* Enthaltsamkeit *f*.

abstemious [əb'stiːmiəs] *adj* mäßig, enthaltsam.

abstract ['abstrakt] *adj* abstrakt, theoretisch. **abstraction** *n* Abstraktion *f*.

absurd [əb'səːd] *adj* unsinning, lächerlich. **absurdity** *n* Unsinn *m*.

abundance [ə'bʌndəns] *n* Überfluß *m*, Reichtum *m*. **abundant** *adj* reichlich. **abundant in** reich an.

abuse [ə'bjuːz; *n* ə'bjuːs] *v* mißbrauchen; (*insult*) beleidigen. *n* Mißbrauch *m*; Beschimpfung *f*. **abusive** *adj* beleidigend.

abyss [ə'bɪs] *n* Abgrund *m*. **abysmal** *adj* abgrundtief; (*fig*) grenzenlos.

academy [ə'kadəm í] *n* Akademie *f*; (*private school*) Internat *m*. **academic** *adj* akademisch.

accede [ak'siːd] *v* (*agree*) zustimmen (+ *dat*), (*join*) beitreten (+ *dat*); (*throne*) besteigen.

accelerate [ak'sɛləreɪt] *v* (*mot*) gasgeben; (*make quicker*) beschleunigen; (*go faster*) schneller werden. **acceleration** *n* Beschleunigung *f*. **accelerator** *n* Gaspedal *neut*.

accent ['aksənt] *n* Akzent *m*. **accentuate** *v* betonen.

accept [ak'sɛpt] *v* akzepieren, annehmen; (*agree*) zusagen (+ *dat*). **acceptable** *adj* annehmbar. **acceptance** *n* Annahme *f*.

access ['aksɛs] *n* Zutritt *m*, Zugang *m*. **accessible** *adj* erreichbar.

accessory [ak'sɛsəri] *n* (*mot*) Zubehörteil *m*; (*law*) Mitschuldige(r).

accident ['aksidənt] *n* (*mishap*) Unfall *m*; (*chance*) Zufall *m*. **accidental** *adj* zufällig.

acclaim [ə'kleɪm] *v* zujubeln (+ *dat*). *n* (*also* **acclamation**) Beifall *m*, Lob *neut*.

acclimatize [ə'klaɪmətaɪz] *v* angewöhnen, akklimatisieren.

accolade ['akəleɪd] *n* Auszeichnung *f*.

accommodate [ə'kɒmədeɪt] *n* (*put up*) unterbringen; (*help*) aushelfen. **accommodating** *adj* hilfreich. **accommodation** *n* Unterkunft *f*.

accompany [ə'kʌmpəni] *v* begleiten. **accompaniment** *n* Begleitung *f*. **accompanist** *n* Begleiter(in).

accomplice [ə'kʌmplɪs] *n* Mittäter *m*.

accomplish [ə'kʌmplɪʃ] *v* vollbringen, vollenden. **accomplished** *adj* gebildet, gewandt. **accomplishment** *n* Durchführung, Vollendung *f*.

accord [ə'kɔːd] *v* übereinstimmen. *n* Übereinstimmung *f*, Einklang *m*. **of one's own accord** freiwillig. **in accordance with** gemäß (+ *dat*): *in accordance with the rules* den Regeln gemäß. **accordingly** *adv* dementsprechend, deswegen. **according to** laut (+ *gen*).

accordion [ə'kɔːdiən] *n* Akkordeon *neut*.

accost [ə'kɒst] *v* ansprechen.

account [ə'kaunt] *n* (*bill*) Rechnung *f*; (*bank, etc*) Konto *neut*; (*report*) Bericht *m*. **accounts** *pl n* Bücher *pl*. **current account** Scheckkonto *neut*. **savings account** Sparkonto *neut*. **on account** auf Konto. **on**

account of wegen (+ *gen*), *auf Grund* (+ *gen*). **on no account** auf keinen Fall. **take into account** berücksichtigen. **v account for** erklären. **accountable** *adj* verantwortlich. **accountant** *n* Buchhalter *m*.

accrue [ə'kruː] *v* auflaufen.

accumulate [ə'kjuːm juleɪt] *v* anhäufen, sich häufen. **accumulation** *n* Anhäufung *f*.

accurate ['akjɪrət] *adj* genau, exakt; (*correct*) richtig. **accuracy** *n* Genauigkeit *f*.

accuse [ə'kjuːz] *v* anklagen. **the accused** der/die Angeklagte(r). **accusation** *n* Anklage *f*. **accusative** *n* Akkusativ *m*.

accustom [ə'kʌstəm] *v* **become accustomed to** sich gewöhnen an. **accustomed** *adj* gewöhnlich, üblich.

ace [eɪs] *n* (*cards*) As *neut*. *adj* (*coll*) erstklassig.

ache [eɪk] *n* Schmerz *m*. *v* schmerzen, weh tun.

achieve [ə'tʃiːv] *v* durchführen, vollbringen; (*reach*) erlangen. **achievement** *n* Vollendung *f*, (*success*) Erfolg *m*.

acid ['asid] *n* Säure *f*. *adj* sauer. **acid rain** saurer Regen *m*.

acknowledge [əkˈnɒlidʒ] *v* anerkennen; (*admit*) zugeben. **acknowledge receipt** Empfang bestätigen. **acknowledgment** *n* Anerkennung *f*.

acne ['akni] *n* Pickel *m*, Akne *f*.

acorn ['eɪkɔːn] *n* Eichel *f*.

acoustic [ə'kuːstik] *adj* akustisch. **acoustics** *pl n* Akustik *f sing*.

acquaint [ə'kweɪnt] *v* bekannt machen. **be acquainted with** kennen (+ *acc*). **get acquainted with** kennenlernen (+ *acc*). **acquaintance** *n* Bekannte(r).

acquiesce [akwiˈes] *v* sich fügen. **acquiescence** *n* Ergebung *f*. **acquiescent** *adj* fügsam.

acquire [ə'kwaɪə] *v* erwerben, bekommen. **acquisition** *n* Erwerb *m*. **acquisitive** habsüchtig, gierig.

acquit [ə'kwɪt] *v* (*law*) freisprechen. **acquittal** *n* Freisprechung *f*.

acrid ['akrid] *adj* scharf, beißend.

acrimony ['akrimənɪ] *n* Bitterkeit *f*. **acrimonious** *adj* bitter, beißend.

acrobat ['akəbat] *n* Akrobat *m*. **acrobatic** *adj* akrobatisch. **acrobatics** *pl n* Akrobatik *f sing*.

acronym ['akrənim] *n* Akronym *neut*.

across [ə'krɒs] *adv* hinüber, herüber. *prep* (quer) über (+ *acc*), jenseits (+ *gen*), auf der anderen Seite.

act [akt] *v* handeln, tun; (*behave*) sich verhalten; (*theatre*) (eine Rolle) spielen. **act on** wirken auf. *n* Handlung, Tat *f*; (*law*) Gesetz *neut*; (*theatre*) Aufzug *m*. **acting** *adj* amtierend; *n* (*theatre*) Spielen *neut*. **actor** *n* Schauspieler *m*. **actress** *n* Schauspielerin *f*.

action ['akʃən] *n* Handlung *f*; (*deed*) Tat *f*; (*effect*) Wirkung *f*; (*law*) Klage *f*; (*battle*) Gefecht *neut*.

active ['aktiv] *adj* tätig, aktiv. **activate** *v* aktivieren. **activist** *n* Aktivist *m*. **activity** *n* Tätigkeit *f*. **activities** *pl n* Unternehmungen *pl*.

actual ['aktʃuəl] *adj* wirklich, eigentlich, tatsächlich. **actually** *adv* wirklich, tatsächlich. *interj* eigentlich.

actuate ['aktjueɪt] *v* in Gang bringen.

acupuncture ['akjupʌŋktʃə] *n* Akupunktur *f*.

acute [ə'kjuːt] *adj* scharf, heftig; (*angle*) spitz; (*person*) scharfsinnig; (*med*) akut.

adamant ['adəm ənt] *adj* unnachgiebig.

Adam's apple [adəm 'zapl] *n* Adamsapfel *m*.

adapt [ə'dapt] *v* anpassen; verändern. **adapted to** geeignet für. **adaptable** *adj* anpassungsfähig. **adaptation** *n* (*theatre*) Bearbeitung *f*. **adaptor** *n* (*for plug*) Zwischenstecker *m*.

add [ad] *v* (*figures*) addieren; (*word, sentence*) hinzufügen. **add up** addieren. **addition** *n* (*math*) Addition *f*; (*something added*) Zugabe *f*, Zutat *m*. **in addition** außerdem. **in addition to** zusätzlich zu. **additional** *adj* zusätzlich, weiter. **additive** *n* Zusatz *m*.

addendum [ə'dendəm] *n* Zusatz *m*.

adder ['adə] *n* (*snake*) Natter *m*.

addict ['adikt; *v* ə'dikt] *n* Süchtige(r); (*coll*) Fanatiker *m*. **drug addict** Rauschgiftsüchtige(r). **addicted** *adj* süchtig. **addiction** *n* Sucht *f*. **addictive** *adj* suchterzeugend; süchtig machend.

additive ['aditiv] *n* Zusatzmittel *neut*.

address [ə'dres] *v* (*letter*) adressieren; (*person*) anreden. *n* Adresse *f*, Anschrift *f*; (*speech*) Anrede *f*. **address book** Adreßbuch *neut*. **addressee** *n* Empfänger *m*.

adenoids ['adənɔidz] *pl n* Polypen *pl*.

adept ['ǝ'dept] *adj* geschickt, erfahren.

adequate ['ædɪkwǝt] *adj* (*quantity*) ausreichend, genügend; (*quality*) annehmbar.

adhere [ǝd'hɪǝ] *v* **adhere to** haften *or* kleben an (+ *dat*); (*belief, etc.*) festhalten an (+ *dat*). klebrig, haftend. **adhesive tape** Klebeband *neut*. **adherent** *n* Anhänger *m*.

adjacent [ǝ'dʒeɪsǝnt] *adj* angrenzend.

adjective ['ædʒɪktɪv] *n* Adjektiv *neut*, Eigenschaftswort *neut*.

adjoin [ǝ'dʒoɪn] *v* angrenzen (an). **adjoining** *adj* angrenzend, anliegend.

adjourn [ǝ'dʒǝ:n] *v* vertagen. **adjournment** *n* Vertagung *f*.

adjudicate [ǝ'dʒu:dɪkeɪt] *v* Recht sprechen, entscheiden. **adjudicator** *n* Schiedsrichter *m*.

adjust [ǝ'dʒʌst] *v* anpassen; berichtigen; (*tech*) einstellen. **adjust to** sich anpassen an. **adjustable** *adj* einstellbar. **adjustment** *n* Anpassung, Einstellung *f*.

ad-lib ['æd'lɪb] *adv* frei. *v* improvisieren.

administer [ǝd'mɪnɪstǝ] *v* verwalten. **administer justice** Recht sprechen. **administration** *n* Verwaltung *f*. **administrative** *adj* Verwaltungs-. **administrator** *n* Verwalter *m*.

admiral ['ædmǝrǝl] *n* Admiral *m*.

admire [ǝd'maɪǝ] *v* bewundern, hochschätzen. **admirable** *adj* bewundernswert. **admiration** *n* Bewunderung *f*.

admission [ǝd'mɪʃǝn] *n* Eintritt *m*; (*acknowledgment*) Zugeständnis *neut*.

admit [ǝd'mɪt] *v* (*let in*) hereinlassen, zulassen; (*concede*) zugeben. **admittance** *n* Zutritt, Eintritt *m*. **no admittance** Zutritt verboten.

adolescence [ædǝ'lesns] Jugend *f*. **adolescent** *adj* jugendlich. *n* Jugendliche(r).

adopt [ǝ'dopt] *v* (*child*) adoptieren; (*idea*) annehmen, übernehmen. **adoption** *n* Adoption *f*; Übernahme *f*.

adore [ǝ'do:] *v* lieben; (*rel*) verehren. **adorable** *adj* entzückend. **adoration** *n* Verehrung *f*.

adorn [ǝ'do:n] *v* schmücken. **adornment** *n* Schmuck *m*.

adrenaline [ǝ'drenǝlɪn] *n* Adrenalin *neut*.

adrift [ǝ'drɪft] *adj*, *adv* (*naut*) treibend; (*fig*) hilflos.

adroit [ǝ'droɪt] *adj* gewandt, geschickt.

adulation [ædju'leɪʃǝn] *n* Lobhudelei *f*.

adult ['ædʌlt] *n* Erwachsene(r). *adj* erwachsen; (*animal, plant*) ausgewachsen.

adulterate [ǝ'dʌlǝreɪt] *v* verfälschen. **adulteration** *n* Verfälschung *f*.

adultery [ǝ'dʌltǝrɪ] *n* Ehebruch *m*. **adulterer** *n* Ehebrecher (in).

advance [ǝd'va:ns] *v* vorwärts gehen, vorrücken; (*make progress*) Fortschritte machen; (*cash*) vorschießen; (*cause*) fördern; (*tech*) vorstellen. *n* Vorrücken *neut*, Fortschritt *m*; Vorschuß *m*. **in advance** im voraus. **advancement** *n* Beförderung *f*.

advantage [ǝd'va:ntɪdʒ] *n* Vorteil *m*. **take advantage of** ausnutzen (+*acc*). **advantageous** *adj* vorteilhaft.

advent ['ædvǝnt] *n* Ankunft *f*; (*rel*) Advent *m*.

adventure [ǝd'ventʃǝ] *n* Abenteuer *m*. **adventurer** *n* Abenteurer *m*. **adventurous** *adj* gewagt.

adverb ['ædvǝ:b] *n* Adverb *neut*, Umstandswort *neut*.

adversary ['ædvǝsǝrɪ] *n* Gegner *m*.

adverse ['ædvǝ:s] *adj* widrig, ungünstig. **adversity** *n* Mißgeschick *neut*, Not *f*.

advertise ['ædvǝtaɪz] *v* anzeigen. **advertisement** *n* Anzeige *f*. **advertising** *n* Reklame, Werbung *f*.

advise [ǝd'vaɪz] *v* (be)raten, empfehlen; (*comm*) benachrichtigen. **advisable** *adj* ratsam. **adviser** *n* Berater *m*. **advice** *n* Rat *m*, Ratschlag *m*; (*comm*) Avis *neut*.

advocate ['ædvǝkeɪt] *v* befürworten.

aerial ['eǝrɪǝl] *n* Antenne *f*. *adj* Luft-.

aerobics [eǝ'rǝubɪks] *n* Aerobic *neut*.

aerodynamics [eǝrǝdaɪnæmɪks] *n* Aerodynamik *f*.

aeronautics [eǝrǝ'no:tɪks] *n* Aeronautik *f*, Flugwesen *neut*.

aeroplane ['eǝrǝpleɪn] *n* Flugzeug *neut*.

aerosol ['eǝrǝsol] *n* Sprühdose *f*, Spray *neut*.

aesthetic [is'θetɪk] *adj* ästhetisch.

affair [ǝ'feǝ] *n* Angelegenheit *f*, Sache *f*; (*love affair*) (Liebes) Affäre *f*.

affect[1] [ǝ'fekt] *v* (*influence*) (ein) wirken auf, beeinflussen. **affected** *adj* (*moved*) bewegt.

affect[2] [ǝ'fekt] *v* (*pretend*) vorgeben. **affectation** *n* Affektation *f*. **affected** *adj* geziert.

affection [ǝ'fekʃǝn] *n* Zuneigung *f*, Liebe *f*. **affectionate** *adj* liebevoll.

affiliated [ǝ'fɪlɪeɪtɪd] *adj* angeschlossen. **affiliated company** Tochtergesellschaft *f*.

affiliation *n* Verbindung *f*, Mitgliedschaft *f*.

affinity [əˈfɪnəti] *n* Zuneigung *f*; (*chem*) Affinität *f*.

affirm [əˈfɜːm] *v* behaupten. **affirmation** *n* Behauptung *f*. **affirmative** *adj* bestätigend.

affix [əˈfiks] *v* befestigen, ankleben (an).

afflict [əˈflikt] *v* betrüben. **affliction** *n* Leiden *neut*.

affluent [ˈafluənt] *adj* wohlhabend, reich. **affluence** *n* Wohlstand *m*.

afford [əˈfɔːd] *v* sich leisten (können); (*allow*) gewähren.

affront [əˈfrʌnt] *v* beleidigen. *n* Beleidigung *f*.

afloat [əˈfləut] *adj, adv* schwimmend; (*boat*) auf dem Meere.

afoot [əˈfut] *adv* im Gang.

aforesaid [əˈfɔːsed] *adj* vorher erwähnt.

afraid [əˈfreid] *adj* ängstlich, erschrocken, bange. **be afraid of** Angst haben vor. **be afraid to** sich scheuen. *I am afraid I must … ich muß leider …*

afresh [əˈfreʃ] *adv* von neuem, noch einmal.

Africa [ˈafrikə] *n* Afrika *neut*. **African** *n* Afrikaner(in); *adj* afrikanisch.

aft [ɑːft] *adj* Achter-. *adv* achtern.

after [ˈɑːftə] *conj* nachdem. *prep* nach, hinter. *adv* später, nachher. *adj* (*naut*) Achter-. **after all** schließlich. **shortly after** kurz danach.

after-effect *n* Nachwirkung *f*.

afterlife [ˈɑːftəlaif] *n* Leben nach dem Tode *neut*.

aftermath [ˈɑːftəmaθ] *n* Auswirkung *f*.

afternoon [ˌɑːftəˈnuːn] *n* Nachmittag *m*. **good afternoon!** guten Tag!

aftershave [ˈɑːftəʃeiv] *n* Rasierwasser *neut*.

after-taste *n* Nachgeschmack *m*.

aftershave [ˈɑːftəʃeiv] *n* Rasierwasser *neut*.

afterthought [ˈɑːftəθɔːt] *n* nachträglicher Einfall *m*.

afterwards [ˈɑːftəwədz] *adv* nachher, später, danach.

again [əˈgen] *adv* wieder, noch einmal, nochmals; (*moreover*) ferner. **again and again** immer wieder.

against [əˈgenst] *prep* gegen. **as against** im Vergleich zu.

age [eidʒ] *n* (*person*) Alter *neut*; (*era*) Zeitalter *neut*. **age group** Altersgruppe *f*. **at the age of …** im Alter von. … **of age** volljährig. **old age** (hohes) Alter *neut*. *v* alt werden. **aged** *adj* (*elderly*) betagt. *aged five years* fünf Jahre alt. **under age** minderjährig.

agency [ˈeidʒənsi] *n* Agentur *f*.

agenda [əˈdʒendə] *n* Tagesordnung *f*.

agent [ˈeidʒənt] *n* Agent *m*, Vermittler *m*; (*chem*) Wirkstoff *m*.

aggravate [ˈagrəveit] *v* verschlimmern; (*coll*) ärgern. **aggravation** *n* Verschlimmerung *f*; Ärger *m*.

aggregate [ˈagrigət] *adj* gesamt, ganz. *n* Summe *f*.

aggression [əˈgreʃən] *n* Angriff *m*, Aggression *f*. **aggressive** *adj* aggresiv. **aggressor** *n* Angreifer *m*.

aghast [əˈgɑːst] *adj* entsetzt.

agile [ˈadʒail] *adj* agil, flink. **agility** *n* Flinkheit *f*.

agitate [ˈadʒiteit] *v* schütteln. **agitated** *adj* beunruhigt. **agitation** *n* Beunruhigung *f*.

agnostic [agˈnostik] *n* Agnostiker *m*. **agnosticism** *n* Agnostizismus *m*.

ago [əˈgou] *adv* vor: *a year ago* vor einem Jahr. **a moment ago** soeben. **a long time ago** schon lange her. **a short time ago** vor kurzem.

agog [əˈgog] *adj* gespannt.

agony [ˈagəni] *n* Qual *f*, Agonie *f*. **agonize over** sich quälen über.

agree [əˈgriː] *v* (*concur*) übereinstimmen, einverstanden sein; (*date, etc.*) vereinbaren; (*consent*) zustimmen; (*be in agreement*) einig sein. *eggs do not agree with me* ich kann Eier nicht vertragen. **agreed!** einverstanden! **agreeable** *adj* angenehm. **agreement** *n* Übereinstimmung *f* (*written*) Abkommen *neut*.

agriculture [ˈagrikʌltʃə] *n* Landwirtschaft *f*. **agricultural** *adj* landwirtschaftlich.

aground [əˈgraund] *adv* **run aground** stranden.

ahead [əˈhed] *adv* vorwärts. **straight ahead** gerade aus. **go ahead** fortfahren.

aid [eid] *n* Hilfe *f*. *v* helfen (+ *dat*).

AIDS [eidz] *n* Aids *neut*.

aim [eim] *v* (*gun*) richten; (*intend*) zielen. *n* Ziel *neut*. **aimless** *adj* ziellos.

air [eə] *n* Luft *f*; (*appearance*) Aussehen

neut; (*music*) Lied *neut*. *v* (*laundry*) trocknen; (*views*) bekanntmachen. **go by air** fliegen. **airy** *adj* luftig.

airbed ['əəbed] *n* Luftmatratze *f*.

airborne ['əəboːn] *adj* in der Luft; Luft-.

air-conditioned *adj* klimatisiert. **air-conditioning** *n* Klimaanlage *f*.

air-cooled *adj* (*mech*) luftgekühlt.

aircraft ['əəkraːft] *n* Flugzeug *neut*.

airfield ['əəfiːld] *n* Flugplatz *m*.

air force *n* Luftwaffe *f*.

air lift *n* Luftbrücke *f*.

airline ['əəlain] *n* Luftverkehrsgesellschaft *f*. **airline passenger** Fluggast *m*.

airmail ['əəmeil] *n* Luftpost *f*. **by airmail** mit Luftpost.

airport ['əəpoːt] *n* Flughafen *m*.

air-raid *n* Luftangriff *m*.

air steward *n* Steward *m*. **air stewardess** *n* Stewardeß *f*.

airtight ['əətait] *adj* luftdicht.

air traffic controller *n* Fluglotse *m*.

aisle [ail] *n* Gang *m*.

ajar [ə'dʒaː] *adj* halboffen.

akin [ə'kin] *adj* **akin to** ähnlich (+ *dat*).

alabaster ['abbəstə] *n* Alabaster *m*.

à la carte [aɬaˈkaːt] *adv* nach der Speisekarte, à la carte.

alarm [ə'laːm] *n* Alarm *m*; (*unrest*) Beunruhigung *f*. *v* beunruhigen. **alarm clock** Wecker *m*.

alas [ə'las] *interj* leider! o weh!

albatross ['abətros] *n* Albatros *m*.

albino [albiːnou] *n* Albino *m*.

album ['abəm] *n* Album *neut*.

alchemy ['akəm] *m* Alchimie *f*. **alchemist** *n* Alchimist *m*.

alcohol ['akəhol] *n* Alkohol *m*. **alcoholic** *adj* alkoholisch. *n* Alkoholiker *m*. **alcoholism** *n* Alkoholismus *m*. **non-alcoholic** *adj* alkoholfrei.

alcove ['akouv] *n* Nische *f*.

alderman ['oːldəmən] *n* Ratsherr *m*.

ale [eil] *m* Bier *neut*.

alert [ə'bːt] *adj* wachsam, munter. *v* warnen. **on the alert** auf der Hut.

algebra ['aldʒibrə] *n* Algebra *f*.

alias ['eiliəs] *adv* sonst ... genannt, alias. *n* Deckname *m*.

alibi ['aibai] *n* Alibi *neut*.

alien ['eiliən] *n* Fremde(r), Ausländer *m*. *adj* fremd. **alienate** *v* entfremden. **alienation** *n* Entfremdung *f*.

alight[1] [ə'lait] *v* (*from bus*) aussteigen.

alight[2] [ə'lait] *adj*, *adv* brennend, in Flammen. **set alight** entflammen.

align [ə'lain] *v* ausrichten. **alignment** *n* Ausrichtung *f*.

alike [ə'laik] *adj*, *adv* gleich.

alimentary canal [alim entəri] *n* Nahrungskanal *m*.

alimony ['alim əni] *n* Unterhalt *m*, Alimente *pl*.

alive [ə'laiv] *adj* lebend, am Leben. **alive with** wimmelnd von.

alkali ['alkəlai] *n* Alkali *neut*. **alkaline** *adj* alkalisch.

all [oːl] *adj* alle, sämtliche. *pl pron* alles, das Ganze. *adv* ganz. **all over** vorbei. **all gone** alle, weg. **above all** vor allem. **all at once** auf einmal. **at all** überhaupt. **all day** den ganzen Tag. **all right** in Ordnung, okay.

allay [ə'lei] *v* beruhigen.

allege [ə'ledʒ] *v* angeben, behaupten. **alleged** *adj* angeblich. **allegation** *n* Behauptung *f*.

allegiance [ə'liːdʒəns] *n* Treue *f*.

allegory ['aligəri] *n* Allegorie *f*. **allegorical** *adj* allegorisch.

allergy ['alədʒi] *n* Allergie *f*. **allergic** *adj* allergisch (gegen).

alleviate [ə'liːvieit] *v* erleichtern.

alley ['ali] *n* Gasse *f*. **bowling alley** Kegelbahn *f*.

alliance [ə'laiəns] *n* (*pol*) Bündnis *neut*. **form an alliance** ein Bündnis schließen.

allied ['alaid] *adj* verbündet, alliiert.

alligator ['aligeitə] *n* Alligator *m*.

alliteration [əlitə'reiʃən] *n* Alliteration *f*. **alliterative** *adj* alliterierend.

allocate ['aləkeit] *v* zuteilen.

allot [ə'lot] *v* (*distribute*) zuteilen; (*assign*) bestimmen. **allotment** *n* Zuteilung *f*; (*garden patch*) Schrebergarten *m*.

allow [ə'lau] *v* erlauben, gestatten. **allow for** berücksichtigen. **will you allow me** (*to*)? darf ich? **allowance** *n* Erlaubnis *f*; (*money*) Rente *f*.

alloy ['aloi; *v* ə'loi] *n* Legierung *f*. *v* legieren.

allude [ə'luːd] *v* **allude to** anspielen auf (+ *acc*). **allusion** *n* Anspielung *f*.

allure [ə'ljuə] n Reiz m. v verlocken. **alluring** adj verlockend.

ally ['alai; v ə'lai] n Verbündete(r); (pol) Alliierte(r). **v ally oneself with** sich verbünden mit. **the Allies** die Alliierten.

almanac ['o:lm ənak] n Jahrbuch neut, Almanach m.

almighty [o:lm ait] adj allmächtig; (coll) gewaltig. **the Almighty** der Allmächtige.

almond ['a:m ənd] n Mandel f.

almost ['o:lm oust] adv fast, beinahe.

alms [a:m z] pl n Almosen neut sing.

aloft [ə'bft] adv (be) oben; (go) nach oben.

alone [ə'bun] adj, adv allein. **leave alone** bleiben lassen. **leave me alone!** laß mich in Ruhe!

along [ə'bŋ] prep entlang (+ acc): along the coast die Küste entlang. adv vorwärts, weiter; mit: come along mitkommen. **along with** zusammen mit. **get along with someone** mit jemandem gut auskommen. **alongside** prep neben (+ acc or dat); (ship) längseits (+ gen).

aloof [ə'lu:f] adj zurückhaltend.

aloud [ə'laud] adv laut. **read aloud** vorlesen.

alphabet ['aləbit] n Alphabet neut. **alphabetical** adj alphabetisch.

Alps [alps] pl n Alpen pl. **alpine** adj Alpen-.

already [o:lredi] adv schon, bereits.

Alsatian [alseʃən] n (dog) Schäferhund m. adj elsässisch.

also ['o:lsou] adv auch, ebenfalls; (moreover) ferner.

altar ['o:ltə] n Altar m.

alter ['o:ltə] v (modify) (ab-, ver)ändern; (become changed) sich (ver)ändern. **alteration** n (Ab-, Ver)Änderung f; (building) Umbau m.

alternate [o:ltə:nət; v'o:ltəneit] adj abwechselnd. v abwechseln.

alternative f. [o:ltə:nətiv] adj ander. n Alternative f. **there is no alternative** es gibt keine andere Möglichkeit.

although [o:lðou] conj obwohl, obgleich, wenn auch.

altitude ['altitju:d] m Höhe f.

alto ['altou] n Alt m, Altstimme f.

altogether [o:ltə'geðə] adv insgesamt, im ganzen; völlig.

altruistic [altru'istik] adj altruistisch.

aluminium [alju'm inəm] n Aluminium neut.

always ['o:lweiz] adv immer, stets; schon immer.

am [am] V **be.**

amalgamate [ə'm algəm eit] v (tech) amalgamieren; (fig) vereinigen.

amass [ə'm as] v aufhäufen.

amateur ['am ətə] n Amateur m. adj Amateur-.

amaze [ə'm eiz] v erstaunen, verblüffen. **amazed at** erstaunt über. **amazement** n Erstaunen neut. **amazing** adj erstaunlich; (coll) sagenhaft.

ambassador [am 'basədə] n Botschafter m.

amber ['am bə] n Bernstein m. adj bernsteinfarb, gelb.

ambidextrous [am bidekstrəs] adj beidhändig.

ambiguous [am 'bigjuəs] adj zweideutig; unklar.

ambition [am 'biʃən] n Ehrgeiz m, Ambition f. **ambitious** adj ehrgeizig, ambitiös.

ambivalence [am 'bivələns] n Ambivalenz f. **ambivalent** adj ambivalent.

amble ['am bl] v schlendern.

ambulance ['am bjuləns] n Krankenwagen m.

ambush ['am buʃ] n Hinterhalt m. v aus dem Hinterhalt überfallen.

ameliorate [ə'm i:liəreit] v (make better) verbessern; (get better) besser werden. **amelioration** n Verbesserung f.

amenable [ə'm i:nəbl] adj zugänglich; (accountable) verantwortlich.

amend [ə'm end] v (ab)ändern; ergänzen, richtigstellen. **make amends for** wiedergutmachen. **amendment** n (to a motion) Ergänzung f.

amenities [ə'm i:nitiz] pl n Vorzüge pl, moderne Einrichtungen pl.

America [ə'm erikə] n Amerika neut. **American** n Amerikaner(in); adj amerikanisch.

amethyst ['am əθist] n Amethyst m.

amiable ['eim əbl] adj freundlich, liebenswürdig.

amicable ['am ikəbl] adj freundschaftlich, friedlich.

amid [ə'm id] prep mitten unter (+ dat).

amiss [ə'm is] adj verkehrt, nicht richtig.

take amiss übelnehmen.

ammonia [əˈmoʊnɪə] n Ammoniak neut.

ammunition [æmjuˈnɪʃən] n Munition f.

amnesia [æmˈniːzɪə] n Gedächtnisverlust m.

amnesty [ˈæmnəstɪ] n Amnestie f.

amoeba [əˈmiːbə] n Amöbe f.

among [əˈmʌŋ] prep unter, zwischen (+ dat); bei (+ dat). **among other things** unter anderem. **among ourselves/yourselves/themselves** miteinander, untereinander.

amoral [eɪˈmɒrəl] adj amoralisch.

amorous [ˈæmərəs] adj verliebt; liebevoll.

amorphous [əˈmɔːfəs] adj (chem) amorph; formlos.

amount [əˈmaʊnt] n (of money) Betrag m, Summe f; (quantity) Menge f. **amount to** betragen. it amounts to the same es läuft auf das gleiche hinaus.

ampere [ˈæmpeə] n Ampere neut.

amphibian [æmˈfɪbɪən] n Amphibie f. **amphibious** adj amphibisch; (vehicle) Amphibien-.

amphitheatre [ˈæmfɪθɪətə] n Amphitheater neut; (lecture room) Hörsaal m.

ample [ˈæmpl] adj ausreichend, reichlich.

amplify [ˈæmplɪfaɪ] v verstärken. **amplification** n Verstärkung f. **amplifier** n Verstärker m.

amputate [ˈæmpjuteɪt] v amputieren. **amputation** n Amputation f.

amuse [əˈmjuːz] v belustigen, amüsieren; (entertain) unterhalten. **be amused by** or **about** lustig finden. **amusing** adj lustig, unterhaltend. **amusement** n Unterhaltung f. **amusement arcade** Spielhalle f.

anachronism [əˈnækrənɪzəm] n Anachronismus m. **anachronistic** adj anachronistisch.

anaemia [əˈniːmɪə] n Anämie, Blutarmut f. **anaemic** adj anämisch, blutarm.

anaesthetic [ænəsˈθetɪk] n Betäubungsmittel neut. **under anaesthetic** unter Narkose. **anaesthetize** v betäuben.

anagram [ˈænəgræm] n Anagramm neut.

analogy [əˈnælədʒɪ] n Ähnlichkeit f, Analogie f. **analogous** adj analog, ähnlich.

analysis [əˈnæləsɪs] n Analyse f. **analyse** v analysieren. **analytical** adj analytisch.

anarchy [ˈænəkɪ] n Anarchie f. **anarchist** Anarchist m.

anathema [əˈnæθəmə] n (rel) Kirchenbann m. that is anathema to me das ist mir ein Greuel.

anatomy [əˈnætəmɪ] n Anatomie f. **anatomical** adj anatomisch.

ancestor [ˈænsestə] n Vorfahr m, Ahn m.

anchor [ˈæŋkə] n Anker m. v befestigen. **ride at anchor** vor Anker liegen. **weigh anchor** den Anker lichten.

anchovy [ˈæntʃəvɪ] n Anschovis f.

ancient [ˈeɪnʃənt] adj alt, uralt; aus alter Zeit, antik.

ancillary [ænˈsɪlərɪ] adj zusätzlich, Hilfs-.

and [ænd] conj und.

anecdote [ˈænɪkdoʊt] n Anekdote f.

anemone [əˈnemənɪ] n Anemone f.

anew [əˈnjuː] adv von neuem, wieder.

angel [ˈeɪndʒəl] n Engel m. **angelic** adj engelhaft.

angelica [ænˈdʒelɪkə] n Angelika f.

anger [ˈæŋgə] n Zorn m, Ärger m. v ärgern. **in anger** im Zorn. **angry** adj ärgerlich, zornig. **be angry** sich ärgern, böse sein.

angina [ænˈdʒaɪnə] n Angina f.

angle¹ [ˈæŋgl] n Winkel m, Ecke f; (coll) Gesichtspunkt m. **be at an angle to** einen Winkel bilden mit.

angle² [ˈæŋgl] v angeln (nach). **angler** n Angler m. **angling** n Angeln neut.

anguish [ˈæŋgwɪʃ] n Qual f.

angular [ˈæŋgjulə] adj winkelig, eckig.

animal [ˈænɪməl] n Tier neut. adj tierisch, animalisch. **animal fat** Tierfett neut. **animal kingdom** Tierreich neut. **animal-rights activist** (militanter)Tierschützer(in) m, f.

animate [ˈænɪmeɪt] v beleben; begeistern. **animated** adj lebhaft. **animated cartoon** Zeichentrickfilm m.

animosity [ænɪˈmɒsətɪ] n Feindseligkeit f.

aniseed [ˈænɪsiːd] n Anis m.

anisette [ænɪˈzet] n Anisett f.

ankle [ˈæŋkl] n (Fuß)Knöchel m.

annals [ˈænlz] pl n Annalen pl.

annex [əˈneks; n ˈæneks] n (to building) Anbau m. v (country) annektieren. **annexation** n Annexion f.

annihilate [əˈnaɪəleɪt] v vernichten. **annihilation** n Vernichtung f.

anniversary [ænɪˈvɜːsərɪ] n Jahrestag m. **wedding anniversary** Hochzeitstag m.

annotate [ˈænəteɪt] v kommentieren.

annotation n Anmerkung f.

announce [ə'nauns] v ankündigen, ansagen, anzeigen. **announcement** n Ankündigung f, Ansage f; (radio) Durchsage f. **announcer** n (radio) Ansager m.

annoy [ə'nɔɪ] v belästigen ärgern. **be annoyed at** or **with** sich ärgern über (+ acc). **annoyance** n Belästigung f.

annual ['ænjuəl] adj jährlich; Jahres-. n (book) Jahrbuch neut; (plant) einjährige Pflanze f.

annul [ə'nʌl] v annullieren. **annulment** n Annullierung f.

anode ['ænoud] n Anode f.

anomaly [ə'noməli] n Anomalie f.

anonymous [ə'noniməs] adj anonym, ungenannt.

anorak ['ænəræk] n Anorak m.

anorexia [ænə'reksə] n Anorexie f.

another [ə'nʌðə] pron, adj (a different) ein anderer; (an additional) noch ein. **one another** einander, sich.

answer ['ɑːnsə] n Antwort f; (solution) Lösung f. v antworten, erwidern. **answer back** unverschämt antworten. **answer for** verantwortlich sein für. **answerable** adj verantwortlich. **answering machine** n Anrufbeantworter m.

ant [ænt] n Ameise f.

antagonize [æn'tægənaɪz] v reizen, entfremden. **antagonist** n Gegner m, Feind m. **antagonistic** adj feindselig.

antecedent [æntɪ'siːdənt] adj früher.

antelope ['æntɪloup] n Antilope f.

antenatal [æntɪ'neɪtl] adj vor der Geburt, pränatal, vorgeburtlich. **antenatal care** Schwangerschaftsvorsorge f.

antenna [æn'tenə] m (insect) Fühler m; (radio) Antenne f.

anthem ['ænθəm] n Hymne f. **national anthem** Nationalhymne f.

anthology [æn'θolədʒi] n Anthologie f.

anthropology [ænθrə'polədʒi] n Anthropologie f. **anthropological** adj anthropologisch.

anti-aircraft [æntɪˈɛəkrɑːft] adj Fliegerabwehr-. **anti-aircraft gun** Fliegerabwehrkanone f.

antibiotic [æntɪbaɪ'ɒtɪk] n Antibiotikum neut. adj antibiotisch.

antibody ['æntɪbɒdi] n Antikörper m.

anticipate [æn'tɪsɪpeɪt] v (expect) erwarten; (foresee) voraussehen. **anticipation** n Erwartung f. **in anticipation of** in Erwartung (+ gen).

anticlimax [æntɪˈklaɪmæks] n Enttäuschung f.

anticlockwise [æntɪˈklɒkwaɪz] adj, adv dem Uhrzeigersinn entgegen.

antics ['æntɪks] pl n Possen pl.

anticyclone [æntɪˈsaɪkloun] n Hochdruckgebiet neut.

antidepressant [æntɪdɪˈpresnt] n Antidepressivum neut.

antidote ['æntɪdout] n Gegenmittel (gegen) neut.

antifreeze ['æntɪfriːz] n Frostschutzmittel neut.

antipathy [æn'tɪpəθi] n Antipathie f, Abneigung f.

antique [æn'tiːk] adj antik, altertümlich. n Antiquität f. **antiquated** adj veraltet. **antiquity** n Altertum neut.

anti-Semitic [æntɪsə'mɪtɪk] adj antisemitisch.

antiseptic [æntɪˈseptɪk] n Antiseptikum neut. adj antiseptisch.

antisocial [æntɪˈsouʃəl] adj gesellschaftsfeindlich; (person) unfreundlich.

antithesis [æn'tɪθəsɪs] n Gegensatz m.

antler ['æntlə] n Geweihsprosse f.

antonym ['æntənɪm] n Antonym neut.

anus ['eɪnəs] n After m.

anvil ['ænvɪl] n Amboß m.

anxious ['æŋkʃəs] adj (worried) beunruhigt, besorgt; (desirous) begierig (nach). **be anxious to do something** gespannt sein, etwas zu tun. **anxiety** n Angst f, Besorgnis f.

any ['eni] pron irgendein, welche. adv etwas. any faster schneller, etwas schneller. any more? noch mehr? do you want any? wollen sie welche? I haven't any money ich habe kein Geld. I can't do it any longer ich kann es nicht mehr machen. **anybody** pron (irgend) jemand; (everybody) jeder. **anyhow** adv jedenfalls. **anyone** pron V **anybody**. **anything** pron (irgend) etwas; (everything) alles. **anytime** adv jederzeit. **anyway** adv jedenfalls, sowieso. **anywhere** adv irgendwo (hin); (everywhere) überall.

apart [ə'pɑːt] adv auseinander, getrennt. **apart from** abgesehen von.

apartheid [ə'paːteit] n Apartheid f.

apartment [ə'paːtmənt] n Wohnung f.

apathy ['apəθi] n Apathie f. **apathetic** adj apathisch.

ape [eip] n Affe m. v nachäffen.

aperitive [ə'peritiv] n Aperitif m.

aperture ['apətjuə] n Öffnung f; (phot) Blende f.

apex ['eipeks] n Spitze f.

aphid ['eifid] n Blattlaus f.

aphrodisiac [afrə'diziak] n Aphrodisiakum neut.

apiece [ə'piːs] adv (per person) pro Person; (for each article) pro Stück.

apology [ə'polədʒi] n Entschuldigung f. **apologetic** adj entschuldigend. **apologize** sich entschuldigen.

apoplexy ['apəpleksi] n Schlaganfall m.

apostle [ə'posl] n Apostel m.

apostrophe [ə'postrəfi] n Apostroph m, Auslassungszeichen neut.

appal [ə'poːl] v entsetzen. **appalling** adj entsetzlich.

apparatus [apə'reitəs] n Apparat m, Gerät neut.

apparent [ə'parənt] adj (obvious) offenbar; (seeming) scheinbar. **apparently** allem Anschein nach.

apparition [apə'rijən] n Erscheinung f, Geist m.

appeal [ə'piːl] n Appell m, dringende Bitte f; (charm) Anziehungskraft f; (law) Berufung f. v **appeal against** (law) Berufung einlegen gegen. **appeal for** dringend bitten um. **appeal to** (turn to) appellieren, sich wenden an; (please) gefallen (+ dat). **appealing** adj reizvoll.

appear [ə'piə] v (seem) scheinen; (become visible, present itself) erscheinen; (crop up) auftauchen. **appearance** n Erscheinen neut; (look) Anschein m.

appease [ə'piːz] v beruhigen; (hunger) stillen. **appeasement** n Beruhigung f.

appendix [ə'pendiks] n (in book) Anhang m; (anat) Blinddarm m. **appendicitis** n Blinddarmentzündung f.

appetite ['apitait] n Appetit m. **appetizer** n Appetitshappen m. **appetizing** adj appetitlich.

applaud [ə'ploːd] v Beifall klatschen (+ dat); applaudieren (+ dat); (fig) loben.

apple ['apl] n Apfel m. **apple juice** Apfelsaft m. **apple tree** Apfelbaum m. **apple sauce** Apfelmus neut.

appliance [ə'plaiəns] n Gerät neut.

applicable ['aplikəbl] adj zutreffend.

applicant ['aplikənt] n Kandidat m.

apply [ə'plai] v anwenden; (be valid) gelten. **apply for** (job) sich bewerben um. **apply to** sich wenden an. **apply oneself to** sich bemühen um. **application** n Anwendung f; (job) Bewerbung f. **applied** adj angewandt.

appoint [ə'point] v anstellen, ernennen. **appointed** adj vereinbart. **well appointed** gut ausgestattet. **appointment** n Anstellung f; (meeting) Verabredung f.

apportion [ə'poːjən] v zuteilen.

appraisal [ə'preizl] n Schätzung f.

appreciable [ə'priːjəbl] adj merkbar.

appreciate [ə'priːjieit] v schätzen; (understand) verstehen; (be grateful for) dankbar sein für; (increase in value) im Wert steigen. **appreciation** n (gratitude) Anerkennung f; (in value) Wertzuwachs m. **appreciative** adj anerkennend.

apprehend [apri'hend] v (understand) begreifen; (seize) verhaften. **apprehensive** adj angstvoll.

apprentice [ə'prentis] n Lehrling m. **apprenticeship** n Lehre f.

approach [ə'proutj] v (come near) sich nähern; (a place) nähern; (someone) sich wenden an. n Herankommen neut; (attitude) Einstellung f; (access) Zugang m. **approachable** adj zugänglich.

appropriate [ə'prouprət; v ə'prouprieit] adj geeignet (+ dat). v sich aneignen.

approve [ə'pruːv] v (agree) zustimmen; (pass, endorse) billigen, genehmigen. **approve of** billigen. **approved** adj bewährt. **approval** n Billigung f, Genehmigung f. **on approval** auf Probe.

approximate [ə'proksimət] adj ungefähr. **approximately** adv ungefähr, etwa.

apricot ['eiprikot] n Aprikose f.

April ['eiprəl] n April m.

apron ['eiprən] n Schürze f.

apt [apt] adj (remark) passend. **apt at** geschickt in. **be apt to do something** geneigtsein, etwas zu tun. **aptitude** n (gift) Begabung f.

aqualung ['akwəlʌŋ] n Unterwasseratmungsgerät neut.

aquarium [əˈkwɛərɪəm] n Aquarium neut.
Aquarius [əˈkwɛərɪəs] n Wassermann m.
aquatic [əˈkwætɪk] n Wasser-.
aqueduct [ˈakwɪɪdʌkt] n Aquädukt m.
Arab [ˈarəb] n Araber m. adj or **Arabian**, **Arabic** arabisch. **Arabic** n arabische Sprache f.
arable [ˈarəbl] adj **arable land** Ackerland neut.
arbitrary [ˈaːbɪtrərɪ] adj willkürlich.
arbitrate [ˈaːbɪtreɪt] v entscheiden. **arbitration** n Schiedspruch m. **arbitrator** n Schiedsrichter m.
arc [aːk] n Bogen m.
arcade [aˈkeɪd] n Arkade f.
arch [aːtʃ] n (architecture) Bogen m. v (sich) wölben. adj Erz-. **archway** n Bogengang m.
archaeology [aːklɒˈbdʒɪ] n Archäologie f. **archaeological** adj archäologisch. **archaeologist** n Archäologe m.
archaic [aˈkeɪɪk] adj altertümlich.
archbishop [aːtʃˈbɪʃəp] n Erzbischof m.
archduke [aːtʃˈdjuːk] n Erzherzog m.
archer [ˈaːtʃə] n Bogenschütze m. **archery** n Bogenschießen neut.
archetype [ˈaːkɪtaɪp] n Vorbild neut; (psychol) Archetyp m.
archipelago [aːkɪpeˈlægou] n Archipel m.
architect [ˈaːkɪtekt] n Architekt m. **architecture** n Architektur f.
archives [ˈaːkaɪvz] pl n Archiv neut sing.
ardent [ˈaːdənt] adj eifrig, begeistert.
ardour [ˈaːdə] n Eifer m.
arduous [ˈaːdjʊəs] adj mühsam, anstrengend.
are [aː] V **be**.
area [ˈɛərə] n (measurement) Fläche f; (region) Gebiet neut. Zone f.
arena [əˈriːnə] n Arena neut.
argue [ˈaːgjuː] v streiten; (case) diskutieren; (maintain) behaupten. **argument** n Streit m; (reasoning) Argument neut. **argumentative** adj streitlustig.
arid [ˈarɪd] adj trocken, dürr.
Aries [ˈɛəriːz] n Widder m.
*arise [əˈraɪz] v (come into being) entstehen; (get up) aufstehen.
arisen [əˈrɪzn] V **arise**.
aristocracy [arɪstokəsi] n Adel m, Aristokratie f. **aristocrat** n Aristokrat m. **aristocratic** adj aristokratisch.

arithmetic [əˈrɪθmətɪk] n Arithmetik f. **arithmetical** adj arithmetisch.
arm¹ [aːm] n Arm m. (of chair) Seitenlehne f. **arm in arm** Arm in Arm. **with open arms** mit offenen Armen.
arm² [aːm] n (weapon) Waffe f. v bewaffnen. **arms race** Wettrüsten neut. **coat of arms** Wappen neut. **armed forces** Streitkräfte pl.
armament [ˈaːməmənt] n Kriegsausrüstung f.
armchair [ˈaːmtʃeə] n Sessel, Lehnstuhl m.
armistice [ˈaːmɪstɪs] n Waffenstillstand m.
armour [ˈaːmə] n (suit of) Rüstung f; (of ship, tank) Panzerung f. **armoured** adj gepanzert.
armpit [ˈaːmpɪt] n Achselhöhle f.
army [ˈaːmɪ] n Armee f, Heer neut. **join the army** zum Militär gehen.
aroma [əˈroumə] n Aroma neut, Duft m. **aromatherapy** n Aromatherapie f.
arose [əˈrouz] V **arise**.
around [əˈraund] adv ringsherum, rundherum; auf allen Seiten; (nearby) in der Nähe. prep um… herum, rings um; (approximately) ungefähr. **look around (for)** sich umsehen (nach). **turn around** sich umdrehen.
arouse [əˈrauz] v wecken, entfachen, aufwecken; (suspicion, sexually) erregen.
arrange [əˈreɪndʒ] v (put in order) anordnen; (meeting) verabreden; (holidays) festsetzen. (see to it) arrangieren, einrichten; (music) bearbeiten. **arrangement** n Anordnung f; (agreement) Vereinbarung f; (music) Bearbeitung f. **make arrangements** Vorbereitungen treffen.
array [əˈreɪ] n Aufstellung f.
arrears [əˈrɪəz] pl n Rückstände pl. **in arrears** im Rückstand m.
arrest [əˈrest] v (thief) verhaften; (halt) anhalten; n Verhaftung f. **under arrest** in Haft, verhaftet. **arresting** adj fesselnd.
arrive [əˈraɪv] v ankommen; (fig) gelangen. **arrival** n Ankunft f. **late arrival** Spätankömmling m.
arrogance [ˈarəgəns] n Hochmut m. **arrogant** adj hochmütig, eingebildet.
arrow [ˈarou] n Pfeil m.
arse [aːs] n (vulg) Arsch m.
arsenal [ˈaːsənl] n Arsenal neut.
arsenic [ˈaːsnɪk] n Arsenik neut.
arson [ˈaːsn] n Brandstiftung f. **arsonist** n

Brandstifter *m*.

art [ɑːt] *n* Kunst *f*. **arts** *pl* Geisteswissen-
schaften *pl*. **arts and crafts** Kunstgewerbe
neut sing. **art gallery** Kunstgalerie *f*. **art
school** Kunstschule *f*. **work of art**
Kunstwert *neut*.

artefact [ˈɑːtɪfækt] *n* Artefakt *neut*.

artery [ˈɑːtəri] *n* Arterie *f*.

arthritis [ɑːˈθraitis] *n* Arthritis *f*.

artichoke [ˈɑːtɪtʃouk] *n* Artischocke *f*.

article [ˈɑːtɪkl] *n* Artikel *m*; *(newspaper)*
Zeitungsartikel *m*, Bericht *m*. **article of
clothing** Bekleidungstück *neut*.

articulate [ɑːˈtɪkjʊlət] *adj*. **be articulate**
sich gut ausdrücken.

articulated lorry [ɑːˈtɪkjʊleitid] *n*
Sattelschlepper *m*.

artifice [ˈɑːtɪfis] *n* Trick *m*.

artificial [ɑːtɪˈfiʃəl] *adj (manmade)* künstlich, Kunst-; *(affected)* affektiert. **artificial intelligence (AI)** künstliche
Intelligenz *f*. **artificial respiration** künstliche Atmung *f*.

artillery [ɑːˈtɪləri] *n* Artillerie *f*.

artisan [ɑːtɪˈzan] *n* Handwerker *m*.

artist [ˈɑːtɪst] *n* Künstler *m*; *(painter)* Maler
m. **artiste** *n* Artist(in). **artistic** *adj* künstlerisch.

as [az] *conj, prep (while)* als, während; *(in
the way that)* wie, sowie; *(since)* da, weil; *(in
role of)* als. **as ... as** (eben)so ... wie. **as far
as** soweit. **as if** als ob. **as long as** solange.
as soon as sobald. **as it were** sozusagen.
as well auch.

asbestos [azˈbestos] *n* Asbest *m*.

ascend [əˈsend] *v* aufsteigen. **ascendant**
adj vorherrschend. **ascent** *n* Aufstieg *m*.
Ascension *n* Himmelfahrt *f*.

ascertain [asəˈtein] *v* feststellen.

ascetic [əˈsetik] *adj* askethisch. *n* Asket *m*.

ash¹ [aʃ] *n (cinder)* Asche *f*. **ashtray** *n*
Aschenbecher *neut*.

ash² [aʃ] *n (tree)* Esche *f*.

ashamed [əˈʃeimd] *adj* **be ashamed** sich
schämen.

ashore [əˈʃoː] *adv* am Ufer. **go ashore** an
Land gehen.

Ash Wednesday *n* Aschermittwoch *m*.

Asia [ˈeʃə] *n* Asien *neut*. **Asian** *n* Asiat *m*;
adj asiatisch.

aside [əˈsaid] *adv* beiseite. **aside from**
außer. **step aside** zur Seite treten. **turn**

aside from sich wegwenden von.

ask [ɑːsk] *v (to question)* fragen; *(request)* bitten. **ask a question** eine Frage stellen.

askew [əˈskjuː] *adv* verschoben, schief.

asleep [əˈsliːp] *adj, adv* **be asleep** schlafen.
fall asleep einschlafen.

asparagus [əˈspærəgəs] *n* Spargel *m*.

aspect [ˈaspekt] *n (appearance)* Aussehen
neut; (of a problem) Aspekt *m*.

asphalt [ˈasfalt] *n* Asphalt *m*.

asphyxiate [əsˈfiksieit] *v* ersticken. **asphyx-
iation** *n* Erstickung *f*.

aspic [ˈaspik] *n* Aspik *m*.

aspire [əˈspaiə] *v* **aspire to** streben nach.
aspiring *adj* hochstrebend.

aspirin [ˈasprin] *n* Aspirin *neut*.

ass [as] *n* Esel *m*.

assail [əˈseil] *v* angreifen. **assailant** *n*
Angreifer *m*.

assassin [əˈsasin] *n* Attentäter *m*, Mörder *m*.
assassinate *v* ermordern. **assassination** *n*
Ermordung *f*.

assault [əˈsoːlt] *v* angreifen, überfallen. *n*
Angriff *m*. **indecent assault**
Sittlichkeitsverbrechen *neut*.

assemble [əˈsembl] *v (congregate)* sich versammeln; *(put together)* montieren, zusam-
menbauen; *(bring together)* versammeln.
assembly *n (people)* Versammlung *f; (tech)*
Montage *f*. **assembly hall** Aula *f*. **assembly line** Fließband *neut*.

assent [əˈsent] *v* zustimmen (+*dat*). *n*
Zustimmung *f*.

assert [əˈsəːt] *v (insist on)* bestehen auf;
(declare) erklären. **assertion** *n* Behauptung
f. **(self-)assertive** *adj* selbstsicher.

assess [əˈses] *v (for tax)* bewerten; *(estimate)*
schätzen. **assessment** *n* Bewertung *f*.

asset [ˈaset] *n* Vorteil *m*. **assets** *pl*
Vermögen *neut sing*.

assiduous [əˈsidjuəs] *adj* fleißig.

assign [əˈsain] *v* zuteilen, bestimmen.
assignment *n* Aufgabe *f*.

assimilate [əˈsimileit] *v* aufnehmen. **assimilation** *n* Aufnahme *f*.

assist [əˈsist] *v* helfen (+*dat*). **assistance** *n*
Hilfe *f*. **assistant** *n* Helfer *m*. **sales assistant** Verkäufer *m*.

associate [əˈsousieit] *v*
verbinden. *n* Kollege *m*, Mitarbeiter *m*;
(comm) Partner *m*. **association** *n (club)*
Verein *m*, Verband *m*; *(link)* Verbindung *f*.

assorted [əˈsɔːtɪd] *adj* verschiedenartig, gemischt. **assortment** *n* Sortiment *neut*.

assume [əˈsjuːm] *v* (*suppose*) annehmen; (*take over*) übernehmen.

assure [əˈʃuə] *v* (*convince*) versichern (+ *dat*), versprechen; (*ensure*) sicherstellen. **assurance** *n* (*assertion*) Versicherung *f*; (*confidence*) Selbstsicherheit *f*. **life assurance** Lebensversicherung *f*.

asterisk [ˈæstərɪsk] *n* Sternchen *neut*.

asthma [ˈæsmə] *n* Asthma *neut*.

astonish [əˈstonɪʃ] *v* erstaunen, verblüffen. **be astonished (at)** erstaunt sein (über), sich wundern (über). **astonishing** *adj* erstaunlich. **astonishment** *n* Erstaunen *neut*.

astound [əˈstaund] *v* bestürzen, erstaunen.

astray [əˈstreɪ] *adv* **go astray** in die Irre gehen. **lead astray** vom rechten Weg abführen.

astride [əˈstraɪd] *adv* rittlings. *prep* rittlings auf (+*dat*).

astringent [əˈstrɪndʒənt] *adj* zusammenziehend.

astrology [əˈstrolədʒɪ] *n* Astrologie *f*. **astrologer** *n* Astrologe *m*. **astrological** *adj* astrologisch.

astronaut [ˈæstrənɔːt] *n* Astronaut *m*.

astronomy [əˈstronəmɪ] *n* Astronomie *f*. **astronomer** *n* Astronom *m*. **astronomical** *adj* astronomisch.

astute [əˈstjuːt] *adj* scharfsinnig.

asunder [əˈsʌndə] *adv* auseinander.

asylum [əˈsaɪləm] *n* Asyl *neut*. **lunatic asylum** Irrenanstalt *f*. **political asylum** politisches Asyl *neut*.

at [æt] *prep* (*place*) in, zu, bei, an, auf; (*time*) um, zu, in; (*age, speed*) mit; (*price*) zu. **at school** in der Schule. **at four o'clock** um vier Uhr. **at my house** bei mir. **at home** zuhause. **at (age) 65** mit 65. **at Christmas** zu Weihnachten. **at peace** in Frieden.

ate [et] *V* **eat**.

atheist [ˈeɪθiːst] *n* Atheist *m*.

Athens [ˈæθinz] *n* Athen *neut*.

athlete [ˈæθliːt] *n* Athlet *m*. **athletic** *adj* athletisch. **athletics** *n* (Leicht)Athletik *f*.

Atlantic [ətˈlæntɪk] *n* Atlantik *m*.

atlas [ˈætləs] *n* Atlas *m*.

atmosphere [ˈætm əsfɪə] *n* Atmosphäre *f*. **atmospheric** *adj* atmosphärisch, Luft-.

atom [ˈætəm] *n* Atom *neut*. **atomic** *adj* Atom-. **atomic bomb** Atombombe *f*. **atomic power** Atomkraft *f*. **atomic reactor** Atomreaktor *m*.

atone [əˈtoun] *v* **atone for** büßen, wiedergutmachen. **atonement** *n* Buße *f*.

atrocious [əˈtrouʃəs] *adj* grausam, brutal; (*coll*) scheußlich. **atrocity** *n* Greueltat *f*.

attach [əˈtætʃ] *v* (*affix*) befestigen, anhängen; (*connect*) anschließen; (*to a letter*) beifügen. **be attached to** mögen, lieb haben. **attach oneself to** sich anschließen an. **attachment** *n* (*liking*) Anhänglichkeit *f*; (*fixture*) Anschluß *m*.

attaché [əˈtæʃeɪ] *n* Attaché. **attaché case** Aktentasche *f*.

attack [əˈtæk] *v* angreifen; (*criticize*) tadeln, kritisieren. *n* Angriff *m*. **heart attack** Herzanfall *m*.

attain [əˈteɪn] *v* erreichen, gelangen zu. **attainable** *adj* erreichbar.

attempt [əˈtempt] *v* versuchen, wagen. *n* Versuch *m*.

attend [əˈtempt] *v* versuchen, wagen. *n* Versuch *m*.

attend [əˈtend] *v* (*school*) besuchen; (*meeting*) beiwohnen (+*dat*); (*lecture*) hören. **attend to** sich kümmern um. **attendance** *n* Anwesenheit *f*. **good attendance** gute Teilnahme *f*. **attendant** *n* Wächter(in).

attention [əˈtenʃən] *n* Aufmerksamkeit *f*; (*care*) Pflege *f*; (*machine*) Wartung *f*. **pay attention to** aufpassen auf. **stand at attention** Haltung annehmen.

attic [ˈætɪk] *n* Dachkammer *f*.

attire [əˈtaɪə] *n* Kleidung *f*. *v* kleiden.

attitude [ˈætɪtjuːd] *n* Einstellung *f*, Verhalten *neut*.

attorney [əˈtɜːnɪ] *n* (*lawyer*) Rechtsanwalt *m*. **power of attorney** Vollmacht *f*.

attract [əˈtrækt] *v* anziehen; (*attention*) erregen. **attraction** *n* Anziehung *f*; (*charm*) Reiz *m*, Anziehungskraft *f*. **attractive** *adj* attraktiv.

attribute [əˈtrɪbjuːt; *n* ˈætrɪbjuːt] *v* zuschreiben (+*dat*). *n* Eigenschaft *f*. **attributable** *adj* zuzuschreiben (+*dat*).

attrition [əˈtrɪʃən] *n* Abnutzung *f*. **war of attrition** Zermürbungskrieg *m*.

aubergine [ˈoubəʒiːn] *n* Aubergine *f*.

auburn [ˈoːbən] *adj* kastanienbraun.

auction [ˈoːkʃən] *n* Auktion *f*, Versteigerung *f*. *v* versteigern. **auctioneer** *n* Versteigerer *m*.

audacious [ɔːˈdeɪʃəs] *adj* kühn. **audacity** *n* (*boldness*) Wagemut *m*; (*cheek*) Frechheit *f*.

audible [ˈɔːdəb] *adj* hörbar.

audience [ˈɔːdɪəns] *n* (*people*) Publikum *neut*, Zuhörer *pl*; (*interview*) Audienz *f*.

audiovisual [ɔːdɪəʊˈvɪʒuəl] *adj* audiovisuell.

audit [ˈɔːdɪt] *v* (Rechnungen) prüfen. *n* Rechnungsprüfung *f*. **auditor** *n* Rechnungsprüfer *m*.

audition [ɔːˈdɪʃən] *n* (*theatre*) Sprech-, Hörprobe *f*. *v* eine Hörprobe abnehmen.

auditorium [ɔːdɪˈtɔːrəm] *n* Hörsaal *m*.

augment [ɔːgˈment] *v* vermehren; (*grow*) zunehmen.

August [ˈɔːgəst] *n* August *m*.

aunt [aːnt] *n* Tante *f*.

au pair [ou ˈpeə] *n* Au-pair-Mädchen *neut*.

aura [ˈɔːrə] *n* Aura *f*; (*med*) Vorgefühl *neut*.

auspicious [ɔːˈspɪʃəs] *adj* günstig.

austere [ɔːˈstɪə] *adj* (*person*) streng; (*surroundings*) nüchtern. **austerity** *n* Strenge *f*.

Australia [ɔːˈstreɪljə] *n* Australien *neut*. **Australian** *n* Australier(in); *adj* australisch.

Austria [ˈɔːstrə] *n* Österreich *neut*. **Austrian** *n* Österreicher(in); *adj* österreichisch.

authentic [ɔːˈθentik] *adj* echt, authentisch. **authenticity** *n* Echtheit *f*.

author [ˈɔːθə] *n* (*writer*) Schriftsteller *m*, Autor *m*; (*of a particular item*) Verfasser *m*.

authority [ɔːˈθorɪti] *n* Autorität *f*; (*expert*) Fachmann *m*. **on good authority** aus guter Quelle. **the authorities** die Behörden *pl*. **authoritarian** *adj* autoritär.

authorize [ˈɔːθəraiz] *v* genehmigen, bevollmächtigen. **authorization** *n* Genehmigung *f*.

autism [ˈɔːtizəm] *n* Autismus *m*. **autistic** *adj* (*person*) autistisch.

autobiography [ɔːtoubaɪˈogrəfi] *n* Autobiographie *f*.

autocratic [ɔːtouˈkratik] *adj* autokratisch.

autograph [ˈɔːtəgraːf] *n* Autogramm *neut*. *v* unterschreiben.

automatic [ɔːtəˈmatik] *adj* automatisch, selbsttätig. **automatic dialling** automatische Wahl *f*. **automatic transmission** Automatik *f*.

automobile [ˈɔːtəm əbiːl] *n* Wagen *m*, Auto *neut*.

autonomous [ɔːˈtonəm əs] *adj* autonom, unabhängig. **autonomy** *n* Autonomie *f*.

autopsy [ˈɔːtopsi] *n* Autopsie *f*.

autumn [ˈɔːtəm] *n* Herbst *m*. **autumnal** *adj* herbstlich, Herbst-.

auxilliary [ɔːgˈzɪljər] *adj* Hilfs-, Zusatz-, zusätzlich. *n* Hilfskraft *f*.

avail [əˈveɪl] *n* **to no avail** nutzlos. *v* **avail oneself of** Gebrauch machen von, sich bedienen (+*gen*).

available [əˈveɪbl] *adj* (*obtainable*) erhältlich; (*usable*) verfügbar. **be available** zur Verfügung stehen. **availability** *n* Erhältlichkeit *f*.

avalanche [ˈavəlaːnʃ] *n* Lawine *f*.

avant-garde [avãˈgaːd] *adj* avantgardistisch. *n* Avantgarde *f*.

avarice [ˈavərɪs] *n* Geiz *m*. **avaricious** *adj* geizig.

avenge [əˈvendʒ] *v* rächen. **avenge oneself on** sich rächen an.

avenue [ˈavinjuː] *n* Allee *f*.

average [ˈavərɪdʒ] *n* Durchschnitt *m*. *adj* durchschnittlich, Durchschnitts-. **on average** im Durchschnitt.

averse [əˈvəːs] *adj* abgeneigt. **aversion** *n* Abneigung *f*.

avert [əˈvəːt] *v* (*gaze*) abwenden; (*danger*) verhindern.

aviary [ˈeɪvər] *n* Vogelhaus *neut*.

aviation [eɪvɪˈeɪʃən] *n* Luftfahrt *f*. **aviator** *n* Flieger *m*.

avid [ˈavil] *adj* gierig (auf). **avidity** *n* Begierde *f*.

avocado [avəˈkaːdou] *n* Avocado(birne) *f*.

avoid [əˈvoid] *v* vermeiden; (*person*) aus dem Wege gehen (+ *dat*). **avoidable** *adj* vermeidbar.

await [əˈweɪt] *v* erwarten.

*awake [əˈweɪk] *v* (*wake up*) aufwachen; (*rouse*) wecken; (*arouse*) erwecken. **be awake** wach sein. **wide awake** munter. **awaken** *v* erwecken.

award [əˈwoːd] *v* verleihen. *n* Preis *m*.

aware [əˈweə] *adj* bewußt (+ *gen*). **awareness** *n* Bewußtsein *neut*.

away [əˈweɪ] *adv* weg, fort. *adj* (*absent*) abwesend. *she is away* sie ist verreist.

awe [ɔː] *n* Ehrfurcht *f*. **awesome** *adj* (*impressive*) imponierend; (*frightening*) erschreckend.

awful ['ɔːfʊl] *adj* furchtbar.

awhile [ə'waɪl] *adv* eine Weile, eine Zeitlang.

awkward ['ɔːkwəd] *adj* (*clumsy*) ungeschickt, linkisch; (*embarrassing*) peinlich; (*contrary*) widerspenstig.

awning ['ɔːnɪŋ] *n* Markise *f.*

awoke [ə'wəʊk] *V* **awake**.

awoken [ə'wəʊkn] *V* **awake**.

axe *or US* **ax** [aks] *n* Axt *f.*

axiom ['aksɪəm] *n* Axiom *neut.*

axis ['aksɪs] *n* Achse *f.*

axle ['aksl] *n* Achse *f.*

B

babble ['babl] *v* plappern; (*water*) plätschern.

baboon [bə'buːn] *n* Pavian *m.*

baby ['beɪbɪ] *n* Baby *neut*, Säugling *m.* **baby carriage** Kinderwagen *m.* **babyish** *adj* kindisch. **babysit** *v* babysitten. **babysitter** *n* Babysitter(in) *m, f.*

bachelor ['batʃələ] *n* Junggeselle *m.*

back [bak] *n* (*anat*) Rücken *m*; (*rear*) Rückseite *f*; (*football*) Verteidiger *m. adj* hinter, Hinter-. *adv* zurück. *v* (*bet on*) wetten auf; (*support*) unterstützen; (*reverse*) rückwärts fahren. **back out** *v* sich zurückziehen. **back up** *v* (*comp*) sicherstellen.

backache ['bakeɪk] *n* Rückenschmerz *m.*

backbone ['bakbəʊn] *n* Rückgrat *neut*, Wirbelsäule *f.*

backdate [ˌbak'deɪt] *v* zurückdatieren.

backer ['bakə] *n* Förderer *m.*

backfire [ˌbak'faɪə] *v* (*car*) fehlzünden; (*plan*) fehlschlagen.

background ['bakɡraʊnd] *n* Hintergrund *m.*

backhand ['bakhand] *n* (*sport*) Rückhandschlag *m.*

backlash ['baklaʃ] *n* (politische) Reaktion *f.*

backlog ['bakløɡ] *n* Rückstand *m.*

backside ['baksaɪd] *n* Hinterteil *neut*, Hintern *m.*

backstage ['baksteɪdʒ] *adj, adv* hinter den Kulissen.

backstroke ['bakstrəʊk] *n* Rückenschwimmen *neut.*

backup ['bakʌp] *n* (*support*) Unterstützung *f*; (*comp*) Datensicherung *f*, Backup *neut.* **backup system** Bereitschaftssystem *neut.*

backward ['bakwəd] *adj* zurückgeblieben.

backwards ['bakwədz] *adv* zurück, rückwärts.

backwater ['bakwɔːtə] *n* Stauwasser *neut.*

backyard [bakˈjɑːd] *n* Hinterhof *m.*

bacon ['beɪkən] *n* (Schinken)Speck *m.*

bacteria [bakˈtɪərɪə] *pl n* Bakterien *pl.*

bad [bad] *adj* schlecht, schlimm; (*naughty*) böse; (*food*) faul, verfault. **bad-tempered** mißgelaunt.

bade [bad] *V* **bid**.

badge [badʒ] *n* Abzeichen *neut.*

badger ['badʒə] *n* Dachs *m. v* plagen.

badminton ['badmɪntən] *n* Federballspiel *neut.*

baffle ['bafl] *v* verblüffen.

bag [baɡ] *n* Beutel *m*, Sack *m*; (*paper*) Tüte *f*; (*handbag*) Tasche *f.* **baggage** *n* Gepäck *neut.* **baggy** *adj* bauschig. **bagpipes** *pl n* Dudelsack *m sing.*

bail¹ [beɪl] *n* (*security*) Kaution *f. v* gegen Kaution freilassen.

bail² *or* **bale** [beɪl] *v* **bail out** (*boat*) ausschöpfen; (*from aeroplane*) abspringen; (*help*) aushelfen.

bailiff ['beɪlɪf] *n* Gerichtsvollzieher *m.*

bait [beɪt] *n* Köder *m. v* ködern; (*tease*) quälen.

bake [beɪk] *v* backen. **baker** *n* Bäcker *m.* **bakery** Bäckerei *f.*

balance ['baləns] *n* Gleichgewicht *neut*; (*scales*) Waage *f*; (*of account*) Saldo *m*; (*amount left*) Rest *m.* **balance sheet** Bilanz *f. v* ausgleichen.

balcony ['balkənɪ] *n* Balkon *m.*

bald [bɔːld] *adj* kahl.

bale¹ [beɪl] *n* Ballen *m.*

bale² [beɪl] *V* **bail²**.

ball¹ [bɔːl] *n* (*sport*) Ball *m*; (*sphere*) Kugel *f.*

ball² [bɔːl] *n* (*dance*) Ball *m.*

ballad ['baləd] *n* Ballade *f.*

ballast ['baləst] *n* Ballast *neut.*

ball bearing *n* Kugellager *neut.*

ballet ['baleɪ] *n* Ballett *neut.* **ballet dancer** Balletttänzer(in).

ballistic [bə'listik] *adj* ballistisch.

balloon [bə'luːn] *n* Ballon *m*; (*toy*) Luftballon *m*.

ballot [ˈbalət] *n* Abstimmung *f*.

ball-point pen *n* Kugelschreiber *m*.

ballroom [ˈboːlrum] *n* Tanzsaal *m*.

balmy [ˈbaːmi] *adj* sanft, lindernd.

bamboo [bamˈbuː] *n* Bambus *m*.

ban [ban] *v* verbieten. *n* Verbot *neut*.

banal [bəˈnaːl] *adj* banal.

banana [bəˈnaːnə] *n* Banane *f*.

band¹ [band] *n* Gruppe *f*; (*music*) Band *f*, Kapelle *f*; (*criminals*) Bande *f*. *v* **band together** sich vereinen.

band² [band] *n* (*strip*) Band *neut*, Binde *f*.

bandage [ˈbandiʒ] *n* Bandage *f*, Binde *f*. *v* bandagieren.

bandit [ˈbandit] *n* Bandit *m*.

bandy [ˈbandi] *adj* krummbeinig. *v* **bandy words** streiten.

bang [baŋ] *n* Knall *m*. *v* (*sound*) knallen; (*strike*) schlagen; (*door*) zuknallen.

bangle [ˈbaŋgl] *n* (Arm)Spange *f*.

banish [ˈbaniʃ] *v* verbannen.

banister [ˈbanistə] *n* Treppengeländer *neut*.

banjo [ˈbandʒou] *n* Banjo *neut*.

bank¹ [baŋk] *n* (*river*) Ufer *neut*; (*sand*) Bank *f*.

bank² [baŋk] *n* (*comm*) Bank *f*. *v* (*money*) auf die Bank bringen. **bank on** sich verlassen auf. **bank account** *n* Bankkonto *neut*. **banker** *n* Bankier *m*. **banker's card** Scheckkarte *f*. **bank holiday** *n* Feiertag *m*. **banknote** *n* Banknote *f*.

bankrupt [ˈbaŋkrʌpt] *adj* bankrott. *n* Bankrotteur *m*. **go bankrupt** Bankrott machen. **bankruptcy** Bankrott *m*.

banner [ˈbanə] *n* Banner *neut*.

banquet [ˈbaŋkwit] *n* Bankett *neut*.

banter [ˈbantə] *v* necken. *n* Neckerei *f*.

baptism [ˈbaptizəm] *n* Taufe *f*. **baptize** *v* taufen.

bar [baː] *n* (*drink*) Bar *f*; (*rod*) Stange *f*, Barre *f*; (*chocolate*) Tafel *f*. **bar code** Streifencode *m*, Streifenkode *m*, Streifenetikett *neut*. *v* (*door*) verriegeln; (*ban*) verbieten.

barbarian [baːˈbeərən] *n* Barbar *m*. **barbaric** *adj* barbarisch.

barbecue [ˈbaːbikjuː] *n* Barbecue *neut*. *v* am Spieß braten.

barbed wire [baːbd] *n* Stacheldraht *m*.

barber [ˈbaːbə] *n* Barbier *m*, Friseur *m*.

barbiturate [baːˈbitjurət] *n* Barbitursäure *f*.

bare [beə] *adj* nackt; (*trees*) kahl; (*empty*) leer; (*mere*) bloß. *v* entblößen. **barefoot** *adj* barfuß. **bare-headed** *adj* mit bloßem Kopf. **barely** *adv* kaum.

bargain [ˈbaːgin] *n* (*good buy*) Gelegenheitskauf *m*. (*deal*) Geschäft *neut*. *v* feilschen. **collective bargaining** tarifverhandlungen *pl*. **into the bargain** obendrein.

barge [baːdʒ] *n* Lastkahn *m*. *v* **barge in** hereinstürzen.

baritone [ˈbaritoun] *n* Bariton *m*.

bark¹ [baːk] *v* (*dog*) bellen. *n* Bellen *neut*.

bark² [baːk] *n* (*tree*) Rinde *f*.

barley [ˈbaːli] *n* (*crop*) Gerste *f*; (*in soup*) Graupen *pl*.

barmaid [ˈbaːmeid] *n* Barmädchen *neut*.

barman [ˈbaːman] *n* Barmann *m*.

barn [baːn] *n* Scheune *f*.

barometer [bəˈromitə] *n* Barometer *neut*.

baron [ˈbarən] *n* Baron *m*.

baronet [ˈbarənit] *n* Baronet *m*.

baroque [bəˈrok] *adj* barock.

barracks [ˈbarəks] *n* Kaserne *f*.

barrage [ˈbaraːʒ] *n* (*dam*) Damm *m*; (*mil*) Sperrfeuer *neut*; (*of questions*) Flut *f*.

barrel [ˈbarəl] *n* Faß *neut*.

barren [ˈbarən] *adj* ruchtbar; (*desolate*) wüst.

barricade [barikeid] *n* Barrikade *f*. *v* verbarrikadieren.

barrier [ˈbariə] *n* Schranke *f*.

barrister [ˈbaristə] *n* Rechtsanwalt *m*.

barrow [ˈbarou] *n* Schubkarren *m*.

bartender [ˈbaːtendə] *n* Barmann *m*.

barter [ˈbaːtə] *n* Tauschhandel *m*. *v* tauschen; (*haggle*) feilschen.

base¹ [beis] *n* (*bottom*) Fuß *m*, Boden *m*; (*basis*) Basis *f*; (*mil*) Stützpunkt *m*; (*chem*) Base *f*. *v* gründen. **be based on** basieren auf (+*dat*).

base² [beis] *adj* (*vile*) gemein.

baseball [ˈbeisboːl] *n* Baseball *m*.

basement [ˈbeismənt] *n* Kellergeschoß *neut*.

bash [baʃ] *v* (*heftig*) schlagen. **have a bash!** versuch's mal!

bashful [ˈbaʃful] *adj* schüchtern.

basic ['beisik] *adj* grundsätzlich, Grund-. **basically** *adv* im Grunde.

basil ['baz] *n* Basilienkraut *neut*.

basin ['beisin] *n* (*washbasin, river basin*) Becken *neut*; (*dish*) Schale *f*.

basis ['beisis] *n* Basis *f*, Grundlage *f*.

bask [bask] *v* sich sonnen.

basket ['ba:skit] *n* Korb *m*. **basketball** *n* Basketball *m*.

bass[1] [beis] *n* (*music*) Baß *m*. **bass guitar** Baßgitarre *f*. **double bass** Kontrabaß *m*.

bass[2] [bas] *n* Seebarsch *m*.

bassoon [bə'su:n] *n* Fagott *neut*.

bastard ['ba:stəd] *n* Bastard *m*; (*derog*) Schweinehund *m*.

baste [beist] *v* (*meat*) mit Fett begießen.

bastion ['bastʃən] *n* Bollwerk *neut*.

bat[1] [bat] *n* (*sport*) Schlagholz *neut*. *v* schlagen *without batting an eyelid* ohne mit der Wimper zu zucken.

bat[2] [bat] *n* (*zool*) Fledermaus *f*.

batch [batʃ] *n* Stoß *m*.

bath [ba:θ] *n* Bad *neut*. *v* baden. **have** *or* **take a bath** ein Bad nehmen. **bathroom** *n* Badezimmer *neut*. **bathtub** *n* Badewanne *f*. **baths** *pl n* Schwimmbad *neut sing*.

baton ['batn] *n* (*music*) Taktstock *m*.

battalion [bə'taljən] *n* Bataillon *neut*.

batter[1] ['batə] *v* (*strike*) verprügeln.

batter[2] ['batə] *n* (*cookery*) Schlagteig *m*.

battery ['batəri] *n* Batterie *f*. **battery farm** Legebatterie *f*.

battle ['batl] *n* Schlacht *f*; (*fig*) Kampf *m*. *v* kämpfen. **battlefield** *n* Schlachtfeld *neut*. **battleship** Schlachtschiff *neut*.

bawl [bo:l] *v* brüllen, heulen.

bay[1] [bei] *n* (*coast*) Bai *f*, Bucht *f*.

bay[2] [bei] *n* **keep at bay** abwehren.

bay[3] [bei] *n* (*tree*) Lorbeer *m*. **bay leaf** Lorbeerblatt *neut*.

bayonet ['beiənit] *n* Bajonett *neut*. *v* bajonettieren.

bay window *n* Erkerfenster *neut*.

bazaar [bə'za:] *n* Basar *m*.

***be** [bi:] *v* sein; (*be situated*) liegen, stehen. *v aux* (*in passive*) werden. **There is/are** es gibt. *the book is on the table* das Buch liegt auf dem Tisch. *I want to be an engineer* ich will Ingenieur werden. *how much is that car?* wieviel kostet der Wagen

beach [bi:tʃ] *n* Strand *m*. *v* (*boat*) auf den Strand setzen.

beacon ['bi:kən] *n* Leuchtfeuer *neut*.

bead [bi:d] *n* Perle *f*.

beak [bi:k] *n* Schnabel *m*.

beaker ['bi:kə] *n* Becher *m*.

beam [bi:m] *n* (*wood*) Balken *m*; (*light*) Strahl *m*. *v* strahlen.

bean [bi:n] *n* Bohne *f*.

***bear**[1] [beə] *v* (*carry, yield*) tragen, (*tolerate*) ertragen, leiden; (*child*) gebären. **bring pressure to bear on** Druck ausüben auf. **bear right** sich nach rechts halten.

bear[2] [beə] *n* (*zool*) Bär *m*.

beard [biəd] *n* Bart *m*.

bearing ['beəriŋ] *n* (*posture*) Haltung *f*; (*relation*) Beziehung *f*; (*tech*) Lager *neut*. **bearings** *pl n* Orientierung *f sing*.

beast [bi:st] *n* Tier *neut*; (*cattle*) Vieh *neut*; (*person*) Bestie *f*. **beastly** *adj* (*coll*) scheußlich.

***beat** [bi:t] *v* schlagen. *n* (*stroke*) Schlag *m*; (*music*) Rhythmus *m*; (*policeman's*) Revier *neut*.

beaten ['bi:tn] *V* beat.

beautiful ['bju:təful] *adj* schön. **beautifully** *adv* ausgezeichnet. **beauty** *n* Schönheit *f*.

beaver ['bi:və] *n* Biber *m*.

became [bi'keim] *V* become.

because [bi'koz] *conj* weil. **because of** wegen (+*gen*).

***become** [bi'kʌm] *v* werden. **becoming** *adj* passend.

bed [bed] *n* Bett *neut*; (*garden*) Beet *neut*. **bed and breakfast** (*service*) Zimmer *neut* mit Frühstück, (*establishment*) (private) Frühstückspension *f*. **river bed** Flußbett *neut*. **seabed** *n* Meeresboden *m*. **bedclothes** *pl n* Bettwäsche *f sing*. **bedridden** *adj* bettlägerig. **bedroom** *n* Schlafzimmer *neut*. **bedsitter** *n* Einzimmerwohnung *f*. **bedspread** *n* Bettdecke *f*. **bedtime** *n* Schlafenzeit *f*.

bee [bi:] *n* Biene *f*.

beech [bi:tʃ] *n* Buche *f*.

beef [bi:f] *n* Rindfleisch *neut*. **beefburger** *n* Hamburger *m*.

beehive ['bi:haiv] *n* Bienenstock *m*.

been [bi:n] *V* be.

beer [biə] *n* Bier *neut*.

beetle ['bi:tl] *n* Käfer *m*.

beetroot ['biːtruːt] n rote Bete f.

before [bɪfɔː] conj bevor, ehe; prep vor; adv (time) zuvor, früher; (ahead) voran. **beforehand** adv im voraus.

befriend [bɪfrend] v befreunden.

beg [beg] v (for money) betteln; (beseech) bitten. **beggar** n Bettler m.

began [bɪgan] V **begin.**

***begin** [bɪgɪn] v beginnen, anfangen. **beginner** n Anfänger m. **beginning** n Anfang m, Beginn m.

begrudge [bɪgrʌdʒ] v mißgönnen.

begun [bɪgʌn] V **begin.**

behalf [bɪhaːf] n **on behalf of** im Namen von. **on my behalf** um meinetwillen.

behave [bɪheɪv] v sich verhalten, sich betragen; (behave well) sich gut benehmen. **behave yourself!** benimm dich! **behaviour** n Benehmen neut, Verhalten neut.

behind [bɪhaɪnd] prep hinter. adv (in the rear) hinten; (back) zurück; (behind schedule) im Rückstand. n (coll) Hinterteil neut. **behindhand** adv im Rückstand.

***behold** [bɪhould] v sehen, betrachten. **beholder** m Betrachter m.

beige [beʒ] adj beige.

being ['biːɪŋ] n (existence) (Da)Sein neut; (creature) Wesen neut, Geschöpf neut. **for the time being** einstweilen. **come into being** enstehen. **human being** Mensch m.

Belarus ['belərʌs] n Belarußland, Weißrußland neut. **Belarussian** n Belarusse m, Belarussin f; adj belarussisch

belated [bɪleɪtɪd] adj verspätet.

belch [beltʃ] v rülpsen; (fumes) ausspeien. n Rülpsen neut.

belfry ['belfrɪ] n Glockenturm m.

Belgium ['beldʒəm] n Belgien neut. **Belgian** n Belgier(in). adj belgisch.

belief [bɪliːf] n Glaube m; (conviction) Überzeugung f. **believe** v glauben (+dat). **believe in** glauben an (+ acc). **believable** adj glaublich. **believer** n Gläubige(r).

bell [bel] n Glocke f; (on door) Klingel m.

belligerent [bɪliːdʒərənt] adj (country) kriegführend; (person) aggressiv.

bellow ['belou] v brüllen. n Gebrüll neut.

bellows ['belouz] n Blasebalg m.

belly ['belɪ] n Bauch m.

belong [bɪlɒŋ] v gehören (+dat); (be a member) angehören (+dat). **belongings** pl n

Eigentum neut sing; Sachen pl.

beloved [bɪlʌvɪd] adj geliebt. n Geliebte(r).

below [bɪlou] prep unter. adv unten.

belt [belt] n Gürtel m. v (coll) verprügeln. **belt up!** halt die Klappe!

bemused [bɪmjuːzd] adj verwirrt.

bench [bentʃ] n Bank f; (work table) Arbeitstisch m.

***bend** [bend] v biegen; (be bent) sich beugen. n Kurve f.

beneath [bɪniːθ] prep unter.

benefactor ['benəfaktə] n Wohltäter m. **benefactress** n Wohltäterin f.

beneficent [bɪnefɪsənt] adj wohltätig.

beneficial [benəˈfɪʃəl] adj vorteilhaft, nützlich.

benefit ['benəfɪt] n Nutzen m, Gewinn m. v nützen. **benefit from** Nutzen ziehen aus.

benevolence [bɪnevələns] n Wohltätigkeit f. **benevolent** adj wohltätig.

benign [bɪnaɪn] adj gütig; (tumour) gutartig.

bent [bent] V **bend.** adj krumm, verbogen; (dishonest) unehrlich. **be bent on** versessen sein auf (+acc).

bequeath [bɪkwiːð] v vermachen.

beret ['bereɪ] n Baskenmütze f.

berry ['berɪ] n Beere f.

berserk [bəˈsəːk] adj **go berserk** wild werden, toben, (coll) ausflippen.

berth [bəːθ] n (mooring) Liegeplatz m; (bunk) Koje f. **give a wide berth to** einen weiten Bogen machen um (+acc).

beside [bɪsaɪd] prep neben. **be beside oneself with** außer sich sein vor (+dat). **besides** prep außer. adv außerdem.

besiege [bɪsiːdʒ] v belagern.

best [best] adj best. adv am besten, bestens. n das Beste. **do one's best** sein Bestes tun. **at best** höchstens. **best man** Trauzeuge m.

bestial ['bestɪəl] adj bestialisch.

bestow [bɪstou] v **bestow upon** schenken (+ dat).

bestseller [best'selə] n Bestseller m.

bet [bet] v wetten. n Wette f.

betray [bɪtreɪ] v verraten. **betrayal** n Verrat m.

better ['betə] adj, adv besser. n das Bessere. v verbessern. **get the better of** übertreffen. **better oneself** sich verbessern.

between [bɪˈtwiːn] *prep* zwischen. *adv* dazwischen. **between you and me** unter uns.

beverage [ˈbevərɪdʒ] *n* Getränk *neut.*

*beware [bɪˈweə] *v* sich hüten vor (+ *dat*). **beware of the dog** Vorsicht Vorsicht–bissiger Hund!

bewilder [bɪˈwɪldə] *v* verwirren, verblüffen.

beyond [bɪˈjɒnd] *prep* uber ... hinaus, jenseits (+ *gen*); mehr als. *adv* jenseits, darüber hinaus. **beyond compare** unvergleichlich. *he is beyond help* ihm ist nicht mehr zu helfen.

bias [ˈbaɪəs] *n* Neigung *f.* **biased** *adj* voreingenommen.

bib [bɪb] *n* Latz *m.*

Bible [ˈbaɪb] *n* Bibel *f.*

bibliography [bɪblɪˈɒɡrəfɪ] *n* Bibliographie *f.*

biceps [ˈbaɪseps] *n* Bizeps *m.*

bicker [ˈbɪkə] *v* zanken.

bicycle [ˈbaɪsɪkl] *n* Fahrrad *neut.*

*bid [bɪd] *v* (*offer*) bieten; (*cards*) reizen. *n* (*offer*) Angebot *neut*; (*attempt*) Versuch *m.* **bid someone welcome** jemanden willkommen heißen. **bidder** *n* Bieter *m.*

bidden [ˈbɪdn] *V* bid.

bidet [ˈbiːdeɪ] *n* Bidet *neut.*

biennial [baɪˈenɪəl] *adj* zweijährig.

big [bɪɡ] *adj* groß. **big-headed** *adj* eingebildet. **big-headed** *adj* großherzig.

bigamy [ˈbɪɡəmɪ] *n* Bigamie *f.*

bigot [ˈbɪɡət] *n* Frömmler *m.* **bigoted** *adj* bigott. **bigotry** *n* Bigotterie *f.*

bikini [bɪˈkiːnɪ] *n* Bikini *m.*

bilateral [baɪˈlætərəl] *adj* bilateral.

bilingual [baɪˈlɪŋɡwəl] *adj* zweisprachig.

bill¹ [bɪl] *n* (*in restaurant*) Rechnung *f*; Banknote *f*; (*comm*) Wechsel *m*; (*pol*) Gesetzentwurf *m*; (*poster*) Plakat *neut. v* fakturieren. **billboard** *n* Plakattafel *f.*

bill² [bɪl] *n* (*beak*) Schnabel *m.*

billiards [ˈbɪljədz] *n* Billard *neut.*

billion [ˈbɪljən] *n* Billion *f*; (*US*) Milliarde *f.*

bin [bɪn] *n* Kiste *f*; (*dustbin*) Mülleimer *m.*

binary [ˈbaɪnərɪ] *adj* binär.

*bind [baɪnd] *v* (*tie*) binden; (*oblige*) verpflichten. **binding** *adj* bindend. *n* (*book*) Einband *m.*

binge [bɪndʒ] *n* (*eating*) Fressorgie *f*; (*drinking*) Besäufnis *f*, Zechgelage, Saufgelage *neut.*

binoculars [bɪˈnɒkjuləz] *pl n* Feldstecher *m.*

biodegradable [ˌbaɪəudɪˈɡreɪdəb] *adj* biologisch abbaubar.

biography [baɪˈɒɡrəfɪ] *n* Biographie *f.* **biographer** *n* Biograph *m.* **biographical** *adj* biographisch.

biology [baɪˈɒlədʒɪ] *n* Biologie *f.* **biological** *adj* biologisch. **biologist** *n* Biologe *m.*

birch [bəːtʃ] *n* Birke *f*; (*rod*) Birkenrute *f.*

bird [bəːd] *n* Vogel *m.*

Biro® [ˈbaɪrəu] *n* Kugelschreiber *m*, (*fam*) Kuli *m.*

birth [bəːθ] *n* Geburt *f.* **date of birth** Geburtsdatum *neut.* **birth certificate** Geburtsurkunde *f.* **birth control** Geburtenregelung *f.* **birthday** Geburtstag *m.* **birthmark** Muttermal *neut.*

biscuit [ˈbɪskɪt] *n* Biskuit *m*, Keks *m.*

bisexual [baɪˈseksjuəl] *adj* bisexuell.

bishop [ˈbɪʃəp] *n* Bischof *m.*

bison [ˈbaɪsən] *n* Bison *m.*

bit¹ [bɪt] *V* **bite**. *n* (*morsel*) Bißchen, Stückchen *neut*: *a bit of bread* ein Stückchen Brot. *a bit frightened* ein bißchen ängstlich.

bit² [bɪt] *n* (*harness*) Gebiß *neut*; (*drill*) Bohreisen *neut.*

bitch [bɪtʃ] *n* Hündin *f*; (*woman*) Weibsstück *neut.*

*bite [baɪt] *v* beißen. *n* (*mouthful*) Bissen *m*; (*wound*) Biß *m.* **bite to eat** Imbiß *m.*

bitten [ˈbɪtn] *V* **bite**.

bitter [ˈbɪtə] *v* bitter; (*weather*) scharf. **to the bitter end** bis zum bitteren Ende. **bitterness** *n* Bitterkeit *f.*

bizarre [bɪˈzaː] *adj* bizarr, seltsam.

black [blæk] *adj* schwarz. *n* (*colour*) Schwarz *neut*; (*person*) Schwarze(r).

blackberry [ˈblækbərɪ] *n* Brombeere *f.*

blackbird [ˈblækbəːd] *n* Amsel *f.*

blackboard [ˈblækbɔːd] *n* Wandtafel *f.*

blackcurrant [ˌblækˈkʌrənt] *n* schwarze Johannisbeere *f.*

blacken [ˈblækn] *v* schwarz machen.

black eye *n* blaues Auge *neut.*

blackhead [ˈblækhed] *n* Mitesser *m.*

blackleg [ˈblækleɡ] *n* Streikbrecher *m.*

blackmail [ˈblækmeɪl] *n* Erpressung *f.* **blackmailer** *n* Erpresser *m.*

black market *n* schwarzer Markt *m.* **black marketeer** Schwarzhändler *m.*

black out v (*darken*) verdunkeln; (*faint*) ohnmächtig werden. **black-out** n Verdunkelung f; Ohnmachtsanfall m; (*elec*) Stromausfall m.

black pudding n Blutwurst f.

blacksmith ['blæksmiθ] n Schmied m.

bladder ['blædə] n Blase f.

blade [bleid] n (*razor, knife*) Klinge f; (*grass*) Halm m; (*tech*) Blatt neut; (*propellor*) Flügel m.

blame [bleim] v tadeln, die Schuld geben (+ dat). n Schuld f, Tadel m. *I am to blame for this* ich bin daran schuld. **blameless** adj untadelig.

blancmange [blə'mõʒ] n Pudding m.

bland [blænd] adj sanft, mild.

blank [blæŋk] adj leer, unausgefüllt. n (*form*) Formular neut; (*cartridge*) Platzpatrone f. **blank cheque** Blankoscheck m.

blanket ['blæŋkit] n Decke f. adj Gesamt-, allgemein.

blare [bleə] v schmettern. n Schmettern neut.

blaspheme [blæs'fiːm] v lästern. **blasphemy** n Gotteslästerung f.

blast [blɑːst] n Explosion f; (*of wind*) (heftiger) Windstoß m. v sprengen.

blatant ['bleitənt] adj offenkundig.

blaze [bleiz] n Brand neut, Feuer neut. v lodern.

blazer ['bleizə] n Blazer m.

bleach [bliːtʃ] v bleichen. n Bleichmittel neut.

bleak [bliːk] adj kahl; (*fig*) trostlos.

bleat [bliːt] v (*sheep*) blöken; (*goat*) meckern. n Blöken neut, Meckern neut.

bled [bled] V **bleed**.

***bleed** [bliːd] v bluten; (*brakes, radiators*) entlüften. **bleeding** adj blutend.

blemish ['blemiʃ] n Makel m.

blend [blend] v mischen. n Mischung f.

bless [bles] v segnen. **blessing** n Segen m.

blew [bluː] V **blow**[1].

blight [blait] n Verschandelung f, (*crops*) Braunfäule f. v vereiteln.

blind [blaind] adj blind; (*corner*) unübersichtlich. n (*window*) Rouleau neut. v blenden; (*fig*) verblenden. **blind alley** Sackgasse f. **blindfold** v die Augen verbinden (+ dat). adv mit verbundenen Augen.

blink [bliŋk] v blinzeln.

bliss [blis] n Wonne f. **blissful** glückselig.

blister ['blistə] n Blase f.

blizzard ['blizəd] n Schneesturm m.

blob [blɔb] n Tropfen m.

bloc [blɔk] n Block m.

block [blɔk] n (*wood*) Klotz m; (*stone*) Block m; (*US*) Häuserblock m; (*in pipe*) Verstopfung f; (*barrier*) Sperre f. v blockieren; verstopfen. **writing block** Schreibblock m. **blockade** n Blockade f. **blockage** n Verstopfung f.

bloke [bləuk] n Kerl m.

blond [blɔnd] adj blond. **blonde** n Blondine f.

blood [blʌd] n Blut neut. **in cold blood** kaltblütig. **blood clot** Blutgerinnsel neut. **blood pressure** Blutdruck m. **blood test** Blutuntersuchung f. **bloodthirsty** adj blutdurstig. **blood transfusion** Blutübertragung f. **blood vessel** Blutgefäß neut. **bloody** adj blutig; (*coll*) verdammt.

bloom [bluːm] v blühen. n Blüte f.

blossom ['blɔsəm] n Blüte f. v blühen.

blot [blɔt] n Fleck m; (*of ink*) Tintenklecks m. v (*make dirty*) beschmieren. **blot out** auslöschen.

blotch [blɔtʃ] n Fleck m; Klecks m.

blotting paper n Löschpapier neut.

blouse [blauz] n Bluse f.

***blow**[1] [bləu] v blasen; (*of wind*) wehen; (*fuse*) durchbrennen. **blow-dry** v (*hair*) föhnen. **blow over** vorbeigehen. **blow up** (*explode*) sprengen. **blow the horn** (*mot*) hupen. **blow one's nose** sich die Nase putzen.

blow[2] [bləu] n Schlag m; (*misfortune*) Unglück neut.

blowlamp ['bləulæmp] n Lötlampe f.

blown [bləun] V **blow**[1].

blowout ['bləuaut] n (*mot*) geplatzter Reifen m, Reifenpanne f.

blubber ['blʌbə] n Walfischspeck m.

blue [bluː] adj blau; (*depressed*) niedergeschlagen. n Blau neut. **bluebell** n Glockenblume f. **blueberry** n Heidelbeere f. **bluebottle** n Schmeißfliege f. **blue chip** (*stock exchange*) Spitzenpapier neut; adj Spitzen-. **the blues** Blues m sing.

bluff [blʌf] v bluffen. n Bluff m.

blunder ['blʌndə] n (dummer) Fehler m,

Schnitzer *m*. *v* (*stumble*) stolpern; (*make mistake*) einen Schnitzer machen.

blunt [blʌnt] *adj* stumpf. *v* stumpf machen; (*enthusiasm*) abstumpfen.

blur [blɜː] *v* verwischen, verschmieren. **blurred** *adj* verschwommen.

blush [blʌʃ] *v* erröten. *n* Erröten *neut*.

boar [bɔː] *n* Eber *m*. **wild boar** Wildschwein *m*.

board [bɔːd] *n* (*wooden*) Brett *neut*; (*comm*) Aufsichtsrat *m*. *v* (*train*) einsteigen in (+ *acc*). **board and lodging** Unterkunft und Verpflegung *f*. **boarding house** Pension *f*. **boarding school** Internat *neut*.

boast [bəust] *v* prahlen, angeben. *n* Prahlerei *f*. **boaster** *n* Prahler *m*.

boat [bəut] *n* Boot *neut*. **in the same boat** in der gleichen Lage.

bob [bob] *v* sich auf-und abbewegen; (*hair*) kurz schneiden.

bobbin ['bobin] *n* Spule *f*.

bobsleigh ['bobslei] *n* Bobsleigh *m*.

bodice ['bodis] *n* Mieder *neut*.

body ['bodi] *n* Körper, Leib *m*; (*corpse*) Leiche *f*; (*of people*) Gruppe *f*; (*car*) Karosserie *f*. **bodily** *adj* körperlich.

bog [bog] *n* Sumpf *m*. *v* **get bogged down** steckenbleiben. **boggy** *adj* sumpfig.

bogus ['bəugəs] *adj* falsch, unecht.

bohemian [bə'hiːmiən] *adj* (*fig*) zigeunerhaft, ungebunden. *n* (*fig*) Bohemien *m*.

boil[1] [boil] *v* kochen. **boiler** *n* Kessel *m*. **boiling** *adj* kochend.

boil[2] [boil] *n* (*sore*) Furunkel *m*.

boisterous ['boistərəs] *adj* ungestüm, laut.

bold [bəuld] *adj* kühn, keck; (*cheeky*) frech; (*typeface*) fett. **boldness** *n* Kühnheit *f*.

bollard ['bolɑːd] *n* Poller *m*.

bolster ['bəulstə] *n* Kissen *neut*. **bolster up** (*fig*) unterstützen.

bolt [bəult] *n* (*door*) Riegel *m*; (*screw*) Bolzen *m*; (*lightning*) Blitzstrahl *m*; (*cloth*) Rolle *f*. *v* (*door*) verriegeln; (*attach with bolts*) anbolzen; (*food*) hinunterschlingen; (*dash*) (*hastig*) fliehen.

bomb [bom] *n* Bombe *f*. *v* bombardieren. **go down a bomb** einen Bombenerfolg haben. **bombard** *v* bombardieren. **bombardment** *n* Beschießung *f*. **bomber** *n* (*aeroplane*) Bombenflugzeug *neut*. **bombing** *n* Bombenangriff *m*.

bond [bond] *n* (*tie*) Bindung *f*; (*comm*) Schuldschein *m*.

bone [bəun] *n* Knochen *m*, Bein *neut*; (*fish*) Gräte *f*. *v* (*meat*) die Knochen entfernen aus; (*fish*) entgräten.

bonfire ['bonfaiə] *n* Gartenfeuer *neut*.

bonnet ['bonit] *n* Haube *f*; (*mot*) Motorhaube *f*.

bonus ['bəunəs] *n* Bonus *m*.

bony ['bəuni] *adj* knochig.

book [buk] *n* Buch *neut*; (*notebook*) Heft *neut*. *v* (*record*) buchen; (*reserve*) reservieren. **bookcase** *n* Bücherschrank *m*. **booking office** Fahrkartenschalter *m*. **bookkeeping** *n* Buchhaltung *f*. **bookmaker** *n* Buchmacher *m*. **bookshop** *n* Buchhandlung *f*.

boom [buːm] *n* (*sound*) Dröhnen *neut*; (*econ*) Konjunktur *f*; (*naut*) Baum *m*. *v* dröhnen.

boost [buːst] *v* Auftrieb geben (+ *dat*), (*tech*) verstärken. *n* Auftrieb *m*.

boot [buːt] *n* Stiefel *m*; (*mot*) Kofferraum *m*. *v* **boot up** (*comp*) booten, starten.

booth [buːð] *n* Bude *f*. **telephone booth** Telephonzelle *f*.

booze [buːz] (*coll*) *v* saufen. *n* alkoholisches Getränk *neut*. **boozer** *n* Säufer *m*.

border ['bɔːdə] *n* (*of country*) Grenze *f*; (*edge*) Rand *m*. *v* grenzen. **borderline** *n* Grenze *f*. **borderline case** Grenzfall *m*.

bore[1] [bɔː] *V* **bear**[1].

bore[2] [bɔː] *v* (*drill*) bohren; (*a hole*) ausbohren; (*cylinder*) ausschleifen. *n* Kaliber *neut*.

bore[3] [bɔː] *v* (*weary*) langweilen. *n* langweiliger Mensch *m*. **be bored** sich langweilen. **boredom** *n* Langeweile *f*. **boring** *adj* langweilig.

born [bɔːn] *adj* geboren. *she was born blind* sie ist von der Geburt blind.

borne [bɔːn] *V* **bear**[1].

borough ['bʌrə] *n* Stadtbezirk *m*.

borrow ['borəu] *v* borgen, entleihen. **borrower** *n* Entleiher *m*.

Bosnia ['bozniə] *n* Bosnien *neut*. **Bosnian** *n* Bosnier(in) *adj* bosnisch.

bosom ['buzəm] *n* Busen *m*. **bosom friend** Busenfreund *m*.

boss [bos] *n* Boß, Chef *m*. *v* **boss around** herumkommandieren. **bossy** *adj* herrisch.

botany ['botəni] *n* Botanik *f*. **botanical** *adj*

botanisch. **botanical gardens** botanischer Garten *m*. **botanist** *n* Botaniker *m*.

both [bouθ] *adj, pron* beide(s). *both (of the) dogs* beide Hunde. **both ... and** sowohl ... als *or* wie auch.

bother ['boðə] *v (disturb)* belästigen, stören; *(take trouble)* sich Mühe geben. *n* Belästigung *f*. **bothersome** *adj* lästig.

bottle ['botl] *n* Flasche *f*. **bottle bank** Altglasbehälter *m*. **bottleneck** *n (fig)* Engpaß *m*. **bottle opener** *n* Flaschenöffner *m*. *v* in Flaschen füllen. **bottled** *adj* in Flaschen, Flaschen-.

bottom ['botəm] *n* Boden *m*; *(coll: anat)* Hintern *m*. *adj* **bottom gear** erster Gang *m*.

bough [bau] *n* Ast *m*.

boulder ['bouldə] *n* Felsbrocken *m*.

bounce [bauns] *v (of ball)* hochspringen; *(of cheque)* platzen. **bounce around** herumhüpfen. **bouncer** *n (coll)* Rausschmeißer *m*.

bought [bo:t] *V* buy.

bound¹ [baund] *V* **bind**.

bound² [baund] *n (leap)* Sprung *m*, Satz *m*. *v* springen.

bound³ [baund] *n (limit)* Grenze *f*. **out of bounds** betreten verboten!

bound⁴ [baund] *adj* **bound for** unterwegs nach. **outward/homeward bound** auf der Ausreise/Heimreise.

bound⁵ [baund] *adj (obliged)* verpflichtet. *He is bound to win* er wird bestimmt gewinnen.

boundary ['baundəri] *n* Grenze *f*.

bouquet [bu:kei] *n (flowers)* Blumenstrauß *m*; *(of wine)* Blume *f*.

bourgeois ['buəʒwɑ:] *adj* bourgeois. *n* Bourgeois *m*. **bourgeoisie** *n* Bourgeoisie *f*.

bout [baut] *n (of illness)* Anfall *m*; *(fight)* Kampf *m*.

bow¹ [bau] *v (lower head)* sich verbeugen. *n* Verbeugung *f*.

bow² [bou] *n (music, archery)* Bogen *m*; *(ribbon)* Schleife *f*.

bow³ [bau] *n* Bug *m*.

bowels ['bauəlz] *pl n* Darm *m sing*; Eingeweide *pl*. **open** *or* **move one's bowels** sich entleeren.

bowl¹ [boul] *n (basin)* Schüssel *f*, Schale *f*.

bowl² [boul] *v (ball)* werfen. *n* Holzkugel *f*. **bowls** *n* Kegelspiel *neut*. **play bowls** kegeln.

box¹ [boks] *n (container)* Schachtel *f*, Kasten *m*; *(theatre)* Loge *f*; *(court)* Stand *m*.

box² [boks] *v (sport)* boxen. **box someone's ears** jemanden ohrfeigen. **boxer** *n* Boxer *m*. **boxing** *n* Boxen *neut*.

Boxing Day *n* zweiter Weihnachtsfeiertag *m*.

box office *n (theatre)* Kasse *f*.

boy [boi] *n* Junge *m*, Knabe *m*. **boyfriend** *n* Freund *m*. **boyhood** *n* Jugend *f*. **boyish** *adj* knabenhaft.

boycott ['boikot] *n* Boykott *m*. *v* boykottieren.

bra [brɑ:] *n* Büstenhalter *m*, BH *m*.

brace [breis] *n* Paar *neut*; *(tech)* Stütze *f*. *v* stützen. **braces** *pl n* Hosenträger *pl*.

bracelet ['breislit] *n* Armband *neut*.

bracing ['breisiŋ] *adj* erfrischend.

bracken ['brakən] *n* Farnkraut *neut*.

bracket ['brakit] *n (parenthesis)* Klammer *f*; *(support)* Träger *m*.

brag [brag] *v* prahlen, angeben. **braggart** *n* Prahler *m*.

braid [breid] *n (hair)* Flechte *f*, Zopf *m*; *(trimming)* Tresse *f*.

braille [breil] *n* Brailleschrift *f*.

brain [brein] *n* Gehirn *neut*; Verstand *m*; Intelligenz *f*. **brainwashing** *n* Gehirnwäsche *f*. **brainwave** *n* Geistesblitz *m*. **brainy** *adj* klug.

braise [breiz] *v* schmoren.

brake [breik] *n* Bremse *f*. *v* bremsen. **brake pedal** Bremspedal *neut*.

bramble ['brambl] *n (bush)* Brombeerstrauch *m*; *(berry)* Brombeere *f*.

bran [bran] *n* (Weizen)Kleie *f*.

branch [brɑ:ntʃ] *n* Zweig *m*; *(of bank)* Zweigstelle *f*; *(department)* Abteilung *f*. *v* **branch off** abzweigen.

brand [brand] *n (of goods)* Marke *f*; *(cattle)* Brandzeichen *neut*. *v (name)* brandmarken. **brand-new** *adj* nagelneu. **brand name** Markenname *m*.

brandish ['brandiʃ] *v* schwingen.

brandy ['brandi] *n* Weinbrand *m*.

brass [brɑ:s] *n* Messing *neut*; *(music)* Blasinstrumente *pl*. *adj* Messing-.

brassiere ['brasə] *n* Büstenhalter *m*.

brave [breiv] *adj* mutig, tapfer. *v* trotzen. **bravery** *n* Mut *m*, Tapferkeit *f*.

brawl [brɔ:l] *n* Rauferei *f*. *v* raufen.

brawn [brɔːn] n Muskelkraft f. (cookery) Sülze f.

brazen ['breɪzn] adj (fig) unverschämt.

breach [briːtʃ] n Bruch m; (mil) Bresche f. v durchbrechen; (law) übertreten. **breach of contract** Vertragsbruch m. **breach of the peace** Friedensbruch m.

bread [bred] n Brot neut. v (cookery) panieren. **bread and butter** Butterbrot neut. **breadwinner** n Brotverdiener m.

breadth [bredθ] n Breite f, Weite f.

*****break** [breɪk] v brechen; (coll) kaputt machen; (law) übertreten; (promise) nicht halten; (day) anbrechen. n Bruch m; (gap) Lücke f; (rest) Pause f; (opportunity) Chance f. **break away** sich losreißen. **break down** (mot) eine Panne haben; (person) zusammenbrechen. **break in** (burgle) einbrechen; (animal) abrichten. **break out** ausbrechen. **break up** zerbrechen; (school) in die Ferien gehen.

breakable ['breɪkəbl] adj zerbrechlich.

breakage ['breɪkɪdʒ] n Bruchschaden m.

breakdown ['breɪkdaun] n (mot) Panne f. **nervous breakdown** Nervenzusammenbruch m.

breakfast ['brekfəst] n Frühstück neut. v frühstücken.

breakthrough ['breɪkθruː] n Durchbruch m.

breast [brest] n Brust f, Busen m. **breastbone** n Brustbein neut. **breast-stroke** n Brustschwimmen neut.

breath [breθ] n Atem m. **out of breath** außer Atem.

breathe [briːð] v atmen. **breathe in** einatmen. **breathe out** ausatmen.

bred [bred] V **breed**.

*****breed** [briːd] v (increase) sich vermehren; (animals) züchten; (fig) erzeugen. n (of dog) Rasse f. **breeding** n Zucht f; (education) Erziehung f.

breeze [briːz] n Brise f.

brew [bruː] v brauen. n Bräu neut. **brewery** n Brauerei f.

bribe [braɪb] v bestechen. n Bestechungsgeld neut. **bribery** n Bestechung f.

brick [brɪk] n Ziegelstein m. **bricklayer** n Maurer m.

bride [braɪd] n Braut f. **bridal** adj bräutlich, hochzeitlich. **bridegroom** n

Bräutigam m. **bridesmaid** n Brautjungfer f.

bridge¹ [brɪdʒ] n Brücke f; (violin) Steg m. v überbrücken.

bridge² [brɪdʒ] n (card game) Bridge neut.

bridle ['braɪdl] n Zaum m.

brief [briːf] adj kurz. v instruieren. **briefcase** n Aktentasche f. **briefing** n Anweisung f. **briefly** adv kurz. **briefs** pl n Slip m sing.

brigade [brɪgeɪd] n Brigade f. **brigadier** n Brigadegeneral m.

bright [braɪt] adj hell, leuchtend; (clever) klug. **brighten** v aufheitern. **brightness** n Glanz m (tech) Beleuchtungsstärke f.

brilliance ['brɪljəns] n Glanz m, Brillanz f. **brilliant** adj glänzend, brillant; (clever) scharfsinnig.

brim [brɪm] n Rand m; (hat) Krempe f.

brine [braɪn] n Salzwasser neut. **in brine** eingepökelt, Salz-.

*****bring** [brɪŋ] v bringen. **bring about** veranlassen. **bring along** mitbringen. **bring down** herunterbringen; (prices) herabsetzen. **bring up** (child) erziehen; (vomit) erbrechen.

brink [brɪŋk] n Rand m.

briquette [brɪket] n Brikett n.

brisk [brɪsk] adj schnell, lebhaft.

bristle ['brɪsl] n Borste f.

Britain ['brɪtn] n (Great Britain) Großbritannien neut. **British** adj britisch. **the British** die Briten. **Briton** n Brite m, Britin f.

brittle ['brɪtl] adj spröde.

broad [brɔːd] adj breit. **broadly** adv im allgemeinen.

broadcast ['brɔːdkɑːst] v übertragen. n Sendung f. **broadcasting** n Rundfunk m. **broadcasting corporation** n Rundfunkgesellschaft f.

brochure ['brəʊʃuə] n Broschüre f.

broke [brəʊk] V **break**. adj (coll) pleite.

broken ['brəʊkn] V **break**.

broker ['brəʊkə] n Makler m.

bronchitis [brɒŋ'kaɪtɪs] n Bronchitis f.

bronze [brɒnz] n Bronze f. adj aus Bronze, Bronze-; (colour) bronzefarben.

brooch [brəʊtʃ] n Brosche f.

brood [bruːd] n Brut f. v brüten. **broody** adj brütig.

brook [brʊk] n Bach m.

broom [bruːm] n Besen m; (bot) Ginster m.
broomstick n Besenstiehl m.

broth [brɒθ] n Brühe f.

brothel [brɒθl] n Bordell neut.

brother [brʌðə] n Bruder m. **Smith Bros.**
Gebrüder Smith. **brothers and sisters**
Geschwister pl. **brotherhood** n
Bruderschaft f. **brother-in-law** n Schwager
m. **brotherly** adj brüderlich.

brought [brɔːt] V **bring**.

brow [brau] n (forehead) Stirn f; (eyebrow)
Augenbraue f; (of hill) Bergkuppe f.

brown [braun] adj braun. n Braun neut. v
bräunen.

Brownie Guide [brauni] n junge
Pfadfinderin f.

browse [brauz] v weiden; (in book) durchblättern; (Internet) browsen. **browser** n
(Internet) Web-browser m.

bruise [bruːz] n blaue Flecke f, Quetschung
f. v quetschen.

brunch [brʌntʃ] n Gabelfrühstück neut,
Brunch m.

brunette [bruːnet] adj brünett. n Brünette
f.

brush [brʌʃ] n Bürste f; (paintbrush) Pinsel
m; (undergrowth) Unterholz neut. v bürsten.
brush past vorbeistreichen.

brusque [brusk] adj brüsk.

Brussels [brʌsəlz] n Brüssel neut. **Brussels
sprouts** Rosenkohl m.

brute [bruːt] n Tier neut; (person) brutaler
Mensch m. **brutal** adj brutal. **brutality** n
Brutalität f.

BSE n BSE f.

bubble [bʌbl] n Blase f. v sprudeln. **bub-
bly** adj sprudelnd.

buck[1] [bʌk] n Bock m; (US coll) Dollar m.
pass the buck den schwarzen Peter weitergeben.

buck[2] [bʌk] v bocken. **buck up** (hurry) sich
beeilen; (cheer up) munter werden.

bucket [bʌkit] n Eimer m. **bucketful** n
Eimervoll m.

buckle [bʌkl] n Schnalle f. v anschnallen.

bud [bʌd] n Knospe f. v knospen. **nip in
the bud** im Keim ersticken. **budding** adj
angehend.

Buddhist [budist] adj buddhistisch. n
Buddhist(in) m, f. **Buddhism** n
Buddhismus m.

buddy [bʌdi] n (coll) Kumpel m.

budge [bʌdʒ] v (sich) bewegen.

budgerigar [bʌdʒərigaː] n Wellensittich
m.

budget [bʌdʒit] n Budget neut. v bud-
getieren.

buffalo [bʌfəlou] n Büffel m; (bison) Bison
m.

buffer [bʌfə] n Puffer m.

buffet[1] [bʌfit] n (blow) Schlag m. v stoßen.

buffet[2] [bufei] n (meal) Büffett neut.

bug [bʌg] n Wanze f; (comp)
Programmfehler m. v (coll) ärgern.

buggy [bʌgi] n Kinderwagen m.

bugle [bjuːgl] n Signalhorn neut.

*****build** [bild] v bauen. n Körperbau m.
build up aufbauen. **builder** n Baumeister
m. **building** n Gebäude neut, Haus neut.
built-in adj eingebaut.

built [bilt] V **build**.

bulb [bʌlb] n (flower) Zwiebel f; (lamp)
Glühbirne f. **bulbous** adj zwiebelförmig.

Bulgaria [bʌlgeərə] n Bulgarien neut.
Bulgarian adj bulgarisch; n Bulgare m,
Bulgarin f.

bulge [bʌldʒ] v anschwellen. n Schwellung
f, Ausbauchung f.

bulimia [buːlimiə] n Bulimie f, Ess-Brech-
Sucht f.

bulk [bʌlk] n Masse f; (greater part)
Hauptteil m. **bulky** adj umfangreich.

bull [bul] n (cattle) Stier m; (animal) Bulle f;
(coll; nonsense) Quatsch m. **bulldog** n
Bulldogge m. **bulldozer** n Bulldozer m.
bullfight n Stierkampf m.

bullet [bulit] n (Gewehr) Kugel f.

bulletin [bulətin] n Bulletin neut.

bullion [buliən] n Gold-, Silberbarren pl.

bully [buli] v einschüchtern. n Tyrann m.

bum [bʌm] n (tramp) Bummler m,
Landstreicher m.

bump [bʌmp] v Stoßen (gegen). n Stoß m;
(on the head) Beule f. **bumper** n (of car)
Stoßstange f. adj **bumper crop**
Rekordernte f.

bun [bʌn] n (hair) Haarknoten m; (cake)
Kuchen m; (bread roll) Brötchen neut.

bunch [bʌntʃ] n Bündel neut. **bunch of
flowers** Blumenstrauß m. **bunch of
grapes** Weintraube f. **bunch of keys**
Schlüsselbund m.

bundle [bʌndl] n Bündel neut. v zusammenbündeln.

bungalow [ˈbʌŋɡəbu] n Bungalow m.

bungle [ˈbʌŋɡ] v verpfuschen. **bungler** n Pfuscher.

bunion [ˈbʌnjən] n entzündeter Fußballen m.

bunk [bʌŋk] n Koje f. **bunk beds** Etagenbett neut sing. v **bunk off** (play truant) schwänzen.

bunker [ˈbʌŋkə] n Bunker m; (golf) Sandgrube f.

buoy [bɔi] n Boje f.

burden [ˈbəːdn] n Last f. v belasten.

bureau [ˈbjuərou] n Büro neut; (desk) Schreibtisch m.

bureaucracy [bjuˈrɔkrəsi] n Bürokratie f. **bureaucrat** n Bürokrat m. **bureaucratic** adj bürokratisch.

burglar [ˈbəːɡlə] n Einbrecher m. **burglary** n Einbruchsdiebstahl m.

burial [ˈberəl] n Beerdigung f, Begräbnis neut.

*****burn** [bəːn] v brennen; (set alight) verbrennen. n Brandwunde f. **burn oneself** (or **one's fingers**) sich (die Finger) verbrennen.

burnt [bəːnt] V **burn**. adj (food) angebrannt.

burrow [ˈbʌrou] n (of rabbit) Bau m. v graben.

*****burst** [bəːst] v platzen. n (of shooting) Feuerstoß m; (of speed) Spurt m. **burst out laughing/crying** in Lachen/Tränen ausbrechen. **burst tyre** geplatzter Reifen m.

bury [ˈberi] v begraben; (one's hands, face) vergraben.

bus [bʌs] n Bus m, Autobus m. **bus driver** Busfahrer m. **bus conductor** Busschaffner m. **bus stop** Bushaltestelle f.

bush [buʃ] n Busch m. **bushy** adj buschig.

business [ˈbiznis] n Geschäft neut. **that's none of your business** das geht dich nichts an. **businessman** n Geschäftsmann m. **businesswoman** n Geschäftsfrau f.

bust¹ [bʌst] n (breasts) Busen m; (sculpture) Büste f.

bust² [bʌst] (coll) adj (bankrupt) pleite; (broken) kaputt. v zerbrechen, kaputt machen.

bustle [ˈbʌsl] n Aufregung f. v **bustle about** herumsausen.

busy [ˈbizi] n (occupied) beschäftigt; (hardworking) fleißig; (telephone) besetzt. v busy

oneself with sich beschäftigen mit.

but [bʌt] conj aber. prep außer. adv (merely) nur. **not only ... but also** nicht nur ... sondern auch. **nothing but** nichts als. **but for** ohne.

butane [ˈbjuːtein] n Butan neut.

butcher [ˈbutʃə] n Fleischer m, Metzger m. **butcher's shop** Metzgerei f, Fleischerei f.

butler [ˈbʌtlə] n Butler m.

butt¹ [bʌt] n (thick end) dickes Ende neut; (of cigarette) Stummel m.

butt² [bʌt] n (of jokes) Zielscheibe f.

butt³ [bʌt] v (with the head) mit dem Kopf stoßen. n Kopfstoß.

butter [ˈbʌtə] n Butter f. v mit Butter bestreichen. **butter someone up** (coll) jemanden Honig um den Bart schmieren.

buttercup [ˈbʌtəkʌp] n Butterblume f.

butterfly [ˈbʌtəflai] n Schmetterling m.

buttocks [ˈbʌtəks] pl n Gesäß neut sing.

button [ˈbʌtn] n Knopf m. v (zu)knöpfen. **buttonhole** n Knopfloch neut.

buttress [ˈbʌtris] n Strebepfeiler m.

*****buy** [bai] v kaufen. **buy in** einkaufen. **buyer** n Käufer(in).

buzz [bʌz] v summen. n Summen neut. **buzzer** n Summer m.

by [bai] prep (close to) bei, neben; (via) über; (past) an ... vorbei; (before) bis; (written by) von. adv vorbei. **by day** bei tage. **by bus** mit dem Bus. **by that** (mean, understand) damit. **by and by** nach und nach. **by-election** Nachwahl f. **bypass** n Umgehungstraße f. **by-product** n Nebenprodukt neut. **bystander** n Zuschauer m.

byte [bait] n (comp) Byte neut.

C

cab [kab] n (taxi) Taxi neut; (horsedrawn) Droschke f; (in truck) Fahrerhaus neut.

cabaret [ˈkabərei] n Kabarett neut.

cabbage [ˈkabidʒ] n Kohl m, Kraut neut.

cabin [ˈkabin] n Hütte f; (naut) Kabine f.

cabinet [ˈkabinit] n Schrank m; (pol) Kabinett neut. **cabinet-maker** n Möbeltischler m.

cable ['keɪbl] n (elec, telegram) Kabel neut; (rope) Tau neut, Seil neut. cable address Telegrammanschrift f. cable railway Drahtseilbahn f. cable television Kabelfernsehen neut.

cache [kaʃ] n (arms) Waffenlager neut; (computing) Cache m, Cachespeicher m.

cackle ['kakl] v gackern. n Gegacker neut.

cactus ['kaktəs] n Kaktus m.

caddie ['kadi] n Golfjunge m.

cadence ['keɪdəns] n (music) Kadenz f. cadenza n Kadenz f.

cadet [kə'det] n Kadett m.

Caesarean section [sɪzeəriən] n Kaiserschnitt m. be born by Caesarean durch Kaiserschnitt geboren werden.

café ['kafeɪ] n Café neut.

cafeteria [kafə'tɪərə] n Selbstbedienungsrestaurant neut.

caffeine ['kafiːn] n Koffein neut.

cage [keɪʒ] n Käfig m. v in einen Käfig sperren.

cake [keɪk] n Kuchen m; (soap) Tafel f. v be caked with mud vor Schmutz starren.

calamine ['kaləmaɪn] n Galmei m.

calamity [kə'lamətɪ] n Unheil neut, Katastrophe f.

calcium ['kalsɪəm] n Kalzium neut.

calculate ['kalkjuleɪt] v kalkulieren, berechnen. calculating adj berechnend. calculation n Berechnung f. calculator n (mech) Rechner m.

calendar ['kaləndə] n Kalender m.

calf¹ [kaːf] n (young cow) Kalb neut. calfskin n Kalbleder neut.

calf² [kaːf] n (anat) Wade f. calf muscle Wadenmuskel m.

calibre ['kalɪbə] n Kaliber neut.

call [koːl] v rufen; anrufen; (a doctor) holen; (regard as) halten für. n Ruf m; (phone) Anruf m; (demand) Aufforderung f. call for verlangen. call off (cancel) absagen. callbox n Telefonzelle f. caller n (visitor) Besucher m; (phone) Anrufer m. calling n Berufung f. call-up n Einberufung f.

callous ['kaləs] adj gefühllos, herzlos.

calm [kaːm] adj ruhig. n Ruhe, Stille f; (naut) Windstille f. v or calm down (sich) or beruhigen.

calorie ['kalərɪ] n Kalorie f.

camcorder ['kam koːdə] n Camcorder m.

came [keɪm] V come.

camel ['kaməl] n Kamel neut. camelhair n Kamelhaar neut.

camera ['kamərə] n Kamera f, Fotoapparat m. cameraman n Kameramann m.

camouflage ['kaməflaːʒ] n Tarnung f; (zool) Schutzfärbung f. v tarnen.

camp [kamp] n Lager neut. v lagern; (go camping) campen, zelten. camp bed Feldbett neut. camp site Campingplatz m. camper n Camper m. camper van Wohnmobil neut. camping n Camping neut.

campaign [kam'peɪn] n (mil, pol) Feldzug m; Kampagne f. v campaign for (fig) werben um, kämpfen für.

campus ['kampəs] n Universitätsgelände neut.

camshaft ['kamʃaːft] n Nockenwelle f.

*can¹ [kan] v (be able) können; (be allowed, may) dürfen.

can² [kan] n (tin) Dose f, Büchse f. v konservieren.

Canada ['kanədə] n Kanada neut. Canadian adj kanadisch; n Kanadier(in).

canal [kə'nal] n Kanal m.

canary [kə'neərɪ] n Kanarienvogel m.

cancel ['kansəl] v (meeting) absagen; (arrangement) aufheben; (stamp) entwerten; (cross out) durchstreichen. cancellation n Absage f; Aufhebung f.

cancer ['kansə] n (med) Krebs m. Cancer (astrol) Krebs m. breast cancer Brustenkrebs m. lung cancer Lungenkrebs m.

candid ['kandɪd] adj offen, ehrlich.

candidate ['kandɪdət] n Kandidat m.

candle ['kandl] n Kerze f. candle light n Kerzenlicht neut. candlestick Leuchter m.

candour ['kandə] n Offenheit f; Ehrlichkeit f.

candy ['kandɪ] n Kandiszucker m; (US: sweet) Bonbon neut.

cane [keɪn] n (walking stick) Spazierstock m. sugar cane Zuckerrohr m. cane sugar Rohrzucker m.

canine ['keɪnaɪn] adj Hunde-, Hunds-. canine tooth Eckzahn m.

canister ['kanɪstə] n Kanister m.

cannabis ['kanəbɪs] n Haschisch neut.

cannibal ['kanɪbəl] n Kannibale m.

cannon ['kænən] *n* Kanone *f.*

canoe [kə'nuː] *n* Kanu *neut.* *v* Kanu fahren.

canon ['kænən] *n* Domherr *m;* (*rule*) Kanon *m.*

can opener *n* Büchsenöffner *m.*

canopy ['kænəpɪ] *n* Baldachin *m.*

canteen [kæn'tiːn] *n* (*restaurant*) Kantine *f.*

canter ['kæntə] *n* Handgalopp *m.* *v* Handgalopp reiten.

canton ['kæntən] *n* Kanton *m.*

canvas ['kænvəs] *n* Segeltuch *neut;* (*artist's*) Leinwand *f.*

canvass ['kænvəs] *v* werben.

canyon ['kænjən] *n* Cañon *m,* Schlucht *f.*

cap [kæp] *n* (*hat*) Kappe *f,* Mütze *f;* (*lid*) Kappe *f.* *v* (*fig*) übertreffen. **capped-rate mortgage** Hypothek (*f*) mit Zinsobergrenze.

capable ['keɪpəbl] *adj* (*able to do something*) fähig (zu); (*skilled*) begabt. **capability** *n* Fähigkeit *f.*

capacity [kə'pæsətɪ] *n* (*volume*) Inhalt *m;* (*of ship*) Laderaum *m;* (*talent*) Talent *m.* **in the capacity of** als. *filled to capacity* voll (besetzt).

cape¹ [keɪp] *n* (*cloak*) Cape *neut,* Umhang *m.*

cape² [keɪp] *n* (*geog*) Kap *neut.*

caper¹ ['keɪpə] *n* Kapriole *f.* *v* kapriolen.

caper² ['keɪpə] *n* (*cookery*) Kaper *f.*

capital ['kæpɪtl] *n* (*city*) Hauptstadt *f;* (*comm*) Kapital *neut. adj* (*main*) Haupt-; (*comm*) Kapital-; (*splendid*) großartig. **capitalism** *n* Kapitalismus *m.* **capitalist** *n* Kapitalist *m. adj* kapitalistisch. **capital punishment** Todesstrafe *m.*

capitulate [kə'pɪtjuleɪt] *v* kapitulieren (vor).

capricious [kə'prɪʃəs] *adj* launenhaft.

Capricorn ['kæprɪkɔːn] *n* Steinbock *m.*

capsize [kæp'saɪz] *v* kentern.

capsule ['kæpsjuːl] *n* Kapsel *f.*

captain ['kæptɪn] *n* (*mil*) Hauptmann *m;* (*naut*) Kapitän *m;* (*sport*) Mannschaftsführer *m. v* (*sport*) führen.

caption ['kæpʃən] *n* (*picture*) Erklärung *f;* (*heading*) Überschrift *f.*

captive ['kæptɪv] *n* Gefangene(r). *adj* gefangen. **captivity** *n* Gefangenschaft *f.* **captor** *n* Fänger *m.*

capture ['kæptʃə] *v* gefangennehmen; (*animal*) einfangen. *n* Genangennahme *f.*

car [kɑː] *n* (*mot*) Wagen *m,* Auto *neut;* (*rail*) Wagen *m.* **by car** mit dem Auto. **car-boot sale** Kofferraumflohmarkt *m.*

caramel ['kærəmel] *n* Karamel *m.*

carat ['kærət] *n* Karat *neut.*

caravan ['kærəvæn] *n* (*mot*) Wohnwagen *m;* (*oriental*) Karawane *f.*

caraway ['kærəweɪ] *n* Kümmel *m.*

carbohydrate [kɑːbə'haɪdreɪt] *n* Kohlehydrat *neut.*

carbon ['kɑːbən] *n* Kohlenstoff *m.* **carbon copy** Durchschlag *m.* **carbon dioxide** Kohlendioxid *neut;* (*in drinks*) Kohlensäure *f.* **carbon dating** C-14 Datierung *f.* **carbon emissions** Kohlendioxidemission *f.* **carbon paper** Kohlepapire *neut.*

carburettor ['kɑːbjuretə] **carburetor** *n* Vergaser *m.*

carcass ['kɑːkəs] *n* Kadaver *m.*

card [kɑːd] *n* Karte *f.* **cardboard** *n* Pappe *f.* **cardboard box** Pappschachtel *f.* **card game** Kartenspiel *neut.* **card index** Kartei *f.*

cardiac ['kɑːdɪæk] *adj* Herz-.

cardigan ['kɑːdɪgən] *n* Wolljacke *f.*

cardinal ['kɑːdənl] *n* Kardinal *m. adj* grundsätzlich.

care [keə] *n* (*carefulness*) Sorgfalt *f;* (*looking after*) Pflege *f;* (*worry*) Sorge *f.* **take care** sich hüten; achtgeben. **take care of** (*look after*) pflegen; (*see to*) erledigen. *v* **care about** sich kümmern um. **care for** (*look after*) pflegen; (*see to*) sorgen für; (*like*) mögen. **carefree** *adj* sorgenfrei. **careful** *adj* sorgfältig; (*cautious*) vorsichtig. **carefulness** *n* Sorgfalt *f;* Vorsicht *f.* **careless** *adj* unachtsam, nachlässig. **carelessness** *n* Nachlässigkeit *f.*

career [kə'rɪə] *n* Laufbahn *f,* Karriere *f.*

caress [kə'res] *v* liebkosen. *n* Liebkosung *f;* Kuß *m.*

cargo ['kɑːgou] *n* Fracht *f.* **cargo plane** Transportflugzeug *neut.* **cargo ship** Frachtschiff *neut.*

Caribbean [kærɪ'biən] *n* Karibik *f.*

caricature ['kærɪkətjuə] *n* Karikatur *f. v* karikieren.

carnal ['kɑːnl] *adj* fleischlich.

carnation [kɑː'neɪʃən] *n* Nelke *f.*

carnival ['kɑːnɪvl] *n* Karneval *m,* Fasching *m.*

carnivorous [kɑː'nɪvərəs] *adj* fleischfressend.

carol [ˈkærəl] n Weihnachtslied neut.

carpenter [ˈkɑːpəntə] n Zimmermann m, Tischler m. **carpentry** n Zimmerhandwerk neut.

carpet [ˈkɑːpɪt] n Teppich m. v mit einem Teppich belegen.

carriage [ˈkærɪdʒ] n (rail) (Eisenbahn) Wagen m; (transport) Transport f; (posture) Haltung f. **carriageway** Fahrbahn f.

carrier [ˈkærə] n Träger m; (med) Keimträger m; (comm) Spediteur m. **carrier bag** Tragebeutel m.

carrot [ˈkærət] n Mohrrübe f, Möhre f.

carry [ˈkærɪ] v tragen; (transport) befördern. **carry out** ausführen. **carry cot** Tragbettchen neut.

cart [kɑːt] n Karren m.

cartilage [ˈkɑːtəlɪdʒ] n Knorpel m.

cartography [kɑːˈtɒɡrəfɪ] n Kartographie f.

carton [ˈkɑːtən] n Karton m.

cartoon [kɑːˈtuːn] n Karikatur f; (film) Trickfilm m. **cartoonist** n Karikaturenzeichner m.

cartridge [ˈkɑːtrɪdʒ] n Patrone f. **cartridge paper** Zeichenpapier neut.

carve [kɑːv] v (in wood) schnitzen; (in stone) meißeln; (meat) vorschneiden. **carving** n Schnitzerei f.

cascade [kæskeɪd] n Kaskade f.

case¹ [keɪs] n (affair, instance) Fall m; (law) Sache f. **in case** falls. **in case of** im Falle (+gen). **in any case** auf jeden Fall.

case² [keɪs] n (suitcase) Koffer m; (for cigarettes, camera) Etui neut; (tech) Gehäuse neut.

cash [kæʃ] n Bargeld neut. v einlösen. **cash on delivery** per Nachnahme. **pay cash** bar zahlen. **cash desk** Kasse f. **cash dispenser** Geldautomat m.

cashier [kaˈʃə] n Kassierer(in).

cashmere [kæʃˈmə] n Kaschmir m.

casing [ˈkeɪsɪŋ] n Gehäuse neut.

casino [kəˈsiːnou] n Kasino neut.

casket [ˈkɑːskɪt] n Kästchen neut; (coffin) Sarg m.

casserole [ˈkæsəroul] n (vessel) Kasserolle f; (meal) Schmorbraten m. v schmoren.

cassette [kəˈset] n Kassette f. **cassette recorder** Kassettenrecorder m.

cassock [ˈkæsək] n Soutane f.

*cast [kɑːst] v werfen; (metal) gießen; (theatre) besetzen. n (theatre) Besetzung f.

caste [kɑːst] n Kaste f.

castle [ˈkɑːsl] n Burg f, Schloß neut; (chess) Turm m. v (chess) rochieren.

castor oil [ˈkɑːstə] n Möbelrolle f.

castrate [kəˈstreɪt] v kastrieren. **castration** n Kastration f.

casual [ˈkæʒuəl] adj beiläufig; (careless) nachlässig; (informal) leger. **casual labour** Gelegenheitsarbeit f.

casualty [ˈkæʒuəltɪ] n Verletzte(r). **casualties** pl n (mil) Ausfälle pl. **casualty department** Unfallstation f.

cat [kæt] n Katze f. **tom cat** Kater m.

catalogue [ˈkætəlɒɡ] n Katalog m.

catalyst [ˈkætəlɪst] n Katalysator m. **catalytic converter** n Katalysator m, Kat m.

catamaran [kætəmˈæran] n Katamaran neut.

catapult [ˈkætəpʌlt] n Katapult neut.

cataract [ˈkætərakt] n (med) grauer Star m; Wasserfall m.

catarrh [kəˈtɑː] n Katarrh m.

catastrophe [kəˈtæstrəfɪ] n Katastrophe f. **catastrophic** adj katastrophal.

*catch [kætʃ] v fangen; (bus, train) nehmen, erreichen; (surprise) ertappen; (illness) sich zuziehen. n Fang m.

category [ˈkætəɡərɪ] n Katagorie f. **categorical** adj kategorisch.

cater [ˈkeɪtə] v **cater for** versorgen. **catering** n Bewirtung f.

caterpillar [ˈkætəpɪlə] n Raupe f. **caterpillar track** Gleiskette f.

cathedral [kəˈθiːdrəl] n Dom m, Kathedrale f.

cathode [ˈkæθoud] n Kathode f.

catholic [ˈkæθəlɪk] adj (rel) katholisch; universal. n Katholik(in). **Roman Catholic** römisch-katholisch.

catkin [ˈkætkɪn] n Kätzchen neut.

cattle [ˈkætl] pl n Vieh neut sing, Rindvieh neut sing. **cattle shed** Viehstall m.

catty [ˈkætɪ] adj (coll) gehässig.

caught [kɔːt] V **catch**.

cauliflower [ˈkɒliflauə] n Blumenkohl m.

cause [kɔːz] n Ursache f; (reason) Grund m; (interests) Sache f. v verursachen, veranlassen.

causeway [ˈkɔːzweɪ] n Damm m.

caustic [ˈkɔːstɪk] adj ätzend; (fig) beißend.

caution [ˈkɔːʃən] n Vorsicht f. v warnen

(vor). **cautious** *adj* vorsichtig.

cavalry ['kævəlrɪ] *n* Kavallerie *f*.

cave [keɪv] *n* Höhle *f*. *v* **cave in** einstürzen. **cavern** *n* Höhle *f*.

caviar ['kævɪɑː] *n* Kaviar *m*.

cavity ['kævətɪ] *n* Hohlraum *m*; (*in tooth*) Loch *neut*.

CCTV *n* Fernsehüberwachungsanlage *f*.

CD *n* CD *f*.

CD-ROM [siːdiːˈrɒm] *n* CD-ROM *f*.

cease [siːs] *v* aufhören; (*fire*) einstellen. **ceasefire** *n* Feuereinstellung *f*. **ceaseless** *adj* unaufhörlich.

cedar ['siːdə] *n* Zeder *f*.

ceiling ['siːlɪŋ] *n* Decke *f*; (*fig*) Höchstgrenze *f*.

celebrate ['selɪbreɪt] *v* Feiern. **celebrated** *adj* berühmt. **celebration** *n* Feier *f*. **celebrity** *n* Berühmtheit *f*; (*person*) Prominente *m*, *f*.

celery ['selərɪ] *n* Sellerie *m*.

celestial [sə'lestɪəl] *adj* himmlisch.

celibacy ['selɪbəsɪ] *n* Zölibat *neut* or *m*, Ehelosigkeit *f*. **celibate** *adj* ehelos.

cell [sel] *n* Zelle *f*.

cellar ['selə] *n* Keller *m*.

cello ['tʃeləu] *n* Cello *neut*.

cellophane ['seləfeɪn] *n* Zellophan *neut*.

cellular ['seljulə] *adj* zellular.

cement [sə'ment] *n* Zement *m*. *v* zementieren; (*fig*) binden.

cemetery ['semɪtrɪ] *n* Friedhof *m*.

cenotaph ['senətɑːf] *n* Ehrenmal *neut*.

censor ['sensə] *n* Zensor *m*. *v* zensieren. **censorship** *n* Zensur *f*.

censure ['senʃə] *n* Tadel *m*. *v* tadeln.

census ['sensəs] *n* Volkszählung *f*.

cent [sent] *n* Cent *m*. **per cent** Prozent *neut*.

centenary [sen'tiːnərɪ] *n* Hundertjahrfeier *f*.

centigrade ['sentɪgreɪd] *adv* Celsius.

centimetre ['sentɪmiːtə] *n* Zentimeter *neut*.

centipede ['sentɪpiːd] *n* Tausendfuß *m*.

centre ['sentə] *n* Zentrum *neut*, Mittelpunkt *m*. *adj* Zentral-, Mittel-. *v* **centre around** sich drehen um. **centre on** sich konzentrieren auf. **centre forward** (*sport*) Mittelstürmer *m*. **centre half** Mittelläufer *m*. **centre of gravity** Schwerpunkt *m*. **centrepiece** *n* Tafelaufsatz *m*. **central** *adj* zentral, Zentral-. **Central America**

Mittelamerika *neut*. **central heating** Zentralheizung *f*. **central station** Hauptbahnhof *m*.

centrifugal [sen'trɪfjugəl] *adj* zentrifugal. **centrifugal force** Zentrifugalkraft *f*.

century ['sentʃurɪ] *n* Jahrhundert *neut*.

ceramic [sə'ræmɪk] *adj* keramisch. **ceramics** *n* Keramik *f*.

cereal ['sɪərɪəl] *n* Getreide *neut*. **breakfast cereal** Getreideflocken *pl*.

ceremony ['serɪmənɪ] *n* Zeremonie *f*. **ceremonial** *adj* zeremoniell. **ceremonious** *adj* zeremoniös.

certain ['səːtn] *adj* bestimmt, gewiß; (*sure*) sicher. **for certain** bestimmt. **certainly** *adv* sicherlich, gewiß. **certainty** *n* Sicherheit *f*.

certificate [sə'tɪfɪkət] *n* Bescheinigung *f*. **certification** *n* Bescheinigung *f*. **certify** *v* bestätigen.

cervix ['səːvɪks] *n* (*anat*) Gebärmutterhals *m*.

cesspool ['sespuːl] *n* Senkgrube *f*.

chafe [tʃeɪf] *v* reiben.

chaffinch ['tʃæfɪntʃ] *n* Buchfink *m*.

chain [tʃeɪn] *n* Kette *f*. *v* anketten. **chain reaction** Kettenreaktion *f*. **chain smoker** Kettenraucher *m*. **chainstore** *n* Kettenladen *m*.

chair [tʃeə] *n* Stuhl *m*; (*armchair*) Sessel *m*; (*at meeting*) Vorsitz *m*. *v* (*meeting*) den Vorsitz führen. **chairlift** *n* Sesselbahn *f*. **chairman** *n* Vorsitzende(r).

chalet ['ʃæleɪ] *n* Chalet *neut*.

chalk [tʃɔːk] *n* Kreide *f*. *v* mit Kreide schreiben.

challenge ['tʃælɪndʒ] *n* Aufforderung *f*; (*objection*) Einwand *m*. *v* auffordern; (*question*) bestreiten. **challenger** *n* Herausforderer *m*.

chamber ['tʃeɪmbə] *n* Kammer *f*. **chamber music** Kammermusik *f*. **chamber pot** Nachttopf *m*.

chameleon [kə'miːlɪən] *n* Chamäleon *neut*.

chamois [ʃæm'wɑː] *n* Gemse *f*; (*leather*) Sämischleder *neut*.

champagne [ʃæm'peɪn] *n* Champagner *m*.

champion ['tʃæmpɪən] *n* (*sport*) Meister *m*, Sieger *m*; (*defender*) Verfechter *m*. *v* (*cause*) verfechten. **championship** *n* Meisterschaft *f*.

chance [tʃɑːns] *n* Zufall *m*; (*opportunity*)

Gelegenheit f; (*possibility*) Chance f,
Möglichkeit f. v riskieren. **by chance** zufällig. **stand a chance** Chancen haben. **take
a chance** sein Glück versuchen. **no
chance!** keine Spur!.

chancellor [ˈtʃɑːnsəl] n Kanzler m.

chandelier [ʃandəˈliə] n Kronleuchter m.

change [tʃeɪndʒ] v (*modify*) (ab-,ver)ändern;
(*exchange*) (aus)tauschen; (*become changed*)
sich (ver)ändern; (*trains*) umsteigen;
(*clothes*) sich umziehen; (*money*) wechseln.
change gear schalten. **change into** (sich)
verwandeln in. **change over to** übergehen
zu. n (Ab-, Ver)Änderung f; (Ver)Wandlung
f; (*small change*) Kleingeld neut. **change of
life** Wechseljahre pl. **for a change** zur
Abwechselung. **changeable** adj veränderlich. **changeless** adj unveränderlich.

channel [ˈtʃanl] n Kanal m; (*fig*) Weg m. v
lenken. **through official channels** durch
die Instanzen. **Channel Tunnel** der
Kanaltunnel. **English Channel** der
Ärmelkanal.

chant [tʃɑːnt] v intonieren. n Gesang m.

chaos [ˈkeɪɒs] n Chaos neut; (*mess*)
Durcheinander neut.

chap[1] [tʃap] v (*skin*) rissig machen; (*become
chapped*) aufspringen.

chap[2] [tʃap] n (*coll*) Kerl m.

chapel [ˈtʃapl] n Kapelle f.

chaperon [ˈʃapərəʊn] n Anstandsdame f. v
begleiten.

chaplain [ˈtʃaplɪn] n Kaplan m.

chapter [ˈtʃaptə] n Kapitel neut; (*branch*)
Ortsgruppe f.

char[1] [tʃɑː] v (*burn*) verkohlen.

char[2] [tʃɑː] n (*cleaning lady*) Putzfrau f.

character [ˈkarəktə] n Charakter m; (*personality*) Persönlichkeit f; (*theatre*) Person f;
(*reputation*) Ruf m; (*letter*) Buchstabe m.
characteristic n Kennzeichen neut; adj
charakteristisch. **characterize** v charakterisieren.

charcoal [ˈtʃɑːkəʊl] n Holzkohle f; (*for
drawing*) Reißkohle f.

charge [tʃɑːdʒ] n (*cost*) Preis m; (*of firearm*)
Ladung f; (*mil*) Angriff m; (*law*) Anklage f;
(*elec*) Ladung f. v (*firearm, battery*) laden;
(*price*) verlangen; (*attack*) angreifen. **be in
charge of** verantwortlich sein für. **bring a
charge against** anklagen. **charge card**
Kreditkarte f.

chariot [ˈtʃarɪət] n Streitwagen m.

charisma [kəˈrɪzmə] n Charisma neut.
charismatic adj charismatisch.

charity [ˈtʃarəti] n Nächstenliebe f,
Wohltätigkeit f; (*organization*)
Wohlfahrtseinrichtung f. **charitable** adj
wohltätig f.

charm [tʃɑːm] n (*personal*) Scharm m, Reiz
m; (*magic word*) Zauberwort neut; (*trinket*)
Amulett neut. v entzücken. **charming**
entzückend, scharmant.

chart [tʃɑːt] n (*naut*) Seekarte f; Diagramm
neut.

charter [ˈtʃɑːtə] n Verfassungsurkunde f;
(*naut, aero*) Charter m. v chartern. adj
Charter-.

chase [tʃeɪs] v verfolgen, jagen. n
Verfolgung f, Jagd f.

chasm [ˈkazəm] n Abgrund m.

chassis [ˈʃasi] n Fahrgestell neut.

chaste [tʃeɪst] adj keusch. **chastity** n
Keuschheit f.

chastise [tʃasˈtaɪz] v strafen.

chat [tʃat] v plaudern, sich unterhalten. n
Plauderei f. **chatroom** n (*Internet*)
Quasselzimmer neut, Chat-Room m.

chatter [ˈtʃatə] v schnattern; (*teeth*) klappern. n Geschnatter neut; Klappern neut.

chauffeur [ˈʃəʊfə] n Chauffeur m.

chauvinism [ˈʃəʊvɪnɪzəm] n Chauvinismus
m. **chauvinist** n Chauvinist m.

chav [tʃav] n (*derog*) Proll m, Asi m.

cheap [tʃiːp] adj billig, preiswert; (*base*)
gemein.

cheat [tʃiːt] v betrügen. n Betrüger m,
Schwindler m.

check [tʃek] v (*inspect*) prüfen, kontrollieren; (*hinder*) (ver)hindern; (*look up*) nachsehen; (*tick*) abhaken. **check in** sich
anmelden. **check out** (*hotel*) abreisen. n
Kontrolle f; (*bill*) Rechnung f; (*cheque*)
Scheck m; (*chess*) Schach m; (*pattern*) Karo
neut. **checklist** n Kontrolliste f.

checkmate n Schachmatt neut. **checkpoint** Kontrollpunkt m. **check-up** n (*med*)
ärztliche Untersuchung f.

cheek [tʃiːk] n (*anat*) Wange f, Backe f;
(*impudence*) Frechheit f. **cheeky** adj frech.

cheer [tʃɪə] v jubeln; (*applaud*) zujubeln (+
dat); (*encourage*) aufmuntern. **cheer up** aufmuntern. n Beifallsruf m, Hurra neut.
cheers! interj prost! **cheerful** adj fröhlich.
cheerio! interj tschüs!

cheese [tʃiːz] n Käse m. **cheesecake** n Käsekuchen m. **cheesecloth** n Musselin m.

cheetah [ˈtʃiːtə] n Gepard m.

chef [ʃef] n Küchenchef m.

chemical [ˈkemɪkl] adj chemisch. **chemicals** pl n Chemikalien f pl **chemical weapons** C-Waffen f pl.

chemist [ˈkemɪst] n Chemiker m; (dispensing chemist) Apotheker m. **chemist's shop** Apotheke f.

chemistry [ˈkemɪstrɪ] n Chemie f.

cheque [tʃek] n Scheck m. **chequebook** n Scheckbuch neut. **cheque card** Scheckkarte f.

cherish [ˈtʃerɪʃ] v (feeling) hegen; (person) lieb haben.

cherry [ˈtʃerɪ] n Kirsche f; (tree) Kirschbaum m.

chess [tʃes] n Schach neut. **chessboard** n Schachbrett neut. **chessman** n Schachfigur f.

chest [tʃest] n (anat) Brust f; (container) Kiste f; (trunk) Truhe f. that's a weight off my chest da fällt mir ein Stein vom Herzen.

chestnut [ˈtʃesnʌt] n (sweet chestnut) (Eß)Kastanie f; (horse chestnut) (Roß) Kastanie f; (tree) Kastanienbaum m; (brown horse) Braune(r) m.

chew [tʃuː] v kauen. **chewing gum** Kaugummi m.

chick [tʃɪk] n Küken neut. **chicken** n Huhn neut; (for eating) Hähnchen neut. adj (coll) feige. **chicken soup** Hühner-brühe f.

chicory [ˈtʃɪkərɪ] n Zichorie f; (salad plant) Chicorée f.

chief [tʃiːf] n (pl-s) Chef m, Leiter m; (of tribe) Häuptling m. adj Haupt-, erster. **chieftain** m Häuptling m.

chilblain [ˈtʃɪlbleɪn] n Frostbeule f.

child [tʃaɪld] n (pl-ren) Kind neut. **with child** schwanger. **childbirth** n Entbindung f. **childhood** n Kindheit f. **childish** adj kindisch. **childlike** adj kindlich. **childminder** n Kinderhüter(in) m, f.

Chile [ˈtʃɪlɪ] n Chile neut. **Chilean** adj chilenisch; n Chilene m, Chilenin f.

chill [tʃɪl] n Kältegefühl neut; (fever) Schüttelfrost m. **chilled** adj (drink) gekühlt. **chilly** adj fröstelnd.

chilli [ˈtʃɪlɪ] n Cayennepfeffer m.

chime [tʃaɪm] v (bell) läuten. n Geläut neut.

chimney [ˈtʃɪmnɪ] n Schornstein m. **chimney sweep** Schornsteinfeger m.

chimpanzee [tʃɪmpənˈziː] n Schimpanse m.

chin [tʃɪn] n Kinn neut.

china [ˈtʃaɪnə] n Porzellan neut. adj Porzellan-. **china clay** Kaolin neut.

China [ˈtʃaɪnə] n China neut. **Chinese** adj chinesisch; n Chinese m, Chinesin f.

chink¹ [tʃɪŋk] n (fissure) Ritze f, Spalt m.

chink² [tʃɪŋk] v (sound) klirren. n Klirren neut.

chip [tʃɪp] n Splitter m; (comp) Chip m. **chips** pl Pommes frites pl; (crisps) Chips pl. **chipped** adj (china) angestoßen.

chiropodist [kɪˈrɒpədɪst] n Fußpfleger(in). **chiropody** n Fußpflege f.

chirp [tʃəːp] v zirpen. n Gezirp neut. **chirpy** adj munter.

chisel [ˈtʃɪzl] n Meißel m. v meißeln.

chivalrous [ˈʃɪvəlrəs] adj ritterlich. **chivalry** n Ritterlichkeit f.

chives [tʃaɪvz] pl n Schnittlauch m sing.

chlorine [ˈklɔːriːn] n Chlor neut. **chlorinate** v chlorieren.

chlorophyll [ˈklɒrəfɪl] n Chlorophyll neut.

chocolate [ˈtʃɒkələt] n Schokolade f. adj (colour) schokoladenbraun.

choice [tʃɔɪs] n Wahl f; (selection) Auswahl f. adj auserlesen.

choir [ˈkwaɪə] n Chor m. **choirboy** n Chorknabe m.

choke [tʃəʊk] v ersticken, würgen; (throttle) erwürgen. n (mot) Starterklappe f.

cholera [ˈkɒlərə] n Cholera f.

cholesterol [kəˈlestərɒl] n Cholesterin neut.

*choose [tʃuːz] v wählen; (select) auswählen; (prefer) vorziehen. **choosy** adj wählerisch.

cholesterol [kəˈlestərɒl] n Cholesterin neut.

chop¹ [tʃɒp] v (food) zerhacken; (wood) spalten. n Kotelett neut.

chop² [tʃɒp] v **chop and change** schwanken, wechseln.

chopsticks [ˈtʃɒpstɪks] pl n Eßstäbchen pl.

chord [kɔːd] n (music) Akkord m.

chore [tʃɔː] n lästige Pflicht f.

choreographer [kɒrɪˈɒɡrəfə] n Choreograph m. **choreography** n Choreographie f.

chorus [ˈkɔːrəs] n Chor m; (of song) Refrain m.

chose [tʃəuz] V choose.

chosen ['tʃəuzn] V choose.

Christ [kraist] n Christus m.

christen ['krisn] v taufen. **christening** n Taufe f.

Christian ['kristʃən] adj christlich. n Christ m, Christin f. **Christian name** Vorname m. **Christianity** n Christentum neut.

Christmas ['krisməs] n Weihnachten pl. **Christmas card** Weihnachtskarte f. **Christmas present** Weihnachtsgeschenk neut. **Christmas tree** Weihnachtsbaum m.

chrome [krəum] n (plating) Verchromung f. adj (yellow) chromgelb. **chrome-plated** adj verchromt.

chromium ['krəumiəm] n Chrom neut.

chronic ['kronik] adj (med) chronisch.

chronicle ['kronikl] n Chronik f.

chronological [kronə'bdʒikəl] adj chronologisch.

chrysalis ['krisəlis] n Puppe f.

chrysanthemum [kri'sanθəməm] n Chrysantheme f.

chubby ['tʃʌbi] adj pausbäckig.

chuck [tʃʌk] v (coll) werfen.

chuckle ['tʃʌkl] v glucksen, kichern. n Kichern neut.

chunk [tʃʌŋk] n Klumpen m, Stück neut.

church [tʃəːtʃ] n Kirche f. **church-goer** n Kirchgänger m. **churchyard** n Kirchhof m.

churn [tʃəːn] n (butter) Butterfaß neut; (milk) Milchkanne f. v (fig) aufwühlen.

chute [ʃuːt] n Rutsche f.

cider ['saidə] n Apfelwein m.

cigar [si'gaː] n Zigarre f.

cigarette [sigə'ret] n Zigarette f. **cigarette end** Zigarettenstümmel m. **cigarette lighter** n Feuerzeug neut.

cinder ['sində] n Zinder m.

cine camera ['sini] n Filmkamera f.

cinema ['sinəmə] n Kino neut.

cinnamon ['sinəmən] n Zimt m.

circle ['səːkl] n Kreis m; (theatre) Rang m. v umkreisen. **circular** adj kreisförmig, rund. **circulate** v zirkulieren, umlaufen; (send round) in Umlauf setzen. **circulation** n Umlauf m; (blood) Kreislauf m.

circuit ['səːkit] n Umlauf m; (elec) Stromkreis m.

circumcise ['səːkəm saiz] v beschneiden. **circumcision** n Beschneidung f.

circumference [sə'kʌm fərəns] n Umfang m.

circumscribe ['səːkəm skraib] v umschreiben.

circumstance ['səːkəm stans] n Umstand m. **under the circumstances** unter diesen Umständen. **under no circumstances** auf keinen Fall.

circus ['səːkəs] n Zirkus m.

cistern ['sistən] n Zisterne f.

cite [sait] v zitieren.

citizen ['sitizn] n Bürger(in); (of country) Staatsangehörige(r). **citizenship** n Staatsangehörigkeit f.

citrus ['sitrəs] adj **citrus fruit** Zitrusfrucht f.

city ['siti] n Stadt f.

civic ['sivik] n städtisch.

civil ['sivl] adj (polite) höflich, freundlich; (not military) Zivil-. **civility** n Höflichkeit f. **civil engineer** Bauingenieur m. **civil rights** Bürgerrechte pl.

civilian [sə'viljən] adj Zivil-. n Zivilist m.

civilization [sivilai'zeiʃən] n Zivilisation f. **civilize** v zivilisieren. **civilized** adj zivilisiert.

clad [klad] adj bekleidet; (tech) umkleidet.

claim [kleim] v verlangen, Anspruch erheben auf. n Anspruch m; (right) Anrecht neut. **claimant** n Antragsteller m.

clairvoyant [kleə'voiənt] n Hellseher(in).

clam [klam] n Muschel f.

clamber ['klambə] v klettern.

clammy ['klami] adj feucht, klebrig.

clamour ['klamə] n Geschrei neut. v clamour for rufen nach.

clamp [klamp] n Klammer f, Krampe f. v verklammern; (car wheel) eine Radkralle an einem Auto anbringen. **clamp down on** unterdrücken.

clan [klan] n Sippe f.

clandestine [klan'destin] adj heimlich.

clang [klaŋ] n Schall m, Klirren neut. v schallen, klirren.

clank [klaŋk] n Gerassel neut; Klappern neut. v rasseln, klappern.

clap [klap] v (applaud) klatschen, Beifall spenden (+ dat); (hit) schlagen, klapsen. n (tap) Klaps m. **clapper** n (bell) Klöppel m. **clapping** n Klatschen neut.

claret ['klarət] n Rotwein m, Bordeaux m.

clarify ['klærɪfaɪ] v klären. **clarification** n Klärung f.

clarinet [klærə'net] n Klarinette f. **clarinettist** n Klarinettist m.

clash [klæʃ] v kollidieren, zusammenprallen; (argue) sich streiten; (colours) nicht zusammenpassen. n Knall m; (conflict) Konflikt m.

clasp [klɑːsp] v umklammern; n Haspe f, Klammer f.

class [klɑːs] n Klasse f; (lesson) Stunde f. v klassieren. **class-conscious** adj klassenbewußt. **classroom** n Klassenzimmer f. **classy** adj (coll) klasse, erstklassig.

classic ['klæsɪk] adj klassisch. **classic** pl n die alten Sprachen pl. **classical** adj klassisch. **classicism** n Klassik f.

classify ['klæsɪfaɪ] v klassifizieren. **classification** n Klassifizierung f.

clatter ['klætə] v klappern. n Klappern neut.

clause [klɔːz] n (in document) Klausel f.

claustrophobia [klɔːstrə'foubiə] n Platzangst f.

claw [klɔː] n Kralle f. Klaue f. v zerkratzen.

clay [kleɪ] n Lehm m, Ton m.

clean [kliːn] adj rein, sauber; (paper) weiß. adv ganz. v reinigen, putzen, saubermachen. **clean up** aufräumen. **come clean** gestehen. **cleaner** n (woman) Putzfrau f. **cleaning** n Reinigen neut. **cleanness** n Sauberkeit f. **cleanly** adj reinlich. **clean-shaven** adj glattrasiert.

cleanse [klenz] v reinigen.

clear [klɪə] adj klar; (sound, meaning) deutlich, klar; (road, way) frei; (glass) durchsichtig. v räumen; (table) abräumen; (road) freimachen; (forest) roden; (authorize) freigeben. **clearance** n Räumung f; (authorization) Freigabe f; (tech) Spielraum m. **clearcut** adj (fig) eindeutig. **clearing** n Lichtung f. **clearly** adv offensichtlich.

clef [klef] n Notenschlüssel m.

clench [klentʃ] v (fist) zusammenballen.

clergy ['klɜːdʒi] n Klerus m. **clergyman** n Geistliche(r) m; Kleriker m.

clerical ['klerɪkəl] adj geistlich. **clerical work** Büroarbeit f.

clerk [klɑːk] n Büroangestellte(r); (sales clerk) Verkäufer(in).

clever ['klevə] adj klug, gescheit; (crafty) raffiniert. **cleverness** n Klugheit f.

cliché ['kliːʃeɪ] n Klischee neut.

click [klɪk] n Klicken neut; (comp) Mausklick m. v klicken; (comp) anklicken.

client ['klaɪənt] n Kunde m, Kundin f. **clientele** n Kundschaft f.

cliff [klɪf] n Klippe f.

climate ['klaɪmət] n Klima neut. **climate change** Klimawandel m

climax ['klaɪmæks] n Höhepunkt m.

climb [klaɪm] v klettern; (ascend) steigen; (mountain) besteigen. n Aufstieg m. **climb up** hinaufklettern auf. **climb down** hinabsteigen. **climber** n (mountaineer) Bergsteiger m. **climbing** n (mountaineering) Bergsteigen neut.

***cling** [klɪŋ] v sich klammern (an); (fig) hängen (an).

clinic ['klɪnɪk] n Klinik f. **clinical** adj klinisch.

clink [klɪŋk] n Klirren neut. v klirren.

clip¹ [klɪp] v (hair) schneiden; (dog) scheren; (ticket) knipsen. **clipping** n (newspaper) Zeitungsausschnitt m.

clip² [klɪp] n (fastener) Klammer f, Klemme f. v **clip together** zusammenklammern.

clitoris ['klɪtərɪs] n Kitzler m, Klitoris f.

cloak [klouk] n Umhang m. **cloakroom** n Garderobe f; (WC) Toilette f.

clock [klɒk] n Uhr f. **clockwise** adj, adv im Uhrzeigersinn. **clockwork** n Uhrwerk neut.

clog [klɒg] n Holzschuh m. v verstopfen.

cloister ['klɔɪstə] n Kreuzgang m.

clone [kloun] n Klon m. v klonen, (fig) nachmachen.

close¹ [klouz] v zumachen, schließen. n Ende neut; Schluß m. **close down** eingehen. **closed** adj (shop) geschlossen; (road) gesperrt.

close² [klous] adj nahe; (intimate) vertraut; (careful) genau; (weather) schwül. adv knapp. **close to** in der Nähe (+ gen or von). **close together** dicht zusammen. that was close! das war knapp! **closely** adv genau, gründlich. **close-up** Nahaufnahme f.

closet ['klɒzɪt] n Schrank m.

clot [klɒt] n Klümpchen neut; (of blood) Blutgerinnsel neut. v gerinnen.

cloth [klɒθ] n (material) Stoff m, Tuch neut; (for wiping) Lappen m.

clothe [klouð] v (be)kleiden. **clothes** pl n Kleider pl. **clothes brush** Kleiderbürste f.

clothes line Wäscheleine f. **clothes peg** Wäscheklammer f. **clothing** n Kleidung f.

cloud [klaud] n Wolke f. **cloud over** sich

bewölken.

clove[1] [kbuv] *n* (*spice*) Gewürznelke *f*.

clove[2] [kbuv] *n* **clove of garlic** Knoblauchzehe *f*.

clover ['kbuvə] *n* Klee *m*.

clown [klaun] *n* Clown *m*.

club [klʌb] *n* (*association*) Klub *m*, Verein *m*; (*weapon*) Keule *f*; (*golf*) Golfschläger *m*. **clubfoot** *n* Klumpfuß *m*.

clue [klu:] *n* Spur *f*, Anhaltspunkt *m*. I haven't a clue ich habe keine Ahnung *f*.

clump [klʌmp] *n* Klumpen *neut*; (*of bushes*) Gebüsch *neut*.

clumsy ['klʌm zi] *adj* unbeholfen, linkisch.

clung [klʌŋ] *V* **cling**.

cluster ['klʌstə] *n* Traube *f*. *v* **cluster around** schwärmen um.

clutch [klʌtʃ] *n* (*fester*) Griff *m*; (*mot*) Kupplung *f*. *v* sich festklammern an. **clutch at** greifen nach.

clutter ['klʌtə] *n* Unordnung *f*, Durcheinander *neut*. *v* vollstopfen.

coach [koutʃ] *n* Kutsche *f*; (*rail*) Wagen *m*; (*sport*) Trainer *m*. *v* eintrainieren.

coagulate [kou'agjuleit] *v* gerinnen.

coal [koul] *n* Kohle *f*. **coal-mine** Kohlenbergwerk *neut*.

coalition [kouə'liʃən] *n* (*pol*) Koalition *f*.

coarse [ko:s] *adj* grob; (*vulg*) ordinär.

coast [koust] *n* Küste *f*. **coastal** *adj* Küsten-. **coastline** *n* Küstenlinie *f*.

coat [kout] *n* Mantel *m*; (*of animal*) Fell *neut*, Pelz *m*; (*of paint*) Anstrich *m*. *v* bestreichen. **coated** *adj* überzogen. **coathanger** *n* Kleiderbügel *m*. **coating** *n* Überzug *m*.

coax [kouks] *v* beschwatzen.

cobbler ['koblə] *n* Schuster *m*.

cobra ['koubrə] *n* Kobra *neut*.

cobweb ['kobweb] *n* Spinngewebe *neut*.

cocaine [kə'kein] *n* Kokain *neut*.

cock[1] [kok] *n* (*male chicken*) Hahn *m*; (*male bird*) Männchen *neut*.

cock[2] [kok] *v* (*gun*) spannen; (*ears*) spitzen.

cockle ['kokl] *n* (*shellfish*) Herzmuschel *f*.

cockpit ['kokpit] *n* Kanzel *f*, Kabine *f*.

cockroach ['kokroutʃ] *n* Küchenschabe *f*.

cocktail ['kokteil] *n* Cocktail *neut*.

cocoa ['koukou] *n* Kakao *m*.

coconut ['koukənʌt] *n* Kokosnuß *m*.

cocoon [kə'ku:n] *n* Kokon *m*, Puppe *f*.

cod [kod] *n* Kabeljau *m*.

code [koud] *n* Kode *m*.

codeine ['koudi:n] *n* Kodein *neut*.

coeducation [kouedju'keiʃən] *n* Gemeinschaftserziehung *f*.

coerce [kou'ə:s] *v* zwingen. **coercion** *n* Zwang *m*.

coexist [kouig'zist] *v* koexistieren. **coexistence** *n* Koexistenz *f*.

coffee ['kofi] *n* Kaffee *m*. **coffee bar** Café *neut*.

coffin ['kofin] *n* Sarg *m*.

cog [kog] *n* Radzahn *neut*. **cogwheel** *n* Zahnrad *neut*.

cognac ['konjak] *n* Kognak *m*.

cohabit [kou'habit] *v* (*ehelich*) zusammenwohnen.

coherent [kou'hiərənt] *adj* zusammenhängend.

coil [koil] *n* Rolle *f*; *v* aufwickeln.

coin [koin] *n* Münze *f*. *v* prägen. **coinbox** *n* (*phone*) Münzfernsprecher *m*.

coincide [kouin'said] *v* zusammenfallen; (*agree*) übereinstimmen. **coincidence** *n* Zufall *m*. **coincidental** *adj* zufällig.

colander ['koləndə] *n* Durchschlag *m*.

cold [kould] *adj* kalt. *I am/feel cold* mir ist kalt. *n* Kälte *f*; (*med*) Erkältung *f*. **catch cold** sich erkälten. **in cold blood** kaltblütig. **coldly** *adv* (*fig*) gefühllos, unfreundlich. **cold store** Kühlhaus *neut*.

coleslaw ['koulslo:] *n* Krautsalat *m*.

colic ['kolik] *n* Kolik *f*.

collaborate [kə'labəreit] *v* zusammenarbeiten. **collaboration** *n* zusammenarbeit *f*. **collaborator** *n* Mitarbeiter *m*; (*in war*) Kollaborateur *m*.

collapse [kə'laps] *v* einstürzen; (*person*) zusammenbrechen. *n* Einsturz *m*; (*fig, med*) Zusammenbruch *m*. **collapsible** *adj* zusammenklappbar.

collar ['kolə] *n* Kragen *m*; (*for dog*) Halsband *m*. **collarbone** *n* Schlüsselbein *neut*.

colleague ['koli:g] *n* Kollege *m*, Kollegin *f*.

collect [kə'lekt] *v* sammeln; (*fetch*) abholen; (*taxes*) einnehmen; (*come together*) zusammenkommen. **collect call** (*phone*) R-Gespräch *neut*. **collected** *adj* (*calm*) gefaßt. **collection** *n* Sammlung *f*; (*rel*) Kollekte *f*; (*mail*) Leerung *f*. **collective** *adj* kollektiv. **collective bargaining** Tarifverhandlungen *pl*. **collector** *n* Sammler *m*; (**of**

taxes) Einnehmer *m*.

college ['kɒlɪdʒ] *n* Hochschule *f*; (*at Oxford, etc.*) College *neut*. **technical college** Realschule *f*.

collide [kə'laɪd] *v* kollidieren, zusammenprallen.

colloquial [kə'ləukwəl] *adj* umgangssprachlich.

Cologne [kə'bun] *n* Köln *neut*. **eau de Cologne** Kölnischwasser *neut*.

colon ['kəulən] *n* (*anat*) Dickdarm *m*; (*gram*) Doppelpunkt *m*.

colonel ['kɜːnl] *n* Oberst *m*.

colony ['kɒlənɪ] *n* Kolonie *f*. **colonial** *adj* Kolonial-. **colonialism** Kolonialismus *m*. **colonize** *v* kolonisieren.

colossal [kə'bsəl] *adj* kolossal, riesig.

colour ['kʌlə] *n* Farbe *f*; (*fig*) Ton *m*, Charakter *m*. **colours** *pl* Fahne *f sing*. *v* färben (*also fig*), kolorieren. **colour bar** Rassenschranke *f*. **colour-blind** *adj* farbenblind. **coloured** *adj* farbig. **coloured man/woman** Farbige(r). **colour film** Farbfilm *m*. **colourful** *adj* farbig, bunt. **colour television** Farbfernsehen *neut*.

colt [kəult] *n* Fohlen *neut*.

column ['kɒləm] *n* Säule *f*; (*in newspaper*) Spalte *f*; (*mil*) Kolonne *f*. **columnist** *n* Kolumnist *m*.

coma ['kəumə] *n* Koma *f*.

comb [kəum] *n* Kamm *m*. *v* kämmen; (*fig*) durchkämmen.

combat ['kɒmbæt] *v* bekämpfen. *n* Kampf *m*, Gefecht *neut*.

combine [kəm'baɪn; *n* 'kɒmbaɪn] *v* vereinigen, verbinden; (*come together*) sich vereinigen. *n* Konzern *m*. **combine harvester** Mähdrescher *m*.

combustion [kəm'bʌstʃən] *n* Verbrennung *f*. **combustible** *adj* brennbar.

****come** [kʌm] *v* kommen. **come about** geschehen. **come across** stoßen auf. **come back** zurückkommen. **come from** herkommen von stammen aus. **come near** sich nähern. **come on** weiterkommen; (*make progress*) fortschreiten. **come on!** los!; weiter! **come out** herauskommen. **come through** durchkommen. **come to** (*arrive at*) ankommen an, gelangen an; (*amount to*) sich belaufen auf; (*regain consciousness*) zu sich kommen. **comeback** *n* Comeback *neut*.

comedy ['kɒmədɪ] *n* Komödie *f*. **comedian** *n* Komiker *m*.

comet ['kɒmɪt] *n* Komet *m*.

comfort ['kʌmfət] *n* Bequemlichkeit *f*, Komfort *m*; (*solace*) Trost *m*. *v* trösten. **comfortable** *adj* bequem; (*room, etc.*) komfortabel.

comic ['kɒmɪk] *adj* komisch, lustig; (*theatre*) Komödien-. *n* (*person*) Komiker *m*; (*paper*) Comic *neut*. **comical** *adj* komisch.

comma ['kɒmə] *n* Komma *neut*.

command [kə'maɪnd] *n* (*order*) Befehl *m*; (*mil*) Oberbefehl *m*; (*mastery*) Beherrschung *f*. *v* (*instruct*) befehlen; (*be in charge of*) kommandieren. **commander** *n* Befehlshaber *m*; (*mil*) Kommandant *m*. **commandment** *n* Gebot *neut*. **commando** *n* Kommando *neut*.

commemorate [kə'meməreɪt] *v* gedenken (+*gen*), feiern. **commemoration** *n* Gedächtnisfeier *f*.

commence [kə'mens] *v* beginnen, anfangen. **commencement** *n* Beginn *m*, Anfang *m*.

commend [kə'mend] *v* (*praise*) loben; (*entrust*) anvertrauen. **commendable** *adj* lobenswert.

comment ['kɒment] *n* (*remark*) Bemerkung *f*; (*annotation*) Anmerkung *f*. *v* kommentieren, Bemerkungen machen. **commentary** *n* Reportage *f*. **commentator** *n* Kommentator *m*.

commerce ['kɒmɜːs] *n* Handel *m*, Kommerz *m*. **commercial** *adj* kommerziell, geschäftlich, Handels-; *n* (*TV*) Werbesendung *f*. **commercialize** *v* kommerzialisieren.

commiserate [kə'mɪzəreɪt] *v* **commiserate with** bemitleiden.

commission [kə'mɪʃən] *n* Auftrag *m*; (*committee*) Kommission *f*; (*fee*) Provision *f*; (*mil*) Offizierspatent *neut*. *v* (*person*) beauftragen; (*thing*) bestellen. **commissioner** *n* Bevollmächtigte(r).

commit [kə'mɪt] *v* (*offence*) begehen. **commit oneself** sich verpflichten. **commitment** *n* Verpflichtung *f*.

committee [kə'mɪtɪ] *n* Ausschuß *m*, Kommission *f*.

commodity [kə'mɒdətɪ] *n* Ware *f*. **commodities** *pl* Grundstoffe *pl*.

common ['kɒmən] *adj* gemein, gemeinsam; (*abundant*) weit verbreitet; (*vulg*) gemein, ordinär. **Common Agricultural**

Policy (CAP) Gemeinsame Agrarpolitik (GAP) *f.* **Common Market** Gemeinsamer Markt *m.* **commonplace** *adj* alltäglich. **commonsense** *n* gesunder Menschenverstand *m.*

commotion [kə'm oʊʃən] *n* Erregung *f,* Aufruhr *m.*

commune ['kom juːn] *n* Kommune *f,* Gemeinschaft *f.*

communicate [kə'm juːnɪkeɪt] *v* mitteilen; (*illness*) übertragen. **communicative** *adj* gesprächig. **communication** *n* Kommunikation *f;* (*message*) Mitteilung *f.* **communications** *pl n* Verkehrswege *pl.*

communism ['kom jʊnɪzəm] *n* Kommunismus *m.* **communist** *adj* kommunistisch. *n* Kommunist(in).

community [kə'm juːnətɪ] *n* Gemeinschaft *f.*

commute [kə'm juːt] *v* (*travel*) pendeln; (*a sentence*) herabsetzen. **commuter** *n* Pendler *m.*

compact[1] [kəm 'pakt] *adj* kompakt, dicht. **compact disc** (Audio-)CD *f.*

compact[2] ['kom pakt] *n* (*agreement*) Vertrag *m,* Pakt *m.*

companion [kəm 'panjən] *n* Begleiter(in); Genosse *m,* Genossin *f.* **companionable** *adj* gesellig. **companionship** *n* Gesellschaft *f.*

company ['kʌm pənɪ] *n* Gesellschaft *f;* (*firm*) Gesellschaft *f,* Firma *f;* (*theatre*) Truppe *f;* (*mil*) Kompanie *f.*

compare [kəm 'peə] *v* vergleichen; (*match up to*) sich vergleichen lassen. **comparable** *adj* vergleichbar. **comparative** *adj* relativ; (*gram*) steigernd. **comparatively** *adv* verhältnismäßig. **comparison** *n* Vergleich *m.* **in comparison with** im Vergleich zu.

compartment [kəm 'paːtm ənt] *n* Abteilung *f.*

compass ['kʌm pəs] *n* Kompaß *m.* **pair of compasses** Zirkel *m.*

compassion [kəm 'paʃən] *n* Mitleid *neut.* **compassionate** *adj* mitleidig.

compatible [kəm 'patəbl] *adj* vereinbar.

compel [kəm 'pel] *v* zwingen.

compensate ['kom pənseɪt] *v* (*money*) entschädigen; (*balance out*) ausgleichen. **compensation** *n* Entschädigung *f;* Ausgleich *m.*

compete [kəm 'piːt] *v* konkurrieren, sich bewerben; (*take part*) teilnehmen. **competition** *n* Wettbewerb *m;* (*comm*)

Konkurrenz *f.* **competitive** *adj* konkurrenzfähig. **competitor** *n* (*sport*) Teilnehmer(in); (*comm*) Konkurrent(in).

compile [kəm 'paɪl] *v* kompilieren.

complacent [kəm 'pleɪsnt] *adj* selbstzufrieden.

complain [kəm 'pleɪn] *v* klagen. **complain about/to** sich beschweren über/bei. **complaint** *n* Klage *f,* Beschwerde *f.*

complement ['kom pləm ənt] *n* Ergänzung *f. v* ergänzen; (*go together*) zusammenpassen. **complementary** *adj* komplementär.

complete [kəm 'pliːt] *v* vollenden, vervollständigen; (*form*) ausfüllen. *adj* vollständig, vollendet. **completely** *adv* völlig, vollständig, ganz und gar. **completion** *n* Vollendung *f.*

complex ['kom pleks] *adj* kompliziert. *n* (*psychol*) Komplex *m.*

complexion [kəm 'plekʃən] *n* Teint *m.*

complicate ['kom plɪkeɪt] *v* verwickeln, komplizieren. **complicated** *adj* kompliziert. **complication** *n* Komplikation *f,* Schwierigkeit *f.*

compliment ['kom pləm ənt] *n* Kompliment *neut. v* komplimentieren. **complimentary** *adj* höflich, artig. **complimentary ticket** Freikarte *f.*

comply [kəm 'plaɪ] *v* sich fügen. **comply with** (*rules*) sich halten an; (*request*) erfüllen.

component [kəm 'pounənt] *n* Bestandteil *m.*

compose [kəm 'pouz] *v* komponieren. **composed** *adj* gefaßt. **be composed of** bestehen aus. **composer** *n* Komponist *m.* **composite** *adj* zusammengesetzt. **composition** *n* Komposition *f;* (*piece of music*) (Musik)Stück *neut.*

compost ['kom post] *n* Kompost *m.*

composure [kəm 'pouʒə] *n* Gefaßtheit *f.*

compound ['kom paund] *n* Zusammensetzung *f;* (*chem*) Verbindung *f; adj* zusammengesetzt, gemischt.

comprehend [kom prɪhend] *v* verstehen, begreifen. **comprehensible** *adj* verständlich. **comprehension** *n* Verständnis.

comprehensive [kom prɪhensɪv] *adj* umfassend. **comprehensive school** *n* Gesamtschule *f.*

compress [kəm 'pres; *n* 'kompres] *v* verdichten, zusammendrücken. *n* (*med*)

Kompresse f. **compressed** adj zusammengedrückt. **compressed air** Preßluft f. **compression** n Verdichtung f. **compressor** n Verdichter m.

comprise [kəm'praɪz] v bestehen aus.

compromise ['kɒm prəm aɪz] n Kompromiß m or neut. v einen Kompromiß schließen; (expose) kompromittieren.

compulsion [kəm'pʌlʃən] n Zwang m. **compulsive** adj Zwangs-. **compulsory** adj Zwangs-.

compunction [kəm'pʌŋkʃən] n Gewissensbisse pl, Reue f.

computer [kəm'pjuːtən] n Computer m. **computing** n elektronische Datenverarbeitung (EDV) f.

comrade ['kɒm rɪd] n Genosse m, Genossin f; Kamerad(in). **comradeship** n Kameradschaft f.

concave [kɒn'keɪv] adj konkav, Hohl-.

conceal [kən'siːl] v verbergen, verstecken; (fact, etc.) verschweigen.

concede [kən'siːd] v zugeben, einräumen; (right) bewilligen.

conceit [kən'siːt] n Einbildung f, Eitelkeit f. **conceited** adj eingebildet.

conceive [kən'siːv] v (plan) erdenken; (child) empfangen; (thoughts) fassen. **conceive of** sich vorstellen (+ acc). **conceivable** adj denkbar, vorstellbar.

concentrate ['kɒnsəntreɪt] v konzentrieren. **concentrate on** sich konzentrieren auf. **concentrated** adj konzentriert. **concentration** n Konzentration f.

concentric [kɒn'sentrɪk] adj konzentrisch.

concept ['kɒnsept] n Begriff m, Idee f. **conception** n Vorstellung f; (of child) Empfängnis f.

concern [kən'səːn] v betreffen, angehen; (worry) beunruhigen. n (worry) Besorgnis f, Sorge f; (interest) Interesse neut; (comm) Betrieb m. **concern oneself with** sich befassen mit. **as far as I am concerned** von mir aus. that's not your concern! das geht Sie nichts an! **concerning** adj betreffend.

concert ['kɒnsət] n Konzert neut.

concerted [kən'səːtid] adj konzertiert.

concerto [kən'tʃəːtou] n Konzert neut.

concession [kən'seʃən] n Konzession f. **concessionnaire** n Konzessionär m.

conciliate [kən'sɪlieit] v versöhnen. **concili-**

ation n Versöhnung f. **conciliatory** adj versöhnlich.

concise [kən'saɪs] adj kurz, knapp.

conclude [kən'kluːd] v schließen. **conclude that** den Schluß ziehen, daß. **conclusive** adj (evidence) schlüssig.

concoct [kən'kokt] v zusammenbrauen.

concrete ['kɒnkrɪt] adj konkret; (made of concrete) Beton-. n Beton m.

concussion [kən'kʌʃən] n (med) Gehirnerschütterung f.

condemn [kən'dem] v verurteilen. **condemnation** n Verurteilung f.

condense [kən'dens] v kondensieren. **condensation** n Kondensation f. **condensed milk** Kondensmilch f.

condescend [kondɪ'send] v sich herablassen. **condescending** adj herablassend. **condescension** n Herablassung f.

condition [kən'dɪʃən] n (state) Zustand m; (requirement) Bedingung f, Voraussetzung f. **conditions** pl Umstände pl. **on condition that** unter der Bedingung, daß. **out of condition** (sport) in schlechter Form. **conditional** adj bedingt. **conditioner** n (hair) Haarspülung f.

condolence [kən'douləns] n Beileid neut.

condom ['kɒndom] n Kondom neut.

condone [kən'doun] v verzeihen.

conducive [kən'djuːsɪv] adj förderlich.

conduct [kən'dʌkt; n 'kɒndʌkt] v führen; (orchestra) dirigieren; (elec) leiten. **conduct oneself** sich verhalten. n Führung f; (behaviour) Verhalten neut.

conductor [kən'dʌktə] n (music) Dirigent m; (bus) Schaffner(in).

cone [koun] n (shape) Kegel m; (ice cream) Waffeltüte f; (bot) Zapfen m.

confectioner [kən'fekʃənə] n Süßwärenhändler m. **confectionery** n Süßwaren pl.

confederation [kən,fedə'reʃən] n Bund m.

confer [kən'fəː] v (bestow) verleihen; (discuss) konferieren. **conference** n Konferenz f.

confess [kən'fes] v bekennen, gestehen; (rel) beichten. **confession** n Geständnis neut; (rel) Beichte f. **confessional** n Beichtstuhl m.

confetti [kən'feti] n Konfetti pl.

confide [kən'faɪd] v anvertrauen. **confide in** vertrauen (+ dat). **confidence** n

Vertrauen *neut*; (*in oneself*) Selbstvertrauen *neut*. **confident** *adj* zuversichtlich; selbstsicher. **confidential** *adj* vertraulich.

confine [kən'faɪn] *v* (*limit*) beschränken; (*lock up*) einsperren. **confinement** *n* (*in prison*) Haft *f*; (*childbirth*) Niederkunft *f*.

confirm [kən'fəːm] *v* bestätigen; (*rel*) konfirmieren. **confirmation** *n* Bestätigung *f*; Konfirmation *f*.

confiscate ['kɒnfɪskeɪt] *v* beschlagnahmen. **confiscation** *n* Beschlagnahme *f*.

conflict ['kɒnflɪkt; *v* kən'flɪkt] *n* Konflikt *m*, Streit *m*. *v* widerstreiten (+ *dat*). **conflict of interests** Interessenkonflikt *m*. **conflicting** *adj* widerstreitend.

conform [kən'fɔːm] *v* (*tally*) übereinstimmen (mit); (*to rules*) sich fügen (+*dat*). **conformist** *n* Konformist.

confound [kən'faund] *v* (*surprise*) erstaunen; (*mix up*) verwechseln. **confound it!** verdammt!

confront [kən'frʌnt] *v* konfrontieren; (*enemy*) entgegentreten (+*dat*). **confrontation** *n* Konfrontation *f*.

confuse [kən'fjuːz] *v* (*mix up*) verwechseln (mit); (*perplex*) verwirren. **confused** *adj* (*person*) verwirrt; (*situation*) verworren. **confusion** *n* Verwirrung *f*.

congeal [kən'dʒiːl] *v* gerinnen.

congenial [kən'dʒiːnɪəl] *adj* freundlich, gemütlich.

congenital [kən'dʒenɪtl] *adj* angeboren.

congested [kən'dʒestɪd] *adj* überfüllt. **congestion** *n* Stauung *f*; (*traffic*) Verkehrsstauung *f*.

conglomeration [kən‚glɒmə'reɪʃən] *n* Anhäufung *f*, Konglomerat *neut*.

congratulate [kən'grætjuleɪt] *v* beglückwünschen. **congratulations** *pl n* Glückwünsche *pl*.

congregate ['kɒŋgrɪgeɪt] *v* sich versammeln. **congregation** *n* Versammlung *f*.

congress ['kɒŋgres] *n* Kongreß *m*. **congressman/woman** Abgeordnete(r).

conifer ['kɒnɪfə] *n* Nadelbaum *m*. **coniferous** *adj* Nadel-.

conjecture [kən'dʒektʃə] *n* Vermutung *f*.

conjugal ['kɒndʒugəl] *adj* ehelich.

conjugate ['kɒndʒugeɪt] *v* (*gramm*) konjugieren.

conjunction [kən'dʒʌŋkʃən] *n* Vereinigung *f*; (*gramm, astrol*) Konjunktion *f*.

conjunctivitis [kən‚dʒʌŋktɪ'vaɪtɪs] *n* Bindehautentzündung *f*.

conjure ['kʌndʒə] *v* **conjure up** heraufbeschwören. **conjurer** *n* Zauberkünstler *m*. **conjuring trick** Zauberkunststück *neut*.

connect [kə'nekt] *v* verbinden; (*phone, etc.*) anschließen. **connection** *n* Verbindung *f*; (*phone, rail*) Anschluß *m*. **in connection with** im Zusammenhang mit.

connoisseur [kɒnə'səː] *n* Kenner *m*.

connotation [kɒnə'teɪʃən] *n* Nebenbedeutung *f*.

conquer ['kɒŋkə] *v* erobern, besiegen; (*fig*) überwinden, beherrschen. **conqueror** *n* Eroberer *m*. **conquest** *n* Eroberung *f*.

conscience ['kɒnʃəns] *n* Gewissen *neut*.

conscientious [kɒnʃɪenʃəs] *adj* pflichtbewußt.

conscious ['kɒnʃəs] *adj* bewußt. **consciousness** *n* Bewußtsein *neut*.

conscript ['kɒnskrɪpt] *v* einziehen. *n* Wehrpflichtige(r). **conscription** *n* Wehrpflicht *f*.

consecrate ['kɒnsɪkreɪt] *v* weihen.

consecutive [kən'sekjutɪv] *adj* aufeinanderfolgend.

consensus [kən'sensəs] *n* Übereinstimmung *f*.

consent [kən'sent] *v* zustimmen (+*dat*). *n* Zustimmung *f*.

consequence ['kɒnsɪkwəns] *n* Folge *f*, Konsequenz *f*. **of no consequence** unbedeutend. **consequently** *adv* folglich.

conserve [kən'səːv] *v* erhalten; (*energy*) sparen. **conservation** *n* Schutz *m*, Erhaltung *f*. **conservative** *adj* konservativ; *n* Konservative(r). **conservatory** *n* Treibhaus *neut*; (*music*) Musikhochschule *f*.

consider [kən'sɪdə] *v* (*think about*) überlegen; (*regard as*) halten für. **considerate** *adj* rücksichtsvoll. **consideration** *n* (*thought*) Überlegung *f*; (*thoughtfulness*) Rücksicht *f*. **considering** *prep* in Anbetracht (+*gen*).

consign [kən'saɪn] *v* versenden. **consignee** *n* Empfänger *m*. **consignment** *n* Sendung *f*. **consignor** *n* Absender *m*.

consist [kən'sɪst] *v* **consist of** bestehen aus. **consistency** *n* (*of substance*) Dichte *f*. **consistent** *adj* konsequent. **consistent with** vereinbar mit.

console [kən'soul] *v* trösten. **consolation** *n*

Trost *m*. **consolation prize** Trostpreis *m*.

consolidate [kən'sɒlɪdeɪt] *v* stärken; *(comm)* konsolidieren. **consolidation** *n* Stärkung *f*.

consommé [kən'sɒmeɪ] *n* Fleischbrühe *f*.

consonant ['kɒnsənənt] *n* Konsonant *m*.

conspicuous [kən'spɪkjuəs] *adj (visible)* sichtbar; *(striking)* auffallend.

conspire [kən'spaɪə] *v* sich verschwören. **conspiracy** *n* Verschwörung *f*. **conspirator** *n* Verschwörer *m*.

constable ['kʌnstəbl] *n* Polizist *m*.

constant ['kɒnstənt] *adj* beständig, konstant; *(continual)* dauernd. **constantly** *adv* ständig.

constellation [kɒnstə'leɪʃən] *n* Sternbild *neut*.

constipation [kɒnstɪpeɪʃən] *n* (Darm) Verstopfung *f*.

constituency [kən'stɪtjuənsɪ] *n* Wahlkreis *m*. **constituent** *n* Wähler *m*.

constitute ['kɒnstɪtjuːt] *v* bilden, darstellen. **constitution** *n* (pol) Grundgesetz *m*, Verfassung *f*; *(of person)* Konstitution *f*.

constrain [kən'streɪn] *v* zwingen. **constraint** *n* Zwang *m*, Druck *m*.

constrict [kən'strɪkt] *v* zusammendrücken, einengen.

construct [kən'strʌkt] *v* bauen, konstruieren; *(argument)* aufstellen. **construction** *n* Bau *m*, Konstruktion *f*. **constructive** *adj* konstruktiv.

consul ['kɒnsəl] *n* Konsul *m*. **consulate** *n* Konsulat *neut*.

consult [kən'sʌlt] *v* zu Rate ziehen, konsultieren; *(book)* nachsehen in. **consultant** *n* Berater *m*. **consultation** *n* Konsultation *f*. **consulting room** Sprechzimmer *neut*.

consume [kən'sjuːm] *v* verzehren; *(money, time)* verbrauchen. **consumer** *n* Verbraucher *m*.

contact ['kɒntækt] *n* Verbindung *f*, Kontakt *m*. *v* sich in Verbindung setzen mit. **be in contact with** in Verbindung stehen mit.

contagious [kən'teɪdʒəs] *adj* ansteckend.

contain [kən'teɪn] *v* enthalten; *(feelings)* beherrschen. **contain oneself** sich beherrschen. **container** *n* Behälter *m*; *(for goods transport)* Container *m*. **container ship** Containerschiff *m*.

contaminate [kən'tæmɪneɪt] *v* verseuchen. **contamination** *n* Verseuchung *f*.

contemplate ['kɒntəmpleɪt] *v (observe)* nachdenklich betrachten; *(think about)* nachdenken über; *(doing something)* vorhaben. **contemplation** *n* Betrachtung *f*; Nachdenken *neut*.

contemporary [kən'tempərərɪ] *adj* zeitgenössisch; *(modern)* modern. *n* Zeitgenosse *m*.

contempt [kən'tempt] *n* Verachtung *f*. **contemptible** *adj* verächtlich. **contemptuous** *adj* voller Verachtung *f*.

contend [kən'tend] *v* kämpfen; *(assert)* behaupten.

content[1] ['kɒntent] *n* Inhalt *m*. **contents** *pl* Inhalt *m sing*. **table of contents** Inhaltsverzeichnis *neut*.

content[2] [kən'tent] *adj* zufrieden. **contentment** *n* Zufriedenheit *f*.

contention [kən'tenʃən] *n* Streit *m*; *(assertion)* Behauptung *f*.

contest ['kɒntest; *v* kən'test] *n* Wettkampf *m*. *v* bestreiten. **contestant** *n* Bewerber(in).

context ['kɒntekst] *n* Zusammenhang *m*.

continent ['kɒntɪnənt] *n* Festland *neut*, Kontinent *m*. **continental** *adj* Kontinental-.

contingency [kən'tɪndʒənsɪ] *n* Eventualität *f*.

continue [kən'tɪnjuː] *v* fortfahren, weitermachen; *(something)* fortsetzen; *(go further)* weitergehen. **continual** *adj* wiederholt. **continually** *adv* immer wieder. **continuation** *n* Fortsetzung *f*. **continuous** *adj* beständig.

contort [kən'tɔːt] *v* verdrehen. **contortion** *n* Verdrehung *f*. **contortionist** *n* Schlangenmensch *m*.

contour ['kɒntuə] *n* Umrißlinie *f*.

contraband ['kɒntrəband] *n* Schmuggelware *f*.

contraception [kɒntrə'sepʃən] *n* Empfängnisverhütung *f*. **contraceptive** *adj* empfängnisverhütend. *n* empfängnisverhütendes Mittel *neut*.

contract ['kɒntrækt; *v* kən'trækt] *n* Vertrag *m*. *v (become smaller)* sich zusammenziehen; *(illness)* sich zuziehen. **contraction** *n* Zusammenziehung *f*. **contractor** *n (building)* Bauunternehmer *m*.

contradict [kɒntrə'dɪkt] *v* widersprechen. **contradiction** *n* Widerspruch *m*. **contradictory** *adj* sich widersprechend.

contralto [kən'trɑːlou] n (*voice*) Alt m; (*singer*) Altistin f.

contraption [kən'træpʃən] n komisches Ding neut.

contrary [kən'trɛəri; *opposite*] 'kontrəri] adj (*person*) widerspenstig; (*opposite*) entgegengesetzt. n Gegenteil m. **on the contrary** im Gegenteil.

contrast [kən'trɑːst; n 'kontrɑːst] v (*compare*) vergleichen. **contrast with** kontrastieren mit. n Kontrast m. **in contrast to** im Gegensatz zu.

contravene [kontrə'viːn] v verstoßen gegen. **contravention** n Verstoß m.

contribute [kən'trɪbjuːt] v beitragen; (*money*) spenden. **contribution** n Beitrag m. **contributor** n Beitragende(r); (*to newspaper, etc.*) Mitarbeiter m.

contrive [kən'traɪv] v (*plan*) ausdenken. *I contrived to meet him* es gelang mir, ihn zu treffen.

control [kən'troul] v (*curb*) zügeln; (*machine*) steuern. n Leitung f. **controls** pl n Steuerung f. **under/out of control** unter/außer Kontrolle.

controversial [kontrə'vəːʃəl] adj umstritten. **controversy** n Streitfrage f, Kontroverse f.

convalesce [konvə'les] v genesen, gesund werden. **convalescence** n Genesungszeit f.

convection [kən'vekʃən] n Konvektion f.

convenience [kən'viːnjəns] n Bequemlichkeit f; (*advantage*) Vorteil m. **public convenience** Bedürfnisanstalt f. **convenient** adj (*suitable*) passend; (*time*) gelegen; (*advantageous*) vorteilhaft.

convent ['konvənt] n Kloster neut; (*school*) Klosterschule f.

convention [kən'venʃən] n (*meeting*) Tagung f; (*agreement*) Konvention f; (*custom*) Brauch m, Konvention f. **conventional** adj Konventionell.

converge [kən'vəːdʒ] v konvergieren.

converse [kən'vəːs] v sich unterhalten, sprechen. **conversation** n Unterhaltung f, Gespräch neut.

convert [kən'vəːt; n 'konvəːt] v umwandeln; (*rel*) bekehren. n Bekehrte(r). **conversion** n Umwandlung f; (*rel*) Bekehrung f.

convertible [kən'vəːtəbl] adj um-, verwandelbar. n (*mot*) Kabrio(lett) neut.

convex ['konveks] adj konvex.

convey [kən'veɪ] v (*goods*) befördern; (*news*) übermitteln. **conveyance** n (*law*) Übertragung f; (*vehicle*) Fahrzeug neut.

convict [kən'vɪkt; n 'konvɪkt] v verurteilen. n Verurteilte(r). **conviction** n (*belief*) Überzeugung f; (*law*) Verurteilung f.

convince [kən'vɪns] v überzeugen. **convincing** adj überzeugend.

convivial [kən'vɪvjəl] adj fröhlich, heiter.

convoy ['konvoɪ] n (*mil*) Konvoi m.

convulsion [kən'vʌlʃən] n Zuckung f.

cook [kuk] v kochen; (*a meal*) zubereiten. n Koch m. Köchin f. **cooker** n Herd m. **cookery** n Küche f. **cookery book** Kochbuch neut. **cooking** n Küche f.

cool [kuːl] adj kühl. v abkühlen. **cooled** adj gekühlt. **coolness** n Kühle.

coop [kuːp] n Hühnerkäfig m. v **coop up** einsperren.

cooperate [kou'opəreɪt] v zusammenarbeiten. **cooperation** n Zusammenarbeit f, Kooperation f. **cooperative** adj (*helpful*) hilfsbereit; kooperativ. n Genossenschaft f, Kooperative f.

coordinate [kou'oːdineɪt] v koordinieren. n (*math*) Koordinate f. **coordination** n Koordination f.

cope [koup] v **cope with** fertigwerden mit.

copious ['koupiəs] adj reichlich.

copper[1] ['kopə] n (*metal*) Kupfer neut. adj kupfern; (*colour*) kupferfarben.

copper[2] ['kopə] n (*coll*) Polyp m.

copulate ['kopjuːleɪt] v sich paaren. **copulation** n Paarung f.

copy ['kopi] n Kopie f; (*book*) Exemplar neut; (*newspaper*) Nummer f. v kopieren. **copyright** n Copyright neut.

coral ['korəl] n Koralle f.

cord [koːd] n Schnur f.

cordial ['koːdjəl] adj herzlich.

cordon ['koːdn] n Absperrkette f. v **cordon off** absperren.

corduroy ['koːdərɔɪ] n Kord m.

core [koː] n (*apple*) Kernhaus neut. v entkernen. **to the core** durch und durch.

cork [koːk] n (*material*) Kork m; (*for bottle*) Korken m, Pfropfen m. adj korken. **corkscrew** n Korkenzieher m.

corn[1] [koːn] n Korn neut, Getreide neut; (*maize*) Mais m; (*wheat*) Weizen m.

corn[2] [koːn] n (*on foot*) Hühnerauge neut.

corner ['kɔːnə] *n* Ecke *f*, Winkel *m*; *(mot)* Kurve *f*; *(sport)* Eckball *m*. *v* in die Enge treiben.

cornet ['kɔːnɪt] *n* *(music)* Kornett *neut*; *(ice cream)* Eistüte *f*.

coronary ['kɔːrənəri] *adj* koronar. **coronary thrombosis** Koronarthrombose *f*.

coronation [kɔrə'neɪʃən] *n* Krönung *f*.

coroner ['kɔːrənə] *n* Leichenbeschauer *m*.

corporal¹ ['kɔːpərəl] *adj* körperlich. **corporal punishment** Prügelstrafe *f*.

corporal² ['kɔːpərəl] *n* *(mil)* Obergefreite(r) *m*.

corporate ['kɔːpərət] *adj* gemeinsam; *(comm)* Firmen-, korporativ.

corporation [kɔːpə'reɪʃən] *n* Körperschaft *f*; *(city authorities)* Gemeinderat *m*.

corps [kɔː] *n* Korps *neut*.

corpse [kɔːps] *n* Leiche *f*.

correct [kə'rekt] *adj* richtig; *(proper)* korrekt. *v* korrigieren. **correction** *n* Korrektur *f*.

correlation [kɔrə'leɪʃən] *n* Wechselbeziehung *f*.

correspond [kɔrə'spond] *v* entsprechen (+*dat*); *(write)* korrespondieren. **correspondence** *n* Entsprechung *f*; Korrespondenz *f*. **corresponding** *adj* entsprechend.

corridor ['kɔridɔː] *n* Gang *m*.

corrode [kə'roud] *v* zerfressen; *(become corroded)* rosten. **corrosion** *n* Korrosion *f*.

corrupt [kə'rʌpt] *v* bestechen. *adj* bestechlich, korrupt. **corruption** *n* Bestechung *f*, Korruption *f*.

corset ['kɔːset] *n* Korsett *neut*.

cosmetic [kɔz'metik] *adj* kosmetisch. **cosmetic surgery** chirurgische Kosmetik *f*. **cosmetics** *pl n* Schönheitsmittel *pl*.

cosmic ['kɔzmik] *adj* kosmisch.

cosmopolitan [kɔzmə'pɔlitən] *adj* kosmopolitisch.

*cost [kɔst] *v* kosten. *n* Preis *m*, Kosten *pl*. **costs** Unkosten *pl*. **cost of living** Lebenshaltungskosten *pl*.

costume ['kɔstjuːm] *n* Kostüm *neut*.

cosy ['kouzi] *adj* gemütlich.

cot [kɔt] *n* Kinderbett *neut*.

cottage ['kɔtidʒ] *n* Hütte *f*, Häuschen *neut*. **cottage cheese** Hüttenkäse *m*.

cotton ['kɔtn] *n* Baumwolle *f*. *adj* Baumwoll-. **cotton wool** Watte *f*.

couch [kautʃ] *n* Couch *f*.

cough [kɔf] *n* Husten *m*. *v* husten.

could [kud] *V* **can**.

council ['kaunsəl] *n* Rat *m*. **council house** Sozialwohnung *f*. **councillor** *n* Rat *m*.

counsel ['kaunsəl] *v* beraten. *n* Rat *m*.

count¹ [kaunt] *v* zählen; *(be valid)* gelten. *n* *(number)* (Gesamt)Zahl *f*. **count on** rechnen mit.

count² [kaunt] *n* *(noble)* Graf *m*.

counter¹ ['kauntə] *n* *(shop)* Ladentisch *m*, Theke *f*; *(bank)* Schalter *m*; *(game)* Spielmarke *f*.

counter² ['kauntə] *adv* entgegen. *adj* entgegengesetzt. *v* entgegnen.

counteract [kauntə'rakt] *v* entgegenwirken (+*dat*).

counterattack ['kauntərə,tak] *n* Gegenangriff *m*.

counter-clockwise *adj*, *adv* dem Uhrzeigersinn entgegen.

counterfeit ['kauntəfit] *adj* gefälscht. *v* fälschen.

counterfoil ['kauntə,fɔil] *n* Kontrollabschnitt *m*.

counterpart ['kauntə,paːt] *n* Gegenstück *neut*.

countess ['kauntis] *n* Gräfin *f*.

country ['kʌntri] *n* Land *neut*; *(homeland)* Heimat *f*; *(pol)* Land *neut*, Staat *m*. *adj* Land-. **in the country** auf dem Lande. **country house** Landhaus *neut*. **country man** *n* Landmann *m*. **fellow countryman** Landsmann *m*. **countryside** Landschaft *f*.

county ['kaunti] *n* Grafschaft *f*.

coup [kuː] *n* Coup *m*; *(pol)* Staatsstreich *m*. **coup de grâce** Gnadenstoß *m*.

couple ['kʌpl] *n* Paar *neut*; *(married couple)* Ehepaar *neut*. **a couple of** ein paar.

coupon ['kuːpon] *n* Coupon *m*, Gutschein *m*.

courage ['kʌridʒ] *n* Mut *m*, Tapferkeit *f*. **courageous** *adj* mutig, tapfer.

courier ['kuriə] *n* Kurier *m*; *(tour guide)* Reiseleiter(in).

course [kɔːs] *n* Lauf *m*; *(study)* Kurs(us) *m*; *(race)* Bahn *f*; *(of action)* Richtung *m*. *v* laufen. **of course** natürlich, selbstverständlich. **in the course of** im Laufe (+*gen*).

court [kɔːt] *n* *(royal)* Hof *m*; *(law)* Gericht *neut*. *v* *(lover)* werben um. **court martial**

Kriegsgericht *neut*. **court-martial** *v* vor ein Kriegsgericht stellen. **court-room** *n* Gerichtssaal *m*. **courtyard** *n* Hof *m*.

courtesy ['kɜːtəsɪ] *n* Höflichkeit *f*. **courteous** *adj* höflich.

cousin ['kʌzn] *n* Cousin *m*, Vetter *m*; Kusine *f*, Base *f*.

cove [kouv] *n* Bucht *f*.

cover ['kʌvə] *v* (be)decken; (*extend over*) sich erstrecken über; (*include*) einschließen. *n* (*lid*) Deckel *m*; (*of book*) (Schutz) Umschlag *m*. **covering** *n* (Be)Deckung *f*.

cow [kau] *n* Kuh *f*. *v* einschüchtern. **cowshed** *n* Kuhstall *m*.

coward ['kauəd] *n* Feigling *m*. **cowardice** *n* Feigheit *f*. **cowardly** *adj* feige.

cower ['kauə] *v* kauern.

coy [kɔɪ] *adj* spröde.

crab [krab] *n* Krebs *m*.

crack [krak] *n* (*slit*) Spalt *m*, Riß *m*; (*sound*) Krach *m*. *v* krachen; (*break*) brechen; (*nut*) knacken; (*egg*) aufschlagen; (*joke*) reißen. **crack up** (*coll*) zusammenbrechen. **cracker** *n* (*firework*) Knallfrosch *m*; (*Christmas*) Knallbonbon *m*; (*biscuit*) Keks *m*.

crackle ['krak] *v* knistern. *n* Knistern *neut*.

cradle ['kreɪdl] *n* Wiege *f*. *v* wiegen.

craft [krɑːft] *n* (*trade*) Handwerk *neut*, Gewerbe *neut*; (*skill*) Kunstfertigkeit *f*; (*ship*) Schiff *neut*. **craftsman** *n* Handwerker *m*, Künstler *m*. **crafty** *adj* schlau, listig.

cram [kram] *v* hineinstopfen; (*study*) pauken.

cramp [kramp] *n* (*med*) Krampf *m*; (*clamp*) Krampe *f*. *v* hemmen.

cranberry ['kranbərɪ] *n* Preiselbeere *f*.

crane [kreɪn] *n* Kran *m*; (*bird*) Kranich *m*.

crank [kraŋk] *n* Kurbel *f*; (*odd person*) Kauz *m*. *v* aukurbeln. **crankshaft** *n* Kurbelwelle *f*.

crap [krap] *n* (*vulg*) Scheiße *f*.

crash [kraʃ] *n* (*sound*) Krach *m*; (*mot*) Zusammenstoß *m*; (*aero*) Absturz *m*. *v* stürzen (gegen); (*sound*) krachen. **crash helmet** *n* Sturzhelm *m*.

crate [kreɪt] *n* Kiste *f*.

crater ['kreɪtə] *n* Krater *m*.

cravat [krə'vat] *n* Halstuch *neut*, Krawatte *f*.

crave [kreɪv] *v* erbitten. **crave for** sehnen nach. **craving** *n* Sehnsucht *f*.

crawl [krɔːl] *v* kriechen. *n* Kriechen *neut*;

(*swimming*) Kraulstil *m*.

crayfish ['kreɪfɪʃ] *n* Flußkrebs *m*.

crayon ['kreɪən] *n* Farbstift *m*.

craze [kreɪz] *n* (*coll*) Manie *f*. **crazy** *adj* verrückt.

creak [kriːk] *v* knarren. *n* Knarren *neut*.

cream [kriːm] *n* Sahne *f*, Rahm *m*; (*skin*) Creme *f*. **cream-coloured** *adj* cremefarben. **creamy** *adj* sahnig.

crease [kriːs] *n* Falte *f*, Kniff *m*. *v* falten.

create [krɪ'eɪt] *v* erschaffen; (*cause*) verursachen. **creation** *n* Schöpfung *f*; (*product*) Werk *neut*. **creative** *adj* schöpferisch. **creator** *n* Schöpfer *m*. **creature** *n* Lebewesen *neut*, Geschöpf *neut*.

crèche [kreʃ] *n* Kinderhort *m*.

credentials [krɪ'denʃəlz] *pl n* (*identity papers*) Ausweispapiere *pl*.

credible ['kredəbl] *adj* glaubhaft, glaubwürdig.

credit ['kredɪt] *n* (*comm*) Guthaben *neut*, Kredit *m*. *v* Glauben schenken (+*dat*). **on credit** auf Kredit. **take the credit for** sich als Verdienst anrechnen. **creditable** *adj* rühmlich. **credit card** Kreditkarte *f*. **creditor** *n* Gläubiger *m*.

credulous ['kredjuləs] *adj* leichtgläubig.

creed [kriːd] *n* Bekenntnis *neut*, Kredo *neut*.

***creep** [kriːp] *v* kriechen, schleichen. *n* Kriechen *neut*.

cremate [krɪ'meɪt] *v* einäschern. **cremation** *n* Einäscherung *f*. **crematorium** *n* Krematorium *neut*.

crept [krept] *V* creep.

crescent ['kresnt] *n* Mondsichel *f*.

cress [kres] *n* Kresse *f*.

crest [krest] *n* (*of mountain*) Bergkamm *m*; (*of wave*) Wellenkamm *m*; (*coat of arms*) Wappen *neut*.

crevice ['krevɪs] *n* Spalte *f*, Sprung *m*.

crew [kruː] *n* Besatzung *f*, Mannschaft *f*.

crib [krɪb] *n* Kinderbett *neut*.

cricket¹ ['krɪkɪt] *n* (*insect*) Grille *f*.

cricket² ['krɪkɪt] *n* Kricket *neut*.

crime [kraɪm] *n* Verbrechen *neut*. **criminal** *adj* verbrecherisch, kriminell. *n* Verbrecher(in).

crimson ['krɪmzn] *n* Karmesinrot *neut*.

cringe [krɪndʒ] *v* sich ducken.

crinkle ['krɪŋkl] *v* kraus machen. *n* Kräuselung *f*. **crinkly** *adj* kraus.

cripple ['krɪpl] n Krüppel m. v lähmen.

crisis ['kraɪsɪs] n (pl -ses) Krise f.

crisp [krɪsp] adj knusprig. **crisps** pl n Chips pl. **crispy** adj knusprig.

criterion [kraɪtɪərɪən] n (pl -a) Kriterium neut.

critic ['krɪtɪk] n Kritiker m. **critical** adj kritisch. **criticism** Kritik f. **criticize** v kritisieren.

croak [krouk] v (person, crow) krächzen; (frog) quaken. n Krächzen neut; Quaken neut.

Croatia [krou'eɪʃə] n Kroatien neut. **Croatian** n Kroate m, Kroatin f. adj kroatisch.

crochet ['krouʃeɪ] v häkeln. **crochet hook** Häkelnadel f. **crochet work** Häkelarbeit f.

crockery ['krokərɪ] n Geschirr neut.

crocodile ['krokədaɪl] n Krokodil neut.

crocus ['kroukəs] n Krokus m.

crook [kruk] n (shepherd's) Hintenstab m; (villain) Gauner m. **crooked** adj gekrümmt; (dishonest) krumm.

crop [krop] n (harvest) Ernte f; (whip) Reitpeitsche f. v (cut) stutzen. **crop up** auftauchen.

croquet ['kroukeɪ] n Krocket neut.

cross [kros] n Kreuz neut; (crossbreed) Kreuzung f. adj Quer-; (annoyed) böse, ärgerlich. v kreuzen, überqueren. **cross over** hinübergehen. **cross one's mind** einfallen (+dat). **crossbow** n Armbrust f. **crossbeed** n Kreuzung f. **cross-country** adj Gelände-. **cross-examination** n Kreuzverhör m. **cross-eyed** adj schielend. **crossing** n Kreuzung f; (rail) Bahnübergang m; (border) Überfahrt f. **cross-legged** adj mit überschlagenen Beinen. **cross-reference** n Kreuzverweisung f. **crossroads** n Straßenkreuzung f; (fig) Scheideweg m. **cross-section** n Querschnitt m. **crosswind** n Seitenwind m. **crossword** n Kreuzworträtsel neut.

crotchet ['krotʃɪt] n (music) Viertelnote f.

crouch [krautʃ] v sich ducken.

crow [krou] n Krähe f. v krähen. **crow's feet** Krähenfüße pl. **crow's nest** (naut) Mastkorb m.

crowd [kraud] n Menge. v **crowd around** sich drängen um. **crowded** adj gedrängt.

crown [kraun] n Krone f. v krönen.

crucial ['kru:ʃəl] adj kritisch, entscheidend.

crucifixion [,kru:sɪfɪkʃən] n Kreuzigung f. **crucify** v kreuzigen.

crude [kru:d] adj roh; (person) grob. **crude oil** Rohöl neut. **crudeness** n Roheit f.

cruel ['kru:əl] adj grausam. **cruelty** n Grausamkeit f.

cruise [kru:z] v (boat) kreuzen; (aircraft) fliegen. n Kreuzfahrt. f. **cruiser** n (naut) Kreuzer m.

crumb [krʌm] n Krume f; (coll) Brocken m.

crumble ['krʌmbl] v zerkrümeln. **crumbly** adj krümelig.

crumple ['krʌmpl] v zerknittern.

crunch [krʌntʃ] v knirschen. n Knirschen neut. **cruncy** adj knusprig.

crusade [kru:'seɪd] n Kreuzzug m. **crusader** n Kreuzfahrer m.

crush [krʌʃ] v zerdrücken; unterdrücken. n Gedränge neut. **crushing** adj Überwältigend.

crust [krʌst] n Kruste f.

crustacean [krʌ'steɪʃən] n Krustentier neut.

crutch [krʌtʃ] n Krücke f.

cry [kraɪ] v (shout) schreien; (weep) weinen. n Schrei m, Ruf m. **cry out** aufschreien. **a far cry from** ein weiter Weg von.

crypt [krɪpt] n Krypta f.

crystal ['krɪstl] n Kristall m.

cub [kʌb] n Junge(s) neut; (fox, wolf) Welpe m; (scout) Wölfling m.

cube [kju:b] n Würfel m; (math) Kubikzahl f. **cubic** adj würfelförmig. **cubic centimetre** Kubikzentimeter neut. **cubic capacity** (mot) Hubraum m.

cubicle ['kju:bɪkl] n Kabine f.

cuckoo ['kuku:] n Kuckuck m.

cucumber ['kju:kʌm bə] n Gurke f.

cuddle ['kʌdl] v herzen, liebkosen.

cue¹ [kju:] n (theatre) Stichwort neut.

cue² [kju:] n (billiards) Bilardstock m.

cuff¹ [kʌf] n (shirt) Manschette f; (trousers) AUfschlag m. **cufflink** n Manschettenknopf m.

cuff² [kʌf] n Ohrfeige. f, Klaps m. v klapsen.

culinary ['kʌlɪnərɪ] adj kulinarisch, Küchen-.

culminate ['kʌlmɪneɪt] v kulminieren. **culmination** n Höhepunkt m.

culprit ['kʌlprɪt] n Täter m.

cult [kʌlt] n Kult m.

cultivate ['kʌltɪveɪt] v bebauen, kultivieren; (fig) pflegen. **cultivation** n Kulture f.

culture ['kʌltʃə] n Kultur f. **cultural** adj kulturell.

cumbersome ['kʌm bəsəm] adj sperrig, schwer zu handhaben.

cumin ['kjuːm in] n Kreuzkümmel m.

cunning ['kʌniŋ] adj schlau, listig. n List f.

cup [kʌp] n Tasse f; (trophy) Pokal m. **cup final** Pokalendspiel neut. **cup tie** Pokalspiel neut.

cupboard ['kʌbəd] n Schrank m.

curate ['kjuərət] n Unterpfarrer m.

curator [kjuə'reitə] n Konservator m.

curb [kəːb] v zügeln. n Zaum m; (kerb) Bordstein m.

curdle ['kəːdl] v gerinnen.

cure [kjuə] v (illness) heilen; (smoke) räuchern; (salt) einsalzen. n heilmittel neut.

curfew ['kəːfjuː] n Ausgehverbot m.

curious ['kjuəriəs] adj (inquisitive) neugierig; (odd) seltsam. **curiosity** n Neugier f.

curl [kəːl] n Locke f, Kräuselung f. v (sich) kräuseln. **curly** adj lockig, kraus.

currant ['kʌrənt] n Korinthe f.

currency ['kʌrənsi] n (money) Währung f.

current ['kʌrənt] adj (present) gegenwärtig; (common) gebräuchlich, üblich. n Strom m. **current account** Scheckkonto neut. **current events** Zeitgeschehen neut. **currently** adv zur Zeit.

curriculum [kə'rikjuləm] n Lehrplan, Studienplan m. **curriculum vitae** Lebenslauf m.

curry ['kʌri] n Curry neut. **curry powder** Curry(pulver) neut. **curry sauce** Currysoße f.

curse [kəːs] v verfluchen; (swear) fluchen. n Fluch m.

cursor ['kəːsə] n Kursor m.

curt [kəːt] adj knapp, barsch.

curtail [kəː'teil] v abkürzen. **curtailment** n Abkürzung f; Einschränkung f.

curtain ['kəːtn] n Gardine f; (theatre) Vorhang m.

curtsy ['kəːtsi] n Knicks m. v knicksen.

curve [kəːv] n Kurve f. v sich biegen. **curved** adj bogenförmig, gekrümmt.

cushion ['kuʃən] n Kissen neut. v polstern.

custard ['kʌstəd] n Vanillesoße f.

custody ['kʌstədi] n Aufsicht f; (arrest) Haft f.

custom ['kʌstəm] n (habit) Gewohnheit f; (tradition) Brauch m. (customers) Kundschaft

f. **customary** adj gewöhnlich. **customer** n Kunde m, Kundin f. **customs** n Zoll m. **customs duty** Zoll m. **customs official** Zollbeamte(r) m.

*****cut** [kʌt] n Schnitt m; (wound) Schnittwunde f; (in wages) Kürzung f; (coll: share) Anteil m. v schneiden; (prices) herabsetzen; (wages) kürzen. **cut and paste** (comp) ausschneiden und einfügen. **cut off** (phone) trennen. **cutting edge** (fig) der führende Stand (z.B. der Technik).

cute [kjuːt] adj (coll) niedlich.

cuticle ['kjuːtikl] n Oberhaut f; (on nail) Nagelhaut f.

cutlery ['kʌtləri] n Besteck neut.

cutlet ['kʌtlit] n Kotelett neut.

cyberspace ['saibəspeis] n Cyberraum, virtueller Raum m.

cycle ['saikl] n Zyklus m; (bicycle) Fahrrad neut. v radfahren. **cycling** n Radsport m. **cyclist** n Radfahrer(in).

cyclone ['saikloun] n Zyklon m.

cylinder ['silində] n Zylinder m. **cylinder block** Motorblock m. **cylinder capacity** Hubraum m. **cylinder head** Zylinderkopf m.

cymbals ['sim bəlz] pl n Becken neut sing.

cynic ['sinik] n Zyniker(in). **cynical** adj zynisch. **cynicism** Zynismus m.

cypress ['saiprəs] n Zypresse f.

Cyprus ['saiprəs] n Zypern neut. **Cypriot** n Zypriot(in); adj zypriotisch.

cyst [sist] n Zyste f.

Czech [tʃek] nm, adj tschechisch; n (people) Tscheche m. Tschechin f. **Czech Republic** Tschechische Republik f.

D

dab [dab] v betupfen. n Tupfen m.

dabble ['dabl] v plätschern. he dabbles in art er beschäftigt sich nebenbei mit Kunst. **dabbler** n Dilettant m.

dad [dad] n Vati m, Papa m.

daffodil ['dafədil] n Narzisse f.

daft [daːft] adj (coll) blöd(e), doof.

dagger ['dagə] n Dolch m.

daily ['deili] adj, adv täglich. **daily paper**

Tageszeitung f.

dainty ['deɪntɪ] adj (person) niedlich; (food) lecker.

dairy ['deərɪ] n Molkerei f. **dairy produce** Milchprodukte pl.

daisy ['deɪzɪ] n Gänseblümchen neut.

dam [dam] n Damm m. v eindämmen.

damage ['damɪdʒ] v beschädigen; verletzen. n Schaden m. **damages** pl n (compensation) Schadenersatz m sing.

damn [dam] v verdammen. interj verdammt!

damp [damp] adj feucht. n Feuchtigkeit f. **dampen** v befeuchten.

damson ['damzən] n Pflaume f.

dance [daːns] n Tanz m. v tanzen. **dancer** n Tänzer(in). **dance hall** Tanzsaal m. **dancing** n Tanz m; Tanzen neut.

dandelion ['dandɪˈtressdaːn] n Löwenzahn m.

dandruff ['dandrəf] n Schuppen pl.

Dane [deɪn] n Däne m, Dänin f. **Danish** adj dänisch.

danger ['deɪndʒə] n Gefahr f. **in** (or out of) **danger** in/außer Gefahr. **dangerous** adj gefährlich.

dangle ['daŋgl] v baumeln; baumeln lassen.

dare [deə] v wagen, riskieren; (challenge) herausfordern. **daring** adj wagemutig; (risky) gewagt; n Mut m.

dark [daːk] adj finster; (esp colour) dunkel. n Dunkelheit f. **in the dark** im Dunkeln; (fig) nicht im Bilde. **darken** v (sich) verdunkeln. **darkness** n Dunkelheit f. Finsternis f. **darkroom** n Dunkelkammer f.

darling ['daːlɪŋ] n Liebling m. adj lieb.

darn [daːn] v stopfen. **darning** n Stopfen neut.

dart [daːt] v schießen, sausen; n Pfeil m. **darts** pl n (game) (Pfeilwerfen) neut sing.

dash [daʃ] v (smash) zerschlagen; (rush) stürzen. n (punctuation) Gedankenstrich m; (rush) Stürzen neut; (addition) Schuß m. **dashboard** n Armaturenbrett neut. **dashing** adj schneidig.

data ['deɪtə] pl n Daten pl. **data processing** Datenverarbeitung f.

date¹ [deɪt] n Datum neut; (appointed day) Termin m; (with someone) Verabredung f. v (letter) datieren. **dated** adj altmodisch.

date² [deɪt] n (fruit) Dattel f.

dative ['deɪtɪv] n Dativ m.

daughter ['dɔːtə] n Tochter f. **daughter-in-law** n Schwiegertochter f.

daunt [dɔːnt] v entmutigen.

dawdle ['dɔːdl] v trödeln.

dawn [dɔːn] n Tagesanbruch m; (Morgen)Dämmerung f; (fig) Anfang m. v dämmern (also fig).

day [deɪ] n Tag m. **daylight** Tageslicht neut.

daze [deɪz] v betäuben. **dazed** adj benommen.

dazzle ['dazl] v blenden.

dead [ded] adj tot. **dead man/woman** Tote(r). **the dead** die Toten pl. **deaden** v dämpfen. **dead certain** todsicher. **dead end** Sackgasse f; (fig) totes Geleise neut. **deadline** n Termin m.

deaf [def] adj taub. **deaf aid** Hörgerät neut. **deaf mute** Taubstumme(r). **deafen** v taub machen.

*****deal** [diːl] n Geschäft neut. v handeln; (cards) austeilen. **deal with** (attend to) sich befassen mit; (resolve) erledigen. **a great/good deal of** viel. **dealer** n Händler m; (cards) Kartengeber m. **dealings** pl n Beziehungen pl.

dealt [delt] v **deal.**

dean [diːn] n Dekan m.

dear [dɪə] adj (beloved) lieb; (expensive) teuer. (in letters) Dear Mr. Smith Lieber Herr Smith, Sehr geehrter Herr Smith. n Liebling m. **dearly** adv herzlich.

death [deθ] n Tod m; (case of death) Todesfall m. **deathbed** n Sterbebett neut. **death penalty** Todesstrafe f.

debase [dɪˈbeɪs] v entwerten.

debate [dɪˈbeɪt] n Debatte f. v debattieren, diskutieren.

debit ['debɪt] n Soll neut; Lastschrift f. v belasten.

debris ['debriː] n Schutt m, Trümmer pl.

debt [det] n Schuld f. **in debt** verschuldet. **debtor** n Schuldner m.

decade ['dekeɪd] n Jahrzehnt neut

decadence ['dekədəns] n Dekadenz f. **decadent** adj dekadent.

decaffeinated [dɪˈkafɪneɪtɪd] adj koffeinfrei, entkoffeiniert.

decanter [dɪˈkantə] n Karaffe f.

decapitate [dɪˈkapɪteɪt] v enthaupten. **decapitation** n Enthauptung f.

decay [dɪkeɪ] v verfallen. n Verfall m. **tooth decay** Karies f.

deceased [dɪsiːst] adj verstorben. **the deceased** der/die Verstorbene.

deceit [dɪsiːt] n Täuschung, Betrug m. **deceitful** adj betrügerisch.

deceive [dɪsiːv] v täuschen.

December [dɪsɛmbə] n Dezember m.

decent ['diːsənt] adj (respectable) anständig; (kind) freundlich. **decency** n Anstand m.

deceptive [dɪsɛptɪv] adj täuschend.

decibel ['desɪbel] n Dezibel neut.

decide [dɪsaɪd] v entscheiden; (make up one's mind) sich entscheiden. **decided** adj entschieden. **decision** n Entscheidung f; (of committee) Beschluß m. **make a decision** eine Entscheidung treffen. **decisive** adj entscheidend.

deciduous [dɪsɪdjuːəs] adj (trees) Laub-.

decimal ['desɪməl] adj Dezimal-.

decipher [dɪsaɪfə] v entziffern.

deck [dek] n Deck neut; (of cards) Pack neut. **deckchair** n Liegestuhl m.

declare [dɪkleə] v erklären. **declaration** n Erklärung f.

decline [dɪklaɪn] v ablehnen; (gram) deklinieren.

decode [diːkoud] v dekodieren, entschlüsseln.

decommission [ˌdiːkəmˈʃən] v (tech) stillegen; (mil) Waffen abgeben.

decompose [ˌdiːkəmˈpouz] v zerfallen.

decor ['deɪkoː] n Ausstattung f.

decorate ['dekəˌreɪt] v schmücken; (room) tapezieren; (mil) auszeichnen. **decoration** n Verzierung f; (of room) Dekoration f; (mil) Orden m.

decoy ['diːkoɪ] n Lockvogel m.

decrease [diːkriːs] v (make less) vermindern; (become less) abnehmen. n Abnahme f.

decree [dɪkriː] n Erlaß m.

decrepit [dɪkrepɪt] adj hinfällig.

dedicate ['dedɪkeɪt] v widmen; (rel) weihen. **dedication** n (book) Widmung f; (to duty, etc.) Hingabe f; (rel) Einweihung f.

deduce [dɪdjuːs] v schließen (aus).

deduct [dɪdʌkt] v abziehen. **deduction** n Abzug m.

deed [diːd] n Tat f; (document) Urkunde f.

deep [diːp] adj tief. **deep freeze** Tiefkühlschrank m. **deep-frozen** adj tiefgekühlt, Tiefkühl-.

deer [dɪə] n Hirsch m.

deface [dɪfeɪs] v entstellen.

default [dɪfoːlt] n Unterlassung f. v (with payments) in Verzug kommen.

defeat [dɪfiːt] v schlagen, besiegen. n Niederlage f.

defect ['diːfekt; v dɪˈfekt] n Fehler m, Defekt m. v (pol) überlaufen. **defective** adj fehlerhaft, defektiv.

defence [dɪfens] n Verteidigung f. **defenceless** adj schutzlos.

defend [dɪfend] v verteidigen. **defendant** n Angeklagte(r). **defender** n Verteidiger m. **defensive** adj defensiv, Verteidigungs-.

defer [dɪfoː] v (postpone) verschieben. **defer to** (yield to) nachgeben (+dat). **deferment** n Verschiebung f.

defiance [dɪfaɪəns] n Trotz m. **defiant** adj trotzig, unnachgiebig.

deficiency [dɪfɪʃəns] n Unzulänglichkeit f, Mangel m. **deficient** adj (defective) defektiv, mangelhaft; (inadequate) unzulänglich.

deficit ['defɪsɪt] n Defizit neut, Fehlbetrag m.

define [dɪfaɪn] v definieren, genauerklären. **(well) defined** adj deutlich. **definite** adj klar, deutlich. **definitely** adv bestimmt. **definition** n Erklärung f, Definition f; (phot) Schärfe f.

deflate [dɪfleɪt] v die Luft ablassen aus. **deflation** (pol) Deflation f.

deflect [dɪflekt] v (missile) ablenken; (blame) (auf andere) abwälzen.

deform [dɪfoːm] v deformieren, entstellen. **deformed** adj deformiert, verformt. **deformity** n Mißbildung f.

defraud [dɪfroːd] v betrügen.

defrost [dɪˈfrost] v abtauen.

deft [deft] adj flink.

defunct [dɪfʌŋkt] adj verstorben; (fig) nicht mehr bestehend.

defuse [diːfjuːz] v entschärfen.

defy [dɪfaɪ] v (resist) trotzen; (challenge) herausfordern.

degenerate [dɪdʒenəˌreɪt; adj dɪˈdʒenərɪt] v degenerieren. adj degeneriert.

degrade [dɪgreɪd] v erniedrigen, entehren. **degradation** n Erniedrigung f. **degrading** adj erniedrigend.

degree [dɪgriː] n Grad m. **to a high degree** in hohem Maße.

dehydrate [di:'haidreit] v trocknen. **dehydrated** adj getrocknet, Trocken-.

deign [dein] v gewähren, sich herablassen, geruhen (etwas zu tun).

dejected [didʒektid] adj niedergeschlagen.

delay [di:lei] v (postpone) aufschieben. n Verzögerung f, Aufschub m. **be delayed** (train, etc.) Verspätung haben. **without delay** unverzüglich.

delegate ['deleget; 'delegit] v delegieren. n Delegierte(r). **delegation** m Delegation f.

delete [di:li:t] v tilgen, streichen.

deliberate [di'libərət; v di'libəreit] adj (intentional) absichtlich. v nachdenken. **deliberately** adv absichtlich. **deliberation** n Überlegung f.

delicate ['delikət] adj (fragile) zart; (fine) fein; (situation) heikel. **delicacy** n Zartheit f; (food) Delikatesse f.

delicatessen [,delikə'tesn] n Delikatessenhandlung f, Feinkostgeschäft neut.

delicious [di:liʃəs] adj köstlich.

delight [di:lait] n Freude f, Vergnügen neut. v erfreuen. **delighted** adj erfreut, entzückt. **delightful** adj entzückend.

delinquency [di:liŋkwənsi] n Straffälligkeit f. **delinquent** adj delinquent. n Delinquent m.

delirious [di:liriəs] adj in Delirium. **delirium** n Delirium neut, Fieberwahn m.

deliver [di:livə] v (goods) (aus)liefern; (rescue) befreien; (a woman in childbirth) entbinden. **deliverance** n Befreiung f. **delivery** n (Aus)Lieferung f; Entbindung f.

delta ['deltə] n Delta neut.

delude [di:lu:d] v täuschen. **delusion** n Täuschung f.

deluge ['delju:dʒ] n Flut f.

delve [delv] v **delve into** erforschen.

demand [di:ma:nd] v verlangen. n Verlangen neut; (for a commodity, etc.) Nachfrage f. **on demand** auf Verlangen. **demanding** adj anspruchsvoll, anstrengend, mühsam.

demean [di:mi:n] v **demean oneself** sich erniedrigen.

demented [di:mentid] adj wahnsinnig.

democracy [di:mokrəsi] n Demokratie f. **democrat** n Demokrat m. **democratic** adj demokratisch.

demolish [di:moliʃ] v abbrechen. **demolition** n Abbruch m.

demon ['di:mən] n Teufel m.

demonstrate ['demənstreit] v demonstrieren. **demonstration** n Demonstration f.

demoralize [di:m orə,laiz] v demoralisieren. **demoralization** n Demoralisation f.

demote [di:m out] v degradieren, zurückstufen.

demure [di:m juə] adj bescheiden.

den [den] n Höhle f; (room) Bude f.

denial [di:naiəl] n Leugnung f.

denim ['denim] adj Denim-. **denims** pl n Jeans pl.

Denmark ['denma:k] n Dänemark neut.

denomination [di,nominei'ʃən] n (rel) Bekenntnis neut; (of banknote) Nennwert m. **denominator** n Nenner m. **common denominator** gemeinsamer Nenner m.

denote [di:nout] v bezeichnen.

denounce [di:nauns] v brandmarken.

dense [dens] adj dicht, dick, **density** n Dichte f.

dent [dent] n Beule f. v einbeulen.

dental ['dentl] adj Zahn-.

dentist ['dentist] n Zahnarzt m. **dentistry** n Zahnheilkunde f.

denture ['dentʃə] n (künstliches) Gebiß neut.

denude [di:nju:d] v entblößen.

denunciation [di,nʌnsi'eiʃən] n Denunziation f.

deny [di:nai] v leugnen; (responsibility) ablehnen; (allegation) dementieren. **deny oneself** sich versagen.

deodorant [di:'oudərənt] n Desodorans neut.

depart [di:pa:t] v abfahren; (fig) abweichen. **departure** n (person) Weggehen neut; (train) Abfahrt f; (aeroplane) Abflug m.

department [di:pa:tm ənt] n Abteilung f; (pol) Ministerium neut. **department store** Warenhaus neut.

depend [di:pend] v **depend on** abhängen von; (rely on) sich verlassen auf. **it (all) depends** es kommt darauf an. **dependable** adj zuverlässig. **dependant** n Familienangehörige(r). **dependent** adj abhängig (+von).

depict [di:pikt] v schildern.

deplete [di:pli:t] v erschöpfen. **depletion** n Erschöpfung f.

deplore [di:plo:] v bedauern. **deplorable**

adj bedauernswert.

deport [dɪˈpɔːt] *v* deportieren. **deport oneself** sich verhalten. **deportation** *n* Deportation *f.* **deportment** *n* Haltung *f.*

depose [dɪˈpəʊz] *v* absetzen.

deposit [dɪˈpɒzɪt] *v* deponieren. *n (surety)* Kaution *f; (down payment)* Anzahlung *f; (sediment)* Niederschlag *m.* **deposit account** Sparkonto *neut.*

depot [ˈdepəʊ] *n* Depot *neut.*

depraved [dɪˈpreɪvd] *adj* lasterhaft, verworfen.

depreciate [dɪˈpriːʃɪeɪt] *v* an Wert verlieren. **depreciation** *n* Wertminderung *f.*

depress [dɪˈpres] *v* niederdrücken, deprimieren. **depressed** *adj* deprimiert. **depressing** *adj* deprimierend. **depression** *n* Depression *f.*

deprive [dɪˈpraɪv] *v* berauben.

depth [depθ] *n* Tiefe *f.* **in depth** gründlich.

deputy [ˈdepjʊtɪ] *n* Stellvertreter *m. adj* stellvertretend.

derail [dɪˈreɪl] *v* entgleisen. **derailment** *n* Entgleisen *neut.*

derelict [ˈderɪlɪkt] *adj (building)* baufällig.

deride [dɪˈraɪd] *v* verspotten. **derision** *n* Spott *m.* **derisory** *adj* spöttisch.

derive [dɪˈraɪv] *v* ableiten; *(originate)* stammen; *(gain)* gewinnen. **derivation** *n* Herkunft *f.*

derogatory [dɪˈrɒgətərɪ] *adj* geringschätzig.

descend [dɪˈsend] *v* hinabsteigen; *(from train)* aussteigen. **be descended from** abstammen von. **descendant** *n* Nachkomme *m.* **descent** *n* Abstieg *m;* Abstammung *f.*

describe [dɪˈskraɪb] *v* beschreiben. **description** *n* Beschreibung *f.*

desert[1] [ˈdezət] *n* Wüste *f.*

desert[2] [dɪˈzɜːt] *n (something deserved)* Verdienst *neut.* **deserts** *pl* Lohn *m sing.*

desert[3] [dɪˈzɜːt] *v* verlassen; *(mil)* desertieren. **deserter** *n* Deserteur *m.* **desertion** *n* Verlassen *neut; (mil)* Desertion *f.*

deserve [dɪˈzɜːv] *v* verdienen.

design [dɪˈzaɪn] *n* Entwurf *m; (drawing)* Zeichnung *f; (pattern)* Muster *neut. v* entwerfen, planen. **designer** *n* Designer(in) *m, f; (fashion)* Modeschöpfer(in) *m, f.* **designer label** Modemarke *f.*

designate [ˈdezɪgneɪt] *n* bezeichnen. **designation** *n* Bezeichnung *f.*

desire [dɪˈzaɪə] *v* wünschen, begehren; *(ask for)* wollen. *n* Wunsch *m; (sexual)* Begierde *f.* **desirous of** begierig nach.

desk [desk] *n* Schreibtisch *m.*

desolate [ˈdesəbt] *v* wüst, öde; *(person)* trostlos.

despair [dɪˈspeə] *v* verzweifeln. *n* Verzweiflung *f.*

desperate [ˈdespərət] *adj* verzweifelt; *(situation)* hoffnungslos.

despicable [dɪˈspɪkəbl] *adj* verächtlich.

despise [dɪˈspaɪz] *v* verachten.

despite [dɪˈspaɪt] *prep* trotz (+*gen*).

despondent [dɪˈspɒndənt] *adj* mutlos.

despot [ˈdespɒt] *n* Gewaltherrscher *m,* Despot *m.* **despotism** *n* Despotismus *m.*

dessert [dɪˈzɜːt] *n* Nachtisch *m.* **dessert spoon** Dessertlöffel *m.*

destiny [ˈdestənɪ] *n* Schicksal *neut.* **destined** *adj* ausersehen, bestimmt. **destination** *n (post)* Bestimmungsort *m; (travel)* Reiseziel *neut.*

destitute [ˈdestɪtjuːt] *adj* notleidend, bedürftig.

destroy [dɪˈstrɔɪ] *v* zerstören, vernichten. **destroyer** *n* Zerstörer *m.* **destruction** *n* Zerstörung *f.* **destructive** *adj* zerstörerisch.

detach [dɪˈtætʃ] *v* losmachen, abtrennen. **detached** *adj (house)* Einzel-; *(fig)* objektiv. **detachment** *n* Objektivität *f; (mil)* Abteilung *f.*

detail [ˈdiːteɪl] *n* Einzelheit *f,* Detail *neut.* **further details** Näheres *neut;* nähere Angaben *pl. v* detaillieren **detailed** *adj* eingehend.

detain [dɪˈteɪn] *v* aufhalten; *(arrest)* verhaften.

detect [dɪˈtekt] *v* entdecken. **detection** *n* Aufdeckung *f.* **detective** *n* Detektiv *m.* **detective story** Kriminalroman *m.*

détente [deɪˈtɑːnt] *n* Entspannung *f.*

detention [dɪˈtenʃən] *n (law)* Haft *m; (school)* Nachsitzen *neut.*

deter [dɪˈtɜː] *v* abschrecken.

detergent [dɪˈtɜːdʒənt] *n* Reinigungsmittel *neut.*

deteriorate [dɪˈtɪərəreɪt] *v* sich verschlechtern. **deterioration** *n* Verschlechterung *f.*

determine [dɪˈtɜːmɪn] *v* bestimmen;

(*decide*) sich entschließen. **determined** *adj* entschlossen. **determination** *n* Entschlossenheit *f*.

detest [dɪˈtest] *v* hassen, verabscheuen. **detestable** *adj* abscheulich.

detonate [ˈdetəneɪt] *v* detonieren.

detour [ˈdiːtuə] *n* Umweg *m*.

detract [dɪˈtrakt] *v* **detract from** beeinträchtigen.

detriment [ˈdetrɪmənt] *n* Schaden *m*, Nachteil *m*. **detrimental (to)** *adj* schädlich (für).

devalue [diːˈvaljuː] *v* abwerten. **devaluation** *n* Abwertung *f*.

devastate [ˈdevəsteɪt] *v* verwüsten. **devastating** *adj* vernichtend. **devastation** *n* Verwüstung *f*.

develop [dɪˈveləp] *v* (sich) entwickeln. **developer** *n* Entwickler *m*. **developing** *adj* Entwicklungs-. **development** *n* Entwicklung *f*.

deviate [ˈdiːvɪeɪt] *v* abweichen. **deviation** *n* Abweichung *f*.

device [dɪˈvaɪs] *n* Gerät *neut*, Vorrichtung *f*; (*trick*) Trick *m*.

devil [ˈdevl] *n* Teufel *m*. **talk of the devil** den Teufel an die Wand malen. **devilish** *adj* teuflisch.

devious [ˈdiːvɪəs] *adj* weitschweifig; (*dishonest*) krumm, unaufrichtig.

devise [dɪˈvaɪz] *v* ausdenken, erfinden.

devoid [dɪˈvɔɪd] *adj* **devoid of** ohne, freivon.

devolution [ˌdiːvəˈluːʃən] *n* Dezentralisation *f*.

devote [dɪˈvout] *v* widmen, hingeben. **devoted** *adj* ergeben. **be devoted to someone** sehr an jemandem hängen. **devotee** *n* Anhänger(in). **devotion** *n* Ergebenheit *f*.

devour [dɪˈvauə] *v* verschlingen.

devout [dɪˈvaut] *adj* fromm, andächtig.

dew [djuː] *n* Tau *m*.

dexterous [ˈdekstrəs] *adj* gewandt, flink. **dexterity** *n* Gewandtheit *f*.

diabetes [ˌdaɪəˈbiːtɪz] *n* Zuckerkrankheit *f*. **diabetic** *adj* zuckerkrank. *n* Diabetiker *m*.

diagnose [ˌdaɪəgˈnouz] *v* diagnostizieren, erkennen. **diagnosis** *n* Diagnose *f*. **diagnostic** *adj* diagnostisch.

diagonal [daɪˈægənəl] *adj* diagonal. *n* Diagonale *f*.

diagram [ˈdaɪəgram] *n* Diagramm *neut*, Schaubild *neut*.

dial [ˈdaɪəl] *n* (*phone*) Wählscheibe *f*. *v* wählen. **dialling tone** Amtszeichen *neut*.

dialect [ˈdaɪəlekt] *n* Dialekt *m*.

dialogue [ˈdaɪəlog] *n* Dialog *m*.

diameter [daɪˈæmɪtə] *n* Durchmesser *m*.

diamond [ˈdaɪəmənd]n Diamant *m*; (*cards*) Karo *neut*; (*sport*) Spielfeld *neut*. *adj* diamanten.

diaper [ˈdaɪəpə] *n* Windel *f*.

diaphragm [ˈdaɪəfram] *n* (*anat*) Zwerchfell *neut*; (*contraceptive*) (Okklusiv)Pessar *neut*.

diarrhoea [ˌdaɪəˈriə] *n* Durchfall *m*.

diary [ˈdaɪəri] *n* Tagebuch *neut*.

dice [daɪs] *pl n* Würfel *pl*. *v* (*cookery*) in Würfel schneiden.

dickhead [ˈdɪkhed] *n* (*impol*) Arschgeige *f*.

dictate [dɪkˈteɪt] *v* diktieren. **dictating machine** Diktiergerät *neut*. **dictation** *n* Diktat *neut*. **dictator** *n* Diktator *m*. **dictatorial** *adj* diktatorisch. **dictatorship** *n*.

dictionary [ˈdɪkʃənəri] *n* Wörterbuch *neut*.

did [dɪd] *v* **do**.

die [daɪ] *v* sterben. **die away** schwächer werden. **die out** aussterben.

diesel [ˈdiːzəl] *adj* Diesel-. **diesel engine** Dieselmotor *m*.

diet [ˈdaɪət] *n* Kost *f*, Nahrung *f*; (*for weight loss*) Abmagerungskur *f*; (*for convalescence, etc.*) Diät *f*, Schonkost *f*. *v* eine Abmagerungskur machen.

differ [ˈdɪfə] *v* sich unterscheiden; (*think differently*) anderer Meinung sein. **difference** *n* Unterschied *m*. **different** *adj* verschieden, unterschiedlich; (*another*) ander. **differential** *adj* unterschiedlich. *n* (*mot*) Differentialgetriebe *neut*.

difficult [ˈdɪfikəlt] *adj* schwer, schwierig. **difficulty** *n* Schwierigkeit *f*.

*dig [dɪg] *v* graben. **dig up** ausgraben.

digest [daɪˈdʒest; *n* ˈdaɪdʒest] *v* verdauen. *n* Auslese *f*. **digestible** *adj* verdaulich. **digestion** *n* Verdauung *f*.

digit [ˈdɪdʒit] *n* (*figure*) Ziffer *f*; (*finger*) Finger *m*; (*toe*) Zehe *f*. **digital** *adj* digital, Digital-.

dignified [ˈdɪgnɪfaɪd] *adj* würdevoll.

dignity [ˈdɪgnəti] *n* Würde *f*.

digress [daɪˈgres] *v* abschweifen. **digression** *n* Abschweifung *f*.

digs [dɪgz] *pl n* (*coll*) Bude *f sing*.

dilapidated [dɪˈlæpɪdeɪtɪd] *adj* baufällig.

dilate [daɪˈleɪt] *v* (sich) weiten.

dilemma [dɪˈlemə] *n* Dilemma *neut*. **be in a dilemma** in der Klemme sitzen.

diligence [ˈdɪlɪdʒəns] *n* Fleiß *m*. **diligent** *adj* fleißig, gewissenhaft.

dilute [daɪˈluːt] *v* (*with water*) verwässern; verdünnen. *adj* (*also* **diluted**) verwässert.

dim [dɪm] *adj* trübe; (*light, vision*) schwach; (*coll: stupid*) dumm. *v* verdunkeln.

dimension [dɪˈmenʃən] *n* Dimension *f*. **dimensions** *pl* Ausmaße *pl*.

diminish [dɪˈmɪnɪʃ] *v* (sich) vermindern. **diminishing** *adj* abnehmend.

diminutive [dɪˈmɪnjutɪv] *adj* winzig.

dimple [ˈdɪmpl] *n* Grübchen *neut*.

din [dɪn] *n* Lärm *m*, Getöse *neut*.

dine [daɪn] *v* speisen, essen. **diner** *n* (*person*) Tischgast *m*; (*rail*) Speisewagen *m*; (*restaurant*) Speiselokal *neut*. **dining car** Speisewagen *m*. **dining room** Eßzimmer *neut*. **dining table** Eßtisch *n*.

dinghy [ˈdɪŋgɪ] *n* Dingi *neut*, Beiboot *neut*. **rubber dinghy** Schlauchboot *neut*.

dingy [ˈdɪndʒɪ] *adj* trübe.

dinner [ˈdɪnə] *n* Abendessen *neut*; (*at midday*) Mittagessen *neut*; (*public*) Festessen *neut*. **dinner jacket** Smoking *m*. **dinner party** Diner *neut*.

dinosaur [ˈdaɪnəsɔː] *n* Dinosaurier *m*.

dip [dɪp] *v* (ein)tauchen; (*slope down*) sich senken. **dip one's lights** (*mot*) abblenden. *n* Senkung *f*; (*bathe*) Bad *neut*. **dip switch** Abblendschalter *m*.

diploma [dɪˈpləumə] *n* Diplom *neut*.

diplomacy [dɪˈpləuməsɪ] *n* Diplomatie *f*. **diplomat** *n* Diplomat *m*. **diplomatic** *adj* diplomatisch.

dipstick [ˈdɪpstɪk] *n* (*mot*) Ölmeßstab *m*.

dire [daɪə] *adj* schrecklich; (*urgent*) dringend.

direct [dɪˈrekt] *adj* direkt. *v* dirigieren, leiten; (*aim*) richten; (*give directions*) den Weg zeigen (+*dat*); (*order*) anweisen. **direct debit** Bankeinzug *m*. **direction** *n* Richtung *f*; Leitung *f*; **directions** *pl* (*for use*) Gebrauchsanweisung *f sing*; (*instructions*) Anweisungen *pl*. **directly** *adv* (*immediately*) unmittelbar; (*straight towards*) direkt, gerade. **director** *n* Direktor *m*, Leiter *m*; (*theatre, film*) Regisseur *m*. **(telephone) directory** *n* Telefonbuch *neut*.

dirt [dɜːt] *n* Schmutz *m*, Dreck *m*. **dirt cheap** spottbillig. **dirty** *adj* schmutzig, dreckig.

disability [dɪsəˈbɪlɪtɪ] *n* Körperbehinderung *f*. **disability pension** Invalidenrente *f*.

disadvantage [dɪsədˈvɑːntɪdʒ] *n* Nachteil *m*. **disadvantageous** *adj* ungünstig, unvorteilhaft.

disagree [dɪsəˈgriː] *v* nicht übereinstimmen; (*argue*) sich streiten. **disagreeable** *adj* unangenehm. **disagreement** *n* Meinungsverschiedenheit *f*.

disappear [dɪsəˈpɪə] *v* verschwinden. **disappearance** *n* Verschwinden *neut*.

disappoint [dɪsəˈpɔɪnt] *v* enttäuschen. **disappointed** *adj* enttäuscht. **disappointing** *adj* enttäuschend. **disappointment** *n* Enttäuschung *f*.

disapprove [dɪsəˈpruːv] *v* **disapprove of** mißbilligen. **disapproval** *n* Mißbilligung *f*.

disarm [dɪsˈɑːm] *v* entwaffnen; (*pol*) abrüsten. **disarmament** *n* Abrüstung *f*. **disarming** *adj* entwaffnend.

disaster [dɪˈzɑːstə] *n* Katastrophe *f*, Unglück *neut*. **disastrous** *adj* katastrophal.

disband [dɪsˈbænd] *v* (sich) auflösen.

disc [dɪsk] *n* Scheibe *f*; (*record*) Schallplatte *f*. **disc jockey** Disk-Jockey *m*.

discard [dɪsˈkɑːd] *v* ablegen.

disc brake *n* Scheibenbremse *f*.

discern [dɪˈsɜːn] *v* (*perceive*) wahrnehmen; (*differentiate*) unterscheiden. **discernible** *adj* wahrnehmbar. **discerning** *adj* einsichtig.

discharge [dɪsˈtʃɑːdʒ] *v* (*dismiss*) entlassen; (*gun*) abschießen; (*duty*) erfüllen; (*ship*) entladen; (*of wound*) eitern. *n* (*med*) Ausfluß *m*.

disciple [dɪˈsaɪpl] *n* Jünger *m*.

discipline [ˈdɪsɪplɪn] *n* Disziplin *f*. *v* disziplinieren; (*train*) schulen.

disclaim [dɪsˈkleɪm] *v* ablehnen. **disclaimer** *n* Dementi *neut*.

disclose [dɪsˈkləuz] *v* enthüllen. **disclosure** *n* Bekanntmachung *f*.

disco [ˈdɪskəu] *n* Disco *f*.

discolour [dɪsˈkʌlə] *v* (sich) verfärben. **discoloration** *n* Verfärbung *f*.

discomfort [dɪsˈkʌmfət] *n* Unbehagen *neut*.

disconcert [dɪskənˈsɜːt] *v* aus der Fassung bringen.

disconnect [dɪskəˈnekt] *v* trennen; (*elec*) abschalten.

disconsolate [dɪskonsəbt] *adj* trostlos.

discontinue [dɪskən'tɪnjuː] *v* aufhören; (*something*) einstellen.

discord ['dɪskoːd] *n* (*disagreement*) Zwietracht *f*; (*music*) Diskordanz *f*. **discordant** *adj* diskordant.

discotheque ['dɪskætek] *n* Diskothek *f*.

discount ['dɪskaunt] *v* (*ignore*) außer Acht lassen. *n* Rabatt *m*.

discourage [dɪskʌrɪdʒ] *v* entmutigen; (*dissuade*) abraten. **discouraging** *adj* entmutigend.

discover [dɪskʌvə] *v* entdecken. **discoverer** *n* Entdecker *m*. **discovery** *n* Entdeckung *f*.

discredit [dɪskredɪt] *v* in Verruf bringen.

discreet [dɪskriːt] *adj* diskret, verschwiegen.

discrepancy [dɪskrepənsɪ] *n* Widerspruch *m*, Diskrepanz *f*.

discretion [dɪskreʃən] *n* Diskretion *f*, Takt *m*. *at your discretion* nach Ihrem Gutdünken.

discriminate [dɪskrɪmɪneɪt] *v* unterscheiden. **discriminate** (*against*) diskriminieren. **discriminating** *adj* anspruchsvoll. **discrimination** *n* (*racial, etc.*) Diskriminierung *f*.

discus ['dɪskəs] *n* Diskus *m*.

discuss [dɪskʌs] *v* besprechen, diskutieren; (*in writing*) behandeln. **discussion** *n* Besprechung *f*, Diskussion *f*.

disease [dɪziːz] *n* Krankheit *f*. **diseased** *adj* krank.

disembark [dɪsɪm'baːk] *v* an Land gehen.

disengage [dɪsɪn'geɪdʒ] *v* sich losmachen. *disengage the clutch* auskuppeln.

disfigure [dɪsfɪgə] *v* entstellen. **disfigurement** *n* Entstellung *f*.

disgrace [dɪsgreɪs] *n* Schande *f*. *v* Schande bringen über. **disgraceful** *adj* schändlich.

disgruntled [dɪsgrʌntld] *adj* mürrisch.

disguise [dɪsgaɪz] *v* verkleiden; (*voice*) verstellen. *n* Verkleidung *f*. *in disguise* verkleidet.

disgust [dɪsgʌst] *n* Ekel *m* (vor). *v* anekeln. **disgusting** *adj* ekelhaft, widerlich.

dish [dɪʃ] *n* Schüssel *f*, Schale *f*; (*meal*) Gericht *neut*. *dishes pl* **Geschirr** *neut sing*. *wash the dishes* abspülen. **dishcloth** *n* (*for drying*) Geschirrtuch *neut*; (*for mopping*) Lappen *m*.

dishearten [dɪshaːtn] *v* entmutigen.

dishevelled [dɪʃevəld] *adj* in Unordnung; (*hair*) zerzaust.

dishonest [dɪsonɪst] *adj* unehrlich, unaufrichtig. **dishonesty** *n* Unehrlichkeit *f*. **dishonour** *n* Unehre *f*, Schande *f*. *v* schänden. **dishonourable** *adj* unehrenhaft.

dishwasher ['dɪʃwoʃə] *n* Geschirrspülmaschine *f*.

disillusion [dɪsɪluːʒən] *v* ernüchtern, desillusionieren. *be disillusioned about* die Illusion verloren haben über.

disinfect [dɪsɪnfekt] *v* desinfizieren. **disinfectant** *n* Desinfektionsmittel *neut*.

disinherit [dɪsɪnherɪt] *v* enterben.

disintegrate [dɪsɪntɪgreɪt] *v* (sich) auflösen, (sich) zersetzen. **disintegration** *n* Auflösung *f*.

disinterested [dɪsɪntrɪstɪd] *adj* unparteiisch.

disjointed [dɪsdʒoɪntɪd] *adj* unzusammenhängend.

disk [dɪsk] *n* (*comp*) Diskette *f*. *disk drive* Diskettenlaufwerk *neut*.

dislike [dɪslaɪk] *v* nicht mögen. *n* Abneigung *f* (gegen).

dislocate ['dɪsləkeɪt] *v* verrenken. **dislocation** *n* Verrenkung *f*.

dislodge [dɪsbdʒ] *v* verschieben.

disloyal [dɪsbɪəl] *adj* untreu. **disloyalty** *n* Untreue *f*.

dismal ['dɪzməl] *adj* trübe, niederdrückend.

dismantle [dɪsmantl] *v* abmontieren.

dismay [dɪsmeɪ] *v* bestürzen. *n* Bestürzung *f*, Angst *f*.

dismiss [dɪsmɪs] *v* wegschicken; (*employee*) entlassen; (*idea*) ablehnen. **dismissal** *n* Entlassung *f*.

dismount [dɪsmaunt] *v* absteigen.

disobey [dɪsəbeɪ] *v* nicht gehorchen (+ *dat*). **disobedience** *n* Ungehorsam *m*. **disobedient** *adj* ungehorsam.

disorder [dɪsoːdə] *n* Unordnung *f*; (*med*) Störung *f*.

disorganized [dɪsoːgənaɪzd] *adj* unordentlich.

disown [dɪsoun] *v* ableugnen; (*child*) verstoßen.

disparage [dɪsparɪdʒ] *v* herabsetzen. **disparaging** *v* geringschätzig.

disparity [dɪsˈpærɪt] n Unterschied m.

dispassionate [dɪsˈpæʃənɪt] adj unparteiisch.

dispatch [dɪsˈpætʃ] v absenden; (person) entsenden. n Versand m, Abfertigung f; (report) Meldung f.

dispel [dɪsˈpel] v vertreiben.

dispense [dɪsˈpens] v ausgeben. **dispense with** verzichten auf. **dispenser** n Verteiler m. **dispensing chemist** Apotheker(in).

disperse [dɪsˈpəːs] v zerstreuen.

displace [dɪsˈpleɪs] v versetzen; (replace) ersetzen; (water) verdrängen. **displacement** n (naut) Wasserverdrängung f.

display [dɪsˈpleɪ] v zeigen; (goods, etc.) auslegen. n (goods) Auslage f; (feelings) Zurschaustellung f; (parade) Entfaltung f.

displease [dɪsˈpliːz] v mißfallen (+ dat). **displeased** adj ärgerlich. **displeasure** n Mißfallen neut.

dispose [dɪsˈpouz] v **dispose of** (get rid of) beseitigen, wegwerfen; (have at disposal) verfügen uber. **disposed** adj geneigt. **disposable** adj zum Wegwerfen; Einweg-. **disposal** n Beseitigung f. **have at one's disposal** zur Verfügung haben. **be at someone's disposal** jemandem zur Verfügung stehen. **disposition** n Natur f, Art f.

disproportion [dɪsprəˈpoːʃən] n Mißverhältnis neut. **disproportionate** adj unverhältnismäßig.

disprove [dɪsˈpruːv] v widerlegen.

dispute [dɪsˈpjuːt] v (contest) bestreiten; (argue) disputieren. n Streit m. **trade dispute** Arbeitsstreitigkeit f.

disqualify [dɪsˈkwolɪfaɪ] v disqualifizieren, ausschließen. **disqualification** n Disqualifikation f.

disregard [dɪsrəˈgaːd] v nicht beachten.

disrepute [dɪsrəˈpjuːt] n Verruf m. **bring into disrepute** in Verruf bringen. **disreputable** adj (notorious) verrufen.

disrespect [dɪsrəˈspekt] n Respektlosigkeit f. **disrespectful** adj respektlos.

disrupt [dɪsˈrʌpt] v stören, unterbrechen. **disruption** n Störung f.

dissatisfied [dɪsatɪsfaɪd] adj unzufrieden.

dissect [dɪsekt] v sezieren.

dissent [dɪsent] n abweichende Meinung. v anderer Meinung sein.

dissident [ˈdɪsɪdənt] n Dissident m.

dissimilar [dɪsɪmɪlə] v unähnlich.

dissipate [ˈdɪspeɪt] v (heat, energy) abführen, ableiten; (time, talent) vergeuden, verzetteln, verschwenden.

dissociate [dɪsousɪeɪt] v **dissociate oneself from** sich lossagen von.

dissolve [dɪzolv] v (sich) auflösen; (meeting) aufheben.

dissuade [dɪsweɪd] v abraten (+ dat).

distance [ˈdɪstəns] n Ferne f, Entfernung f. (gap) Abstand m. **in the distance** in der Ferne. **keep one's distance** Abstand halten. **distant** adj fern, entfernt.

distaste [dɪsteɪst] n Abneigung f. **distasteful** adj unangenehm.

distended [dɪstendɪd] adj ausgedehnt.

distil [dɪstɪl] v destillieren. **distillery** n Brennerei f.

distinct [dɪstɪŋkt] adj (different) verschieden; (clear) deutlich, ausgeprägt. **distinction** n (difference) Unterschied m; (merit) Würde f. **of distinction** von Rang. **gain a distinction** sich auszeichnen. **distinctive** adj kennzeichnend.

distinguish [dɪstɪŋgwɪʃ] v unterscheiden; (perceive) erkennen. **distinguish oneself** sich auszeichnen. **distinguishable** adj erkennbar. **distinguished** adj hervorragend.

distort [dɪstoːt] v verdrehen; (truth) entstellen. **distortion** n Verdrehung f.

distract [dɪstrakt] v ablenken. **distracted** adj verwirrt, außer sich. **distraction** n Ablenkung f; (amusement) Unterhaltung f; (madness) Wahnsinn m.

distraught [dɪstroːt] adj verwirrt, bestürzt.

distress [dɪstres] n Not f; (suffering) Leid neut, Qual f. v betrüben, quälen. **distress signal** Notsignal m.

distribute [dɪstrɪbjuːt] v verteilen. **distribution** n Verteilung f. **distributor** n Verteiler m.

district [ˈdɪstrɪkt] n Gebiet neut, Gegend f; (of town) Viertel neut; (administrative) Bezirk m. adj Bezirks-. **district attorney** Staatsanwalt m.

distrust [dɪstrʌst] v mißtrauen (+dat). n Mißtrauen neut.

disturb [dɪstəːb] v stören; (worry) beunruhigen. **disturbance** n Störung f. **disturbances** pl (pol) Unruhen pl. **disturbing** adj beunruhigend.

disused [dɪsˈjuːzd] *adj* außer Gebrauch.

ditch [dɪtʃ] *n* Wassergraben *m*. *v* (coll) im Stich lassen.

dither [ˈdɪðə] *v* zaudern. **in a dither** verdattert.

ditto [ˈdɪtou] *adv* ebenfalls, dito. **ditto mark** Wiederholungszeichen *neut*.

divan [dɪvan] *n* Divan *m*, Sofa *neut*.

dive [daɪv] *v* tauchen; (from board) einen Kopfsprung machen; (aero) stürzen. *n* Tauchen *neut*; Kopfsprung *m*; (aero) Sturzflug *m*. **diver** *n* Taucher *m*.

diverge [daɪvəːdʒ] *v* auseinandergehen.

diverse [daɪvəːs] *adj* verschieden.

divert [daɪvəːt] *v* ableiten; (traffic) umleiten. **diversion** *n* Ablenkung *f*; (mot) Umleitung *f*. **diversity** *n* Verschiedenheit *f*.

divide [dɪvaɪd] *v* (sich) teilen.

dividend [ˈdɪvidend] *n* Dividende *f*.

divine [dɪvaɪn] *adj* göttlich. *v* erraten.

division [dɪvɪʒən] *n* Teilung *f*; (math, mil) Division *f*; (comm) Abteilung *f*.

divorce [dɪvoːs] *n* (Ehe)Scheidung *f*. *v* scheiden. **divorced** *adj* geschieden. **get divorced** sich scheiden lassen. **divorcee** *n* Geschiedene(r).

divulge [daɪvʌldʒ] *v* preisgeben.

dizzy [ˈdizi] *adj* schwindlig. **dizziness** *n* Schwindel *m*.

***do** [duː] *v* tun, machen. **that will do!** (that's enough) das genügt! **that won't do** (that's no good) das geht nicht! **How do you do?** Guten Tag! *I could do with the money* ich könnte das Geld gut gebrauchen. **do away with** abschaffen. **do in** (coll) umbringen. **do up** (coll) überholen. **do without** verzichten auf.

DNA *n* DNS (Deoxyribonukleinsäure) *f*.

docile [ˈdousaɪl] *adj* fügsam.

dock[1] [dok] *n* Dock *neut*. **docks** *pl* Hafenanlagen *pl*. *v* (ship) docken.

dock[2] [dok] *n* (law) **in the dock** auf der Anklagebank *f*.

dock[3] [dok] *v* (cut) stutzen; (pay) kürzen.

doctor [ˈdoktə] *n* (of medicine) Arzt *m*, Ärztin *f*; (as title) Doktor *m*.

doctrine [ˈdoktrin] *n* Lehre *f*.

document [ˈdokjumənt] *n* Urkunde *f*, Dokument *neut*. **documents** *pl* Papiere *pl*. *v* urkundlich belegen. **documentary** *adj* urkundlich. *n* Lehrfilm *m*.

dodge [dodʒ] *v* beiseitespringen; (avoid) ausweichen. *n* Knitt *m*.

dodgy [ˈdodʒi] *adj* (coll) fragwürdig, zwielichtig.

doe [dou] *n* (deer) Ricke *f*, Damtier *neut*; (rabbit) Häsin *f*.

dog [dog] *n* Hund *m*. **dog-eared** *adj* mit Eselsohren. **dogged** *adj* hartnäckig. **dog kennel** Hundehütte *f*.

dogma [ˈdogmə] *n* Dogma *neut*. **dogmatic** *adj* dogmatisch.

do-it-yourself [ˌduːɪtjɔːˈself] *adj* zum Selbermachen; Bastler-.

dole [doul] *n* Stempelgeld *neut*. **go on the dole** stempeln gehen. *v* **dole out** verteilen.

doll [dol] *n* Puppe *f*.

dollar [ˈdolə] *n* Dollar *m*.

dolphin [ˈdolfin] *n* Delphin *m*.

domain [dəˈmein] *n* Bereich *neut*.

dome [doum] *n* Kuppel *f*.

domestic [dəˈmestik] *adj* häuslich, Haus-; (national) inländisch, Innen-. **domestic animal** Haustier *neut*. **domesticate** *v* (tame) zähmen.

dominate [ˈdomineit] *v* beherrschen. **dominant** *adj* (vor)herrschend; (music, biol) dominant. **domination** *n* Herrschaft *f*.

domineering [ˌdomiˈniəriŋ] *adj* herrisch.

dominion [dəˈminjun] *n* Herrschaft *f*; (country) Dominion *neut*.

domino [ˈdominou] *n* Dominostein *m*. **dominoes** *pl* Dominospiel *neut sing*.

don [don] *v* (clothes) anziehen; (hat) aufsetzen.

donate [dəˈneit] *v* stiften, spenden. **donation** *n* Spende *f*, Stiftung *f*. **donor** *n* Spender *m*.

done [dʌn] *v* **do**.

donkey [ˈdoŋki] *n* Esel *m*.

doodle [ˈduːdl] *v* kritzeln. *n* Gekritzel *neut*.

doom [duːm] *n* Verhängnis *neut*. **doomed** *adj* verloren.

door [doː] *n* Tür *f*. **out of doors** draußen. **doorbell** Türklingel *f*. **doorhandle** *n* Türgriff *m*. **doorway** *n* Türöffnung *f*; Torweg *m*.

dope [doup] *n* (coll) Rauschgift *neut*. *v* (sport) dopen.

dormant [ˈdoːmənt] *adj* schlafend.

dormitory [ˈdoːmitəri] *n* Schlafsaal *m*. (US: student house) Wohnheim *m*.

dormouse ['dɔːˌmaʊs] *n* Haselmaus *f*.

dose [dəʊs] *n* Dosis *f*. *v* dosieren.

dot [dɒt] *n* Punkt *m*. **dot com** Internetfirma *f*. **dot matrix** Punktraster *neut*.

dote [dəʊt] *v* **dote on** vernarrt sein in.

dotted ['dɒtɪd] *adj* ubersät (mit). **dotted line** punktierte Linie *f*.

double ['dʌbl] *adj* doppelt, Doppel-. *adv* doppelt, zweimal. *n* das Doppelte; (*film*) Double *neut*. **doubles** *n* (*sport*) Doppelspiel *neut*. *v* verdoppeln; (*fold*) falten. **double-barrelled** *adj* doppelläufig. **double-bass** Kontrabaß *m*. **double-cross** *v* betrügen. **double-decker** Doppeldecker *m*. **double meaning** Zweideutigkeit *f*.

doubt [daʊt] *n* Zweifel *m*. *v* bezweifeln. **doubt whether** zweifeln, ob. **doubtful** *adj* zweifelhaft. **doubtless** *adv* ohne Zweifel, zweifellos.

dough [dəʊ] *n* Teig *m*. **doughnut** *n* Krapfen *m*.

dove [dʌv] *n* Taube *f*.

dowdy ['daʊdɪ] *adj* schäbig, schlampig.

down¹ [daʊn] *adv* hinab, herab; hinunter, herunter; unten. *I went down the road* ich ging die Straße hinunter. **up and down** auf und ab.

down² [daʊn] *n* (*feathers*) Daunen *pl*.

down-and-out [daʊnən'aʊt] *n* Penner(in) *m, f*.

downcast ['daʊnˌkaːst] *adj* niedergeschlagen.

downfall ['daʊnˌfɔːl] *n* Sturz *m*.

downhearted [ˌdaʊn'haːtɪd] *adj* mutlos.

downhill [ˌdaʊn'hɪl] *adv* bergab.

download [ˌdaʊn'bʊd] *v* (*comp*) herunterladen. *n* Download *m*.

downmarket [ˌdaʊn'maːkɪt] *adj* in der unteren Preislage.

downpour ['daʊnˌpɔː] *n* Wolkenbruch *m*.

downright ['daʊnˌraɪt] *adv* völlig, höchst.

downsize ['daʊnˌsaɪz] *v* den Personalbestand verringern.

Down's syndrome *n* Downsyndrom *neut*.

downstairs [ˌdaʊn'steəz] *adv* unten. *she came downstairs* sie kam nach unten.

downstream [ˌdaʊn'striːm] *adv* stromabwärts.

downtrodden ['daʊnˌtrɒdn] *adj* unterworfen.

downward ['daʊnwəd] *adj* Abwärts-, sinkend.

downwards ['daʊnwədz] *adv* abwärts.

dowry ['daʊərɪ] *n* Mitgift *f*.

doze [dəʊz] *v* dösen. *n* Schläfchen *neut*.

dozen ['dʌzn] *n* Dutzend *neut*.

drab [dræb] *adj* eintönig, farblos.

draft [draːft] *n* (*plan*) Konzept *neut*, Entwurf *m*; (*comm*) Tratte *f*; (*mil*) Aushebung *f*. *v* entwerfen; (*mil*) ausheben.

drag [dræg] *v* schleppen, schleifen. **drag on** sich in die Länge ziehen.

dragon ['drægən] *n* Drache *m*. **dragonfly** *n* Libelle *f*.

drain [dreɪn] *n* Abfluß *m*; (*fig*) Belastung *f*. *v* ablassen; (*water*) ableiten; (*fig*) erschöpfen. **drainage** *n* Entwässerung *f*. **drainpipe** *n* Abflußrohr *neut*.

drama ['draːmə] *n* Drama *neut*. **dramatic** *adj* dramatisch. **dramatize** *v* dramatisieren.

drank [dræŋk] *v* drink.

drape [dreɪp] *v* drapieren. *n* (*curtain*) Vorhang *m*. **draper** *n* Tuchhändler *m*.

drastic ['dræstɪk] *adj* drastisch.

draught *or US* **draft** [draːft] *n* Zug *m*; (*naut*) Tiefgang *m*. **draughts** *n* Damespiel *neut*. **draught beer** Bier vom Faß. **draughtsman** *n* Zeichner *m*. **draughty** *adj* zugig.

*draw [drɔː] *v* ziehen; (*curtain*) zuziehen; (*picture*) zeichnen; (*money*) abheben; (*public*) anziehen; (*water*) schöpfen; (*sport*) unentschieden spielen. *n* (*lottery*) Ziehung *f*; (*sport*) Unentschieden *neut*. **draw near** sich nähern. **draw up** (*document*) ausstellen. **drawback** *n* Nachteil *m*. **drawbridge** *n* Zugbrücke *f*. **drawer** *n* Schublade *f*. **drawing** *n* Zeichnung *f*. **drawing pin** Heftzwecke *f*. **drawing room** Salon *m*.

drawl [drɔːl] *v* schleppend sprechen.

drawn [drɔːn] *v* draw.

dread [dred] *n* Furcht *f*, Angst *f*. *v* Angst haben vor. **dreadful** *adj* furchtbar.

*dream [driːm] *n* Traum *m*. *v* träumen. **dreamer** *n* Träumer *n* **dreamy** *adj* träumerisch.

dreamt [dremt] *v* dream.

dreary ['drɪərɪ] *adj* trübe, düster.

dredge [dredʒ] *v* (*river*) ausbaggern. **dredger** *n* Bagger *m*.

dregs [dregz] *pl n* Bodensatz *m sing*; (*fig*)

Abschaum *m sing.*

drench [drentʃ] *v* durchnässen.

dress [dres] *v* (sich) anziehen; *(wound)* verbinden. *n (clothes)* Kleidung *f*; *(woman's)* Kleid *neut.* **dress designer** Modezeichner *m.* **dresser** *n (furniture)* Küchenschrank *m.* **dressing** *n (salad)* Soße *f*; *(med)* Verband *m.* **dressing gown** Morgenrock *m.* **dressing room** *(theatre)* Garderobe *f.* **dressing table** Toilettentisch *m.* **dressmaking** *n* Damenschneiderei *f.* **dress suit** Gesellschaftsanzug *m.*

drew [druː] *v* draw.

dribble ['dribl] *v* tröpfeln; *(football)* dribbeln. *n* Tröpfeln *neut.*

drier ['draiə] *n* Trockner *m.*

drift [drift] *v* treiben; *(coll)* sich treiben lassen. *n (snow)* Verwehung *f*; *(tendency)* Tendenz *f.* **drifter** *n (person)* Vagabund *m.*

drill [dril] *n* Bohrmaschine *f*; *(training)* Drill *m. v (holes)* bohren; *(train)* trainieren, drillen.

***drink** [driŋk] *v* trinken; *(animal, coll)* saufen. *n* Getränk *neut*; *(cocktail, etc.)* Drink *m.* **drinker** *n* Trinker *m (coll)* Säufer *m.*

drip [drip] *v* tropfen, triefen. *n* Tropfen *m* **drip-dry** *adj* bügelfrei. **dripping** *adj* triefend. *n* Schmalz *neut.*

***drive** [draiv] *v* treiben; *(vehicle)* fahren. *n* Fahrt *f*; *(tech)* Antrieb *m*; *(mil)* Kampagne *f.* **drive mad** verrückt machen. **drive-in** *n (cinema)* Autokino *neut.*

drivel ['drivl] *v* sabbern, geifern. *n* Quatsch *m.*

driver ['draivə] *n* Fahrer *m*, Chauffeur *m.* **driver's license** Führerschein *m.*

driving ['draiviŋ] *adj* Treib-; *(mot)* Fahr-; *(rain)* heftig. *n* Fahren *neut.* **driving lessons** Fahrunterricht *m.* **driving licence** Führerschein *m.* **driving school** Fahrschule *f.* **driving test** Fahrprüfung *f.*

drizzle ['drizl] *n* Sprühregen *m. v* nieseln.

drone [droun] *v* summen. *n* Drohne *f.*

droop [druːp] *v* (schlaff) herunterhängen; *(flower)* welken.

drop [drop] *n (of water)* Tropfen *m*; *(fall)* Fall, Sturz *m. v (fall)* fallen; *(let fall)* fallen lassen; *(passenger)* absetzen; *(bomb)* abwerfen. **drop in** vorbeikommen. **drop off (to sleep)** einschlafen. **drop-out** *n* Dropout *m*, Aussteiger(in) *m, f.*

drought [draut] *n* Dürre *f.*

drove [drouv] *v* drive.

drown [draun] *v* ertrinken. **drown out** übertönen.

drowsy ['drauzi] *adj* schläfrig.

drudge [drʌdʒ] *n* Packesel *m.* **drudgery** *n* Plackerei *f.*

drug [drʌg] *n (medicinal)* Droge *f*; *(narcotic)* Rauschgift *neut. v* betäuben. **drug addict** Rauschgiftsüchtige(r).

drum [drʌm] *n* Trommel *f. v* trommeln. **drummer** *n* Trommler *m.* **drumstick** *n* Trommelstock *m.*

drunk [drʌŋk] *v* drink. *adj* betrunken; *(coll)* besoffen. **get drunk** sich betrinken; *(coll)* besoffen werden. **drunken** *adj* betrunken. **drunkard** *n* Trinker *m*; *(coll)* Säufer. **drunkenness** *n* Betrunkenheit *f.*

dry [drai] *adj* trocken; *(wine)* herb. *v* trocknen. **dry up** austrocknen; *(dishes)* abtrocknen. **dry-clean** *v* chemisch reinigen. **dry cleaner** chemische Reinigung *f.* **dry dock** Trockendock *neut.* **dry land** fester Boden *m.*

dual ['djuəl] *adj* doppelt. **dual carriageway** zweispurige Hauptverkehrstraße *f.* **dual-purpose** *adj* Mehrzweck-.

dubbed ['dʌbd] *adj (film)* synchronisiert.

dubious ['djuːbiəs] *adj* zweifelhaft, dubiös.

duchess ['dʌtʃis] *n* Herzogin *f.*

duck¹ [dʌk] *n* Ente *f.*

duck² [dʌk] *v* sich ducken; *(under water)* untertauchen.

duct [dʌkt] *n* Kanal *m.*

dud [dʌd] *adj* wertlos. *n* Niete *f*, Versager *m.*

due [djuː] *adj (suitable)* gebührend; *(payment)* fällig. *the train is due at 7 o'clock* der Zug soll (planmäßig) um 7 Uhr ankommen. *adv* **due east** genau nach Osten. **due to** infolge (+ *gen*). **in due course** zur rechten Zeit. *I am due to* ich muß.

duel ['djuəl] *n* Duell *neut.*

duet [dju'et] *n* Duett *neut.*

dug [dʌg] *v* dig.

duke [djuːk] *n* Herzog *m.*

dull [dʌl] *adj (colour)* matt, düster; *(pain)* dumpf; *(boring)* langweilig, uninteressant; *(stupid)* dumm. **dullness** *n* Düsterkeit *f*, Trübe *f. v* abstumpfen.

duly ['djuːli] *adv* gebührend, ordnungsgemäß.

dumb [dʌm] *adj* stumm; (*coll: stupid*) doof. **deaf and dumb** taubstumm. **dumbfound** *v* verblüffen.

dummy ['dʌm] *n* (*baby's*) Schnuller *m*; (*tailor's*) Schneiderpuppe *f*; (*imitation*) Attrappe *f*.

dumb [dʌm p] *n* Müllhaufen *m*, Müllkippe *f*. *v* abladen.

dumpling ['dʌm plɪŋ] *n* Knödel *m*, Kloβ *m*.

dunce [dʌns] *n* Dummkopf *m*.

dune [djuːn] *n* Düne *f*.

dung [dʌŋ] *n* Mist *m*.

dungeon ['dʌndʒən] *n* Kerker *m*.

duplicate ['djuːplɪkət; *n* 'djuːplɪkeɪt] *n* Duplikat *neut*. *v* verdoppeln; (*make copies*) vervielfältigen, kopieren. *adj* doppelt. **duplication** *n* Verdoppelung *f*. **duplicator** *n* Vervielfältigungsmaschine *f*.

durable ['djʊərəbl] *adj* dauerhaft.

duration [djuːreɪʃən] *n* Dauer *f*.

during ['djʊrɪŋ] *prep* während (+ *gen*).

dusk [dʌsk] *n* (Abend)Dämmerung *f*. **dusky** *adj* düster.

dust [dʌst] *n* Staub *m*. *v* abstauben. **dustbin** *n* Mülleimer *m*. **dustcart** Müllwagen *m*. **duster** *n* Staubtuch *neut*. **dustman** *n* Müllabfuhrmann *m*. **dusty** *adj* staubig.

duty ['djuːtɪ] *n* Pflicht *f*; (*task*) Aufgabe *f*; (*tax*) Zoll *m*, Abgabe *f*. **off/on duty** auβer/im Dienst. **duty-free** *adj* zollfrei. **dutiful** *adj* pflichtbewuβt.

Dutch [dʌtʃ] *adj* holländisch. **Dutchman** *n* Holländer *m*. **Dutchwoman** *n* Holländerin *f*.

duvet ['duːveɪ] *n* Federbett *neut*.

DVD *n* DVD (digitale Videoplatte) *f*.

dwarf [dwoːf] *n* Zwerg *m*. *adj* zwergenhaft.

***dwell** [dwel] *n* wohnen. **dwell on** bleiben bei. **dwelling** *n* Wohnung *f*.

dwelt [dwelt] *v* dwell.

dwindle ['dwɪndl] *v* abnehmen.

dye [daɪ] *n* Farbstoff *m*. *v* färben.

dyke [daɪk] *n* Deich *m*, Damm *m*.

dynamic [daɪnæm ɪk] *adj* dynamisch. **dynamics** *n* Dynamik *f*.

dynamite ['daɪnəm aɪt] *n* Dynamit *neut*.

dynamo ['daɪnəm oʊ] *n* Dynamo *n*.

dynasty ['dɪnəstɪ] *n* Dynastie *f*.

dysentery ['dɪsəntrɪ] *n* Ruhr *f*.

dyslexia [dɪsleksə] *n* Legasthenie *f*, Wortblindheit *f*.

dyspepsia [dɪspepsə] *n* Verdauungsstörung *f*.

E

each [iːtʃ] *adj*, *pron* jeder, jede, jedes. *adv* je. **each other** einander, sich.

eager ['iːgə] *adj* eifrig. **eagerness** Eifer *m*.

eagle ['iːgl] *n* Adler *m*.

ear¹ [ə] *n* (*anat*) Ohr *neut*; (*hearing*) Gehör *neut*. **earache** *n* Ohrenschmerzen *pl*. **eardrum** *n* Trommelfell *neut*. **earlobe** *n* Ohrläppchen *neut*. **earring** *n* Ohrring *m*. **earshot** *n* **within/out of earshot** in/auβer Höweite.

ear² [ə] *n* (*of corn*) Ähre *f*.

earl [əːl] *n* Graf *m*.

early ['əːlɪ] *adj*, *adv* früh; (*soon*) bald.

earn [əːn] *v* verdienen. **earnings** *pl n* Einkommen *neut sing*.

earnest ['əːnɪst] *adj* ernsthaft. **n in earnest** im Ernst.

earth [əːθ] *n* Erde *f*. *v* (*elec*) erden. **earthly** *adj* irdisch. **earthenware** *n* Steingut *neut*. **earthquake** *n* Erdbeben *neut*. **earthworm** *n* Regenwurm *m*.

earwig ['əwɪg] *n* Ohrwurm *m*.

ease [iːz] *n* Leichtigkeit *f*; (*comfort*) Behagen *neut*. *v* erleichtern. **at ease** behaglich. **with ease** ohne Mühe.

easel ['iːzl] *n* Staffelei *f*.

east [iːst] *n* Osten *m*. *adj also* **easterly** östlich, Ost-. *adv also* **eastwards** nach Osten; ostwärts. **eastern** *adj* östlich; orientalisch.

Easter ['iːstə] *n* Ostern *neut*.

easy ['iːzɪ] *adj* leicht. **easily** *adv* leicht, mühelos; (*by far*) bei weitem. **easy-going** *adj* ungezwungen.

***eat** [iːt] *v* essen; (*of animals*) fressen.

eaten ['iːtn] *v* eat.

eavesdrop ['iːvzdrop] *v* lauschen.

ebb [eb] *n* Ebbe *f*; (*fig*) Tiefstand *m*. *v* verebben.

ebony ['ebənɪ] *n* Ebenholz *neut*.

eccentric [ɪksentrɪk] *adj* exzentrisch. *n* Sonderling *m*.

ecclesiastical [ɪkliːzɪ'astɪk] *adj* kirchlich.

echo ['ekou] *n* Echo *neut*. *v* widerhallen.

eclipse [iklips] *n* Finsternis *f*. *v* verfinstern; (*fig*) in den Schatten stellen.

ecology [ikoləd3ɪ] *n* Ökologie *f*. **ecological** *adj* ökologisch.

economy [ikonəm ɪ] *n* Wirtschaft *f*; (*thrift*) Sparsamkeit *f*. **economic** *adj* ökonomisch, wirtschaftlich, Wirtschafts-. **economical** *adj* sparsam, wirtschaftlich. **economics** *n* Volkswirtschaft *f*. **economist** *n* Volkswirtschaftler *m*. **economize** *v* sparen (an).

ecstasy ['ekstəsɪ] *n* Ekstase *f*; (*drug*) Ecstasy *f*. **ecstatic** *adj* ekstatisch.

eczema ['eksɪm ə] *n* Ekzem *neut*.

edge [ed3] *n* Rand *m*. **on edge** nervös.

edible ['edəbl] *adj* eßbar.

edit ['edɪt] *v* redigieren. **edition** *n* Ausgabe *f*. **editor** *n* Redakteur *m*.

editorial [edɪtoːrɪəl] *adj* Redaktions-. *n* Leitartikel *m*.

educate ['edjukeɪt] *n* erziehen, ausbilden. **education** *n* Bildung *f*, Erziehung *f*; (*system*) Schulwesen *neut*. **educational** *adj* pädagogisch.

eel [iːl] *n* Aal *m*.

eerie ['ɪərɪ] *adj* unheimlich.

effect [ifekt] *n* Wirkung *f*; (*impression*) Eindruck *m*. **have an effect on** wirken auf. **in effect** in Wirklichkeit. **effective** *adj* wirksam. **effectiveness** *n* Wirksamkeit *f*.

effeminate [ifem nət] *adj* weibisch.

effervesce [efəves] *v* sprudeln. **effervescent** *adj* sprudelnd.

efficiency [ifɪʃənsɪ] *n* Leistungsfähigkeit *f*. **efficient** *adj* (*person*) tüchtig; (*effective*) wirksam; (*machine*) leistungsfähig.

effigy ['efɪd3ɪ] *n* Abbild *neut*.

effort ['efət] *n* Anstrengung *f*, Mühe *f*. **make an effort** sich anstrengen. **make every effort** sich alle Mühe geben. **effortless** *adj* mühelos.

egg [eg] *n* Ei *neut*. *v* **egg on** reizen. **boiled egg** gekochtes Ei *neut*. **fried egg** Spiegelei *neut*. **scrambled egg** Rührei *neut*. **egg cup** Eierbecher *m*. **eggshell** *n* Eierschale *f*.

ego ['igou] *n* Ich *neut*. **egoism** *n* Egoismus *m*. **egoist** *n* Egoist *m*.

Egypt ['idʒɪpt] *n* Ägypten *neut*. **Egyptian** *adj* ägyptisch; *n* Ägypter(in).

eiderdown ['aɪdədaun] *n* Federbett *neut*.

eight [eɪt] *adj* acht. *n* Acht *f*. **eight** *adj*

acht; *n* Achtel *neut*.

eighteen [eɪtiːn] *adj* achtzehn. **eighteenth** *adj* achtzehnt.

eighty ['eɪtɪ] *adj* achtzig. **eightieth** *adj* achtzigst.

either ['aɪðə] *pron* einer (eine, eines) von beiden. **on either side** auf beiden Seiten. **either ... or ...** entweder ... oder ....

ejaculate [idʒakjuleɪt] *v* (*utter*) ausstoßen; ejakulieren.

eject [idʒekt] *v* ausstoßen.

eke [iːk] *v* **eke out** (*add to*) ergänzen.

elaborate [ilabərət; *v* iˈlabəreɪt] *adj* ausführlich, genau ausgearbeitet. *v* **elaborate on** eingehend erörtern. **elaboration** *n* Ausarbeitung *f*.

elapse [ilaps] *v* vergehen.

elastic [ilastɪk] *adj* elastisch. **elastic band** Gummiband *neut*.

elated [ileɪtɪd] *adj* begeistert, froh.

elbow ['elbou] *n* Ellbogen *m*.

elder[1] ['eldə] *adj* älter. *n* Ältere(r).

elder[2] ['eldə] *n* (*tree*) Holunder *m*.

elderly ['eldəlɪ] *adj* älter.

eldest ['eldɪst] *adj* ältest. *n* Älteste(r).

elect [ilekt] *v* wählen. **election** *n* Wahl *f*. **elector** *n* Wähler *m*. **electorate** *n* Wählerschaft *f*.

electric [əˈlektrɪk] *adj also* **electrical** elektrisch. **electrical engineering** Elektrotechnik *f*. **electric blanket** Heizdecke *f*. **electric chair** elektrischer Stuhl *m*. **electric cooker** Elektroherd *neut*. **electrician** *n* Elektriker *m*. **electricity** *n* Strom *m*, Elektrizität *f*.

electrify [əˈlektrɪfaɪ] *v* elektrifizieren. **electrifying** *adj* (*fig*) elektrisierend.

electronic [eləktronɪk] *n* elektronisch. **electronics** *n* Elektronik *f sing*.

elegant ['eləgənt] *adj* elegant.

element ['eləm ənt] *n* Element *neut*. **elementary** *adj* elementar.

elephant ['eləfənt] *n* Elefant *m*.

elevate ['eliveɪt] *v* heben; (*promote*) erheben. **elevation** *n* Hochheben *neut*; (*promotion*) Erhebung *f*. **elevator** *n* Aufzug *m*.

eleven [ilevn] *adj* elf. **eleventh** *adj* elft.

eligible ['elɪd3əbl] *adj* wählbar. **be eligible in Frage kommen. **be eligible for** berechtigt sein zu. **eligibility** *n* Eignung *f*.

eliminate [ɪlɪm ineɪt] n beseitigen; (*sport*) ausscheiden. **elimination** n Beseitigung f; Ausscheidung f.

élite [eɪlitɪ] n Elite f.

ellipse [ɪlɪps] n Ellipse f. **elliptical** *adj* elliptisch.

elm [eɪm] n Ulme f.

elocution [eb'kju:ʃən] n Sprechkunde f.

elope [ɪloup] v entlaufen. **elopement** n Entlaufen neut.

eloquent [ˈeɪbkwənt] *adj* (*person*) redegewandt. **eloquence** n Redegewandtheit f.

else [eɪs] *adv* sonst. **anyone else?** sonst noch jemand? **someone else** jemand anders. **nothing else** nichts weiter. **elsewhere** *adv* anderswo, woanders.

elucidate [ɪlu:sɪdeɪt] v aufklären. **elucidation** n Aufklärung f.

elude [ɪlu:d] v entgehen (*dat*).

emaciated [ɪmeɪsɪeɪtɪd] *adj* abgemagert.

e-mail [ˈim eɪl] n E-mail f, neut, (*system*) E-post. f. v (*person*) eine E-mail (an jemanden) schicken/senden.

emanate [ˈem əneɪt] v ausströmen (aus); (*fig*) herstammen (von).

emancipate [ɪmansɪpeɪt] v befreien, emanzipieren. **emancipated** *adj* emanzipiert. **emancipation** n Befreiung f.

embalm [ɪn'baːm] v einbalsamieren.

embankment [ɪn'baŋkmənt] n Damm m; (*road*) Uferstraße f.

embargo [ɪn'baːgou] n Handelssperre f.

embark [ɪn'baːk] v sich einschiffen (nach); (*fig*) sich einlassen (in).

embarrass [ɪn'barəs] v in Verlegenheit bringen. **be embarrassed** verlegen sein. **embarrassment** n Verlegenheit f.

embassy [ˈem bəsɪ] n Botschaft f.

embellish [ɪn'belɪʃ] v verzieren.

embers ['embəz] pl n Glut f sing.

embezzle [ɪn'bezl] v unterschlagen. **embezzlement** n Unterschlagung f.

embitter [ɪn'bɪtə] v verbittern.

emblem [ˈem bləm] n Sinnbild neut.

embody [ɪn'bodɪ] v verkörpern. **embodiment** n Verkörperung f.

embossed [ɪn'bost] *adj* erhaben.

embrace [ɪn'breɪs] v umarmen; (*include*) umfassen. n Umarmung f.

embroider [ɪn'brɔɪdə] v (be)sticken; (*story*) ausschmücken. **embroidery** n Stickerei f.

embryo [ˈem brɪou] n Embryo m.

emerald [ˈem ərəld] n Smaragd m. **emerald green** smaragdgrün.

emerge [ɪmɜːdʒ] v (*from water*) auftauchen; (*appear*) hervorkommen. **emergence** n Auftauchen neut.

emergency [ɪmɜːdʒənsɪ] n Notfall m. *adj* Not-. **emergency exit** Notausgang m.

emigrate [ˈem ɪgreɪt] v auswandern. **emigration** n Auswanderung f. **emigrant** n Auswanderer m.

eminent [ˈem ɪnənt] *adj* hervorragend, erhaben: **eminence** n Erhöhung f.

emit [ɪmɪt] v von sich geben. **emission** n Ausstrahlung f, Emission f.

emotion [ɪmouʃən] n Gefühl neut. **emotional** *adj* Gefühls-; (*excitable*) erregbar; (*full of feeling*) gefühlvoll. **emotive** *adj* gefühlserregend.

empathy [ˈem pəθɪ] n Einfühlung f.

emperor [ˈem pərə] n Kaiser m.

emphasis [ˈem fəsɪs] n (pl -ses) Nachdruck m. **emphasize** v betonen, unterstreichen. **emphatic** *adj* nachdrücklich.

empire [ˈem paɪə] n Reich neut.

empirical [ɪn'pɪrɪkəl] *adj* empirisch.

employ [ɪn'plɔɪ] v (*use*) verwenden; (*appoint*) anstellen. **be employed** beschäftigt or tätig sein. **employee** n Angestellte(r); (*as opposed to employer*) Arbeitnehmer m. **employer** n Arbeitgeber m. **employment** n Arbeit f, Beschäftigung f.

empower [ɪn'pauə] v ermächtigen.

empress [ˈem prɪs] n Kaiserin f.

empty [ˈem ptɪ] *adj* leer. v leeren. **emptiness** n Leere f.

emulate [ˈem jʊleɪt] v nacheifern (*dat*).

emulsion [ɪm ʌlʃən] n Emulsion f. **emulsify** v emulgieren.

enable [ɪneɪbl] v ermöglichen.

enact [ɪnakt] v verordnen; (*law*) erlassen.

enamel [ɪnam əl] n Emaille f; (*teeth*) Zahnschmelz m. v emaillieren.

enamour [ɪnam ə] v **be enamoured of** verliebt sein in.

encase [ɪn'keɪs] v umschließen.

enchant [ɪn'tʃaːnt] v entzücken. **enchanting** *adj* entzückend. **enchantment** n Zauber m, Entzücken neut.

encircle [ɪn'sɜːkl] v umringen.

enclose [inˈkləʊz] v einschließen; (*in letter*) beifügen. **enclosed** *adj* (*in letter*) beigefügt. **enclosure** n Einzäunung f; (*in letter*) Anlage f.

encompass [inˈkʌm pəs] v umfassen.

encore [ˈɒŋkɔː] *interj* noch einmal! n Zugabe f.

encounter [inˈkaʊntə] v treffen; (*difficulties*) stoßen auf. n Begenung f; (*mil*) Gefecht neut.

encourage [inˈkʌridʒ] v ermutigen; (*promote*) fördern. **encouragement** n Ermutigung f.

encroach [inˈkrəʊtʃ] v eindringen (in). **encroachment** n Eingriff m.

encyclopedia [insaikɒˈpiːdiə] n Enzyklopädie f.

end [end] n Ende *neut*; (*finish*) Schluß m; (*purpose*) Zweck m. v beend(ig)en; (*come to an end*) zu Ende gehen. **ending** n Ende neut. **endless** *adj* unendlich.

endanger [inˈdeindʒə] v gefährden.

endearing [inˈdɪərɪŋ] *adj* liebenswert.

endeavour [inˈdevə] v sich anstrengen, versuchen. n Versuch m, Bestrebung f.

endemic [enˈdem ik] *adj* endemisch.

endive [ˈendiv] n Endivie f.

endorse [inˈdɔːs] v indossieren; (*approve of*) billigen. **endorsement** n Vermerk m; Billigung f.

endow [inˈdaʊ] v stiften. **endowed with** begabt mit. **endowment** n Ausstattung f, Stiftung f.

endure [inˈdjʊə] v ertragen. **enduring** *adj* beständig.

enemy [ˈenəm i] n Feind m. *adj* Feind-.

energy [ˈenədʒi] n Energíe f. **energetic** *adj* energisch.

enforce [inˈfɔːs] v durchsetzen. **enforcement** n Durchsetzung f.

engage [inˈgeidʒ] v (*employ*) anstellen; (*tech*) einschalten; (*enemy*) angreifen. **engaged** *adj* (*to be married*) verlobt; (*occupied*) besetzt. **get engaged** sich verloben. **engagement** n (*to marry*) Verlobung f; (*appointment*) Verabredung f.

engine [ˈendʒin] n Motor m; (*rail*) Lokomotive f. **engine driver** Lokomotivführer m.

engineer [endʒiˈnɪə] n Ingenieur m. v (*fig*) organisieren. **engineering** n Technik f.

England [ˈiŋgənd] n England *neut*.

English [ˈiŋliʃ] *adj* englisch. **(the) English (language)** (das) Englisch(e), die englische Sprache. *I am English* ich bin Engländer(in). **English Channel** Ärmelkanal m. **Englishman** n Engländer m. **Englishwoman** n Engländerin f. **English-speaking** *adj* englischsprechend.

engrave [inˈgreiv] v gravieren. **engraving** n Stich m.

engrossed [inˈgrəʊst] *adj* vertieft.

engulf [inˈgʌlf] v (*overcome*) überwältigen.

enhance [inˈhains] v verstärken.

enigma [inigm ə] n Rätsel neut. **enigmatic** *adj* rätselhaft.

enjoy [inˈdʒɔi] v genießen, Freude haben an. **enjoy oneself** sich (gut) unterhalten. **enjoyment** n Freude f. **enjoy yourself!** viel spaß/Vergnügen!

enlarge [inˈlaidʒ] v (sich) vergrößern. **enlargement** n Vergrößerung f.

enlighten [inˈhin] v aufklären. **enlightened** *adj* aufgeklärt. **enlightenment** n Aufklärung f.

enlist [inˈlist] v (*help*) in Anspruch nehmen; (*in army*) sich melden.

enmity [ˈenm əti] n Feindseligkeit f.

enormous [inoːm əs] *adj* riesig, ungeheuer.

enough [inʌf] *adv* genug. **be enough** genügen. **have enough of something** (*be tired of*) etwas satt haben.

enquire [inˈkwaiə] *adv* sich erkundigen, fragen. **enquiry** n Nachfrage f.

enrage [inˈreidʒ] v wütend machen. **enraged** *adj* wütend.

enrich [inˈritʃ] v bereichern.

enrol [inˈrəʊl] v einschreiben; (*in club*) als Mitglied aufnehmen; (*oneself*) beitreten (*dat*). **enrolment** n Aufnahme f.

ensign [ˈensain] n (*naut*) (Schiffs)Flagge f.

enslave [inˈsleiv] n versklaven.

ensue [inˈsjuː] v (darauf) folgen. **ensuing** *adj* daraufolgend.

en suite [ˈɒnswiːt] *adj* mit Bad und WC.

ensure [inˈʃʊə] v gewährleisten, sichern.

entail [inˈteil] v mit sich bringen.

entangle [inˈtaŋgl] v verstricken. **entangled** *adj* verstrickt.

enter [ˈentə] v (*go in*) eintreten; (*a room*) hineintreten in; (*in book*) einschreiben; (*sport*) sich anmelden.

enterprise [ˈentəpraiz] n (*concern*)

Unternehmen *neut*; (*initiative*) Initiative *f*. **private enterprise** freie Wirtschaft *f*. **enterprising** *adj* unternehmungslustig.

entertain [,entə'teɪn] *v* (*amuse*) unterhalten; (*feelings*) hegen; (*as guests*) gastlich bewirten. **entertaining** *adj* unterhaltsam. **entertainment** *n* Unterhaltung *f*.

enthral [ɪn'θrɔːl] *v* entzücken. **enthralling** *adj* entzückend.

enthusiasm [ɪn'θuːziˌazəm] *n* Begeisterung *f*, Enthusiasmus *m*. **enthusiastic** *adj* begeistert, enthusiastisch.

entice [ɪn'taɪs] *v* verlocken. **enticement** *n* Anreiz *m*. **enticing** *adj* verlockend.

entire [ɪn'taɪə] *adj* ganz. **entirely** *adv* ganz, völlig, durchaus. **entirety** *n* Gesamtheit *f*.

entitle [ɪn'taɪtl] *v* berechtigen (zu).

entity [entəti] *n* Wesen *neut*.

entrails [entreɪlz] *pl n* Eingeweide *pl*.

entrance[1] [entrəns] *n* (*going in, fee*) Eintritt *m*; (*way in*) Eingang *m*.

entrance[2] [ɪn'trɑːns] *v* entzücken.

entrant [entrənt] *n* (*sport*) Teilnehmer(in); (*for exam*) Kandidat *m*.

entreat [ɪn'triːt] *v* ernstlich bitten. **entreaty** *n* Bitte *f*.

entrenched [ɪn'trentʃt] *v* **become entrenched** sich festsetzen.

entrepreneur [,ɒntrəprə'nəː] *n* Unternehmer *m*.

entrust [ɪn'trʌst] *v* (*thing*) anvertrauen (*dat*); (*person*) betrauen (mit).

entry [entri] *n* Eintritt *m*; (*into country*) Einreise *f*; (*comm*) Posten *m*; (*theatre*) Auftritt *m*. **no entry** Eintritt verboten.

entwine [ɪn'twaɪn] *v* umwinden.

enunciate [ɪnʌnsieɪt] *v* aussagen; (*state*) ausdrücken.

envelop [ɪn'veləp] *v* einwickeln; (*fig*) umhüllen.

envelope [envə,loup] *n* Umschlag *m*.

enviable [enviəbl] *adj* beneidenswert.

envious [enviəs] *adj* neidisch (*of* auf). **be envious of** beneiden.

environment [ɪn'vaɪərənmənt] *n* Umgebung *f*. **the environment** Umwelt *f*. **environmental** *adj* Umwelt-, ökologisch.

envisage [ɪn'vɪzɪdʒ] *v* sich vorstellen.

envoy [envɔɪ] *n* Bote *m*.

envy [envi] *v* beneiden. *n* Neid *m*.

enzyme [enzaɪm] *n* Enzym *neut*.

epaulet [epəˌlet] *n* Epaulette *f*.

ephemeral [ɪfem'ərə] *adj* vergänglich.

epic [epɪk] *adj* (*poetry*) episch; heldenhaft. *n* Heldengedicht *neut*.

epicure [epɪkˌjuə] *n* Feinschmecker *m*.

epidemic [epɪdem'ɪk] *n* Epidemie *f*. *adj* epidemisch.

epilepsy [epɪlepsi] *n* Epilepsie *f*. **epileptic** *adj* epileptisch; *n* Epileptiker(in).

epilogue [epɪlɒg] *n* Epilog *m*.

Epiphany [ɪpifəni] *n* Epiphanias *neut*.

episcopal [ɪpiskəpə] *adj* bischöflich.

episode [epɪsoud] *n* Episode *f*.

epitaph [epɪtɑːf] *n* Grabschrift *f*.

epitome [ɪpitəm'i] *n* Inbegriff *m*.

epoch [iːpɒk] *n* Epoche *f*.

equable [ekwəbl] *adj* (*person*) gelassen.

equal [iːkwəl] *adj* gleich (+ *dat*). **be equal to** gleichen (+ *dat*); (*be able*) gewachsen sein (+ *dat*). **equal in size** von gleicher Größe. *n* Gleichgestellte(r). *v* gleichen (+ *dat*), gleich sein (+ *dat*). **equality** *n* Gleichheit *f*; (*pol*) Gleichberechtigung *f*. **equalize** *v* gleichmachen. **equally** *adv* ebenso, in gleichem Maße.

equanimity [ekwə'nɪmˌəti] *n* Gleichmut *m*.

equate [ɪkweɪt] *v* gleichstellen. **equation** *n* Gleichung *f*.

equator [ɪkweɪtə] *n* Äquator *m*. **equatorial** *adj* äquatorial.

equestrian [ɪkwestriən] *adj* Reit-, Reiter-.

equilateral [,iːkwɪlatərə] *adj* gleichseitig.

equilibrium [,iːkwɪlɪbriəm] *n* Gleichgewicht *neut*.

equinox [ekwɪnɒks] *n* Tagundnachtgleiche *f*.

equip [ɪkwɪp] *v* ausrüsten, ausstatten. **equipment** *n* Ausrüstung *f*, Einrichtung *f*.

equity [ekwəti] *n* Billigkeit *f*; (*law*) Billigkeitsrecht *f*.

equivalent [ɪkwɪvələnt] *adj* gleichwertig. **be equivalent to** gleichkommen (*dat*). *n* Gegenstück *neut*.

era [iːərə] *n* Epoche *f*, Ära *f*.

eradicate [ɪradɪkeɪt] *v* ausrotten. **eradication** *n* Ausrottung *f*.

erase [ɪreɪz] *v* ausradieren, tilgen. **eraser** *n* Radiergummi *m*.

erect [ɪrekt] *v* errichten. *adj* aufrecht. **erection** *n* Errichtung *f*; (*anat*) Erektion *f*.

ermine [əːmɪn] *n* Hermelin *m*.

erode [ɪˈroud] *v* zerfressen. **erosion** *n* Zerfressung *f*.

erotic [ɪˈrotɪk] *adj* erotisch. **eroticism** *n* Erotik *f*.

err [əː] *v* sich irren.

errand [ˈerənd] *n* (Boten)Gang *m*.

erratic [ɪˈratɪk] *adj* unberechenbar.

error [ˈerə] *n* Fehler *m*, Irrtum *m*; (*of compass*) Abweichung *f*; (*oversight*) Versehen *neut*. **erroneous** *adj* irrtümlich.

erudite [ˈerudaɪt] *adj* gelehrt.

erupt [ɪˈrʌpt] *v* (*volcano*) ausbrechen. **eruption** *n* Ausbruch *m*; (*skin*) Hautausschlag *m*.

escalate [ˈeskəˌleɪt] *v* (*a war*) steigern, eskalieren. **escalation** *n* Eskalation *f*. **escalator** *n* Rolltreppe *f*.

escalope [ˈeskəˌlɒp] *n* Schnitzel *neut*.

escape [ɪˈskeɪp] *v* entkommen (+ *dat*); (*fig*) entgehen (+ *dat*). *n* Flucht *f*; (*of liquid*) Ausfluß *m*. **have a narrow escape** mit knapper Not entkommen. **escapism** *n* Realitätsflucht *f*, Eskapismus *m*.

escort [ˈeskɔːt; *n* ˈeskɔːt] *v* begleiten. *n* (*mil*) Eskorte *f*.

esoteric [esəˈterik] *adj* esoterisch.

especial [ɪˈspeʃəl] *adj* besonder, speziell. **especially** *adv* besonders.

espionage [ˈespiˌɒnɑːʒ] *n* Spionage *f*.

esplanade [espləˈneɪd] *n* Esplanade *f*.

essay [ˈeseɪ] *n* (*school*) Aufsatz *m*; (*literary*) Essay *m*.

essence [ˈesns] *n* Wesen *neut*; (*extract*) Essenz *f*.

essential [ɪˈsenʃəl] *adj* Wesentlich; (*indispensable*) unentbehrlich, unbedingt notwendig. **essentially** *adv* im wesentlichen.

establish [ɪˈstablɪʃ] *v* einrichten, aufstellen; (*a fact*) feststellen; (*found*) gründen. **establishment** *n* Gründung *f*; (*comm*) Unternehmen *neut*.

estate [ɪˈsteɪt] *n* (*of deceased*) Nachlaß *m*; (*of noble*) Landsitz *m*. **housing estate** Siedlung *f*. **real estate** Immobilien *pl*. **estate agent** Grundstücksmakler *m*. **estate car** Kombiwagen *m*.

esteem [ɪˈstiːm] *n* Achtung *f*. *v* hochschätzen.

estimate [ˈestɪmeɪt; *n* ˈestɪmət] *v* schätzen (auf). *n* (Ab)Schätzung. **estimation** *n* Ansicht (*opinion*) *f*.

Estonia [eˈstounɪə] *n* Estland *neut*.

Estonian *n* Este *m*, Estin *f*; *adj* estnisch, estländisch.

estuary [ˈestjʊərɪ] *n* (Fluß)Mündung *f*.

eternal [ɪˈtəːnl] *adj* ewig. **eternity** *n* Ewigkeit *f*.

ether [ˈiːθə] *n* Äther *m*. **ethereal** *adj* ätherisch.

ethical [ˈeθɪkl] *adj* ethisch, sittlich. **ethics** *n* Ethik *f*.

ethnic [ˈeθnɪk] *adj* ethnisch, Volks-.

etiquette [ˈetɪket] *n* Etikette *f*.

etymology [etɪmˈɒlədʒɪ] *n* Etymologie *f*.

EU *n* EU (Europäische Union) *f*.

Eucharist [ˈjuːkərɪst] *n* heilige Messe *f*.

eunuch [ˈjuːnək] *n* Eunuch *m*, Verschnittene(r) *m*.

euphemism [ˈjuːfəmˌizəm] *n* Euphemismus *m*. **euphemistic** *adj* beschönigend.

euphoria [juˈfɔːrɪə] *n* Wohlbefinden *neut*, Euphorie *f*.

euro [ˈjʊəroʊ] *n* Euro *m*. **Eurozone** *n* Eurozone *f*.

Europe [ˈjʊərəp] *n* Europe *neut*. **European** *adj* europäisch; *n* Europäer(in). **European Community** Europäische Gemeinschaft (EG) *f*. **European Union** Europäische Union (EU) *f*.

euthanasia [juːθəˈneɪzɪə] *n* Euthanasie *f*, Gnadentod *m*.

evacuate [ɪˈvakjuˌeɪt] *v* (*depart*) aussiedeln; (*empty*) entleeren; (*people*) evakuieren. **evacuation** *n* Evakuierung *f*.

evade [ɪˈveɪd] *v* ausweichen, entgehen (+ *dat*); (*tax*) hinterziehen.

evaluate [ɪˈvaljuˌeɪt] *v* abschätzen. **evaluation** *n* Abschätzung *f*.

evangelical [ˌiːvanˈdʒelɪkə] *adj* evangelisch. **evangelism** *n* Evangelismus *m*. **evangelist** *n* Evangelist *m*.

evaporate [ɪˈvapəˌreɪt] *v* verdampfen. **evaporated milk** Kondensmilch *f*. **evaporation** *n* Verdampfung *f*.

evasion [ɪˈveɪʒən] *n* Ausweichen *neut*. **tax evasion** Steuerhinterziehung *f*. **evasive** *adj* ausweichend. **evasive action** Ausweichmanöver *neut*.

eve [iːv] *n* Vorabend *m*. **Christmas Eve** Heiliger Abend *m*. **New Year's Eve** Sylvesterabend *m*.

even [ˈiːvən] *adj* eben, gerade. *v* sogar. *even bigger* noch größer. **even more** noch mehr. **not even** nicht einmal. **even if** wenn auch. **even-handed** adj unparteiisch.

evening ['iːvnɪŋ] n Abend m. **in the evening** abends, am Abend. **this evening** heute abend. **evening dress** Gesellschaftsanzug m. **evening meal** Abendessen neut.

event [ɪˈvent] n Ereignis neut; (sport) Disziplin f. **in the event of** im Falle (+ gen). **eventful** adj ereignisvoll.

ever ['evə] adv je(mals); (always) immer. *have you ever been to Berlin?* sind Sie schon einmal in Berlin gewesen? **ever so** sehr. **for ever** für immer. **evergreen** adj immergrün. **everlasting** adj ewig.

every ['evrɪ] adj jede; alle pl. **every day** jeden Tag. **every one** jeder einzelne. **every other day** jeden zweiten Tag. **every so often** hin und wieder. **everybody/everyone** pron jeder. **everything** pron alles. **everywhere** adv überall.

evict [ɪˈvɪkt] n exmittieren. **eviction** n Exmission f.

evidence ['evɪdəns] v Zeugnis neut; Beweis m. **give evidence** Zeugnis ablegen. v beweisen.

evil ['iːvl] adj übel, böse. n Übel neut, Böse neut.

evoke [ɪˈvouk] v hervorrufen.

evolve [ɪˈvolv] v (sich) entwickeln. **evolution** n Entwicklung f; (biol) Evolution f.

ewe [juː] n Mutterschaf neut.

exacerbate [ɪgˈzæsəˌbeit] v verschlimmern.

exact [ɪgˈzækt] adj genau, exakt. v verlangen; (payment) eintreiben. **exacting** adj anspruchsvoll. **exactly** adv genau.

exaggerate [ɪgˈzædʒəˌreit] v übertreiben. **exaggerated** adj übertrieben. **exaggeration** n Übertreibung f.

exalt [ɪgˈzolt] v erheben; (praise) preisen. **exaltation** n (joy) Wonne f. **exalted** adj erhaben; (excited) aufgeregt.

exam [ɪgˈzæm] n Examen neut, öffentliche Prüfung f.

examine [ɪgˈzæm in] v untersuchen, prüfen; (law) verhören. **examination** n Prüfung f; (inspection) Untersuchung f. **medical examination** ärztliche Untersuchung f.

example [ɪgˈzaːm pl] n Beispiel neut. **for example** zum Beispiel. **set an example** ein Beispiel geben.

exasperate [ɪgˈzaːspəˌreit] v zum Verzweifeln bringen. **exasperation** n Verzweiflung f.

excavate ['ekskəˌveit] v ausgraben. **excavation** n Ausgrabung f. **excavator** n (mech) Bagger m.

exceed [ɪkˈsiːd] v überschreiten. **exceedingly** adv höchst.

excel [ɪkˈsel] v sich auszeichnen. **excellence** n Vorzüglichkeit f. **Excellency** n Exzellenz f. **excellent** adj ausgezeichnet, vorzüglich.

except [ɪkˈsept] prep außer. **except for** abgesehen von. v ausschließen. **exception** n Ausnahme f. **take exception to** übelnehmen.

excerpt ['eksəːpt] n Auszug m.

excess [ɪkˈses] n Übermaß neut, Überfluß m (an). adj Über-. **excess fare** Zuschlag m. **excessive** adj übermäßig.

exchange [ɪksˈtʃeindʒ] v (aus-, um)tauschen; (money) wechseln. n Austausch m; (phone) Zentrale f. **foreign exchange** Devisen pl. **exchange rate** Wechselkurs m.

exchequer [ɪksˈtʃekə] n Schatzamt neut.

excise ['eksaiz] v (cut out) herausschneiden. **excise duty** indirekter Steuer m.

excite [ɪkˈsait] v erregen, aufregen. **get excited** sich aufregen. **excitement** n Aufregung f.

exclaim [ɪkˈskleim] v ausrufen. **exclamation** n Ausruf m. **exclamation mark** Ausrufungszeichen neut.

exclude [ɪkˈskluːd] v ausschließen. **exclusive** adj ausschließlich; (fashionable) exklusiv. **exclusive of** also **excluding** ausschließlich. **exclusion** n Ausschluß m.

excommunicate [ekskəˈmjuːnikeit] v exkommunizieren. **excommunication** n Exkommunikation f.

excrement ['ekskəm ənt] n Exkrement neut, Kot m.

excrete [ɪkˈskriːt] v ausscheiden. **excretion** n Ausscheidung f.

excruciating [ɪkˈskruːʃieitɪŋ] adj peinigend.

excursion [ɪkˈskəːʃən] n Ausflug m.

excuse [ɪkˈskjuːz] n Ausrede f. v entschuldigen, verzeihen. **excuse me!** Verzeihung!

ex-directory [eksdɪˈrektəri] adj nicht im Telefonbuch zu finden.

execute ['eksikjuːt] v (carry out) ausführen; (person) hinrichten. **execution** n Ausführung f; Hinrichtung f. **executioner** n Henker m. **executor** n

Testamentvollstrecker *m*.

executive [ig'zekjutiv] *adj* vollziehend. *n* (*comm*) Geschäftsführer *m*.

exemplify [ig'zemplifai] *v* als Beispiel dienen für.

exempt [ig'zempt] *v* befreien (von). *adj* **exempt from** frei von.

exercise ['eksəsaiz] *n* Übung *f*; (*of duty*) Ausübung *f*. *v* üben; (*wield*) ausüben. **physical exercise** Leibesübung *f*. **exercise book** Schulheft *neut*.

exert [ig'zə:t] *v* ausüben. **exert oneself** sich anstrengen. **exertion** *n* Anstrengung *f*.

exhale [eksheil] *v* ausatmen.

exhaust [ig'zo:st] *v* erschöpfen. **exhausted** *adj* erschöpft. **exhausting** *adj* anstrengend. **exhaustion** *n* Erschöpfung *f*. *n* **exhaust (gases)** Abgase *pl*. **exhaust pipe** Auspuffrohr *neut*.

exhibit [ig'zibit] *v* zeigen; (*goods*) ausstellen. **exhibition** *n* Ausstellung *f*. **exhibitor** *n* Aussteller *m*.

exhilarate [ig'ziləreit] *v* erheitern. **exhilarated** *adj* angeregt, heiter. **exhilarating** erheiternd. **exhilaration** *n* Erheiterung *f*.

exile ['eksail] *n* Verbannung *f*; (*person*) Verbannte(r). *v* verbannen.

exist [ig'zist] *v* existieren, sein. **existence** Dasein *neut*, Existenz *f*. **existing** bestehend.

exit ['egzit] *n* Ausgang. *v* abtreten.

exodus ['eksədəs] *n* Auswanderung *f*; (*coll*) allgemeiner Ausbruch *m*.

exonerate [ig'zonəreit] *v* freisprechen (von).

exorbitant [ig'zo:bitənt] *adj* übermäßig.

exorcize ['ekso:saiz] *v* austreiben.

exotic [ig'zotik] *adj* exotisch, fremdartig.

expand [ikspand] *v* (sich) ausdehnen; (*develop*) entwickeln, erweitern. **expanse** *n* Weite *f*, weite Fläche *f*. **expansion** *n* Ausdehnung *f*; (*of firm*) Erweiterung *f*; (*pol*) Expansion *f*.

expatriate [eks'peitrieit; *n* eks'peitriət] *v* ausbürgern. *n* im Ausland Lebende(r).

expect [ikspekt] *v* erwarten; (*support*) annehmen. *She is expecting* sie ist in anderen Umständen. **expectation** *n* Erwartung *f*.

expedient [ikspi:diənt] *adj* zweckdienlich. *n* Notbehelf *m*.

expedition [ˌekspidiʃən] *n* Expedition *f*.

expel [ikspel] *v* ausstoßen; (*from school*) ausschließen.

expenditure [ikspendiʃə] *n* Ausgabe *f*.

expense [ikspens] *n* (Geld)Ausgabe *f*. **expenses** *pl* Unkosten *pl*. **at my expense** auf meine Kosten. **at the expense of** zum Schaden von. **expensive** *adj* teuer, kostspielig.

experience [ikspiəriəns] *n* Erfahrung *f*; (*event*) Erlebnis *neut*. *v* erfahren, erleben. **experienced** *adj* erfahren.

experiment [iksperimənt] *m* Experiment *neut*, Probe *f*. *v* experimentieren. **experimental** *adj* Experimental-.

expert ['ekspə:t] *n* Fachmann *m*, Sachkundige(r). *adj* geschickt, gewandt. **expertise** *n* Sachkenntnis *f*.

expire [ikspaiə] *v* (*breathe out*) ausatmen; (*lapse*) verfallen; (*die*) sterben. **expiry** *n also* **expiration** Ablauf *m*.

explain [iksplein] *v* erklären. **explanation** *n* Erklärung *f*. **explanatory** *adj* erklärend. **be self-explanatory** sich von selbst verstehen.

explicit [iksplisit] *adj* deutlich, ausdrücklich.

explode [iksploud] *v* explodieren. **explosion** *n* Explosion *f*.

exploit[1] ['eksploit] *n* Heldentat *f*, Abenteuer *m*.

exploit[2] [iksploit] *v* ausbeuten. **exploitation** *n* Ausbeutung *f*.

explore [iksplo:] *v* erforschen. **explorer** *n* (Er)Forscher *m*. **exploration** *n* Erforschung *f*. **exploratory** *adj* forschend, Forschungs-.

exponent [ikspounənt] *n* (*person*) Verfechter *m*.

export [ikspo:t; *n* 'ekspo:t] *v* exportieren. *n* Export *m*. **exportation** *n* Ausfuhr *f*. **exporter** *n* Exporteur *m*. **export trade** *n* Exporthandel *m*.

expose [ikspouz] *v* aussetzen; (*phot*) belichten; (*impostor*) aufdecken. **exposed** *adj* (*unprotected*) ungeschützt. **be exposed to** ausgesetzt sein (+ *dat*). **exposure** *n* (*phot*) Belichtung *f* (*med*) Unterkühlung *f*.

express [ikspres] *v* ausdrücken. *adj* Eil-, Schnell-. **express letter** Eilbrief *m*. **express train** D-zug *m*. **expression** *n* Ausdruck *m*. **expressionism** *n* Expressionismus *m*. **expressionless** *adj* ausdruckslos. **expressive** *adj* ausdrucksvoll. **expressly** *adv* ausdrücklich.

expulsion [ɪk'spʌʃən] n Ausweisung f.

exquisite ['ekswɪzɪt] adj ausgezeichnet; (pain) heftig.

extend [ɪk'stend] v ausdehnen; (develop) erweitern; (hand) ausstrecken; (cover area) sich erstrecken. **extension** n Erweiterung f; (comm) Verlängerung f; (phone) Nebenanschluß; (building) Anbau m. **extensive** adj ausgedehnt. **extent** n Umfang m. **to a certain extent** bis zu einem gewissen Grade.

exterior [ɪk'stɪərɪə] adj äußer, Außen-. n das Äußere; (appearance) äußeres Ansehen neut.

exterminate [ɪk'stəːmɪneɪt] v ausrotten. **extermination** n Ausrottung f.

external [ɪk'stəːnl] adj äußer, äußerlich, Außen-.

extinct [ɪk'stɪŋkt] adj ausgestorben; (volcano) ausgebrannt. **become extinct** aussterben. **extinction** n Aussterben neut.

extinguish [ɪk'stɪŋgwɪʃ] v (aus)löschen. (fire) **extinguisher** Feuerlöscher m.

extort [ɪk'stɔːt] v erpressen. **extortion** n Erpressung f. **extortionate** adj erpresserisch. **extortionate price** Wucherpreis m.

extra ['ekstrə] adj zusätzlich, Extra-. adv besonders. **extras** pl n (expenses) Sonderausgaben pl; (accessories) Sonderzubehörteile pl.

extract [ɪk'strakt; n 'ekstrakt] v ausziehen; (tooth) ziehen; (numerals) gewinnen. n Auszug m. **extraction** n Ausziehen neut; (tooth, minerals) Extraktion f.

extradite ['ekstrədaɪt] v ausliefern. **extradition** n Auslieferung f.

extramural [ˌekstrə'mjʊərəl] adj außerplanmäßig.

extraordinary [ɪk'strɔːdənəri] adj außerordentlich, seltsam.

extravagant [ɪk'stravəgənt] adj verschwenderisch; (exaggerated) übertrieben.

extreme [ɪk'striːm] adj höchst, letzt; (fig) extrem; n Extrem m, äußerste Grenze f. **extremism** n Extremismus m. **extremist** n Extremist m.

extricate ['ekstrɪkeɪt] v herauswickeln.

extrovert ['ekstrəvəːt] adj (psychol) extravertiert. n Extravertierte(r).

exuberance [ɪg'zjuːbərəns] n Übermut m. **exuberant** adj übermütig.

exude [ɪg'zjuːd] v ausschlagen; ausstrahlen.

exultation [ˌegzʌl'teɪʃən] n Jubel m.

eye [aɪ] n Auge neut; (of needle) Öse f. v anschauen.

eyeball ['aɪbɔːl] n Augapfel m.

eyebrow ['aɪbrau] n Augenbraue f.

eye-catching ['aɪkatʃɪŋ] adj auffallend.

eyelash ['aɪlaʃ] n Wimper f.

eyelid ['aɪlɪd] n Augenlid neut.

eye shadow n Lidschatten m.

eyesight ['aɪsaɪt] m Sehkraft f.

eyewitness ['aɪwɪtnɪs] n Augenzeuge m.

F

fable ['feɪbl] n Fabel f.

fabric ['fabrɪk] n Stoff m, Gewebe neut. **fabricate** v herstellen; (fig) erfinden.

fabulous ['fabjʊləs] adj fabelhaft, sagenhaft.

façade [fə'saːd] n Fassade f.

face [feɪs] n Gesicht neut; (of clock) Zifferblatt neut; (surface) Oberfläche f; (cheek) Stirn f. **pull faces** Fratzen schneiden. v gegenüberstehen; (fig) entgegentreten; (of house, etc.) liegen nach.

facet ['fasɪt] n Facette f; (fig) Aspekt m.

facetious [fə'stiːʃəs] adj scherzhaft.

facial ['feɪʃl] adj Gesichts-.

facile ['fasaɪl] adj (easy) leicht; (superficial) oberflächlich. **facilitate** v erleichtern. **facility** n Leichtigkeit f. **facilities** pl n Einrichtungen pl.

facing ['feɪsɪŋ] prep gegenüber. n Verkleidung f.

facsimile [fak'sɪmɪli] n Faksimile neut.

fact [fakt] n Tatsache f; (reality) Wirklichkeit f. **in fact** in der Tat, tatsächlich.

faction ['fakʃən] n Faktion f.

factor ['faktə] n Faktor m; (comm) Agent m.

factory ['faktəri] n Fabrik f. **factory worker** Fabrikarbeiter(in).

fad [fad] n Mode f.

fade [feɪd] v verschießen, verblassen; (flower) verwelken; (sound) schwinden. **faded** adj verschossen.

fag [fag] n (coll: tiresome job) Plackerei f. **fagged** adj erschöpft.

fail [feɪl] v fehlschlagen, scheitern; (to do something) unterlassen; (in exam) durchfallen; (let down) im Stich lassen. n **without fail** unbedingt.

faint [feɪnt] adj (colour) blaß; (sound) leise; (memory) schwach. v ohnmächtig werden. n Ohnmacht f.

fair¹ [feə] adj (hair) hell, blond; (beautiful) schön; (just) gerecht, fair. **fair chance** aussichtsreiche Chance f. **play fair** fair spielen. **fair and square** offen und ehrlich. **fairly** adv (quite) ziemlich.

fair² [feə] n Messe f; (funfair) Jahrmarkt m. **fairground** Messegelände neut; Rummelplatz m.

fairy ['feərɪ] n Fee f. adj feenhaft, Feen-. **fairy tale** Märchen neut.

faith [feɪθ] n Vertrauen neut; (belief) Glaube m. **faithful** adj treu; (accurate) getreu. **yours faithfully** hochachtungsvoll.

fake [feɪk] v fälschen. n Fälschung f; (person) Schwindler. adj vorgetäuscht.

falcon ['fɔːlkən] n Falke m.

*fall [fɔːl] n Sturz m, Fall m; (fig) Untergang m. v fallen; (prices) abnehmen; (curtain) niedergehen; (fortress) eingenommen werden. **fall asleep** einschlafen. **fall back** sich zurückziehen. **fall down** (person) hinfallen; (building) einstürzen. **fall for** (person) sich verknallen in; (trick) sich hereinlegen lassen. **fall in love with** sich verlieben in. **fall into** geraten in. **fall out with** zanken mit. **fall through** durchfallen.

fallacy ['faləsɪ] n Trugschluß m.

fallen ['fɔːlən] v fall.

fallible ['falɪbl] adj fehlbar.

fall-out ['fɔːlaut] n Niederschlag m.

fallow ['faləu] adj fahl.

false [fɔːls] adj falsch; (person) untreu; (thing) gefälscht. **false alarm** blinder Alarm m. **false start** Fehlstart m. **falsehood** n Lüge f. **falsify** fälschen.

falter ['fɔːltə] v stolpern, (hesitate) zögern; (courage) versagen.

fame [feɪm] n Ruhm m, Berühmtheit f.

familiar [fə'mɪljə] adj bekannt; (informal) ungezwungen. **familiarity** n Vertrautheit f.

family ['famǝlɪ] n Familie f; (bot, zool) Gattung f. adj Familien-.

famine ['famɪn] n Hungersnot f.

famished ['famɪʃt] n **be famished** großen Hunger haben.

famous ['feɪməs] adj berühmt. **famously** adv (coll) glänzend.

fan¹ [fan] n (hand) Fächer m; (mot, elec) Ventilator m. **fan belt** n Keilriemen m.

fan² [fan] n (admirer) Fan m.

fanatic [fə'natɪk] n Fanatiker(in). **fanatical** adj fanatisch.

fancy ['fansɪ] n Neigung f (zu); (fantasy) Phantasie f. **take a fancy to** eingenommen sein für. v gern haben; adj schick. **fancy dress** Maskenkostüm m.

fanfare ['fanfeə] n Fanfare f.

fang [faŋ] n Fangzahn m; (of snake) Giftzahn m.

fantastic [fan'tastɪk] adj phantastisch; (coll) sagenhaft, toll.

fantasy ['fantəsɪ] n Phantasie f.

far [fɑː] adj fern, entfernt. adv fern, weit. **as far as** bis (nach). **by far** bei weitem. **far and near** nahe und fern. **far better** viel besser. **far off** weit weg. **on the far side** auf der anderen Seite.

farce [fɑːs] n Posse f; (fig) Farce f.

fare [feə] n Fahrpreis m; (food) Kost f. v ergehen.

farewell [feə'wel] interj lebe wohl! n Lebewohl neut. adj Abschieds-. **bid farewell to** Abschied nehmen von.

far-fetched [ˌfɑː'fetʃt] adj weit hergeholt.

farm [fɑːm] n Bauernhof m. **dairy farm** Meierei f. **poultry farm** Geflügelfarm f. v Landwirtschaft betreiben; (land) bebauen. **farm out** (work) weitergeben. **farmer** n Landwirt m, Bauer m. **farmhouse** n Bauernhaus neut. **farming** n Landwirtschaft f. **farmworker** Landarbeiter(in).

far-sighted [ˌfɑː'saitɪd] adj weitsichtig.

fart [fɑːt] n (vulg) Furz m. v furzen.

farther ['fɑːðə] adj, adv weiter, ferner.

farthest ['fɑːðɪst] adj fernst, weitest. adv am weitesten.

fascinate ['fasɪneɪt] v faszinieren. **fascinating** adj fesselnd. faszinieren. **fascination** n

Bezauberung f, Faszination f.

fascism [ˈfæʃɪzəm] n Faschismus m. **fascist** adj faschistisch. n Faschist m.

fashion [ˈfæʃən] n Mode f; (manner) Art (und Weise) f. **in fashion** modisch. **out of fashion** unmodisch. v bilden, gestalten. **fashionable** adj modisch. **fashion-conscious** adj modebewußt. **fashion show** Modeschau f.

fast¹ [fɑːst] adj, adv (quick) schnell, rasch; (firm) fest; (colour) echt. my watch is fast meine Uhr geht vor. **fast food** Fastfood neut.

fast² [fɑːst] v fasten. n Fasten neut.

fasten [ˈfɑːsn] v befestigen, festbinden; (door) verriegeln. **fastener** n Verschluß m.

fastidious [fəˈstɪdiəs] adj wählerisch, anspruchsvoll.

fat [fæt] adj (person) dick, fett; (greasy) fett, fettig. n Fett neut.

fatal [ˈfeitl] adj tödlich. **fatalistic** adj fatalistisch. **fatality** n Todesfall m.

fate [feit] n Schicksal neut. **fateful** adj verhängnisvoll.

father [ˈfɑːðə] n Vater m. v zeugen. **Father Christmas** der Weihnachtsmann. **father-in-law** n Schwiegervater m. **fatherland** n Vaterland neut.

fathom [ˈfæðəm] n Faden m. v sondieren; (fig) eindringen in.

fatigue [fəˈtiːg] n Ermüdung f. v ermüden. **fatiguing** adj mühsam, ermüdend.

fatuous [ˈfætjuəs] adj albern.

fault [fɔːlt] n Fehler m; (tech) Störung f; (blame) Schuld f. It's my fault es ist meine Schuld. Whose fault is this? wer ist daran schuld? **at fault** im Unrecht. **find fault (with)** tadeln.

fauna [ˈfɔːnə] n Fauna f.

favour [ˈfeivə] n Gunst f; (kindness) Gefallen m. **in favour of** zugunsten von (or + gen). **be in favour of** einverstanden sein mit. **in his favour** zu seinen Gunsten. **find favour with** Gunst finden bei. Do me a favour and … Tun sie nur den Gefallen und …. **favourable** adj günstig. **favourite** adj Lieblings-; n Liebling m; (sport) Favorit m.

fawn [fɔːn] n Rehkalb neut. adj rehfarbig.

fax [fæks] n (message) Fax neut; (machine) Faxgerät neut. v (document) faxen.

fear [fiə] n Furcht f, Angst f. **fears** pl n

Befürchtungen pl. v sich fürchten (vor), Angst haben (vor). **fearful** adj (person) ängstlich; (thing) furchtbar. **fearless** adj furchtlos. **fearsome** adj schrecklich.

feasible [ˈfiːzəbl] adj möglich. **feasibility** n Möglichkeit f.

feast [fiːst] n Fest neut; (meal) Festessen neut. v sich ergötzen (von).

feat [fiːt] n Kunststück neut.

feather [ˈfeðə] n Feder f. **featherweight** n Federgewicht neut.

feature [ˈfiːtʃə] n (of face) Gesichtszug m; (characteristic) Eigenschaft f, Kennzeichen neut; (newspaper) Feature neut. v darstellen. **feature film** Spielfilm m.

February [ˈfebruəri] n Februar m.

fed [fed] v feed.

federal [ˈfedərəl] adj Bundes-; (Swiss) eidgenössisch. **Federal Republic of Germany** Bundesrepublik Deutschland. **federalism** n Föderalismus m. **federalist** n Föderalist m. **federation** n Bundesstaat m; (organization) Verband m.

fee [fiː] n Gebühr f. **school fees** Schulgeld neut sing.

feeble [ˈfiːbl] adj schwach, kraftlos. **feeble-minded** adj schwachsinnig. **feebleness** n Schwachheit f.

*feed [fiːd] v essen; (of animals) fressen; (cattle) füttern; (person) zu essen geben; (tech) zuführen. n Futter neut; (tech) Zufuhr f. **be fed up with** (coll) satt haben, die Nase voll haben. **feedback** n Rückkopplung; (fig) Rückwirkung. **feeding** n Nahrung f; (animals) Fütterung f.

*feel [fiːl] v (sich) fühlen; (detect, sense) empfinden; (pulse) betasten. I feel cold mir is kalt. I feel better es geht mir besser. It feels hard es fühlt sich hart an. I don't feel like working ich habe keine Lust zur Arbeit. n (atmosphere) Stimmung f. **feeler** n Fühler m. **feeling** n Gefühl neut. **hurt someone's feelings** jemanden verletzen.

feet [fiːt] v foot.

feign [fein] v simulieren.

feint [feint] n Täuschungsmanöver neut.

feline [ˈfiːlain] adj Katzen-.

fell¹ [fel] v fall.

fell² [fel] v (tree) fällen.

fellow [ˈfebu] n Genosse m, Genossin f; (coll) Kerl m. **fellow-countryman** n Landsmann m. **fellow men** Mitmenschen *pl.* **fellowship** *n* Kameradschaft *f*; Gesellschaft *f*.

felony ['feləni] *n* Schwerverbrechen *neut*. **felon** *n* Schwerverbrecher *m*.

felt¹ [felt] *v* feel.

felt² [felt] *n* Filz *m*.

female ['fiːmeil] *adj* weiblich. *n* Weib *neut*; *(of animals)* Weibchen *neut*.

feminine ['feminin] *adj* weiblich. *n (gramm)* Femininum *neut*. **femininity** *n* Weiblichkeit *f*.

feminism ['feminizəm] *n* Frauenrechtlertum *neut*. **feminist** *n* Frauenrechtler(in), Feminist(in).

fence [fens] *n* Zaun *m*. *v (sport)* fechten. **fence in** *or* **off** einzäunen.

fend [fend] *v* **fend off** abwehren. **fend for oneself** sich allein durchschlagen.

fender ['fendə] *n (fireguard)* Kaminvorsetzer *m*; *(US)* Kotflügel *m*.

fennel ['fenl] *n* Fenchel *m*.

ferment [fə'ment; *n* 'fəːment] *v* gären (lassen). *n (fig)* Unruhe *f*. **fermentation** *n* Gärung *f*.

fern [fəːn] *n* Farn *m*.

ferocious [fə'rouʃəs] *adj* wild, grausam; *(dog)* bissig. **ferocity** *n* Wildheit *f*.

ferret ['ferit] *n* Frettchen *neut*. *v* **ferret out** ausforschen. **ferret about** herumsuchen.

ferry ['feri] *n* Fähre *f*. *v* übersetzen.

fertile ['fəːtail] *adj* fruchtbar. **fertility** *n* Fruchtbarkeit *f*. **fertilization** *n* Befruchtung *f*; *(of land)* Düngung *f*. **fertilize** *v* befruchten; *(land)* düngen. **fertilizer** *n* Düngemittel *neut*.

fervent ['fəːvənt] *adj* glühend, eifrig.

fester ['festə] *v* verfaulen; *(wound)* eitern.

festival ['festəvəl] *n* Fest *neut*.

festive ['festiv] *adj* festlich. **festivity** *n* Fröhlichkeit *f*.

fetch [fetʃ] *v* holen; *(collect)* abholen; *(price)* erzielen. **fetching** *adj* reizend.

fête [feit] *n* Gartenfest *neut*.

fetid ['fiːtid] *adj* übelriechend.

fetish ['fetiʃ] *n* Fetisch *m*.

fetter ['fetə] *v* fesseln. **fetters** *pl n* Fessel *f sing*.

feud [fjuːd] *n* Fehde *f*. *v* sich befehden.

feudal ['fjuːdl] *adj* feudal, Lehns-. **feudalism** *n* Feudalismus *m*.

fever ['fiːvə] *n* Fieber *neut*. **feverish** *adj* fiebrig; *(activity)* fieberhaft.

few [fjuː] *adj, pron* wenige. **a few** einige, ein paar.

fiancé [fɔnsei] *n* Verlobte(r) *m*. **fiancée** *n* Verlobte *f*.

fiasco [fiaskou] *n* Fiasko *neut*, Mißerfolg *m*.

fib [fib] *n* Flunkerei *f*. *v* flunkern. **fibber** *n* Flunkerer *m*.

fibre ['faibə] *n* Faser *f*. **fibreglass** *n* Glasfiber *f*.

fickle ['fikl] *adj* unbeständig. **fickleness** *n* Unbeständigkeit *f*.

fiction ['fikʃən] *n* Erdichtung *f*; *(as genre)* Erzählungsliteratur *f*. **work of fiction** Roman *m*. **fictitious** *adj* fiktiv. **fictitious character** erfundene Person *f*.

fiddle ['fidl] *v* tändeln, spielen. *n* Schwindel *m*; *(violin)* Fiedel *f*. **fiddler** *n (violinist)* Fiedler *m*.

fidelity [fideəti] *n* Treue *f*.

fidget ['fidʒit] *v* zappeln. **fidgety** *adj* zappelig.

field [fiːld] *n* Feld *neut*; *(mining)* Flöz *neut*; *(fig: sphere)* Bereich *m*. **field glasses** Feldstecker *m*. **fieldwork** *n* Feldforschung *f*.

fiend [fiːnd] *n* Teufel *m*; *(evil person)* Unhold *m*. **fiendish** *adj* teuflisch.

fierce [fiəs] *adj* wild, grausam. **fierceness** *n* Wildheit *f*.

fiery ['faiəri] *adj* feurig.

fifteen [fiftiːn] *adj* fünfzehn. **fifteenth** *adj* fünfzehnt.

fifth [fifθ] *adj* fünft. *n* Fünftel *neut*.

fifty ['fifti] *adj* fünfzig. **fiftieth** *adj* fünfzigst. **fifty-fifty** *adv* halb und halb.

fig [fig] *n* Feige *f*; *(tree)* Feigenbaum *m*.

*fight [fait] *v* kämpfen; *(fig)* bekämpfen. **have a fight** sich streiten. *n* Kampf *m*; *(quarrel)* Streit *m*; *(brawl)* Schlägerei *f*. **fighter** *n* Kämpfer(in) *m*, *f*; *(aircraft)* Jäger *m*, Jagdflugzeug *neut*.

figment ['figmənt] *n* Erzeugnis der Phantasie *neut*.

figure ['figə] *n (number)* Ziffer *f*; *(of person)* Figur *f*; *(diagram)* Zeichnung *f*, Diagramm *neut*. **figure of speech** Redewendung *f*. *v (appear)* auftreten; *(coll: reckon)* meinen. **figure out** ausrechnen.

filament ['filəmənt] *n (elec)* Glühfaden *m*.

file¹ [fail] *n (documents)* Akte *f*; *(folder)* Mappe *f*; *(row)* Reihe *f*; *(comp)* Datei *f*. *v (let-*

ters) ablegen; (*suit*) vorlegen; (*mil*) difilieren. **filing cabinet** Aktenschrank *m*. **filing clerk** Registrator *m*.

file² [faɪl] *n* (*tool*) Feile *f*. *v* feilen.

filial ['fɪlɪəl] *adj* Kindes-.

fill [fɪl] *v* (an)füllen; (*with objects*) vollstopfen; (*tooth*) plombieren; (*hole*) zustopfen; (*become full*) sich füllen. **fill up** auffüllen; (*mot*) auftanken.

fillet ['fɪlɪt] *n* Filet *neut*.

film [fɪlm] *n* Film *m*. *v* filmen. **make a film** einen Film drehen.

filter ['fɪltə] *n* Filter *m or neut*. *v* filtrieren. **filter-tip** *n* Filtermundstück *neut*.

filth [fɪlθ] *n* Dreck *m*, Schmutz *m*. **filthy** *adj* dreckig, schmutzig; (*indecent*) unflätig; (*weather*) scheußlich.

fin [fɪn] *n* Flosse *f*.

final ['faɪnl] *adj* letzt, End-; (*definitive*) endgültig. *n* (*sport*) Endspiel *neut*. **finals** *pl n* (*exams*) Abschlußprüfung *f sing*. **finale** *n* Finale *neut* **finalist** *n* Endspielteilnehmer(in). **finalize** *v* abschließen. **finally** *adv* schließlich, zum Schluß.

finance [faɪnæns] *n* Finanzwesen *neut*. *v* finanzieren. **finances** *pl n* Finanzen *pl*. **financial** *adj* finanziell, Finanz-.

finch [fɪntʃ] *n* Fink *m*.

***find** [faɪnd] *v* finden. **find guilty** für schuldig erklären. **find oneself** sich befinden. **find out** herausfinden; (*a person*) ertappen. *n* Fund *m*. **findings** *pl n* Beschluß *m sing*.

fine¹ [faɪn] *adj* fein; (*weather*) schön; (*splendid*) gut, herrlich; (*hair*) dünn; (*point*) spitz; (*clothes*) elegant.

fine² [faɪn] *n* Geldstrafe *f*. *v* mit einer Geldstrafe belegen.

finesse [fɪnɛs] *n* Feinheit *f*; (*cards*) Schneiden *neut*.

finger ['fɪŋgə] *n* Finger *m*. *v* betasten. **fingernail** *n* Fingernagel *m*. **fingerprint** *n* Fingerabdruck *m*.

finish ['fɪnɪʃ] *v* aufhören, zu Ende gehen; beenden; (*complete*) vollenden; (*food*) aufessen; (*drink*) auftrinken. *n* Ende *neut*; Schluß *m*. **finished** *adj* fertig.

finite ['faɪnaɪt] *adj* endlich.

Finland ['fɪnlənd] *n* Finnland *neut*. **Finn** *n* Finne *m*, Finnin *f*. **Finnish** *adj* finnisch.

fir [fəː] *n* Tannenbaum *m*.

fire [faɪə] *n* Feuer *neut*; Brand *m*. **catch fire** Feuer fangen. **set fire to** in Brand stecken. *v* (*a gun*) abfeuern; (*with a gun*) schießen; (*mot*) zünden.

fire alarm *n* Feueralarm *m*; (*device*) Feuermelder *m*.

firearms ['faɪərɑːmz] *pl n* Schußwaffen *pl*.

fire brigade *n* Feuerwehr *f*.

fire drill *n* Feueralarmübung *f*.

fire engine *n* Feuerwehrauto *neut*.

fire escape *n* Nottreppe *f*.

fire extinguisher *n* Feuerlöscher *m*.

fire-guard *n* Kaminvorsetzer *m*.

fireman ['faɪəmən] *n* Feuerwehrmann *m*.

fireplace ['faɪəpleɪs] *n* Kamin *m*.

fireproof ['faɪəpruːf] *adj* feuerfest.

fireside ['faɪəsaɪd] *n* Kamin *m*. *adj* häuslich.

fire station *n* Feuerwache *f*.

firewood ['faɪəwud] *n* Brennholz *neut*.

firework ['faɪəwəːk] *n* Feuerwerkskörper *m*. **fireworks** *pl n* Feuerwerk *neut sing*.

firing squad *n* Exekutionskommando *neut*.

firm¹ [fəːm] *adj* fest, hart; (*resolute*) entschlossen. **firm friends** enge Freunde *pl*.

firm² [fəːm] *n* Firma *f*.

first [fəːst] *adj* erst. **first name** Vorname *m*. *adv or* **firstly** erstens, zuerst, zunächst. **at first** zuerst. **come first** (*sport*) gewinnen. **first aid** erste Hilfe. **first-class** *adj* erstklassig.

fiscal ['fɪskəl] *adj* fiskalisch. **fiscal year** Finanzjahr *neut*.

fish [fɪʃ] *n* Fisch *m*; *v* fischen; (*in river*) angeln. **fishbone** *n* Gräte *f*. **fisherman** *n* Fischer. **fishhook** *n* Angelhaken *m*. **fishing** *n* Fischen *neut*, Angeln *neut*. **fishing boat** Fischerboot *neut*. **fishing rod** Angelrute *f*. **fishmonger** *n* Fischhändler *m*. **fishy** *n* (*coll: suspicious*) verdächtig.

fission ['fɪʃən] *n* Spaltung *f*.

fissure ['fɪʃə] *n* Spalt *m*.

fist [fɪst] *n* Faust *m*.

fit¹ [fɪt] *adj* (*suitable*) geeignet, angemessen; (*healthy*) gesund; (*sport*) fit, in guter Form. *n* (*clothes*) Sitz *m*. *v* (*clothes*) sitzen; (*insert*) einsetzen. **fit in** sich einfügen. **fit into** sich hineinpassen in. **fitness** *n* Gesundheit *f*; (*sport*) Fitneß *f*. **fitted kitchen** Einbauküche *f*. **fitted sheet** Spannbetttuch *neut*. **fitter** *n* (*mech*) Monteur *m*. **fitting**

adj passend, angebracht. **fittings** *pl n* Zubehör *neut sing.*

fit² [fɪt] *n* (*med*) Anfall *m*.

five [faɪv] *adj* fünf.

fix [fɪks] *v* befestigen (an); (*arrange*) bestimmen; (*eyes*) richten (auf); (*repair*) reparieren. *n* (*coll*) Klemme *f*; (*drugs*) Fix *m*.

fizz [fɪz] *v* zischen, sprudeln. **fizzy** *adj* sprudelnd, sprudel-.

flabbergast ['flæbəgaːst] *v* verblüffen.

flabby ['flæbɪ] *adj* schlaff.

flag¹ [flæg] *n* Fahne *f*; (*naut*) Flagge *f*. **flag down** stoppen.

flag² [flæg] *v* (*wane*) nachlassen.

flagrant ['fleɪgrənt] *adj* offenkundig.

flagstone ['flægstoun] *n* Steinplatte *f*, Fliese *f*.

flair [fleə] *n* natürliche Begabung *f*, feine Nase *f*.

flake [fleɪk] *n* (*snow, cereals*) Flocke *f*; (*thin piece*) Schuppe *f*. *v* **flake off** sich abschuppen.

flamboyant [flæm͵bɔɪənt] *adj* auffallend.

flame [fleɪm] *n* Flamme *f*. **burst into flames** in Flammen aufgehen. **old flame** alte Flamme *f*.

flamingo [flə'mɪŋgou] *n* Flamingo *m*.

flan [flæn] *n* Torte *f*.

flank [flæŋk] *n* Flanke *f*. *v* flankieren.

flannel ['flænl] *n* (*material*) Flanell *m*; (*facecloth*) Waschlappen *m*.

flap [flæp] *n* Klappe *f*; (*of skin, etc.*) Lappen *m*. *v* flattern.

flare [fleə] *v* flackern; (*dress*) sich bauschen. **flare up** aufflackern. *n* (*naut*) Lichtsignal *neut*; (*of dress*) Ausbauchung *f*.

flash [flæʃ] *n* Blitz *m*; (*phot*) Blitzlicht *neut*. **news flash** Kurznachricht *f*. *v* aufblitzen; (*fig*) sich blitzartig bewegen. **flashback** *n* Rückblende *f*. **flashbulb** *n* Blitzlichtlampe *f*. **flasher** *n* (*mot*) Blinker *m*. **flashlight** *n* Taschenlampe *f*. **flashy** *adj* auffällig.

flask [flaːsk] *n* Flasche *f*; (*laboratory*) Glaskolben *m*. **vacuum flask** Warmflasche *f*.

flat¹ [flæt] *adj* platt, flach; (*level*) eben; (*refusal*) glatt. **fall flat** ein glatter Versager sein.

flat² [flæt] *n* Wohnung *f*.

flatter ['flætə] *v* schmeicheln. **flattering** *adj* schmeichelnd. **flattery** *n* Schmeichelei *f*.

flatulence ['flætjʊləns] *n* Blähsucht *f*.

flaunt [flɔːnt] *v* paradieren mit, prunken mit.

flautist ['flɔːtɪst] *n* Flötist(in).

flavour ['fleɪvə] *n* Geschmack *m*. *v* würzen. **flavouring** *n* Würze *f*.

flaw [flɔː] *n* (*crack*) Sprung *m*; (*defect*) Makel *m*. **flawless** *adj* tadellos.

flax [flæks] *n* Flachs *m*.

flea [fliː] *n* Floh *m*.

fleck [flek] *n* Flecken *neut*. *v* tüpfeln.

fled [fled] *v* **flee**.

*flee [fliː] *v* fliehen.

fleece [fliːs] *n* Vlies *neut*; (*clothing*) Fleece *neut*, Webpelz *m*. *v* (*coll*) schröpfen. **fleecy** *adj* flockig.

fleet [fliːt] *n* Flotte *f*.

fleeting ['fliːtɪŋ] *adj* flüchtig.

Flemish ['flemɪʃ] *adj* flämisch.

flesh [fleʃ] *n* Fleisch *neut*. **flesh-coloured** *adj* fleischfarben. **fleshly** *adj* fleischlich. **fleshy** *adj* fleischig.

flew [fluː] *v* **fly¹**.

flex [fleks] *n* Schnur *f*. *v* biegen; (*muscles*) zusammenziehen. **flexibility** *n* Biegsamkeit *f*. **flexible** *adj* biegsam, flexibel.

flick [flɪk] *v* schnellen, schnippen. *n* Schnippchen *neut*.

flicker ['flɪkə] *v* flackern. *n* Flackern *neut*.

flight¹ [flaɪt] *n* (*flying*) Flug *m*. **flight of stairs** Treppe *f*. **flighty** *adj* launisch.

flight² [flaɪt] *n* (*fleeing*) Flucht *f*.

flimsy ['flɪmzɪ] *adj* dünn, schwach.

flinch [flɪntʃ] *v* zurückschrecken (vor).

*fling [flɪŋ] *v* schleudern, werfen. **fling away** wegwerfen. **fling open** aufreißen.

flint [flɪnt] *n* Feuerstein *m*.

flip [flɪp] *v* klapsen, schnellen. *n* Klaps *m*.

flippant ['flɪpənt] *adj* leichtfertig, keck.

flirt [fləːt] *v* flirten. **flirtatious** *adj* kokett.

flit [flɪt] *v* flitzen.

float [flout] *v* schwimmen, treiben; (*boat*) flott sein. *n* (*angling*) Kokschwimmer *m*. **floating** *adj* schwimmend.

flock [flɔk] *n* (*sheep*) Herde *f*; (*birds*) Flug *m*. *v* sich scharen.

flog [flɔg] *v* peitschen, prügeln. **flogging** *adj* Prügelstrafe *f*.

flood [flʌd] *n* Flut *f*. *v* fluten.

floor [flɔː] n (Fuß)Boden m; (storey) Stock m. v (coll) verblüten.

flop [flɒp] v plumpsen; (fail) versagen. n (failure) Niete f, Versager m. **floppy** adj schlapp. **floppy disk** n (comp) Diskette f.

flora ['flɔːrə] m Flora f. **floral** adj Blumen-.

florist ['flɒrist] n Blümenhändler m.

flounder ['flaundə] v herumplatschen, stolpern.

flour ['flauə] n Mehl neut. **flour mill** n Mühle f. **floury** adj mehlig.

flourish ['flʌriʃ] v (thrive) gedeihen. n Schörkel m.

flout [flaut] v verspotten.

flow [fləu] v fließen, strömen. n Fluß m; (fig) Strom m.

flower ['flauə] n (plant) Blume f; (bloom) Blüte f. v blüten. **flowerbed** n Blumenbeet neut. **flowerpot** n Blumentopf m. **flowerseller** n Blumenverkäufer(in). **flowery** adj blumenreich.

flown [fləun] v **fly¹**.

flu [fluː] n Grippe f.

fluctuate ['flʌktjueit] v schwanken. **fluctuation** n Schwankung f.

flue [fluː] n Abzugsrohr neut.

fluent ['fluːənt] adj fließend.

fluff [flʌf] n Flaum m, Federflocke f. v (coll) verpfuschen. **fluffy** adj flaumig, flockig.

fluid ['fluːid] n Flüssigkeit f. adj flüssig.

fluke [fluːk] n (coll) Dusel m.

flung [flʌŋ] v **fling**.

fluorescent [fluə'resnt] adj fluoreszierend. **fluorescent light** Leuchtstofflampe f.

fluoride ['fluəraid] n Fluorid neut.

flush¹ [flʌʃ] v (blush) erröten; (WC) spülen. **flush out** ausspülen. n Erröten neut. **flushed** adj erregt.

flush² [flʌʃ] adj (level) glatt. **be flush** (coll) bei Kasse sein.

fluster ['flʌstə] v nervös machen, verwirren. **in a fluster** ganz verwirrt.

flute [fluːt] n Flöte f. **flute-player** n Flötenspieler(in).

flutter ['flʌtə] v flattern. n Flattern neut.

flux [flʌks] n Fluß m; (tech) Schmelzmittel neut. **in flux** in Fluß.

***fly¹** [flai] v fliegen; (time) entfliehen; (flee) fliehen; (goods) im Flugzeug befördern. n (in trousers) Hosenschlitz m. **flyer** n (aero) Flieger m. **flying** n Fliegen neut; adj

fliegend. **flying saucer** fliegende Untertasse f. **flying visit** Stippvisite f. **flyover** n Überführung f. **flywheel** n Schwungrad neut.

fly² [flai] n (insect) Fliege f.

foal [fəul] n Fohlen neut.

foam [fəum] n Schaum m. v schäumen. **foam rubber** Schaumgummi m. **foaming** adj schäumend.

fob off [fɒb] v abspeisen. **fob someone off with something** jemanden mit etwas prellen.

focal ['fəukəl] adj fokal. **focal point** Brennpunkt m.

fodder ['fɒdə] n Futter neut.

foe [fəu] n Feind m.

fog [fɒg] n Nebel m. **foggy** adj neblig. **foghorn** n Nebelhorn m. **foglamp** n Nebelscheinwerfer m.

foible ['fɒibl] n Schwäche f.

foil¹ [fɒil] v vereiteln, verhindern.

foil² [fɒil] n (metal) Folie f.

foist [fɒist] v **foist something on someone** jemandem etwas andrehen.

fold¹ [fəuld] v (sich) falten; (paper) kniffen; (arms) kreuzen; (business) eingehen. n Falte f; Kniff m. **folder** n (for papers) Mappe f.

fold² [fəuld] n (for sheep) Pferch m.

foliage ['fəuliidʒ] n Laub neut.

folk [fəuk] n Leute pl. **folks** pl n (relations) Verwandte pl. **folk dance** Volkstanz m. **folklore** n Folklore f. **folk song** Volkslied neut.

follow ['fɒləu] v folgen (+ dat); (instructions) sich halten an; (profession) ausüben. **as follows** folgendermaßen. **follow from** sich ergeben aus. **follow up** verfolgen.

folly ['fɒli] n Narrheit f.

fond [fɒnd] adj zärtlich; (hopes) kühn. **be fond of** gern or lieb haben. **fondness** n Vorliebe f.

fondle ['fɒndl] v streicheln.

font¹ [fɒnt] n Taufbecken m.

font² [fɒnt] n (typeface) Schriftart, Schrift f.

food [fuːd] n Lebensmittel pl, Essen neut. **food and drink** Essen und Trinken neut. **food processor** Küchenmaschine f. **foodstuff** n Nahrungsmittel pl.

fool [fuːl] n Narr m, Närrin f, Tor m. v zum Narren halten; betrügen. **fool around** herumalbern. **foolish** adj albern, dumm. **foolishness** n Torheit f.

foot [fʊt] *n* (*pl* **feet**) Fuß *m*; (*of bed, page*) Fußende *neut*. **on foot**. zu Fuß. **football** *n* (*game*) Fußballspiel *neut*; (*ball*) Fußball *m*. **foothills** *pl n* Vorgebirge *neut sing*. **foothold** *n* Halt *m*. **gain a foothold** Fuß fassen. **footnote** *n* Anmerkung *f*. **footpath** *n* Fußweg *m*. **footprint** *n* (Fuß)Spur *f*. **footstep** *n* Schritt *m*. **footwear** *n* Schuhzeug *neut*.

for [fɔː] *prep* für. *conj* denn. **leave for London** nach London abreisen. **for fun** aus Spaß. **for joy** vor Freude. **stay for three weeks** drei Wochen bleiben. **what for?** wozu?

forage [ˈfɒrɪdʒ] *n* Furage *f*. *v* furagieren.

forbade [fəˈbad] *v* **forbid**.

***forbear** [fɔːˈbeə] *v* sich enthalten (+ *gen*).

***forbid** [fɔːˈbɪd] *v* verbieten. **forbidden** *adj* verboten. **forbidding** *adj* bedrohlich.

forbidden [fɔːˈbɪdn] *v* **forbid**.

force [fɔːs] *n* Kraft *f*; (*violence*) Gewalt *f*. *v* (*compel*) zwingen; (*a door*) aufbrechen. **by force** gewaltsam. **in force** (*current*) in Kraft. **armed forces** Streitkräfte *pl*. **police force** Polizei *f*. **forced** *adj* gekünstelt. **forceful** *adj* eindringlich. **forcible** *adj* gewaltsam. **forcibly** *adv* zwangsweise.

forceps [ˈfɔːseps] *pl n* Zange *f sing*.

ford [fɔːd] *n* Furt *f*. *v* durchwaten.

fore [fɔː] *adj* Vorder-. **come to the fore** hervortreten.

forearm [ˈfɔːrɑːm] *n* Unterarm *m*.

forebear [ˈfɔːbə] *n* Vorfahr *m*.

foreboding [fɔːˈbəʊdɪŋ] *n* Vorahnung *f*.

***forecast** [ˈfɔːkɑːst] *v* voraussagen. *n* Voraussage *f*. **weather forecast** Wettervorhersage *f*.

forecourt [ˈfɔːkɔːt] *n* Vorhof *m*.

forefather [ˈfɔːfɑːðə] *n* Vorfahr *m*.

forefinger [ˈfɔːfɪŋɡə] *n* Zeigefinger *m*.

forefront [ˈfɔːfrʌnt] *n* **in the forefront** im Vordergrund.

foreground [ˈfɔːɡraʊnd] *n* Vordergrund *m*.

forehand [ˈfɔːhand] *n* (*sport*) Vorhandschlag *m*.

forehead [ˈfɒrɪd] *n* Stirn *f*.

foreign [ˈfɒrən] *adj* fremd, ausländisch, Auslands-. **foreign body** Fremdkörper *m*. **foreign language** Fremdsprache *f*. **foreign minister** Außenminister *m*. **foreign policy** Außenpolitik *f*. **foreigner** *n* Fremde(r), Ausländer(in).

foreleg [ˈfɔːleg] *n* Vorderbein *neut*.

foreman [ˈfɔːmən] *n* Vorarbeiter *m*, Aufseher *m*; (*jury*) Sprecher *m*.

foremost [ˈfɔːməʊst] *adj* vorderst. **first and foremost** zu allererst.

forename [ˈfɔːneɪm] *n* Vorname *m*.

forensic [fəˈrensɪk] *adj* forensisch.

forerunner [ˈfɔːrʌnə] *n* Vorgänger *m*.

***foresee** [fɔːˈsiː] *v* voraussagen.

foresight [ˈfɔːsaɪt] *n* Vorsorge *f*.

foreskin [ˈfɔːskɪn] *n* Vorhaut *m*.

forest [ˈfɒrɪst] *n* Forst *m*, Wald *m*. **forest fire** Waldbrand *m*.

forestall [fɔːˈstɔːl] *v* zuvorkommen (+ *dat*).

foretaste [ˈfɔːteɪst] *n* Vorgeschmack *m*.

***foretell** [fɔːˈtel] *v* vorhersagen.

forethought [ˈfɔːθɔːt] *n* Vorbedacht *m*.

forever [fɔːˈevə] *adv* immer, ständig.

forword [ˈfɔːwɜːd] *n* Vorwort *neut*.

forfeit [ˈfɔːfɪt] *v* verwirken. *n* Verwirkung *f*. *adj* verwirkt.

forgave [fəˈɡeɪv] *v* **forgive**.

forge [fɔːdʒ] *v* (*metal*) schmieden; (*plan*) ersinnen; (*document*) fälschen. *n* Schmiede *f*. **forgery** *n* Fälschung *f*. **forgery** *n* Fälschung *f*.

***forget** [fəˈɡet] *v* vergessen. **forgetful** *adj* vergeßlich.

***forgive** [fəˈɡɪv] *v* verzeihen, vergeben. **forgiveness** *n* Verzeihung *f*. **forgiving** *adj* versöhnlich.

forgiven [fəˈɡɪvn] *v* **forgive**.

***forgo** [fɔːˈɡəʊ] *v* verzichten auf.

forgot [fəˈɡɒt] *v* **forget**.

forgotten [fəˈɡɒtn] *v* **forget**.

fork [fɔːk] *n* Gabel *f*; (*in road*) Gabelung *f*. *v* **fork out** (*coll: pay*) blechen.

forlorn [fəˈbːn] *adj* verlassen, hilflos.

form [fɔːm] *n* Gestalt *f*, Form *f*; (*to fill out*) Formular *neut*. **on form** in Form. *v* bilden.

formal [ˈfɔːməl] *adj* formell.

format [ˈfɔːmat] *n* Format *neut*. *v* (*comp*) formatieren.

formation [fɔːˈmeɪʃən] *n* Bildung *f*; (*geol, mil*) Formation *f*.

former [ˈfɔːmə] *adj* vorig; (*one-time*) ehemalig; (*of two*) jene(r). **formerly** *adv* früher.

formidable [ˈfɔːmɪdəbl] *adj* furchtbar.

formula [ˈfɔːmjulə] *n* (*pl* -**ae**) Formel *f*;

(*med*) Rezept *neut*. **formulate** *v* formulieren. **formulation** *n* Formulierung *f*.

***forsake** [ʃəˈseɪk] *v* (*person*) verlassen.

forsaken [ʃəˈseɪkn] *v* **forsake**.

forsook [ʃəˈsuk] *v* **forsake**.

fort [fɔːt] *n* Festung *f*.

forte [ˈfɔːteɪ] *adv* (*music*) laut. *n* Stärke *f*.

forth [fɔːθ] *adv* (*place*) hervor; (*time*) fort. **and so forth** und so weiter *or* fort. **back and forth** hin und her.

fortify [ˈfɔːtɪfaɪ] *v* (*mil*) befestigen; (*hearten*) ermutigen; (*food*) anreichern. **fortification** *n* Befestigung *f*; (*fortress*) Festung *f*.

fortitude [ˈfɔːtɪtjuːd] *n* Mut *m*.

fortnight [ˈfɔːtnaɪt] *n* vierzehn Tage. **fortnightly** *adj* vierzehntägig. *adv* alle vierzehn Tage.

fortress [ˈfɔːtrɪs] *n* Festung *f*.

fortuitous [fɔːˈtjuːɪtəs] *adj* zufällig.

fortune [ˈfɔːtʃən] *n* Glück *neut*; (*fate*) Schicksal *neut*; (*wealth*) Vermögen *neut*. **fortunate** *adj* glücklich. **fortunately** *adv* glücklicherweise.

forty [ˈfɔːtɪ] *adj* vierzig.

forum [ˈfɔːrəm] *n* Forum *neut*.

forward [ˈfɔːwəd] *adj* vorder, Vorder-; (*impudent*) vorlaut. *adv* vorwärts. *v* (*goods*) spedieren; (*letter*) nachschicken. *n* (*sport*) Stürmer *m*.

fossil [ˈfɒsl] *n* Fossil *neut*.

foster [ˈfɒstə] *v* pflegen; (*feelings*) Legen. *adj* Pflege-. **foster home** Pflegestelle *f*. **foster parents** Pflegeeltern *pl*.

fought [fɔːt] *v* **fight**.

foul [faul] *adj* (*dirty*) schmutzig; (*disgusting*) widerlich; (*weather*) schlecht. *v* verschmutzen. *n* (*sport*) Regelverstoß *m*.

found[1] [faund] *v* **find**.

found[2] [faund] *v* gründen. **be founded on** beruhen auf. **foundation** *n* (*of building*) Grundmauer *f*; (*of institute, firm, etc.*) Gründung *f*; (*basis*) Grundlage *f*; (*institute*) Stiftung *f*. **founder** *n* Gründer *m*.

foundry [ˈfaundrɪ] *n* Gießerei *f*.

fountain [ˈfauntɪn] *n* Springbrunnen *m*. **fountain pen** Füllfeder *f*.

four [fɔː] *adj* vier. **four-by-four** *n* (*car*) Geländefahrzeug *neut*. **fourth** *adj* viert; *n* Viertel *neut*.

fourteen [fɔːˈtiːn] *adj* vierzehn.

fowl [faul] *n* Haushuhn *neut*.

fox [fɒks] *n* Fuchs *m*. *v* (*coll*) täuschen.

foyer [ˈfɔɪeɪ] *n* Foyer *neut*.

fraction [ˈfrakʃən] *n* Bruchteil *m*; (*math*) Bruch *m*.

fracture [ˈfraktʃə] *n* (*med*) Knochenbruch *m*. *v* zerbrechen.

fragile [ˈfradʒaɪl] *adj* zerbrechlich.

fragment [ˈfragmənt] *n* Bruchstück *neut*, Brocken *m*.

fragrance [ˈfreɪgrəns] *n* Duft *m*, Aroma *neut*. **fragrant** *adj* duftig, wohlriechend.

frail [freɪl] *adj* schwach, gebrechlich. **frailty** *n* Schwäche *f*.

frame [freɪm] *n* Rahmen *m*. *v* einrahmen. **spectacle frame** Brillengestell *neut*.

France [frɑːns] *n* Frankreich *neut*.

franchise [ˈfrantʃaɪz] *n* (*pol*) Wahlrecht *neut*; (*comm*) Konzession *f*.

frank [fraŋk] *adj* offen, freimütig. **frankly** *adv* frei, offen. **frankness** *n* Freimut *m*.

frantic [ˈfrantɪk] *adj* wild, rasend.

fraternal [frəˈtəːnl] *adj* brüderlich.

fraud [frɔːd] *n* Betrug *m*; (*person*) Schwindler(in). **fraudulent** *adj* betrügerisch.

fraught [frɔːt] *adj* voll. **fraught with danger** gefahrvoll.

fray[1] [freɪ] *v* (sich) ausfransen.

fray[2] [freɪ] *n* Rauferei *f*.

freak [friːk] *n* (*of nature*) Mißbildung *f*; (*event, storm*) Ausnahmeerscheinung *f*. *adj* anormal. **freak out** *v* ausflippen.

freckle [ˈfrekl] *n* Sommersprosse *f*.

free [friː] *adj* frei; kostenlos. *v* befreien. freimachen. **free and easy** ungezwungen. **free-range egg** Freilandei *neut*. **free speech** Redefreiheit *f*. **free will** freier Wille *m*. **freedom** *n* Freiheit. **freely** *adv* reichlich.

freelance [ˈfriːlɑːns] *n* freier Schriftsteller *m*. *adj* freiberuflich tätig.

freemason [ˈfriːmeɪsn] *n* Freimaurer *n*.

***freeze** [friːz] *v* (*water*) frieren; (*food*) tiefkühlen. **freeze to death** erfrieren. *I'm freezing* ich friere. *n* (*comm*) Stopp *m*. **freezer** *n* Tiefkühltruhe *f*. **freezing point** Gefrierpunkt *m*.

freight [freɪt] *n* Fracht *f*; (*freight costs*) Frachtgebühr *f*.

French [frentʃ] *adj* französisch. **Frenchman** *n* Franzose *m*. **Frenchwoman**

n Französin f. **French horn** Waldhorn *neut.* **French window** Verandatür f.

frenzy ['frenzɪ] *n* Raserei f.

frequency ['friːkwənsɪ] *n* Frequenz f. **frequent** *adj* häufig, frequent; *v* häufig besuchen. **frequently** *adv* öfters, häufig.

fresco ['freskou] *n* Fresko *neut.*

fresh [freʃ] *adj* frisch; (*water*) süß; (*air*) erfrischend; (*cheeky*) frech. **fresh water** Süßwasser *neut.* **freshen** *v* auffrischen. **freshness** *n* Frische f.

fret [fret] *v* sich Sorgen machen.

friar ['fraɪə] *n* Mönch *m.*

friction ['frɪkʃən] *n* Reibung f.

Friday ['fraɪdeɪ] *n* Freitag *m.* **Good Friday** Karfreitag *m.*

fridge [frɪdʒ] *n* Kühlschrank *m.*

fried [fraɪd] *adj* gebraten. **fried egg** Spiegelei *neut.* **fried potatoes** Bratkartoffeln.

friend [frend] *n* Freund(in). **make friends with** sich befreunden mit. **friendly** *adj* freundlich, freundschaftlich. **friendship** *n* Freundschaft f.

frieze [friːz] *n* Fries *m.*

frigate ['frɪgɪt] *n* Fregatte f.

fright [fraɪt] *n* Schreck *m* **frighten** *v* erschrecken. **frightening** *adj* erschreckend. **frightened** *adj* erschrocken. **be frightened of** Angst haben vor. **frightful** *adj* schrecklich.

frigid ['frɪdʒɪd] *adj* frigid. **frigidity** *n* Frigidität f.

frill [frɪl] *n* Rüsche, Krause f. **frilly** *adj* gekräuselt.

fringe [frɪndʒ] *n* Franse f; (*edge*) Randzone f; (*hair*) Pony *neut.* **fringe benefits** Nebenbezüge *pl.*

frisk [frɪsk] *v* herumhüpfen; (*search*) absuchen. **frisky** *adj* munter, lebhaft.

fritter ['frɪtə] *v* **fritter away** verzetteln.

frivolity [frɪvolɪtɪ] *n* Leichtfertigkeit f. **frivolous** *adj* (*person*) leichtfertig; (*worthless*) nichtig.

frizz [frɪz] *v* (sich) kräuseln. **frizzy** *adj* kraus.

fro [frou] *adv* **to and fro** auf und ab, hin und her.

frock [frok] *n* Kleid *neut.*

frog [frog] *n* Frosch *m.*

frolic ['frolɪk] *n* Spaß *m*, Posse f. **frolicsome** *adj* lustig, ausgelassen.

from [from] *prep* von; (*place*) aus, von; (*to judge from*) nach. *Where are you from?* Wo kommen Sie her?

front [frʌnt] *n* Vorderseite f, vorderer Teil *m*; (*mil, pol*) Front f; (*fa, cade*) Fassade f. *adj* Vor-, Vorder-. **front door** Haustür f. **front room** Vorderzimmer *neut.* **in front of** vor.

frontier ['frʌntɪə] *n* Grenze f.

frost [frost] *n* Frost *m.* *v* (*cookery*) glasieren. **frostbite** *n* Erfrieren *neut;* (*wound*) Frostbeule f. **frostbitten** *adj* erfroren. **frosty** *adj* frostig.

froth [froθ] *n* Schaum *m.* **frothy** *adj* schäumig.

frown [fraun] *n* Stirnrunzeln *neut.* *v* die Stirn runzeln. **frown on** mißbilligen.

froze [frouz] *v* **freeze.**

frozen ['frouzn] *v* **freeze.** *adj* gefroren; (*comm*) eingefroren; (*food*) tiefgekühlt. **frozen over** zugefroren.

frugal ['fruːgəl] *adj* sparsam.

fruit [fruːt] *n* Obst *neut*, Früchte *pl*; (*result, yield*) Frucht f. **fruitful** *adj* fruchtbar. **fruition** *n* Erfüllung f. **fruitless** *adj* fruchtlos. **fruit machine** Spielautomat *neut.* **fruit salad** Obstsalat *m.* **fruit tree** Obstbaum *m.* **fruity** *adj* würzig.

frustrate [frʌ'streɪt] *v* vereiteln, frustrieren. **frustrated** *adj* vereitelt, frustriert. **frustration** *n* Vereitelung f, Frustration f.

fry [fraɪ] *v* (in der Pfanne) braten. **frying-pan** *n* Bratpfanne f.

fuchsia ['fjuːʃə] *n* Fuchsia f.

fudge [fʌdʒ] *n* Karamelle f.

fuel ['fjuəl] *n* Brennstoff; (*for engines*) Treibstoff *m*; (*mot*) Benzin *neut.* *v* tanken. **fuel gauge** Treibstoffmesser *m.* **fuel oil** Brennöl *neut.*

fugitive ['fjuːdʒɪtɪv] *adj* flüchtig. *n* Flüchtling *m.*

fulcrum ['fʌlkrəm] *n* Drehpunkt *m.*

fulfil [fulfɪl] *v* erfüllen. **fulfilment** *n* Erfüllung f; (*satisfaction*) Befriedigung f.

full [ful] *adj* voll; (*after meal*) satt. *adv* direkt, gerade. **pay in full** voll bezahlen. **write out in full** ausschreiben. **full-grown** *adj* ausgewachsen. **full moon** Vollmond *m.* **fullness** *n* Fülle f. **full stop** Punkt *m.* **full-time** *adj* ganztägig. **fully** *adv* voll, völlig.

fumble ['fʌmbl] *v* umhertasten. **fumble with** herumfummeln an.

fume [fjuːm] v dampfen; (coll) wütend sein. n Dunst m, Dampf m. **fumigate** v ausräuchern.

fun [fʌn] n Spaß m. **it's fun** es macht Spaß. **for fun** aus Spaß. **in fun** zum Scherz. **have fun** sich amüsieren. **have fun!** viel Spaß/vergnügen! **make fun of** sich lustig machen über.

function ['fʌŋkʃən] n Funktion f; (task) Aufgabe f; (gathering) Veranstaltung f. v (tech) funktionieren; tätig sein. **functional** adj funktionell, zweckmäßig. **functionary** n Beamte(r).

fund [fʌnd] n Fonds m; (fig) Vorrat m. v fundieren.

fundamental [fʌndə'm ent] adj grundlegend, grundsätzlich.

funeral ['fjuːnərəl] n Begräbnis neut.

fungus ['fʌŋɡəs] n (pl -i) Pilz m.

funnel ['fʌnl] n Trichter m; (ship) Schornstein m.

funny ['fʌni] adj (amusing) komisch, lustig, spaßhaft; (strange) komisch, seltsam. **funny-bone** n Musikantenknochen m.

fur [fəː] n Pelz m; (on tongue) Belag m; (in boiler) Kesselstein m. **fur coat** Pelzmantel m. **furry** adj pelzartig, Pelz-; belegt.

furious ['fjuəriəs] adj wütend.

furnace ['fəːnis] n (Brenn)Ofen m.

furnish ['fəːniʃ] v (a room) möblieren; (supply) versehen, ausstatten. **furnishings** pl n Möbel pl.

furniture ['fəːnitʃə] n Möbel pl.

furrow ['fʌrou] n Furche f.

further ['fəːðə] adj, adv weiter. **until further notice** bis auf weiteres. v fördern. **furthermore** adv ferner, überdies. **furthest** adj weitest; adv am weitestem.

furtive ['fəːtiv] adj (person) hinterlistig; (action) verstohlen.

fury ['fjuəri] n Wut f.

fuse [fjuːz] n (elec) Sicherung f; (explosives) Zünder m. v (join, melt) (ver)schmelzen; (elec) sichern; (elec: blow a fuse) durchbrennen. **fuse box** Sicherungskasten m.

fuselage ['fjuːzəˌlɑːʒ] n Rumpf m.

fusion ['fjuːʒən] n Verschmelzung f.

fuss [fʌs] n Getue, Theater neut. **make a fuss** viel Wesens machen (um). **fussy** adj kleinlich.

futile ['fjuːtail] adj zwecklos, wertlos. **futility** n Zwecklosigkeit f.

future ['fjuːtʃə] n Zukunft f. adj künftig. **in future** in Zukunft. **futures** pl n (comm) Termingeschäfte pl. **futuristic** adj futuristisch.

fuzz [fʌz] n Fussel f. **fuzzy** adj (hair) kraus; (vision) verschwommen.

G

gabble ['gabl] v schwätzen.

gable ['geibl] n Giebel m. **gabled** adj gegiebelt.

gadget ['gadʒit] n Apparat m, Gerät neut.

Gaelic ['geilik] adj gälisch.

gag[1] [gag] v knebeln. n Knebel m.

gag[2] [gag] (coll: joke) n Witz m. v einen Witz reißen.

gaiety ['geiəti] n Heiterkeit f.

gain [gein] n Gewinn m. v gewinnen; (of clock) vorgehen. **gain on** einholen. **gains** pl n (comm) Profit m.

gait [geit] n Gang m.

gala ['gaːlə] n Festlichkeit f.

galaxy ['galəksi] n Sternsystem neut; (ours) Milchstraße f.

gale [geil] n heftiger Wind m, Sturmwind m.

gallant ['galənt] adj tapfer; (courteous) ritterlich. **gallantry** n Tapferkeit f; Ritterlichkeit f.

gall bladder [goːl] n Gallenblase f.

galleon ['galiən] n Gallone f.

gallery ['galəri] n Galerie f.

galley ['gali] n Galeere f; (kitchen) Schiffsküche f.

gallon ['galən] n Gallone f.

gallop ['galəp] n Galopp m. v galoppieren.

gallows ['galouz] n Galgen m.

gallstone ['goːlstoun] n Gallenstein m.

galore [gə'loː] adv in Hülle und Fülle.

galvanize ['galvənaiz] v galvanisieren, verzinken; (fig: stimulate) anspornen (zu).

gamble ['gambl] v um Geld spielen. **gamble on** wetten auf. **gamble with** aufs Spiel setzen. **gambler** n Spieler m. **gambling** n Spielen (um Geld) neut, Wagnis neut.

game [geim] n Spiel neut; (hunting) Wild

neut. **give the game away** den Plan verraten. *adj (leg)* lahm. **be game for** bereit sein zu. **gamekeeper** *n* Wildhüter *m.*

gammon ['gamən] *n* (geräucherter) Schinken *m.*

gang [gaŋ] *n (criminals)* Bande *f;* *(workers)* Kolonne *f.* **v gang up** sich zusammenrotten. **gangster** *n* Gangster *m.*

gangrene ['gaŋgriːn] *n* Brand *m.*

gangway ['gaŋweɪ] *n (theatre)* Gang *m;* *(naut)* Laufplanke *f.*

gaol [dʒeɪl] *v* jail.

gap [gap] *n* Lücke *f.*

gape [geɪp] *v* klaffen; *(person)* gähnen.

garage ['garɑːdʒ] *n* Garage *f;* *(mot: workshop)* Autowerkstatt *f.* **v** in eine Garage einstellen *or* unterbringen.

garbage ['gɑːbidʒ] *n* Müll *m.* **garbage can** Müllkasten *m.*

garble ['gɑːbl] *v* verstümmeln.

garden ['gɑːdn] *n* Garten *m.* **v** im Garten arbeiten. **gardening** *n* Gartenbau *m.* **garden party** Gartenfest *neut.*

gargle ['gɑːgl] *v* gurgeln. *n* Mundwasser *neut.*

gargoyle ['gɑːgoɪl] *n (arch)* Wasserspeier *m.*

garish ['geərɪʃ] *adj (colour)* grell, knallbunt.

garland ['gɑːlənd] *n* Girlande *f,* Blumengewinde *neut.* **v** bekränzen.

garlic ['gɑːlik] *n* Knoblauch *m.*

garment ['gɑːmənt] *n* Kleidungsstück *neut.*

garnish ['gɑːnɪʃ] *v (cookery)* garnieren. *n* Garnierung *f.*

garrison ['garɪsn] *n* Garnison *f.* **v** *(town)* besetzen; *(troops)* in Garnison legen.

garter ['gɑːtə] *n* Strumpfband *neut.*

gas [gas] *n* Gas *neut, (US: petrol)* Benzin *neut.* **step on the gas** Gas geben. **v** *(poison)* vergasen; *(slang: chatter)* schwätzen. **gasbag** *n (coll)* Windbeutel *m.* **gas cooker** Gasherd *m.* **gas fire** Gasheizung *f.*

gash [gaʃ] *v* aufschneiden. *n* klaffende Wunde *f.*

gasket ['gaskit] *n* Dichtung *f.*

gas main *n* Gasleitung *f.*

gas meter *n* Gasmesser *m.*

gasoline ['gasəliːn] *n (US)* Benzin *neut.*

gasp [gɑːsp] *v* keuchen. *n* **Keuchen** *neut.*

gas station *n* Tankstelle *f.*

gastric ['gastrik] *adj* gastrisch, Magen-.

gate [geɪt] *n* Tor *neut.*

gâteau ['gatoʊ] *n* Torte *f.*

gateway ['geɪtweɪ] *n* Torweg *m.*

gather ['gaðə] *v* sammeln; *(people)* (sich) versammeln; *(flowers, etc.)* lesen; *(dress)* raffen; *(deduce)* schließen (aus). **gathering** *n* Versammlung *f.*

gaudy ['gɔːdi] *adj (colours)* grell, bunt.

gauge [geɪdʒ] *v* abmessen; *(judge)* schätzen. *n* Normalmaß *neut;* *(rail)* Spurweite *f.* **pressure gauge** Druckmesser *m.*

gaunt [gɔːnt] *adj* mager.

gauze [gɔːz] *n* Gaze *f.*

gave [geɪv] *V* **give.**

gay [geɪ] *adj (colours)* bunt; *(person)* heiter, lustig; *(slang: homosexual)* schwul, warm. *n* Homosexuelle *m,* Schwule *m.*

gaze [geɪz] *v* starren (auf). *n* (starrer) Blick *neut.*

gazelle [gə'zel] *n* Gazelle *f.*

gazetteer [gazə'tə] *n* Namensverzeichnis *neut.*

gear [gɪə] *n (mot)* Gang *m;* *(gear wheel)* Zahnrad *neut;* *(equipment)* Gerät *neut,* Ausrüstung *f.* **in gear** eingeschaltet. **change gear** *(up or down)* Gang herauf *or* herab setzen. **gearbox** *n* Getriebe(gehäuse) *neut.*

geek [giːk] *n (coll) (comp)* Stubengelehrte *m, f,* Computerversessene *m, f;* *(general)* Streber *m.*

geese [giːs] *V* goose.

gel [dʒel] *n* Gel *neut.*

gelatine ['dʒelətiːn] *n* Gelatine *f;* *(explosive)* Sprenggelatine *f.*

gelignite ['dʒelignaɪt] *n* Gelatinedynamit *neut.*

gem [dʒem] *n* Edelstein *m,* Gemme *f.*

Gemini ['dʒemɪnaɪ] *n* Zwillinge *pl.*

gender ['dʒendə] *n* Geschlecht *neut;* *(gramm)* Genus *neut.*

gene [dʒiːn] *n* Gen *neut,* Erbeinheit *f.*

genealogy [dʒiːnɪ'alədʒɪ] *n* Genealogie *f.* **genealogist** *n* Genealoge *m.*

general ['dʒenərəl] *adj* allgemein. *n* General *m.* **in general** im Allgemeinen. **General Assembly** Generalversammlung *f.* **general election** allgemeine Wahlen *pl.* **general practitioner** Arzt/Ärztin für Allgemeinmedizin *m, f.*

generate ['dʒenəreɪt] *v* erzeugen, verursachen. **generator** *n* Generator *m,*

Stromerzeuger *m.* **generation** *n*
Generation *f*, Zeitalter *m*; (*production*)
Erzeugung *f*.

generic [dʒɪnerɪk] *adj* allgemein, generell.

generous [dʒenərəs] *adj* großzügig, freigebig. **generosity** *n* Großzügigkeit *f*.

genetic [dʒɪnetɪk] *adj* genetisch, Entstehungs-. **genetics** *n* Genetik *f*. **genetically modified** *adj* gentechnisch verändert; **genetically modified (GM) food** *n* Genfood *neut*.

Geneva [dʒɪnɪvə] *n* Genf *neut*. **Lake Geneva** der Genfer See *m*.

genial [dʒɪnɪəl] *adj* freundlich, herzlich. **geniality** *n* Freundlichkeit *f*.

genital [dʒenɪtl] *adj* Geschlechts-. **genitals** *pl n* Geschlechtsteile *pl*.

genitive [dʒenɪtɪv] *n* Genitiv *m*.

genius [dʒɪnɪəs] *n* Genie *neut*; (*talent*) Begabung *f*.

genocide [dʒenəsaɪd] *n* Völkermord *m*.

genteel [dʒenˈtiːl] *adj* wohlerzogen, vornehm.

gentle [dʒentl] *adj* sanft, mild. **gentleman** *n* Herr *m*. **gentleness** *n* Mildheit *f*.

gentry [dʒentrɪ] *n* Landadel *m*.

gents [dʒents] *n* (*sign*) Herren *pl*.

genuine [dʒenjuɪn] *adj* echt, wahr. **genuineness** *n* Wahrheit *f*, Echtheit *f*.

genus [dʒiːnəs] *n* Gattung *f*, Sorte *f*.

geography [dʒɒɡrəfɪ] *n* Erdkunde *f*, Geographie *f*. **geographical** *adj* geographisch. **geographer** *n* Geograph(in).

geology [dʒɪɒlədʒɪ] *n* Geologie *f*. **geologist** *n* Geologe *m*.

geometry [dʒɪɒmətrɪ] *n* Geometrie *f*. **geometric** *adj* geometrisch.

germanium [dʒəˈreɪnɪəm] *n* Geranie *f*.

geriatric [dʒerɪætrɪk] *adj* geriatrisch. **geriatrics** *n* Geriatrie *f*.

germ [dʒəːm] *n* Keim *m*, Bakterie *f*.

German measles *n* Röteln *pl*.

Germany [dʒəːmənɪ] *n* Deutschland *neut*. **German** *adj* deutsch; *n* Deutsche(r); (language) Deutsch *neut*. **Federal Republic of Germany** *n* Bundesrepublik Deutschland (BRD) *f*; **German Democratic Republic** *n* Deutsche Demokratische Republik (DDR) *f*.

germinate [dʒəːmɪneɪt] *v* Keimen. **germination** *n* Keimen *neut*.

gesticulate [dʒeˈstɪkjʊleɪt] *v* wilde Gesten machen.

gesture [dʒestʃə] *n* Geste *f*. *v* eine Geste machen.

*****get** [get] *v* (*obtain*) bekommen, erhalten; (*become*) werden. **get hold of** bekommen. **get in** einsteigen. **get married** sich verheiraten. **get off** aussteigen. **get ready** vorbereiten.

geyser [ɡiːzə] *n* Geiser *m*.

ghastly [ɡaːstlɪ] *adj* schrecklich, furchtbar.

gherkin [ɡəːkɪn] *n* Essiggurke *f*.

ghetto [ɡetou] *n* Getto *neut*.

ghost [ɡoust] *n* Gespenst *neut*, Geist *m*. **ghostly** *adj* gespenstisch.

giant [dʒaɪənt] *n* Riese *m*. *adj* riesenhaft.

gibberish [dʒɪbərɪʃ] *n* Quatsch *m*.

gibe [dʒaɪb] *v* spotten (über). *n* Spott *m*.

giblets [dʒɪblɪts] *pl n* Hühnerklein *neut*.

giddy [ɡɪdɪ] *adj* schwind(e)lig. **giddiness** *n* Schwindel *m*.

gift [ɡɪft] *n* Geschenk *neut*; (*talent*) Begabung *f*. **gifted** *adj* begabt.

gigantic [dʒaɪɡæntɪk] *adj* riesenhaft, gigantisch.

giggle [ɡɪɡl] *v* kichern. *n* Gekicher *neut*.

gill [ɡɪl] *n* (*fish*) Kieme *f*.

gilt [ɡɪlt] *adj* vergoldet. *n* Vergoldung *f*.

gimmick [ɡɪmɪk] *n* Trick *m*.

gin [dʒɪn] *n* Gin *m*, Wacholderschnapps *m*.

ginger [dʒɪndʒə] *n* Ingwer *m*. **gingerbread** *n* Pfefferkuchen *m*. **ginger-haired** *adj* rothaarig.

gingerly [dʒɪndʒəlɪ] *adv* vorsichtig.

gipsy [dʒɪpsɪ] *n* Zigeuner(in). *adj* Zigeuner.

giraffe [dʒɪraːf] *n* Giraffe *f*.

*****gird** [ɡəːd] *v* umgürten, umlegen.

girder [ɡəːdə] *n* Träger *m*, Tragbalken *m*.

girdle [ɡəːdl] *n* Gurt *m*. *v* umgürten.

girl [ɡəːl] *n* Mädchen *neut*. **girlfriend** *n* Freundin *f*. **girlhood** *n* Mädchenjahre *pl*. **girlish** *adj* mädchenhaft.

girt [ɡəːt] *v* gird.

girth [ɡəːθ] *n* Umfang *m*; (*horse*) Gurt *m*.

gist [dʒɪst] *n* Wesentliche. *neut*, Hauptpunkt *m*.

*****give** [ɡɪv] *v* geben; (*gift*) schenken (*hand over*) überreichen. *n* Elastizität *f*. **give away** (*betray*) verraten. **give back** zurückgeben. **give in** nachgeben. **give up** aufgeben.

given [ɡɪvn] *v* give. *adj* (an)gegeben.

glacier [ɡlæsɪə] *n* Gletscher *m*.

glad [glæd] *adj* froh, fröhlich, glücklich. **gladness** *n* Fröhlichkeit, Glücklichkeit *f*.

glamour [glæmə] *n* bezaubernde Schönheit *f*. **glamorous** *adj* bezaubernd.

glance [glɑːns] *v* (flüchtig) blicken, einen Blick werfen. *n* flüchtiger Blick *m*.

gland [glænd] *n* Drüse *f*. **glandular** *adj* drüsig, Drüsen-. **glandular fever** *n* Drüsenfieber *m*.

glare [gleə] *v* grell leuchten; (*stare*) starren. **glare at** anstarren. *n* blendendes Licht *neut*. **glaring** *adj* (*colour*) grell; (*error*) krass.

glass [glɑːs] *n* Glas *neut*. **glasses** *pl* Brille *f sing*. **glassfibre** *n* Glaswolle *f*.

glaze [gleiz] *n* Glasur *f*. *v* verglasen; (*windows*) mit Glasscheiben versehen. **glazier** *n* Glaser *m*.

gleam [gliːm] *n* Schimmer *m*. *v* schimmern.

glean [gliːn] *v* (nach)lesen.

glee [gliː] *n* Fröhlichkeit *f*. **gleeful** *adj* fröhlich.

glib [glib] *adj* zungenfertig.

glide [glaid] *v* gleiten. **glider** *n* Segelflugzeug *neut*.

glimmer ['glimə] *n* Schimmer *m*. *v* schimmern.

glimpse [glimps] *n* flüchtiger Blick. *v* erspähen.

glint [glint] *n* Glitzern *neut*. *v* glitzern.

glisten ['glisn] *n* Glanz *m*. *v* glänzen.

glitter ['glitə] *n* Funkeln *neut*. *v* funkeln.

gloat [glout] *v* sich hämisch freuen über. **gloating** *n* Schadenfreude *f*.

globe [gloub] *n* (Erd)Kugel *f*. **global** *adj* global. **global positioning system (GPS)** globales Positionsbestimmungssystem *neut*. **global warming** Erderwärmung *f*. **globular** *adj* kugelförmig.

gloom [gluːm] *n* Düsternis *f*, Dunkelheit *f*; (*mood*) Trübsinn *m*. **gloomy** *adj* düster.

glory ['gloːri] *n* Ruhm *m*, Ehre *f*. *v* sich freuen. **glorify** *v* verherrlichen. **glorious** *adj* glorreich, herrlich.

gloss [glos] *n* Glanz *m*. *v* polieren. **gloss paint** Ölfarbe *f*. **gloss over** vertuschen.

glossary ['glosəri] *n* Glossar *neut*, (spezielles) Wortverzeichnis *neut*.

glove [glʌv] *n* Handschuh *m*. **fit like a glove** passen wie angegossen.

glow [glou] *n* Glühen *neut*. *v* glühen.

glucose ['gluːkous] *n* Traubenzucker *m*.

glue [gluː] *n* Klebstoff *neut*. *v* kleben.

glum [glʌm] *adj* mürrisch.

glut [glʌt] *n* Überfluß *m*; (*comm*) Überangebot *neut*. *v* sättigen.

glutton ['glʌtən] *n* Vielfraß *m*. **gluttonous** *adj* gefräßig. **gluttony** *n* Gefräßigkeit *f*.

GM *adj* gentechnisch verändert. **GM food** Genfood *neut*.

gnaried [nɑːld] *adj* knorrig.

gnash [næʃ] *v* knirschen.

gnat [næt] *n* Mücke *f*.

gnaw [noː] *v* nagen an (+ *dat*).

gnome [noum] *n* Zwerg *m*, Gnom *m*.

*go [gou] *v* gehen; (*travel*) fahren, reisen; (*machine*) funktionieren, in Betrieb sein; (*time*) vergehen; (*coll: become*) werden. **go ahead** fortfahren. **go away** weggehen; (*travel*) verreisen. **go down** hinuntergehen; (*price*) fallen. **go out** hinausgehen; (*fire*) erlöschen. **go up** hinaufgehen; (*prices*) steigen. **have a go at** einen Versuch machen mit. **it's no go!** es geht nicht!

goad [goud] *n* Stachelstock *m*. *v* antreiben.

goal [goul] *n* Ziel *neut*; (*sport*) Tor *m*. **goalkeeper** *n* Torwart *m*.

goat [gout] *n* Ziege *f*.

gobble ['gobl] *v* **gobble (down)** (*food*) hinunterschlingen. **gobble up** verschlingen.

goblin ['goblin] *n* Kobold *m*.

god [god] *n* Gott *m*. **thank God!** Gott sei dank! **godchild** *n* Patenkind *neut*. **goddaughter** *n* Patentochter *f*. **goddess** *n* Göttin *f*. **godfather** *n* Pate *m*. **godmother** *n* Patin *f*. **godsend** *n* Glücksfall *m*. **godson** *n* Patensohn *m*.

goggles ['goglz] *pl n* Schutzbrille *f sing*.

gold [gould] *n* Gold *neut*. **golden** *adj* golden. **goldfish** *n* Goldfisch *m*. **gold leaf** *n* Blattgold *neut*. **gold mine** Goldgrube *f*. **gold-plated** *adj* vergoldet. **goldsmith** *n* goldschmied.

golf [golf] *n* Golf(spiel) *neut*. **golfclub** *n* Golfschläger *m*. **golf course** Golfplatz *m*. **golfer** *n* Golfspieler *m*.

gondola ['gondələ] *n* Gondel *f*.

gone [gon] *v* go.

gong [gon] *n* Gong *m*.

gonorrhoea [gonə'riə] *n* (*med*) Gonorrhöe *f*.

good [gud] *adj* gut; (*pleasant*) angenehm;

(child) brav. n Gute neut, Wohl neut. **good afternoon** guten Tag. **goodbye** interj auf Wiedersehen. **good evening** guten Abend. **good for nothing** nichts Wert. **good-for-nothing** n Taugenichts m. **good-looking** adj gut aussehend. **good morning** guten Morgen. **good night** gute Nacht. **do (someone) good** (jemanden) wohltun. **it's no good** es nützt nichts. **goodness** n Güte f. **goods** pl n Güter pl.

Good Friday n Karfreitag m.

goose [guːs] n (pl **geese**) Gans f.

gooseberry ['guzbən] n Stachelbeere f. **play gooseberry** Anstandswauwau spielen.

gore [goː] n Blut neut. v aufspießen.

gorge [goːdʒ] n (geog) Schlucht f. v **gorge oneself** (coll) sich vollessen.

gorgeous ['goːdʒəs] adj Wunderschön, prachtvoll.

gorilla [gə'rib] n Gorilla m.

gorse [goːs] n Stechginster m.

gory [goːr] adj blutig.

gospel ['gospəl] n Evangelium neut.

gossip ['gosip] n Geschwätz neut; (person) Klatschbase f. v schwätzen.

got [got] v get.

Gothic ['goθik] adj gotisch.

gotten ['gotn] v get.

gouge [gaudʒ] v aushöhlen. n Hohleisen neut.

goulash ['guːlaʃ] n Gulasch neut.

gourd [guəd] n Kürbis m.

gourmet ['guəm ei] n Feinschmecker m.

gout [gaut] n Gicht f. **gouty** gichtkrank, gichtisch.

govern ['gʌvən] v (country) regieren; (determine) bestimmen; (tech) regeln. **governess** n Gouvernante f. **government** n Regierung f. **governmental** adj Regierungs-. **governor** n Gouverneur m.

gown [gaun] n Kleid neut.

GP n Arzt/Ärztin f. für Allgemeinmedizin m, f.

grab [grab] v ergreifen, (an)packen. n (plötzlicher) Griff m.

grace [greis] n Gnade f, Güte f; (prayer) Tischgebet neut. **14 days' grace** 14 Tage Aufschub. **Your Grace** Eure Hoheit. **graceful** adj anmutig. **gracious** adj angenehm, gnädig.

grade [greid] n Grad m, Stufe f; (comm)

Qualität f; (US) (Schul)Klasse f; (slope) Gefälle neut. v sortieren, einordnen.

gradient ['greidiənt] n Gefälle neut.

gradual ['gradjuəl] adj stufenweise, allmählich.

graduate ['gradjuət; v 'gradjueit] n Graduierte(r); (high school) Absolvent(in). v abstufen; (university) promovieren. **graduation** n. Promovierung f; (high school) Absolvieren neut; (ceremony) Schulentlassungsfeier f.

graffiti [grə'fiːti] pl n Graffiti neut sing.

graft[1] [graːft] n (bot) Pfropfreis neut; (med) Transplantat neut. v pfropfen; transplantieren.

graft[2] [graːft] n Korruption f.

grain [grein] n Getreide neut, Korn neut; (sand, etc.) Körnchen neut; (wood) n Maserung f. **grainy** adj körnig.

gram [gram] n Gramm neut.

grammar ['gramə] n Grammatik f. **grammatical** adj grammatisch. **grammar school** Gymnasium neut.

gramophone ['gramə əfoun] n Plattenspieler m. **gramophone record** (Schall)Platte f.

granary ['granəri] n Kornkammer f.

grand [grand] adj groß, großartig. **grand piano** Flügel m. **grandeur** n Erhabenheit f.

grand-dad n also **grandpa** (coll) Opa m.

grand-daughter n Enkelin f.

grandfather ['gran,faːðə] n Großvater m.

grandma ['granmaː] n also **granny** (coll) Oma f.

grandmother ['gran,mʌðə] n Großmutter f.

grandparents ['gran,peərənts] pl n Großeltern pl.

grandson ['gransʌn] n Enkel m.

grandstand ['granstand] n Haupttribüne f.

grand total n Gesamtbetrag m.

granite ['granit] n Granit m.

grant [graːnt] v gewähren; (admit) zugestehen. n (student) Stipendium neut; (subsidy) Subvention f, Zuschuß m.

granule ['granjuːl] n Körnchen neut. **granular** adj körnig, granuliert.

grape [greip] n (Wein)Traube f. **grapevine** n Rebstock m.

grapefruit ['greipfruːt] n Grapefruit neut, Pampelmuse f.

graph [graf] n graphische Darstellung f,

Schaubild *neut*. **graphics** *n* (*comp*) graphische Datenverarbeitung *f*.

grapple ['græpl] *v* sich auseinandersetzen (mit), ringen (mit).

grasp [graːsp] *v* greifen, packen; (*understand*) begreifen. *n* Griff *m*. **grasping** *adj* habgierig.

grass [graːs] *n* Gras *neut*; (*lawn*) Rasen *m*. *v* (*coll*) pfeifen.

grate[1] [greit] *n* (Feuer)Rost *m*, Gitter *neut*.

grate[2] [greit] *v* (*cookery*) reiben; (*teeth*) knirschen. **grate on one's nerves** auf die Nerven gehen.

grateful ['greitful] *adj* dankbar.

gratify ['grætifai] *v* befriedigen. **gratification** *n* Befriedigung *f*. **gratitude** *n* Dankbarkeit *f*.

gratuity [grə'tjuːəti] *n* Trinkgeld *neut*.

grave[1] [greiv] *n* Grab *neut*. **gravedigger** *n* Totengräber *m*. **gravestone** *n* Grabstein *m*. **graveyard** *n* Friedhof *m*.

grave[2] [greiv] *adj* ernsthaft, schwerwiegend.

gravel ['grævəl] *n* Kies *m*. **gravelpit** *n* Kiesgrube *f*.

gravity ['grævəti] *n* Schwerkraft *f*; (*seriousness*) Ernsthaftigkeit *f*, Ernst *m*.

gravy ['greivi] *n* (Braten)Soße *f*.

graze[1] [greiz] *n* (*med*) Abschürfung *f*. *v* abschürfen; (*touch*) leicht berühren.

graze[2] [greiz] *v* (*animal*) (ab)weiden. **grazing** *n* Weide *f*.

grease [griːs] *n* Fett *neut*, Schmalz *neut*; (*tech, mot*) Schmiere *f*. *v* schmieren.

great [greit] *adj* groß; (*important*) bedeutend; (*coll*) großartig, toll. **greatly** *adv* in hohem Maße. **great-grandparents** *pl n* Urgroßeltern *pl*. **greatness** *n* Größe *f*.

Great Britain *n* Großbritannien *neut*.

Greece [griːs] *n* Griechenland *neut*. **Greek** *adj* griechisch; *n* Grieche *m*, Griechin *f*.

greed [griːd] *n* Gier *f* (nach). **greedy** *adj* gierig.

green [griːn] *adj* grün. *n* Grün *neut*. **greenfly** *n* grüne Blattlaus *f*. **greengage** *n* Reineclaude *f*. **greengrocer's** *n* Obst- und Gemüseladen *m*. **greenhouse** *n* Treibhaus *neut*. **greenhouse effect** Treibhauseffekt *m*. **greens** *pl n* (*cookery*) Grünzeug *neut*.

Greenland ['griːnlənd] *n* Grönland *neut*. **Greenlander** *n* Grönländer *m*.

greet [griːt] *v* grüßen, begrüßen. **greeting** *n* Gruß *m*, Begrüßung *f*.

gregarious [grigeəriəs] *adj* gesellig.

grenade [grə'neid] *n* Granate *f*.

grew [gruː] *v* grow.

grey [grei] *adj* grau; (*gloomy*) trübe. *n* **Grau** *neut*. **greyhound** *n* Windhund *m*.

grid [grid] *n* Gitter *neut*; (*network*) Netz *neut*.

grief [griːf] *n* Trauer *f*. **grievance** *n* Beschwerde *f*. **grieve** *v* trauern.

grill [gril] *v* grillen; (*question*) einem strengen Verhör unterziehen; (*coll: person*) ausquetschen. *n* Bratrost *m*, Grill *m*.

grille [gril] *n* Gitter *neut*.

grim [grim] *adj* (*person*) grimmig, verbissen; (*prospect*) schlimm, hoffnungslos.

grimace [grim eis] *n* Grimasse *f*. *v* Grimassen schneiden.

grime [graim] *n* Schmutz *m*, Ruß *m*.

grin [grin] *n* Lächeln *neut*, Grinsen *neut*. *v* lächeln, grinsen.

***grind** [graind] *v* mahlen; (*knife*) schleifen; (*teeth*) knirschen. *n* (*coll*) Plackerei *f*. **grinder** *n* (*coffee, etc.*) Mühle *f*.

grip [grip] *v* (an)packen, festhalten. *n* Griff *m*.

gripe [graip] *v* zwicken. *n* Kolik *f*; Bauchschmerzen *pl*.

grisly ['grizli] *adj* gräßlich.

gristle ['grisl] *n* Knorpel *m*. **gristly** *adj* knorpelig.

grit [grit] *n* Splitt *m*; (*coll*) Mut *m*, Entschlossenheit *f*. **grit one's teeth** die Zähne zusammenbeißen.

groan [groun] *n* Stöhnen *neut*. *v* stöhnen.

grocer ['grousə] *n* Lebensmittelhändler *m*. **grocer's shop** Lebensmittelgeschäft *neut*. **groceries** *pl n* Lebensmittel *pl*.

groin [groin] *n* (*anat*) Leistengegend *f*.

groom [gruːm] *n* (*of bride*) Bräutigam *m*; (*for horse*) (Pferde)Knecht *m*. *v* pflegen. **well groomed** gepflegt.

groove [gruːv] *n* Rinne *f*, Furche *f*.

grope [group] *v* tasten (nach). **gropingly** *adv* tastend, vorsichtig.

gross [grous] *adj* grob; (*comm*) Brutto-; (*fat*) dick. *n* Gros *neut*. **Gross National Product** (GNP) Bruttosozialprodukt *neut*. **gross weight** Bruttogewicht *n*.

grotesque [grə'tesk] *adj* grotesk.

grotto ['grotou] *n* Grotte *f*.

ground¹ [graʊnd] v **grind**.

ground² [graʊnd] n Boden m, Erde f. v (aero) still legen. **ground floor** Erdgeschoß neut. **grounds** pl (of house) Anlagen pl; (coffee) Bodensatz m; (reason) Grund m.

group [gruːp] n Gruppe f. v gruppieren.

grouse¹ [graʊs] n Birkhuhn neut.

grouse² [graʊs] v (coll: grumble) meckern. n Beschwerde f.

grove [grouv] n Hain m.

grovel ['grɒvl] v kriechen (vor). **grovelling** adj kriecherisch.

*grow [grou] v wachsen; (become) werden; (plants) züchten. **grow better** sich bessern. **grow old** alt werden. **grow out of** (clothes) herauswachsen aus; (habit) entwachsen (+ dat); (arise from) entstehen aus. **grow up** heranwachsen. **grower** n Züchter. **growing** adj wachsend. **growth** n Wachstum neut; (increase) Zunahme f; (med) Gewächs neut.

grown [groun] v **grow**. adj erwachsen. **grown-up** Erwachsene(r).

grub [grʌb] n Mode f; (slang: food) Futter neut. **grubby** adj schmutzig, dreckig.

grudge [grʌdʒ] v mißgönnen. n Mißgunst f.

gruelling ['gruəliŋ] adj mörderisch.

gruesome ['gruːsəm] adj grausam.

gruff [grʌf] adj barsch.

grumble ['grʌmbl] v schimpfen, murren. n Murren neut.

grumpy ['grʌmpi] adj mürrisch.

grunt [grʌnt] n Grunzen neut. v grunzen.

guarantee [garən'tiː] n Garantie f, Gewährleistung f. v garantieren, gewährleisten. **guarantor** n Gewährsmann m.

guard [gaːd] n Wächter m, Wache f. v (be)schützen, bewachen. **guard against** sich hüten vor. **on one's guard** auf der Hut. **guard of honour** Ehrenwache f.

guerrilla [gə'rilə] n Guerillakämpfer m. **guerilla warfare** Guerillakrieg m.

guess [ges] n Schätzung f, Vermutung f. v schätzen, vermuten. **guesswork** n Mutmaßung f.

guest [gest] n Gast m. **guest house** Pension f. **guestroom** Fremdenzimmer neut.

guide [gaid] n Führer m; (book) Handbuch neut. v führen, leiten. **guide book**

Reiseführer m. **guidelines** pl n Leitlinien f pl; (advice) Rat m.

guild [gild] n Gilde f, Vereinigung f.

guillotine ['gilətiːn] n Guillotine f; (for paper) Papierschneidemaschine f. v guillotinieren.

guilt [gilt] n Schuld f; (feeling of) Schuldgefühl neut. **guilty** adj schuldig. **guilty conscience** schlechtes Gewissen neut. **find guilty** für schuldig erklären.

guinea pig ['gini] n Guinee f. **guinea pig** Meerschweinchen neut; (fig: in experiment) Versuchskaninchen neut.

guitar [gi'taː] n Gitarre f. **guitarist** n Gitarrenspieler(in).

gulf [gʌlf] n Golf m.

gull [gʌl] n Möwe f.

gullet ['gʌlit] n Schlund m.

gullible ['gʌləbl] adj naiv, leichtgläubig. **gullibility** n Leichtgläubigkeit f.

gully ['gʌli] n Rinne f.

gulp [gʌlp] v hinunterschlucken. n Schluck m.

gum¹ [gʌm] n (glue) Klebstoff m; (from tree) Gummi neut; (sweet) Gummibonbon neut. **chewing gum** Kaugummi neut. v kleben.

gum² [gʌm] n (in mouth) Zahnfleisch neut.

gun [gʌn] n Gewehr neut; (hand gun) Pistole f; (large) Kanone f. **stick to one's guns** nicht nachgeben. v **gun down** erschießen.

gurgle ['gəːgl] n Gurgeln neut. v gurgeln.

gush [gʌʃ] v hervorquellen, entströmen. n Strom m, Guß m. **gushing** adj überschwenglich.

gust [gʌst] n Bö neut. v blasen.

gusto ['gʌstou] n Schwung m. **with gusto** eifrig.

gut [gʌt] n Darm m. **guts** pl Eingeweide pl; (coll) Mut m.

gutter ['gʌtə] n (roof) Dachrinne; (street) Gosse f. **gutter press** Schmutzpresse f.

guy¹ [gai] n (coll) Kerl m.

guy² [gai] n Halteseil neut. **guy-rope** n Spannschnur f.

gymnasium [dʒim'neizəm] n Turnhalle f. **gymnast** n Turner(in). **gymnastic** adj gymnastisch. **gymnastics** n Gymnastik f.

gynaecology [gainə'kɒlədʒi] n Frauenheilkunde f, Gynäkologie f. **gynaecologist** n Frauenarzt m, Gynäkologe m. **gynaecological** adj gynäkologisch.

gypsum [ˈdʒɪpsəm] n Gips m.

gyrate [ˌdʒaɪˈreɪt] v wirbeln.

gyroscope [ˈdʒaɪrəˌskoup] n Giroskop neut.

H

haberdasher [ˈhabədaʃə] n Kurzwarenhändler m. **haberdasher** n Kurzwaren pl.

habit [ˈhabɪt] n Gewohnheit f. **be in the habit of** gewöhnt sein. **habitual** adj gewohnt, üblich.

habitable [ˈhabɪtəbl] adj bewohnbar. **habitat** n Heimat f. **habitation** n Wohnung f. **unfit for human habitation** für Wohnzwecke ungeeignet.

hack¹ [hak] v (zer)hacken. **hack into** (comp) hacken in. **hacker** n (comp) Hacker m. **hacksaw** n Metallsäge f.

hack² [hak] n (horse) Mietpferd neut. Gaul m; (writer) Lohnschreiber m.

hackneyed [ˈhaknɪd] adj abgedroschen banal.

had [had] V have.

haddock [ˈhadək] n Schellfisch m.

haemorrhage [ˈhem ərɪdʒ] n Blutung f, Blutsturz m. v bluten.

haemorrhoids [ˈhem əroɪdz] pl n Hämorrhoiden pl.

haggard [ˈhagəd] adj hager, verstört.

haggle [ˈhagl] v feilschen.

Hague [heɪg] n Den Haag m.

hail¹ [heɪl] n Hagel m. v hageln. **hailstone** n Hagelkorn neut. **hailstorm** n Hagelschauer m.

hail² [heɪl] v (greet) begrüßen; (call up) zurufen. **hail from** herkommen von.

hair [heə] n (single) Haar neut; (person's) Haar neut, Haare pl. **hairy** adj behaart, haarig.

hairbrush [ˈheəbrʌʃ] n Haarbürste f.

haircut [ˈheəkʌt] n Haare schnitt m. **have a haircut** sich die Haare schneiden lassen.

hair-do n Frisur f.

hairdresser [ˈheəˌdresə] n Friseur m, Friseuse f.

hair-dryer [ˈheəˌdraɪə] n Haartrockner m.

hair-net n Haarnetz neut.

hairpin [ˈheəpɪn] n Haarnadel f.

hair-raising [ˈheəˌreɪzɪŋ] adj aufregend.

hake [heɪk] n Seehecht m.

half [haːf] n Hälfte f. adj halb. adv halb, zur Hälfte; (almost) beinahe. **at half price** zum halben Preis.

half-and-half adv halb-und-halb.

half-back [ˈhaːfbak] n Läufer m.

half-baked [ˌhaːfˈbeɪkt] adj (idea) halbfertig, nicht durchgedacht.

half-breed [ˈhaːfbriːd] n Mischling m.

half-brother [ˈhaːfbrʌðə] n Halbbruder m.

half-hearted [ˌhaːfˈhaːtɪd] adj gleichgültig, lustlos.

half-hour [ˌhaːfˈauə] n halbe Stunde f. **half-hourly** adv jede halbe Stunde.

half-mast [ˌhaːfˈmaːst] n **at half-mast** halbmast.

half-sister [ˈhaːfˌsɪstə] n Halbschwester f.

half-term [ˌhaːfˈtəːm] n Semesterhalbzeit f.

half-time [ˌhaːfˈtaɪm] n Halbzeit f.

halfway [ˌhaːfˈweɪ] adv in der Mitte, halbwegs.

halfwit [ˈhaːfwɪt] n Schwachkopf m. **half-witted** adj dumm, blöd.

halibut [ˈhalɪbət] n Heilbutt m.

hall [hoːl] n Halle f, Saal m; (entrance) Diele f, Flur m. **hall of residence** Studentenheim neut. **hall porter** Hotelportier m.

hallmark [ˈhoːlmaːk] n Feingehaltsstempel m; (characteristic) Kennzeichen neut.

hallowed [ˈhaloud] adj verehrt.

Hallowe'en [habuˈiːn] n Abend vor Allerheiligen m.

hallucinate [həˈluːsɪneɪt] v halluzinieren. **hallucination** n Halluzination f.

halo [ˈheɪbu] n Glorienschein m.

halt [hoːlt] n Halt m, Pause f; (railway) Haltestelle f. v Pause machen; (put a stop to) halten lassen.

halter [ˈhoːltə] n Halfter f.

halve [haːv] v halbieren; (reduce) auf die Hälfte reduzieren.

ham [ham] n Schinken m. **(radio) ham** Radio-amateur m.

hamburger [ˈham bəːgə] n Frikadelle f.

hamlet [ˈham lɪt] n Dörfchen neut.

hammer [ˈham ə] n Hammer m. v hämmern. **hammer and tongs** (coll) mit aller Kraft.

hammock [ˈham ək] n Hängematte f.

hamper¹ ['ham pə] v behindern, hemmen.

hamper² ['ham pə] n Packkorb m, Eßkorb m.

hamster ['ham stə] n Hamster m.

hamstring ['ham strɪŋ] n Knieflechse f. v (coll) lähmen.

hand [hand] n Hand f; (of clock) Zeiger m. v (give) geben. **at** or **to hand** zur Hand. **hand in** einreichen. **hand out** austeilen. **hand over** übergeben. **in hand** im Gange. **on the one hand … on the other hand** … einerseits … anderseits ….

handbag ['handbag] n Handtasche f.

handbook ['handbuk] n Handbuch neut; (travel) Reiseführer m.

handbrake ['handbreɪk] n Handbremse f.

handcream ['handkrɪm] n Handcreme f.

handcuff ['handkʌf] v Handschellen anlegen (+ dat). **handcuffs** pl n Handschellen pl.

handful ['handfuː] n Handvoll f.

handicap ['handikap] n Behinderung f; (sport) Handikap neut. v (horse) extra belasten; (person) hemmen. **handicapped** adj (med, etc.) behindert.

handicraft ['handikraːft] n Handwerk neut.

handiwork ['handiwəːk] n Handarbeit f.

handkerchief ['haŋkətʃif] n Taschentuch neut.

handle ['handl] n Griff m; (door) (Tür)Klinke f. v anfassen, handhaben; (deal with) behandeln, sich befassen mit. **handlebar** n Lenkstange f. **handling** n Behandlung f.

handmade [,handm eid] adj mit der Hand gemacht.

hand-out ['handaut] n Almosen neut; (leaflet) Prospekt m, Werbezettel m.

hand-pick [hand'pik] v (sorgfältig) auswählen.

handrail ['handreil] n Geländer neut.

handshake ['handʃeik] n Händedruck m.

handsome ['hansəm] adj schön, stattlich.

handstand ['hand,stand] n Handstand m.

hand-towel n Handtuch neut.

handwriting ['hand,raitiŋ] n (Hand)Schrift f.

handy ['handi] adj greifbar, zur Hand; (adroit) geschickt, gewandt.

*hang [haŋ] v hängen; (person) erhängen. n (of a dress) Sitz m. **get the hang of** beherrschen, begreifen. **hang on** (phone) am Apparat bleiben. **hang up** (phone) auflegen; (picture, coat) aufhängen.

hanger ['haŋə] n Flugzeughalle f.

hanger ['haŋə] n (for clothes) Kleiderbügel m.

hangover ['haŋouvə] n (coll) Kater m.

hanker ['haŋkə] v sich sehnen (nach). **hankering** n Verlangen neut.

haphazard [,hap'hazəd] adj zufällig.

happen ['hapən] v geschehen, vorkommen. **happen upon** finden. **happen along** erscheinen. **happening** n Ereignis neut.

happy ['hapi] adj glücklich, zufrieden. **happy-go-lucky** adj sorglos. **happiness** n Glück neut, Glückseligkeit f.

harass ['harəs] v quälen, aufreiben. **harassment** n Schikanierung f; (sexual) sexuelle Belästigung f.

harbour ['haːbə] n Hafen m. v (protect) beherbergen.

hard [haːd] adj hart; (difficult) schwer, schwierig; (callous) gefühllos. **hard-boiled** adj hartgekocht; (coll) hartnäckig. **hard drive** (comp) Festplattenlaufwerk neut. **hard-pressed** adj in schwerer Bedrängnis. **hard shoulder** (motorway) Standspur f, Abstellstreifen m. **hard up** (coll) schlecht bei Kasse. **hard-of-hearing** adj schwerhörig.

harden ['haːdn] v härten, hart machen; (become hard) hart werden.

hardly ['haːdli] adj kaum. **hardly ever** fast nie.

hardware ['haːdweə] n Eisenwaren pl; (comp) Hardware f.

hardy ['haːdi] adj kräftig, abgehärtet; (plant) winterfest.

hare [heə] n Hase m.

haricot ['harikou] n weiße Bohne f.

hark [haːk] v horchen. interj hör mal!

harm [haːm] v schaden (+ dat), verletzen. n Schaden m, Leid neut. **harmful** adj schädlich. **harmfulness** n Schädlichkeit f. **harmless** adj harmlos. **harmlessness** n Harmlosigkeit f.

harmonic [haːm onik] adj harmonisch.

harmonica [haːm onikə] n Mundharmonika f.

harmonious [haːm ouniəs] adj harmonisch, wohlklingend.

harmonize ['haːm ənaiz] v harmonisieren.

harmonization n Harmonisierung f.

harmony ['haːmənɪ] n Harmonie f; (agreement) Einklang m, Übereinstimmung f.

harness ['haːnɪs] n (Pferde)Geschirr neut. v spannen; (fig) nutzbar machen.

harp [haːp] n Harfe f. v **harp on** (coll) dauernd reden von.

harpoon [haːˈpuːn] n Harpune f. v harpunieren.

harpsichord ['haːpsɪkoːd] n Cembalo neut.

harrowing ['harouɪŋ] adj qualvoll, schrecklich.

harsh [haːʃ] adj hart; (voice) rauh; (strict) streng. **harshness** n Strenge f, Härte f.

harvest ['haːvɪst] n Ernte f. (time) Erntezeit f. v ernten, einbringen. **harvester** n (mech) Mähdrescher f. **Harvest Festival** Erntedankfest neut.

hash [haʃ] n Haschee neut. **make a hash of** (coll) verpfuschen.

hashish ['haʃiʃ] n Haschisch neut.

hash key n (telephone) Rautentaste f.

hassle ['hasl] n lästiger Kram m. v. belästigen. **hassle-free** adj streßfrei, mühelos. **it's no hassle!** (es macht) keine Umstände!

haste [heɪst] n Eile f. **make haste** sich beeilen. **hasten** v sich beeilen; beschleunigen. **hasty** adj eilig; (rushed) übereilt. **hastiness** Voreiligkeit f.

hat [hat] n Hut m. **eat one's hat** einen Besen fressen. **keep under one's hat** für sich halten.

hatch[1] [hatʃ] v ausbrüten. **hatch a plot** ein Komplott schmieden.

hatch[2] [hatʃ] n (naut) Luke f; (serving) Servierfenster neut.

hatchet ['hatʃɪt] n Beil neut. **bury the hatchet** das Kriegsbeil begraben.

hate [heɪt] v hassen, verabscheuen. n also **hatred** Haß m, Abscheu m. **hateful** adj hassenswert.

haughty ['hoːtɪ] adj hochmutig. **haughtiness** n Hochmut m.

haul [hoːl] v ziehen, schleppen. n (coll: booty) Fang m. **haulage** n Transport m, Spedition f. **haulier** n Transportunternehmer m, Spediteur m.

haunch [hoːntʃ] n Hüfte f; (of animal) Keule f, Lende f.

haunt [hoːnt] v (ghost) spuken in. **haunted** adj gespenstig.

*have [hav] v haben. I have to go ich muß

gehen. I will have it repaired ich werde es reparieren lassen. I have got a car ich habe ein Auto. he's had it es ist aus mit ihm. **be had** (be cheated) reingelegt sein. **have a tooth out** sich einen Zahn ziehen lassen. **have it out with** sich auseinandersetzen mit.

haven ['heɪvn] n Hafen m; (fig) Asyl neut.

havoc ['havək] n Verheerung f. **play havoc with** verheeren.

hawk [hoːk] n Habicht m, Falke m.

hawthorn ['hoːθoːn] n Hagedorn m.

hay [heɪ] n Heu neut. **make hay** Heu machen, heuen. **hay fever** Heuschnupfen m. **haystack** n Heuschober m.

haywire ['heɪwaɪə] adj (coll) kaputt. **go haywire** kaputtgehen.

hazard ['hazəd] n (danger) Gefahr f; (risk) Risiko neut; (chance) Zufall m; (golf) Hindernis neut. v aufs Spiel setzen, wagen. **hazardous** adj gefährlich, riskant. **hazard warning lights** (car) Warnblinkanlage f.

haze [heɪz] n Dunst m, leichter Nebel m; (fig) Verschwommenheit f. **hazy** adj dunstig; verschwommen.

hazel ['heɪzl] n Haselstrauch m. adj (colour) nußbraun. **hazelnut** n Haselnuß f.

he [hiː] pron er.

head [hed] n Kopf m; (leader) Leiter m; (top) Spitze f. v leiten, führen. **head for** zugehen nach. **head off** umlenken. **per head** pro Kopf. **by a head** um eine Kopflänge f.

headache ['hedeɪk] n Kopfweh neut, Kopfschmerzen pl.

headfirst [ˌhedˈfəːst] adj kopfüber.

heading ['hedɪŋ] n Titel m, Überschrift f.

headlamp ['hedlamp] n Scheinwerfer m.

headland ['hedlənd] n Landzunge f, Landspitze f.

headline ['hedlaɪn] n Schlagzeile f.

headlong ['hedloŋ] adv kopfüber; ungestüm, blindlings.

headmaster [ˌhedˈmaːstə] n (Schul)Direktor n. **headmistress** n Direktorin f, Vorsteherin f.

head office n Hauptsitz m, Hauptverwaltung f.

headphones ['hedfounz] pl n Kopfhörer m sing.

headquarters [ˌhedˈkwoːtəz] n (mil) Hauptquartier neut; (comm) Hauptsitz m.

headrest ['hedrest] n Kopfstütze f.

headscarf ['hedska:f] n Kopftuch neut.

headstrong ['hedstrɒŋ] adj eigensinnig.

head waiter n Ober(kellner) m.

headway ['hedweɪ] n Fortschritte pl. **make headway** vorankommen, Fortschritte machen.

heal [hi:l] v heilen. **healer** n Heiler m. **healing** n Heilung f. adj heilend, heilsam.

health [helθ] n Gesundheit f. **your health!** zum Wohl! **health insurance** Krankenversicherung f. **health resort** Kurort m. **healthy** adj gesund.

heap [hi:p] n Haufe(n) m. v häufen. heaps better (coll) viel besser. **heap up** anhäufen.

*hear [hɪə] v hören; (listen) zuhören. **hearing** n Gehör neut; (law) Verhör neut. **hearing aid** Horgerät neut. **hearsay** n Hörensagen neut. **preliminary hearing** Voruntersuchung f.

heard [hɜ:d] V hear.

hearse [hɜ:s] n Leichenwagen m.

heart [ha:t] n Herz neut. **change of heart** Gesinnungswechsel m.

heart attack n Herzanfall m.

heartbeat ['ha:tbi:t] n Herzschlag m.

heart-breaking ['ha:tbreɪkɪŋ] adj herzzerbrechend. **heart-broken** adj untröstlich.

heartburn ['ha:tbɜ:n] n Sodbrennen neut.

heart failure n Herzschlag m.

heartfelt ['ha:tfelt] adj tiefempfunden.

hearth [ha:θ] n Kamin m.

hearty ['ha:tɪ] adj herzlich. **heartily** adv herzlich, von Herzen.

heat [hi:t] n Hitze f, Wärme f; (sport) Vorlauf m. **in the heat of passion** (law) im Affekt. v hitzen. **heated** adj (fig) erregt. **heating** n Heizung f. **heatproof** adj hitzebeständig. **heat-stroke** n Hitzschlag m. **heatwave** n Hitzewelle f.

heath [hi:θ] n Heide f.

heathen ['hi:ðn] n Heide m. adj heidnisch, unzivilisiert.

heather ['heðə] n Heidekraut neut.

heave [hi:v] v hieven; hochheben; (sigh) ausstoßen; (anchor) lichten. n Heben neut.

heaven ['hevn] n Himmel m. **go to heaven** in den Himmel kommen. **move heaven and earth** (fig) Himmel und Erde in Bewegung setzen. **for heaven's sake** um Himmels Willen. **heavenly** adj himmlisch. **heavenly body** Himmelskörper m.

heavy ['hevɪ] adj schwer, schwerwiegend; (mood) träge; (book) langweilig. **heaviness** n Schwere f; (mood) Schwerfälligkeit f. **heavy-duty** adj Hochleistungs-. **heavyweight** n (sport) Schwergewichtler m.

Hebrew ['hi:bru:] n Hebräer m. adj hebräisch.

heckle ['hekl] v durch Fragen belästigen. **heckler** n Zwischenrufer m.

hectare ['hekta:] n Hektar neut.

hectic ['hektɪk] adj hektisch.

hedge [hedʒ] n Hecke f, Heckenzaun m. **hedgerow** n Hecke f.

hedgehog ['hedʒhɒg] n Igel m.

heed [hi:d] v achtgeben auf. n Beachtung. **heedful** adj achtsam. **heedless** adj achtlos.

heel [hi:l] n Ferse f; (of shoe) Absatz m. v (shoes) mit Absätzen versehen. **take to one's heels** die Beine in die Hand nehmen. **down-at-heel** adj (fig) schäbig. **well-heeled** adj wohlhabend.

hefty ['heftɪ] adj kräftig.

heifer ['hefə] n Färse f.

height [haɪt] n Höhe f; (person) Größe f; (fig) Höhepunkt m. **heighten** v verstärken.

heir [eə] n Erbe m. **heiress** n Erbin f. **heirloom** n Erbstück neut.

held [held] V hold[1].

helicopter ['helɪkɒptə] n Hubschrauber m.

hell [hel] n Hölle f. interj zum Teufel! **to hell with** zum Teufel mit. **hellish** adj höllisch.

hello [hə'bu] interj Guten Tag; (on telephone) hallo!

helm [helm] n Steuer neut, Ruder neut. **helmsman** n Steuermann m.

helmet ['helmɪt] n Helm m.

help [help] v helfen (+ dat). n Hilfe f. I can't help it ich kann nichts dafür, ich kann nicht anders. help yourself bedienen Sie Sich! **helper** n Helfer(in). **helpful** adj hilfreich. **helping** n Portion f. **helpless** adj hilflos.

hem [hem] n Saum m. v säumen. **hem in** einengen.

hemisphere ['hemɪsfɪə] n Halbkugel f, Hemisphäre f.

hemp [hemp] n Hanf m.

hen [hen] n Huhn neut.

hence [hens] adv von hier; (therefore) deshalb, daher. a week hence in einer Woche. **henceforth** fortan, von jetzt an.

henna ['henə] *n* Henna *f.*

henpecked ['henpekt] *adj* **henpecked husband** Pantoffelheld *m.*

her [hə:] *pron (acc)* sie; *(dat)* ihr. *poss adj* ihr.

herald ['herəld] *n* Herold *m. v (fig)* einleiten. **heraldic** *adj* heraldisch, Wappen-. **heraldry** *n* Heraldik *f,* Wappenkunde *f.*

herb [hə:b] *n* Kraut *n.* **herbal** *adj* Kräuter-. **herbalist** *n* Kräuterkenner(in).

herd [hə:b] *n* Herde *f. v* hüten, zusammentreiben.

here [hɪə] *adv* hier; *(to here)* hierher. **hereafter** *adv* in Zukunft. **herewith** *adv* hiermit.

hereditary [hɪredətəri] *adj* erblich. **heredity** *n* Vererbung *f,* Erblichkeit *f.*

heresy ['herəsi] *n* Ketzerei *f.* **heretic** *n* Ketzer(in). **heretical** *adj* Ketzerisch.

heritage ['heritidʒ] *n* Erbe *neut,* Erbgut *neut.*

hermit ['hə:m it] *n* Eremit *m.* **hermitage** *n* Klause *f.*

hernia ['hə:niə] *n* Bruch *m.*

hero ['hiərou] *n* Held *m.* **heroine** *n* Heldin *f.* **heroic** *adj* heroisch, heldenmutig. **heroism** *n* Heldentum *neut.*

heron ['herən] *n* Reiher *m.*

herring ['heriŋ] *n* Hering *m.* **herringbone** *n (pattern)* Fischgrätenmuster *neut.* **pickled herring** Rollmops *m.*

hers [hə:z] *poss pron* ihrer *m,* ihre *f,* ihres *neut.* **herself** *pron (reflexive)* sich; selbst. **by herself** allein.

hesitate ['heziteit] *v* zögern. **hesitant** *adj* zögernd. **hesitation** *n* Zögern *neut,* Bedenken *neut.*

heterosexual [hetərə'sekʃuəl] *adj* heterosexuell.

*hew [hju:] *v* hauen.

hewn [hju:n] *V* hew.

hexagon ['heksəgən] *n* Sechseck *neut.*

heyday ['heidei] *n* Höhepunkt *m,* Blütezeit *f.*

hi [hai] *interj (coll)* grüß Dich!

hiatus [haieitəs] *n* Lücke *f.*

hibernate ['haibəneit] *v* Winterschlaf halten. **hibernation** *n* Winterschlaf *m.*

hiccup ['hikʌp] *n* Schluckauf *m,* Schlucken *m. v* den Schluckauf haben.

hid [hid] *V* hide¹.

hidden ['hidn] *V* hide¹.

*hide¹ [haid] *v (conceal)* verstecken, verbergen; *(keep secret)* verheimlichen.

hide² [haid] *n (skin)* Fell *neut,* Haut *f.*

hideous ['hidiəs] *adj* abscheulich, schrecklich.

hiding¹ ['haidiŋ] *n* Versteck *neut.* **be in hiding** sich versteckt halten.

hiding² ['haidiŋ] *n (thrashing)* Prügel *neut.*

hierarchy ['haiəra:ki] *n* Hierarchie *f,* Rangordnung *f.* **hierarchical** *adj* hierarchisch.

high [hai] *adj* hoch; *(wind)* stark.

highbrow ['haibrau] *adj* intellektuell. *n* Intellektuelle(r).

hi-fi ['haifai] *adj* hi-fi. *n* Hi-Fi.

high frequency *n* Hochfrequenz *f.*

high jump *n* Hochsprung *m.*

highland ['hailənd] *n* Bergland *neut.*

highlight ['hailait] *n* Höhepunkt *m.*

highly ['haili] *adv* höchst, in hohem Grad, stark. **highly strung** überempfindlich.

highness ['hainis] *n* Höhe *f.* **Your Highness** Eure Hoheit.

highpitched [,haipitʃt] *adj* hoch.

high point *n* Höhepunkt *m.*

high-rise building *n* Hochhaus *neut.*

high-spirited *adj* lebhaft, temperamentvoll.

high street *n* Hauptstraße *f.*

high-tech [,haitek] *or* **hi-tech** *adj* Hi-tech-.

high tide *n* Hochwasser *neut.*

highway ['haiwei] *n* Landstraße *f.*

hijack ['haidʒak] *v (aeroplane)* entführen. *n* Entführung *f.* **hijacker** *n* Entführer *m,* Hijacker *m.*

hike [haik] *v* wandern. *n* Wanderung *f.* **hiker** *n* Wanderer *m.*

hilarious [hilɛəriəs] *adj* lustig. **hilarity** *n* Lustigkeit *f.*

hill [hil] *n* Hügel *m,* Berg *m.* **hillside** *n* Hang *m.* **hilltop** *n* Bergspitze *f.*

him [him] *pron (acc)* ihn; *(dat)* ihm. **himself** *pron (reflexive)* sich; selbst. **by himself** allein.

hind [haind] *adj* hinter, Hinter-. **hindsight** *n* **with hindsight** im Rückblick.

hinder ['hində] *v* (ver)hindern. **hindrance** *n* Hindernis *neut,* Hinderung *f.*

Hindu [hin'du:] *n* Hindu *m.* *adj* Hindu-.

hinge [hɪndʒ] n Scharnier neut, Gelenk neut. **to hinge on** abhängen (von).

hint [hɪnt] n Wink m. v andeuten.

hip [hɪp] n Hüfte f. **hip-bone** n Hüftbein neut. **hip-joint** n Hüftgelenk neut.

hippopotamus [hɪpə'potəm əs] n Nilpferd neut.

hire [haə] v (ver)mieten; (staff) anstellen. n Miete f. **hire-car** n Mietwagen m. **hire purchase** Ratenkauf m. **hire-purchase agreement** Teilzahlungsvertrag m.

his [hɪz] poss adj sein. poss pron seiner m, seine f, seines neut.

hiss [hɪs] v zischen. n Zischen neut.

history ['hɪstərɪ] n Geschichte f. **history book** Geschichtsbuch neut. **historian** n Historiker(in). **historic** adj historisch. **historical** adj historisch, geschichtlich.

*****hit** [hɪt] v schlagen, stoßen. n Schlag m, Stoß m; (record) Schlager m. **make a hit** (fig) Erfolg haben. **hard hit** schwer getroffen. **hit upon** zufällig finden.

hitch [hɪtʃ] v befestigen; (horse) anspannen. n (problem) Haken m. **hitchhike** v per Anhalter fahren.

hi-tech [haɪtek] V **high-tech.**

hitherto [hɪðə'tuː] adv bisher.

HIV n HIV m. **HIV-positive** adj HIV-positiv.

hive [haɪv] n Bienenkorb m. v **hive off** abzweigen.

hoard [hɔːd] n Schatz m, Hort m. v sammeln, hamstern.

hoarding ['hɔːdɪŋ] n Reklamewand f.

hoarse [hɔːs] adj rauh, heiser.

hoax [hoʊks] n Falschmeldung f. v zum Besten haben.

hobble ['hobl] v hinken, hoppeln; (horse) fesseln.

hobby ['hobɪ] n Hobby neut. **hobby horse** n Steckenpferd neut.

hock¹ [hok] n (joint) Sprunggelenk neut.

hock² [hok] n (wine) Rheinwein m.

hockey ['hokɪ] n Hockey neut.

hoe [hoʊ] n Hacke f. v hacken.

hog [hog] n (Schlacht) Schwein neut; (coll) Vielfraß m. **go the whole hog** aufs Ganze gehen.

hoist [hɔɪst] v hochziehen. n Aufzug m, Kran m.

hoity-toity [hɔɪtɪtɔɪtɪ] adj hochnäsig.

*****hold¹** [hoʊld] v halten; (contain) enthalten. n Halt m, Griff m; (fig) Einfluß m. **hold back** zurückhalten. **hold down** (job) behalten. **hold up** (delay) aufhalten; (rob) überfallen. **hold-up** n (traffic) Stockung f; (robbery) Überfall m.

hold² [hoʊld] n (naut) Frachtraum m, Schiffsraum m.

holder ['hoʊldə] n (owner) Inhaber m.

holding ['hoʊldɪŋ] n (land) Grundbesitz m, Guthaben neut. **holding company** Dachgesellschaft f.

hole [hoʊl] n Loch neut.

holiday ['holədɪ] n Feiertag m, Ruhetag m. **holidays** pl Ferien pl, Urlaub m sing. **go on holiday** verreisen, in die Ferien gehen, auf Urlaub gehen. **holidaymaker** n Feriengast m, Urlauber(in).

holistic [hou'lɪstɪk] adj holistisch, ganzheitlich.

Holland ['holənd] n Holland neut, die Niederlände pl.

hollow ['holoʊ] n Höhle f, Loch neut. adj hohl, leer. v (aus)höhlen. **hollowness** n Hohlheit f, Leerheit f.

holly ['holɪ] n Steckpalme f.

holster ['hoʊlstə] n Pistolenhalfter f.

holy ['hoʊlɪ] adj heilig.

homage ['homɪdʒ] n Huldigung f. **do** or **pay homage** huldigen.

home [hoʊm] n Heim neut, Haus neut, Zuhause neut; (institution) Heim neut. **at home** zu Hause. **at home with** vertraut mit. make yourself at home mach dich bequem. go home nach Hause gehen. **hammer home** (nail) fest einschlagen. adj häuslich; (national) inner, Innen-. **home affairs** innere Angelegenheiten pl. **home market** Binnenmarkt m. **homecoming** n Heimkehr f. **homeland** n Heimat f, Vaterland neut. **homeless** adj obdachlos. **homely** adj heimisch, gemütlich. **be homesick** Heimweh haben. **homesickness** n Heimweh neut. **homeward** adj Heim-; adv heimwärts. **homework** n Hausaufgaben pl.

homeopathic [hom ə'paθɪk] adj homöopathisch.

home page n (Internet) Homepage, Startseite f.

homicide ['hom ɪsaɪd] n Mord m; (person) Mörder m.

homogeneous [hom ə'dʒɪnɪəs] adj gleichartig, homogen.

homosexual [hom ə'sekʃuə] *adj* homosexuell. *n* Homosexuelle(r). **homosexuality** *n* Homosexualität *f*.

honest ['onɪst] *adj* ehrlich, aufrecht. **honesty** *n* Ehrlichkeit *f*, Aufrichtigkeit *f*.

honey ['hʌnɪ] *n* Honig *m*; (*darling*) Liebling *m*, Schatz *m*. **honey-bee** *n* Honigbiene *f*. **honeycomb** *n* Honigwabe *f*. **honeymoon** *n* Hochzeitsreise *f*.

honeysuckle ['hʌnɪsʌkl] *n* Geißblatt *neut*.

honour ['onə] *n* Ehre *f*; (*reputation*) guter Ruf *m*. **honours** *pl* Auszeichnungen *pl*. *v* (ver)ehren; (*cheque*) einlösen. **honourable** *adj* ehrenvoll; (*in titles*) ehrenwert.

hood [hud] *n* Kapuze *f*; (*US: on car*) Motorhaube *f*; (*coll*) Gangster *m*. **hoodwink** *v* täuschen.

hoof [huːf] *n* Huf *m*.

hook [huk] *n* Haken *m*. *v* haken **hook up** (*coll*) anschließen.

hooligan ['huːlɪgən] *n* Rowdy *m*. **hooliganism** *n* Rowdytum *neut*.

hoop [huːp] *n* Reif(en) *m*.

hoot [huːt] *v* hupen. *n* Hupen *neut*.

Hoover® ['huːvə] *n* Staubsauger *m*.

hop¹ [hop] *v* hüpfen. *n* Sprung *m*.

hop² [hop] *n* (*bot*) Hopfen *m*.

hope [houp] *v* hoffen (auf). *n* Hoffnung *f*. **hopeful** *adj* hoffnungsvoll; (*promising*) vielversprechend. **hopefully** *adv* hoffentlich. **hopeless** *adj* hoffnungslos. **hopelessness** *n* Hoffnungslosigkeit *f*.

horde [hoːd] *n* Horde *f*.

horizon [hə'raɪzn] *n* Horizont *m*. **horizontal** *adj* waagerecht, horizontal.

hormone ['hoːm oun] *n* Hormon *neut*.

horn [hoːn] *n* Horn *neut*; (*mot*) Hupe *f*. **horned** *adj* gehörnt. **horn-rimmed spectacles** Hornbrille *f*. **horny** *adj* (*hands*) schwielig.

hornet ['hoːnɪt] *n* Hornisse *f*.

horoscope ['horəskoup] *n* Horoskop *neut*.

horrible ['horɪbl] *adj* schrecklich, fürchterlich.

horrid ['horɪd] *adj* scheußlich, abscheulich.

horrify ['horɪfaɪ] *v* erschrecken, entsetzen. **horrifying** *adj* entsetzlich.

horror ['horə] *n* Entsetzen *neut*, Grausen *neut*. **horror-stricken** *adj* von Grausen gepackt.

hors d'oeuvre [oː'dəːvr] *n* Vorspeise *f*.

horse [hoːs] *n* Pferd *neut*, Roß *neut*. **on horseback** zu Pferd. **horse chestnut** Roßkastanie *f*. **horseman** *n* Reiter *m*. **horsepower (hp)** Pferdestärke (PS) *f*. **horse race** *n* Pferderennen *neut*. **horseradish** *n* Meerrettich *m*.

horticulture ['hoːtɪkʌlʃə] *n* Gartenbau *m*.

hose [houz] *n* (*stockings*) Strümpfe *pl*; (*tech, mot*) Schlauch *m*; (*in garden*) Gartenschlauch *m*.

hosiery ['houzəri] *pl n* Strumpfwaren *pl*.

hospitable [ho'spɪtəb] *adj* gastfreundlich.

hospital ['hospɪtl] *n* Krankenhaus *neut*, Klinik *f*.

hospitality [,hospɪ'talɪtɪ] *n* Gastfreundschaft *f*.

host¹ [houst] *n* Gastgeber *m*, Wirt *m*.

host² [houst] *n* (*large number*) Masse *f*, Menge *f*.

hostage ['hostɪdʒ] *n* Geisel *m*, *f*.

hostel ['hostəl] *n* Herberge *f*. **student hostel** Studentenheim *neut*. **youth hostel** Jugendherberge *f*. **hostelry** *n* Wirtshaus *neut*.

hostess ['houstɪs] *n* Gastgeberin *f*, Wirtin *f*; (*air hostess*) Stewardeß *f*.

hostile ['hostaɪl] *adj* feindlich, feindselig (gegen). **hostility** *n* Feindseligkeit *f*, Feindschaft *f*.

hot [hot] *adj* heiß; (*food, drink*) warm. **hot-dog** *n* (heißes) Würstchen. **hot meal** warme Mahlzeit. **hot-water bottle** Wärmflasche *f*.

hotel [hou'tel] *n* Hotel *neut*, Gasthof *m*. **hotel register** *n* Fremdenbuch *neut*. **hotelier** *n* Hotelier *m*.

hound [haund] *n* Jagdhund *m*. *v* jagen, verfolgen.

hour ['auə] *n* Stunde *f*. **after hours** nach Geschäftsschluß. **for hours** stundenlang. **hourglass** *n* Sanduhr *f*. **hourly** *adj, adv* stündlich. **hourly wage** Stundenlohn *m*.

house [haus; *v* hauz] *n* Haus *neut*; (*theatre*) Publikum *neut*. **House of Commons** Unterhaus *neut*. **House of Lords** Oberhaus *neut*. **House of Representatives** Abgeordnetenhaus *neut*. *v* unterbringen.

houseboat ['hausbout] *n* Hausboot *neut*.

household ['haushould] *n* Haushalt *m*.

housekeeper ['hauskɪpə] *n* Haushälterin *f*. **housekeeping** *n* Haushaltung *f*. **housekeeping money** Haushaltsgeld *neut*.

housemaid ['hausm eɪl] n Dienstmächen neut. **housemaid's knee** (med) Kniescheibenentzündung f.

house-warming ['hauswɔːm ɪŋ] n Einzugsfest neut.

housewife ['hauswaɪf] n Hausfrau f.

housework ['hauswɜːk] n Hausarbeit f.

housing ['hauzɪŋ] n Unterbringung f, Wohnung f; (tech) Gehäuse neut. **housing estate** Siedlung f.

hovel ['hovəl] n Schuppen m.

hover ['hovə] v schweben. **hovercraft** n Luftkissenfahrzeug neut.

how [hau] adv wie. **how do you do?** guten Tag. **how are you?** wie geht es Ihnen? **how much** or **how many** wieviel. **however** adv aber, jedoch; (in whatever way) wie auch immer.

howl [haul] v heulen. n Heulen neut.

hub [hʌb] n Nabe f; (fig) Mittelpunkt m. **hub cap** Radkappe f.

huddle ['hʌdl] v sich zusammendrängen. **huddled** adj kauernd.

hue [hjuː] n Farbe f, Färbung f.

huff [hʌf] n **in a huff** gekränkt, beleidigt.

hug [hʌg] v umarmen. n Umarmung f.

huge [hjuːdʒ] adj riesig, riesengroß.

hulk [hʌlk] n (naut) Hulk m.

hull [hʌl] n (naut) Rumpf m; (of seed, etc.) Hülse f, Schale f. v enthülsen.

hum [hʌm] v summen, brummen. n Summen neut, Brummen neut.

human ['hjuːm ən] adj menschlich. **human being** Mensch m. **human nature** Menschheit f, menschliche Natur f. **humane** adj human. **humanist** n Humanist(in). **humanitarian** adj menschenfreundlich. **humanity** n Menschheit f.

humble ['hʌm bl] adj demütig, bescheiden; (lowly) niedrig. **humiliate** v demütigen. **humiliating** adj demütigend. **humility** n Demut f, Bescheidenheit f.

humdrum ['hʌm drʌm] adj langweilig, alltäglich.

humid ['hjuːm ɪd] adj feucht. **humidity** n Feuchtigkeit f.

humour ['hjuːm ə] n Humor m; (mood) Stimmung f, Laune f. v (person) nachgeben (+ dat). **sense of humour** Humor m. **humorous** adj lustig, humorvoll.

hump [hʌm p] n Buckel m. v (coll: carry) schleppen. **humpback** n Bucklige(r). **humpbacked** adj bucklig.

hunch [hʌntʃ] n (coll) Vorahnung f.

hundred ['hʌndrəd] adj hundert. n Hundert neut. **hundredth** adj hundertst; n Hundertstel neut. **hundredweight** Zentner m.

hung [hʌŋ] V hang.

Hungary ['hʌŋgərɪ] n Ungarn neut. **Hungarian** adj ungarisch; n Ungar(in).

hunger ['hʌŋgə] n Hunger m. v hungern. **hunger for** sehnen nach. **hungry** adj hungrig. **be hungry** Hunger haben.

hunt [hʌnt] n Jagd f, Jagen neut; (for person) Verfolgung f. v jagen; verfolgen. **hunter** n Jäger m; (horse) Jagdpferd neut. **hunting** n Jagd f.

hurdle ['hɜːdl] n Hürde f; (fig) Hindernis neut.

hurl [hɜːl] v werfen.

hurricane ['hʌrɪkən] n Orkan m. **hurricane lamp** Sturmlaterne f.

hurry ['hʌrɪ] v eilen, sich beeilen; (something) beschleunigen. n Eile f, Hast f. **hurry up** mach schnell! **hurried** adj eilig, übereilt.

*hurt [hɜːt] v (injure) verletzen; (ache) schmerzen, weh tun; (offend) kränken, verletzen. n Verletzung f; Schmerzen neut. **hurtful** adj schädlich.

hurtle ['hɜːtl] v stürzen, sausen.

husband ['hʌzbənd] n (Ehe)Mann m. v (resources) sparsam umgehen mit. **husbandry** n Landwirtschaft f.

hush [hʌʃ] n Stille f, Ruhe f. v beruhigen.

husk [hʌsk] n Hülse f. v enthülsen.

husky ['hʌskɪ] adj (voice) rauh, heiser.

hussar [həˈzaː] n Husar m.

hustle ['hʌsl] v drängen. **hustle and bustle** Gedränge neut.

hut [hʌt] n Hütte f.

hutch [hʌtʃ] n Stall m.

hyacinth ['haɪəsɪnθ] n Hyazinthe f.

hybrid ['haɪbrɪd] n Kreuzung f, Mischling m. adj Misch-.

hydraulic [haɪdrɔːlɪk] adj hydraulisch.

hydrocarbon [ˌhaɪdrouˈkaːbən] n Kohlenwasserstoff m.

hydro-electric [ˌhaɪdrouɪlektrɪk] adj hydroelektrisch.

hydrogen ['haɪdrədʒən] n Wasserstoff m.

hydrogen bomb Wasserstoffbombe f.
hydrogen peroxide Wasserstoffsuperoxyd neut.

hyena [haɪnə] n Hyäne f.

hygiene ['haɪʒiːn] n Hygiene f, Gesundheitspflege f. **hygienic** adj hygienisch.

hymn [hɪm] n Kirchenlied neut, Hymne f. **hymnbook** n Gesangbuch neut.

hype [haɪp] n (coll) Reklameschwindel m.

hyperactive [haɪpərˈaktiv] adj hyperaktiv.

hypermarket ['haɪpəmaːkɪt] n Großmarkt m.

hypersensitive [haɪpəˈsɛnsətɪv] adj überempfindlich.

hyphen ['haɪfən] n Bindestrich m.

hypnosis [hɪpˈnəʊsɪs] n Hypnose f. **hypnotic** adj hypnotisch. **hypnotist** n Hypnotiseur m. **hypnotize** v hypnotisieren.

hypochondria [haɪpəˈkɒndrə] n Hypochondrie f. **hypochondriac** adj hypochondrisch. n Hypochonder m.

hypocrisy [hɪpokəsi] n Heuchelei f. **hypocrite** n Heuchler(in). **hypocritical** adj heuchlerisch.

hypodermic [haɪpəˈdəːmɪk] adj subkutan. **hypodermic syringe** Spritze f.

hypothesis [haɪpɒθəsɪs] n (pl -ses) Hypothese f. **hypothetical** adj hypothetisch.

hysterectomy [hɪstəˈrɛktəmɪ] n Hysterektomie f.

hysteria [hɪstɪərə] n Hysterie f. **hysterical** adj hysterisch; (coll: funny) zum Schreien komisch.

I

I [aɪ] pron ich.

ice [aɪs] n Eis neut. v (cookery) mit Zuckerguß überziehen. **ice age** Eiszeit f. **iceberg** n Eisberg m. **icebox** n Kühlschrank m. **ice cream** Eis neut. **ice cube** Eiswürfel m. **ice hockey** Eishockey neut. **icing** n Zuckerguß m. **icy** adj eisig.

Iceland ['aɪslənd] n Island neut. **Icelandic** adj isländisch. **Icelander** n Isländer(in).

icicle ['aɪsɪkl] n Eiszapfen m.

icon ['aɪkɒn] n Ikone f.

idea [aɪdɪə] n Idee f; (concept) Begriff m. I've no idea Ich habe keine Ahnung.

ideal [aɪdɪəl] n Ideal neut. adj ideal. **idealism** n Idealismus neut. **idealist** n Idealist m. **idealistic** adj idealistisch. **ideally** adv idealerweise.

identical [aɪdɛntɪkl] adj identisch.

identify [aɪdɛntɪfaɪ] v identifizieren; (recognize) erkennen. **identification** n Identifizierung f; (pass) Ausweis m.

identity [aɪdɛntɪtɪ] n Identität f. **identity card** Personalausweis m. **identity papers** Ausweispapiere pl.

ideology [aɪdɪˈɒlədʒɪ] n Ideologie f. **ideological** adj ideologisch. **ideologist** n Ideologe m, Ideologin f.

idiom ['ɪdɪəm] n Mundart f, Idiom neut. **idiomatic** adj idiomatisch.

idiosyncrasy [ˌɪdɪəˈsɪŋkrəsɪ] n Eigenart f. **idiosyncratic** adj eigenartig.

idiot ['ɪdɪət] n (coll) Idiot m, Dummkopf m; (med) Blödsinnige(r). **idiocy** n Blödsinn m.

idle ['aɪdl] adj (person) faul, untätig; (words, etc.) eitel, unnütz. **idleness** n Faulheit f. **idler** n Faulenzer m.

idol ['aɪdl] n Idol neut. **idolize** v vergöttern.

idyllic [ɪdɪlɪk] adj idyllisch.

if [ɪf] conj wenn, falls; (whether) ob. **even if** selbst wenn. **if only** wenn ... nur. **if not** falls nicht. **if so** in dem Fall.

ignite [ɪɡˈnaɪt] v (ent)zünden.

ignition [ɪɡˈnɪʃən] n Zündung f. **ignition key** Zündschlüssel m.

ignorant ['ɪɡnərənt] adj unwissend; (uneducated) ungebildet. **be ignorant of** nicht wissen or kennen. **ignorance** n Unkenntnis f.

ignore [ɪɡˈnɔː] v ignorieren, unbeachtet lassen.

ill [ɪl] adj (sick) krank; (bad) schlimm, böse. **fall ill** krank werden. **ill-at-ease** adj unbehaglich. **ill-bred** schlecht erzogen. **ill-disposed** adj bösartig. **ill-fated** adj unselig. **ill feeling** n Mißgunst f; böses Blut neut. **ill-natured** adj boshaft. **illness** n Krankheit f. **ill-treat** v mißhandeln.

illegal [ɪliːɡəl] adj illegal, gesetzwidrig. **illegality** n Ungesetzlichkeit f.

illegible [ɪlɛdʒəbl] adj unleserlich. **illegibility** n Unleserlichkeit f.

illegitimate [ˌɪlɪdʒɪtɪmɪt] *adj* (*child*) unehelich; (*unlawful*) ungesetzlich.

illicit [ɪlɪsɪt] *adj* unzulässig, gesetzwidrig.

illiterate [ɪlɪtərɪt] *adj* analphabetisch, ungebildet. *n* Analphabet(in).

illogical [ɪlɒdʒɪkəl] *adj* unlogisch.

illuminate [ɪluːmɪneɪt] *v* erleuchten. **illuminated** *adj* beleuchtet. **illumination** *n* Beleuchtung *f*.

illusion [ɪluːʒən] *n* Illusion *f*. **illusory** *adj* illusorisch.

illustrate [ɪləstreɪt] *v* (*book*) illustrieren; (*idea*) erklären. **illustration** *n* Illustration *f*, Bild *n*.

illustrious [ɪlʌstrəs] *adj* berühmt.

image [ɪmɪdʒ] *n* Bild *neut*. (*idea*) Vorstellung *f*; (*public*) Image *neut*. **imagery** *n* Symbolik *f*.

imagine [ɪmædʒɪn] *v* sich vorstellen *or* denken. **imaginable** *adj* denkbar. **imaginary** *adj* eingebildet, Schein-. **imagination** *n* Phantasie *f*. **imaginative** *adj* phantasiereich.

imbalance [ɪmbæləns] *n* Unausgeglichenheit *f*.

imbecile [ɪmbəsiːl] *n* Schwachsinnige(r). *adj* schwachsinnig.

imitate [ɪmɪteɪt] *v* nachahmen, imitieren. **imitation** *n* Nachahmung *f*; *adj* künstlich, Kunst-.

immaculate [ɪmækjulɪt] *adj* makellos.

immaterial [ˌɪmətɪərɪəl] *adj* belanglos.

immature [ˌɪmətʃuə] *adj* unreif, unentwickelt. **immaturity** *n* Unreife *f*.

immediate [ɪmiːdɪət] *adj* unmittelbar, direkt. **immediately** *adv* sofort.

immense [ɪmens] *adj* riesig, ungeheuer.

immerse [ɪməːs] *v* versenken, tauchen. **immersion** *n* Versunkenheit *f*, Immersion *f*. **immersion heater** Tauchsieder *m*.

immigrate [ɪmɪgreɪt] *v* einwandern. **immigrant** *n* Einwanderer *m*, Einwanderin *f*. **immigration** *n* Einwanderung *f*.

imminent [ɪmɪnənt] *adj* drohend.

immobile [ɪmoubaɪl] *adj* bewegungslos, unbeweglich. **immobility** *n* Unbeweglichkeit *f*. **immobilize** *v* unbeweglich machen. **immobilizer** *n* (*car*) Wegfahrsperre *f*.

immodest [ɪmɒdɪst] *adj* schamlos.

immoral [ɪmɒrəl] *adj* unsittlich, unmoralisch. **immorality** *n* Sittenlosigkeit *f*.

immortal [ɪmɔːtl] *adj* unsterblich, ewig. **immortality** *n* Unsterblichkeit *f*.

immovable [ɪmuːvəbl] *adj* unbeweglich.

immune [ɪmjuːn] *adj* immun (gegen). **immunity** *n* Immunität *f*. **immunization** *n* Impfung *f*.

imp [ɪmp] *v* Kobold *m*.

impact [ɪmpækt] *n* Anprall *m*, Stoß *m*; (*effect*) Wirking *f*, Einfluß *m*.

impair [ɪmpeə] *v* beeinträchtigen. **impairment** *n* Beeinträchtigung *f*.

impart [ɪmpaːt] *v* gegen, erteilen.

impartial [ɪmpaːʃəl] *adj* unparteiisch. **impartiality** *n* Unparteilichkeit *f*.

impassable [ɪmpaːsəbl] *adj* ungangbar, unpassierbar.

impasse [æmpaːs] *n* Sackgasse *f*.

impassive [ɪmpæsɪv] *adj* ungerührt.

impatient [ɪmpeɪʃənt] *adj* ungeduldig. **impatience** *n* Ungeduld *f*.

impeach [ɪmpiːtʃ] *v* anklagen. **impeachment** *n* Anklage *f*.

impeccable [ɪmpekəbl] *adj* tadellos. **impeccability** *n* Tadellosigkeit *f*.

impede [ɪmpiːd] *v* (be)hindern. **impediment** *n* Verhinderung *f*. **speech impediment** Sprachfehler *m*.

impel [ɪmpel] *v* (an)treiben. **impelled** *adj* gezwungen.

impending [ɪmpendɪŋ] *adj* bevorstehend, drohend.

imperative [ɪmperətɪv] *adj* dringend notwendig. *n* (*gramm*) Imperativ *m*.

imperfect [ɪmpəːfɪkt] *adj* unvollkommen. fehlerhaft. **imperfection** *n* (*blemish*) Fehler *m*.

imperial [ɪmpɪərɪəl] *adj* kaiserlich. **imperialism** *n* Imperialismus *m*. **imperialist** *adj* imperialistisch.

imperil [ɪmperɪl] *v* gefährden.

impermanent [ɪmpəːmənənt] *adj* unbeständig.

impersonal [ɪmpəːsənl] *adj* unpersönlich. **impersonality** *n* Unpersönlichkeit *f*.

impersonate [ɪmpəːsəneɪt] *v* sich ausgeben als.

impertinent [ɪmpəːtɪnənt] *adj* frech, unverschämt. **impertinence** *n* Frechheit *f*, Unverschämtheit *f*.

impervious [ɪmpəːvɪəs] *adj* undurchdringlich.

impetuous [ɪm'petjʊəs] *adj* ungestüm, impulsiv. **impetuosity** *n* Ungestüm *neut.*

impetus ['ɪmpətəs] *n* Antrieb *m*, Schwung *m.*

impinge [ɪm'pɪndʒ] *v* eingreifen (in), stoßen (an).

implement ['ɪmplɪmənt; *v* 'ɪmplɪment] *n* Werkzeug *neut*, Gerät *neut. v* durchführen.

implicate ['ɪmplɪkeɪt] *v* hineinziehen. **implication** *n* Bedeutung *f*, Konsequenz *f.*

implicit [ɪm'plɪsɪt] *adj* (*tacit*) unausgesprochen; (*unquestioning*) absolut. **implicitly** *adv* unbedingt.

implore [ɪm'plɔː] *v* dringend bitten. **imploring** *adj* flehentlich.

imply [ɪm'plaɪ] *v* bedeuten.

impolite [ɪmpə'laɪt] *adj* unhöflich. **impoliteness** *n* Unhöflichkeit *f.*

import [ɪm'pɔːt] *v* einführen, importieren. *n* Einfuhr *f*, Import *m*. **importer** *n* Importeur *m*, Einfuhrhändler *m*. **imports** *pl n* Importwaren *pl.*

importance [ɪm'pɔːtəns] *n* Wichtigkeit *f*, Bedeutung *f*. **important** *adj* wichtig.

impose [ɪm'pəʊz] *v* auferlegen. **impose upon** mißbrauchen. **imposing** *adj* imponierend. **imposition** *n* Auferlegung *f*; (*unreasonable demand*) Zumutung *f.*

impossible [ɪm'posəbl] *adj* unmöglich. **impossibility** *n* Unmöglichkeit *f.*

impostor [ɪm'postə] *n* Betrüger(in).

impotent ['ɪmpətənt] *adj* impotent. **impotence** *n* Impotenz *f.*

impound [ɪm'paʊnd] *v* beschlagnahmen.

impoverish [ɪm'povərɪʃ] *v* arm machen. **impoverished** *adj* verarmt.

impractical [ɪm'præktɪkəl] *adj* unpraktisch.

impregnate ['ɪmpregneɪt] *v* befruchten, schwanger machen; (*fabric, wood, etc.*) imprägnieren. **impregnable** *adj* uneinnehmbar.

impress [ɪm'pres] *v* beeindrucken. **impression** *n* Eindruck *m*; (*book*) Auflage *f*. **impressionism** *n* (*painting*) Impressionismus *m.*

imprint [ɪm'prɪnt; *n* 'ɪmprɪnt] *v* aufdrücken (auf); (*fig*) einprägen in. *n* Stempel *m*; (*fig*) Eindruck *m.*

imprison [ɪm'prɪzn] *v* einsperren. **imprisonment** *n* Haft *f*, Gefangenschaft *f.*

improbable [ɪm'probəbl] *adj* unwahrscheinlich. **improbability** *n*
Unwahrscheinlichkeit *f.*

impromptu [ɪm'promptjuː] *adj* improvisiert.

improper [ɪm'propə] *adj* unpassend, unsittlich.

improve [ɪm'pruːv] *v* verbessern; (*become better*) sich verbessern, besser werden. **improvement** *n* Verbesserung *f.*

improvise ['ɪmprəvaɪz] *v* improvisieren. **improvisation** *n* Improvisierung *f.*

impudent ['ɪmpjʊdənt] *adj* frech, unverschämt. **impudence** *n* Unverschämtheit *f.*

impulse ['ɪmpʌls] *n* Antrieb *m*, Drang *m*. **impulsive** *adj* impulsiv.

impure [ɪm'pjʊə] *adj* unrein. **impurity** *n* Unreinheit *f*; (*extraneous substance*) fremde Bestandteile *pl.*

in [ɪn] *prep* (*place*) in, an auf; (*time*) in, während. (*into*) in ... hinein *or* herein. **in the street** auf der Straße. **in the evening** abends. **in bad weather** bei schlechtem Wetter. **in three days' time** nach drei Tagen. **in that** insofern als. **be in** (*at home*) zu Hause sein.

inability [ɪnə'bɪlɪti] *n* Unfähigkeit *f*. **inability to pay** Zahlungsunfähigkeit *f.*

inaccessible [ɪnæk'sesəbl] *adj* unzugänglich, unerreichbar. **inaccessibility** *n* Unzugänglichkeit *f.*

inaccurate [ɪn'ækjʊrɪt] *adj* ungenau; (*incorrect*) falsch. **inaccuracy** *n* Ungenauigkeit *f*; Fehler *m.*

inactive [ɪn'æktɪv] *adj* untätig. **inactivity** *n* Untätigkeit *f.*

inadequate [ɪn'ædɪkwɪt] *adj* ungenügend, mangelhaft. **inadequacy** *n* Unzulänglichkeit *f*, Mangelhaftigkeit *f.*

inadvertent [ɪnəd'vɜːtənt] *adj* unabsichtlich, versehentlich.

inane [ɪn'eɪn] *adj* leer, albern.

inanimate [ɪn'ænɪmət] *adj* leblos.

inarticulate [ɪnɑː'tɪkjʊlɪt] *adj* undeutlich. **be inarticulate** sich nicht gut ausdrücken können.

inasmuch [ɪnəz'mʌtʃ] *conj* **inasmuch as** da.

inaudible [ɪn'ɔːdəbl] *adj* unhörbar.

inaugurate [ɪn'ɔːgjʊreɪt] *v* (*feierlich*) eröffnen. **inauguration** *n* (feierliche) Eröffnung *f*. **inaugural** *adj* Einführungs-.

inborn [ɪn'bɔːn] *adj* angeboren.

incapable [ɪn'keɪpəbl] *adj* unfähig. **inca-**

pacity n Unfähigkeit f.

incapacitate [inkə'pæsiteit] v unfähig machen, untauglich machen.

incendiary [in'sendiəri] adj Brand-. **incendiary bomb** Brandbombe f.

incense¹ ['insens] n Weihrauch m.

incense² [in'sens] v wütend machen.

incentive [in'sentiv] n Ansporn m; (bonus) Leistungsanreiz m.

incessant [in'sesənt] adj ständig, unaufhörlich.

incest ['insest] n Blutschande f. **incestuous** adj blutschänderisch.

inch [intʃ] n Zoll m.

incident ['insidənt] n Vorfall m, Ereignis neut.

incinerator [in'sinə,reitə] n Verbrennungsofen m. **incinerate** v verbrennen. **incineration** n Verbrennung f.

incite [in'sait] v anregen. **incitement** n Anregung f, Aufreizung f.

incline [in'klain] v neigen; (slope) abfallen. **inclination** n Neigung f. **inclined** adj geneigt.

include [in'klu:d] v einschließen. **included** adj (in price) inbegriffen. **inclusive** adj einschließlich. **inclusive of** also **including** einschließlich. **inclusion** n Einbeziehung f.

incognito [,inkog'ni:tou] adv inkognito.

incoherent [,inkə'hiərənt] adj inkonsequent; (speech) unklar.

income ['inkʌm] n Einkommen neut, Einkünfte pl. **income tax** Einkommensteuer f. **income tax return** Einkommensteuererklärung f.

incompatible [inkəm'pætəbl] adj unvereinbar. **incompatibility** n Unvereinbarkeit f.

incompetent [in'kompitənt] adj unfähig. **incompetence** n Unfähigkeit f.

incomplete [,inkəm'pli:t] adj unvollständig.

incomprehensible [in,komprihensəbl] adj unbegreiflich.

inconceivable [inkən'si:vəbl] adj unfaßbar. **inconceivability** n Unfaßbarkeit f.

inconclusive [inkən'klu:siv] adj ohne Beweiskraft.

incongruous [in'kongruəs] adj unangemessen.

inconsiderate [,inkən'sidərit] adj rücksichtslos, besinnungslos.

inconsistent [,inkən'sistənt] adj inkon-

sequent; (person) unbeständig. **inconsistency** n Widerspruch m.

inconspicuous [inkən'spikjuəs] adj unauffällig.

incontinence [in'kontinəns] n (med) Inkontinenz f.

inconvenient [inkən'vi:njənt] adj ungelegen. **inconvenience** n Ungelegenheit f. v stören, lästig sein (+ dat).

incorporate [in'kɔ:pəreit] v (combine) vereinigen; (comm) inkorporieren; (contain, include) enthalten. **incorporation** n (comm) Gründung f.

incorrect [inkə'rekt] adj unrichtig; (inexact) ungenau.

increase [in'kri:s] v zunehmen; (in number) sich vermehren; (prices) steigen. n Vermehrung f, Zunahme f; Steigerung f; (wages) Lohnerhöhung f. **increasingly** adv immer mehr.

incredible [in'kredəbl] adj unglaublich. **incredibility** n Unglaublichkeit f. **incredibly** adv unglaublicherweise; (coll: extremely) unglaublich.

incredulous [in'kredjuləs] adj skeptisch, ungläubig. **incredulity** n Skepsis f.

increment ['inkrəmənt] n Zunahme f.

incriminate [in'krimineit] v beschuldigen. **incrimination** n Beschuldigung f.

incubate ['inkju,beit] v ausbrüten. **incubation** n Ausbrütung f. **incubator** n (for babies) Brutkasten m.

incur [in'kə:] v sich zuziehen. **incur debts** Schulden machen. **incur losses** Verluste erleiden.

incurable [in'kjuərəbl] adj unheilbar.

indebted [in'detid] adj verschuldet.

indecent [in'di:snt] adj unanständig. **indecency** n Unanständigkeit f.

indeed [in'di:d] adv tatsächlich, wirklich.

indefinite [in'definit] adj unbestimmt. **indefinitely** adv auf unbestimmte Zeit.

indelible [in'deləbl] adj unauslöschlich; (ink) wasserfest.

indemnify [in'demnifai] v entschädigen. **indemnity** n Entschädigung f.

indent [in'dent] v (type) einrücken. **indentation** n Einrückung f.

independence [indi'pendəns] n Unabhängigkeit f, Selbstständigkeit f. **independent** adj unabhängig, selbstständig; (pol) parteilos; n (pol) Unabhängige(r).

indescribable [ɪndɪskraɪbəbl] *adj*
unbeschreiblich.

indestructible [ɪndɪstrʌktəbl] *adj* unzer-
störbar.

index ['ɪndeks] *n* (*in book*) Register *neut*;
(*file*) Kartei *f*; (*cost of living*) Index *m*. **index
finger** Zeigefinger *m*.

India ['ɪndɪə] *n* Indien *neut*. **Indian** *adj*
indisch; (*American*) indianisch; *n* Inder(in);
(*American*) Indianer(in). **Indian ink**
chinesische Tusche *f*. **Indian summer**
Nachsommer *m*.

indicate ['ɪndɪkeɪt] *v* anzeigen; (*hint*)
andeuten. **indication** *n* Anzeichen *neut*;
(*idea*) Andeutung *f*; (*information*) Angabe;
(*med*) Indikation *f*. **indicative** *adj*
anzeigend. **indicator** *n* (*sign*) Zeichen *neut*;
(*mot*) Richtungsanzeiger *m*, Blinker *m*.

indict [ɪndaɪt] *v* anklagen (wegen). **indict-
ment** *n* Anklageschrift *f*.

indifferent [ɪndɪfərənt] *adj* gleichgültig;
(*poor quality*) mittelmäßig. **indifference** *n*
Gleichgültigkeit *f*, Mittelmäßigkeit *f*.

indigenous [ɪndɪdʒɪnəs] *adj* einheimisch.

indigestion [ɪndɪdʒestʃən] *n*
Verdauungsstörung *f*. **indigestible** *adj*
unverdaulich.

indignant [ɪndɪgnənt] *adj* empört. **indignation** *n* Empörung *f*.

indignity [ɪndɪgnətɪ] *n* Demütigung *f*.

indirect [ɪndɪrekt] *adj* indirekt.

indiscreet [ɪndɪskriːt] *adj* indiskret, taktlos.
indiscretion *n* Vertrauensbruch *m*,
Indiskretion *f*.

indiscriminate [ɪndɪskrɪmɪnɪt] *adj* rücksichtslos. **indiscriminately** *adv* ohne
Unterschied.

indispensable [ɪndɪspensəbl] *adj* unerläßlich, unentbehrlich. **indispensability** *n*
Unerläßlichkeit *f*, Unentbehrlichkeit *f*.

indisposed [ɪndɪspouzd] *adj* indisponiert,
unpäßlich.

indisputable [ɪndɪspjuːtəbl] *adj* unbestreitbar.

indistinct [ɪndɪstɪŋkt] *adj* unklar.

individual [ɪndɪvɪdjuəl] *n* Individuum *neut*,
Person *f*. *adj* einzeln, persönlich, individuell. **individualist** *n* Individualist(in). **indi-
viduality** *n* Individualitäat *f*, Eigenart *f*.
individually *adv* einzeln.

indoctrinate [ɪndɒktrɪneɪt] *v* unterweisen.
indoctrination *n* Unterweisung *f*.

indolent ['ɪndələnt] *adj* lässig. **indolence** *n*
Lässigkeit *f*.

indoor ['ɪndoː] *adj* Haus-, Zimmer-. **indoor
swimming pool** Hallenbad *neut*. **indoors**
adv im Haus; (*go*) ins Haus.

induce [ɪndjuːs] *v* (*cause*) verursachen; (*persuade*) überreden. **inducement** *n* Anreiz *m*.

indulge [ɪndʌldʒ] *v* (*a person*) nachgeben
(+ *dat*); (*oneself*) verwöhnen. **indulgence** *n*
Nachsicht *f*; Verwöhnung *f*. **indulgent** *adj*
nachsichtig.

industry ['ɪndəstrɪ] *n* Industrie *f*. **industrial** *adj* industriell. **industrialist** *n*
Industrielle(r). **industrious** *adj* fleißig.

inebriated [ɪnibrɪeɪtɪd] *adj* betrunken.

inedible [ɪnedɪbl] *adj* nicht eßbar.

inefficient [ɪnɪfɪʃənt] *adj* unfähig; (*thing*)
unwirksam. **inefficiency** *n*
Leistungsunfähigkeit *f*.

inept [ɪnept] *adj* albern. **ineptitude** *n*
Albernheit *f*.

inequality [ɪnɪkwɒlətɪ] *n* Ungleichheit *f*.

inert [ɪnəːt] *adj* inaktiv; (*person*) schlaff.
inertia *n* Trägheit *f*.

inevitable [ɪnevɪtəbl] *adj* unvermeidlich.
inevitability *n* Unvermeidlichkeit *f*.

inexpensive [ɪnɪkspensɪv] *adj* billig,
preiswert.

inexperienced [ɪnɪkspɪərɪənst] *adj* unerfahren.

infallible [ɪnfælbl] *adj* unfehlbar. **infalli-
bility** *n* Unfehlbarkeit *f*.

infamous ['ɪnfəməs] *adj* schändlich.
infamy *n* Schande *f*.

infancy ['ɪnfənsɪ] *n* frühe Kindheit *f*. **be
still in its infancy** noch in den Kinder-
schuhen stecken. **infant** (*baby*) Säugling
m; (*small child*) Kleinkind *neut*. **infantile**
adj kindisch.

infantry ['ɪnfəntrɪ] *n* Infanterie *f*. **infantryman** *n* Infanterist *m*.

infatuated [ɪnfætjueɪtɪd] *adj* vernarrt (in).
infatuation *n* Vernarrtheit *f*.

infect [ɪnfekt] *v* infizieren, anstecken.
infection *n* Infizierung *f*, Ansteckung *f*
infectious *adj* ansteckend.

infer [ɪnfəː] *v* folgern. **inference** *n* (*conclusion*) Schlußfolgerung *f*.

inferior [ɪnfɪərə] *adj* minderwertig. **inferiority** *n* Minderwertigkeit *f*. **inferiority
complex** Minderwertigkeitskomplex *m*.

infernal [ɪnfəːnl] *adj* höllisch; (*coll*) verdammt. **inferno** n Inferno neut.

infertile [in'ə:tail] adj unfruchtbar. **infertility** n Unfruchtbarkeit f.

infest [in'fest] v heimsuchen, plagen. **infestation** n Plage f.

infidelity [,infideliti] n Untreue f.

infiltrate [in'filtreit] v einsickern in; (pol) unterwandern. **infiltration** n Einsickern neut; Unterwanderung f. **infiltrator** n Unterwanderer m.

infinite ['infinit] adj unendlich. **infinity** n Unendlichkeit f. **infinitesimal** adj winzig.

infinitive [in'finitiv] n (gramm) Infinitiv m, Nennform f.

infirm [in'ə:m] adj schwach. **infirmary** n Krankenhaus neut. **infirmity** n Krankheit f.

inflame [in'fleim] v entzünden; (fig) erregen. **inflamed** (med) entzündet. **inflammable** adj brennbar. **inflammation** n Entzündung f. **inflammatory** adj (fig) aufrührerisch.

inflate [in'fleit] v aufblasen; (price) übermäßig steigern. **inflatable** adj aufblasbar. **inflated** adj aufgebläht; (fig) aufgeblasen; (price) überhöht. **inflation** n Aufgeblasenheit; (comm) Inflation f. **inflationary** adj inflationistisch.

inflection [in'flekʃən] n Biegung f; (of voice) Modulation f.

inflict [in'flikt] v (blow) versetzen; (pain) zufügen; (burden) aufbürden. **infliction** n Zufügung f; (burden) Last f.

influence ['influəns] n Einfluß m; (power) Macht f. v beeinflussen, Einfluß ausüben auf. **influential** adj einflußreich.

influenza [,influ'enzə] n Grippe f.

influx ['inflaks] n Zustrom m.

inform [in'fo:m] v benachrichtigen, unterrichten. **inform against** anzeigen.

informal [in'fo:m l] adj informell. **informality** n Ungezwungenheit f.

information [,infə'meʃən] n Auskunft f, Information f, Nachricht f; (data) Angaben pl. **information bureau** Auskunftsbüro neut. **information technology** (IT) Informationstechnologie f. **informative** adj lehrreich. **informed** adj informiert. **informer** n Angeber(in).

infra-red [,infə'red] adj infrarot.

infringe [in'frindʒ] v verstoßen gegen; (rights) verletzen. **infringement** n

Verletzung f.

infuriate [in'fjuərieit] v wütend machen. **infuriated** adj wütend.

ingenious [in'dʒi:niəs] adj (person) erfinderisch; (device) raffiniert, ausgeklügelt. **ingenuity** n Erfindungsgabe f.

ingot ['iŋgət] n Barren m.

ingrained [in'greind] adj tief eingewurzelt.

ingratiate [in'greiʃieit] v **ingratiate oneself with** sich bei jemandem einschmeicheln. (impol) jemandem hinten reinkriechen; jemandem Zucker in den Arsch blasen.

ingredient [in'gri:diənt] n Zutat f.

inhabit [in'habit] v bewohnen. **inhabitable** adj bewohnbar. **inhabitant** n Einwohner(in).

inhale [in'heil] v einatmen. **inhalation** n Einatmung f. **inhaler** n Inhaliergerät neut.

inherent [in'hiərənt] adj angeboren.

inherit [in'herit] v erben. **inheritance** n Erbe neut. **inherited** adj ererbt. **inheritor** n Erbe m, Erbin f.

inhibit [in'hibit] v hemmen; (prevent) hindern. **inhibition** n Hemmung f.

inhospitable [inhə'spitəb] adj ungastlich.

inhuman [in'hju:m ən] adj unmenschlich. **inhumanity** n Unmenschlichkeit f.

iniquitous [in'ikwətəs] adj (unjust) ungerecht; (sinful) frevelhaft. **iniquity** n Ungerechtigkeit f, (sin) Sünde f.

initial [in'iʃl] adj anfänglich, Anfangs-. n Anfangsbuchstabe m. **initials** pl n Monogramm neut. **initially** adv am Anfang.

initiate [in'iʃieit] v einführen (in); (start) beginnen. n Eingeweihte(r). **initiation** n Einweihung.

initiative [in'iʃətiv] n Initiative f. **take the initiative** die Initiative ergreifen. **initiator** n Anstifter m.

inject [in'dʒekt] v einspritzen. **injection** n **give/have an injection** eine Spritze geben/bekommen.

injure ['indʒə] v verletzen. **injured party** Geschädigte(r). **injurious** adj schädlich. **injury** n Verletzung f, Wunde f.

injustice [in'dʒʌstis] n Unrecht neut, Ungerechtigkeit f.

ink [iŋk] n Tite f, Tusche f. **inkblot** n Tintenklecks m. **inkjet printer** Tintenstrahldrucker m. **inkwell** n

Tintenfaß *neut.*

inkling ['ɪŋklɪŋ] *n* Ahnung *f.*

inland ['ɪnlənd] *adj* Binnen-. **Inland Revenue** Steuerbehörde *f.*

in-laws ['ɪnˌlɔːs] *pl n* angeheiratete Verwandte *pl.* **daughter-in-law** Schwiegertochter *f.* **father-in-law** Schwiegervater *m.* **mother-in-law** Schwiegermutter *f.* **son-in-law** Schwiegersohn *m.*

*****inlay** ['ɪnleɪ] *v* einlegen. *n* eingelegte Arbeit *f;* (*dentistry*) Plombe *f.*

inlet ['ɪnlet] *n* Meeresarm *m.*

inmate ['ɪnmeɪt] *n* Insasse *m,* Insassin *f.*

inn [ɪn] *n* Gasthof *m,* Wirtshaus *neut.* **innkeeper** *n* Gastwirt(in).

innate [ɪˈneɪt] *adj* angeboren. **innately** *adv* von Natur.

inner ['ɪnə] *adj* inner, Innen-. **inner city** Innenstadt *f.* **innermost** *adj* innerst.

innocent ['ɪnəsnt] *adj* unschuldig, schuldlos. **innocence** *n* Unschuld *f,* Schuldlosigkeit *f.*

innocuous [ɪnokjuəs] *adj* harmlos, unschädlich.

innovation [ɪnəˈveɪʃən] *n* Neuerung *f.* **innovator** *n* Neuerer *m.*

innuendo [ɪnjuˈendou] *n* Stichelei *f.*

innumerable [ɪnjuːmˈərəbl] *adj* zahllos, unzählig.

inoculate [ɪnokjuleɪt] *v* (ein)impfen. **inoculation** *n* Impfung *f.*

inorganic [ɪnoːˈganɪk] *adj* unorganisch.

input ['ɪnput] *n* Eingabe *f,* Input *m.*

inquest ['ɪnkwest] *n* gerichtliche Untersuchung *f.*

inquire [ɪnˈkwaɪə] *v* sich erkundigen (nach). **inquiry** *n* Anfrage *f;* (*examination*) Untersuchung *f,* Prüfung *f.* **inquiry office** Auskunftsbüro *neut.*

inquisition [ɪnkwɪˈzɪʃən] *n* Untersuchung *f;* (*rel*) Ketzergericht *neut.*

inquisitive [ɪnˈkwɪzətɪv] *adj* neugierig.

insane [ɪnˈseɪn] *adj* geisteskrank; (*coll*) verrückt. **insanity** *n* Geisteskrankheit *f.*

insatiable [ɪnˈseɪʃəbl] *adj* unersättlich. **insatiability** *n* Unersättlichkeit *f.*

inscribe [ɪnˈskraɪb] *v* (auf)schreiben. **inscription** *n* Beschriftung *f;* (*in book*) Widmung *f.*

insect ['ɪnsekt] *n* Insekt *neut.* **insecticide** *n* Insektizid *neut.*

insecure [ɪnsɪˈkjuə] *adj* unsicher. **insecurity** *n* Unsicherheit *f.*

inseminate [ɪnˈsem ɪneɪt] *v* befruchten. **insemination** *n* Befruchtung *f.*

insensible [ɪnˈsensəbl] *adj* gefühllos; (*unconscious*) bewußtlos.

insensitive [ɪnˈsensətɪv] *adj* unempfindlich. **insensitivity** *n* Unempfindlichkeit *f.*

inseparable [ɪnˈsepərəbl] *adj* untrennbar.

insert [ɪnˈsəːt; *n* ˈɪnsəːt] *v* einfügen, einsetzen. *n* Beilage *f.* **insertion** *n* Einsatz *m.*

inshore [ɪnˈʃoː] *adj* Küsten-. *adv* zur Küste hin.

inside [ɪnˈsaɪd] *adj* inner, Innen-. *adv* (*be*) drinnen; (*go*) nach innen. *prep* in, innerhalb; (*into*) in ... hinein. *n* Innenseite *f,* Innere *neut.* **insides** (*intestines*) Eingeweide *pl.*

insidious [ɪnˈsɪdɪəs] *adj* heimtückisch.

insight ['ɪnsaɪt] *n* Einblick *m;* (*understanding*) Verständnis *neut.*

insignificant [ɪnsɪgˈnɪfɪkənt] *adj* unbedeutend, unwichtig. **insignificance** *n* Bedeutungslosigkeit *f.*

insincere [ɪnsɪnˈsɪə] *adj* unaufrichtig. **insincerity** *n* Unaufrichtigkeit *f.*

insinuate [ɪnˈsɪnjueɪt] *v* zu verstehen geben, andeuten. **insinuation** *n* Andeutung *f.*

insipid [ɪnˈsɪpɪd] *adj* fade.

insist [ɪnˈsɪst] *v* bestehen (auf). **insistence** *n* Bestehen *neut.* **insistent** *adj* beharrlich.

insolent ['ɪnsələnt] *adj* unverschämt, frech. **insolence** *n* Unverschämtheit *f,* Frechheit *f.*

insoluble [ɪnˈsoljubl] *adj* unauflöslich; (*problem*) unlösbar.

insolvent [ɪnˈsolvənt] *adj* zahlungsunfähig.

insomnia [ɪnˈsom nɪə] *n* Schlaflosigkeit *f.*

inspect [ɪnˈspekt] *v* untersuchen, besichtigen. **inspection** *n* Untersuchung *f.* Besichtigung *f.* **inspector** *n* Inspektor *m.*

inspire [ɪnˈspaɪə] *v* inspirieren, begeistern; (*give rise to*) anregen. **inspiration** *n* Inspiration *f,* Anregung *f.* **inspiring** *adj* anregend.

instability [ɪnstəˈbɪlɪtɪ] *n* Unbeständigkeit *f.*

install [ɪnˈstoːl] *v* einsetzen, einrichten. **installation** *n* Einrichtung *f.*

instalment [ɪnˈstoːlmənt] *n* Rate *f.* **instalment plan** Teilzahlungssystem *neut.*

instance ['ɪnstəns] *n* (*case*) Fall *f;* (*example*)

Beispiel *neut*. **for instance** zum Beispiel (z.B.).

instant ['instənt] *n* Augenblick *m*. *adj* sofortig. **instant coffee** Pulverkaffee *m*. **instantaneous** *adj* augenblicklich. **instantly** *adv* sofort.

instead [in'sted] *adv* statt dessen. **instead of** (an)statt (+ *gen*).

instep ['instep] *n* Rist *m*, Spann *m*.

instigate ['instigeit] *v* anstiften. **instigation** *n* Anstiftung *f*. **instigator** *n* Anstifter(in).

instil [in'stil] *v* (*teach*) beibringen (+ *dat*).

instinct ['instiŋkt] *n* (Natur)Trieb *m*, Instinkt *m*. **instinctive** *adj* instinktiv; (*automatic*) unwillkürlich.

institute ['institju:t] *n* Institut *neut*. *v* einführen; (*found*) gründen. **institution** *n* Institut *neut*; (*home*) Anstalt *f*; (*foundation*) Stiftung *f*.

instruct [in'strʌkt] *v* unterweisen; (*teach*) unterrichten. **instruction** *n* Vorschrift *f*; (*teaching*) Unterrichtung *f*. **instructive** *adj* lehrreich. **instructor** *n* Lehrer(in). **instructions for use** Gebrauchsanweisung *f*.

instrument ['instrəmənt] *n* Instrument *neut*; (*tool*) Werkzeug *neut*; (*means*) Mittel *neut*. **instrumental** *adj* (*helpful*) förderlich. **be instrumental in** durchsetzen.

insubordinate [insə'bɔːdənət] *adj* widersetzlich. **insubordination** *n* Widersetzlichkeit *f*.

insufficient [insə'fʃənt] *adj* unzureichend. **insufficiency** *n* Unzulänglichkeit *f*.

insular ['insjələ] *adj* insular. **insularity** *n* Beschränktheit *f*.

insulate ['insjəleit] *v* isolieren. **insulation** *n* Isolierung *f*. **insulating tape** Isolierband *neut*.

insulin ['insjulin] *n* Insulin *neut*.

insult [in'sʌlt; *n* 'insʌlt] *v* beleidigen, beschimpfen. *n* Beleidigung *f*. **insulting** *adj* beleidigend.

insure [in'ʃuə] *v* versichern. **insurance** *n* Versicherung *f*. **insurance broker** Versicherungsmakler *m*. **insurance policy** Versicherungspolice *f*. **insurance premium** Versicherungsprämie *f*.

insurmountable [insə'mauntəbl] *adj* unüberwindlich.

insurrection [insə'rekʃən] *n* Aufstand *m*.

intact [in'takt] *adj* unberührt.

intake ['inteik] *n* Aufnahme *f*, Einlaß *m*.

intangible [in'tandʒəbl] *adj* unfaßbar.

integral ['intigrəl] *adj* wesentlich; (*math*) Integral-.

integrate ['intigreit] *v* integrieren; (*people*) eingliedern. **integration** *n* Integration *f*; Eingliederung *f*. **integrity** *n* Integrität *f*; (*completeness*) Vollständigkeit *f*.

intellect ['intilekt] *n* Intellekt *m*. **intellectual** *adj* intellektuell; *n* Intellektuelle(r).

intelligent [in'telidʒənt] *adj* intelligent. **intelligence** *n* Intelligenz *f*; (*information*) Information *f*; (*secret service*) Geheimdienst *m*.

intelligible [in'telidʒəbl] *adj* verständlich, klar.

intend [in'tend] *v* beabsichtigen, die Absicht haben.

intense [in'tens] *adj* stark, intensiv; (*colour*) tief; (*person*) ernsthaft. **intensely** *adj* (*highly*) äußerst. **intensify** *v* verstärken. **intensity** *n* Stärke *f*. **intensive** *adj* intensiv.

intent[1] [in'tent] *n* Absicht *f*, Vorsatz *m*. **to all intents and purposes** im Grunde.

intent[2] [in'tent] *adj* **intent on** versessen auf.

intention [in'tenʃən] *n* Absicht *f*; (*plan*) Vorhaben *neut*; (*aim*) Ziel *neut*; (*meaning*) Sinn *m*. **intentional** *adj* absichtlich.

inter [in'tə:] *v* beerdigen. **interment** *n* Beerdigung *f*.

interact [intər'akt] *v* aufeinander wirken. **interaction** *n* Wechselwirkung *f*.

interactive [intər'aktiv] *adj* interaktiv.

intercede [intə'si:d] *v* sich verwenden (bei). **intercession** *n* Fürsprache *f*.

intercept [intə'sept] *v* abfangen. **interception** *n* Abfangen *neut*.

interchange [intə'tʃeindʒ] *n* Austausch *m*; (*roads*) (Autobahn) Kreuz/Dreieck *neut*. *v* austauschen.

intercom ['intəkɔm] *n* Sprechanlage *f*.

intercourse ['intəkɔːs] *n* Verkehr *m*, Umgang *m*. **sexual intercourse** Geschlechtsverkehr *m*.

interest ['intrist] *n* Interesse *neut*; (*comm*) Zinsen *pl*; (*advantage*) Vorteil *m*. **interest rate** Zinssatz *m*. **interested** *adj* interessiert; (*biased*) beteiligt. **interesting** *adj* interessant.

interfere [intə'fiə] *v* (*person*) sich einmischen; (*adversely affect*) stören. **inter-ference** *n* Einmischung *f*; Störung *f*. **inter-fering** *adj* lästig, störend.

interim ['intərim] *n* Zwischenzeit *f*. *adj* vorläufig.

interior [in'tiəriə] *n* Innere *neut*. *adj* inner, Binnen-.

interjection [‚intə'dʒekʃən] *n* Ausruf *m*; (*gramm*) Interjektion *f*.

interlock [intə'bk] *v* ineinandergreifen. **interlocking** *adj* verzahnt.

interlude ['intəlu:d] *n* (*interval*) Pause *f*.

intermediate [‚intə'mi:diət] *adj* Zwischen-. **intermediary** *n* Vermittler *m*.

interminable [in'tə:m inəbl] *adj* endlos.

intermission [‚intə'm ʃən] *n* Pause *f*, Unterbrechung *f*. **without intermission** pausenlos.

intermittent [‚intə'm itənt] *adj* stoßweise, periodisch.

intern [in'tə:n] *v* internieren. *n* Assistentenarzt *m*. **internment** *n* Internierung *f*.

internal [in'tə:nl] *adj* inner; (*domestic*) Innen-, Inlands-; (*within organization*) intern.

international [‚intə'næʃənl] *adj* international.

Internet ['intənet] *n* Internet *neut*. **Internet service provider** Internetdienstanbieter *m*.

interpose [‚intə'pouz] *v* dazwischenstellen. **interposition** *n* Zwischenstellung *f*.

interpret [in'tə:prit] *v* dolmetschen; (*explain*) auslegen; (*theatre, music*) interpretieren. **interpreter** *n* Dolmetscher(in); Interpret(in). **interpretation** *n* Dolmetschen *neut*; Auslegung *f*; Interpretation *f*.

interrogate [in'terəgeit] *v* verhören. **interrogation** *n* Verhör *neut*. **interrogator** *n* Fragesteller *m*.

interrogative [‚intə'rogətiv] *adj* fragend; (*gramm*) Frage-. *n* (*gramm*) Interrogativ *m*.

interrupt [‚intə'rʌpt] *v* unterbrechen. **interruption** *n* Unterbrechung *f*.

intersect [‚intə'sekt] *v* schneiden. **intersection** *n* Kreuzungspunkt *m*; (*mot*) Kreuzung *f*.

intersperse [‚intə'spə:s] *v* verstreuen.

interval ['intəvəl] *n* Zwischenraum *m*; (*break*) Pause *f*; (*timespan*) Abstand *m*; (*music*) Tonabstand *m*.

intervene [‚intəvi:n] *v* (*interfere*) ein-greifen; (*come between*) dazwischentreten. **intervention** *n* Intervention *f*, Eingreifen *neut*.

interview ['intəvju:] *n* Interview *neut*. *v* interviewen. **interviewee** *n* Interviewte(r). **interviewer** *n* Interviewer *m*.

intestine [in'testin] *n* Darm *m*. **intestines** *pl* Eingeweide *pl*. **intestinal** *adj* Darm-.

intimate[1] ['intim ət] *adj* vertraut. **intimacy** *n* Vertrautheit *f*.

intimate[2] ['intim eit] *v* andeuten. **intimation** *n* Andeutung *f*, Wink *m*.

intimidate [in'tim ieit] *v* einschüchtern. **intimidation** *n* Einschüchterung *f*.

into ['intu] *prep* in (+ *acc*) hinein/herein. **be into** (*coll*) sich interessieren für. **get into** (*difficulties, etc.*) geraten in. **look into** (*investigate*) untersuchen.

intolerable [in'tolərəbl] *adj* unerträglich.

intolerant [in'tolərənt] *adj* intolerant. **intolerance** *n* Intoleranz *f*.

intonation [‚intə'neiʃən] *n* Intonation *f*. **intone** *v* intonieren.

intoxicate [in'toksikeit] *v* berauschen. **intoxicated** *adj* berauscht; (*drunk*) betrunken. **intoxication** *n* Rausch *m*.

intransitive [in'trænsitiv] *adj* (*gramm*) intransitiv.

intravenous [‚intrə'vi:nəs] *adj* intravenös.

intrepid [in'trepid] *adj* unerschrocken.

intricate [in'trikət] *adj* kompliziert. **intricacy** *n* Kompliziertheit *f*.

intrigue ['intri:g ; v in'tai:g] *n* Intrige *f*. *v* faszinieren; (*plot*) intrigieren. **intriguing** *adj* faszinierend.

intrinsic [in'trinsik] *adj* wesentlich.

introduce [‚intrə'dju:s] *v* einführen; (*person*) vorstellen. **introduction** *n* Einführung *f*; (*in book*) Einleitung *f*, Vorwort *neut*; Vorstellung *f*. **introductory** *adj* einleitend. **letter of introduction** Empfehlungsbrief *m*.

introspective [‚intrə'spektiv] *adj* selbst-prüfend. **introspection** *n* Selbstprüfung *f*.

introvert ['intrəvə:t] *n* introvertierter Mensch *m*. **introverted** *adj* introvertiert.

intrude [in'tru:d] *v* hineindrängen; (*interfere*) sich einmischen. **intruder** *n* Eindringling *m*. **intrusion** *n* Eindrängen *neut*; Einmischung *f*. **intrusive** *adj* zudringlich; (*nuisance*) lästig.

intuition [ˌintjuːˈʃən] n Intuition f. **intuitive** adj intuitiv.

inundate [ˈinʌndeit] v überschwemmen. **inundation** n Überschwemmung f; Flut f.

invade [inˈveid] v überfallen. **invader** n Eindringling m. **invasion** n Einfall m, Invasion f.

invalid¹ [ˈinvəlid] n Kranke(r), Invalide m.

invalid² [inˈvalid] adj ungültig. **invalidate** v fürungültig erklären. **invalidation** n Ungültigkeitserklärung f. **invalidity** n Ungültigkeit f.

invaluable [inˈvaljuəbl] adj unschätzbar.

invariable [inˈveərəbl] adj konstant, unveränderlich. **invariably** adv ausnahmslos.

invective [inˈvektiv] n Beschimpfung f.

invent [inˈvent] v erfinden. **invention** n Erfindung f. **inventor** n Erfinder(in). **inventive** adj erfinderisch, einfallsreich, erfindungsreich.

inventory [ˈinvəntri] n Inventar neut, Bestandsverzeichnis neut; (stocktaking) Bestandsaufnahme f.

invert [inˈvəːt] v umkehren. **inversion** n Umkehrung f.

invertebrate [inˈvəːtibrət] adj wirbellos. n wirbelloses Tier neut.

invest [inˈvest] v investieren, anlegen. **investment** n Investition f, Anlage f. **investor** n Kapitalanleger m.

investigate [inˈvestigeit] v untersuchen. **investigation** n Untersuchung f. **investigator** n Prüfer(in).

invigorating [inˈvigəreitiŋ] adj stärkend.

invincible [inˈvinsəbl] adj unüberwindlich. **invincibility** n Unüberwindlichkeit f.

invisible [inˈvizbl] adj unsichtbar. **invisibility** n Unsichtbarkeit f.

invite [inˈvait] v einladen. **invitation** n Einladung f. **inviting** adj verlockend.

invoice [ˈinvɔis] n Rechnung f. v in Rechnung stellen.

invoke [inˈvouk] v anrufen. **invocation** n Anrufung f.

involuntary [inˈvoləntəri] adj unwillkürlich; (unintentional) unabsichtlich.

involve [inˈvolv] v (entail) mit sich bringen; (draw into) hineinziehen. **involved** adj verwickelt. **involvement** n Verwicklung f; Rolle f.

inward [ˈinwəd] adj inner. adv also

inwards nach innen. **inwardly** adv im Innern.

iodine [ˈaiədin] n Jod neut.

ion [ˈaiən] n Ion neut.

IOU n Schuldschein m.

IQ n IQ (Intelligenzquotient) m.

irate [aiˈreit] adj wütend.

Ireland [ˈaiələnd] n Irland neut. **Irish** adj irisch. **Irishman/woman** n Irländer(in), Ire m, Irin f.

iris [ˈaiəris] n (eye) Iris f; (flower) Schwertlilie f.

irk [əːk] v ärgern. **irksome** adj ärgerlich.

iron [ˈaiən] n Eisen neut; (ironing) Bügeleisen neut. adj eisern. v bügeln. **Iron Curtain** Eiserner Vorhang m. **ironing board** n Bügelbrett neut. **ironmonger** n Eisenwarenhändler m.

irony [ˈaiərəni] n Ironie f. **ironic** adj ironisch.

irrational [iˈraʃən] adj unlogisch; (unreasonable) unvernünftig. **irrationality** n Unvernunft f.

irredeemable [iridiːm əbl] adj untilgbar; (beyond improvement) unverbesserlich.

irregular [iˈregjulə] adj unregelmäßig. **irregularity** n Unregelmäßigkeit f.

irrelevant [iˈreləvənt] adj belanglos. **irrelevance** n Belanglosigkeit f.

irreparable [iˈrepərəbl] adj nicht wiedergutzumachen.

irresistible [ˌiriˈzistəbl] adj unwiderstehlich.

irrespective [ˌiriˈspektiv] adj abgesehen (von), ohne Rücksicht (auf).

irresponsible [ˌiriˈsponsəbl] adj unverantwortlich, verantwortungslos. **irresponsibility** n Unverantwortlichkeit f, Verantwortungslosigkeit f.

irrevocable [iˈrevəkəbl] adj unwiderruflich.

irrigate [ˈirigeit] v bewässern. **irrigation** n Bewässerung f.

irritate [ˈiriteit] v reizen. **irritable** adj reizbar. **irritant** n Reizmittel neut. **irritation** n Reizung f.

Islam [ˈizlɑːm] n Islam m. **Islamic** adj islamisch.

island [ˈailənd] n Insel f. **islander** n Inselbewohner(in).

isolate [ˈaisəleit] v isolieren. **isolated** adj abgesondert; (lonely) einsam. **isolated case** Einzelfall m. **isolation** n Isolierung f; Einsamkeit f. **isolationism** n

Isolationismus *m*.

issue ['ʃuː] *n* Frage *f*; (*newspaper*) Ausgabe *f*; (*offspring*) Nachkommenschaft *f*. *v* ausgeben; (*orders*) erteilen.

isthmus ['ɪsm əs] *n* Landenge *f*.

it [ɪt] *pron* (*nom, acc*) es; (*dat*) ihm.

IT *n* Informationstechnologie *f*.

italic [ɪtalɪk] *adj* kursiv. **italics** *pl n* Kursivschrift *f sing*. **in italics** kursiv gedruckt.

Italy ['ɪtəlɪ] *n* Italien *neut*. **Italian** *adj* italienisch; *n* Italiener(in).

itch [ɪtʃ] *v* jucken. *n* Jucken *neut*.

item ['aɪtəm] *n* Gegenstand *m*; (*on agenda*) Punkt *m*; (*in newspaper*) Artikel *m*. **itemize** *v* verzeichnen.

itinerary [aɪtɪnərərɪ] *n* Reiseplan *m*.

its [ɪts] *poss adj* sein, ihr. **itself** *pron* sich; selbst. **by itself** von selbst.

ivory ['aɪvərɪ] *n* Elfenbein *neut*.

ivy ['aɪvɪ] *n* Efeu *m*.

J

jab [dʒab] *n* Stoß *m*, Stich *m*; (*coll: injection*) Spritze *f*. *v* Stechen.

jack [dʒak] *n* (*mot*) (Wagen)Heber *m*; (*cards*) Bube *m*. **v jack up** aufbocken.

jackal ['dʒakoːl] *n* Schakal *m*.

jackdraw ['dʒakdoː] *n* Dohle *f*.

jacket ['dʒakɪt] *n* Jacke *f*; (*book*) (Schutz)Umschlag *m*.

jack-knife ['dʒaknaɪf] *n* Klappmesser *neut*.

jackpot ['dʒakpot] *n* Jackpot *m*.

jade [dʒeɪd] *n* Nephrit *m*, Jade *m*.

jaded ['dʒeɪdɪd] *adj* erschöpft, abgemattet.

jagged ['dʒagɪd] *adj* zackig.

jaguar ['dʒagjuə] *n* Jaguar *m*.

jail [dʒeɪl] *n* Gefängnis *neut*. *v* ins Gefängnis werfen, einsperren. **jailer** *n* (Gefängnis)Wärter *m*.

jam¹ [dʒam] *v* einklemmen, verstopfen. **jam on the brakes** heftig auf die Bremse treten. **jam-packed** *adj* vollgestopft. *n* Engpaß *m*, Klemme *f*. **traffic jam** (Verkehrs)Stockung *f*, Vorkehrsstau *m*.

jam² [dʒam] *n* Marmelade *f*.

janitor ['dʒanɪtə] *n* Hauswart *m*, Pförtner *m*.

January ['dʒanjuərɪ] *n* Januar *m*.

Japan [dʒə'pan] *n* Japan *neut*. **Japanese** *adj* japanisch; *n* Japaner(in).

jar¹ [dʒaː] *n* Glass *neut*.

jar² [dʒaː] *v* kreischen. **jar on one's nerves** einem auf die Nerven gehen. **jarring** *adj* mißtönend.

jargon ['dʒaːgən] *n* Jargon *m*, Kauderwelsch *neut*.

jasmine ['dʒazm ɪn] *n* Jasmin *m*.

jaundice ['dʒoːndɪs] *n* Gelbsucht *f*. **jaundiced** *adj* gelbsüchtig; (*fig*) neidisch, voreingenommen.

jaunt [dʒoːnt] *n* Ausflug *m*. *v* einen Ausflug machen. **jaunty** *adj* lebhaft, flott.

javelin ['dʒavəlɪn] *n* Speer *m*.

jaw [dʒoː] *n* Kiefer *m*. **jawbone** *n* Kinnbacken *m*.

jazz [dʒaz] *n* Jazz *m*. **jazz band** Jazzkapelle *f*, Jazzband *f*.

jealous ['dʒeləs] *adj* eifersüchtig. **jealousy** *n* Eifersucht *f*.

jeans [dʒiːnz] *pl n* Jeans *pl*.

jeep [dʒiːp] *n* Jeep *m*.

jeer [dʒɪə] *v* spotten. **jeer at** verspotten. **jeering** *adj* höhnisch.

jelly ['dʒelɪ] *n* Gelee *neut*. **jellyfish** *n* Qualle *f*.

jeopardize ['dʒepədaɪz] *v* gefährden. **jeopardy** *n* Gefahr *f*.

jerk [dʒəːk] *v* stoßen, rücken. *n* Ruck *m*, Stoß *m*; (*coll*) Vollidiot *m*. **jerkily** *adv* stoßweise.

jersey ['dʒəːzɪ] *n* Pullover *m*; (*fabric*) Jersey *m*.

Jerusalem [dʒə'ruːsələm] *n* Jerusalem *neut*.

jest [dʒest] *n* Scherz *m*. *v* scherzen. **jesting** *adj* scherzhaft. **jestingly** *adv* in Spaß.

jet [dʒet] *n* (*liquid*) Strahl *m*; (*tech*) Düse *f*; (*aero*) Düsenflugzeug *neut*. **jet-black** *adj* rabenschwarz. **jet engine** Düsenmotor *m*. **jet-propelled** *adj* mit Düsenantrieb.

jettison ['dʒetɪsn] *v* abwerfen; (*discard*) wegwerfen.

jetty ['dʒetɪ] *n* Landungssteg *m*, Mole *f*.

Jew [dʒuː] *n* Jude *m*, Judin *f*. **Jewish** *adj* jüdisch.

jewel ['dʒuːəl] *n* Edelstein *m*, Juwel *neut*; (*fig*) Perle *f*. **jeweller** *n* Juwelier *m*. **jew-**

ellery n Schmuck m.

jig [dʒɪɡ] n Gigue f. v eine Gigue tanzen.

jigsaw [ˈdʒɪɡsɔː] n Puzzlespiel neut, Geduldspiel neut.

jilt [dʒɪlt] v sitzenlassen.

jingle [ˈdʒɪŋɡl] n (sound) Geklingel neut; (radio, etc.) Werbelied neut. v klingeln.

jinx [dʒɪŋks] n Unheil neut. v verhexen.

jittery [ˈdʒɪtəri] adj verängstigt.

job [dʒob] n Arbeit f; (post) Stelle f; (task) Aufgabe f. **jobless** adj arbeitslos.

jockey [ˈdʒoki] n Jockei m.

jocular [ˈdʒokjulə] adj scherzhaft.

jodhpurs [ˈdʒodpəz] pl n Reithose f.

jog [dʒoɡ] v stoßen; (run) trotten. n Stoß m. **jog trot** n Trott m.

join [dʒoin] v verbinden, vereinigen; (club, etc.) beitreten (+ dat). (come together) zusammenkommen. n Verbindungsstelle f; (seam) Naht f. **join in** mitmachen. **joiner** n Tischler m. **joinery** Tischlerarbeit f.

joint [dʒoint] n (anat) Gelenk neut: Verbindung f; (cookery) Braten m; (slang: place) Lokal neut. adj Gesamt-. **jointed** adj gegliedert. **jointly** adv gemeinsam.

joist [dʒoist] n Querbalken m, Träger m.

joke [dʒouk] n Witz m, Scherz m. v scherzen. **joker** n Spaßvogel m; (cards) Joker m. **jokingly** adv im Spaß.

jolly [ˈdʒoli] adj lustig. **jolliness** n Lustigkeit f.

jolt [dʒoult] n Stoß m. v stoßen.

jostle [ˈdʒosl] v anstoßen. n Stoß m.

jot [dʒot] n Jota neut. v **jot down** notieren.

journal [ˈdʒəːnl] n Zeitschrift f; (diary) Tagebuch neut. **journalism** n Zeitungswesen neut. **journalist** n Journalist(in).

journey [ˈdʒəːni] n Reise f. v (ver)reisen.

jovial [ˈdʒouviəl] adj lustig, jovial. **joviality** n Lustigkeit f.

joy [dʒoi] n Freude f, Wonne f. **joyride** v (car) eine Spritztour machen. **joystick** n (aircraft) Steuerknüppel m; (computer games) Joystick m. **joyful** adj erfreut. **joyfulness** n Fröhlichkeit f.

jubilant [ˈdʒuːbilənt] adj jubelnd, frohlockend. **jubilation** n Jubel m, Frohlocken neut.

jubilee [ˈdʒuːbiliː] n Jubiläum neut; (celebration) Jubelfest neut.

Judaism [ˈdʒuːdeiizəm] n Judentum neut.

judge [dʒʌdʒ] n (law) Richter; (expert) Kenner m. v beurteilen; (value) (ein)schätzen. **judgment** n Beurteilung f; (law) Urteil neut.

judicial [dʒuːˈdiʃəl] adj gerichtlich. **judiciary** n Gerichtswesen neut.

judicious [dʒuːˈdiʃəs] adj wohlüberlegt; (reasonable) vernünftig.

judo [ˈdʒuːdou] n Judo neut.

jug [dʒʌɡ] n Krug m, Kanne f.

juggernaut [ˈdʒʌɡənɔːt] n Moloch m; (mot) Fernlastwagen m.

juggle [ˈdʒʌɡl] v jonglieren. **juggler** n Jongleur m.

jugular [ˈdʒʌɡjulə] n Drosselader f.

juice [dʒuːs] n Saft m. **juicy** adj saftig.

jukebox [ˈdʒuːkboks] n Jukebox f.

July [dʒuˈlai] n Juli m.

jumble [ˈdʒʌm bl] n Durcheinander neut. v durcheinander bringen. **jumble sale** Basar m, Ramschverkauf m.

jump [dʒʌm p] n Sprung m. v springen; (be startled) zusammenzucken. **jump at the chance** die Gelegenheit ergreifen. **jumpy** adj nervös.

jumper [ˈdʒʌm pə] n Pullover m.

junction [ˈdʒʌŋkʃən] n (road) Kreuzung f; (rail) Knotenpunkt m.

juncture [ˈdʒʌŋkʃə] n Augenblick m. **at this juncture** an dieser Stelle, zu dieser Zeit.

June [dʒuːn] n Juni m.

jungle [ˈdʒʌŋɡl] n Dschungel m.

junior [ˈdʒuːniə] adj junior, jünger. **junior school** Grundschule f.

juniper [ˈdʒuːnipə] n Wacholder m.

junk¹ [dʒʌŋk] n Trödel m. **junk food** Fastfood neut. **junk mail** (comp) unerwünschte E-mail. **junk shop** Trödelladen m.

junk² [dʒʌŋk] n (naut) Dschunke f.

junta [ˈdʒʌntə] n Junta f.

Jupiter [ˈdʒuːpitə] n Jupiter m.

jurisdiction [dʒuərisˈdikʃən] n Gerichtsbarkeit f.

jury [ˈdʒuəri] n die Geschworene pl; (quiz, etc.) Jury f. **trial by jury** Schwurgerichtsverhandlung f. **juror** n Geschworene(r).

just [dʒʌst] adv (recently) gerade, eben; (only) nur; (exactly) genau. **just about** so ungefähr. **just as good** ebenso gut. **just a little** ein ganz klein wenig. *adj* gerecht.

justly *adv* mit Recht, gerecht.

justice ['dʒʌstɪs] *n* Gerechtigkeit *f*; (*judge*) Richter *m*. **Justice of the Peace** Friedensrichter *m*.

justify ['dʒʌstɪfaɪ] *v* rechtfertigen. **justification** *n* Rechtfertigung *f*. **justifiable** *adj* berechtigt.

jut [dʒʌt] *v* **jut out** hervorragen.

jute [dʒuːt] *n* Jute *f*.

juvenile ['dʒuːvənaɪl] *adj* jugendlich. **juvenile court** Jugendgericht *neut*. **juvenile delinquent** jugendlicher Straftäter *m*. **juvenile delinquency** Jugendkriminalität *f*.

juxtapose [ˌdʒʌkstə'pouz] *v* nebeneinanderstellen.

K

kaleidoscope [kə'laɪdəskoup] *n* Kaleidoskop *neut*.

kangaroo [kaŋgə'ruː] *n* Känguruh *neut*.

karate [kə'raːti] *n* Karate *neut*.

kebab [kɪbab] *n* Kebab *m*.

keel [kiːl] *n* Kiel *m*.

keen [kiːn] *adj* (*sharp*) scharf; (*hearing*) fein; (*enthusiastic*) eifrig. **keenness** *n* Eifer *f*.

*****keep** [kiːp] *v* halten, behalten; haben; (*remain*) bleiben; (*preserve, store*) aufbewahren; (*of food*) sich halten; (*support*) versorgen. **keep away** fernhalten. **keep fit** sich gesund erhalten. **keep in mind** im Gedächtnis behalten. **keep on** fortfahren. **keep out!** Eintritt verboten! **keep up with** Schritt halten mit. **keeper** *n* Wächter *m*; (*animals*) Züchter *m*. **be in keeping with** passen zu. **keepsake** *n* Andenken *neut*.

keg [keg] *n* Faß *neut*.

kennel ['kenl] *n* Hundehütte *f*.

kept [kept] *V* **keep**.

kerb [kəːb] *n* Straßenkante *f*.

kernel ['kəːnl] *n* Kern *m*.

kerosene ['kerəsiːn] *n* Petroleum *neut*.

ketchup ['ketʃəp] *n* Ketchup *m*.

kettle ['ketl] *n* Kessel *m*. **kettledrum** *n* Pauke *f*. **a pretty kettle of fish** eine

schöne Bescherung. **a different kettle of fish** was ganz anderes.

key [kiː] *n* Schlüssel *m*; (*piano, typewriter*) Taste *f*; (*music*) Tonart *f*. **keyboard** *n* Tastatur *f*. **keyring** *n* Schlüsselring *m*. **key in** (*comp*) eintasten.

khaki ['kaːki] *adj* khaki.

kick [kɪk] *v* mit dem Fuß treten *or* stoßen. *n* Fußtritt *m*; (*football*) Schuß *m*; (*fig*) Schwung *m*. **kick-off** *n* Anstoß *m*. **kick off** anstoßen.

kid[1] [kɪd] *n* (*goat*) Zicklein *neut*; (*leather*) Ziegenleder *neut*; (*child*) Kind *neut*.

kid[2] [kɪd] *v* (*coll*) auf den Arm nehmen.

kidnap ['kɪdnap] *v* entführen. **kidnapper** *n* Entführer *m*, Kidnapper *m*.

kidney ['kɪdni] *n* Niere *f*. **kidney bean** weiße Bohne *f*. **kidney stone** Nierenstein *m*.

kill [kɪl] *v* töten, umbringen; (*animals*) schlachten. **kill oneself laughing** sich totlachen. **killer** *n* Mörder *m*. **killing** *n* Tötung *f*. *adj* tötend.

kiln [kɪln] *n* Brennofen *m*.

kilo ['kiːlou] *n* Kilo *neut*.

kilobyte ['kɪləbaɪt] *n* Kilobyte *neut*.

kilogram ['kɪlɡram] *n* Kilogramm *neut*.

kilometre ['kɪləmiːtə] *n* Kilometer *m*.

kin [kɪn] *n* Verwandte *pl*. **next of kin** nächste(r) Verwandte(r).

kind[1] [kaɪnd] *adj* freundlich, gütig. **kindly** *adj* gütig. **kindness** *n* Güte *f*.

kind[2] [kaɪnd] *n* Sorte *f*, Art *f*; (*species*) Gattung *f*. **all kinds of** allerlei. **in kind** in Waren.

kindergarten ['kɪndəɡaːtn] *n* Kindergarten *m*, Krippe *f*.

kindle ['kɪndl] *v* entzünden.

kindly ['kaɪndli] *adv* freundlicherweise. **Will you kindly shut the door!** Seien Sie bitte so gut, die Tür zu schließen!

kindred ['kɪndrɪd] *n* Verwandtschaft *f*.

kinetic [kɪn'etik] *adj* kinetisch. **kinetics** *n* Kinetik *f*.

king [kɪŋ] *n* König *m*. **kingdom** *n* Königreich *neut*. **animal kingdom** Tierreich *neut*. **king-size(d)** *adj* übergroß, riesengroß.

kink [kɪŋk] *n* Knick *m*. *v* knicken.

kiosk ['kiɔsk] *n* Kiosk *m*. **telephone kiosk** Telephonzelle *f*.

kipper ['kɪpə] *n* Bückling *m*, Räucherhering *m*.

kiss [kɪs] n Kuß m, Küßchen neut. v küssen. **kiss goodbye** einen Abschiedskuß geben (+dat). **kiss my arse!** (impol) Du kannst mich....

kit [kɪt] n Ausrüstung f; (mil) Gepäck neut.

kitchen ['kɪtʃin] n Küche f. **kitchenette** n Kochnische f.

kite [kaɪt] n Drachen m; (bird) Gabelweihe f.

kitten ['kɪtn] n Kätzchen neut.

kitty ['kɪti] n Kasse f.

kleptomaniac [kleptə'meɪniak] n Kleptomane m.

knack [nak] n Kniff m, Trick m. **get the knack of** den Dreh heraushaben (+ gen).

knapsack ['napsak] n Rucksack m.

knave [neɪv] n Schurke m; (cards) Bube m.

knead [niːd] v kneten.

knee [niː] n Knie neut. **kneecap** n Knieschiebe f.

*kneel [niːl] v knien.

knelt [nelt] V **kneel**.

knew [njuː] V **know**.

knickers ['nɪkəz] pl n Schlüpfer m sing; Höschen neut sing.

knife [naɪf] n Messer neut. v (er)stechen.

knight [naɪt] n Ritter m; (chess) Springer m. **knighthood** Rittertum neut. **knightly** adj ritterlich.

*knit [nɪt] v stricken; (brow) rünzein. **knitted** adj Strick-. **knitting** n Strickzeug neut. **knitting needle** Stricknadel f. **knitwear** n Strickwaren pl.

knob [nob] n Knopf m, Griff m.

knobbly ['nobli] adj knorrig.

knock [nok] v (strike) schlagen; (on door) klopfen; (criticize) heruntermachen. n Schlag m; Klopfen neut. **knock off** (coll: steal) klauen; (work) Feierabend machen. **knock out** k.o. schlagen.

knot [not] n Knoten m; (in wood) Ast m. v knoten.

*know [nou] v wissen; (be acquainted with) kennen; (know how to) können; (understand) verstehen. **know-all** n Besserwisser m, (vulg) Klugscheißer m. **know-how** n Knowhow neut. **knowing** adj geschickt; (sly) schlau. **knowingly** adv absichtlich. **be in the know** Bescheid wissen. **known** adj bekannt.

knowledge ['nolidʒ] n Kenntnis f. **knowledgeable** adj kenntnisreich.

known [noun] V **know**.

knuckle ['nʌkl] n Fingerknöchel m. **knuckle down** eifrig herangehen. **knuckle under** nachgeben.

L

label ['leɪbl] n Zettel m; (sticky) Klebezettel neut; (luggage) Anhängezettel neut. v mit einem Zettel versehen; (fig) bezeichnen.

laboratory [ə'borətəri] n Labor neut. **laboratory assistant** Laborant(in).

labour ['leɪbə] n Arbeit; (work-force) Arbeitskräfte pl; (birth) Wehen pl. v (schwer) arbeiten, sich anstrengen. **laboured** adj schwerfällig; (style) mühsam. **labourer** n (ungelernter) Arbeiter m.

laburnum [lə'bəːnəm] n Goldregen m.

labyrinth ['labərinθ] n Labyrinth neut.

lace [leɪs] n Spitze f; (shoe) Schnur f. v schnüren. **lacy** adj Spitzen-.

lacerate ['lasəreɪt] v zerreißen. **laceration** n Zerreißung f.

lack [lak] v mangeln (an). n Mangel m. **be lacking** fehlen.

lackadaisical [lakə'deɪzikl] adj schlapp.

lacquer ['lakə] n Lack m. v lackieren.

lad [lad] n Junge m, Bursche m.

ladder ['ladə] n Leiter f; (stocking) Laufmasche f. **ladder-resistant** adj maschenfest.

laden ['leɪdn] adj beladen.

ladle ['leɪdl] n Schöpflöffel m. v ausschöpfen.

lady ['leɪdi] n Dame f. **Ladies** n (sign) Damen pl. **ladies' man** Frauenheld m. **ladybird** Marienkäfer m. **lady-in-waiting** n Hofdame f. **ladylike** adj damenhaft.

lag¹ [lag] v **lag behind** zurückbleiben. n Zeitabstand m.

lag² [lag] v (cover) verkleiden.

lager ['laːgə] n Lagerbier neut.

lagoon [lə'guːn] n Lagune f.

laid [leɪd] V **lay¹**.

lain [leɪn] V **lie²**.

lair [leə] n Lager neut.

laity ['leɪti] n Laienstand m.

lake [leɪk] n (Binnen) See m.

lamb [læm] n Lamm neut; (meat) Lammfleisch neut.

lame [leɪm] adj lahm, hinkend; (excuse) schwach. v lahm machen. **lameness** n Lahmheit f; Schwäche f.

lament [ə'ment] v (weh)klagen; (regret) bedauern. n Klagelied neut. **lamentable** adj beklagenswert; bedauerlich. **lamentation** n Jammer m.

laminate ['læmɪneɪt] v schichten. **laminated** adj beschichtet.

lamp [læmp] n Lampe f; (street) Laterne f. **lamplight** n Lampenlicht neut. **lamp-post** n Laternenpfahl m. **lampshade** n Lampenschirm m.

lance [lɑːns] n Lanze f. v (med) mit einer Lanzette eröffnen, aufstechen. **lance corporal** n Hauptgefreiter(r) m.

land [lænd] n Land neut. v an Land gehen; (aircraft) landen; (goods) abladen. **landing** n Landung f; (stairs) Treppenabsatz m. **landing craft** Landungsboot neut. **landing stage** Landesteg m.

landlady ['lændleɪdɪ] n Wirtin f.

landlord ['lændlɔːd] n (Gast-)Wirt m.

landmark ['lændmɑːk] n Wahrzeichen neut; (milestone) Markstein m.

landowner ['lændəʊnə] n Grundbesitzer m.

landscape ['lændskeɪp] n Landschaft f. **landscape gardener** Kunstgärtner m. **landscape gardening** Kunstgärtnerei f. **landscape painter** Landschaftsmaler(in).

landslide ['lændslaɪd] n Erdrutsch m; (pol) Erdrutschsieg m. adj (pol) überwältigend.

lane [leɪn] n (country) (Feld) Weg m, Pfad m; (town) Gasse f; (mot) Spur f. (sport) Rennbahn f.

language ['læŋgwɪdʒ] n Sprache f; (style) Stil m, Redeweise f. **bad language** Schimpfworte pl. **foreign language** Fremdsprache f.

languish ['læŋgwɪʃ] v schmachten.

lanky ['læŋkɪ] adj schlaksig.

lantern ['læntən] n Laterne f.

lap¹ [læp] n (anat) Schoß m; (circuit) Runde f. **laptop** n (comp) Laptop m.

lap² [læp] v (drink) auflecken.

lapel [ə'pel] n Revers m or neut.

lapse [læps] n Versehen neut; (mistake) Irrtum m; (time) Zeitspanne f. v (time) vergehen; (from faith) abfallen.

larceny ['lɑːsənɪ] n Diebstahl m.

larch [lɑːtʃ] n Lärche f.

lard [lɑːd] n Schmalz neut. v spicken. **larding needle** Sticknadel f.

larder ['lɑːdə] n Speisekammer f.

large [lɑːdʒ] adj groß; (considerable) beträchtlich. **at large** auf freiem Fuß m. **large as life** in Lebensgröße. **large-scale** adj Groß-. **largesse** n Freigebigkeit f. **largely** adv weightened. **largeness** n Größe f.

lark¹ [lɑːk] n (bird) Lerche f.

lark² [lɑːk] n Spaß m. v **lark about** Possen treiben.

larva ['lɑːvə] n Larve f. **larval** adj Larven-.

larynx ['lærɪŋks] n Kehlkopf m. **laryngitis** n Kehlkopfentzündung f.

laser ['leɪzə] n Laser m. **laser beam** Laserstrahl m. **laser printer** Laserdrucker m.

lash [læʃ] v (whip) peitschen; (tie) festbinden. n Peitschenschnur f; (eyelash) Wimper f. **lash out** ausschlagen.

lass [læs] n Mädchen neut, Mädel neut.

lassitude ['læsɪtjuːd] n Mattigkeit f.

lasso [læ'suː] n Lasso m. v mit einem Lasso fangen.

last [lɑːst] adj letzt. **at last** endlich, schließlich. **last but not least** nicht zuletzt. **last year** im vorigen Jahr. adv also **lastly** zuletzt. v (time) dauern; (supply) ausreichen; (be preserved) (gut) halten. **lasting** adj anhaltend, dauernd.

latch [lætʃ] n Klinke f. v einklinken. **latch onto** (understand) spitzkriegen.

late [leɪt] adj spät; (tardy) verspätet; (decreased) selig; (former) ehemalig. **be late** Verspätung haben. **lately** adv neuerdings. **lateness** n Verspätung f. **later** adj später. **latest** adj spätest; (newest) neuest. **at the latest** spätestens.

latent ['leɪtənt] adj latent.

lateral ['lætərəl] adj seitlich. **laterally** adv seitwärts.

lathe [leɪð] n Drehbank f.

lather ['lɑːðə] n Seifenschaum m. v schäumen; (beat) verprügeln.

Latin ['lætɪn] adj lateinisch. n Latein neut.

Latin America n Lateinamerika neut. **Latin-American** adj lateinamerikanisch.

latitude ['lætɪtjuːd] n Breite f; (fig) Spielraum m. **latitudinal** adj Breiten-.

latrine [lə'triːn] n Klosett neut, Latrine f.

latter ['lætə] *adj* letzt. **latterly** *adv* neuerdings.

lattice ['lætɪs] *n* Gitter *neut*. (*pattern*) Gitterwerk *neut*.

Latvia ['lætvɪə] *n* Lettland *neut*. **Latvian** *n* Lette *m*, Lettin *f*; *adj* lettisch.

laugh [lɑːf] *v* lachen. **laugh at** sich lustig machen über. **laugh off** mit einem Scherz abtun. **laughable** *adj* lächerlich. *n* Lachen *neut*. **laughter** Gelächter *neut*.

launch [lɔːntʃ] *n* (*boat*) Barkasse *f*; (*of boat*) Stapellauf *m*; (*of rocket*) Abschuß *m*; (*start*) Start *m*. *v* (*boat*) vom Stapel lassen; (*fig*) in Gang setzen.

launder ['lɔːndə] *v* waschen. **launderette** *n* Waschsalon *m*. **laundry** *n* Wäscherei *f*; (*washing*) Wäsche *f*.

laurel ['lɒrəl] *n* Lorbeer *m*.

lava ['lɑːvə] *n* Lava *f*.

lavatory ['lævətərɪ] *n* Klosett *neut*, Toilette *f*.

lavender ['lævɪndə] *n* Lavendel *m*. *adj* (*colour*) lavendelfarben.

lavish ['lævɪʃ] *adj* verschwenderisch. **lavishness** *n* Verschwendung *f*.

law [lɔː] *n* (*single law*) Gesetz *neut*; (*system*) Recht *neut*; (*study*) Jura *pl*. **law-abiding** *adj* friedlich. **law court** Gerichtshof *m*. **lawful** *adj* rechtsmäßig, gesetzlich. **lawless** *adj* gesetzwidrig. **lawsuit** *n* Prozeß *m*. **lawyer** *n* Rechtsanwalt *m*

lawn [lɔːn] *n* Rasen *m*; (*fabric*) Batist *m*. **lawnmower** *n* Rasenmäher *m* **lawn tennis** Tennis *neut*.

lax [læks] *n* locker.

laxative ['læksətɪv] *n* Abführmittel *neut*.

*lay¹ [leɪ] *v* legen; (*put down*) setzen, stellen; (*table*) decken. **laid-back** *adj* gelassen, locker. **lay down** hinlegen; (*law*) vorschreiben. **lay off** (*dismiss*) entlassen.

lay² [leɪ] *adj* Laien-. **layman** *n* Laie *m*.

lay-by ['leɪbaɪ] *n* Parkstreifen *m*.

layer ['leɪə] *n* Schicht *f*.

lazy ['leɪzɪ] *adj* faul. **laze** *v* faulenzen. **laziness** *n* Faulheit *f*. **lazybones** *n* Faulpelz *m*.

*lead¹ [liːd] *v* leiten, führen. **leader** *n* Führer *m*, **Leiten** *m*; (*in newspaper*) Leitartikel *m*. **leadership** *n* Führerschaft *f*. **leading** *adj* führend, Haupt-. *n* (*dog's*) Leine *f*; (*theatre*) Hauptrolle *f*; (*cable*) Schnur *f*; (*hint*) Hinweis *m*.

lead² [led] *n* Blei *neut*; (*in pencil*) Bleistiftmine *f*.

leaf [liːf] *n* Blatt *neut*. **leaflet** *n* (*pamphlet*) Prospekt *m*. *v* **leaf through** durchblättern. **leafy** *adj* belaubt.

league [liːg] *n* (*association*) Bund *neut*; (*sport*) Liga *f*.

leak [liːk] *n* Leck *neut*; (*pol*) Durchsickern *neut*. *v* lecken; durchsickern. **leakage** *n* Lecken *neut*. **leaky** *adj* leck.

*lean¹ [liːn] *v* (*sich*) lehnen. **lean on** sich stützen auf; (*rely on*) sich verlassen auf. **learning** *n* Neigung *f*.

lean² [liːn] *adj* mager.

leant [lent] *V* **lean¹**.

*leap [liːp] *v* hüpfen, springen. *n* Sprung *m*. **look before you leap** erst wägen, dann wagen. **by leaps and bounds** sprunghaft. **leapfrog** *n* Bockspringen *neut*. **leap year** Schaltjahr *neut*.

leapt [lept] *V* **leap**.

*learn [lɜːn] *v* lernen; (*find out*) erfahren. **learned** *adj* gelehrt. **learner** *n* Anfänger *m*; (*driver*) Fahrschüler(in). **learning** *n* Wissen *neut*.

learnt [lɜːnt] *V* **learn**.

lease [liːs] *n* Mietvertrag *m*, Pachtvertrag *m*. *v* (ver)mieten, pachten. **leaseholder** *n* Pächter(in).

leash [liːʃ] *n* Leine *f*.

least [liːst] *adj* (*smallest*) kleinst; (*slightest*) geringst. **at least** mindestens. **not in the lest** nicht im geringsten.

leather ['leðə] *n* Leder *neut*. *adj* ledern. **leathery** *adj* lederartig.

*leave¹ [liːv] *v* verlassen, lassen; (*go away*) (ab-, ver)reisen, weggehen. **leave off** aufhören. **leave out** auslassen. **left-luggage office** Gepäckaufbewahrung *f*.

leave² [liːv] *n* (*permission*) Erlaubnis *f*; (*holiday*) Urlaub *m*. **take one's leave of** Abschied nehmen von.

lecherous ['letʃərəs] *adj* wollustig. **lechery** *n* Wollust *f*.

lectern ['lektən] *n* Lesepult *neut*.

lecture ['lektʃə] *n* Vortrag *m*, Vorlesung *f*. *v* einen Vortrag halten. **lecture** *n* Dozent *m*. **lecture hall** Hörsaal *m*.

led [led] *V* **lead¹**.

ledge [ledʒ] *n* Sims *m* or *neut*.

ledger ['ledʒə] *n* Hauptbuch *neut*.

lee [liː] *n* (*naut*) Leeseite *f*.

leech [liːtʃ] *n* Blutegel *m*.

leek [liːk] *n* Porree *m*.

leer [lɪə] *n* anzügliches Grinsen. *v* anzüglich grinsen.

leeway ['liːweɪ] *n* Abtrift *f*; *fig* Spielraum *m*.

left¹ [left] *V* **leave¹**.

left² [left] *adj* link. *adv* (nach) links. **on the left** links. **left-handed** *adj* linkshändig. **left-wing** *adj* Links-.

leg [leg] *n* Bein *neut*; *(cookery)* Keule *f*; *(sports)* Lauf *m*. **be on one's last legs** auf dem letzten Loch pfeifen. **leggy** *adj* langbeinig.

legacy ['legəsɪ] *n* Legat *neut*.

legal ['liːgəl] *adj* gesetzlich, rechtlich. **legality** *n* Gesetzlichkeit *f*. **legalize** *v* legalisieren.

legend ['ledʒənd] *n* Sage *f*, Legende *f*. **legendary** *adj* sagenhaft, legendär.

legible ['ledʒəbl] *adj* leserlich. **legibility** *n* Leserlichkeit *f*.

legion ['liːdʒən] *n* Legion *f*. **legionary** *n* Legionär *m*.

legislate ['ledʒɪsleɪt] *v* Gesetze geben. **legislation** *n* Gesetzgebung *f*. **legislative** *adj* gesetzgebend. **legislator** *n* Gesetzgeber *m*.

legitimate [lə'dʒɪtɪmət] *adj* rechtmäßig; *(child)* ehelich; *(justified)* berechtigt. **legitimacy** *n* Rechtmäßigkeit; Ehelichkeit *f*.

leisure ['leʒə] *n* Freizeit *f*. **leisurely** *adv* ohne Hast; *adj* gemächlich.

lemon ['lemən] *n* Zitrone *f*. *adj* zitronengelb. **lemonade** *n* Zitronenlimonade *f*. **lemon squeezer** Zitronenpresse *f*.

***lend** [lend] *v* (ver)leihen. **lend a hand** helfen. **lending library** Leihbibliothek *f*.

length [leŋθ] *n* Länge *f*; *(of cloth)* Stück *neut*; *(time)* Dauer *f*. **at length** *(in detail)* ausführlich; *(at last)* schließlich. **lengthen** *v* (sich) verlängern. **lengthways** *adv* längs. **lengthy** *adj* übermäßig lang.

lenient ['liːnɪənt] *adj* nachsichtig (gegenüber). **leniency** Nachsicht *f*.

lens [lenz] *n* Linse *f*; *(photographic)* Objektiv *neut*.

lent [lent] *V* **lend**.

Lent [lent] *n* Fastenzeit *f*.

lentil ['lentɪl] *n* Linse *f*.

Leo ['liːou] *n* Löwe *m*. **leonine** *adj* Löwen-.

leopard ['lepəd] *n* Leopard *m*.

leper ['lepə] *n* Leprakranke(r). **leprosy** *n* Lepra *f*.

lesbian ['lezbɪən] *adj* lesbisch. *n* Lesbierin *f*.

less [les] *adv* weniger. *adj* geringer. *prep* minus. **lessen** *v* (sich) vermindern. **lesser** *adj* kleiner, geringer.

lesson ['lesn] *n* *(in school)* Stunde *f*; *(warning)* Warnung *f*. **lessons** *pl* Unterricht *m sing*.

lest [lest] *conj* damit ... nicht.

***let** [let] *v* lassen; *(rooms, etc.)* vermieten. **let's go** gehen wir. **let alone** *(not annoy)* in Ruhe lassen; *(much less)* geschweige denn **let down** enttäuschen, im Stich lassen. **let go** gehen lassen. **let go of** loslassen. **let up** *(coll)* nachlassen.

lethal ['liːθəl] *adj* tödlich.

lethargy ['leθədʒɪ] *n* Lethargie *f*. **lethargic** *adj* lethargisch.

letter ['letə] *n* Brief *m*; *(of alphabet)* Buchstabe *m*. **letter box** Briefkasten *m*.

lettuce ['letɪs] *n* Kopfsalat *m*.

leukaemia [luː'kiːmɪə] *n* Leukämie *f*.

level ['levl] *adj* gerade, eben; *(equal)* gleich. **level crossing** Bahnübergang *m*. **level-headed** *adj* nüchtern. **draw level with** einholen; *v* ebnen; *(make equal)* gleichmachen. *n* Ebene *f*, Niveau *neut*.

lever ['liːvə] *n* Hebel *m*.

levy ['levɪ] *n* Abgabe *f*. *v* erheben.

lewd [luːd] *adj* lüstern. **lewdness** *n* Lüsternheit *f*.

liable ['laɪəbl] *adj* *(responsible)* verantwortlich. **be liable to** neigen zu. **liability** *n* Verantwortlichkeit. **limited liability** *(comm)* mit beschränkter Haftung. **be liable for** haften für. **liable to prosecution** strafbar.

liaise [lɪ'eɪz] *v* sich (mit jemandem) in Verbindung setzen.

liaison [lɪ'eɪzɒn] *n* Verbindung *f*; *(love affair)* (Liebes)Verhältnis *neut*.

liar ['laɪə] *n* Lügner(in).

libel ['laɪbl] *n* Verleumdung *f*. *v* *(schriftlich)* verleumden. **libellous** *adj* verleumderisch.

liberal ['lɪbərəl] *adj* liberal; *(generous)* großzügig. *n* Liberale(r). **liberalize** *v* liberalisieren.

liberate ['lɪbəreɪt] *v* befreien. **liberation** *n* Befreiung *f*. **liberator** *n* Befreier *m*.

liberty ['lɪbətɪ] *n* Freiheit *f*. **at liberty** frei.

Libra ['liːbrə] *n* Waage *f*.

library ['laɪbrərɪ] *n* Bibliothek *f*, Bücherei *f*. **librarian** *n* Bibliothekar(in).

libretto [lɪ'bretou] *n* Libretto *neut*,

Textbuch *neut*.

lice [laɪs] *V* louse.

licence ['laɪsəns] *n* Genehmigung *f*, Lizenz *f*. **driving licence** Führerschein *m*. **marriage licence** Eheerlaubnis *f*. **license** *v* genehmigen. **licensed** *adj* konzessioniert.

lichen ['laɪkən] *n* Flechte *f*.

lick [lɪk] *v* lecken; (*coll: defeat*) besiegen; (*flames*) züngeln. *n* Lecken *neut*.

lid [lɪd] *n* Deckel *m*; (*eyelid*) Lid *neut*.

lie¹ [laɪ] *n* Lüge *f*. *v* lügen.

*lie² [laɪ] *v* liegen. **lie down** sich hinlegen. **lie in** (*coll*) sich ausschlafen.

lieutenant [əftenənt] *n* Leutnant *m*.

life [laɪf] *n* Leben *neut*. **lifebelt** *n* Rettungsgürtel *m*. **lifebuoy** *n* Rettungsgurt *m*. **lifeboat** *n* Rettungsboot *neut*. **lifeguard** *n* Bademeister *m*. **life insurance** Lebensversicherung *f*. **life jacket** Schwimmweste *f*. **lifeless** *adj* leblos. **lifelike** *adj* naturgetreu. **life-size** *adj* lebensgroß. **lifestyle** *n* Lebensstil *m*, Lebensweise *f*. **lifetime** *n* Lebenszeit *f*.

lift [lɪft] *n* Aufzug *m*, Fahrstuhl *m*. *v* (auf)heben. **give a lift to** (im Auto) mitnehmen.

*light¹ [laɪt] *n* Licht *neut*; (*lamp*) Lampe *f*; (*for cigarette*) Feuer *neut*. *v* anzünden.

light² [laɪt] *adj* leicht; (*colour*) hell.

lighten¹ ['laɪtn] *v* (*reduce weight*) erleichtern, leichter machen.

lighten² ['laɪtn] *v* (*brighten*) sich erhellen, heller werden.

lighter ['laɪtə] *n* (*cigarette*) Feuerzeug *neut*.

lighthouse ['laɪthaus] *n* Leuchtturm *m*.

lighting ['laɪtɪŋ] *n* Beleuchtung *f*.

lightning ['laɪtnɪŋ] *n* Blitz *m*. **lightning conductor** Blitzableiter *m*. **flash of lightning** Blitzschlag *m*.

light ['laɪtweɪt] weight *adj* leicht. *n* Leichtgewichtler *m*.

light-year ['laɪtjə] *n* Lichtjahr *neut*.

like¹ [laɪk] *adj* gleich (+*dat*), ähnlich (+*dat*). *prep* wie. *what's it like?* wie ist es? **like-minded** *adj* gleichgesinnt. **likewise** *adv* gleichfalls.

like² [laɪk] *v* gern haben; mögen. *do you like it? gefällt es Ihnen?* (*food*) schmeckst (Ihnen). **likeable** *adj* liebenswürdig. **liking** *n* Zuneigung *f*; (*taste*) Geschmack *m*.

likely ['laɪkli] *adj* wahrscheinlich. **likelihood** *n* Wahrscheinliehkeit *f*.

lilac ['laɪlək] *n* (*colour*) Lila *neut*. *adj* lilafarben.

lily ['lɪli] *n* Lilie *f*.

limb [lɪm] *n* Glied *neut*. **limbs** *pl* Gliedmaßen *pl*.

limbo ['lɪm bou] *n* (*rel*) Vorhölle *f*. **in limbo** (*fig*) in der Schwebe, in Vergessenheit.

lime¹ [laɪm] *n* (*mineral*) Kalk *neut*.

lime² [laɪm] *n* (*tree*) Linde *f*, Lindenbaum *m*; (*fruit*) Limonelle *f*.

limit ['lɪmit] *n* Grenze *f*, Schranke *f*. *v* begrenzen, beschränken. **limited** *adj* beschränkt; (*comm*) mit beschränkter Haftung.

limousine ['lɪm ə,zɪn] *n* Limousine *f*.

limp¹ [lɪm p] *v* hinken. *n* Hinken *neut*.

limp² [lɪm p] *adj* schlaff.

line [laɪn] *n* Linie *f*, Strich *m*; (*row*) Reihe *f*; (*of print*) Zeile *f*; (*washing*) Leine *f*; (*wrinkle*) Falte *f*. *v* linieren; (*coat, etc.*) füttern. **lineage** *n* Abstammung *f*. **linear** *adj* Linear-.

linen ['lɪnin] *n* Leinen *neut*. **bed linen** Wäsche *f*.

liner ['laɪnə] *n* (*ship*) Linienschiff *neut*, Überseedampfer *m*.

linesman ['laɪnzm an] *n* Linienrichter *m*.

linger ['lɪŋgə] *v* verweilen. **lingering** *adj* (*illness*) schleichend.

lingerie ['læʒərɪ] *n* (Damen)Unterwäsche *f*.

linguist ['lɪŋgwist] *n* Linguist(in). **linguistic** *adj* linguistisch. **linguistics** *n* Linguistik *f*.

lining ['laɪnɪŋ] *n* Futter *neut*, Fütterung *f*.

link [lɪŋk] *n* (*of chain*) Glied *neut*; (*connection*) Verbindung *f*. *v* verbinden. **link arms** sich einhaken (bei).

linoleum [lɪnouləm] *n* Linoleum *neut*.

linseed ['lɪn,sɪd] *n* Leinsamen *m*. **linseed oil** Leinöl *neut*.

lint [lɪnt] *n* Zupfleinen *neut*.

lion ['laɪən] *n* Löwe *m*. **lioness** *n* Löwin *f*. **lion's share** Löwenanteil *m*.

lip [lɪp] *n* Lippe *f*; (*edge*) Rand *m*; (*coll: impudence*) Frechheit *f*. **lip service** Lippendienst *m*. **lipstick** *n* Lippenstift *m*.

liqueur [lɪkjuə] *n* Likör *m*.

liquid ['lɪkwid] *n* Flüssigkeit *f*. *adj* flüssig. **liquidate** *v* (*comm*) liquidieren. **liquidation** *n* Liquidierung *f*. **liquidator** *n* Liquidator *m*. **liquidity** *n* Flüssigkeit *f*.

liquor ['lɪkə] *n* alkoholisches Getränk *neut*.

liquorice ['lɪkərɪs] n Lakritze f.

lisp [lɪsp] n Lispeln neut. v lispeln.

list[1] [lɪst] n Liste f, Verzeichnis neut. v verzeichnen.

list[2] [lɪst] n (naut) Schlagseite f. v Schlagseite haben.

listen ['lɪsn] v hören auf, zuhören (+dat). **listener** n Zuhörer m. **listening device** Abhörgerät neut.

listless ['lɪstlɪs] adj lustlos.

lit [lɪt] V **light**[1].

litany ['lɪtəni] n Litanei f.

literacy ['lɪtərəsi] n die Fähigkeit, lesen und schreiben zu können f. **literate** adj gelehrt. **be literate** lesen und schreiben können.

literal ['lɪtərəl] adj buchstäblich.

literary ['lɪtərəri] adj literarisch.

literature ['lɪtrətʃə] n Literatur f.

lithe [laɪð] adj geschmeidig.

Lithuania [ˌlɪθjuˈeɪnjə] n Litauen neut. **Lithuanian** n Litauer(in); adj litauisch.

litigation [ˌlɪtiˈgeɪʃən] n Prozeß m.

litre ['lɪtə] n Liter neut.

litter ['lɪtə] n (rubbish) Abfall m; (stretcher) Tragbahre f; (animals) Wurf m. **litter bin** Abfallkorb m.

little ['lɪtl] adj klein. adv wenig. **a little** ein bißchen, ein wenig.

liturgy ['lɪtədʒi] n Liturgie f.

live[1] [lɪv] v leben; (reside) wohnen.

live[2] [laɪv] adj (alive) lebendig; (radio, etc.) live; (electricity) stromführend. **live broadcast** Livesendung f.

livelihood ['laɪvlihud] n Lebensunterhalt m.

lively ['laɪvli] adj lebhaft. **liveliness** n Lebhaftigkeit f.

liver ['lɪvə] n Leber f.

livestock ['laɪvstok] n Vieh neut.

livid ['lɪvid] adj (coll: angry) wütend.

living ['lɪvɪŋ] adj lebendig, am Leben. n Lebensunterhalt m. **make a living** sein Brot verdienen. **living room** Wohnzimmer neut.

lizard ['lɪzəd] n Eidechse f.

load [loud] n Last f, Belastung f. v (be)laden.

loaf[1] [louf] n Laib m, Brot neut.

loaf[2] [louf] v **loaf around** faulenzen. **loafer** n Bummler m, Faulenzer m.

loan [loun] n Anleihe f; (credit) Darlehen neut. v leihen.

loathe [louð] v hassen, nicht ausstehen können. **loathing** n Abscheu m. **loathsome** adj abscheulich.

lob [lob] v (sport) lobben. n Lob m.

lobby ['lobi] n Vorhalle f; (pol) Interessengruppe f.

lobe [loub] n Lappen m.

lobster ['lobstə] n Hummer m.

local ['loukəl] adj örtlich, Orts-. n Ortsbewohner m. **local government** Gemeindeverwaltung f. **locality** n Ort m. **localize** v lokalisieren.

locate [ləˈkeɪt] v ausfindig machen. **location** n Standort m.

lock[1] [lok] n Schloß neut; (canal) Schleuse f. v verschließen. **lock in** einsperren. **lock out** aussperren. **lock up** verschließen.

lock[2] [lok] n (of hair) Locke f.

locker ['lokə] n Schließfach neut.

locket ['lokit] n Medaillon neut.

locomotive [ˌloukəˈmoutiv] n Lokomotive f, Lok f.

locust ['loukəst] n Heuschrecke f.

lodge [lodʒ] v (a person) unterbringen; (complaint) einreichen. n (hunting) Jagdhütte f. **lodger** n Untermieter m. **lodgings** pl Wohnung f sing, Zimmer neut sing.

loft [loft] n (Dach)Boden m. **lofty** adj hoch.

log [log] n Klotz m; (naut) Log neut. v (naut) loggen, ins Logbuch eintragen. **log off** (comp) sich ausloggen. **log on** (comp) sich einloggen.

logarithm ['logərəðəm] n Logarithmus m.

loggerheads ['logəhedz] pl n **be at loggerheads with** in den Haaren liegen mit.

logic ['lodʒik] n Logik f. **logical** adj logisch.

loins [loinz] pl n Lenden pl. **loincloth** n Lendentuch neut.

loiter ['loitə] v schlendern. **loiterer** n Schlenderer m.

lollipop ['lolipop] n Lutscher m.

London ['lʌndən] n London neut.

lonely ['lounli] adj einsam. **loneliness** n Einsamkeit f.

long[1] [loŋ] adj lang.

long[2] [loŋ] v sich sehnen (nach).

long-distance adj Fern-.

longevity [lonˈdʒevəti] n Langlebigkeit f.

longing ['loŋiŋ] n Sehnsucht f.

longitude ['londʒɪtjuːd] n Länge f. **longitu-**

dinal adj Längen-.

long-playing record n Langspielplatte f.

long-term adj langfristig.

long-wave adj Langwelle-.

long-winded adj langatmig.

loo [luː] (coll) Klo neut.

look [lʊk] n (glance) Blick m; (appearance) Aussehen neut; (expression) Miene f. v schauen, blicken, gucken (auf); (appear) aussehen. **look after** aufpassen auf; (care for) sorgen für. **look for** suchen. **look forward** to sich freuen auf. **look into** untersuchen. **look out!** paß auf!

loom[1] [luːm] v **loom up** aufragen.

loom[2] [luːm] n Webstuhl m, Webmaschine f.

loop [luːp] n Schleife f, Schlinge f. v eine Schleife machen.

loophole [ˈluːphoul] n Lücke f.

loose [luːs] adj schlaff, locker; (free) los. **loosen** v lösen, lockern. **loose change** Kleingeld neut. **loose translation** freie Übersetzung f.

loot [luːt] n Beute f. v plündern. **looter** n Plünderer m. **looting** n Plünderung f.

lop [lɒp] v **lop off** abhacken.

lopsided [ˌlɒpˈsaidid] adj schief.

lord [lɔːd] n Herr m; (noble) Edelmann m. **House of Lords** Oberhaus neut.

lorry [ˈlɒri] n Lastkraftwagen (Lkw) m.

*****lose** [luːz] v verlieren; (clock) nachgehen. **lose one's way** sich verlieren. **loser** n Verlierer(in). **loss** n Verlust m; (decrease) Abnahme f. **dead loss** (coll) Niete f, Versager m.

lost [lɒst] V **lose**.

lot [lɒt] n Los neut; (fate) Schicksal neut; (land) Bauplatz m. **draw lots** Lose ziehen. **a lot of** viel, eine Menge.

lotion [ˈloʊʃən] n Lotion f.

lottery [ˈlɒtəri] n Lotterie f.

lotus [ˈloʊtəs] n Lotos m.

loud [laud] adj laut; (colour) schreiend. **loudmouth** n Maulheld m. **loudness** n Lautstärke f. **loudspeaker** n Lautsprecher m.

lounge [laundʒ] n Wohnzimmer neut; (hotel) Foyer neut. v faulenzen.

louse [laus] n (pl lice) Laus f. **lousy** adj (slang) saumäßig.

love [lʌv] n Liebe f; (person) Liebling m;

(sport) null. v lieben. **love doing something** etwas gern tun. **love affair** Liebesaffäre f. **loveless** adj lieblos. **love letter** Liebesbrief m. **loveliness** n Schönheit f. **lovely** adj lieblich, schön. **lover** n Liebhaber(in), Geliebte(r). **lovesick** adj liebeskrank. **loving** adj liebevoll.

low [loʊ] adj niedrig; (deep) tief; (sad) niedergeschlagen; (base) ordinär. **low-fat** adj fettarm, mager. **low tide** Niedrigwasser neut. **lowly** adj bescheiden.

lower [ˈloʊə] v senken, niederlassen; (fig) erniedrigen.

loyal [ˈlɔiəl] adj treu. **loyalty** n Treue f.

lozenge [ˈlɒzindʒ] n Pastille f.

lubricate [ˈluːbrikeit] v schmieren, ölen. **lubricant** n Schmiermittel neut. **lubrication** n Schmierung f.

lucid [ˈluːsid] adj deutlich, klar.

luck [lʌk] n (happiness, fortune) Glück neut; (fate) Schicksal neut; (chance) Zufall m. **luckily** adv glücklicherweise. **lucky** adj glücklich.

lucrative [ˈluːkrətiv] adj gewinnbringend.

ludicrous [ˈluːdikrəs] adj lächerlich.

lug [lʌg] v (carry, drag) schleppen.

luggage [ˈlʌgidʒ] n Gepäck neut. **luggage rack** Gepäcknetz neut.

lukewarm [ˈluːkwɔːm] adj lauwarm.

lull [lʌl] n (pause) Pause f; (calm) Stille f.

lullaby [ˈlʌləbai] n Wiegenlied neut.

lumbago [lʌmˈbeigou] n Hexenschuß m, Lumbago f.

lumber[1] [ˈlʌmbə] n (timber) Bauholz neut; (junk) Plunder m. **lumber room** Rumpelkammer f.

lumber[2] [ˈlʌmbə] v schwerfällig gehen.

luminous [ˈluːminəs] adj leuchtend.

lump [lʌmp] n Klumpen m, Beule f. **lump sugar** Würfelzucker m. **lump sum** Pauschalsumme f. v **lump together** zusammenfassen. **lumpy** adj klumpig.

lunar [ˈluːnə] adj Mond-.

lunatic [ˈluːnətik] n Wahnsinnige(r). **lunacy** n Wahnsinn m.

lunch [lʌntʃ] n Mittagessen neut. v zu Mittag essen. **lunchtime** Mittagspause f.

lung [lʌŋ] n Lunge f. **lung cancer** Lungenkrebs m.

lunge [lʌndʒ] v losstürzen (auf).

lurch[1] [ləːtʃ] v taumeln.

lurch² [bːtʃ] *n* leave in the lurch im Stich lassen.

lure [luə] *v* (an)locken. *n* Köder *m*.

lurid ['luəriid] *adj* grell.

lurk [bːk] *v* lauern.

luscious ['lʌʃəs] *adj* köstlich, lecker.

lush [lʌʃ] *adj* saftig.

lust [lʌst] *n* Wollust *f*, Begierde *f*. *v* lust after begehren. **lustful** *adj* lüstern.

lustre ['lʌstə] *n* Glanz *m*. **lustrous** *adj* strahlend.

lute [luːt] *n* Laute *f*.

Luxembourg ['lʌksəm,bəːg] *n* Luxemburg *neut*.

luxury ['lʌkʃəri] *n* Luxus *m*; (*article*) Luxusartikel *m*. **luxuriant** *adj* üppig. **luxurious** *adj* luxuriös.

lynch [lintʃ] *v* lynchen.

lynx [links] *n* Luchs *m*.

lyrical ['lirkəl] *adj* lyrisch.

lyrics ['lirks] *pl n* Lyrik *f sing*, Text *m sing*.

M

mac [mak] *n* Regenmantel *m*.

macabre [mə'kaːbr] *adj* grausig.

macaroni [makə'rouni] *n* Makkaroni *pl*.

mace¹ [meis] *n* Amtsstab *m*.

mace² [meis] *n* (*cookery*) Muskatblüte *f*.

machine [mə'ʃiːn] *n* Maschine *f*. *v* maschinell herstellen. **machine gun** Maschinengewehr *neut*. **machinery** *n* Maschinerie *f*. **machine tool** Werkzeugmaschine *f*. **machinist** *n* Maschinenarbeiter(in).

mackerel ['makrəl] *n* Makrele *f*.

mackintosh ['makin,tɒʃ] *n* Regenmantel *m*.

mad [mad] *adj* wahnsinnig, verrückt; (*angry*) wütend. **madhouse** *n* Irrenhaus *neut*. **madly** *adv* wie verrückt. **madman** *n* Verrückte(r) *m*. **madness** *n* Wahnsinn *m*.

madam ['madəm] *n* gnädige Frau *f*.

made [meid] *V* **make**.

magazine [,magə'ziːn] *n* (*publication*) Zeitschrift *f*, Illustrierte *f*; (*also warehouse, rifle*) Magazin *neut*.

maggot ['magət] *n* Made *f*. **maggoty**

adj madig.

magic ['madʒik] *n* Zauberei *f*. *adj also* **magical** Zauber-, zauberhaft. **magician** *n* Zauberer *m*; (*entertainer*) Zauberkünstler *m*.

magistrate ['madʒistreit] *n* Friedensrichter *m*.

magnanimous [mag'naniməs] *adj* großmütig. **magnanimity** *n* Großmut *f*.

magnate ['magneit] *n* Magnat *m*.

magnet ['magnət] *n* Magnet *m*. **magnetic** *adj* magnetisch. **magnetism** *n* Magnetismus *m*; (*fig*) Anziehungskraft *f*. **magnetize** *v* magnetisieren.

magnificent [mag'nifisnt] *adj* prächtig. **magnificence** *n* Pracht *f*.

magnify ['magnifai] *v* vergrößern. **magnifying glass** Lupe *f*. **magnification** *n* Vergrößerung *f*.

magnitude ['magnitjuːd] *n* Größe *f*, Ausmaß *neut*.

magnolia [mag'nouliə] *n* Magnolie *f*.

magpie ['magpai] *n* Elster *f*.

mahogany [mə'hogəni] *n* (*wood*) Mahagoni *neut*. *adj* Mahagoni-.

maid [meid] *n* Mädchen *neut*; (*servant*) Dienstmädchen *neut*. **old maid** alte Jungfer *f*.

maiden ['meidən] *n* Mädchen *neut*. **maiden name** Mädchenname *m*. **maiden speech** Jungfernrede *f*.

mail [meil] *n* Post *f*. *v* schicken, absenden. **mailbox** Briefkasten *m*. **mail-order company** Versandhaus *neut*. **mailboat** *n* Paketboot *neut*.

maim [meim] *v* lähmen.

main [mein] *adj* Haupt-, hauptsächlich. **mains** *pl n* (*gas, water*) Hauptleitung *f*; (*elec*) Netz *neut sing*. **mainstay** *n* (*fig*) Hauptstütze *f*. **mainstream** *n* Durchschnitt *m*. **main street** Hauptstraße *f*.

maintain [mein'tein] *v* erhalten; behaupten. **maintenance** *n* Erhaltung *f*; (*tech, mot*) Wartung *f*.

maisonette [meizə'net] *n* Wohnung *f*.

maize [meiz] *n* Mais *m*.

majesty ['madʒəsti] *n* Majestät *f*. **His/Her/Your Majesty** Seine/Ihre/Eure Majestät. **majestic** *adj* majestätisch.

major ['meidʒə] *n* (*mil*) Major *m*; (*music*) Dur *neut*. *adj* (*significant*) bedeutend; (*greater*) größer. **majority** *n* Mehrheit *f*; (*law*) Mündigkeit *f*.

*make [m eɪk] v machen; (*produce*) herstellen; (*force*) zwingen; (*build*) bauen; (*reach*) erreichen. n (*brand*) Marke f; (*type*) Art f. **make good** (*succeed*) Erfolg haben. **make out** vergeben. **makeover** n geschniegeltes Aussehen neut. **makeshift** adj Behelfs-. **make-up** n Schminke f.

maladjusted [m aˈdʒʌstɪd] adj verhaltensgestört.

malaria [m əˈlɛərə] n Malaria f.

male [m eɪl] n Mann m; (*animals*) Männchen neut. adj männlich. **male nurse** Krankenpfleger m.

malevolent [m əˈlevələnt] adj mißgünstig. **malevolence** n Mißgunst f.

malfunction [m alfʌŋkʃən] n Funktionsstörung f.

malice [ˈm alɪs] n Böswilligkeit. **malicious** adj böswillig.

malignant [m əˈlɪgnənt] adj böswillig; (*med*) bösartig.

malinger [m əˈlɪŋgə] v sich krank stellen, simulieren.

mall [m ɔːl] n Einkaufszentrum neut.

mallet [ˈm alɪt] n Schlegel m.

malnutrition [m alnjuˈtrɪʃən] n Unterernährung f.

malt [m ɔːlt] n Malz neut.

Malta [ˈm ɔːltə] n Malta neut. **Maltese** n Malteser(in); adj maltesisch.

maltreat [m altriːt] v mißhandeln, schlecht behandeln. **maltreatment** n schlechte Behandlung f.

mammal [ˈm am əl] n Säugetier neut.

mammoth [ˈm am əθ] n Mammut neut. adj riesig.

man [m an] n (*pl* men) Mann m; (*human*) Mensch m. v bemannen. **manliness** n Mannhaftigkeit f. **manly** adj mannhaft. **manslaughter** n Totschlag m.

manage [ˈm anɪdʒ] v (*control*) leiten, führen; (*cope*) zurechtkommen, auskommen. **management** n Geschäftsleitung f, Direktion f. **manager** n Leiter m, Manager m.

mandarin [ˈm andərɪn] n Mandarin m; (*fruit*) Mandarine f.

mandate [ˈm andeɪt] n Mandat neut. **mandatory** adj verbindlich.

mandolin [ˈm andəlɪn] n Mandoline f.

mane [m eɪn] n Mähne f.

maneuver [m əˈnuːvə] n (*US*) Manöver neut. v manövrieren.

manage [m eɪndʒ] n Räude f.

mangle¹ [ˈm aŋgl] n (Wäsche)Mangel f. v mangeln.

mangle² [m aŋgl] v (*disfigure*) verstümmeln.

manhandle [m anˈhandl] v grob behandeln, mißhandeln.

mania [m eɪnə] n Manie f. **maniac** n Wahnsinnige(r). **manic** adj manisch.

manicure [ˈm anɪkjə] n Maniküre f. v maniküren. **manicurist** n Maniküre f.

manifest [ˈm anɪfest] adj offenbar. v erscheinen. **manifestation** n Offenbarung f; (*symptom*) Anzeichen neut.

manifesto [m anɪfestou] n Manifest neut.

manifold [ˈm anɪfould] adj mannigfaltig.

manipulate [m əˈnɪpjuleɪt] v manipulieren. **manipulation** n Manipulation f.

mankind [m anˈkaɪnd] n Menschheit f.

man-made [m anˈm eɪd] adj künstlich.

manner [ˈm anə] n (*way*) Art f, Weise f; (*behaviour*) Manier f, Benehmen neut. **mannered** adj manieriert. **mannerism** n Manierismus m.

manoeuvre [m əˈnuːvə] n Manöver neut. v manövrieren.

manor [ˈm anə] n Herrensitz m, Herrenhaus neut.

manpower [ˈm anˌpauə] n Arbeitskräfte pl.

mansion [ˈm anʃən] n (herrschaftliches) Wohnhaus neut.

mantelpiece [ˈm antlpiːs] n Kaminsims m or neut.

manual [ˈm anjuəl] adj manuell, Hand-. n Handbuch neut.

manufacture [m anjuˈfaktʃə] v herstellen, erzeugen. n Herstellung f, Erzeugung f. **manufacturer** n Hersteller m, Fabrikant m.

manure [m əˈnjuə] n Dünger m, Mist m. v düngen.

manuscript [ˈm anjuskrɪpt] n Manuskript neut. adj handschriftlich.

many [ˈm enɪ] adj viele. **how many?** wieviele? **many times** oft. **a good many** ziemlich viele.

map [m ap] n (Land)Karte f; (*of town*) Stadtplan m. v eine karte machen von.

maple [ˈm eɪpl] n Ahorn m.

mar [m aː] v verderben, beeinträchtigen.

marathon [ˈm arəθən] n Marathonlauf m. adj Marathon-.

marble [ˈm aːbl] n Marmor m; (*toy*)

Marmel f.

march [mɑːtʃ] n Marsch m. v marschieren. **march past** vorbeimarschieren an.

March [mɑːtʃ] n März m.

marchioness [mɑːʃəˈnes] n Marquise f.

mare [meə] n Stute f.

margarine [mɑːdʒəˈriːn] n Margarine f.

margin [ˈmɑːdʒɪn] n Rand m; (limit) Grenze f; (profit) Gewinnspanne f. **marginal** adj Rand-; (slight) geringfügig.

marguerite [mɑːɡəˈriːt] n Gänseblümchen neut.

marigold [ˈmærɪɡould] n Ringelblume f.

marijuana [mærɪwɑːnə] n Marihuana neut.

marina [məˈriːnə] n Yachthafen m.

marinade [mærɪneɪd] v marinieren. n Marinade f.

marine [məˈriːn] adj See-, Meeres-. n (shipping) Marine f; (mil) Marineinfanterist m. **mariner** n Matrose m.

marital [ˈmærɪtl] adj ehelich. **marital status** Familienstand m.

maritime [ˈmærɪtaɪm] adj See-, Schiffahrts-.

marjoram [ˈmɑːdʒərəm] n Majoran m.

mark¹ [mɑːk] n Marke f, Zeichen neut; (school) Note f; (stain) Fleck m; (distinguishing feature) Kennzeichen neut. v bezeichnen; (note) notieren, vermerken. **marked** adj markant, ausgeprägt. **markedly** adv ausgesprochen.

mark² [mɑːk] n (currency) Mark f.

market [ˈmɑːkɪt] n Markt m. v auf den Markt bringen. **marketing** n Marketing neut. **market place** Marktplatz m. **market research** Marktforschung f.

marmalade [ˈmɑːməleɪd] n Orangenmarmelade f.

maroon¹ [məˈruːn] adj (colour) rotbraun.

maroon² [məˈruːn] v (naut) aussetzen.

marquee [mɑːˈkiː] n großes Zelt neut.

marquess [ˈmɑːkwis] n Marquis m.

marriage [ˈmærɪdʒ] n Heirat f, Ehe f; (wedding) Hochzeit f; (ceremony) Trauung f. **marriage certificate** Trauschein m.

marrow [ˈmærou] n (of bone) Mark neut; (vegetable) Eierkürbis m. **marrowbone** n Markknochen m.

marry [ˈmæri] v heiraten; (get married) sich verheiraten mit. **married couple** Ehepaar neut.

Mars [mɑːz] n Mars m. **Martian** adj Mars-;

n Marsbewohner m.

marsh [mɑːʃ] n Sumpf m. **marshy** adj sumpfig.

marshal [ˈmɑːʃəl] n Marschall m. v einordnen; (troops) aufstellen.

martial [ˈmɑːʃəl] adj militärisch, Kriegs-.

martin [ˈmɑːtin] n Mauerschwalbe f.

martyr [ˈmɑːtə] n Märtyrer(in). **martyrdom** n Martyrium neut.

marvel [ˈmɑːvəl] n Wunder neut. v staunen (über). **marvellous** adj wunderbar.

marzipan [mɑːzɪpan] n Marzipan neut.

mascara [maˈskɑːə] n Wimperntusche f.

mascot [ˈmæskət] n Maskottchen neut.

masculine [ˈmæskjulin] adj männlich; (manly) mannhaft; (of woman) männisch. n (gramm) Maskulinum m. **masculinity** n Männlichkeit f, Mannhaftigkeit f.

mash [mæʃ] v zerquetschen. **mashed potatoes** Kartoffelpüree neut.

mask [mɑːsk] n Maske f. v maskieren.

masochist [ˈmæsəkist] n Masochist m. **masochism** n Masochismus m.

mason [ˈmeisn] n Maurer m. **masonic** adj Freimaurer-. **masonry** n Mauerwerk neut.

masquerade [mæskəˈreid] n Maskerade f. v sich ausgeben (als).

mass¹ [mæs] n Masse f. v sich ansammeln. adj Massen-. **the masses** die breite Masse. **mass meeting** Massenversammlung f. **mass-produce** v serienmäßig herstellen. **mass production** Massenherstellung f.

mass² [mæs] n (rel) Messe f.

massacre [ˈmæsəkə] n Massaker neut, Blutbad neut. v massakrieren.

massage [ˈmæsɑːʒ] n Massage f. v massieren. **masseur** n Masseur m. **masseuse** n Masseuse f.

massive [ˈmæsiv] adj massiv.

mast [mɑːst] n Mast m.

mastectomy [mæˈstektəmi] n Brustamputation f.

master [ˈmɑːstə] n Herr m; (school) Lehrer m; (artist) Meister m. v meistern. **masterful** adj meisterhaft. **masterpiece** n Meisterwerk neut. **mastery** n Beherrschung f.

masturbate [ˈmæstəbeit] v onanieren, (coll) wichsen. **masturbation** n Onanie f.

mat [mæt] n Matte f; (beer) Untersetzer m. **matted** adj mattiert.

match¹ [m atʃ] n Streichholz *neut.*

match² [m atʃ] n (*equal*) Gleiche(r); (*sport*) Spiel *neut.* v anpassen. **meet one's match** seinen Meister finden. **matching** *adj* zusammengehörig, übereinstimmend. **matchless** *adj* unvergleichlich.

mate [m eɪt] n (*friend*) Kamarad(in); (*chess*) (Schach)Matt *neut*; (*animal*) Männchen *neut*, Weibchen *neut*; (*naut*) Schiffsoffizier *m.* v sich paaren; (*chess*) matt setzen.

material [m ə'tərɪə] n Stoff *m. adj* materiell; (*important*) wesentlich. **materials** *pl* Werkstoffe *pl.* **materialist** n Materialist *m.* **materialistic** *adj* materialistisch.

maternal [m ə'tə:n] *adj* mütterlich; mütterlicherseits. **maternal grandfather** Großvater. **maternity** n Mutterschaft *f.* **maternity dress** Umstandskleid *neut.* **maternity home** Entbindungsheim *neut.*

mathematics [m aθə'matiks] n Mathmatik *f.* **mathematical** *adj* mathematisch. **mathematician** n Mathematiker *m.*

matinee ['m atineɪ] n Matinee *f.*

matins ['m atɪnz] n Frühgottesdienst *m.*

matrimony ['m atrɪm ənɪ] n Ehestand *m*, Ehe *f.* **matrimonial** *adj* ehelich, Ehe-.

matrix ['m eɪtrɪks] n Matrix *f.*

matron ['m eɪtrən] n (*school*) Hausmutter *f*; (*nurse*) Oberin *f.*

matter ['m atə] n Stoff *m*, Materie *f*; (*affair*) Sache *f*; (*pus*) Eiter *m.* v von Bedeutung sein. *what's the matter?* was ist los? *it doesn't matter* es macht nichts. **matter-of-fact** *adj* sachlich.

mattress ['m atrɪs] n Matratze *f.*

mature [m ə'tjuə] *adj* reif. v reifen. **maturity** n Reife *f.*

maudlin ['m ɔ:dlɪn] *adj* weinerlich.

maul [m ɔ:] v zerreißen.

mausoleum [m ɔ:sə'lɪəm] n Mausoleum *neut*, Grabmal *neut.*

mauve [m ouv] *adj* malvenfarben.

maxim ['m aksɪm] n Grundsatz *m.*

maximize ['m aksɪn aɪz] v maximieren.

maximum ['m aksɪn əm] n Maximum *neut. adj* Höchst-, Maximal-.

*may [m eɪ] v mögen, können. *may I?* darf ich? **may be** *adv* vielleicht.

May [m eɪ] n Mai *m.* **mayday** (*SOS*) Maydaysignal *neut.*

mayonnaise [ˌm eə'neɪz] n Mayonnaise *f.*

mayor [m eə] n Bürgermeister *m.* **mayoress** n Bürgermeisterin *f.*

maze [m eɪz] n Labyrinth *neut*, Irrgarten *m.*

me [m ɪ] *pron* (*acc*) mich; (*dat*) mir.

meadow ['m edou] n Wiese *f.*

meagre ['m ɪgə] *adj* mager, dürr.

meal¹ [m ɪ] n Mahlzeit *f*, Essen *neut.*

meal² [m ɪ] n (*flour*) Mehl *neut.*

*mean¹ [m ɪn] v (*word, etc.*) bedeuten; (*person*) meinen; (*intend*) vorhaben, beabsichtigen.

mean² [m ɪn] *adj* (*slight*) gering; (*base*) gemein; (*tight-fisted*) geizig. **meanness** n Gemeinheit *f.*

mean³ [m ɪn] n Durchschnitt *m. adj* mittler, Durchschnitts-.

meander [m andə] v sich winden. n Windung *f.*

meaning ['m ɪnɪŋ] n (*significance*) Bedeutung *f*; (*sense*) Sinn *m.* **meaningful** *adj* bedeutsam. **meaningless** *adj* sinnlos.

means [m ɪnz] n Mittel *neut.* **by means of** durch, mittels. **by no means** auf keinen Fall. **by all means** selbstverständlich.

meant [m ent] V **mean¹**.

meanwhile ['m ɪnwaɪl] *adv* mittlerweile.

measles ['m ɪzlz] n Masern *pl.* **German measles** Röteln *pl.*

measure ['m eʒə] v messen. n Maß *neut.* **measurement** n Messung *f*, Maß *neut.*

meat [m ɪt] n Fleisch *neut.* **meatball** n Fleischklößchen. **meaty** *adj* fleischig.

mechanic [m ɪkanɪk] n Mechaniker *m.* **mechanical** *adj* mechanisch. **mechanics** n Mechanik *f.* **mechanism** n Mechanismus *m.* **mechanize** v mechanisieren.

medal ['m edl] n Medaille *f*, Orden *m.* **medallion** n Schaumünze *f.*

meddle ['m edl] v sich (ein)mischen (in). **meddlesome** *adj* zudringlich.

media ['m ɪdɪə] *pl* n Medien *pl.* **mass media** Massenmedien *pl.*

mediate ['m ɪdɪeɪt] v vermitteln. **mediation** n Vermittlung *f.* **mediator** n Vermittler *m.*

medical ['m edɪkə] *adj* medizinisch, ärztlich. **medical certificate** Krankenschein *m.* **medical student** Medizinstudent *m.* **medicament** n Arzneimittel *neut.* **medicinal** *adj* heilkräftig. **medicine** n Arznei *f*, Arzneimittel *neut*; (*science*) Medizin *f.*

medieval [ˌmediˈiːvəl] *adj* mittelalterlich.

mediocre [ˌmiːdiˈoukə] *adj* mittelmäßig. **mediocrity** *n* Mittelmäßigkeit *f*.

meditate [ˈmedɪteɪt] *v* meditieren; (*reflect*) nachdenken (über). **meditation** *n* (*rel*) Meditation *f*; Nachdenken *neut*.

Mediterranean [ˌmedɪtəˈreɪniən] *n* Mittelmeer *neut*. *adj* Mittelmeer-.

medium [ˈmiːdiəm] *adj* mittler, Mittel-. *n* Mitte *f*; (*spiritualist*) Medium *neut*. **medium-sized** *adj* mittelgroß.

medley [ˈmedli] *n* Gemisch *neut*; (*music*) Potpourri *neut*.

meek [miːk] *adj* mild, sanft. **meekness** *n* Milde *f*, Sanftmut *f*.

*meet [miːt] *v* treffen, begegnen (+*dat*); (*by appointment*) sich treffen (*mit*); (*requirements*) erfüllen; (*call for*) abholen. **meeting** *n* Treffen *neut*; (*session*) Versammlung *f*, Sitzung *f*.

megabyte [ˈmegəbaɪt] *n* Megabyte *neut*.

megaphone [ˈmegəfoun] *n* Megaphon *neut*.

melancholy [ˈmelənkəli] *n* Melancholie *f*, Trübsinn *m*. **melancholic** *adj* melancholisch.

mellow [ˈmelou] *adj* reif; (*person*) freundlich, heiter.

melodrama [ˈmelədrɑːmə] *n* Melodrama *neut*. **melodramatic** *adj* melodramatisch.

melody [ˈmelədi] *n* Melodie *f*. **melodious** *adj* wohlklingend.

melon [ˈmelən] *n* Melone *f*.

melt [melt] *v* schmelzen. **melt away** zergehen. **melting point** Schmelzpunkt *m*.

member [ˈmembə] *n* Mitglied *m*. **Member of Parliament** *n* Abgeordnete *m*, *f* (des britischen Unterhauses). **membership** *n* Mitgliedschaft *f*.

membrane [ˈmembreɪn] *n* Membrane *f*.

memento [məˈmentou] *n* Andenken *neut*.

memo [ˈmemou] *n* (*note*) Notiz *f*; (*message*) Mitteilung *f*.

memoirs [ˈmemwɑːz] *pl n* Memoiren *pl*.

memorable [ˈmemərəbl] *adj* denkwürdig.

memorandum [ˌmeməˈrandəm] *n* (*note*) Notiz *f*; (*message*) Mitteilung *f*.

memorial [məˈmɔːriəl] *n* Denkmal *neut*. *adj* **memorial service** Gedenkgottesdienst *m*.

memory [ˈmeməri] *n* (*power of*) Gedächtnis *neut*; (*of something*) Erinnerung *f*. **memorize** *v* auswendig lernen.

men [men] *V* **man**.

menace [ˈmenis] *n* Drohung *f*. *v* bedrohen. **menacing** *adj* drohend.

menagerie [məˈnadʒəri] *n* Menagerie *f*.

mend [mend] *v* reparieren; (*clothes*) flicken; (*socks, etc.*) stopfen. *n* ausgebesserte Stelle *f*. **on the mend** (*coll*) auf dem Wege der Besserung.

menial [ˈmiːniəl] *adj* niedrig.

menopause [ˈmenəpɔːz] *n* Wechseljahre *pl*, Menopause *f*.

menstrual [ˈmenstruəl] *adj* Menstruations-. **menstruate** *v* die Regel haben, menstruieren. **menstruation** *n* Menstruation *f*, Monatsblutung *f*.

mental [ˈmentl] *adj* geistig, Geistes-; (*slang*) verrückt. **mental deficiency** Schwachsinn *m*. **mental hospital** Nervenheilanstalt *f*. **mental illness** Geisteskrankheit *f*. **mentality** *n* Mentalität *f*, Gesinnung *f*. **mentally ill** geisteskrank.

menthol [ˈmenθəl] *n* Menthol *neut*.

mention [ˈmenʃən] *v* erwähnen. *n* Erwähnung *f*. **don't mention it!** bitte sehr!

menu [ˈmenjuː] *n* Speisekarte *f*, Menü *neut*.

mercantile [ˈmɜːkəntaɪl] *adj* kaufmännisch, Handels-.

mercenary [ˈmɜːsinəri] *adj* gewinnsüchtig, geldgierig. *n* Söldner *m*.

merchandise [ˈmɜːtʃəndaɪz] *n* Waren *pl*, Handelsgüter *pl*. *v* verkaufen.

merchant [ˈmɜːtʃənt] *n* Kaufmann *m*; (*wholesaler*) Großhändler *m*. **merchant navy** Handelsflotte *f*.

mercury [ˈmɜːkjuri] *n* Quecksilber *neut*. **Mercury** *n* Merkur *m*.

mercy [ˈmɜːsi] *n* Erbarmen *neut*, Gnade *f*. **merciful** *adj* barmherzig. **merciless** *adj* erbarmungslos.

mere [miə] *adj* bloß, rein.

merge [mɜːdʒ] *v* verschmelzen; (*comm*) fusionieren. **merger** *n* Fusion *f*.

meridian [məˈridiən] *n* Meridian *m*.

meringue [məˈraŋ] *n* Meringe *f*, Baiser *neut*.

merit [ˈmerit] *n* Verdienst *neut*; (*value*) Wert *m*. *v* verdienen.

mermaid [ˈmɜːmeid] *n* Seejungfrau *f*.

merry [ˈmeri] *adj* lustig, fröhlich. **make merry** feiern. **merry-go-round** *n* Karussell *neut*. **merriment** *n* Lustigkeit *f*

mesh [m eʃ] *n* Masche *f*. *v* ineinandergreifen. **meshed** *adj* maschig.

mesmerize ['m ezn əraiz] *v* hypnotisieren; (*fig*) faszinieren.

mess [m es] *n* Durcheinander *neut*, Unordnung *f*; (*mil*) Messe *f*. *v* beschmutzen. **mess about** herumpfuschen. **mess up** verderben, verpfuschen. **messy** *adj* unordentlich.

message ['m esiʤ] *n* Mitteilung *f*; (*news*) Nachricht *f*. **messenger** *n* Bote *m*.

met [m et] *V* meet.

metabolism [m itabəlizm] *n* Stoffwechsel *m*. **metabolic** *adj* metabolisch.

metal ['m et] *n* Metall *neut*. **metallic** *adj* metallisch. **metallurgy** *n* Metallurgie *f*.

metamorphosis [m etə'm o:əsis] *n* Metamorphose *f*, Verwandlung *f*. **metamorphose** *v* verwandeln.

metaphor ['m etəə] *n* Metapher *f*. **metaphorical** *adj* metaphorisch.

metaphysics [,m etə'fiziks] *n* Metaphysik *f*. **metaphysical** *adj* metaphysisch.

meteor ['m itə] *n* Meteor *m*. **meteoric** *adj* meteorartig, plötzlich.

meteorology [,m itə'rɒləʤi] *n* Meteorologie *f*, Wetterkunde *f*. **meteorological** *adj* meteorologisch, Wetter-.

meter ['m itə] *n* Messer *m*. **gas meter** Gasuhr *f*. **parking meter** Parkuhr *f*.

methane ['m iθein] *n* Methan *neut*.

method ['m eθəd] *n* Methode *f*; (*procedure*) Verfahren *neut*. **methodical** *adj* methodisch.

methylated spirits ['m eθileitid] *n* Brennspiritus *m*.

meticulous [m itikjuləs] *adj* übergenau, peinlich genau.

metre ['m itə] *n* Meter *m* or *neut*. **metric** *adj* metrisch.

metronome ['m etrənoum] *n* Metronom *neut*, Taktmesser *m*.

metropolis [m ə'trɒpəlis] *n* Metropole *f*, Hauptstadt *f*.

Mexico ['m eksikou] *n* Mexiko *neut*. **Mexican** *n* Mexikaner(in); *adj* mexikanisch.

mice [m ais] *V* mouse.

microbe ['m aikroub] *n* Mikrobe *f*.

microchip ['m aikroutʃip] *n* Mikrochip *m*.

microfilm ['m aikrə,film] *n* Mikrofilm *m*.

microphone ['m aikrəfoun] *n* Mikrophon *neut*.

microscope ['m aikrəskoup] *n* Mikroscop *neut*. **microscopic** *adj* mikroscopisch; (*tiny*) verschwindend klein.

microwave ['m aikrə,weiv] *adj* Mikrowellen-.

mid [m id] *adj* mittler, Mittel-. **in mid air** mitten in der Luft. **midday** *n* Mittag *m*.

middle ['m idl] *n* Mitte *f*. *adj* mittler, Mittel-. **middle-aged** *adj* im mittleren Alter. **middle-class** *adj* bürgerlich, bourgeois. **middle classes** Mittelstand *m*.

Middle Ages *pl n* Mittelalter *neut*.

Middle East *n* Naher Osten *m*.

midge [m idʒ] *n* Mücke *f*.

midget ['m idʒit] *n* Zwerg *m*.

midnight ['m idnait] *n* Mitternacht *f*.

midsummer ['m id,sʌm ə] *n* Hochsommer *m*.

midst [m idst] *n* Mitte *f*. **in the midst of** mitten unter (+ *dat*).

midwife ['m idwaif] *n* Hebamme *f*. **midwifery** *n* Geburtshilfe *f*.

might¹ [m ait] *V* may.

might² [m ait] *n* Macht *f*; (*force*) Gewalt *f*.

mighty ['m aiti] *adj* mächtig. *adv* sehr.

migraine ['m igrein] *n* Migräne *f*.

migrant ['m aigrənt] *adj* wandernd. *n* (*worker*) Gastarbeiter(in) *m*, *f*; (*bird*) Zugvogel *m*.

migrate [m aigreit] *v* abwandern. **migration** *n* Wanderung *f*.

mike [m aik] *n* (*coll*) Mikrophon *neut*.

mild [m aild] *adj* mild, sanft. **to put it mildly** gelinde gesagt. **mildness** *n* Sanftheit *f*.

mildew ['m ildju:] *n* Mehltau *m*, Moder *m*.

mile [m ail] *n* Meile *f*. **mileage** *n* Meilenzahl *f*. **milestone** *n* (*fig*) Markstein *m*.

militant ['m ilitənt] *adj* militant, kämpferisch. *n* (*pol*) Radikale(r).

military ['m ilitəri] *adj* militärisch, Militär-, Kriegs-.

milk [m ilk] *n* Milch *f*. *v* melken. **milk tooth** *n* Milchzahn *m*. **milky** *adj* milchig. **Milky Way** Milchstraße *f*.

mill [m il] *n* Mühle *f*; (*works*) Fabrik *f*. *v* mahlen. **run-of-the-mill** *adj* mittelmäßig. **miller** *n* Müller *m*.

millennium [m ileniəm] *n* Jahrtausend *neut*.

milligram ['m ɪlɪgræm] *n* Milligramm *neut.*

millilitre ['m ɪlɪltə] *n* Milliliter *neut.*

millimetre ['m ɪlɪm ɪtə] *n* Millimeter *neut.*

millinery ['m ɪlɪnərɪ] *n* Müte *pl.*

million ['m ɪljən] *n* Million *f.* **millionaire** *n* Millionär *n.* **millionairess** *n* Millionärin *f.*

milometer [m aɪlɒm ɪtə] *n* Meilenzähler *m*, Kilometerzähler *m.*

mime [m aɪn] *n* (*actor*) Mime *m.* *v* mimen.

mimic ['m ɪn ɪk] *v* nachäffen. **mimicry** *n* Nachäffung *f.*

mince [m ɪns] *v* zerhacken. *n* (*mincemeat*) Hackfleisch *neut.* **mincer** *n* Fleischwolf *m.* **mince about** geziert gehen. **mincing** *adj* geziert, affektiert. **not mince one's words** kein Blatt vor den Mund nehmen.

mind [m aɪnd] *n* Geist *m*, Verstand *m*; (*opinion*) Meinung *f.* *v* etwas dagegen haben; (*look after*) aufpassen auf. **change one's mind** die Meinung ändern. **frame of mind** Gesinnung *f*, Stimmung *f.* **make up one's mind** sich entschließen. **mind out!** paß auf! Achtung! **Never mind!** macht nichts! *I don't mind* ist mir egal. **minder** *n* (*bodyguard*) Aufpasser *m.*

mine[1] [m aɪn] *poss pron* meiner *m*, meine *f*, meines *neut*; der, die, das meine *or* meinige. **a friend of mine** ein Freund von mir. **it's mine** es gehört mir.

mine[2] [m aɪn] *n* (*coal, etc.*) Bergwerk *neut*; (*mil*) Mine *f.* *v* minieren. **miner** *n* Bergarbeiter *m.* **minefield** *n* Minenfeld *n.* **mining** *n* Bergbau *m.* **minesweeper** *n* Minensuchboot *neut.*

mineral ['m ɪnərəl] *n* Mineral *neut. adj* mineralisch. **mineral water** Mineralwasser *neut.*

mingle ['m ɪŋgl] *v* (sich) vermischen.

miniature ['m ɪnɪtʃə] *n* Miniatur *f. adj* Klein-.

minibus ['m ɪnɪbʌs] *n* Kleinbus *m.*

minimum ['m ɪnɪm əm] *n* Minimum *neut.* **minimal** *adj* Mindest-, Minimal-.

minister ['m ɪnɪstə] *n* (*pol*) Minister *m*; (*rel*) Pfarrer *m.* **ministry** *n* (*pol*) Ministerium *neut.*

mink [m ɪŋk] *n* Nerz *m.*

minor ['m aɪnə] *adj* kleiner, geringer; (*trivial*) geringfügig. *n* (*under age*) Minderjährige(r); (*music*) Moll *neut.* **minority** *n* Minderheit *f*; (*under age*) Minderjährigkeit *f.*

minstrel ['m ɪnstrəl] *n* Minnesänger *m.*

mint[1] [m ɪnt] *n* (*cookery*) Minze *f.*

mint[2] [m ɪnt] *n* (*money*) Münzanstalt *f. v* münzen.

minuet [m ɪnjuːet] *n* Menuett *neut.*

minus ['m aɪnəs] *prep* weniger, minus. *it's minus 20 degrees* wir haben 20 Grad Kälte.

minute[1] ['m ɪnɪt] *n* Minute *f.* **just a minute!** Moment mal!

minute[2] [m aɪnjuːt] *adj* winzig.

miracle ['m ɪrəkl] *n* Wunder *neut*, Wundertat *f.* **miraculous** *adj* wunderbar. **miraculously** *adv* durch ein Wunder.

mirage ['m ɪraːʒ] *n* Luftspiegelung *f.*

mirror ['m ɪrə] *n* Spiegel *m.* *v* widerspiegeln.

mirth [m əːθ] *n* Fröhlichkeit *f*, Lustigkeit *f.*

misadventure [m ɪsəd'ventʃə] *n* Unfall *m*, Unglück *neut.*

misanthropist [m ɪ'zænθrəpɪst] *n* Menschenfeind *m.* **misanthropic** *adj* menschenfeindlich.

misapprehension [m ɪsæprɪhenʃən] *n* Mißverständnis *neut.*

misbehave [m ɪsbɪheɪv] *v* sich schlecht benehmen. **misbehaviour** *n* schlechtes Benehmen *neut.*

miscalculate [m ɪs'kælkjuleɪt] *v* sich verrechnen.

miscarriage [m ɪskærɪʒ] *n* Fehlgeburt *f.* **miscarriage of justice** Fehlspruch *m*, Rechtsbeugung *f.* **miscarry** *v* eine Fehlgeburt haben; (*go wrong*) mißlingen.

miscellaneous [m ɪsə'leɪnɪəs] *adj* vermischt. *n* Verschiedenes *neut.* **miscellany** *n* Gemisch *neut.*

mischance [m ɪstʃaːns] *n* Unfall *m.*

mischief ['m ɪstʃɪf] *n* Unfug *m.* **mischievous** *adj* schelmisch, durchtrieben. **mischiefmaker** *n* Störenfried *m.*

misconception [m ɪskən'sepʃən] *n* Mißverständnis *neut.*

misconduct [m ɪskɒndʌkt] *n* schlechtes Benehmen *neut.*

misconstrue [m ɪskən'struː] *v* mißdeuten.

misdeed [m ɪsdɪd] *n* Untat *f*, Verbrechen *neut.*

misdemeanour [m ɪsdɪm ɪnə] *n* Vergehen *neut.*

miser ['m aɪzə] *n* Geizhals *m.* **miserly** *adj* geizig. **miserliness** *n* Geiz *m.*

miserable ['m ɪzərəbl] *adj* (*unhappy*)

unglücklich; (*wretched*) elend.

misery ['mɪzərɪ] *n* Elend *neut*, Not *f*.

misfire [mɪsˈfaɪə] *v* versagen; (*mot*) fehlzünden. *n* Versager *m*; Fehlzündung *f*.

misfit ['mɪsfɪt] *n* Einzelgänger *m*.

misfortune [mɪsˈfɔːtʃən] *n* Unglück *neut*.

misgiving [mɪsˈgɪvɪŋ] *n* Zweifel *m*.

misguided [mɪsˈgaɪdɪd] *adj* (*erroneous*) irrig.

mishap ['mɪshap] *n* Unglück *neut*.

*****mishear** [mɪsˈhɪə] *v* sich verhören.

misinterpret [mɪsɪnˈtəːprɪt] *v* mißdeuten.

*****mislay** [mɪsˈleɪ] *v* verlegen.

*****mislead** [mɪsˈliːd] *v* irreführen. **misleading** *adj* irreführend.

misnomer [mɪsˈnoumə] *n* falsche Bezeichnung *f*.

misplace [mɪsˈpleɪs] *v* verlegen. **misplaced** *adj* (*inappropriate*) unangebracht.

misprint ['mɪsprɪnt] *n* Druckfehler *m*.

miss[1] [mɪs] *v* (*shot*) verfehlen; (*train, opportunity*) verpassen, versäumen; (*absent friend*) vermissen. *n* Fehlschuß *m*. **missing** *adj* fehlend; (*person*) vermißt.

miss[2] [mɪs] *n* (*title*) Fräulein *neut*.

missile [mɪsaɪl] *n* Rakete *f*, Geschoß *neut*. **guided missile** Fernlenkrakete *f*.

mission [mɪʃən] *n* Mission *f*; (*task*) Auftrag *m*; (*pol*) Gesandschaft *f*. **missionary** *n* Missionar(in).

mist [mɪst] *n* (feuchter) Dunst *m*, Nebel *m*.

*****mistake** [mɪsˈteɪk] *n* Fehler *m*, Irrtum *m*. *v* verwechseln. **be mistaken** im Irrtum sein.

mister ['mɪstə] *n* Herr *m*.

mistletoe [mɪsltou] *n* Mistel *f*.

mistress ['mɪstrɪs] *n* (*lover*) Mätresse *f*; (*school*) Lehrerin *f*; (*of house or animal*) Herrin *f*.

mistrust [mɪsˈtrʌst] *v* mißtrauen. *n* Mißtrauen *neut*, Argwohn *m*. **mistrustful** *adj* mißtrauisch.

*****misunderstand** [mɪsʌndəˈstand] *v* mißverstehen. **misunderstanding** *n* Mißverständnis *neut*.

misuse [mɪsˈjuːs; *v* misˈjuːz] *v* mißbrauchen. *n* Mißbrauch *m*.

mitigate ['mɪtɪgeɪt] *v* mildern. **mitigating circumstances** strafmildernde Umstände *pl*.

mitre ['maɪtə] *n* Bischofsmütze *f*.

mitten ['mɪtn] *n* Fausthandschuh *m*.

mix [mɪks] *v* (ver)mischen. *n* Mischung *f*.

mix up verwechseln. **mixer** *n* Mixer *m*.

mixture *n* Mischung *f*; (*med*) Mixtur *f*.

moan [moun] *n* Stöhnen *neut*. *v* stöhnen.

mob [mɔb] *n* Pöbel *m*, Gesindel *neut*.

mobile ['moubaɪl] *adj* beweglich; (*motorized*) motorisiert. *n* Mobile *neut*. **mobile phone** Handy *neut*. **mobility** *n* Beweglichkeit *f*. **mobilization** *n* Mobilisierung *f*. **mobilize** *v* mobilisieren.

moccasin ['mɔkəsɪn] *n* Mokassin *m*.

mock [mɔk] *v* verhöhnen, verspotten. *adj* Schein-. **mock trial** Scheinprozeß *m*. **mock-up** *n* Modell *neut*. **mockery** *n* Verhöhnung *f*. (*travesty*) Zerrbild *neut*. **mocking** *adj* spöttisch.

mode [moud] *n* Weise *f*, Methode *f*.

model [mɔdl] *n* Modell *neut*; (*pattern*) Muster *neut*, Vorbild *neut*; (*fashion*) Mannequin *neut*. *adj* vorbildlich, musterhaft. *v* modellieren; (*clothes*) vorführen.

modem ['moudem] *n* Modem *neut*.

moderate ['mɔdərət; *v* 'mɔdəreɪt] *adj* gemäßigt, mäßig. *v* mäßigen. **moderation** *n* Mäßigung *f*. **in moderation** mit Maß.

modern ['mɔdən] *adj* modern. **modernity** *n* Modernität *f*. **modernize** *v* modernisieren. **modernization** *n* Modernisierung *f*.

modest ['mɔdɪst] *adj* bescheiden; (*reasonable*) vernünftig. **modesty** *n* Bescheidenheit *f*.

modify ['mɔdɪfaɪ] *v* abändern, modifizieren. **modification** *n* Abänderung *f*, Modifikation *f*.

modulate ['mɔdjuleɪt] *v* modulieren.

mohair ['mouheə] *n* Mohair *m*.

moist [mɔist] *adj* feucht. **moisture** *n* Feuchtigkeit *f*.

molar ['moulə] *n* Backenzahn *m*.

molasses [məˈlasɪz] *n* Melasse *f*.

mold (*US*) *V* mould.

Moldova [mɔlˈdouvə] *n* (Republik) Moldau *f*. **Moldovan** *n* Moldauer(in) *adj* moldauisch.

mole[1] [moul] *n* (*birthmark*) Muttermal *neut*, Leberfleck *m*.

mole[2] [moul] *n* (*zool*) Maulwurf *m*.

molecule ['mɔlɪkjuːl] *n* Molekül *neut*. **molecular** *adj* molekular.

molest [məˈlest] *v* belästigen.

mollusc ['mɔləsk] *n* Weichtier *neut*.

molt (*US*) *V* moult.

molten ['m ouɩən] *adj* geschmolzen, flüssig.

moment ['m oum ənt] *n* Moment *m*, Augenblick *m*. **momentary** *adj* momentan, augenblicklich.

monarch ['m onək] *n* Monarch(in). **monarchy** *n* Monarchie *f*.

monastery ['m onəstəɪ] *n* Kloster *neut*. **monastic** *adj* kloster-.

Monday ['m ʌndɪ] *n* Montag *m*.

money ['m ʌnɪ] *n* Geld *neut*. **money box** Sparbüchse *f*. **money order** Zahlungsanweisung *f*. **monetary** *adj* Währungs-.

mongrel ['m ʌŋɡrəl] *n* Mischling *m*, Kreuzung *f*.

monitor ['m onɪə] *n* (*TV*) Monitor *m*. *v* überwachen, kontrollieren.

monk [m ʌŋk] *n* Mönch *m*. **monkish** *adj* mönchisch.

monkey ['m ʌŋkɪ] *n* Affe *m*. *v* **monkey around** herumalbern.

monogamy [m ə'nogəm ɪ] *n* Monogamie *f*. **monogamous** *adj* monogam.

monogram ['m onəɡɹam] *n* Monogramm *neut*.

monologue ['m onəlɔɡ] *n* Monolog *m*.

monopolize [m ə'nopəlaɪz] *v* monopolisieren. **monopoly** *n* Monopol *neut*.

monosyllable ['m onəsɪbbl] *n* einsilbiges Wort *neut*.

monotonous [m ə'notənəs] *adj* monoton. **monotony** *n* Monotonie *f*.

monsoon [m on'su:n] *n* Monsun *m*.

monster ['m onstə] *n* Ungeheuer *neut*; (*malformation*) Mißbildung *f*. **monstrous** *adj* ungeheuer.

month [m ʌnθ] *n* Monat *m*. **monthly** *adj* monatlich; *n* (*magazine*) Monatsschrift *f*.

monument ['m onjɪm ənt] *n* Denkmal *neut*. **monumental** *adj* kolossal.

mood [m u:d] *n* Laune *f*, Stimmung *f*. **be in a good/bad mood** guter/schlechter Laune sein. **moody** *adj* launisch.

moon [m u:n] *n* Mond *m*. **full moon** Vollmond *m*. **moonlight** *n* Mondschein *m*.

moor[1] [m uə] *n* Heide *f*, Moor *neut*.

moor[2] [m uə] *v* (*boat*) vertäuen. **mooring** *n* Liegeplatz *m*.

mop [m op] *n* Mop *m*. *v* aufwischen.

mope [m oup] *v* traurig sein, (*coll*) Trübsal blasen.

moped ['m ouped] *n* Moped *neut*.

moral ['m ɔɹəl] *adj* moralisch. *n* (*of story*) Lehre *f*. **morals** *pl* Moral *f sing*, Sitten *pl*. **morale** *n* Morale *f*. **morality** *n* Sittlichkeit *f*. **mores** *pl n* Sitten *pl*.

morbid ['m ɔ:bɪd] *adj* (*fig*) schauerlich.

more [m ɔ:] *adj* mehr; (*in number*) weitere, mehr. *adv* mehr, weiter. *more rapid* schneller. **more and more** immer mehr. **more or less** mehr oder weniger. **once more** noch einmal. **moreover** *adv* überdies, fernerhin.

morgue [m ɔ:ɡ] *n* Leichenhaus *neut*.

morning ['m ɔ:nɪŋ] *n* Morgen *m*, Vormittag *m*. **in the mornings** morgens. **this morning** heute früh.

moron ['m ɔ:ron] *n* Schwachsinnige(r). **moronic** *adj* schwachsinnig.

morose [m ə'rous] *adj* mürrisch.

morphine ['m ɔ:fɪn] *n* Morphium *neut*.

morse code [m ɔ:s] *n* Morsealphabet *neut*.

morsel ['m ɔ:səl] *n* Bissen *m*, Stückchen *neut*.

mortal ['m ɔ:tl] *adj* sterblich; (*wound*) tödlich. **mortality** *n* Sterblichkeit *f*.

mortar ['m ɔ:tə] *n* (*for bricks*) Mörtel *m*; (*mil*) Granatwerfer *m*.

mortgage ['m ɔ:ɡɪdʒ] *n* Hypothek *f*.

mortify ['m ɔ:tɪfaɪ] *v* demütigen. **mortification** *n* Demütigung *f*.

mortuary ['m ɔ:tʃuəɪ] *n* Leichenhaus *neut*.

mosaic [m ə'zeɪk] *n* Mosaik *neut*.

mosque [m osk] *n* Moschee *f*.

mosquito [m ə'skɪtou] *n* Moskito *m*.

moss [m os] *n* Moos *neut*. **mossy** *adj* bemoost.

most [m oust] *adj* die meisten. *adv* äußerst, höchst; am meisten. *n* das Meiste. *most people* die meisten Leute. **at most** höchstens. **mostly** *adv* meistens, größtenteils.

motel [m ou'tel] *n* Motel *neut*.

moth [m oθ] *n* Motte *f*. **mothball** *n* Mottenkugel *f*.

mother ['m ʌðə] *n* Mutter *f*. *v* bemuttern. **on one's mother's side** mütterlicherseits. **mother country** Mutterland *neut*. **motherhood** *n* Mutterschaft *f*. **mother-in-law** Schwiegermutter *f*. **motherless** *adj* mutterlos. **motherly** *adj* mütterlich. **mother-of-pearl** *n* Perlmutt *neut*.

motion ['m oufən] *n* Bewegung *f*; (*pol*) Antrag *m*. *v* zuwinken. **set in motion** in

Gang setzen.

motivate ['m outiveit] v motivieren. **motivation** n Motivierung f.

motif [m ou'ti:f] n Motiv m.

motive ['m outiv] n Beweggrund m.

motor ['m outə] n Motor m. **motor accident** Autounfall m. **motorcar** n Wagen m, Auto neut. **motor cycle** n Mottorrad neut. **motorist** n Autofahrer m.

mottled ['m otld] adj gefleckt.

motto ['m otou] n Motto neut.

mould[1] [m ould] or US **mold** n (tech) Form f; (type) Art f. v bilden, formen; (tech) gießen.

mould[2] [m ould] or US **mold** n (mildew) Schimmel m. **mouldy** adj schimmelig.

moult [m ould] or US **molt** v sich mausern.

mound [m aund] n (Erd)Hügel m.

mount[1] [m aunt] v (horse) besteigen. n (frame) Gestell neut; (horse) Reittier neut.

mount[2] [m aunt] n Berg m, Hügel m.

mountain ['m auntən] n Berg m. **mountain bike** Mountainbike neut; geländetauchliches Fahrrad neut. **mountaineer** n Bergsteiger m.

mourn [m o:n] v trauern (um). **mourning** n Trauer f. **go into mourning** Trauer anlegen.

mouse [m aus] n (pl mice) Maus f. **mouse mat** n Mausmatte f. **mousetrap** n Mausefalle f.

mousse [m u:s] n Kremeis neut.

moustache [m ə'sta:ʃ] or US **mustache** n Schnurrbart m.

mouth [m auθ] n Mund m; (opening) Öffnung f; (river) Mündung f; (animal) Maul neut. **mouthful** n Mundvoll m. **mouthpiece** n Mundstück neut. **mouthwash** n Mundwasser neut.

move [m u:v] v (sich) bewegen; (emotionally) rühren; (house) umziehen. **movable** adj beweglich. **movement** n Bewegung f. **moving** adj rührend. **moving staircase** Rolltreppe f.

movie [m u:vi] n Film m. **go to the movies** ins Kino gehen.

***mow** [m ou] v mähen. **mower** n (Rasen)Mäher m.

mown [m oun] V **mow**.

MP n Abgeordnete m, f.

Mr ['m istə] n Herr m.

Mrs ['m isiz] n Frau f.

Ms [m iz] n Frau.

much [m ʌtʃ] adj, adv viel. **how much?** wieviel?

muck [m ʌk] n (dung) Mist m; (dirt) Dreck m. **mucky** adj schmutzig, dreckig.

mucus ['m ju:kəs] n Schleim m.

mud [m ʌd] n Schlamm m. **muddy** adj schlammig. **mudguard** n Kotflügel m. **mudslinger** n Verleumder(in).

muddle ['m ʌd] n Durcheinander neut, Wirrwarr m. v **muddle through** sich durchwursteln. **muddled** adj konfus.

muff [m ʌf] n Muff m.

muffle ['m ʌfl] v (noise) dämpfen. **muffler** n Schal m; (mot) Schalldämpfer m.

mug [m ʌg] n Krug m, Becher m. v (rob) überfallen. **mugger** n Straßenräuber m. **muggy** adj (weather) schwül.

mulberry ['m ʌlbəri] n Maulbeere f.

mule [m ju:l] n Maulesel m. **mulish** adj störrisch.

multicoloured [,m ʌltikʌləd] adj bunt, vielfarbig.

multiple ['m ʌltipl] adj mehrfach, vielfach.

multiply ['m ʌltiplai] v (sich) vermehren; (math) multiplizieren. **multiplication** v Vermehrung f; (math) Multiplikation f. **multiplicity** n Vielfalt f.

multiracial [,m ʌltireiʃəl] adj gemischtrassig.

multitude ['m ʌltitju:d] n Menge f. **multitudinous** adj zahlreich.

mumble ['m ʌmbl] v murmeln. n Gemurmel neut.

mummy[1] ['m ʌmi] n (embalmed) Mumie f.

mummy[2] ['m ʌmi] n (coll) Mutti f.

mumps [m ʌmps] n Ziegenpeter m.

munch [m ʌntʃ] v schmetzend kauen.

mundane [m ʌn'dein] adj alltäglich, banal.

municipal [m ju:'nisipə] adj städtisch, Stadt-. **municipality** n Stadt f, Stadtbezirk m.

mural ['m juərəl] n Wandgemälde neut.

murder ['m ə:də] n Mord m, Ermordung f. v (er)morden. **murderer** n Mörder m. **murderous** adj mörderisch, tödlich.

murmur ['m ə:m ə] v murmeln. n Murmeln neut.

muscle ['m ʌsl] n Muskel m. **muscular** adj (person) muskulös.

muse [m ju:z] n Muse f. v (nach)denken.

museum [m ju'ziəm] n Museum neut.

mushroom [ˈmʌʃrum] *n* Pilz *m*, Champignon *m*. *v* (*coll*) sich ausbreiten.

music [ˈmjuːzɪk] *n* Musik f. **musical** *adj* musikalisch. **musician** *n* Musiker *m*. **music stand** Notenständer *m*.

musk [mʌsk] *n* Moschus *m*.

musket [ˈmʌskɪt] *n* Flinte f, Muskete f. **musketeer** *n* Musketier *m*.

Muslim [ˈmʌzlɪm] *n* Mohammedaner(in). *adj* mohammedanisch.

muslin [ˈmʌzlɪn] *n* Musselin *m*.

mussel [ˈmʌsl] *n* Muschel f.

***must*¹** [mʌst] *v* müssen.

must² [mʌst] *n* Most *m*. **musty** *adj* muffig, schimmelig.

mustard [ˈmʌstəd] *n* Senf *m*.

muster [ˈmʌstə] *v* antreten lassen. **muster one's courage** sich zusammennehmen. *n* **pass muster** Zustimmung finden.

mutation [mjuːˈteɪʃən] *n* Veränderung f; (*biol*) Mutation f.

mute [mjuːt] *adj* stumm. *n* Stumme(r); (*music*) Sordine f.

mutilate [ˈmjuːtɪleɪt] *v* verstümmeln. **mutilation** *n* Verstümmelung f.

mutiny [ˈmjuːtɪni] *n* Meuterei f. *v* meutern. **mutineer** *n* Meuterer *m*. **mutinous** *adj* meuterisch.

mutter [ˈmʌtə] *v* murmeln.

mutton [ˈmʌtn] *n* Hammelfleisch *neut*.

mutual [ˈmjuːtʃuəl] *adj* gegenseitig.

muzzle [ˈmʌzl] *n* Maul *neut*; (*protection*) Maulkorb *m*.

my [maɪ] *poss adj* mein, meine, mein. **myself** *pron* mich (selbst). **by myself** allein.

mystery [ˈmɪstəri] *n* Rätsel *neut*, Geheimnis *neut*. **mysterious** *adj* geheimnisvoll, mysteriös. **mystic** *n* Mystiker(in). *adj* mystisch. **mysticism** *n* Mystizismus *m*. **mystify** *v* täuschen, verblüffen.

myth [mɪθ] *n* Mythos *m*. **mythical** *adj* mythisch. **mythological** *adj* mythologisch. **mythology** *n* Mythologie f.

N

nag [nag] *v* herumnörgeln an. *n* (*horse*) Gaul *m*. **nagging** *adj* (*pain, etc*.) nagend.

nail [neɪl] *n* Nagel *m*. *v* (an)nageln. **nail down** zunageln. **nailbrush** *n* Nagelbürste f. **nail-file** *n* Nagelfeile f. **nail polish** Nagellack *m*. **nail scissors** Nagelschere f *sing*.

naive [naɪˈiːv] *adj* naiv. **naïveté** *n* Naivität f.

naked [ˈneɪkɪd] *adj* nackt. **nakedness** *n* Nacktheit f.

name [neɪm] *n* Name *m*; (*reputation*) Ruf *m*. **by name** namentlich. **by the name of** namens. *what's your name?* wie heißen Sie? *v* nennen; (*mention*) erwähnen. **namely** *adv* nämlich.

nanny [ˈnani] *n* Kindermädchen *neut*.

nap [nap] *n* Nickerchen *neut*.

napkin [ˈnapkɪn] *n* (*table*) Serviette f.

nappy [ˈnapi] *n* Windel f.

narcotic [naːˈkɒtɪk] *n* Narkotikum *neut*. *adj* narkotisch.

narrate [nəˈreɪt] *v* erzählen. **narration** *n* *also* **narrative** Erzählung f. **narrative** *adj* Erzählungs-. **narrator** *n* Erzähler(in).

narrow [ˈnarou] *adj* eng, schmal; (*fig*) beschränkt. *v* sich verengen. **narrowly** *adv* (*just*) mit Mühe. **narrow-minded** *adj* engstirnig.

nasal [ˈneɪzəl] *adj* Nasen-; (*voice*) nasal.

nasturtium [nəˈstəːʃəm] *n* Kapuzinerkresse f.

nasty [ˈnaːsti] *adj* ekelhaft, widerlich; (*serious*) ernst, schlimm; (*person*) gemein, böse.

nation [ˈneɪʃən] *n* Nation f, Volk *neut*. **national** *adj* national, Volks-. **nationalism** *n* Nationalismus *m*. **nationality** *n* Staatsangehörigkeit f. **nationalization** *n* Verstaatlichung f. **nationalize** *v* verstaatlichen. **national anthem** Nationalhymne f. **National Insurance** Sozialversicherung f. **nationwide** *adj* landesweit.

native [ˈneɪtɪv] *adj* eingeboren. *n* Eingeborene(r).

nativity [nəˈtɪvəti] *n* Geburt f. **nativity play** Krippenspiel *neut*.

natural [ˈnatʃərəl] *adj* natürlich, Natur-. **natural resources** Naturschätze *pl*. **naturalist** *n* Naturforscher *m*. **naturalize** *v* einbürgen.

nature [ˈneɪtʃə] *n* Natur f.

naughty [ˈnoːti] *adj* unartig, ungezogen. **naughtiness** *n* Ungezogenheit f.

nausea ['nɔːzə] n Übelkeit f, Brechreiz m; (seasickness) Seekrankheit f. **nauseating** adj widerlich.

nautical ['nɔːtɪkəl] adj nautisch, Schiffs-. **nautical mile** Seemeile f.

naval ['neɪvəl] adj Flotten-, See-. **naval battle** Seeschlacht f.

navel ['neɪvəl] n Nabel m.

navigate ['navɪgeɪt] v navigieren. **navigable** adj schiffbar. **navigation** n Navigation f. **navigator** n Navigator m.

navy ['neɪvɪ] n Flotte f, Kriegsmarine f. **navy-blue** adj marineblau.

near [nɪə] adj nahe. adv nahe, in der Nähe. prep in der Nähe (von or +gen), nahe an. **nearby** adv in der Nähe; adj nahe gelegen. **nearly** adv fast, beinahe.

neat [niːt] adj ordentlich; (alcohol) rein, unverdünnt. **neatness** n Ordentlichkeit f.

necessary ['nesɪsərɪ] adj nötig, erforderlich. **necessarily** adv notwendigerweise. **necessitate** v erfordern. **necessity** n Notwendigkeit f. **necessities** pl Bedarfsartikel pl.

neck [nek] n Hals m. **neckerchief** n Halstuch neut. **necklace** n Halskette f. **necktie** n Krawatte f.

nectar ['nektə] n Nektar m.

nectarine ['nektərin] n Nektarine f.

née [neɪ] adj geborene.

need [niːd] v Bedürfnis neut, Bedarf m; (necessity) Notwendigkeit f. **if need arise** im Notfall. **needful** adj nötig. **neediness** n Armut f. **needless** adj unnötig. **needy** adj arm.

needle ['niːdl] n Nadel f; (indicator) Zeiger m. v (coll) reizen. **needlework** n Handarbeit f.

negate [nɪgeɪt] v annullieren, verneinen. **negation** n Annullierung f, Verneinung f. **negative** adj negativ; (answer) ablehnend. n (phot) Negativ neut.

neglect [nɪglekt] v vernachlässigen. n Vernachlässigung f.

negligée ['neglɪʒeɪ] n Negligé neut.

negligence ['neglɪdʒəns] n Nachlässigkeit f. **negligent** adj nachlässig. **negligible** adj geringfügig.

negotiate [nɪgoʊʃɪeɪt] v verhandeln. **negotiation** n Verhandlung f. **negotiator** n Vermittler m.

Negro ['niːgrəʊ] n Neger m. adj Neger-.

Negress n Negerin f.

neigh [neɪ] v wiehern. n Wiehern neut.

neighbour ['neɪbə] n Nachbar(in). **neighbourhood** n Nachbarschaft f. **neighbourly** adj freundlich.

neither ['naɪðə] adj, pron kein (von beiden). **neither ... nor ...** weder ... noch ....

neon ['nɪon] n Neon neut.

nephew ['nefjuː] n Neffe m.

nepotism ['nepətɪzəm] n Vetternwirtschaft f.

nerd [nəːd] (coll) Computerfreak m.

nerve [nəːv] n Nerv m; (cheek) Frechheit f. **nerves** pl Nervosität f sing. **nervous** adj Nerven-; (on edge) nervös. **nervousness** n Nervosität f. **nervy** adj nervös. **nerveracking** nervenaufreibend.

nest [nest] n Nest neut. v nisten.

nestle ['nesl] v sich anschmiegen.

net[1] [net] n Netz neut; (fabric) Tüll m. v fangen.

net[2] [net] adj (comm) netto, Netto-. **net amount** Nettobetrag m. **net price** Nettopreis m. **net profit** Reingewinn m.

Net [net] n (Internet) Internet neut.

Netherlands ['neðələndz] pl n Niederlände pl.

nettle ['netl] n Nessel f. v ärgern. **nettle rash** Nesselausschlag m. **grasp the nettle** die Schwierigkeit anpacken.

neurosis [njuˈrəʊsɪs] n Neurose f. **neurotic** adj neurotisch; n Neurotiker(in).

neuter ['njuːtə] adj (gramm) sächlich. n Neutrum neut. v (male) kastrieren; (female) sterilisieren.

neutral ['njuːtrəl] adj neutral. n (mot) Leerlauf m. **neutrality** n Neutralität f. **neutralize** v neutralisieren.

never ['nevə] adv nie, niemals. **neverending** adj endlos. **never-failing** adj unfehlbar. **nevermore** adv nimmermehr. **nevertheless** adv nichtsdestoweniger.

new [njuː] adj neu; (strange) unbekannt. **newborn** adj neugeboren. **newcomer** n Neuankömmling m. **new-fangled** adj neumodisch. **newish** adj ziemlich neu. **newly** adv neulich. **newly-wed** adj jungvermählt. **newness** n Neuheit f. **news** pl n Nachrichten pl. **newspaper** n Zeitung f. **newsagent** n Zeitungshändler m. **news flash** Kurznachricht f. **newsstand** n Zeitungskiosk m **newsworthy** adj aktuell.

newt [njuːt] n Wassermolch m.

New Testament n Neujahr neut. **New Year's Day** Neujahr neut. **New Year's Eve** Sylvester neut.

next [nekst] adj nächst, nächstfolgend; adv gleich daran, nächstens. prep neben, bei. **next door** nebenan.

nib [nib] n (Füllfeder)Spitze f.

nibble ['nibl] v nagen, knabbern (an). n Nagen neut, Knabbern neut; (morsel) Happen m.

nice [nais] adj nett; (kind) freundlich. **nicely** adv nett. **nicety** n Feinheit f.

niche [niʃ] n Nische f.

nick [nik] v einkerben; (coll: catch) erwischen. n Kerbe f; (coll) Gefängnis neut; Polizeiwache f.

nickel [nikl] n Nickel neut; (US) Fünfcentstück neut. adj Nickel-. **nickel-plated** adj vernickelt.

nickname ['nikneim] n Spitzname m.

nicotine ['nikətiːn] n Nikotin neut.

niece [niːs] n Nichte f.

niggle ['nigl] v trödeln.

night [nait] n Nacht f; (evening) Abend m. **all night** die ganze Nacht. **goodnight** gute Nacht. **nightclub** n Nachtlokal neut. **nightdress** n Nachthemd neut. **nightly** adj nächtlich. **nightmare** n Alptraum m. **nighttime** n Nacht f.

nightingale ['naitiŋgeil] n Nachtigall f.

nil [nil] n Null f.

nimble ['nimbl] adj flink. **nimbleness** n Gewandtheit f.

nine [nain] adj neun. n Neun f. **ninth** adj neunt; n Neuntel neut.

nineteen [nain'tiːn] adj neunzehn. n Neunzehn f. **nineteenth** adj neunzehnt.

ninety ['nainti] adj neunzig. n Neunzig f. **ninetieth** adj neunzigst.

nip [nip] v kneifen, zwicken. **nip in the bud** im Keim ersticken.

nipple ['nipl] n Brustwarze f; (baby's bottle) Lutscher m; (tech) Nippel m.

nit [nit] n Niß f, Nisse f.

nitrogen ['naitrədʒən] n Stickstoff m.

no [nou] adv nein. adj kein. **on no account** auf keinen Fall. **in no way** keineswegs. **no more** nicht mehr. **no smoking** Rauchen verboten. **no-smoking compartment** Nichtraucher m.

noble ['noubl] adj edel, adlig. **nobility** n Adel m, Adelsstand m. **nobleman** n Edelmann m.

nobody ['noubodi] pron niemand, keiner.

nocturnal [nok'təːnəl] adj nächtlich, Nacht-.

nod [nod] v nicken. n Nicken neut. **nod off** einschlafen.

noise [noiz] n Lärm m, Geräusch neut. **noiseless** adj geräuschlos. **noisy** adj laut.

nomad ['noum ad] n Nomade m, Nomadin f. **nomadic** adj nomadisch.

nominal ['nom inl] adj nominell, Nenn-.

nominate ['nom ineit] v ernennen. **nomination** n Ernennung f.

nominative ['nom inətiv] n (gramm) Nominativ m.

nonchalant ['nonʃələnt] adj unbekümmert. **nonchalance** n Gleichgültigkeit f.

nondescript ['nondiskript] adj nichtssagend.

none [nʌn] pron kein; (person) niemand. adv keineswegs.

nonentity [non'entəti] n Unding neut; (coll: person) Null f.

nonetheless [nʌnðə'les] adv nichtsdestoweniger.

nonplussed [non'plʌst] adj verblüfft.

nonsense ['nonsəns] n Unsinn m. interj Unsinn! Quatsch! **nonsensical** adj sinnlos. **stand no nonsense** sich nichts gefallen lassen.

non-smoker [non'sm oukə] n Nichtraucher(in). **non-smoking compartment** Nichtraucher(abteil) m.

non-stick [non'stik] adj mit Antihaftbeschichtung.

non-stop [non'stop] adj pausenlos; (train) durchgehend.

noodles ['nuːdlz] pl n Nudeln pl.

noon [nuːn] n Mittag m. **at noon** zu Mittag.

no-one ['nouwʌn] pron keiner, niemand.

noose [nuːs] n Schlinge f.

nor [noː] adj noch. **nor do I** ich auch nicht.

norm [noːm] n Norm f. **normal** adj normal. **normality** n Normalität f. **normalize** v normalisieren. **normally** adv normalerweise.

north [noːθ] n Norden m. adj also **northerly, northern** nördlich, Nord-. adv also

northwards nach Norden, nordwärts. **North America** Nordamerika *neut.* **north-east** *n* Nordosten *m.* **Northern Ireland** Nordirland *neut.* **North Pole** Nordpol *m.* **north-west** *n* Nordwesten *m.*

Norway ['nɔːweɪ] *n* Norwegen *neut.* **Norwegian** *adj* norwegisch; *n* Norweger(in).

nose [nouz] *n* Nase *f.* **nosy** *adj* (*coll*) neugierig.

nostalgia [nɒˈstældʒə] *n* Nostalgie *f.* **nostalgic** *adj* wehmütig.

nostril ['nɒstrəl] *n* Nasenloch *neut.*

not [nɒt] *adv* nicht. **not a** kein. **is it not?** *or* **isn't it?** nicht wahr?

notch [nɒtʃ] *n* Kerbe *f.* *v* einkerben.

note [nout] *n* Vermerk *m,* Notiz *f;* (*letter*) Zettel *m;* (*music*) Note *f;* (*money*) Schein *m;* (*importance*) Bedeutung *f.* *v* merken. **take notes** Notizen machen.

nothing ['nʌθiŋ] *pron* nichts. *n* Nichts *neut.* **nothing but** nichts als.

notice ['noutis] *n* Notiz *f;* (*law*) Kündigung *f.* *v* bemerken. **period of notice** Kündigungsfrist *f.* **take notice (of)** achtgeben (auf). **give notice** kündigen. **until further notice** bis auf weiteres. **noticeable** *adj* bemerkenswert. **noticeboard** *n* Anschlagtafel *f.*

notify ['noutifai] *v* melden, benachrichtigen. **notification** *n* Meldung *f;* Benachrichtigung *f.*

notion ['noufən] *n* Begriff *m.* **have no notion** keine Ahnung haben.

notorious [nouˈtɔːriəs] *adj* notorisch, anrüchig.

notwithstanding [nɒtwɪðˈstandiŋ] *prep* trotz (+*gen*).

nougat ['nuːgaː] *n* Nugat *m.*

nought [nɔːt] *n* Null *f.* **come/bring to nought** zunichte kommen/bringen.

noun [naun] *n* Hauptwort *neut.*

nourish ['nʌrɪʃ] *v* (er)nähren. **nourishing** *adj* nahrhaft. **nourishment** *n* Ernährung *f.*

novel ['nɒvəl] *adj* neu, neuartig. *n* Roman *m.* **novelist** *n* Romanschriftsteller(in). **novelty** *n* Neuheit *f.*

November [nəˈvembə] *n* November *m.*

novice ['nɒvis] *n* Anfänger(in); (*rel*) Novize *m, f.*

now [nau] *adv* jetzt, nun; (*straightaway*) sofort. **now and again** ab und zu, hin und wieder. **nowadays** *adv* heutzutage.

nowhere ['nouweə] *adv* nirgends, nirgendwo. **from nowhere** aus dem Nichts.

noxious ['nɒkʃəs] *adj* schädlich.

nozzle ['nɒzl] *n* Schnauze *f,* Ausguß *m.*

nuance ['njuːãs] *n* Nuance *f,* Schattierung *f.*

nuclear ['njuːklɪə] *adj* Kern-. **nuclear energy** Atomkraft *f.* **nuclear reactor** Kernreaktor *m.*

nucleus ['njuːklɪəs] *n* Kern *m.*

nude ['njuːd] *adj* nackt. **nudist** *n* Nudist(in). **nudity** *n* Nacktheit *f.*

nudge [nʌdʒ] *n* Rippenstoß *m.* *v* leicht anstoßen.

nugget ['nʌgit] *n* Goldklumpen *m.*

nuisance ['njuːsns] *n* Ärgernis *neut.*

null [nʌl] *adj* nichtig, ungültig. **null and void** null und nichtig.

numb [nʌm] *adj* starr, erstarrt. *v* taub machen.

number ['nʌmbə] *n* Nummer *f;* (*amount*) Anzahl *f;* (*figure*) Ziffer *f.* *v* numerieren. **number-plate** *n* Nummernschild *neut.* **numeral** *n* Ziffer *f.* **numerous** *adj* zahlreich.

nun [nʌn] *n* Nonne *f.*

nurse [nəːs] *n* Krankenschwester *f,* Krankenpfleger(in). *v* pflegen; (*feed baby*) stillen. **nursemaid** *n* Kindermädchen *neut.* **nursing** *n* Krankenpflege *f.* **nursing home** Privatklinik *f.*

nursery ['nəːsəri] *n* (*in house*) Kinderzimmer *neut;* (*institution*) Krippe *f,* Kindertagesstätte *f;* (*bot*) Gärtnerei *f.* **nurseryman** *n* Pflanzenzüchter *m.* **nursery rhyme** *n* Kinderlied *neut,* Kinderreim *m.* **nursery school** *n* Kindergarten *m.*

nurture ['nəːtʃə] *v* erziehen.

nut [nʌt] *n* Nuß *f;* (*for bolt*) Mutter *f.* **nutcracker** Nußknacker *m.* **nuts** *adj* (*coll*) verrückt. **nutmeg** *n* Muskatnuß *f.*

nutrient ['njuːtriənt] *n* Nährstoff *m.* *adj* nährend. **nutrition** *n* Ernährung *f.* **nutritious** *adj* nahrhaft.

nuzzle ['nʌzl] *v* sich schmiegen (an).

nylon ['naɪlɒn] *n* Nylon *neut.* **nylons** *pl* Strümpfe *pl.*

nymph [nimf] *n* Nymphe *f.*

O

oak [ouk] *n* Eiche *f*, *(wood)* Eichenholz *neut.* **oaken** *adj* eichen.

oar [o:] *n* Ruder *neut.* Riemen *m.* **oarsman** *n* Ruderer *m.*

oasis [ou'eisis] *n* *(pl -ses)* Oase *f.*

oath [ouθ] *n* Eid *m;* *(swear word)* Fluch *m.*

oats [outs] *pl n* Hafer *m sing.* **oatmeal** *n* Hafermehl *neut.*

obedient [ə'bi:diənt] *adj* gehorsam. **obedience** *n* Gehorsam *m.*

obese [ə'bi:s] *adj* fettleibig. **obesity** *n* Fettleibigkeit *f.*

obey [ə'bei] *v* gehorchen (+*dat*); *(an order)* befolgen.

obituary [ə'bitjuəri] *n* Todesanzeige *f.*

object ['obʒikt; *v* əb'ʒekt] *n* Gegenstand *m;* *(aim)* Ziel *neut;* *(gramm)* Objekt *neut. money is no object* Geld spielt keine Rolle. **objective** *adj* objektiv. *v* einwenden (gegen). **objection** *n* Einwand *m*, Einspruch *m.* **objectionable** *adj* unangenehm.

oblige [ə'blaidʒ] *v* *(coerce)* zwingen. **be obliged to do something** etwas tun müssen. **much obliged!** besten Dank! **obligation** *n* Verpflichtung *f.* **obligatory** *adj* verbindlich.

oblique [ə'bli:k] *adj* schräg.

obliterate [ə'blitəreit] *v* auslöschen, tilgen. **obliteration** *n* Auslöschung *f*, Vertilgung *f.*

oblivion [ə'bliviən] *n* Vergessenheit *f.* **oblivious (to)** *adj* blind (gegen).

oblong ['obloŋ] *n* Rechteck *neut. adj* rechtickig.

obnoxious [əb'nokʃəs] *adj* gehässig.

oboe ['oubou] *n* Oboe *f.* **oboist** *n* Oboist(in).

obscene [əb'si:n] *adj* obszön. **obscenity** *n* Obszönität *f*, Unzüchtigkeit *f.*

obscure [əb'skjuə] *adj* *(dark)* dunkel, düster; *(meaning, etc.)* obskur, udeutlich.

obscurity *n* Dunkelheit *f*; Undeutlichkeit *f.*

observe [əb'zə:v] *v* beobachten; *(remark)* bemerken. **observer** *n* Beobachter *m.* **observation** *n* Beobachtung *f*; Bemerkung *f.*

obsess [əb'ses] *v* quälen, heimsuchen. **obsessed** *adj* besessen. **obsession** *n*

Besessenheit *f.* **obsessive** *n* *(person)* Zwangsneurotiker(in); *adj* besessen.

obsolescent [obsə'lesnt] *adj* veraltend. **obsolescence** *n* Veralten *neut.*

obsolete ['obsəli:t] *adj* überholt, veraltet.

obstacle ['obstək] *n* Hindernis *neut.*

obstetrics [ob'stetriks] *n* Geburtshilfe *f.* **obstetrician** *n* Geburtshelfer(in).

obstinate ['obstinət] *adj* hartnäckig. **obstinacy** *n* Hartnäckigkeit *f.*

obstruct [əb'strʌkt] *v* versperren, blockieren; *(hinder)* hemmen. **obstruction** *n* Versperrung *f*; Hemmung *f*; *(obstacle)* Hindernis *neut.*

obtain [əb'tein] *v* erhalten, bekommen. **obtainable** *adj* erhältlich.

obtrusive [əb'tru:siv] *adj* aufdringlich.

obtuse [əb'tju:s] *adj* stumpf.

obvious ['obviəs] *adj* offensichtlich, deutlich. **obviously** *adv* selbstverständlich, natürlich.

occasion [ə'keiʒən] *n* Gelegenheit *f*; *(possibility)* Möglichkeit *f*; *(cause)* Anlaß *m.* **occasional** *adj* gelegentlich.

occult ['okʌlt] *adj* okkult. **the occult** okkulte Wissenschaften *pl.*

occupy ['okjupai] *v* *(person)* beschäftigen; *(house)* bewohnen; *(mil)* besetzen. **occupied** *adj* *(phone booth, etc.)* besetzt. **occupant** *n* Bewohner(in). **occupation** *n* Beschäftigung *f*; *(profession)* Beruf *m*; *(mil)* Besatzung *f.* **occupational** *adj* beruflich.

occur [ə'kə:] *v* vorkommen. *it occurs to me* es fällt mir ein. **occurrence** *n* Ereignis *neut.*

ocean ['ouʃən] *n* Ozean *m*, Meer *neut.* **oceanic** *adj* ozeanisch. **ocean-going** *adj* Hochsee-.

ochre ['oukə] *adj* ockerfarbig.

octagon ['oktəgən] *n* Achteck *neut.* **octagonal** *adj* achteckig.

octave ['oktiv] *n* Oktave *f.*

October [ok'toubə] *n* Oktober *m.*

octopus ['oktəpəs] *n* Tintenfisch *m.*

oculist ['okjulist] *n* Augenarzt *m.*

odd [od] *adj* *(strange)* seltsam; *(numbers)* ungerade. **oddity** *n* Seltsamkeit *f.* **oddly (enough)** seltsamerweise. **oddments** *pl n* Reste *pl.* **oddness** *n* Seltsamkeit *f.* **odds** *pl n* (Gewinn)Chancen *pl.* **at odds with** uneins mit. **odds and ends** Krimskrams *m.*

ode [oud] *n* Ode *f.*

odious ['oudiəs] *adj* verhaßt.

odour ['oudə] n Geruch m. **odourless** adj geruchlos.

oesophagus [i'sɒfəgəs] n Speiseröhre f.

of [ɒv] prep von or gen.

off [ɒf] prep fort, weg. adv weg, entfernt; ab. adj (food) verdorben, nicht mehr frisch. **go off** weggehen; (food) verderben. **take off** (clothes) ausziehen; (holiday) frei nehmen. **switch off** ausschalten. **off and on** ab und zu. **off duty** dienstfrei.

offal ['ɒfl] n Innereien pl.

offend [ə'fend] v kränken, beleidigen. **offender** n Missetäter(in). **offence** n Vergehen neut, Verstoß m. **take offence (at)** Anstoß nehmen (an). **offensive** adj widerwärtig; n (mil) Angriff m.

offer ['ɒfə] v (an)bieten. n Angebot neut. **on offer** im Angebot. **offering** n (gift) Spende f.

offhand [ɒf'hand] adj lässig.

office ['ɒfɪs] n Büro neut; (official position or department) Amt neut. **officer** n (mil) Offizier. **take office** das Amt antreten. **office staff** Büropersonal neut.

official [ə'fɪʃəl] n Beamte(r). adj amtlich; (report, function) offiziell. **officially** adv offiziell.

officious [ə'fɪʃəs] adj aufdringlich.

offing ['ɒfɪŋ] n **in the offing** in Sicht, drohend.

off-licence ['ɒflaisns] n Wein- und Spirituosenhandlung f.

off-line [ɒf'lain] adj, adv (Internet) offline.

off-peak [ɒf'piːk] adj außerhalb der Hauptverkehrszeit.

off-putting ['ɒfputiŋ] adj abstoßend.

off-road vehicle ['ɒfroud] n Geländefahrzeug neut. Fahrzeug/Auto mit Allradantrieb neut.

off-season [ɒf'siːzn] n stille Saison f.

offset [ɒf'set; n 'ɒfset] v ausgleichen. n (printing) Offsetdruck m.

offshore ['ɒfʃoː] adj Küsten-. adv von der Küste entfernt, auf dem Meere.

offside [ɒf'said] adj abseits.

offspring ['ɒfspriŋ] n Nachkommenschaft f.

offstage ['ɒfsteidʒ] adv hinter den Kulissen.

often ['ɒfn] adv oft, häufig.

ogre ['ougə] n Ungeheuer neut, Riese m.

oil [ɔil] n Öl n; (petroleum) Erdöl neut. v ölen. **oilfield** Ölfeld neut. **oil-paint** n Ölfarbe f. **oil-painting** n Ölgemalde neut. **oily** adj fettig.

ointment ['ɔintmənt] n Salbe f.

old [ould] adj alt. **grow old** alt werden. five years old fünf Jahre alt. **old age** Alter neut. **old-fashioned** adj altmodisch:

olive ['ɒliv] n Olive f. **olive-green** adj olivgrün. **olive branch** n Ölzweig m. **olive oil** Olivenöl neut. **olive tree** Ölbaum m.

Olympics [ə'limpiks] pl n Olympische Spiele pl, Olympiade f.

omelette ['ɒmlit] n Omelett neut.

omen ['oumən] n Vorzeichen neut. **ominous** adj verhängnisvoll, drohend.

omit [ou'mit] v auslassen; (to do something) unterlassen. **omission** n Unterlassung f.

omnipotent [ɒm'nipətənt] adj allmächtig. **omnipotence** n Allmacht f.

on [ɒn] prep (position) an, auf; (concerning) über. adv (forward) fort, weiter. **have on** one bei sich haben. **on fire** in Brand. **on foot** zu Fuß. **on time** pünktlich. **put on** (clothes) anziehen; (manner) affektieren. **switch on** einschalten.

once [wʌns] adv, conj einmal. **at once** sofort. **once and for all** ein für allemal. **all at once** auf einmal, plötzlich.

one [wʌn] adj ein, eine, ein. n Eins f. pron man. **oneself** pron sich (selbst). **by oneself** allein. **one-off** adj einmalig. **one-piece** adj einteilig. **one-way street** Einbahnstraße f.

ongoing [ɒn'gouiŋ] adj laufend, dauernd, permanent.

onion ['ʌnjən] n Zwiebel f.

on-line [ɒn'lain] adj, adv Online-, online.

onlooker ['ɒnlukə] n Zuschauer(in).

only ['ounli] adj einzig. adv nur; (with times) erst. conj jedoch. **only just** gerade. **not only ... but also** ... nicht nur ... sondern auch ….

onset ['ɒnset] n Anfang m.

onslaught ['ɒnslɔːt] n Angriff m.

onus ['ounəs] n Last f, Verpflichtung f.

onward ['ɒnwəd] adv vorwärts, weiter.

ooze [uːz] v (aus)sickern.

opal ['oupəl] n Opal m.

opaque [ə'paik] adj undurchsichtig.

open ['oupən] v öffnen, aufmachen; (book) aufschlagen; (event, shop) eröffnen; (begin) anfangen. adj offen, auf. **open-air** adj

Freiluft-. **in the open air** im Freien. **with open arms** herzlich. **open-handed** adj freigiebig. **opening** n Öffnung f. (shop) Eröffnung f. **openminded** adj aufgeschlossen.

opera ['ɒpərə] n Oper f. **opera house** Oper f, Opernhaus neut. **opera singer** Opernsänger(in). **operatic** adj Opern-.

operate ['ɒpəreɪt] v funktionieren, laufen; (med, tech, comm) operieren. **operation** n Arbeitslauf m, Betrieb m; Operation f. **operative** adj tätig, wirksam; n Arbeiter m.

ophthalmic [ɒfθalmik] adj Augen-. **ophthalmologist** n Augenarzt m. **ophthalmology** n Ophthalmologie f.

opinion [ə'pɪnjən] n Meinung f, Ansicht f. **in my opinion** meines Erachtens. **opinion poll** Meinungsumfrage f.

opium ['oupɪəm] n Opium neut.

opponent [ə'pounənt] n Gegner(in).

opportune [ɒpə'tjuːn] adj rechtzeitig. **opportunist** n Opportunist(in).

opportunity [ɒpə'tjuːnəti] n Gelegenheit f; (possibility) Möglichkeit f. **take the opportunity** die Gelegenheit ergreifen.

oppose [ə'pouz] v bekämpfen, sich widersetzen (+dat). **opposed** adj feindlich (gegen). **as opposed to** im Vergleich zu. **opposing** adj (ideas) widerstreitend. **opposition** n Widerstand m; (pol) Opposition f.

opposite ['ɒpəzɪt] adj gegenüberliegend. n Gegenteil neut.

oppress [ə'prɛs] v unterdrücken. **oppression** n Unterdrückung f. **oppressive** adj bedrückend; (weather) schwül.

opt [ɒpt] v sich entscheiden (für).

optical ['ɒptɪk] adj optisch. **optician** n Optiker m. **optics** n Optik f.

optimism ['ɒptɪmɪzəm] n Optimismus m. **optimist** n Optimist(in). **optimistic** adj optimistisch.

optimum ['ɒptɪməm] n Optimum neut. adj optimal.

option ['ɒpʃən] n Wahl f; (comm) Option f. **have no option (but to)** keine andere Möglichkeit haben (, als zu). **optional** adj wahlfrei.

opulent ['ɒpjulənt] adj opulent, üppig. **opulence** n Opulenz f, Üppigkeit f.

or [ɔː] conj oder. **or else** sonst.

oracle ['ɒrəkl] n Orakel neut.

oral ['ɔːrəl] adj mündlich; (med) oral. n mündliche Prüfung f.

orange ['ɒrɪndʒ] n Apfelsine f, Orange f. adj orange.

orator ['ɒrətə] n Redner m. **oration** n Rede f. **oratory** n Redekunst f.

orbit ['ɔːbɪt] n Umlaufbahn f. v umkreisen.

orchard ['ɔːtʃəd] n Obstgarten m.

orchestra ['ɔːkəstrə] n Orchester neut. **orchestral** adj Orchester-, orchestral.

orchid ['ɔːkɪd] n Orchidee f.

ordain [ɔːˈdeɪn] v ordinieren, weihen; (decree) anordnen.

ordeal [ɔːˈdiːl] n schwere Prüfung f.

order ['ɔːdə] n Ordnung f; (series) Reihenfolge f; (comm) Bestellung f, Auftrag m; (command) Befehl m; (rel) Orden m. v (comm) bestellen; (command) befehlen. **put in order** ordnen. **in order to** ... um ... zu ...

orderly ['ɔːdəli] adj ordentlich. n (med) Sanitäter m.

ordinal ['ɔːdɪnl] adj Ordinal-.

ordinary ['ɔːdənəri] adj gewöhnlich, normal. **out-of-the-ordinary** außerordentlich. **ordinarily** adv normalerweise.

ore [ɔː] n Erz neut.

oregano [ɒrɪˈɡaːnou] n Origanum neut.

organ ['ɔːɡən] n Organ neut; (music) Orgel f. **organist** n Organist(in).

organic [ɔːˈɡanɪk] adj organisch; (food) Bio-, biologisch.

organism ['ɔːɡənɪzəm] n Organismus m.

organize ['ɔːɡənaɪz] v organisieren. **organization** n Organisation f; (association) Verband m. **organizer** n Organisator m.

orgasm ['ɔːɡazəm] n Orgasmus m.

orgy ['ɔːdʒi] n Orgie f.

orient ['ɔːrɪənt] v orientieren. **the Orient** Morgenland neut, Orient m. **oriental** adj orientalisch; n Orientale m, Orientalin f.

orientate ['ɔːrɪənteɪt] v orientieren. **orientation** n Orientierung f.

origin ['ɒrɪdʒɪn] n Ursprung f; Herkunft f, Entstehung f. **original** adj ursprünglich; (unusual) originell; n Original neut. **originality** n Originalität f. **originate** v entstehen.

ornament ['ɔːnəmənt] n Ornament neut. v verzieren, schmücken. **ornamental** adj ornamental.

ornate [ɔːˈneɪt] adj reich verziert.

ornithology [ɔːnɪˈθɒlədʒɪ] n Ornithologie f, Vogelkunde f. **ornithologist** n Ornithologe m, Ornithologin f.

orphan [ˈɔːfən] n Waise f, Waisenkind neut. v verwaisen. **orphanage** n Waisenhaus neut.

orthodox [ˈɔːθədɒks] adj orthodox.

orthopaedic [ɔːθəˈpiːdik] adj orthopädisch. **orthopaedics** n Orthopädie f.

oscillate [ˈɒsɪleɪt] v oszillieren, schwingen. **oscillation** n Schwingung f.

ostensible [ɒˈstensəbl] adj scheinbar.

ostentatious [ɒstenˈteɪʃəs] adj großtuerisch. **ostentation** n Prahlerei f.

osteopath [ˈɒstəpæθ] n Osteopath(in).

ostracize [ˈɒstrəsaɪz] v verbannen.

ostrich [ˈɒstrɪʃ] n Strauß m.

other [ˈʌðə] adj, pron ander. **other than** anders als. **each other** einander. **somebody or other** irgend jemand. **one after the other** einer/eine/eins nach dem/der andern.

otherwise [ˈʌðəwaɪz] adv sonst.

otter [ˈɒtə] n Otter m.

*ought [ɔːt] v sollen. you ought to do it Sie sollten es tun.

ounce [auns] n Unze f.

our [auə] adj unser. **Our Father** Vaterunser neut. **ours** poss pron unsere. **ourselves** uns (selbst).

oust [aust] v vertreiben.

out [aut] adv aus, hinaus, heraus; (outside) draußen. **come out** herauskommen; (book, etc.) erscheinen. **go out** hinausgehen. **out of the question** ausgeschlossen. **out-of-date** adj veraltet.

outboard [ˈautbɔːd] adj Außenbord-. n Außenbordmotor m.

outbreak [ˈautbreɪk] n Ausbruch m.

outbuilding [ˈautbɪldɪŋ] n Nebengebäude neut.

outburst [ˈautbəːst] n Ausbruch m.

outcast [ˈautkɑːst] n Ausgestoßene(r).

outcome [ˈautkʌm] n Ergebnis neut.

outcry [ˈautkraɪ] n Aufschrei m.

outdated [autˈdeɪtɪd] adj (practice) überholt; (clothes) veraltet.

*outdo [autˈduː] v übertreffen.

outdoor [ˈautdɔː] adj Außen-. **outdoor swimming pool** Freibad neut. **outdoors** adv draußen.

outer [ˈautə] adj äußer, Außen-. **outer garments** Oberkleidung f. **outer space** Weltraum m.

outfit [ˈautfɪt] n Ausstattung f; (coll: team) Mannschaft f. **outfitter** n (Herren)Ausstatter m.

outgoing [ˈautgouɪŋ] adj (pol) abtretend; (friendly) gesellig.

*outgrow [autˈgrou] v hinauswachsen über; (clothes) herauswachsen aus.

outhouse [ˈauthaus] n Anbau m, Nebengebäude neut.

outing [ˈautɪŋ] n Ausflug m.

outlandish [autˈlændɪʃ] adj seltsam, grotesk.

outlaw [ˈautlɔː] n Vogelfreie(r). v ächten.

outlay [ˈautleɪ] n Auslage f, Ausgabe f.

outlet [ˈautlɪt] n Auslaß m.

outline [ˈautlaɪn] n Umriß m. v umreißen.

outlive [autˈlɪv] v überleben.

outlook [ˈautluk] n Aussicht f; (attitude) Auffassung f.

outlying [ˈautlaɪɪŋ] adj entlegen.

outnumber [autnʌm bə] v (zahlenmäßig) überlegen sein (+dat).

outpatient [ˈautpeɪʃənt] n ambulanter Patient m.

outpost [ˈautpoust] n Vorposten m.

output [ˈautput] n Leistung f, Output m; (comp) Ausgabe f.

outrage [ˈautreɪdʒ] n Schande f. **outraged** adj beleidigt, schockiert. **outrageous** adj frevelhaft.

outright [autˈraɪt; adv autˈraɪt] adj, adv ganz, völlig; (immediately) sogleich, auf der Stelle.

outside [autˈsaɪd; adv autˈsaɪd] n Äußere neut, Außenseite f. adj äußer, Außen-. prep außerhalb (+gen). adv (go) hinaus; (be) draußen. **outsider** n Außenseiter(in).

outsize [ˈautsaɪz] adj übergroß. n Übergröße f.

outskirts [ˈautskəːts] pl n Umgebung f sing, Staatrand m sing.

outspoken [autˈspoukən] adj freimütig.

outstanding [autˈstandɪŋ] adj hervorragend; (not settled) unerledigt.

outstrip [autˈstrip] v überholen.

outward [ˈautwəd] adj äußer. adv also **outwards** nach Außen. **outward-bound** adj auf der Ausreise. **outwardly** adv äußerlich.

outweigh [autˈweɪ] v überwiegen.

outwit [autˈwɪt] v überlisten.

oval [ˈouvəl] n Oval neut. adj oval.

ovary [ˈouvəri] n Eierstock m.

ovation [ouˈveɪʃən] n Ovation f, Beifallssturm m.

oven [ˈʌvn] n (cookery) Backofen m; (industrial, etc.) Ofen m.

over [ˈouvə] adv über, hinüber, herüber; (finished) zu Ende; (during) während; (too much) allzu. prep über; (more than) mehr als. **over and over again** immer wieder. **over there** drüben. **all over England** in ganz England. it's all over es ist aus.

overall [ˈouvərɔːl] adj gesamt. adv insgesamt. n also **overalls** pl Overall m, Schutzanzug m.

overbalance [ouvəˈbaləns] v umkippen.

overbearing [ouvəˈbeərɪŋ] adj anmaßend, arrogant.

overboard [ˈouvəbɔːd] adv über Bord.

overcast [ouvəˈkaːst] adj bedeckt, bewölkt.

overcharge [ouvəˈtʃaːdʒ] v zuviel verlangen von.

overcoat [ˈouvəkout] n Mantel m.

*****overcome** [ouvəˈkʌm] v überwinden. adj (with emotion) tief bewegt.

overcrowded [ouvəˈkraudɪd] adj überfüllt.

*****overdo** [ouvəˈduː] v übertreiben. **overdo it** zu weit gehen. **overdone** adj (cookery) übergar.

overdose [ˈouvədous] n Überdosis f.

*****overdraw** [ouvəˈdrɔː] v überziehen. **overdraft** n (Konto)Überziehung f.

overdrive [ˈouvədraɪv] n Schongang m.

overdue [ouvəˈdjuː] adj überfällig; (train) verspätet.

overestimate [ouvəˈestɪmeɪt] v überschätzen.

overexpose [ouvəɪkˈspouz] v (phot) überbelichten.

overfill [ouvəˈfɪl] v überfüllen.

overflow [ouvəˈflou; n ˈouvəflou] v überlaufen. n Überlauf m.

overgrown [ouvəˈgroun] adj überwachsen.

*****overhang** [ouvəˈhaŋ; n ˈouvəhaŋ] v überhängen. n Überhang m.

overhaul [ouvəˈhɔːl] v überholen. n Überholung f.

overhead [ouvəˈhed] adj obenliegend. **overheads** pl n allgemeine Unkosten pl.

*****overhear** [ouvəˈhɪə] v (zufällig) hören.

overheat [ouvəˈhiːt] v überheizen; (mot) heißlaufen.

overjoyed [ouvəˈdʒɔɪd] adj entzückt, außer sich vor Freude.

overland [ouvəˈland] adj Überland-.

overlap [ouvəˈlap; n ˈouvəlap] v sich überschneiden (mit). n Überscheiden neut, Übergreifen neut.

*****overlay** [ouvəˈleɪ; n ˈouvəleɪ] v bedecken, belegen. n Auflage f, Bedeckung f.

overleaf [ouvəˈliːf] adv umseitig, umstehend.

overload [ouvəˈboud; n ˈouvəloud] v überbelasten. n Überbelastung f.

overlook [ouvəˈlʊk] v (room, etc.) überblicken; (let pass) nicht beachten.

overnight [ouvəˈnaɪt] adv über Nacht. **stay overnight** übernachten. adj Nacht-. **overnight case** Handkoffer m.

overpower [ouvəˈpauə] v überwältigen.

overrate [ouvəˈreɪt] v überschätzen.

overrule [ouvəˈruːl] v zurückweisen; (person) überstimmen.

*****overrun** [ouvəˈrʌn] v überschwemmen, überlaufen.

overseas [ouvəˈsiːz] adv in Übersee. adj überseeisch, Übersee-.

overseer [ˈouvəsɪə] n Vorarbeiter m.

overshadow [ouvəˈʃadou] v überschatten.

*****overshoot** [ouvəˈʃuːt] v hinausschießen über.

oversight [ˈouvəsaɪt] n Versehen neut.

*****oversleep** [ouvəˈsliːp] v sich verschlafen.

overspill [ˈouvəspɪl] n Überschuß m.

overt [ouˈvəːt] adj offenkundig.

*****overtake** [ouvəˈteɪk] v überholen.

*****overthrow** [ouvəˈθrou; n ˈouvəθrou] v (um)stürzen. n Umsturz m.

overtime [ˈouvətaɪm] n Überstunden pl. **work overtime** Überstunden machen.

overtone [ˈouvətoun] n Nuance f.

overture [ˈouvətjuə] n (music) Ouvertüre f.

overturn [ouvəˈtəːn] v umkippen.

overweight [ouvəˈweɪt] adj (zu) dick, fettleibig.

overwhelm [ouvəˈwelm] v überwältigen. **overwhelming** adj überwältigend.

overwork [ouvəˈwəːk] v (sich) überanstrengen.

overwrought [ouvəˈrɔːt] adj nervös, überreizt.

ovulate ['ovjuleɪt] v ovulieren. **ovulation** n Ovulation f. **ovum** n Ei neut, Eizelle f.

owe [ou] v schulden; (have debts) Schulden haben. **owing** adj zu zahlen. **owing to** infolge or wegen (+gen).

owl [auɫ] n Eule f.

own [oun] adj eigen. v besitzen; (admit) zugeben. **own up** gestehen. **owner** n Inhaber(in). **ownership** n Besitz m.

ox [oks] n (pl oxen) Ochse m, Rind neut. **oxtail** Ochsenschwanz m.

oxygen ['oksɪdʒən] n Sauerstoff m.

oyster ['oɪstə] n Auster f.

ozone ['ouzoun] n Ozon neut. **ozone layer** Ozongürtel m.

P

pace [peɪs] n (step) Schritt m; (speed) Geschwindigkeit f. Tempo neut. v schreiten. **keep pace with** Schritt halten mit. **pacemaker** n Schrittmacher m; (heart) Herzschrittmacher m.

Pacific [pə'sɪfɪk] n Pazifik m.

pacify ['pasɪfaɪ] v befrieden. **pacifier** n (for baby) Schnuller m. **pacifism** n Pazifismus m. **pacifist** n Pazifist(in).

pack [pak] n Pack m, Packung f; (cards) Spiel neut; (dogs) Meute f. v einpacken; (stuff) vollstopfen. **package** n Paket neut. **packaging** n Verpackung f. **packet** n Packung f, Päckchen neut. **packhorse** n Lastpferd neut.

pact [pakt] n Pakt m, Vertrag m.

pad¹ [pad] n Polster neut; (paper) Block m; (sport) Schützer m; (ink) Stempelkissen neut. **padding** n Polsterung f.

pad² [pad] v trotten.

paddle¹ ['padl] n Paddel neut. v paddeln. **paddle-steamer** n Raddampfer m.

paddle² ['padl] v (wade) planschen, herumpaddeln.

paddock ['padək] n Pferdekoppel f; (on racecourse) Sattelplatz m.

paddyfield ['padɪfiːld] n Reisfeld neut.

padlock ['padlɒk] n Vorhängeschloß neut. v (mit einem Vorhängeschloß) verschließen.

paediatric ['piːdɪatrɪk] adj pädiatrisch. **pae-diatrician** n Kinderarzt m, Kinderärztin f. **paediatrics** n Kinderheilkunde f.

pagan ['peɪgən] adj heidnisch. n Heide m, Heidin f.

page¹ [peɪdʒ] n (book) Seite f.

page² [peɪdʒ] n (boy) Page m.

pageant ['padʒənt] n Festzug m. **pageantry** n Prunk m.

paid [peɪd] V pay.

pail [peɪl] n Eimer m.

pain [peɪn] n Schmerz m, Schmerzen pl; (suffering) Leid neut. v peinigen. **take pains** sich Mühe geben. **on pain of** bei Strafe von. **painful** adj schmerzhaft. **painkiller** n schmerzstillendes Mittel neut. **painless** adj schmerzlos. **painstaking** adj sorgfältig.

paint [peɪnt] n Farbe f, Lack m. v anstreichen; (pictures) malen. **paintbrush** n Pinsel m. **painted** adj bemalt. **painter** n Maler(in). **painting** n Gemälde neut.

pair [peə] n Paar neut; (animals) Pärchen neut; (married couple) Ehepaar neut. v **pair off** paarweise anordnen. **a pair of trousers** eine Hose.

Pakistan [pakɪstaːn] n Pakistan neut. **Pakistani** n Pakistaner(in); adj pakistanisch.

pal [pal] n (coll) Kamerad m, Kumpel m.

palace ['paləs] n Palast m.

palate ['palɪt] n (Vorder)Gaumen m; (taste) Geschmack m. **palatable** adj schmackhaft.

pale [peɪl] adj blaß, bleich. v blaßwerden. **pale ale** helles Bier neut. **paleness** n Blässe f.

palette ['palɪt] n Palette f.

pall¹ [pɔːl] v (become boring) jeden Reiz verlieren.

pall² [pɔːl] n (for coffin) Leichentuch neut; (fig) Hülle f. **pall-bearer** n Sargträger m.

palm¹ [paːm] n (of hand) Handfläche f. **palmist** n Handwahrsager(in). **palmistry** n Handlesekunst f.

palm² [paːm] n (tree) Palme f.

palpitate ['palpɪteɪt] v (heart) unregelmäßigschlagen; (tremble) beben, zittern.

pamper ['pampə] v verwöhnen.

pamphlet ['pamflɪt] n Broschüre f.

pan [pan] n Pfanne f.

pancreas ['paŋkrɪəs] n Bauchspeicheldrüse f.

panda ['pandə] n Panda m.

pander ['pændə] v nachgeben (+ *dat*).

pane [peɪn] n (Fenster)Scheibe f.

panel ['pænl] n Tafel f; (*door*) Füllung f; (*dress*) Einsatzstück m; (*instrument*) Armaturenbrett neut. v täfeln. **panelling** n Täfelung f.

pang [pæŋ] n (*of remorse*) Gewissensbisse pl.

panic ['pænɪk] n Panik f. v hinreißen (zu). **panic-stricken** adj von panischer Angst erfüllt. **panicky** adj überängstlich.

pannier ['pænɪə] n (Trag)Korb m; (*motorcycle*) Satteltasche f.

panorama [ˌpænəˈrɑːm ə] n Panorama neut, Rundblick m. **panoramic** adj panoramisch.

pansy ['pænzi] n Stiefmütterchen neut.

pant [pænt] v keuchen, schnaufen.

panther ['pænθə] n Panther m.

panties ['pæntiz] pl n (*coll*) Schlüpfer m sing, Höschen neut sing.

pantomime ['pæntəm aɪm] n Pantomime f.

pantry ['pæntri] n Speiseschrank m.

pants [pænts] pl n (*trousers*) Hose f sing; (*underpants*) Unterhose f sing. **pantyhose** Strumpfhose f.

papal ['peɪpl] adj päpstlich.

paper ['peɪpə] n Papier neut; (*newspaper*) Zeitung f; (*scientific*) Abhandlung f. v (*a room*) tapezieren. **paperback** n Taschenbuch neut. **paper bag** Tüte f. **paper-clip** n Büroklammer f. **paper-thin** adj hauchdünn. **paperweight** n Briefbeschwerer m. **paperwork** n Büroarbeit f.

paprika ['pæprɪkə] n Paprika m.

par [pɑː] n Nennwert m, (*golf*) Par neut. **on a par with** gleich (+ *dat*).

parable ['pærəbl] n Parabel f.

parachute ['pærəʃuːt] n Fallschirm m. v mit dem Fallschirm abspringen.

parade [pəˈreɪd] n Parade f. v (*march past*) vorbeimarschieren. **parade ground** Paradeplatz m.

paradise ['pærədaɪs] n Paradies neut.

paradox ['pærədɒks] n Paradox neut. **paradoxical** adj paradox.

paraffin ['pærəfɪn] n Paraffin neut.

paragon ['pærəgən] n Muster neut, Vorbild neut.

paragraph ['pærəgrɑːf] n Absatz m.

parallel ['pærəlel] n Parallele f. adj parallel.

v entsprechen (+ *dat*).

paralyse ['pærəlaɪz] v paralysieren. **paralysed** adj gelähmt. **paralysis** n (*pl* -ses) Lähmung f, Paralyse f. **paralytic** adj paralytisch; (*coll*) besoffen.

paramedic [ˌpærəˈmedɪk] n Rettungsassistent(in).

paramilitary [ˌpærəˈmɪlɪtəri] adj paramilitärisch.

paramount ['pærəmaunt] adj äußerst wichtig, überragend.

paranoia [ˌpærəˈnɔɪə] n Paranoia f. **paranoid** adj paranoid.

parapet ['pærəpɪt] n Brüstung f.

paraphernalia [ˌpærəfəˈneɪliə] n Zubehör neut.

paraphrase ['pærəfreɪz] n Umschreibung f. Paraphrase f. v umschreiben.

paraplegia [ˌpærəˈpliːdʒə] n Paraplegie f. **paraplegic** adj paraplegisch.

parasite ['pærəsaɪt] n Parasit m, Schmarotzer m. **parasitic** adj parasitisch.

parasol ['pærəsɒl] n Sonnenschirm m.

paratrooper ['pærəˌtruːpə] n Fallschirmjäger m.

parcel ['pɑːsl] n Paket neut, Päckchen neut; (*of land*) Parzelle f. **parcel post** Paketpost f. **parcels office** Gepäckabfertigung f. **parcel out** austeilen.

parch [pɑːtʃ] v dörren. **parched** adj ausgetrocknet; (*coll*) sehr durstig.

parchment ['pɑːtʃmənt] n Pergament neut.

pardon ['pɑːdn] n Verzeihung f. v verzeihen (+ *dat*); (*law*) begnadigen. **I beg your pardon** or **pardon me** Verzeihung! **pardonable** adj verzeihlich.

pare [peə] v schälen; (*prices, costs, etc.*) herabsetzen, beschneiden.

parent ['peərənt] n Vater m, Mutter f. **parents** pl Eltern pl. **parentage** n Abkunft f. **parental** adj elterlich.

parenthesis [pəˈrenθəsis] n (*pl* -ses) Parenthese f.

parish ['pærɪʃ] n (Kirchen)gemeinde f. adj Gemeinde-.

parity ['pærɪti] n Parität f.

park [pɑːk] n Park m. v (*mot*) parken. **park-and-ride** n Zubringerbus (m) ins Stadtzentrum. **car park** Parkplatz m. **no parking** Parken verboten. **parking place** or **lot** Parkplatz m. **parking light** Standlicht neut. **parking meter** Parkuhr f.

parliament ['pɑːləm ənt] n Parlament neut.
member of parliament Abgeordnete(r),
Parlamentarier m. **parliamentary** adj parlamentarisch, Parlaments-.

parlour ['pɑːlə] n Wohnzimmer neut. **ice-
cream parlour** Eisdiele f.

parochial [pə'rəʊkiə] adj Gemeinde-; (fig)
engstirnig.

parody ['parədi] n Parodie f. v parodieren.

parole [pə'rəʊl] n Bewährung f. **release on
parole** auf Bewährung entlassen.

paroxysm ['parəksizəm] n Anfall m.

parrot ['parət] n Papagei m.

parsley ['pɑːsli] n Petersilie f.

parsnip ['pɑːsnip] n Pastinake f.

parson ['pɑːsn] n Pfarrer m. **parsonage** n
Pfarrhaus neut.

part [pɑːt] n Teil m; (theatre) Rolle f. adj
Teil-. v trennen; (people) sich trennen; (hair)
scheiteln. **for my part** meinerseits. **in
part** teilweise. **take part (in)** v teilnehmen (an), sich an etwas beteiligen.

*partake [pɑːteik] v **partake of** (eat) zu
sich nehmen.

partial ['pɑːʃəl] adj Teil-; (biased) eingenommen. **be partial to** (coll) eine
Vorliebe haben für. **partially** adv teilweise.

participate [pɑː'tisipeit] v teilnehmen (an).
participant n Teilnehmer(in). **participation** n Teilnahme f.

participle ['pɑːtisip] n Partizip neut.

particle ['pɑːtik] n Teilchen neut.

particular [pə'tikjulə] adj besonder,
speziell; (fussy) wählerisch. **particulars** pl
n Einzelheiten pl. **particularly** adv besonders.

parting ['pɑːtiŋ] n Abschied neut; (hair)
Scheitel m.

partisan [pɑːtizan] n Anhänger m.

partition [pɑː'tiʃən] n Aufteilung f,
Trennung f; (wall, etc.) Scheidewand f.

partly ['pɑːtli] adv zum Teil, teils.

partner ['pɑːtnə] n Partner(in). **partnership** n Partnerschaft f.

partridge ['pɑːtridʒ] n Rebhuhn neut.

party ['pɑːti] n (pol, law) Partei f; (social
gathering) Party f. **be a party to** beteiligt
sein an.

pass [pɑːs] v (go past) vorbeigehen(an); (go
beyond) überschreiten, übertreffen; (exam)
bestehen; (of time) vergehen; (time)
vertreiben; (hand) überreichen; (approve)

billigen; (sport) zuspielen. n (travel
document) Zeitkarte f. **pass away** sterben.
pass off (as) ausgeben (als). **pass out** (coll)
ohmächtig werden. **pass up** verzichten
auf.

passage ['pasidʒ] n Durchfahrt f, Reise f;
(in book) Stelle f; (corridor) Gang m; (of time)
Verlauf m.

passenger ['pasindʒə] n Fahrgast m,
Reisende(r); (aeroplane) Fluggast m.

passion ['paʃən] n Leidenschaft f; (anger)
Zorn m; (rel) Passion f. **passionate** adj leidenschaftlich.

passive ['pasiv] adj passiv. **passivity** n
Passivität f.

Passover ['pɑːsəʊvə] n Passahfest neut.

passport ['pɑːspoːt] n (Reise)Paß m.

password ['pɑːswəːd] n Kennwort neut.

past [pɑːst] n Vergangenheit f. adj vergangen. prep nach, über; (in front of) an ... vorbei. **ten past six** zehn (Minuten) nach sechs.
half past six halb sieben. **in the past**
früher.

pasta ['pastə] n Teigwaren pl.

paste [peist] n Paste f; (glue) Klebstoff m. v
kleben.

pastel ['pastə] adj **pastel colour**
Pastellfarbe f.

pasteurize ['pastʃəraiz] v pasteurisieren.

pastime ['pɑːstaim] n Zeitvertreib m.

pastor ['pɑːstə] n Pfarrer m, Pastor m. **pastoral** adj (poetry) Hirten-; (rel) pastoral.

pastry ['peistri] n Teig m; (cake)
Tortengebäck neut.

pasture ['pɑːstʃə] n Weide f, Grasland neut.

pasty[1] ['peisti] adj teigig; (complexion)
bleich.

pasty[2] ['pasti] n Pastete f.

pat [pat] n (leichter) Schlag m. v klopfen,
patschen. **pat on the back** (v) beglückwünschen.

patch [patʃ] n Flicken m, Lappen m; (on
eye) Augenbinde f. v flicken. **patchwork** n
Flickwerk neut. **patchy** adj ungleichmäßig.

pâté ['patei] n Pastete f.

patent ['peitənt] n Patent neut. adj patentiert, Patent-; (obvious) offenkundig. v
patentieren.

paternal [pə'təːn] adj väterlich. **paternal
grandfather** Großvater väterlicherseits.
paternity n Vaterschaft f.

path [pɑːθ] n Weg m, Pfad m. **pathway** n

Weg *m*, Bahn *f*.

pathetic [pə'θetik] *adj* (*moving*) rührend; (*pitiable*) kläglich.

pathology [pə'θolədʒi] *n* Pathologie *f*. **pathological** *adj* pathologisch. **pathologist** *n* Pathologe *m*, Pathologin *f*.

patience ['peɪʃəns] *n* Geduld *f*. **patient** *adj* geduldig, duldsam. *n* Patient(in).

patio ['pætɪəu] *n* Patio *m*.

patriarchal ['peɪtrɪɑːkəl] *adj* patriarchalisch.

patriot ['pætrɪət] *n* Patriot(in). **patriotic** *adj* patriotisch. **patriotism** *n* Patriotismus *m*.

patrol [pə'trəul] *n* Patrouille *f*. *v* durchstreifen. **patrol car** Streifenwagen *m*. **patrolman** *n* Streifenpolizist *m*.

patron ['peɪtrən] *n* Patron *m*, Gönner *m*. **patronage** *n* Gönnerschaft *f*. **patronize** *v* (*theatre*, *restaurant*) besuchen; (*person*) gönnerhaft behandeln. **patronizing** *adj* gönnerhaft.

patter[1] ['pætə] *n* (*rain*) Prasseln *neut*. *v* prasseln.

patter[2] ['pætə] *n* (*speech*) Geplapper *neut*, Rotwelsch *neut*. *v* plappern.

pattern ['pætən] *n* Muster *neut*.

paunch [pɔːntʃ] *n* Wanst *m*. **paunchy** *adj* dickbäuchig.

pauper ['pɔːpə] *n* Arme(r).

pause [pɔːz] *n* Pause *f*. *v* anhalten, zögern.

pave [peɪv] *v* pflastern. **pave the way** den Weg bahnen. **pavement** *n* Bürgersteig *m*.

pavilion [pə'vɪljən] *n* Pavillon *m*.

paw [pɔː] *n* Pfote *f*, Tatze *f*. *v* (*ground*) stampfen auf.

pawn[1] [pɔːn] *n* (*chess*) Bauer *m*.

pawn[2] [pɔːn] *v* verpfänden. **pawnbroker** *n* Pfandleiher *m*.

*****pay** [peɪ] *n* Lohn *m*, Gehalt *neut*. *v* zahlen; (*bill*) bezahlen; (*be worthwhile*) sich lohnen; (*visit*, *compliment*) machen. **pay attention** achtgeben (auf). **pay homage** huldigen (+*dat*). **pay for** bezahlen. **payable** *adj* fällig. **payday** *n* Zahltag *m*. **paying guest** zahlender Gast *m*. **payload** *n* Nutzlast *f*. **payment** *n* (Be)Zahlung *f*; (*cheque*) Einlösung *f*.

pea [piː] *n* Erbse *f*.

peace [piːs] *n* Frieden *m*; (*quiet*) Ruhe *f*. **make one's peace with** sich aussöhnen mit. **leave in peace** in Ruhe lassen. **peace of mind** Seelenruhe *f*. **peace treaty** Friedensvertrag *m*. **peaceable** *adj* friedlich. **peaceful** *adj* ruhig.

peach [piːtʃ] *n* Pfirsich *m*.

peacock ['piːkok] *n* Pfau *m*.

peak [piːk] *n* Spitze *f*, Gipfel *m*. *adj* Höchst-, Spitzen-. **peaked** *adj* spitz.

peal [piːl] *v* (*bells*) läuten. *n* Geläute *neut*. **peal of thunder** Donnerschlag *m*.

peanut ['piːnʌt] *n* Erdnuß *f*.

pear [peə] *n* Birne *f*. **pear-shaped** *adj* birnenförmig.

pearl [pəːl] *n* Perle *f*. *adj* Perlen-.

peasant ['pezənt] *n* Bauer *m*. *adj* bäuerlich.

peat [piːt] *n* Torf *m*.

pebble ['pebl] *n* Kieselstein *m*.

peck [pek] *v* picken, hacken. *n* Picken *neut*; (*kiss*) (flüchtiger) Kuß *m*. **peckish** *adj* (*coll*) hungrig.

peculiar [pɪkjuːlɪə] *adj* (*strange*) seltsam. **peculiar to** eigentümlich (+*dat*). **peculiarity** *n* Eigentümlichkeit *f*.

pedal ['pedl] *n* Pedal *neut*, Fußhebel *m*. *v* (*a bicycle*) fahren.

pedantic [pɪdantɪk] *adj* pedantisch.

peddle ['pedl] *v* hausieren. **peddler** *n* Hausierer *m*.

pedestal ['pedɪstl] *n* Sockel *m*. **put on a pedestal** vergöttern.

pedestrian [pɪdestrɪən] *n* Fußgänger(in). *adj* Fußgänger-; (*humdrum*) langweilig, banal. **pedestrian crossing** Fußgängerübergang *m*. **pedestrian precinct** Fußgängerzone *f*.

pedigree ['pedɪgriː] *n* Stammbaum *m*.

pedlar ['pedlə] *n* Hausierer *m*.

peel [piːl] *n* Schale *f*. *v* schälen. **peeler** *n* Schäler *m*.

peep [piːp] *v* gucken, verstohlen blicken. *n* verstohlener Blick *m*. **peephole** *n* Guckloch *neut*.

peer[1] [piə] *v* (*look*) spähen, gucken.

peer[2] [piə] *n* (*equal*) Ebenbürtige(r); (*noble*) Peer *m*. **peerage** *n* Peerwürde *f*. **peerless** *adj* unvergleichlich.

peevish ['piːvɪʃ] *adj* verdrießlich.

peg [peg] *n* Pflock *m*; (*coathook*) Haken *m*; (*clothes*) Klammer *f*. *v* anpflöcken; (*prices*) festlegen. **off the peg** von der Stange.

pejorative [pə'dʒorətɪv] *adj* herabsetzend.

pelican ['pelɪkən] *n* Pelikan *m*.

pellet ['pelɪt] n Kügelchen neut; (shot) Schrotkorn neut.

pelmet ['pelmɪt] n Falbel f.

pelt¹ [pelt] v (throw) bewerfen.

pelt² [pelt] n (skin) Fell neut. Pelz m.

pelvis ['pelvɪs] n (anat) Becken neut.

pen¹ [pen] n (writing) (Schreib) Feder f, Federhalter m.

pen² [pen] n (animals) Pferch m, Hürde f. v einpferchen.

penal ['piːnl] adj Straf-. **penalize** v bestrafen. **penalty** n (gesetzliche) Strafe f. **penalty kick** Elfmeterstoß m.

penance ['penəns] n Buße f.

pencil ['pensl] n Bleistift m. v pencil in (a date) vorläufig festsetzen. **pencil-sharpener** n Bleistiftspitzer m.

pendant ['pendənt] n Anhänger m.

pending ['pendɪŋ] adj (noch) unentschieden. prep bis.

pendulum ['pendjuləm] n Pendel neut.

penetrate ['penɪtreɪt] v durchdringen, eindringen (in). **penetrating** adj durchdringend. **penetration** n Durchdringen neut.

penguin ['peŋgwɪn] n Pinguin m.

penicillin [penɪsɪlɪn] n Penizillin neut.

peninsula [pə'nɪnsjulə] n Halbinsel f. **peninsular** adj Halbinsel-.

penis ['piːnɪs] n Penis m.

penitent ['penɪtənt] adj bußfertig. n Büßer (in). **penitence** n Buße f.

penknife ['nennaɪf] n Taschenmesser neut.

pen-name n Pseudonym neut.

pennant ['penənt] n Wimpel m.

penny ['peni] n Penny m, Pfennig m. **penniless** adj mittellos.

pension ['penʃən] n Rente f. **pensioner** n Rentner(in).

pensive ['pensɪv] adj gedankenvoll.

pent [pent] adj pent up (feelings) angestaut, zurückgehalten.

pentagon ['pentəgən] n Fünfeck neut. **Pentagon** (US) Pentagon neut. **pentagonal** adj fünfeckig.

penthouse ['penthaus] n Dachwohnung f.

penultimate [pɪnʌltɪmɪt] adj vorletzt.

people ['piːpl] pl n Leute pl, Menschen pl; sing (nation) Volk neut. **people carrier** (mot) Mehrzweckfahrzeug (MZF) neut.

pepper ['pepə] n Pfeffer m. **peppercorn** n Pfefferkorn neut. **peppermint** n

Pfefferminze f. **peppery** adj pfefferig, scharf.

per [pəː] prep pro. **per capita** pro Kopf.

perceive [pə'siːv] v wahrnehmen; (understand) begreifen. **perceptible** adj spürbar. **perception** n Wahrnehmung f. **perceptive** adj (person) scharfsinnig.

per cent adv, n Prozent neut. sixty per cent sechzig Prozent. **percentage** n Prozentsatz m.

perch [pəːtʃ] n Sitzstange f; (fish) Barsch m. v sitzen.

percolate ['pəːkəleɪt] v durchsickern. **percolator** n Kaffeemaschine f.

percussion [pə'kʌʃən] n (music) Schlaginstrumente pl.

perennial [pə'renɪəl] adj beständig; (plant) perennierend. n perennierende Pflanze f.

perfect ['pəːfɪkt; v pə'fekt] adj vollkommen, vollendet, perfekt. v vervollkommnen. **perfection** n Vollkommenheit f. **perfectionist** n Perfektionist(in). **perfectly** adv (coll) ganz, völlig.

perforate ['pəːfəreɪt] v perforieren. **perforation** n Perforation f.

perform [pə'fɔːm] n machen, ausführen; (music, play) aufführen, spielen. n (work, output) Leistung f; (music, theatre) Aufführung f. **performer** n Artist(in).

perfume ['pəːfjuːm] n (fragrance) Duft m; (woman's) Parfüm neut. v parfümieren.

perhaps [pə'haps] adv vielleicht.

peril ['peril] n Gefahr f. **perilous** adj gefährlich.

perimeter [pə'rɪmɪtə] n Umkreis; (outer area) Peripherie f.

period ['pɪərɪəd] n Periode f, Frist f; (lesson) Stunde f; (menstrual) Regel f, Periode f; (full stop) Punkt m. **periodic** adj periodisch. **periodical** n Zeitschrift f. **periodically** adv periodisch, von Zeit zu Zeit.

peripheral [pə'rɪfərəl] adj peripherisch, Rand-; (comp) Peripherie-. **periphery** n Peripherie f.

periscope ['perɪskoup] n Periskop neut.

perish ['perɪʃ] v umkommen, sterben; (materials) verwelken. **perishable** adj leicht verderblich.

perjure ['pəːdʒə] v perjure oneself meineidig werden. **perjurer** n Meineidige(r). **perjury** n Meineid m.

perk¹ [pəːk] v perk up munter werden.

perky *adj* munter.

perk² [pəːk] *n* (*coll: benefit*) Vorteil *m*, (unentgeltliche) Vergünstigung *f*.

perm [pəːm] *n* Dauerwelle *f*.

permanent ['pəːm ənənt] *adj* dauernd, ständig, permanent. **permanence** *n* Permanenz *f*, Ständigkeit *f*.

permeate ['pəːm iːət] *v* durchdringen. **permeable** *adj* durchlässig.

permit [pəːm iː; n 'pəːmit] *v* erlauben, gestatten; (*officially*) zulassen, genehmigen. *n* Genehmigung *f*; (*certificate*) Zulassungsschein *m*. **permissible** *adj* zulässig. **permission** *n* Erlaubnis *f*, Genehmigung *f*. **permissive** *adj* freizügig.

permutation [pəːm juˈteʃən] *n* Permutation *f*.

pernicious [pəˈnʃəs] *adj* bösartig.

perpendicular [pəːpenˈdikjuˌlə] *adj* senkrecht. *n* Senkrechte *f*.

perpetrate ['pəːpitreit] *v* begehen. **perpetration** *n* Begehung *f*. **perpetrator** *n* Täter *m*.

perpetual [pəˈpetʃuəl] *adj* beständig, ewig. **perpetuate** [pəˈpetʃueit] *v* verewigen, fortsetzen.

perplex [pəˈpleks] *v* verwirren, verblüffen. **perplexed** *adj* perplex, verwirrt.

persecute ['pəːsikjuːt] *v* verfolgen. **persecution** *n* Verfolgung *f*. **persecutor** *n* Verfolger(in).

persevere [pəːsiˈvə] *v* beharren, nicht aufgeben. **perseverance** *n* Beharrlichkeit *f*. **persevering** *adj* beharrlich.

persist [pəˈsist] *v* (*person*) beharren (bei); (*thing*) fortdauern. **persistance** *n* Beharren *neut*, Hartnäckigkeit *f*. **persistent** *adj* (*person*) hartnäckig; (*questions, etc.*) anhaltend.

person ['pəːsn] *n* Person *f*. **personal** *adj* persönlich. **personal assistant (PA)** Chefsekretär(in). **personal computer (PC)** Personal-Computer *m*. **personal matter** Privatsache *f*. **personality** *n* Personalität *f*; (*personage*) Persönlichkeit *f*.

personnel [pəːsəˈnel] *n* Personal *neut*, Belegschaft *f*. **personnel department** Personalabteilung *f*. **personnel manager** Personalchef *m*.

perspective [pəˈspektiv] *n* Perspektive *f*.

perspire [pəˈspaə] *v* schwitzen, transpirieren. **perspiration** *n* Schweiß *m*.

persuade [pəˈsweid] *v* überreden; (*convince*) überzeugen. **persuasion** *n* Überredung *f*; Überzeugung *f*. **persuasive** *adj* überredend; überzeugend.

pert [pəːt] *adj* keck.

pertain [pəˈtein] *v* betreffen. **pertaining to** betreffend. **pertinacious** *adj* hartnäckig. **pertinent** *adj* angemessen.

perturb [pəˈtəːb] *v* beunruhigen.

peruse [pəˈruːz] *v* durchlesen.

pervade [pəˈveid] *v* erfüllen, durchdringen. **pervasive** *adj* durchdringend.

perverse [pəˈvəːs] *adj* pervers, widernatürlich. **perversion** *n* Perversion *f*, Verdrehung *f*. **perversion of justice** Rechtsbeugung *f*. **pervert** *v* verdrehen. *n* perverser Mensch *m*.

pest [pest] *n* Schädling *m*; (*coll: person*) lästiger Mensch *m*. **pesticide** *n* Pestizid *neut*.

pester ['pestə] *v* quälen, plagen.

pet [pet] *n* Haustier *neut*; (*darling*) Schätzchen *neut*. *adj* Lieblings-. *v* liebkosen. **pet name** Kosename *m*.

petal ['petl] *n* Blumenblatt *neut*.

petition [pəˈtʃən] *n* Bittschrift *f*.

petrify ['petrifai] *v* versteinen. **petrified** *adj* (*coll*) starr, bestürzt.

petrol ['petrəl] *n* Benzin *neut*. **petrol station** Tankstelle *f*. **petroleum** *n* Erdöl *neut*.

petticoat ['petikout] *n* Unterrock *m*.

petty ['peti] *adj* (*unimportant*) unbedeutend; (*mean*) kleinlich. **petty cash** Kleinkasse *f*.

petulant ['petjulənt] *adj* verdrießlich.

pew [pjuː] *n* Kirchensitz *m*.

pewter ['pjuːtə] *n* Hartzinn *neut*.

phantom ['fantəm] *n* Phantom *neut*, Gespenst *neut*. *adj* Schein-.

pharmacy ['faːm əsi] *n* Apotheke *f*. **pharmacist** *n* Apotheker(in).

pharynx ['fariŋks] *n* Schlundkopf *m*.

phase [feiz] *n* (*tech*) Phase *f*; (*stage*) Stadium *neut*, Etappe *f*.

pheasant ['feznt] *n* Fasan *m*.

phenomenon [fəˈnom ənən] *n* (*pl* -a) Phänomen *neut*. **phenomenal** *adj* phänomenal.

phial ['faəl] *n* Ampulle *f*.

philanthropy [filanθrəpi] *n* Philanthropie *f*. **philanthropic** *adj* philanthropisch, menschenfreundlich. **philanthropist** *n*

Philanthrop, Menschenfreund *m*.

philately [fɪ'lætəlɪ] *n* Briefmarkensammeln *neut*. **philatelist** *n* Briefmarkensammler(in).

philosophy [fɪ'losəfɪ] *n* Philosophie *f*. **philosopher** *n* Philosoph *m*. **philosophical** *adj* philosophisch.

phlegm [flem] *n* Schleim *m*, Phlegma *neut*. **phlegmatic** *adj* phlegmatisch.

phobia ['foubiə] *n* Phobie *f*.

phone [foun] *n* (*coll*) Fernsprecher *m*. *v* anrufen. **phone book** Telefonbuch *neut*. **phone booth** *or* **box** Telefonzelle *f*.

phonetic [fə'netɪk] *adj* phonetisch. **phonetics** *n* Phonetik *f*.

phoney ['founɪ] *adj* (*coll*) falsch, fingiert. *n* Schwindler *m*.

phosphate ['fosfeɪt] *n* Phosphat *neut*.

phosphorescence [fosfə'resəns] *n* Phosphoreszenz *f*. **phosphorescent** *adj* phosphoreszierend.

phosphorus ['fosfərəs] *n* Phosphor *m*.

photo ['foutou] *n* Foto *neut*.

photocopy ['foutou,kopɪ] *n* Fotokopie *f*. *v* fotokopieren.

photogenic [,foutou'dʒenɪk] *adj* fotogen.

photograph ['foutəgrɑːf] *n* Lichtbild *neut*, Foto *neut*. *v* aufnehmen, fotografieren. **photographer** *n* Fotograf *m*. **photographic** *adj* fotografisch. **photography** *n* Fotografie *f*.

phrase [freɪz] *n* (*expression*) Ausdruck *m*, Redewendung *f*; (*music*) Phrase *f*. *v* fassen.

physical ['fɪzɪkəl] *adj* physisch, körperlich. **physical education** Leibeserziehung *f*.

physician [fɪ'zɪʃən] *n* Arzt *m*, Ärztin *f*.

physics ['fɪzɪks] *n* Physik *f*. **physicist** *n* Physiker *m*.

physiology [,fɪzɪə'lodʒɪ] *n* Physiologie *f*. **physiological** *adj* physiologisch.

physiotherapy [,fɪzɪou'θerəpɪ] *n* Physiotherapie *f*.

physique [fɪ'ziːk] *n* Körperbau *m*.

piano [pɪ'ænou] *n* Klavier *neut*. **pianist** *n* Klavierspieler(in).

pick¹ [pɪk] *v* (*choose*) auswählen, (*fruit*) pflücken; (*lock*) knacken. *n* **pick of the bunch** (*coll*) das Beste (von allen). **pick on** quälen, belästigen.

pick² [pɪk] *or* **pickaxe** *n* Spitzhacke *f*.

picket ['pɪkɪt] *n* Pfahl *m*; (*strike*) Streikposten *m*. *v* (*factory, etc.*) Streikposten aufstellen vor.

pickle ['pɪkl] *n* Pökel *m*. *v* einpökeln. **pickled** *adj* gepökelt; (*coll: drunk*) blau. **pickles** *pl n* Eingepökeltes *neut sing*.

picnic ['pɪknɪk] *n* Picknick *neut*.

pictorial [pɪk'toːrɪəl] *adj* Bilder-.

picture ['pɪktʃə] *n* Bild *neut*; (*painting*) Gemälde *neut*; (*film*) Film *m*. *v* (*imagine*) sich vorstellen. **pictures** *pl* Kino *neut sing*. **picture book** Bilderbuch *neut*. **picture postcard** Ansichtskarte *f*.

picturesque [pɪktʃə'resk] *adj* pittoresk.

pidgin ['pɪdʒən] *n* Mischsprache *f*.

pie [paɪ] *n* (*meat*) Pastete *f*; (*fruit*) Torte *f*.

piece [piːs] *n* Stück *neut*; (*part*) Teil *m*; (*paper*) Blatt *neut*. **piece of advice** Ratschlag *m*. **fall to pieces** in Stücke gehen, zerfallen. **go to pieces** zusammenbrechen. *v* **piece together** zusammenstellen. **piecemeal** *adv* stückweise. **piecework** *n* Akkordarbeit *f*.

pier [pɪə] *n* Pier *m*, Kai *m*.

pierce [pɪəs] *v* durchbohren, durchstechen. **piercing** *adj* durchdringend.

piety ['paɪətɪ] *n* Frömmigkeit *f*.

pig [pɪg] *n* Schwein *m*. **pigheaded** *adj* störrisch. **piglet** *n* Schweinchen *neut*. **pigskin** *n* Schweinsleder *neut*. **pigsty** *n* Schweinestall *m*. **pigtail** *n* Zopf *m*.

pigment ['pɪgmənt] *n* Pigment *neut*, Farbstoff *m*. **pigmentation** *n* Pigmentation *f*.

pike [paɪk] *n* (*fish*) Hecht *m*; (*weapon*) Pike *f*, Spieß *m*.

pilchard ['pɪltʃəd] *n* Sardine *f*.

pile¹ [paɪl] *n* (*heap*) Haufen *m*, Stapel *m*. *v* (an)häufen, stapeln. **pile-up** *n* (*mot*) (Massen)Karambolage *f*.

pile² [paɪl] *n* (*post*) Pfahl *m*, Joch *neut*.

pile³ [paɪl] *n* (*of carpet*) Flor *m*.

piles [paɪlz] *pl n* Hämorrhoiden *pl*.

pilfer ['pɪlfə] *v* klauen. **pilferage** *n* Dieberei *f*.

pilgrim ['pɪlgrɪm] *n* Pilger(in). **pilgrimage** *n* Pilgerfahrt *f*, Wallfahrt *f*.

pill [pɪl] *n* Pille *f*, Tablette *f*. **the pill** (*contraceptive*) die Pille.

pillage ['pɪlɪdʒ] *v* (aus)plündern. *n* Plünderung *f*.

pillar ['pɪlə] *n* Pfeiler *m*, Säule *f*. **pillarbox** *n* Briefkasten *m*.

pillion ['pɪlɪən] *n* Soziussitz *m*. **ride pillion**

auf dem Sozius fahren.

pillow ['pɪləʊ] n Kopfkissen *neut*. **pillow case** n Kissenbezug *m*.

pilot ['paɪlət] n Pilot *m*. v steuern, lenken. **pilot light** Zündflamme *f*.

pimento [pɪ'mentəʊ] n Piment *m or neut*.

pimp [pɪmp] n Zuhälter *m*.

pimple ['pɪmpl] n Pustel *f*, Pickel *m*. **pimply** *adj* pickelig.

pin [pɪn] n Stecknadel *f*. v befestigen. **pin down** festnageln. **pincushion** n Nadelkissen *neut*.

PIN [pɪn] n persönliche Geheimnummer *f*, Geheimzahl *f*.

pinafore ['pɪnəfɔː] n Schürze *f*. **pinafore dress** Kleiderrock *m*.

pincers ['pɪnsəz] pl n Zange *f sing*; (*crab's*) Krebsschere *f sing*.

pinch [pɪntʃ] v zwicken, kneifen; (*coll*) klauen. n Kneifen *neut*, Zwicken *neut*; (*salt, etc.*) Prise *f*.

pine¹ [paɪn] n Kiefer *f*, Pinie *f*. **pine cone** n Kiefernzapfen *m*.

pine² [paɪn] v sich sehnen (nach). **pine away** verschmachten.

pineapple ['paɪnæpl] n Ananas *f*.

ping-pong ['pɪŋpɒŋ] n (*coll*) Tischtennis *neut*.

pinion ['pɪnjən] n (*tech*) Ritzel *m*. v fesseln.

pink [pɪŋk] *adj* rosa, blaßrot. n (*flower*) Nelke *f*. v (*mot*) klopfen. **in the pink** kerngesund.

pinnacle ['pɪnəkl] n Spitzturm *m*; (*fig*) Gipfel *m*.

pinpoint ['pɪnpɔɪnt] v ins Auge fassen, hervorheben.

pint [paɪnt] n Pinte *f*.

pioneer [paɪə'nɪə] n Pionier *m*, Bahnbrecher *m*. v den Weg bahnen für. **pioneering** *adj* bahnbrechend.

pious ['paɪəs] *adj* fromm.

pip¹ [pɪp] n (*fruit*) (Obst)Kern *m*.

pip² [pɪp] n (*sound*) Ton *m*; (*mil*) Stern *m*; (*on card*) Auge *neut*; (*on dice*) Punkt *m*.

pipe [paɪp] n Rohr *neut*, Röhre *f*; (*tobacco, music*) Pfeife *f*; (*sound*) Pfeifen *neut*. v (*liquid*) durch Röhren leiten; (*play pipes, etc.*) pfeifen; (*cookery*) spritzen. **pipedream** n Luftschloß *neut*. **pipeline** n Rohrleitung *f*.

piquant ['pɪkənt] *adj* pikant.

pique [piːk] n Groll *m*.

pirate ['paɪərət] n Seeräuber *m*. **piracy** n Seeräuberei *f*.

pirouette [pɪru'et] n Pirouette *f*. v pirouettieren.

Pisces ['paɪsiːz] n Fische *pl*.

piss [pɪs] v (*vulg*) pissen. n Pisse *f*. **take the piss** (**out of someone**) (jemanden) verarschen.

pistachio [pɪstɑːʃɪəʊ] n Pistazie *f*.

pistol ['pɪstl] n Pistole *f*.

piston ['pɪstən] n Kolben *m*.

pit [pɪt] n Grube *f*; (*mining*) Zeche *f*, Bergwerk *neut*. **pitted** *adj* vernarbt; (*corroded*) zerfressen.

pitch¹ [pɪtʃ] v werfen; (*tent*) aufschlagen. n Wurf *m*; (*sport*) Feld *neut*; (*music*) Tonhöhe *f*; (*level*) Grad *m*. **pitcher** n Werfer *m*; (*jug*) Krug *m*. **pitchfork** n Mistgabel *f*.

pitch² [pɪtʃ] n (*tar*) Pech *neut*.

pitfall ['pɪtfɔːl] n Fallgrube *f*, Falle *f*.

pith [pɪθ] n Mark *neut*. **pithy** *adj* markig.

pittance ['pɪtəns] n Hungerlohn *m*.

pituitary [pɪtjuːɪtəri] n Hirnanhangdrüse *f*, Hypophyse *f*.

pity ['pɪti] n Mitleid *neut*. v bemitleiden. *it's a pity* es ist schade, es ist ein Jammer *m*.

pivot ['pɪvət] n Drehpunkt *m*. v sich drehen.

placard ['plækɑːd] n Plakat *neut*.

placate [plə'keɪt] v beschwichtigen.

place [pleɪs] n Platz *m*; (*town, locality*) Ort *m*; (*spot*) Stelle *f*. **go places** (*coll*) es weit bringen. **out-of-places** *adj* (*remark*) unangebracht. **placename** n Ortsname *m*. **place of interest** Sehenswürdigkeit *f*. **take place** stattfinden. v stellen, legen, setzen; (*identify*) identifizieren, erkennen.

placenta [plə'sentə] n Plazenta *f*.

placid ['plæsɪd] *adj* ruhig, gelassen.

plagiarize ['pleɪdʒəraɪz] v plagiieren. **plagiarism** n Plagiat *m*.

plague [pleɪg] n Seuche *f*, Pest *f*. v plagen, quälen.

plaice [pleɪs] n Scholle *f*.

plain [pleɪn] *adj* einfach, schlicht; (*obvious*) klar; (*not pretty*) unansehnlich. *adv* einfach. n Ebene *f*. **plain chocolate** zartbittere Schokolade *f*. **plainly** *adv* offensichtlich. **speak plainly** offen reden.

plaintiff ['pleɪntɪf] n Kläger(in).

plaintive ['pleɪntɪv] *adj* traurig, wehmütig.

plait [plæt] *n* Zopf *m*, Flechte *f*. *v* flechten.

plan [plæn] *n* Plan *m*; (*drawing*) Entwurf *m*, Zeichnung *f*. *v* planen; (*intend*) vorhaben. **according to plan** planmäßig.

plane[1] [pleɪn] *adj* flach, eben. *n* Ebene *f*; (*aeroplane*) Flugzeug *neut*.

plane[2] [pleɪn] *n* (*tool*) Hobel *m*. *v* (ab)hobeln.

planet ['plænɪt] *n* Planet *m*.

plank [plæŋk] *n* Planke *f*, Diele *f*.

plankton ['plæŋktən] *n* Plankton *neut*.

planning ['plænɪŋ] *n* Planung *f*.

plant [plɑːnt] *n* Pflanze *f*; (*factory*) Betrieb *m*, Fabrik *f*. *v* pflanzen. **plantation** *n* Pflanzung *f*.

plaque [plæk] *n* Gedenktafel *f*.

plasma ['plæzmə] *n* Plasma *neut*.

plaster ['plɑːstə] *n* (*med*) Pflaster *neut*; (*of Paris*) Gips *m*. *v* bepflastern. **adhesive plaster** Heftpflaster *neut*. **plaster cast** Gipsabdruck *m*; (*med*) Gipsverband *m*.

plastic ['plæstɪk] *n* Kunststoff *m*. *adj* Kunststoff-.

plate [pleɪt] *n* (*for food*) Teller *m*; (*tech*) Platte *f*, Scheibe *f*. *v* (*metal*) plattieren. **gold-plated** *adj* vergoldet.

plateau ['plætou] *n* Hochebene *f*, Plateau *neut*.

platform ['plætfɔːm] *n* (*rail*) Bahnsteig *m*; (*speaker's*) Tribüne *f*; (*fig: pol*) Parteiprogramm *neut*.

platinum ['plætɪnəm] *n* Platin *neut*.

platonic [plə'tɒnɪk] *adj* platonisch.

platoon [plə'tuːn] *n* (*mil*) Zug *m*.

plausible ['plɔːzəbl] *adj* glaubhaft.

play [pleɪ] *n* Spiel *neut*; (*theatre*) Schauspiel *neut*, Stück *neut*; (*tech*) Spielraum *m*. *v* spielen. **play safe** kein Risiko eingehen. **playboy** *n* Playboy *m*. **player** *n* Spieler(in); (*actor*) Schauspieler(in). **playful** *adj* scherzhaft. **playground** *n* Spielplatz *m*; (*school*) Schulhof *m*. **playing card** Spielkarte *f*. **playing field** Sportplatz *m*. **playmate** *n* Spielkamerad(in). **plaything** *n* Spielzeug *neut*. **playwright** *n* Dramatiker *m*.

plea [pliː] *n* dringende Bitte *f*; (*law*) Plädoyer *neut*.

plead [pliːd] *v* (*law*) plädieren. **plead for** flehen um.

please [pliːz] *v* gefallen (+*dat*), Freude machen (+*dat*). *adv* bitte! **pleasant** angenehm; (*person*) freundlich, nett.

pleased *adj* zufrieden. **pleasing** *adj* angenehm. **pleasurable** *adj* vergnüglich. **pleasure** *n* Vergnügen *neut*.

pleat [pliːt] *n* Falte *f*. *v* in Falten legen.

plebiscite ['plebɪsaɪt] *n* Volksabstimmung *f*, Plebiszit *neut*.

pledge [pledʒ] *n* Pfand *neut*; (*promise*) Versprechen *neut*. *v* versprechen.

plenty ['plentɪ] *n* Fülle *f*, Reichtum *m*. **plenty of** eine Menge, viel.

pleurisy ['pluərɪsɪ] *n* Rippenfellentzündung *f*.

pliable ['plaɪəbl] *adj* biegsam. **pliability** *n* Biegsamkeit *f*.

pliers ['plaɪəz] *pl n* Zange *f sing*.

plight [plaɪt] *n* Notlage *f*.

plimsoll ['plɪmsəl] *n* Turnschuh *m*.

plinth [plɪnθ] *n* Sockel *m*, Plinthe *f*.

plod [plɒd] *v* sich hinschleppen, schwerfällig gehen.

plonk[1] [plɒŋk] *v* **plonk down** hinschmeißen.

plonk[2] [plɒŋk] *n* (*coll*) billiger Wein.

plot[1] [plɒt] *n* Komplott *neut*; (*in novel*) Handlung *f*. *v* sich verschwören; (*on map*) einzeichnen. **plotter** *n* Verschwörer(in).

plot[2] [plɒt] *n* (*land*) Parzelle *f*, Grundstück *neut*.

plough [plau] *n* Pflug *m*; (*astron*) Großer Bär *m*. *v* (um)pflügen. **ploughman** *n* Pflüger *m*.

ploy [plɔɪ] *n* List *f*.

pluck [plʌk] *v* pflücken; (*poultry*) rupfen; (*music*) zupfen. *n* (*courage*) Mut *m*. **plucky** *adj* mutig. **pluck up courage** Mut fassen.

plug [plʌg] *n* (*elec*) Stecker *m*; (*stopper*) Stöpsel *m*. *v* verstopfen; (*coll*) befürworten. **plug in** anschließen, einstecken.

plum [plʌm] *n* Pflaume *f*, Zwetsche *f*.

plumage ['pluːmɪdʒ] *n* Gefieder *neut*.

plumb [plʌm] *n* Senkblei *neut*. *adj* senkrecht. *v* (*sound*) sondieren. **plumber** *n* Klempner *m*. **plumbing** *n* Klempnerarbeit *f*; (*pipes*) Rohrleitungen *pl f*.

plume [pluːm] *n* Feder *f*; (*of smoke*) Streifen *m*.

plummet ['plʌmɪt] *v* abstürzen.

plump[1] [plʌmp] *adj* (*fat*) rundlich, mollig. **plumpness** *n* Rundlichkeit *f*.

plump² [plʌmp] v (*fall*) plumpsen. **plump for** sich entscheiden für.

plunder ['plʌndə] v plündern. n (*spoils*) Beute f.

plunge [plʌndʒ] v tauchen; (*fall*) stürzen. n Sturz m.

pluperfect [pluːˈpəfɪkt] n (*gramm*) Vorvergangenheit f.

plural ['pluərəl] adj Plural-. n Plural m, Mehrzahl f.

plus [plʌs] prep plus. adj Plus-. n Plus neut.

plush [plʌʃ] adj (*fig*) luxuriös.

Pluto ['pluːtou] n Pluto m.

ply¹ [plai] v (*trade*) ausüben; (*travel*) verkehren.

ply² [plai] n (*of yarn*) Strähne f. **plywood** n Sperrholz neut.

pneumatic [njuːmˈatik] adj pneumatisch. **pneumatic tyre** n Luftreifen m. **pneumatic drill** Preßluftbohrer m.

pneumonia [njuːˈmounə] n Lungenentzündung f.

poach¹ [poutʃ] v (*cookery*) pochieren. **poached egg** verlorenes Ei neut.

poach² [poutʃ] v wildern. **poacher** n Wilddieb m.

pocket ['pokit] n Tasche f. adj Taschen-. v in die Tasche stecken, einstecken. **to be in pocket** gut bei Kasse sein. **pocket-knife** n Taschenmesser neut. **pocket-money** n Taschengeld neut.

pod [pod] n Schote f.

podcast ['podkaːst] n Podcast m, Podcasting neut.

podgy ['podʒi] adj (*coll*) mollig, dick.

poem ['pouim] n Gedicht neut. **poet** n Dichter m. **poetess** n Dichterin f. **poetic** adj poetisch, dichterisch. **poetry** n Dichtkunst f. (*poems*) Gedichte f.

poignant ['poinjənt] adj schmerzlich; (*wit*) scharf; (*grief*) bitter.

point [point] n (*tip*) Spitze f; (*place, spot*) Punkt m; (*in time*) Zeitpunkt m; (*main thing*) Hauptsache f. **be on the point of doing** eben tun wollen. **point of view** Standpunkt m. **points** pl n (*rail*) Weichen pl. **that's the point!** das is es ja! **there's no point in** es hat keinen Zweck, zu. v spitzen; (*indicate*) zeigen; (*mit dem Finger*) zeigen. **point out** hinweisen auf. **pointed** adj zugespitzt; (*remark*) treffend, beißend. **pointless** adj sinnlos.

poise [poiz] n Haltung f; (*calmness*) Gelassenheit f.

poison ['poizən] n Gift neut. v vergiften. **poisoner** n Giftmörder(in). **poisonous** adj giftig.

poke [pouk] n Stoß m, Puff m. v stoßen; (*fire*) schüren.

poker¹ ['poukə] n (*for fire*) Feuerhaken m.

poker² ['poukə] n (*gambling*) Poker(spiel) neut.

Poland ['poulənd] n Polen neut. **Pole** n Pole m, Polin f. **Polish** adj polnisch.

polar ['poulə] adj polar. **polar bear** Eisbär m.

pole¹ [poul] n (*geog*) Pol m. **pole star** n Polarstern m.

pole² [poul] n Pfosten m, Pfahl m; (*telegraph, etc.*) Stange f. **pole-vault** n Stabhochsprung m.

police [pəˈliːs] n Polizei f. n (polizeilich) überwachen. adj polizeilich, Polizei-. **police force** Polizei f. **policeman** n Polizist m, Schutzmann m. **police station** Polizeiwache f, Polizeirevier neut.

policy¹ ['poləsi] n Politik f; (*personal*) Methode f.

policy² ['poləsi] n (*insurance*) Police f.

polio ['pouliou] n Kinderlähmung f.

polish ['poliʃ] n Politur f; (*floors, furniture*) Bohnerwachs neut; (*shoes*) Schuhcreme f. v polieren; (*furniture*) bohnern; (*shoes*) wichsen. **polished** adj poliert; (*fig*) fein, elegant. **polisher** n polierer m.

polite [pəˈlait] adj höflich. **politeness** n Höflichkeit f.

politics ['politiks] n Politik f. **political** adj politisch. **political correctness** politische Korrektheit f. **politically correct** politisch korrekt. **politician** n Politiker m.

polka ['polkə] n Polka f.

poll [poul] n (*voting*) Abstimmung f; (*opinion poll*) Meinungsumfrage f.

pollen ['polən] n Pollen m, Blütenstaub m. **pollinate** v befruchten.

pollute [pəˈluːt] v verschmutzen, verunreinigen. **pollution** n (*environmental*) Umweltverschmutzung f.

polo ['poulou] n Polo neut. **polo-neck** n Rollkragen m.

polygamy [pəˈligəm] n Polygamie f. **polygamous** adj polygam.

polygon ['poligən] n Polygon neut.

polytechnic [ˌpɒlɪˈteknɪk] n Polytechnikum neut.

polythene [ˈpɒlɪθiːn] n Polyäthylen neut. adj **polythene bag** Plastiktüte f.

pomegranate [ˈpɒmɪɡranɪt] n Granatapfel m.

pomp [pɒmp] n Prunk m, Pracht f. **pomposity** n Bombast m. **pompous** adj bombastisch.

pond [pɒnd] n Teich m.

ponder [ˈpɒndə] v nachdenken (über). **ponderous** adj schwer; (movement) schwerfällig.

pong [pɒŋ] n Gestank f. v miefen.

pony [ˈpəʊnɪ] n Pony neut, Pferdchen neut. **pony-tail** Pferdeschwanz m.

poodle [ˈpuːdl] n Pudel m.

poof [puːf] n (derog) Schwule(r) m.

pool¹ [puːl] n (pond) Teich m; (blood, etc.) Lache f; (swimming) (Schwimm)Bad neut.

pool² [puːl] n (game) Pool m; (fund) Kasse f. v (resources) vereinigen. **football pools** Fußballtoto m.

poor [pʊə] adj arm, bedürftig; (earth) dürr; (bad) schlecht. **the poor** die Armen pl. **poorly** adj (coll) krank, unwohl.

pop¹ [pɒp] n Knall m, Puff m; (drink) Limonade f. v knallen; (burst) platzen. **pop in** schnell vorbeikommen. **pop up** (appear) auftauchen.

pop² [pɒp] adj **pop music** Popmusik f. **pop song** Schlager m.

pope [pəʊp] n Papst m.

poplar [ˈpɒplə] n Pappel f.

poppy [ˈpɒpɪ] n Mohn m.

popular [ˈpɒpjʊlə] adj populär; (well-liked) beliebt; (of the people) Volks-. **popularity** n Popularität f.

population [ˌpɒpjʊˈleɪʃən] n Bevölkerung f. **populate** v bevölkern. **populous** adj volkreich.

porcelain [ˈpɔːslɪn] n Porzellan neut. adj Porzellan-.

porch [pɔːtʃ] n Vorhalle neut.

porcupine [ˈpɔːkjʊpaɪn] n Stachelschwein neut.

pore¹ [pɔː] n Pore f.

pore² [pɔː] v **pore over** eifrig studieren, brüten über.

pork [pɔːk] n Schweinefleisch neut. **pork butcher** Schweineschlächter m. **pork**

chop Schweinskotelett neut. **roast pork** Schweinebraten m.

pornography [pɔːˈnɒɡrəfɪ] n Pornographie f. **pornographic** adj pornographisch; (film, book) Porno-.

porous [ˈpɔːrəs] adj porös.

porpoise [ˈpɔːpəs] n Tümmler m.

porridge [ˈpɒrɪdʒ] n Haferflockenbrei m. **porridge oats** Haferflocken pl.

port¹ [pɔːt] n (harbour) Hafen m; (town) Hafenstadt f; (comp) Port m. **port of call** Anlaufhafen m.

port² [pɔːt] n (naut) Backbord neut. adj Backbord-.

port³ [pɔːt] n (wine) Portwein m.

portly [ˈpɔːtlɪ] adj wohlbeleibt.

portable [ˈpɔːtəbl] adj tragbar. **portable radio** Kofferradio neut.

portent [ˈpɔːtent] n Omen neut, Vorzeichen f. **portentous** adj ominös.

porter [ˈpɔːtə] n (rail, etc.) Gepäckträger m.

portfolio [pɔːtˈfəʊlɪəʊ] n Mappe f; (pol) Portefeuille neut. **minister without portfolio** Minister ohne Geschäftsbereich m.

porthole [ˈpɔːthəʊl] n Luke f.

portion [ˈpɔːʃən] n (food) Portion f; (share) (An)Teil m.

portrait [ˈpɔːtrət] n Porträt neut. **portray** v malen; (fig) schildern. **portrayal** n Porträt neut, Schilderung f.

Portugal [ˈpɔːtʃʊɡəl] n Portugal neut. **Portuguese** adj portugiesisch; n Portugiese m, Portugiesin f.

pose [pəʊz] n Pose f. v sitzen, posieren; (problem) stellen. **pose as** sich ausgeben als. **poseur** n poseur f.

posh [pɒʃ] adj vornehm.

position [pəˈzɪʃən] n Position f, Stellung f; (situation) Lage f; (attitude) Standpunkt m; (standing) Rang m. v stellen.

positive [ˈpɒzətɪv] adj positiv.

possess [pəˈzes] v besitzen. **possessed** adj besessen. **possession** n Besitz m. **take possession of** in Besitz nehmen. **possessive** adj (person) besitzgierig. **possessor** n Inhaber(in).

possible [ˈpɒsəbl] adj möglich; (imaginable) eventuell. **possibility** n Möglichkeit f. **possibly** adv möglicherweise.

post¹ [pəʊst] n (pole) Pfahl m, Pfosten m. **deaf as a post** stocktaub.

post² [pəʊst] n (mil) Posten m; (job)

Stelle *f. v* aufstellen.

post³ [pəust] *n (mail)* Post *f.* **by post** per Post. **postage stamp** Briefmarke *f.* **postcard** *n* Postkarte *f.* **postman** *n* Briefträger *m.* **post office** Postamt *neut. v* zur Post bringen; *(send)* (mit der Post) schicken. **keep someone posted** jemanden auf dem laufenden halten. **postage** *n* Porto *neut,* Postgebühr *f.* **postal** *adj* Post-.

poste restante [pəust'testāt] *adv* postlagernd.

poster ['pəustə] *n* Plakat *neut.*

posterior [po'stɜrə] *adj* später, hinter. *n* Hintern *m.*

posterity [po'steɪətɪ] *n* Nachwelt *f.*

postgraduate [pəust'gradjuɪt] *n* Doktorand(in).

post-haste *adv* schnellstens.

posthumous ['postjm əs] *adj* postum.

post-mortem [pəustm ɔːtəm] *n* Autopsie *f.*

post-natal [pəusneɪt] *adj* postnatal.

postpone [pəuspoun] *v* verschieben. **postponement** *n* Verschiebung *f.*

postscript ['pəuskrɪpt] *n* Postskriptum *neut.*

postulate ['postjʊleɪt] *v* voraussetzen, annehmen.

posture ['postʃə] *n* (Körper)Haltung *f.*

post-war *adj* Nachkriegs-.

pot [pot] *n* Topf *m; (tea, coffee)* Kanne *f. v (coll)* schießen. **go to pot** vor die Hunde gehen. **pot-bellied** *adj* dickbauchig.

potassium [pə'tasɪm] *n* Kalium *neut.*

potato [pə'teɪtou] *n* Kartoffel *f.* **boiled potatoes** Salzkartoffeln *pl.* **chipped** *or* **french-fried potatoes** Pommes frites *pl.* **roast** *or* **fried potatoes** Bratkartoffeln *pl.*

potent ['poutənt] *adj* stark; *(sexually)* potent. **potency** *n* Stärke *f.* Potenz *f.*

potential [pə'tenʃəl] *adj* möglich, potential. *n* Potential *neut.*

pothole ['pothoul] *n* Höhle *f.*

potion ['pouʃən] *n* Arzneitrank *m.* **love potion** Liebestrank *m.*

potluck ['potlʌk] *n* **take potluck with** *(coll)* probieren, es riskieren mit/bei.

potted ['potɪd] *adj (meat)* eingemacht; *(plant)* Topf-; *(version)* gekürzt.

potter ['potə] *v* **potter around** herumhantieren, herumbasteln.

pottery ['potərɪ] *n* Töpferwaren *pl,*

Steingut *neut.*

potty ['potɪ] *n* Töpfchen *neut.*

pouch [pautʃ] *n* Beutel *m.*

poultice ['poultɪs] *n* Breiumschlag *m.*

poultry ['poultrɪ] *n* Geflügel *neut.*

pounce [pauns] *v* springen, sich stürzen. *n* Sprung *m,* Satz *m.*

pound¹ [paund] *v* zerstampfen; *(hit)* hämmern, klopfen.

pound² [paund] *n (currency, weight)* Pfund *neut.*

pour [poː] *v* gießen. **pour out** *(a liquid)* ausgießen; *(drink)* einschenken; *(come out)* herausströmen. **pouring** *adj (rain)* strömend.

pout [paut] *v* schmollen, maulen.

poverty ['povətɪ] *n* Armut *f.* **poverty-stricken** *adj* verarmt.

powder ['paudə] *n* Pulver *neut; (face)* Puder *m. v (face)* pudern. **powder room** Damentoilette *f.* **powdery** *adj* pulverig.

power ['pauə] *n* Macht *f; (tech)* Kraft *f; (elec)* Strom *m. v* betreiben, antreiben. **great power** *(pol)* Großmacht *f.* **powerful** *adj* mächtig. **powerless** *adj* machtlos. **power station** Kraftwerk *neut.*

PR *n* Öffentlichkeitsarbeit *f.*

practicable ['praktɪkəbl] *adj* durchführbar.

practical ['praktɪkl] *adj* praktisch.

practice ['praktɪs] *n* Praxis *f; (exercise)* Übung *f; (custom)* Brauch *m; (procedure)* Verfahren *neut. v see* **practise**.

practise ['praktɪs] *v* üben; *(profession)* ausüben; *(med, law)* praktizieren. **practised** *adj* geübt.

practitioner [prakt'ʃənə] *n* Praktiker *m.* **medical practitioner** praktischer Arzt *m.*

pragmatic [prag'm atɪk] *adj* pragmatisch. **pragmatism** *n* Pragmatismus *m.* **pragmatist** *n* Pragmatiker *m.*

Prague [prɑːg] *n* Prag *neut.*

prairie ['preərɪ] *n* Prärie *f.*

praise [preɪz] *v* loben. *v* Lob *neut.* **praiseworthy** *adj* lobenswert.

pram [pram] *n* Kinderwagen *m.*

prance [prɑːns] *v* tänzeln.

prank [praŋk] *n* Streich *m,* Possen *m.*

prattle ['pratl] *v* plappern, schwatzen. *n* Geplapper *neut,* Geschwätz *neut.*

prawn [prɔːn] *n* Garnele *f.*

pray [preɪ] *v* beten; *(ask)* bitten. **prayer** *n*

Gebet *neut*. **prayerbook** Gebetbuch *neut*.

preach [priːʃ] *v* predigen. **preacher** *n* Prediger(in). **preaching** *n* Lehre *f*.

precarious [prɪkeərəs] *adj* unsicher, gefährlich.

precaution [prɪkoːʃən] *n* Vorkehrung *f*. **precautionary** *adj* vorbeugend.

precede [prɪsɪd] *v* vorhergehen. **precedence** *n* Vorrang *m*. **precedent** *n* Präzedenzfall *m*. **order of precedence** Rangordnung *f*. **preceding** *adj* vorhergehend.

precinct ['priːsɪŋkt] *n* Bezirk *m*. **precincts** *pl* Umgebung *f*.

precious ['preʃəs] *adj* kostbar, wertvoll; (*jewels*) edel. *adv* (*coll*) äußerst.

precipice ['presipis] *n* Abgrund *m*.

precipitate [prɪsɪpiteit] *v* (*bring about*) herbeiführen; (*chem*) Fällen. **precipitation** *n* (*haste*) Hast *f*; (*chem*) Fällung *f*; (*rain, etc.*) Niederschlag *m*.

précis ['preisi] *n* Zusammenfassung *f*. *v* zusammenfassen.

precise [prɪsais] *adj* präzis, genau. **precisely** *adv* genau. **precision** *n* Genauigkeit *f*; (*tech*) Präzision.

preclude [prɪkluːd] *v* ausschließen; (*prevent*) vorbeugen.

precocious [prɪkouʃəs] *adj* frühreif. **precociousness** *n* Frühreife *f*.

preconceive [priːkənstv] *v* vorher ausdenken. **preconception** *n* Vorurteil *neut*.

precondition [priːkəndʃən] *n* Voraussetzung *f*.

precursor [prɪkəːsə] *n* Vorläufer(in). **precursory** *adj* vorausgehend.

predatory ['predətəri] *adj* räuberisch. **predator** *n* Raubtier *neut*.

predecessor ['priːdisesə] *n* Vorgänger(in).

predestine [prɪdestɪn] *v* prädestinieren. **predestination** *n* Vorbestimmung *f*, Prädestination *f*.

predicament [prɪdikəmənt] *n* schwierige Lage *f*.

predicate ['predikət] *n* (*gramm*) Prädikat *neut*. *v* aussagen.

predict [prɪdikt] *v* voraussagen. **predictable** *adj* voraussagbar. **prediction** *n* Voraussage *f*.

predominate [prɪdomineit] *v* vorwiegen. **predominance** *n* Vorherrschaft *f*. **predominant** *adj* vorwiegend.

pre-eminent [prɪem inənt] *adj* hervorragend. **pre-eminence** *n* Überlegenheit *f*.

pre-empt [prɪem pt] *v* zuvorkommen.

preen [priːn] *v* (sich) putzen.

prefabricate [prɪfabrikeit] *v* vorfabrizieren. **prefabricated** *adj* Fertig-.

preface ['prefis] *n* Vorwort *neut*. *v* einleiten.

prefect ['priːfekt] *n* (*pol*) Präfekt *m*; (*school*) Aufsichtsschüler(in).

prefer [prɪfəː] *v* vorziehen, lieber haben. **preferable** *adj* vorzuziehen. **preferably** *adv* am besten. **preference** *n* Vorzug *m*. **preferential** *adj* bevorzugt.

prefix ['priːfiks] *n* Präfix *neut*, Vorsilbe *f*.

pregnant ['pregnənt] *adj* schwanger; (*animals*) trächtig; (*fig*) bedeutend, vielsagend. **pregnancy** *n* Schwangerschaft *f*.

prehistoric [priːhistorik] *adj* vorgeschichtlich. **prehistory** *n* Vorgeschichte *f*.

prejudice ['predʒədis] *n* Vorurteil *neut*. *v* beeinträchtigen; (*person*) beeinflussen. **prejudiced** *adj* voreingenommen. **prejudicial** *adj* nachteilig, schädlich.

preliminary [prɪlim inəri] *adj* vorläufig, Vor-.

prelude ['preljuːd] *n* Vorspiel *neut*, Präludium *neut*.

premarital [priːm arit] *adj* vorehelich.

premature [prem əˈtʃuə] *adj* frühzeitig. **premature birth** Frühgeburt *f*. **prematurity** *n* Frühzeitigkeit *f*.

premeditate [priːm edieit] *v* vorher überlegen. **premediated** *adj* (*crime*) vorsätzlich. **premeditation** *n* Vorbedacht *m*.

premier ['prem iə] *adj* erst. *n* Premierminister *m*.

premiere ['prem iə] *n* Erstaufführung *f*, Premiere *f*.

premise ['prem is] *n* Voraussetzung *f*, Prämisse *f*.

premises ['prem isis] *pl n* Gelände *neut sing*. **business premises** Büro *neut*, Geschäftsräume *pl*. **on the premises** im Hause.

premium ['prim əm] *n* Prämie *f*.

premonition [prem əˈnʃən] *n* Vorahnung *f*.

prenatal [prɪneit] *adj* prenatal, vor der Geburt.

preoccupied [prɪokjupaid] *adj* vertieft (in).

prepare [prɪpeə] *v* vorbereiten; (*food*)

zubereiten; (*produce*) herstellen. **prepare for** sich vorbereiten auf. **preparation** *n* Vorbereitung *f*; (*med*) Präparat *neut*; (*homework*) Hausaufgaben *pl*. **preparatory** *adj* vorbereitend. **prepared** *adj* bereit.

preposition [ˌprepəˈzʃən] *n* Präposition *f*.

preposterous [prɪˈpostərəs] *adj* absurd, lächerlich.

prerequisite [priːˈrekwizit] *n* Voraussetzung *f*.

prerogative [prɪˈrogətiv] *n* Vorrecht *neut*.

prescribe [prɪˈskraib] *v* vorschreiben, anordnen; (*med*) verordnen. **prescription** *n* Verordnung *f*.

present[1] [ˈprezənt] *adj* (*time*) gegenwärtig; (*people*) anwesend; (*things*) vorhanden. *n* Gegenwart *f*. **at the present time** im Moment, zur Zeit. **be present at** Beiwohnen (+*dat*). **presently** *adv* gleich. **presence** *n* (*people*) Anwesenheit *f*, Beisein *neut*; (*things*) Vorhandensein *neut*. **presence of mind** Geistesgegenwart *f*.

present[2] [ˈprezənt; *v* priˈzent] *n* Geschenk *neut*. *v* vorlegen; (*gift*) schenken; (*person*) vorstellen; (*play*) vorführen. **presentation** *n* Vorlegung *f*; Schenkung *f*; Übergabe *f*; Vorführung *f*.

preserve [prɪˈzəːv] *v* bewahren; (*food*) einmachen. **in Konserve f.**

preside [prɪˈzaid] *v* den Vorsitz führen. **preside over** (*meeting*) leiten.

president [ˈprezidənt] *n* Präsident *m*; (*comm*) Generaldirektor *m*. **presidency** *n* (*pol*) Präsidentschaft *f*; (*meeting*) Vorsitz *m*. **presidential** *adj* Präsidenten-.

press [pres] *v* drücken; (*iron*) bügeln. *n* Presse *f*. **press conference** Pressekonferenz *f*. **press stud** Druckknopf *m*. **press-up** *n* Liegestütz *m*. **pressing** *adj* dringend.

pressure [ˈpreʃə] *n* Druck *m*. **pressure cooker** Schnellkochtopf *m*. **pressure gauge** Druckmesser *m*. **pressure group** Interessengruppe *f*. **pressurize** (*aircraft*) auf Normaldruck halten; (*person*) unter Druck setzen.

prestige [preˈstiːʒ] *n* Prestige *neut*. **prestigious** *adj* Prestige-.

presume [prɪˈzjuːm] *v* annehmen; (*dare to*) sich erlauben. **presumably** *adv* vermutlich. **presumption** *n* Vermutung *f*; (*cheek*) Unverschämtheit *f*. **presumptuous** *adj* unverschämt.

pretend [prɪˈtend] *v* vorgeben. **pretend to**

so tun, als ob; (*claim*) Anspruch erheben (auf). **pretence** *n* Vorwand *m*, Anschein *m*. **under false pretences** unter Vorspiegelung falscher Tatsachen. **pretentious** *adj* anmaßend. **pretentiousness** *n* Anmaßung *f*.

pretext [ˈpriːtekst] *n* Vorwand *m*, Ausrede *f*.

pretty [ˈpriti] *adj* hübsch, niedlich. *adv* (*coll*) ziemlich. **prettify** *v* hübsch machen. **prettiness** *n* Schönheit *f*.

prevail [prɪˈveil] *v* (*win*) siegen (über); (*be prevalent*) vorwiegen, vorherrschen. **prevailing** *adj* vorherrschend; (*opinion*) allgemein. **prevalence** *n* Herrschen *neut*. **prevalent** *adj* (vor)herrschend.

prevent [prɪˈvent] *v* verhindern, verhüten. **prevention** *n* Verhütung *f*. **preventive** *adj* vorbeugend. **preventive measure** Vorsichtsmaßnahme *f*.

preview [ˈpriːvjuː] *n* Vorschau *f*, Probeaufführung *f*.

previous [ˈpriːvjəs] *adj* vorhergehend, früher. **previously** *adv* vorher.

prey [prei] *n* Opfer *neut*. *v* **prey on** erbeuten.

price [prais] *n* Preis *m*, Kosten *pl*. *v* den Preis festsetzen für; (*evaluate*) bewerten. **priceless** *adj* unschätzbar. **price-tag** *n* Preiszettel *m*.

prick [prik] *n* Stich *m*. *v* stechen.

prickle [ˈprikl] *n* Stachel *m*, Dorn *m*. *v* prickeln, kribbeln. **prickly** *adj* stachelig; (*person*) reizbar, übellaunig.

pride [praid] *n* Stolz *m*; (*arrogance*) Hochmut *m*; (*lions*) Rudel *neut*. *v* **pride oneself on** stolz sein auf.

priest [priːst] *n* Priester *m*. **priestess** *n* Priesterin *f*. **priesthood** *n* Priesterschaft *f*. **priestly** *adj* priesterlich.

prim [prim] *adj* steif, affektiert. **primness** *n* Steifheit *f*.

primary [ˈpraiməri] *adj* erst, ursprünglich; (*main*) primär, Haupt-; (*basic*) grundlegend. **primary school** Grundschule *f*. **primarily** *adv* hauptsächlich, in erster Linie.

primate [ˈpraimət] *n* (*biol*) Primat *m*.

prime [praim] *adj* erst; (*main*) Haupt-; (*number*) unteilbar; (*best*) erstklassig. **prime minister** Premierminister(in). *n* Blüte *f*. *v* (*gun*) laden; (*paint*) grundieren; (*fig*) vorbereiten. **primer** *n* (*paint*) Grundierfarbe *f*; (*book*) Elementarbuch *neut*. **priming** *n* Vorbereitung.

primeval [praɪm̩iːvḷ] adj urzeitlich.

primitive ['prɪmɪtɪv] adj (early) urzeitlich, Ur-; (crude, unrefined) primitiv. **primitiveness** n Primitivität f.

primrose ['prɪmrəʊz] n Primel f.

prince [prɪns] n (ruler) Fürst m; (king's son) Prinz m. **princely** adj fürstlich. **princess** n Fürstin f, Prinzessin f. **principality** n Fürstentum neut.

principal ['prɪnsəpḷ] adj erst, Haupt-. n Vorsteher(in); (comm) Kapital neut. **principally** adv hauptsächlich.

principle ['prɪnsəpḷ] n Prinzip neut, Grundsatz m; (basis) Grundlage f. **principled** adj mit hohen Grundsätzen.

print [prɪnt] v drucken. **printed matter** Drucksache f. **printer** n (also comp) Drucker m. **printing** n Druck m. **printing press** Druckerei f. n Druck m; (of photograph) Abzug m, Kopie f.

prior ['praɪə] adj früher. adv prior to vor. **priority** n Priorität f; (precedence) Vorrang m.

prise [praɪz] v prise open aufbrechen.

prism ['prɪzm] n Prisma neut.

prison ['prɪzn] n Gefängnis neut. **prisoner** n Gefangene(r), Häftling m.

pristine ['prɪstiːn] adj unberührt, unverdorben.

private ['praɪvət] adj privat; (personal) persönlich. n gemeiner Soldat m. **privacy** n Privatleben neut, Ruhe f.

privet ['prɪvət] n Liguster m.

privilege ['prɪvəlɪdʒ] n Privilegium neut, Sonderrecht neut; (honour) Ehre f. **privileged** adj bevorrechtet. **be privileged to** die Ehre haben, zu.

privy ['prɪvɪ] n Abort m. adj **be privy to** eingeweiht sein in. **privy council** Geheimer Rat m.

prize [praɪz] n Preis m; (lottery) Los neut. adj Preis-. v hochschätzen. **prizegiving** n Preisverleihung f, Prämierung f.

pro [prəʊ] n **the pros and cons** die Vor- und Nachteile, das Pro und Kontra, das Für und Wider.

probable ['prɒbəbḷ] adj wahrscheinlich. **probability** n Wahrscheinlichkeit f.

probation [prəˈbeɪʃn] n Probezeit f; (law) bedingte Freilassung f. **probationary** adj Probe-.

probe [prəʊb] n (tech) Sonde f; (enquiry) Untersuchung f. v **probe into** eindringen in, erforschen.

problem ['prɒbləm] n Problem neut. **problematical** adj problematisch.

proceed [prəˈsiːd] v weitergehen; (continue) fortfahren; (begin) beginnen. **procedure** n Vorgehen neut. **proceedings** pl n (law) Verfahren neut sing. **proceeds** pl n Erlös m sing, Ertrag m sing.

process ['prəʊses] v bearbeiten, verarbeiten. n Verfahren neut, Prozeß m. **processing** n Verarbeitung f.

procession [prəˈseʃn] n Prozession f, Zug m.

proclaim [prəˈkleɪm] v proklamieren, verkünden. **proclamation** n Proklamation f.

procrastinate [prəʊˈkræstɪneɪt] v aufschieben.

procreate ['prəʊkrieɪt] v erzeugen. **procreation** n Zeugung f.

procure [prəˈkjʊə] v beschaffen, besorgen.

prod [prɒd] v stechen, stoßen; (coll: induce) anspornen (zu). n Stich m, Stoß m.

prodigy ['prɒdɪdʒɪ] n Wunder neut; (child) Wunderkind neut. **prodigious** adj riesig, erstaunlich.

produce [prəˈdjuːs] n 'prɒdjuːs] v (goods) erzeugen, herstellen; (submit) vorlegen; (cause, call forth) hervorrufen; (theatre) aufführen; (films) herausbringen. n Erzeugnis neut, Produkte pl. **producer** n Hersteller; (theatre, film) Regisseur m. **product** n Produkt neut, Erzeugnis neut; (result) Ergebnis neut. **production** n Herstellung f, Produktion f; (theatre) Aufführung f; (film) Regie f. **production line** Fließband neut. **productive** adj fruchtbar, leistungsfähig. **productivity** n Leistungsfähigkeit f, Produktivität f.

profane [prəˈfeɪn] adj profan. **profanity** n Fluchen neut.

profess [prəˈfes] v erklären. **profession** n (occupation) Beruf m; (assertion) Beteuerung f. **professional** adj Berufs-, beruflich; (education) fachlich, Fach-.

professor [prəˈfesə] n Professor(in). **professorship** n Lehrstuhl m.

proficient [prəˈfɪʃnt] adj erfahren. **proficiency** n Erfahrenheit f.

profile ['prəʊfaɪl] n Profil neut. v profilieren.

profit ['prɒfɪt] n (comm) Gewinn m, Profit

m; (*advantage*) Vorteil *m*. *v* **profit from** Nutzen ziehen aus. **profitable** *adj* rentabel; (*advantageous*) vorteilhaft. **profiteer** *n* Profitmacher *m*; *v* sich bereichern.

program ['prougræm] *n* (*comp*) Programm *neut*; (US: *broadcast*) Fernsehprogramm *neut*. *v* programmieren. **programmer** *n* Programmgeber(in). **programming** *n* Programmierung *f*.

programme ['prougræm] *n* Programm *neut*; (*TV, radio*: *broadcast*) Sendung *f*. *v* planen.

progress ['prougres] *n* Fortschritt *m*; (*development*) Entwicklung *f*. *v* fortschreiten, sich entwickeln. **in progress** im Gange. **progression** *n* Fortbewegung *f*. **progressive** *adj* fortschrittlich.

prohibit [prə'hibit] *v* verbieten. **prohibition** *n* Verbot *neut*; (*of drinking*) Alkoholverbot *neut*. **prohibitive** *adj* verbietend; (*excessively high*) untragbar.

project ['prodʒekt; *v* prə'dʒekt] *n* Projekt *neut*, Plan *m*; (*school*) Planaufgabe *f*. *v* (*film, etc.*) projizieren; (*plan*) planen. **projection** *n* Projektion *f*. **projector** *n* Projektionsapparat *m*.

proletariat [proulə'teəriət] *n* Proletariat *neut*. **proletarian** *adj* proletarisch. *n* Proletarier(in).

proliferate [prə'lifəreit] *v* sich vermehren, wuchern. **proliferation** *n* Wucherung *f*.

prolific [prə'lifik] *adj* fruchtbar.

prologue ['proulog] *n* Prolog *m*.

prolong [prə'loŋ] *v* verlängern. **prolonged** *adj* anhaltend. **prolongation** *n* Verlängerung *f*.

promenade [promə'naːd] *n* Promenade *f*; (*walk*) Spaziergang *m*. *v* promenieren, spazieren.

prominent ['promi nənt] *adj* (*person*) prominent, maßgebend. **prominence** *n* Prominenz *f*, hervorragende Bedeutung *f*.

promiscuous [prə'miskjuəs] *adj* promiskuitiv. **promiscuity** *n* Promiskuität *f*.

promise ['promis] *n* Versprechen *neut*. *v* versprechen. **promising** *adj* vielversprechend.

promontory ['promntəri] *n* Landspitze *f*.

promote [prə'mout] *v* (*person*) befördern; (*encourage, support*) fördern, Vorschub leisten (+ *dat*); (*comm*) Reklame machen für. **promoter** *n* (*sport*) Promoter *m*. **promo-**

tion *n* Beförderung; (*publicity*) Werbung *f*, Reklame *f*.

prompt [prompt] *adj* sofortig, prompt. *v* (*theatre*) soufflieren; (*cause*) hervorrufen. **promptness** *n* Pünktlichkeit *f*.

prone [proun] *adj* hingestreckt. **prone to** geneigt zu.

prong [proŋ] *n* Zinke *f*. **pronged** *adj* gezinkt.

pronoun ['prounaun] *n* Pronomen *neut*.

pronounce [prə'nauns] *v* aussprechen. **pronouncement** *n* Ausspruch *m*. **pronunciation** *n* Aussprache *f*.

proof [pruːf] *n* Beweis *m*, Nachweis *m*; (*printing*) Korrekturabzug *m*. *adj* undurchlässig, fest. **proof against** sicher vor. **proof-reader** *n* Korrektor(in).

prop¹ [prop] *n* Stütze *f*. *v* **prop up** stützen.

prop² [prop] *n* (*theatre*) Requisit *neut*.

propaganda [propə'gandə] *n* Propaganda *f*. **propagandist** *n* Propagandist(in).

propagate ['propəgeit] *v* fortpflanzen. **propagation** *n* Fortpflanzung *f*.

propel [prə'pel] *v* (an)treiben. **propellant** *n* Treibstoff *m*. **propeller** *n* Propeller *m*.

proper ['propə] *adj* (*fitting*) richtig, passend, geeignet; (*thorough*) ordentlich. **properly** *adv* richtig, wie es sich gehört.

property ['propəti] *n* Eigentum *neut*; (*characteristic*) Eigenschaft *f*; (*real estate*) Immobilien *pl*.

prophecy ['profəsi] *n* Weissagung *f*. **prophesy** *v* prophezeien. **prophet** *n* Prophet *m*. **prophetic** *adj* prophetisch.

proportion [prə'poːʃən] *n* Verhältnis *neut*; (*part*) Anteil *m*; (*measurement*) Ausmaß *neut*. **in proportion to** im Verhältnis zu. **be out of proportion to** in keinem Verhältnis stehen zu. **well-proportioned** *adj* wohlgestaltet. **proportional** *adj* verhältnismäßig, proportional.

propose [prə'pouz] *v* vorschlagen; (*a motion*) beantragen; (*marriage*) einen Heiratsantrag machen (+*dat*). **proposal** *n* Vorschlag *m*; (*offer*) Angebot *neut*; (*marriage*) Heiratsantrag *m*. **proposer** *n* Antragsteller *n*. **proposition** *n* Vorschlag *m*; (*project*) Projekt *neut*, Plan *m*.

proprietor [prə'praiətə] *n* Besitzer(in), Inhaber(in).

propriety [prə'praiəti] *n* Schicklichkeit *f*, Anstand *m*.

propulsion [prə'pʌlʃən] n Antrieb m.
prose [prouz] n Prosa f. adj Prosa-.
prosecute ['prɒsɪkjuːt] v (law) gerichtlich verfolgen. **prosecution** n Verfolgung f; (law) Anklage f.
prospect ['prɒspekt; v prə'spekt] n Aussicht f. v **prospect for** (gold, etc.) graben nach. **prospective** adj künftig, voraussichtlich.
prospectus [prə'spektəs] n (Werbe)-Prospekt m.
prosper ['prɒspə] v gedeihen. **prosperity** n Wohlstand m. **prosperous** adj erfolgreich, wohlhabend.
prostitute ['prɒstɪtjuːt] n Prostituierte f. v prostituieren. **prostitution** n Prostitution f.
prostrate ['prɒstreɪt; v pro'streit] adj hingestreckt. v zu Boden werfen. **prostrate oneself** sich demütigen (vor).
protagonist [prou'tagənist] n Hauptfigur f.
protect [prə'tekt] v (be)schützen. **protection** n Schutz m. **protectionism** n Schutzzollpolitik f. **protective** adj (be)schützend. **protector** n Beschützer m. **protectorate** n Schutzgebiet neut.
protégé ['prɒtəʒeɪ] n Schützling m.
protein ['proutiːn] n Protein neut, Eiweiß neut.
protest ['proutest; v prə'test] n Protest m, Einspruch m. v protestieren, Einspruch erheben(auf).
Protestant ['prɒtistənt] n Protestant(in). adj protestantisch. **Protestantism** n Protestantismus n.
protocol ['proutəkɒl] n Protokoll neut.
prototype ['proutətaip] n Prototyp m.
protractor [prə'traktə] n Winkelmesser m.
protrude [prə'truːd] v herausstehen, hervorstehen.
proud [praud] adj stolz (auf); (arrogant) hochmütig.
prove [pruːv] v beweisen. **prove to be** sich erweisen als.
proverb ['prɒvəːb] n Sprichwort neut. **proverbial** adj sprichwörtlich.
provide [prə'vaid] v versehen, versorgen. **provide for** sorgen für. **provided** conj vorausgesetzt.
provident ['prɒvidənt] adj fürsorglich. **providence** n Vorsehung f. **providential** adj glücklich.
province ['prɒvins] n Provinz f. **provincial**

adj Provinz-, provinzial; (limited, narrow) provinziell.
provision [prə'viʒən] n Vorrichtung f; (regulation) Vorschrift f. **provisions** pl Vorrat m. **provisional** adj vorläufig, provisorisch.
proviso [prə'vaizou] n Vorbehalt m, Klausel f.
provoke [prə'vouk] v (cause) veranlassen; (person) provozieren; (annoy) ärgern. **provocation** n Provokation f; (challenge) Herausforderung f.
prow [prau] n Bug m.
prowess ['prauis] n Tüchtigkeit f.
prowl [praul] v herumstreichen. **prowler** n Herumtreiber m.
proximity [prɒk'sim əti] n Nähe f.
proxy ['prɒksi] n Vollmacht f; (person) Bevollmächtigte(r).
prude [pruːd] n prüder Mensch m. **prudery** n Prüderie f. **prudish** adj prüde.
prudent ['pruːdənt] adj vernünftig, umsichtig. **prudence** n Klugheit f.
prune¹ [pruːn] n Backpflaume f.
prune² [pruːn] v (tree) beschneiden.
pry [prai] v herumschnüffeln. **pry into** die Nase stecken in. **prying** adj neugierig.
psalm [saːm] n Psalm m.
pseudonym ['sjuːdənim] n Pseudonym neut, Deckname m.
psychedelic [,saikə'delik] adj psychedelisch.
psychiatry [saikaiətri] n Psychiatrie f. **psychiatric** adj psychiatrisch. **psychiatrist** n Psychiater(in).
psychic ['saikik] adj psychisch.
psychoanalysis [,saikouə'nalisis] n Psychoanalyse f. **psychoanalyst** n Psychoanalytiker(in).
psychology [saikɒlədʒi] n Psychologie f. **psychological** adj psychologisch. **psychologist** n Psycholog(in).
psychopath ['saikəpaθ] n Psychopath(in).
psychosomatic [,saikəsə'm atik] adj psychosomatisch.
pub [pʌb] n (coll) Kneipe f.
puberty ['pjuːbəti] n Pubertät f, Geschlechtsreife f.
pubic ['pjuːbik] adj Scham-.
public ['pʌblik] adj öffentlich; (national) Volks-, national. n Öffentlichkeit f, Publikum neut. **public house** n Wirtshaus neut. **public school** Privatschule f. **public-**

spirited *adj* gemeinsinnig. **publication** *n* Veröffentlichung f, Publikation f. **publicity** *n* Reklame f, Werbung f. **publicize** *v* veröffentlichen.

publish ['pʌblɪʃ] *v* (*publicize*) veröffentlichen; (*book*) herausbringen. **publisher** *n* Verleger(in), Herausgeber(in); (*firm*) Verlag m. **publishing** *n* Verlagswesen *neut*.

pucker ['pʌkə] *v* runzeln; (*mouth*) spitzen.

pudding ['pudɪŋ] *n* Pudding m. **black pudding** *n* Blutwurst f.

puddle ['pʌdl] *n* Pfütze f, Lache f.

puerile ['pjuərail] *adj* pueril.

puff [pʌf] *n* Hauch m; (*on cigar, etc.*) Zug m. *v* blasen, pusten. **powder puff** Puderquaste f. **puffed-up** *adj* (*coll*) aufgeblasen. **puff pastry** Blätterteig m. **puffy** *adj* angeschwollen.

pull [pul] *v* ziehen; (*tug*) zerren; (*rip*) reißen. *n* Zug m. **pull through** (*survive*) durchkommen.

pulley ['puli] *n* Rolle f.

pullover ['puləuvə] *n* Pullover m.

pulp [pʌlp] *n* Brei m; (*fruit*) Fruchtfleisch *neut*; (*paper*) Pulpe f. **pulpy** *adj* breiig, weich.

pulpit ['pulpit] *n* Kanzel f.

pulsate [pʌlseit] *v* pulsieren. **pulsation** *n* Pulsieren *neut*.

pulse [pʌls] *n* Puls m, Pulsschlag m. *v* pulsieren.

pulverize ['pʌlvəraiz] *v* pulverisieren, zermahlen. **pulverization** *n* Pulverisierung f.

pump [pʌm p] *n* Pumpe f. *v* pumpen.

pumpkin ['pʌm pkin] *n* Kürbis m.

pun [pʌn] *n* Wortspiel *neut*.

punch¹ [pʌntʃ] *n* (*blow*) (Faust)Schlag m. *v* (mit der Faust) schlagen.

punch² [pʌntʃ] *n* (*drink*) Punsch m. **punchbowl** *n* Punschbowle f.

punch³ [pʌntʃ] *n* (*tool*) Locher m. Lochzange f. *v* lochen; (*tickets*) knipsen. **punchcard** *n* Lochkarte f.

punctual ['pʌŋktʃuəl] *adj* pünktlich. **punctuality** *n* Pünktlichkeit f.

punctuate ['pʌŋktʃueit] *v* interpunktieren; (*fig*) unterbrechen. **punctuation** *n* Interpunktion f.

puncture ['pʌŋktʃə] *v* durchstechen, perforieren; (*tyre*) platzen. *n* Loch *neut*; (*tyre*) Reifenpanne f.

pungent ['pʌndʒənt] *adj* scharf.

punish ['pʌnɪʃ] *v* (be)strafen. **punishment** *n* Strafe f.

punk [pʌŋk] *n* Punk m.

puny ['pju:ni] *adj* schwächlich.

pupil¹ ['pju:pl] *n* Schüler(in).

pupil² ['pju:pl] *n* (*eye*) Pupille f.

puppet ['pʌpit] *n* Marionette f. **puppet show** Puppenspiel *neut*, Marionettentheater *neut*.

puppy ['pʌpi] *n* junger Hund m, Welpe m.

purchase ['pə:tʃəs] *n* Einkauf m. *v* (ein)kaufen. **purchaser** *n* Käufer(in).

pure ['pjuə] *adj* rein. **purebred** *adj* reinrassig. **purify** *v* reinigen; (*tech*) klären. **purification** *n* Reinigung f; Klärung f. **purity** *n* Reinheit f.

purée ['pjuərei] *n* Purée *neut*.

purgatory ['pə:gətəri] *n* Fegefeuer *neut*.

purge [pə:dʒ] *v* reinigen, säubern. *n* Reinigung f; (*pol*) Säuberung f.

puritan ['pjuəritən] *n* Puritaner(in). **puritanical** *adj* puritanisch. **puritanism** *n* Puritanismus m.

purl [pə:l] *n* Linksstricken *neut*. *v* linksstricken.

purple ['pə:pl] *adj* purpurn, purpurrot. *n* Purpur m.

purpose ['pə:pəs] *n* Zweck m, Ziel *neut*. **for the purpose of** zwecks (+ *gen*). **on purpose** absichtlich. **purposeful** *adj* zielbewußt. **purposeless** *adj* zwecklos. **purposely** *adv* absichtlich.

purr [pə:] *v* schnurren, summen. *n* Schnurren *neut*.

purse [pə:s] *n* Portemonnaie *neut*, Geldbeutel m; Handtasche f; (*prize*) Börse f. *v* (*lips*) spitzen.

purser ['pə:sə] *n* Zahlmeister m.

pursue [pə'sju:] *v* verfolgen; (*studies*) betreiben; (*continue*) fortfahren in. **pursuit** *n* Verfolgung f; (*activity*) Beschäftigung f; (*of happiness, etc.*) Jagd f, Suche f.

pus [pʌs] *n* Eiter m.

push [puʃ] *n* Stoß m, Schub m. **get the push** (*coll*) entlassen werden. *v* stoßen, schieben; (*button*) drücken; (*in crowd*) drängen. **be pushed for time** keine Zeit haben. **push aside** beiseite schieben. **push open/to** (*door*) auf/zuschieben. **push off** (*coll*) abhauen. **push through** durchsetzen. **pushbike** *m* (*coll*) Rad *neut*. **push-button** *n* Druckknopf m. **pushchair** *n*

Kinderwagen. **pusher** *n* (*drugs*) Pusher *m*.
pushing *adj* aufdringlich.

pussy ['pusɪ] *n* (*coll*) Mieze *f*.

***put** [put] *v* stellen, setzen, legen; (*express*) ausdrücken; (*shot*) werfen. **put away** weglegen. **put back** (*clock*) nachstellen; (*postpone*) aufschieben. **put by** aufsparen. **put down** hinlegen; (*revolt*) unterdrücken; (*animal*) töten. **put off** verschieben; (*discourage*) davon abraten (+ *dat*). **put through** durchführen; (*phone*) verbinden. **put up** (*coll*) unterbringen. **put up with** dulden, ausstehen.

putrid ['pjuːtrɪd] *adj* verfault.

putt [pʌt] *v* putten.

putty ['pʌtɪ] *n* Kitt *m*.

puzzle ['pʌzl] *n* Rätsel *neut*; (*jigsaw*) Puzzlespiel *neut*. *v* verwirren. **puzzlement** *n* Verwirrung *f*. **puzzling** *adj* rätselhaft.

pyjamas [pə'dʒaːməz] *n* Schlafanzug *m*.

pylon ['paɪlən] *n* (*elec*) Leitungsmast *m*.

pyramid ['pɪrəmɪd] *n* Pyramide *f*.

python ['paɪθən] *n* Pythonschlange *f*.

Q

quack[1] [kwak] *n* (*duck*) Quaken *neut*. *v* quaken.

quack[2] [kwak] *n* (*doctor*) Quacksalber *m*. *adj* quacksalberisch.

quadrangle ['kwodræŋgl] *n* Viereck *neut*; Hof *m*. **quadrangular** *adj* viereckig.

quadrant ['kwodrənt] *n* Quadrant *m*.

quadrilateral [kwodrɪ'lætərəl] *adj* vierseitig.

quadruped ['kwodruped] *n* Vierfüßer *m*.

quadruple ['kwod'ruːpl] *adj* vierfach, vierfältig. *v* vervierfachen.

quagmire ['kwagmaɪə] *n* Morast *m*.

quail[1] [kweɪl] *n* (*bird*) Wachtel *f*.

quail[2] [kweɪl] *v* verzagen, den Mut verlieren.

quaint [kweɪnt] *adj* kurios, merkwürdig.

quake [kweɪk] *v* beben. *n* Erdbeben *neut*.

qualify ['kwolɪfaɪ] *v* (sich) qualifizieren; (*limit*) einschränken. **qualification** *n* Qualifikation *f*; Einschränkung *f*. **qualified** *adj* qualifiziert, geeignet; eingeschränkt.

quality ['kwolɪtɪ] *n* Qualität *f*; (*property*) Eigenschaft *f*; (*type*) Sorte *f*. *adj* erstklassig, guter Qualität *f*.

qualm [kwaːm] *n* Skrupel *m*.

quandary ['kwondərɪ] *n* Verlegenheit *f*.

quantify ['kwontɪfaɪ] *v* messen, (quantitativ) bestimmen.

quantity ['kwontətɪ] *n* Quantität *f*, Menge *f*.

quarantine ['kworəntiːn] *n* Quarantäne *f*. *v* unter Quarantäne stellen.

quarrel ['kworəl] *n* Streit *m*, Zank *m*. *v* (sich) streiten, (sich) zanken. **quarrelsome** *adj* streitsüchtig, zankig.

quarry[1] ['kworɪ] *n* (*hunting*) Jagdbeute *f*; (*fig*) Opfer *neut*.

quarry[2] ['kworɪ] *n* Steinbruch *m*. *v* brechen, hauen.

quart [kwoːt] *n* Quart *neut*.

quarter ['kwoːtə] *n* (*fourth, of town, etc.*) Viertel *neut*; (*of year*) Quartal *neut*, Vierteljahr *neut*. *v* vierteln; (*to house*) unterbringen. **quarter of an hour** Viertelstunde *f*. **quarter to/past** Viertel vor/nach. **quarterdeck** *n* Achterdeck *neut*. **quarter-final** *n* Viertelfinale *neut*. **quarterly** *adj* vierteljährlich.

quartet [kwoː'tet] *n* Quartett *neut*.

quartz [kwoːts] *n* Quartz *m*.

quash [kwoʃ] *v* annullieren; (*resistance, etc.*) unterdrücken.

quaver ['kweɪvə] *v* zittern. *n* (*music*) Achtelnote *f*.

quay [kiː] *n* Kai *m*.

queasy ['kwiːzɪ] *adj* übel. *I feel queasy* mir ist übel.

queen [kwɪn] *n* Königin *f*; (*cards, chess*) Dame *f*. **queen bee** Bienenkönigin *f*. **queen mother** Königinmutter *f*.

queer [kwɪə] *adj* seltsam, sonderbar; (*odd*) komisch; (*coll: homosexual*) schwul. *n* (*coll*) Homo *m*, Schwule(r).

quell [kwel] *v* unterdrücken.

quench [kwentʃ] *v* löschen.

query ['kwɪərɪ] *n* Frage *f*, Erkundigung *f*. *v* in Frage stellen.

quest [kwest] *n* Suche *f* (nach).

question ['kwestʃən] *n* Frage *f*. *v* (be)fragen. **put** *or* **ask a question** eine Frage stellen. **out of the question** ausgeschlossen. **the question is** es handelt sich darum. **questionable** *adj* fragwürdig. **questioning** *adj* fragend. *n* Befragung *f.* **questionnaire** *n* Fragebogen *m.*

queue [kjuː] *n* Schlange *f.* *v* Schlange stehen, sich anstellen.

quibble ['kwɪbl] *v* Haare spalten, spitzfindig sein.

quick [kwɪk] *adj* schnell; (*nimble*) flink; (*temper*) hitzig; (*ear, eye*) scharf. **quicken** *v* beschleunigen. **quickness** *n* Schnelligkeit *f.* **quicksand** *n* Treibsand *m.* **quicksilver** *n* Quecksilber *neut.* **quick-tempered** *adj* hitzig, reizbar. **quick-witted** *adj* scharfsinnig.

quid [kwɪd] *n* (*coll*) Pfund *neut.*

quiet ['kwaɪət] *adj* ruhig, still. **quieten** *v* beruhigen. **quietness** *n* Ruhe *f,* Stille *f.*

quill [kwɪl] *n* Feder *f.*

quilt [kwɪlt] *n* Steppdecke *f.*

quinine [kwɪniːn] *n* Chinin *neut.*

quinsy ['kwɪnzi] *n* Mandelentzündung *f.*

quintet [kwɪn'tet] *n* Quintett *neut.*

quirk [kwəːk] *n* Eigenart *f.*

*quit [kwɪt] *v* (*stop*) aufhören; (*leave*) verlassen; (*job*) aufgeben. **notice to quit** Kündigung *f.* **quits** *adj* (*coll*) quitt.

quite [kwaɪt] *adv* (*fairly*) ziemlich; (*wholly*) ganz, durchaus.

quiver[1] ['kwɪvə] *v* zittern.

quiver[2] ['kwɪvə] *n* (*arrows*) Köcher *m.*

quiz [kwɪz] *n* Quiz *neut.* *v* (aus)fragen.

quizzical ['kwɪzɪk] *adj* spöttisch.

quota ['kwoutə] *n* Quote *f,* Anteil *m.*

quote [kwout] *v* zitieren. **quotation** *n* Zitat *f;* (*comm*) Preisangabe *f.* **quotation marks** Anführungszeichen *pl.*

R

rabbi ['ræbaɪ] *n* Rabbiner *m.*

rabbit ['ræbɪt] *n* Kaninchen *neut.* **rabbit hutch** Kaninchenstall *m.*

rabble ['ræbl] *n* Pöbel *m.*

rabies ['reɪbiːz] *n* Tollwut *f.* **rabid** *adj* tollwütig; (*coll: angry*) wütend.

race[1] [reɪs] *n* Rennen *neut,* Wettlauf *m.* *v* um die Wette laufen (mit), rennen. **the races** Pferderennen *pl.* **racecourse** *or* **racetrack** *n* Rennbahn *f.* **racehorse** *n* Rennpferd *neut.* **racing** *n* Pferderennen

neut; *adj* Renn-. **racing driver** Rennfahrer *m.*

race[2] [reɪs] *n* (*group*) Rasse *f.* **racial** *adj* rassisch, Rassen-. **racialism** *or* **racism** *n* Rassismus *m.* **racialist** *or* **racist** *n* Rassist(in); *adj* rassistisch.

rack [ræk] *n* Gestell *neut;* (*luggage*) Gepäcknetz *neut.* *v* **rack one's brains** sich den Kopf zerbrechen.

racket[1] ['rækɪt] *n* (*sport*) Rakett *neut,* Schläger *m.*

racket[2] ['rækɪt] *n* (*noise*) Krach *m,* Trubel *m;* (*coll: swindle*) Schwindel *m.* **racketeer** *n* Schwindler *m,* Gangster *m.*

radar ['reɪdɑː] *n* Radar *m or neut.*

radial ['reɪdiəl] *adj* radial. *n* (*tyre*) Gürtelreifen *m.*

radiant ['reɪdiənt] *adj* strahlend. **radiance** *n* Strahlung *f.*

radiate ['reɪdieɪt] *v* ausstrahlen. **radiation** *n* Strahlung *f.* **radiator** *n* (*house*) Heizkörper *m;* (*mot*) Kühler *m.*

radical ['rædɪkl] *adj* radikal. *n* Radikale(r). **radicalism** *n* Radikalismus *m.*

radio ['reɪdiou] *n* (*set*) Radio *neut;* (*network*) Rundfunk *m.* *v* senden, durchgeben. **radio ham** (*coll*) Funkamateur *m.* **radio station** Sender *m,* Funkstation *f.* **radio wave** Radiowelle *f.*

radioactive [reɪdiou'æktɪv] *adj* radioaktiv. **radioactivity** *n* Radioaktivität *f.*

radiology [reɪdiɒlədʒɪ] *n* Radiologie *f,* Röntgenlehre *f.* **radiologist** *n* Radiologe *m.*

radiotherapy [reɪdiou'θerəpɪ] *n* Radiotherapie *f,* Strahlenbehandlung *f.*

radish ['rædɪʃ] *n* Radieschen *neut.*

radium ['reɪdiəm] *n* Radium *neut.*

radius ['reɪdiəs] *n* Radius *m.*

raffia ['ræfiə] *n* Raffiabast *m.*

raffle ['ræfl] *n* Tombola *f.* *v* verlosen.

raft [rɑːft] *n* Floß *neut.*

rafter ['rɑːftə] *n* Dachsparren *m.*

rag[1] [ræg] *n* Fetzen *m,* Lumpen *m;* (*coll: newspaper*) Blatt *neut.* **rag doll** Stoffpuppe *f.* **ragged** *adj* zerfetzt.

rag[2] [ræg] *v* (*coll: tease*) necken, piesacken.

rage [reɪdʒ] *n* Wut *f.* *v* wüten. **in a rage** wütend. **be all the rage** die große Mode sein.

raid [reɪd] *n* Angriff *m,* Überfall *m;* (*police*) Razzia *f.* *v* überfallen; eine Razzia machen auf.

rail [reɪl] *n* Riegel *m*, Schiene *f*. **by rail** mit der Bahn. **railing** *n* Geländer *neut*. **railway** *or* **railroad** *n* Eisenbahn *f*. **railway station** Bahnhof *m*.

rain [reɪn] *n* Regen *m*. *v* regnen. **rainbow** *n* Regenbogen *m*. **raincoat** *n* Regenmantel *m*. **rainfall** *n* Niederschlag *m*. **rainforest** *n* Regenwald *m*, Urwald *m*. **rainproof** *adj* wasserdicht. **rainstorm** *n* Regenguß. **rainy** *adj* regnerisch.

raise [reɪz] *v* erheben, aufrichten; (*provoke*) hervorrufen; (*money*) beschaffen. *n* (*in pay*) Erhöhung *f*. **raised** *adj* erhöht.

raisin ['reɪzən] *n* Rosine *f*.

rake [reɪk] *n* Rechen *m*. *v* rechen.

rally ['ralɪ] *n* (*meeting*) (Massen) Versammlung *f*; (*mot*) Sternfahrt *f*, Rallye *f*. *v* (wieder) sammeln; (*spirits*) sich erholen. **rally round** sich scharen um.

ram [ram] *n* (*zool*) Widder *m*; (*tech*) Ramme *f*. *v* rammen.

RAM [ram] *n* Direktzugriffsspeicher *m*, RAM *neut*.

ramble ['ram bl] *v* wandern; (*speech*) drauflos reden. *n* Wanderung *f*, Bummel *m*. **rambler** *n* Wanderer *m*; (*rose*) Kletterrose *f*. **rambling** *adj* wandernd; (*speech*) unzusammenhängend, weitschweifig.

ramp [ram p] *n* Rampe *f*.

rampage [ram 'peɪdʒ] *v* (herum)toben.

rampant ['ram pənt] *adj* üppig, wuchernd.

rampart ['ram paːt] *n* Festungswall *m*.

ramshackle ['ram ʃakl] *adj* wackelig.

ran [ran] *V* **run**.

ranch [raːntʃ] *n* Ranch *f*.

rancid ['ransɪd] *adj* ranzig.

rancour ['raŋkə] *n* Erbitterung *f*, Böswilligkeit *f*.

random ['randəm] *adj* zufällig. *n* **at random** wahllos, aufs Geratewohl.

randy ['randɪ] *adj* (*coll*) geil, wollüstig.

rang [raŋ] *V* **ring²**.

range [reɪndʒ] *n* Reihe *f*; (*mountains*) Kette *f*; (*reach*) Tragweite *f*. *v* anordnen; (*vary*) variieren, schwanken; (*rove*) wandern.

rank¹ [raŋk] *n* (*status*) Rang *m*; (*row*) Reihe *f*. *v* **rank with** zählen zu. **the ranks** (*mil*) die Mannschaften *pl*.

rank² [raŋk] *adj* (*plants*) üppig; (*offensive*) widerlich; (*coarse*) grob.

rankle ['raŋkl] *v* nagen.

ransack ['ransak] *v* plündern, durchwühlen.

ransom ['ransəm] *n* Lösegeld *neut*. *v* loskaufen.

rap [rap] *n* Klopfen *neut*; *n* (*music*) Rap *m*. *v* klopfen.

rape [reɪp] *n* Vergewaltigung *f*. *v* vergewaltigen. **rapist** *n* Vergewaltiger *m*.

rapid ['rapɪd] *adj* schnell, rasch. **rapidity** *n* Schnelligkeit *f*. **rapids** *pl n* Stromschnelle *f*.

rapier ['reɪpə] *n* Rapier *neut*.

rapture ['raptʃə] *n* Verzückung *f*, Begeisterung *f*. **rapturous** *adj* hingerissen.

rare¹ ['reə] *adj* selten, rar; (*air*) dünn. **rarely** *adv* selten. **rarity** *n* Seltenheit *f*.

rare² ['reə] *adj* (*cookery*) nicht durchgebraten, englisch.

rascal ['raːskl] *n* Schurke *m*. **rascally** *adj* schurkisch.

rash¹ [raʃ] *n* (*on skin*) Hautausschlag *m*.

rash² [raʃ] *adj* hastig, übereilt. **rashness** *n* Hast *f*.

rasher ['raʃə] *n* (Schinken) Schnitte *f*.

raspberry ['raːzbərɪ] *n* Himbeere *f*.

rat [rat] *n* Ratte *f*. *v* **rat on** (*coll*) verraten.

rate [reɪt] *n* (*comm*) Satz *m*, Kurs *m*; (*charge*) Gebühr *f*; (*speed*) Geschwindigkeit *f*. *v* schätzen. **rates** *pl* Gemeindesteuer *f*. **birth rate** Geburtenziffer *f*. **at any rate** auf jeden Fall. **first-rate** *adj* erstklassig. **second-rate, third-rate**, *etc. adj* minderwertig. **ratings** *pl n* (*TV*) Einschaltquote *f*.

rather ['raːðə] *adv* (*quite*) ziemlich, etwas; (*preferably*) lieber, eher. *I would rather* ich möchte lieber.

ratify ['ratɪfaɪ] *v* ratifizieren. **ratification** *n* Ratifizierung *f*.

ratio ['reɪʃɪou] *n* Verhältnis *neut*.

ration ['raʃən] *n* Ration *f*. *v* rationieren. **rations** *pl* Verpflegung *f sing*.

rational ['raʃənl] *adj* rational, vernünftig. **rationale** *n* Grundprinzip *neut*. **rationalization** *n* Rationalisierung *f*. **rationalize** *v* rationalisieren.

rattle ['ratl] *v* klappern, rasseln. *n* Gerassel *neut*, Klappern *neut*. **rattlesnake** *n* Klapperschlange *f*.

raucous ['rɔːkəs] *adj* rauh, heiser.

ravage ['ravɪdʒ] *v* verwüstern. *n* Verwüstung. **ravages of time** Zahn der Zeit *m*.

rave [reɪv] *v* irre reden, toben, **rave about**

(coll) schwärmen von. **raving** *adj* delirierend. **ravings** *pl n* Fieberwahn *m*, Delirien *pl*.

raven ['reɪən] *n* Rabe *m*.

ravenous ['rævənəs] *adj* heißhungrig.

ravine [rə'viːn] *n* Schlucht *f*.

ravish ['rævɪʃ] *v (delight)* hinreißen; *(rape)* vergewaltigen. **ravishing** *adj* entzückend.

raw [rɔː] *adj* roh; *(voice)* rauh; *(sore)* wund. **rawhide** *n* Rohleder *neut*. **rawness** *n* Rohzustand *m*.

ray [reɪ] *n* Strahl *m*. **ray of light** Lichtstrahl *m*.

rayon ['reɪɒn] *n* Kunstseide *f*.

razor ['reɪzə] *n* Rasiermesser *neut*. **electric razor** Elektrorasierer *m*. **razor blade** Rasierklinge *f*. **razor-sharp** *adj* messerscharf.

re [riː] *prep* mit Bezug auf; bezüglich, betreffs (+ *gen*); *(in letter heading)* Betr.

reach [riːtʃ] *v (arrive at)* erreichen; *(stretch to)* sich erstrecken (bis). *n* Reichweite *f*. **reach (out) for** reichen *or* greifen nach.

react [ri'ækt] *v* reagieren. **reaction** *n* Reaktion *f*. **reactionary** *adj* reaktionär; *n* Reaktionär(in).

***read** [riːd] *v* lesen; *(interpret)* auslegen, deuten. **read aloud** vorlesen. **read through** durchlesen. **readable** *adj* leserlich; *(worth reading)* lesenswert. **reader** *n* Leser(in); *(university)* Dozent *m*. **readership** *n* Leserkreis *m*. **reading** *n* Lesen *neut*; *(public)* Vorlesung *f*. **reading matter** Lektüre *f*.

readjust [riːə'dʒʌst] *v* wider in Ordnung bringen; *(tech)* wieder einstellen; *(person)* (sich) wieder anpassen (an). **readjustment** *n* Wiederanpassung *f*.

ready ['redi] *adj* bereit, fertig; *(quick)* prompt. **get** *or* **make ready** sich vorbereiten; *(thing)* fertig machen. **readiness** *n* Bereitschaft *f*. **ready-made** *adj* Fertig-. **ready-reckoner** *n* Rechentabelle *f*. **readily** *adv* ohne weiteres.

real [riəl] *adj* wirklich, wahr; *(genuine)* echt. **real estate** Immobilien *pl*. **realism** *n* Realismus *m*. **realist** *n* Realist(in). **realistic** *adj* realistisch. **reality** *n* Wirklichkeit *f*, Realität *f*. **reality TV** *n* Reality-Show *f*. **really** *adv* tatsächlich, in der Tat; *(very, actually)* wirklich.

realize ['riəlaɪz] *v* begreifen, erkennen; *(bring about)* verwirklichen. **realizable** *adj*

durchführbar. **realization** *n* Erkenntnis *f*; Verwirklichung *f*.

realm [relm] *n* Königreich *neut*; *(sphere)* Gebiet *neut*.

reap [riːp] *v* ernten, mähen. **reaper** *n* Mäher(in).

reappear [riːə'pɪə] *v* wieder erscheinen. **reappearance** *n* Wiedererscheinen *neut*.

rear¹ [riə] *adj* hinter, Hinter-. *n* Hinterseite *f*, Rückseite *f*. **rear lamp** Schlußlicht *neut*. **rear wheel** Hinterrad *neut*.

rear² [riə] *v (child)* erziehen; *(animals)* züchten.

rearrange [riːə'reɪndʒ] *v* neu ordnen, umordnen; *(date, etc.)* ändern. **rearrangement** *n* Neuordnung *f*; Änderung *f*.

reason ['riːzn] *n* Grund *m*; *(good sense)* Vernunft *f*. *v* folgern. **for this reason** aus diesem Grund. **by reason of** wegen (+ *gen*). **reason with** zu überzeugen versuchen. **reasonable** *adj* vernünftig. **reasonableness** *n* Vernünftigkeit. **reasonably** *adv* vernünftigerweise; *(fairly)* ziemlich. **reasoning** *n* Schlußfolgerung *f*, Argument *neut*.

reassure [riːə'ʃuə] *v* beruhigen. **reassurance** *n* Beruhigung *f*.

rebate ['riːbeɪt] *n* Rabatt *m*.

rebel ['rebl] *n* Rebell(in), Aufrührer(in). *adj* aufrührerisch. *v* rebellieren. **rebellion** *n* Aufstand *m*. **rebellious** *adj* aufrührerisch.

reboot [riː'buːt] *v* neu booten.

rebound [rɪ'baund; *n* 'riː'baund] *v* zurückprallen. *n* Rückprall *m*.

rebuff [rɪ'bʌf] *v* abweisen. *n* Abweisung *f*.

***rebuild** [riː'bɪld] *v* wiederaufbauen.

rebuke [rɪ'bjuːk] *v* zurechtweisen, rüffeln. *n* Rüffel *m*.

recall [rɪ'kɔːl] *v (call back)* zurückrufen; *(remember)* sich erinnern an. *n* Rückruf *m*; Erinnerung *f*.

recap ['riːkæp] *v* kurz zusammenfassen. *n* Zusammenfassung *f*.

recede [rɪ'siːd] *v* zurückgehen, zurückweichen.

receipt [rə'siːt] *n (of letter)* Empfang *m*; *(of goods)* Annahme *f*; *(bill)* Quittung *f*. **receipts** *pl* Einnahmen *pl*. **acknowledge receipt** Empfang bestätigen.

receive [rə'siːv] *v* empfangen, bekommen. **receiver** *n (phone)* Hörer *m*; *(comm)* Konkursverwalter *m*; *(radio)* Empfänger *m*.

receivership n Konkursverwaltung f.
recent ['ri:snt] adj neu, modern, neulich
entstanden. **recently** adv neulich, vor
kurzem.
receptacle [rə'septəkl] n Behälter m, Gefäß
neut.
reception [rə'sepʃən] n Empfang m. **recep-
tionist** n Empfangsdame f. **reception
room** Empfangszimmer neut.
recess [rises] n Pause f, Unterbrechung f;
(holiday) Ferien pl; (niche) Nische f.
recession [rə'seʃən] n (comm) Rezession f.
recharge [ri:'tʃɑːdʒ] v (battery) wieder
aufladen.
recipe ['resəpi] n Rezept neut.
recipient [rə'sipiənt] n Empfänger(in).
reciprocate [rə'siprəkeit] v erwidern. **reciprocal** adj gegenseitig. **reciprocation** n
Erwiderung f.
recite [rə'sait] v vortragen, rezitieren.
piano/song recital Klavier-/Liederabend
m.
reckless ['rekləs] adj rücksichtslos. **reck-
lessness** n Rücksichtslosigkeit f.
reckon ['rekən] v rechnen, zählen; (believe)
meinen. **reckon on** sich verlassen auf.
reckon with rechnen mit. **reckoning** n
Abrechnung f.
reclaim [ri:kleim] v (ask for back) zurück-
fordern; (land from sea) gewinnen.
recline [ri:klein] v sich zurücklehnen (an).
recluse [rə'klu:s] n Einsiedler(in).
recognize ['rekəgnaiz] v (wieder) erkennen;
(acknowledge) anerkennen; (concede)
zugeben. **recognition** n (Wieder)Erkennen
neut; Anerkennung f. **recognizable** adj
erkennbar.
recoil [rə'koil; n 'ri:koil] v zurückprallen; (in
fear) zurückschrecken. n Rückprall m.
recollect [rekə'lekt] n sich erinnern an. **rec-
ollection** n Erinnerung f.
recommence [ri:kə'mens] v wieder beginnen.
recommend [rekə'mend] v empfehlen. **to
be recommended** empfehlenswert. **recommendation** n Empfehlung f;
(suggestion) Vorschlag m.
recompense ['rekəmpens] n Belohnung f. v
belohnen.
reconcile ['rekənsail] v versöhnen. **reconcile oneself to** sich abfinden mit. **recon-
cilable** adj vereinbar (mit). **reconciliation**

n Versöhnung f.
reconstruct [ri:kən'strʌkt] v wiederaufbauen; (events) rekonstruieren. **reconstruc-
tion** n Wiederaufbau m; Rekonstruktion f.
record [rə'kɔːd; n 'rekɔːd] v (film, tape)
aufnehmen; (write down) aufschreiben, eintragen. n (disc) Schallplatte f; (of proceedings, etc.) Protokoll neut, Bericht m; (sport)
Rekord m. **break the record** den Rekord
brechen. **off the record** inoffiziell.
recorder n (music) Blockflöte f. **recording**
n Aufnahme f. **record-player** n
Plattenspieler m.
recount [ri:kaunt] v (narrate) erzählen.
recoup [ri:ku:p] v (loss) wieder einholen.
recover [rə'kʌvə] v zurückgewinnen; (get
better) sich erholen. **recovery** n
Zurückgewinnung f; Erholung f.
recreation [rekri:eiʃən] n Erholung f,
Entspannung f. **recreation ground** n
Spielplatz neut.
recrimination [rikrimi:neiʃən] n
Gegenbeschuldigung f.
recruit [rə'kru:t] n Rekrut m. v rekrutieren.
recruitment n Rekrutierung f.
rectangle ['rektaŋgl] n Rechteck neut. **rectangular** adj rechteckig.
rectify ['rektifai] v richtigstellen, korrigieren; (elec) gleichrichten. **rectification**
n Richtigstellung f, Korrektur f.
rectum ['rektəm] n Mastdarm m. **rectal** adj
rektal.
recuperate [rə'kju:pəreit] v sich erholen.
recuperation n Erholung f.
recur [ri:kəː] v wieder auftreten, sich
wiederholen. **recurrence** n
Wiederauftreten neut. **recurrent** adj
wiederkehrend.
recycle [ri:'saikl] v wiederverwerten. **recycling** n Wiederverwertung f, Recycling
neut.
red [red] adj rot. n Rot neut. **Red Cross**
Rotes Kreuz neut. **red tape** Amtsschimmel
m. **redden** v erröten, rot werden. **redness** n
Röte f. **red-handed** adj auf frischer Tat.
redeem [rə'di:m] v (pledge) einlösen; (prisoner) loskaufen; (promise) einhalten.
redemption n Ablösung f; Rückkauf m.
redevelop [ri:di:veləp] v neu entwickeln;
(town) umbauen.
redress [rə'dres] n (legal) Rechtshilfe f;
(compensation) Wiedergutmachung f. v
wiedergutmachen. **redress the balance**

das Gleichgewicht wiederherstellen.

reduce [rə'djuːs] *v* vermindern, verringern; (*prices*) herabsetzen; (*tech*) reduzieren; (*slim*) eine Abmagerungskur machen. **in reduced circumstances** verarmt. **reduction** *n* Verminderung *f*; Herabsetzung *f*; (*tech*) Reduktion *f*.

redundant [rə'dʌndənt] *adj* überflüssig; (*jobless*) arbeitslos. **be made redundant** entlassen werden. **redundancy** *n* Überflüssigkeit *f*; (*worker*) Entlassung *f*.

reed [riːd] *n* Rohr *neut*; (*music*) (Rohr)Blatt *neut*. **reedy** *adj* (*voice*) piepsig.

reef [riːf] *n* (Felsen)Riff *neut*.

reek [riːk] *v* stinken (nach). *n* Gestank *m*.

reel¹ [riːl] *n* Spule *f*; (*cotton*) Rolle *f*.

reel² [riːl] *v* taumeln, schwanken.

refectory [rə'fektəri] *n* Speisesaal *m*; (*university*) Mensa *f*.

refer [rə'fəː] *v* **refer to** hinweisen auf, sich beziehen auf; (*mention*) erwähnen; (*a book*) nachschlagen in. **reference** *n* Bezug *m*, Hinweis *m*; Erwähnung *f*; (*in book*) Verweis *m*. **with reference to** in Bezug auf, hinsichtlich (+*gen*). **reference book** Nachschlagewerk *neut*.

referee [refə'riː] *n* Schiedsrichter *m*.

referendum [refə'rendəm] *n* Volksentscheid *m*.

refill [riː'fil; *n* 'riːfil] *v* nachfüllen. *n* (*for pen*) Ersatzmine *f*.

refine [rə'fain] *v* (*tech*) raffinieren; (*improve*) verfeinern. **refined** *adj* raffiniert; (*person*, *etc.*) kultiviert **refinement** *n* Verfeinerung *f*; (*good breeding*) Kultiviertheit *f*. **refinery** *n* Raffinerie *f*.

reflation [rə'fleiʃn] *n* Wirtschaftsbelebung *f*.

reflect [rə'flekt] *v* widerspiegeln; (*consider*) nachdenken. **reflection** *n* Widerspiegelung *f*. (*thought*) Überlegung *f*; (*remark*) Bemerkung *f*. **reflective** *adj* zurückstrahlend; (*thoughtful*) nachdenklich. **reflector** *n* (*mot*) Rückstrahler *m*.

reflex ['riːfleks] *n* Reflex *m*.

reform [rə'foːm] *n* Reform *f*, Verbesserung *f*. *v* reformieren, (ver)bessern. **reformation** *n* Verbesserung *f*; (*history*) Reformation *f*. **reformatory** *n* Besserungsanstalt *f*. **reformed** *adj* verbessert. **reformer** *n* Reformer(in).

refract [rə'frakt] *v* brechen.

refrain¹ [rə'frein] *v* **refrain from** sich

enthalten (+*gen*).

refrain² [rə'frein] *n* Refrain *m*.

refresh [rə'freʃ] *v* erfrischen; (*memory*) auffrischen. **refresher course** Wiederholungskurs *m*. **refreshing** *adj* erfrischend. **refreshment** *n* Erfrischung *f*. **refreshments** *pl* Imbiß *m sing*.

refrigerator [rə'fridʒəreitə] *n* Kühlschrank *m*. **refrigerate** *v* kühlen. **refrigeration** *n* Kühlung *f*.

refuel [riː'fjuːəl] *v* tanken.

refuge ['refjuːdʒ] *n* Zuflucht *f*, Schutz *m*. **refugee** *n* Flüchtling *m*.

refund ['riːfʌnd; *v* ri'fʌnd] *n* Rückvergütung *f*. *v* zurückzahlen.

refuse¹ [rə'fjuːz] *v* ablehnen, verweigern. **refusal** *n* Verweigerung *f*, Ablehnung *f*.

refuse² ['refjuːs] *n* Abfall *m*, Müll *m*. **refuse collection** Müllabfuhr *f*.

refute [ri'fjuːt] *v* widerlegen.

regain [ri'gein] *v* wiedergewinnen.

regal ['riːgəl] *adj* königlich.

regard [rə'gaːd] *v* ansehen, betrachten. *n* (*esteem*) (Hoch)Achtung *f*; (*consideration*) Rücksicht *f*, Hinblick *m*. **in this regard** in dieser Hinsicht. **with regard to** in bezug auf. **as regards** was ... betrifft. **regarding** *prep* hinsichtlich (+*gen*), bezüglich (+*gen*). **regardless** *adj* ohne Rücksicht (auf).

regatta [rə'gatə] *n* Regatta *f*.

regent ['riːdʒənt] *n* Regent(in).

regime [rei'ʒiːm] *n* Regime *f*.

regiment ['redʒimənt] *n* Regiment *neut*.

region ['riːdʒən] *n* Gebiet *neut*, Gegend *f*. **in the region of** etwa, ungefähr. **regional** *adj* regional, örtlich.

register ['redʒistə] *v* registrieren; (*report*) sich eintragen lassen. *n* Register *neut*. **registered** *adj* eingetragen. **registered letter** Einschreibebrief *m*. **send by registered post** per Einschreiben schicken. **registered trademark** eingetragenes Warenzeichen *neut*. **registrar** *n* (*births, etc.*) Standesbeamte(r); (*hospital, etc.*) Direktor *m*. **registration** *n* Registrierung *f*. **registration number** (*mot*) polizeiliches Kennzeichen *neut*. **registry office** Standesamt *neut*.

regress [ri'gres] *v* zurückgehen. **regression** *n* Regression *f*. **regressive** *adj* rückläufig.

regret [rə'gret] *v* bedauern. *n* Reue *f*, Bedauern *neut*. **regrettable** *adj* bedauer-

lich. **regretfully** adv leider, bedauerlicher-
weise.

regular ['regjʊlə] adj regelmäßig; (normal)
gewöhnlich; (correct) ordnungsgemäß. **regular (customer)** Stammgast m. **regularity**
n Regelmäßigkeit f.

regulate ['regjʊleɪt] v regeln, ordnen. **regulation** n (rule) Vorschrift f; (tech) Regelung
f. **regulator** n Regler m.

rehabilitate [ri:hə'bɪliteɪt] n rehabilitieren.
rehabilitation n Rehabilitation f.

rehearse [rə'hɜːs] v proben. **rehearsal** n
Probe f.

reign [reɪn] n Regierung(szeit) f. v regieren,
herrschen.

reimburse [ri:ɪm'bɜːs] v (person) entschädigen. **reimbursement** n Entschädigung f.

rein [reɪn] n Zügel m.

reincarnation [ri:ɪnkɑː'neɪʃən] n
Reinkarnation f, Wiederverkörperung f.

reindeer ['reɪndɪə] n Ren(tier) neut.

reinforce [ri:ɪn'fɔːs] v verstärken; (concrete)
armieren. **reinforcement** n Verstärkung f.

reinstate [ri:ɪn'steɪt] v wiedereinsetzen.
reinstatement n Wiedereinsetzung f.

reinvest [ri:ɪn'vest] v wiederinvestieren.

reissue [ri:'ʃuː] v neu herausgeben. n
Neuausgabe f.

reject [rə'dʒekt; n 'ri:dʒekt] v ablehnen, verwerfen. **rejection** n Ablehnung f,
Verwerfung f. n Ausschußartikel m.

rejoice [rə'dʒɔɪs] v sich freuen. **rejoicing**
adj froh; n Freude f.

rejoin [rə'dʒɔɪn] v sich wieder anschließen;
(reply) erwidern. **rejoinder** n Erwiderung f.

rejuvenate [rə'dʒuːvəneɪt] v verjüngen.
rejuvenation n Verjüngung f.

relapse [rə'læps] v zurückfallen; (med) einen
Rückfall bekommen. n Rückfall m.

relate [rə'leɪt] v (tell) erzählen; (link)
verbinden. **related** adj verwandt. **relating
to** in bezug auf.

relation [rə'leɪʃn] n Verhältnis neut; (business) Beziehung f; (person) Verwandte(r).
relationship n Verhältnis neut; (family)
Verwandtschaft f.

relative ['relətɪv] n Verwandte(r). adj relativ, verhältnismäßig. **relatively** adv verhältnismäßig. **relativity** n Relativität f.

relax [rə'læks] v entspannen. **relaxation** n
Entspannung f.

relay ['riːleɪ; v ri'leɪ] n (race) Staffellauf m;

(tech) Relais neut. v weitergeben.

release [rə'liːs] v freilassen, entlassen; (film,
etc.) freigeben; (news) bekanntgeben; (let
go) loslassen. n Entlassung f; Freigabe f.

relent [rə'lent] v nachgiebig werden.
relentless adj unbarmherzig.

relevant ['reləvənt] adj erheblich, relevant;
(appropriate) entsprechend. **relevance** n
Relevanz f.

reliable [rɪ'laɪəbl] adj zuverlässig. **reliability** n Zuverlässigkeit f. **reliance** n
Vertrauen neut.

relic ['relɪk] n Überbleibsel neut; (rel)
Reliquie f.

relief [rə'liːf] n Erleichterung f; (mil)
Ablösung f; (help) Hilfe f; (geog) Relief neut.
tax relief Steuerbegünstigung f.

relieve [rə'liːv] v erleichtern; (from burden)
entlasten; (person) ablösen; (reassure)
beruhigen.

religion [rə'lidʒən] n Religion f. **religious**
adj religiös.

relinquish [rə'lɪŋkwɪʃ] v aufgeben, verzichten auf.

relish ['relɪʃ] v sich erfreuen an. n (fig)
Vergnügen neut; (sauce) Soße f.

relocate [ˌriːbuː'keɪt] v verlegen (production)
verlagern.

reluctant [rə'lʌktənt] adj widerwillig. **be
reluctant to do** ungern tun. **reluctance** n
Widerstreben neut. **reluctantly** adv
ungern.

rely [rə'laɪ] v sich verlassen (auf).

remain [rə'meɪn] v bleiben; (be left over)
übrigbleiben. **remains** pl n Überreste pl;
(person) die sterblichen Überreste pl.
remainder n Rest m, Restbestand m.
remaining adj übriggebliebenen.

remand [rə'mɑːnd] v in Untersuchungshaft
zurückschicken.

remark [rə'mɑːk] n Bemerkung f. v
bemerken. **remarkable** adj
bemerkenswert.

remarry [ri'mæri] v wieder heiraten.

remedy ['remədi] n Gegenmittel neut;
(med) Heilmittel neut. v berichtigen.

remember [rɪm em bə] v sich erinnern an.
remember me to your mother grüße deine
Mutter von mir. **remembrance** n
Erinnerung f.

remind [rə'm aɪnd] v erinnern (an); (someone to do something) mahnen. **reminder** n

Mahnung f.

reminiscence [ˌrem əˈnɪsəns] n Erinnerung f. **be reminiscent of** erinnern an.

remiss [rəˈmɪs] adj nachlässig.

remit [rəˈmɪt] v überweisen. **remittance** n Überweisung f.

remnant [ˈremnənt] n (Über)Rest m, Überbleibsel neut.

remorse [rəˈmɔːs] n Gewissensbisse pl, Reue f. **remorseful** n reumütig. **remorseless** adj unbarmherzig.

remote [rəˈmout] adj fern, entfernt. **remote control** Fernsteuerung f, Fernbedienung f. **remoteness** n Ferne f.

remove [rəˈmuːv] v beseitigen, entfernen; (move house) umziehen. **removal** n Beseitigung f; Umzug m. **remover** n (Möbel)Spediteur m.

remunerate [rəˈmjuːnəreɪt] v belohnen. **remuneration** n Lohn m, Vergütung f.

renaissance [rəˈneɪsəns] n Renaissance f.

rename [riːˈneɪm] v umbenennen.

render [ˈrendə] v (make) machen; (give back) wiedergeben; (service) leisten.

rendezvous [ˈrɒndɪvuː] n Verabredung f, Stelldichein neut.

renegade [ˈrenɪɡeɪd] n Abtrünnige(r). adj abtrünnig.

renew [rəˈnjuː] v erneuern; (contract) verlängern. **renewable** adj erneuerbar. **renewal** n Erneuerung f.

renounce [rɪˈnauns] v verzichten auf; (person) verleugnen; (beliefs) abschwören.

renovate [ˈrenəveɪt] v erneuern, renovieren. **renovation** n Renovierung f, Erneuerung f.

renown [rəˈnaun] n Ruhm m, Berühmtheit f. **renowned** adj berühmt.

rent [rent] n Miete f. v mieten; (let) vermieten. **rental** n Mietbetrag m.

renunciation [rɪnʌnsɪˈeɪʃən] n (rejection) Ablehnung f.

reopen [riːˈoupən] v wieder öffnen; (shop, etc.) wiedereröffnen.

reorganize [riːˈɔːɡənaɪz] v reorganisieren, neugestalten. **reorganization** n Reorganisation f.

rep [rep] n (coll: representative) Vertreter(in).

repair [rɪˈpeə] v reparieren, ausbessern; (clothes) flicken. n Reparatur f. **in good repair** in gutem Zustand. **in need of repair** reparaturbedürftig. **repair kit**

Flickzeug neut. **reparation** n Wiedergutmachung f.

repartee [repɑːˈtiː] n Schlagabtausch m.

repatriate [riːˈpatrieɪt] v repatriieren. **repatriation** n Repatriierung f.

***repay** [rɪpeɪ] v zurückzahlen; (kindness) erwidern. **repayable** adj rückzahlbar. **repayment** n Rückzahlung f.

repeal [rəˈpiːl] v aufheben, widerrufen. n Aufhebung f.

repeat [rəˈpiːt] v wiederholen. n Wiederholung f. **repeated** adj wiederholt.

repel [rəˈpel] v abweisen. **repellent** adj abstoßend, widerlich.

repent [rəˈpent] v bereuen. **repentance** n Reue f. **repentant** adj bußfertig.

repercussions [riːpəˈkʌʃənz] pl n Rückwirkungen pl.

repertoire [ˈrepətwɑː] n Repertoire neut.

repetition [repəˈtɪʃn] n Wiederholung f. **repetitive** adj sich wiederholend.

replace [rəˈpleɪs] v ersetzen. **replacement** n Ersatz m. **replacement part** Ersatzteil neut.

replay [ˈriːpleɪ] n (sport) Wiederholungsspiel neut; (tape) Wiedergabe f.

replenish [rəˈplenɪʃ] v ergänzen.

replica [ˈreplɪkə] n Kopie f.

reply [rəˈplaɪ] v antworten, erwidern. n Antwort f. Erwiderung f. **reply to** (person) antworten (+dat); (question, letter) antworten auf. **in reply to** in Erwiderung auf.

report [rəˈpɔːt] n Bericht m; (factual statement) Meldung f. v berichten; (denounce) melden; (present oneself) sich melden. **reporter** n Reporter m.

repose [rəˈpouz] n Ruhe f. v ruhen.

represent [reprəˈzent] v darstellen; (act as representative) vertreten. **representation** n Darstellung f; Vertretung f. **representative** n Vertreter(in). adj (typical) typisch.

repress [rəˈpres] v unterdrücken; (psychol) verdrängen. **repression** n Unterdrückung f; Verdrängung f.

reprieve [rəˈpriːv] v begnadigen. n Strafaufschub m; (fig) Gnadenfrist f.

reprimand [ˈreprɪmɑːnd] v rügen. n Rüge f. Verweis m.

reprint [riːˈprɪnt; n ˈriːprɪnt] v neu drucken. n Neudruck m.

reprisal [rəˈpraɪzəl] n Repressalie f.

reproach [ɪə'prəʊtʃ] n Vorwurf m, Tadel m. v Vorwürfe machen (+ dat). **reproachful** adj vorwurfsvoll.

reproduce [ɪːprə'djuːs] v (sich) fortpflanzen; (copy) kopieren. **reproduction** n Fortpflanzung f; (copy) Reproduktion f.

reproof [ɪə'pruːf] n Verweis m, Rüge f. **reprove** v rügen.

reptile ['rɛptaɪl] n Reptil neut, Kriechtier neut.

republic [ɪə'pʌblɪk] n Republik f. **republican** adj republikanisch; n Republikaner(in).

repudiate [ɪə'pjuːdieɪt] v zurückweisen, nicht anerkennen. n Nichtanerkennung f.

repugnant [ɪə'pʌgnənt] adj widerlich, widerwärtig.

repulsion [ɪə'pʌlʃn] n Abscheu m. **repulsive** adj widerwärtig, abscheulich.

repute [ɪə'pjuːt] n Ruf m. **reputation** n Ruf m. **reputed** adj angeblich. **be reputed** betrachtet sein (als).

request [rɪkw est] n Bitte f. v bitten (um). **on request** auf Wunsch.

requiem ['rɛkwɪəm] n Requiem neut.

require [ɪə'kwaɪə] v (need) brauchen; (person) verlangen (von); (call for) erfordern. **be required** erforderlich sein. **requirement** n Anforderung f; (need) Bedürfnis neut.

requisite ['rɛkwɪzɪt] adj erforderlich, notwendig.

re-route [ɪiː'ruːt] v umleiten.

resale [rɪ'seɪl] n Weiterverkauf m.

rescue ['rɛskjuː] v retten, befreien. n Rettung f. **come to the rescue of** zur Hilfe kommen (+ dat). **rescuer** n Retter m.

research [rɪsəː'tʃ] n Forschung f. v forschen. **researcher** n Forscher m.

resemble [ɪə'zɛmbl] v ähnlich sein (+ dat). **resemblance** n Ähnlichkeit f.

resent [rɪzɛnt] v übelnehmen. **resentful** adj ärgerlich (auf). **resentment** n Groll m, Unwille m.

reserve [ɪə'zəːv] v reservieren (lassen). n Reserve f; (for animals) Schutzgebiet neut; (sport) Ersatzmann m. **reserved** adj reserviert. **reservation** n Vorbehalt m; Reservierung f.

reservoir ['rɛzəvwaː] n Reservoir neut.

reside [ɪə'zaɪd] v wohnen. **residence** n Wohnung f; (domicile) Wohnsitz m. **resident** adj wohnhaft. **residential** adj Wohn-.

residue ['rɛzɪdjuː] n Rest m, Rückstand m. **residual** adj übrig, Rest-.

resign [ɪə'zaɪn] v zurücktreten. **resign oneself to** sich abfinden mit. **resignation** n Rücktritt m; (mood) Resignation f. **hand in one's resignation** seinen Rücktritt einreichen. **resigned** adj resigniert, ergeben.

resilient [ɪə'zɪliənt] adj elastisch; (person) unverwüstlich.

resin ['rɛzɪn] n Harz neut.

resist [ɪə'zɪst] v widerstehen. **resistance** n Widerstand m. **resistant** adj widerstehend, beständig.

*resit [rɪ'sɪt] v (exam) wiederholen.

resolute ['rɛzəluːt] adj entschlossen. **resolution** n (determination) Entschlossenheit f; (decision) Beschluß m.

resolve [ɪə'zɒlv] v (problem) lösen; (tech) auflösen; (decide) beschließen. n (determination) Entschlossenheit f. **resolved** adj entschlossen.

resonant ['rɛzənənt] adj widerhallend; (voice) volltönend. **resonance** n Resonanz f.

resort [ɪə'zɔːt] n (hope) Ausweg m; (place) Ferienort m; (use) Anwendung f. **seaside resort** Seebad neut. v **resort to** zurückgreifen auf.

resound [ɪə'zaʊnd] v widerhallen.

resource [ɪə'zɔːs] n Mittel neut. **natural resources** Bodenschätze pl. **resourceful** adj findig.

respect [ɪə'spɛkt] v (hoch)achten; (take account of) berücksichtigen. n (for person) Hochachtung f, Respekt m; Rücksicht f. **in this respect** in dieser Hinsicht. **respectable** adj ansehnlich, respektabel. **respectful** adj achtvoll. **respective** adj entsprechend. **respectively** adv beziehungsweise.

respiration [rɛspə'reɪʃn] n Atmung f.

respite ['rɛspaɪt] n **without respite** ohne Unterlaß.

respond [ɪə'spɒnd] v **respond to** (question) antworten (auf); (react) reagieren (auf). **response** n Antwort f; Reaktion f.

responsible [ɪə'spɒnsəbl] adj verantwortlich. **responsibility** n Verantwortung f; (commitment) Verpflichtung f.

rest¹ [rɛst] n Ruhe f. **day of rest** Ruhetag m. **have a rest** sich ausruhen. **without rest** unaufhörlich. v ruhen. **rested** adj ausgeruht. **restful** adj ruhig. **restive** adj unruhig. **restless** *adj* ruhelos. **restlessness** *n* Unruhe *f*.

rest² [rest] *n* (*remainder*) Rest *m*.

restaurant ['restrɒnt] *n* Restaurant *neut*, Gaststätte *f*. **restaurant car** Speisewagen *m*.

restore [rə'stɔː] *v* wiederherstellen. **restoration** *n* Wiederherstellung *f*; (*of painting, etc.*) Restauration *f*.

restrain [rə'strein] *v* zurückhalten. **restrained** *adj* zurückhaltend. **restraint** *n* Zurückhaltung *f*; (*limitation*) Einschränkung *f*.

restrict [rə'strikt] *v* einschränken, beschränken. **restricted** *adj* eingeschränkt, beschränkt. **restriction** *n* Einschränkung *f*, Beschränkung *f*. **restrictive** *adj* einschränkend.

result [rə'zʌlt] *n* Ergebnis *neut*, Resultat *neut*; (*consequence*) Folge *f*. *v* sich ergeben. **result in** enden mit. **resultant** *adj* daraus enstehend.

resume [rə'zjuːm] *v* wieder beginnen; (*work*) wieder aufnehmen. **resumption** *n* Wiederaufnahme *f*.

résumé ['reizum ei] *n* Resümee *neut*; (*US; curriculum vitae*) Lebenslauf *m*.

resurgence [rəs'dʒəns] *n* Wiederaufstieg *m*.

resurrect [rezə'rekt] *v* (*thing*) ausgraben, wieder einführen. **resurrection** *n* Auferstehung *f*.

resuscitate [rə'sʌsəteit] *v* wiederbeleben. **resuscitation** *n* Wiederbelebung *f*.

retail ['riːteil] *n* Einzelhandel *m*. *adj* Einzelhandels-. **retail price** Ladenpreis *m*. **retail shop** Einzelhandelsgeschäft *neut*. *v* im Einzelhandel verkaufen. **retailer** *n* Einzelhändler(in).

retain [rə'tein] *v* behalten. **retention** *n* Beibehaltung *f*.

retaliate [rə'talieit] *v* sich rächen. **retaliation** *n* Vergeltung *f*. **relaliatory** *adj* Vergeltungs-.

retard [rə'tɑːd] *v* hindern. **retarded** *adj* zurückgeblieben.

retch [retʃ] *v* würgen.

reticent ['retisənt] *adj* schweigsam. **reticence** *n* Schweigsamkeit *f*, Zurückhaltung *f*.

retina ['retinə] *n* Netzhaut *f*.

retinue ['retinjuː] *n* Gefolge *neut*.

retire [rə'taiə] *v* sich zurückziehen; (*from work*) in den Ruhestand treten. **retired** *adj* pensioniert. **retirement** *n* Ruhestand *m*; (*resignation*) Rucktritt *m*. **retiring** *adj* zurückhaltend.

retort¹ [rə'tɔːt] *v* (scharf) erwidern. *n* (schlagfertige) Antwort *f*.

retort² [rə'tɔːt] *n* (*vessel*) Retorte *f*.

retrace [riː'treis] *v* zurückverfolgen.

retract [rə'trakt] *v* (*draw in*) einziehen; (*take back*) zurücknehmen, widerrufen. **retractable** *adj* einziehbar.

retrain [riː'trein] *v* umschulen.

retreat [rə'triːt] *v* sich zurückziehen. *n* Rückzug *m*; (*place*) Zufluchtsort *m*.

retrieve [rə'triːv] *v* wiederfinden, herausholen. **retriever** *n* Apporthund *m*.

retrograde ['retəgreid] *adj* rückläufig.

retrospect ['retrəspekt] *n* Rückblick *m*. **in retrospect** rückschauend. **retrospective** *adj* rückwirkend.

return [rə'təːn] *v* zurückkommen, wiederkehren; (*give back*) zurückgeben; (*answer*) erwidern. *n* Rückkehr *f*; (*ticket*) Rückfahrkarte *f*; (*comm*) Ertrag *m*. **tax return** Steuererklärung *f*. **many happy returns** herzlichen Glückwunsch.

reunite [riːjuˈnait] *v* wiedervereinigen. **reunion** *n* Wiedervereinigung *f*; (*meeting*) Treffen *neut*.

rev [rev] *v* (*coll: mot*) auf Touren bringen. **revs** *pl n* Drehzahl *f sing*.

reveal [rə'viːl] *v* enthüllen, offenbaren; (*display*) zeigen. **revealing** *adj* aufschlußreich. **revelation** *n* Enthüllung *f*, Offenbarung *f*.

revel ['revl] *v* feiern. **revel in** schwelgen in. **reveller** *n* Feiernde(r). **revelry** *n* Festlichkeit *f*.

revenge [rə'vendʒ] *n* Rache *f*. *v* rächen. **take revenge on** sich rächen an.

revenue ['revinjuː] *n* Einnahmen *pl*.

reverberate [rə'vəːbəreit] *v* (*sound*) widerhallen. **reverberation** *n* Widerhall *m*.

reverence ['revərəns] *n* Verehrung *f*, Ehrfurcht *f*. **revere** *v* (ver)ehren. **reverend** *adj* ehrwürdig. **reverent** *adj* ehrerbietig.

reverse [rə'vəːs] *v* umkehren; (*mot*) rückwarts fahren. *n* (*opposite*) Gegenteil *neut*; (*of coin, etc.*) Rückseite *f*; (*mot*) Rückwärtsgang *m*. **reverse-charge call** R-Gespräch *neut*. **reversible** *adj* (*coat*) wendbar; (*law*) umstoßbar.

revert [rə'vəːt] *v* zurückkehren.

review [rəˈvjuː] n Nachprüfung f; (*magazine*) Rundschau f; (*troops*) Parade f. v nachprüfen. **reviewer** n Kritiker m.

revise [rəˈvaiz] v revidieren; (*book*) überarbeiten. **revision** n Revision f; Überarbeitung f.

revive [rəˈvaiv] v wiederbeleben. **revival** n Wiederbelebung f; (*play*) Wiederauffürung f.

revoke [rəˈvouk] n widerrufen. **revocable** adj widerruflich. **revocation** n Widerruf m.

revolt [rəˈvoult] n Aufruhr m, Aufstand m. v revoltieren, sich empören; (*disgust*) abstoßen. **revolting** adj abstoßend.

revolution [revəˈluːʃən] n (pol) Revolution f; (*turning*) Umdrehung f, Rotation f. **revolutions per minute** Drehzahl f. **revolutionary** adj revolutionär; n Revolutionär(in).

revolve [rəˈvolv] v (sich) drehen. **revolver** n Revolver m. **revolving** adj drehbar.

revue [rəˈvjuː] n Revue f.

revulsion [rəˈvʌlʃən] n Ekel m.

reward [rəˈwoːd] n Belohnung f; v belohnen. **rewarding** adj lohnend.

rewire [riːˈwaiə] v mit neuen Leitungen versehen.

rhetoric [ˈretərik] n Rhetorik f; (*empty*) Redeschwall m. **rhetorical** adj rhetorisch.

rheumatism [ˈruːmətizəm] n Rheumatismus m. **rheumatic** adj rheumatisch.

rhinoceros [rainosərəs] n Nashorn neut.

rhododendron [roudəˈdendrən] n Rhododendron m or neut.

rhubarb [ˈruːbaːb] n Rhabarber m.

rhyme [raim] n Reim m. v reimen. **nursery rhyme** Kinderreim n.

rhythm [ˈriðəm] n Rhythmus m. **rhythmic** adj rhythmisch.

rib [rib] n Rippe f. **ribbed** adj (*material*) gerippt.

ribbon [ˈribən] n Band neut; (*typewriter*) Farbband neut. **ribbons** pl (*rags*) Fetzen pl. **ribboned** adj gestreift.

rice [rais] n Reis m.

rich [ritʃ] adj reich, wohlhabend; (*earth*) fruchtbar; (*food*) schwer. **rich man/woman** Reiche(r). **the rich** die Reichen. **riches** pl n Reichtum m. **richness** n Reichtum m; (*food*) Schwere f; (*finery*) Pracht f.

rickety [ˈrikəti] adj (*wobbly*) wackelig.

*****rid** [rid] v befreien, frei machen. **be rid of** los sein (+acc). **get rid of** loswerden (+acc). **good riddance to him!** Gott sei Dank ist man ihn los!

ridden [ˈridn] V ride.

riddle [ˈridl] n Rätsel neut.

riddled [ˈridld] adj durchlöchert.

*****ride** [raid] v reiten; (*bicycle, motor cycle*) fahren. **riding whip** Reitpeitsche f. n Ritt m; Fahrt f. **take for a ride** (*coll*) übers Ohr hauen. **rider** n Reiter(in); (*cycle*) Fahrer(in). **riding** n Reitsport m.

ridge [ridʒ] n Kamm m, Grat m; (*roof*) First m.

ridicule [ˈridikjuːl] n Spott m. v verspotten, lächerlich machen. **ridiculous** adj lächerlich.

rife [raif] adj **be rife** vorherrschen, grassieren. **rife with** voll von.

rifle[1] [ˈraifl] n (*gun*) Gewehr neut. **rifle range** Schießstand m.

rifle[2] [ˈraifl] v ausplündern.

rift [rift] n Spalte f, Riß m.

rig [rig] n Takelung f; (*coll*) Vorrichtung f, Anlage f. v auftakeln. **rig out** (*coll*) ausstatten. **rigging** n Takelwerk neut.

right [rait] adj (*correct*) recht, richtig; (*proper*) angemessen; (*right-hand*) recht. **all right** in Ordnung. **be right** (*thing*) recht sein; (*person*) recht haben. **feel all right** sich wohl befinden. **right-handed** adj rechtshändig. **right-wing** adj Rechts-. adv (*correctly*) recht, richtig; (*completely*) ganz; (*to the right*) (nach) rechts. **right away** sofort. n Recht neut. **right of way** (*mot*) Vorfahrt f. v berichtigen. **rightly** adv mit Recht.

righteous [ˈraitʃəs] adj rechtschaffen, gerecht.

rigid [ˈridʒid] adj starr, steif; (*person*) streng, unbeugsam. **rigidity** n Starrheit f.

rigmarole [ˈrigmərəul] n (*coll*) Theater neut.

rigour [ˈrigə] n Strenge f, Härte f. **rigorous** adj streng.

rim [rim] n Rand m.

rind [raind] n (*cheese*) Rinde f; (*bacon*) Schwarte f.

ring[1] [riŋ] n Ring m; (*comm*) Kartell neut. **wedding ring** n Trauring m. **ringleader** n Rädelsführer m.

*ring² [rɪŋ] v (sound) läuten, Klingeln; (echo) widerhallen. n (Glocken)Klang m, Klingeln neut. **there's a ring at the door** es klingelt. **ring (up)** (coll: phone) anrufen. **ring-ing** n Läuten neut.

rink [rɪŋk] n (ice) Eisbahn f.

rinse [rɪns] v ausspülen. n Spülung f.

riot [ˈraɪət] n Aufruhr m, Tumult m. v randalieren. **rioter** n Aufrührer(in). **riotous** adj aufrührerisch; (laughter) zügellos.

rip [rɪp] v reißen, zerreißen. n Riß m. **rip-cord** n Reißleine f. **rip-off** n (swindle) Nepp m, Schwindel m.

ripe [raɪp] adj reif. **ripen** v reifen, reif werden.

ripple [ˈrɪpl] n Kräuselung f; (noise) Platschern neut. v (sich) kräuseln.

*rise [raɪz] v sich erheben; (get up) aufstehen; (meeting) vertagen; (prices) steigen. n Aufstieg m; (prices) Steigen neut; (increase) Zuwachs m; (pay) Erhöhung f. **give rise to** hervorrufen, veranlassen. **rising** adj steigend.

risen [ˈrɪzn] V rise.

risk [rɪsk] n Risiko neut; (danger) Gefahr f. v riskieren. **take a risk** ein Risiko eingehen. **risky** adj riskant.

rissole [ˈrɪsoul] n Boulette f, Frikadelle f.

rite [raɪt] n Ritus m, Zeremonie f.

ritual [ˈrɪfjuəl] n Ritual neut. adj rituell.

rival [ˈraɪvəl] n Rivale m, Rivalin f. adj rivalisierend. v rivalisieren or wetteifern mit. **rivalry** n Rivalität f.

river [ˈrɪvə] n Fluß m. **down river** stromabwärts. **up river** stromaufwärts. **riverside** n Flußufer neut; adj Ufer-.

rivet [ˈrɪvɪt] n Niet m. v vernieten; (captivate) fesseln.

road [roud] n Straße f; (esp. fig) Weg m. **main road** Landstraße f. **on the road to** auf dem Wege zu. **road accident** Verkehrsunfall m. **road block** Straßensperre f. **road rage** aggressive Fahrweise f. **road sign** Straßenschild neut. **roadworks** pl n Straßenbauarbeiten pl.

roam [roum] v (umher)wandern.

roar [rɔː] v brüllen; (person) laut schreien; (wind) toben. n Gebrüll neut. **roaring** adj (coll) enorm, famos.

roast [roust] v braten, rösten. n Braten m.

rob [rɒb] v rauben. **robber** n Räuber m. **robbery** n Raub m.

robe [roub] n Talar m. **bathrobe** Bademantel m. v kleiden.

robin [ˈrɒbin] n Rotkehlchen neut.

robot [ˈroubot] n Roboter m.

robust [rəˈbʌst] adj robust, kräftig. **robustness** n Robustheit f.

rock¹ [rɒk] n (stone) Fels m, Felsen m; (naut) Klippe f. **steady as a rock** felsenfest. **on the rocks** (fig) gescheitert; (drink) mit Eis. **rockery** n Steingarten m. **rocky** adj felsig.

rock² [rɒk] v schaukeln; (baby) wiegen. **rocking-horse** n Schaukelpferd neut. **rock 'n' roll** n Rock and Roll m.

rocket [ˈrɒkit] n Rakete f. v hochschießen.

rod [rɒd] n Rute f.

rode [roud] V ride.

rodent [ˈroudənt] n Nagetier neut.

roe [rou] n Rogen m.

rogue [roug] n Schurke m. **roguish** adj schurkisch.

role [roul] n Rolle f.

roll [roul] v rollen. **roll out** ausrollen. **roll over** sich herumdrehen. **roll up** aufwickeln, aufrollen. **roller** n Walze f. **roller blind** Rouleau neut. **roller-skate** n Rollschuh. **rolling-pin** n Nudelholz neut. **rollneck** n Rollkragen m. n Rolle f; (bread) Brötchen neut; (meat) Roulade f. **roll-call** n Namensaufruf m.

romance [rouˈmans] n Romanze f. **romantic** romantisch. n Romantiker(in).

Rome [roum] n Rom neut. **Roman** adj römisch. n Römer(in). **Roman Catholic** römisch-katholisch.

romp [romp] v sich herumbalgen. **romp through** leicht hindurchkommen.

roof [ruːf] n (pl -s) Dach neut. v bedachen. **roofing** n Dachwerk neut.

rook¹ [rʊk] n Saatkrähe f. v (coll) schwindeln, betrügen.

rook² [rʊk] n (chess) Turm m.

room [ruːm] n (house) Zimmer neut; (space) Raum m, Platz m. v logieren (bei). **rooms** pl Wohnung f. **room-mate** n Zimmergenosse m, -genossin f. **roomy** adj geräumig.

roost [ruːst] n Hühnerstall m. v (bird) auf der Stange sitzen, schlafen. **rooster** n Hahn m.

root¹ [ruːt] n Würzel f; (source) Quelle f. **take root** Wurzel schlagen. **rooted** adj eingewürzelt. **rootless** adj wurzellos.

root² [ruːt] v **root for** (pigs) wühlen nach.

root out ausgraben.

rope [rəup] n Seil neut; (naut) Tau neut. v festbinden. **know the ropes** sich auskennen. **ropeladder** n Strickleiter f. **ropy** adj (coll) kläglich, schäbig.

rosary ['rəuzəri] n Rosenkranz m.

rose¹ [rəuz] V **rise**.

rose² [rəuz] n Rose f. **rosebush** n Rosenstrauch m. **rose-coloured** adj rosenrot. **through rose-coloured spectacles** durch eine rosarote Brille. **rosette** n Rosette f. **rosy** adj rosig.

rosemary ['rəuzməri] n Rosmarin m.

rot [rɒt] v verfaulen. n Fäulnis f; (nonsense) Quatsch m. **rotten** adj faul, verfault; (corrupt) morsch, faul. **rottenness** n Fäule f. **rotter** n (coll) Schweinehund m.

rota ['rəutə] n Turnus m.

rotate [rəu'teit] v sich drehen, rotieren; (crops) wechseln lassen. **rotary** adj rotierend, kreisend. **rotation** n Umdrehung f, Rotation f; (crops, etc.) Abwechselung f. **rotor** n Rotor m.

rouge [ruːʒ] n (make-up) Rouge neut.

rough [rʌf] adj rauh; (sea) stürmisch; (hair) struppig; (person) grob, roh; (approximate) ungefähr. **roughage** n Ballaststoffe pl. **roughen** v aufrauhen. **roughly** adv ungefähr. **roughness** n Rauhheit f.

roulette [ruːˈlet] n Roulette f.

round [raund] adj rund. adv rundherum. n Runde f. v runden; (corner) (herum)fahren um. **round off** abrunden. **round up** (cattle) zusammentreiben; (criminals) ausheben. **round trip** (Hinund) Rückfahrt f. **roundabout** n Karussel neut; (mot) Kreisverkehr m; adj weitschweifig. **roundly** adv gründlich. **roundness** n Rundheit f.

route [ruːt] n Weg m, Route f.

routine [ruːˈtiːn] n Routine f. adj üblich.

rove [rəuv] v herumwandern. **rover** n Wanderer m.

row¹ [rəu] n Reihe f. **in rows** reihenweise.

row² [rəu] v (boat) rudern. **rowing** n Rudern neut; (sport) Rudersport m. **rowing boat** Ruderboot neut.

row³ [rau] n (quarrel) Streit m; (noise) Krach m. v sich streiten, zanken.

rowdy ['raudi] adj lärmend, flegelhaft. n Rowdy m.

royal ['rɔiəl] adj königlich. **royalist** n Royalist m. **royalty** n Königtum neut. **roy-**

alties pl Tantieme f.

rub [rʌb] v reiben. **rub off** abreiben. **rub out** (erase) ausradieren. n Reiben neut.

rubber ['rʌbə] n Gummi m; (eraser) Radiergummi m. **rubber band** Gummiband neut. **rubber stamp** Gummistempel m.

rubbish ['rʌbiʃ] n Abfall m, Müll m; (nonsense) Quatsch m. **rubbishy** adj wertlos.

rubble ['rʌbl] n Trümmer pl, Schutt m.

ruby ['ruːbi] n Rubin m. adj (colour) rubinrot.

rucksack ['rʌksæk] n Rucksack m.

rudder ['rʌdə] n Ruder neut.

rude [ruːd] adj grob, unverschämt; (rough) roh, wild. **rudeness** n Grobheit f; Roheit f.

rudiment ['ruːdimənt] n Rudiment neut. **rudiments** pl Grundlagen pl.

rueful ['ruːfəl] adj kläglich, traurig. **ruefulness** n Traurigkeit f.

ruff [rʌf] n Krause f; (bird's) Halskrause f.

ruffian ['rʌfiən] n Schurke m, Raufbold m.

ruffle ['rʌfl] v kräuseln. n Krause f.

rug [rʌg] n (floor) Vorleger m; (blanket) Wolldecke f.

rugby ['rʌgbi] n Rugby neut.

rugged ['rʌgid] adj wild, rauh; (face) runzelig. **ruggedness** n Rauheit f.

ruin ['ruːin] n Verfall m, Vernichtung f; (building) Ruine f. v vernichten, ruinieren. **ruins** pl Trümmer pl. **ruinous** adj ruinierend.

rule [ruːl] n Regel f; (pol) Regierung f; (drawing) Lineal neut. **rule of thumb** Faustregel f. v (govern) regieren; (decide) entscheiden. **ruler** n (pol) Herrscher(in); (drawing) Lineal neut. **ruling** adj herrschend; n Entscheidung f.

rum [rʌm] n Rum m.

Rumania [ruːˈmeiniə] n Rumänien neut. **Rumanian** n Rumäne m, Rumänin f; adj rumänisch.

rumble ['rʌmbl] v poltern, knurren. n Dröhnen neut, Gepolter neut.

rummage ['rʌmiʤ] v **rummage through** durchsuchen, herumwühlen in.

rumour ['ruːmə] n Gerücht neut.

rump [rʌmp] n Hinterteil neut. **rump steak** Rumpsteak neut.

*run [rʌn] v rennen, laufen; (river) fließen; (machine) laufen, in Gang sein; (nose) laufen. **run away** weglaufen. **run down**

(*person*) heruntermachen. **run-down** *adj* erschöpft. **run out** zu Ende laufen. **run out of** knapp werden mit. **run over** (flüchtig) durchsehen. **runway** *n* Rollbahn *f*. *n* Lauf *m*, Rennen *neut*. **in the long run** auf die Dauer. **on the run** auf der Flucht. **runner** *n* Läufer(in). **running** *adj* laufend; (*water*) fließend.

rung[1] [ɪʌŋ] *V* **ring**[2].

rung[2] [ɪʌŋ] *n* Sprosse *f*.

rupture ['ɪʌptʃə] *n* Bruch *m*. *v* brechen, zerreißen.

rural ['ɪuərəl] *adj* ländlich, Land-.

rush[1] [ɪʌʃ] *v* stürzen, rasen. *n* Stürzen *neut*. **be in a rush** es eilig haben. **rush hour** Hauptverkehrszeit *f*.

rush[2] [ɪʌʃ] *n* (*bot*) Binse *f*.

rusk [ɪʌsk] *n* Zwieback *m*.

Russia ['ɪʌʃə] *n* Rußland *neut*. **Russian** *adj* russisch; *n* Russe *m*, Russin *f*.

rust [ɪʌst] *n* Rost *m*. *v* rosten, rostig werden. **rust-coloured** *adj* rostfarben. **rust-proof** *adj* rostfrei. **rusty** *adj* rostig.

rustic ['ɪʌstik] *adj* ländlich, bäuerlich. *n* Bauer *m*.

rustle ['ɪʌsl] *v* rascheln, rauschen. *n* Rascheln *neut*.

rut [ɪʌt] *n* Furche *f*. **be stuck in a rut** beim alten Schlendrian verbleiben.

ruthless ['ɪuːθlis] *adj* unbarmherzig, rücksichtslos. **ruthlessness** *n* Unbarmherzigkeit *f*.

rye [ɪaɪ] *n* Roggen *m*.

S

Sabbath ['sabəθ] *n* Sabbat *m*.

sabbatical [sə'batɪkəl] *adj* **sabbatical year** Urlaubsjahr *neut*.

sable ['æbl] *n* Zobel *m*; (fur) Zobelpelz *m*. *adj* Zobel-.

sabotage ['sabətaːʒ] *n* Sabotage *f*. *v* sabotieren. **saboteur** *n* Saboteur *m*.

sabre ['seɪbə] *n* Säbel *m*.

saccharin ['sakərin] *n* Saccharin *neut*.

sachet ['saʃeɪ] *n* Kissen *neut*, Täschchen *neut*.

sack [sak] *n* Sack *m*. *v* entlassen. **get the**

sack (*coll*) entlassen werden.

sacrament ['sakrəm ənt] *n* Sakrament *neut*. **sacramental** *adj* sakramental.

sacred ['seɪkrɪd] *adj* heilig.

sacrifice ['sakrifaɪs] *v* opfern. *n* Opfer *neut*. **sacrificial** *adj* Opfer-.

sacrilege ['sakrəlɪdʒ] *n* Sakrileg *neut*. **sacrilegious** *adj* gotteslästerlich.

sad [sad] *adj* traurig. **sadden** *v* traurig machen. **sadness** *n* Traurigkeit *f*.

saddle ['sadl] *n* Sattel *m*, (*meat*) Rücken *m*. *v* satteln; (*with task*) belasten. **saddlebag** *n* Satteltasche *f*. **saddler** *n* Sattler *m*.

sadism ['seɪdɪzəm] *n* Sadismus *m*. **sadist** *n* Sadist(in). **sadistic** *adj* sadistisch.

safe [seɪf] *adj* (*secure*) sicher; (*not dangerous*) ungefährlich; (*careful*) vorsichtig; (*dependable*) verläßlich. *n* Safe *m*, Geldschrank *m*. **safe and sound** gesund und munter. **safe conduct** Geleitbrief *m*. **safeguard** *n* Sicherung *f*, Vorsichtsmaßnahme *f*. **safety** *n* Sicherheit *f*. **safety belt** Sicherheitsgurt *m*. **safety pin** Sicherheitsnadel *f*.

saffron ['safən] *n* Safran *m*. *adj* safrangelb.

sag [sag] *v* absacken, herabhängen.

saga ['saːgə] *n* Saga *f*.

sage[1] [seɪdʒ] *adj* weise. *n* Weise(r). **sagacious** *adj* scharfsinnig, klug. **sagacity** *n* Klugheit *f*.

sage[2] [seɪdʒ] *n* (*bot*) Salbei *f*.

Sagittarius [sadʒɪteərɪəs] *n* Schütze *m*.

sago ['seɪgou] *n* Sago *m*.

said [sed] *V* say.

sail [seɪl] *n* Segel *neut*. *v* segeln; (*depart*) fahren. **sailing** *n* Segelsport *m*. **sailing boat** *n* Segelboot *neut*. **sailor** *n* Matrose *m*.

saint [seɪnt] *n* Heilige(r). **saintliness** *n* Heiligkeit *f*. **saintly** *adj* fromm.

sake [seɪk] *n* **for the sake of** wegen (+*gen*), um ... (+*gen*) willen. **for heaven's sake** um Himmels willen. **for my sake** um meinetwillen.

salad ['saləd] *n* Salat *m*. **salad dressing** Salatsoße *f*.

salami [sə'laːm] *n* Salami *f*.

salary ['saləri] *n* Gehalt. *neut*. **salaried employee** Gehaltsempfänger(in). **salary increase** Gehaltserhöhung *f*.

sale [seɪl] *n* Verkauf *m*; (*end of season*) Schlußverkauf *m*. **on** *or* **for sale** zu verkaufen. **sales** *pl* Absatz *m*, Umsatz *m*. **sales department** Verkaufsabteilung *f*.

salesgirl or **saleswoman** n Verkäuferin.
salesman n Verkäufer m; (travelling)
Geschäftsreisende(r).
saline ['seɪlaɪn] adj salzig. **salinity** n
Salzigkeit f.
saliva [sə'laɪvə] n Speichel m. **salivary** adj
Speichel-.
sallow ['saləu] adj bläßlich.
salmon ['sam ən] n Lachs m. adj (colour)
lachsrot.
salon ['salɒn] n Salon m.
saloon [sə'luːn] n Saal m, Salon m; (bar)
Kneipe f, Ausschank m.
salt [sɔːlt] n Salz neut. v salzen; (pickle) einsalzen. **salt beef** gepökeltes Rindfleisch
neut. **salt cellar** Salzfäßchen neut. **salted**
adj gesalzen. **saltiness** n Salzigkeit f. **salt
water** Salzwasser neut. **salty** adj salzig.
salute [sə'luːt] v grüßen. n Gruß m; (of guns)
Salut m.
salvage ['salvɪdʒ] n Bergung f, Rettung f. v
bergen, retten.
salvation [salveɪʃən] n Rettung f, Heil neut.
Salvation Army Heilsarmee f.
same [seɪm] pron, adj derselbe, dieselbe,
dasselbe; der/die/das gleiche. **all the same**
trotzdem. **it's all the same to me** es ist
mir gleich or egal. **the same old story** die
alte Leier f. **sameness** n Gleichheit f;
(monotony) Eintönigkeit f.
sample ['saːm pl] n Muster neut, Probe f. v
probieren.
sanatorium [sanə'tɔːrɪəm] n Sanatorium
neut.
sanction ['saŋkʃən] n Sanktion f. v billigen.
sanctity ['saŋktətɪ] n Heiligkeit f.
sanctuary ['saŋktʃuərɪ] n Heiligtum neut;
(place of safety) Asyl neut.
sand [sand] n Sand m. v sand down
abschmirgeln. **sandbag** n Sandsack m.
sandbank n Sandbank f. **sandpaper** n
Sandpapier neut. **sand-pit** n Sandgrube f.
sandy adj sandig.
sandal ['sandl] n Sandale f.
sandwich ['sanw ɪdʒ] n Sandwich neut.
sane [seɪn] adj geistig gesund. **sanity** n
geistige Gesundheit f.
sang [saŋ] V **sing**.
sanitary ['sanɪtərɪ] adj hygienisch. **sanitary towel** Damenbinde f. **sanitation** n
Sanierung f. sanitäre Einrichtungen pl.
sank [saŋk] V **sink**.

Santa Claus ['santə,klɔːz] n der
Weihnachtsmann.
sap [sap] n Saft m. **sapling** n junger Baum
m.
sapphire ['safaɪə] n Saphir m.
sarcasm ['saːkazəm] n Sarkasmus m. **sarcastic** adj sarkastisch, höhnisch.
sardine [saː'diːn] n Sardine f.
sardonic [saː'dɒnɪk] adj sardonisch,
zynisch.
sash¹ [saʃ] n (garment) Schärpe f.
sash² [saʃ] n (window) Fensterrahmen m.
sash window Fallfenster neut.
sat [sat] V **sit**.
satchel ['satʃəl] n Schulmappe f.
satellite ['satəlaɪt] n Satellit m; (pol)
Satellitenstaat m. **satellite dish**
Satellitenantenne f.
satin ['satɪn] n Satin m. adj Satin-.
satire ['sataɪə] n Satire f. **satirical** adj
satirisch. **satirist** n Satiriker(in).
satisfy ['satɪsfaɪ] v befriedigen. **satisfaction**
n Befriedigung f; (contentment)
Zufriedenheit f. **satisfactory** adj befriedi-
gend. **satisfied** adj zufrieden.
saturate ['satʃəreɪt] v sättigen. **saturation**
n Sättigung f.
Saturday ['satədɪ] n Sonnabend m, Samstag
m.
Saturn ['satən] n Saturn m. **saturnine** adj
(person) stillschweigend, verdrießlich.
sauce [sɔːs] n Soße f; (cheek) Frechheit f.
sauce-boat n Soßenschüssel f.
saucepan ['sɔːspən] n Kochtopf m,
Kasserolle f.
saucer ['sɔːsə] n Untertasse f. **flying
saucer** fliegende Untertasse f.
saucy ['sɔːsɪ] adj frech, keck.
sauna [sɔːnə] n Sauna f.
saunter [sɔːntə] v schlendern.
sausage ['sɒsɪdʒ] n Wurst f.
savage ['savɪdʒ] adj (animal) wild; (tribe,
etc.) primitiv, barbarisch; (behaviour) brutal,
roh. n Wilde(r). **savageness** n Wildheit f.
savagery n Unzivilisiertheit f.
save¹ [seɪv] v (rescue) (er)retten; (money)
sparen; (avoid) ersparen; (time) gewinnen;
(protect) schützen. n (football) Abwehr f.
saving n Ersparnis f. **savings** pl Ersparnisse
pl. **savings account** Sparkonto neut. **savings bank** Sparkasse f. **savings book**

Sparbuch *neut.*

save² [seɪv] *prep, conj* außer (+ *dat*), mit Ausnahme von (+ *dat*).

saviour ['seɪvə] *n* Retter *m.*

savoir-faire [sæwɑ:'fɛə] *n* Gewandtheit *f*, Feingefühl *neut.*

savoury ['seɪvəri] *adj* wohlschmeckend, würzig. *n* (*piquant*) Vorspeise *f.*

saw¹ [sɔ:] *V* see¹.

*saw² [sɔ:] *n* Sägen. *f. v* sägen. **sawdust** *n* Sägemehl *neut.* **sawmill** *n* Sägewerk *neut.*

sawn [sɔ:n] *V* saw².

saxophone ['sæksəfoun] *n* Saxophon *neut.* **saxophonist** *n* Saxophonist(in).

*say [seɪ] *v* sagen; (*maintain*) behaupten. **saying** *n* Sprichwort *neut.* **have one's say** seine Meinung äußern. **it goes without saying** selbstverständlich.

scab [skab] *n* Schorf *m*; (*strike-breaker*) Streikbrecher *m.*

scaffold ['skafəld] *n* (*execution*) Schafott *m.* **scaffolding** *n* Baugerüst *neut*, Gestell *neut.*

scald [skɔ:ld] *v* verbrühen. *n* Verbrühung *f.* **scalding** *adj* brühheiß.

scale¹ [skeɪl] *n* (*fish, etc.*) Schuppe *f*; (*kettle*) Kesselstein *m. v* schuppen. **scaly** *adj* schuppig.

scale² [skeɪl] *n* also **scales** *pl* Waage *f.*

scale³ [skeɪl] *n* (*gradation*) Skala *f*; (*music*) Tonleiter *f*; (*proportion*) Maßstab *m. v* (*climb*) erklettern. **to scale** maßstabgetreu. **scale model** maßstabgetreues Modell *neut.*

scallop ['skaləp] *n* Kammuschel *f.*

scalp [skalp] *n* Kopfhaut *f*; (*as trophy*) Skalp *m. v* skalpieren.

scalpel ['skalpəl] *n* Skalpell *neut.*

scampi ['skampi] *pl n* Scampi *pl.*

scan [skan] *v* (*carefully*) prüfen, genau untersuchen; (*briefly*) (flüchtig) überblicken. **scanner** *n* (*comp*) Scanner *m.*

scandal ['skandl] *n* Skandal *m.* **scandalize** *v* schockieren. **scandalous** *adj* skandalös. **scandalmonger** *n* Lästermaul *neut.*

scant [skant] *adj* knapp, spärlich. **scanty** *adj* knapp; (*insufficient*) unzulänglich.

scapegoat ['skeɪpgout] *n* Sündenbock *m.*

scar [skɑ:] *n* Narbe *f. v* vernarben.

scarce [skɛəs] *adj* knapp, selten. **scarcely** *adv* kaum. **scarcity** *n* Mangel *m.*

scare [skɛə] *v* erschrecken, in Schrecken versetzen. *n* Schreck *m.* **scarecrow** *n*

Vogelscheue *f.* **scary** *adj* erschreckend.

scarf [skɑ:f] *n* Halstuch *neut*, Schal *m.*

scarlet ['skɑ:lit] *adj* scharlachrot. **scarlet fever** Scharlachfieber *neut.*

scathing ['skeɪðiŋ] *adj* (*fig*) verletzend, beißend.

scatter ['skatə] *v* (ver)streuen; bestreuen (mit). **scatterbrain** *n* Wirrkopf *n.*

scavenge ['skavindʒ] *v* durchsuchen, herumwühlen (in). **scavenger** *n* (*zool*) Aasfresser *m.*

scene [si:n] *n* Szene *f*; (*situation*) Ort *m.* **scenery** *n* Landschaft *f*; (*theatre*) Bühnenbild *neut.* **scenic** *adj* malerisch.

scent [sent] *n* Duft *m*; (*perfume*) Parfüm *neut. v* (*smell*) riechen; (*perfume*) parfümieren. **scented** *adj* parfümiert.

sceptic ['skeptik] *n* Skeptiker(in). **sceptical** *adj* skeptisch. **scepticism** *n* Skeptizismus *m.*

sceptre ['septə] *n* Zepter *neut.*

schedule ['ʃedju:l] *n* Plan *m*; (*list*) Verzeichnis *neut*; (*trains*) Fahrplan *m. v* planen. **scheduled flight** Linienflug *m*, fahrplanmäßiger Flug *m.*

scheme [ski:m] *n* Schema *neut*; (*plan*) Plan *m*, Programm *neut. v* (*coll*) intrigieren. **schemer** *n* Ränkeschmied *m.*

schizophrenia [skitsə'fri:niə] *n* Schizophrenie *f.* **schizophrenic** *adj* schizophren; *n* Schizophrene(r).

scholar ['skolə] *n* Gelehrte(r); (*pupil*) Schüler(in). **scholarly** *adj* gelehrt. **scholarship** *n* Gelehrsamkeit *f*; (*grant*) Stipendium *neut.*

scholastic [skə'lastik] *adj* akademisch.

school¹ [sku:l] *n* Schule *f. v* schulen. **schoolboy** *n* Schüler *m.* **schoolgirl** *n* Schülerin *f.* **schooling** *n* Unterricht *m.* **schoolteacher** *n* Lehrer(in).

school² [sku:l] *n* (*fish*) Zug *m*; (*whales*) Schar *f.*

schooner ['sku:nə] *n* Schoner *m*; (*glass*) Humpen *m.*

sciatica [saiatikə] *n* Ischias *m or neut.*

science ['saiəns] *n* Wissenschaft *f*; (*natural science*) Naturwissenschaft *f.* **scientific** *adj* wissenschaftlich. **scientist** *n* Wissenschaftler(in).

scissors ['sizəz] *pl n* Schere *f sing.*

scoff¹ [skof] *v* spotten (über). *n* Spott *m*, Hohn *m.*

scoff² [skɒf] v (coll: eat) fressen, hinunterschlingen.

scold [skəʊld] v schimpfen. **give a scolding** ausschelten (+ acc).

scone [skɒn] n Teegebäck neut.

scoop [sku:p] n Schaufel f, Schöpfer m; (newspaper) (sensationelle) Erstmeldung f. v schöpfen.

scooter [ˈsku:tə] n Roller m.

scope [skəʊp] n Umfang m, Gebiet neut.

scorch [skɔ:tʃ] v verbrennen. **scorching** adj (weather) brennend.

score [skɔ:] n (score) Punktzahl f, Spielergebnis neut; (20) zwanzig (Stück); (music) Partitur f. v (points) zählen, machen. **know the score** (coll) Bescheid wissen. **scoreboard** n Anzeigetafel f.

scorn [skɔ:n] n Verachtung f, Spott m. v verachten. **scornful** adj verächtlich.

scorpion [ˈskɔ:pjən] n Skorpion m.

Scotland [ˈskɒtlənd] n Schottland neut. **Scotch** n (schottischer) Whisky m. **Scotsman** n Schotte m. **Scotswoman** n Schottin f. **Scottish** adj schottisch.

scoundrel [ˈskaʊndrəl] n Schurke m, Schuft m.

scour¹ [skaʊə] v (clean) scheuern, schrubben. **scourer** n Scheuerlappen m.

scour² [skaʊə] v (search) durchsuchen.

scout [skaʊt] n (mil) Späher m; (boy scout) Pfadfinder m.

scowl [skaʊl] v finster (an)blicken. n finsterer Blick m.

scramble [ˈskræmbl] v krabbeln, klettern; (eggs) rühren. **scramble for** balgen um. **scrambled egg(s)** Rührei neut.

scrap [skræp] n (piece) Stück neut, Fetzen m; (metal) Schrott m; (fight) Prügelei f. v (metal) verschrotten; (plan) verwerfen. **scrapbook** n Sammelalbum neut, Einklebebuch neut. **scrap merchant** Schrotthändler m. **scrapyard** n Schrottplatz m.

scrape [skreɪp] v schaben, kratzen. n Kratzen neut; (coll) Klemme f.

scratch [skrætʃ] v (zer)kratzen. n Kratzstelle f, Riß m; (wound) Schramme f. **scratchy** adj kratzend.

scrawl [skrɔ:l] v kritzeln. n Gekritzel neut.

scream [skri:m] n Schrei m. v schreien. **it's a scream** es ist zum Schreien.

screech [skri:tʃ] n Gekreisch neut; (cry) (durchdringender) Schrei m. v kreischen.

screen [skri:n] n (Schutz)Schirm m, (Schutz)Wand f; (film) Leinwand f; (TV, comp) Bildschirm m. v abschirmen. **screening** n (med) Untersuchung f; (security) Überprüfung f. **screenplay** n Drehbuch neut. **screen-saver** n (comp) Bildschirmschoner m.

screw [skru:] n Schraube f. v schrauben. **screwdriver** n Schraubenzieher m.

scribble [ˈskrɪbl] n Gekritzel neut. v kritzeln. **scribbler** n Kritzler m.

script [skrɪpt] n Schrift f; (handwriting) Handschrift f; (film) Drehbuch neut. **scripture** [ˈskrɪptʃə] n Heilige Schrift f.

scroll [skrəʊl] n Schriftrolle f; (decoration) Schnörkel m. v (comp) scrollen.

scrounge [skraʊndʒ] v (coll) schmarotzen, schnorren. **scrounger** n Schmarotzer m.

scrub¹ [skrʌb] v schrubben, scheuern. n Schrubben neut. **scrubbing brush** n Scheuerbürste f.

scrub² [skrʌb] n (bush) Gestrüpp neut, Busch m.

scruffy [ˈskrʌfɪ] adj schäbig.

scruple [ˈskru:pl] n Skrupel m. **scrupulous** adj peinlich, voller.

scrutiny [ˈskru:tənɪ] n (genaue) Untersuchung f. **scrutinize** v genau untersuchen.

scuffle [ˈskʌfl] n Rauferie f. v sich raufen.

sculpt [skʌlpt] v formen, schnitzen. **sculptor** n Bildhauer m. **sculpture** n Skulptur f.

scum [skʌm] n Abschaum m.

scurf [skə:f] n Schorf m; (dandruff) Schuppen pl.

scurvy [ˈskə:vɪ] n Skorbut m.

scuttle [ˈskʌtl] n Kohleneimer m.

scythe [saɪð] n Sense f. v (ab)mähen.

sea [si:] n See f, Meer neut. **at sea** auf See. **all at sea** (coll) perplex, im Dunkeln. **on the high seas** auf hoher see. **go to sea** zur See gehen.

seabed [ˈsi:bed] n Meeresgrund m.

sea front n Strandpromenade f.

seagoing [ˈsi:gəʊɪŋ] adj Hochsee-.

seagull [ˈsi:gʌl] n Möwe f.

seahorse [ˈsi:hɔ:s] n Seepferdchen neut.

seal¹ [si:l] n Siegel neut. v besiegeln. **seal off** (area, street) abriegeln, absperren. **seal up** versiegeln. **sealing wax** Siegellack m.

seal² [si:l] n (zool) Robbe f, Seehund m. **seal-**

skin *n* Seehundsfell *neut.*

sea-level *n* Meeresspiegel *m.*

sea-lion *n* Seelöwe *m.*

seam [siːm] *n* Saum *m*, Naht *f*; (*minerals*) Flöz *neut. v* säumen.

seaman ['siːmən] *n* Seemann *m*, Matrose *m.* **seamanlike** *adj* seemännisch. **seamanship** *n* Seemannskunst *f.*

search [səːtʃ] *v* suchen, forschen (nach); (*for criminal*) fahnden (nach); (*person, place*) durchsuchen (nach). **search engine** (*comp*) Suchmaschine *f*, Suchroboter *m.* **searchlight** *n* Scheinwerfer *m.* **search party** Suchtrupp *m.* **search warrant** Haussuchungsbefehl *m. n* Suche *f*; Untersuchung *f.* **searcher** *n* Sucher *m*, Forscher *m.* **searching** *adj* (*enquiry*) gründlich.

sea-shore *n* Seeküste *f.*

seasick ['siːsik] *adj* seekrank. **seasickness** *n* Seekrankheit *f.*

seaside ['siːsaid] *n* See *f.* **at the seaside** an der See. **to the seaside** an die See. **seaside town** Küstenstadt *f.*

season ['siːzn] *n* Jahreszeit *f*; (*comm*) Saison *f. v* (*cookery*) würzen; (*wood*) ablagern. **seasonal** *adj* saisonbedingt. **seasoning** *n* Würze *f.* **season-ticket** *n* Zeitkarte *f*; (*theatre*) Abonnement *neut.*

seat [siːt] *n* Sitz *m*; (*train, theatre*) Platz *m*; (*residence*) Wohnsitz *m. v* setzen. *please be seated!* bitte setzen Sie sich! **seating** *n* Sitzgelegenheit *f.*

seaweed ['siːwiːd] *n* Tang *m*, Alge *f.*

seaworthy ['siːwəːði] *adj* seetüchtig.

secluded [siklüːdid] *adj* abgelegen. **seclusion** *n* Zurückgezogenheit *f.*

second¹ ['sekənd] *n* (*time*) Sekunde *f. wait a second!* moment mal!

second² ['sekənd] *adj* zweit; (*next*) nächst, folgend. *adv* an zweiter Stelle. *n* Zweite(r). **for the second time** zum zweiten Mal. **on second thoughts** bei näherer Überlegung. **play second fiddle** die Nebenrolle spielen. **secondary** *adj* nebensächlich, sekundär. **secondary school** Sekundarschule *f.* **second-best** *adj* zweitbest. **second-class** *adj* zweitrangig. **second-hand** *adj* gebraucht, Gebraucht-. **secondly** *adv* zweitens. **second-rate** *adj* minderwertig.

secret ['siːkrit] *adj* geheim, heimlich. **keep secret** geheimhalten. *n* Geheimnis *neut.* **in secret** *or* **secretly** *adv* heimlich. **secrecy** *n*

Verborgenheit *f*, Heimlichkeit *f.* **secretive** *adj* verschlossen. **secretiveness** *n* Verschlossenheit *f.*

secretary ['sekrətəri] *n* Sekretär(in). **secretarial** *adj* Sekretär-. **secretary general** Generalsekretär *m.*

secrete [sikriːt] *v* absondern. **secretion** *n* Absonderung *f.*

sect [sekt] *n* Sekte *f.* **sectarian** *adj* sektiererisch.

section ['sekʃən] *n* (*part*) Teil *m*; (*of firm*) Abteilung *f*; (*of book, document*) Abschnitt *m. v* **section off** abteilen.

sector ['sektə] *n* Sektor *m.*

secular ['sekjuːlə] *adj* weltlich. **secularism** *n* Säkularismus *f.*

secure [sikjuːə] *adj* sicher. *v* sichern; (*affix*) festmachen (an); (*procure*) sich beschaffen. **security** *n* Sicherheit *f*; (*bond*) Bürgschaft *f.* **securities** *pl* (*comm*) Wertpapiere *pl.*

sedate [sideit] *adj* ruhig, gelassen. **sedateness** *n* Gelassenheit *f.* **sedative** *n* Beruhigungsmittel *neut.* **sedation** *n* (Nerven)Beruhigung *f.*

sediment ['sedimənt] *n* Sediment *neut.* **sedimentation** *n* Sedimentation *n.*

seduce [sidjuːs] *v* verführen. **seducer** *n* Verführer *m.* **seduction** *n* Verführung *f.* **seductive** *adj* verlockend.

*see¹ [siː] *v* sehen; (*understand*) einsehen, verstehen; (*consult*) konsultieren, besuchen. **see home** (*person*) nach Hause begleiten. **seeing that** da. **see through** (*understand*) durchschauen; (*finish*) zu Ende führen. **see to** sich kümmern um. **see to it that** darauf achten, daβ. **wait and see** abwarten.

see² [siː] *n* Bistum *neut.*

seed [siːd] *n* Same *m*; (*pip*) Kern *m.* **seedy** *adj* schäbig.

*seek [siːk] *v* suchen. **seeker** *n* Sucher(in).

seem [siːm] *v* scheinen. **seeming** *adj* scheinbar. **seemly** *adj* schicklich.

seen [siːn] *V* **see¹.**

seep [siːp] *v* (durch)sickern.

seesaw ['siːsɔː] *n* Wippe *f. v* schaukeln.

seethe [siːð] *v* sieden. **seething** *adj* (*coll*) wütend.

segment ['segmənt] *n* Abschnitt *m*, Segment *neut.*

segregate ['segrigeit] *v* trennen, absondern. **segregation** *n* Absonderung *f*; (*racial*) Rassentrennung *f.*

seize [stz] v ergreifen. **seize up** festfahren. **seizure** n Ergreifung f; (med) Anfall m.

seldom ['seldəm] adv selten.

select [sə'lekt] v auswählen, auslesen. adj exklusiv. **selected** adj ausgewählt. **selection** n Auswahl f. **selective** adj auswählend.

self [self] n Selbst neut, Ich neut.

self-adhesive adj selbstklebend.

self-assured adj selbstsicher. **self-assurance** n Selbstsicherheit f.

self-catering adj für Selbstversorger.

self-centred adj ichbezogen.

self-confident adj selbstbewußt, selbstsicher. **self-confidence** n Selbstbewußtsein neut.

self-conscious adj gehemmt, befangen. **self-consciousness** n Befangenheit f.

self-contained adj (flat) separat; (person) zurückhaltend.

self-control n Selbstbeherrschung f.

self-defence n Selbstverteidigung f.

self-denial n Selbstverleugnuang f.

self-discipline n Selbstdisziplin f.

self-employed adj selbständig.

self-esteem n Selbstachtung f.

self-evident adj selbstverständlich.

self-important adj wichtigtuerisch.

self-indulgent adj selbstgefällig.

self-interest n Eigennutz m. **self-interested** adj eigennützig.

selfish ['selfɪʃ] adj selbstisch, selbstsüchtig. **selfishness** n Egoismus m.

selfless ['selflis] adj selbstlos.

self-made adj **self-made man** Emporkömmling m.

self-pity n Selbstmitleid neut.

self-portrait n Selbstporträt neut.

self-respect n Selbstachtung f.

self-righteous adj selbstgerecht.

self-sacrifice n Selbstaufopferung f. **self-sacrificing** adj aufopferungsvoll.

selfsame ['selfseɪm] adj ebenderselbe, ebendieselbe, ebendasselbe.

self-satisfied adj selbstzufrieden.

self-service adj Selbstbedienung f. adj Selbstbedienungs-.

self-sufficient adj unabhängig; (person) selbstgenügsam.

self-will n Eigensinn m. **self-willed** adj eigensinnig.

*****sell** [sel] v verkaufen. **seller** n Verkäufer(in). **sell out** (betray) verraten. **sold out** ausverkauft.

Sellotape® ['seləteɪp] n Tesa-Film m.

semantic [sə'mantɪk] adj semantisch. **semantics** n Semantik f.

semaphore ['seməfɔː] n Semaphor m.

semen ['siːmən] n Samen m, Sperma neut.

semicircle ['semɪsɜːkl] n Halbkreis m. **semicircular** adj halbkreisförmig.

semicolon [semɪ'kəulən] n Strichpunkt m.

semi-detached (house) adj halbfreistehend.

semifinal [semɪ'faɪnl] n Vorschlußrunde f; Halbfinale neut.

seminal ['semɪnl] adj Samen-; (influential) einflußreich, wichtig.

seminar ['semɪnɑː] n Seminar neut.

semiprecious [semɪ'preʃəs] adj halbedel.

semi-skimmed adj halbentrahmt.

semolina [semə'liːnə] n Grieß m; (pudding) Grießbrei m.

senate ['senɪt] n Senat m. **senator** n Senator m. **senatorial** adj senatorisch.

*****send** [send] v schicken, senden. **send away** fortschicken. **send for** (person) schicken nach. **send off** (letter) absenden. **send-off** n Abschiedsfeier f. **sender** n Absender(in).

senile ['siːnaɪl] adj senil. **senility** n Senilität f.

senior ['siːnɪə] adj älter; (school) Ober-. n Ältere(r). **senior citizen** Senior(in).

sensation [sen'seɪʃən] n Gefühl neut, Empfindung f; (excitement) Sensation f. **sensational** adj sensationell. **sensationalism** n Effekthascherei f.

sense [sens] n Sinn m; (feeling) Gefühl neut. **common sense** Vernunft f. **make sense** sinnvoll sein. **sense of humour** Sinn für Humor m. v empfinden, spüren. **senseless** adj sinnlos.

sensible ['sensəbl] adj vernünftig. **sensibility** n Sensibilität f. **sensibleness** n Vernünftigkeit f.

sensitive ['sensɪtɪv] adj empfindlich (gegen). **sensitivity** n Empfindlichkeit f; (appreciativeness) Sensibilität f, Feingefühl neut.

sensual ['sensjuəl] adj sinnlich. **sensuality** n Sinnlichkeit f.

sensuous ['sensjɔəs] *adj* sinnlich. **sensuousness** *n* Sinnlichkeit *f*.

sent [sent] *V* **send**.

sentence ['sentəns] *n* Satz *m*; (*punishment*) Strafe *f*, Urteil *neut. v* verurteilen.

sentiment ['sentɪmənt] *n* Empfindsamkeit *f*; (*feeling*) Gefühl *neut.* **sentiments** *pl* Meinungen *pl*, Gesinnung *f sing.* **sentimental** *adj* sentimental. **sentimentality** *n* Sentimentalität *f*.

sentry ['sentrɪ] *n* Wachposten *m*.

separate ['sepərət; *v* 'sepəreit] *adj* getrennt. *v* trennen; (*couple*) sich trennen. **separable** *adj* trennbar. **separateness** *n* Getrenntheit *f*. **separation** *n* Trennung *f*.

September [sep'tem bə] *n* September *m*.

septic ['septik] *adj* septisch.

sequel ['sɪkwəl] *n* (*novel, etc.*) Fortsetzung *f*; (*consequence*) Folge *f*.

sequence ['sɪkwəns] *n* (Reihen)Folge *f*, Reihe *f*; (*film*) Szene *f*. **sequential** *adj* (aufeinander)folgend.

sequin ['sɪkwɪn] *n* Paillette *f*.

Serbia ['sɜːbə] *n* Serbien *neut.* **Serbian** *n* Serbe *m*, Serbin *f*; *adj* serbisch.

serenade [serə'neɪd] *n* Serenade *f*.

serene [sə'rɪn] *adj* heiter, gelassen. **serenity** *n* Heiterkeit *f*.

serf [sɜːf] *n* Leibeigene(r). **serfdom** *n* Leibeigenschaft *f*.

sergeant ['sɑːdʒənt] *n* (*mil*) Feldwebel *m*; (*police*) Wachtmeister *m*.

serial ['sɪərɪəl] *n* (*book*) Fortsetzungsroman *m*; (*TV, radio*) Sendereihe *f*. *adj* Fortsetzungs-. **serial number** Seriennummer *f*.

series ['sɪəriːz] *n* Serie *f*.

serious ['sɪərɪəs] *adj* ernst(haft); (*illness*) gefährlich. **seriously** *adv* ernstlich, im Ernst; (*injured*) schwer. **seriousness** *n* Ernst *m*.

sermon ['sɜːm ən] *n* Predigt *f*.

serpent ['sɜːpənt] *n* Schlange *f*.

serum ['sɪərəm] *n* Serum *neut*.

servant ['sɜːvənt] *n* Diener(in). **domestic servant** Hausangestellte(r). **public servant** *n* Beamte(r), Beamtin *f*.

serve [sɜːv] *v* dienen (+*dat*); (*customer*) bedienen; (*food*) servieren; (*tennis*) aufschlagen. **serve no purpose** nichts nützen. **it serves him right** es geschieht ihm recht. **server** *n* (*comp*) (File-)Server *m*.

service ['sɜːvɪs] *n* Dienst *m*; (*shop, restaurant*) Bedienung *f*; (*after-sales*) Kundendienst *m*; (*mot*) Inspektion; (*favour*) Gefallen *m*; (*church*) Gottesdienst *m*. **military service** Wehrdienst *m*. **service station** Tankstelle *f*. *v* (*mot*) warten, überholen. **serviceable** *adj* brauchbar.

serviette [sɜː'vɪet] *n* Serviette *f*.

servile ['sɜːvaɪl] *adj* servil. **servility** *n* Unterwürfigkeit *f*.

session ['seʃən] *n* Sitzung *f*; (*university*) Semester *neut*.

*set [set] *v* setzen, stellen; (*date, etc.*) festsetzen; (*table*) decken; (*sun*) untergehen; (*become solid*) gerinnen. **set aside** aufheben. **setback** *n* Rückschlag *m*. **set fire to** in Brand stecken. **set off** (*on journey*) sich auf den Weg machen, aufbrechen. **set one's heart on** sein Herz hängen an. **set to** darangehen. **setting** *n* Hintergrund *m*. *n* Satz *m*; (*crockery*) Service *f*; (*radio*) Apparat *m*; (*clique*) Kreis *m*, Clique *f*.

settee [se'tɪ] *n* Sofa *neut*.

settle ['setl] *v* (*arrange*) festsetzen; (*dispute*) schlichten; (*debt*) bezahlen; (*come to rest*) sich niederlassen; (*subside*) sich senken; (*in place*) sich ansiedeln. **settle down** (*calm down*) sich beruhigen; (*in place*) sich niederlassen. **settle for** (*coll*) annehmen. **settle in** sich einleben. **settle up** bezahlen. **settled** *adj* abgemacht, erledigt. **settlement** *n* (*place*) Siedlung *f*; (*agreement*) Übereinkommen *neut.* **settler** *n* Siedler(in).

seven ['sevn] *adj* sieben. *n* Sieben *f*. **seventh** *adj* siebt, siebent; *n* Siebtel *neut*.

seventeen [sevn'tɪn] *adj* siebzehn. *n* Siebzehn *f*. **seventeenth** *adj* siebzehnt.

seventy ['sevntɪ] *adj* siebzig. *n* Siebzig *f*.

sever ['sevə] *v* trennen. **severance** *n* Trennung *f*. **severance pay** Abfindungsentschädigung *f*.

several ['sevrəl] *adj* mehrere; (*separate*) getrennt. **severally** *adv* getrennt.

severe [sə'vɪə] *adj* streng, hart; (*weather*) rauh; (*difficult*) schwierig. **severity** *n* Strenge *f*; Härte *f*; (*seriousness*) Ernst *m*.

*sew [sou] *v* nähen. **sewing** *n* Näharbeit *f*. **sewing machine** Nähmaschine *f*.

sewage ['sjuːɪdʒ] *n* Abwasser *neut.* **sewer** *n* Abwasserkanal *m*. **sewerage** *n* Kanalisation *f*.

sewn [soun] *V* **sew**.

sex [sɛks] n Geschlecht neut, Sex m. adj Geschlechts-, sexual. **sexist** adj sexistisch. **sexual** adj sexual. **sexual intercourse** Geschlechtsverkehr m. **sexuality** n Sexualität f. **sexy** adj sexy.

sextet [sɛksˈtɛt] n Sextett neut.

shabby [ˈʃabɪ] adj schäbig.

shack [ʃak] n Hütte f.

shackle [ˈʃakl] v fesseln. **shackles** pl n Fesseln pl.

shade [ʃeɪd] n Schatten m. v beschatten; (protect) schützen; (drawing) schattieren. **shading** n Schattierung f. **shady** adj schattig; (dubious) fragwürdig.

shadow [ˈʃadoʊ] n Schatten m. **without a shadow of doubt** ohne den geringsten Zweifel. **shadow cabinet** Schattenkabinett neut. **shadowy** adj schattig.

shaft [ʃaːft] n (handle) Schaft m; (lift) Schacht m; (tech) Welle f.

shaggy [ˈʃagɪ] adj zottig.

*****shake** [ʃeɪk] v schütteln; (shock) erschüttern; (tremble) zittern; (hand) drücken. **shake hands** with die Hand geben (+dat). **shake off** (coll) loswerden. n Schütteln neut. **shaky** adj wackelig.

shall [ʃal] v (to form future) werden; (implying permission) sollen, dürfen. I shall go ich werde gehen. shall I go? soll ich gehen?

shallot [ʃəˈbɒt] n Schalotte f.

shallow [ˈʃabu] adj flach, seicht; (superficial) oberflächlich, seicht. **shallows** pl n Untiefe f. **shallowness** n Seichtheit f.

sham [ʃam] n Betrug m; (person) Schwindler m. adj falsch.

shambles [ˈʃambl̩z] n Durcheinander neut.

shame [ʃeɪm] n Scham f, Schamgefühl neut; (scandal) Schande f. **it's a shame that ...** schade, daß ... **shame-faced** adj verschämt. **shamefacedness** n Verschämtheit f. **what a shame!** (wie) Schade! v schämen. **shameful** adj schändlich. **shamefulness** n Schändlichkeit f. **shameless** adj schamlos. **shamelessness** n Schamlosigkeit f.

shampoo [ʃamˈpuː] n Shampoo neut, Haarwaschmittel neut. v shampooieren.

shamrock [ˈʃamrɒk] n Kleeblatt neut.

shanty[1] [ˈʃantɪ] n (hut) Hütte f. **shanty town** Elendsviertel neut.

shanty[2] [ˈʃantɪ] n (song) Matrosenlied neut.

shape [ʃeɪp] n Gestalt f, Form f. v gestalten, formen. **shaped** adj geformt. **shapeless** adj

formlos. **shapelessness** n Formlosigkeit f. **shapely** adj wohlgeformt.

share [ʃeə] n (An)Teil m; (comm) Aktie f. v teilen. **shareholder** n Aktionär m.

shark [ʃaːk] n Hai(fisch) m.

sharp [ʃaːp] adj scharf; (pointed) spitz; (outline) deutlich. adv (coll) pünktlich. **look sharp!** mach schnell! **sharpen** v (knife) schleifen; (pencil) spitzen. **sharpeyed** adj scharfsichtig. **sharpness** n Schärfe f. **sharpshooter** n Scharfschütze m. **sharpwitted** adj scharfsinnig.

shatter [ˈʃatə] v zerschmettern; (glass) zersplittern. **shattered** adj (coll) erschüttert.

shave [ʃeɪv] v (sich) rasieren. **clean-shaven** adj glattrasiert. **shaving brush** Rasierpinsel m. **shaving soap** Rasierseife f. **shaving foam** Rasierschaum m. n Rasur f. **shaver** n Rasierapparat m.

shawl [ʃɔːl] n Schal m.

she [ʃiː] pron sie.

sheaf [ʃiːf] n (pl sheaves) Garbe f.

*****shear** [ʃɪə] v scheren. **shears** pl n Schere f sing. **shearer** n Scherer m. **shearing** n Schur f.

sheath [ʃiːθ] n Scheide f. **sheathe** v (sword) in die Scheide stecken. **sheathed** adj (tech) verkleidet.

*****shed**[1] [ʃed] v (tears, blood) vergießen; (leaves) abwerfen.

shed[2] [ʃed] n (hut) Schuppen m; (cows) Stall m.

sheen [ʃiːn] n Glanz m, Schimmer m.

sheep [ʃiːp] n (pl sheep) Schaf neut. **sheepdog** n Schäferhund. **sheepskin** n Schaffell neut. **sheepish** adj einfältig, verlegen.

sheer [ʃɪə] adj (pure) bloß; (steep) steil.

sheet [ʃiːt] n (bed) Bettuch neut, (Bett)Laken neut; (paper, metal) Blatt neut.

shelf [ʃelf] n (pl shelves) Regal neut, Fach neut. **on the shelf** sitzengeblieben.

shell [ʃel] n Schale f; (snail) Schneckenhaus neut; (mil) Granate f. **shellfish** n Schalentier neut. **shell-shock** n Kriegsneurose f. v (egg) schälen; (nuts) enthülsen. **shelling** n (mil) Artilleriefeuer neut.

shelter [ˈʃeltə] n Obdach neut; (little hut) Schutzhütte f. v beschützen; (take shelter) Schutz suchen.

shelve [ʃelv] v (plan) auf die lange Bank schieben, aufschieben.

shepherd [ˈʃepəd] n Schäfer m, Hirt m. **shepherdess** n Schäferin f, Hirtin f.

sheriff [ˈʃerif] n Sheriff m.

sherry [ˈʃeri] n Sherry m.

shield [ʃiːld] n Schild m; (fig) Schutz m. v beschirmen.

shift [ʃift] v (sich) verschieben; (get rid of) beseitigen; (coll: move fast) schnell fahren; (gear) schalten. n Verschiebung f; (work) Schicht f. **shifty** adj schlau.

shimmer [ˈʃimə] n Schimmer m. v schimmern.

shin [ʃin] n Schienbein neut. v **shin up** hinaufklettern.

*****shine** [ʃain] v scheinen, leuchten; (shoes) putzen. n Glanz m. **shiny** glänzend, strahlend.

shingle [ˈʃiŋgl] n (on beach) Strandkies m.

shingles [ˈʃiŋglz] n (med) Gürtelrose f.

ship [ʃip] n Schiff neut. **shipowner** n Reeder m. **shipwreck** n Schiffbruch m **be shipwrecked** Schiffbruch erleiden. **shipyard** n Werft f. v verschiffen, spedieren. **shipment** n Verladung f. **shipper** n Spediteur m.

shirk [ʃəːk] v sich drücken (vor). **shirker** n Drückeberger(in).

shirt [ʃəːt] n Hemd neut. **shirty** adj (coll) verdrießlich.

shit [ʃit] n (vulg) Scheiße f. v scheißen. **shitty** adj beschissen.

shiver [ˈʃivə] v zittern. n Zittern neut.

shoal [ʃoul] n Schwarm m, Zug m.

shock [ʃok] v (impact) Stoß m, Anprall m; (fright) Schreck m, Schock m; (med) Nervenschock m; (elec) Schlag m. v schockieren, entsetzen. **shocked** adj schockiert. **shocking** adj schockierend.

shod [ʃod] V **shoe**.

shoddy [ˈʃodi] adj schäbig.

*****shoe** [ʃuː] n Schuh m; (horse) Hufeisen neut. **shoe-horn** n Schuhlöffel m. **shoelace** n Schnürsenkel m. v beschuhen. **shoemaker** n Schuhmacher m.

shone [ʃon] V **shine**.

shook [ʃuk] V **shake**.

*****shoot** [ʃuːt] v schießen; (hit) anschießen; (kill) erschießen; (film) drehen. **shoot down** (aeroplane) abschießen. **shooting** n (game, etc.) Jagd f. **shooting star** Sternschnuppe f.

shop [ʃop] n Laden m, Geschäft neut; (factory) Werkstatt f. **shop assistant** Verkäufer(in). **shopkeeper** n Ladenbesitzer m. **shop-lifting** n Ladendiebstahl m. **shopsteward** n Betriebstrat m. **shop-window** n Schaufenster neut. v (also **go shopping**) einkaufen gehen. **shopper** n Einkäufer(in). **shopping** n Einkäufe pl.

shore [ʃoː] n Küste f, Strand m.

shorn [ʃoːn] V **shear**.

short [ʃoːt] adj kurz; (person) klein. adv plötzlich. **short of** knapp an.

shortage [ˈʃoːtidʒ] n Mangel m, Knappheit f.

shortbread [ˈʃoːtbred] n Mürbekuchen m.

short-circuit n Kurzschluß m. v kurzschließen.

shortcoming [ˈʃoːtkʌmiŋ] n Fehler m, Unzulänglichkeit f.

short cut n Abkürzung f.

shortfall [ˈʃoːtfoːl] n Fehlmenge f.

shorthand [ˈʃoːthand] n Kurzschrift f. **shorthand typist** Stenotypist(in).

short list v in die engere Wahl ziehen.

short-lived adj kurzlebig.

shortly [ˈʃoːtli] adv bald, in kurzer Zeit.

short-sighted adj kurzsichtig. **shortsightedness** n Kurzsichtigkeit f.

shorts [ʃoːts] pl n kurze Hose f sing.

short-tempered adj reizbar.

short-term adj kurzfristig.

short-time adj **short-time work** Kurzarbeit f.

short-wave adj Kurzwellen-.

shot [ʃot] V **shoot**. n Schuß m; (pellets) Schrot m; (sport) Kugel f; (films) Aufnahme f; (injection) Spritze f. adj (coll) erschüttert. **have a shot** (coll) versuchen. **shotgun** n Schrotflinte f. **shot put** Kugelstoß m.

should [ʃud] v sollen. I should go ich sollte gehen. I should like (to) Ich möchte.

shoulder [ˈʃouldə] n Schulter f, Achsel f. **shoulder-blade** n Schulterblatt neut.

shout [ʃaut] v rufen, schreien. n Schrei m, Ruf m. **shouting** n Geschrei neut.

shove [ʃʌv] v schieben, stoßen. n Stoß m, Schub m.

*****show** v zeigen; (goods, etc.) ausstellen. **showcase** n Schaukasten m. **showman** n Schausteller m. **show off** angeben, sich großtun. **show-off** n Angeber m, Großtuer m. **showpiece** n Paradestück neut. **showroom** n Ausstellungsraum m. n Ausstellung f; (*theatre*) Vorstellung f. **mere show** *leerer Schein m.*

shower ['ʃauə] n (*rain*) Schauer m; (*bath*) Dusche f. v sich duschen.

shown [ʃoun] V **show**.

shred [ʃred] n Fetzen m. v zerfetzen. **not a shred of** keine Spur von.

shrew [ʃruː] n Spitzmaus f; (*woman*) zankisches Weib *neut*.

shrewd [ʃruːd] adj scharfsinnig, schlau. **shrewdness** n Scharfsinn m.

shriek [ʃriːk] n Schrei, Gekreisch *neut*. v schreien, kreischen.

shrill [ʃril] adj schrill, gellend.

shrimp [ʃrimp] n Garnele f.

shrine [ʃrain] n Schrein m. *shrink [ʃriŋk] v einschrumpfen. **shrink from** zurück-weichen von. **shrinkage** n Schrumpfung f.

shrivel ['ʃrivl] v runzelig werden, schrumpfen.

shroud [ʃraud] n Leichentuch *neut*. v (*fig*) umhüllen.

Shrove Tuesday [ʃrouv] n Fastnachtsdienstag m.

shrub [ʃrʌb] n Strauch m, Busch m. **shrubbery** n Gebüsch *neut*.

shrug [ʃrʌg] v zucken. n (Achsel)Zucken *neut*.

shrunk [ʃrʌŋk] V **shrink**.

shudder ['ʃʌdə] v schaudern. n Schauder m.

shuffle ['ʃʌfl] v (mit den Füßen) scharren, schlurfen; (*cards*) mischen. n Schlurfen *neut*; (*cards*) (Karten)Mischen *neut*.

shun [ʃʌn] v vermeiden.

shunt [ʃʌnt] v (*rail*) rangieren.

*shut [ʃʌt] v schließen, zumachen; (*book*) zuklappen. **shut down** stillegen. **shut off** abstellen. **shut out** aussperren. **shut up** (*be silent*) den Mund halten. adj geschlossen, zu.

shutter ['ʃʌtə] n Fensterladen m; (*phot*) Verschluß m.

shuttle ['ʃʌtl] n Pendelverkehr m.

shuttlecock ['ʃʌtlkok] n Federball m.

shy [ʃai] adj schüchtern. v (*horse*) scheuen. **shy away from** zurückschrecken vor. **shyness** n Schüchternheit f.

sick [sik] adj krank. *I feel sick* mir ist übel. **sick humour** schwarzer Humor m. **sicken** v erkranken; (*disgust*) anekeln. **sickening** adj ekelhaft. **sick leave** Krankheitsurlaub m. **sickly** adj kränklich. **sickness** n

Krankheit f; (*vomiting*) Erbrechen *neut*.

sickle ['sikl] n Sichel f.

side [said] n Seite f; (*edge*) Rand m; (*team*) Mannschaft f. adj seitlich, Seiten-. **sideboard** n Buffet *neut*. **sideboards** *or* **sideburns** pl n Koteletten pl. **sidelight** n (*mot*) Standlicht *neut*. **sideline** n Nebenbeschäftigung f. **sidelong** adj seitlich. **sideshow** n Jahrmarktsbude f. **siding** n Nebengleis *neut*.

sidle ['saidl] v sich schlängeln. **sidle up to** heranschleichen an.

siege [siːdʒ] n Belagerung f. **lay siege to** belagern.

sieve [siv] n Sieb *neut*. v (durch)sieben.

sift [sift] v (durch)sieben; (*evidence, etc.*) sorgfältig überprüfen.

sigh [sai] v seufzen. n Seufzer m.

sight [sait] n (*power of*) Sehvermögen *neut*; (*instance of seeing*) Anblick m; (*range of vision*) Sehkraft f; (*of gun*) Visier *neut*; (*place of interest*) Sehenswürdigkeit f. **at sight** (*comm*) bei Sicht. **at first sight** beim ersten Anblick. **sighted** adj sichtig. **sightless** adj blind. **go sightseeing** die Sehenswürdigkeiten besichtigen.

sign [sain] n Zeichen *neut*; (*noticeboard, etc.*) Schild *neut*. v unterschreiben. **sign on** (*comp*) Programm beginnen; (*as unemployed*) stempeln gehen. **signwriter** n Schriftmaler m. **signpost** n Wegweiser m.

signal ['signəl] n Signal *neut*. v signalisieren.

signature ['signətʃə] n Unterschrift f. **signature tune** Kennmelodie f. **signatory** n Unterzeichner m; (*pol*) Signatar m.

signify ['signifai] v bedeuten. **significance** n Bedeutung f. **significant** adj wichtig.

silence ['sailəns] n Ruhe f, Stille f; (*absence of talking, etc.*) Schweigen *neut*. v zum Schweigen bringen.

silent ['sailənt] adj still, ruhig; stillschweigend. **be** *or* **fall silent** schweigen. **silent film** Stummfilm m.

silhouette [silu'et] n Silhouette f.

silicon chip ['silikən] n Siliciumchip m.

silk [silk] n Seide f. adj Seiden-.

sill [sil] n Fensterbrett *neut*; (*door*) Schwelle f.

silly ['sili] adj dumm, albern. **silly season** Sauregurkenzeit f.

silt [silt] n Schlamm m. v **silt up** verschlammen.

silver ['sɪlvə] n Silber neut. adj silbern, Silber-. **silver plate** Tafelsilber neut. **silver-plated** adj versilbert.

similar ['sɪmɪlə] adj ähnlich (+dat). **similarity** n Ähnlichkeit f. **similarly** adv gleichermaßen.

simile ['sɪmɪlɪ] n Gleichnis neut.

simmer ['sɪmə] v leicht kochen (lassen).

simple ['sɪmpl] adj einfach. **simple-minded** adj einfältig. **simpleton** n Einfaltspinsel m. **simplicity** n Einfachheit f. **simplify** v vereinfachen. **simply** adv einfach.

simulate ['sɪmjuleɪt] v simulieren. **simulation** n Simulation f. **simulator** n Simulator m.

simultaneous [ˌsɪməlteɪnjəs] adj gleichzeitig.

sin [sɪn] n Sünde f. v sündigen. **sinful** adj sündig. **sinner** n Sünder(in).

since [sɪns] prep seit. I've been living here since 1960 ich wohne hier seit 1960. conj (time) seit(dem); (because) da. adv seitdem, seither; (in the meantime) inzwischen.

sincere [sɪn'sɪə] adj aufrichtig, ehrlich. **yours sincerely** mit freundlichen Grüßen. **sincerity** n Aufrichtigkeit f.

sinew ['sɪnjuː] n Sehne f. **sinewy** adj sehnig.

*sing [sɪŋ] v singen. **singer** n Sänger(in). **singing** n Singen neut, Gesang m.

singe [sɪndʒ] v (ver)sengen.

single ['sɪŋgl] adj einzig; (individual) einzeln; (room, bed, etc.) Einzel-; (unmarried) ledig. v single out auslesen. **single parent** n Alleinerziehende m, f. **single ticket** einfache Fahrkarte f. **single-handed** adj eigenhändig. **single-minded** adj zielstrebig. **singly** adv einzeln, allein.

singular ['sɪŋgjulə] adj einzigartig; (gramm) im Singular. n (gramm) Singular m.

sinister ['sɪnɪstə] adj drohend, unheilvoll.

*sink [sɪŋk] v sinken; (cause to sink) senken. n Spülbecken neut.

sinuous ['sɪnjuəs] adj gewunden, sich windend.

sinus ['saɪnəs] n (Nasen) Nebenhöhle f. **sinusitis** n Nebenhöhlenentzündung f.

sip [sɪp] v nippen an, schlürfen. n Schlückchen neut.

siphon ['saɪfən] n Heber m; (soda) Siphon m. v aushebern.

sir [səː] n (mein) Herr. **Dear Sir** (in letters) sehr geehrter Herr!

siren ['saɪərən] n Sirene f.

sirloin ['səːlɔɪn] n Lendenstück neut.

sister ['sɪstə] n Schwester f; (nurse) Oberschwester f. **sister-in-law** n Schwägerin f. adj Schwester-. **sisterly** adj schwesterlich.

*sit [sɪt] v sitzen; (exam) machen; (hen) brüten. **sit down** sich (hin)setzen. **sitting** n Sitzung f. **sitting duck** leichtes Opfer neut. **sitting-room** n Wohnzimmer neut.

sitcom ['sɪtkɒm] n Fernsehkomödie f.

site [saɪt] n Stelle f. **building site** Baustelle f. v placieren.

situation [sɪtjuˈeɪʃən] n Lage f; (state of affairs) Situation f, (Sach)Lage f; (job) Stelle f, Posten m. **situated** adj gelegen.

six [sɪks] adj sechs. n Sechs f. **sixth** adj sechst; n Sechstel neut. **sixth form** Prima f.

sixteen [sɪksˈtiːn] adj sechzehn. n Sechzehn f.

sixty ['sɪkstɪ] adj sechzig. n Sechzig f.

size [saɪz] n Größe f. v **size up** (coll) abschätzen.

sizzle ['sɪzl] v zischen.

skate[1] [skeɪt] n (ice) Schlittschuh m; (roller) Rollschuh m. v Schlittschuh/Rollschuh laufen. **skateboard** n Skateboard neut. **skater** n Eisläufer(in); Rollschuhläufer(in).

skate[2] [skeɪt] n (fish) Rochen m.

skeleton ['skelɪtn] n Skelett neut, Knochengerüst neut. **skeleton key** Dietrich m.

sketch [sketʃ] n Skizze f; (theatre) Sketch m. v skizzieren. **sketchy** adj oberflächlich.

skewer ['skjuə] n Fleischspieß m. v spießen.

ski [skiː] n Ski m. v Ski laufen. **ski slope** n Skiabfahrt f. **skier** n Skiläufer(in), Skifahrer(in). **skiing** n Skilaufen neut, Skifahren neut.

skid [skɪd] v schleudern. n Schleudern neut.

skill [skɪl] n (skilfulness) Geschicklichkeit f, Gewandtheit f; (expertise) Fachkenntnis f. **skilled** adj geschickt. **skilled worker** Facharbeiter m. **skilful** adj geschickt.

skim [skɪm] v abschöpfen; (milk) entrahmen. **skim through** (read) überfliegen. **skim milk** Magermilch f.

skimp [skɪmp] v geizen (mit); (work) nachlässig machen.

skin [skɪn] n Haut f; (animal) Fell neut, Pelz m; (fruit) Schale f, Rinde f. **skin-deep** adj

oberflächlich. **skin-diving** n Schwimm-
tauchen neut. **skinflint** n Geizhals m.
skin-tight adj hauteng. v enthäuten.
skinny adj mager.

skip [skɪp] v hüpfen; (with rope) seilsprin-
gen; (miss) auslassen. **skip through** (read)
überfliegen. n Sprung m. **skipping-rope** n
Hüpfseil neut.

skipper ['skɪpə] n (coll: naut) Kapitän m.

skirmish ['skəːmɪʃ] n Gefecht neut.

skirt [skəːt] n Rock m. v (go around)
herumgehen um. **skirting board**
Wandleiste f.

skittle ['skɪtl] n Kegel m. **play skittles**
kegeln. **skittle alley** Kegelbahn f.

skull [skʌl] n Schädel m. **skull-cap** n
Käppchen neut.

skunk [skʌŋk] n Skunk m, Stinktier neut.

sky [skaɪ] n Himmel m. **sky-blue** adj him-
melblau. **sky-high** adj, adv himmelhoch.
skylark n Lerche f. **skylight** n Dachfenster
neut. **skyscraper** n Hochhaus neut,
Wolkenkratzer m.

slab [slab] n (stone) (Stein)Platte f; (chocolate) Tafel f.

slack [slak] adj schlaff, locker; (person)
nachlässig; (trade) flau. **slacken** v lockern,
entspannen; (pace, etc.) vermindern.
slacker n (person) Drückeberger(in). **slack-
ness** n Schlaffheit f.

slacks [slaks] pl n Hose f sing.

slag [slag] n Schlacke f. **slagheap** n Halde f.

slalom ['slɑːləm] n Slalom m.

slam [slam] v (door) zuknallen; (criticize)
(jemanden) herunterputzen. n Knall m.

slander ['slɑːndə] n Verleumdung f. v verleumden. **slanderer** n Verleumder m. **slanderous** adj verleumderisch.

slang [slaŋ] n Jargon m. v beschimpfen.

slant [slɑːnt] n Schräge f; (attitude)
Einstellung f. v schräg liegen. **slant-eyed**
adj mit schräggestellten Augen. **slanting**
adj schräg.

slap [slap] v klapsen, schlagen. n Klaps m,
Schlag m. **slapdash** adj schlampig.

slash [slaʃ] v schlitzen, zerfetzen. n Schnitt
m, Schlitz m.

slat [slat] n Latte f, Leiste f.

slate [sleɪt] n Schiefer m; (writing)
Schiefertafel f; (on roof) Dachschiefer m. v
(coll) heftig tadeln, kritisieren.

slaughter ['slɔːtə] v schlachten. n

Schlachten neut. **slaughterhouse** n
Schlachthaus neut. **slaughterer** n
Schlächter m.

slave [sleɪv] n Sklave m, Sklavin f. **slave-
driver** n Leuteschinder m. v **slave away**
schuften. **slavery** n Sklaverei f. **slavish** adj
sklavisch.

sleaze n (pol) Filz m. **sleazy** adj schäbig.

sledge [sledʒ] n Schlitten m.

sledgehammer ['sledʒ,hamə] n
Schmiedehammer m, Schlägel m.

sleek [sliːk] adj glatt. **sleekness** n Glätte f.

*****sleep** [sliːp] v schlafen; (spend the night)
übernachten. n Schlaf m. **go to sleep** einschlafen. **sleeper** n Schläfer(in); (railway)
Schwelle f. **sleeping bag** Schlafsack m.
sleeping car Schlafwagen m. **sleeping
policeman** (speed hump) Fahrbahnhöcker
m. **sleepless** adj schlaflos. **sleeplessness** n
Schlaflosigkeit f. **sleepwalker** n
Nachtwandler m. **sleepy** adj schläfrig,
müde.

sleet [sliːt] n Schneeregen m.

sleeve [sliːv] n Ärmel m. **sleeved** adj mit
Ärmeln. **sleeveless** adj ärmellos.

sleigh [sleɪ] n Schlitten m.

slender ['slendə] adj schlank, schmal. **slen-
derness** n Schlankheit f.

slept [slept] V sleep.

slice [slaɪs] n Scheibe f, Schnitte f. v aufschneiden. **sliced** adj geschnitten, in
Scheiben. **slicer** n Schneidemaschine f.

slick [slɪk] adj glatt; (person) raffiniert.
slicker n Gauner m.

slid [slɪd] V slide.

*****slide** [slaɪd] v gleiten, rutschen. **slide rule**
Rechenschieber m. **sliding door**
Schiebetür f. **sliding scale** gleitende Skala
f. n (phot) Dia(positiv) neut; (playground)
Schlitterbahn f.

slight [slaɪt] adj gering, unbedeutend,
klein; (person) schmächtig, dünn. **not in
the slightest** nicht im geringsten. v
(person) kränken. n Beleidigung f. **slightly**
adv leicht, ein bißchen.

slim [slɪm] adj schlank, dünn; (chance, etc.)
gering. v eine Schlankheitskur machen,
abnehmen. **slimness** n Schlankheit f.

slime [slaɪm] n Schleim m. **slimy** adj
schleimig.

*****sling** [slɪŋ] n (weapon) Schleuder m; (arm)
Schlinge f. v schleudern.

*slink [slɪŋk] v schleichen.

slip [slɪp] n Fehltritt m; (underskirt) Unterrock m. v gleiten, rutschen. **slip away** sich davonmachen. **slip off** (clothes) ausziehen. **slip on** (clothes) anziehen. **slip up** sich irren, sich vertun. **slipknot** n Laufknoten m. **slipshod** adj schlampig.

slipper ['slɪpə] n Pantoffel m.

slippery ['slɪpərɪ] adj schlüpfrig, glitschig; (person) aalglatt.

*slit [slɪt] n Schlitz m. v aufschlitzen. **sliteyed** adj schlüpfrig.

slither ['slɪðə] v rutschen, schlittern. **slithery** adj schlüpfrig.

slobber ['slɒbə] v sabbern, geifern. n Geifer m. **slobbery** adj sabbernd.

sloe [sləu] n Schlehe f.

slog [slɒg] v hart schlagen; (work hard) schuften. n (harter) Schlag m.

slogan ['sləugən] n Slogan m, Schlagwort neut.

slop [slɒp] v verschütten. n Pfütze f. **slops** pl n Abwasser neut.

slope [sləup] n Abhang m. v abfallen. **sloping** adj schräg.

sloppy ['slɒpɪ] adj matschig; (slapdash) schlampig. **sloppiness** n Matschigkeit f; Schlampigkeit f.

slot [slɒt] n Schlitz m; (for coin) Münzeinwurf m.

slouch [slautʃ] v latschen. **slouching** adj latschig.

Slovakia [sləu'vakɪə] n Slowakei f. **Slovakian** n Slowake m, Slowakin f; adj slowakisch.

Slovenia [sləu'vinə] n Slowenien neut. **Slovenian** n Slowene m, Slowenin f; adj slowenisch.

slovenly ['slʌvnlɪ] adj schlampig.

slow [sləu] adj langsam; (boring) langweilig. v also **slow down** or **up** (sich) verlangsamen. **slow-down** n Verlangsamung f. **slow motion** Zeitlupentempo neut. **slowness** n Langsamkeit f; (wits) Schwerfälligkeit f.

sludge [slʌdʒ] n Schlamm m.

slug [slʌg] n Schnecke f.

sluggish ['slʌgɪʃ] adj träge, schwerfällig; (river) langsam fließend. **sluggishness** n Schwerfälligkeit f.

sluice [slu:s] n Schleuse f. v ausspülen.

slums [slʌmz] pl n Elendsviertel neut.

slumber ['slʌmbə] v schlummern. n Schlummer m.

slump [slʌmp] v hinplumpsen; (prices) stürzen. n (comm) Geschäftsrückgang m, Wirtschaftskrise f.

slung [slʌŋ] V **sling**.

slunk [slʌŋk] V **slink**.

slur [slə:] v (words) verschlucken, undeutlich aussprechen. n Vorwurf m.

slush [slʌʃ] n Matsch m; (snow) Schneematsch m; (sentimentality) Schmalz m. **slushy** adj matschig; schmalzig.

slut [slʌt] n Schlampe f. **sluttish** adj schlampig.

sly [slaɪ] adj schlau, hinterhältig. **slyness** n Schlauheit f.

smack¹ [smak] n Klaps m, Klatsch m. v schlagen, einen Klaps geben (+ dat).

smack² [smak] n (flavour) Geschmack m. v schmecken (nach).

small [smɔ:l] adj klein; (number, extent) gering. **small ad** n Annonce (in der Zeitung) f. **small change** Kleingeld neut. **small talk** Geplauder neut. **smallness** n Kleinheit f.

smallpox ['smɔ:lpɒks] n Pocken pl.

smart [smɑ:t] adj schick, gepflegt; (coll: clever) gescheit, raffiniert. **smart aleck** (coll) Naseweis m, Besserwisser m, (vulg) Klugscheißer m. v (suffer) leiden. **smarten up** zurechtmachen.

smash [smaʃ] v zerschmettern, zerschlagen; (enemy, etc.) vernichten. n (mot) Zusammenstoß m. **smash hit** Bombenerfolg m. **smashing** adj (coll) toll, sagenhaft.

smear [smə] v (be)schmieren. n (Schmutz) Fleck m; (med) Abstrich m. **smear campaign** Verleumdungskampagne f, Rufmordkampagne f.

*smell [smel] n Geruch m; (pleasant) Duft m. v riechen. **smell of** riechen nach. **smelly** adj übelriechend.

smelt [smelt] V **smell**.

smile [smaɪl] v lächeln. n Lächeln neut. **smiling** adj lächelnd.

smirk [smə:k] v schmunzeln.

smock [smɒk] n Kittel m.

smog [smɒg] n Smog m, Rauchnebel m.

smoke [sməuk] v rauchen; (meat, fish) räuchern. n Rauch m. **smokescreen** n Nebelvorhang m. **smokestack** n Schornstein m. **smoker** n Raucher(in);

(*train*) Raucherabteil *m*. **smoking** *n* Rauchen *neut*. **no smoking** Rauchen verboten.

smooth [smuːð] *adj* glatt. **smoothness** *n* Glätte *f*. **smooth-tongued** *adj* schmeichlerisch. *v* glätten.

smother ['smʌðə] *v* ersticken; (*with gifts, etc*.) überhäufen.

smoulder ['smouldə] *v* schwelen.

smudge [smʌdʒ] *n* Schmutzfleck *m*, Klecks *m*. *v* beschmutzen.

smug [smʌg] *adj* selbstgefällig.

smuggle ['smʌgl] *v* schmuggeln. **smuggler** *n* Schmuggler *m*. **smuggling** *n* Schmuggel *m*.

snack [snak] *n* Imbiß *m*. **snack bar** Imbißstube *f*.

snag [snag] *n* (*difficulty*) Haken *m*.

snail [sneil] *n* Schnecke *f*. **at a snail's pace** im Schneckentempo.

snake [sneik] *n* Schlange *f*.

snap [snap] *v* (*break*) (zer)brechen; (*dog*) schnappen; (*noise*) knacken; (*phot*) knipsen. **snap at** (*person*) anschnauzen. **snapdragon** *n* Löwenmaul *neut*. **snap-fastener** *n* Druckknopf *m*. **snapshot** *n* Schnappschuß *m*. **snappy** *adj* (*coll*) schnell, lebhaft.

snare [sneə] *n* Schlinge *f*. *v* fangen.

snare drum *n* Schnarrtrommel *f*.

snarl [snaːl] *n* Knurren *neut*. *v* knurren.

snatch [snatʃ] *v* schnell ergreifen. **snatch at** greifen nach.

sneak [sniːk] *v* schleichen; (*tell tales*) petzen. *n* Petzer *m*. **sneakers** *pl n* Turnschuhe *pl*. **sneaking** *adj* heimlich. **sneaky** *adj* heimtückisch.

sneer [sniə] *v* spötteln (über). *v* höhnisch lächeln. *n* Hohnlächeln *neut*.

sneeze [sniːz] *v* niesen. *n* Niesen *neut*.

sniff [snif] *v* schnüffeln. *n* Schnüffeln *neut*.

snigger ['snigə] *v* kichern. *n* Kichern *neut*.

snip [snip] *v* schneiden. *n* Schnitt *m*.

snipe [snaip] *n* Schnepfe *f*. *v* aus dem Hinterhalt schießen. **sniper** *n* Heckenschütze *m*.

snivel ['snivl] *v* wimmern. **snivelling** *adj* weinerlich.

snob [snob] *n* Snob *m*. **snobbery** *n* Snobismus *m*. **snobbish** *adj* snobistisch.

snooker ['snuːkə] *n* Snooker *neut*.

snoop [snuːp] *v* herumschnüffeln. *n* Schnüffler *m*.

snooty ['snuːti] *adj* hochnäsig.

snooze [snuːz] *n* Nickerchen *neut*. *v* ein Nickerchen machen.

snore [snoː] *v* schnarchen. *n* Schnarchen *neut*.

snorkel ['snoːkəl] *n* Schnorchel *m*.

snort [snoːt] *n* Schnauben *neut*. *v* schnauben.

snout [snaut] *n* Schnauze *f*.

snow [snou] *n* Schnee *m*. **snowball** *n* Schneeball *m*; *v* (*develop*) lawinenartig anwachsen. **snowboard** *n* Snowboard *neut*. **snowdrift** *n* Schneewehe *f*. **snowdrop** *n* Schneeglöckchen *neut*. *v* schneien.

snub [snʌb] *n* Rüffel *m*, Verweis *m*. *v* rüffeln. *adj* stumpf.

snuff [snʌf] *n* Schnupftabak *m*. **take snuff** schnupfen.

snug [snʌg] *adj* gemütlich, bequem.

snuggle ['snʌg] *v* sich schmiegen (an).

so [sou] *adv* so; (*very*) sehr. *conj* also, daher. **so that** damit. *so am/do I* ich auch. **so what?** na und? *I think so* ich glaube schon.

soak [souk] *v* durchtränken; (*washing*) einweichen. **soaking wet** triefend naß.

soap [soup] *n* Seife *f*. *v* (ein)seifen. **soapy** *adj* seifig. **soapy water** Seifenwasser *neut*.

soar [soː] *v* (*fly up*) hochfliegen; (*rise*) hoch aufsteigen.

sob [sob] *v* schluchzen. *n* Schluchzen *neut*.

sober ['soubə] *adj* nüchtern. *v* **sober up** nüchtern werden. **sobriety** *n* Nüchternheit *f*.

sociable ['souʃəbl] *adj* gesellig. **sociability** *n* Geselligkeit *f*.

social ['souʃəl] *adj* (*animals*) gesellig; (*gathering*) gesellschaftlich, gesellig; (*of society*) Gesellschafts-, Sozial-, gesellschaftlich. **social security** Sozialversicherung *f*. **social services** soziale Einrichtungen *pl*. **social worker** Sozialarbeiter(in). **socialism** *n* Sozialismus *m*. **socialist** *n* Sozialist(in).

society [sə'saiəti] *n* Gesellschaft *f*.

sociology [sousiɔlɔdʒi] *n* Soziologie *f*. **sociological** *adj* soziologisch. **sociologist** *n* Soziologe *m*.

sock [sok] *n* Socke *f*.

socket ['sokit] *n* (*elec*) Steckdose *f*; (*eye*) Höhle *f*; (*bone*) Gelenkpfanne *f*.

soda ['soudə] *n* Soda; *also* **soda water**

Soda(wasser) *neut.*

sodden ['sɒdn] *adj* durchnäßt.

sofa ['soufə] *n* Sofa *neut.*

soft [sɒft] *adj* weich; *(voice, etc.)* leise; *(gentle)* sanft, mild. **soften** *v* weich machen *or* werden; *(water)* enthärten. **soft-hearted** *adj* weichherzig. **software** *n* Software *f.*

soggy ['sɒgi] *adj* feucht.

soil[1] [sɔil] *n* Boden *m*, Erde *f.*

soil[2] [sɔil] *n (dirt)* Schmutz *m. v* beschmutzen.

solar ['soulə] *adj* Sonnen-.

sold [sould] *V* **sell**.

solder ['sɒldə] *v* löten. *n* Lot *neut.* **soldering iron** Lötkolben *m.*

soldier ['souldʒə] *n* Soldat *m.*

sole[1] [soul] *adj (only)* einzig, alleinig.

sole[2] [soul] *n (of shoe)* Sohle *f. v* besohlen.

sole[3] [soul] *n (fish)* Seezunge *f.*

solemn ['sɒləm] *adj* feierlich; *(person)* ernst. **solemnity** *n* Feierlichkeit *f.*

solicitor [sə'lisitə] *n (law)* Anwalt *m.*

solicitous [sə'lisitəs] *adj* fürsorglich; *(eager)* eifrig.

solid ['sɒlid] *adj (not liquid)* fest; *(pure)* massiv. **solidarity** *n* Solidarität *f.* **solidify** *v* fest werden.

solitary ['sɒlitəri] *adj (person)* einsam; *(single)* einzeln.

solitude ['sɒlitjuːd] *n* Einsamkeit *f.*

solo ['soulou] *n* Solo *neut. adj* Solo-, Allein-. *adv* allein. **soloist** *n* Solist(in).

solstice ['sɒlstis] *n* Sonnenwende *f.*

solve [sɒlv] *v* lösen. **soluble** *adj* löslich; *(problem)* lösbar. **solution** *n* Lösung *f.* **solvent** *n* Lösungsmittel *neut; adj (comm)* zahlungsfähig.

sombre ['sɒmbə] *adj* düster.

some [sʌm] *adj (several)* einige; *(a little)* etwas; *(some ... or other)* (irgend)ein; *(approx.)* ungefähr. **somebody** *or* **someone** *pron* jemand. **some day** eines Tages. **something** *pron* etwas. **sometime** *adv* irgendwann. **sometimes** *adv* manchmal. **somewhat** *adv* ziemlich. **somewhere** *adv* irgendwo(hin).

somersault ['sʌməsɔːlt] *n* Purzelbaum *m. v (person)* einen Purzelbaum schlagen; *(thing)* sich überschlagen.

son [sʌn] *n* Sohn *m.* **son-in-law** *n* Schwiegersohn *m.*

sonata [sə'nɑːtə] *n* Sonata *f.*

song [sɒŋ] *n* Lied *neut*, Gesang *m.* **songbird** *n* Singvogel *m.*

sonic ['sɒnik] *adj* Schall-. **sonic barrier** Schallgrenze *f.*

sonnet ['sɒnit] *n* Sonett *neut.*

soon [suːn] *adv* bald. **as soon as** sobald. **as soon as possible** so bald wie möglich. **sooner** *adv* früher.

soot [sut] *n* Ruß *m.* **sooty** *adj* rußig.

soothe [suːð] *v* beruhigen; *(pain)* lindern. **soothing** *adj* lindernd, besänftigend.

sophisticated [sə'fistikeitid] *adj (person)* kultiviert; *(machinery, etc.)* kompliziert, hochentwickelt. **sophistication** *n* Kultiviertheit *f.*

sopping ['sɒpiŋ] *adj* patschnaß.

soprano [sə'prɑːnou] *n* Sopranistin *f; (voice)* Sopran *m. adj* Sopran-.

sordid ['sɔːdid] *adj* schmutzig, gemein.

sore [sɔː] *adj* wund; *(inflamed)* entzündet; *(coll: annoyed)* verärgert. *n* Wunde *f.* **sorely** *adv* äußerst. **soreness** *n* Empfindlichkeit *f.*

sorrow ['sɒrou] *n* Kummer *m*, Leid *neut; (regret)* Reue *f.* **sorrowful** *adj* betrübt, traurig.

sorry ['sɒri] *adj* traurig, betrübt; *(sight, etc.)* jämmerlich, traurig. *interj* Verzeihung! **I am sorry** es tut mir leid. **I am/feel sorry for you** Sie tun mir leid.

sort [sɔːt] *n* Sorte *f*, Art *f; (brand)* Marke *f.* **all sorts of** allerlei. **a sort of** eine Art. **sort of (coll)** gewissermaßen. **that sort of thing** so etwas. *v* sortieren.

soufflé ['suːflei] *n* Auflauf *m.*

sought [sɔːt] *V* **seek**. **sought-after** *adj* gesucht.

soul [soul] *n* Seele *f.* **not a soul** kein Mensch. **soul-destroying** *adj* seelentötend. **soulful** *adj* seelenvoll. **soulless** *adj* seelenlos.

sound[1] [saund] *n* Schall *m; (noise)* Geräusch *neut*, Klang *m.* **soundproof** *adj* schalldicht. **sound wave** Schallwelle *f. v* klingen. **sound the alarm** den Alarm schlagen. **sound the horn** hupen. **soundless** *adj* geräuschlos.

sound[2] [saund] *adj (healthy)* gesund; *(safe)* sicher; *(reasoning)* stichhaltig.

sound[3] [saund] *v* loten, sondieren.

soup [suːp] *n* Suppe *f*, Brühe *f.*

sour [sauə] *adj* sauer.

source [sɔːs] n Quelle f.

south [sauθ] n Süden m. adj also **souther-ly, southern** südlich, Süd-. adv also **south-wards** nach Süden, südwärts. **South Africa** Südafrika neut. **South America** Südamerika neut. **south-east-n** Südosten. **South Pole** Südpol m. **southwest** n Südwesten m.

souvenir [suːvəˈnɪə] n Andenken neut.

sovereign [ˈsɔvrɪn] n Souverän m. adj souverän. **sovereignty** n Souveränität f.

Soviet Union [ˈsouvɪət] n Sowjetunion f.

***sow¹** [sou] v säen; (field) besäen. **sower** n Säer m.

sow² [sau] n Sau f.

sown [soun] V **sow¹**.

soya [ˈsɔɪə] n Sojabohne f.

spa [spaː] n Badekurort m.

space [speis] n Raum m; (gap) Zwischenraum m, Abstand m; (astron) Weltraum m. **space flight** Raumflug m. **spaceship** n Raumschiff neut. **space shut-tle** Raumfähre f. v (räumlich) einteilen. **spacious** adj geräumig.

spade¹ [speid] n Spaten m. **spadework** n (fig) Vorarbeit f.

spade² [speid] n (cards) Pik neut.

Spain [spein] n Spanien neut. **Spaniard** n Spanier(in). **Spanish** adj spanisch.

spam [spam] n (Internet) Spam m.

span [span] n (arch) Spannweite f; (time) Zeitspanne f.

spaniel [ˈspanjəl] n Spaniel m.

spank [spaŋk] v verhauen, prügeln.

spanner [ˈspanə] n Schraubenschlüssel m.

spare [speə] adj Ersatz-; (over) übrig; (thin) hager, dürr. **spare time** Freizeit f. **spare tyre** Ersatzreifen m. **spare rib** Rippenspeer m. v (pains, expense) scheuen; (give) übrig haben (für); (feelings, etc.) verschonen. **sparing** adj sparsam. n also **spare part** Ersatzteil m.

spark [spaːk] n Funke m. v funkeln. **spark** or **sparking plug** Zündkerze f.

sparkle [ˈspaːkl] v funkeln, glänzen. n Funkeln neut, Glanz m. **sparkler** n Wunderkerze f. **sparkling** adj funkelnd; (wine) schäumend.

sparrow [ˈsparou] n Spatz m, Sperling m.

sparse [spaːs] adj spärlich, dünn. **sparse-ness** n Spärlichkeit f.

spasm [ˈspazəm] n (med) Krampf m; (fig)

Anfall m. **spasmodic** adj (fig) sprunghaft.

spastic [ˈspastik] adj spastisch. n Spastiker(in).

spat [spat] V **spit¹**.

spate [speit] n **a spate of** eine Flut von.

spatial [ˈspeiʃl] adj räumlich.

spatula [ˈspatjələ] n Spachtel m.

spawn [spɔːn] n Laich m. v (eggs) ablegen; (fig) hervorbringen.

***speak** [spiːk] v sprechen, reden. **speak out** frei herausreden. **speak to** reden mit. **speak up** laut sprechen. **speak up for** sich einsetzen für. **speaker** n Redner m.

spear [spɪə] n Speer m. v aufspießen.

special [ˈspeʃəl] adj besonder, speziell; (train, case) Sonder-. **specialist** n Fachmann m. **speciality** n Spezialität f. **specialization** n Spezialisierung f. **special-ize** v spezialisieren. **specially** adv beson-ders.

species [ˈspiːʃiːz] n Art f; (biol) Spezies f.

specify [ˈspesifai] v spezifizieren, im einzeln angeben. **specific** adj spezifisch. **specifica-tions** n pl (tech) technische Daten pl.

specimen [ˈspesimin] n Muster neut, Probe f.

speck [spek] n Fleck m. **speckle** v flecken.

spectacle [ˈspektəkl] n Schauspiel neut. **spectacles** pl Brille f sing. **spectacular** adj sensationell.

spectator [spekˈteitə] n Zuschauer(in).

spectrum [ˈspektrəm] n Spektrum neut.

speculate [ˈspekjuleit] v nachdenken; (comm) spekulieren. **speculation** n Mutmaßung f, Annahme f; (comm) Spekulation f. **speculative** adj spekulativ. **speculator** n Spekulant m.

sped [sped] V **speed**.

speech [spiːtʃ] n Sprache f; (a talk) Rede f. **make a speech** eine Rede halten.

***speed** [spiːd] n Geschwindigkeit f, Tempo neut. v rasen, eilen; (exceed limit) (zu) schnell fahren. **speed up** beschleunigen. **speed limit** Geschwindigkeitsbegrenzung f. **speedboat** n Schnellboot neut. **speedometer** n Tachometer m. **speedy** adj schnell.

***spell¹** [spel] v (name the letters in) buch-stabieren; (signify) bedeuten. **how do you spell…?** wie schreibt man …? **spell out** (fig) deutlich erklären. **spelling** n Rechtschreibung f.

spell² [spel] n (magic) Zauber m, Zauberspruch m. **cast a spell on** bezaubern. **spellbound** adj fasziniert.

spell³ [spel] n (period) Periode f, Weile f.

spelt [spelt] V **spell¹**.

***spend** [spend] v (money) ausgeben; (time) verbringen. **spending money** Taschengeld neut. **spendthrift** n Verschwender(in); adj verschwenderisch.

spent [spent] V **spend**.

sperm [spə:m] n Sperma neut.

sperm whale n Pottwal m.

spew [spju:] v (vulg) sich erbrechen, kotzen. **spew out** ausspeien.

sphere [sfiə] n Kugel f; (fig) Bereich m. **spherical** adj kugelförmig.

spice [spais] n Gewürz neut. v würzen. **spiced** adj gewürzt. **spicy** adj pikant, scharf.

spider ['spaidə] n Spinne f. **spider's web** Spinngewebe neut. **spidery** adj spinnenartig.

spike [spaik] n Spitze f, Dorn m.

***spill** [spil] v verschütten; (blood) vergießen. n (coll) Sturz, Fall m.

spilt [spilt] V **spill**.

***spin** [spin] v (thread, web) spinnen; (turn) (herum)wirbeln, spinnen; (washing) schleudern. n (coll: in car, etc.) Spazierfahrt f. **spin doctor** (pol) Ideengeber(in), PR-Berater(in). **spin-dryer** n Wäscheschleuder f. **spin-off** n Nebenprodukt neut; (econ) Ausgliederung f. **spinning wheel** Spinnrad neut.

spinach ['spinitʒ] n Spinat m.

spindle ['spindl] n Spindel f. **spindly** adj spindeldürr.

spine [spain] n (thorn, etc.) Stachel m; (anat) Rückgrat neut, Wirbelsäule f. **spiny** adj stachelig.

spinster ['spinstə] n unverheiratete Frau f; (elderly) alte Jungfer f.

spiral ['spaiərəl] adj schraubenförmig, spiral. **spiral staircase** Wendeltreppe f. n Spirale f.

spire ['spaiə] n Turmspitze f.

spirit ['spirit] n Geist m. **spirits** pl (drinks) Spirituosen pl, Alkohol m. **high spirits** Frohsinn m, gehobene Stimmung f. **v spirit away** hinwegzaubern. **spirited** adj lebhaft. **spiritual** adj geistig, geistlich.

***spit¹** [spit] n (saliva) Spucke f, Speichel m.

v spucken.

spit² [spit] n (roasting) (Brat)Spieß m; (geog) Landzunge f.

spite [spait] n Boshaftigkeit f. **in spite of** trotz (+ gen). **spiteful** adj boshaft.

splash [splaʃ] v (be)spritzen. n Spritzen neut; (mark) Fleck m.

spleen [spli:n] n Milz f.

splendid ['splendid] adj prächtig, herrlich. **splendour** n Pracht f.

splice [splais] v (ropes) spleißen; (tapes, films) zusammenfügen.

splint [splint] n Schiene f. **splinter** n Splitter m. v zersplittern. **splinter group** Splittergruppe f.

***split** [split] v (zer)spalten, sich spalten. **split up** sich trennen. **split hairs** Haarspalterei treiben. **splitting headache** rasende Kopfschmerzen pl. n Spalt m, Riß m. adj gespalten.

splutter ['splʌtə] v stottern.

***spoil** [spɔil] v verderben; (child) verwöhnen. **spoils** pl n Beute f. **spoil-sport** n Spielverderber(in).

spoke¹ [spouk] V **speak**.

spoke² [spouk] n (wheel) Speiche f.

spoken ['spoukn] V **speak**.

spokesman ['spouksmən] n Sprecher m.

sponge [spʌndʒ] n Schwamm m. v **sponge down** (mit einem Schwamm) abwaschen. **sponge-cake** n Sandtorte f. **sponger** n (coll) Schmarotzer m. **spongy** adj schwammig.

sponsor ['sponsə] n Förderer m, Schirmherr m; (radio, TV) Sponsor m. v unterstützen, fördern. **sponsorship** n Schirmherrschaft f.

spontaneous [spon'teinjəs] adj spontan. **spontaneity** n Freiwilligkeit f, Spontaneität f.

spool [spu:l] n Spule f.

spoon [spu:n] n Löffel m. v **spoon out** auslöffeln. **spoon-feed** v verhätscheln. **spoonful** n Löffelvoll m.

sporadic [spə'radik] adj verstreut, sporadisch.

sport [spɔ:t] n Sport m; (fun) Spaß m. **play sports** Sport treiben. **sportscar** n Sportwagen m. **sportsman** n Sportler m. **sportswoman** n Sportlerin f. v scherzen; (wear) tragen. **sporting** adj sportlich.

spot [spot] n (mark) Fleck m; (place) Stelle f; (pimple) Pickel m. **spot check** Stichprobe f.

spotlight n Scheinwerfer m. **spotless** adj fleckenlos. v beflecken; (notice) entdecken, erspähen. **spotted** adj fleckig. **spotty** adj pickelig.

spouse [spaʊs] n Gatte m, Gattin f, Gemahl(in).

spout [spaʊt] n Tülle f, Schnauze f. v (coll) deklamieren.

sprain [spreɪn] n Verrenkung f. v verrenken.

sprang [spraŋ] V spring.

sprawl [sprɔːl] v (person) sich rekeln; (town) sich ausbreiten.

spray[1] [spreɪ] v (be)sprühen. n (aerosol, etc.) Sprühdose f, Spray m; (sea) Schaum m.

spray[2] [spreɪ] n (of flowers) Blütenzweig m.

***spread** [spred] v ausbreiten; (butter, etc.) streichen; (rumour) (sich) verbreiten. n Ausbreitung f; (extent) Umfang m, Spanne f; (for bread) Aufstrich m. **spreadsheet** n Arbeitsblatt neut, Tabelle f.

spree [spriː] n (shopping) Einkaufsbummel m.

sprig [sprig] n Schößling m.

sprightly ['spraɪtlɪ] adj lebhaft, munter.

***spring** [sprɪŋ] n (season) Frühling m; (tech) Feder f; (water) Brunnen m, Quelle f. **springboard** n Sprungbrett neut. v springen. **spring a leak** ein Leck bekommen. **springing** n Federung f. **springy** adj elastisch.

sprinkle ['sprɪŋkl] v sprenkeln. **sprinkler** n Brause f. **a sprinkling of** ein bißchen.

sprint [sprɪnt] n Sprint m. v sprinten. **sprinter** n Sprinter m.

sprout [spraʊt] v sprießen. n Sprößling m. **(Brussels) sprouts** Rosenkohl m sing.

spruce [spruːs] n (tree) Fichte f.

sprung [sprʌŋ] V spring.

spur [spəː] n Sporn m; (fig) Ansporn m. v (horse) die Sporen geben (+ dat); (fig) anspornen.

spurious ['spjʊərɪəs] adj falsch, unecht.

spurn [spəːn] v zurückweisen.

spurt [spəːt] v (water) hervorspritzen. n (sport) Spurt m.

spy [spaɪ] v (espy) erspähen; (pol) spionieren. n Spion(in). **spy-glass** n Fernglas neut. **spying** n Spionage f.

squabble ['skwobl] v sich zanken. n Kabbelei f, Zank m.

squad [skwod] n Gruppe f; (mil) Zug m;
(police) Kommando neut. **flying squad** Überfallkommando neut. **squad car** Streifenwagen m.

squadron ['skwodrən] n (naut) Geschwader neut; (aero) Staffel f. **squadron leader** Major m.

squalid [skwolid] adj schmutzig. **squalor** n Schmutz m.

squall [skwɔːl] n heftiger Windstoß m; (storm) Gewitter neut.

squander ['skwondə] v verschwenden, vergeuden.

square [skweə] n Quadrat neut, Viereck neut; (in town) Platz m. adj viereckig, quadratisch.

squash [skwoʃ] n (people) Gedränge neut; (game) Squash neut. v zerquetschen. **fruit squash** Fruchtsaft m.

squat [skwot] v hocken; (ein Haus) unberechtigt besetzen. adj gedrungen. **squatter** n Squatter m.

squawk [skwɔːk] n Kreischen neut. v kreischen.

squeak [skwiːk] v (wheel, etc.) quietschen; (mouse, etc.) piepsen. n Quietschen neut; Piepsen neut. **squeaky** adj quietschend.

squeal [skwiːl] v schreien, quieken; (criminal) pfeifen. n Schrei m, Quieken neut.

squeamish ['skwiːmɪʃ] adj überempfindlich. **squeamishness** n Überempfindlichkeit f.

squeeze [skwiːz] v drücken; (fruit) auspressen, ausquetschen. n Druck m. **credit squeeze** Kreditbeschränkung f. **squeezer** n Presse f.

squid [skwɪd] n Tintenfisch m.

squiggle ['skwɪgl] n Kritzelei f.

squint [skwɪnt] n Schielen neut. v schielen. **squint-eyed** adj schielend.

squire ['skwaɪə] n Junker m, Gutsherr m.

squirm [skwəːm] v sich winden.

squirrel ['skwɪrəl] n Eichhörnchen neut.

squirt [skwəːt] v spritzen. n Spritze f.

stab [stab] v (kill) erstechen. n Stich m. **stab wound** Stichwunde f. **make a stab at** versuchen.

stabilize ['steɪbɪlaɪz] v stabilisieren. **stability** n Stabilität f. **stabilization** n Stabilisierung f.

stable[1] ['steɪbl] n Stall m. v einstallen. **stable-lad/man** n Stallknecht m.

stable[2] ['steɪbl] adj stabil.

staccato [stə'kɑːtou] *adj, adv* staccato.

stack [stak] *n* Schober *m*; (*wood, etc.*) Stapel *m*. *v* aufschobern.

stadium ['steidɪəm] *n* Stadion *neut*.

staff [stɑːf] *n* (*stick*) Stock *m*; (*work force*) Personal *neut*; (*mil*) Stab *m*. *adj* Personal-; stabs-.

stag [stag] *n* Rothirsch *m*. **stag party** Herrengesellschaft *f*.

stage [steidʒ] *n* (*of development, etc.*) Stufe *f*, Stadium *neut*; (*theatre*) Bühne. **stage fright** Lampenfieber *neut*. **stage-manager** *n* Inspizient *m*. *v* (*play*) aufführen; (*fig*) veranstalten.

stagger ['stagə] *v* schwanken, taumeln; (*amaze*) verblüffen. **staggering** *adj* taumelnd; phantastisch.

stagnant ['stagnənt] *adj* stillstehend, stagnierend. **stagnate** *v* stagnieren. **stagnation** *n* Stagnation *f*.

staid [steid] *adj* gesetzt, seriös.

stain [stein] *adj* Fleck *m*; (*for wood, etc.*) Färbung *f*. *v* beflecken; fäben. **stainless** *adj* (*steel*) rostfrei.

stair [steə] *n* Treppenstufe *f*. (**flight of**) **stairs** Treppe *f*. **stair-carpet** *n* Treppenläufer *m*.

stake[1] [steik] *n* (*post*) Pfahl *m*, Pfosten *m*. **stake a claim** (**to**) Anspruch erheben (auf).

stake[2] [steik] *n* (*betting*) Einsatz *m*; (*share*) Anteil *m*. *v* (*money*) setzen. **put at stake** aufs Spiel setzen.

stale [steil] *adj* (*bread*) alt, altbacken; (*beer, etc.*) abgestanden; (*thing*) abgedroschen.

stalemate ['steilmeit] *n* (*chess*) Patt *neut*; (*fig*) Stillstand *m*. *v* pattsetzen.

stalk[1] [stɔːk] *n* (*bot*) Stiel *m*.

stalk[2] [stɔːk] *v* sich anpirschen an.

stall[1] [stɔːl] *n* (*stable*) Stand *m*; (*market*) Bude *f*. **stalls** *pl* (*theatre*) Parkett *neut sing*. *v* (*engine*) aussetzen; (*car*) stehenbleiben.

stall[2] [stɔːl] *v* (*delay*) ausweichen, Ausflüchte machen.

stallion ['staljən] *n* Hengst *m*.

stamina ['stam inə] *n* Durchhaltevermögen *neut*, Ausdauer *f*.

stammer ['stam ə] *v* stottern, stammeln. *n* Stottern *neut*, Gestammel *neut*. **stammerer** *n* Stotterer *m*. **stammering** *adj* stotternd.

stamp [stam p] *v* (*with foot*) stampfen; (*rubber stamp*) stempeln; (*letters*) frankieren. *n*

Stempel *m*; (*letter*) Briefmarke *f*. **stamp album** Briefmarkenalbum *neut*. **stamp collector** Briefmarkensammler *m*.

stampede [stam 'piːd] *n* wilde Flucht *f*.

*****stand** [stand] *n* (*sales, etc.*) Bude *f*, Stand *m*; (*attitude*) Standpunkt *m*; (*for spectators*) (Zuschauer)Tribüne *f*; (*resistance*) Widerstand *m*. *v* stehen. *I can't stand him* ich kann ihn nicht ausstehen. *I can't stand it* ich kann es nicht aushalten. **as things stand** unter den Umständen. *my offer stands* mein Angebot gilt noch. **stand aside** beiseite treten. **stand back** zurücktreten. **stand by** (*be loyal to*) treu bleiben (+*dat*). **stand for** (*mean*) bedeuten, stehen für; (*tolerate*) sich gefallen lassen; (*parliament*) kandidieren. **stand in for** einspringen für. **stand up** aufstehen. **stand up to** sich verteidigen gegen. **standby** *n* Stütze *f*; (*alert*) Alarmbereitschaft *f*. **standing** *n* Stand *m*, Rang *m*. **standing order** (*bank*) Dauerauftrag *m*. **stand-offish** *adj* hochmütig.

standard ['standəd] *n* Standard *m*, Norm *f*. (*flag*) Standarte *f*. *adj* Normal-; (*usual*) gewöhnlich, normal. **standardize** *v* normen, standardisieren. **standardization** *n* Normung *f*.

stank [staŋk] *V* stink.

stanza ['stanzə] *n* Strophe *f*, Stanza *f*.

staple[1] ['steipl] *n* Heftklammer *f*. *v* heften. **stapler** *n* Heftmaschine *f*.

staple[2] [steipl] *adj* Haupt-.

star [stɑː] *n* Stern *m*; (*films, etc.*) Star *m*. **starlight** *n* Sternenlicht *neut*. *v* die Hauptrolle spielen. **starring** in der Hauptrolle. **starry** *adj* (*sky*) Sternen-; (*night*) sternhell.

starboard ['stɑːbəd] *n* Steuerbord *neut*. *adj* Steuerbord-.

starch [stɑːtʃ] *n* (Wäsche)Stärke *f*. *v* stärken. **starched** *adj* gestärkt. **starchy** *adj* (*person*) steif, förmlich.

stare [steə] *n* starrer Blick *m*, Starrblick *m*. *v* starren. **stare at** anstarren.

stark [stɑːk] *adj* kahl, öde. *adv* **stark naked** splitternackt. **stark-staring mad** total verrückt.

starling ['stɑːlŋ] *n* Star *m*.

start [stɑːt] *v* anfangen, beginnen; (*leave*) abfahren; (*arise*) entstehen; (*sport*) starten (lassen); (*engine*) anlassen; (*jump*) hochschrecken. *n* Anfang *m*, Beginn *m*;

(*sport*) Start *m*; (*journey*) Abreise *f*. **from the start** vom Anfang an. **starter** *n* (*sport*) Start *m*. **starter motor** Anlaßmotor *m*.

startle ['sta:tl] *v* erschrecken, überraschen. **startling** *adj* erschreckend.

starve [sta:v] *v* verhungern. **starvation** *n* Hungern *neut*, Verhungern *neut*.

state [steit] *n* (*pol*) Staat *m*; (*condition*) Zustand *m*; (*situation*) Lage *f*. *v* erklären, behaupten. *adj* Staats-, staatlich. **stated** *adj* angegeben. **stateless** *adj* staatenlos. **stately** *adj* stattlich. **statement** *n* Erklärung *f*. **statement of account** Kontoauszug *m*. **statesman** *n* Staatsmann *m*. **statesmanship** *n* Staatskunst *f*.

static ['statik] *adj* statisch. *n* statische Elekrizität *f*.

station ['steiʃən] *n* Platz *m*, Posten *m*; (*rail*) Bahnhof *m*; (*standing*) Stand *m*. **station master** Bahnhofsvorsteher *m*. **station wagon** Kombi(wagen) *m*. *v* stationieren.

stationary ['steiʃənər] *adj* stillstehend, stationär.

stationer ['steiʃənə] *n* Schreibwarenhändler *m*. **stationery** *n* Schreibwaren *pl*; (*office*) Büromaterial *neut*.

statistics [stə'tistiks] *n* Statistik *f*. **statistical** *adj* statistisch.

statue ['statju:] *n* Standbild *neut*, Statue *f*.

stature ['statʃə] *n* Körpergröße *f*, Statur *f*; (*moral, etc.*) Kaliber *neut*.

status ['steiəs] *n* Status *m*; (*rank*) Stand *m*, Rang *m*. **status quo** Status quo *m*. **status symbol** Statussymbol *neut*.

statute ['statju:t] *n* Gesetz *neut*. **statutory** *adj* gesetzlich (vorgeschrieben).

staunch [stɔ:ntʃ] *adj* getreu, zuverlässig.

stay [stei] *v* bleiben; (*in hotel*) logieren, unterkommen; (*with friends, etc.*) zu Besuch sein (bei). **stay the night** übernachten. **stay behind** zurückbleiben. **stay in** zu Hause bleiben. *n* Aufenthalt *m*; Besuch *m*.

steadfast ['stedfa:st] *adj* fest, treu.

steady ['stedi] *adj* sicher, fest, stabil; (*regular*) regelmäßig, gleichmäßig; (*cautious*) vorsichtig. *v* festigen. **steady on!** langsam!, vorsichtig! **steadiness** *n* Festigkeit *f*, Sicherheit *f*.

steak [steik] *n* Steak *neut*.

***steal** [sti:l] *v* stehlen. **steal away** sich davonstehlen.

stealthy ['stelθi] *adj* heimlich. **stealth** *n*

Heimlichkeit *f*.

steam [sti:m] *n* Dampf *m*. *v* dampfen; (*food*) dünsten. **steam-boiler** *n* Dampfkessel *m*. **steamer** *n* (*naut*) Dampfer *m*, Dampfschiff *neut*; (*cookery*) Dampfkochtopf *m*. **steam-roller** *n* Dampfwalze *f*; *v* (*opposition*) niederwalzen. **steamy** *adj* dampfig.

steel [sti:l] *n* Stahl *m*. *adj* stählern, Stahl-. **steelworks** *pl n* Stahlwerk *neut sing*. **steely** hart.

steep[1] [sti:p] *adj* steil, jäh; (*coll: improbable*) unwahrscheinlich; (*prices*) gepfeffert.

steep[2] [sti:p] *v* (*soak*) einweichen.

steeple ['sti:pl] *n* Kirchturm *m*, Spitzturm *m*.

steeplechase ['sti:plʧeis] *n* Steeplechase *f*. **steeplejack** *n* Turmarbeiter *m*.

steer [stiə] *v* steuern, lenken. **steering column** Lenksäule *f*. **steering lock** Lenkradschloß *m*. **steering wheel** Lenkrad *neut*, Steuer *neut*.

stem[1] [stem] *n* (*stalk*) Stiel *m*; (*line of descent*) Stamm *m*. *v* **stem from** stammen von, zurückgehen auf.

stem[2] [stem] *v* eindämmen; (*blood*) stillen.

stench [stentʃ] *n* Gestank *m*.

stencil ['stensl] *n* Schablone *f*. *v* schablonieren.

step [step] *v* treten, schreiten. *n* Schritt *m*; (*measure*) Maßnahme *f*; (*stage, gradation*) Stufe *f*. **step by step** Schritt für Schritt. **step on it** (*coll*) Gas geben. **step aside** zur seite treten. **step-ladder** *n* Trittleiter *f*. **stepping-stone** *n* Trittstein *m*; (*fig*) Sprungbrett *neut*.

stepbrother ['stepbrʌðə] *n* Stiefbruder *m*.

stepdaughter ['stepdɔ:tə] *n* Stieftochter *f*.

stepfather ['stepfa:ðə] *n* Stiefvater *m*.

stepmother ['stepmʌðə] *n* Stiefmutter *f*.

stepsister ['stepsistə] *n* Stiefschwester *f*.

stepson ['stepsʌn] *n* Stiefsohn *m*.

stereo ['steriou] *n* Stereoanlage *f*. *adj* Stereo-. **stereophonic** *adj* stereophonisch.

stereotyped ['steriətaipt] *adj* stereotyp.

sterile ['sterail] *adj* steril. **sterility** *n* Sterilität *f*.

sterling ['stə:liŋ] *n* Sterling *m*.

stern[1] [stə:n] *adj* streng, hart. **sternness** *n* Strenge *f*, Härte *f*.

stern[2] [stə:n] *n* (*naut*) Heck *neut*.

stethoscope ['steθəskoup] *n* Stethoskop *neut*.

stew [stjuː] *n* Eintopfgericht *neut*. *v* schmoren. **stewed** *adj* geschmort.

steward [stjuəd] *n* (*ship, aeroplane*) Steward *m*; (*race, etc.*) Ordner *m*. **stewardess** *n* Stewardeß *f*.

stick¹ [stik] *n* (*wood*) Stock *m*; (*hockey*) Schläger *m*.

***stick²** [stik] *v* (*with glue, etc.*) kleben *or* heften (an); (*pointed instrument*) stecken; **sticker** (*badge*) *n* Aufkleber *m*. **stick out** (*tongue*) herausstrecken; (*protrude*) hervorstehen. **stick to** (*remain with*) bleiben bei. **stick up for** sich einsetzen für. **be stuck** steckenbleiben. **stuck-up** *adj* hochnäsig. **sticking plaster** Heftpflaster *neut*. **sticky** *adj* klebrig.

stiff [stif] *adj* steif, starr; (*drink*) stark; (*difficult*) schwierig. *n* (*coll*) Leiche *f*. **stiffen** *v* (ver)steifen, (ver)stärken. **stiffnecked** *adj* halsstarrig. **stiffness** *n* Steife *f*, Starrheit *f*.

stifle [ˈstaifl] *v* ersticken. **stifling** *adj* zum Ersticken.

stigma [ˈstigmə] *n* Brandmal *neut*, Stigma *neut*.

stile [stail] *n* Zauntritt *m*.

still¹ [stil] *adj* (immer)noch. *conj* und doch, dennoch. *v* beruhigen. **still birth** Totgeburt *f*. **stillborn** *adj* totgeboren. **stillness** *n* Stille *f*.

still² [stil] *n* (*for spirits*) Brennerei *f*.

stilt [stilt] *n* Stelze *f*. **stilted** *adj* gespreizt.

stimulus [ˈstimjuləs] *n* (*pl* -i) Stimulus *m*. **stimulant** *n* Reizmittel *neut*. **stimulate** *v* anregen. **stimulating** *adj* anregend. **stimulation** *n* Anreiz *m*.

***sting** [stiŋ] *v* (*insect*) stechen; (*be painful*) brennen; (*remark*) kränken. *n* Stich *m*. **stinging** *adj* brennend; schmerzend. **stinging nettle** Brennessel *f*.

stingy [ˈstindʒi] *adj* geizig.

***stink** [stiŋk] *v* stinken, übel riechen. *n* Gestank *m*; (*coll: scandal*) Skandal *m*.

stint [stint] *v* knausern mit. *n* (*of work*) Schicht *f*.

stipulate [ˈstipjuleit] *v* festsetzen; (*insist on*) bestehen auf. **stipulation** Bedingung *f*.

stir [stəː] *v* (*liquids*) (an)rühren; (*move*) sich rühren *or* bewegen; (*excite*) aufrühren, bewegen. *n* Rühren *neut*; (*sensation*) Sensation *f*. **stirring** *adj* aufregend.

stirrup [ˈstirəp] *n* Steigbügel *m*.

stitch [stitʃ] *n* Stich *m*; (*knitting*) Masche *f*; (*pain*) Stechen *m*. *v* nähen. **stitch up** vernähen. **stitching** *n* Näherei *f*.

stoat [stout] *n* Hermelin *neut*.

stock [stok] *n* (*of goods*) Vorrat *m*, Lager *neut*; (*cookery*) Brühe; (*descent*) Stamm *m*. **stocks** *pl* (*comm*) Aktien *pl*. **stockbroker** *n* Börsenmakler *m*. **stock exchange** Börse *f*. **stockpile** *v* aufstapeln. **stock-still** *adj* bewegungslos. **stocktaking** *n* Bestandaufnahme *f*. *v* (*goods*) führen, vorrätig haben.

stocking [ˈstokiŋ] *n* Strumpf *m*.

stocky [ˈstoki] *adj* stämmig, untersetzt.

stodge [stodʒ] *n* schwerverdauliches Zeug *neut*. **stodgy** *adj* schwer(verdaulich).

stoical [ˈstouik] *adj* stoisch.

stoke [stouk] *v* schüren. **stoker** *n* Heizer *m*.

stole¹ [stoul] *V* **steal**.

stole² [stoul] *n* Stola *f*.

stolen [ˈstoulən] *V* **steal**.

stomach [ˈstʌmək] *n* Magen *m*; (*coll: abdomen*) Bauch *m*; (*taste for*) Appetit (zu) *f*. *v* ertragen. **stomach-ache** *n* Magenschmerzen *pl*.

stone [stoun] *n* Stein *m*; (*fruit*) Kern *m*. *adj* steinern, Stein-. *v* (*fruit*) entkernen; (*to death*) steinigen. **stone age** Steinzeit *f*. **stoned** *adj* (*coll*) besoffen. **stone-deaf** *adj* stocktaub. **stonemason** *n* Steinmetz *m*. **stony** *adj* steinig.

stood [stud] *V* **stand**.

stool [stuːl] *n* Hocker *m*, Stuhl *m*; (*med*) Stuhlgang *m*.

stoop [stuːp] *v* sich bücken; (*posture*) gebeugt gehen. *n* Beugen *neut*, krumme Haltung *f*.

stop [stop] *v* (*activity*) aufhören; (*motion*) anhalten, stoppen; (*clock*) stehenbleiben; (*put a stop to*) einstellen; (*bus, train*) anhalten; (*pipe, etc.*) verstopfen. *n* Halt *m*, Stillstand *m*; (*break*) Pause *f*; (*bus*) Haltestelle *f*. **stopover** *n* (*aero*) Zwischenlandung *f*. **stop-watch** *n* Stoppuhr *f*. **stoppage** *n* Stillstand *m*. **stopper** *n* Stöpsel *m*.

store [stoː] *v* aufbewahren. *n* Vorrat *m*, Lager *neut*; (*shop*) Laden *m*. **storecard** *n* Kaufhauskarte *f*. **storekeeper** *n* (*shop*) Ladenbesitzer *m*. **storage** *n* Lagerung *f*.

storey [ˈstoːri] *n* Stockwerk *neut*. **four-storied** *adj* vierstöckig.

stork [stoːk] *n* Storch *m*.

storm [stoːm] *n* Sturm *m*, Unwetter *neut*;

(*thunderstorm*) Gewitter *neut*. **stormtossed** *adj* sturmgepeitscht. *v* stürmen. **storm-troops** Sturmtruppen *pl*. **stormy** *adj* stürmisch.

story ['stɔːrɪ] *n* Geschichte f, Erzählung f. **to cut a long story short** um es ganz kurz zu sagen. **story-book** *n* Märchenbuch *neut*. **story-teller** *n* Erzähler(in).

stout [staut] *adj* dick, beleibt; (*strong*) kräftig. *n* dunkles Bier *neut*, Malzbier *neut*.

stove [stouv] *n* Ofen *m*; (*cooking*) Kochherd *m*. **stove-pipe** Ofenrohr *neut*.

stow [stou] *v* verstauen. **stowaway** blinder Passagier *m*.

straddle ['stradl] *v* (*sitting*) rittlings sitzen auf.

straggle ['stragl] *v* umherstreifen. **straggle behind** nachhinken. **straggler** *n* Nachzügler *m*.

straight [streɪt] *adj* gerade; (*hair*) glatt; (*candid*) offen, freimütig. *adv* gerade, direkt. **get straight** (*clarify*) klarstellen. **think straight** logisch denken. **straight on** *or* **ahead** gerade aus. **straightaway** *adv* sofort. **straighten** *v* gerademachen. **straighten out** (*put in order*) in Ordnung bringen. **straightforward** *adj* (*thing*) einfach, schlicht; (*person*) offen, aufrichtig. *n* (*sport*) Gerade f.

strain¹ [streɪn] *v* spannen; (*muscle*) zerren; (*tech*) verzerren; (*filter*) sieben, filtern. **strain oneself** sich (über)anstrengen. *n* Überanstrengung f; (*emotional*) Streß *m*, Anspannung f; (*med*) Zerrung f. **strained** *adj* (*relations, etc.*) gespannt.

strain² [streɪn] *n* (*race*) Abstammung f, Rasse f.

straits [streɪts] *pl n* Straße f, Meerenge f. **dire straits** Notlage f. **strait-jacket** *n* Zwangsjacke f.

strand¹ [strand] *n* (*rope*) Strang *m*; (*hair*) Strähne f; (*thought*) Faden *m*.

strand² [strand] *n* (*shore*) Strand *m*, Ufer *neut*. *v* stranden. **stranded** *adj* gestrandet.

strange [streɪndʒ] *adj* (*odd*) seltsam, sonderbar; (*alien*) fremd. **strangeness** *n* Seltsamkeit f; Fremdartigkeit f. **stranger** *n* Fremde(r). **be a stranger to** nicht vertraut sein mit. **strangely** *adv* seltsamerweise.

strangle ['straŋgl] *v* erwürgen, erdrosseln. **stranglehold** *n* Würgegriff *m*.

strap [strap] *n* Riemen *m*; (*dress*) Träger *m*. *v* festschnallen. **strapless** *adj* trägerlos.

strapping *adj* stramm.

strategy ['stratədʒɪ] *n* Strategie f. **strategic** *adj* strategisch.

stratum ['strɑːtəm] *n* (*pl* -a) Schicht f.

straw [strɔː] *n* Stroh *neut*; (*single*) Strohhalm *m*; (*drinking*) Trinkhalm *m*. *adj* Stroh-. **straw hat** Strohhut *m*.

strawberry ['strɔːbərɪ] *n* Erdbeere f.

stray [streɪ] *v* sich verirren; (*from path, etc.*) abgehen (von); (*attention*) wandern. *adj* verirrt. *n* verirrtes Tier *neut*.

streak [striːk] *n* Streifen *neut*; (*in character*) Einschlag *m*. **streak of lightning** Blitzstrahl *m*. *v* streifen; (*race, fly*) rasen, sausen. **streaked** *adj* gestreift.

stream [striːm] *n* Bach *m*; (*current*) Strom *m*, Strömung f. *v* strömen. **streamer** *n* (*party*) Papierschlange f. **streamline** *v* (*fig*) rationalisieren. **streamlined** *adj* windschnittig.

street [striːt] *n* Straße f. **streetcar** *n* Straßenbahn f. **street lamp** Straßenlaterne f. **street-walker** *n* Straßendirne f.

strength [streŋθ] *n* Stärke f, Kraft f, Kräfte *pl*; (*liquids*) Stärke f; (*mil*) Macht f, Schlagkraft f. **strengthen** *v* (ver)stärken. **strengthening** *n* Verstärkung f.

strenuous ['strenjuəs] *adj* anstrengend.

stress [stres] *n* (*emphasis*) Nachdruck *m*; (*psychological*) Streß *m*; (*pronunciation*) Akzent *m*. *v* betonen. **stressful** *adj* belastend.

stretch [stretʃ] *v*. (aus)strecken, ausdehnen; (*person*) sich strecken; (*e.g. land, town*) sich erstrecken. *n* (*time*) Zeitspanne f; (*place*) Strecke f. **stretcher** *n* Tragbahre f. **stretchy** *adj* dehnbar.

stricken ['strɪkən] *adj* (*sickness*) befallen (von); (*emotion*) ergriffen (von).

strict [strɪkt] *adj* streng. **strictness** *n* Strenge f.

stridden ['strɪdn] *V* **stride**.

*****stride** [straɪd] *v* schreiten. *n* Schritt *m*. **make great strides** Fortschritte machen. **get into one's stride** in Schwung kommen.

strident ['straɪdənt] *adj* grell.

strife [straɪf] *n* Kampf *m*.

*****strike** [straɪk] *v* schlagen; (*target*) treffen; (*workers*) streiken; (*match*) entzünden. **it strikes me** es fällt mir ein. **strike off** streichen von. *n* Schlag *m*, Stoß *m*; (*labour*)

Streik *m*. **striking** *adj* auffallend.

*string [strɪŋ] *n* Schnur *f*, Bindfaden *m*; (*instrument*) Saite *f*. **strings** *pl* (*mus*) Streicher *pl*. *v* (*instrument*) besaiten. **string together** verknüpfen. **stringed instrument** Streichinstrument *neut*.

stringent ['strɪndʒənt] *adj* streng. **stringency** *n* Strenge *f*.

strip¹ [strɪp] *v* abziehen; (*clothes*) ausziehen.

strip² [strɪp] *n* (*narrow piece*) (schmaler) Streifen *m*.

stripe [straɪp] *n* Streifen *m*, Strich *m*. *v* streifen. **striped** *adj* gestreift.

*strive [straɪv] *v* (*for*) streben (nach); (*to do*) sich anstrengen (zu).

striven ['strɪvn] *V* **strive**.

strode [stroud] *V* **stride**.

stroke¹ [strouk] *n* (*blow*) Schlag *m*; (*pen*) Strich *m*; (*med*) Schlaganfall *m*.

stroke² [strouk] *v* streicheln.

stroll [stroul] *v* schlendern. *n* Bummel *m*, Spaziergang *m*.

strong [strɒŋ] *adj* (*person, thing*) stark; (*person*) kräftig; (*flavour, etc.*) scharf. **be going strong** wohlauf sein. **strong-room** *n* Tresor *m*. **strong-willed** *adj* willensstark. **strongly** *adv* kräftig.

strove [strouv] *V* **strive**.

struck [strʌk] *V* **strike**.

structure ['strʌktʃə] *n* Struktur *f*. **structural** *adj* strukturell.

struggle ['strʌgl] *v* kämpfen, ringen. *n* Kampf *m*.

strum [strʌm] *v* klimpern (auf).

strung [strʌŋ] *V* **string**.

strut¹ [strʌt] *v* (herum)stolzieren. **strutting** *adj* prahlerisch.

strut² [strʌt] *n* Stütze *f*, Spreize *f*.

stub [stʌb] *n* Stumpf *m*; (*cheque*) Kontrollabschnitt *m*, Talon *m*; (*cigarette*) (Zigaretten)Stummel *m*. *v* **stub out** ausdrücken.

stubble ['stʌbl] *n* Stoppel *f*; (*beard*) Stoppeln *pl*. **stubbly** *adj* stoppelig.

stubborn ['stʌbən] *adj* hartnäckig, eigensinnig. **stubbornness** *n* Hartnäckigkeit *f*.

stuck [stʌk] *V* **stick²**.

stud¹ [stʌd] *n* Beschlagnagel *m*; (*button*) Knopf *m*.

stud² [stʌd] *n* (*farm*) Gestüt *neut*; (*horse*)

Zuchthengst *m*.

student ['stjuːdənt] *n* Student(in); (*at school, also fig*) Schüler(in).

studio ['stjuːdiou] *n* Studio *neut*.

study ['stʌdɪ] *n* Studium *neut*; (*piece of research, etc.*) Studie *f*, Untersuchung *f*; (*room*) Studierzimmer *neut*. *v* studieren.

stuff [stʌf] *n* Stoff *m*; (*coll*) Zeug *neut*, Kram *m*. *v* vollstopfen; (*taxidermy*) ausstopfen; (*cookery*) füllen. **stuffing** *n* Füllung *f*.

stuffy ['stʌfɪ] *adj* (*air*) dumpf, schwül; (*thing*) langweilig; (*person*) pedantisch; (*nose*) verstopft.

stumble [stʌmbl] *v* stolpern. **stumbling block** *n* Hindernis *neut*.

stump [stʌmp] *n* Stumpf *m*. *v* (*coll*) verblüffen. **stumpy** *adj* stumpfartig.

stun [stʌn] *v* betäuben; (*fig*) bestürzen. **stunning** *adj* (*coll*) phantastisch.

stung [stʌŋ] *V* **sting**.

stunk [stʌŋk] *V* **stink**.

stunt¹ [stʌnt] *v* (*growth*) hindern, hemmen. **stunted** *adj* verkümmert.

stunt² [stʌnt] *n* (*feat*) Kunststück *neut*.

stupid ['stjuːpɪd] *adj* dumm, blöd. **stupidity** *n* Dummheit *f*.

stupor ['stjuːpə] *n* Erstarrung *f*; (*dullness*) Stumpfsinn *m*.

sturdy ['stəːdɪ] *adj* robust, kräftig.

sturgeon ['stəːdʒən] *n* Stör *m*.

stutter ['stʌtə] *n* Stottern *neut*. *v* stottern. **stutterer** *n* Stotterer *m*.

sty [staɪ] *n* Schweinestall *m*.

style [staɪl] *n* Stil *m*. *v* (*name*) benennen; (*shape*) formen. **latest style** neueste Mode *f*. **hairstyle** *n* Frisur *f*. **stylish** *adj* elegant.

stylus ['staɪləs] *n* Griffel *m*; (*record-player*) Nadel *f*.

suave [swaːv] *adj* weltmännisch, zuvorkommend.

subconscious [sʌb'kɒnʃəs] *adj* unterbewußt. *n* das Unterbewußte *neut*.

subcontract [sʌbkən'trækt] *n* Nebenvertrag *m*. **subcontractor** *n* Unterkontrahent *m*.

subdue [səb'djuː] *v* unterwerfen. **subdued** *adj* (*person*) zurückhaltend; (*lights*) gedämpft.

subject ['sʌbdʒɪkt; *v* səb'dʒekt] *n* (*school, etc.*) Fach *neut*; (*theme*) Thema *neut*, Gegenstand *m*; (*gramm*) Subjekt *neut*; (*citizen*) Staatsangehörige(r). *adj* (*to ruler*) untertan (+*dat*); (*liable*) geneigt (zu); (*exposed*) ausgesetzt (+*dat*). *v* unterwerfen; (*expose*) aussetzen (+*dat*). **subjection** *n* Unterwerfung *f*. **subjective** *adj* subjektiv.

subjunctive [səb'dʒʌŋktiv] *n* Konjunktiv *m*.

*sublet [sʌb'let] *n* untervermieten.

sublime [sə'blaɪm] *adj* sublim, erhaben.

submarine ['sʌbm əriːn] *n* Unterseeboot (U-Boot) *neut*. *adj* Untersee-.

submerge [səb'm əːdʒ] *v* (ein)tauchen. **submerged** *adj* untergetaucht.

submit [səb'm ɪt] *v* sich unterwerfen; (*maintain*) behaupten; (*hand in*) einreichen, vorlegen. **submission** *n* Unterwerfung *f*; (*documents*) Vorlage *f*. **submissive** *adj* gehorsam.

subnormal [sʌb'nɔːm əl] *adj* (*child, etc.*) minderbegabt.

subordinate [sə'bɔːdinət] *v* unterordnen. *adj* untergeordnet. *n* Untergebene(r).

subscribe [səb'skraɪb] *v* (*money*) zeichnen. **subscribe to** (*newspaper*) abonnieren auf; (*view, etc.*) billigen. **subscriber** *n* Abonnent(in); (*phone*) Teilnehmer(in). **subscription** *n* Abonnement *neut*.

subsequent ['sʌbsɪkw ənt] *adj* (nach)folgend. **subsequently** *adv* nachher, hinterher.

subservient [səb'sə:vɪənt] *adj* unterwürfig. **subservience** *n* Unterwürfigkeit *f*.

subside [səb'saɪd] *v* (*noise, etc.*) nachlassen, abnehmen; (*sink*) sich senken. **subsidence** *n* (Boden)Senkung *f*.

subsidiary [səb'sɪdɪərɪ] *adj* Hilfs-, Neben-. *n* (*company*) Tochtergesellschaft.

subsidize ['sʌbsɪdaɪz] *v* subventionieren. **subsidy** *n* Subvention *f*.

subsist [səb'sɪst] *v* existieren. **subsist on** sich ernähren von. **subsistence** *n* Existenz *f*.

substance ['sʌbstəns] *n* Substanz *f*, Stoff *m*; (*of argument, etc.*) Gehalt *neut*, Kern *m*. **substantial** *adj* beträchtlich. **substantiate** *v* begründen.

substitute ['sʌbstɪtjuːt] *n* Ersatz *m*; (*sport*) Ersatzspieler(in). *adj* Ersatz-. *v* ersetzen. **substitution** *n* Einsetzung *f*.

subtitle ['sʌbtaɪtl] *n* Untertitel *m*.

subtle ['sʌtl] *adj* fein, subtil. **subtlety** *n* Feinheit *f*.

subtract [səb'trakt] *v* abziehen. **subtraction** *n* Abziehen *neut*; (*thing subtracted*) Abzug *m*.

suburb ['sʌbə:b] *n* Vorort *m*. **suburban** *adj* Vororts-; (*coll: provincial*) kleinstädtisch.

subvert [səb'vəːt] *v* (*government*) stürzen; (*morals*) untergraben. **subversion** *n* Sturz *m*; Untergrabung *f*. **subversive** *adj* umstürzlerisch.

subway ['sʌbweɪ] *n* (*in UK*) Fußgängerunterführung *f*; (*in US*) U-Bahn *f*.

succeed [sək'siːd] *v* (*follow*) folgen auf, nachfolgen (+*dat*); (**be successful**) Erfolg haben, erfolgreich sein; gelingen (*impers*). *I succeeded in doing it* es gelang mir, es zu tun. **success** *n* Erfolg *m*. **successful** *adj* erfolgreich. **succession** *n* Reihenfolge *f*, Folge *f*. **successive** *adj* (aufeinander)folgend. **successor** *n* Nachfolger(in).

succinct [sək'sɪŋkt] *adj* kurz(gefaßt).

succulent ['sʌkjulənt] *adj* saftig. *n* (*bot*) Sukkulente *f*. **succulence** *n* Saftigkeit *f*.

succumb [sə'kʌm] *v* nachgeben (+*dat*).

such [sʌtʃ] *adj* solch, derartig. *such a big house* ein so großes Haus. **no such thing** nichts dergleichen. **such as** wie zum Beispiel. **as such** an sich. **such is life** so ist das Leben.

suck [sʌk] *v* saugen; (*sweet, thumb*) lutschen. **sucker** *n* (*coll*) Gimpel *m*; (*bot*) Wurzelschößling *m*. **sucking pig** *n* Spanferkel *neut*. **suckle** *v* stillen. **suckling** *n* Säugling *m*.

suction ['sʌkʃən] *v* Saugwirkung *f*, Sog *m*.

sudden ['sʌdən] *adj* plötzlich. **suddenness** *n* Plözlichkeit *f*.

suds [sʌdz] *n* Seifenlauge *f*.

sue [suː] *v* verklagen (auf).

suede [sweɪd] *n* Wildleder *neut*.

suet ['suːɪt] *n* Nierenfett *neut*, Talg *m*.

suffer ['sʌfə] *v* leiden (an). **sufferer** *n* Leidende(r). **suffering** *n* Leiden *neut*; *adj* leidend (an).

sufficient [sə'fɪʃənt] *adj* genügend, ausreichend.

suffocate ['sʌfəkeɪt] *v* ersticken. **suffocating** *adj* erstickend. **suffocation** *n* Ersticken *neut*.

sugar ['ʃugə] *n* Zucker *m*. *v* zuckern; süßen. **sugar cane** *n* Zuckerrohr *neut*. **sugared** *adj* gezuckert. **sugary** *adj* süßlich; (*fig*) zuckersüß.

suggest [sə'dʒest] *v* vorschlagen; (*maintain*) behaupten; (*indicate*) hindeuten auf. **suggestion** n Vorschlag m; (trace) Spur f. **suggestive** adj anzüglich, zweideutig. **be suggestive of** deuten auf.

suicide ['suːɪsaɪd] n Selbstmord m. **suicidal** adj selbstmörderisch.

suit [suːt] n (man's) Anzug m; (woman's) Kostüm neut; (cards) Farbe f; (law) Klage f. **follow suit** dasselbe tun. **suitcase** n Handkoffer m. v (an)passen; (clothes) (gut) stehen (+dat); (food) bekommen (+dat). **suitable** adj geeignet, passend.

suite [swiːt] n (furniture) Garnitur f; (rooms) Zimmerflucht f.

sulk [sʌlk] v schmollen, trotzen. **sulky** adj mürrisch, schmollend.

sullen ['sʌlən] adj mürrisch.

sulphur ['sʌlfə] n Schwefel m. **sulphurous** adj schwefelig; (fig) hitzig.

sultan ['sʌltən] n Sultan m.

sultana [sʌltaːnə] n (dried fruit) Sultanine f.

sultry ['sʌltri] adj schwül. **sultriness** n Schwüle f.

sum [sʌm] n Summe f; (money) Betrag m; (calculation) Rechenaufgabe f. v **sum up** zusammenfassen.

summarize ['sʌməraiz] v zusammenfassen. **summary** n Zusammenfassung f.

summer ['sʌmə] n Sommer m. adj sommerlich, Sommer-. **summerhouse** n Gartenhaus neut. **summery** adj sommerlich.

summit ['sʌmit] n Gipfel m. **summit conference** Gipfelkonferenz f.

summon ['sʌmən] v aufrufen, kommen lassen; (meeting) einberufen; (courage) fassen. **summons** n Berufung f; (law) (Vor)Ladung f. **take out a summons against** vorladen lassen.

sump [sʌmp] n Ölwanne f.

sumptuous ['sʌmptʃuəs] adj prächtig, kostspielig.

sun [sʌn] n Sonne f. v **sun oneself** sich sonnen.

sunbathe ['sʌnbeið] v ein Sonnenbad nehmen, sich sonnen.

sunbeam ['sʌnbiːm] n Sonnenstrahl m.

sunburn ['sʌnbəːn] n Sonnenbrand m. **sunburnt** adj sonnenverbrannt.

sundae ['sʌndei] n Eisbecher m.

Sunday ['sʌndi] n Sonntag m. **Sunday best** Sonntagskleider pl.

sundial ['sʌndaiəl] n Sonnenuhr f.

sundry ['sʌndri] pl adj verschiedene, diverse. **sundries** pl n Verschiedenes neut sing.

sunflower ['sʌn,flauə] n Sonnenblume f.

sung [sʌŋ] V sing.

sun-glasses pl n Sonnenbrille f sing.

sunk [sʌŋk] V sink.

sunlight ['sʌnlait] n Sonnenlicht neut.

sunny ['sʌni] adj sonnig.

sunrise ['sʌnraiz] n Sonnenaufgang m.

sunroof ['sʌnruːf] n (auto) Schiebedach neut.

sunset ['sʌnset] n Sonnenuntergang m.

sunshine ['sʌnʃain] n Sonnenschein m.

sunstroke ['sʌnstrouk] n Sonnenstich m.

sun-tan n (Sonnen)Bräune f.

super ['suːpə] adj (coll) prima.

superannuation [,suːpərænjuˈeiʃən] n (contribution) Altersversicherungsbeitrag m; (pension) Pension f. **superannuated** adj pensioniert.

superb [suːˈpəːb] adj herrlich, prächtig.

supercilious [,suːpəˈsiliəs] adj herablassend, hochmütig.

superficial [,suːpəˈfiʃəl] adj oberflächlich.

superfluous [suːˈpəːfluəs] adj überflüssig.

superhuman [,suːpəˈhjuːmən] adj übermenschlich.

superimpose [,suːpərimˈpouz] v legen (auf); (add) hinzufügen (zu). **superimposed** adj darübergelegt.

superintendent [,suːpərinˈtendənt] n Inspektor m, Vorsteher m.

superior [suːˈpiəriə] adj überlegen; (higher) höherliegend; (quality) hervorragend, erlesen. n Überlegene(r). **mother superior** Oberin f. **superiority** n Überlegenheit f.

superlative [suːˈpəːlətiv] adj unübertrefflich, hervorragend. n Superlativ m.

supermarket [,suːpəmˈaːkit] n Supermarkt m.

supernatural [,suːpəˈnatʃərə] adj übernatürlich. n das Übernatürliche neut.

supersede [,suːpəˈstid] v ersetzen.

supersize [,suːpəˈsaiz] n übergroße Portion f.

supersonic [,suːpəˈsonik] adj Überschall-.

superstition [suːpəˈstiʃən] n Aberglaube m. **superstitious** adj abergläubig.

supervise ['suːpəvaiz] v beaufsichtigen, kontrollieren. **supervision** n

Beaufsichtigung f, Kontrolle f. **supervisor** n Aufseher m, Kontrolleur m. **supervisory** adj Aufsichts-.

supper ['sʌpə] n Abendessen neut.

supple ['sʌpl] adj geschmeidig, biegsam. **suppleness** n Geschmeidigkeit f.

supplement ['sʌpləmənt] n Ergänzung f; (newspaper) Beilage f. **supplementary** adj ergänzend, Zusatz-.

supply [sə'plai] v liefern, versorgen; (a need) decken. n Lieferung f. (stock) Vorrat m; (water, electricity, etc.) Versorgung f. **supply and demand** Angebot und Nachfrage. **supplies** pl n Zufuhren pl. **supplier** n Lieferant m.

support [sə'pɔːt] v tragen, stützen; (withstand) ertragen; (family) unterhalten; (cause) befürworten. n (tech) Stütze f; Unterstützung f. **supporter** n Anhänger m.

suppose [sə'pouz] v annehmen, sich vorstellen; (believe, think) meinen. **supposed** adj angenommen. **be supposed to** sollen. **supposition** n Vermutung f, Annahme f.

suppository [sə'pozitəri] n (Darm-) Zäpfchen neut.

suppress [sə'pres] v unterdrücken; (truth) verheimlichen. **suppression** n Unterdrückung f; Verheimlichung f.

supreme [su'priːm] adj oberst, höchst. **supremacy** n Obergewalt neut.

surcharge ['səːtʃɑːdʒ] n Zuschlag m.

sure [ʃuə] adj sicher, gewiß. adv (coll) sicherlich. **for sure** gewiß. **make sure** sich vergewissern. **you can be sure** du kannst dich darauf verlassen. **sure-fire** adj todsicher. **surely** adv sicherlich. **sureness** n Sicherheit f. **surety** n Bürge f.

surf [səːf] n Brandung f. v wellenreiten; (Internet) surfen. **surfboard** n Wellenreiterbrett neut. **surfer** n Wellenreiter(in); (Internet) Surfer(in).

surface ['səːfis] n Oberfläche f. adj oberflächlich. v auftauchen. **surface mail** gewöhnliche Post f.

surfeit ['səːfit] n Übermaß neut. v übersättigen.

surge [səːdʒ] n (water) Woge f; (emotion) Aufwallung f. v (waves) branden; (crowd) (vorwärts)drängen.

surgeon ['səːdʒən] n Chirurg m. **surgery** n Chirurgie f; (consulting room) Sprechzimmer neut. **surgical** adj chirurgisch.

surly ['səːli] adj verdrießlich, mürrisch. **surliness** n Verdrießlichkeit f.

surmount [sə'maunt] v überwinden. **surmountable** adj überwindlich.

surname ['səːneim] n Familienname m, Zuname m.

surpass [sə'pɑːs] v übertreffen. **surpass oneself** sich selbst übertreffen.

surplus ['səːpləs] n Überschuß m. adj überschüssig.

surprise [sə'praiz] v überraschen. n Überraschung f. adj unerwartet. **surprised** adj überrascht. **surprising** adj erstaunlich.

surrealism [sə'riːlizəm] n Surrealismus m. **surrealist** n Surrealist(in). **surrealistic** adj surrealistisch.

surrender [sə'rendə] v sichergeben, kapitulieren; (office) aufgeben; (prisoner) ausliefern. n Kapitulation f; Auslieferung f.

surreptitious [ˌsʌrəp'tiʃəs] adj erschlichen; (stealthy) heimlich.

surround [sə'raund] v umgeben, umringen. n Einfassung f. **surrounding** adj umgebend. **surroundings** pl n Umgebung f.

surveillance [səːˈveiləns] n Überwachung f.

survey ['səːvei; v sə'vei] n Überblick m; (land, house, etc.) Vermessung f; (questionnaire) Umfrage f. v überblicken; vermessen. **surveyor** n Landmesser m.

survive [sə'vaiv] v (outlive) überleben; (continue to exist) weiterleben, weiterbestehen. **survival** n Überleben neut. **survivor** n Überlebende(r).

susceptible [sə'septəbl] adj anfällig, empfänglich (für). **susceptibility** n Anfälligkeit f, Empfänglichkeit f.

suspect [sə'spekt; n 'sʌspekt] v verdächtigen; (believe) vermuten. n Verdachtsperson f. adj verdächtig.

suspend [sə'spend] v aufhängen; (person) suspendieren; (regulation) (zeitweilig) aufheben. **suspended** adj ausgesetzt, verschoben. **suspender** n Strumpfhalter m. **suspenders** pl (for trousers) Hosenträger pl. **suspense** n Spannung f. **suspension** n (mot) Federung f; (person) Suspension f. **suspension bridge** Hängebrücke f. **suspension railway** Schwebebahn f.

suspicion [sə'spiʃən] n Verdacht m; (mistrust) Mißtrauen neut; (trace) Spur f. **suspicious** adj mißtrauisch; (behaviour) verdächtig. **suspiciousness** n

Mißtrauen *neut.*

sustain [sə'steɪn] *v* (*suffer*) erleiden; (*family*) ernähren. **sustained** *adj* anhaltend. **sustenance** *n* Ernährung *f.*

suture ['suːtʃə] *n* Naht *f. v* vernähen.

swab [swɒb] *n* (*med*) Abstrich *m.*

swagger ['swægə] *v* (herum)stolzieren. **swaggering** *adj* stolzierend.

swallow[1] ['swɒbu] *v* schlucken. *n* Schluck *m.*

swallow[2] ['swɒbu] *v* (*bird*) Schwalbe *f.*

swam [swæm] *V* swim.

swamp [swɒmp] *n* Sumpf *m*, Moor *neut. v* überschwemmen. **swampy** *adj* sumpfig.

swan [swɒn] *n* Schwan *m.*

swank [swæŋk] *v* protzen, prahlen. **swanky** *adj* protzig.

swap [swɒp] *v* (aus)tauschen. *n* Tausch *m.*

swarm [swɔːm] *n* Schwarm *m. v* schwärmen.

swarthy ['swɔːðɪ] *adj* dunkelhäutig, schwärzlich.

swat [swɒt] *v* zerquetschen.

sway [sweɪ] *v* schwanken, schaukeln. *n* Schwanken *neut;* (*power*) Macht *f*, Einfluß *m.*

*****swear** [sweə] *v* schwören; (*bad language*) fluchen. **swearword** *n* Fluch *m*, Fluchwort *neut.*

sweat [swet] *n* Schweiß *m. v* schwitzen. **sweater** *n* Pullover *m.* **sweaty** *adj* verschwitzt.

swede [swɪd] *n* Kohlrübe *f.*

Sweden ['swɪdn] *n* Schweden *neut.* **Swede** *n* Schwede *m*, Schwedin *f.* **Swedish** *adj* schwedisch.

*****sweep** [swɪp] *v* kehren, fegen; (*mines*) suchen. **sweep aside** beiseite schieben, abtun. **sweepstake** *n* Toto *neut. n* Schornsteinfeger *m.* **make a clean sweep** reinen Tisch machen. **sweeper** *n* Kehrer *m.* **sweeping** *adj* radikal, weitreichend. **sweepings** *pl* Kehricht *m sing.*

sweet [swɪt] *adj* süß; (*kind*) nett. **sweetcorn** Mais *m.* **sweeten** *v* süßen. **sweetener** *n* Süßstoff *m;* (*fig: bribe*) Anreiz *m*, Schmiergeld *neut.* **sweetheart** *n* Schatz *m.* **sweet-tempered** *adj* gutmütig. *n* Bonbon *m;* (*dessert*) Nachspeise *f.* **sweetshop** *n* Süßwarengeschäft *neut.* **sweetness** *n* Süßigkeit *f;* (*person*) Lieblichkeit *f.*

*****swell** [swel] *v* (auf)schwellen. *n* (*sea*) Wellengang *m. adj* (*coll*) prima. **swelling** *n* (*med*) Schwellung *f.*

swelter ['sweltə] *v* vor Hitze kochen. **sweltering** *adj* schwül.

swept [swept] *V* sweep.

swerve [swɜːv] *v* ausscheren.

swift [swɪft] *n* (*zool*) Segler *m. adj* schnell, rasch. **swift-footed** *adj* schnellfüßig. **swiftness** *n* Schnelligkeit *f.*

swill [swɪl] *n* Schweinefutter *neut. v* spülen.

*****swim** [swɪm] *v* schwimmen. **my head is swimming** mir ist schwindlig. *n* Schwimmen *neut*, Bad *neut.* **in the swim** auf dem laufenden. **swimmer** *n* Schwimmer(in). **swimming** *n* Schwimmen *neut.* **swimming pool** Schwimmbad *neut.*

swindle ['swɪndl] *v* betrügen. *n* Schwindel *m*, Betrug *m.* **swindler** *n* Schwindler(in).

swine [swaɪn] *n* (*pl* swine) Schwein *neut.*

*****swing** [swɪŋ] *v* schwingen. *n* (*child's*) Schaukel *f.* **swing a door open/shut** eine Tür auf/zustoßen.

swipe [swaɪp] *v* hauen; (*coll: steal*) klauen. *n* Hieb *m.*

swirl [swɜːl] *v* wirbeln. *n* Wirbel *m.*

swish [swɪʃ] *v* rascheln. *n* Rascheln *neut.*

Swiss [swɪs] *n* Schweizer(in). *adj* schweizerisch. **Swiss German** Schweizerdeutsch *neut.*

switch [swɪtʃ] *n* Schalter *m;* (*change*) Wechsel *m;* (*whip*) Rute *f.* **on/off-switch** *n* Ein/Ausschalter *m. v* (*change*) wechseln. **switchboard** *n* (*phone*) Vermittlung *f.* **switch on** einschalten. **switch off** ausschalten. **switch over to** übergehen zu.

Switzerland ['swɪtsələnd] *n* die Schweiz *f.*

swivel ['swɪvl] *v* (sich) drehen.

swollen ['swəulən] *V* swell. *adj* geschwollen. **swollen-headed** *adj* eingebildet, aufgeblasen.

swoop [swuːp] *v* niederschießen, sich stürzen (auf).

swop [swɒp] *V* swap.

sword [sɔːd] *n* Schwert *neut.* **swordfish** *n* Schwertfisch *m.* **swordsman** *n* Fechter *m.*

swore [swɔː] *V* swear.

sworn [swɔːn] *V* swear. *adj* vereidigt; (*enemy*) geschworen.

swot [swɒt] *v* (*coll*) büffeln, pauken. *n* Büffler *m.*

swum [swʌm] *V* swim.

swung [swʌŋ] *V* swing.

sycamore [ˈsɪkəmɔː] n Sykamore f.
syllable [ˈsɪləbl] n Silbe f.
syllabus [ˈsɪləbəs] n Lehrplan m.
symbol [ˈsɪmbl] n Sinnbild neut, Symbol neut. **symbolic** adj sinnbildlich, symbolisch (für). **symbolism** n Symbolik f. **symbolize** v symbolisieren.
symmetry [ˈsɪmɪtri] n Symmetrie f. **symmetrical** adj symmetrisch.
sympathy [ˈsɪmpəθi] n Mitleid neut, Mitgefühl neut. **sympathetic** adj mitleidend.
symphony [ˈsɪmfəni] n Sinfonie f. **symphonic** adj sinfonisch.
symposium [sɪmˈpouzɪəm] n Symposion neut.
symptom [ˈsɪmptəm] n Symptom neut. **symptomatic** adj symptomatisch.
synagogue [ˈsɪnəgog] n Synagoge f.
synchromesh [ˈsɪŋkroumeʃ] n Synchrongetriebe neut.
synchronize [ˈsɪŋkrənaɪz] v synchronisieren.
syndicate [ˈsɪndɪkɪt] n Syndikat neut. **syndication** n Syndikatsbildung f.
syndrome [ˈsɪndroum] n (med) Syndrom neut.
synonym [ˈsɪnənɪm] n Synonym neut. **synonymous** adj synonym.
synopsis [sɪˈnopsis] n (pl -ses) Synopse f, Zusammenfassung f. **synoptic** adj synoptisch.
syntax [ˈsɪntaks] n Syntax f. **syntactic** adj syntaktisch.
synthesis [ˈsɪnθisis] n (pl -ses) Synthese f. **synthetic** adj synthetisch, Kunst-.
syphilis [ˈsɪfɪlɪs] n Syphilis f.
syringe [sɪˈrɪndʒ] n Spritze f.
syrup [ˈsɪrəp] n Sirup m, Zuckersaft m. **syrupy** adj sirupartig.
system [ˈsɪstəm] n System neut; (geol) Formation f. **systems analyst** n (comp) Systemberater(in). **systematic** adj systematisch.

T

tab [tab] n (in garment) Aufhänger m; (label)

Etikett neut; (coll: bill) Rechnung f.
table [ˈteɪbl] n Tisch m; (math, etc.) Tabelle f. **table of contents** Inhaltsverzeichnis neut. **table-cloth** n Tischtuch neut. **table-spoon** n Eßlöffel m.
table d'hôte [taːblˈdout] n Table d'hôte f.
tablet [ˈtablɪt] n Tablette f; (stone) Tafel f.
taboo [təˈbuː] adj tabu. n Tabu neut.
tacit [ˈtasɪt] adj stillschweigend. **taciturn** adj schweigsam.
tack [tak] n Reißnagel m; (naut) Lavieren neut; (sewing) Heftstich m; v lavieren; heften. **tacky** adj klebrig.
tackle [ˈtakl] n (naut) Takel neut; (equipment, etc.) Zeug neut, Ausrüstung f. v (sport) angreifen; (person) angehen; (problem) anpacken.
tact [takt] n Takt m. **tactful** adj taktvoll. **tactless** adj taktlos.
tactics [ˈtaktiks] pl n Taktik f. **tactical** adj taktisch.
tadpole [ˈtadpoul] n Kaulquappe f.
taffeta [ˈtafɪtə] n Taft m.
tag [tag] n (loop) Anhänger m, (label) Etikett neut. **price-tag** Preiszettel m.
tail [teɪl] n Schwanz m. v (coll: follow) beschatten. **tailback** n (traffic) Stau m. **tail end** Schluß m. **tailcoat** n Frack m. **tail-lamp** n Schlußlicht neut.
tailor [ˈteɪlə] n Schneider m. v schneidern. **tailor-made** adj nach Maß angefertigt.
taint [teɪnt] n Fleck m, Makel m. v verderben.
***take** [teɪk] v nehmen; (something somewhere) bringen; (prisoner) fassen; (photo, exam) machen. how long does it take? wie lange dauert es? wie lange braucht man? **take aback** verblüffen. **take along** mitnehmen. **take away** wegnehmen; (subtract) abziehen. **takeaway** n (shop) Imbißstube f; (food) Essen (neut) zum Mitnehmen. **take back** (retract) zurücknehmen. **take down** (on paper) aufschreiben. **take off** (clothes) ausziehen; (mimic) nachäffen. **take over** übernehmen. **take up** aufnehmen.
taken [ˈteɪkn] V take.
talcum powder [ˈtalkəm] n Talkumpuder m.
tale [teɪl] n Erzählung f. **old wives' tale** Ammenmärchen neut.
talent [ˈtalənt] n Talent neut, Begabung f.

talented *adj* begabt.

talk [tɔːk] *n* Rede *neut*; (*conversation*) Gespräch *neut*; (*chat*) Unterhaltung *f*; (*lecture*) Vortrag *m*. *v* reden, sprechen. **talk over** besprechen. **talkative** *adj* geschwätzig.

tall [tɔːl] *adj* groß, hoch. **tallness** *n* Größe, Höhe *f*. **tall story** unglaubliche Geschichte *f*.

tally [ˈtalɪ] *v* (*coll*) übereinstimmen (mit), entsprechen (+ *dat*).

talon [ˈtalən] *n* Klaue *f*.

tambourine [tam bəˈriːn] *n* Tamburin *neut*.

tame [teɪm] *adj* zahm, gezähmt. *v* zähmen.

tamper [ˈtam pə] *v* herumpfuschen (an), sich einmischen (in).

tampon [ˈtam pon] *n* Tampon *m*.

tan [tan] *v* gerben; (*skin*) sich bräunen. *n* (*colour*) Gelbbraun *neut*; (*skin*) Sonnenbräunung *f*.

tandem [ˈtandəm] *n* Tandem *neut*.

tangent [ˈtandʒənt] *n* Tangente *f*.

tangerine [tandʒəˈriːn] *n* Mandarine *f*.

tangible [ˈtandʒəbl] *adj* greifbar.

tangle [ˈtaŋgl] *n* Gewirr *neut*. *v* verwickeln.

tank [taŋk] *n* Tank *m*, Behälter *m*; (*mil*) Panzer *m*. **tanker** *n* (*ship*) Tanker *m*.

tankard [ˈtaŋkəd] *n* Krug *m*.

tantalize [ˈtantəlaɪz] *v* quälen.

tantamount [ˈtantəm aunt] *adj* **be tantamount to** gleichkommen (+ *dat*).

tantrum [ˈtantrəm] *n* Wutanfall *m*.

tap¹ [tap] *v* leicht schlagen, klopfen. *n* leichter Schlag *m*. **tap-dance** *n* Steptanz *m*.

tap² [tap] *n* Hahn *m*. *v* anzapfen. **taproom** *n* Schankstube *f*.

tape [teɪp] *n* Band *neut*, Streifen *m*; (*recording*) Tonband *neut*; (*sport*) Zielband *m*. *v* heften. **adhesive tape** Klebestreifen. **tape measure** *n* Metermaß *m*. **tape-recorder** *n* Tonbandgerät *neut*. **tape-recording** *n* Bandaufnahme *f*.

taper [ˈteɪpə] *n* (dünne) Wachskerze *f*. *v* spitz zulaufen. **tapered** *adj* spitz (zulaufend).

tapestry [ˈtapəstrɪ] *n* Wandteppich *m*.

tapioca [tapɪˈoukə] *n* Tapioka *f*.

tar [taː] *n* Teer *m*.

tarantula [təˈrantjulə] *n* Tarantel *f*.

target [ˈtaːgɪt] *n* (*sport*) Zielscheibe *f*; (*ambition*) Ziel *neut*.

tariff [ˈtarɪf] *n* (*imports*) Zolltarif *m*; (*price list*) Preisverzeichnis *neut*.

tarmac® [ˈtaːm ak] *n* Asphalt *m*; (*runway*) Rollbahn *f*.

tarnish [ˈtaːnɪʃ] *v* (*metal*) anlaufen; (*reputation*) beflecken.

tarpaulin [taːˈpoːlɪn] *n* Persenning *f*.

tarragon [ˈtarəgən] *n* Estragon *m*.

tart¹ [taːt] *n* Torte *f*; (*prostitute*) Dirne *f*, Nutte *f*.

tart² [taːt] *adj* sauer, herb.

tartan [ˈtaːtən] *n* Tartan *m*, Schottenmuster *neut*.

tartar [ˈtaːtə] *n* Weinstein *m*; (*teeth*) Zahnstein *m*.

task [taːsk] *n* Aufgabe *f*. **take to task** zur Rede stellen.

tassel [ˈtasl] *n* Quaste *f*.

taste [teɪst] *n* Geschmack *neut*; (*sample*) Kostprobe *f*; (*liking*) Neigung *f*. *v* schmecken. **tasteful** *adj* geschmackvoll. **tasteless** *adj* geschmacklos. **tasty** *adj* schmackhaft.

tattered [ˈtatəd] *adj* zerrissen.

tattoo [təˈtuː] *n* Tätowierung *f*. *v* tätowieren.

taught [tɔːt] *V* **teach**.

taunt [tɔːnt] *v* sticheln, verspotten. *n* Stichelei *f*.

Taurus [ˈtɔːrəs] *n* Stier *m*.

taut [tɔːt] *adj* stramm, straff.

tavern [ˈtavən] *n* Taverne *f*, Kneipe *f*.

tax [taks] *n* Steuer *f*. **tax disc** (Kfz-)Steuerplakette *f*. **tax-free** *adj* steuerfrei. **taxpayer** *n* Steuerzahler(in). **tax return** Steuererklärung *f*. *v* besteuern; (*test*) anstrengen. **taxable** *adj* steuerpflichtig.

taxi [ˈtaksɪ] *n* Taxi *neut*. **taxi-driver** *n* Taxifahrer *m*.

tea [tiː] *n* Tee *m*; (*meal*) Abendbrot *neut*. **tea-cloth** *n* Geschirrtuch *neut*. **teacup** *n* Teetasse *f*. **teapot** *n* Teekanne *f*. **teaspoon** *n* Teelöffel *m*.

*****teach** [tiːtʃ] *v* lehren; (*animals*) dressieren. **teacher** *n* Lehrer(in). **teaching** *n* Unterricht *m*. **teachings** *pl* Lehre *f sing*.

teak [tiːk] *n* Teakholz *neut*.

team [tiːm] *n* (*sport*) Mannschaft *f*; (*horses*) Gespann *neut*. *v* **team up** sich zusammentun (mit). **teamwork** *n* Zusammenarbeit *f*.

*****tear¹** [teə] *v* reißen, zerreißen. *n* Riß *m*.

tear away wegreißen. **tear oneself away** sich losreißen.

tear² [tɪə] n Träne f. **tear gas** n Tränengas neut. **tearful** adj weinerlich.

tease [tiːz] v necken.

teat [tiːt] n (bottle) Sauger m; (anat) Brustwarze f; (zool) Zitze f.

technical ['teknikəl] adj technisch. **technician** n Techniker m. **technique** n Technik f. **technological** adj technologisch. **technology** n Technologie f.

tedious ['tiːdiəs] adj langweilig. **tedium** n Langeweile f.

tee [tiː] n (golf) Abschlagstelle f.

teem [tiːm] v wimmeln (von).

teenage ['tiːneidʒ] adj Jugend-. **teenager** n Teenager m.

teeth [tiːθ] V **tooth.**

teethe [tiːð] v zahnen. **teething troubles** (fig) Kinderkrankheiten pl.

teetotal [tiː'toutl] adj abstinent. **teetotaller** n Abstinenzler(in).

telecommunications [ˌtelikəmjuːniˈkeiʃənz] pl n Fernmeldewesen neut sing.

telegram ['teligram] n Telegramm neut. **by telegram** telegraphisch.

telegraph ['teligraːf] n Telegraph m. v telegraphieren. **telegraphic** adj telegraphisch.

telepathy [təˈlepəθi] n Telepathie f, Gedankenübertragung f. **telepathic** adj telepathisch.

telephone ['telifoun] n Fernsprecher m, Telefon neut. v anrufen, telefonieren. **by telephone** telefonisch. **telephone booth** Telefonzelle f. **telephone call** Telefongespräch neut, Anruf m. **telephone directory** Telefonbuch neut. **telephone exchange** (Telefon)Zentrale f. **telephonist** n Telefonist(in).

telescope ['teliskoup] n Fernrohr neut, Teleskop neut. **telescopic** adj teleskopisch.

television ['teliviʒən] n Fernsehen neut. **televize** v (im Fernsehen) übertragen. **on television** im Fernsehen.

telex ['teleks] n Fernschreiber m, Telex neut. v (durch Telex) übertragen.

*****tell** [tel] v sagen; (story) erzählen; (recognize) erkennen. **telltale** n Klatschblase f. **tell the truth** die Wahrheit sagen. **teller** n Kassierer m. **telling** adj wirkungsvoll.

temper ['tempə] n Wut f, Zorn m; (mood) Laune f. **lose one's temper** in Wut geraten. v mildern; (steel) härten. **temperament** n Temperament neut. **temperamental** adj temperamentvoll. **temperance** n Mäßigkeit f. **temperate** adj maßvoll; (climate) gemäßigt. **tempered** adj gehärtet.

temperature ['temprətʃə] n Temperatur f. **have a temperature** Fieber haben. **take (a person's) temperature** die Temperatur messen (+ dat).

tempestuous [tem'pestjuəs] adj stürmisch.

temple¹ ['templ] n (arch) Tempel m.

temple² ['templ] n (anat) Schläfe f.

tempo ['tempou] n Tempo neut.

temporary ['tempərəri] adj provisorisch, vorläufig.

tempt [tempt] v verlocken. **temptation** n Verlockung f. **tempting** adj verlockend; (food) appetitanregend.

ten [ten] adj zehn. n Zehn f. **tenth** adj zehnt; n Zehntel neut.

tenable ['tenəbl] adj haltbar.

tenacious [təˈneiʃəs] adj zäh. **tenacity** n Zähigkeit f.

tenant ['tenənt] n Mieter m. **tenancy** n Mietverhältnis neut.

tend¹ [tend] v (be inclined) neigen (zu), eine Tendenz haben (zu).

tend² [tend] v (care for) bedienen, sich kümmern um.

tendency ['tendənsi] n Tendenz f.

tender¹ ['tendə] adj zart; (affectionate) zärtlich. **tender-hearted** adj weichherzig. **tenderloin** n Filet neut. **tenderness** n Zartheit f; Zärtlichkeit f.

tender² ['tendə] v anbieten; (comm) ein Angebot machen. n Angebot neut.

tendon ['tendən] n Sehne f.

tendril ['tendril] n Ranke f.

tenement ['tenəmənt] n Mietshaus neut.

tennis ['tenis] n Tennis neut. **tennis ball** Tennisball m. **tennis court** Tennisplatz m. **tennis racket** (Tennis)Schläger m.

tenor ['tenə] n Tenor m. adj Tenor-.

tense¹ [tens] adj gespannt. v (sich) straffen. **tensile** adj dehnbar. **tension** n Spannung f.

tense² [tens] n (gramm) Zeitform f, Tempus neut.

tent [tent] n Zelt neut.

tentacle ['tentək] *n* Tentakel *m*, Fühler *m*; (*octupus*) Fangarm *m*.

tentative ['tentətɪv] *adj* versuchend, Versuchs-; (*temporary*) vorläufig. **tentatively** *adv* versuchsweise.

tenterhooks ['tentəhuks] *n* be on tenterhooks wie auf heißen Kohlen sitzen.

tenuous ['tenjuəs] *adj* dünn; (*argument*) schwach.

tepid ['tepɪd] *adj* lauwarm. **tepidness** *n* Lauheit *f*.

term [təːm] *n* (*expression*) Ausdruck *m*; (*period of time*) Frist *f*; (*academic, two per year*) Semester *neut*; (*academic, three per year*) Trimester *neut*. **end of term** (*school*) Schulschluß *m*. **terms** *pl* Bedingungen *pl*. **be on good terms with** gut auskommen mit. **come to terms with** sich abfinden mit.

terminal ['təːm inəl] *adj* End-, Schluß-; (*med*) unheilbar. *n* Terminal *neut*; (*comp*) Datenstation *f*.

terminate ['təːm ineit] *v* beenden; (*contract*) kündigen. **termination** *n* Ende *neut*, Schluß *m*.

terminology [təːm inɔlədʒi] *n* Terminologie *f*.

terminus ['təːm inəs] *n* Endstation *f*.

terrace ['terəs] *n* Terrasse *f*; (*houses*) Häuserreihe *f*.

terrain [tə'rein] *n* Terrain *neut*, Gelände *neut*.

terrestrial [tə'restrəl] *adj* irdisch.

terrible ['terəbl] *adj* schrecklich, furchtbar. **terribleness** *n* Schrecklichkeit *f*, Fürchterlichkeit *f*.

terrier ['teriə] *n* Terrier *m*.

terrify ['terifai] *v* erschrecken. **terrific** *adj* (*coll*) klasse, unwahrscheinlich. **terrified** *adj* erschrocken. **be terrified of** sich fürchten vor.

territory ['teritəri] *n* Gebiet *neut*, Territorium *neut*; (*pol*) Staatsgebiet *neut*. **territorial waters** Hoheitsgewässer *pl*.

terror ['terə] *n* Schrecken *m*, Entsetzen *neut*; (*pol*) Terror *m*. **terrorism** *n* Terrorismus *m*. **terrorist** *n* Terrorist(in); *adj* terroristisch.

test [test] *n* Versuch *m*, Probe *f*; (*examination*) Prüfung *f*. *v* prüfen, erproben. **test-case** *n* Präzedensfall *m*.

testament ['testəm ənt] *n* Testament *neut*.

testicle ['testikl] *n* Hoden *m*.

testify ['testifai] *v* bezeugen.

testimony ['testim əni] *n* Zeugnis *neut*. **testimonial** *n* Zeugnis *neut*, Empfehlungsschreiben *m*.

tetanus ['tetənəs] *n* Wundstarrkrampf *m*, Tetanus *m*.

tether ['teðə] *n* Haltestrick *m*. **be at the end of one's tether** mit seiner Geduld am Ende sein. *v* anbinden.

text [tekst] *n* Text *m*. *v* eine SMS schicken; (*coll*) simsen. **textbook** *n* Lehrbuch *neut*. **text message** SMS-Nachricht *f*. **textual** *adj* textlich.

textile ['tekstail] *n* Gewebe *neut*, Faserstoff *m*. **textiles** *pl* Textilien *pl*.

texture ['tekstjuə] *n* Textur *f*.

than [ðən] *conj* als.

thank [θaŋk] *v* danken (+*dat*), sich bedanken bei. **thanks** *pl n* Dank *m sing*. *interj* danke! **thankful** *adj* dankbar. **thankless** *adj* undankbar. **thank you!** danke! **many thanks!** dankeschön! **thank goodness!** Gott sei Dank!

that [ðat] *adj* der, die, das; jener, jene, jenes. *pron* das; (*who, which*) der, die, das, welch. **that is** (i.e.) das heißt (d.h.). **that's it!** so ist es! **like that** so. **that which** das, was. *the man that I saw* der Mann, den ich sah. **in order that** damit. *conj* daß. *adv* (*coll*) so, dermaßen.

thatch [θatʃ] *n* Dachstroh *neut*. **thatched roof** Strohdach *neut*.

thaw [θɔː] *v* tauen. *n* Tauwetter *neut*.

the [ðə] *art* der, die, das *sing*; die *pl*.

theatre ['θiətə] *n* Theater *neut*; (*operating*) Operationssaal *m*. **theatre-goer** *n* Theaterbesucher(in). **theatrical** *adj* theatralisch.

theft [θeft] *n* Diebstahl *m*.

their [ðeə] *poss adj* ihr, ihre, ihr. **theirs** *pron* der/die/das ihrige. *a friend of theirs* ein Freund von ihnen.

them [ðem] *pron* (*acc*) sie; (*dat*) ihnen.

theme [θiːm] *n* Thema *neut*. **theme park** Themenpark *m*.

then [ðen] *adv* (*at that time*) damals; (*next*) dann, darauf. *conj* also. *adj* damalig.

theology [θi'ɔlədʒi] *n* Theologie *f*. **theologian** *n* Theologe *m*. **theological** *adj* theologisch.

theorem ['θiərəm] *n* Theorem *m*.

theory ['θɪəri] n Theorie f. **theoretical** adj theoretisch. **theorist** n Theoretiker(in). **theorize** v theoretisieren.

therapy ['θerəpɪ] n Therapie f, Behandlung f. **therapeutic** adj therapeutisch. **therapist** n Therapeut(in).

there [ðeə] adv dort, da; (to that place) dahin, dorthin. **here and there** hier und da. **over there** da drüben. **thereabouts** adv so ungefähr. **thereafter** adv danach. **there and back** hin und zurück. **there are** es sind, es gibt. **there is** es ist, es gibt. **up there** da oben. interj na!

thermal ['θə:məl] adj thermal, Wärme-, Thermo-. n (aero) Thermik f.

thermodynamics [θə:moudai'namiks] n Thermodynamik f.

thermometer [θə'mɒmitə] n Thermometer neut.

thermonuclear [θə:mou'njukliə] adj thermonuklear.

Thermos® ['θə:məs] n Thermosflasche f.

thermostat ['θə:məstat] n Thermostat m.

thesaurus [θɪsɔː:rəs] n Thesaurus m.

these [ðiːz] pl adj, pron diese. **one of these days** eines Tages. **these are** dies sind.

thesis ['θiːsis] n (pl -ses) These f, Satz m; (university) Dissertation f.

they [ðeɪ] pl pron sie. **they say** man sagt.

thick [θɪk] adj dick; (hair, woods) dicht; (coll: stupid) dumm. **thicken** v dick machen or werden, (sich) verdicken; (cookery) legieren. **thickness** n Dicke f, Stärke f. **thick-skinned** adj (fig) dickfellig.

thief [θiːf] n (pl thieves) Dieb(in). **thieve** v stehlen. **thievish** adj diebisch.

thigh [θai] n (Ober)Schenkel m. **thighbone** n Schenkelknochen m.

thimble [θimbl] n Fingerhut m.

thin [θin] adj dünn; (person) mager; (weak) schwach. v dünn machen or werden; (cookery) verdünnen. **thinner** n Verdünner m. **thinness** n Dünne f, Magerkeit f. **thinskinned** adj empfindlich.

thing [θiŋ] n Ding neut. **things** pl Sachen pl, Zeug neut sing. **how are things?** wie geht es?

***think** [θiŋk] v denken; (hold opinion) denken, meinen. **think about** denken an; (consider) überlegen, nachdenken über. **think of** (doing) daran denken, vorhaben. **what do you think of it?** was halten sie

davon? I think so ich glaube schon. **think-tank** n Denkfabrik f, Beraterstab m. **thinker** n Denker(in). **thinking** n (opinion) Meinung f.

third [θə:d] adj dritt. n Drittel neut. **third party** Dritte(r). **third-party insurance** Haftpflichtversicherung f. **third-rate** adj (coll) minderwertig.

thirst [θə:st] n Durst (nach) m. **die of thirst** verdursten. v dursten. **thirsty** adj durstig. **be thirsty** Durst haben.

thirteen [θə:'tiːn] adj dreizehn. n Dreizehn f. **thirteenth** adj dreizehnt.

thirty ['θə:ti] adj dreißig. n Dreißig f. **thirtieth** adj dreißigst.

this [ðis] adj (pl these) dieser, diese, dieses. pron dies, das. **like this** so, folgendermaßen. **this morning** heute früh. **this year** dieses Jahr.

thistle ['θisl] n Distel f.

thong [θɒŋ] n (underwear) Tanga m, Stringtanga m.

thorn [θɔ:n] n Dorn m. **thorny** adj dornig.

thorough ['θʌrə] adj gründlich; (person) genau, sorgfältig. **thoroughbred** n Vollblut neut. adj Vollblut-. **thoroughfare** n Durchgangsstraße f. **thoroughness** n Gründlichkeit f.

those [ðouz] pl adj, pron jene.

though [ðou] conj obwohl, obgleich. adv aber, dennoch, jedoch. **as though** als ob. **even though** wenn ... auch.

thought [θɔ:t] V **think**. n Gedanke m; (thinking) Denken neut; (reflection) Überlegung f. **thoughtful** adj gedankenvoll; (considerate) rücksichtsvoll. **thoughtless** adj gedankenlos; rücksichtslos.

thousand ['θauzənd] adj tausend. n Tausend neut. **thousandth** adj tausendst; n Tausendstel neut.

thrash [θraʃ] v verdreschen; (defeat) heftig schlagen. **thrash about** hin und her schlagen. **thrashing** n Prügel pl, Dresche f.

thread [θred] n Faden m; (screw) Gewinde neut. **threadbare** adj fadenscheinig. v (needle) einfädeln; (beads) einreihen. **thread one's way through** sich winden durch.

threat [θret] n Drohung f; (danger) Gefahr f, Bedrohung f. **threaten** v bedrohen; (endanger) gefährden. **threatening** adj drohend.

three [θri:] adj drei. n Drei f. **threecornered** dreieckig. **three-dimensional**

adj dreidimensional. **threefold** *adv*, *adj* dreifach. **three-ply** *adj* dreifach. **three-quarters of an hour** eine Dreiviertelstunde *f*.

thresh [θreʃ] *v* dreschen.

threshold ['θreʃould] *n* (Tür)Schwelle *f*.

threw [θruː] *V* **throw**.

thrift [θrift] *n* Sparsamkeit *f*. **thrifty** *adj* sparsam.

thrill [θril] *v* erregen, begeistern. *n* Zittern *neut*, Erregung *f*. **thriller** *n* Reißer *m*. **thrilling** *adj* sensationell.

thrive [θraiv] *v* gedeihen. **thriving** *adj* blühend.

throat [θrout] *n* Kehle *f*, Rachen *m*; (neck) Hals *m*. **throaty** *adj* rauh.

throb [θrob] *v* pulsieren, klopfen. *n* Pulsieren *neut*.

thrombosis [θrom'bousis] *n* Thrombose *f*.

throne [θroun] *n* Thron *m*.

throng [θroŋ] *n* Gedränge *neut*. *v* sich scharen.

throttle ['θrotl] *v* erwürgen. *n* (tech) Drosselklappe *f*. **open the throttle** (mot) Gas geben.

through [θruː] *prep*, *adv* durch. **fall through** (coll) ins Wasser fallen. **get through** fertig sein mit; (exam) bestehen. **go through with** zu Ende führen. **wet through** durchnäßt. **throughout** *adv* (place) überall in. **throughout the night** die ganze Nacht hindurch. *adj* (ticket, train) durchgehend.

*****throw** [θrou] *v* werfen. **throw away** wegwerfen; (chance) verpassen. **throwback** *n* Rückkehr *f*. **throw up** (coll) kotzen. **throw-in** (sport) Einwurf *m*. *n* Wurf *m*.

thrush [θrʌʃ] *n* Drossel *f*.

*****thrust** [θrʌst] *v* stecken, schieben. *n* Stoß *m*, Hieb *m*; (tech) Schubkraft *f*.

thud [θʌd] *n* (dumpfer) Schlag *m*. *v* dumpf schlagen.

thumb [θʌm] *n* Daumen *m*. *v* **thumb through** durchblättern. **thumb a lift** per Anhalter fahren. **thumbtack** Reißnagel *m*.

thump [θʌmp] *n* Puff *m*, Schlag *m*. *v* puffen.

thunder ['θʌndə] *n* Donner *m*. *v* donnern. **thunderbolt** *n* Blitz *m*. **thunderclap** *n* Donnerschlag *m*. **thunderstorm** *n* Gewitter *neut*. **thunderstruck** *adj* wie vom Blitz getroffen.

Thursday ['θəːzdi] *n* Donnerstag *m*. **on Thursdays** donnerstags.

thus [ðʌs] *adv* so, folgendermaßen. **thus far** bis jetzt, soweit.

thwart [θwoːt] *v* (person) entgegenarbeiten (+ dat); (plan) vereiteln.

thyme [taim] *n* Thymian *m*.

thyroid ['θairoid] *n* Schilddrüse *f*. *adj* Schilddrüsen-.

tiara [tiˈɑːrə] *n* Tiara *f*.

tick¹ [tik] *v* (clock) ticken; (with pen) abhaken. **tick over** (mot) im Leerlauf sein. *n* Ticken *neut*; Häkchen *neut*.

tick² [tik] *n* (parasite) Zecke *f*.

ticket ['tikit] *n* (label) Etikett *neut*, Zettel *m*; (travel) Fahrkarte *f*, Fahrschein *m*; (theatre) Karte *f*. **ticket-collector** *n* Schaffner *m*. **ticket-office** *n* Fahrkarten-schalter *m*.

tickle ['tikl] *v* kitzeln; (fig) amüsieren. *n* Kitzel *m*, Juckreiz *m*. **ticklish** *adj* kitzlig.

tide [taid] *n* Gezeiten *pl*, Ebbe und Flut *f*. **high tide** Flut *f*, Hochwasser *neut*. **low tide** Ebbe *f*, Niedrigwasser *neut*. **tidal** *adj* Gezeiten-, Flut-. **tidal wave** Flutwelle *f*, Tsunami *m*.

tidy ['taidi] *adj* ordentlich, sauber. *v* in Ordnung bringen. **tidy up** aufräumen.

tie [tai] *v* (an)binden, festbinden; (knot) machen; (necktie) binden. **tie in with** übereinstimmen mit. **tie up** verbinden. **be tied up** nicht abkömmlich sein. *n* (necktie) Schlips *m*, Krawatte *m*; (sport) Unentschieden *neut*; (obligation) Verpflichtung *f*, Last *f*.

tier [tiə] *n* Reihe *f*, Rang *m*.

tiger ['taigə] *n* Tiger *m*. **tigress** *n* Tigerin *f*.

tight [tait] *v* fest, stramm; (clothes) eng, knapp; (watertight, etc.) dicht; (in short supply) knapp; (coll: mean) geizig. **tighten** *v* festziehen, straffen. **tight-fisted** *adj* geizig. **tights** *pl n* Strumpfhose *f sing*. **hold tight** festhalten. **sit tight** sitzenbleiben.

tile [tail] *n* (roof) (Dach)Ziegel *m*; (wall) Fliese *f*.

till¹ [til] *V* **until**.

till² [til] *n* (in shop) Kasse *f*.

till³ [til] *v* (land) bebauen, pflügen.

tiller ['tilə] *n* (naut) (Ruder)Pinne *f*.

tilt [tilt] *v* kippen, (sich) neigen. *n* Neigung *f*, Schräglage *f*. **tilt over** umkippen.

timber ['timbə] *n* (Bau)Holz *neut*. **timber forest** Hochwald *m*.

time [taɪm] n Zeit f; (occasion) Mal neut; (era) Zeitalter neut, (music) Takt m. **at all times** stets. **at this time** zu dieser Zeit. **behind the times** rückständig. **have a good time** sich gut unterhalten. **in good time** rechtzeitig. **time limit** Frist f. **timepiece** n Uhr f. **timeshare** n zeitlich verzahnte Ferienwohnung f. **timetable** n (bus, train) Fahrplan m; (school) Stundenplan m. **what time is it?** wieviel Uhr ist es? or wie spät ist es? v (mit der Uhr) messen, zeitlich abstimmen. **timeless** adj ewig. **timely** adj rechtzeitig.

timid ['tɪmɪd] adj ängstlich, schüchtern. **timidity** n Ängstlichkeit f, Schüchternheit f.

tin [tɪn] n Zinn neut; (can) Dose f, Büchse f. adj zinnern, Zinn-. **tin can** Blechdose f. **tin foil** n Stanniol neut. **tin-opener** n Dosenöffner m.

tinge [tɪndʒ] v (leicht) färben. n Färbung f; (fig) Anstrich m.

tingle ['tɪŋgl] v prickeln, kribbeln. n Prickeln neut.

tinker ['tɪŋkə] n Kesselflicker m. v tinker with herumbasteln an.

tinkle ['tɪŋkl] v klingeln. n Klingeln neut, Geklingel neut.

tinsel ['tɪnsəl] n Lametta neut.

tint [tɪnt] n Farbton m. v tönen, leicht färben.

tiny ['taɪni] adj winzig.

tip¹ [tɪp] n (sharp end) Spitze f; (summit) Gipfel m. **tipped** adj (cigarette) Filter-. **on tiptoe** auf den Zehenspitzen.

tip² [tɪp] n (for rubbish) (Müll) Abladeplatz m. v kippen. **tip over** umkippen.

tip³ [tɪp] n (gratuity) Trinkgeld neut; (hint) Wink m, Tip m. v ein Trinkgeld geben (+ dat); einen Tip geben (+ dat). **tip off** n rechtzeitiger Wink m.

tipsy ['tɪpsi] adj (coll) beschwipst.

tire¹ ['taɪə] v ermüden; (become tired) müde werden. **tire out** erschöpfen. **tired** adj müde. **tiredness** n Müdigkeit f. **tireless** adj unermüdlich. **tiresome** adj lästig.

tire² ['taɪə] n (US) V tyre.

tissue ['tɪʃuː] n Gewebe neut; (paper handkerchief) Papiertaschentuch neut. **tissue paper** n Seidenpapier neut.

tit [tɪt] n (bird) Meise f.

title ['taɪtl] n Titel m; (right) Rechtstitel m.

titled adj betitelt. **title-deed** Eigentumsurkunde f. **title-holder** n (sport) Titelverteidiger(in). **title-role** Titelrolle f.

to [tu] prep zu; (motion, travel) nach; (time of day) vor; (in order to) um zu. adv (shut) zu, geschlossen. **to and fro** auf und ab. fix to the wall an die Wand befestigen. **go to bed/the movies/school** ins Bett/ins Kino/in die Schule gehen. **go to Berlin** nach Berlin fahren. I gave it to him ich gab es ihm. **ten to one** (o'clock) zehn vor eins; (odds) zehn gegen eins. **to-do** n Getue neut.

toad [toud] n Kröte f. **toadstool** n Pilz m.

toast [toust] n Toast m; (drink) Trinkspruch m, Toast m. v toasten. **toaster** n Toaster m. **toastmaster** n Toastmeister m.

tobacco [tə'bakou] n Tabak m. **tobacconist** n Tabakhändler m.

toboggan [tə'bogən] n Schlitten m, Rodel(schlitten) m. v rodeln.

today [tə'dei] n, adv heute. **today's** or **of today** heutig, von heute; (of nowadays) der heutigen Zeit.

toddler ['todlə] n Kleinkind neut.

toe [tou] n Zehe f. **on one's toes** auf Draht. **toe-cap** n Kappe f. **toe-nail** n Zehennagel m.

toffee ['tofi] n Karamelle f.

together [tə'geðə] adv zusammen; (at the same time) gleichzeitig. **get together** (coll) sich treffen.

toil [toil] n Mühe f, schwere Arbeit f. v mühselig arbeiten, schuften (an).

toilet ['toilit] n (all senses) Toilette f; (WC) Klosett neut. **toilet-paper** Klosettpapier neut. **toilet soap** Toilettenseife f.

toiletries ['toilitriz] n pl Toilettenartikel m pl.

token ['toukən] n Zeichen neut, Beweis m; (voucher) Gutschein m, Bon m. adj nominell.

told [tould] V tell.

tolerate ['tolbreit] v dulden, tolerieren. **tolerable** adj erträglich. **tolerance** n Toleranz f. **tolerant** adj duldsam, tolerant.

toll¹ [toul] n Zoll m.

toll² [toul] v (bell) läuten.

tomato [tə'maːtou] n (pl **tomatoes**) Tomate f.

tomb [tuːm] n Grabmal neut, Grab neut. **tombstone** n Grabstein m.

tomorrow [tə'morou] n, adv morgen.

tomorrow morning morgen früh. **tomorrow's** or **of tomorrow** morgig, von morgen. **the day after tomorrow** übermorgen.

ton [tʌn] n Tonne f.

tone [toun] n Ton m; (muscle) Tonus m. **tone down** v mildern. **tonal** adj tonal.

tongs [tɒŋz] pl n Zange f sing.

tongue [tʌŋ] n Zunge f; (language) Sprache f. **tongue-tied** adj zungenlahm. **tongue-twister** n Zungenbrecher m.

tonic ['tɒnɪk] adj tonisch, Ton-. **tonic water** Tonic neut. n Tonikum neut.

tonight [tə'naɪt] adv heute abend, heute nacht.

tonsil ['tɒnsɪl] n Mandel f. **tonsillectomy** n Mandelentfernung f. **tonsillitis** n Mandelentzündung f.

too [tuː] adv (excessively) zu, allzu; (as well) auch, ebenfalls.

took [tuk] V take.

tool [tuːl] n Werkzeug neut. **toolbox** n Werkzeugkasten m. **tooling** n Bearbeitung f.

tooth [tuːθ] n (pl teeth) Zahn m. **toothache** n Zahnweh neut. **toothbrush** n Zahnbürste f. **toothless** adj zahnlos. **toothpaste** n Zahnpasta f. **toothpick** n Zahnstocher m.

top¹ [tɒp] n oberes Ende neut, obere Seite f; (hill) Gipfel m; (lid) Deckel m; (page) Kopf m. **on top of** oben auf; (besides) über. **top hat** Zylinder m. **top-heavy** adj kopflastig. **topsoil** n Ackerkrume f. **topless** adj oben ohne. adj oberst, höchst; (chief) Haupt-. v krönen.

top² [tɒp] n (toy) Kreisel m.

topaz ['toupaz] n Topas m.

topic ['tɒpɪk] n Thema neut, Gegenstand m. **topical** adj aktuell.

topography [tə'pɒgrəfi] n Topographie f.

topple ['tɒpl] v (um)kippen.

topsy-turvy [tɒpsɪ'təːvɪ] adv durcheinander, in Unordnung.

torch [tɔːtʃ] n Fackel f; (elec) Taschenlampe f.

tore [tɔː] V tear¹.

torment [tɔː'ment; n 'tɔːment] v quälen. n Qual f. **tormentor** n Quälgeist m.

torn [tɔːn] V tear¹. adj zerrissen.

tornado [tɔː'neɪdou] n Tornado m, Wirbelsturm m.

torpedo [tɔː'piːdou] n Torpedo m.

torrent ['tɒrənt] n Wildbach m; (of abuse, etc.) Strom m, Ausbruch m. **torrential** adj strömend. **torrential rain** Wolkenbruch m.

torso ['tɔːsou] n Torso m.

tortoise ['tɔːtəs] n Schildkröte f. **tortoiseshell** n Schildpatt m.

tortuous ['tɔːtʃuəs] adj gekrümmt.

torture ['tɔːtʃə] n Folter f, Folterung f; Tortur f. v foltern. **torturer** n Folterer m.

Tory ['tɔːrɪ] adj (British pol) konservativ, Tory-; n. Konservative m, f.

toss [tɒs] v (hoch)werfen; (coin) hochwerfen; tossed about by the waves von den Wellen hin und her geworfen. **I don't give a toss** (vulg) das geht mir am Arsch vorbei. **tosser** n (vulg) wichser m.

tot¹ [tɒt] n (whisky, etc.) Schlückchen neut; (child) Knirps m.

tot² [tɒt] v **tot up** zusammenzählen.

total ['toutl] adj total, ganz, Gesamt-. n Summe f, Gesamtbetrag m. **in total** als Ganzes. **totalitarian** adj totalitär. **totalisator** n Totalisator m. v sich belaufen auf; (person) zusammenzählen. **totality** n Gesamtheit f. **totally** adv völlig, total.

totter ['tɒtə] v taumeln, wanken. **tottering** adj wackelig.

touch [tʌtʃ] v anrühren, anfassen; (feel) betasten; (border on) grenzen an; (emotionally) berühren. **touch down** landen. **touch up** (restore) ausbessern. **touching** adj rührend. **touchline** n Marklinie f. **touchstone** n Prüfstein m. n Berührung f, Anrühren neut; (sense) Tastsinn m, (trace) Spur f. **be/keep in touch with** in Verbindung stehen/bleiben mit. **touchy** adj empfindlich, reizbar.

tough [tʌf] adj zäh; (person) zäh, robust; (difficult) schwierig, sauer. **toughen** v zäher machen or werden. **toughness** n Zähigkeit f, Härte f.

toupee ['tuːpeɪ] n Toupet neut.

tour [tuə] n Tour f, Rundreise f, (of inspection) Rundgang m; (theatre) Tournee f. v bereisen. **touring** adj Touren-. **tourism** n Tourismus m. **tourist** n Tourist(in). **tourist office** Verkehrsverein m, Verkehrsbüro neut.

tournament ['tuənəmənt] n Turnier neut.

tout [taut] n Kartenschwärzhändler(in). v **tout for custom(ers)** Kunden anreißen, auf Kundenfang gehen.

tow [təʊ] v bugsieren, schleppen. n Schlepptau neut. **have in tow** im Schlepptau haben. **towline** or **towrope** n Schlepptau neut.

towards [tə'wɔːdz] prep (place) auf ... zu, nach ... hin; (behaviour, attitude) gegen(über). towards midday gegen Mittag.

towel ['taʊəl] n Handtuch neut. **towelling** n Handtuchstoff m.

tower ['taʊə] n Turm m. v (hoch)ragen.

town [taʊn] n Stadt f. adj Stadt-. **town council** Stadtrat m. **town hall** Rathaus neut. **town planning** Stadtplanung f.

toxic ['tɒksik] adj giftig, toxisch. **toxin** n Toxin neut.

toy [tɔi] n Spielzeug neut. **toys** pl Spielwaren pl. v **toy with** spielen mit.

trace [treis] n Spur f. v nachspüren, verfolgen; (draw) pausen, durchzeichnen. **tracing** n Pause f. **tracing paper** Pauspapier neut.

track [trak] n Spur f, Fährte f; (rail) Gleis neut; (road) Weg m, Pfad m; (sport) Bahn f. **track suit** Trainingsanzug m.

tract[1] [trakt] n (land) Strecke f. **digestive tract** Verdauungssystem neut.

tract[2] [trakt] n (treatise) Traktat neut.

tractor ['traktə] n Traktor m.

trade [treid] n Handel m; (job, skill) Gewerbe neut. **trade balance** n Handelsbilanz f. **trade fair** Messe f. **trademark** n Warenzeichen neut. **tradesman** n Lieferant m. **trade union** n Gewerkschaft f. **trade-unionist** n Gewerkschaftler(in). v handeln; (exchange) eintauschen. **trader** n Händler m.

tradition [tə'diʃən] n Tradition f. **traditional** adj traditionell.

traffic ['trafik] n Verkehr m. **traffic jam** Verkehrsstockung f. **trafficker** n Händler m. **traffic lights** Verkehrsampel f sing.

tragedy ['tradʒədi] n (theatre) Tragödie f; (fig) Unglück neut. **tragic** adj tragisch.

trail [treil] n Spur f, Fährte f. v schleifen, (nach)schleppen; (follow) verfolgen; (lag behind) nachhinken.

train [trein] n Zug m; (of dress) Schleppe f. v (person for job, etc.) ausbilden; (sport) trainieren; (child) schulen; (animal) dressieren. **trainee** n Lehrling m. **trainer** n (sport) Trainer m. **training** n Ausbildung f; (sport) Training neut.

trait [treit] n Zug m, Merkmal neut.

traitor ['treitə] n Verräter(in). **traitorous** adj verräterisch.

tram [tram] n Straßenbahn f.

tramp [tramp] n Landstreicher m. v stampfen.

trample ['trampl] v trampeln.

trampoline ['trampəlin] n Trampoline f.

trance [trains] n Trance f.

tranquil ['traŋkwil] adj ruhig, friedlich. **tranquillity** n Ruhe f. **tranquillizer** n Beruhigungsmittel neut.

transact [tran'zakt] v durchführen. **transaction** n Geschäft neut, Transaktion f.

transcend [tran'send] v überschreiten. **transcendental** adj transzendental.

transcribe [tran'skraib] v abschreiben. **transcription** n Abschrift f.

transept ['transept] n Querschiff neut.

transfer [trans'fəː; n 'transfəː] v übertragen; (money) überweisen; (trains) umsteigen. n Übertragung f; Überweisung f; Umsteigen neut; (design) Abziehbild neut. **transferable** adj übertragbar. **transferred-charge call** R-Gespräch neut.

transform [trans'fɔːm] v umwandeln. **transformation** n Umwandlung f. **transformer** n (elec) Transformator m.

transfuse [trans'fjuːz] v (blood) übertragen. **transfusion** n (blood) Blutübertragung f.

transient ['tranziənt] adj vorübergehend.

transistor [tran'zistə] n Transistor m.

transit ['transit] n Durchfahrt f; (of goods) Transport f. adj Durchgangs-. **in transit** unterwegs.

transition [tran'ziʃən] n Übergang m. **transitional** adj Übergangs-.

transitive ['transitiv] adj transitiv.

translate [trans'leit] v übersetzen. **translation** n Übersetzung f. **translator** n Übersetzer(in).

translucent [trans'luːsnt] adj lichtdurchlässig.

transmit [tranz'mit] v übersenden; (radio, TV) senden. **transmitter** n (radio, TV) Sender m. **transmission** n (mot) Getriebe neut; (radio, TV) Sendung f.

transparent [trans'peərənt] adj durchsichtig, transparent; (fig) offensichtlich. **transparency** n Durchsichtigkeit f; (phot) (Dia)Positiv neut.

transplant [trans'plaint; n 'transplaint] v

verpflanzen; (*med*) transplantieren. *n* (*operation*) Transplantation *f*; (*actual organ*) Transplantat *neut*. **transplantation** *n* Verpflanzung *f*.

transport [trænspo:t; *n* 'trænspo:t] *v* befördern, transportieren. *n* Beförderung *f*, Transport *m*. **transportable** *adj* transportierbar. **transportation** *n* Transport *m*.

transpose [trænspouz] *v* umstellen, versetzen.

transverse ['trænzvə:s] *adj* quer, Quer-.

trap [træp] *n* Falle *f*. **lay a trap** eine Falle stellen. **shut your trap!** (*impol*) halt die Klappe! **trapdoor** *n* Falltür *f*. *v* fangen. **trapper** *n* Trapper *m*.

trapeze [trə'pi:z] *n* Trapez *neut*.

trash [træʃ] *n* Abfall *m*; (*film, book, etc.*) Kitsch *m*. **trash-can** *n* Abfalleimer *m*. **trashy** *adj* wertlos.

trauma ['trɔ:m ə] *n* Trauma *neut*. **traumatic** *adj* traumatisch.

travel ['trævl] *v* reisen. *n* Reisen *neut*. **travel agency** Reisebüro *neut*. **traveller** Reisende(r). **travelling** *adj* Reise-. **travelling expenses** Reisespesen *pl*.

travesty ['trævəst] *n* Travestie *f*.

trawl [trɔ:l] *n* Grundschleppnetz *neut*, Trawl *neut*. **trawler** *n* Trawler *m*.

treachery ['tretʃəri] *n* Verrat *m*. **treacherous** *adj* verräterisch; (*dangerous*) gefährlich.

treacle ['tri:kl] *n* Sirup *m*, Melasse *f*.

*tread [tred] *n* Tritt *m*, Schritt *m*; (*tyre*) Profil *neut*; (*ladder*) Sprosse *f*. *v* treten. **treadmill** *n* Tretmühle *f*.

treason ['tri:zn] *n* Verrat *m*.

treasure ['treʒə] *n* Schatz *m*. *v* hochschätzen. **treasurer** *n* Schatzmeister(in); (*club*) Kassenwart *m*. **treasury** *n* Schatzkammer *f*. **Treasury** *n* (*pol*) Finanzministerium *neut*.

treat [tri:t] *v* behandeln. **treat someone to something** jemandem zu etwas einladen. *n* (*coll*) Genuß *m*, Vergnügen *neut*. **treatment** *n* Behandlung *f*.

treatise ['tri:tiz] *n* Abhandlung *f*.

treaty ['tri:ti] *n* Vertrag *m*, Pakt *m*.

treble ['trebl] *adj* dreifach; (*music*) Diskant-. *v* (sich) verdreifachen.

tree [tri:] *n* Baum *m*. **family tree** Stammbaum *m*.

trek [trek] *n* Treck *m*. *v* trecken.

trellis ['trelis] *n* Gitter *neut*, Gitterwerk *neut*.

tremble ['trembl] *v* zittern. *n* Zittern *neut*.

tremendous [trə'mendəs] *adj* enorm, kolossal; (*coll: excellent*) ausgezeichnet.

tremor ['trem ə] *n* Beben *neut*.

trench [trentʃ] *n* Graben *m*; (*mil*) Schützengraben *m*. **trench coat** *n* Trenchcoat *m*.

trend [trend] *n* Tendenz *f*, Trend *m*. **trendy** *adj* (neu)modisch.

trespass ['trespəs] *v* unbefugt betreten. **trespasser** *n* Unbefugte(r). **trespassers will be prosecuted** Eintritt bei Strafe verboten.

trestle ['tresl] *n* Gestell *m*.

trial ['traiəl] *n* Probe *f*, Versuch *m*; (*legal*) Prozeß *m*. *adj* Probe-. **on trial** vor Gericht.

triangle ['traiæŋgl] *n* Dreieck *neut*; (*music*) Triangel *m*. **triangular** *adj* dreieckig.

tribe [traib] *n* Stamm *m*. **tribal** *adj* Stammes-. **tribesman** *n* Stammesangehörige(r).

tribunal [traibju:nl] *n* Gerichtshof *m*, Tribunal *neut*.

tributary ['tribjutəri] *n* Nebenfluß *m*.

tribute ['tribju:t] *n* Tribut *m*. **pay tribute** (*fig*) Anerkennung zollen.

trick [trik] *n* Trick *m*, Kniff *m*; (*practical joke*) Streich *m*; (*cards*) Stich *m*. *adj* Trick-. *v* betrügen. **trickery** *n* Betrügerei *f*. **trickster** *n* Schwindler(in). **tricky** *adj* knifflig.

trickle ['trikl] *v* tröpfeln, sickern. *n* Tröpfeln *neut*.

tricycle ['traisikl] *n* Dreirad *neut*.

tried [traid] *adj* erprobt, bewährt.

trifle ['traifl] *n* Kleinigkeit *f*; (*cookery*) Trifle *m*, (süßer) Auflauf *m*. **a trifle** ein bißchen. *v* spielen. **trifling** *adj* belanglos.

trigger ['trigə] *n* Abzug *m*. **pull the trigger** abdrücken. *v* **trigger off** auslösen.

trigonometry [trigə'nom ətri] *n* Trigonometrie *f*.

trilby ['trilbi] *n* weicher Filzhut *m*.

trim [trim] *adj* gepflegt, nett; (*slim*) schlank. *v* zurechtmachen; (*hair, etc.*) ausputzen, beschneiden. **trimming** *n* Verzierung *f*.

trinket ['trinkit] *n* Schmuckstück *neut*.

trio ['tri:ou] *n* Trio *neut*.

trip [trip] *n* Reise *f*, Ausflug *m*; (*stumble*) Fehltritt *m*, Stolpern *neut*. *v* stolpern; (*dance*) tänzeln, trippeln. **trip up** (*someone else*) ein Bein stellen (+ *dat*). **tripper** *n*

Ausflügler(in).

tripe [traɪp] n Kaldaunen pl; (coll: nonsense) Quatsch m.

triple ['trɪpl] adj dreifach, Drei-. v verdreifachen. **triplet** n Drilling m. **triplex glass** Sicherheitsglas neut.

tripod ['traɪpɒd] n Dreifuß m; (phot) Stativ neut.

trite [traɪt] adj platt, banal.

triumph ['traɪəmf] n Triumph m; Sieg m. v triumphieren. **triumphal** adj Triumph-, Sieger-. **triumphant** adj triumphierend, siegreich.

trivial ['trɪvjəl] adj geringfügig, trivial. **triviality** n Trivialität f.

trod [trɒd] V tread.

trodden ['trɒdn] V tread.

trolley ['trɒlɪ] n (supermarket) Einkaufswagen m; (tea) Servierwagen m; (airport, etc.) Kofferkuli m; (tram) Straßenbahn f. **trolleybus** n O-Bus m.

trombone [trɒm'boun] n Posaune f. **trombonist** n Posaunist(in).

troop [truːp] n Trupp m. **troops** pl Truppen pl. **trooping the colour** Fahnenparade f.

trophy ['troufɪ] n (sport) Preis m; (mil, hunting) Trophäe f.

tropic ['trɒpɪk] n Wendekreis m. **tropics** pl Tropen pl. **tropical** adj tropisch.

trot [trɒt] n Trott m, Trab m. v trotten, traben.

trouble ['trʌbl] n Schwierigkeiten pl; (effort) Mühe f; (burden) Belästigung f; (tech) Störung f. v beunruhigen, stören. **troubles** pl (pol) Unruhe f, Aufruhr f. **be in trouble** Schwierigkeiten haben. **be troubled** bekümmert sein. **get into trouble** Ärger bringen (+ dat) or bekommen. **take (the) trouble** sich die Mühe gelen. **troublemaker** n Unruhestifter(in). **troubleshooter** n Störungssucher(in). **troublesome** adj lästig.

trough [trɒf] n Trog m.

trousers ['trauzəz] pl n Hose f sing.

trout [traut] n Forelle f.

trowel ['trauəl] n Kelle f; (gardening) Pflanzenheber m.

truant ['truːənt] n Schwänzer(in). **play truant** (die Schule) schwänzen. **truancy** n Schwänzerei f.

truce [truːs] n Waffenstillstand m.

truck [trʌk] n (road) Lastkraftwagen (Lkw) m; (rail) Güterwagen m. **truckdriver** n Lastwagenfahrer m.

trudge [trʌdʒ] v sich mühsam schleppen.

true [truː] adj wahr; (genuine) echt; (loyal) treu; (rightful) rechtmäßig. **true to life** wirklichkeitsgetreu. **truism** n Binsenwahrheit f. **truly** adv wirklich, in der Tat. **yours truly** hochachtungsvoll.

truffle ['trʌfl] n Trüffel f.

trump [trʌmp] n Trumpf m. **trump card** Trumpfkarte f. v (über)trumpfen. **trumped up** falsch, erdichtet.

trumpet ['trʌmpɪt] n Trompete f. v trompeten. **trumpeter** n Trompeter m.

truncheon ['trʌntʃən] n Knüppel m.

trunk [trʌŋk] n (tree) Baumstamm m; (anat) Leib m; (case) Schankkoffer m. **trunks** pl Badehose f sing. **trunk-call** Ferngespräch neut. **trunk-road** Fernstraße f.

truss [trʌs] n (med) Bruchband neut. v zusammenbinden; (cookery) dressieren.

trust [trʌst] v trauen (+ dat); (hope) hoffen. n Vertrauen neut; (expectation) Erwartung f; (comm) Trust m. **hold in trust** als Treuhänder verwalten. **trustee** n Treuhänder m. **trusting** adj vertrauensvoll. **trustworthy** adj vertrauenswürdig. **trusty** adj treu.

truth [truːθ] n Wahrheit f. **truthful** adj wahr, wahrhaftig. **truthfulness** n Wahrhaftigkeit f.

try [traɪ] v (attempt) versuchen; (test, sample) probieren; (law) vor Gericht stellen, verhandeln gegen (wegen). **try on** (clothes) anprobieren. **try out** probieren. n Versuch m. **trying** adj peinlich, schwierig; (person) belästigend.

tsar [zɑː] n Zar m.

T-shirt ['tʃəːt] n T-shirt neut.

tub [tʌb] n (Bade) Wanne f; (barrel) Faß neut, Tonne f. **tubby** adj (coll) rundlich.

tuba ['tjuːbə] n Tuba f.

tube [tjuːb] n Rohr neut, Röhre f; (of tyre) (Luft)Schlauch m; (coll: underground railway) U-Bahn f.

tuber ['tjuːbə] n Knolle f.

tuberculosis [tjubəːkjuˈbusis] n Tuberkulose f.

tuck [tʌk] n Einschlag m. v **tuck in** (shirt) einstecken; (food) einhauen, zugreifen; (sheet) feststecken; (person) warm zudecken.

Tuesday ['tjuːzdɪ] n Dienstag m. **on**

Tuesdays dienstags.

tuft [tʌft] n Büschel neut, Schopf m.

tug [tʌg] v ziehen, zerren; (boat) schleppen. n Zerren neut, Zug m; (boat) Schlepper m, Bugsierdampfer m.

tuition [tjuː'ʃən] n Unterricht m.

tulip ['tjuːlip] n Tulpe f.

tumble ['tʌm bl] v hinfallen, umstürzen. **tumbledown** adj baufällig. **tumble-dryer** (Wäsche)Trockner m. n Fall m, Sturz m. **tumbler** n Glas neut.

tummy ['tʌm i] n (coll) Bauch m, Bäuchlein neut. **tummy-ache** n Bauchweh neut.

tumour ['tjuːm ə] n Geschwulst f, Tumor m.

tumult ['tjuːm ʌlt] n Tumult m, Lärm m. **tumultuous** adj stürmisch.

tuna ['tjuːnə] n Thunfisch m.

tune [tjuːn] n Melodie f. **in/out of tune** gestimmt/verstimmt. **to the tune of** (coll) im Ausmaß von. v (ab)stimmen. **tune in to** einstellen auf. **tuneful** adj melodisch, wohlklingend. **tuner** n (pianos, etc.) Stimmer m.

tunic ['tjuːnik] n (school) Kittel m. (mil) Uniformrock m.

tunnel ['tʌnl] n Tunnel m, Unterführung f. v **tunnel through** einen Tunnel bauen durch.

tunny ['tʌni] V tuna.

turban ['təːbən] n Turban m.

turbine ['təːbain] n Turbine f.

turbot ['təːbət] n Steinbutt m.

turbulent ['təːbjulənt] adj unruhig, stürmisch. **turbulence** n Turbulenz f.

tureen [tə'riːn] n Terrine f.

turf [təːf] n Rasen m; (sport) Turf m, Rennbahn f. v **turf out** (coll) hinausschmeißen.

turkey ['təːki] n (cock) Truthahn m; (hen) Truthenne f.

Turkey ['təːki] n die Türkei f. **Turk** n Türke m, Türkin f. **Turkish** adj türkisch.

turmeric ['təːm ərik] n Gelbwurz f.

turmoil ['təːm oil] n Aufruhr m.

turn [təːn] v (sich) drehen; (become) werden. **turn around** or **round** (person) sich umdrehen; (thing) herumdrehen. **turn back** umkehren. **turn down** (offer) ablehnen; (radio) leiser stellen. **turning** n (mot) Abzweigung f. **turning point** Wendepunkt m. **turn left/right** links/rechts abbiegen. **turn loose**

freilassen. **turn off** (light) ausschalten; (radio) abstellen; (mot) abbiegen. **turn on** einschalten. **turn out** (expel) ausweisen; (produce) herstellen. **turn-out** n (spectators) Teilnahme f. **turn over** (sich) umdrehen. **turnover** n (comm) Umsatz m. **turnstile** n Drehkreuz neut. **turntable** n (records) Plattenteller m. **turn up** (appear) auftauchen; (radio) lauter stellen. **turnup** n (trousers) Umschlag m. n Umdrehung f; (change of direction) Wendung f. it's my turn ich bin an der Reihe. **do someone a good turn** jemandem einen Gefallen tun.

turnip ['təːnip] n (weiße) Rübe f.

turpentine ['təːpəntain] n Terpentin neut.

turquoise ['təːkwoiz] n Türkis m. adj (colour) türkisblau.

turret ['tʌrit] n Türmchen neut; (gun) Geschützturm m, Panzerturm m.

turtle ['təːtl] n Schildkröte f. **turtle dove** Turteltaube f.

tusk [tʌsk] n Stoßzahn m.

tussle ['tʌsl] n Balgerei f, Ringen neut. v sich balgen, kämpfen.

tutor ['tjuːtə] n Privatlehrer m; (university) Tutor m.

tuxedo [tʌk'siːdou] n Smoking m.

tweed [twiːd] n Tweed m.

tweezers ['twiːzəz] pl n Pinzette f sing.

twelve [twelv] adj zwölf. n Zwölf f. **twelfth** adj zwölft.

twenty ['twenti] adj zwanzig. n Zwanzig f. **twentieth** adj zwanzigst.

twice [twais] adv zweimal. **twice as much** zweimal so viel. **think twice about** sich gründlich überlegen.

twiddle ['twidl] v herumdrehen, spielen mit.

twig [twig] n Zweig m.

twilight ['twailait] n (Abend)Dämmerung f, Zwielicht neut. adj Zwielicht-.

twin [twin] n Zwilling m. adj Zwillings-. **twin-cylinder engine** Zweizylindermotor m.

twine [twain] n Bindfaden m, Schnur f. v (threads) zusammendrehen. **twine around** winden um, umranken.

twinge [twindʒ] n Stich m, Stechen neut. **twinge of conscience** Gewissensbiß m. v zwicken, kneifen.

twinkle ['twiŋkl] v glitzern, funkeln; (eyes) blinzeln. n Glitzern neut; Blinzeln neut. **in**

a twinkle im Nu.

twirl [twə:l] v wirbeln. n Wirbel m.

twist [twɪst] v (sich) drehen, (sich) winden; (meaning) verdrehen; (features) verzerren. **twist one's ankle** sich den Fuß verrenken. **twisted** adj (person) verschroben. **twisting** adj sich windend. n Drehung f, Windung f; (in story) Wendung f.

twit [twɪt] n (coll) Dummkopf m.

twitch [twɪtʃ] v zucken. n Zucken neut.

twitter ['twɪtə] v zwitschern. n Gezwitscher neut, Zwitschern neut.

two [tuː] adj zwei. **two-faced** adj heuchlerisch. **twofold** adj zweifach. **two-stroke engine** Zweitaktmotor m. n Zwei f; (pair) Paar neut.

tycoon [taɪkuːn] n Industriemagnat m.

type [taɪp] n Typ m, Sorte f, Klasse f; (person) Typ m; (print) Druck m, Druckschrift f. v (mit der Maschine) schreiben, tippen. **typed** adj maschinengeschrieben. **typeface** n Schriftart f. **typewriter** n Schreibmaschine f. **typing error** Tippfehler m. **typist** n Typist(in).

typhoid ['taɪfɔɪd] n Typhus m.

typhoon [taɪfuːn] n Taifun m.

typical ['tɪpɪkəl] adj typisch. **typify** v verkörpern.

tyrant ['taɪərənt] n Tyrann(in). **tyrannical** adj tyrannisch. **tyrannize** v tyrannisieren. **tyranny** n Tyrannei f.

tyre ['taɪə] or US **tire** n Reifen m.

U

ubiquitous [juːbɪkwɪtəs] adj überall zu finden(d).

udder ['ʌdə] n Euter neut.

UFO n Ufo (abbr. for unbekanntes Flugobjekt) neut.

ugly ['ʌglɪ] adj häßlich. **ugliness** n Häßlichkeit f.

Ukraine [juːkreɪn] n die Ukraine f. **Ukrainian** n Ukrainer(in); adj ukrainisch.

ulcer ['ʌlsə] n Geschwür neut.

ulterior [ʌltɪərɪə] adj **ulterior motives** Hintergedanken pl.

ultimate ['ʌltɪmət] adj allerletzt;

(conclusive) endgültig, entscheidend. **ultimately** adv schließlich. **ultimatum** n Ultimatum neut.

ultrasound ['ʌltrəsaund] n Ultraschall m. **ultrasound scan** Ultraschalluntersuchung f.

ultraviolet [ʌltrə'vaɪələt] adj ultraviolett.

umbilical [ʌm'bɪlɪkəl] n Nabelschnur f.

umbrella [ʌm'brɛlə] n Regenschirm m.

umlaut ['umlaut] n Umlaut m.

umpire [ʌm'paɪə] n Schiedsrichter m.

umpteen [ʌm'ptiːn] adj zahllos. **umpteen times** x-mal.

unable [ʌn'eɪbl] adj unfähig. **be unable** nicht können.

unacceptable [ʌnək'septəbl] adj unannehmbar.

unaccompanied [ʌnə'kʌmpənɪd] adj unbegleitet; (music) ohne Begleitung.

unanimous [juːnanɪməs] adj einstimmig. **unanimity** n Einstimmigkeit f.

unannounced [ʌnə'naunst] adj unangekündigt.

unarmed [ʌn'aːmd] adj unbewaffnet.

unassuming [ʌnə'sjuːmɪŋ] adj bescheiden.

unattractive [ʌnə'traktɪv] adj reizlos, nicht anziehend.

unauthorized [ʌn'oːθəraɪzd] adj unbefugt.

unavoidable [ʌnə'vɔɪdəbl] adj unvermeidlich.

unaware [ʌnə'wɛə] adj **be unaware of** sich nicht bewußt sein (+ gen). **unawares** adv **take unawares** überraschen.

unbalanced [ʌn'balənst] adj unausgeglichen; (mentally disturbed) geistesgestört.

unbearable [ʌn'bɛərəbl] adj unerträglich.

unbelievable [ʌnbɪ'liːvəbl] adj unglaublich. **unbeliever** n Ungläubige(r). **unbelieving** adj ungläubig.

***unbend** [ʌn'bend] v (person) freundlicher werden. **unbending** adj unbeugsam.

unborn [ʌn'bɔːn] adj ungeboren.

unbounded [ʌn'baundɪd] adj unbegrenzt, grenzenlos.

unbreakable [ʌn'breɪkəbl] adj unzerbrechlich.

unbridled [ʌn'braɪdld] adj zügellos.

unbroken [ʌn'brəukn] adj (continuous) ununterbrochen.

uncalled-for [ʌn'kɔːldfɔː] adj unangebracht.

uncanny [ʌnˈkanɪ] adj unheimlich.

uncertain [ʌnˈsəːtn] adj unsicher, ungewiß. **uncertainty** n Unsicherheit f, Ungewißheit f.

uncle [ˈʌŋkl] n Onkel m.

unclean [ʌnˈkliːn] adj unrein.

uncomfortable [ʌnˈkʌmfətəbl] adj unbequem; (fact, etc.) beunruhigend.

uncommon [ʌnˈkomən] adj ungewöhlich, selten. **uncommonly** adv (extremely) außerordentlich.

unconditional [ʌnkənˈdiʃənl] adj bedingungslos, uneingeschränkt.

unconfirme [ʌnkənˈfəːmd]d adj unbestätigt.

unconscious [ʌnˈkonʃəs] adj (unknowing) unbewußt; (med) bewußtlos. **unconsciousness** n Bewußtlosigkeit f.

uncontrollable [ʌnkənˈtrəubl] adj unbeherrscht, unkontrollierbar.

unconventional [ʌnkənˈvenʃənl] adj unkonventionell.

unconvinced [ʌnkənˈvinst] adj nicht überzeugt. **unconvincing** adj nicht überzeugend.

uncooked [ʌnˈkukt] adj roh, ungekocht.

uncork [ʌnˈkɔːk] v entkorken.

uncouth [ʌnˈkuːθ] adj ungehobelt, unfein.

uncover [ʌnˈkʌvə] v aufdecken.

uncut [ʌnˈkʌt] adj (gem) ungeschliffen; (grass) ungemäht; (book) unabgekürzt.

undecided [ʌndiˈsaidid] adj (thing) unentschieden; (person) unentschlossen.

undeniable [ʌndiˈnaiəbl] adj unbestreitbar.

under [ˈʌndə] prep unter; (less than) weniger als. **under age** minderjährig. **under construction** im Bau. **under cover of** im Schutz (+ gen). adv unten. **go under** zugrunde gehen. adj Unter-.

undercharge [ʌndəˈtʃaːdʒ] v zu wenig berechnen.

underclothes [ˈʌndəkbuðz] pl n Unterwäsche f sing.

undercoat [ˈʌndəkout] n Grundierung f, Grundanstrich m.

undercover [ʌndəˈkʌvə] adj Geheim-.

*****undercut** [ʌndəˈkʌt] v (comm) unterbieten.

underdeveloped [ʌndədiˈveləpt] adj unterentwickelt. **underdeveloped country** Entwicklungsland neut.

underdone [ʌndəˈdʌn] adj (meat) nicht durchgebraten.

underestimate [ʌndəˈestimeit] adj unterschätzen.

underexpose [ʌndərikˈspouz] v unterbelichten. **underexposure** n Unterbelichtung f.

underfoot [ʌndəˈfut] adv am Boden.

*****undergo** [ʌndəˈgou] v erleben; (operation) sich unterziehen (+ dat).

undergraduate [ʌndəˈgradjuət] n Student(in).

underground [ˈʌndəgraund; adv ʌndəˈgraund] adj unterirdisch, Untergrund-; (pol) geheim, Untergrund-. n (rail) Untergrundbahn f, (coll) U-Bahn f. adv unter der Erde. **go underground** (hide) untertauchen.

undergrowth [ˈʌndəgrouθ] n Unterholz neut.

underhand [ʌndəˈhand] adj heimlich, hinterlistig.

*****underlie** [ʌndəˈlai] v zugrunde liegen (+ dat).

underline [ʌndəˈlain] v unterstreichen; (stress) betonen.

undermine [ʌndəˈmain] v unterminieren, untergraben.

underneath [ʌndəˈniːθ] prep unter, unterhalb. adv unten, darunter.

underpants [ˈʌndəpants] pl n Unterhose f sing.

underpass [ˈʌndəpaːs] n Unterführung f.

underprivileged [ʌndəˈpriviliʒd] adj benachteiligt.

underrate [ʌndəˈreit] v unterschätzen.

*****understand** [ʌndəˈstand] v verstehen. **understandable** adj verständlich. **understanding** n Verständnis neut; (agreement) Verständigung f; adj verständnisvoll.

understate [ʌndəˈsteit] v untertreiben. **understatement** n Untertreibung f.

understudy [ˈʌndəstʌdi] n Ersatzschauspieler(in).

*****undertake** [ʌndəˈteik] v übernehmen. **undertaker** n Leichenbestatter m. **undertaking** n Unternehmen neut; (promise) Versprechen neut.

undertone [ˈʌndətoun] n Unterton m.

underwear [ˈʌndəweə] n Unterwäsche f.

underweight [ʌndəˈweit] adj untergewichtig.

underworld ['ʌndəwɜːld] n Unterwelt f.

*underwrite [ʌndə'raɪt] v unterzeichnen, versichern. **underwriter** n Versicherer m.

undesirable [ʌndɪ'zaɪərəbl] adj nicht wünschenswert, unerwünscht.

*undo [ʌn'duː] v (package) öffnen, aufmachen; (coat, knot) aufknöpfen; (work) zunichte machen. **undoing** n Ruin m, Vernichtung f.

undoubted [ʌn'dautɪd] adj unbestritten. **undoubtedly** adv ohne Zweifel.

undress [ʌn'dres] v (sich) ausziehen. **undressed** adj unbekleidet.

undue [ʌn'djuː] adj übermäßig, übertrieben; (improper) ünschicklich. **unduly** adv übertrieben.

undulate ['ʌndjuleɪt] v wogen, wallen. **undulation** n Wallen neut.

unearth [ʌn'ɜːθ] v ausgraben; (fig) ans Tageslicht bringen.

uneasy [ʌn'iːzɪ] adj (person) beunruhigt, ängstlich; (feeling) unbehaglich.

uneducated [ʌn'edjukeɪtɪd] adj ungebildet.

unemployed [ʌnem'plɔɪd] adj arbeitslos. **unemployment** n Arbeitslosigkeit f.

unending [ʌn'endɪŋ] adj endlos.

unequal [ʌn'iːkwəl] adj ungleich. **unequalled** adj unübertroffen.

uneven [ʌn'iːvn] adj uneben. **unevenness** n Unebenheit f.

uneventful [ʌnɪ'ventfəl] adj ereignislos.

unexpected [ʌneks'pektɪd] adj unerwartet.

unfailing [ʌn'feɪlɪŋ] adj unfehlbar.

unfair [ʌn'feə] adj ungerecht, unfair. **unfairness** n Unbilligkeit f.

unfaithful [ʌn'feɪθfəl] adj untreu. **unfaithfulness** n Untreue f.

unfamiliar [ʌnfə'mɪljə] adj unbekannt.

unfasten [ʌn'faːsn] v aufmachen, losbinden.

unfit [ʌn'fɪt] adj ungeeignet; (sport) nicht fit.

unfold [ʌn'fould] v (sich) entfalten.

unforeseen [ʌnfɔː'siːn] adj unvorhergesehen.

unforgettable [ʌnfə'getəbl] adj unvergeßlich.

unfortunate [ʌn'fɔːtʃənət] adj unglücklich; (regrettable) bedauerlich. n Unglückliche(r). **unfortunately** adv unglücklicherweise, leider.

unfurnished [ʌn'fɜːnɪʃd] adj unmöbliert.

ungrateful [ʌn'greɪtfəl] adj undankbar.

unhappy [ʌn'hapɪ] adj unglücklich; (with something) unzufrieden. **unhappily** adv leider. **unhappiness** n Unglück neut.

unhealthy [ʌn'helθɪ] adj (person) ungesund; (damaging to health) gesundheitsschädlich.

unhurt [ʌn'hɜːt] adj unverletzt.

unicorn ['juːnɪkɔːn] n Einhorn m.

uniform ['juːnɪfɔːm] n Uniform f, Dienstkleidung f. adj einförmig, gleichförmig. **uniformity** n Gleichheit f.

unify ['juːnɪfaɪ] v vereinigen. **unification** n Vereinigung f.

unilateral [juːnɪ'latərəl] adj einseitig.

uninhabited [ʌnɪn'habɪtɪd] adj unbewohnt. **uninhabitable** adj unbewohnbar.

unintelligible [ʌnɪn'telɪdʒəbl] adj unverständlich.

uninterested [ʌn'ɪntrɪstɪd] adj uninteressiert. **uninteresting** adj uninteressant.

union ['juːnjən] n Vereinigung f; (pol) Staatenbund m; (agreement) Eintracht f; (trade union) Gewerkschaft f. **unionize** v gewerkschaftlich organisieren.

unique [juː'niːk] adj einzigartig; (only) einzig.

unison ['juːnɪsn] n Einklang m.

unit ['juːnɪt] n Einheit f.

unite [juː'naɪt] v (sich) vereinigen. **united** adj vereint, vereinigt. **unity** n Einheit f; (accord) Einigkeit f.

United Kingdom n Vereinigtes Königreich.

United Nations pl n Vereinte Nationen.

United States of America n Vereinigte Staaten von Amerika.

universe ['juːnɪvɜːs] n Weltall neut, Universum neut. **universal** adj universal.

university [juːnɪ'vɜːsətɪ] n Universität f, Hochschule f. adj Universitäts-, Hochschul-.

unjust [ʌn'dʒʌst] adj ungerecht.

unkempt [ʌn'kempt] adj ungepflegt.

unkind [ʌn'kaɪnd] adj unfreundlich. **unkindness** n Unfreundlichkeit f.

unknown [ʌn'noun] adj unbekannt. n das Unbekannte.

unlawful [ʌn'lɔːfəl] adj rechtswidrig, unzulässig.

unleaded [ʌn'ledɪd] adj (petrol) bleifrei.

unless [ʌn'les] *conj* wenn ... nicht, es sei denn.

unlike [ʌn'laik] *adj, prep* unähnlich, *(in contrast to)* im Gegensatz zu. **unlikely** *adv* unwahrscheinlich.

unload [ʌn'bud] *v* *(goods)* abladen; *(truck, etc.)* entladen.

unlock [ʌn'lɒk] *v* aufschließen, öffnen. **unlocked** *adj* unverschlossen.

unlucky [ʌn'lʌki] *adj* unglücklich.

unmarried [ʌn'm arid] *adj* ledig, unverheiratet.

unnatural [ʌn'natʃərəl] *adj* unnatürlich.

unnecessary [ʌn'nesəsəri] *adj* unnötig, nicht notwendig.

unobtainable [ʌnəb'teinəbl] *adj* unerhältlich.

unoccupied [ʌn'okjupaid] *adj* unbesetzt; *(house)* unbewohnt; *(person)* unbeschäftigt.

unofficial [ʌnə'fʃəl] *adj* inoffiziell.

unorthodox [ʌn'ɔːθədoks] *adj* unorthodox.

unpack [ʌn'pak] *v* auspacken.

unpleasant [ʌn'pleznt] *adj* unangenehm. **unpleasantness** *n* Unannehmlichkeit *f.*

unplug [ʌn'plʌg] *v* den Stecker herausziehen.

unpopular [ʌn'popjulə] *adj* unbeliebt.

unprecedented [ʌn'presidentid] *adj* unerhört.

unpretentious [ʌnprɪtenʃəs] *adj* anspruchslos.

unravel [ʌn'ravəl] *v* auftrennen; *(fig)* enträtseln.

unreal [ʌn'rɪl] *adj* unwirklich. **unrealistic** *adj* unrealistisch.

unreasonable [ʌn'rɪzənəbl] *adj* übertrieben, übermäßig; *(person)* unvernünftig.

unrelenting [ʌnrɪlentɪŋ] *adj* unerbittlich.

unreliable [ʌnrɪlaiəbl] *adj* unzuverlässig. **unreliability** *n* Unzuverlässigkeit *f.*

unrest [ʌn'rest] *n* Unruhe *f.*

unruly [ʌn'ruːli] *adj* unlenksam.

unsafe [ʌn'seif] *adj* unsicher, gefährlich.

unsatisfactory [ʌnsatisfaktəri] *adj* unbefriedigend. **unsatisfied** *adj* unzufrieden.

unscrew [ʌn'skruː] *v* aufschrauben.

unsettle [ʌn'setl] *v* beunruhigen. **unsettled** *adj* unruhig.

unsightly [ʌn'saitli] *adj* unansehnlich.

unskilled [ʌn'skild] *adj* ungelernt.

unsound [ʌn'saund] *adj* *(advice, etc.)* unzuverlässig. **of unsound mind** geistesgestört.

unspeakable [ʌn'spiːkəbl] *adj* unbeschreiblich; *(horrible)* scheußlich, entsetzlich.

unstable [ʌn'steibl] *adj* nicht fest, schwankend; *(person)* labil.

unsteady [ʌn'stedi] *adj* wackelig, unsicher.

unsuccessful [ʌnsək'sesfəl] *adj* erfolglos.

unsuitable [ʌn'suːtəbl] *adj* ungeeignet.

untangle [ʌn'taŋgl] *v* entwirren.

untidy [ʌn'taidi] *adj* unordentlich. **untidiness** *n* Unordentlichkeit *f.*

untie [ʌn'tai] *v* losbinden.

until [ən'til] *prep, conj* bis. **not until** erst.

untoward [ʌntə'wɔːd] *adj* ungünstig.

untrue [ʌn'truː] *adj* unwahr, falsch; *(friend)* untreu. **untruth** *n* Unwahrheit *f,* Falschheit *f.* **untruthful** *adj* unwahr, unaufrichtig.

unusual [ʌn'juːʒuəl] *adj* ungewöhnlich, außergewöhnlich.

unwell [ʌn'wel] *adj* unwohl.

unwieldy [ʌn'wiːldi] *adj* unhandlich.

***unwind** [ʌn'waind] *v* loswickeln, abspulen; *(rest)* sich entspannen, (sich) ausruhen.

unworthy [ʌn'wəːði] *adj* unwürdig.

unwrap [ʌn'rap] *v* auswickeln.

up [ʌp] *prep* auf, hinauf. *adv* auf, hoch; hinauf, herauf; *(out of bed)* auf; *(sun)* aufgegangen. *it's up to me* es liegt an mir. **up to now** bis jetzt. **up for trial** vor Gericht. **what's up?** was ist los?

upbringing ['ʌpbrɪŋ] *n* Erziehung *f.*

update [ʌp'deit] *v* modernisieren; *(book)* neu bearbeiten.

upgrade [ʌp'greid; *n* 'ʌpgreid] *v* *(tech)* aufrüsten, verbessern. *n* *(comp)* Upgrade *neut.*

upheaval [ʌp'hiːvl] *n* Umwälzung *f.*

uphill [ʌp'hil] *adv* bergauf. *adj* *(fig)* mühsam.

***uphold** [ʌp'hould] *v* unterstützen, billigen.

upholster [ʌp'houlstə] *v* (auf)polstern. **upholsterer** *n* Polsterer *m.* **upholstery** *n* Polsterung *f.*

upkeep ['ʌpkiːp] *n* Instandhaltung *f;* *(cost)* Unterhaltskosten *pl.*

uplift [ʌp'lift] *v* erbauen.

upmarket [ʌp'm aːkit] *adj* exklusiv, in der

gehobenen Preislage.

upon [ə'pɒn] *prep* auf. **once upon a time** es war einmal.

upper ['ʌpə] *adj* ober, höher. **uppermost** *adj* oberst, höchst. *n* (*shoe*) Oberleder *neut*.

upright ['ʌpraɪt] *adj, adv* gerade, aufrecht; (*honest*) aufrecht, aufrichtig.

uprising ['ʌpraɪzɪŋ] *n* Aufstand *m*.

uproar ['ʌprɔː] *n* Aufruhr *m*, Tumult *m*.

uproot [ʌp'ruːt] *v* ausreißen, entwurzeln.

*upset [ʌp'sɛt; *n* 'ʌpsɛt] *v* (*person*) bestürzen, beunruhigen; (*plan*) vereiteln; (*tip over*) umkippen. *adj* bestürzt, außer Fassung; (*stomach*) verstimmt. *n* (*stomach*) Verstimmung *f*.

upshot ['ʌpʃɒt] *n* Ergebnis *neut*.

upside down [ʌpsaɪdaun] *adv* verkehrt herum, mit dem Kopf nach unten. **turn upside down** sich auf den Kopf stellen.

upstairs [ʌp'stɛəz] *adv* (*go*) nach oben, die Treppe hinauf; (*be*) oben. *adj* (*room*) obere(r).

upstream [ʌp'striːm] *adv* stromaufwärts.

uptight ['ʌptaɪt] *adj* (*coll*) nervös, aufgeregt.

up-to-date [ʌptə'deɪt] *adj* modern, aktuell.

upward ['ʌpwəd] *adj* nach oben (gerichtet). **upward glance** Blick nach oben *m*. *adv also* **upwards** aufwärts, nach oben.

uranium [ju'reɪnɪəm] *n* Uran *neut*.

Uranus ['juə'reɪnəs] *n* Uranus *m*.

urban ['əːbən] *adj* städtisch, Stadt-. **urbanization** *n* Verstädterung *f*. **urbanize** *v* verstädtern.

urchin ['əːtʃɪn] *n* (*boy*) Bengel *m*.

urge [əːdʒ] *v* (*implore*) (dringend) bitten, raten (+ *dat*); (*insist on*) betonen, bestehen auf. **urge on** antreiben. *n* Drang *m*, (An)Trieb *m*.

urgent ['əːdʒənt] *adj* dringend. **urgency** *n* Dringlichkeit *f*.

urine ['juːrɪn] *n* Urin *m*, Harn *m*. **urinal** *n* Urinbecken *neut*, Pissoir *neut*. **urinary** *adj* Urin-. **urinate** *v* urinieren.

urn [əːn] *n* Urne *f*.

us [ʌs] *pron* uns. **both of us** wir beide. **all of us** wir alle.

usage ['juːzɪdʒ] *n* Brauch *m*, Gebrauch *m*.

use [juːz; *n* juːs] *v* benutzen, gebrauchen; (*apply*) anwenden; (*coll: exploit*) ausbeuten. *n* Gebrauch *m*, Verwendung *f*. **be of use** von Nutzen sein, helfen. **for the use of** zum Nutzen von. **it's no use** es hilft nichts. **make use of** Gebrauch machen von. **use up** verbrauchen. *I used to live here* ich wohnte (früher) hier. *she used to say* sie hat immer gesagt, sie pflegte zu sagen. **useful** *adj* nützlich, brauchbar. **usefulness** *n* Nützlichkeit *f*. **useless** *adj* nutzlos, unnütz. **user** *n* Benutzer(in). **user-friendly** *adj* (*comp*) benutzerfreundlich. **uselessness** *n* Nutzlosigkeit *f*.

usher ['ʌʃə] *n* Platzanweiser(in). *v* **usher in** (*fig*) einleiten.

usual ['juːʒuəl] *adj* üblich, gewöhnlich. **usually** *adv* gewöhnlich, normalerweise.

usurp [juː'zəːp] *v* gewaltsam nehmen, usurpieren. **usurpation** *n* Usurpation *f*. **usurper** *n* Usurpator *m*.

utensil [juː'tɛnsl] *n* Gerät *neut*, Werkzeug *neut*; (*pl*) Utensilien *pl*.

uterus ['juːtərəs] *n* Gebärmutter *f*, Uterus *m*. **uterine** *adj* Gebärmutter-.

utility [juː'tɪlətɪ] *n* Nutzen *m*. **public utility** öffentlicher Versorgungsbetrieb *m*.

utilize ['juːtɪlaɪz] *v* verwenden. **utilization** *n* Verwendung *f*.

utmost ['ʌtm oust] *adj* äußerst. **do one's utmost** sein möglichstes tun.

utter¹ ['ʌtə] *v* äußern, aussprechen. **utterance** *n* Äußerung *f*.

utter² ['ʌtə] *adj* rein, bloß, höchst.

U-turn ['juːtəːn] *n* Wende *f*; (*pol*) Kehrtwendung *f*.

V

vacant ['veɪkənt] *adj* leer. **vacancy** *n* Leere *f*; (*job*) freie Stelle. **vacate** *v* verlassen; (*seat*) freimachen. **vacation** *n* Urlaub *m*.

vaccine ['vaksɪn] *n* Impfstoff *m*. **vaccinate** *v* impfen. **vaccination** *n* Impfung *f*.

vacillate ['vasɪleɪt] *v* schwanken. **vacillation** *n* Schwanken *neut*.

vacuum ['vakjum] *n* Vakuum *neut*. **vacuum-cleaner** *n* Staubsauger *m*. *v* (*coll*) mit dem Staubsauger reinigen. **vacuous** *adj* leer.

vagina [və'dʒaɪnə] *n* Scheide *f*, Vagina *f*.

vagrant ['veɪɡrənt] *n* Vagabund *m*,

Landstreicher *m.*

vague [veɪɡ] *adj* vage, undeutlich; (*person*) zerstreut. **vagueness** *n* Verschwommenheit *f.*

vain [veɪn] *adj* (*person*) eitel, eingebildet; (*thing*) eitel, leer; (*effort*) vergeblich. **in vain** umsonst, vergeblich.

valiant ['valɪənt] *adj* tapfer, heroisch.

valid ['valɪd] *adj* gültig. **validate** *v* für gültig erklären. **validity** *n* Gültigkeit *f.*

valley ['valɪ] *n* Tal *neut.*

value ['valjuː] *n* Wert *neut.* **value-added tax (VAT)** Mehrwertsteuer (Mwst) *f. v* (*establish value of*) einschätzen; (*treasure*) bewerten. **valuable** *adj* wertvoll, kostbar. **valuables** *pl n* Wertsachen *pl.* **valuation** *n* Schätzung *f.* **valued** *adj* hochgeschätzt. **valueless** *adj* wertlos.

valve [valv] *n* Ventil *neut;* (*anat*) Klappe *f;* (*elec*) Röhre *f.*

vampire ['vampaɪə] *n* Vampir *m.*

van [van] *n* Lastwagen *m,* Lieferwagen *m.* **luggage van** Gepäckwagen *m.*

vandal ['vandl] *n* Vandale *m,* Vandalin *f.* **vandalism** *n* Vandalismus *m.*

vanilla [və'nɪlə] *n* Vanille *f.*

vanish ['vanɪʃ] *v* verschwinden. **vanishing cream** Tagescreme *f.*

vanity ['vanətɪ] *n* Eitelkeit *f.* **vanity bag** Kosmetiktasche *f.*

vapour ['veɪpə] *n* Dampf *m.* **vaporize** *v* verdampfen.

varicose veins ['varɪkous] *pl n* Krampfadern *pl.*

varnish ['vaːnɪʃ] *n* Lack *m,* Firnis *m. v* lackieren.

vary ['veərɪ] *v* (*modify*) (ab)ändern, variieren; (*become changed*) sich ändern, variieren. **variable** *adj* veränderlich. **variation** *n* Veränderung; (*music, biology*) Variation *f.* **varied** *adj* verschiedenartig, abwechslungsvoll. **variety** *n* Verschiedenheit, Mannigfaltigkeit *f;* (*species*) Art *f,* Varietät *f.* **variety show** Varieté *neut.* **various** *adj* verschieden; (*several*) mehrere. **varying** *adj* wechselnd, unterschiedlich.

vase [vaːz] *n* Vase *f.*

vasectomy [və'sektəm ɪ] *n* Vasektomie *f.*

vast [vaːst] *adj* ungeheuer, riesig; (*wide*) weit, ausgedehnt. **vast majority** überwiegende Mehrheit *f.* **vast numbers of**

zahllos(e). **vastly** *n* gewaltig. **vastness** *n* Weite *f.*

vat [vat] *n* großes Faß *neut.*

VAT [ˌviːeɪtiː *also* vat] *n* MwSt (Mehrwertsteuer) *f.*

vault¹ [voːlt] *n* (*ceiling*) Gewölbe *neut;* (*cellar*) Keller *m;* (*safe*) Stahlkammer *f.*

vault² [voːlt] *v* (*jump*) springen (über). *n* Sprung *m.* **vaulting-horse** *n* Sprungpferd *neut.*

veal [viːl] *n* Kalbfleisch *neut.*

veer [vɪə] *v* sich drehen; (*mot*) ausscheren.

vegan ['viːɡən] *adj* vegan, strikt vegetarisch. *n* Veganer(in) *m, f.*

vegetable ['vedʒtəbl] *n* Gemüse *neut. adj* pflanzlich. **vegetarian** *n* Vegetarier(in); *adj* vegetarisch. **vegetation** *n* Pflanzenwuchs *m,* Vegetation *f.*

vehement ['viːəmənt] *adj* heftig, gewaltig.

vehicle ['viːɪkl] *n* Fahrzeug *neut;* (*medium*) Mittel *neut,* Vehikel *neut.*

veil [veɪl] *n* Schleier *m. v* verschleiern. **veiled** *adj* verschleiert.

vein [veɪn] *n* Vene *f;* (*mood*) Stimmung *f;* (*in rock*) Ader *f.* **veined** *adj* geädert.

velocity [və'bsətɪ] *n* Geschwindigkeit *f.*

velvet ['velvɪt] *n* Samt *m. adj* Samt-. **velvety** *adj* samtweich, samtartig.

vending machine ['vendɪŋ] *n* (Verkaufs)Automat *m.*

veneer [və'nɪə] *n* Furnier *neut;* (*fig*) Anstrich *m. v* furnieren.

venerate ['venəreɪt] *v* verehren, bewundern. **venerable** *adj* ehrwürdig. **veneration** *n* Verehrung *f.*

venereal disease [və'nɪərɪəl] *n* Geschlechtskrankheit *f.*

Venetian blind [və'niːʃən] *n* Jalousie *f.*

vengeance ['vendʒəns] *n* Rache *f.* **take vengeance on** sich rächen an. **vengeful** *adj* rachsüchtig.

venison ['venɪsn] *n* Reh *neut,* Wildbret *neut.*

venom ['venəm] *n* (Tier)Gift *neut.* **venomous** *adj* giftig.

vent [vent] *n* Öffnung *f,* Luftloch *neut;* (*in jacket*) Schlitz *m. v* lüften; (*feelings*) freien Lauf lassen (+ *dat*), äußern.

ventilate ['ventɪleɪt] *v* ventilieren, lüften. **ventilation** *n* Ventilation *f,* Lüftung *f.* **ventilator** *n* Ventilator *m,* Lüftung-sanlage *f.*

venture ['ventʃə] *n* (*risk*) Risiko *neut,* Wagnis *neut;* (*undertaking*) Unternehmen *neut. v* wagen.

venue ['venjuː] *n* Schauplatz *m*; (*meeting place*) Treffpunkt *m*.

Venus ['viːnəs] *n* Venus *f*.

verb [vəːb] *n* Verbum *neut*, Zeitwort *neut*. **verbal** *adj* mündlich. **verbalize** *v* formulieren. **verbatim** *adv* wortwörtlich. **verbose** *adj* wortreich.

verdict ['vəːdikt] *n* Urteil *neut*.

verge [vəːdʒ] *n* Rand *m*, Grenze *f*; (*grass*) Grasstreifen *m*. **verge on** grenzen an.

verify ['verifai] *v* beweisen, bestätigen, beglaubigen. **verification** *n* Beglaubigung *f*.

vermin ['vəːmin] *pl n* Schädlinge *pl*.

vermouth ['vəːməθ] *n* Wermut *m*.

vernacular [və'nakjulə] *n* Volkssprache *f*.

versatile ['vəːsətail] *adj* (*person*) vielseitig. **versatility** *n* Vielseitigkeit *f*.

verse [vəːs] *n* (*stanza*) Strophe *f*; (*line*) Vers *m*; (*poetry*) Poesie *f*, Dichtung *f*. **versed** *adj* versiert.

version ['vəːʃən] *n* Fassung *f*, Version *f*; (*Bible, etc.*) Übersetzung *f*.

versus ['vəːsəs] *prep* gegen.

vertebra ['vəːtibrə] *n* (*pl* -ae) Wirbel *m*. **vertebral column** Wirbelsäule *f*. **vertebrate** *n* Wirbeltier *neut*.

vertical ['vəːtikl] *adj* senkrecht, lotrecht. *n* Senkrechte *f*.

vertigo ['vəːtigou] *n* Schwindelgefühl *neut*.

very ['veri] *adj* sehr. **very best** allerbest. *that very day* an ebendemselben Tag. *at the very beginning* gerade am Anfang.

vessel ['vesl] *n* Gefäß *neut*; (*ship*) Schiff *neut*.

vest [vest] *n* (*undershirt*) Unterhemd *neut*; (*waistcoat*) Weste *f*.

vestige ['vestidʒ] *n* Spur *f*.

vestments ['vestmənts] *pl n* (*rel*) Amtstracht *f*.

vestry ['vestri] *n* Sakristei *f*.

vet [vet] *n* (*animals*) Tierarzt *m*. *v* prüfen, überholen.

veteran ['vetərən] *n* Veteran *m*.

veterinary ['vetərinəri] *n* Tierarzt *m*.

veto ['viːtou] *n* Veto *neut*, Einspruch *m*. *v* Veto einlegen gegen.

vex [veks] *v* ärgern, belästigen. **vexation** *n* Ärger *m*. **vexed** *adj* ärgerlich; (*question*) strittig.

via [vaiə] *prep* über.

viable ['vaiəbl] *adj* lebensfähig; (*practicable*) durchführbar.

viaduct ['vaiədʌkt] *n* Viadukt *m*.

vibrate [vaibreit] *v* vibrieren. **vibration** *n* Vibrieren *neut*, Vibration *f*.

vicar ['vikə] *n* Pfarrer *m*. **vicarage** *n* Pfarrhaus *neut*.

vicarious [vi'keəriəs] *adj* aus zweiter Hand.

vice¹ [vais] *n* (*evil*) Laster *neut*, Untugend *f*.

vice² [vais] *n* (*tool*) Schraubstock *m*, Zwinge *f*.

vice-chancellor [vais'tʃaːnsələ] *n* (*university*) Rektor *m*.

vice-president [vais'prezidənt] *n* Vizepräsident *m*.

vice versa [vaisvəːsə] *adv* umgekehrt.

vicinity [vi'siniti] *n* Nähe *f*, Nachbarschaft *f*.

vicious ['viʃəs] *adj* bösartig, gemein; (*blow, etc*) heftig, gewaltig. **vicious circle** Teufelskreis *m*. **viciousness** *n* Gemeinheit *f*.

victim ['viktim] *n* Opfer *neut*. **victimize** *v* ungerecht behandeln.

victor ['viktə] *n* Sieger(in). **victorious** *adj* siegreich. **victory** *n* Sieg *m*.

video ['vidiou] *adj* Video-. *v* auf Videoband aufnehmen. **videocassette** *n* Videokassette *f*. **videoconference** *n* Videokonferenz *f*. **videorecorder** *n* Videorecorder *m*.

videotape ['vidiouteip] *n* Videoband *neut*.

view [vjuː] *n* Ausblick *m*, Aussicht *f*; (*picture, opinion*) Ansicht *f*. **in view** in Sicht. **viewfinder** *n* Sucher *m*. **viewpoint** *n* Gesichtspunkt *m*, Standpunkt *m*. **with a view to** mit der Absicht, zu. *v* ansehen, betrachten. **viewer** *n* (*TV*) Zuschauer(in).

vigil ['vidʒil] *n* Wachen *neut*. **keep vigil** wachen. **vigilance** *n* Wachsamkeit *f*. **vigilant** *adj* wachsam.

vigour ['vigə] *n* Kraft *f*, Vitalität *f*. **vigorous** *adj* kräftig, energisch.

vile [vail] *adj* gemein, ekelerregend, widerlich.

villa ['vilə] *n* Villa *f*.

village ['vilidʒ] *n* Dorf *neut*. *adj* dörflich, Dorf-. **villager** *n* Dorfbewohner(in).

villain ['vilən] *n* Schurke *m*; (*coll*) Schelm *m*. **villainous** *adj* schurkisch. **villainy** *n* Schurkerei *f*.

vindictive [vin'diktiv] *adj* rachsüchtig. **vindictiveness** *n* Rachsucht *f*.

vine [vaɪn] *n* Rebe *f*, Weinstock *m*. **vineleaf** *n* Weinblatt *m*. **vineyard** *n* Weinberg *m*. **viniculture** *n* Weinbau *m*.

vinegar ['vɪnɪɡə] *n* Essig *m*. **vinegary** *adj* sauer.

vintage ['vɪntɪdʒ] *n* Weinernte *f*; *(particular year)* Jahrgang *m*.

vinyl ['vaɪnl] *n* Vinyl *neut. adj* Vinyl-.

viola [vɪoʊlə] *n* Viola *f*.

violate ['vaɪəleɪt] *v* *(law)* übertreten; *(woman)* vergewaltigen. **violation** *n* Übertretung *f*.

violence ['vaɪələns] *n* Gewalt *f*, Gewalttätigkeit *f*. **violent** *adj* *(blow)* heftig, gewaltig; *(person, action)* gewaltsam.

violet ['vaɪəlɪt] *n* Veilchen *neut. adj* violett.

violin [vaɪə'lɪn] *n* Geige *f*, Violine *f*. **violinist** *n* Geiger(in).

viper ['vaɪpə] *n* Viper *f*, Natter *f*.

virgin ['və:dʒɪn] *n* Jungfrau *f. adj* jungfräulich; *(soil)* unbebaut. **virginity** *n* Jungfernschaft *f*.

Virgo ['və:ɡoʊ] *n* Jungfrau *f*.

virile ['vɪraɪl] *adj* männlich, kräftig. **virility** *n* Männlichkeit *f*.

virtual ['və:tʃuə] *adj* praktisch; *(comp)* virtuell. **virtual reality** virtuelle Realität (VR) *f*. **virtually** *adv* praktisch.

virtue ['və:tʃu:] *n* Tugend *f*. **by virtue of** wegen (+ *gen*). **virtuous** *adj* tugendhaft, rechtschaffen.

virtuoso [və:tjʊ'ouzou] *n* Virtuose *m*, Virtuosin *f*. **virtuosity** *n* Virtuosität *f*.

virus ['vaɪərəs] *n* Virus *neut*.

visa ['vi:zə] *n* Visum *neut*.

viscount ['vaɪkaunt] *n* Vicomte *m*.

viscous ['vɪskəs] *adj* zähflüssig. **viscosity** *n* Viskosität *f*.

visible ['vɪzəbl] *adj* sichtbar. **visibility** *n* Sichtbarkeit *f*. **visibly** *adj* offenbar.

vision ['vɪʒən] *n* *(power of sight)* Sehvermögen *neut*; *(insight)* Einsicht *f*; *(mystical, etc.)* Vision *f*. **field of vision** Blickfeld *neut*. **visionary** *adj* phantastisch; *n* Hellseher(in).

visit ['vɪzɪt] *v* besuchen. *n* Besuch *m*. **visitation** *n* Besuchen *neut*. **visiting** *adj* Besuchs-. **visitor** *n* Besucher(in). **visitor's book** Gästebuch *neut*.

visor ['vaɪzə] *n* Visier *neut*; *(peak)* Schirm *m*.

visual ['vɪʒuəl] *adj* visuell. **visual aids** Anschauungsmaterial *neut*. **visualize** *v*

vergegenwärtigen.

vital ['vaɪtl] *adj* lebenswichtig. **vitality** *n* Lebenskraft *f*.

vitamin ['vɪtəmɪn] *n* Vitamin *neut*.

vivacious [vɪveɪʃəs] *adj* lebhaft, munter. **vivacity** *n* Lebhaftigkeit *f*.

vivid ['vɪvɪd] *adj* *(description)* lebendig; *(colour)* leuchtend; *(imagination)* lebhaft.

vixen ['vɪksn] *n* Füchsin *f*.

vocabulary [və'kæbjʊlərɪ] *n* Wortschatz *m*; *(glossary)* Wörterverzeichnis *neut*.

vocal ['voukəl] *adj* stimmlich; *(music)* Vokal-. **vocal cords** *pl* Stimmbänder *pl*. **vocalist** *n* Sänger(in).

vocation [vou'keɪʃən] *n* *(rel)* Berufung *f*; *(occupation)* Beruf *m*. **vocational** *adj* Berufs-.

vociferous [və'sɪfərəs] *adj* brüllend, lärmend.

vodka ['vodkə] *n* Wodka *m*.

voice [vɔɪs] *n* Stimme *f*. *v* ausdrücken, äußern. **voicemail** *n* Voicemail *f*.

void [vɔɪd] *adj* leer; *(invalid)* nichtig, ungültig.

volatile ['volətaɪl] *adj* flüchtig; *(person)* wankelmütig, sprunghaft.

volcano [vol'keɪnou] *n* Vulkan *m*. **volcanic** *adj* vulkanisch. **volcanic eruption** Vulkanausbruch *m*.

volley ['volɪ] *n* *(mil)* Salve *f*; *(tennis)* Flugschlag *m*.

volt [voult] *n* Volt *neut*. **voltage** *n* Spannung *f*.

volume ['voljum] *n* Volumen *neut*, Inhalt *m*; *(book)* Band *m*; *(noise level)* Lautstärke *f*.

voluntary ['voləntrɪ] *adj* freiwillig.

volunteer [volən'tɪə] *n* Freiwillige(r). *adj* Freiwilligen-. *v* sich freiwillig melden.

voluptuous [və'lʌptʃuəs] *adj* wollüstig. **voluptuousness** *n* Wollust *f*.

vomit ['vomɪt] *v* (sich) erbrechen.

voodoo ['vu:du:] *n* Wodu *m*.

voracious [və'reɪʃəs] *adj* gierig.

vote [vout] *n* *(individual)* Stimme *f*; *(right to vote)* Stimmrecht *neut*; *(election)* Abstimmung *f*, Wahl *f*. **vote of no confidence** Mißtrauensvotum *neut*. *v* abstimmen. **vote for** stimmen für. **voter** *n* Wähler(in).

vouch [vautʃ] *v* (sich) bürgen für. **voucher** *n* Gutschein *m*. **vouchsafe** *v* gewähren.

vow [vau] n Gelübde neut. v schwören, geloben.

vowel ['vauəl] n Vokal m. adj vokalisch.

voyage ['voiidʒ] n Reise f. v reisen. **voyager** n Reisende(r).

vulgar ['vʌlɡə] adj vulgär, ordinär. **vulgarity** n Ungezogenheit f.

vulnerable ['vʌlnərəbl] adj verwundbar.

vulture ['vʌltʃə] n Geier m.

W

wad [wod] n Bausch m; (money) Rolle f.

waddle ['wodl] v watscheln.

wade [weid] v waten.

wafer ['weifə] n Waffel f; (rel) Hostie f. **wafer-thin** adj hauchdünn.

waffle ['wofl] n Waffel f.

waft [woft] v wehen.

wag [waɡ] v **wag one's head** mit dem Kopf wackeln. **wag one's tail** wedeln.

wage [weidʒ] n also **wages** Lohn m. **wage agreement** Tarifvertrag m. **wage-earner** n Lohnempfänger(in). **wage freeze** n Lohnstopp m. **wage-packet** n Lohntüte f. v (war) führen.

waggle ['waɡl] v wackeln (mit).

wagon ['waɡən] n Wagen m; (rail) Waggon m.

waif [weif] n verwahrlostes Kind neut.

wail [weil] v jammern, wehklagen. **wailing** n Jammern neut.

waist [weist] n Taille f. **waistband** n Bund m. **waistcoat** n Weste f.

wait [weit] v warten. **no waiting** Parken verboten. **wait and see** abwarten. **wait for** warten auf. **waiting-room** n Wartesaal m. **wait on** bedienen. n Wartezeit f. **waiter** n Kellner m. **waitress** n Kellnerin f.

waive [weiv] v verzichten auf.

***wake** [weik] v also **waken** or **wake up** aufwachen, erwachen; (awaken) (auf)-wecken, erwecken. **wakeful** adj wachsam. **waking** adj wach.

walk [wo:k] v laufen, (zu Fuß) gehen. **walk out** streiken. **walk out on** im Stich lassen. **walk-over** n leichter Sieg m, Spaziergang m. n Spaziergang m; (path) Weg m. **go for a**

walk einen Spaziergang machen, spazierengehen. **walk of life** Lebensstellung f.

wall [wo:l] n Mauer f; (internal) Wand f. **wallpaper** n Tapete f; v tapezieren.

wallet ['wolit] n Brieftasche f, Geldtasche f.

wallop ['woləp] v prügeln. n (heftiger) Schlag m.

wallow ['wolou] v sich wälzen.

walnut ['wo:lnʌt] n Walnuß f.

walrus ['wo:lrəs] n Walroß neut.

waltz [wo:ls] n Walzer m. v Walzer tanzen, walzen.

wand [wond] n Rute f; (magic) Zauberstab m.

wander ['wondə] v wandern. **wander about** umherwandern. **wanderlust** n Wanderlust f. **wanderer** n Wanderer m. **wandering** n Wandern neut. adj wandernd.

wane [wein] v abnehmen.

wangle ['waŋɡl] v organisieren, (hinten-herum) beschaffen. **wangler** n Schieber m.

want [wont] v wollen; (need) benötigen; (wish) wünschen. **wants** pl n Bedürfnisse pl. **wanted** adj gesucht. **be found wanting** den Erwartungen nicht entsprechen.

wanton ['wontən] adj lüstern; (cruelty, etc.) rücksichtslos.

war [wo:] n Krieg m. **be at war with** Kriegführen mit. **prisoner-of-war** Kriegsgefangene(r). **war crime** n Kriegsverbrechen neut. **warfare** n Kriegführung f. **warlike** adj kriegerisch. **war memorial** Kriegerdenkmal neut.

warble ['wo:bl] v trillern.

ward [wo:d] n (town) Bezirk n; (hospital) Station f; (of court) Mündel neut. v **ward off** abwehren. **warden** n Vorsteher m. **warder** n Gefängniswärter m.

wardrobe ['wo:droub] n Kleiderschrank m; (clothes) Garderobe f.

wares [weəz] pl n Waren pl.

warehouse ['weəhaus] n Lager(haus) neut.

warm [wo:m] adj warm. **warm-blooded** adj warmblütig. **warm-hearted** adj warmherzig. v (auf)wärmen. **warm up** v (become warm) warm werden; (engine) warmlaufen (lassen). **warmish** adj lauwarm. **warmth** n Wärme f.

warn [wo:n] v warnen. **warn off** verwarnen. **warning** n Warnung f. adj warnend. **warning light** Warnlicht neut. **warning**

triangle (*auto*) Warndreieck *neut.*

warp [wɔːp] *v* sich verziehen, krumm werden. **warped** *adj* verzogen.

warrant ['wɔrənt] *n* Vollmacht *f*, Berechtigung *f*. **warrant of arrest** Haftbefehl *m*.

warren ['wɔrən] *n* Kaninchengehege *neut.*

warrior ['wɔriə] *n* Krieger *m.*

wart [wɔːt] *n* Warze *f.*

wary ['wɛəri] *adj* vorsichtig, behutsam. **wary of** auf der Hut vor.

was [wɒz] *V* be.

wash [wɒʃ] *v* waschen; (*oneself*) sich waschen; (*dishes*) spülen. **washbasin** *n* Waschbecken *neut.* **wash down** abwaschen. **washed-out** *adj* verblaßt; (*coll*) ermüdet. **washed-up** *adj* (*coll*) ruiniert, fertig. **washing** *n* (*laundry*) Wäsche *f.* **washing machine** Waschmaschine *f.* **washing powder** Waschmittel *neut.* **wash up** (ab)spülen, abwaschen. *n* Waschen *neut*, Wäsche *f*, **washable** *adj* waschecht.

washer *n* (*tech*) Scheibe *f*, Dichtungsring *m.*

wasp [wɒsp] *n* Wespe *f.* **waspish** *adj* reizbar.

waste [weist] *v* verschwenden, vergeuden. **waste away** abnehmen, verfallen. *n* Verschwendung *f*; (*rubbish*) Abfall *m.* **waste of time** Zeitverschwendung *f. adj* (*land*) wüst; Abfall-. **lay waste** verwüsten. **waste-bin** *n* Abfalleimer *m.* **waste-paper basket** *n* Papierkorb *neut.* **wasteful** *adj* verschwenderisch.

watch [wɒtʃ] *v* (*guard*) bewachen; (*observe*) zusehen, beobachten; (*pay attention to*) achtgeben auf. **watch out!** paß auf! **watch out for** auf der Hut sein vor. **watch television** fernsehen. *n* Wache *f*; (*wristwatch*) Armbanduhr *f.* **keep watch** Wache halten. **watchdog** *n* Wachhund *m.* **watchman** *n* Wächter *m.* **watchful** *adj* wachsam.

water ['wɔːtə] *n* Wasser *neut.* *v* wässern. **water down** verwässern.

water-closet *n* (Wasser)Klosett *neut*, WC *neut.*

water-colour *n* Aquarell *neut. adj* Aquarell-.

watercress ['wɔːtəkrɛs] *n* Brunnenkresse *f.*

waterfall ['wɔːtəfɔːl] *n* Wasserfall *m.*

watering-can *n* Gießkanne *f.*

water-lily *n* Seerose *f*, Wasserlilie *f.*

waterlogged ['wɔːtəlɒgd] *adj* vollgesogen.

watermark ['wɔːtəmɑːk] *n* (*in paper*) Wasserzeichen *neut.*

water-melon *n* Wassermelone *f.*

water-mill *n* Wassermühle *f.*

waterproof ['wɔːtəpruːf] *adj* wasserdicht. *n* Regenmantel *m.* *v* imprägnieren.

watershed ['wɔːtəʃɛd] *n* Wasserscheide *f.*

water-ski *n* Wasserski *m.* *v* Wasserski fahren.

watertight ['wɔːtətait] *adj* wasserdicht; (*argument*) unanfechtbar.

water-way *n* Wasserstraße *f.*

waterworks ['wɔːtəwɜːks] *pl n* Wasserwerk *neut sing.*

watery ['wɔːtəri] *adj* wässerig; (*eyes*) tränend.

watt [wɒt] *n* Watt *neut.* **wattage** *n* Wattleistung *f.*

wave [weiv] *n* Welle *f*; (*gesture*) Wink *m.* **waveband** *n* Wellenband *neut.* **wavelength** *n* Wellenlänge *f.* *v* winken; (*hair*) in Wellen legen. **wavy** *adj* wellig; (*hair*) gewellt.

waver ['weivə] *v* schwanken.

wax[1] [waks] *n* Wachs *neut.* *v* (*floor*) bohnern. **waxen** *adj* wächsern. **waxwork** *n* Wachsfigure *f.*

wax[2] [waks] *v* (*increase*) wachsen; (*become*) werden.

way [wei] *n* Weg *m*; (*direction*) Richtung *f*; (*method*) Art *f*, Weise *f*; (*respect*) Hinsicht *f*, Beziehung *f.* **by the way** übrigens. **on the way** unterwegs. **out-of-the-way** *adj* abgelegen; (*odd*) ungewöhnlich.

*****waylay** [wei'lei] *v* auflauern (+*dat*).

wayward ['weiwəd] *adj* eigensinnig. **waywardness** *n* Eigensinn *m.*

we [wiː] *pl pron* wir.

weak [wiːk] *adj* schwach; (*liquids*) dünn. **weak-minded** *adj* charakterschwach. **weaken** *v* schwächen. *n* Schwächling *m.* **weakly** *adj, adv* schwächlich. **weakness** *n* Schwäche *f*; (*disadvantage*) Nachteil *m*; (*liking*) Vorliebe *f*, Faible *neut.*

wealth [wɛlθ] *n* Reichtum *m*; (*fortune*) Vermögen *neut.* **wealthy** *adj* reich, wohlhabend.

wean [wiːn] *v* entwöhnen.

weapon ['wɛpən] *n* Waffe *f.*

*****wear** [wɛə] *v* tragen; (*wear out*) abnutzen; (*become worn*) abgenutzt werden; *n* Tragen *neut*; (*wear and tear*) Abnutzung *f*, Verschleiß *m*. **wear off** (*fig*) sich verlieren. **wear out** (*person*) ermüden.

weary ['wɪərɪ] *adj* müde; (*task*) lästig. *v* ermüden; (*become tired of*) müde werden (+ *gen*). **weariness** *n* Müdigkeit *f*. **wearisome** *adj* ermüdend, langweilig.

weasel ['wɪːzl] *n* Wiesel *neut*.

weather ['weðə] *n* Wetter *neut*. **weather-beaten** *adj* verwittert. **weathercock** *n* Wetterhahn *m*. **weather forecast** Wettervorhersage *f*. **weatherman** *n* (*coll*) Meteorologe *m*. **weather-proof** *adj* wetter-fest.

*****weave** [wɪːv] *v* weben. **weave into** ein-flechten in. **weaving** *n* Weberei *f*; *adj* Web-.

web [web] *n* (*spider's*) Spinngewebe *neut*. **(World Wide) Web** *n* (*comp*) Web *neut*. **weblog** *n* Blog *neut*, Online-Tagebuch *neut*. **website** *n* Website *f*. **webbed foot** Schwimmfuß *m*. **webbing** *n* Gewebe *neut*. **web-footed** *adj* schwimmfüßig.

wedding ['wedɪŋ] *n* Hochzeit *f*. **wedding cake** Hochzeitskuchen *m*. **wedding day** Hochzeitstag *m*. **wedding ring** Trauring *m*.

wedge [wedʒ] *n* Keil *m*; (*of cheese*) Ecke *f*. **wedge-shaped** *adj* keilförmig. *v* einkeilen.

Wednesday ['wenzdɪ] *n* Mittwoch *m*. **on Wednesdays** mittwochs.

weed [wɪːd] *n* Unkraut *neut*. *v* (Unkraut) jäten. **weedy** *adj* (*coll*) schmächtig.

week [wɪːk] *n* Woche *f*. **weekday** *n* Wochentag *m*. **weekend** *n* Wochenende *neut*. **weekly** *adj* wöchentlich; *n* (*magazine*) Wochenzeitschrift *f*.

*****weep** [wɪːp] *v* weinen. **weeping** *adj* weinend; *n* Weinen *neut*. **weeping willow** Trauerweide *f*.

weigh [weɪ] *v* wiegen. **weigh one's words** seine Worte abwägen. **weigh up** ab-schätzen. **weight** *n* Gewicht *neut*. **carry weight with** viel gelten bei. **lose weight** abnehmen. **put on weight** zunehmen. **weight-lifting** *n* Gewichtheben *neut*. **weighty** *adj* schwerwiegend.

weir [wɪə] *n* Wehr *neut*.

weird [wɪəd] *adj* unheimlich.

welcome ['welkəm] *n* Willkommen *neut*. *adj, interj* willkommen. **you're welcome** (*coll*) bitte, nichts zu danken. *v* willkom-men heißen; (*fig*) begrüßen.

weld [weld] *v* (ver)schweißen. *n* Schweißstelle *f*, Schweißnaht *f*. **welder** *n*

Schweißer *m*. **welding** *n* Schweißen *neut*.

welfare ['welfeə] *n* Wohlfahrt *f*. **welfare state** Wohlfahrtsstaat *m*.

well¹ [wel] *n* (*for water*) Brunnen *m*, Quelle *f*.

well² [wel] *adv* gut. **as well** auch. **as well as** sowohl … als auch. **you may well ask** du kannst wohl fragen. *adj* (*healthy*) wohl, gesund. **feel well** sich wohl fühlen. **I'm not well** mir ist nicht wohl. *interj* na, schön.

well-being *n* Wohlergehen *neut*.

well-behaved *adj* artig.

well-bred *adj* wohlerzogen.

well-built *adj* gut gebaut; (*person*) kräftig gebaut.

well-done *adj* (*meat*) gut durchgebraten.

wellingtons ['welɪŋtənz] *pl n* Gummistiefel *pl*.

well-known *adj* (wohl)bekannt.

well-meaning *adj* wohlmeinend.

well-off *adj* wohlhabend.

well-paid *adj* gut bezahlt.

well-spoken *adj* höflich.

well-to-do *adj* wohlhabend.

well-worn *adj* abgenutzt; (*phrase*) abge-droschen.

went [went] *V* **go**.

wept [wept] *V* **weep**.

west [west] *n* Westen *m*. *adj also* **westerly** westlich, West-. *adv also* **westwards** nach Westen; westwärts. **western** *adj* westlich; *n* Wildwestfilm *m*. **West Indies** Westindische Inseln *f pl*, Karibik *f*. **West Indian** karibisch.

wet [wet] *adj* naß. **wet through** durchnäßt. **wet weather** Regenwetter *neut*. *n* Nässe *f*. *v* anfeuchten, naßmachen. **wetness** *n* Nässe *f*.

whack [wak] *v* schlagen, verhauen. *n* Schlag *m*.

whale [weɪl] *n* Wal *m*, Walfisch *m*. **whaler** *n* Walfänger *m*. **whaling** *n* Walfang *m*.

wharf [woːf] *n* Kai *m*.

what [wot] *pron* was. **so what?** na und? **what about …?** wie wäre es mit …? **what-ever** *pron* was auch immer. **nothing whatever** *pron* was auch immer. **nothing whatever** überhaupt nichts. **what for?** wozu? **what's up?** was ist los? **what's your name?** wie heißt du? *or* (*polite*) wie ist Ihr Name? *adj* was für ein, welch.

wheat [wiːt] n Weizen m.

wheel [wiːl] n Rad neut; (steering) Lenkrad neut. **at the wheel** am Steuer. v rollen. **wheelbarrow** n Schubkarren m. **wheelchair** n Rollstuhl m. **wheel clamp** n Radkralle f; Parkkralle f

wheeze [wiːz] n Keuchen neut; (coll) Plan m. v keuchen, schnaufen.

whelk [welk] n Wellhornschnecke f.

when [wen] adv (question) wann. conj (with past tense) als; (with present tense) wenn. **whenever** conj wann auch immer.

where [weə] adv, conj wo; (motion) wohin. **where from?** woher? **where to?** wohin? where do you come from? wo kommen Sie her? where are you going? wo gehen Sie hin? **whereabouts** adv wo; n Verbleib m. **whereas** conj wohingegen, während. **whereby** adv wodurch, womit. **whereupon** adv woraufhin. **wherever** adv wo auch immer.

whether [weðə] conj ob.

which [witʃ] pron (question) welch; (the one that) welch, der/die/das.

whiff [wif] n Hauch m.

while [wail] conj während; (whereas) wogegen. n Weile f. **a long while ago** schon lange her. **for a while** eine Zeitlang. **in a while** bald. v **while away the time** sich die Zeit vertreiben.

whim [wim] n Laune f, Einfall m.

whimper [wimpə] n Wimmer neut. v wimmern.

whimsical [wimzikl] adj launenhaft.

whine [wain] n Gewinsel neut. v winseln. **whining** adj weinerlich.

whip [wip] n Peitsche f. v peitschen; (cream) schlagen. **whipped cream** Schlagsahne f. **whipping** n Peitschen neut. **whip-round** n (coll) Geldsammlung f.

whippet [wipit] n Whippet m.

whirl [wəːl] n Wirbel m. v wirbeln. **whirlwind** n Wirbelwind m.

whisk [wisk] n Schneebesen m. v schlagen. **whisk away/off** v wegzaubern.

whiskers [wiskəz] pl n (animals) Schnurrhaare pl; (man's) Barthaare pl.

whisky [wiski] n Whisky m.

whisper [wispə] v flüstern. n Flüstern neut.

whist [wist] n Whist neut.

whistle [wisl] v pfeifen. n Pfiff m; (instrument) Pfeife f.

white [wait] adj weiß; (pale) blaß. **white bread** Weißbrot neut. **white-collar crime** Wirtschaftskriminalität f. **white-collar worker** Büroangestellte m, f. **white lie** Notlüge f. **white man** Weiße(r) m. **whitewash** v tünchen. **white wine** Weißwein m. n Weiß neut; (person) Weiße(r). **whiten** v weiß machen; (bleach) bleichen. **whiteness** n Weiße f.

whiting [waitiŋ] n Weißfisch m.

Whitsun [witsn] n Pfingsten neut sing.

whiz [wiz] v zischen.

who [huː] pron (question) wer; (the one which, that) wer, welch, der/die/das. **whoever** pron wer auch immer.

whole [houl] adj ganz; (undamaged) heil, unverletzt. n das Ganze neut; (collective) Gesamtheit f. **on the whole** im großen und ganzen. **wholefood** n Vollwertkost f. **wholefood shop** Bioladen m.

whole-hearted adj rückhaltlos.

wholemeal [houlmiːl] adj Vollkorn-.

wholesale [houlseil] adv en gros; (fig) unterschiedslos. adj Großhandels-. n Großhandel m. **wholesaler** n Großhändler m.

wholesome [houlsəm] adj bekömmlich, gesund.

whom [huːm] pron (question) (acc) wen, (dat) wem; (that, the one whom) den, dem.

whooping cough [huːpiŋ] n Keuchhusten m.

whore [hoː] n Hure f. v huren.

whose [huːz] pron (question) wessen; (of whom) dessen, deren. whose is this? wem gehört dies?

why [wai] adv warum. interj nun, ja. **that is why** deshalb. **the reason why** der Grund, weshalb.

wick [wik] n Docht m.

wicked [wikid] adj böse. **wickedness** n Bosheit f.

wicker [wikə] adj Weiden-, Korb-. **wickerwork** n Korbwaren pl.

wicket [wikit] n (gate) Pförtchen neut.

wide [waid] adj breit. adv weit. **far and wide** weit und breit. **wide awake** hellwach. **widespread** adj weitverbreitet. **widely** adv weit. **widely known** allgemein bekannt. **widen** v breiter machen or werden. **wideness** n Breite f.

widow [widou] n Witwe f. **widowed** adj

verwitwet. **widower** n Witwer m. **widowhood** n Witwenstand m.

width [wiːθ] n Breite f, Weite f.

wield [wiːld] v (*weapon*) handhaben; (*influence*) ausüben.

wife [waif] n (pl **wives**) Frau f.

wig [wig] n Perücke f.

wiggle [wigl] v wackeln. n Wackeln neut.

wild [waild] adj wild; (*coll: angry*) wütend. **be wild about** (*coll*) schwärmen für. **wildcat strike** wilder Streik m. **wild flower** Feldblume f. **Wildness** n Wildheit f.

wilderness [wildənəs] n Wüste f.

wilful [wilfəl] adj eigensinnig. **wilfulness** n Eigensinn m.

will¹ [wil] v (*to form future*) werden; (*expressing wish or determination*) wollen.

will² [wil] n Wille m; (*testament*) Testament neut. **will-power** n Willenskraft f.

willing [wiliŋ] adj bereit. **willingly** adv bereitwillig. **willingness** n Bereitschaft f.

willow [wilou] n Weide f.

wilt [wilt] v verwelken.

wily [waili] adj schlau, listig.

*win [win] v gewinnen; (*mil*) siegen. n Sieg m.

wince [wins] v zusammenzucken. n (Zusammen)Zucken neut.

winch [wintʃ] n Winde f.

wind¹ [wind] n Wind m. **wind farm** Windpark m, Windfarm f. **wind instrument** Blasinstrument neut.

*wind² [waind] v (sich) winden; (*yarn*) aufwickeln; (*clock*) aufziehen. **wind up** (*come to a close*) Schluß machen. (*business*) auflösen. **winder** n Winde f. **winding** adj sich windend, schlängelnd.

windlass [windləs] n Winde f.

windmill [windmil] n Windmühle f.

windpipe [windpaip] n Luftröhre f.

window [windou] n Fenster neut; (*ticket office, etc.*) Schalter m; (*shop*) Schaufenster neut. **window-box** n Blumenkasten m. **window-frame** n Fensterrahmen m. **window-pane** n Fensterscheibe f. **window-shopping** n Schaufensterbummel m. **window-sill** n Fensterbrett neut.

windscreen [windskriːn] n Windschutzscheibe f. **windscreen wiper** Scheibenwischer m.

windsurfing [windsəːfiŋ] n Windsurfen neut.

windy [windi] adj windig.

wine [wain] n Wein m. **wine bar** Weinstube f. **wineglass** n Weinglas neut.

wing [wiŋ] n Flügel m. (*theatre*) Kulisse f; (*mot*) Kotflügel m. **on the wing** im Fluge. **winged** adj geflügelt. **winger** n (*sport*) Außenstürmer m. **wing-nut** n Flügelmutter f.

wink [wiŋk] n Zwinkern neut. v **wink at** zuzwinkern (+dat).

winkle [wiŋkl] n Strandschnecke f.

winner [winə] n Sieger(in), Gewinner(in). **winnings** pl n Gewinn m sing.

winter [wintə] n Winter m. v überwintern. **wintry** adj winterlich.

wipe [waip] v wischen. **wipe out** (*destroy*) ausrotten. **wipe up** (*dishes*) abtrocknen. **wiper** n Wischer m.

wire [waiə] n Draht m; (*telegram*) Telegramm neut. **wire netting** Maschendraht m. v (*house, etc.*) Leitungen legen in. **wireless** n Radio neut. **wiring** n Leitungsnetz neut.

wiry [waiəri] adj (*person*) sehnig, zäh, (*hair*) borstig.

wisdom [wizdəm] n Weisheit f. **wisdom tooth** n Weisheitszahn m.

wise [waiz] adj weise, klug. **wise guy** (*coll*) Besserwisser m. **wise man/woman** Weise(r).

wish [wiʃ] v wünschen. **wish for** sich wünschen. *I wish to know* ich möchte wissen. **wished-for** adj erwünscht. n Wunsch m.

wisp [wisp] n (*hair*) Strähne f. **wispy** adj (*hair*) wuschelig.

wistful [wistfəl] adj sehnsüchtig. **wistfulness** n Sehnsucht f.

wit [wit] n Witz m, Esprit m. **wits** pl Verstand m.

witch [witʃ] n Hexe f. **witchcraft** n Hexerei f. **witch-doctor** n Medizinmann m.

with [wið] prep mit; (*among people*) bei. **weep with joy** vor Freude weinen. **stay with** bleiben bei.

*withdraw [wiðdrɔː] v (sich) zurückziehen; (*remark*) zurücknehmen; (*money*) abheben. **withdrawal** n Zurückziehung f; Zurücknahme f; Abhebung f. **withdrawn** adj zurückgezogen.

wither [wiðə] v verdorren, verwelken.

withered *adj* welk.

*withhold [wɪðˈhoʊld] *v* zurückhalten.

within [wɪðˈɪn] *prep* innerhalb (+*gen*). *adv* darin, innen. **within a short time** binnen kurzem.

without [wɪðˈaʊt] *prep* ohne (+*acc*).

*withstand [wɪðˈstænd] *v* widerstehen (+*dat*).

witness [ˈwɪtnɪs] *n* Zeuge *m*, Zeugin *f*. **bear witness to** Zeuge ablegen von. **witness-box** *n* Zeugenstand *m*. *v* bezeugen; (*be present at*) erleben, sehen.

witty [ˈwɪtɪ] *adj* witzig. **witticism** *n* Witz *m*.

wizard [ˈwɪzəd] *n* Zauberer *m*. **wizardry** *n* Zauberei *f*.

WMD *n* MVW (Massenvernichtungswaffen) *f pl*.

wobble [ˈwɒbl] *v* wackeln, schwanken. *n* Wackeln *neut*. **wobbly** *adj* wackelig.

woke [wəʊk] *V* **wake**.

woken [ˈwəʊkn] *V* **wake**.

wolf [wʊlf] *n* (*pl* **wolves**) Wolf *m*. *v* (*gobble*) verschlingen. **she-wolf** *n* Wölfin *f*.

woman [ˈwʊmən] *n* (*pl* **women**) Frau *f*. **woman doctor** Ärztin *f*. **womanly** *adj* weiblich, fraulich.

womb [wuːm] *n* Gebärmutter *f*.

won [wʌn] *V* **win**.

wonder [ˈwʌndə] *n* (*marvel*) Wunder *neut*; (*astonishment*) Erstaunen *neut*, Verwunderung *f*. **no wonder** kein Wunder. *v* (*be surprised*) sich wundern; (*ask oneself, muse*) sich fragen, gespannt sein. **wonderful** *adj* wunderbar. **wondrous** *adj* erstaunlich.

wonky [ˈwɒŋki] *adj* wackelig.

wood [wʊd] *n* Holz *neut*; (*forest*) Wald *m*. **wooden** *adj* hölzern, Holz-.

woodcock [ˈwʊdkɒk] *n* Waldschnepfe *f*.

woodpecker [ˈwʊdpekə] *n* Specht *m*.

wood-pigeon *n* Ringeltaube *f*.

woodwind [ˈwʊdwɪnd] *n* Holzblasinstrument *neut*; Holzbläser *m*.

woodwork [ˈwʊdwɜːk] *n* Holzarbeit *f*, Tischlerei *f*.

woodworm [ˈwʊdwɜːm] *n* Holzwurm *m*.

woody [ˈwʊdi] *adj* Holz-, holzig; (*countryside*) Wald-, waldig.

wool [wʊl] *n* Wolle *f*. **woollen** *adj* wollen, Woll-. **woolly** *adj* wollig.

word [wɜːd] *n* Wort *neut*. **break/keep one's word** sein Wort brechen/halten. **word processing** Textverarbeitung *f*. **word processor** Textverarbeiter *m*. **wording** *n* Fassung *f*. **wordy** *adj* wortreich, langatmig.

wore [wɔː] *V* **wear**.

work [wɜːk] *n* Arbeit *f*; (*piece of work, art, music, etc.*) Werk *neut*. **works** *pl* Werk *neut*. *v* arbeiten; (*of machine*) laufen, funktionieren; (*succeed*) klappen; (*land*) bebauen; (*metal*) schmieden; (*operate (machine)*) bedienen. **work off** (*debt*) abarbeiten; (*feelings*) abreagieren. **work out** ausrechnen. **out of work** arbeitslos. **worked-up** *adj* aufgeregt, aufgebracht. **worker** *n* Arbeiter(in). **working** *adj* Arbeits-; (*person*) berufstätig. **working class** Arbeiterklasse *f*; *adj* Arbeiter-. **in working order** betriebsfähig. **working party** Arbeitsgruppe *f*. **workman** *n* Handwerker *m*. **workstation** *n* Datenstation *f*. **work-to-rule** *n* Bummelstreik *m*.

workaholic [ˌwɜːkəˈhɒlɪk] *n* Arbeitssüchtige(r).

world [wɜːld] *n* Welt *f*. **not for all the world** nicht um alles in der Welt. **the world to come** das Jenseits *neut*. **world champion** Weltmeister(in). **world-famous** *adj* weltberühmt. **worldly-wise** *adj* weltklug. **world-wide** *adj* weitverbreitet. **worldly** *adj* irdisch.

worm [wɜːm] *n* Wurm *m*.

worn [wɔːn] *v* **wear**. *adj* (*worn out*) abgenutzt. **worn out** *adj* (*thing*) abgenutzt; (*person*) todmüde.

worry [ˈwʌri] *v* (*bother*) beunruhigen; (*be worried*) sich Sorgen machen, sich beunruhigen. *n* Sorge *f*, Besorgnis *f*. **worrying** *adj* beunruhigend. **worried** *adj* beunruhigt, besorgt.

worse [wɜːs] *adj, adv* schlimmer, schlechter. **worse and worse** immer schlechter. **worsen** *v* (sich) verschlechtern *or* verschlimmern.

worship [ˈwɜːʃɪp] *n* Anbetung *f*, Verehrung *f*; (*in church*) Gottesdienst *m*. *v* anbeten, verehren. **worshipful** *adj* ehrwürdig. **worshipper** *n* Anbeter(in).

worst [wɜːst] *adj* schlechtest, schlimmst. *adv* am schlechtesten *or* schlimmsten. **at the worst** im schlimmsten Falle. **worst-case scenario** GAU (größter anzunehmender Unfall) *m*.

worsted ['wʊstɪd] n Kammgarn neut.

worth [wə:θ] n Wert m. adj wert. it's worth ten marks es ist zehn Mark wert. it's not worth it es lohnt sich nicht. **worthless** adj wertlos. **worthwhile** adj der Mühe wert. **worthy** adj würdig, wert.

would [wʊd] v (to form conditional) würde, würdest, etc. (used to) pflegte, pflegtest, etc; (expressing desire, volition) wollte, wolltest, etc. he would go (if) er würde gehen(wenn). I would like ich möchte. he would come in the summer er pflegte im Sommer zu kommen. he would not come er wollte durchaus nicht kommen.

wound[1] [waʊnd] V **wind**[2].

wound[2] [wu:nd] n Wunde f. v verwunden. **wounded** adj verletzt.

wove [wouv] V **weave**.

woven ['wouvn] V **weave**.

wrangle ['ræŋgl] v zanken, streiten. n Zank m, Streit m.

wrap [ræp] v wickeln. **wrap up** einwickeln. n Schal m. **wrapper** n Umschlag m. **wrapping** n Verpackung f. **wrapping paper** n Einwickelpapier neut.

wreath [ri:θ] n Kranz m.

wreck [rek] n wrack neut; (naut) Schiffbruch m. v zerstören. **wreckage** n Trümmer pl.

wren [ren] n Zaunkönig m.

wrench [rentʃ] v zerren, ziehen. n (tool) Schraubenschlüssel m.

wrestle ['resl] v ringen. **wrestler** n Ringer m. **wrestling** n Ringkampf m, Ringen neut.

wretch [retʃ] n Elende(r), armes Wesen neut. **wretched** adj unglücklich, elend.

wriggle ['rɪgl] v sich schlängeln. n Schlängeln neut.

***wring** [rɪŋ] v (hands) ringen; (clothes) auswringen. **wringer** n Wringermaschine f. **wringing wet** triefend naß.

wrinkle ['rɪŋkl] n (face, brow) Runzel f, Falte f; (paper) Knitter m. **wrinkled** adj runzlig.

wrist [rɪst] n Handgelenk neut. **wristwatch** n Armbanduhr f.

writ [rɪt] n (law) (Vor)Ladung f. **Holy Writ** Heilige Schrift f.

***write** [raɪt] v schreiben. **write down** aufschreiben. **write off** v abschreiben. **write-off** n (after car accident) Totalschaden m. **write out** (cheque) ausstellen. **writer** n Schriftsteller(in). **writing** n Schreiben neut.

in writing schriftlich. **writing-paper** n Schreibpapier neut.

written ['rɪtn] V **write**. adj schriftlich.

writhe [raɪð] v sich winden.

wrong [rɒŋ] adj (incorrect) falsch; (bad, immoral) unrecht. **be wrong** sich irren, unrecht haben. what's wrong with ...? was ist los mit ...? that was wrong of you das war unrecht von dir. **go wrong** (mech) kaputtgehen; (plan) schiefgehen. **get it wrong** es ganz falsch verstehen. **wrongdoer** n Missetäter(in). **wrongdoing** n Missetat f. **wrongly** adv mit Unrecht.

wrote [rout] V **write**.

wrought iron [rɔ:taɪən] n Schweißeisen neut.

wrung [rʌŋ] V **wring**.

wry [raɪ] adj verschroben.

X

xenophobia [ˌzenəˈfoubiə] n Fremdenfeindlichkeit f.

Xerox® ['zɪərɒks] n Fotokopiergerät neut. v fotokopieren.

X-ray [eksreɪ] n Röntgenstrahl m; (picture) Röntgenbild neut. v röntgen. adj Röntgen-.

xylophone ['zaɪləfoun] n Xylophon neut.

Y

yacht [jɒt] n Jacht f. **yachting** n Segeln neut.

yank [jæŋk] v (coll) heftig ziehen (an). n Ruck m.

yap [jæp] v kläffen; (coll) schwätzen. n Kläffen neut.

yard[1] [jɑ:d] n (measure) Yard neut. **yardstick** n Maßstab m.

yard[2] [jɑ:d] n Hof m.

yarn [jɑ:n] n Garn neut; (story) Gechichte f.

yawn [jɔ:n] n Gähnen neut. v gähnen.

year [jə] n Jahr neut. 5 years old fünf Jahre alt. **for years** jahrelang. **yearbook** n

Jahrbuch *neut.* **yearly** *adj* jährlich.

yearn [jɜːn] *v* sich sehnen (nach). **yearning** *n* Sehnsucht *f*.

yeast [jiːst] *n* Hefe *f*.

yell [jel] *v* (gellend) aufschreien. *n* Schrei *m*.

yellow ['jeləu] *adj* gelb. *n* Gelb *neut*.

yelp [jelp] *v* jaulen. *n* Jaulen *neut*.

yes [jes] *adv* ja, jawohl. **yes-man** *n* Jasager *m*.

yesterday ['jestədi] *n, adv* gestern. **yesterday morning** gestern früh. **yesterday's** *or* **of yesterday** gestrig, von gestern. **the day before yesterday** vorgestern.

yet [jet] *adv* noch, immer noch. *conj* aber.

yew [juː] *n* Eibe *f*.

yield [jiːld] *n* Ertrag *m*. **yielding** *adj* ergiebig.

yob [jɒb] *n* (*coll*) Rowdy *m*.

yoga ['jəugə] *n* Joga *m*.

yoghurt ['jɒgət] *n* Joghurt *m*.

yoke [jəuk] *n* Joch *m*. *v* verbinden.

yolk [jəuk] *n* Eidotter *m*, Eigelb *neut*.

yonder ['jɒndə] *adv* da, dort drüben. *adj* jene(r).

you [juː] *pron* (*fam sing*) du; (*fam pl*) ihr; (*polite sing or pl*) Sie; (*impers, one*) man. *acc*: dich; euch; Sie; einen. *dat*: dir; euch; Ihnen; einem.

young [jʌŋ] *adj* jung. *n* (Tier)Junge *pl*. **young children** kleine Kinder *pl*.

your [jɔː] *adj* (*fam sing*) dein; (*fam pl*) euer; (*polite sing or pl*) Ihr; (*impers, one's*) sein. **yours** (der/die/das) deine *or* eure *or* Ihre *or* seine. *a friend of yours* ein Freund von dir.

youth [juːθ] *n* Jugend *f*; (*lad*) Jüngling *m*. *adj* Jugend-. **youth hostel** Jugendherberge *f*. **youthful** *adj* jugendlich, jung.

Yugoslavia [juːgou'slɑːvjə] *n* Jugoslawien *neut*. **Yugoslav** *n* Jugoslawe *m*, Jugoslawin *f*. *adj* jugoslawisch.

Z

zap [zap] *v* (*coll: channel-hop*) zappen.

zeal [ziːl] *n* Eifer *m*. **zealous** *adj* eifrig.

zebra ['zebrə] *n* Zebra *neut*. **zebra crossing** *n* Zebrastreifen *m*.

zero ['zɪərou] *n* Null *f*.

zest [zest] *n* Lust *f*, Begeisterung *f*.

zigzag ['zigzag] *adj* Zickzack-. *n* Zickzack *m*.

zinc [ziŋk] *n* Zink *neut*.

zip [zip] *n also* **zipper** Reißverschluß *m*. **zip code** Postleitzahl *f*.

zodiac ['zoudiæk] *n* Tierkreis *m*. **signs of the zodiac** Tierkreiszeichen *pl*.

zone [zoun] *n* Zone *f*.

zoo [zuː] *n* Zoo *m*. **zoological** *adj* zoologisch. **zoologist** *n* Zoologe *m*. **zoology** *n* Zoologie *f*, Tierkunde *f*.

zoom [zuːm] *v* summen, brummen; (*coll: rush*) sausen; (*prices*) Hochschnellen. **zoom lens** Zoom (objektiv) *neut*.

German – Englisch

A

Aal [aːl] m (pl -e) eel.

ab [ap] adv off; prep (abwärts, nach unten) from; (weg, fort) from. **ab und zu** now and again, from time to time. **auf und ab** up and down, to and fro.

abänderlich [ˈapɛndərliç] adj variable. **abändern** v change, modify. **Abänderung** f modification; (Pol) amendment.

abarbeiten [ˈaparbaitən] (Schuld) work off; (Werkzeug) wear out. **sich die Finger abarbeiten** work one's fingers to the bone.

Abbau [ˈapbau] m (unz.) demolition; (Personal) reduction of staff, staff-cut. **abbauen** v demolish; (Personal) cut.

abbestellen [ˈapbəʃtɛlən] v cancel.

*****abbiegen** [ˈapbiːgən] v deflect, turn aside; (Straße) bend; (Mot) turn off.

Abbild [ˈapbilt] neut image, likeness. **abbilden** v illustrate, depict. **Abbildung** f illustration, drawing.

abblenden [ˈapblɛndən] v (Mot) dip one's headlights.

*****abbrechen** [ˈapbrɛçən] v break off; (Blumen, Obst) pick; (abbauen) demolish; (Lager) break.

*****abbringen** [ˈapbriŋən] v dissuade, put off; (entfernen) remove.

Abbruch [ˈapbrux] m (unz.) (Haus) demolition; (Einstellung) stop, cessation.

abdanken [ˈapdaŋkən] v (König) abdicate; (Beamter) resign. **Abdankung** f (pl -en) abdication; resignation.

abdecken [ˈapdɛkən] v uncover; (Tisch) clear; (schützen) shield, cover; (Verlust) make good.

abdichten [ˈapdiçtən] v seal up; (wasserdicht machen) make watertight.

Abdomen [apˈdoːmən] neut abdomen. **abdominal** adj abdominal.

abdrehen [ˈapdreːən] v unscrew, twist off; (Hals) wring.

Abdruck [ˈapdruk] m reprint, new impression; (Finger-) print. **abdrucken** v print.

abdrücken [ˈapdrykən] v (Pistole) fire.

Abend [ˈaːbənt] m (pl -e) evening. **gestern abend** yesterday evening, last night. **–brot** or **–essen** neut supper, dinner. **–land** neut West, Occident. **–mahl** neut Holy Communion. **abends** adv in the evening(s).

Abenteuer [ˈaːbəntɔyər] neut (pl -) adventure. **abenteuerlich** adj adventurous. **Abenteurer** m adventurer.

aber [ˈaːbər] conj but; (jedoch) however. das ist aber schrecklich! that's just awful!

Aberglaube [ˈaːbərglaubə] m superstition. **abergläubisch** adj superstitious.

aberkennen [ˈapɛrkɛnən] v deprive, dispossess.

abermals [ˈaːbərmals] adv again, once more.

*****abfahren** [ˈapfaːrən] v set off, depart; (Mot) drive off. **Abfahrt** f departure; (Ski) descent, downhill run.

Abfall [ˈapfal] 1 (unz.) falling off, decline; (Neigung) slope. 2 m waste, rubbish. **–eimer**

m dustbin. **abfallen** *v* fall off, decline.
abfällig *adj* disparaging.

abfassen ['apfasən] *v* compose, draw up,
formulate. **Abfassung** *f* wording.

abfertigen ['apfɛrtɪgən] *v* (*Güter*) (prepare
for) dispatch; (*Fahrzeug*) check over, prepare (for departure); (*Kundschaft*) see to.

abfinden ['apfɪndən] *v* pay off. **sich
abfinden mit** come to terms with (*auch
fig*) **Abfindung** *f* (*pl* -en) settlement, agreement.

*****abfliegen** ['apfliːgən] fly away; (*Flugzeug*)
take off.

*****abfließen** ['apfliːsən] flow away, drain off.

Abflug ['apfluːk] *m* (*Flugzeug*) take-off.

Abfluß ['apfluss] *m* outflow, draining off.
-rohr *neut* waste-pipe.

Abfuhr ['apfuːr] *m* removal. **abführen** *v*
lead away; (*Wärme, Energie*) dissipate.
Abführmittel *n* laxative.

Abgabe ['apgaːbə] *f* delivery, handing
over; (*Steuer*) tax, duty. **Abgaben** *pl*
(*Verkauf*) sales. **abgabenfrei** *adj* tax-free,
duty-free.

Abgang ['apgaŋ] *m* (*Zug, usw.*) departure;
(*Abtreten*) retirement; (*Verlust*) loss, depreciation.

Abgas ['apgaːs] *neut* exhaust gas.

*****abgeben** ['apgeːbən] *v* give up, hand
over; (*Stimme*) cast.

abgedroschen ['apgədrɔʃən] *adj* commonplace, hackneyed.

abgegriffen ['apgəgrɪfən] *adj* (*Münze*)
worn; (*Buch*) dog-eared, well-thumbed.

*****abgehen** ['apgeːən] *v* go away, depart;
(*Straße*) branch off; (*Knopf, usw.*) come off.

abgemacht ['apgəm axt] *adj* agreed.

Abgeordnete(r) ['apgəɔːrdnətə (r)] delegate; (*Parlament*) Member of Parliament;
(*US*) congressman. **Abgeordnetenhaus**
neut parliament; (*GB*) House of Commons.

abgesehen ['apgəzːən] *prep* **abgesehen
von** apart from, except for.

abgestanden ['apgəʃtandən] *adj* stale;
(*Bier, usw.*) flat.

abgestorben ['apgəʃtɔrbən] *adj* numb.

Abgott ['apgɔt] *m* idol.

abgrenzen ['apgrɛntsən] *v* (*Gebiete*) limit,
mark off. **Abgrenzung** *f* demarcation, definition.

Abgrund ['apgrunt] *m* abyss.

abhalten ['aphaltən] *v* keep away; (*hindern*)

hinder, stop; (*Versammlung, usw.*) hold.

Abhandlung ['aphandlʊŋ] *f* essay, written
report.

Abhang ['aphaŋ] *m* slope.

abhauen ['aphauən] *v* cut off; (*umg.*) go
away, (*umg.*) buzz off.

abhelfen ['aphɛlfən] *v* remedy, correct.

abholen ['apholːən] *v* call for, pick up.

abhören ['aphøː rən] *v* (*Platte*) listen to;
(*Gespräch*) eavesdrop on; (*Telef*) monitor,
listen in, tap; (*Zeugen*) question.
Abhörgerät *neut* (electronic) listening
device, bug.

Abitur [abiˈtuːr] *neut* school-leaving exam,
'A'-levels.

abkanzeln ['apkantsəln] *v* scold, reprimand.

abkehren ['apkeːrən] *v* sweep up. **sich
abkehren** turn away.

abknöpfen ['apknœ pfən] *v* unbutton.

Abkommen ['apkɔm ən] *neut* (*pl* -) agreement, settlement.

abkühlen ['apkyːlən] *v* cool, cool off.

Abkunft ['apkunft] *f* descent, lineage.

abkürzen ['apkyrtsən] *v* shorten; (*Wort*)
abbreviate. **Abkürzung** *f* abbreviation;
(*Weg*) short cut.

*****abladen** ['aplaːdən] *v* unload.

Ablauf ['aplauf] *m* (*Abfluß*) outlet, drain;
(*Verlauf*) sequence of events; (*Ende*) expiry,
end. **ablaufen** *v* drain, flow off; (*Zeit*)
elapse; (*Schuhe*) wear out.

ablegen ['apleːgən] *v* put down; (*Kleider*)
take off; (*Gewohnheiten*) give up.

ablehnen ['apleːnən] *v* reject, refuse;
(*Einladung*) decline. **Ablehnung** *f* (*pl* -en)
refusal.

ableiten ['aplaɪtən] *v* divert, lead away;
(*Flüssigkeit*) draw off; (*Wärme*) dissipate.
Ableitung *f* diversion.

ablenken ['aplɛŋkən] *v* turn away, divert,
deflect.

abliefern ['apliːfərn] *v* deliver.
Ablieferung *f* delivery.

ablösen ['apløː zən] *v* (*Person*) relieve,
replace; (*Schuld*) settle; (*loslösen*) loosen,
free. **Ablösung** *f* relief; loosening.

abmachen ['apm axən] *v* detach; (*Geschäft*)
arrange, agree about. **Abmachung** *f* (*pl*
-en) arrangement, agreement.

abmelden ['apm ɛldən] *v* **sich abmelden** *v*
give notice (of one's departure).

*abmessen ['apm ɛsən] v measure off; (*Grundstück*) survey; (*Worte*) weigh. **Abmessung** f measurement, dimension.

Abnahme ['apnaːm ə] f (*pl* -n) reduction, decrease; (*Entfernung*) removal.

*abnehmen ['apneːm ən] v take off, take away; (*sich vermindern*) decrease; (*schlanker werden*) lose weight, grow slim. **Abnehmer** m (*pl* -) customer, consumer.

Abneigung ['apnaiɡuŋ] f dislike, aversion.

abnorm [ap'nɔrm] *adj* abnormal. **Abnormität** f (*pl* -en) abnormality.

abnutzen ['apnutsən] v wear out. **Abnutzung** f wear (and tear).

Abonnement [abɔn'mã] *neut* (*pl* -s) subscription. **Abonnent** m (*pl* -en) subscriber. **abonnieren** v subscribe.

Abort [a'bɔrt] m (*pl* -e) lavatory.

abquälen ['apkvɛːlən] v **sich abquälen** take great pains.

abraten ['apraːtən] v advise against, dissuade from.

abräumen ['aprɔym ən] v clear away.

abrechnen ['aprɛçnən] v settle; (*abziehen*) deduct. **abrechnen mit** settle up with.

Abrede ['apreːdə] f agreement. **in Abrede stellen** deny. **abreden** v agree.

abreiben ['apraibən] v rub off; (*trocknen*) rub down.

Abreise ['apraizə] f departure. **abreisen** v depart, leave.

*abreißen ['apraisən] v tear off; (*Haus*) demolish, tear down; (*sich ablösen*) break off.

Abrieb ['aprip] m abrasion, wear.

*abrufen ['apruːfən] v cancel, call off; (*Person*) recall.

abrüsten ['aprystən] v disarm. **Abrüstung** f disarmament.

Absage ['apzaːɡə] f (*pl* -n) refusal. **absagen** v cancel, call off; (*Einladung*) decline, refuse.

Absatz ['apzats] **1** m (*Pause*) stop, break; (*Schuh*) heel; paragraph. **2** m (*unz.*) (*Waren*) sales (*pl*), turnover.

abschaffen ['apʃafən] v abolish, do away with. **Abschaffung** f abolition.

abschalten ['apʃaltən] v switch off.

abschätzen ['apʃɛtsən] v estimate, appraise. **Abschätzung** f estimate, assessment.

Abscheu ['apʃɔy] m or f horror, revulsion.

abscheulich *adj* horrible, revolting.

abschicken ['apʃikən] v send off or away.

Abschied ['apʃiːt] m (*pl* -e) departure, leaving. **Abschied nehmen von** say goodbye to, take one's leave of.

*abschießen ['apʃiːsən] v (*Gewehr*) fire; (*Flugzeug*) shoot down.

Abschlag ['apʃlaːk] m reduction, rebate. **abschlagen** v strike off; (*ablehnen*) refuse.

*abschließen ['apʃliːsən] v lock up; (*Geschäft, Vertrag*) conclude, settle; end, close.

Abschluß ['apʃlus] m conclusion; (*Geschäft, Vertrag*) settlement. **–prüfung** f final exam(s), finals.

abschnallen ['apʃnalən] v unbuckle.

*abschneiden ['apʃnaidən] v cut off.

Abschnitt ['apʃnit] m section, part; (*Kontroll-*) counterfoil.

abschrauben ['apʃraubən] v unscrew.

abschrecken ['apʃrɛkən] v scare off, deter. **–d** *adj* deterrent. **Abschreckung** f deterrence. **–smittel** *neut* deterrent.

*abschreiben ['apʃraibən] v copy out, write out; (*Verlust, usw.*) abschreiben; (*plagiieren*) plagiarize.

Abschrift ['apʃrift] f copy.

Abschuß ['apʃus] m (*Gewehr*) firing; (*Flugzeug*) shooting down.

*absehen ['apzɛːən] v see, perceive; (*voraussehen*) foresee. **absehbar** *adj* within sight; (*Zeit*) foreseeable.

abseilen ['apzailən] v abseil.

abseits ['apzaits] *adv* aside.

*absenden ['apzɛndən] v send (off). **Absender** m sender.

absetzen ['apzɛtsən] v set down; (*verkaufen*) sell; (*entlassen*) dismiss; (*aussteigen lassen*) drop off.

Absicht ['apziçt] f (*pl* -en) intention, purpose. **absicht||lich** *adj* deliberate; *adv* on purpose, deliberately. **–slos** *adj* unintentional.

absolut [apzo'luːt] *adj* absolute.

absondern ['apzɔndərn] v isolate, cut off, separate; (*Med, Bot*) secrete. **Absonderung** f (*pl* -en) isolation.

absorbieren [apzɔrbiːrən] v absorb. **Absorption** f absorption.

abspeisen ['apʃpaizən] v fob off.

absperren ['apʃpɛrən] v block off; (*Gas, Strom*) cut off; (*Straße*) block, cordon off.

abspielen [ˈapʃpiːlən] v (Schallplatte, usw.) play; (Musik) sight-read; (Ball) pass.

***abspringen** [ˈapʃprɪŋən] v jump down (from), jump off; (Flugzeug) bale out; (Splitter) chip or break off; (Farbe) flake off.

abspülen [ˈapʃpyːlən] v wash, wash up. **Abspülwasser** neut dishwater.

abstammen [ˈapʃtam ən] v be descended from. **Abstammung** f descent, lineage.

Abstand [ˈapʃtant] m distance. **Abstand halten** keep one's distance.

abstatten [ˈapʃtatən] v (Besuch) pay; (Dank) give.

***absteigen** [ˈapʃtaigən] v climb down, descend; (vom Pferd) dismount.

abstellen [ˈapʃtɛ ən] v (Gerät, Licht) turn off; (niederlegen) put down; (Mot) park.

Abstieg [ˈapʃtiːk] m (pl -e) descent.

abstimmen [ˈapʃtim ən] v vote. (Instrument, Radio) tune. **sich abstimmen** agree. **aufeinander abstimmen** collate, coordinate. **abstimmung** f vote, poll.

Abstinenz [apstɪnɛnts] f abstinence; (Alkohol) teetotalism. **–ler** m (pl -) abstainer; teetotaller.

abstoßend [ˈapʃtoːsənt] adj repulsive, repellent.

abstrakt [apˈstrakt] adj abstract.

Absturz [ˈapʃturts] m fall; (Flugzeug) crash; (Abgrund) precipice. **abstürzen** v fall, plummet; (Flugzeug) crash.

absurd [apˈzurt] adj absurd.

Abszeß [apstsɛs] m (pl Abszesse) abcess.

Abt [apt] m (pl Äbte) abbott. **Abtei** f (pl -en) abbey.

Abteil [apˈtail] neut (pl -e) compartment. **abteilen** v separate, divide off. **Abteilung** f (auch Mil) division; (einer Firma) department. **–sleiter** m head of department.

Äbtissin [ɛpˈtisin] f (pl -nen) abbess.

***abtreiben** [ˈapˌtraibən] v drive away; (Med) abort. **Abtreibung** f (pl -en) (induced) abortion.

Abtritt [ˈaptrɪt] m departure; (Theater) exit.

abtrocknen [ˈapˌtrɔknən] v wipe dry; (Geschirr) wipe up, dry.

abtrünnig [ˈaptrʏnic] adj disloyal, rebellious.

***abtun** [ˈaptuːn] put aside; (Kleider) take off; (erledigen) close, settle; (Tier) put down.

abwälzen [ˈapvɛltsən] v deflect (Kritik, Schuld).

abwandeln [ˈapvandəln] v vary. **Abwandlung** f variation.

abwarten [ˈapvartən] v wait for, expect; wait and see.

abwärts [ˈapvɛrts] adv downwards, down.

abwaschen [ˈapvaʃən] v wash off; (Geschirr) wash up.

Abwasser [ˈapvasər] neut waste water, effluent.

abwechseln [ˈapvɛksəln] v take turns; (wechseln) change, vary. **–d** adj alternating. adv alternately, in turns. **Abwechslung** f change.

Abwehr [ˈapveːr] f defence; (Widerstand) resistance. **abwehren** v ward off; (Feind) repel.

***abweichen** [ˈapvaiçən] v deviate. **–d** adj discrepant, anomalous; (Meinung) dissenting.

***abweisen** [ˈapvaisən] v turn away, refuse; (Bewerber) turn down. **–d** adj unfriendly, dismissive.

***abwenden** [ˈapvɛndən] v turn away or aside; (Gefahr) avert, prevent.

***abwerfen** [ˈapvɛrfən] v throw off; (Bomben) drop; (Zinsen) yield.

abwerten [ˈapvɛrtən] v devalue. **Abwertung** f devaluation.

abwesend [ˈapveːzənt] adj absent; (zerstreut) absent-minded. **Abwesenheit** f absence.

abzahlen [ˈaptsaːlən] v pay off.

abzählen [ˈaptsɛːlən] v count; (Geld) count out.

abzäunen [ˈaptsɔynən] v fence off.

Abzeichen [ˈaptsaiçən] neut badge; (Kennzeichen) mark.

***abziehen** [ˈaptsiːən] v draw off, remove; (Math) subtract; (fortgehen) go away, withdraw.

Abzug [ˈaptsuːk] m departure; (Geld) deduction; (Foto) print; (Abdruck) copy.

abzweigen [ˈaptsvaigən] v branch off. **Abzweigung** f (pl -en) branch; (Mot) turning.

ach! [ax] interj oh! ah!

Achse [ˈaksə] f (pl -n) (Rad) axle; (Math, Pol) axis.

Achsel [ˈaksəl] f (pl -n) shoulder. **–bein** neut shoulder-blade. **–höhle** f armpit. **–zucken** neut (pl -) shrug (of the shoulders).

acht [axt] adj eight. **(heute) vor acht**

Tagen a week ago (today).
Acht [axt] *f* (*unz.*) attention. **außer acht lassen** ignore, disregard. **sich in acht nehmen** be careful, take care. **acht‖en** *v* esteem. **–en auf** pay attention to, heed. **–geben** *v* pay attention. **–los** *adj* careless. **–sam** *adj* attentive. **Achtung** *f* attention; (*Wertschätzung*) esteem; *interj* watch out! look out!
achtzig [ˈaxtsɪç] *adj* eighty.
ächzen [ˈɛçtsən] *v* groan.
Acker [ˈakər] *m* (*pl* **Äcker**) field. **–bau** *m* agriculture, farming.
addieren [aˈdiːrən] *v* add (up). **Addiermaschine** *f* adding machine.
Adel [ˈaːdəl] *m* nobility, aristocracy. **ad(e)lig** *adj* noble, aristocratic. **Ad(e)lige(r)** noble(man), aristocrat.
Ader [ˈaːdər] *f* (*pl* **-n**) blood vessel; vein, artery.
Adjektiv [ˈatjktiːf] *neut* (*pl* **-e**) adjective.
Adler [ˈaːdlər] *m* (*pl* **-**) eagle.
Admiral [atmiˈraːl] *m* (*pl* **-e**) admiral. **–ität** *f* admiralty.
adoptieren [adɔpˈtiːrən] *v* adopt. **Adoptiv-** adopted, adoptive.
Adrenalin [adrenaˈliːn] *neut* adrenaline.
Adresse [aˈdrɛsə] *f* (*pl* **-n**) address. **Adreßbuch** *neut* address book, directory. **adressieren** *v* address.
Advokat [atvoˈkaːt] *m* (*pl* **-en**) lawyer.
Aerobic [ɛːˈroːbik] *neut* aerobics.
Affäre [aˈfɛːrə] *f* (*pl* **-n**) affair; (*Liebes-*) (love) affair.
Affe [ˈafə] *m* (*pl* **-n**) ape, monkey.
affektiert [afkˈtiːrt] *adj* affected, conceited.
äffen [ˈɛfən] *v* ape, imitate.
Afrika [ˈaːfrika] *neut* Africa. **Afrikaner** *m* African. **afrikanisch** *adj* African.
After [ˈaftər] *m* (*pl* **-**) anus.
Agent [aˈgɛnt] *m* (*pl* **-en**) agent. **–ur** *f* (*pl* **-en**) agency.
Agnostiker [aˈgnɔstikər] *m* (*pl* **-**) agnostic. **agnostisch** *adj* agnostic.
Ägypten [ɛˈgyptən] *neut* Egypt. **Ägypter** *m* (*pl* **-**) Egyptian. **ägyptisch** *adj* Egyptian.
Ahn [aːn] *m* (*pl* **-en**) ancestor.
ähneln [ˈɛːnəln] *v* look like, resemble.
ahnen [ˈaːnən] *v* suspect, guess.
ähnlich [ˈɛːnlɪç] *adj* like, similar (to). **Ähn-**

lichkeit *f* (*pl* **-en**) likeness, similarity.
Ahorn [ˈaːhɔrn] *m* (*pl* **-e**) maple.
Ähre [ˈɛːrə] *f* (*pl* **-n**) ear (of corn).
Aids [eidz] *neut* AIDS.
Akadem‖ie [akadeˈmiː] *f* (*pl* **-n**) academy; (*Hochschule, Fachschule*) college. **–iker** *m* (*pl* **-**) university graduate. **akademisch** *adj* academic.
Akkord [aˈkɔrt] *m* (*pl* **-e**) agreement; (*Musik*) chord. **–arbeit** *f* piece-work.
Akrobat [akroˈbaːt] *m* (*pl* **-en**) acrobat. **akrobatisch** *adj* acrobatic.
Akronym [akroˈnyːm] *neut* (*pl* **-e**) acronym.
Akt [akt] *m* (*pl* **-e**) act, action, deed; document; (*Kunst*) nude.
Akte [ˈaktə] *f* (*pl* **-n**) file, dossier. **zu den Akten legen** file (away). **Akten‖schrank** *m* filing cabinet. **–tasche** *f* briefcase.
Aktie [ˈaktsiə] *f* (*pl* **-n**) share. **Aktien‖gesellschaft** *f* joint-stock company. **–makler** *m* stockbroker.
Aktionär [aktsioˈnɛːr] *m* (*pl* **-e**) shareholder.
aktiv [akˈtiːf] *adj* active. **–ieren** *v* activate.
aktuell [aktuˈɛl] *adj* current, contemporary, up-to-date.
Akzent [akˈtsɛnt] *m* (*pl* **-e**) accent.
akzeptieren [aktsɛpˈtiːrən] *v* accept.
Alarm [aˈlarm] *m* (*pl* **-e**) alarm. **alarm‖bereit** *adj* standing by, on the alert. **–ieren** *v* alarm.
albern [ˈalbərn] *adj* silly, foolish.
Album [ˈalbum] *neut* (*pl* **Alben**) album.
Alge [ˈalgə] *f* (*pl* **-n**) seaweed.
Algebra [ˈalgebra] *f* algebra.
Alimente [aliˈmɛntə] *pl* alimony *sing*.
Alkohol [alkoˈhoːl] *m* (*pl* **-e**) alcohol. **alkoholfrei** *adj* non-alcoholic. **Alkoholiker** *m* alcoholic. **alkoholisch** *adj* alcoholic.
all [al] *pron, adj* all. **All** *neut* universe. **alle** *pl* all; everybody *sing*. **alle beide** both. **wir alle** we all, all of us. **die Milch ist alle** the milk is all gone. **alle zwei Tage** every other day. **alles** everything. **alledem** *pron* **trotz alledem** nevertheless.
Allee [aˈleː] *f* (*pl* **-n**) avenue.
Allegorie [alegoˈriː] (*pl* **-n**) allegory. **allegorisch** *adj* allegorical.
allein [aˈlain] *adj, adv* alone; (*ohne Hilfer*) (by) oneself. *conj* but. **alleinstehend** *adj* (*Haus*) detached; (*Person*) single.
allemal [ˈaləmaːl] *adv* always. **ein für alle-**

mal once and for all.

allenfalls ['alənfals] *adv* if need be; (*höchstens*) at most.

aller||best ['alərbɛst] *adj* very best, best of all. **–dings** *adv* certainly, surely, indeed. **–erst** *adj* first of all, very first. **–höchst** *adj* supreme, highest of all. **–lei** *adj* (*undeklinierbar*) various, all kinds of. **–liebst** *adj* (most) delightful, dearest. **–wenigst** *adj* very least.

allezeit ['alətsait] *adv* always, at any time.

allgemein ['algəm ain] *adj* common, general. **im allgemeinen** in general.

Alliierte(r) [ali:rtə (r)] *m* ally.

alljährlich ['alj:rlɪç] *adj* annual.

allmächtig [alm ɛçtɪç] *adj* all-powerful, almighty.

allmählich ['alm ɛ:lɪç] *adj* gradual.

Allradantrieb [alra:tantr ɪp] *m* four-wheel drive. **Auto mit Allradantrieb** 4x4, 4WD.

allseitig ['alzaitɪç] *adj* universal, comprehensive.

alltäglich ['alt:klɪç] *adj* everyday, *adv* every day.

allzu ['altsu:] *adv* much too, all too.

Almanach ['alm anax] *m* (*pl* -e) almanac.

Alpen ['alpən] *pl* Alps *pl*.

Alphabet [alfa'be:t] *neut* (*pl* -e) alphabet. **alphabetisch** *adj* alphabetical.

Alptraum ['alptraum] *m* nightmare.

als [als] *conj* as; (*da, zu der Zeit*) when; (*nach Komparativen*) than. **als ob** as if. **nichts als** nothing but. *als dein Freund möchte ich sagen ...* as your friend, I would like to say *... als ich noch ein Kind war* when I was a child.

also ['alzo] *conj* so, therefore.

alt [alt] *adj* old.

Alt [alt] *m* (*unz.*) alto (voice).

Altar [alta:r] *m* (*pl* Altäre) altar.

Alter ['altər] *neut* (*unz.*) age; (*hohes Alter*) old age. **Alters||fürsorge** *f* care of the aged. **–heim** *neut* old people's home. **altersschwach** *adj* (*Person*) senile, feeble. **Altertum** *neut* (*unz.*) antiquity. **altertümlich** *adj* ancient, archaic.

Altglasbehälter [altgl:sbə'hɛltər] *m* (*pl* -) bottle bank.

Aluminium [alu'm ɪnium] *neut* aluminium.

am [am] *prep* + *art* an dem.

Amboß ['am bɔs] *m* (*pl* Ambosse) anvil.

Ameise ['am aizə] *f* (*pl* -n) ant.

Amerika [am e:rɪka] *neut* America. **Amerikaner** *m* American. **amerikanisch** *adj* American.

Ampel ['am pəl] *f* (*pl* -n) (*Verkehrs-*) traffic light; (*Hängelampe*) hanging lamp.

Amsel ['am zəl] *f* (*pl* -n) blackbird.

Amt [am t] *neut* (*pl* Ämter) office; (*Stellung*) official position, post; (*Telef*) exchange. **das Auswärtige Amt** the Foreign Office. **das Amt antreteten** take office. **amtieren** *v* officiate. **amtlich** *adj* official. **Amts||geheimnis** *neut* offical secret. **–gericht** *neut* district court. **–zeichen** *neut* dial tone.

amüsant [am y'zant] *adj* amusing. **amüsieren** *v* amuse. **sich amüsieren** amuse or enjoy oneself.

an [an] *prep* at; (*nahe*) near; (*auf*) on. *adv* on. *an diesem Tag* on this day. *an diesem Ort* at this place. *der Ort, an dem* the place where. *an der Wand* on the wall. *an die Tür klopfen* knock at or on the door. *von heute an* from today. *von jetzt an* from now on. *sie hat nichts an* she has nothing on.

analog [ana'lo:k] *adj* analagous. **Analogie** *f* analogy. **analogisch** *adj* analogous.

Analphabet [analfa'be:t] *m* (*pl* -en) illiterate.

Analyse [ana'ly:zə] *f* (*pl* -n) analysis. **analysieren** *v* analyse. **Analytiker** *m* analyst. **analytisch** *adj* analytical.

Ananas ['ananas] *f* (*pl* -se) pineapple.

Anarchie [anar'çi:] *f* (*pl* -n) anarchy. **Anarchist** *m* (*pl* -en) anarchist.

Anatomie [anato'm i:] *f* (*pl* -n) anatomy. **anatomisch** *adj* anatomical.

Anbau ['anbau] **1** *m* (*unz.*) cultivation, tillage. **2** *m* extension, annexe.

*anbeißen ['anbaisən] *v* bite into; (*Fisch*) bite, take the bait.

anbelangen ['anbəlaŋən] *v* concern, relate to. *was mich anbelangt* as to me, as far as I am concerned.

anbeten ['anbe:tən] *v* worship, adore.

*anbieten ['anbi:tən] *v* offer.

Anblick ['anblɪk] *m* sight, view; (*Aussehen*) appearance. **anblicken** *v* look at, gaze at.

*anbrechen ['anbrɛçən] *v* (*Essen, Vorrat*) break into, begin; (*Tag*) dawn, break; (*Nacht*) fall.

*anbrennen ['anbrɛnən] (*Speisen*) burn;

(*Zigarette, Lampe*) light.

*anbringen ['anbrɪŋən] v bring, place; (*befestigen*) attach; (*Klage*) lodge, bring.

Anbruch ['anbrʊx] m (*unz.*) beginning. *bei Anbruch der Nacht* at nightfall.

Andacht ['andaxt] f (*pl* **-en**) devotion.

Andenken ['andɛŋkən] neut (*pl* -) memory, remembrance; (*Erinnerungstück*) souvenir.

ander ['andər] adj, pron other, different. **ein andermal** adv another time.

ändern ['ɛndərn] v alter, change. **Änderung** f (*pl* **-en**) alteration, change.

ander||thalb ['andərthalp] adj one-and-a-half. **–nfalls** adv otherwise, else. **–s** adv differently. **–seits** adv on the other hand. **–swo** adv elsewhere.

andeuten ['andɔytən] v indicate, point to; (*anspielen*) imply, suggest, allude to. **Andeutung** f indication; suggestion, allusion.

andrehen ['andreːən] v turn on, switch on; (*Mot*) start up; (*umg.*) wangle, fix up.

andrer ['andrər] pron **anderer**. V **ander**.

aneignen ['anaɪgnən] v **sich aneignen** appropriate; (*Kenntnisse*) acquire. **Aneignung** f (*pl* **-en**) appropriation; acquisition.

aneinander [anaɪn'andər] adv to or against one another, together. **–liegend** adj neighbouring, adjacent. **–schließen** v join together.

*anerkennen ['anɛrkɛnən] v recognize, acknowledge. **Anerkennung** f recognition, approval.

*anfahren ['anfaːrən] v begin (to move); (*bringen*) convey, carry; (*ankommen*) arrive; (*zusammenstoßen*) drive into. **Anfahrt** f arrival; (*Zufahrtsstraße*) drive.

Anfall ['anfal] m attack.

Anfang ['anfaŋ] m beginning, start. **anfangen** v begin, start. **Anfänger** m (*pl* -) beginner. **anfangs** adv at first, initially. **Anfangsbuchstabe** m (*pl* **-n**) initial letter.

anfassen ['anfasən] v touch; (*ergreifen*) hold, grasp; (*Aufgabe*) set or go about.

*anfecht||en ['anfɛçtən] v contest, dispute; (*beunruhigen*) trouble; (*Versuchung*) tempt. **-bar** adj questionable, contestable.

Anforderung ['anfɔrdərʊŋ] f demand, claim; (*Bedürfnis*) requirement.

Anfrage ['anfraːgə] f inquiry.

anfühlen ['anfyːlən] v touch, feel. **sich**

anfühlen feel (to the touch).

anführen ['anfyːrən] v lead, command; (*Worte*) quote, state; (*täuschen*) trick, deceive. **Anführungszeichen** pl quotation marks.

anfüllen ['anfʏlən] v fill (up).

Angabe ['angaːbə] f declaration, statement. **-n** pl specifications, data. **nähere Angaben** details, particulars.

*angeben ['angeːbən] v state, declare; (*anzeigen*) inform against; (*vorgeben*) pretend; (*prahlen*) brag, boast, show off. **Angeber** m (*pl* -) informer; (*Prahler*) show off, boaster. **angeblich** adj supposed, alleged.

angeboren ['angəboːrən] adj innate, inherent.

Angebot ['angəboːt] neut (*pl* **-e**) offer. **Angebot und Nachfrage** supply and demand.

*angehen ['angeːən] v begin; (*angreifen*) attack; (*betreffen*) concern. *das geht mich nichts an* that is none of my business.

angehören ['angəhøː rən] v belong (to). **Angehörige(r)** member.

Angeklagte(r) ['angəklaːktə (r)] (*Jur*) (the) accused, defendant.

Angelegenheit ['angəleːgənhaɪt] f matter, concern, business.

angeln ['aŋəln] v fish, angle. **Angeln** neut angling, fishing. **Angelrute** f fishing rod.

Angelsachse ['aŋəlzaksə] m Anglo-Saxon. **angelsächsisch** adj Anglo-Saxon.

angemessen ['angəm ɛsən] adj proper, suitable.

angenehm ['angəneːm] adj pleasant, agreeable.

angenommen ['angənɔm ən] adj supposing, assuming.

angesehen ['angəzeːən] adj respected.

Angesicht ['angəzɪçt] neut face, countenance. **angesichts** prep considering, in view of.

Angestellte(r) ['angəʃtɛlə (r)] employee, office worker.

angewandt ['angəvant] adj applied, practical.

angewöhnen ['angəvøː nən] v accustom. **sich angewöhnen** get used to, make a habit of. **Angewohnheit** f habit, custom.

Angler ['aŋ lər] m (*pl* -) angler, fisherman.

*angreifen ['angraɪfən] v (*anfassen*) take

hold of; (*feindlich*) attack; (*unternehmen*) set about. **Angreifer** *m* (*pl* -) aggressor, attacker.

angrenzen ['angrɛntsən] *v* border on, adjoin.

Angriff ['angrɪf] *m* attack. **angriffslustig** *adj* aggressive.

Angst [aŋst] *f* (*pl* **Ängste**) fear, anxiety. **Angst haben vor** be afraid of.

ängst||igen ['ɛŋstɪgən] *v* frighten. **–lich** *adj* fearful, timid; (*peinlich*) scrupulous, (over-)careful.

*anhaben ['anhaːbən] *v* wear, have on.

Anhalt ['anhalt] *m* support, prop; (*fig*) clue. **anhalten** *v* stop; (*andauern*) continue, last. **Anhalter** *m* hitchhiker. **per Anhalter fahren** hitchhike.

Anhang ['anhaŋ] *m* appendix, supplement. **anhängen** *v* hang on, attach; (*hinzufügen*) add. **Anhänger** *m* follower; (*Fußball*) supporter; (*Mot*) trailer. **Anhängeschloß** *neut* padlock. **anhänglich** *adj* affectionate.

Anhöhe ['anhœːə] *f* (low) hill.

anhören ['anhœːrən] *v* listen (to).

Ankauf ['ankauf] *m* purchase. **ankaufen** *v* purchase, buy.

Anker ['aŋkər] *m* (*pl* -) anchor. **den Anker lichten/werfen** weigh/cast anchor. **ankern** *v* anchor.

Anklage ['anklaːgə] *f* accusation, charge. **–bank** *f* dock. **anklagen** *v* accuse. **Ankläger** *m* plaintiff.

Anklang ['anklaŋ] *m* approval, recognition; (*Spur*) touch, echo.

anknüpfen ['anknypfən] *v* fasten (on), tie (on); (*fig*) take up, establish.

*ankommen ['ankɔmən] *v* arrive; (*abhängen*) depend (on). **es kommt darauf an** it depends.

ankündigen ['ankyndɪgən] *v* announce, publicize. **Ankündigung** *f* announcement.

Ankunft ['ankunft] *f* (*pl* **Ankünfte**) arrival.

Anlage ['anlaːgə] *f* installation; (*Entwurf*) plan, layout; (*Gewehr*) park, gardens *pl*; (*Brief*) enclosure; (*Begabung*) talent; (*Neigung*) tendency, susceptibility; (*Komm*) investment; (*Fabrik*) plant, works.

anlangen ['anlaŋən] *v* (*ankommen*) arrive; (*betreffen*) concern.

Anlaß ['anlas] *m* (*pl* **Anlässe**) occasion, cause. **Anlaß geben** cause, give rise to. **anlassen** *v* leave on; (*Mot*) start. **anläßlich** *prep* on the occasion of. **Anlasser** *m* (*pl* -)

(*Mot*) starter-motor.

Anlauf ['anlauf] *m* start; (*kurzer Lauf*) run, dash. **anlaufen** *v* run at, rush at; (*Hafen*) put into; (*wachsen*) rise, increase.

anlegen ['anleːgən] *v* put on *or* against; (*Gewehr*) aim at; (*gründen*) found; (*Geld*) invest; (*Schiff*) lie alongside.

Anleihe ['anlaːə] *f* (*pl* -n) loan.

Anleitung ['anlaɪtuŋ] *f* instruction.

*anliegen ['anliːgən] *v* (*Schiff*) lie beside; (*Kleidung*) fit well. **Anliegen** *neut* (*pl* -) request. **anliegend** *adj* adjoining.

anlocken ['anlɔkən] *v* entice, attract.

anmachen ['anmaxən] *v* attach; (*Speisen*) prepare; (*Feuer*) kindle; (*Licht*) turn on.

Anmarsch ['anmarʃ] *m* advance, approach. **anmarschieren** *v* advance on, march on.

anmaßen ['anmaːsən] *v* **sich anmaßen, zu** presume to, take it upon oneself to. **Anmaßung** *f* presumptuousness.

anmelden ['anmɛldən] *v* announce, report. **sich anmelden** *v* report; (*polizeilich*) register (with the police). **Anmeldung** *f* announcement; (*polizeilich*) registration.

anmerken ['anmɛrkən] *v* note, observe. **Anmerkung** *f* note, observation.

Anmut ['anmuːt] *f* grace, charm, elegance. **anmutig** *adj* graceful.

annähern ['annɛːərn] *v* bring closer; (*ähnlich machen*) make similar. **sich annähern** approach. **annähernd** *adj* approaching. *adv* almost, close to.

Annahme ['annaːmə] *f* (*pl* -n) acceptance; (*Vermutung*) assumption.

*annehm||en ['anneːmən] *v* accept, take; (*vermuten*) assume, suppose. **–bar** *adj* acceptable.

anonym [ano'nyːm] *adj* anonymous. **Anonymität** *f* anonymity.

anordnen ['anɔrdnən] *v* put in order, arrange; (*befehlen*) direct, command. **Anordnung** *f* arrangement; (*Befehl*) order, instruction.

Anorexie [anɔrɛksˈiː] *f* anorexia.

anpacken ['anpakən] *v* grasp, seize.

anpassen ['anpasən] *v* fit, adapt. **sich anpassen** *v* adapt, adjust. **Anpassung** *f* adaptation, adjustment. **anpassungsfähig** *adj* adaptable. **Anpassungsfähigkeit** *f* adaptability.

anrechnen ['anrɛçnən] *v* charge; (*hochschätzen*) value, esteem highly.

Anrede [ˈanrɛːdə] *f* speech, address. **anreden** *v* address, speak to.

anregen [ˈanreːgən] *v* stimulate, incite; (*geistig*) excite, inspire. **–d** *adj* exciting. **Anregung** *f* excitement.

anrichten [ˈanriçtən] *v* (*Schaden*) cause, do; (*Essen*) prepare.

anrüchig [ˈanrʏçiː] *adj* notorious, infamous.

Anruf [ˈanruːf] *m* call, shout; (*Telef*) call. **anrufen** *v* call, hail; (*Telef*) ring up, call.

anrühren [ˈanryːrən] *v* touch, handle; (*Küche*) stir.

ans [ans] *prep+art* **an das**.

Ansage [ˈanzaːgə] *f* announcement; (*Kartenspiel*) bidding. **ansagen** *v* announce, declare; bid. **Ansager** *m* (*pl* -) announcer.

ansammeln [ˈanzam əln] *v* collect. **sich ansammeln** gather. **Ansammlung** *f* collection, accumulation; (*Menge*) crowd, gathering.

Ansatz [ˈanzats] *m* (*Anfang*) start, beginning; (*Zusatzstück*) (added) piece, fitting. **–punkt** *m* starting point.

anschaffen [ˈanʃafən] *v* procure, obtain.

anschalten [ˈanʃaltən] *v* switch, turn on.

anschau||en [ˈanʃauən] *v* look at, view. **–lich** *adj* obvious, evident.

Anschein [ˈanʃain] *m* (*unz.*) (outer) appearance. **allem Anschein nach** to all appearances.

Anschlag [ˈanʃlaːk] *m* (*Med*) stroke, attack; (*Plakat*) poster; (*Kosten-*) estimate; (*Angriff*) (criminal) attack, outrage.

*anschließen [ˈanʃliːsən] *v* connect; (*anketten*) chain up. **–d** *adj* subsequent.

Anschluß [ˈanʃlus] *m* connection; (*pol*) annexation.

anschnallen [ˈanʃnalən] *v* fasten, buckle.

Anschove [anˈʃoːvə] *f* (*pl* -n), **Anschovis** *f* (*pl* -) anchovy.

Anschrift [ˈanʃrift] *f* (postal) address.

anschuldigen [ˈanʃuldigən] *v* accuse (of), charge (with).

*ansehen [ˈanzeːən] *v* look at, consider. **Ansehen** *neut* appearance; (*Hochachtung*) respect, esteem. **ansehnlich** *adj* notable.

ansetzen [ˈanzɛtsən] *v* put on, attach; (*Gewicht*) put on; (*anfangen*) begin; (*versuchen*) try.

Ansicht [ˈanziçt] *f* view, sight; (*Meinung*) opinion.

Anspiel [ˈanʃpiːl] *neut* (*Tennis*) service; (*Fußball*) kick-off. **anspielen** *v* play first; (*Tennis*) serve; (*Fußball*) kick off. **anspielen auf** hint at, allude to. **Anspielung** *f* (*pl* -en) allusion.

ansprechen [ˈanʃprɛçən] speak to, address; (*auf der Straße, usw.*) accost.

Anspruch [ˈanʃprux] *m* claim. **Anspruch haben auf** have a right to. **in Anspruch nehmen** lay claim to, claim; (*Zeit*) take up. **Ansprüche stellen** make demands. **anspruchsvoll** *adj* demanding.

Anstalt [ˈanʃtalt] *f* (*pl* -en) (*Heim*) institution; (*Schule*) institute; (*Vorbereitung*) arrangement.

Anstand [ˈanʃtant] *m* (*unz.*) decency. **anständig** *adj* decent, proper. **Anstandsdame** *f* chaperone.

anstatt [anˈʃtat] *prep* instead of. **anstattdaß** rather than.

anstecken [ˈanʃtɛkən] *v* pin on (to); (*Ring*) put on; (*Med*) infect; (*Feuer*) light. **–d** *adj* infectious. **Ansteckung** *f* infection.

anstellen [ˈanʃtɛlən] *v* carry out, do; (*Person*) appoint, employ; (*Mot*) start; (*Radio*) switch on. **Anstellung** *f* appointment.

anstiften [ˈanʃtiftən] *v* cause, instigate.

Anstoß [ˈanʃtoːs] *m* impulse; (*Sport*) kick-off. **Anstoß geben/nehmen** give/take offence (*US* offence). **anstoßen** *v* knock against; (*Haus, usw.*) adjoin.

anstrengen [ˈanʃtrɛŋən] *v* strain, exert; (*Prozeß*) bring in. **sich anstrengen** strain or exert oneself; make an effort.

Antarktika [anˈtarktika] *f* Antarctica. **Antarktis** *f* Antarctic. **antarktisch** *adj* antarctic.

antasten [ˈantastən] *v* touch, handle; (*Thema*) touch on; (*Recht, usw.*) injure.

Anteil [ˈantail] *m* share, portion; (*Mitgefühl*) sympathy. **–nahme** *f* sympathy.

Antenne [anˈtɛnə] *f* (*pl* -n) aerial.

Antibiotikum [antiˈbioːtikum] *neut* (*pl* -biotika) antibiotic.

Antidepressivum [antidɛprɛsˈiːvum] *neut* (*pl* -depressiven) (*med*) antidepressive.

Antihaftbeschichtung [antihaftbəˈʃiçtuŋ] *f* (*pl* -en) non-stick coating.

antik [anˈtik] *adj* ancient, classical.

Antikörper [ˈantikœrpər] *m* antibody.

Antiquität [antikviˈtɛːt] *f* (*pl* -en) antique.

–enhändler m antique dealer.

antisemitisch [antize'm ɪtʃ] adj anti-Semitic.

Antiseptikum [antɪsɛptɪkum] m (pl -septika) antiseptic. **antiseptisch** adj antiseptic.

Antrag ['antraːk] m (pl **Anträge**) offer, proposal; (Pol) motion. **einen Antrag stellen** propose a motion. **Antragsteller** m applicant; (Pol) mover (of a motion).

*****antreffen** ['antrɛfən] v encounter.

*****antreiben** ['antraɪbən] v drive, propel; (Person) urge; (ans Ufer) drift ashore.

*****antreten** ['antreːtən] v (Amt) enter, take over; (Reise) set out on.

Antrieb ['antriːp] m drive, impulse; (Tech) drive. **aus eigenem Antrieb** of one's own free will.

Antritt ['antrɪt] m beginning; (Amt) entrance.

*****antun** ['antuːn] v (Kleidung) put on; (Verletzung) do, inflict.

Antwort ['antvort] f (pl -en) answer, reply. **antworten** v answer, reply (to).

anvertrauen ['anfɛrtrauən] v entrust.

Anwalt ['anvalt] m (pl **Anwälte**) (defending) lawyer, solicitor.

anwärmen ['anvɛrm ən] v warm (up).

*****anweisen** ['anvaɪzən] v (zuweisen) assign; (anleiten) direct, show; (Geld) transfer. **Anweisung** f instruction, order; (Geld) remittance, transfer.

*****anwend||en** ['anvɛndən] v employ, use; (Gewalt, Methode, Wissenschaft, usw.) apply. **–bar** adj applicable. **Anwendung** f. application.

anwesend ['anveːzənt] adj present. **Anwesenheit** f presence.

Anzahl ['antsaːl] f number. **Anzahlung** f deposit, down payment.

Anzeichen ['antsaɪçən] neut mark, sign.

Anzeige ['antsaɪgə] f (pl -n) announcement; (Inserat) advertisement; (bei der Polizei) report. **–blatt** neut advertiser, advertising journal. **anzeig||en** v announce; (person) inform against, report (to the police). **–epflichtig** adj notifiable.

*****anziehen** ['antsiːən] v (Kleider) put on; (Schraube) tighten; (Person) dress; (heranlocken) attract. **sich anziehen** get dressed. **anziehend** adj attractive. **Anziehung** f attraction. **–skraft** f power of attraction;

(Person) attractiveness.

Anzug ['antsuːk] **1** m (unz.) approach. **2** m suit.

anzünden ['antsyndən] v light, ignite.

Apfel ['apfəl] m (pl **Äpfel**) apple. **–baum** m apple tree. **–garten** m apple orchard. **–kuchen** m apple cake. **–mus** neut apple sauce. **–saft** m apple juice. **–sine** f orange. **–wein** m cider.

Apostel [a'pɔstəl] m (pl -) apostle. **–geschichte** f Acts of the Apostles.

Apostroph [apo'stroːf] m (pl -e) apostrophe.

Apotheke [apo'teːkə] f (pl -n) chemist's (shop), pharmacy. **–r** m (pl -) chemist, pharmacist. **–rkunst** f pharmacy, pharmaceutics.

Apparat [apa'raːt] m (pl -e) apparatus; (Vorrichtung) appliance, device; (Foto) camera; (Telef) telephone, handset. **am Apparat!** speaking! **am Apparat bleiben** hold the line.

appellieren [apɛ'liːən] v appeal.

Appetit [apɛ'tiːt] m (pl -e) appetite.

Aprikose [aprikoːzə] f (pl -n) apricot.

April [a'prɪl] m (pl -e) April. **der erste April** April Fools' Day.

Aquarell [akva'rɛl] neut (pl -e) water-colour.

Aquarium [a'kvaːrɪum] neut (pl **Aquarien**) aquarium.

Äquator [ɛ'kvaːtɔr] m equator. **äquatorial** adj equatorial.

Arab||er ['aːrabər] m (pl -) Arab. **–ien** neut Arabia. **arabisch** adj Arab, Arabian.

Arbeit ['arbaɪt] f (pl -en) work; (Beschäftigung) job. **arbeiten** v work. **Arbeiter** m worker, workman. **–klasse** f working class. **Arbeitgeber** m employer. **Arbeits||amt** neut employment office. **–erlaubnis** f work permit. **arbeits||fähig** adj able to work. **–los** adj unemployed. **–losenunterstützung** f. unemployment benefit. **–losigkeit** f unemployment.

Arbeitssüchtige(r) ['arbaɪtszyçtɪç(ər)] (pl (die) -n) workaholic.

Archäolog||ie [arçɔb'giː] f archaeology. **–e** m archaeologist. **archäologisch** adj archaeological.

Architekt [arçɪtɛkt] m (pl -en) architect. **–ur** f (pl -en) architecture.

Archiv [arçiːf] neut (pl -e) archives pl, records pl.

arg [aɾk] *adj* bad, evil; (*ernst*) serious.

Ärger ['ɛɾɡəɾ] *m* (*unz.*) (*Verdruß*) annoyance, irritation; (*Zorn*) anger. **ärgerlich** *adj* (*Person*) angry, annoyed; (*Sache*) annoying. **ärgern über** be angry about.

Argument [aɾɡu'm ɛnt] *neut* (*pl* -e) argument, reasoning.

Argwohn ['aɾkvoːn] *m* (*unz.*) distrust, suspicion. **argwöhnisch** *adj* suspicious, mistrustful.

Aristokrat [aɾistoˈkɾaːt] *m* (*pl* -en) aristocrat. **-ie** *f* aristocracy. **aristokratisch** *adj* aristocratic.

Arithmetik [aɾitmˈeːtik] *f* arithmetic. **arithmetisch** *adj* arithmetical.

Arktis ['aɾktis] *f* Arctic. **arktisch** *adj* arctic.

arm [aɾm] *adj* poor. **-arm** *adj* poor in .... **nikotinarm** *adj* low-nicotine.

Arm [aɾm] *m* (*pl* -e) arm; (*Fluß*) branch, tributary.

Armaturenbrett [aɾm aˈtuːɾənbɾɛt] *neut* dashboard, instrument panel.

Armband ['aɾm bant] *neut* bracelet. **-uhr** *f* (wrist)watch.

Armee [aɾm eː] *f* (*pl* -n) army.

Ärmel ['ɛm əl] *m* (*pl* -) sleeve. **-kanal** *m* English Channel.

ärmlich ['ɛm liç] *adj* poor, miserable.

armselig ['aɾm zeːliç] *adj* wretched, miserable.

Arm||sessel *m* armchair. **-stuhl** *m* armchair.

Armut ['aɾm uːt] *f* poverty.

Arrest [aˈɾɛst] *m* (*pl* -e) arrest, detention.

Arsch [aɾʃ] *m* (*pl* **Ärsche**) (*vulg*) arse. **-geige** *f* (*vulg*) dickhead.

Art [aɾt] *f* (*pl* -en) type, kind, sort; (*Weise*) way, method; (*Biol*) species; (*Brauch*) habit.

artig ['aɾtiç] *adj* (*kind*) good, well-behaved.

Autismus [] *m* autism. **autistisch** *adj* autistic.

-artig [-aɾtiç] *adj* -like.

Artikel [aɾˈtiːkəl] *m* (*pl* -) article.

Artillerie [aɾtiˈlˈɾiː] *f* (*pl* -n) artillery.

Artischocke [aɾtiˈʃɔkə] *f* (*pl* -n) artichoke.

Artist [aɾˈtist] *m* (*pl* -en) artiste.

Arznei [aɾtsˈnai] *f* (*pl* -en) medicine, medicament, drug. **-mittel** *neut* medicine.

Arzt [aɾtst] *m* (*pl* **Ärzte**) doctor, physician. **Arzt für Allgemeinmedizin** general practitioner (GP).

Ärztin ['ɛɾtstin] *f* (*pl* -nen) (woman) doctor. **ärztlich** *adj* medical.

As [as] *neut* (*pl* -se) ace.

Asbest [asˈbɛst] *m* asbestos.

Asche ['aʃə] *f* (*pl* -n) ash. **-nbecher** *m* ashtray.

Aspekt [asˈpɛkt] *m* (*pl* -e) aspect.

Asphalt [asˈfalt] *m* asphalt, tarmac.

Assistent [asisˈtɛnt] *m* (*pl* -en) assistant.

Ast [ast] *m* (*pl* **Äste**) bough, branch.

ästhetisch [ɛsˈteːtʃ] *adj* aesthetic.

Astronaut [astroˈnaut] *m* (*pl* -en) astronaut. **-ik** *f* astronautics. **astronautisch** *adj* astronautical.

Astronom [astroˈnoːm] *m* (*pl* -en) astronomer. **-ie** *f* astronomy. **astronomisch** *adj* astronomical.

Asyl [aˈzyːl] *neut* (*pl* -e) asylum.

Atelier [atəˈljeː] *neut* (*pl* -s) studio.

Atem ['aːtəm] *m* (*pl* -) breath. **Atem holen** take breath.

Atheis||mus [ateˈismus] *m* atheism. **-t** *m* (*pl* -en) atheist.

Äther ['ɛːtəɾ] *m* ether. **ätherisch** *adj* ethereal.

Athlet [atˈleːt] *m* (*pl* -en) athlete. **-ik** *f* athletics. **athletisch** *adj* athletic.

Atlantik [atˈlantik] *m* Atlantic (Ocean).

Atlas¹ ['atlas] *m* (*pl* **Atlanten**) (*Buch*) atlas.

Atlas² *m* (*pl* -se) (*Stoff*) satin.

atmen ['aːtmən] *v* breathe.

Atmosphäre [atm osˈfɛːɾə] *f* (*pl* -n) atmosphere.

Atmung ['aːtmuŋ] *f* respiration, breathing. **-sapparat** *m* respirator.

Atom [aˈtoːm] *neut* (*pl* -e) atom. **-abfall** *m* atomic waste. **-antrieb** *m* nuclear propulsion. **-bombe** *f* atom bomb. **-kraft** *f* nuclear power. **-kraftwerk** *f* nuclear power station.

Attentat [atɛnˈtaːt] *neut* (*pl* -e) assassination (attempt). **Attentäter** *m* assassin, assailant.

ätzen ['ɛtsən] *v* corrode; (*Med*) cauterize; (*Kupferstich*) etch. **-d** *adj* corrosive, caustic.

Aubergine [obɛɾˈʒiːnə] *f* (*pl* -n) aubergine.

auch [aux] *conj* also, too; (*sogar*) even; (*tatsächlich*) indeed, but. **nicht nur ... sondern auch** ... not only ... but also .... **sowohl ... als auch** ... both ... and .... **auch wenn** even if, (even) though. *ich* *auch!* me too! *ich auch nicht* nor me, me neither. *was er auch sagen mag* whatever he may say. **wer auch immer** whoever.

Audienz [audiɛnts] *f (pl -en)* audience, interview.

auf [auf] *prep* on. *adv* up; *(offenstehend)* open. **auf und ab** up and down. *auf den Tisch stellen* put on the table. *auf dem Tisch finden* find on the table. *auf die Schule gehen* go to school. *auf der Schule sein* be at school. *auf deutsch* in German. **auf einmal** at once.

Aufbau [aufbau] *m (unz.)* building, construction; structure.

aufbessern [aufbɛsən] *v* improve; *(Gehalt)* increase. **Aufbesserung** *f* improvement; *(Gehalt)* increase, rise.

aufbewahren [aufbəva:rən] *v* store (up), keep. **Aufbewahrung** *f* storage, safekeeping.

*aufblasen [aufbla:zən] *v* blow up, inflate.

aufblicken [aufblıkən] *v* look up.

aufbrauchen [aufbrauxən] *v* use up.

*aufbrechen [aufbrɛçən] *v* break open; *(Knospen, Wunden)* open; *(abreisen)* set off.

*aufbringen [aufbrıŋən] *v* bring up, raise; *(ärgern)* imitate, provoke.

Aufbruch [aufbrux] *m* departure, start.

aufdecken [aufdɛkən] *v* uncover, reveal; *(Tisch)* spread. **Aufdeckung** *f* revealing, unveiling.

aufdrehen [aufdre:ən] *v* switch *or* turn on; *(Schraube)* unscrew.

aufdringlich [aufdrıŋlıç] *adj* intrusive, importunate.

aufeinander [aufain'andər] *adv* (one) after another; *(gegeneinander)* one against the other. **–folgen** *v* follow (one after another). **–folgend** *adj* successive. **–stoßen** *v (Mot)* collide; *(Meinungen)* clash. **–treffen** *v* meet.

Aufenthalt [aufənthalt] *m (pl -e)* (kurze Wartezeit) delay, stop; (längerer Besuch usw.) stay. **–serlaubnis** *f* residence permit.

auferlegen [aufɛrle:gən] *v* impose.

*auferstehen [aufɛrʃte:ən] *v* rise from the dead. **Auferstehung** *f* resurrection.

*auffahren [auffa:rən] *v* rise, go up; *(herauffahren)* draw up; *(aufspringen)* start, jump; *(zornig werden)* flare up; *(wagen)* collide. **Auffahrt** *f* ascent; *(in den Himmel)* Ascension; *(Zufahrtsweg)* drive.

*auffallen [auffalən] *v* strike, come to

one's attention. *es fiel mir ein* it struck me, I realized. **auffallend** *or* **auffällig** *adj* striking, remarkable.

auffassen [auffasən] *v* pick up; *(begreifen)* understand; *(deuten)* interpret. **Auffassung** *f* comprehension; *(Auslegung)* interpretation; *(Meinung)* opinion.

*auffliegen [auffli:gən] *v* fly up; *(Flugzeug)* take off; *(Tür)* fly open; *(explodieren)* explode.

auffordern [auffɔrdən] *v* challenge; *(einladen)* ask, invite. **Aufforderung** *f* challenge; *(Recht)* summons; *(Einladung)* invitation, request.

*auffressen [auffrɛsən] *v* devour.

auffrischen [auffrıʃən] *v* freshen up; *(Kenntnisse)* refresh.

aufführen [auffy:rən] *v (Theater)* put on, perform; *(Film)* show; *(Konzert)* give; *(zitieren)* cite; *(aufbauen)* erect. **Aufführung** *f* performance; *(Film)* showing; *(Benehmen)* behaviour.

Aufgabe [aufga:bə] *f* task, duty; *(Übergabe)* handing in.

Aufgang [aufgaŋ] *m* rise, ascent.

*aufgeben [aufge:bən] *v* give up; *(Gepäck)* check in.

aufgeblasen [aufgəbla:zən] *adj* arrogant, conceited.

aufgeklärt [aufgəklɛ:rt] *adj* enlightened.

aufgelegt [aufgəle:kt] *adj* inclined, in the mood. **gut/schlecht aufgelegt** in a good/bad mood.

aufgeregt [aufgərɛ:kt] *adj* excited.

aufgeschlossen [aufgəʃɔsən] *adj* enlightened, open-minded.

*aufhalten [aufhaltən] *adj* keep open; *(anhalten)* stop; *(hinhalten)* delay. **sich aufhalten** stay.

*aufhängen [aufhɛŋən] *v* hang up.

*aufheben [aufhe:bən] *v* lift, raise; *(aufbewahren)* store, keep; *(abschaffen)* abolish, cancel. **Aufhebung** *f* raising, abolition.

aufheitern [aufhaitən] *v* cheer up. **sich aufheitern** *(Wetter)* brighten up.

aufhören [aufhø:rən] *v* stop, cease.

aufklären [aufklɛ:rən] *v (Person)* enlighten; *(Sache)* clarify, explain. **Aufklärung** *f* clarification; *(the)* Enlightenment.

aufkleben [aufkle:bən] *v* stick on, paste on.

aufknöpfen [aufknœpfən] *v* unbutton.

*aufkommen [ˈaʊfkʌm ən] **v** arise.
aufkommen für take responsibility for.

*aufladen [ˈaʊfaːdən] **v** load.

Auflage [ˈaʊfaːgə] **f** (*Buch*) edition;
(*Zeitung*) circulation.

*auflassen [ˈaʊfasən] **v** leave open.

Auflauf [ˈaʊfaʊf] **m** riot; (*Speise*) trifle, soufflé. **auflaufen** **v** run up; (*Schiff*) run
aground; (*Geld*) increase.

auflegen [ˈaʊfleːgən] **v** put on; (*Buch*) print,
publish; (*Telef*) hang up.

auflösbar [ˈaʊfløː ːzbaːr] **adj** soluble.
auflösen **v** (*Knoten*) loosen; (*in Wasser,
usw.*) dissolve; (*Rätsel*) solve; (*Vertrag*) cancel; (*Geschäft*) close down; (*Ehe*) break up.
Auflösung **f** loosening; solution; cancellation; closure; break-up.

*aufmachen [ˈaʊfm axən] **v** open; (*Knoten,
Knöpfe*) undo. **sich aufmachen** set off.
Aufmachung **f** outward appearance.

aufmerksam [ˈaʊfm ɛrkzam] **adj** attentive.
**jemanden auf etwas aufmerksam
machen** draw something to someone's
attention. **Aufmerksamkeit** **f** attentive-
ness, attention.

aufmuntern [ˈaʊfm untərn] **v** encourage,
cheer up.

Aufnahme [ˈaʊfnaːm ə] **f** (*pl* **-n**) taking up;
(*Foto*) shot, picture; (*Tonband, usw.*) recording; (*Zulassung*) admission; (*Empfang*)
reception. **aufnahmefähig** **adj** receptive.
Aufnahmeprüfung **f** entrance exam.

*aufnehmen [ˈaʊfneːm ən] **v** take up;
(*zulassen*) admit; (*empfangen*) receive;
(*Radio*) pick up; (*Foto*) photograph;
(*Protokoll, Tonband*) record.

aufopfern [ˈaʊfɒpfərn] **v** sacrifice.

aufpassen [ˈaʊfpasən] **v** pay attention; (*vorsichtig sein*) take care. **aufpassen auf** take
care of, look after.

Aufprall [ˈaʊfpral] **m** (*pl* **-e**) impact, collision. **aufprallen** **v** strike, collide.

aufputzen [ˈaʊfpʊtsən] **v** dress up, adorn;
(*reinigen*) clean up.

aufräumen [ˈaʊfrɔym ən] **v** tidy up, clean
up; (*wegschaffen*) clear away. **Aufräumung**
f cleaning up.

aufrecht [ˈaʊfrɛçt] **adj** upright, erect; (*fig*)
upright, honest. **–erhalten** **v** maintain,
keep up.

aufregen [ˈaʊfreːgən] **v** excite, upset. **sich
aufregen** get excited *or* upset. **Aufregung**

f excitement, agitation.

aufrichten [ˈaʊfrɪçtən] **v** erect, set up;
(*trösten*) console.

aufrichtig [ˈaʊfrɪçtɪç] sincere, honest.
Aufrichtigkeit **f** sincerity, honesty.

aufrücken [ˈaʊfrʏkən] **v** move up;
(*Dienstgrad*) be promoted.

Aufruf [ˈaʊfruː f] **m** call, appeal. **aufrufen** **v**
call out.

Aufruhr [ˈaʊfruː r] **m** (*pl* **-e**) tumult;
(*Erhebung*) revolt. **aufrühren** **v** stir up;
(*Erhebung*) incite to revolt. **Aufrührer** **m**
(*pl* **-**) agitator, rebel. **aufrührerisch** **adj**
rebellious, riotous.

aufrüsten [ˈaʊfrʏstən] **v** (re)arm; (*tech*)
upgrade. **Aufrüstung** **f** (re)armament.

aufs [aʊfs] **prep** + **art** auf das.

aufsagen [ˈaʊfzaːgən] **v** recite, repeat.

Aufsatz [ˈaʊfzats] **m** essay; (*Tech*) top
(piece); (*Tafel-*) centre-piece.

*aufsaugen [ˈaʊfzaʊgən] **v** suck up. **–d** **adj**
absorbent.

*aufschieben [ˈaʊfʃiːbən] **v** push open; (*fig*)
put off, delay, procrastinate.
Aufschiebung **f** postponement, delay.

Aufschlag [ˈaʊfʃlaːk] **m** surcharge, extra
charge; (*Hose*) turn-up; (*Jacke*) lapel;
(*Auftreffen*) impact; (*Tennis*) service. **aufschlagen** **v** (*Preis*) raise; (*Stoff*) turn up;
(*auftreffen*) hit; (*Buch*) open, consult;
(*Tennis*) serve.

*aufschließen [ˈaʊfʃliːsən] **v** open up,
unlock; (*erklären*) explain.

Aufschluß [ˈaʊfʃlʊs] **m** unlocking;
(*Erklärung*) explanation. **aufschlußreich**
adj informative.

*aufschneiden [ˈaʊfʃnaɪdən] **v** cut open;
(*Fleisch*) carve.

Aufschnitt [ˈaʊfʃnɪt] **m** (cold) sliced meat.

Aufschrei [ˈaʊfʃraɪ] **m** scream, shriek; (*fig*)
outcry.

*aufschreiben [ˈaʊfʃraɪbən] **v** write down,
note.

Aufschrift [ˈaʊfʃrɪft] **f** (*Briefumschlag*)
address; (*Etikett*) labelling, information;
(*Inschrift*) inscription.

Aufschub [ˈaʊfʃuː p] **m** delay, deferment.

Aufschwung [ˈaʊfʃvʊŋ] **m** swinging up,
rising up; (*Komm*) boom, upturn (in
economy).

*aufsehen [ˈaʊfzeː ən] **v** look up. **Aufsehen**
neut (*unz.*) stir, sensation. **Aufseher** **m** (*pl* **-**)

overseer, inspector.

aufsetzen [ˈaʊfzɛtsən] v put on; (*Schriftliches*) draft, draw up.

Aufsicht [ˈaʊfziçt] f supervision, control; (*Verantwortung*) charge, care. **–srat** m board of directors.

*****aufspringen** [ˈaʊfʃprɪŋən] v spring up; (*Tür*) fly open; (*Riß*) crack, open.

Aufstand [ˈaʊfʃtant] m revolt, rebellion.

aufstapeln [ˈaʊfʃtaːpəln] v stack up, pile up.

aufstauen [ˈaʊfʃtaʊən] v dam (up).

*****aufstehen** [ˈaʊfʃteːən] v stand up; (*morgens, usw.*) get up, rise; (*revoltieren*) revolt; (*offenstehen*) stand open.

*****aufsteigen** [ˈaʊfʃtaɪɡən] v climb up, ascend, rise; (*Pferd*) mount.

aufstellen [ˈaʊfʃtɛlən] v set up; (*Kandidat*) nominate; (*Mil*) draw up; (*Theorie, usw.*) propose, advance.

Aufstieg [ˈaʊfʃtiːk] m ascent, rise.

aufsuchen [ˈaʊfzuːxən] v (*Arzt, Gasthaus*) visit; (*Person*) visit, look up.

auftanken [ˈaʊftaŋkən] v refuel.

auftauchen [ˈaʊftaʊxən] v (*aus Wasser*) emerge; (*fig*) turn up, crop up.

auftauen [ˈaʊftaʊən] v thaw (out), melt.

aufteilen [ˈaʊftaɪlən] v divide up; (*verteilen*) share out.

Auftrag [ˈaʊftraːk] m (*pl* **Aufträge**) (*Komm*) order; (*Aufgabe*) task. **auftragen** v (*Farbe*) apply; (*Essen*) serve. **Auftrag‖geber** m customer, purchaser. **–nehmer** m contractor, supplier.

*****auftreiben** [ˈaʊftraɪbən] v (*auffinden*) hunt out, find; (*Staub*) stir up; (*Geld*) raise.

*****auftreten** [ˈaʊftreːtən] v come forward, appear.

Auftritt [ˈaʊftrɪt] m (*Szene*) scene; (*Schauspieler*) appearance, entrance.

*****auftun** [ˈaʊftuːn] v open.

aufwachen [ˈaʊfvaxən] v wake up.

*****aufwachsen** [ˈaʊfvaksən] v grow up.

Aufwand [ˈaʊfvant] m (*unz.*) expenditure.

aufwärmen [ˈaʊfvɛrmən] v (*Sport*) warm up; (*speisen*) heat up.

aufwärts [ˈaʊfvɛrts] *adv* up(wards).

aufwecken [ˈaʊfvɛkən] v wake up.

*****aufwend‖en** [ˈaʊɡvɛndən] v (*Geld*) spend; (*Zeit*) devote; (*Energie*) expend. **–ig** *adj* expensive. **Aufwendung** f expenditure.

*****aufwerfen** [ˈaʊfvɛrfən] v throw up.

aufwerten [ˈaʊfvɛrtən] v raise the value of, revalue. **Aufwertung** f revaluation.

*****aufwinden** [ˈaʊfvɪndən] v wind up; (*mit der Winde*) winch up.

aufwirbeln [ˈaʊfvɪrbəln] v whirl up.

aufwischen [ˈaʊfvɪʃən] v wipe up.

aufwühlen [ˈaʊfvyːlən] v root up; (*fig*) stir up, agitate.

aufzählen [ˈaʊftsɛːlən] v count out.

aufzeichnen [ˈaʊftsaɪçnən] v sketch; (*niederschreiben*) write down.

*****aufziehen** [ˈaʊftsiːən] v (*Kind, Tier, Flagge*) raise; (*Vorhang*) open; (*Pflanze*) grow; (*necken*) tease.

Aufzug [ˈaʊftsuːk] m lift, (*US*) elevator; (*Festzug*) procession, parade; (*Theater*) act.

Augapfel [ˈaʊkapfəl] m eyeball.

Auge [ˈaʊɡə] *neut* (*pl* **–n**) eye. **unter vier Augen** in private, **ins Auge fallen** be conspicuous, catch the eye. **Augen‖arzt** m oculist, ophthalmologist. **–blick** m moment, instant. **–braue** f eyebrow. **–lid** *neut* eyelid. **–loch** *neut* eye socket.

August [aʊˈɡʊst] m (*pl* **–e**) August.

Aula [ˈaʊla] f (*pl* **Aulen**) (great) hall.

Au-pair-Mädchen [oˈpɛːm ɛːtçən] *neut* au-pair girl.

aus [aʊs] *prep* from. *adv* out; (*vorbei*) over, finished. *aus London* from London. *aus dem Fenster* out of the window. *aus Liebe zu* for love of. *aus Holz* (made) of wood, wooden. *von mir aus* as far as I'm concerned. *es ist aus* it's over.

ausarbeiten [ˈaʊsarbaɪtən] v work out; (*vervollkommnen*) perfect, finish off. **Ausarbeitung** f working out; finishing off, completion.

ausarten [ˈaʊsaːrtən] v degenerate.

ausatmen [ˈaʊsaːtm ən] v exhale, breathe out.

ausbaggern [ˈaʊsbaɡərn] v dredge.

Ausbau [ˈaʊsbaʊ] m (*pl* **–ten**) extension; (*Fertigstellung*) completion.

ausbauchen [ˈaʊsbaʊxən] v bulge. **Ausbauchung** f bulge.

ausbessern [ˈaʊsbɛsərn] v repair, mend.

Ausbeute [ˈaʊsbɔʏtə] f profit, gain; (*Ernte*) crop, yield. **ausbeuten** v exploit. **Ausbeut‖er** m exploiter. **–ung** f exploitation.

ausbilden [ˈaʊsbɪldən] v educate; (*Lehrling*)

train; (*gestalten*) develop, shape.

Ausbildung f education; training; (*Gestaltung*) development, shaping.

*ausbleiben ['ausblaibən] v stay away; (*aufhören*) stop.

Ausblick ['ausblɪk] m view; (*fig*) prospect, outlook.

*ausbrechen ['ausbrɛçən] v break out.

ausbreiten ['ausbraitən] v spread (out), stretch (out), extend.

Ausbruch ['ausbrʊx] m outbreak; (*vom Gefängnis*) escape, break-out; (*Zorn, Vulkan*) eruption.

ausbrüten ['ausbry:tən] v hatch.

Ausdauer ['ausdauər] f endurance, perseverance. **ausdauern** v persevere, endure.

ausdehnen ['ausde:nən] v extend; (*Metall*) expand. **Ausdehnung** f extension; expansion.

*ausdenken ['ausdɛŋkən] v invent, think out; (*sich vorstellen*) imagine.

ausdrehen ['ausdre:ən] v turn off, switch off; (*Gelenk*) dislocate.

Ausdruck ['ausdrʊk] m expression, phrase. **ausdrück||en** f express; (*auspressen*) squeeze out. **–lich** adj express, explicit. **ausdrucks||los** adj expressionless, vacant. **–voll** adj expressive.

auseinander [ausain'andər] adv apart. **–bauen** v take apart, dismantle. **–fallen** v fall to pieces. **–gehen** v break up; (*sich trennen*) part. **–nehmen** v take apart. **–setzen** v explain. **Auseinandersetzung** f (*vigorous*) discussion; (*Streit*) argument.

auserlesen ['ausɛrlɛ:zən] adj selected.

ausersehen ['ausɛrzeən] v choose, select.

auserwählen ['ausɛrvɛ:ən] v choose, select.

*ausfahren ['ausfa:rən] v drive out; (*Person*) take for a drive or walk. **Ausfahrt** f exit; (*Ausflug*) excursion; (*Ausfahren*) departure.

Ausfall ['ausfal] m loss; (*Fehlbetrag*) deficiency, deficit; (*Ergebnis*) result; (*Mil*) attack, sally. **ausfallen** v fall out; (*unterbleiben*) fail, be wanting; attack.

ausfertigen ['ausfɛrtigən] v (*Schriftliches*) draw up; (*ausstellen*) issue.

ausfindig ['ausfɪndɪç] adj **ausfindig machen** find out.

Ausflug ['ausflu:k] m excursion, outing.

ausfragen ['ausfra:gən] v question, interrogate.

Ausfuhr ['ausfu:r] f (*pl* -en) export.

ausführ||en ['ausfy:rən] v carry out, perform; (*Waren*) export; (*erklären*) explain, set out (in detail). **–bar** adj feasible. **–lich** adj detailed, extensive; adv in full.

Ausführung f execution, performance; (*Darstellung*) explanation.

ausfüllen ['ausfʏlən] v fill; (*Formular*) fill out.

Ausgabe ['ausga:bə] f expenditure, expense; (*Buch*) edition.

Ausgang ['ausgaŋ] m going out; (*Tür*) way out, exit; (*Ergebnis*) result, issue; (*freier Tag*) day off.

*ausgeben ['ausge:bən] v (*Geld*) spend; (*herausgeben*) distribute; (*Karten*) deal. **sich ausgeben für** pose as.

ausgeglichen ['ausgəglɪçən] adj (well-)balanced.

*ausgehen ['ausge:ən] v go out; (*enden*) come to an end; (*Vorrat*) run out. **Ausgehverbot** neut curfew.

ausgelassen ['ausgəlasən] adj wild, unrestrained, boisterous.

ausgemacht ['ausgəm axt] adj agreed, settled.

ausgenommen ['ausgənɔm ən] prep except for.

ausgeprägt ['ausgəprɛ:kt] adj marked, distinct.

ausgerechnet ['ausgərɛçnət] adv precisely, just.

ausgeschlossen ['ausgəʃlɔsən] adj impossible, out of the question.

ausgesprochen ['ausgəʃprɔxən] adj pronounced, distinct. adv distinctly, very.

ausgewachsen ['ausgəvaksən] adj fullgrown.

ausgezeichnet ['ausgətsaiçnət] adj excellent.

*ausgießen ['ausgi:sən] v pour out.

Ausgleich ['ausglaiç] m (*pl* -e) settlement; (*Entschädigung*) compensation; (*Sport*) equalizer. **ausgleichen** v equalize, make even; (*Verlust*) compensate; (*Konto*) balance.

Ausguß ['ausgʊs] m outlet; (*Kanne*) spout.

*aushalten ['aushaltən] v bear, endure; (*durchhalten*) persevere.

*ausheben ['aushe:bən] v pull out, lift out; (*Truppen*) enlist. **Aushebung** f enlistment; (*Wehrdienst*) conscription.

*aushelfen ['aushɛlfən] v help (out), assist.

Aushilfe ['aushilfə] f (temporary) help, assistance.

aushöhlen ['aushœ:lən] v hollow out, excavate.

*auskennen ['auskɛnən] v sich auskennen (umg.) know what's what; (in einer Sache) know well.

auskleiden ['ausklaidən] v line. sich auskleiden undress.

*auskommen ['auskɔmən] v (mit etwas) manage or cope with; (mit einer Person) get on well with.

Auskunft ['auskunft] f (pl Auskünfte) information.

auslachen ['auslaxən] v laugh at.

*ausladen ['auslaːdən] v unload.

Auslage ['auslaːgə] f display; (Schaufenster) shop window. **–n** pl expenses pl.

Ausland ['auslant] neut foreign country or countries. **ins** or **im Ausland** abroad. **Ausländer** m (pl -), **Ausländerin** f (pl -nen) foreigner. **ausländisch** adj foreign.

*auslassen ['auslasən] v omit, leave out; (Butter) melt; (Kleider) let down. **Auslassung** f omission; (Äußerung) utterance. **–szeichen** neut apostrophe.

Auslauf ['auslauf] m outflow; (Schiff) sailing, departure; (Bewegungsfreiheit) room to move. **auslaufen** v run out; (Schiff) put to sea.

ausleeren ['auslɛːrən] v empty. **Ausleerung** f emptying, draining.

auslegen ['auslɛːgən] v lay out; (Geld) spend; (erklären) explain, interpret. **Auslegung** f display; (Erklärung) interpretation.

Auslese ['auslɛːzə] f (pl -n) selection; (Wein) choice wine. **auslesen** v select; (Buch) read to the end.

ausliefern ['auslifərn] v deliver; (Verbrecher) extradite. **Auslieferung** f delivery; extradition.

auslösen ['auslœːzən] v loosen; (Gefangene) ransom; (veranlassen) cause, spark off.

ausmachen ['ausm axən] v (Feuer, Licht) put out; (betragen) amount to; (verabreden) agree, fix. **das macht nichts aus** that doesn't matter.

Ausmaß ['ausm aːs] neut scale, extent.

Ausnahme ['ausnaːmə] f (pl -n) exception. **mit Ausnahme von** excepting, with the exception of. **–fall** m exception, special case. **–zustand** m (Pol) state of emergency. **ausnahmslos** adj without exception. **–weise** adv by way of exception, just for once.

*ausnehmen ['ausnɛːm ən] v take out; (ausschließen) exclude, make an exception of.

ausnutzen ['ausnutsən] v take advantage of.

auspacken ['auspakən] v unpack.

ausprobieren ['ausprɔbiːrən] v try (out), test.

Auspuff ['auspuf] m (pl -e) exhaust. **–rohr** neut exhaust pipe. **–topf** m silencer.

ausradieren ['ausradiːrən] v erase, rub out.

ausräumen ['ausrɔym ən] v clear out, clean out.

ausrechnen ['ausrɛçnən] v calculate, work out. **Ausrechnung** f calculation.

Ausrede ['ausrɛːdə] f excuse.

ausreichen ['ausraiçən] v be enough or sufficient. **–d** adj sufficient, enough.

Ausreise ['ausraizə] f outward journey; (Grenzübertritt) departure, exit. **ausreisen** v depart.

ausrichten ['ausriçtən] v adjust, align; (durchsetzen) accomplish, do; (Botschaft) convey.

ausrotten ['ausrɔtən] v stamp out, root out.

Ausruf ['ausruːf] m cry, exclamation; (Bekanntmachung) proclamation. **ausrufen** v cry out, exclaim; (Namen) call out. **Ausrufung** f exclamation. **–szeichen** neut exclamation mark.

ausruhen ['ausruːən] v rest.

ausrüsten ['ausrystən] v equip; (Mil) arm. **Ausrüstung** f equipment; (Mil) armament.

Aussage ['auszaːgə] f (pl -n) statement, declaration; (Jur) evidence, testimony. **aussagen** v declare, state; (Jur) give evidence, make a statement, testify.

ausschalten ['ausʃaltən] v switch off; (fig) exclude.

Ausschank ['ausʃaŋk] m (Ausgabe) service (of alcoholic drinks); (Kneipe) bar, pub. **Ausschank über die Straße** off-sales, off-licence.

*ausscheiden ['ausʃaidən] v withdraw, retire; (absondern) separate. **Ausscheidung** f withdrawal; separation.

ausschicken ['ausʃɪkən] *v* send out.

ausschiffen ['ausʃɪfən] *v* disembark, land. **Ausschiffung** *f* disembarkation.

ausschimpfen ['ausʃɪmpfən] *v* scold, abuse.

*****ausschlafen** ['ausʃlaːgən] *v* lie in, sleep until completely rested.

Ausschlag ['ausʃlaːk] *m* (*Med*) rash; (*Bot*) shoot; (*Zeiger*) deflection. **ausschlagen** *v* knock out; (*ablehnen*) refuse; (*Pferd*) kick out.

*****ausschließen** ['ausʃliːsən] *v* shut out, lock out; (*fig*) exclude. **ausschließlich** *adj* exclusive; *prep* excluding, exclusive of. **Ausschließung** *f* exclusion; (*Arbeiter*) lockout.

*****ausschneiden** ['ausʃnaidən] *v* cut out.

Ausschnitt ['ausʃnɪt] *m* (*Teil*) section; (*Zeitung*) press cutting; (*Kleid*) low neckline.

ausschöpfen ['ausʃœpfən] *v* (*Wasser*) scoop out; (*Boot*) bail out; (*Möglichkeiten*) exhaust.

*****ausschreiben** ['ausʃraibən] *v* write out, copy out; (*Formular*) fill out; (*ankündigen*) announce.

Ausschreitung ['ausʃraituŋ] *f* excess, transgression.

Ausschuß ['ausʃus] **1** *m* committee, board. **2** *m* (*unz.*) (*Abfall*) refuse, rejects *pl*.

ausschweifen ['ausʃvaifən] *v* (*moralisch*) lead a dissolute life; (*von Thema*) digress. **Ausschweifung** *f* debauchery, immorality; digression.

*****aussehen** ['auszeːən] *v* appear, look. *sie sieht hübsch aus* she looks pretty. *es sieht nach Regen aus* it looks like rain.

außen ['ausən] *adv* (to the) outside, outwards. **Außenbordmotor** *m* outboard motor.

*****aussenden** ['auszɛndən] *v* send out; (*Strahlen*) emit; (*Radio*) transmit.

Außen||handel *m* foreign trade. **–läufer** *m* wing-half. **–minister** *m* foreign minister. **–politik** *f* foreign policy; (*allgemein*) foreign affairs. **–seite** *f* outside. **–seiter** outsider. **–stürmer** *m* wing (forward).

außer ['ausər] *prep* (*räumlich*) out of, outside; (*ausgenommen*) except. **außer Betrieb** out of order.

äußer ['ɔysər] *adj* external, exterior, outer.

außer||dem *adv* besides. **–halb** *adv, prep* outside.

äußerlich ['ɔysərlɪç] *adj* external.

äußern ['ɔysərn] *v* express, utter; (*zeigen*)

manifest, reveal.

außerordentlich [ausər'ɔrdəntlɪç] *adj* extraordinary.

äußerst ['ɔysərst] *adj* the utmost.

aussetzen ['auszɛtsən] *v* (*Pflanze*) plant out; (*Kind*) abandon; (*Tier*) set free; (*Geld*) offer; (*einer Gefahr, dem Spott, usw.*) expose (to); (*aufhören*) stop; (*Mot*) stall.

Aussicht ['auszɪçt] *f* outlook, prospect; (*Blick*) view. **aussichts||los** *adj* unpromising, hopeless. **–voll** *adj* promising.

aussondern ['auszɔndərn] (*auswählen*) select; excrete. **Aussonderung** *f* separation; selection; excretion.

ausspeien ['ausʃpaiən] *v* spit out; (*Rauch*) belch out.

Aussprache ['ausʃpraːxə] *f* pronunciation.

*****aussprechen** ['ausʃprɛçən] *v* pronounce.

Ausspruch ['ausʃprux] *m* remark, saying; (*Jur*) verdict.

ausspülen ['ausʃpyːlən] *v* wash out, rinse.

Ausstand ['ausʃtant] *m* strike.

ausstatten ['ausʃtatən] *v* equip, furnish; (*Tochter*) provide with a dowry. **Ausstattung** *f* (*pl* **-en**) equipment, outfit; dowry.

*****ausstehen** ['ausʃteːən] *v* be missing; (*Geld*) be owed; (*ertragen*) endure, bear. *ich kann ihn nicht ausstehen* I can't stand him.

*****aussteigen** ['ausʃtaigən] *v* get off, alight.

ausstellen ['ausʃtɛlən] *v* display, exhibit; (*Paß, Urkunde*) issue; (*Quittung*) write out. **Aussteller** *m* (*pl* **-**) exhibiter. **Ausstellung** *f* exhibition; issue; writing out.

*****aussterben** ['ausʃtɛrbən] *v* die out.

Ausstieg ['ausʃtiːg] *m* (*pl* **-e**) exit door.

ausstoßen ['ausʃtoːsən] *v* push out, thrust out; (*Schrei*) give.

ausstrahlen ['ausʃtraːlən] *v* radiate.

ausstrecken ['ausʃtrɛkən] *v* stretch out, extend.

*****ausstreichen** ['ausʃtraiçən] *v* (*Wort*) strike out, cross out; (*Teig*) roll out.

ausströmen ['ausʃtrøːmən] *v* (*Flüssigkeit*) pour out; (*Gas*) escape.

aussuchen ['auszuːxən] *v* search (out), select.

Austausch ['austauʃ] *m* exchange. **austauschen** *v* exchange.

austeilen ['austailən] *v* distribute, share out.

Auster ['austər] f (pl -n) oyster.
Austrag ['austraːk] m (pl Austräge) decision, end, result. **austragen** v carry out; (Kampf) decide; (Post) deliver.
Australi||en [au'straːliən] neut Australia. **-er** m (pl -), **-erin** f (pl -nen) Australian. **australisch** adj Australian.
*austreiben ['austraibən] v expel.
*austreten ['austreːtən] v leave, withdraw (from); (Schuhe, usw.) wear out.
*austrinken ['austrɪŋkən] v drain, drink off.
Austritt ['austrɪt] m leaving, departure.
ausüben ['ausyːbən] v practise; (Druck, Einfluß) exert; (Macht) wield. **-d** adj practising. **Ausübung** f practice, exercise.
Ausverkauf ['ausfɛrkauf] m (clearance) sale. **ausverkauft** adj sold out.
Auswahl ['ausvaːl] f choice, selection.
Auswanderer ['ausvandərər] m emigrant. **auswandern** v emigrate. **Auswanderung** f emigration.
auswärtig ['ausvɛrtɪç] adj foreign. **das Auswärtige Amt** the Foreign Office.
auswärts ['ausvɛrts] adv outwards; (nach draußen) outside.
auswechseln ['ausvɛksəln] v change (for), exchange.
Ausweg ['ausveːk] m way out.
*ausweichen ['ausvaiçən] v make way for; (Frage) evade, dodge. **-d** adj evasive, elusive. **Ausweichung** f evasion.
Ausweis ['ausvais] m (pl -e) identity card or papers; (Paß) passport. **ausweisen** v expel, turn out. **Ausweisung** f expulsion.
auswendig ['ausvɛndɪç] adj external. **auswendig lernen** learn by heart.
*auswerfen ['ausvɛrfən] v throw out; (Anker) cast.
auswirken ['ausvɪrkən] v obtain. **sich auswirken auf** have an effect on. **Auswirkung** f effect.
auswischen ['ausvɪʃən] v wipe out.
Auswuchs ['ausvuks] m growth; (Nebenerscheinung) (unwelcome) product, side-effect.
auszahlen ['austsaːlən] v pay out. **Auszahlung** f payment.
auszeichnen ['austsaiçnən] v (Ware) label; (ehren) honour; (hervorheben) distinguish, mark out. **sich auszeichnen** distinguish oneself. **Auszeichnung** f distinction, honour, award.

*ausziehen ['austsiːən] v pull out, extract; (Person) undress; (aus einer Wohnung) move out. **sich ausziehen** undress.
Auszug ['austsuːk] m removal; (Abmarsch) departure; (Exzerpt) excerpt.
authentisch [au'tɛntɪʃ] adj authentic.
Autismus ['autɪsmus] m autism. **autistisch** adj autistic.
Auto ['auto] neut (pl -s) car, automobile. **-ausstellung** f motor show. **-bahn** f motorway. **-fahrer** m driver, motorist.
Autogramm [auto'gram] neut (pl -e) autograph.
Automat [auto'maːt] m (pl -en) vending machine. **automatisch** adj automatic. **automatisieren** v automate.
autonom [auto'noːm] adj autonomous.
Autor ['autɔr] m (pl -en) author.
autoritär [autori'tɛːr] adj authoritarian. **Autorität** f authority.
Auto||unfall m road accident. **-vermietung** f car hire.
avantgardistisch [avãgar'dɪstɪʃ] adj avant-garde.
Axt [akst] f (pl Äxte) axe.

B

Baby ['beːbi] neut (pl -s) baby.
Bach [bax] m (pl Bäche) stream, brook.
Backbord ['bakbɔrt] neut (naut) port (side).
Backe ['bakə] f (pl -n) cheek.
backen ['bakən] v bake.
Bäcker ['bɛkər] m (pl -) baker. **-ei** f (pl -en) bakery.
Back||ofen m oven. **-pulver** neut baking powder. **-stein** m brick.
Bad [baːt] neut (pl Bäder) bath; (Badeort) spa. **Bade||anstalt** f baths, swimming pool. **-anzug** m bathing costume. **-hose** f bathing trunks pl. **baden** v bathe. **Bade||wanne** f bath tub. **-zimmer** neut bathroom. **mit Bad und WC** en suite.
Bagger ['bagər] m (pl -) dredger, excavator. **baggern** v dredge, excavate.
Bahn [baːn] f (pl -en) railway; (Weg) path. **-brecher** m pioneer. **bahmen** v **den Weg bahnen** pave the way (for). **Bahn||hof** m

(railway) station. **–steig** m (railway) platform.

Bahre ['baːrə] f (pl **-n**) stretcher; (Toten-) bier.

Bai [bai] f (pl **-en**) (Bucht) bay.

Bajonett [bajɔ'nɛt] neut (pl **-e**) bayonet.

Bakterium [bak'teːrium] neut (pl **Bakterien**) bacterium (pl **-a**).

balancieren [balɑ̃'siːrən] v balance.

bald [balt] adv soon. **-ig** adj early, quick. **-möglichst** adv as soon as possible.

Balken ['balkən] m (pl -) beam.

Balkon [nalkõ:] m (pl **-e**) balcony.

Ball¹ [bal] m (pl **Bälle**) ball.

Ball² m (pl **Bälle**) (Tanz) dance, ball.

Ballade [ba'laːdə] f (pl **-n**) ballad.

ballen ['balən] v (Faust) clench. **sich ballen** cluster, clump together.

Ballen ['balən] m (pl -) bale, bundle; (Anat) palm. **-entzündung** f bunion.

Ballett [ba'lɛt] neut (pl **-e**) ballet. **Balletttänzer** m (pl -), **-tänzerin** f (pl **-nen**) ballet dancer. **Balletteuse** f (pl **-n**) ballerina.

Ballistik [ba'listik] f (unz.) ballistics. **ballistisch** adj ballistic.

Ballon [ba'lɔ̃:] m (pl **-e**) balloon.

Balsam ['balzaːm] m (pl **-e**) balsam; (fig) balm. **balsamieren** v embalm.

baltisch ['baltʃ] adj baltic.

Bambus ['bam bus] m (pl **-se**) bamboo.

Banane [ba'naːnə] f (pl **-n**) banana.

Band¹ [bant] **1** neut (pl **Bänder**) tape; (Haar) ribbon; (Anat) ligament; (Radio) waveband. **2** neut (pl **-e**) bond, tie.

Band² m (pl **Bände**) (Buch) volume.

Band³ [bɛnt] f (pl **-s**) (Jazz) band.

Bandage [ban'daːʒə] f (pl **-n**) bandage. **bandagieren** v bandage.

Bandaufnahme ['bantaufnaːm ə] f tape recording.

Bande ['bandə] f (pl **-n**) gang, bandit.

bändigen ['bɛndiɡən] v tame, subdue; (Wut) control.

Bandit [ban'diːt] m (pl **-en**) bandit.

Bandscheibe ['bantʃaibə] f (Anat) disc. **-nverfall** m slipped disc.

bang(e) ['baŋ ə)] adj afraid, anxious. **bangen** v be afraid or anxious.

Bank¹ [baŋk] f (pl **Bänke**) (zum Sitzen) bench, seat.

Bank² f (pl **-en**) (Komm) bank.

Bankett [baŋ'kɛt] neut (pl **-e**) banquet.

bankrott [baŋ'rɔt] adj bankrupt. **Bankrott** m (pl **-e**) bankruptcy. **Bankrott machen** go bankrupt. **Bankrotteur** m (pl **-e**) bankrupt.

Bank||konto neut bank account. **-note** f banknote.

Bann [ban] m (pl **-e**) ban; (Kirche) excommunication; (Zauber) spell.

bar [baːr] adj bare; (Geld) ready, in cash. **für bare Münze nehmen** accept, take at face value.

Bar [baːr] f (pl **-s**) bar, tavern.

Bär [bɛːr] m (pl **-en**) bear.

Barbar [barˈbaːr] m (pl **-en**) barbarian. **Barbarei** f (pl **-en**) barbarism. **barbarisch** adj barbarian.

barfuß ['baːrfuːs] adv barefoot. **barfüßig** adj barefoot.

Bargeld ['baːrɡɛlt] neut cash.

Bariton ['bariton] m (pl **-e**) baritone.

Barmädchen ['baːrm ɛtʃən] neut barmaid.

barmherzig [barm 'hɛrtsiç] adj merciful, compassionate. **Barmherzigkeit** f mercifulness, mercy.

Barock [ba'rɔk] neut or m baroque. **barock** adj baroque.

Barometer [ba'rom ɛtər] neut barometer.

Baron [ba'rɔːn] m (pl **-e**) baron. **-in** f (pl **-nen**) baroness.

Barre ['baːrə] f (pl **-n**) bar; (Gold) ingot.

Barriere [barɪ:rə] f (pl **-n**) barrier, gate.

barsch [baʃ] adj rude, brusque.

Bart [baːrt] m (pl **Bärte**) beard.

bärtig ['bɛːrtiç] adj bearded.

Base¹ ['baːzə] f (pl **-n**) (female) cousin.

Base² f (pl **-n**) alkali, base.

Basel ['baːzə] neut Basle, Bâle.

basieren [ba'ziːrən] v be based (on). **Basis** f (pl **Basen**) basis (pl **-ses**), base.

Baß [bas] m (pl **Bässe**) bass. **-geige** f double-bass.

Bassist [ba'sist] m (pl **-en**) (Sänger) bass (singer); (Baßgeigenspieler) double-bass (player).

Bastard ['bastart] m (pl **-e**) bastard.

basteln ['bastəln] v put together, rig up; (umg.) do-it-yourself. **er bastelt gern** he loves to tinker around. **Bastler** m (pl -) handyman, tinkerer.

Bataillon [bataˈlϳ̈ːn] *neut* (*pl* -e) battalion.

Batterie [batəˈrɪ] *f* (*pl* -n) battery.

Bau [bau] **1** *m* (*unz.*) building, construction; (*Getreide, usw.*) cultivation, growing. **2** *m* (*pl* -e) (*Bergwerk*) mine; (*Tiere*) burrow. **3** *m* (*pl* -ten) building. **-arbeiter** *m* construction worker.

Bauch [baux] *m* (*pl* Bäuche) belly, abdomen. **bauchig** *adj* bellied, bulging, convex. **Bauchweh** *neut or* **Bauschmerzen** *pl* stomach-ache.

bauen [ˈbauən] build; (*Bot*) grow, cultivate.

Bauer [ˈbauər] *m* (*pl* -n) (small) farmer, peasant; (*Schach*) pawn.

Bäuerin [ˈbɔyərin] *f* (*pl* -nen) farmer's wife, peasant woman. **bäuerlich** *adj* rustic, rural.

Bauern||haus *neut* farmhouse. **-hof** *m* farm(yard).

baufällig [ˈbaufɛliç] *adj* dilapidated. **Bau||genossenschaft** *f* building society. **-ingenieur** *m* structural or civil engineer. **-stelle** *f* building site.

Baum [baum] *m* (*pl* Bäume) tree; (*Schiff*) boom. **-garten** *m* orchard. **-wolle** *f* cotton.

Bayer [ˈbaiər] *m* (*pl* -) Bavarian. **-n** *neut* Bavaria. **bay(e)risch** *adj* Bavarian.

beabsichtigen [bəˈapzɪçtigən] *v* intend, propose.

beachten [bəˈaxtən] *v* pay attention to. **beachtungswert** *f* noteworthy. **Beachtung** *f* attention, notice.

Beamte(r) [bəˈam tə (r)] *m*, **Beamtin** *f* (*Staats-*) civil servant, official; (*Privat-*) officer, representative.

beängstigen [bəˈɛŋstigən] *v* worry, frighten.

beanspruchen [bəˈanʃpruxən] *v* claim, demand; (*person*) make demands on. **Beanspruchung** *f* claim; (*Belastung*) strain, load.

*beantragen [bəˈantraːgən] *v* propose.

beantworten [bəˈantvɔrtən] *v* answer, reply to.

bearbeiten [bəˈarbaitən] *v* work on; (*Metall, Holz, Land*) work; (*Buch*) edit, revise; (*Musik*) arrange; (*Theaterstück*) adapt. **Bearbeiter** *m* editor, reviser; arranger. **Bearbeitung** *f* working; (*Verbesserung*) revision, adaptation; (*Musik*) arrangement.

beaufsichtigen [bəˈaufzɪçtigən] *v* supervise, control. **Beaufsichtigung** *f* supervision, control.

*beauftragen [bəˈaufraːgən] *v* commission, authorize. **Beauftragte(r)** *m* deputy, agent.

bebauen [bəˈbauən] *v* (*Gelände*) build on; (*Land*) cultivate. **bebaute Fläche** *f* builtup area.

beben [ˈbeːbən] *v* tremble, shake.

Becher [ˈbɛçər] *m* (*pl* -) tumbler, glass. **-glas** *neut* (laboratory) beaker.

Becken [ˈbɛkən] *neut* (*pl* -) basin; (*Anat*) pelvis; (*Musik*) cymbal.

bedacht [bəˈdaxt] *adj* thoughtful, mindful. **Bedacht** *m* consideration; (*Überlegung*) deliberation. **bedächtig** *adj* thoughtful, careful.

Bedarf [bəˈdarf] *m* (*unz.*) need; (*Nachfrage*) demand.

bedauerlich [bəˈdauərliç] *adj* regrettable, unfortunate. **bedauern** *v* (*Sache*) regret, deplore; (*Person*) be or feel sorry for.

bedecken [bəˈdɛkən] *v* cover. **bedeckt** *adj* (*Himmel*) overcast. **Bedeckung** *f* (*pl* -en) cover(ing).

*bedenken [bəˈdɛŋkən] *v* consider, think over. **sich bedenken** deliberate, weigh the consequences (of).

bedeuten [bəˈdɔytən] *v* mean, signify. **-d** *adj* important. **Bedeutung** *f* meaning; (*Wichtigkeit*) significance, importance. **bedeutungs||los** *adj* meaningless. **-voll** *adj* significant.

bedienen [bəˈdiːnən] *v* serve, wait on; (*Maschine*) operate, work. **Bedienung** *f* service; (*Maschine*) operation; (*Diener*) staff, servants *pl*.

bedingt [bəˈdɪŋkt] *adj* conditional, limited. **Bedingung** *f* (*pl* -en) condition.

Bedrängnis [bəˈdrɛŋnis] *f* (*pl* -se) distress, trouble.

bedrohen [bəˈdroːən] *v* threaten. **Bedrohung** *f* (*pl* -en) threat.

*bedürfen [bəˈdyrfən] *v* need, require. **Bedürfnis** *neut* (*pl* -se) need, requirement. **Bedürfnisanstalt** *f* public toilet.

beeilen [bəˈailən] *v* **sich beeilen** hurry.

beeindrucken [bəˈaindrukən] *v* impress.

beeinflussen [bəˈainfluːsən] *v* influence, have an influence or effect on.

beeinträchtigen [bəˈaintrɛçtigən] *v* reduce, inhibit, be detrimental to.

beendigen [bə'ɛndɪɡən] v end, finish.
Beendigung f end, termination.

Beerdigung [bə'eːɐdɪɡuŋ] f burial, funeral.

Beere ['beːɐə] f (pl -n) berry.

Beet [beːt] neut (pl -e) bed; (Blumen-)
flowerbed; (Gemüse) vegetable patch.

befähigen [bə'fɛːɪɡən] v enable, make fit.
befähigt adj able, qualified. **Befähigung** f
(pl -en) capacity, fitness.

befahrbar [bə'faːɐbaːɐ] adj passable, usable.
befahren v travel or drive on.

*****befallen** [bə'falən] v befall; (Krankheit)
attack, strike.

befangen [bə'faŋən] adj shy, self-
conscious; (parteiisch) biased.

befassen [bə'fasən] v **sich befassen mit**
engage in, occupy oneself with.

*****befehlen** [bə'feːlən] v command, order.
Befehl m (pl -e) command, order.
Befehlshaber m (pl -) commander, com-
manding officer.

befestigen [bə'fɛstɪɡən] v fasten; (stärken)
strengthen; (Mil) fortify. **Befestigung** f (pl
-en) fastening; strengthening; (Mit) fortification.

*****befinden** [bə'fɪndən] v find. **sich befin-
den**, be, be situated; (Person) be, find oneself. **sich wohl befinden** feel well.
befindlich adj present, to be found.

beflecken [bə'flɛkən] v stain, soil.

befolgen [bə'fɔlɡən] v obey, follow.

befördern [bə'fœ dəm] v convey, dispatch;
(Rang) promote. **Beförderung** f (pl -en)
transport, conveyance; promotion.

befragen [bə'fraːɡən] v question. **sich
befragen** enquire, inquire.

befreien [bə'fraɪən] v liberate, free.
Befreier m (pl -) liberator. **Befreiung** f (pl
-en) liberation; (Entlastung) exemption.

befreunden [bə'frɔyndən] v **sich befreunden mit** make friends with. **befreundet**
adj friendly (with); intimate. **eng befreundet sein mit** be a close friend of.

befriedigen [bə'friːdɪɡən] v satisfy. **-d** adj
satisfactory. **Befriedigung** f (pl -en) satisfaction.

befruchten [bə'frʊxtən] v fertilize;
(anregen) stimulate. **Befruchtung** f (pl -en)
fertilization.

befugen [bə'fuːɡən] v authorize, empower.
Befugnis f (pl -se) authority, right.

befürchten [bə'fyːrçtən] v fear; (vermuten)

suspect. **Befürchtung** f (pl -en) fear, apprehension.

befürworten [bə'fyːɐvɔrtən] v recommend,
advocate.

begabt [bə'ɡaːpt] adj talented, gifted.
Begabung f talent, gift.

begatten [bə'ɡatən] v **sich begatten**
mate, copulate. **Begattung** f (pl -en) mating, copulation.

*****begeben** [bə'ɡeːbən] v **sich begeben** go,
proceed; (verzichten) renounce, give up.

begegnen [bə'ɡeːɡnən] v meet, encounter.
Begegnung f (pl -en) meeting, encounter.

*****begehen** [bə'ɡeːən] (Unrecht) commit, do;
(gehen auf) walk on.

begehren [bə'ɡeːrən] v desire, covet.

begeistern [bə'ɡaɪstəm] v inspire, fill with
enthusiasm. **begeistert** adj inspired,
enthusiastic. **Begeisterung** f enthusiasm.

Begier [bə'ɡiːɐ] f (unz.), also **Begierde** f (pl
-n) desire, craving. **begierig** adj desirous,
covetous.

begießen [bə'ɡiːsən] v water, sprinkle;
(Braten) baste.

Beginn [bə'ɡɪn] m (unz.) beginning. **beginnen** v begin.

beglaubigen [bə'ɡlaʊbɪɡən] v certify,
attest. **Beglaubigung** f (pl -en) certification.

begleiten [bə'ɡlaɪtən] v accompany.
Begleit|ler m (pl -) attendant; (Musik)
accompanist. **-schreiben** neut covering letter. **-ung** f (pl -en) attendants pl, escort;
(Musik) accompaniment.

beglücken [bə'ɡlʏkən] v make happy.
beglückwünschen v congratulate.
Beglückwünschung f (pl -en) congratulations pl.

begnadigen [bə'ɡnaːdɪɡən] v pardon.

begnügen [bə'ɡnyːɡən] v **sich begnügen
mit** content oneself with, be satisfied with.

*****begraben** [bə'ɡraːbən] v bury. **Begräbnis**
neut (pl -se) burial, funeral.

*****begreifen** [bə'ɡraɪfən] v understand,
grasp, apprehend. **begreiflich** adj comprehensible.

begrenzt [bə'ɡrɛntst] adj restricted, limited.

Begriff [bə'ɡrɪf] m (pl -e) concept, idea.
Begriffsvermögen neut comprehension.

begründen [bə'ɡrʏndən] v found, establish; (Behauptung) substantiate. **Begründer**

m founder.

begrüßen [bə'gryːsən] *v* greet, welcome.

begünstigen [bə'gynstɪɡən] *v* (*vorziehen*) favour; (*fördern*) promote, further.

begütert [bə'gyːtərt] *adj* wealthy, well-to-do.

begütigen [bə'gyːtɪɡən] *v* placate, appease.

behäbig [bə'hɛːbɪç] *adj* (*beleibt*) portly, corpulent; (*bequem, langsam*) comfortable.

behagen [bə'haːɡən] *v* please, suit. **Behagen** *neut* (*pl -*) ease, comfort. **behaglich** *adj* comfortable, at ease.

*****behalten** [bə'haltən] *v* keep, retain; (*im Gedächtnis*) remember. **Behälter** *m* (*pl -*) container; (*Flüssigkeiten*) tank.

behandeln [bə'handəln] *v* treat, handle. **Behandlung** *f* treatment, handling; (*Med*) treatment, therapy.

beharren [bə'harən] *v* persist. **beharrlich** *adj* persistent, pertinacious.

behaupten [bə'hauptən] *v* maintain, asset, state. **Behauptung** *f* (*pl -en*) statement, assertion.

behend(e) [bə'hɛnt, bə'hɛndə] *adj, also* **behendig** nimble, agile. **Behendigkeit** *f* agility.

beherbergen [bə'hɛrbɛrɡən] *v* rule, govern.

beherrschen [bə'hɛrʃən] *v* (*Zorn, usw.*) control; (*meistern, können*) master. **sich beherrschen** control oneself. **Beherrschung** *f* rule, control; mastery.

beherzigen [bə'hɛrtsɪɡən] *v* take to heart.

behilflich [bə'hɪlflɪç] *adj* helpful.

behindern [bə'hɪndərn] *v* hinder, obstruct. **Behinderung** *f* (*pl -en*) hindrance.

Behörde [bə'hoːrdə] *f* (*pl -n*) authority, authorities *pl*.

behüten [bə'hyːtən] *v* guard, protect. **Behüter** *m* (*pl -*) protector, guard.

bei [bai] *prep* at; (*neben*) near. **bei mir** at (my) home; (*in der Tasche*) on me. **bei Herrn Schmidt** at Herr Schmidt's (house). **bei der Post arbeiten** work for the Post Office. **bei der Hand nehmen** take by the hand. **beim Aussteigen** while *or* when getting out. **bei Nacht** at night. **bei Tag** during the day. **bei der Arbeit** at work. **bei weitem** by far. **bei Shakespeare** in Shakespeare.

*****beibehalten** [ˈbaibəhaltən] *v* retain; keep.

*****beibringen** [ˈbaibrɪŋən] *v* bring forward;

(*Verlust, Wunde*) inflict; (*lehren*) teach.

Beichte [ˈbaiçtə] *f* (*pl -n*) (*Rel*) confession. **beichten** *v* confess. **Beichtvater** *m* confessor.

beide [ˈbaidə] *adj, pron* both. **alle beide** both. **einer von beiden** either of two. **in beiden Fällen** in either case. **wir beide** both of us. **zu beiden Seiten** on both sides. **beider||lei** *adj* of both sorts. **–seitig** *adj* mutual, reciprocal. **–seits** *adv* mutually. **beidhändig** *adj* ambidextrous.

Beifahrer [ˈbaifaːrər] *m* (*pl -*) passenger.

Beifall [ˈbaifal] *m* (*unz.*) applause; (*Billigung*) approval. **Beifall klatschen** applaud.

beifügen [ˈbaifyːɡən] *v* enclose, attach.

*****beigeben** [ˈbaiɡeːbən] *v* add. **klein beigeben** draw in one's horns, yield.

Beigeschmack [ˈbaiɡəʃmak] *m* (after)taste; (*fig*) tinge.

Beihilfe [ˈbaihɪlfə] *f* financial aid, subsidy; (*Jur*) aiding and abetting.

*****beikommen** [ˈbaikɔmən] *v* get at, get near, reach.

Beil [bail] *neut* (*pl -e*) (*Holz*) hatchet; (*Fleisch*) cleaver.

Beilage [ˈbaiːlaːɡə] *f* enclosure, insert; (*Zeitung*) supplement.

beiläufig [ˈbaiːlɔyfɪç] *adj* incidental. *adv* incidentally, by the way.

beilegen [ˈbaiːleːɡən] *v* add; (*zuschreiben*) attribute, ascribe; (*schlichten*) settle.

Beileid [ˈbaiːlait] *neut* (*unz.*) condolence.

beiliegend [ˈbaiːliːɡənt] *adj* enclosed.

beim [baim] *prep + art* **bei dem**.

*****beimessen** [ˈbaimɛsən] *v* attribute, credit with.

Bein [bain] *neut* (*pl -e*) leg; (*Knochen*) bone.

beinah(e) [ˈbainaːə] *adv* almost, nearly.

Beiname [ˈbaina:mə] *m* nickname. **mit dem Beinamen ... known as ..., called ....**

beirren [bəˈirən] *v* **sicht nicht beirren lassen** stick to one's opinions, not be misled.

beisammen [baiˈzamən] *adv* together.

Beischlaf [ˈbaiʃla:f] *m* (sexual) intercourse.

beiseite [baiˈzaitə] *adv* to one side, aside. **–legen** *v* put aside or by.

Beispiel [ˈbaiʃpiːl] *neut* (*pl -e*) example. **zum Beispiel** for example *or* instance. **beispielsweise** *adv* for instance, as an example.

*****beißen** [ˈbaisən] *v* bite. **beißend** *adj* biting;

(*Säure*) caustic. **Beißllzahn** *m* incisor. **–zange** *f* pincers.

Beistand ['baɪʃtant] *m* help, assistance.

*beistehen ['baɪʃteːən] *v* help, assist.

beistimmen ['baɪʃtɪm ən] *v* agree, consent. **Bestimmung** *f* agreement, consent.

Beitrag ['baɪtraːk] *m* (*pl* **Beiträge**) contribution; (*Klub*) subscription. **beitragen** *v* contribute. **Beiträger** *m* (*pl* -) contributor.

*beitreten ['baɪtreːtən] *v* join; (*Meinung*) agree to, accept.

Beiwagen ['baɪvaːgən] *m* sidecar.

beiwohnen ['baɪvoːnən] *v* be present at, attend; (*beischlafen*) have sex with.

beizeiten [baɪtsaɪtən] *adv* early.

beizen ['baɪtsən] *v* (*Holz*) stain; (*Metall*) etch; (*Fleisch*) salt, pickle.

bejahen [bə'jaːən] *v* affirm, agree to.

bejahrt [bə'jaːrt] *adj* aged.

bekämpfen [bə'kɛm pfən] *v* fight (against), combat.

bekannt [bə'kant] *adj* known. **bekannt werden mit** become acquainted with. **sich bekanntmachen mit** acquaint oneself with. **Bekanntlle(r)** acquaintance. **–gabe** *f* announcement, notification. **bekanntllgeben** *v* make known, disclose. **–lich** *adv* as is well known. **Bekanntschaft** *f* acquaintance.

bekehren [bə'keːrən] *v* convert. **Bekehrllte(r)** *m*. **–ung** *f* conversion.

*bekennen [bə'kɛnən] *v* acknowledge, confess. **Bekenntnis** *neut* (*pl* -**se**) confession; (*Glaube*) faith, creed.

beklagen [bə'klaːgən] *v* lament, deplore. **–swert** *adj* lamentable. **Baklagte(r)** *m* accused, defendant.

bekleiden [bə'klaɪdən] *v* clothe; (*beziehen*) coat; (*Amt*) occupy. **Bekleidung** *f* clothing; (*Material*) coating.

*beklemmen [bə'klɛm ən] *v* oppress, frighten; (*ersticken*) stifle. **Angst beklemmt mich** I am seized by fear.

*bekommen [bə'kɔm ən] *v* obtain, get, receive; (*Zug*) catch; (*Krankheit*) catch, get. **bekömmlich** *adj* wholesome, beneficial.

bekräftigen [bə'krɛftɪgən] *v* confirm, strengthen.

bekreuzigen [bə'krɔʏtsɪgən] *v* **sich bekreuzigen** cross oneself.

bekümmern [bə'kym ərn] *v* trouble, distress. **bekümmert sein** be anxious or troubled.

bekunden [bə'kʊndən] *v* state; (*zeigen*) show, manifest.

*beladen [bə'laːdən] *v* load.

Belag [bə'laːk] *m* (*pl* **Beläge**) covering, coating; (*Aufstrich*) spread. **Butterbrot mit Belag** sandwich.

belagern [bə'laːgərn] *v* besiege. **Belagerung** *f* siege.

belangen [bə'laŋən] *v* concern; (*Jur*) prosecute. **belanglos** *adj* unimportant.

Belarus, Belarußland ['bɛlarʊs] *neut* Belarus. **Belarusse** *m*, **Belarussin** *f* Belarussian. **belarussisch** *adj* Belarussian.

belasten [bə'lastən] *v* burden; (*Konto*) debit, charge; (*Jur*) accuse.

belästigen [bə'lɛstɪgən] *v* pester, bother; (*sexuell*) harass; (*umg*) bug. **Belästigung** *f* bother, annoyance.

Belastung [bə'lastʊŋ] *f* (*pl* -**en**) load; (*Konto*) debit, charge.

*belaufen [bə'laʊfən] *v* **sich belaufen auf** amount to, total.

belauschen [bə'laʊʃən] *v* eavesdrop on, listen to (secretly).

beleben [bə'leːbən] *v* animate; (*Med*) revive. **belebt** *adj* animated, lively; (*Ort*) crowded, bustling. **Belebllheit** *f* liveliness. **–ung** *f* animation; revival.

Beleg [bə'leːk] *m* (*pl* -**e**) proof, evidence; (*Urkunde*) voucher. **belegen** *v* cover; (*Platz*) reserve; (*Kursus*) enrol for; (*Brot*) spread. **belegtes Brötchen** filled roll, sandwich. **Belegschaft** *f* personnel, staff.

belehren [bə'leːrən] *v* instruct, teach.

beleibt [bə'laɪpt] *adj* portly, stout.

beleidigen [bə'laɪdɪgən] *v* insult. **beleidigend** *adj* insulting, offensive. **Beleidigung** *f* (*pl* -**en**) insult.

beleuchten [bə'bʏçtən] *v* illuminate, light (up). **Beleuchtung** *f* lighting, illumination.

Belgien ['bɛlɡjən] *neut* Belgium. **Belgier** *m* (*pl* -), **Belgierin** *f* (*pl* -**nen**) Belgian. **belgisch** *adj* Belgian.

belichten [bə'lɪçtən] *v* (*Foto*) expose. **Belichtung** *f* (*pl* -**en**) exposure. **Belichtungsmesser** *m* light meter.

belieben [bə'liːbən] *v* (*gefallen*) please; (*wünschen*) like, wish. **Belieben** *neut* pleasure, will. **nach Belieben** at will, as you like. **beliebig** *adj* any (you like), whatever. **beliebt** *adj* loved, popular.

bellen ['bɛlən] v bark.

belohnen [bə'lo:nən] v reward, recompense. **Belohnung** f reward, recompense.

belüften [bə'lyftən] v ventilate. **Belüftung** f ventilation.

belustigen [bə'lʊstɪgən] v amuse. **Belustigung** f amusement.

bemächtigen [bə'm ɛçtɪgən] v **sich bemächtigen** seize, take possession of.

bemerkbar [bə'm ɛrkbaːr] adj noticeable, observable. **bemerken** v notice; (sagen) remark. **–swert** adj remarkable, noteworthy. **Bemerkung** f (pl -en) remark.

*bemessen [bə'm ɛsən] v measure. adj restricted.

bemitleiden [bə'm ɪtlaidən] v pity, feel sorry for.

bemühen [bə'm y:ən] v trouble (oneself), take pains. **Bemühen** neut or **Bemühung** f (pl -en) effort, exertion.

benachbart [bə'naxbaːrt] adj neighbouring.

benachrichtigen [bə'naxrɪçtɪgən] v inform. **Benachrichtigung** f report.

benannt [bə'nant] adj named.

*benehmen [bə'ne:m ən] v **sich benehmen** behave. **Benehmen** neut behaviour.

beneiden [bə'naidən] v envy.

*benennen [bə'nɛnən] v name, call. **Benennung** f (pl -en) name, title.

Bengel ['bɛŋəl] m (pl -) brat, little rascal.

benommen [bə'nɔm ən] adj confused.

benötigen [bə'nœ :tɪgən] v need, require.

benutzen [bə'nutsən] v use, make use of. **Benutzung** f use, employment.

Benzin [bɛn'tsi:n] neut petrol, (US) gasoline. **–uhr** f petrol or fuel gauge. **–verbrauch** m fuel consumption.

beobachten [bə'o:baxtən] v observe, watch; (bemerken) notice. **Beobachter** m (pl -) observer, onlooker. **–tung** f (pl -en) observation.

bepflanzen [bə'pflantsən] v plant.

bequem [bə'kve:m] adj comfortable; (mühelos) convenient. **bequemlich** adj lazy, comfort-loving.

*beraten [bə'ra:tən] v advise. **sich beraten** confer. **beratend** adj advisory. **Berater** m adviser, counsellor. **Beraterstab** m team of advisors, think tank. **Beratung** f consultation.

berauben [bə'raubən] v rob or deprive of.

berauschen [bə'rauʃən] v intoxicate.

berechenbar [bə'rɛçənba:r] adj calculable. **berechnen** v calculate, evaluate. **berechnend** adj (Person) selfish, calculating. **Berechnung** f calculation, evaluation.

berechtigen [bə'rɛçtɪgən] v entitle, authorize. **berechtigt** adj entitled. **Berechtigung** f authorization, entitlement.

bereden [bə're:dən] v persuade. **beredsam** adj eloquent.

Bereich [bə'raiç] m (pl -e) region, domain; (fig) field, sphere, realm.

bereichern [bə'raiçərn] v enrich. **sich bereichern** acquire wealth, get rich.

bereit [bə'rait] adj ready, prepared. **bereiten** v prepare, make ready. **bereit ‖ halten** v keep in readiness. **–machen** v make ready. **Bereitschaft** f readiness. **bereit ‖ stehen** v be ready. **-stellen** v make ready, prepare. **Bereitung** f (pl -en) preparation. **bereitwillig** adj ready.

Bereitschaftssystem [bə'raiʃaftszys'e:m] neut (pl -e) (comp) back-up system.

bereuen [bə'rɔyən] v regret, repent.

Berg [bɛrk] m (pl -e) mountain. **bergab** adv downhill. **Bergarbeiter** m miner. **bergauf** adv uphill. **Bergbau** m mining.

*bergen ['bɛrgən] v conceal; (schützen) protect; (Güter) recover.

Bergführer ['bɛrkfy:rər] m mountain guide.

bergig ['bɛrgɪç] adj mountainous, hilly.

Berg ‖ leute pl miners. **-mann** m miner. **bergmännisch** adj mining. **Berg ‖ rutsch** m landslide. **-steigen** neut mountain climbing. **-steiger** m (mountain) climber, mountaineer.

Bergung ['bɛrguŋ] f (pl -en) rescue; (Schiff) salvage. **-sarbeiten** f pl salvage or rescue operations.

Bergwerk ['bɛrkvɛrk] neut mine, pit.

Bericht [bə'rɪçt] m (pl -e) report, account. **berichten** v report, give an account. **Berichterstatter** m (pl -) reporter; (Radio) commentator, correspondent.

berichtigen [bə'rɪçtɪgən] v correct, amend; (Schulden) pay. **Berichtigung** f correction; (Schulden) settlement.

beritten [bə'rɪtən] adj mounted.

Bernstein ['bɛrnʃtain] m amber.

berüchtigt [bə'ryçtɪçt] adj notorious, infamous.

berücksichtigen [bə'rʏkzɪçtɪɡən] v keep in mind, consider, take account of. **Berücksichtigung** f consideration.

Beruf [bə'ruːf] m (pl -e) occupation, job, profession; (Gewerbe) trade. **beruf||en** v appoint; (kommen lassen) summon, send for. **–lich** adj professional, vocational. **Beruf||ausbildung** f vocational training. **–krankheit** f occupational disease. **–schule** f vocational school, technical college. **berufstätig** adj employed. **Berufstätigkeit** f employment, professional activity. **Berufung** f (pl -en) appointment; (Jur) appeal.

beruhen [bə'ruːən] v rest (on), be founded (on).

beruhigen [bə'ruːɪɡən] v pacify, calm. **beruhigend** adj calming. **Beruhigung** f calming, pacification. **Beruhigungsmittel** neut sedative.

berühmt [bə'rʏːm t] adj famous, celebrated. **Berühmtheit** f fame; (Person) celebrity.

berühren [bə'rʏːrən] v touch, handle; (angrenzen) border; (angehen) concern; (erwähnen) touch on.

besäen [bə'zɛːən] v sow.

besänftigen [bə'zɛnftɪɡən] v soothe, calm (down).

Besatzung [bə'zatsuŋ] f (Mil) garrison; (Schiff, Flugzeug) crew; (Pol) occupation. **-szone** f occupied area (of a country).

Besäufnis [bə'zɔyfnɪs] f (pl -se) binge (Alkohol).

beschädigen [bə'ʃɛːdɪɡən] v damage. **Beschädigung** f damage.

beschaffen [bə'ʃafən] v get, procure. adj constituted.

beschäftigen [bə'ʃɛftɪɡən] v employ; (zutun geben) occupy, keep busy. **beschäftigt** adj employed; occupied, busy. **Beschäftigung** f (pl -en) employment, occupation.

beschämen [bə'ʃɛːm ən] v shame.

beschatten [bə'ʃatən] v shade; (verfolgen) shadow.

beschauen [bə'ʃauən] v look at; (prüfen) examine, look over. **Beschauer** m (pl -) spectator, inspector. **beschaulich** adj contemplative.

Bescheid [bə'ʃaɪt] m (pl -e) information; (Entscheidung) decision, ruling. **Bescheid geben/sagen** give information, inform. **Bescheid wissen** know the situation, be well informed.

bescheinigen [bə'ʃaɪnɪɡən] v certify, attest. **Bescheinigung** f (pl -en) certificate; (Quittung) receipt.

beschenken [bə'ʃɛnkən] v give a present to, present (with).

bescheren [bə'ʃeːrən] v give presents. **Bescherung** f giving (of presents). **eine schöne Bescherung** a fine mess.

*beschießen [bə'ʃiːsən] v fire on, shell. **Beschießung** f shelling, bombardment.

beschimpfen [bə'ʃɪm pfən] v insult.

Beschlag [bə'ʃlaːk] m (pl Beschläge) clasp, catch; (Jur) seizure. **in Beschlag nehmen** seize, confiscate. **beschlagen** v cover, fit; (Pferd) shoe. **Beschlagnahme** f (pl -n) confiscation, seizure. **beschlagnahmen** v seize, confiscate.

beschleunigen [bə'ʃlɔynɪɡən] v accelerate. **Beschleunigung** f acceleration.

*beschließen [bə'ʃliːsən] v decide, resolve; (beendigen) terminate, end.

Beschluß [bə'ʃlus] m (pl Beschlüsse) decision, resolution; (Ende) end, close.

beschmutzen [bə'ʃm utsən] v dirty, soil.

*beschneiden [bə'ʃnaɪdən] v cut, prune, clip; (Kind) circumcize. **Beschneidung** f circumcision.

beschränken [bə'ʃrɛnkən] v restrict, limit. **beschränkt** adj limited, confined. **Beschränkung** f limitation.

*beschreiben [bə'ʃraɪbən] v describe. **Beschreibung** f description.

beschuldigen [bə'ʃuldɪɡən] v accuse. **Beschuldigte(r)** m accused, defendant. **Beschuldigung** f accusation.

beschützen [bə'ʃʏtsən] v protect.

Beschwerde [bə'ʃveːrdə] f (pl -n) complaint. **beschweren** v burden. **sich beschweren über** complain about. **beschwerlich** adj troublesome; (mühselig) tedious.

beschwichtigen [bə'ʃvɪçtɪɡən] v appease, pacify. **Beschwichtigung** f allaying, appeasement.

beschwipst [bə'ʃvɪpst] adj (umg.) tipsy.

*beschwören [bə'ʃvøːrən] v swear (on oath); (Person) implore, beg; (Erinnerungen, Geister) conjure up.

*besehen [bə'zeːən] v look at, inspect.

beseitigen [bə'zaɪtɪɡən] v remove, get rid of, eliminate; (Schwierigkeiten) overcome.

Beseitigung f removal, elimination.
Besen ['be:zən] m (pl -) broom.
besessen [bə'zɛsən] adj possessed.
besetzen [bə'zɛtsən] v (Platz) occupy, take;
(Mil) occupy; (Kleid) trim, decorate; (Posten)
fill. **besetzt** adj (Theater) full; (Platz) taken;
(WC) occupied, engaged; (Telef) engaged.
Besetzung f occupation; (Theater) casting.
besichtigen [bə'zɪçtɪɡən] v inspect, view.
Besichtigung f inspection;
(Sehenswürdigkeiten) sightseeing.
besiedeln [bə'zi:dəln] v colonize.
besiegen [bə'zi:ɡən] v conquer.
*besinnen [bə'zɪnən] v sich besinnen
remember, recollect. **Besinnen** neut reflection, consideration. **Besinnung** f contemplation; (Bewußtsein) consciousness.
besinnunglos adj unconscious, senseless.
Besitz [bə'zɪts] m (pl -e) possession.
besitzen v possess, own. **Besitzer** m (pl -)
owner.
besoffen [bə'zɔfən] adj (vulg) drunk.
Besoldung [bə'zɔlduŋ] f (pl -en) salary,
wages pl.
besonder [bə'zɔndər] adj special, particular. **besonders** adv especially, particularly.
nichts Besonderes nothing special, not up
to much.
besonnen [bə'zɔnən] adj sensible, prudent.
Besonnenheit f prudence.
besorgen [bə'zɔrɡən] v take care of, see to;
(beschaffen) obtain. **Besorgnis** f (pl -se)
apprehension, anxiety. **besorgniser-
regend** adj giving cause for worry. **besorgt**
adj anxious, worried. **Besorgung** f (pl -en)
management; (Einkauf) purchase.
bespannen [bə'ʃpanən] v (verkleiden) cover;
(Fahrzeug) harness; (Musik) string.
Bespannung f (pl -en) covering; (Pferde)
team (of horses).
*besprechen [bə'ʃprɛçən] v discuss; (Buch,
Film) review. **Besprechung** f discussion;
(Buch, Film) review.
besser ['bɛsər] adj better. **desto besser** so
much the better. **um so besser** all the better. **er ist besser dran** he is better off.
bessern v improve, make better.
Besserung f (pl -en) improvement.
best [bɛst] adj best. **am besten** adv best.
aufs Beste in the best possible way. **besten
Dank!** many thanks!
Bestand [bə'ʃtant] m (pl Bestände) contin-
uance, duration; (Vorrat) stock, supply.

beständig [bə'ʃtɛndɪç] adj constant, lasting.
Bestandteil [bə'ʃtanttail] m component,
part.
bestärken [bə'ʃtɛrkən] v strengthen;
(bestätigen) confirm. **Bestärkung** f
strengthening; confirmation.
bestätigen [bə'ʃtɛ:tɪɡən] v confirm, verify.
bestätigend adj confirmatory.
Bestätigung f (pl -en) confirmation.
bestatten [bə'ʃtatən] v bury. **Bestattung** f
(pl -en) funeral, burial.
*bestechen [bə'ʃtɛçən] v bribe, corrupt.
bestechlich adj corrupt, bribable.
Bestechung f bribery, corruption.
Besteck [bə'ʃtɛk] neut (pl -e) cutlery; knife,
fork, and spoon; (Med) (medical) instruments pl.
*bestehen [bə'ʃte:ən] v exist, be; (überstehen) undergo; (Examen) pass; (fortdauern)
endure, survive. **bestehen auf** insist on.
bestehen aus consist of.
*besteigen [bə'ʃtaiɡən] v climb, ascend;
(Pferd) mount. **Besteigung** f ascent;
mounting.
bestellen [bə'ʃtɛlən] v (Waren) order;
(Zimmer) reserve; (Boden) clutivate.
Bestellung f order; reservation; cultivation.
bestenfalls ['bɛstənfals] adv at best.
bestens adv in the best manner.
besteuern [bə'ʃtɔyərn] v tax. **Besteuerung**
f taxation.
Bestie ['bɛstə] f (pl -n) beast.
bestimmen [bə'ʃtɪmən] v determine, fix;
(ernennen) appoint. **bestimmt** adj definite,
certain. **Bestimmung** f determination;
(Vorschrift) regulation; (Ernennung) appointment.
bestrafen [bə'ʃtra:fən] v punish.
Bestrafung f punishment.
Bestrahlung [bə'ʃtra:luŋ] f radiation; (Med)
radiotherapy.
bestreben [bə'ʃtre:bən] v sich bestreben
strive, endeavour. **Bestreben** neut or
Bestrebung f endeavour, exertion.
*bestreiten [bə'ʃtraitən] v dispute, contest.
bestürmen [bə'ʃtʏrmən] v assault, storm.
bestürzen [bə'ʃtʏrtsən] v startle, disconcert.
bestürzt adj taken aback, dismayed.
Besuch [bə'zu:x] m (pl -e) visit, call. **Besuch
haben** have visitors. **ich bin zu Besuch hiet**

I am visiting, I am a visitor. **besuchen** v visit, see; (*Schule*) go to, attend. **Besucher** *m* (*pl* -) visitor, caller; (*Gast*) guest.

betagt [bə'taːkt] *adj* aged, elderly.

betasten [bə'tastən] v finger, touch.

betätigen [bə'tɛːtɪɡən] v put into action; (*Maschine*) operate; (*Bremse*) apply. **sich betätigen** occupy oneself, work; (*activ sein*) be active, participate. **Betätigung** *f* operation; (*Teilnahme*) participation.

betäuben [bə'ɔybən] v stun; (*narkotisieren*) anaesthetize. **Betäubung** *f* anaesthesia. **Betäubungsmittel** *neut* anaesthetic.

Bete ['beːtə] *f* beet, beetroot.

beteiligen [bə'taɪlɪɡən] v give a share to. **sich beteiligen** participate in. **beteiligt sein an** be involved in. **Beteiligung** *f* (*pl* -en) participation; (*Anteil*) share.

beten ['beːtən] v pray.

beteuern [bə'ɔyən] v affirm, declare; (*Unschuld*) protest. **Beteuerung** *f* (*pl* -en) affirmation, declaration.

Beton [be'tõ] *m* concrete.

betonen [bə'toːnən] v stress, emphasize. **Betonung** *f* stress, emphasis.

Betracht [bə'traxt] *m* (*unz.*) consideration. **außer Betracht lassen** leave aside, not consider. **in Betracht ziehen** take into consideration. **betrachten** v look at; (*ansehen als*) consider. **beträchtlich** *adj* considerable. **Betrachtung** *f* consideration.

Betrag [bə'traːk] *m* (*pl* **Beträge**) amount. **betragen** v amount to. **sich betragen** behave. **Betragen** *neut* behaviour.

betrauen [bə'traʊən] v entrust.

Betreff [bə'trɛf] *m* (*unz.*) **in Betreff** with regard to, concerning. **betreff||en** v concern; (*befallen*) befall; (*erwischen*) surprise. **-end** *adj* in question. *prep* concerning. **-s** *prep* concerning, re:.

*****betreiben** [bə'traɪbən] v carry on, follow; (*Studien*) pursue; (*Maschine*) operate.

*****betreten** [bə'treːtən] v tread on; (*eintreten*) enter. *adj* surprised, disconcerted.

Betrieb [bə'triːp] *m* (*pl* -e) firm, concern, business; (*Wirken*) running; (*Verkehr*) bustle, activity. **außer Betrieb** out of order. **in Betrieb** in operation, working, in use. **in Betrieb setzen** put into operation. **Betriebs||anlage** *f* industrial plant, works. **-anweisung** *f* operating instructions *pl*. **-führer** *m* works manager. **-kosten** *pl* operating costs. **-rat** *m* works council.

-unfall *m* industrial accident.

*****betrinken** [bə'trɪŋkən] v **sich betrinken** get drunk.

betroffen [bə'trɔfən] *adj* perplexed, disconcerted.

betrüben [bə'tryːbən] v grieve, depress. **betrübt** *adj* sad.

Betrug [bə'truːk] *m* (*unz.*) fraud, swindle, deception. **betrügen** v cheat, deceive. **Betrüger** *m* (*pl* -) cheat, swindler. **betrügerisch** *adj* deceitful.

betrunken [bə'trʊŋkən] *adj* drunk. **Betrunkenheit** *f* drunkenness.

Bett [bɛt] *neut* (*pl* -en) bed. **ins Bett gehen** go to bed. **-decke** *f* bedspread.

betteln ['bɛtəln] v beg.

bettlägerig ['bɛtlɛːɡərɪç] *adj* bedridden.

Bettler ['bɛtlər] *m* (*pl* -) beggar.

Bett||wäsche *f* bed linen. **-zeug** *neut* bedding.

beugen ['bɔyɡən] v bend; (*Gramm*) inflect. **sich beugen** bow; (*sich fügen*) submit. **Beugung** *f* bow, bend(ing).

Beule ['bɔylə] *f* (*pl* -n) swelling, lump; (*Metall*) dent.

beunruhigen [bə'ʊnruːɪɡən] v disturb, make anxious. **beunruhigt sein** be anxious or alarmed. **Beunruhigung** *f* agitation, uneasiness.

beurkunden [bə'uːrkundən] v certify, attest. **Beurkundung** *f* certification.

beurlauben [bə'uːrlaʊbən] v grant leave to, send on holiday.

beurteilen [bə'uːrtaɪlən] v judge. **Beurteilung** *f* judgment.

Beute ['bɔytə] *f* (*unz.*) booty, loot.

Beutel ['bɔytəl] *m* (*pl* -) bag; (*Geld*) purse; (*Zool*) pouch. **beuteln** v be baggy, bulge. **Beuteltier** *neut* marsupial.

bevölkern [bə'fœlkərn] v populate. **dicht/ spärlich bevölkert** densely/sparsely populated. **Bevölkerung** *f* population.

bevollmächtigen [bə'fɔlmɛçtɪɡən] v authorize. **bevollmächtigt** *adj* authorized. **Bevollmächtigte(r)** *m* authorized agent or representative; (*Jur*) attorney.

bevor [bə'foːr] *conj* before.

*****bevorstehen** [bə'foːrʃteːən] v be imminent, be at hand.

bevorzugen [bə'foːrtsuːɡən] v favour, prefer.

bewachen [bə'vaxən] v guard.

bewaffnen [bə'vafnən] v arm. **bewaffnet** adj armed. **Bewaffnung** f armament.

bewahren [bə'vaːʀən] v keep, preserve.

bewähren [bə'vɛːʀən] v sich **bewähren** prove true, **bewährt** adj tried, proved.

Bewahrung [bə'vaːʀuŋ] f (pl -en) preservation.

Bewährung [bə'vɛːʀuŋ] f trial, test; (Jur) probation. **-sfrist** f probation (period).

bewältigen [bə'vɛltigən] v overpower; (Schwierigkeit) master, overcome.

bewässern [bə'vɛsəm] v irrigate. **Bewässerung** f irrigation.

*bewegen [bə'veːgən] v move; (rühren) move, touch; (überreden) persuade. **sich bewegen** move. **Beweggrund** m motive. **beweglich** adj movable, mobile. **bewegt** adj excited; (gerührt) touched, moved. **Bewegung** f (pl -en) motion, movement; (Rührung) emotion. **in Bewegung setzen** set in motion.

Beweis [bə'vais] m (pl -e) proof, evidence. **beweisen** v prove, demonstrate. **Beweisführung** f reasoning, demonstration. **-stück** neut (piece of) evidence, exhibit.

bewerben [bə'vɛrbən] v sich **bewerben um** apply for. **Bewerber** m applicant, candidate. **Bewerbung** f application, candidacy.

bewerkstelligen [bə'vɛrkʃtɛligən] v accomplish, achieve.

bewerten [bə'vɛːʀtən] v value, rate.

bewilligen [bə'viligən] v allow, grant. **Bewilligung** f (pl -en) grant, permission.

bewirken [bə'viʀkən] v bring about, cause.

bewirten [bə'viʀtən] v entertain. **bewirtschaften** v manage, administer. **Bewirtung** f hospitality.

bewohnbar [bə'voːnbaːʀ] adj inhabitable. **bewohnen** v live in, inhabit. **Bewohner** m (pl -) inhabitant, resident.

bewölken [bə'vœlkən] v sich **bewölken** (Himmel) become cloudy. **bewölkt** adj overcast, cloudy.

Bewunderer [bə'vundəʀəʀ] m (pl -) admirer. **bewundern** v admire. **bewundernswert** adj admirable. **Bewunderung** f admiration.

bewußt [bə'vust] adj conscious, deliberate; (klar) aware, conscious. ich bin mir meines Fehlers bewußt I am aware of my mistake.

Bewußtheit f awareness. **bewußtlos** adj unconscious. **Bewußtllosigkeit** f unconsciousness. **-sein** neut consciousness. **zu Bewußtsein kommen** regain consciousness.

bezahlen [bə'tsaːlən] v pay for; (Rechnung) pay. **Bezahlung** f payment, settlement.

bezaubern [bə'tsaubəʀn] v enchant, charm, bewitch. **Bezauberung** f spell.

bezeichnen [bə'tsaiçnən] v designate; (Zeichen) mark. **Bezeichnung** f (Beschreibung) description; (Name) designation; (Zeichen) mark.

bezeugen [bə'tsɔygən] v testify (to), provide evidence of.

*beziehen [bə'tsiːən] v cover; (Geige) string; (Wohnung) move into; (Posten) take up; (Gehalt) draw; (erhalten, kaufen) procure. **das Bett frisch beziehen** change the sheets. **sich beziehen auf** refer to, relate to. **Beziehung** f relation(ship). **in Beziehung auf** with regard or respect to. **beziehungsweise** adv respectively, or.

Bezirk [bə'tsiʀk] m (pl -e) district, area.

Bezug [bə'tsuːk] m (pl Bezüge) covering; (Kopfkissen) pillow-case; (Waren) supply, purchase. **bezüglich** prep concerning, relating to. **mit Bezug auf** regarding, re.

bezweifeln [bə'tsvaifəln] v doubt.

*bezwingen [bə'tsviŋən] v conquer, overcome. **sich bezwingen** control or restrain oneself.

Bibel ['biːbəl] f (pl -n) Bible. **-stelle** f (biblical) text or passage.

Biber ['biːbəʀ] m (pl -) beaver.

Bibliographie [biblioɡʀa'fiː] f (pl -n) bibliography. **bibliographisch** adj bibliographic.

Bibliothek [biblio'teːk] f (pl -en) library. **-ar** m (pl -e) librarian.

biblisch ['biːbliʃ] adj biblical.

bieder ['biːdəʀ] adj honest, upright, respectable. **Biedermann** m honest man or fellow.

*biegen ['biːgən] v bend; (beim Fahren, usw.) turn. **biegsam** adj supple; (f-ügsam) yielding. **Biegung** f (pl -en) bend; curve.

Biene ['biːnə] f (pl -n) bee. **Bienenllstich** m bee sting; (Kuchen) almond pastry. **-stock** m beehive. **-wabe** f honeycomb. **-zucht** f beekeeping. **-züchter** m beekeeper.

Bier [biːʀ] neut (pl -e) beer. **-faß** neut beer barrel, cask. **-garten** m beer garden.

Biest [biːst] *neut* (*pl* -er) beast; (*fig*) brute.

***bieten** ['biːtən] *v* offer; (*Versteigerung*) bid.

Bigamie [biga'miː] *f* bigamy. **bigamisch** *adj* bigamous.

bigott [bi'gɔt] *adj* bigoted.

Bikini [bi'kiːni] *m* (*pl* -s) bikini.

Bilanz [bi'lants] *f* (*pl* -en) balance (sheet), annual accounts.

Bild [bilt] *neut* (*pl* -er) picture; (*Buch*) illustration; (*Vorstellung*) idea.

bilden ['bildən] *v* form, shape; (*erziehen*) educate; (*darstellen*) constitute.

Bilder||buch *neut* picture book. **–galerie** *f* (picture) gallery. **Bild||feld** *neut* field of vision. **–hauer** *m* sculptor. **bildhübsch** *adj* very pretty, lovely. **Bildnis** *neut* (*pl* -se) image, likeness. **bildsam** *adj* plastic, flexible; (*fig*) docile. **Bildsäule** *f* statue. **Bildschirm** *m* screen. **Bildschirmschoner** *m* (*comp*) screensaver.

Bildung ['bilduŋ] *f* (*pl* -en) formation; (*Erziehung*) education.

Billard ['biljart] *neut* (*pl* -e) billiards; (*Tisch*) billiard table. **–stock** *m* cue.

Billett [bil'jɛt] *neut* (*pl* -s or -e) ticket; (*Zettel*) note.

billig ['biliç] *adj* cheap, inexpensive; (*gerecht*) fair. **-en** *v* approve. **Billig||keit** *f* cheapness, fairness. **–ung** *f* approval.

Billion [bil'joːn] *f* (*pl* -en) billion, (*US*) trillion.

Bimsstein ['bimsʃtain] *m* pumice stone.

binär [bi'nɛːr] *adj* binary.

Binde ['bində] *f* (*pl* -n) bandage; (*Arm*) sling. **–haut** *f* conjunctiva.

***binden** ['bindən] *v* bind, tie. **Bind||estrich** *m* hyphen. **–faden** *m* string. **–ung** *f* binding; (*Verpflichtung*) obligation.

binnen ['binən] *prep* within. **Binnenhandel** *m* internal trade.

Biograph [bio'graːf] *m* (*pl* -en) biographer. **-ie** *f* biography. **biographisch** *adj* biographical.

Biologe [bio'loːgə] *m* (*pl* -n) biologist. **Biologie** *f* biology. **biologisch** *adj* biological. **biologisch abbaubar** biodegradable.

Birke ['birkə] *f* (*pl* -n) birch.

Birne ['birnə] *f* (*pl* -n) pear; (*Glühbirne*) light-bulb.

bis [bis] *prep* (*räumlich*) as far as, (up) to; (*zeitlich*) until, till, to. *conj* until, till. **bis an, bis nach,** *or* **bis zu** up to, as far as. **bis**

jetzt until now. **bis morgen** by tomorrow; (*Gruß*) see you tomorrow.

Bischof ['biʃɔf] *m* (*pl* **Bischöfe**) bishop. **bischöflich** *adj* episcopal.

bisher [bis'heːr] *adv* until now, hitherto. **-ig** *adj* until now, previous.

Biß [bis] *m* (*pl* Bisse) bite. **ein bißchen** a bit, a little.

bisweilen [bis'vailən] *adv* occasionally, sometimes.

bitte ['bitə] *interj* please. **Bitte** *f* request. **bitten** *v* request, ask; (*anflehen*) beg, implore.

bitter ['bitər] *adj* bitter. **Bitter||keit** *f* bitterness. **–salz** *neut* Epsom salts. **bittersüß** *adj* bittersweet.

Bizeps ['biːtsɛps] *m* (*pl* -e) biceps.

Blamage [bla'maːʒə] *f* (*pl* -n) disgrace. **blamieren** *v* disgrace, compromise.

blank [blaŋk] *adj* bright, polished; (*rein*) clean; (*bloß*) bare.

blanko ['blaŋko] *adj* blank. **Blankoscheck** *m* blank cheque.

Blase ['blaːzə] *f* (*pl* -n) bubble; (*Haut*) blister; (*Harn*) bladder. **blasen** *v* blow.

blasiert [bla'ziːrt] *adj* blasé, conceited.

Blasinstrument ['blaːsinstrument] *neut* wind instrument.

blaß [blas] *adj* pale. **Blässe** *f* paleness, pallor. **bläßlich** *adj* pale, palish.

Blatt [blat] *neut* (*pl* Blätter) leaf; (*Papier*) sheet; (*Zeitung*) newspaper; (*Klinge*) blade. **blätterabwerfend** *adj* deciduous. **blättern** *v* (*Buch*) leaf through. **Blätterteig** *m* puff pastry. **Blatt||grün** *neut* chlorophyll. **–laus** *f* greenfly, aphid.

blau [blau] *adj* blue; (*umg.*) drunk. **blaues Auge** black eye. **Blau** *neut* blue.

Blech [blɛç] *neut* (*pl* -e) sheet metal, tin. **–bläser** *pl* (*Musik*) brass (section). **–dose** *f* tin-can.

blecken ['blɛkən] show, bare (teeth).

Blei [blai] *neut* (*pl* -e) lead. **bleifrei** *adj* (*Benzin*) unleaded.

***bleiben** ['blaibən] *v* remain, stay. **bleiben bei** keep or stick to.

bleich [blaiç] *adj* pale, faded. **Bleiche** *f* paleness. **bleichen** *v* black; (*farblos werden*) grow pale, fade. **Bleich||mittel** *neut* bleach(ing agent). **–sucht** *f* anaemia. **bleichsüchtig** *adj* anaemic.

Bleistift ['blaiʃtift] *m* (*pl* -e) pencil.

Blende ['blɛndə] f (pl -n) blind, shutter; (Foto) shutter. **blenden** v blind, dazzle. **-d** adj dazzling, brilliant.

Blick [blɪk] m (pl -e) glance, look; (Aussicht) view. **blicken** v look.

blind [blɪnt] adj blind. **Blind||darm** m (Anat) appendix. **-darmentzündung** f appendicitis. **-e(r)** m blind man. **-enhund** m guide dog. **-enschrift** f braille. **-gänger** m dud (bomb or shell). **-heit** f blindness. **blindlings** adv blindly.

blinken ['blɪŋkən] v sparkle, twinkle, glitter. **Blinker** m (Mot) indicator. **Blinklicht** neut flashing light.

blinzeln ['blɪntsəln] v blink, wink.

Blitz [blɪts] m (pl -e) lightning. **blitzen** v flash, emit flashes. **Blitzlicht** neut (Foto) flash, flashlight. **blitz||sauber** adj spruce, very clean. **-schnell** adj quick as lightning. **Blitzschlag** m flash of lightning.

Block [blɔk] m (pl Blöcke) block; (Papier) pad. **-ade** f blockade, embargo. **-flöte** f (Musik) recorder. **blockieren** v blockade, block. **Blockschrift** f block letters.

blöd(e) [blø:t, 'blø:də] adj silly, daft. **Blöd||heit** f stupidity, silliness. **-sinn** m idiocy. **blödsinnig** adj idiotic, silly.

blöken ['blø:kən] v bleat.

blond [blɔnt] adj blond, fair-haired. **Blondine** f blonde.

bloβ [blo:s] adj bare, simple, adv only, merely.

Blöβe ['blø:sə] f nakedness; (fig) weakness.

bloβlegen ['blo:sle:gən] v reveal, expose.

blühen ['bly:ən] v bloom, flower. **blühend** adj blooming; (fig) flourishing.

Blume ['blu:mə] f (pl -n) flower; (Wein) bouquet. **Blumen||beet** neut flowerbed. **-blatt** neut petal. **-kohl** m cauliflower. **-muster** neut floral pattern. **-strauβ** m bunch of flowers, bouquet. **-topf** m flowerpot. **-zwiebel** f bulb.

Bluse ['blu:zə] f (pl -n) blouse.

Blut [blu:t] neut blood. **-druck** m blood pressure. **blutdürstig** adj bloodthirsty.

Blüte ['bly:tə] f (pl -n) blossom, bloom.

bluten ['blu:tən] v bleed. **Blut||gefäβ** neut blood vessel. **-gerinnsel** neut blood clot. **-gruppe** f blood group. **blutig** adj bloody. **Blut||übertragung** f blood transfusion. **-untersuchung** f blood test.

Bö [bœ:] f (pl -en) squall, gust of wind.

Bock [bɔk] m (pl Böcke) (Schaf-) ram; (Ziegen-, Reh-) buck; (Sport) horse. **bockig** adj obstinate. **Bockwurst** f saveloy, large Frankfurter.

Boden ['bo:dən] m (pl Böden) (Erde) ground; (Fuβ-) floor; (Dach-) loft; (Fluβ-, Meeres-) bottom, bed. **bodenlos** adj bottomless.

Bogen ['bo:gən] m (pl -) curve, arch; (Waffe, auch für Geige) bow. **-schieβen** neut archery. **-schütze** m archer.

Bohne ['bo:nə] f (pl -n) bean.

bohren ['bo:rən] v bore, drill. **Bohrer** m (pl -) borer, drill. **Bohrmaschine** f drill.

Boje ['bo:jə] f (pl -n) buoy.

Bollwerk ['bɔlvɛrk] neut (pl -e) bulwark.

Bolzen ['bɔltsən] m (pl -) peg; (Tech) bolt; (Pfeil) arrow, bolt.

bombardieren [bɔmbaː'diːrən] v bombard.

Bombe ['bɔmbə] f (pl -n) bomb. **Bomben||angriff** m bombing raid. **-anschlag** m (terrorist) bombing. **-flugzeug** neut bomber.

Bonbon [bõ'bõ] neut (pl -s) sweet, (US) candy.

Boot [bo:t] neut (pl -e) boat.

Bord¹ [bɔrt] neut (pl -e) board.

Bord² m (pl -e) edge, rim. **an Bord gehen** go aboard, board.

Bordell [bɔr'dɛl] neut (pl -e) brothel.

borgen ['bɔrgən] v (entleihen) borrow; (verleihen) lend. **Borger** m (pl -) (Entleiher) borrower; (Verleiher) lender.

Borke ['bɔrkə] f (pl -n) bark.

Börse ['bœ:rzə] f (pl -n) stock exchange; (Beutel) purse. **-nmakler** m stockbroker.

Borste ['bɔrstə] f (pl -n) bristle.

bös(e) ['bœ:zə] adj bad; (Mensch) wicked; (Geist) evil; (Kind) naughty; (wütend) cross. **bösartig** adj malicious; (Med) malignant. **Böse** neut mischief; m evil person, devil.

boshaft ['bo:shaft] adj malicious, spiteful.

Bosnien ['bɔsniən] neut Bosnia. **Bosnier(in)** Bosnian. **bosnisch** adj Bosnian.

Boβ [bɔs] m (pl Bosse) boss.

böswillig ['bø:svɪlɪç] adj malicious, malevolent. **Böswilligkeit** f malice.

Botanik [bo'ta:nɪk] f botany. **-er** m (pl -) botanist. **botanisch** adj botanical.

Bote ['boːtə] *m* (*pl* -n) messenger. **Botllengang** *m* errand. **–schaft** *f* message; (*Gesandschaft*) embassy. **–schafter** *m* ambassador.

Bottich ['bɔtiç] *m* (*pl* -e) tub, vat.

Bowle ['boːlə] *f* (*pl* -n) (*Getränk*) punch, fruit cup; (*Gefäß*) punchbowl.

boxen ['bɔksən] *v* box. **Boxer** *m* (*pl* -) boxer. **Boxkampf** *m* boxing match.

brach [braːx] *adj* fallow, untilled.

Branche ['brãʃə] *f* (*pl* -n) (*Geschäftszweig*) line of business, trade; (*Abteilung*) department.

Brand [brant] *m* (*pl* Brände) fire, blaze; (*Med*) gangrene; (*Bot*) mildew. **–bombe** *f* incendiary bomb. **brandmarken** *v* brand, stigmatize. **Brandllstifter** *m* arsonist, fire-raiser. **–stiftung** *f* arson.

Brandung ['brandʊŋ] *f* (*pl* -en) surf, breakers *pl*.

Branntwein ['brantvain] *m* brandy.

***braten** ['braːtən] *v* roast; (*in der Pfanne*) fry; (*auf dem Rost*) grill. **Braten** *m* roast (meat), joint. **Bratllfisch** *m* fried fish. **–hähnchen** *neut* roast chicken. **–kartoffeln** *pl* fried potatoes. **–pfanne** *f* frying pan. **–wurst** *f* fried sausage.

Bräu [brɔy] *neut* brew (*Brauerei*) brewery.

Brauch [braux] *m* (*pl* Bräuche) custom, usage. **brauchbar** *adj* serviceable; usable; (*nützlich*) useful. **brauchen** *v* need, require; (*gebrauchen*) use.

brauen ['brauən] *v* brew. **Brauerei** *f* brewery.

braun [braun] *adj* brown. **Braun** *neut* brown.

Braunfäule ['braunfɔylə] *f* blight (*Pflanzen*).

Braunschweig ['braunʃvaik] *neut* Brunswick.

Brause ['brauzə] *f* (*pl* -n) (*Dusche*) shower; (*Gießkanne*) rose; (*Limonade*) lemonade, pop. **–bad** *neut* shower.

Braut [braut] *f* (*pl* Bräute) (*am Hochzeitstag*) bride; (*Verlobte*) fiancée.

Bräutigam ['brɔytigam] *m* bridegroom.

Brautlljungfer *f* bridesmaid. **–kleid** *neut* wedding dress.

bräutlich ['brɔytliç] *adj* bridal.

brav [braːf] *adj* honest, worthy; (*tapfer*) brave; (*artig*) good, well-behaved.

***brechen** ['brɛçən] *v* break; (*Marmor*) quarry. **Bahn brechen** (*fig*) blaze a trail.

Brechllbohne *f* French bean. **–mittel** *neut* emetic.

Brei [brai] *m* (*pl* -e) paste, pulp.

breit [brait] *adj* broad, wide. **Breite** *f* breadth, width; (*Geog*) latitude.

Bremse¹ ['brɛmzə] *f* (*pl* -n) brake. **bremsen** *v* brake. **Bremsllicht** *f* brake light, stop light. **–pedal** *neut* brake pedal.

Bremse² *f* (*pl* -n) horse-fly.

brennbar ['brɛnbaːr] *adj* combustible, inflammable. **brennen** *v* burn; (*Branntwein*) distill. **Brennllerei** *f* distillery. **–nessel** *f* stinging nettle. **–punkt** *m* focus. **–stoff** *m* fuel.

Brett [brɛt] *neut* (*pl* -er) board; (*Regal*) shelf.

Brezel ['breːtsəl] *f* (*pl* -n) pretzel.

Brief [briːf] *m* (*pl* -e) letter. **–kasten** *m* letterbox. **–kopf** *m* letterhead. **brieflich** *adj* written. **Briefllmarke** *f* (postage) stamp. **–tasche** *f* wallet, pocket book. **–träger** *m* postman.

Brigade [brigaːdə] *f* (*pl* -n) brigade.

brillant [briljant] *adj* brilliant.

Brille ['brilə] *f* (*pl* -n) spectacles, glasses; (*Schutz*) goggles.

***bringen** ['brɪŋən] *v* bring; (*mitnehmen, begleiten*) take; (*Zeitung*) print, publish; (*Theater*) present, put on. **es weit bringen** do well, go far. **ans Licht bringen** bring to light.

Brite ['britə] *m* (*pl* -n), **Britin** *f* (*pl* -nen) Briton.

bröckelig ['brœkəliç] *adj* crumbly. **bröckeln** *v* crumble.

Brocken ['brɔkən] *m* (*pl* -) crumb; (*pl*) scraps, bits and pieces.

Brombeere ['brɔmbeːrə] *f* blackberry. **Brombeerstrauch** *m* blackberry bush, bramble.

Bronze ['brõsə] *f* (*pl* -n) bronze. **bronzefarben** *adj* bronze(-coloured).

Brosche ['brɔʃə] *f* (*pl* -n) brooch.

Broschüre [brɔʃyːrə] *f* (*pl* -n) brochure.

Brot [broːt] *neut* (*pl* -e) bread; (*Laib*) loaf. **Brötchen** ['brøːtçən] *neut* bread roll.

Brotllschnitte *f* slice (of bread). **–verdiener** *m* bread-winner.

Bruch [brux] *m* (*pl* Brüche) break; (*Knochen*) fracture; (*Math*) fraction; (*Versprechen, Vertrag*) breech; (*Gesetz*) violation, breech. **bruchfest** *adj* unbreakable.

brüchig [ˈbrʏçɪç] *adj* brittle.
Bruch||landung *f* crash landing. **–stück** *neut* fragment. **–teil** *m* fraction.
Brücke [ˈbrʏkə] *f* (*pl* -n) bridge.
Bruder [ˈbruːdər] *m* (*pl* Brüder) brother.
brüderlich [ˈbrʏdəːrlɪç] *adj* brotherly. **Brüderschaft** *f* brotherhood.
Brühe [ˈbryːə] *f* (*pl* -n) broth; (*Suppengrundlage*) stock. **brühen** *v* scald. **brühheiß** *adj* boiling hot.
brüllen [ˈbrʏlən] *v* bellow; (*Sturm, Raubtier*) roar. **Brüllfrosch** *m* bullfrog.
brummen [ˈbrʊm ən] growl; (*Insekten*) buzz, hum; (*mürrisch sein*) grumble; (*umg.*) go to prison, do time.
brünett [brʏˈnɛt] *adj* brunette, dark brown. **Brünette** *f* brunette.
Brunnen [ˈbrʊnən] *m* (*pl* -) well; (*Quelle*) spring.
Brunst [brʊnst] *f* (*pl* Brünste) lust, ardour; (*Tier*) heat. **brünstig** *adj* lusty; (*Tier*) in heat.
Brüssel [ˈbrʏsə] *neut* Brussels.
Brust [brʊst] *f* (*pl* Brüste) breast, chest; (*Frauen*) breast. **–kasten** *m* chest. **–krebs** *m* breast cancer. **–schwimmen** *neut* breaststroke. **–warze** *f* nipple.
brutal [brʊˈtaːl] *adj* brutal.
brüten [ˈbrʏtən] *v* brood.
brutto [ˈbrʊto] *adj* gross. **Bruttogewicht** *neut* gross weight. **Bruttosozialprodukt** *neut* gross national product.
BSE *f* BSE.
Bube [ˈbuːbə] *m* (*pl* -n) boy, lad; (*Karten*) jack, knave.
Buch [buːx] *neut* (*pl* Bücher) book.
Buche [ˈbuːxə] *f* (*pl* -n) beech (tree).
buchen [ˈbuːxən] *v* record, enter (in a book).
Bücherei [ˈbyçəːraɪ] *f* (*pl* -en) library. **Bücherschrank** *m* bookcase.
Buchfink [buˈçfɪŋk] *m* chaffinch.
Buch||halter *m* book-keeper. **–haltung** *f* book-keeping; accounts department. **–händler** *m* bookseller. **–handlung** *f* bookshop. **–macher** *m* bookmaker.
Büchse [ˈbʏksə] *f* (*pl* -n) box; (*Blechdose*) tin, can; (*Gewehr*) rifle.
Buchstabe [ˈbuːxʃtaːbə] *f* (*pl* -n) letter (of the alphabet). **buchstabieren** *v* spell. **Buchstabierung** *f* spelling. **buchstäblich** *adj* literal.

Bucht [buxt] *f* (*pl* -en) bay.
Buckel [ˈbuːkə] *m* (*pl* -) hump, mound; (*am Rücken*) humpback. **buckelig** *adj* hunchbacked.
bücken [ˈbʏkən] *v* sich bücken stoop, bow.
Buddhismus [bʊˈdɪsm us] *m* Buddhism. **Buddhist(in)** Buddhist. **buddhistisch** *adj* Buddhist.
Bude [ˈbuːdə] *f* (*pl* -n) booth; (*Markt*) stall; (*umg.*) lodgings, digs, room(s).
Budget [bʏˈdʒɛː] *neut* (*pl* -s) budget.
Büfett [bʏˈfɛt] *neut* (*pl* -s) sideboard, dresser. **kaltes Büfett** cold buffet.
Büffel [ˈbʏfə] *m* (*pl* -) buffalo.
Bug [buːk] *m* (*pl* -e) (*Schiff*) bow; (*Flugzeug*) nose; (*Pferd*) shoulder.
Bügel [ˈbyːgə] *m* (*pl* -) hoop, handle; (*Kleider* -) hanger; (*Steig* -) stirrup. **–brett** *neut* ironing board. **–eisen** *neut* iron. **bügelt** *adj* permanent press, non-iron. **bügeln** *v* iron.
bugsieren [bʊgˈziːən] *v* tow. **Bugsierer** *m* tugboat.
Bühne [ˈbyːnə] *f* (*pl* -n) stage. **Bühnen||bild** *neut* set, scenery. **–dichter** *m* playwright. **–deutsch** *neut* high German, standard German.
Bulgare [bʊlˈgaːrə] *m* (*pl* -n), **Bulgarin** *f* (*pl* -nen) Bulgarian. **Bulgarien** *neut* Bulgaria. **bulgarisch** *adj* Bulgarian.
Bulimie [bulimiˈ] *f* bulimia.
Bulle [ˈbʊlə] *m* (*pl* -n) bull; (*umg.*) cop.
Bummel [ˈbumə] *m* (*pl* -) stroll. **bummeln** *v* stroll; (*nichts tun*) loaf, loiter. **Bummel||streik** *m* work-to-rule, go-slow. **–zug** *m* slow train, local (train).
Bund[1] [bunt] *neut* (*pl* -e) bundle; (*Schlüssel, Radieschen, usw.*) bunch.
Bund[2] *m* (*pl* Bünde) band; (*Verein*) association, league; (*Staat*) federation.
Bündel [ˈbʏndə] *neut* (*pl* -) bundle, bunch. **bündeln** bundle (up).
Bundes||bahn *f* federal railway, German railway. **–haus** parliament buildings. **–präsident** *m* federal president. **–rat** *m* (*BRD, Österreich*) upper house (of parliament); (*Schweiz*) (Swiss) government. **–republik Deutschland (BRD)** *f* Federal Republic of Germany. **–tag** *m* German parliament, federal parliament. **–staat** *m* federal state.

Bündnis ['byntnɪs] *neut* (*pl* -se) alliance.
Bunker ['bunkər] *m* (*pl* -) bunker.
bunt [bunt] *adj* brightly coloured, gay.
Bürde ['byːrdə] *f* (*pl* -n) burden.
Burg [burk] *f* (*pl* -en) castle; (*Festung*) fort.
Bürge ['byrgə] *m* (*pl* -n) surety, guarantor. **bürgen** *v* guarantee, vouch for; (*Jur*) stand bail for.
Bürger ['byrgər] *m* (*pl* -) citizen; (*Stadt*) townsman; bourgeois. **–krieg** *m* civil war. **bürgerlich** *adj* bourgeois, middle-class; (*Küche*) simple, plain; (*zivil*) civilian. **Bürgerllmeister** *m* mayor. **–recht** *neut* civil rights. **–schaft** *f* citizenry, citizens. **–stand** *m* middle class(es). **–steig** *m* pavement, (*US*) sidewalk.
Bürgschaft ['byrgʃaft] *f* (*pl* -en) surety, bond.
Büro [by'roː] *neut* (*pl* -s) office. **–klammer** *f* paperclip. **–krat** *m* (*pl* -en) bureaucrat. **–kratie** *f* bureaucracy. **bürokratisch** *adj* bureaucratic.
Bursche ['burʃə] *m* (*pl* -n) lad, fellow.
Bürste ['byrstə] *f* (*pl* -n) brush. **bürsten** *v* brush.
Busch [buʃ] *m* (*pl* **Büsche**) bush, shrub.
Büschel ['byʃəl] *neut* (*pl* -) bunch; (*Haare*) tuft.
buschig ['buʃiç] *adj* bushy.
Busen ['buːzən] *m* (*pl* -) breast. **–freund** *m* bosom friend.
Buße ['buːsə] *f* (*pl* -n) penance; (*Geld*) fine. **büßen** ['bysən] *v* do penance (for).
Büste ['bystə] *f* (*pl* -n) bust. **–nhälter** *m* brassière.
Butter ['butər] *f* (*unz.*) butter. **–blume** *f* buttercup. **–brot** *neut* (slice of) bread and butter. **–brotpapier** *neut* greaseproof paper.
Byte ['baɪt] *neut* (*pl* - or -s) (*comp*) byte.

C

Cache ['kaʃ] *m* (*pl* -s) (*comp*) cache.
Café [ka'feː] *neut* (*pl* -s) café, coffee house.
Camcorder ['kam kɔːtər] *m* (*pl* -) camcorder.
campen ['kɛm pən] *v* camp. **Camper** *m* camper. **Camping** *neut* camping. **–platz** *m* camp(ing) site.
Caravan ['karavaːn] *m* (*pl* -s) caravan; (*Kombiwagen*) estate car.
CD *f* (*pl* -s) CD, compact disc. **CD-ROM** *f* (*pl* -s) CD-ROM.
Cellist [tʃɛ'list] *m* (*pl* -en), **Cellistin** *f* (*pl* -nen) cellist. **Cello** *neut* cello.
Cembalo ['tʃɛm baloː] *neut* (*pl* -s) harpsichord.
Champagner [ʃam 'panjər] *m* (*pl* -) champagne.
Champignon ['ʃam pɪnjɔ] *m* (*pl* -s) mushroom.
Chance ['ʃãːsə] *f* (*pl* -n) chance. **Chancengleichheit** *f* equality of opportunity.
Chaos ['kaːɔs] *neut* (*unz.*) chaos. **chaotisch** *adj* chaotic.
Charakter ['karaktər] *m* (*pl* -e) character. **charakterisieren** *v* characterize. **charakteristisch** *adj* characteristic.
Charisma [ka'rɪsmaː] *neut* charisma. **charismatisch** *adj* charismatic.
Chauffeur [ʃɔ'fœːr] *m* (*pl* -e) driver. chauffeur.
Chaussee [ʃo'seː] *f* (*pl* -n) highway, main road.
Chef [ʃɛf] *m* (*pl* -s) boss, head; (*Arbeitgeber*) employer.
Chemie [çe'miː] *f* (*unz.*) chemistry. **Chemikalien** *f pl* chemicals. **Chemiker** *m* (*pl* -) (industrial *or* research) chemist. **chemisch** *adj* chemical. **–e Reinigung** *f* dry cleaning.
China ['çiːnaː] *neut* China. **Chinese** *m* (*pl* -n), **Chinesin** *f* (*pl* -nen) Chinese (person). **chinesisch** *adj* Chinese.
Chirurg [çɪrurk] *m* (*pl* -en) surgeon. **–ie** *f* surgery. **chirurgisch** *adj* surgical.
Chlor [kloːr] *neut* (*unz.*) chlorine. **Chloroform** *neut* chloroform. **Chlorophyll** *neut* chlorophyll. **Chlorwasser** *neut* chlorinated water.
Cholera ['koleraː] *f* (*unz.*) cholera.
Cholesterin [ko'lɛstəriːn] *neut* cholesterol.
Chor [koːr] *m* (*pl* **Chöre**) choir; (*Gesang*) chorus. **–direktor** *m* choirmaster.
Christ [krɪst] *m* (*pl* -en) Christian. **christlich** *adj* Christian. **Christllnacht** *f* Christmas Eve. **–us** *m* Christ.
Chrom [kroːm] *neut* (*unz.*) chromium; (*Verchromung*) chrome, chrome-plating.

chromiert *adj* chrome-plated.

Chronik ['kroːnɪk] *f* (*pl* -en) chronicle. **chronisch** *adj* chronic.

Computer [kɔmˈpjuːtər] *m* (*pl* -) computer. **–versessene** *m, f* (*pl* -n) nerd, geek.

Coupé [kuˈpeː] *neut* (*pl* -s) railway carriage.

Cousin [kuˈzɛ̃] *m* (*pl* -s) (male) cousin. **-e** *f* (female) cousin.

Creme [kreːm] *f* (*pl* -s) cream; (*Süßspeise*) cream pudding; (*Hautsalbe*) handcream, skincream.

C-Waffen ['tseːvafən] *f pl* chemical weapons.

Cyberraum ['tsaɪbərˈraum] *m* cyberspace.

D

da [daː] *adv* (*örtlich*) there; (*zeitlich*) then. *conj* because, since. **da draußen/drinnen** out/in there. **da sein** be present. **da bin ich** here I am. **da siehst Du!** see! **da hingegen** whereas.

dabei [daˈbaɪ] *adv* close (by), near; (*bei diesem*) thereby; (*außerdem*) moreover. **dabei sein** be present. **es bleibt dabei** that is or remains settled. **was ist dabei?** what does it matter? **dabei sein, es zu tun** be on the point of doing it. **dabei bleiben** stick to one's opinion.

Dach [dax] *neut* (*pl* Dächer) roof. **–boden** *m* attic. **–fenster** *neut* skylight. **–gesellschaft** *f* holding company. **–kammer** *f* attic, garret. **–rinne** *f* gutter.

Dachs [daks] *m* (*pl* -e) badger. **–hund** *m* dachshund.

Dachziegel ['daxtsiːgəl] *m* roof tile.

dadurch [daˈdurç] *adv* for this reason, in this way. **dadurch daß** because, since.

dafür [daˈfyːr] *adv* for that; (*Gegenleistung*) in return. **dafür sein** be in favour of (it). **er kann nichts dafür** he can't help it.

dagegen [daˈgeːgən] *adv* against it; (*Vergleich*) in comparison. *conj* on the contrary, however, *ich habe nichts dagegen* I have no objections. *er stimmt dagegen* he is voting against it.

daher [daˈheːr] *adv* from there. *conj* hence, accordingly. **daher kommt es** hence it follows. **daher, daß** since, because.

dahin [daˈhɪn] *adv* there, to that place.

dahinten [daˈhɪntən] *adv* back there.

dahinter [daˈhɪntər] *adv* behind it or that. **–kommen** *v* find out (about it), get to the bottom of it. **–stecken** *v* lie behind, be the cause.

damals ['daːmaːls] *adv* then, at that time.

Dame ['daːmə] *f* (*pl* -n) lady; (*Karten*) queen. **–brett** *neut* draughtboard, (*US*) checker-board. **Damen‖binde** *f* sanitary towel. **–toilette** *f* ladies' lavatory. **–wäsche** *f* lingerie. **Dame‖spiel** *neut* draughts. **–stein** *m* draughtsman, (*US*) checker.

Damm [dam] *m* (*pl* Dämme) dam; dike; (*Bahn-, Straßen-*) embankment.

dämmen ['dɛm ən] *v* dam (up).

dämmern ['dɛm ərn] *v* (*morgens*) dawn, grow light; (*abends*) grow dark. **es dämmert** dawn is breaking. **Dämmerung** *f* (*pl* -en) (*morgens*) dawn; (*abends*) twilight, dusk.

Dampf [dam pf] *m* (*pl* Dämpfe) steam, vapour. **dampfen** *v* steam; (*Rauch*) smoke, fume.

dämpfen ['dɛm pfən] *v* (*Ofen*) damp down; (*Schall*) muffle; (*Licht*) soften; (*Küche*) steam.

Dampf‖‖er ['dam pfər] *m* (*pl* -) steamer, steamship. **–kessel** *m* boiler. **–kochtopf** *m* pressure cooker. **–maschine** *f* steam engine. **–schiff** *neut* steamship, steamer.

danach [daˈnaːx] *adv* after it; (*darauf*) afterwards; (*entsprechend*) accordingly.

Däne ['dɛːnə] *m* (*pl* -n), **Dänin** (-nen) Dane. **Dänemark** *neut* Denmark. **dänisch** *adj* Danish.

daneben [daˈneːbən] *adv* beside (it); (*außerdem*) besides.

Dank [daŋk] *m* (*unz.*) thanks. **dankbar** *adj* grateful, thankful. **Dankbarkeit** *f* gratitude. **danken** *v* thank.

dann [dan] *adv* then.

daran [daˈran] *adv* on or at or by it. **nahe daran sein zu** be on the point of. **nahe daran** close by. **gut daran sein** be well off.

darauf [daˈrauf] *adv* on it; (*nachher*) afterwards. **es kommt darauf an (ob)** it depends (whether). *wie kommt er darauf?* why does he think so?

daraus [daˈraus] *adv* out of it, from it. *es ist nichts daraus geworden* nothing has come of that.

*darbieten ['daːrbiːtən] *v* offer, present.

darein [da'raɪn] *adv* in(to) it; *(hierin)* there-in.

darin [da'rɪn] *adv* in it, within; *(hierin)* therein.

darlegen ['daːrleːgən] *v* explain, expound. **Darlegung** *f* explanation.

Darlehen ['daːrleːən] *neut* (*pl* -) loan.

Darm [darm] *m* (*pl* **Därme**) intestines *pl*. **–verstopfung** *f* constipation.

darstellen ['daːrʃtɛlən] *v* represent. **Darsteller** *m* (*Theater*) actor, performer. **Darstellung** *f* exhibition.

darüber [da'ryːbər] *adv* over it; *(davon)* about it; *(hinüber)* across. **darüber hinaus** over and above that, furthermore.

darum [da'rum] *adv* around *or* about it, for it. *conj* therefore.

darunter [da'runtər] *adv* under *or* beneath it; *(dazwischen)* among them; *(weniger)* less.

das [das] *art* the. *pron* which, that.

Dasein ['daːzaɪn] *neut* (*unz.*) existence, being; *(Vorhandensein)* presence. **Daseinskampf** *m* struggle for existence.

daβ [das] *conj* that.

Daten ['daːtən] *neut pl* data *pl*. **–sicherung** *f* (*comp*) backup. **–verarbeitung** *f* data processing.

datieren [da'tiːrən] *v* date.

Datum ['daːtum] *neut* (*pl* **Daten**) date; *(Tatsache)* datum, fact.

Dauer ['dauər] *f* (*unz.*) period (of time), duration. **–auftrag** *m* (*Bank*) standing order. **dauerhaft** *adj* lasting, durable. **Dauerkarte** *f* season ticket. **dauern** *v* last, continue. **-d** *adj* lasting, permanent. **Dauerwelle** *f* perm, permanent wave.

Daumen ['daum ən] *m* (*pl* -) thumb.

Daunendecke ['daunəndɛkə] *f* eiderdown, continental quilt.

davon [da'fɔn] *adv* of *or* from it; *(weg)* away; *(darüber)* about it. **–kommen** *v* escape. **sich davonmachen** *v* (*umg.*) make one's escape, slide off.

davor [da'foːr] *adv* (*örtlich*) before it, in front of it; *(zeitlich)* before that *or* then. **Angst haben davor** be afraid of it. **eine Stunde davor** an hour earlier.

dawider [da'vɪdər] *adv* against it.

dazu [da'tsuː] *adv* to it; *(Zweck)* for this (purpose), to that end; *(überdies)* in addition.

dazwischen [da'tsvɪʃən] *adv* between *or* among them. **–treten** *v* intervene.

Debatte [de'batə] *f* (*pl* -n) debate. **debattieren** *v* debate.

Debet ['deːbɛt] *neut* (*pl* -s) debit.

Debüt [de'byː] *neut* (*pl* -s) début.

Deck [dɛk] *neut* (*pl* -e) deck.

Decke ['dɛkə] *f* (*pl* -n) cover(ing); *(Bett)* blanket; *(Zimmer)* ceiling. **–I** *m* lid. **decken** *v* cover; set (the table). **Deck‖mantel** *m* pretext. **–name** *m* pseudonym. **–ung** *f* cover(ing); *(Verteidigung)* protection.

definieren [defɪ'niːrən] *v* define. **definitiv** *adj* definite.

Defizit ['deːfɪtsɪt] *neut* (*pl* -e) deficit.

degenerieren [degene'riːrən] *v* degenerate.

degradieren [degra'diːrən] *v* demote.

dehnbar ['deːnbaːr] *adj* elastic, malleable; *(Begriff)* loose, vague. **Dehnbarkeit** *f* elasticity, malleability. **dehnen** *v* stretch. **Dehnung** *f* stretching, expansion.

Deich [daɪç] *m* (*pl* -e) dike.

Deichsel ['daɪksə] *f* (*pl* -n) shaft, pole, **deichseln** *v* (*umg.*) wangle.

dein [daɪn] *adj* your. *pron* yours. **deinerseits** *adv* on *or* for your part. **deinesgleichen** *pron* your likes, people like you. **deinethalben, deinetwegen,** *or* **deinetwillen** *adv* for your sake. **deinige** *pron* **der die, das deinige** yours.

dekadent [deka'dɛnt] *adj* decadent. **Dekadenz** *f* decadence.

Dekan [de'kaːn] *m* (*pl* -e) dean.

deklamieren [dekla'miːrən] *v* declaim.

deklarieren [dekla'riːrən] *v* declare.

Deklination [deklinatsioːn] *f* (*pl* -en) declension. **deklinieren** *v* decline.

dekodieren [deko'diːrən] *v* decode.

Dekor [de'koːr] *m* (*pl* -s) decoration(s). **dekorieren** *v* decorate.

Dekret [de'kreːt] *neut* (*pl* -e) decree.

delegieren [dele'giːrən] *v* delegate. **Delegierte(r)** *m* delegate.

delikat [deli'kaːt] *adj* (*Person, Angelegenheit*) delicate; *(Speise)* delicious. **Delikatesse** *f* (*pl* -n) delicacy.

Delikatessenhandlung [delikatɛsənhandluŋ] *f* (*pl* -en) delicatessen.

Delikt [de'lɪkt] *neut* (*pl* -e) crime.

Delphin [dɛl'fiːn] *m* (*pl* -e) dolphin.

dem [deːm] *art* to the. *pron* to this *or* that (one); *(wem)* to whom, to which.

Dementi [deˈmɛnti] *neut* (*pl* **-s**) (official) denial. **dementieren** *v* deny.

demgemäß [ˈdeːm gəm ɛːs] *adv* accordingly.

Demission [dem isˈoːn] *f* (*pl* **-en**) resignation. **demissionieren** *v* resign.

demnach [deːm naːx] *adv* accordingly.

demnächst [ˈdeːm nɛːçst] *adv* shortly, soon.

Demokrat [dem oˈkraːt] *m* (*pl* **-en**) democrat. **-ie** *f* democracy. **demokratisch** *adj* democratic.

demolieren [dem oˈliːən] *v* demolish.

Demonstrant [dem ɔnˈstrant] *m* (*pl* **-en**) demonstrator. **Demonstration** *f* (*pl* **-en**) demonstration. **demonstrieren** *v* demonstrate. **demonstrativ** *adj* demonstrative.

Demut [ˈdeːm uːt] *f* (*unz.*) humility. **demütig** *adj* humble. **-en** *v* humiliate, humble. **Demütigung** *f* (*pl* **-en**) humiliation.

demzufolge [ˈdeːm tsuˈfɔlgə] *adv* accordingly. *pron* according to which.

den [deːn] *art* the. *pl* to the. *pron* whom, which. *pl* to these. **denen** *pron* to whom *or* which.

Denkart [ˈdɛŋkaːrt] *f* way of thinking. **denk||bar** *adj* conceivable, thinkable. **-en** *v* think. **Denk||en** *neut* thinking, thought. **-er** *m* (*pl* **-**) thinker. **-fabrik** *f* think tank. **-freiheit** *f* freedom of thought. **-mal** *neut* monument. **denkwürdig** *adj* memorable. **Denkzettel** *m* lesson, punishment.

dennoch [ˈdɛnnɔx] *conj* nevertheless.

Denunziant [denuntsiant] *m* (*pl* **-en**) informer. **denunzieren** *v* denounce, inform against.

Depesche [deˈpɛʃə] *f* (*pl* **-n**) telegram, dispatch.

deponieren [depoˈniːən] *v* deposit.

Depot [deˈpoː] *neut* (*pl* **-s**) warehouse, storehouse, depot.

Depression [depreˈsioːn] *f* (*pl* **-en**) depression. **depressiv** *adj* depressed.

deprimieren [depriˈmiːən] *v* depress. **-d** *adj* depressing.

der [deːr] *art* the; (to) the; *pl* of the. *pron* who, which; (to) whom *or* which.

derart [ˈdeːraːrt] *adv* in such a way, so. **-ig** *adj* of such a type, such, of that kind.

derb [dɛrp] *adj* crude, coarse; (*Person*) rough, tough. **Derbheit** *f* crudeness;

(*Person*) roughness.

deren [ˈdeːrən] *pron* whose, of which. **derenthalben, derentwegen** *or* **derentwillen** *adv* on whose account, for whose sake.

dergleichen [deːrˈglaɪçən] *adv* suchlike, of the kind.

derjenige [ˈdeːrjeːnigə] **diejenige, dasjenige** *pron* he who, she who, that which.

dermaßen [ˈdeːrmaːsən] *adv* to such a degree, in such a way.

derselbe [deːrˈzɛlbə] *pron* **dieselbe, dasselbe** the same.

derzeitig [ˈdeːrtsaɪtiç] *adj* present; (*damalig*) of that time.

des [dɛs] *art* of the.

desgleichen [dɛsˈglaɪçən] *adv* likewise.

deshalb [ˈdɛshalp] *adv* therefore.

Desillusion [dɛzilluzioːn] *f* disillusionment.

Desinfektion [dɛzinfɛktsioːn] *f* disinfection. **-smittel** *neut* disinfectant. **desinfizieren** *v* disinfect.

dessen [ˈdɛsən] *pron* whose, of which.

destillieren [dɛstiliːən] *v* distil.

desto [ˈdɛsto] *adv* the, all the, so much. **je ... desto** ... the ... the ....

deswegen [ˈdɛsveːgən], **deswillen** *adv* therefore.

Detail [deˈtaɪ] *neut* (*pl* **-s**) detail, item. **-geschäft** *neut* retail firm *or* business. **-handel** *m* retail trade. **detaillieren** *v* detail, particularize.

deuten [ˈdɔytən] *v* explain, interpret. **deuten auf** point to, indicate, suggest. **deutlich** *adj* clear, plain. **Deutlichkeit** *f* clearness, distinctness.

deutsch [dɔytʃ] *adj* German. **Deutsch** *neut* German (language). **Deutsche(r)** German. **Deutschland** *neut* Germany.

Devise [deˈviːzə] *f* (*pl* **-n**) motto; *pl* foreign currency *or* exchange. **Devisenkurs** *m* rate of exchange.

Dezember [deˈtsɛmbər] *m* (*pl* **-**) December.

dezimal [detsimaːl] *adj* decimal.

Dia [ˈdiːa] *neut* (*pl* **-s**), *also* **Diapositiv** slide, transparency.

Dialekt [diaˈlɛkt] *m* (*pl* **-e**) dialect.

Dialog [diaˈloːk] *m* (*pl* **-e**) dialogue.

Diamant [diaˈmant] *m* (*pl* **-en**) diamond. **diamanten** *adj* diamond.

Diät [diːɛːt] *f* (*pl* **-en**) diet.

dich [dɪç] *pron sing* you.

dicht [dɪçt] *adj* dense; (*Wald, Nebel, Stoff*) thick; (*nahe*) close (by); (*wasserdicht*) watertight.

dichten[1] ['dɪçtən] *v* seal, make watertight *or* airtight.

dichten[2] *v* write (poetry); (*erträumen*) invent. **Dichter** *m* (*pl* -), **Dichterin** *f* (*pl* -nen) poet. **dichterisch** *adj* poetic.

Dichtheit ['dɪçthaɪt] *or* **Dichtigkeit** *f* density.

Dichtung ['dɪçtuŋ] *f* poetry, literature.

dick [dɪk] *adj* think; (*Person*) fat. **Dick‖darm** *m* large intestine. **-e** *f* fatness, thickness. **-icht** *neut* thicket.

die [diː] *art* the; *pron* who, which.

Dieb [diːp] *m* (*pl* -e) thief. **diebisch** *adj* thieving. **Diebstahl** *m* theft.

Diele ['diːlə] *f* (*pl* -n) board, plank; (*Vorraum*) hall, vestibule; (*Eis*-) ice-cream parlour. **Dielenbrett** *neut* floorboard.

dienen ['diːnən] *v* serve. **Diener** *m* (*pl* -), **Dienerin** *f* (*pl* -nen) servant. **Dienerschaft** *f* servants *pl*, domestics *pl*. **Dienst** *f* (*pl* -e) service; (*Amt*) duty.

Dienstag ['diːnstaːk] *m* Tuesday.

Dienst‖entlassung *f* dismissal. **-grad** *m* rank. **-leistung** *f* service. **dienstlich** *adj*, *adv* official(ly). **Dienst‖mädchen** *neut* (serving) maid. **-pflicht** *f* conscription. **-stunden** *f pl* working hours. **-wohnung** *f* official residence.

dieser ['diːzər] **diese, dieses** *pron*, *adj* this. **dies‖jährig** *adj* this year's. **-mal** *adv* this time. **-seits** *adv* on this side.

Dietrich ['diːtrɪç] *m* (*pl* -e) skeleton key.

diffizil [dɪfiˈtsiːl] *adj* difficult, awkward.

Diktat [dɪkˈtaːt] *neut* (*pl* -e) dictation. **Diktator** *m* (*pl* -en) dictator. **diktatorisch** *adj* dictatorial. **Diktatur** *f* (*pl* -en) dictatorship. **diktieren** *v* dictate. **Diktiergerät** *neut* dictaphone, dictating machine.

Diner [diˈneː] *neut* (*pl* -s) dinner, dinner party.

Ding [dɪŋ] *neut* (*pl* -e) thing. **vor allen Dingen** above all. **Dingelchen** *neut* (pretty) little thing. **Dingsbums** *neut* (*umg.*) what's-its-name, what's-his-name.

Diplom [diˈploːm] *neut* (*pl* -e) diploma. **-at** *m* (*pl* -en) diplomat. **-atie** *f* diplomacy. **diplomatisch** *adj* diplomatic. **Diplomingenieur** *m* graduate engineer.

dir [diːr] *pron sing* to you.

Direktzugriffsspeicher [diːˈrɛktsuːɡrɪf-ʃpaɪçər] *m* (*comp*) RAM (random access memory).

Dirigent [diriˈɡɛnt] *m* (*pl* -en) (*Musik*) conductor. **dirigieren** *v* conduct.

Dirne ['dɪrnə] *f* (*pl* -n) prostitute, whore; wench.

Disco [dɪskoː] *f* (*pl* -s) disco.

Diskette [dɪsˈkɛtə] *f* (*pl* -n) disk. **Diskettenlaufwerk** *neut* (*pl* -e) disk drive.

diskontieren [dɪskɔnˈtiːrən] *v* discount. **Diskontsatz** *m* bank-rate.

Diskothek [dɪskoˈteːk] *f* (*pl* -en) disco(theque).

diskriminieren [dɪskrimiˈniːrən] *v* discriminate (against). **Diskriminierung** *f* discrimination.

Diskussion [dɪskuˈsioːn] *f* (*pl* -en) discussion. **diskutieren** *v* discuss.

disponieren [dɪspoˈniːrən] *v* arrange, dispose (of). **disponieren über** have at one's disposal.

Dissident [dɪsiˈdɛnt] *m* (*pl* -en) dissident, dissenter.

Distel ['dɪstəl] *f* (*pl* -n) thistle.

Disziplin [dɪstsiˈpliːn] *f* (*pl* -en) discipline. **disziplinarisch** *adj* disciplinary. **Disziplinarverfahren** *neut* disciplinary action.

D-Mark ['deːm ark] *f* (*pl* -) (West) German mark.

DNS *f* DNA (deoxyribonucleic acid).

doch [dɔx] *conj* nevertheless, yet, but; *adv* indeed, oh yes.

Docht [dɔxt] *m* (*pl* -e) wick.

Dock [dɔk] *neut* (*pl* -e) dock. **-arbeiter** *m* docker, (*US*) longshoreman.

Dogge ['dɔɡə] *f* (*pl* -n) Great Dane; bulldog.

Dogma ['dɔɡm a] *f* (*pl* **Dogmen**) Dogma. **dogmatisch** *adj* dogmatic.

Doktor ['dɔktɔr] *m* (*pl* -en) doctor. **-arbeit** *f* doctoral *or* PhD thesis. **-at** *neut* doctorate, PhD.

Dolch [dɔlç] *m* (*pl* -e) dagger.

dolmetschen ['dɔlmɛtʃən] *v* interpret. **Dolmetscher** *m* interpreter.

Dom [doːm] *m* (*pl* -e) cathedral. **-herr** *m* canon. **-pfaff** (*Zool*) *m* bullfinch.

Domino ['doːm ino] *neut* (*pl* -s) dominoes.

–stein *m* domino.

Donau ['do:nau] *f* Danube.

Donner ['dɔnər] *m* (*pl* -) thunder. **donnern** *v* thunder.

Donnerstag ['dɔnərstaːk] *m* Thursday.

Donnerwetter ['dɔnərvɛtər] *neut* thunderstorm. *interj* damn!

doof [do:f] *adj* (*umg.*) daft, dumb, stupid.

Doppel ['dɔpəl] *neut* (*pl* -) duplicate. **Doppel-** *adj* double-. **Doppel‖bett** *neut* double bed. **–ehe** *f* bigamy. **–gänger** *m* ghostly double; doppelgänger **doppeln** *v* double. **Doppel‖punkt** *m* colon. **–sinn** *m* ambiguity. **doppelt** *adj* double(d).

Dorf [dɔrf] *neut* (*pl* Dörfer) village. **–bewohner** *m* villager.

Dorn [dɔrn] *m* (*pl* -en) thorn. **–röschen** *neut* Sleeping Beauty.

Dorsch [dɔrʃ] *m* (*pl* -e) cod.

dort [dɔrt] *adv* there. **–her** *adv* (from) there. **–herum** *adv* around there. **–hin** *adv* (to) there. **–ig** *adj* of that place.

Dose ['do:zə] *f* (*pl* -n) tin, box; (*Konserven-*) tin, can. **Dosenöffner)** *m* tin-opener, can-opener.

dosieren [do'zi:rən] *v* measure out (a dose of). **Dosis** *f* (*pl* Dosen) dose.

Dotter ['dɔtə] *m* (*pl* -) (egg) yolk.

Download [daun'loud] *m* (*pl* -s) (*comp*) download.

Downsyndrom [daun'zyndroːm] *neut* Down's syndrome.

Dozent [do'tsɛnt] *m* (*pl* -en) university or college lecturer.

Drache ['draxə] *m* (*pl* -n) dragon.

Drachen ['draxən] *m* (*pl* -) kite.

Draht [draːt] *m* (*pl* Drähte) wire, (*Kabel*) cable. **–anschrift** *f* telegraphic address. **–seil** *neut* cable. **–seilbahn** *f* cable car, funicular.

Drama ['draːma] *neut* (*pl* Dramen) drama. **–tiker** *m* (*pl* -) dramatist. **dramatisch** *adj* dramatic.

dran [dran] *V* daran.

Drang [draŋ] *m* (*pl* Dränge) drive, urge; (*Druck*) pressure.

drängeln ['drɛŋəln] *v* jostle, shove.

drängen ['drɛŋən] *v* press, urge.

drapieren [dra'piːrən] *v* drape.

drastisch ['drastiʃ] *adj* drastic.

drauf [drauf] *V* darauf.

draußen ['drausən] *adv* outside, out of doors.

Dreck [drɛk] *m* (*unz.*) filth, dirt; (*Kot*) excrement; (*Kleinigkeit*) trifle. **dreckig** *adj* filthy, dirty.

Dreh [dreː] *m* (*pl* -e) turn. **den Dreh heraushaben** get the hang or knack of it. **–bank** *f* lathe. **–buch** *neut* film-script, scenario. **drehen** *v* turn, rotate. **Dreh‖punkt** *m* pivot. **–ung** *f* (*pl* -en) turn, rotation, revolution. **–zahl** *f* revolutions per minute, rpm.

drei [drai] *adj* three. **Dreieck** *neut* triangle. **dreieckig** *adj* triangular. **dreifach** *adj* triple, treble. **Dreifuß** *m* tripod. **dreimal** *adv* three times. **Dreirad** *neut* tricycle.

dreißig ['draisiç] *adj* thirty.

dreist [draist] *adj* cheeky, impudent.

dreiviertel ['draifirtəl] *adj* three-quarter. *adv* three-quarters. **Dreiviertelstunde** *f* three-quarters of an hour.

dreizehn ['draitseːn] *adj* thirteen.

***dreschen** ['drɛʃən] *v* thresh.

dressieren [drɛ'siːrən] *v* train.

Drillich ['drɪlɪç] *m* (*pl* -e) (*Stoff*) drill, canvas.

Drilling ['drɪlɪŋ] *m* (*pl* -e) triplet.

drin [drɪn] *V* darin.

***dringen** ['drɪŋən] *v* penetrate. **dringen auf** insist on. **dringen in** implore, urge.

dritte ['drɪtə] *adj* third. **Drittel** *neut* (*pl* -) third.

Droge ['droːgə] *f* (*pl* -n) drug. **Drogerie** *f* (*pl* -n) chemist's (shop), pharmacy. **Drogist** *m* (*pl* -en) pharmacist, chemist.

drohen ['droːən] *v* threaten. **–d** *adj* threatening; (*Gefahr, usw.*) impending, imminent.

Drohne ['droːnə] *f* (*pl* -n) drone.

dröhnen ['drøː nən] *v* roar; (*Kanone*) boom; (*Donner*) rumble.

Drohung ['droːuŋ] *f* (*pl* -en) threat.

Droschke ['drɔʃkə] *f* (*pl* -n) taxi; (*Pferde-*) cab.

Drossel ['drɔsəl] *f* (*pl* -n) (*Vogel*) thrush; (*Mot*) throttle. **–ader** *f* jugular vein. **drosseln** *v* throttle.

drüben ['dryːbən] *adv* over there.

Druck¹ [drʊk] *m* (*pl* Drücke) pressure.

Druck² *m* (*pl* -e) print; (*Auflage*) impression. **drucken** *v* print.

drücken ['drʏkən] v press, push; (*Hand*) shake; (*bedrücken*) oppress. **sich drücken** get out of, avoid.

Druck||er ['drʊkər] m (pl -) printer. **–erei** f (pl **-en**) printing plant, press. **–fehler** m misprint. **–knopf** m push button; (*Kleidung*) snap fastener. **–luft** f compressed air. **–messer** m pressure gauge. **–sache** f printed matter. **–schrift** f publication; (*Buchstaben*) block letter.

drum [drʊm] V **darum**.

drunter ['drʊntər] V **darunter**.

Drüse ['dryːzə] f (pl **-n**) gland.

Dschungel ['dʒʊŋəl] m (pl -) jungle.

du [duː] pron you.

Dübel ['dyːbəl] m (pl -) dowel, wall-plug.

ducken ['dʊkən] v humble, humiliate. **sich ducken** duck; (*fig*) cower.

Dudelsack ['duːdəlzak] m bagpipes pl.

Duell [du'ɛl] neut (pl **-e**) duel. **–ant** m duellist.

Duett [du'ɛt] neut (pl **-e**) duet.

Duft [dʊft] m (pl **Düfte**) fragrance, aroma; (*Blumen*) scent. **dufte** adj (*umg.*) splendid, fine. **duften** v smell (sweet), be fragrant. **–d** adj fragrant, aromatic.

dulden ['dʊldən] v endure; (*erlauben*) tolerate, allow. **duldsam** adj tolerant, patient.

dumm [dʊm] adj stupid. **–heit** f stupidity; (*Tat*) foolish action, blunder. **–kopf** m idiot, fool.

dumpf [dʊmpf] adj (*Klang*) dull, hollow, muffled; (*schwül*) close, sultry; (*muffig*) musty.

Düne ['dyːnə] f (pl **-n**) dune.

Düngemittel ['dyŋəm ɪtəl] neut fertilizer. **düngen** v fertilize, manure. **Dünger** m manure.

dunkel ['dʊŋkəl] adj dark; (*düster*) gloomy, dim; (*ungewiß*) obscure. **Dunkel||heit** f darkness, obscurity. **–kammer** f (*Foto*) darkroom. **dunkeln** v **es dunkelt** it is growing dark.

Dünkel ['dyŋkəl] m arrogance.

dünn [dyn] adj thin. **Dünn||darm** m small intestine.

Dunst [dʊnst] m (pl **Dünste**) haze, mist. **dunsten** v steam.

dünsten ['dynstən] v steam; (*Küche*) stew.

Dur [duːr] neut (*Musik*) major (key).

durch [dʊrç] prep through; (*mittels*) by, through; (*Zeit*) during. adv through(out).

durch Zufall by chance. **durch und durch** thoroughly.

durchaus [dʊrç'aus] adv completely, thoroughly.

durchblättern [dʊrç'blɛtərn] v leaf through, skim through.

durchbohren ['dʊrçboːrən] v pierce, bore through.

***durchbrechen** ['dʊrçbrɛçən] v break through. **Durchbruch** m break-through; (*Öffnung*) breach.

***durchdringen** ['dʊrçdrɪŋən] v penetrate; ['drɪŋən] (*durchsickern*) permeate.

durcheinander [dʊrçaɪn'andər] adv in confusion, in disorder, in a mess. **Durcheinander** neut muddle. **durcheinanderbringen** v muddle up; (*aufregen*) upset, excite.

Durchfahrt ['dʊrçfaːrt] f passage; (*Tor*) gate. **keine Durchfahrt** no thoroughfare.

Durchfall ['dʊrçfal] m failure; (*Med*) diarrhoea. **durchfallen** v fall through; (*Prüfung*) fail.

durchführen ['dʊrçfyːrən] v carry out, perform; (*begleiten*) lead through. **Durchführung** f implementation, execution.

Durchgabe ['dʊrçgaːbə] f transmission.

Durchgang ['dʊrçgaŋ] m passage.

durchgeben ['dʊrçgeːbən] v transmit, pass on.

durchgehen ['dʊrçgeːən] v walk or go through, (*fliehen*) run away; (*durchdringen*) penetrate. **–d** adj continuous; (*Zug*) through.

***durchkommen** ['dʊrçkɔm ən] v come or pass through.

***durchlaufen** ['dʊrçlaufən] v run through.

durchleuchten [dʊrç'lɔyçtən] v (*Med*) x-ray.

durchmachen ['dʊrçm axən] v endure, live through.

Durchmesser ['dʊrçm ɛsər] m diameter.

Durchreise ['dʊrçraɪzə] f journey through, passage, transit.

durchs [dʊrçs] prep + art **durch das**.

Durchsage ['dʊrçzaːgə] f announcement. **durchsagen** v announce.

Durchschlag ['dʊrçʃlaːk] m carbon (copy); (*Sieb*) strainer, sieve. **–papier** neut carbon paper.

Durchschnitt ['dʊrçʃnɪt] m cutting

through; (*Querschnitt*) cross-section; (*Mittelwert*) mean, average. **durchschnittlich** *adj* average. **Durchschnittsmensch** *m* average person, man in the street.

Durchschrift ['durçʃrɪft] *f* (carbon) copy.

*****durchsehen** ['durçzeːən] *v* look or see through; (*prüfen*) look through or over.

Durchsicht ['durçzɪçt] *f* (*pl* -en) perusal, inspection. **durchsichtig** *adj* transparent.

durchsuchen ['durçzuːxən] *v* search.

durchtrieben [durçtriːbən] *adj* cunning, sly.

*****durchwinden** ['durçvɪndən] *v* **sich durchwinden** struggle through.

*****durchziehen** ['durçtsiːən] *v* pass through; (*etwas durch etwas*) pull or draw through; [-tsiːən] traverse; (*durchdringen*) fill, permeate.

*****dürfen** ['dyrfən] *v* be allowed or permitted to, may. **darf ich?** may I? **wenn ich bitten darf** if you please. **du darfst nicht** you may or must not.

dürftig ['dyrftɪç] *adj* needy, poor. **Dürftigkeit** *f* poverty.

dürr [dyr] *adj* arid, dry; (*hager*) lean. **Dürre** *f* drought; (*Magerkeit*) leanness.

Durst [durst] *m* thirst. **durstllen** *v* be thirsty. **-ig** *adj* thirsty. **-stillend** *adj* thirst-quenching.

Dusche ['duʃə] *f* (*pl* -n) shower. **duschen** *v* shower, have or take a shower.

Düse ['dyːzə] *f* (*pl* -n) jet, nozzle. **Düsenll antrieb** *m* jet propulsion. **-flugzeug** *neut* jet (plane).

düster ['dyːstər] *adj* dark; (*fig*) gloomy.

Dutzend ['dutsənt] *neut* (*pl* -e) dozen.

duzen ['duːtsən] *v* address familiarly (using **du**), be on first-name terms with.

DVD *f* DVD.

Dynamik [dyˈnaːmɪk] *f* dynamics. **dynamisch** *adj* dynamic.

Dynamit [dynaˈmiːt] *neut* (*unz.*) dynamite.

Dynamo [dyˈnaːmo] *m* (*pl* -s) dynamo.

Dynastie [dynasˈtiː] *f* (*pl* -n) dynasty.

D-Zug ['deːtsuk] *m* (*pl* -Züge) express train.

E

Ebbe ['ɛbə] *f* (*pl* -n) ebb; (*Niedrigwasser*) low tide. **ebben** *v* ebb.

eben ['eːbən] *adj* level, even. *adv* just. *ich war eben abgereist* I had just left. **eben deswegen** for that very reason. **Ebenbild** *neut* image. **ebenbürtig** *adj* equal (in rank). **Ebene** *f* (*pl* -n) plain; (*Math*) plane. **ebenfalls** *adv* likewise. **Ebenllheit** *f* evenness, smoothness. **-holz** *neut* ebony. **ebenso** *adv* just so. **-gut** *adv* just as well. **-viel** *adv* just as much.

Eber ['eːbər] *m* (*pl* -) boar.

ebnen ['eːbnən] *v* level, smooth.

Echo ['ɛço:] *neut* (*pl* -s) echo.

echt [ɛçt] *adj* genuine, real. **Echtheit** *f* genuineness, authenticity.

Eck [ɛk] *neut* (*pl* -e) corner. **-ball** *m* corner (kick). **-e** *f* corner, angle. **eckig** *adj* angular. **Eckzahn** *m* eyetooth.

edel ['eːdəl] *adj* noble. **Edelllmann** *m* nobleman. **-metall** *neut* precious metal. **-stein** *m* precious stone, gemstone.

Edikt [eˈdɪkt] *neut* (*pl* -e) edict.

Efeu ['eːfɔy] *m* ivy.

Effekten [ɛˈfɛktən] *pl* effects, personal belongings; (*Komm*) bonds, shares. **Effekthascherei** *f* sensationalism. **effektlliv** *adj* effective, actual. **-voll** *adj* effective.

egal [eˈgaːl] *adj* equal, (all) the same. *das ist mir ganz egal* it's all the same to me.

Egoismus [egoˈɪsmus] *m* (*pl* Egoismen) selfishness, egotism. **Egoist** *m* egotist. **egoistisch** *adj* egotistic, selfish.

ehe ['eːə] *conj, adv* before. **-malig** *adj* former.

Ehe ['eːə] *f* (*pl* -n) marriage. **-brecher** *m* adulterer. **-brecherin** *f* adulteress. **ehebrecherisch** *adj* adulterous. **Ehellbruch** *m* adultery. **-frau** *f* wife, married woman. **ehelllich** *adj* matrimonial, conjugal. **-los** *adj* unmarried, single. **Ehellmann** *m* husband. **-paar** *neut* married couple.

eher ['eːər] *adv* sooner; (*lieber*) rather.

Ehre ['eːrə] *f* (*pl* -n) honour. **ehren** *v* honour. **-haft** *adj* honourable. **Ehrenmal** *neut* war memorial. **ehrenvoll** *adj* honourable.

Ehrfurcht ['eːrfurçt] *f* awe. **ehrfürchtig** *adj* full of awe or reverence.

Ehr||gefühl *neut* sense of honour, self-respect. **–geiz** *m* ambition. **ehrgeizig** *adj* ambitious.

ehrlich ['eːrlɪç] *adj* honest, sincere. **Ehrlichkeit** *f* honesty. **ehrlos** *adj* dishonourable. **Ehrung** *f (pl* **-en**) honour, award. **ehrwürdig** *adj* venerable.

Ei [aɪ] *neut (pl* **-er**) egg. **–abstoßung** *f* ovulation. **–dotter** *m* yolk.

Eiche ['aɪçə] *f (pl* **-n**) oak. **Eich||el** *f* acorn. **–hörnchen** *neut* squirrel.

Eid [aɪt] *m (pl* **-e**) oath. **einen Eid ablegen** swear an oath.

Eidechse ['aɪdɛksə] *f (pl* **-n**) lizard.

Eidgenosse *m* confederate. **–nschaft** *f* confederacy; (*Schweiz*) Switzerland. **eidgenössisch** *adj* confederate; (*schweizerisch*) Swiss.

Eier||becher ['aɪərbɛçər] *m* eggcup. **–kuchen** *m* omelette. **–schale** *f* eggshell. **–stock** *m* ovary.

Eifer ['aɪfər] *m (unz.)* fervour, zeal. **–sucht** *f* jealousy. **eifersüchtig** *adj* jealous. **eifrig** *adj* eager, zealous. **Eifrigkeit** *f* zeal.

Eigelb ['aɪgɛlp] *neut (pl* **-e**) (egg) yolk.

eigen ['aɪgən] *adj* own; (*eigentümlich*) particular; (*eigenartig*) peculiar. **sich etwas zu eigen machen** get or acquire something. **etwas auf eigene Faust unternehmen** do something of one's own accord.

Eigenart *f (pl* **-en**) peculiarity. **eigenartig** *adj* peculiar.

eigen||händig *adj* by oneself. **–mächtig** *adj* arbitrary.

Eigen||name *m* proper name. **–nutz** *m* self-interest.

Eigenschaft *f (pl* **-en**) quality, attribute, trait. **–swort** *neut* adjective.

Eigensinn *m* obstinacy. **eigensinnig** *adj* obstinate, headstrong.

eigen||ständig *adj* independent. **–süchtig** *adj* egoistic.

eigentlich ['aɪgəntlɪç] *adv* actually, really. *adj* real, actual.

Eigentum ['aɪgəntuːm] *neut (pl* **Eigentümer**) property. **Eigentümer** *m* owner. **eigentümlich** *adj* peculiar.

eignen ['aɪgnən] *v* **sich eignen für** or **zu** be suited for.

Eil||bote ['aɪlboːtə] *m (pl* **-n**) courier, express messenger. **–brief** *m* express letter.

Eile ['aɪlə] *f* haste, hurry. **eilen** *v* hurry, has-ten. **eilig** *adj* hasty, fast. **Eil||sendung** *f.* (*Post*) special delivery. **–zug** *m* fast train, limited-stop train.

Eimer ['aɪmər] *m (pl* **-**) bucket, pail.

ein [aɪn], **eine, ein** *art* a, an. *pron, adj* one.

einander [aɪn'andər] *pron* each other, one another.

einatmen ['aɪnɑːtmən] *v* inhale, breathe in. **Einatmung** *f* inhalation.

Einbahnstraße ['aɪnbaːnʃtraːsə] *f* one-way street.

einbalsamieren [aɪnbalˈzaːmiːrən] *v* embalm.

Einband ['aɪnbant] *m* binding, cover (of book).

Einbau ['aɪnbau] *m* installation. **einbauen** *v* install, build in; (*fig*) incorporate (into).

*einbegreifen ['aɪnbəgraɪfən] *v* include, comprise. **mit einbegriffen** included.

*einbiegen ['aɪnbiːgən] *v* bend in; (*Straße*) turn into.

einbilden ['aɪnbɪldən] *v* **sich einbilden** imagine. **Einbildung** *f* imagination; (*Dünkel*) conceit. **–svermögen** *neut* (power of) imagination.

Einblick ['aɪnblɪk] *m* insight.

*einbrechen ['aɪnbrɛçən] *v* break open; (*Haus*) break into, burgle. **Einbrecher** *m* burglar. **Einbruch** *m* break-in, burglary; (*Mil*) invasion. **–sdiebstahl** *m* burglary.

einbürgern ['aɪnbyrgərn] *v* naturalize. **sich einbürgern** become naturalized; (*Wort, usw.*) come into use, gain acceptance. **Einbürgerung** *f* naturalization.

eindeutig ['aɪndɔytɪç] *adj* unequivocal, clear.

*eindringen ['aɪndrɪŋən] *v* enter by force; (*Mil*) invade. **eindringlich** *adj* urgent.

Eindruck ['aɪndrʊk] *m* impression. **eindrücken** *v* press in. **sich eindrücken** leave an impression. **eindrucksvoll** *adj* impressive.

einerlei ['aɪnərlaɪ] *adj* of one kind. **est ist einerlei** it makes no difference.

einerseits ['aɪnərzaɪts] *adv* on (the) one hand.

einfach ['aɪnfax] *adj* simple; (*nicht doppelt*) single. **Einfachheit** *f* simplicity.

*einfahren ['aɪnfaːrən] *v* drive in; (*Mot*) run in; (*einbringen*) bring in. **Einfahrt** *f* entrance, way in; (*Hineinfahren*) arrival, entrance.

Einfall ['aɪnfal] *m* idea, inspiration; (*Mil*) invasion, assault. **einfallen** *v* fall in; (*idee*) occur (to). *es fällt mir ein* it strikes me.

einfältig ['aɪnfɛltɪç] *adj* naive, artless. **Einfältigkeit** *f* naivety, artlessness.

einfetten ['aɪnfɛtən] *v* grease, lubricate.

***einfinden** ['aɪnfɪndən] *v* sich einfinden appear, turn up.

***einflechten** ['aɪnflɛçtən] *v* interweave; (*Wort*) put in.

Einflug ['aɪnfluːk] *m* incursion; (*Aero*) approach.

Einfluß ['aɪnflus] *m* influence. **einflußreich** *adj* influential.

einförmig ['aɪnfœrmɪç] *adj* monotonous, uniform.

einfügen ['aɪnfyːɡən] *v* fit in.

einfühlen ['aɪnfyːlən] *v* sich einfühlen in empathize with, get into the spirit of. **Einfühlung** *f* empathizing, empathy.

Einfuhr ['aɪnfuːr] *f* (*pl* -en) import. **einführen** *v* bring in; (*Waren*) import; (*Gebrauch*) introduce. **Einfuhrhandel** *m* import trade. **Einführung** *f* introduction. **Einfuhrverbot** *neut* import ban.

Eingang ['aɪnɡaŋ] *m* way in; (*Ankunft*) arrival; (*Einleitung*) introduction.

eingebildet ['aɪnɡəbɪldət] *adj* conceited; (*erfunden*) imaginary.

eingeboren ['aɪnɡəboːrən] *adj* native; (*angeboren*) innate. **Eingeborene(r)** *m* native.

Eingebung ['aɪnɡeːbʊŋ] *f* (*pl* -en) inspiration.

***eingehen** ['aɪnɡeːən] *v* go *or* enter into; (*aufhören*) stop; (*welken*) decay; (*Risiko*) run; (*zustimmen*) agree. **-d** *adj* thorough, detailed.

eingemacht ['aɪnɡəmaxt] *adj* bottled; canned; (*Fleisch*) potted.

eingenommen ['aɪnɡənɔmən] *adj* biased (in favour of).

Eingeweide ['aɪnɡəvaɪdə] *neut* (*pl* -) intestines *pl*, entrails *pl*.

Eingeweihte(r) ['aɪnɡəvaɪtə(r)] *m* (*pl* -) initiate.

eingewöhnen ['aɪnɡəvøːnən] *v* accustom. **sich eingewöhnen** become accustomed (to).

***eingießen** ['aɪnɡiːsən] *v* pour in *or* out.

eingliedern ['aɪnɡliːdərn] *v* incorporate; (*einordnen*) classify. **Eingliederung** *f* incor-

poration; classification.

***eingreifen** ['aɪnɡraɪfən] *v* catch (hold of); (*einmischen*) interfere. **Eingriff** *m* catch; interference; (*Übergriff*) encroachment.

***einhalten** ['aɪnhaltən] *v* restrain, check; observe; stop.

einhändig ['aɪnhɛndɪç] *adj* with one hand. **-en** *v* hand in.

einheimisch ['aɪnhaɪmɪʃ] *adj* native, indigenous.

Einheit ['aɪnhaɪt] *f* (*pl* -en) unit; (*Pol*) unity. **einheitlich** *adj* uniform.

einholen ['aɪnhoːlən] *v* collect; (*einkaufen*) shop, buy; (*erreichen*) catch up with.

einig ['aɪnɪç] *adj* united, at one. **einig sein** be in agreement. **-en** *v* unite. **sich einigen** agree.

einiger ['aɪnɪɡər] **einige, einiges** *pron* some, any. **einigermaßen** *adv* to some extent.

Einigkeit *f* (*unz.*) unity; (*Eintracht*) agreement. **Einigung** *f* unification; agreement.

einjährig ['aɪnjɛːrɪç] *adj* one-year-old; (*Bot*) annual.

einkassieren ['aɪnkasiːrən] *v* cash (in).

Einkauf ['aɪnkauf] *m* (*pl* Einkäufe) purchase. **Einkaufszentrum** *neut* (*pl* -zentren) shopping centre, mall. **einkaufen** *v* buy, purchase. **einkaufen gehen** go shopping.

einkehren ['aɪnkeːrən] *v* call in (at).

Einklang ['aɪnklaŋ] *m* (*pl* Einklänge) harmony.

***einkommen** ['aɪnkɔmən] *v* come in, arrive. **Einkommen** *neut* income.

einkreisen ['aɪnkraɪzən] *v* encircle.

Einkünfte ['aɪnkynftə] *pl* revenue, income *sing*.

***einladen** ['aɪnlaːdən] *v* invite. **Einladung** *f* (*pl* -en) invitation.

Einlage ['aɪnlaːɡə] *f* (*pl* -n) lining, filler; (*Brief*) enclosure; (*Geld*) deposit.

Einlaß ['aɪnlas] *m* (*pl* Einlässe) admission; (*Öffnung*) inlet. **einlassen** *v* let in, admit.

***einlaufen** ['aɪnlaufən] *v* arrive; (*Wasser*) run in.

einleben ['aɪnleːbən] *v* sich einleben in accustom oneself to.

einlegen ['aɪnleːɡən] *v* enclose, insert; (*Beschwerde*) file; (*Fleisch*) salt, pickle.

einleiten ['aɪnlaɪtən] *v* introduce, initiate; (*beginnen*) start. **Einleitung** *f* introduction.

einlösen ['aɪnløːzən] v redeem. **Einlösung** f payment, redemption.

einmachen ['aɪnmaxən] v (Obst) preserve, bottle.

einmal ['aɪnmaːl] adv once. **auf einmal** all at once. **noch einmal** (once) again. **nicht einmal** not even. **-ig** adj unique.

Einmarsch ['aɪnmarʃ] m (pl **Einmärsche**) marching in, entry. **einmarschieren** v enter, march in (to).

einmischen ['aɪnmɪʃən] v **sich einmischen in** interfere or meddle in.

einmünden ['aɪnmyndən] v run or flow (into), join.

Einnahme ['aɪnnaːmə] f (pl -n) receipts pl, takings pl, revenue.

*einnehmen ['aɪnneːmən] v take (in); (Geld) receive.

Einöde ['aɪnøːdə] f (pl -n) desert, wasteland.

einölen ['aɪnøːlən] v oil.

einordnen ['aɪnɔrdnən] v order, arrange; (Mot) get in lane.

einpacken ['aɪnpakən] v pack, wrap up.

einpökeln ['aɪnpøːkəln] v pickle.

einprägen ['aɪnprɛːgən] v imprint. **jemandem etwas einprägen** impress something on somebody.

einrahmen ['aɪnraːmən] v frame.

einräumen ['aɪnrɔymən] v tidy up, put away; (zugeben) concede; (einrichten) furnish; (Platz) vacate, give up.

Einrede ['aɪnreːdə] f (pl -n) objection. **einreden** v persuade; (widersprechen) contradict.

einreichen ['aɪnraɪçən] v hand over or in.

Einreise ['aɪnraɪzə] f (pl -n) entry.

einrichten ['aɪnrɪçtən] v arrange, set up; (gründen) establish; (Zimmer) furnish. **Einrichtung** f establishment; arrangement; (Anstalt) institution; (Zimmer) fittings pl, furnishings pl.

einrücken ['aɪnrykən] v enter.

eins [aɪns] pron one.

einsam ['aɪnzaːm] adj lonely, solitary. **Einsamkeit** f loneliness.

Einsatz ['aɪnzats] m (pl **Einsätze**) insertion; insert, filling; (Spiel) stake; (Mil) mission, operation.

einschalten ['aɪnʃaltən] v switch on; (einfügen) insert, put in. **Einschaltung** f switching on; insertion.

einschiffen ['aɪnʃɪfən] v bring on board, load (into a ship). **sich einschiffen** go on board, embark.

*einschlafen ['aɪnʃlaːfən] v go to sleep, fall asleep.

Einschlag ['aɪnʃlaːk] m (pl **Einschläge**) impact; (Umschlag) wrapper. **einschlagen** v drive in, break; (einwickeln) wrap; (Weg) take, follow; (Hände) shake hands; (zustimmen) agree.

*einschließen ['aɪnʃliːsən] v lock up or in; (umfassen) comprise, include; (umzingeln) encircle. **einschließlich** adj inclusive; prep including, inclusive of. **Einschluß** m (pl **Einschlüsse**) inclusion.

einschmeicheln ['aɪnʃmaɪçəln] v **sich einschmeicheln bei** ingratiate oneself with.

einschränken ['aɪnʃrɛnkən] v restrict, limit. **Einschränkung** f restriction, limitation.

Einschreibebrief ['aɪnʃraɪbəbriːf] m registered letter. **einschreiben** v register; (eintragen) inscribe, write in. **per Einschreiben** adv (by) registered mail. **Einschreibung** f registration.

einschüchtern ['aɪnʃyçtərn] v intimidate.

*einsehen ['aɪnzeːən] v inspect, look over; (prüfen) examine; (begreifen) realize.

einseitig ['aɪnzaɪtɪç] adj one-sided; (Pol) unilateral.

einsenden ['aɪnzɛndən] v send in.

einsetzen ['aɪnzɛtsən] v set in, put in; (Amt) install; begin; (Geld) deposit.

Einsicht ['aɪnzɪçt] f (pl -en) insight; (Verständnis) understanding. **einsichtsvoll** adj judicious, sensible.

Einsiedler ['aɪnziːdlər] m (pl -) hermit.

einspannen ['aɪnʃpanən] v (Pferd) harness; (mit Rahmen) stretch.

einsperren ['aɪnʃpɛrən] v lock in or up; (Gefängnis) imprison, jail.

einspritzen ['aɪnʃprɪtsən] v inject.

Einspruch ['aɪnʃprux] m (pl **Einsprüche**) objection, protest. **Einspruch erheben gegen** raise an objection against.

einst [aɪnst] adv (Vergangenheit) once, at one time; (Zukunft) some day, one day.

einstecken ['aɪnʃtɛkən] v put in; (in die Tasche) pocket.

*einsteigen ['aɪnʃtaɪgən] v (Auto, Schiff, usw.) get in, get on, board.

einstellen ['aɪnʃtɛlən] v cease, stop; (tech) adjust; (phot) focus; (radio, usw.) tune. **–bar**

adj adjustable. **Einstellung** *f* stop, suspension; adjustment; (*Ansicht*) attitude.

einstig ['aɪnstɪç] *adj* former.

einstimmen ['aɪnʃtɪm ən] *v* agree; join (in). **einstimmig** *adj* unanimous.

einstmalig ['aɪnstm aːlɪç] *adj* former.

einstöckig ['aɪnʃtœ kɪç] *adj* one-storeyed.

***einstoßen** ['aɪnʃtoːsən] *v* push *or* drive in(to); (*Tür*) knock *or* break down.

einströmen ['aɪnʃtrœ ːm ən] *v* flow *or* stream in(to).

einstufen ['aɪnʃtuː fən] *v* classify, grade.

einstürmen ['aɪnʃtʏrm ən] *v* rush in; (*angreifen*) attack.

Einsturz ['aɪnʃtʊrts] *m* (*pl* **Einstürze**) downfall, collapse. **einstürzen** *v* collapse; (*niederreißen*) knock down, demolish.

einstweilen ['aɪnstvaɪlən] *adv* meanwhile, for the time being. **einstweilig** *adj* temporary, provisional.

eintägig ['aɪntɛːgɪç] *adj* one-day.

Eintausch ['aɪntaʊʃ] *m* exchange. **eintauschen** *v* exchange, trade.

einteilen ['aɪntaɪlən] *v* divide up, classify; (*Skala*) graduate; (*Arbeit*) plan out.

eintönig ['aɪntøː nɪç] *adj* monotonous.

Eintopf ['aɪntɔpf] *m* stew, casserole.

Eintracht ['aɪntraxt] *f* (*urz.*) harmony, unity.

Eintrag ['aɪntraːk] *m* (*pl* **Einträge**) (*Komm*) entry; (*Schaden*) damage. **eintragen** *v* carry in; (*einschreiben*) enter; (*einbringen*) yield. **einträglich** *adj* profitable. **Eintragung** *f* entry.

***eintreten** ['aɪntreːtən] *v* come in; (*eindrücken*) kick in; (*beitreten*) join; (*geschehen*) occur.

Eintritt ['aɪntrɪt] *m* entrance; (*Anfang*) beginning. **–skarte** *f* admission ticket.

einverleiben ['aɪnfɛrlaɪbən] *v* incorporate.

einverstanden ['aɪnfɛrʃtandən] *adj* in agreement. **einverstanden sein mit** agree with, approve of.

Einwand ['aɪnvant] *m* (*pl* **Einwände**) objection. **einwandfrei** *adj* perfect, faultless.

Einwanderer ['aɪnvandərər] *m* (*pl* -) immigrant. **einwandern** *v* immigrate. **Einwanderung** *f* immigration.

einwärts ['aɪnvɛrts] *adv* inwards.

einwechseln ['aɪnvɛksəln] *v* change; exchange.

Einwegflasche ['aɪnveːkflaʃə] *f* nonreturnable bottle.

einweichen ['aɪnvaɪçən] *v* soak, steep.

einweihen ['aɪnvaɪən] *v* inaugurate; (*Person*) initiate; (*Kirche*) consecrate. **Einweihung** *f* inauguration; initiation; consecration.

Einwendung ['aɪnvɛndʊŋ] *f* (*pl* -**en**) objection.

einwickeln ['aɪnvɪkəln] *v* wrap (up).

einwilligen ['aɪnvɪlɪgən] *v* consent, agree. **Einwilligung** *f* consent.

einwirken ['aɪnvɪrkən] *v* **einwirken auf** influence, affect. **Einwirkung** *f* influence.

Einwohner ['aɪnvoːnər] *m* (*pl* -) inhabitant.

Einzahl ['aɪntsaːl] *f* (*unz.*) (*Gramm*) singular.

einzahlen ['aɪntsaːlən] *v* pay in, deposit.

Einzel||erscheinung ['aɪntsəlɛrʃaɪnʊŋ] *f* (isolated) phenomenon. **–fall** *m* individual case. **–handel** *m* retail trade. **–handelsgeschäft** *neut* retail shop. **–händler** *m* retailer. **–haus** *neut* detached house. **–heit** *f* detail. **–kind** *neut* only child. **einzeln** *adj* single; (*getrennt*) isolated; (*alleinstehend*) detached. **einzelstehend** *adj* detached. **Einzelzimmer** *neut* single room.

einziehen ['aɪntsiːən] *v* pull *or* draw in; (*einkassieren*) collect; (*beschlagnahmen*) confiscate; (*Rekruten*) draft; (*Wohnung*) move in.

einzig ['aɪntsɪç] *adj* only, single.

Einzug ['aɪntsuːk] *m* entry, entrance; (*Wohnung*) moving in.

Eis [aɪs] *neut* (*unz.*) ice; (*Speise*) icecream. **–bahn** *f* ice/skating rink. **–bär** *m* polar bear. **–bein** *neut* knuckle of pork. **–berg** *m* iceberg.

Eischale ['aɪʃaːlə] *f* eggshell.

Eisen ['aɪzən] *neut* (*pl* -) iron. **–bahn** *f* railway. **–händler** *m* ironmonger. **–waren** *f pl* ironmongery.

eisern ['aɪzərn] *adj* iron.

eisig ['aɪzɪç] *adj* icy. **eiskalt** *adj* ice-cold.

Eis||lauf *m* skating. **–läufer** *m* (*pl* -) skater. **–laufbahn** *f* skating rink. **–meer** *neut* polar sea. **–regen** *m* freezing rain. **–tüte** *f* icecream cone/cornet. **–vogel** *m* kingfisher. **–würfel** *m* ice cube. **–zapfen** *m* icicle.

eitel ['aɪtəl] *adj* vain. **Eitelkeit** *f* vanity.

Eiter ['aɪtər] *m* (*unz.*) pus. **eitern** *v* fester, suppurate.

Eiweiß ['aɪvaɪs] *neut* (*pl* -**e**) egg-white; protein; albumen. **–stoff** *m* protein.

Ekel ['eːkəl] *m* (*unz.*) disgust, repugnance. **ekelhaft** *adj* loathsome, disgusting. **sich ekeln** be disgusted by.

Ekzem [ɛkˈtseːm] *neut* (*pl* -e) eczema.

elastisch [eˈlastʃ] *adj* elastic.

Elefant [eleˈfant] *m* (*pl* -en) elephant.

elegant [eleˈgant] *adj* elegant. **Eleganz** *f* elegance.

elektrifizieren [elektrifiˈtsiːrən] *v also* **elektrisieren** electrify. **Elektriker** *m* electrician. **elektrisch** *adj* electric(al). **Elektrizität** *f* electricity.

Elektro||gerät [eˈlɛktrogəˌrɛːt] *neut* electric appliance. **–installateur** *m* electrician. **–motor** *m* electric motor.

Elektronik [elɛkˈtroːnik] *f* electronics. **elektronisch** *adj* electronic.

Elektrotechnik [elɛktroˈtɛçnik] *f* electrical engineering.

Element [eleˈmɛnt] *neut* (*pl* -e) element; (*Zelle*) battery. **elementar** *adj* elementary.

elend ['eːlɛnt] *adj* miserable. **Elend** *neut* misery. **–sviertel** *neut* slums *pl*.

elf [ɛlf] *pron, adj* eleven.

Elf [ɛlf] *m* (*pl* -en) elf, fairy.

elfte [ɛlftə] *adj* eleventh.

Elfenbein ['ɛlfənbain] *neut* (*unz.*) ivory.

Elite [eˈliːtə] *f* (*pl* -n) elite.

Ellbogen ['ɛlboːgən] *m* (*pl* -) elbow.

Ellipse [ɛˈlipsə] *f* (*pl* -n) ellipse. **elliptisch** *adj* elliptical.

Elsaß ['ɛlzas] *neut* Alsace. **Elsässer** *m* (*pl* -), **Elsässerin** *f* (*pl* -nen) Alsatian. **elsäsisch** *adj* Alsatian.

Elster ['ɛlstər] *f* (*pl* -n) magpie.

Eltern ['ɛltərn] *pl* parents. **elterlich** *adj* parental.

Email [eˈm aːj] *neut* (*pl* -s) enamel.

E-mail ['iːmeil] *neut, f* (*pl* -s) e-mail. **ein(e) E-mail (an jemanden) schicken/senden** e-mail someone.

emanzipieren [em antsipiːrən] *v* emancipate. **Emanzipation** *f* emancipation.

Empfang [ɛmˈpfaŋ] *m* (*pl* **Empfänge**) welcome, reception. **empfangen** *v* welcome. receive; (*Kind*) conceive. **Empfänger** *m* receiver. **empfänglich** *adj* susceptible. **Empfängnis** *f* conception. **–verhütung** *f* contraception.

*empfehlen [ɛmˈpfeːlən] *v* recommend.

–swert *adj* to be recommended. **Empfehlung** *f* recommendation. **–sschreiben** letter of recommendation.

empfinden [ɛmˈpfindən] *v* feel. **empfindlich** *adj* sensitive; (*reizbar*) touchy. **Empfindung** *f* feeling; (*Wahrnehmung*) perception.

empor [ɛmˈpoːr] *adv* up(wards). **–ragen** *v* tower (up/over). **–streben** *v* struggle up(wards).

empören [ɛmˈpøːrən] *v* shock, revolt; (*erregen*) stir up. **sich empören** rebel.

emsig ['ɛm ziː] *adj* diligent, industrious.

Ende ['ɛndə] *neut* (*pl* -n) end.

endemisch [ɛnˈdeːm ʃ] *adj* endemic.

enden ['ɛndən] *v* finish, end. **endgültig** *adj* final. **–lich** *adv* finally, at last; (*beschränkt*) finite. **–los** *adj* endless, infinite.

End||punkt *m* end (point). **–spiel** *neut* (*Sport*) final. **–station** *f* terminus. **–zweck** *m* (ultimate) goal *or* purpose.

Energie [enɛrˈgiː] *f* (*pl* -n) energy. **–krise** energy crisis. **energisch** *adj* energetic.

eng [ɛŋ] *adj* narrow; (*dicht*) tight, close; (*Freund*) close. **Enge** *f* narrowness; tightness; (*Klemme*) difficulty.

Engel ['ɛŋəl] *m* (*pl* -) angel. **engelhaft** *adj* angelic.

England ['ɛŋlant] *neut* England. **Engländer** *m* (*pl* -) Englishman. **Engländerin** *f* (*pl* -nen) Englishwoman, *ich bin Engländer(in)* I am English. **englisch** adj English.

Engpaß ['ɛŋpas] *m* narrow pass; (*verkehr*) bottleneck; (*Klemme*) difficulty, tight spot.

engros [ãˈgroː] *adv* wholesale.

engstirnig ['ɛŋʃtirniç] *adj* narrow-minded.

Enkel ['ɛŋkəl] *m* (*pl* -) grandson. **–in** *f* granddaughter. **–kind** *neut* grandchild.

enorm [eˈnɔrm] *adj* enormous.

entarten [ɛntaˈrtən] *v* degenerate. **Entartung** *f* degeneracy, degeneration.

entbehrlich [ɛntˈbeːrliç] *adj* dispensable, (to) spare.

*entbinden [ɛntˈbindən] *v* release, set free; (*eine Frau*) deliver. **Entbindung** *f* release, setting free; (*Geburt*) delivery.

entblößen [ɛntˈbløːsən] *v* uncover; (*berauben*) deprive, rob.

entdecken [ɛntˈdɛkən] *v* discover. **Entdecker** *m* discoverer. **Entdeckung** *f* discovery.

Ente ['ɛntə] *f* (*pl* -n) duck; (*Falschmeldung*,

Lüge) hoax, canard.

entehren [ɛntˈeːɐn] *v* dishonour, disgrace.

enteignen [ɛntˈaignən] *v* expropriate, dispossess. **Enteignung** *f* expropriation; seizure.

enterben [ɛntˈɛrbən] *v* disinherit.

*****entfallen** [ɛntˈfalən] *v* fall *or* slip from; *(Gedächtnis)* slip, escape.

entfalten [ɛntˈfaltən] *v* unfold; *(zeigen)* display. *(Mil)* deploy; **Entfaltung** *f* unfolding; display; deployment; development.

entfernen [ɛntˈfɛrnən] *v* remove. **sich entfernen** go away, withdraw. **Entfernung** *f* distance; *(Wegbringen)* removal.

entflammen [ɛntˈflamən] *v* inflame, kindle.

*****entfliehen** [ɛntˈfliːən] *v* flee from.

entfremden [ɛntˈfrɛmdən] *v* alienate, estrange. **Entfremdung** *f* alienation, estrangement.

entführen [ɛntˈfyːrən] *v* abduct; *(Flugzeug)* hijack. **Entführer** *m* abductor, kidnapper; hijacker. **Entführung** *f* abduction, kidnapping; hijacking.

entgegen [ɛntˈgeːgən] *prep* against, contrary to; *(hinzu)* towards, *adv* towards. **–kommen** *v* meet; *(Kompromiß)* make concessions. **–sehen** *v* look forward to. **–treten** *v* move towards; *(widerstehen)* oppose. **–wirken** *v* work against.

entgegnen [ɛntˈgeːgnən] *v* retort, answer back.

*****entgehen** [ɛntˈgeːən] *v* escape from.

Entgelt [ɛntˈgɛlt] *neut (unz.)* compensation.

entgiften [ɛntˈgiftən] *v* decontaminate.

entgleisen [ɛntˈglaizən] *v* be *or* become derailed. **Entgleisung** *f* derailment.

entgräten [ɛntˈgrɛːtən] *v* bone; fillet (fish).

enthaaren [ɛntˈhaːrən] *v* remove hair from, depilate.

*****enthalten** [ɛntˈhaltən] *v* hold, contain. **sich enthalten** refrain (from). **enthaltsam** *adj* abstemious. **Enthaltung** *f* abstention.

enthaupten [ɛntˈhauptən] *v* behead, decapitate.

enthüllen [ɛntˈhylən] *v* uncover, reveal.

Enthusiasmus [ɛntuˈziasmʊs] *m (unz.)* enthusiasm. **enthusiastisch** *adj* enthusiastic.

entkernen [ɛntˈkɛrnən] *v (Obst)* stone.

entkleiden [ɛntˈklaidən] *v (Person)* undress,

strip; *(wegnehmen)* diverst. **sich entkleiden** undress.

entkoffeiniert [ɛntkofaˈiniːrt] *adj* decaffeinated, decaf.

*****entkommen** [ɛntˈkomən] *v* escape.

entkuppeln [ɛntˈkʊpəln] *v* disconnect; *(Mot)* declutch.

entladen [ɛntˈlaːdən] *v* unload; *(Gewehr, Batterie)* discharge.

entlang [ɛntˈlaŋ] *prep, adv* along. **–fahren** *v* travel along. **–gehen** walk along.

*****entlassen** [ɛntˈhasən] *v* dismiss, discharge, *(umg.)* fire, sack; *(Gefangene)* release. **entlassen werden** be dismissed, *(coll)* get the sack. **Entlassung** *f* dismissal, discharge; release.

entlasten [ɛntˈlastən] *v* unburden; *(erleichtern)* relieve; *(Bank)* credit; *(Verdachtsperson)* clear, exonerate.

entleeren [ɛntˈleːrən] *v* empty. **sich entleeren** relieve oneself.

entlegen [ɛntˈleːgən] *adj* remote.

entmilitarisieren [ɛntmilitariˈziːrən] *v* demilitarize.

entmutigen [ɛntˈmuːtigən] *v* discourage. **Entmutigung** *f* discouragement.

Entnahme [ɛntˈnaːmə] *f (unz.)* taking *or* drawing out; *(Geld)* withdrawal; *(Strom)* use.

entnazifizieren [ɛntnatsifiˈtsiːrən] *v* denazify.

*****entnehmen** [ɛntˈneːmən] *v* take away *or* out; *(folgern)* conclude, infer; *(Geld)* withdraw; *(Strom)* use. **Entnehmer** *m (Komm)* drawer (of bills); *(Strom)* user.

entrahmen [ɛntˈraːmən] *v* skim (milk).

entrüsten [ɛntˈrystən] *v* irritate, anger. **Entrüstung** *f* indignation, anger.

entsagen [ɛntˈzaːgən] *v* renounce, give up.

entschädigen [ɛntˈʃɛːdigən] *v* compensate. **Entschädigung** *f* compensation.

entschärfen [ɛntˈʃɛrfən] *v* defuse.

Entscheid [ɛntˈʃait] *m (pl -e)* decision. **entscheiden** *v* decide. **sich entscheiden** decide, resolve, make up one's mind. **entscheidend** *adj* decisive. **Entscheidung** *f* decision; *(Urteil)* sentence.

entschieden [ɛntˈʃiːdən] *adj* determined, resolute. *adv* decidedly. **Entschiedenheit** *f* determination.

*****entschließen** [ɛntˈʃliːsən] *v* **sich entschließen** decide, determine.

entschlossen [ɛntʃbsən] *adj* determined, resolute.

Entschluß [ɛntʃlus] *m* (*pl* **Entschlüsse**) decision. **–kraft** *f* power of decision, decisiveness.

entschlüsseln [ɛntʃlysəln] *v* decipher, decode.

entschuldigen [ɛntʃuldɪgən] *v* excuse, pardon. **sich entschuldigen** apologize, excuse oneself. **entschuldigen Sie!** excuse me! **Entschuldigung** *f* apology; *interj* I'm sorry! pardon me!

entsetzen [ɛntzɛtsən] *v* horrify, appal; (*von einem Posten*) dismiss; (*Mil*) relieve. **Entsetzen** *neut* horror. **entsetzlich** *adj* dreadful, horrible. **entsetzt** *adj* horrified, shocked.

entspannen [ɛntʃpanən] *v* relax, release. **sich entspannen** relax, calm down. **Entspannung** *f* relaxation; (*Pol*) détente.

*****entsprechen** [ɛntʃprɛçən] *v* correspond (to); (*Anforderung*) comply with. **entsprechend** *adj* corresponding, appropriate.

*****entspringen** [ɛntʃprɪŋən] *v* escape from, run away from.

entstammen [ɛntʃtam ən] *v* descend (from).

*****entstehen** [ɛntʃteːən] *v* arise, originate. **Entstehung** *f* origin.

enttäuschen [ɛntɔyʃən] *v* disappoint. **enttäuscht** *adj* disappointed. **Enttäuschung** *f* disappointment.

entvölkern [ɛntfœ kərn] *v* depopulate.

*****entwachsen** [ɛntvaksən] *v* grow out of.

entwaffnen [ɛntvafnən] *v* disarm.

entwässern [ɛntvɛsərn] *v* drain; (*austrocknen*) dehydrate. **Entwässerung** *f* drainage; dehydration.

entweder [ɛntveːdər] *conj* either.

*****entweichen** [ɛntvaɪçən] *v* escape.

entweihen [ɛntvaɪən] *v* desecrate, profane.

*****entwerfen** [ɛntvɛrfən] *v* design, plan; (*skizzieren*) sketch; (*Fassung*) draft, draw up.

entwerten [ɛntvɛrtən] *v* devalue; (*Briefmarke*) cancel. **Entwertung** *f* devaluation; cancellation.

entwickeln [ɛntvɪkəln] *v* develop. **sich entwickeln** develop. **Entwicklung** *f* development. **Entwicklungs‖land** *neut* developing country. **–lehre** *f* theory of evolution.

entwirren [ɛntvɪrən] *v* disentangle.

entwischen [ɛntvɪʃən] *v* slip *or* steal away from.

entwürdigen [ɛntvyrdɪgən] *v* degrade, debase.

Entwurf [ɛntvurf] *m* (*pl* **Entwürfe**) desingn, plan; (*Skizee*) sketch; (*Fassung*) draft.

entwurzeln [ɛntvurtsəln] *v* uproot; (*vernichten*) eradicate.

*****entziehen** [ɛnttsɪən] *v* take away, withdraw; (*rauben*) deprive.

entziffern [ɛnttsɪfərn] *v* decipher, make out.

entzücken [ɛnttsʏkən] *v* delight, enchant. **Entzücken** *neut* delight, enchantment. **entzückt** *adj* delighted, enchanted. **entzückend** *adj* delightful, enchanting.

entzündbar [ɛnttsʏntbaːr] *adj* inflammable. **entzünden** *adj* kindle, light. **sich entzünden** catch fire. **Entzündung** *f* ignition; (*med*) inflammation.

entzwei [ɛnttsvaɪ] *adv* in two, asunder. **–brechen** *v* break in two.

Enzyklopädie [ɛntsʏkbpɛˈdiː] *f* (*pl* **-n**) encyclopedia.

Epidemie [epideˈmiː] *f* (*pl* **-n**) epidemic. **epidemisch** *adj* epidemic.

Epilepsie [epiˈlɛpsiː] *f* (*unz.*) epilepsy. **Epileptiker** *m* epileptic. **epileptisch** *adj* epileptic.

Episode [epiˈzoːdə] *f* (*pl* **-n**) episode.

er [ɛr] *pron* he.

erachten [ɛˈraxtən] *v* think, consider. **Erachten** *neut* opinion, judgment. **meines Erachtens** in my opinion.

Erbarmen [ɛrˈbam ən] *neut* (*unz.*) pity, compassion. **erbärmlich** *adj* pitiful, pitiable. **erbarmungs‖los** *adj* merciless, pitiless. **–voll** *adj* compassionate, merciful.

erbauen [ɛrˈbauən] *v* build, erect.

Erbe [ˈɛrbə] *m* (*pl* **-n**) heir; *neut* (*unz.*) inheritance. **Erbeinheit** *f* gene. **erben** *v* inherit. **Erb‖fehler** *m* hereditary defect. **–feind** *m* traditional enemy. **–gut** *neut* inheritance; (*Erbhof*) ancestral estate. **erblich** *adj* hereditary.

erbittern [ɛrˈbɪtərn] *v* embitter. **erbittert** *adj* embittered, bitter.

erblassen [ɛrˈblasən] *v* grow pale.

erblicken [ɛrˈblɪkən] *v* glimpse, catch sight of.

erblinden [ɛrˈblɪndən] *v* blind.

*erbrechen [ɛrˈbrɛçən] v **sich erbrechen** vomit.

Erbschaft [ˈɛrpʃaft] v (pl -en) legacy, inheritance.

Erbse [ˈɛrpsə] f (pl -n) pea.

Erd||beben [ˈɛːrtbeːbən] neut (pl -) earthquake. **–beere** f strawberry. **–boden** m earth, soil.

Erde [ˈeːrdə] v (pl -n) earth. **erden** v (Strom) earth.

*erdenken [ɛrˈdɛŋkən] v think of, think out; (erfinden) invent.

Erdgas neut natural gas.

erdichten [ɛrˈdɪçtən] v fabricate, invent. **Erdichtung** f fabrication, invention.

Erd||kreis m globe, earth. **–kunde** f geography. **erdkundlich** adj geographic(al). **Erd||nuß** f peanut. **–öl** neut oil, petroleum.

erdrosseln [ɛrˈdrɔsəln] v strangle.

erdulden [ɛrˈdʊldən] v endure.

ereignen [ɛrˈaignən] v **sich ereignen** happen. **Ereignis** neut event, occurrence.

*erfahren [ɛrˈfaːrən] v experience; (hören, lernen) learn, hear of. adj experienced, proficient. **Erfahrung** f experience.

erfassen [ɛrˈfasən] v seize; (einschließen) include; (begreifen) understand, grasp.

*erfinden [ɛrˈfɪndən] v invent. **Erfinder** m inventor. **erfinderisch** adj inventive. **Erfindung** f invention.

Erfolg [ɛrˈfɔlk] m (pl -e) success; (Ergebnis) result, outcome. **Erfolg haben** achieve success, succeed. **erfolgen** v result, follow. **erfolg||los** adj unsuccessful. **–reich** adj successful.

erforderlich [ɛrˈfɔrdərlɪç] adj necessary. **erfordern** v require, need; (verlangen) demand. **Erfordernis** neut necessity; (Voraussetzung) requirement.

erforschen [ɛrˈfɔrʃən] v investigate. **Erforsch||er** m investigator. **–ung** f investigation.

erfreuen [ɛrˈfrɔyən] v delight. **sich erfreuen an** enjoy, take delight in. **erfreulich** adj gratifying. **erfreut** adj gratified.

*erfrieren [ɛrˈfriːrən] v freeze to death. **Erfrierung** f frostbite.

erfrischen [ɛrˈfrɪʃən] v refresh. **–d** adj refreshing. **Erfrischung** f refreshment.

erfüllen [ɛrˈfʏlən] v fill; (Aufgabe) carry out; (Bitte, Forderung) comply with, fulfil.

Erfüllung f accomplishment, fulfilment.

ergänzen [ɛrˈgɛntsən] v supplement, add to; (vervollständigen) complete, **Ergänzung** f supplement; completion.

*ergeben [ɛrˈgeːbən] v yield. **sich ergeben** surrender; (folgen) result. **Ergebenheit** f devotion; (Fügsamkeit) submissiveness. **Ergebnis** neut result.

*ergehen [ɛrˈgeːən] v (Gesetz) be promulgated, come out.

ergiebig [ɛrˈgiːbiç] adj productive, profitable.

*ergreifen [ɛrˈgraifən] v grasp, seize; (rühren) touch, move (deeply). **–d** adj touching, affecting. **Ergreifung** f seizure.

erhaben [ɛrˈhaːbən] adj exalted, sublime.

*erhalten [ɛrˈhaltən] v receive, obtain; (bewahren) preserve, maintain. **erhältlich** adj available, obtainable. **Erhaltung** f preservation, maintenance.

*erheben [ɛrˈheːbən] v lift up; (Einspruch) raise. **sich erheben** rise (up). **Anspruch erheben auf** lay claim to. **erheblich** adj considerable. **Erhebung** f uprising.

erheitern [ɛrˈhaitərn] v cheer up; (unterhalten) amuse. **sich erheitern** (Himmel) brighten, clear up.

erhitzen [ɛrˈhɪtsən] v heat (up); (Person) inflame.

erhöhen [ɛrˈhøːən] v raise, heighten. **Erhöhung** f raising, heightening.

erholen [ɛrˈhoːlən] v **sich erholen** recover, get better; (sich ausruhen) rest. **Erholung** f recovery; rest; (Unterhaltung) recreation.

erinnern [ɛrˈɪnərn] v remind. **sich erinnern an** remember. **Erinnerung** f (pl -en) memory, remembrance.

erkälten [ɛrˈkɛltən] v cool. **sich erkälten** catch (a) cold. **Erkältung** f (pl -en) (Med) cold.

erkennbar [ɛrˈkɛnbaːr] adj recognizable. **erkennen** v recognize; (Fehler) acknowledge; (merken) perceive.

Erkenntnis¹ [ɛrˈkɛntnɪs] neut (pl -se) judgment, sentence.

Erkenntnis² f (pl -se) recognition; (Einsicht) understanding.

Erkenn||ung [ɛrˈkɛnuŋ] f (pl -en) recognition. **–ungswort** neut password. **–ungszeichen** neut distinguishing mark.

Erkerfenster [ˈɛrkərfɛnstər] neut bay window.

Ersatz | 263

erklären [ɛʁˈklɛːʁən] v explain; (*aussprechen*) declare. **sich erklären** declare oneself. **Erklärung** f explanation; declaration.

erkranken [ɛʁˈkʁaŋkən] v fall ill, become sick.

erkundigen [ɛʁˈkʊndɪɡən] v **sich erkundigen (nach)** inquire (about). **Erkundigung** f inquiry.

erlangen [ɛʁˈlaŋən] v obtain, acquire; (*erreichen*) get to, reach.

Erlaß [ɛʁˈlas] m (pl **Erlässe**) decree, edict.

*erlassen [ɛʁˈlasən] v issue; (*befreien*) release, absolve.

erlauben [ɛʁˈlaubən] v permit. **Erlaubnis** f permission.

erläutern [ɛʁˈlɔʏtəʁn] v explain, elucidate. **Erläuterung** f explanation; pl commentary, notes.

erleben [ɛʁˈleːbən] v live through, experience. **Erlebnis** neut (pl -se) experience.

erledigen [ɛʁˈleːdɪɡən] v take care of, deal with; (*beenden*) finish (off). **erledigt** adj settled; (*erschöpft*) exhausted. **Erledigung** f (pl -en) carrying out, execution.

erlegen [ɛʁˈleːɡən] v kill.

erleichtern [ɛʁˈlaɪçtəʁn] v ease, aid, lighten. **Erleichterung** f (pl -en) relief.

*erleiden [ɛʁˈlaɪdən] v suffer, undergo.

erlernen [ɛʁˈlɛʁnən] v learn, acquire.

Erlös [ɛʁˈløːs] m (pl -e) proceeds pl.

*erlöschen [ɛʁˈløʃən] v go or die out.

ermächtigen [ɛʁˈmɛçtɪɡən] v authorize, empower.

ermahnen [ɛʁˈmaːnən] v admonish.

Ermangelung [ɛʁˈmaŋəlʊŋ] f (pl -) **in Ermangelung** in the absence or default (of).

ermäßigen [ɛʁˈmɛːsɪɡən] v reduce, lower. **Ermäßigung** f reduction.

ermitteln [ɛʁˈmɪtəln] v ascertain, find out.

ermöglichen [ɛʁˈmøːklɪçən] v enable, render possible.

ermorden [ɛʁˈmɔʁdən] v murder, assassinate.

ermüden [ɛʁˈmyːdən] v tire out; grow tired.

ermuntern [ɛʁˈmʊntəʁn] v encourage, cheer up.

ermutigen [ɛʁˈmuːtɪɡən] v encourage. **Ermutigung** f encouragement.

ernähren [ɛʁˈnɛːʁən] v feed, nourish. **sich ernähren** support oneself. **Ernährer** m

breadwinner. **Ernährung** f nourishment.

*ernennen [ɛʁˈnɛnən] v appoint, designate. **Ernennung** f appointment.

erneuern [ɛʁˈnɔʏəʁn] v renew; renovate, restore. **Erneuerung** f renewal; renovation. **erneut** adj repeated; adv again.

erniedrigen [ɛʁˈniːdʁɪɡən] v lower; (*degradieren*) degrade, humble. **sich erniedrigen** v demean oneself.

ernst [ɛʁnst] adj serious, grave. **Ernst** m seriousness, gravity. **im Ernst** in earnest. **ernsthaft** adj earnest, serious. **–lich** adj serious.

Ernte [ˈɛʁntə] f (pl -n) harvest; (*Wein*) vintage. **ernten** v harvest, reap.

ernüchtern [ɛʁˈnʏçtəʁn] v disillusion, disenchant; (*vom Rausch*) sober (up). **sich ernüchtern** sober up. **Ernüchterung** f disillusionment; sobering up.

Eroberer [ɛʁˈoːbəʁəʁ] m (pl -) conqueror. **erobern** v conquer. **Eroberung** f conquest.

eröffnen [ɛʁˈœfnən] v open; (*anfangen*) open, begin. **Eröffnung** f opening, beginning.

erörtern [ɛʁˈœʁtəʁn] v discuss. **Erörterung** f discussion.

Erotik [eˈʁoːtɪk] f (unz.) eroticism. **erotisch** adj erotic.

erpressen [ɛʁˈpʁɛsən] v (*Sache*) extort; (*Person*) blackmail. **Erpresser** m blackmailer. **erpresserisch** adj extortionate. **Erpressung** f blackmail, extortion.

erproben [ɛʁˈpʁoːbən] v try (out), test. **Erprobung** f trial, test.

*erraten [ɛʁˈʁaːtən] v guess.

errechnen [ɛʁˈʁɛçnən] v calculate.

erregen [ɛʁˈʁeːɡən] v excite; (*hervorrufen*) create, produce. **erregbar** adj excitable. **erregend** adj exciting. **erregt** adj excited. **Erregung** f excitement.

erreichen [ɛʁˈʁaɪçən] v attain, reach. **erreichbar** adj attainable. **Erreichung** f attainment.

errichten [ɛʁˈʁɪçtən] v erect, build; (*gründen*) set up, establish.

erröten [ɛʁˈʁøːtən] v blush.

Errungenschaft [ɛʁˈʁʊŋənʃaft] f (pl -en) achievement.

Ersatz [ɛʁˈzats] m (unz.) substitute; (*Wiedergutmachung*) compensation; (*Nachschub*) reinforcements pl. **–kaffee** m coffee substitute. **–rad** neut spare wheel.

–spieler m (*Sport*) substitute. **–teil** neut spare part.

***erschaffen** [ɛr'ʃafən] v create. **Erschaffer** m creator. **Erschaffung** f creation.

***erscheinen** [ɛr'ʃainən] v appear. **Erscheinung** f phenomenon; (*Aussehen*) appearance.

***erschießen** [ɛr'ʃiːsən] v shoot (dead). **Erschießungskommando** neut firing squad.

***erschließen** [ɛr'ʃliːsən] v open up; (*folgern*) infer, deduce.

erschöpfen [ɛr'ʃœpfən] v exhaust, use up; (*Person*) exhaust, tire out. **erschöpft** adj exhausted. **Erschöpfung** f exhaustion.

***erschrecken** [ɛr'ʃrɛkən] v scare, frighten; be frightened or scared. **Erschrecken** neut fright. **erschreckend** adj frightening.

erschrocken [ɛr'ʃrɔkən] adj frightened, terrified. **Erschrockenheit** f fright, terror.

erschüttern [ɛr'ʃʏtərn] v shake; (*Person*) shake, disturb, shock. **Erschütterung** f shock.

erschweren [ɛr'ʃvɛːrən] v make (more) difficult, aggravate.

***ersehen** [ɛr'zeːən] v perceive, see.

ersetzen [ɛr'zɛtsən] v replace; (*Schaden*) make good. **ersetzlich** adj replaceable, renewable.

ersichtlich [ɛr'zɪçtlɪç] adj evident.

***ersinnen** [ɛr'zɪnən] v contrive, devise.

ersparen [ɛr'ʃpaːrən] v save.

erst [eːrst] adj first. adv at first; (*nur*) only, just.

erstarren [ɛr'ʃtarən] v stiffen, become rigid; (*Flüssigkeit*) congeal, solidify. **Erstarrung** f stiffness.

erstatten [ɛr'ʃtatən] v restore; (*ersetzen*) replace. **Bericht erstatten** report, make a report. **Erstattung** f restitution.

Erstaufführung ['eːrstaufyːruŋ] f (pl -en) première, first performance.

erstaunen [ɛr'ʃtaunən] v astonish; be astonished. **Erstaunen** neut astonishment, amazement. **erstaunlich** adj astonishing.

erste(r) ['eːrstə (r)] **erste**, **erste(s)** adj first.

erstens ['eːrstəns] adv first(ly).

ersticken [ɛr'ʃtɪkən] v suffocate; (*fig*) stifle. **erstickend** adj suffocating. **Erstickung** f suffocation; stifling.

erst||klassig adj first-class. **–malig** adj for the first time, first-time.

erstrecken [ɛr'ʃtrɛkən] v **sich erstrecken** stretch, extend.

ertappen [ɛr'tapən] v catch, surprise. **auf frischer Tat ertappen** catch red-handed.

Ertrag [ɛr'traːk] m (pl Erträge) profit; (*Boden*) yield. **ertragen** v bear, stand. **erträglich** adj bearable, tolerable.

ertränken [ɛr'trɛŋkən] v (cause to) drown.

***ertrinken** [ɛr'trɪŋkən] v drown, be drowned.

erwachen [ɛr'vaxən] v awake, wake up.

***erwachsen** [ɛr'vaksən] v grow up. **Erwachsene(r)** m adult.

***erwägen** [ɛr'vɛːgən] v consider, weigh. **Erwägung** f consideration.

erwähnen [ɛr'vɛːnən] v mention. **Erwähnung** f mention.

erwärmen [ɛr'vɛːrm ən] v warm, heat.

erwarten [ɛr'vartən] v expect. **über Erwarten** better than expectation. **wider Erwarten** contrary to expectation. **Erwartung** f (pl -en) expectation.

erwecken [ɛr'vɛkən] v awaken; (*erregen*) arouse, rouse.

***erweisen** [ɛr'vaizən] v prove; (*Dienst*) render, do; (*Ehrung*) pay. **sich erweisen als** prove to be.

erweitern [ɛr'vaitərn] v enlarge, widen. extend. **Erweiterung** f (pl -en) extension, enlargement.

Erwerb [ɛr'vɛrp] m (pl -e) acquisition; (*Lohn*) earnings. **erwerben** v acquire; (*Verdienen*) earn. **erwerbstätig** adj (gainfully) employed. **Erwerbung** f acquisition.

erwidern [ɛr'viːdərn] v reply; (*vergelten*) retaliate. **Erwiderung** f reply.

erwischen [ɛr'vɪʃən] v (*Person*) catch.

erwünscht [ɛr'vʏnʃt] adj desired, wished-for.

erwürgen [ɛr'vʏrgən] v strangle.

Erz [eːrts] neut (pl -e) ore.

erzählen [ɛr'tsɛːlən] v tell, relate. **Erzähler** m narrator; story-teller. **erzählerisch** adj narrative. **Erzählung** f story.

Erz||bischof n archbishop. **–engel** m archangel.

erzeugen [ɛr'tsɔygən] v (*herstellen*) produce; (*Strom*) generate; (*Kinder*) procreate. **Erzeuger** m producer; father, procreator. **Erzeugnis** neut product(ion); (*Boden*) produce.

Erz||feind m arch-enemy. **–herzog** m

archduke. **–herzogin** f archduchess.

*erziehen [ɛɐˈtsiːən] v (Tiere, Menschen) bring up; (Bildung) educate. **Erzieher** m educator. **erzieherisch** adj educational. **Erziehung** f upbringing; (Bildung) education.

erzogen [ɛɐˈtsoːgən] adj **gut/schlecht erzogen** well/badly brought up.

es [ɛs] pron it.

Esche [ˈɛʃə] f (pl -n) ash (tree).

Esel [ˈeːzəl] m (pl -) donkey, ass. **eselhaft** adj asinine. **Eselsohr** neut dog-ear (on page).

esoterisch [ezoˈteːrɪʃ] adj esoteric.

Essay [ˈɛseː] m, neut (pl -s) essay.

eßbar [ˈɛsbaɐ] adj edible.

essen [ˈɛsən] v eat. **zu Mittag essen** lunch, have lunch. **zu Abend essen** dine, have supper. **Essen** neut food; (Mahlzeit) meal.

Essig [ˈɛsɪç] m (pl -e) vinegar. **–gurke** f pickled cucumber, gherkin.

Eß||kastanie f sweet chestnut. **–löffel** m tablespoon. **–tisch** m dinner table. **–zimmer** neut dining room.

Estland [ˈɛstlant] neut Estonia. **Este** m, **Estin** f Estonian. **estnisch** adj Estonian.

etablieren [etaˈbliːrən] v establish.

Etage [eˈtaːʒə] f (pl -n) storey, floor. **–nwohnung** f flat, (US) apartment.

Etat [eˈtaː] m (pl -s) budget; (Komm) balance-sheet.

Ethik [ˈeːtɪk] f (unz.) ethics. **ethisch** adj ethical.

ethnisch [ˈeːtnɪʃ] adj ethnic.

Etikett [etɪkɛt] neut (pl -e) tag, label. **Etikette** [etɪkɛtə] f (pl -n) etiquette.

etliche [ˈɛtlɪçə] pron pl some, several.

Etui [ɛtˈviː] neut (pl -s) (small) case; (Zigaretten) cigarette-case; (Brillen) spectacles-case.

etwa [ˈɛtva] adv about, around; (vielleicht) perhaps.

etwas [ˈɛtvas] pron something, anything. adj some, any, a little.

Etymologie [etymoloˈgiː] f (pl -n) etymology.

EU f EU.

euch [ɔyç] pron you; (to) you.

euer [ˈɔyɐ] pl adj your. pron yours.

Eule [ˈɔylə] f (pl -n) owl.

Eunuch [ɔyˈnuːx] m (pl -en) eunuch.

Euro [ˈɔyroː] m (pl - or -s) euro. **Eurozone** f eurozone.

Europa [ɔyˈroːpa] neut Europe. **Europäer** m European. **europäisch** adj European. **Europäische Gemeinschaft (EG)** European Community. **Europäische Union (EU)** European Union.

evakuieren [evakuˈiːrən] v evacuate.

evangelisch [evanˈɡeːlɪʃ] adj Protestant. **Evangelium** neut gospel.

eventuell [evɛntuˈɛl] adj possible. adv possibly, if necessary.

ewig [ˈeːvɪç] adj eternal, everlasting. **auf ewig** for ever. **Ewigkeit** f eternity.

exakt [ɛˈksakt] adj exact, accurate.

Examen [ɛˈksaːmən] neut (pl -, or Examina) exam(ination).

Exempel [ɛˈksɛmpəl] neut (pl -) example.

Exemplar [ɛksɛmˈplaːr] neut (pl -e) specimen; (Buch) copy.

Exil [eˈksiːl] neut (pl -e) exile.

Existenz [ɛksɪsˈtɛnts] f (pl -en) existence; (Unterhalt) livelihood. **existieren** v exist.

exklusiv [ɛkskluˈziːf] adj exclusive, upmarket.

exkommunizieren [ɛkskɔmunitsiːrən] v excommunicate.

exotisch [ɛˈksoːtɪʃ] adj exotic.

Expedition [ɛkspediˈtsioːn] f (pl -en) expedition; (Versendung) dispatching.

Experiment [ɛksperiˈmɛnt] neut (pl -e) experiment. **experimentell** adj experimental. **experimentieren** v experiment.

explodieren [ɛksploˈdiːrən] v explode. **Explosion** f explosion. **explosiv** adj explosive.

Export [ɛksˈpɔrt] m (pl -e) export. **–eur** m exporter. **–handel** m export trade. **exportieren** v export.

extrem [ɛksˈtreːm] adj extreme. **Extrem||ismus** m extremism. **–ist(in)** extremist.

Exzentriker [ɛksˈtsɛntrɪkɐ] m (pl -) eccentric. **exzentrisch** adj eccentric.

F

Fabel [ˈfaːbəl] f (pl -n) fable; (Handlungs-

ablauf) plot. **fabelhaft** *adj* fabulous, marvellous.

Fabrik [fáˈbriːk] *f* (*pl* -en) factory. **-ant** *m* (*pl* -en) manufacturer. **-arbeiter(in)** factory worker. **-at** *neut* (*pl* -e) manufacture. **fabrizieren** *v* manufacture.

Fach [fax] *neut* (*pl* **Fächer**) (*Abteil*) compartment, pigeonhole; (*Wissensgebiet*) subject; speciality. **-arbeiter** *m* skilled worker. **-arzt** *m* medical specialist.

fächeln [ˈfɛçəln] *v* fan. **Fächer** *m* (*pl* -) fan.

Fach||mann *m* specialist. **-schule** *f* technical college *or* school. **-sprache** *f* technical language, jargon. **-wort** *neut* technical term. **-zeitschrift** *f* technical journal.

Fackel [ˈfakəl] *f* (*pl* -n) torch.

fade [ˈfaːdə] *adj* insipid, boring; (*Essen*) tasteless.

Faden [ˈfaːdən] *m* (*pl* **Fäden**) thread.

Fagott [faˈɡɔt] *neut* (*pl* -e) bassoon.

fähig [ˈfɛːiç] *adj* capable, able. **Fähigkeit** *f* (*pl* -en) ability.

fahl [faːl] *adj* pale, sallow.

Fahne [ˈfaːnə] *f* (*pl* -n) flag, standard; (*mil*) colours. **Fahnen||flucht** *f* desertion. **-flüchtige(r)** *m* deserter. **-stock** *m* flagstaff.

Fahrbahn [ˈfaːrbaːn] *f* (*Mot*) lane. **-höcker** *m* (*pl* -) speed hump, sleeping policeman. **fahrbar** *adj* passable; (*Wasser*) navigable; (*beweglich*) mobile.

Fähre [ˈfɛːrə] *f* (*pl* -n) ferry.

*fahren [ˈfaːrən] *v* go, travel; (*Mot, Zug*) drive; (*Rad, Motorrad*) ride. **Fahrer** *m* driver.

Fahr||gast *m* passenger. **-geld** *neut* fare. **-gestell** *neut* (*Mot*) chassis; (*Flugzeug*) undercarriage. **-karte** *f* ticket. **-kartenschalter** *m* ticket office.

fahrlässig [ˈfaːrlɛsiç] *adj* careless, negligent.

Fahr||plan *m* timetable. **-preis** *m* fare. **-prüfung** *f* driving test. **-rad** *neut* bicycle. **-schein** *m* ticket. **-schule** *f* driving school. **-stuhl** *m* lift, (*US*) elevator.

Fahrt [faːrt] *f* (*pl* **en**) drive, journey.

Fährte [ˈfɛːrtə] *f* (*pl* -n) track, trail.

Fahrzeug [ˈfaːrtsɔyk] *neut* vehicle. **-mit Allradantrieb** 4x4, off-road vehicle.

Faktur [fakˈtuːr] *f* (*pl* -en) *also* **Faktura** invoice. **fakturieren** *v* invoice.

Fakultät [fakulˈtɛːt] *f* (*pl* -en) faculty.

Falke [ˈfalkə] *m* (*pl* -n) hawk, falcon.

Fall [fal] *m* (*pl* **Fälle**) (*Sturz*) fall;

(*Angelegenheit*) case. **-beil** *neut* guillotine. **-brücke** *f* drawbridge.

Falle [ˈfalə] *f* (*pl* -n) trap, snare; (*umg.*) bed. **in die Falle gehen** go to bed.

*fallen [ˈfalən] *v* fall. **Fallen** *neut* fall, decline.

fällen [ˈfɛlən] *v* cut down; (*Urteil*) pass; (*Chem*) precipitate.

fallig [ˈfɛliç] *adj* due.

falls [fals] *conj* if, in case.

Fall||schirm *m* (*pl* -e) parachute. **-schirmjäger** *m* paratrooper. **-sucht** *f* epilepsy. **-tür** *f* trapdoor.

falsch [falʃ] *adj* false.

fälschen [ˈfɛlʃən] *v* falsify, fake; (*Geld*) counterfeit. **Fälscher** *m* (*pl* -) counterfeiter, forger.

Falschheit [ˈfalʃhait] *f* (*pl* -en) falsehood.

Fälschung [ˈfɛlʃuŋ] *f* (*pl* -en) falsification; (*Geld*) forgery, counterfeiting.

Falte [ˈfaltə] *f* (*pl* -n) crease, fold. **falten** *v* crease; (*zusammenlegen*) fold.

familiär [famiˈljɛːr] *adj* familiar.

Familie [faˈmiːljə] *f* (*pl* -n) family. **-stand** *m* personal *or* marital status. **-zulage** *f* family allowance. **Familien||name** *m* surname.

famos [faˈmoːs] *adj* splendid, excellent.

Fanatiker [faˈnaːtikər] *m* (*pl* -) fanatic. **fanatisch** *adj* fanatical.

Fanfare [fanˈfaːrə] *f* (*pl* -n) fanfare.

Fang [faŋ] *m* (*pl* **Fänge**) catch. **fangen** *v* catch.

Farbe [ˈfarbə] *f* (*pl* -n) colour. **Farbe bekennen** show one's colours; (*Karten*) follow suit.

färben [ˈfɛrbən] *v* colour, tint; (*Stoff*) dye.

farbenblind [ˈfarbənblint] *adj* colour blind. **Farb||fernsehen** *neut* colour television. **-film** *m* colour film. **-stoff** *m* dye. **farbig** *adj* coloured. **Farbiger(r)** *m* coloured (man). **farblos** *adj* colourless.

Fasan [faˈzaːn] *m* (*pl* -e) pheasant.

Fasching [ˈfaʃiŋ] *m* (*pl* -e) carnival.

Faschismus [faˈʃismus] *m* (*unz.*) fascism. **Faschist** *m* (*pl* -en) fascist. **faschistisch** *adj* fascist.

Faser [ˈfaːzər] *f* (*pl* -n) fibre; (*fein*) filament. **-stoff** *m* synthetic fibre, manmade material.

Faß β [fas] *neut* (*pl* **Fässer**) barrel, cask, vat. **-bier** *neut* draught beer.

Fassade [fa'saːdə] *f* (*pl* -n) façade.
fassen ['fasən] *v* grasp, seize; (*begreifen*) understand. **sich fassen** pull oneself together; (*ausdrücken*) express oneself. **Fassung** *f* (*Kleinod*) mounting; (*Gemütsruhe*) composure; (*Wortlaut*) wording; (*Verständnis*) comprehension. **–skraft** *f* (power of) comprehension.

fast [fast] *adv* almost, nearly.

fasten ['fastən] *v* fast. **Fasten** *neut* fasting. **–zeit** *f* Lent. **Fastnacht** *f* Shrove Tuesday.

fatal [fa'taːl] *adj* disastrous; (*peinlich*) awkward.

faul [faul] *adj* rotten; (*person*) lazy. **–en** *v* rot. **–enzen** *v* idle, be lazy. **Faul||enzer** *m* loafer. **–heit** *f* laziness, sloth.

Fäulnis ['fɔʏlnis] *f* rottenness, putrefaction.

Faust [faust] *f* (*pl* Fäuste) fist. **–handschuh** *m* mitten.

Fax [faks] *neut* (*pl* - or -e) fax. **Faxgerät** *neut* fax machine. **faxen** *v* fax.

Februar ['feːbruaːr] *m* (*pl* -e) February.

*fechten ['fɛçtən] *v* fence, fight (with swords).

Feder ['feːdər] *f* (*pl* -n) feather; (*tech*) spring; (*schreiben*) pen. **–bett** *neut* featherbed. **–gewicht** *neut* featherweight. **federleicht** *adj* light as a feather. **Federung** *f* suspension, springs *pl*.

Fee [feː] *f* (*pl* -n) fairy.

fegen ['feːgən] *v* sweep.

Fehde ['feːdə] *f* (*pl* -n) feud.

fehlbar ['feːlbaːr] *adj* fallible. **Fehl||betrag** *m* deficit. **–druck** *m* misprint; (*Briefmarken*) error. **fehlen** *v* (*mangeln*) be missing or lacking; (*abwesend*) be absent; (*irren*) make a mistake. **–d** *adj* missing, absent.

Fehler ['feːlər] *m* (*pl* -) mistake; (*Schwäche*) weakness; (*Mangel*) defect. **fehler||frei** *adj* flawless. **–haft** *adj* faulty, defective.

Fehlgeburt ['feːlgəburt] *f* miscarriage. **Fehl||menge** *f* shortfall. **–tritt** *m* false move or step, slip. **–zündung** *f* (*Mot*) misfire. **fehlschlagen** *v* fail, not succeed.

Feier ['faiər] *f* (*pl* -n) festival. **Feierabend** *m* evening leisure time, free time. **Feierabend machen** finish work (for the day). **feierlich** *adj* solemn, ceremonial. **feiern** *v* celebrate. **Feiertag** *m* holiday; (*Festtag*) festival.

feige ['faigə] *adj* cowardly.

Feige ['faigə] *f* (*pl* -n) fig.

Feig||heit *f* (*unz.*) cowardice. **–ling** *m* coward.

feil [fail] *adj* for sale; (*bestechlich*) venal, corrupt.

Feile ['failə] *f* (*pl* -n) file. **feilen** *v* file.

feilschen ['failʃən] *v* haggle.

fein [fain] *adj* fine.

Feind [faint] *m* (*pl* -e) enemy. **feindlich** *adj* hostile. **Feindschaft** *f* enmity, hostility. **feind/schaftlich** *adj* inimical. **–selig** *adj* hostile.

Fein||gehaltsstempel *m* hallmark (stamp). **–heit** *f* fineness. **–schmecker** *m* gourmet.

Feld [fɛlt] *neut* (*pl* -er) field; (*Schach*) square. **–bau** *m* agriculture. **–blume** *f* wild flower. **–früchte** *f pl* crops. **–herr** *m* commander (-in-chief). **–messer** *m* surveyor. **–zug** *m* campaign.

Fell [fɛl] *neut* (*pl* -e) skin, hide.

Fels [fɛls] *m* (*pl* -en) rock, boulder. **–enklippe** *f* cliff. **–sturz** *m* rockfall.

Femininum [fɛm iniːnum] *neut* (*pl* Feminina) (*Gramm*) feminine (gender).

Fenster ['fɛnstər] *neut* (*pl* -) window.

Ferien ['feːriən] *neut pl* holiday. **in die Ferien gehen** go on holiday. **–kolonie** *f* holiday-camp. **–ort** *m* holiday resort.

Ferkel ['fɛrkəl] *neut* (*pl* -) piglet.

Ferment [fɛrm ɛnt] *neut* (*pl* -e) enzyme, ferment.

fern [fɛrn] *adj* far(away), distant. **–bleiben** *v* stay away. **Ferne** *f* distance. **ferner** *adj* farther; *adv* further; *conj* in addition. **–hin** *adv* in future.

Fern||gespräch *neut* (*phone*) long-distance call. **–glas** *neut* telescope. **–laster** *m* long-distance lorry. **–lenkung** *f* remote control. **–meldedienst** *m* telecommunications. **–rohr** *neut* telescope. **–schreiber** *m* teletype machine; Telex. **–sehapparat** *m* television (set). **–sehen** *neut* television. **–sehen** watch television. **–sprecher** *m* telephone. **–straße** *f* trunkroad. **–zug** *m* long-distance train.

Fernsehkomödie ['fɛrnzeːkoˈmøːdi] *f* (*pl* -n) sitcom.

Fernsehüberwachungsanlage ['fɛrnzeːybərˈvaxuŋsˌanlaːgə] *f* (*pl* -n) closed-circuit television (CCTV).

Ferse ['fɛrzə] *f* (*pl* -n) heel.

fertig ['fɛrtiç] *adj* (*bereit*) ready; (*beendet*)

finished. **–en** v produce. **Fertigkeit** f (pl -en) skill, proficiency. **fertigmachen** v finish; (umg.) beat (into submission).

Fessel ['fɛsə] f (pl -n) fetter, chain. **fesseln** v fetter, chain. **–d** adj fascinating; (bezaubernd) enchanting.

fest [fɛst] adj firm, secure; (dicht) solid.

Fest [fɛst] neut (pl -e) festival. **–essen** neut banquet.

*festhalten ['fɛsthaltən] v hold (tight); (Bild, Buch) portray; (anpacken) seize. **festigen** v make firm or secure. **Festland** neut continent. **festlegen** v lay down, fix, **sich festlegen** commit oneself.

festlich ['fɛstlɪç] adj festive. **Festlichkeit** f festivity.

fest||machen v fasten; (vereinbaren) agree, arrange. **–nehmen** v arrest, capture. **–setzen** v settle, fix. **Festsetzung** f settling, establishment. **fest||stehen** v stand fast. **–stellen** v settle; (herausfinden) establish, ascertain. **Feststellung** f establishment, ascertaining.

Festtag ['fɛstta:k] m holiday.

Festung ['fɛstuŋ] f (pl -en) fortress.

Festzug ['fɛsttsu:k] m procession.

fett [fɛt] adj fat; (schmierig) greasy. **Fett** neut (pl -e) fat; grease. **fettig** adj fatty; greasy.

Fetzen ['fɛtsən] m (pl -) rag, shred.

feucht [fɔyçt] adj damp, moist. **–en** v dampen, moisten. **Feuchtigkeit** f dampness, moisture.

Feuer ['fɔyər] neut (pl -) fire. **–alarm** m fire alarm. **feuer||beständig** or **–fest** adj fireproof. **–gefährlich** adj inflammable. **Feuerlöscher** m fire extinguisher. **feuern** v fire. **Feuer||schaden** m fire damage. **–spritze** f fire engine. **–stein** m flint. **–waffe** f gun. **–wehr** f fire brigade, (US) fire department. **–wehrmann** m fireman. **–zeug** neut (cigarette) lighter.

Feuilleton ['fœ jtɔ̃] neut (pl -s) newspaper supplement, review section.

feurig ['fɔyrɪç] adj fiery.

Fiber ['fi:bər] f (pl -n) fibre.

Fichte ['fɪçtə] f (pl -n) fir, spruce (tree).

Fieber ['fi:bər] neut (pl -) fever. **fieberartig** adj feverish. **fieberhaft** adj feverish.

Fiedel ['fi:dəl] f (pl -n) fiddle, violin. **fiedeln** v (play the) fiddle.

Figur [fi gu:r] f (pl -en) figure; (Schach) piece, chessman.

fiktiv [fɪk'ti:f] adj fictitious.

Filiale [fiːliaːlə] f (pl -n) (Komm) branch.

Film [fɪlm] m (pl -e) film. **Filter** ['fɪltər] m (pl -) filter. **filtrieren** v filter.

Filz [fɪlts] m (pl -e) felt; (Geizhals) miser; (fig.; Korruption in der Politik) sleaze.

Finanz [fi nants] f (pl -en) finance. **–amt** neut tax office, Inland Revenue. **finanziell** adj financial. **Finanzier** m (pl -s) financier. **finanzieren** v finance. **Finanz||jahr** m financial year. **–minister** m finance minister.

*finden ['fɪndən] v find; (glauben) think, believe. **Finder** m (pl -) finder. **findig** adj clever, resourceful.

Finger ['fɪŋər] m (pl -) finger. **–abdruck** m fingerprint. **–hut** m thimble; (Bot) foxglove. **–nagel** m fingernail. **–spitze** f fingertip.

Fink [fɪŋk] m (pl -en) finch.

Finne ['fɪnə] m (pl -), **Finnin** f (pl -nen) Finn. **finnisch** adj Finnish. **Finnland** neut Finland. **Finnländer(in)** f Finn.

finster ['fɪnstər] adj dark; (düster) gloomy; (drohend) foreboding. **Finsternis** f darkness; gloom.

Firma ['fɪrm ə] f (pl Firmen) firm, business. **Firmen-** adj corporate.

Firnis ['fɪrnɪs] m (pl -se) varnish.

Fisch [fɪʃ] m (pl -e) fish. **Fische** pl (Astrol) Pisces. **fischen** v fish. **Fischer** m (pl -) fisherman. **–boot** neut fishing boat. **–ei** f fishing. **–korb** m creel. **–otter** m or f otter. **–reiher** m heron. **–zeug** neut (fishing) tackle.

fix [fɪks] adj firm; (fig) quick.

flach [flax] adj flat, even; (nicht tief) shallow; (uninteressant) dull.

Fläche ['flɛçə] f (pl -n) flatness; (Gebiet) area; (Oberfläche) surface. **–ninhalt** m surface area.

Flachs [flaks] m (unz.) flax.

flackerig ['flakərɪç] adj flickering. **flackern** v flicker, flare.

Flagge ['flagə] f (pl -n) flag.

Flamme ['flam ə] f (pl -n) flame. **flammen** v flame, blaze.

Flanell [fla'nɛl] m (pl -e) flannel.

Flanke ['flaŋkə] f (pl -n) flank. **flankieren** v (out)flank.

Flasche ['flaʃə] *f* (*pl* **-n**) bottle. **Flaschen–**
adj cylindrical. **Flaschenöffner** *m* bottle-
opener.

flattern ['flatərn] *v* flutter.

flau [flau] *adj* weak; (*Getränke*) flat; (*Komm*)
slack, dull.

Flaum [flaum] *m* (*unz.*) down. **flaumig** *adj*
downy.

Flaute ['flautə] *f* (*pl* **-n**) lull, calm;
(*Wirtschaft*) recession.

Flechte ['flɛçtə] *f* (*pl* **-n**) braid; (*Bot*) lichen;
(*Med*) ringworm, herpes. **flechten** *v* braid,
interweave; (*Korb*) weave. **Flechtkorb** *m*
wicker basket.

Fleck [flɛk] *m* (*pl* **-e**) stain, spot; (*Makel*)
blemish, flaw. **flecken** *v* stain.

Fledermaus ['fleːdərm aus] *f* bat.

flehen ['fleːən] *v* implore, entreat (for).
–tlich *adj* imploring.

Fleisch [flaiʃ] *neut* (*unz.*) meat. **–brühe** *f*
(meat) stock. **Fleischer** *m* (*pl* -) butcher. **-ei**
f (*pl* **-en**) butcher's (shop). **fleisch∥farbig**
adj flesh-coloured. **–fressend** *adj* carnivorous. **–ig** *adj* fleshy. **–lich** *adj* carnal.
Fleisch∥topf *m* meat saucepan; (*fig*) flesh-
pot. **–werdung** *f* (*Rel*) Incarnation. **–wolf**
m mincer.

Fleiß [flais] *m* (*unz.*) diligence, industry.
fleißig *adj* industrious, hard-working.

Flick [flik] *m* (*pl* **-en**) patch. **-arbeit** *f* patch-
ing; (*Pfuscherei*) botch. **flicken** *v* mend,
patch.

Fliege ['fliːgə] *f* (*pl* **-n**) fly. **fliegen** *v* fly.
Flieger *m* (*pl* -) aviator, flier. **–abwehr** *f*
anti-aircraft defence.

*fliehen ['fliːən] *v* flee.

Fliese ['fliːzə] *f* (*pl* **-n**) flagstone.

Fließband ['fliːsbant] *neut* conveyor belt,
assembly line. **fließen** *v* flow. **fließend** *adj*
flowing, running, (*sprachkenntnisse*) fluent.

flimmern ['flim ərn] *v* glimmer, twinkle.

flink [fliŋk] *adj* nimble, agile.

Flinte ['flintə] *f* (*pl* **-n**) musket; (*Schrot*) shotgun.

flirten ['flirtən] *v* flirt.

Flitterwochen ['flitərvɔxən] *f pl* honeymoon *sing*.

Flocke ['flɔkə] *f* (*pl* **-n**) flake; (*Wolle, Haar*)
flock, tuft. **flocken** *v* fall in flakes. **flockig**
adj flaky; (*Haar, usw.*) fluffy.

Floh [floː] *m* (*pl* **Flöhe**) flea. **–stich** *m*
fleabite.

Floskel ['flɔskəl] *f* (*pl* **-n**) flowery *or* fine
phrase.

Floß [floːs] *neut* (*pl* **Flöße**) raft.

Flosse ['flɔsə] *f* (*pl* **-n**) fin.

Flöte ['fløːtə] *f* (*pl* **-n**) flute. **flöten** *v* play
the flute. **Flötist(in)** flautist.

flott [flɔt] *adj* brisk; (*Schnell*) fast; (*schick*)
smart; (*schwimmend*) afloat. **Flotte** *f* fleet,
navy.

Flöz [fløːts] *neut* (*pl* **-e**) (*Mineralien*) seam.

Fluch [fluːx] *m* (*pl* **Flüche**) curse;
(*Fluchwort*) swear-word. **fluchen** *v* swear,
curse.

Flucht [fluxt] *f* (*pl* **-en**) flight, escape;
(*Reihe*) row.

flüchtig ['flyçtiç] *adj* fleeting, cursory.
Flüchtling *m* (*pl* **-e**) refugee.

Flug [fluːk] *m* (*pl* **Flüge**) flight, flying;
(*Vögel*) flock. **–bahn** *f* trajectory. **–blatt**
neut handbill, pamphlet.

Flügel ['flyːgəl] *m* (*pl* -) wing; (*Klavier*)
grand piano. **–fenster** *neut* French window.

Flug∥gast *m* air passenger. **–hafen** *m* airport. **–lotse** *m* (*pl* **-n**) air-traffic controller.
neut **–post** *f* air-mail. **–schiff** *m* flying-boat.
–schrift *f* pamphlet. **–wesen** *neut* aviation,
flying. **–zeug** *neut* aeroplane. **–zeughalle** *f*
hanger. **–zeugträger** *m* aircraft-carrier.

flunkern ['fluŋkərn] *v* fib, lie; (*übertreiben*)
exaggerate, brag.

Flur [fluːr] *m* (*pl* **-e**) floor; (*entrance*) hall.

Fluß [flus] *m* (*pl* **Flüsse**) river. **fluß∥**
abwärts *adv* downstream. **–aufwärts** *adv*
upstream. **Flussfisch** *m* fresh-water fish.

flüssig ['flysiç] *adj* liquid. **Flüssigkeit** *f* liquid.

flüstern ['flystərn] *v* whisper.

Flut [fluːt] *f* (*pl* **-en**) flood; (*Hochwasser*)
(high) tide, (*fig*) spate. **Ebbe und Flut** ebb
and flow. **fluten** *v* flood.

Fohlen ['foːlən] *neut* (*pl* -) foal.

Föhn [føːn] *m* (*pl* **-e**) (warm) south wind.

Folge ['fɔlgə] *f* (*pl* **-n**) succession; (*Wirkung*)
consequence. **folgen** *v* follow; (*gehorchen*)
obey. **folgend** *adj* (the) following.
–ermaßen *adv* as follows. **folgerichtig** *adj*
consistent, logical. **folgern** *v* conclude,
infer. **Folgerung** *f* (*pl* **-en**) conclusion,
inference. **folgewidrig** *adj* inconsistent,
illogical. **folglich** *adv* consequently.

Folter ['fɔltər] *f* (*pl* **-n**) torture; (*Gerät*)
rack. **foltern** *v* torture. **Folterung** *f*

torture, torturing.

Fön [fø:n] *m* (*pl* **-e**) hairdrier.

Fonds [fõ:] *m* (*pl* -) fund.

Förderer ['fœːrdərər] *m* (*pl* -) promoter, sponsor. **förderlich** *adj* useful, beneficial.

fordern ['fɔrdərn] *v* demand; (*beanspruchen*) claim.

fördern ['fœːrdərn] *v* further, promote.

Forderung ['fɔrdəruŋ] *f* (*pl* -**en**) demand.

Förderung ['fœːrdəruŋ] *f* (*pl* -**en**) further-ance, advancement; (*Komm*) promotion; (*Kohle*) mining.

Forelle [fo'rɛlə] *f* (*pl* -**n**) trout.

Form [fɔrm] *f* (*pl* -**en**) form; (tech, Kuchen) mould. **in Form** (*sport*) fit, on form. **Formel** *f* (*pl* -**n**) formula. **form**llell *adj* for-mal. -**en** *v* form, shape. -**los** *adj* shapeless, formless. **Formular** *neut* (*pl* -**e**) (question) form, (*US*) blank. **formulieren** *v* formu-late.

forschen ['fɔrʃən] *v* investigate; (*fragen*) inquire; (*Wissenschaft*) do research. **forschend** *adj* searching. **Forscher** *m* (*pl* -) investigator, enquirer; researcher. **Forschung** *f* (*pl* -**en**) investigation; research.

Forst [fɔrst] *m* (*pl* -**e**) forest.

Förster ['fœːrstər] *m* (*pl* -) forestry.

Forstwirtschaft ['fɔrstvirtʃaft] *f* forestry.

fort [fɔrt] *adv* away; (*vorwärts*) forward(s); (*weiter*) on.

fortan [fɔrt'an] *adv* from now on.

***fortbestehen** ['fɔrtbəʃteːən] *v* continue (to exist), live on, survive.

Fortbildung ['fɔrtbilduŋ] *f* further educa-tion.

***fortbleiben** ['fɔrtblaibən] *v* remain away.

fortdauern ['fɔrtdauərn] *v* last, continue. -**d** *adj* continual, incessant.

***fortfahren** ['fɔrtfaːrən] *v* drive away, depart; (*weitermachen*) proceed, continue.

***fortgehen** ['fɔrtgeːən] *v* go away.

fortgeschritten ['fɔrtgəʃritən] *adj* advanced.

***fortkommen** ['fɔrtkɔmən] *v* escape; (*fig*) prosper, make progress.

***fortlaufen** ['fɔrtlaufən] *v* run away; (*fortkommen*) escape; (*weiterlaufen*) con-tinue. -**d** *adj* continuous.

fortleben ['fɔrtleːbən] *v* survive. **Fortleben** *neut* survival; (*nach dem Tode*) afterlife.

fortpflanzen ['fɔrtpflantsən] *v* **sich fortpflanzen** reproduce, multiply; (*Krankheit*) spread.

***fortschreiten** ['fɔrtʃraitən] *v* go forward, proceed.

Fortschritt ['fɔrtʃrit] *m* (*pl* -**e**) progress. **fortschrittlich** *adj* progressive.

fortsetzen ['fɔrtzɛtsən] *v* continue. **Fortsetzung** *f* continuation.

fortwährend ['fɔrtvɛːrənt] *adj* continuous, incessant.

Fossil [fɔ'siːl] *neut* (*pl* -**ien**) fossil.

Foto ['foːto] *neut* (*pl* -**s**) (*umg.*) photo.

Fötus ['føːtus] *m* (*pl* -**se**) foetus.

Fracht [fraxt] *f* (*pl* -**en**) freight. -**brief** *m* consignment *or* dispatch note. -**gut** *neut* cargo, goods. -**schiff** *neut* merchantman.

Frack [frak] *m* (*pl* **Fräcke**) dresscoat, tails. -**hemd** *neut* dress shirt. -**zwang** *m* obliga-tory evening dress, formal dress.

Frage ['fraːgə] *f* (*pl* -**n**) question. -**bogen** *m* questionnaire. **fragen** *v* ask. **Fragezeichen** *neut* question mark. **frag**llich *adj* in ques-tion, doubtful. -**los** *adj* unquestionable.

Fragment [frag'mɛnt] *neut* (*pl* -**e**) fragment.

fragwürdig ['fraːkvurdiç] *adj* questionable, dubious; (*coll*) dodgy, shady.

Fraktion [frak'tsioːn] *f* (*pl* -**en**) (*Pol*) parlia-mentary party, faction.

Fraktur [frak'tuːr] *f* (*pl* -**en**) fracture; (*Druck*) Gothic type *or* script.

frankieren [fraŋ'kiːrən] *v* (*Brief*) stamp; (*Päckchen*) pre-pay. **franko** *adv* post paid.

Frankreich ['fraŋkraiç] *neut* France.

Franse ['franzə] *f* (*pl* -**n**) fringe. **fransig** *adj* fringed; (*ausgefasert*) frayed.

Franzose [fran'tsoːzə] *m* (*pl* -**n**) Frenchman. **Französin** *f* (*pl* -**nen**) Frenchwoman. **französisch** *adj* French.

Fratze ['fratsə] *f* (*pl* -**n**) grimace. **Fratzen-schneiden** make *or* pull faces.

Frau [frau] *f* (*pl* -**en**) woman; (*Ehefrau*) wife; (*Titel*) Mrs, Ms. **Frauen**llarzt *m* gynaecolo-gist. -**befreiung** *f* women's liberation. **frauenhaft** *adj* womanly. **Frauen**llrecht-lerin *f* (*pl* -**nen**) feminist. -**welt** *f* woman-kind, women *pl.*

Fräulein ['frɔylain] *neut* (*pl* -) young lady; (*Titel*) Miss.

frech [frɛç] *adj* cheeky, insolent. **Frechheit** *f* cheek, insolence.

frei [frai] *adj* free; (*nicht besetzt*) vacant,

unoccupied; (*offen*) candid.

Freibad ['fraɪbat] *neut* outdoor swimming pool.

freiberuflich ['fraɪbəruːflɪç] *adj* freelance, self-employed, professional.

Freibrief ['fraɪbriːf] *m* charter.

Freie ['fraɪə] *neut* (*unz.*) outdoors, open air. **im Freien** in the open air.

Freigabe ['fraɪgaːbə] *f* release.

*freigeben ['fraɪgeːbən] *v* set free; (Straße, usw.) open; (*Waren, Arznei*) pass, approve, decontrol. **freigebig** *adj* generous.

Freihandel ['fraɪhandəl] *m* free-trade.

Freiheit ['fraɪhaɪt] *f* (*pl* -en) freedom, liberty. **freiheitlich** *adj* liberal.

Freiherr ['fraɪhɛr] *m* (*pl* -) baron. **-in** *f* (*pl* -nen) baroness.

Freikarte ['fraɪkaːrtə] *f* complimentary ticket.

*freilassen ['fraɪlasən] *v* set free.

freilich ['fraɪlɪç] *adv* certainly, indeed, of course.

freimachen ['fraɪmaxən] *v* deliver (from captivity), release.

Freimaurer ['fraɪmaurər] *m* (*pl* -) freemason.

Freimut ['fraɪmuːt] *m* (*unz.*) candour, frankness, **freimütig** *adj* candid, frank.

*freisprechen ['fraɪʃprɛçən] *v* acquit, discharge.

Freitag ['fraɪtaːk] *m* Friday.

freiwillig ['fraɪvɪlɪç] *adj* voluntary.

Freizeit ['fraɪtsaɪt] *f* leisure time, spare time.

fremd [frɛmt] *adj* strange; (*ausländisch*) foreign. **Fremde(r)** stranger; foreigner. **Fremdenzimmer** *neut* guest room. **-heit** *f* strangeness. **-körper** *m* foreign body. **-sprache** *f* foreign language. **-wort** *neut* foreign word, loan word.

Frequenz [fre'kvɛnts] *f* (*pl* -en) frequency.

*fressen ['frɛsən] *v* eat, devour.

Fressorgie ['frɛsɔrgiə] *f* (*pl* -n) binge (*Essen*).

Freude ['frɔydə] *f* (*pl* -n) joy; (*Vergnügen*) delight. **-ntag** *m* red-letter day. **freudig** *adj* joyful, joyous.

freuen ['frɔyən] *v* give pleasure to. **es freut mich** I am glad *or* pleased. **sich freuen** be glad, rejoice. **sich freuen auf** look forward to.

Freund [frɔynt] *m* (*pl* -e) friend; (*Liebhaber*) boyfriend. **-in** *f* (*pl* -nen) (girl) friend.

freundlich *adj* friendly; (*liebenswürdig*) kind. **-erweise** *adv* kindly. **Freundlichkeit** *f* friendliness. **-schaft** *f* friendship. **freundschaftlich** *adj* friendly.

Frevel ['freːfəl] *m* (*pl* -) sacrilege. **frevelhaft** *adj* sacrilegious.

Friede(n) ['friːdə(n)] *m* (*pl* -) peace. **Friedensbruch** *m* breach of the peace. **-stifter** *m* peacemaker. **-vertrag** *m* peace (treaty). **Friedhof** *m* cemetary. **friedlich** *adj* peaceful.

*frieren ['friːrən] *v* freeze.

Frikadelle [frika'dɛlə] *f* (*pl* -n) rissole.

frisch [frɪʃ] *adj* fresh; (*lebhaft*) lively. **Frische** *f* freshness; liveliness.

Friseur [fri'zøːr] *m*, (*pl* -e) **Friseuse** *f* (*pl* -n) hairdresser; (*nur für Herren*) barber. **frisieren** *v* cut *or* style hair; (*Bücher*) cook, falsify; (*Mot*) soup up. **Frisiersalon** *m* hairdressing salon.

Frist [frɪst] *f* (*pl* -en) period, time; (*Termin*) time limit, deadline.

Frisur [fri'zuːr] *f* (*pl* en) hairstyle; (*umg.*) hairdo.

froh [froː] *adj* glad, cheerful, happy.

fröhlich ['frøːlɪç] *adj* cheerful, joyous. **Fröhlichkeit** *f* cheerfulness.

frohlocken [froː'lɔkən] *v* rejoice. **Frohsinn** *m* gaiety.

fromm [frɔm] *adj* pious, religious.

frömmelnd ['frøːməlnt] *adj* religiose, hypocritical. **Frömmler** *m* hypocritic.

Fronleichnam [froːn'laɪçnaːm] *m* Corpus Christi Day.

Front [frɔnt] *f* (*pl* -en) front, face; (*Pol*) front. **-antrieb** *m* front-wheel drive.

Frosch [frɔʃ] *m* (*pl* Frösche) frog; (*Feuerwerk*) squib, banger.

Frost [frɔst] *m* (*pl* Fröste) frost; (*Kälte*) coldness, chill. **-beule** *f* chilblain. **frostig** *adj* chilly, frosty. **Frostschutzmittel** *neut* antifreeze.

Frucht [fruxt] *f* (*pl* Früchte) fruit. **fruchtbar** *adj* fertile. **Fruchtbarkeit** *f* fertility. **fruchtlos** *adj* fruitless. **Fruchtsaft** *m* fruit juice.

früh [fryː] *adj* early. **Frühe** *f* early hour, early morning. **früher** *adj* earlier; (*ehemalig*) former. **frühestens** *adv* earliest. **Frühgeburt** *f* premature birth. **-jahr** *neut* spring. **-ling** *m* spring. **-reife** *f* precocity. **-stück** *neut* breakfast. **frühstücken** *v* breakfast. **–zeitig** *adj* premature, untimely; (*rechtzeitig*) early, in good time.

Fuchs [fuks] *m* (*pl* Füchse) fox.

Füchsin ['fʏçsɪn] *f* (*pl* **-nen**) vixen.

Fuge ['fuːɡə] *f* (*pl* **-n**) joint; (*Musik*) fugue.

fügen ['fyːɡən] *v* join together; (*ordnen*) dispose. **sich fügen** submit. **fügsam** *adj* submissive, obedient.

fühlen ['fyːlən] *v* touch, feel. **sich fühlen** feel. **sich glücklich fühlen** feel *or* be happy. **Fühlen** *neut* feeling (sense). **Fühler** *m* feeler. **Fühlung** *f* touch.

führen ['fyːrən] *v* lead, direct; (*Waren*) stock, carry; (*Bücher*) keep. **–d** *adj* prominent, leading. **Führer** *m* leader, guide. **–haus** *neut* (*Zug*) driver's cab. **–schaft** *f* leadership. **–schein** *m* driving licence, (*US*) driver's license. **–sitz** *m* driver's *or* pilot's seat. **Führung** *f* command, management.

Fülle ['fʏlə] *f* (*pl* **-n**) abundance, plenty. **Hülle und Fülle** plentiful, in plenty. **füllen** *v* fill (up). **Füll‖feder** *f* fountain pen. **–ung** *f* (*pl* **-en**) filling.

Fundament [fundaˈmɛnt] *neut* (*pl* **-e**) foundation, base.

fünf [fʏnf] *adj* five. **fünft** *adj* fifth. **Fünftel** *neut* fifth. **fünf‖zehn** *pron*, *adj* fifteen.

fungieren [fuŋˈɡiːrən] *v* function (as), act (as).

Funk [fuŋk] *m* (*unz.*) radio, wireless. **–e** *m* (*pl* **-n**) spark. **funkeln** *v* sparkle. **Funk-sendung** *f* (*Radio*) programme transmission.

Funktion [fuŋktsˈloːn] *f* (*pl* **-en**) function. **–är** *m* (*pl* **-e**) functionary. **funktionieren** *v* function.

für [fyːr] *prep* for. **das Für und Wider** for and against, the pros and cons.

Furche ['furçə] *f* (*pl* **-n**) furrow; (*Runzel*) wrinkle. **furchen** *v* furrow.

Furcht [furçt] *f* (*unz.*) fear. **furchtbar** *adj* frightful.

fürchten ['fʏrçtən] *v* fear. **sich fürchten vor** be afraid of. **fürchterlich** *adj* terrible, dreadful.

Furnier [furˈniːr] *neut* (*pl* **-e**) veneer.

Fürsorge ['fyːrzɔrɡə] *f* care; (*Hilfstätigkeit*) welfare work; (*Geld*) social security. **–arbeit** *f* social work.

Fürsprecher ['fyːrʃprɛçər] *m* advocate. **fürsprechen** *v* intercede.

Fürst [fʏrst] *m* (*pl* **-en**) prince. **–in** *f* (*pl*

-nen) princess. **fürstlich** *adj* princely.

Furz [furts] *m* (*pl* Fürze) (*vulg*) fart. **furzen** *v* fart.

Fuß [fuːs] *m* (*pl* Füße) foot. **–ball** *m* football. **–boden** *m* floor. **–bremse** *f* footbrake. **–gänger** *m* pedestrian. **–pflege** *f* chiropody. **–steig** *m* pavement, (*US*) sidewalk. **–tritt** *m* kick; (*Gang*) step. **–volk** *neut* infantry. **–weg** *m* footpath.

Futter ['futər] *neut* (*pl* **-**) feed, fodder; (*Kleider*) lining.

füttern ['fytərn] *v* feed; line. **Fütterung** *f* feeding, fodder; lining.

G

Gabe ['ɡaːbə] *f* (*pl* **-n**) gift.

Gabel ['ɡaːbəl] *f* (*pl* **-n**) fork. **gabeln** *v* fork. **Gabelung** *f* fork, branching.

Gabelfrühstück ['ɡaːbəlfryːʃtyk] *neut* (*pl* **-e**) brunch.

gackern ['ɡakərn] *v* cackle.

gähnen ['ɡɛːnən] *v* yawn.

galant [ɡaˈlant] *adj* polite, gallant.

Galeere [ɡaˈleːrə] *f* (*pl* **-n**) galley.

Galerie [ɡaləˈriː] *f* (*pl* **-n**) gallery.

Galgen ['ɡalɡən] *m* (*pl* **-**) gallows *pl*.

gälisch ['ɡɛːliʃ] *adj* Gaelic.

Galle ['ɡalə] *f* (*pl* **-n**) gall, bile; (*fig*) rancour. **Gallen‖blase** ['ɡalənblaːzə] *f* gallbladder. **–stein** *m* gallstone.

Galopp [ɡaˈlɔp] *m* (*pl* **-e**) gallop. **galoppieren** *v* gallop.

galvanisieren [ɡalvaniˈziːrən] *v* galvanize.

Gang [ɡaŋ] *m* (*pl* Gänge) walk; (*Gangart*) gait; (*Flur*) corridor; (*Essen*) course; (*Mot*) gear. **im Gang** in motion. **Gang‖art** *f* gait. **–schalter** *m* gear lever.

Gans [ɡans] *f* (*pl* Gänse) goose.

Gänse‖blume ['ɡɛnzəbluːm ə] *f* daisy. **–braten** *m* roast goose. **–füßchen** *pl* quotation marks. **–rich** *m* gander.

ganz [ɡants] *adj* whole, all; (*vollständig*) complete. *adv* quite; (*vollends*) fully. **Ganze** *neut* whole.

gar [ɡaːr] *adj* (*Kochen*) done, cooked. *adv* very. **gar nicht** not at all. **gar keiner** none whatever.

Garantie [gaʀanˈtiː] f (pl -n) guarantee.

Garde [ˈgaʀdə] f (pl -n) guard.

Garderobe [gaʀdəˈʀoːbə] f (pl -n) cloakroom; (Kleider) wardrobe.

Gardine [gaʀˈdiːnə] f (pl -n) curtain.

***gären** [ˈgɛːʀən] v ferment.

garnieren [gaʀˈniːən] v garnish; (Kleidung) trim.

Garnison [gaʀnɪˈzoːn] f (pl -en) garrison.

Garnitur [gaʀnɪˈtuːʀ] f (pl -en) (Verzierung) trimming; (Satz) set; (Ausrüstung) equipment.

Garten [ˈgaʀtən] m (pl Gärten) garden. –bau m horticulture. –haus neut summer house. –laube f arbour.

Gärtner [ˈgɛːtnəʀ] m (pl -) gardener. –ei f (pl -en) nursery.

Gärung [ˈgɛːʀʊŋ] f (pl -en) fermentation.

Gas [gaːs] neut (pl -e) gas. –flasche f gas cylinder or bottle. –hebel m accelerator. –hahn m gas cock. –herd m gas cooker.

Gasse [ˈgasə] f (pl -n) alley, lane.

Gast [gast] m (pl Gäste) guest. –arbeiter m (pl -) guest worker, migrant worker. gastfreundlich adj hospitable. Gast||freundschaft f hospitality. –geber m (pl -) host. –geberin f (pl -nen) hostess. –hof m hotel, inn. –mahl neut banquet. –stätte f restaurant, café. –wirt m landlord, innkeeper.

Gatte [ˈgatə] m (pl -n) spouse, husband. gatten v match. **Gattin** f (pl -nen) spouse, wife.

Gattung [ˈgatʊŋ] f (pl -en) sort, kind; (Biol) species.

gaukeln [ˈgaukəln] v perform tricks, juggle.

Gaul [gaul] m (pl Gäule) nag.

Gaumen [ˈgaumən] m (pl -) palate.

Gauner [ˈgaunəʀ] m (pl -) swindler, trickster.

Gaze [ˈgaːzə] f (pl -n) gauze.

Gazelle [gaˈtsɛlə] f (pl -n) gazelle.

geartet [gəˈaːʀtət] adj constituted, composed.

Gebäck [gəˈbɛk] neut (pl -e) pastry, cakes; (Keks) biscuit.

Gebärde [gəˈbɛːʀdə] f (pl -n) gesture.

***gebären** [gəˈbɛːʀən] v give birth to, bear. **Gebärmutter** f womb.

Gebäude [gəˈbɔydə] neut (pl -) building.

***geben** [ˈgeːbən] v give. sich geben relent, abate. es gibt there is/are. was gibt es? what is the matter? sich zufrieden geben

be content. das gibt's nicht! that's impossible! Geben neut giving. Geber m (pl -), Geberin f (pl -nen) giver, donor.

Gebet [gəˈbeːt] neut (pl -e) prayer. –buch neut prayerbook.

Gebiet [gəˈbiːt] neut (pl -e) (Staats-) territory; (Gegend) area, district; (fig) field, sphere.

Gebilde [gəˈbɪldə] neut (pl -) (Erzeugnis) product; (Form) structure, shape.

gebildet [gəˈbɪldət] adj educated, cultured.

Gebirge [gəˈbɪʀgə] neut (pl -) mountain range, mountains pl.

Gebiß [gəˈbɪs] neut (pl Gebisse) (set of) teeth; (Zaum) bit; (künstlich) denture.

Gebläse [gəˈblɛːzə] neut (pl -) blower, bellows pl; (Mot) supercharger.

geboren [gəˈboːʀən] adj born. geborener Hamburger native of Hamburg. Frau Maria Müller, geborene (geb.) Schmidt Mrs. Maria Müller, née Schmidt.

Gebot [gəˈboːt] neut (pl -e) order. die zehn Gebote the Ten Commandments.

Gebrauch [gəˈbʀaux] neut (pl Gebräuche) custom; (Benutzen) use. gebrauchen v use. gebräuchlich adj customary. Gebrauchs||anweisung f or –anleitung f instructions (for use). Gebrauchtwagen m second-hand car.

gebrechlich [gəˈbʀɛçlɪç] adj (Gegenstand) fragile; (Person) frail.

Gebrüder [gəˈbʀydəʀ] m pl brothers. Gebrüder Schmidt Schmidt Bros.

Gebrüll [gəˈbʀyl] neut (unz.) roar, roaring.

Gebühr [gəˈbyːʀ] 1 f (pl -en) fee, charge. 2 f (unz.) decency, propriety. nach Gebühr duly. gebühren v be due. sich gebühren be fitting or decent. gebührend adj seemly, proper.

gebunden [gəˈbundən] adj bound.

Geburt [gəˈbuʀt] f (pl -en) birth. Geburten||beschränkung f or –regelung f birth control. gebürtig adj born (in). Geburts||fehler m congenital defect. –helfer m obstetrician. –helferin f midwife; (Arztin) obstetrician. –hilfe f obstetrics. –mal neut mole. –ort m birthplace. –schein m birth certificate. –tag m birthday.

Gebüsch [gəˈbyʃ] neut (pl -e) (clump of) bushes.

Gedächtnis [gəˈdɛçtnɪs] neut (pl -se) memory. –feier f commemoration. –schwund *m* loss of memory, amnesia.

Gedanke [gə'daŋkə] *m (pl* **-n**) thought. **sich Gedanken machen über** worry about. **gedankenlos** *adj* thoughtless. **gedanklich** *adj* mental.

Gedeck [gə'dɛk] *neut (pl* **-e**) cover, place-setting; menu.

***gedeihen** [gə'daɪn] *v* flourish, thrive.

***gedenken** [gə'dɛŋkən] *v* think (of); *(vorhaben)* intend. **Gendenkfeier** *f* commemoration.

Gedicht [gə'dɪçt] *neut (pl* **-e**) poem. **-sammlung** *f* anthology (of verse).

gediegen [gə'diːgən] *adj (echt)* genuine; *(rein)* pure; *(solide)* solid; *(sorgfältig)* thorough.

Gedränge [gə'drɛŋə] *neut (unz.)* crowd, press; *(Notlage)* difficulty. **gedrängt** *adj* narrow, close; *(Stil)* terse, concise.

gedruckt [gə'drʊkt] *adj* printed.

gedrückt [gə'drʏkt] *adj* depressed.

Geduld [gə'dʊlt] *f* patience. **geduldig** *adj* patient. **Geduldspiel** *neut* puzzle.

geehrt [gə'eːrt] *adj* honoured. **sehr geehrter Herr (Smith)** Dear Sir (Dear Mr Smith).

geeignet [gə'aɪgnət] *adj* suitable, adapted (to).

Gefahr [gə'faːr] *f (pl* **-en**) danger. **gefährden** *v* endanger, jeopardize. **gefährlich** *adj* dangerous. **gefahrllos** *adj* safe, without risk. **-voll** *adj* dangerous.

Gefährte [gə'fɛːrtə] *m (pl* **-n**), **Gefährtin** *f (pl* **-nen**) companion.

***gefallen** [gə'falən] *v* please. **es gefällt mir** I like it. **sich nicht gefallen lassen** not put up with.

Gefallen[1] [gə'falən] *neut (unz.)* pleasure.

Gefallen[2] *m (pl* **-**) favour. **tun Sie mir den Gefallen und ...** Do me the favour of ....

gefällig [gə'fɛlɪç] *adj* pleasing; obliging.

gefangen [gə'faŋən] *adj* captive. **Gefangene(r)** *m* prisoner, captive. **Gefangenschaft** *f* captivity.

Gefängnis [gə'fɛŋnɪs] *neut (pl* **-se**) prison. **-wärter** *m* warder, prison officer.

Gefäß [gə'fɛːs] *neut (pl* **-e**) container, vessel.

gefaßt [gə'fast] *adj* collected, calm, *(bereit)* ready.

Gefecht [gə'fɛçt] *neut (pl* **-e**) fight; combat.

Gefieder [gə'fiːdər] *neut (unz.)* feathers *pl*; plumage.

Geflügel [gə'flyːgəl] *neut (unz.)* poultry.

Gefolge [gə'fɔlgə] *neut (pl* **-**) followers *pl*, entourage.

gefräßig [gə'frɛːsɪç] *adj* voracious, gluttonous.

Gefrier||punkt [gə'friːrpuŋkt] *m* freezing point. **-schutzmittel** *neut* antifreeze.

gefügig [gə'fyːgɪç] *adj* pliant, submissive.

Gefühl [gə'fyːl] *neut (pl* **-e**) feeling. **gefühllos** *adj* unfeeling. **Gefühlssinn** *m* sense of touch. **gefühlvoll** *adj* full of feeling, emotional.

gegebenenfalls [gə'geːbənənfals] *adv* if need be, should the need arise. **Gegebenheit** *f (pl* **-en**) reality.

gegen ['geːgən] *prep* against; *(in Richtung)* towards; *(ungefähr)* about; compared with; *(Tausch)* in exchange for.

Gegen||angriff *m* counterattack. **-besuch** *m* return visit. **-bild** *neut* counterpart.

Gegend ['geːgənt] *f (pl* **-en**) district, area.

gegeneinander ['geːgənaɪnandər] *adv* against one another. **-stoßen** *v* collide.

Gegen||gift *neut* antidote. **-leistung** *f* return (service). **-mittel** *neut* remedy. **-satz** *m* opposite, contrary. **gegenllsätzlich** *adj* opposite, contrary. **-seitig** *adj* reciprocal, mutual. **Gegenllstand** *m* object; *(Thema)* subject. **-stück** *neut* counterpart. **-teil** *neut* opposite, contrary. **im Gegenteil zu** contrary to, in contrast to.

gegenüber ['geːgənyːbər] *adv, prep* opposite. **-liegend** *adj* opposite. **-stehen** *v* stand opposite. **Gegenüberstellung** *f* confrontation; antithesis.

Gegenwart ['geːgənvart] *f (unz.)* present; *(Anwesenheit)* presence. **gegenwärtig** *adj* present, current.

Gegner ['geːgnər] *m (pl* **-**) opponent, enemy. **gegnerisch** *adj* antagonistic, hostile.

Gehalt[1] [gə'halt] *m (unz.)* contents *pl*; *(Wert)* worth, value.

Gehalt[2] *neut (pl* **Gehälter**) salary, pay. **Gehaltsllempfänger** *m* salaried employee. **-erhöhung** *f* rise (in salary).

gehässig [gə'hɛsɪç] *adj* spiteful, malicious.

Gehäuse [gə'hɔyzə] *neut (pl* **-**) case, box; *(Tech)* casing.

geheim [gə'haɪm] *adj* secret. **Geheim||agent** *m* secret agent. **-dienst** *m* secret *or* intelligence service. **geheim-halten** *v* keep secret. **Geheimnis** *neut* (*pl* -se) secret; (*unerklärbar*) mystery. **geheimnisvoll** *adj* mysterious. **Geheim‖polizei** *f* secret police. **–schrift** *f* code, cipher. **geheimtuerisch** *adj* secretive.

*gehen ['geːən] *v* walk, go (on foot); (*Maschine*) go, work. **wie geht es Ihnen?** how are you? **es geht** it's all right. **es geht nicht** it can't be done, that's no good. **sie geht mit ihm** she is going out with him. **an die Arbeit gehen** set to work.

Gehilfe [gə'hilfə] *m* (*pl* -n) assistant, help.

Gehirn [gə'hirn] *neut* (*pl* -e) brain. **–erschütterung** *f* concussion. **–schlag** *m* cerebral apoplexy. **–wäsche** *f* brainwashing.

gehoben [gə'hoːbən] *adj* high, elevated.

Gehör [gə'høːr] *neut* (*unz.*) hearing; (*Musik*) ear.

gehorchen [gə'hɔrçən] *v* obey.

gehören [gə'høːrən] *v* belong (to). **es gehört sich** it is proper *or* fitting. **gehörig** *adj* fit, proper.

gehorsam [gə'hoːrzaːm] *adj* obedient. **Gehorsam** *adj* obedience. **–verweigerung** *f* insubordination.

Geh‖steig ['geːʃtaik] *m* (*pl* -e) pavement. **–werk** *neut* movement, works.

Geier ['gaiər] *m* (*pl* -) vulture.

Geifer ['gaifər] *m* (*unz.*) spittle, slaver; (*fig*) venom. **geifern** *v* slaver; (*fig*) rave, foam with rage.

Geige [gaigə] *f* (*pl* -n) violin, fiddle. **–r** *m* violinist.

Geisel ['gaizəl] *m* (*pl* -) hostage.

Geist [gaist] **1** *m* (*unz.*) mind; (*Witzigkeit*) wit; (*nichtmaterielle Eigenschaften*) spirit. **2** *m* (*pl* -er) (**Genius**) genius; (*Gespenst*) ghost, spirit. **geistesabwesend** *adj* absent-minded. **Geistes‖blitz** *m* brainwave. **–freiheit** *f* freedom of thought. **geisteskrank** *adj* mentally ill, insane. **Geisteskranke(r)** *m* mental patient. **geist‖lig** *adj* intellectual; (*nicht körperlich*) spiritual; (*Getränke*) alcoholic. **–lich** *adj* spiritual, religious; (*kirchlich*) clerical. **Geistliche(r)** *m* cleric, clergyman. **geistreich** *adj* clever, ingenious.

Geiz [gaits] *m* (*unz.*) avarice, miserliness. **geizig** *adj* miserly, avaricious.

Gekicher [gə'kiçər] *neut* (*unz.*) giggling.

Geklapper [ge'klapər] *neut* (*unz.*)

clatter(ing).

Geklimper [gə'klimpər] *neut* (*unz.*) jingling, chinking; (*Instrument*) strumming.

Geklingel [gə'kliŋəl] *neut* (*unz.*) tinkling, ringing.

Gekritzel [gə'kritsəl] *neut* doodle.

gekünstelt [gə'kynstəlt] *adj* artificial, affected.

Gel [ʒɛl] *neut* (*pl* -e) gel.

Gelächter [gə'lɛçtər] *neut* (*pl* -) laughter.

geladen [gə'laːdən] *adj* loaded; (*Batterie*) charged.

Gelände [gə'lɛndə] *neut* (*pl* -) tract of land, area; (*Bau-*) site; (*Sport-*) grounds *pl*. **–fahrzeug** *neut* off-road vehicle. **–lauf** *m* cross-country (running).

Geländer [gə'lɛndər] *neut* (*pl* -) railing, banister.

gelangen [gə'laŋən] *v* reach, arrive at; (*Ziel*) attain.

gelassen [gə'lasən] *adj* calm, composed.

geläufig [gə'bʏfiç] *adj* familiar; (*Sprache*) fluent.

gelaunt [gə'launt] *adj* disposed. **gut gelaunt** sweet-tempered. **schlecht** *or* **übel gelaunt** bad-tempered.

gelb [gɛlp] *adj* yellow. **Gelb** *neut* yellow. **–sucht** *f* jaundice. **gelbsüchtig** *adj* (*Med*) jaundiced.

Geld [gɛlt] *neut* (*pl* -er) money. **–ausgabe** *f* expenditure. **–beutel** *m* purse. **–geber.** *m* financial backer. **geldlich** *adj* pecuniary. **Geld‖nehmer** *m* borrower. **–strafe** *f* fine. **–stück** *neut* coin. **–sucht** *f* avarice.

Gelee [ʒe'leː] *neut* (*pl* -s) jelly.

gelegen [gə'leːgən] *adj* situated; (*günstig*) convenient, opportune. **Gelegenheit** *f* (*pl* -en) opportunity, occasion. **Gelegenheits‖arbeit** *f* casual work. **–kauf** *m* bargain. **gelegentlich** *adj* occasional.

gelehrig [gə'leːriç] *adj* eager to learn; (*klug*) intelligent. **gelehrt** *adj* learned. **Gelehrte(r)** *m* scholar.

Geleit [gə'lait] *neut* (*pl* -) escort, entourage. **–brief** *m* (letter of) safe conduct. **geleiten** *v* escort, accompany.

Gelenk [gə'lɛŋk] *neut* (*pl* -e) joint. **–entzündung** *f* arthritis.

gelernt [gə'lɛrnt] *adj* skilled, trained.

Geliebte(r) [gə'liːptə] *m* beloved, sweetheart.

gelinde [gə'lində] *adj* gentle, mild.

gelingen [gəˈlɪŋən] v succeed, be successful. **es gelingt mir, zu** ... I am able to ....

geloben [gəˈloːbən] v vow, promise solemnly.

*gelten [gɛltən] v be worth, cost; (*gültig sein*) be valid; (*betreffen*) concern. **-d** adj valid. **geltend machen** urge, insist (on).

Gelübde [gəˈlyːpdə] neut (pl -) vow.

Gemach [gəˈm ax] neut (pl **Gemächer**) room, chamber.

Gemahl [gəˈm aːl] m (pl -e) husband. **-in** f (pl **-nen**) wife.

Gemälde [gəˈm ɛːldə] neut (pl -) painting, picture. **-galerie** f picture gallery.

gemäß [gəˈm ɛːs] prep in accordance with. adj suitable.

gemein [gəˈm aɪn] adj common; (*öffentlich*) public; vulgar, low; (*böse*) nasty, mean.

Gemeinde [gəˈm aɪndə] f (pl -n) community; (*Kommune*) municipality, town; (*Kirche*) congregation. **-rat** m local council; (*Person*) councillor. **-schule** f village school. **-steuer** f rates pl.

Gemeine(r) [gəˈm aɪnə (r)] m (*Mil*) private. **Gemeinheit** f meanness, nastiness; (*Tat*) mean trick, piece of spite. **gemeinllnützig** adj charitable. **-sam** adj joint, common, corporate. **Gemeinschaft** f community; (*Komm*) partnership. **-serziehung** f coeducation. **-sschule** f coeducational school.

Gemenge [gəˈm ɛŋə] neut (pl -n) mixture; (*Gewühl*) scuffle.

gemessen [gəˈm ɛsən] adj measured, sedate.

Gemisch [gəˈm ɪʃ] neut (pl -e) mixture. **gemischt** adj mixed.

Gemurmel [gəˈm ʊrm əl] neut (*unz.*) murmuring.

Gemüse [gəˈm yːzə] neut (pl -) vegetable(s). **-gärtner** m market gardener. **-händler** m greengrocer.

Gemüt [gəˈm yːt] neut (pl **-er**) disposition, temperament, heart. **gemütlich** adj comfortable, cosy; (*leutselig*) good-natured. **Gemütlichkeit** f cosiness, comfortableness; good nature.

Gen [gɛn] neut (pl -e) gene.

genannt [gəˈnant] adj named, called.

genau [gəˈnau] adj precise, exact. **Genauigkeit** f precision, exactness.

genehmigen [gəˈneːm ɪgən] v authorize, permit. **Genehmigung** f (pl **-en**) authoriza-

tion, permission.

geneigt [gəˈnaɪkt] adj disposed, inclined.

General [geneˈraːl] m (pl -e) general. **-police** f comprehensive insurance policy. **-probe** f dress rehearsal. **-sekretär** m secretary-general. **-versammlung** f general meeting.

Generation [generatsˈloːn] f (pl **-en**) generation.

*genesen [gəˈneːzən] v recover, convalesce, get better. **Genesung** f recovery. **-sheim** neut convalescent home.

Genetik [geˈneːtɪk] f genetics. **genetisch** adj genetic.

Genf [gɛnf] neut Geneva.

Genfood [ˈgɛnfuːd] neut (pl -s) GM (genetically modified) food.

genial [genˈiaːl] adj (*Person*) brilliant, gifted; (*Sache*) ingenious, inspired.

Genick [gəˈnɪk] neut (pl -e) (nape of the) neck.

Genie [ʒeˈniː] neut (pl -s) genius.

genieren [ʒeˈniːrən] v bother, trouble. **sich genieren** be embarrassed.

genießbar [gəˈniːsbaːr] adj enjoyable; (*Essen, Trinken*) palatable. **genießen** v enjoy; eat; drink. **Genießer** m (pl -) epicure, gourmet.

Genitalien [geniˈtaːlən] pl genitals.

Genosse [gəˈnɔsə] m (pl -n), **Genossin** f (pl **-nen**) comrade; (*Kollege*) colleague. **Genossenschaft** f cooperative (society). **genossenschaftlich** adj cooperative.

genug [gəˈnuːk] adv, adj enough, sufficient(ly). **genügen** v be enough, suffice. **-d** adj sufficient, enough. **genügsam** adj easily satisfied. **Genugtuung** f satisfaction.

Genuß [gəˈnus] m (pl **Genüsse**) pleasure, enjoyment.

Geograph [geoˈgraːf] m (pl **-en**) geographer. **-ie** f geography. **geographisch** adj geographical.

Geologe [geoˈloːgə] m (pl -n) geologist. **Geologie** f geology. **geologisch** adj geological.

Geometrie [geomˈetriː] f (pl -n) geometry. **geometrish** adj geometrical.

Gepäck [gəˈpɛk] neut (*unz.*) baggage, luggage. **-aufbewahrung** f left-luggage office. **-netz** neut luggage rack. **-träger** m porter.

gepflegt [gəˈpfleːkt] adj well-tended; (*Person*) well-groomed, well-dressed.

gepanzert [gə'pantsərt] *adj* armoured.

Gepflogenheit [gə'pfloːgənhaɪt] *f (pl -en)* habit, custom.

Geplapper [gə'plapər] *neut (unz.)* chatter.

Geplauder [gə'plaudər] *neut (unz.)* chat, small talk.

Gepräge [gə'prɛːgə] *neut (pl -)* stamp; *(Münze)* coinage; *(Eigenart)* character.

Geprassel [gə'prasəl] *neut (unz.)* clatter.

gerade [gə'raːdə] *adj* straight; *(direkt)* direct; *(Haltung)* erect; *(Zahl)* even. *adv* just; *(genau)* exactly, precisely; *(direkt)* straight, directly. **-aus** *adv* straight on *or* ahead. **-so** *adv* just so, just the same. **-stehen** *v* stand erect, stand up straight. **-swegs** *adv* immediately; *(ohne Umwege)* directly. **-zu** *adv* directly; *(freimütig)* plainly, flatly; *(durchaus)* sheer, downright. **Geradheit** *f* straightness; *(Ehrlichkeit)* honesty. **gerad‖läufig** *adj* straight. **-zahlig** *adj* even (-numbered).

Geranie [gɛ'raːniə] *f (pl -n)* geranium.

Gerassel [gə'rasəl] *neut (unz.)* clatter, rattle.

Gerät [gə'rɛːt] *neut (pl -e)* tool, implement; *(kompliziert)* instrument; *(Maschine)* device, appliance; *(Radio, TV)* set; *(Ausrüstung)* equipment.

*geraten [gə'raːtən] *v* come upon; *(gelingen)* turn out well; *(gedeihen)* thrive. **in Schwierigkeiten geraten** get into difficulties. **in Zorn geraten** fly into a rage. **über etwas geraten** come across, stumble upon something.

Geratewohl [gə'raːtəvoːl] *neut* **aufs Geratewohl** at random.

geräumig [gə'ɔʏmiç] *adj* roomy, spacious.

Geräusch [gə'ɔʏʃ] *neut (pl -e)* noise.

gerben ['gɛrbən] *v* tan. **Gerber** *m (pl -)* tanner. **Gerberei** *f (pl -en)* tannery.

gerecht [gə'rɛçt] *adj* just, fair; *(geeignet)* suitable. **-fertigt** *adj* justified; *(legitim)* legitimate. **Gerechtigkeit** *f* justice; *(Rechtschaffenheit)* righteousness.

Gerede [gə'reːdə] *neut (unz.)* gossip.

Gericht[1] [gə'rɪçt] *neut (pl -e) (Essen)* dish; *(Gang)* course.

Gericht[2] *neut (pl -e)* law-court; *(fig)* justice, judgment. **gerichtlich** *adj* judicial, legal. **Gerichts‖hof** *m (law)* court. **-kosten** *pl* (legal) costs. **-medizin** *f* forensic medicine. **-saal** *m* courtroom. **-schreiber** *m* clerk (of the court). **-verfahren** *neut* legal proceed-

ings *pl.* **-vollzieher** *m* bailiff.

gerieben [gə'riːbən] *adj* grated.

gering [gə'rɪŋ] *adj* small; *(Vorrat)* short; *(Preis)* low; *(unbedeutend)* unimportant, insignificant. **-fügig** *adj* trivial, insignificant. **-schätzen** *v* think little of, despise. **-schätzig** *adj* disdainful.

gerinnen [gə'rɪnən] *v* congeal; *(Blut)* clot. **Gerinnsel** *neut* clot.

Gerippe [gə'rɪpə] *neut (pl -)* skeleton.

Germane [gɛr'maːnə] *m (pl -n)*, **Germanin** *f (pl -nen)* German; *pl* Germanic (tribes or peoples). **germanisch** *adj* Germanic.

gern(e) ['gɛrn ə] *adv* willingly, gladly, readily. **gern haben** *or* **mögen** be fond of, like. **gern tun** like to do. *ich möchte gern …* I should like … **gut und gern** easily.

Gerste ['gɛrstə] *f* barley.

Geruch [gə'ruːx] *m (pl Gerüche)* smell, odour. **-ssinn** *m* (sense of) smell.

Gerücht [gə'rʏçt] *neut (pl -e)* rumour.

Gerümpel [gə'rʏmpəl] *neut* junk, trash.

Gerüst [gə'rʏst] *neut (pl -e)* scaffolding.

gesamt [gə'zamt] *adj* whole, entire. **Gesamt‖betrag** *m* total (amount). **-heit** *f* whole, totality. **-schule** *f* comprehensive school. **-übersicht** *f* overall view. **-versicherung** *f* comprehensive insurance. **-zahl** *f* total (number).

Gesandte(r) [gə'zantə] *m (pl -n)* ambassador. **Gesandtschaft** *f* embassy.

Gesang [gə'zaŋ] *m (pl Gesänge)* song; *(Singen)* singing. **-buch** *neut* songbook; *(Kirche)* hymnbook.

Gesäß [gə'zɛːs] *neut (pl -e)* seat, bottom.

Geschäft [gə'ʃɛft] *neut (pl -e)* business; *(Laden)* shop; *(Handel)* deal. **das Geschäft blüht** business is booming. **ein unsauberes Geschäft** a dirty business. **ein gutes Geschäft machen** get a bargain. **geschäftlich** *adj* commercial, business. **Geschäfts‖freund** *m* business associate, customer. **-führer** *m* manager; *(Verein)* secretary. **-haus** *neut* firm. **-jahr** *neut* business year. **-mann** *m* businessman. **-raum** *m* or **-räume** *pl* office(s). **geschäftsmäßig** *adj* businesslike. **Geschäfts‖reisende(r)** *m* commercial traveller, representative. **-schluß** *m* closing time. **-stunden** *pl* office hours.

*geschehen [gə'ʃeːən] *v* happen.

gescheit [gə'ʃaɪt] *adj* clever, smart.

Geschenk [gə'ʃɛŋk] *neut* (*pl* -e) present, gift.

Geschichte [gə'ʃɪçtə] *f* (*pl* -n) (*Erzählung*) story; (*Vergangenheit*) history; (*Angelegenheit*) affair. **Geschichtenbuch** *neut* story book. **geschichtlich** *adj* historical. **Geschichts∥buch** *neut* history book. **–forscher** *m* (research) historian. **–schreiber** *m* historian.

Geschick [gə'ʃɪk] *neut* (*pl* -e) aptitude; (*Schicksal*) fate. **–lichkeit** *f* skill. **geschickt** *adj* able, skilful.

geschieden [gə'ʃiːdən] *adj* divorced.

Geschirr [gə'ʃɪr] *neut* (*pl* -e) crockery, dishes; (*Pferde*) harness. **–tuch** *neut* dishcloth. **–spülmaschine** *f* dishwasher.

Geschlecht [gə'ʃlɛçt] *neut* (*pl* -er) sex; (*Art*) kind, sort; (*Familie*) family, house; (*Gramm*) gender. **geschlechtlich** *adj* sexual. **Geschlechts∥krankheit** *f* venereal disease. **–reife** *f* puberty. **–teile** *pl* genitals. **–verkehr** *m* sexual intercourse.

geschlossen [gə'ʃlɔsən] *adj* closed.

Geschmack [gə'ʃmak] *m* (*pl* **Geschmäcke**) taste. **geschmacklos** *adj* tasteless. **Geschmacks∥sache** *f* matter of taste. **–sinn** *m* sense of taste. **geschmackvoll** *adj* tasteful.

Geschnatter [gə'ʃnatər] *neut* (*unz.*) cackling.

Geschöpf [gə'ʃœpf] *neut* (*pl* -e) creature.

Geschoß [gə'ʃɔs] *neut* (*pl* **Geschosse**) projectile, missile; (*Kanone*) shell; (*Stockwerk*) floor, storey.

Geschrei [gə'ʃrai] *neut* (*pl* -e) cry, shouting, crying; (*fig*) fuss, noise.

Geschütz [gə'ʃyts] *neut* (*pl* -e) gun, cannon.

Geschwätz [gə'ʃvɛts] *neut* idle talk, prattle. **geschwätzig** *adj* talkative.

geschweige [gə'ʃvaigə] *conj* **geschweige denn** let alone, to say nothing of.

geschwind [gə'ʃvint] *adj* quick, fast. **Geschwindigkeit** *f* speed, velocity. **Geschwindigkeits∥grenze** *f* speed limit. **–messer** *m* speedometer.

Geschwister [gə'ʃvistər] *pl* brother(s) and sister(s); siblings. *haben Sie Geschwister?* have you any brothers and sisters?

Geschworene(r) [gə'ʃvoːrənə] *m* (*pl* -n) juror. **Geschworenengericht** *neut* (trial by) jury.

Geschwür [gə'ʃvyːr] *neut* (*pl* -e) ulcer, sore.

Geselle [gə'zɛlə] *m* (*pl* -n) comrade, companion; (*Bursche*) lad, fellow; (*gelehrter Handwerker*) journeyman. **gesellig** *adj* sociable. **Gesellschaft** *f* society; (*Firma*) company; (*Verein*) society, association; (*Abend-, usw.*) party, social gathering; (*Begleitung*) company. **gesellschaftlich** *adj* social. **Gesellschaftsanzug** *m* evening dress. **gesellschaftsfeindlich** *adj* antisocial. **Gesellschafts∥kleid** *neut* party dress. **–steuer** *f* corporation tax. **–tanz** *m* society dance, ball.

Gesetz [gə'zɛts] *neut* (*pl* -e) law. **–buch** *neut* statute book, law code. **–entwurf** *m* bill. **gesetzgebend** *adj* legislative. **Gesetzgebung** *f* legislation. **gesetz∥lich** *adj* legal, lawful. **–los** *adj* lawless. **–mäßig** *adj* legal, lawful.

gesetzt [gə'zɛtst] *adj* sedate, quiet.

gesetzwidrig [gə'zɛtsviːdriç] *adj* illegal, unlawful.

Gesicht [gə'ziçt] *neut* (*pl* -er) face; (*Miene*) expression. **Gesichts∥ausdruck** *m* (facial) expression. **–farbe** *f* complexion. **–feld** *neut* field of vision. **–punkt** *m* viewpoint.

gesinnt [gə'zint] *adj* disposed, minded. **Gesinnung** *f* opinion, mind, conviction. **gesinnungslos** *adj* unprincipled.

Gespann [gə'ʃpan] *neut* (*pl* -e) (*Pferden*) (team of) horses.

gespannt [gə'ʃpant] *adj* tense; (*Verhältnis*) strained. **gespannt sein** be eager or anxious.

Gespenst [gə'ʃpɛnst] *neut* (*pl* -er) ghost. **gespenstig** *adj* ghostly.

Gespräch [gə'ʃprɛːç] *neut* (*pl* -e) conversation, talk. **Gespräche** *pl* talks, discussion *sing.* **gesprächig** *adj* talkative.

Gestalt [gə'ʃtalt] *f* (*pl* -en) form, shape; (*Körper-*) figure, build; (*Literatur*) character. **gestalt∥en** *v* form, shape. **–et** *adj* formed, shaped. **–los** *adj* shapeless. **Gestaltung** *f* (*unz.*) shaping, formation.

Geständnis [gə'ʃtɛntnis] *neut* (*pl* -se) confession.

Gestank [gə'ʃtaŋk] *m* stink, stench; (*umg.*) pong.

gestatten [gə'ʃtatən] *v* permit, allow.

Geste ['gɛstə] *f* (*pl* -n) gesture.

*gestehen [gə'ʃteːən] *v* confess.

Gestell [gə'ʃtɛl] *neut* (*pl* -e) (*Rahmen*) frame, stand; (*Bock*) trestle; (*Regal*) shelf; (*Bett-*) bedstead.

gestern ['gɛstərn] *adv* yesterday.

Gesträuch [gəˈʃtrɔyç] *neut* (*unz.*) shrubbery, bushes *pl.*

gestrichen [gəˈʃtrɪçən] *adj* painted. **frisch gestrichen** newly painted; wet paint.

gestrig [ˈgɛstrɪç] *adj* yesterday's.

Gestrüpp [gəˈʃtryp] *neut* undergrowth, scrub.

Gesuch [gəˈzuːx] *neut* (*pl* -e) petition. **gesucht** *adj* in demand; (*Person*) wanted.

gesund [gəˈzunt] *adj* healthy, well. **Gesundheit** *f* health. *interj* bless you! **gesundheitlich** *adj* sanitary. **gesundheitsförderlich** *adj* wholesome, healthy. **Gesundheitslehre** *f* hygiene. **gesundheitsschädlich** *adj* insanitary, unhealthy.

Getränk [gəˈtrɛŋk] *neut* (*pl* -e) drink.

Getreide [gəˈtraɪdə] *neut* (*pl* -) grain, cereals *pl.*

getreu [gəˈtrɔy] *adj* loyal, faithful.

Getriebe [gəˈtriːbə] *neut* (*pl* -) commotion, bustle; (*Tech*) transmission, gears *pl.* **–gehäuse** *neut* gearbox.

getrost [gəˈtroːst] *adj* confident. *adv* without hesitation.

Getto [ˈgetoː] *neut* (*pl* -s) ghetto.

geübt [gəˈypt] *adj* practised, skilful.

Gewächs [gəˈvɛks] *neut* (*pl* -e) plant; (*Med*) growth.

gewachsen [gəˈvaksən] *adj* grown. **gewachsen sein** be equal (to), be up (to).

gewagt [gəˈvaːkt] *adj* bold, daring.

gewählt [gəˈvɛːlt] *adj* select(ed), choice.

Gewähr [gəˈvɛːr] *f* (*unz.*) guarantee, surety. **gewähren** *v* allow, grant, deign. **gewährleisten** *v* guarantee, vouch for.

Gewalt [gəˈvalt] *f* (*pl* -en) force; (*Macht*) power; (*Obrigkeit*) authority; (*Gewalttätigkeit*) violence. **–herrscher** *m* tyrant. **gewalttlig** *adj* forceful, powerful; enormous; (*gewalttätig*) violent. **–los** *adj* powerless. **–sam** *adj* violent; *adv* by force. **–tätig** *adj* violent.

Gewand [gəˈvant] *neut* (*pl* **Gewänder**) garment, robe.

gewandt [gəˈvant] *adj* skilled, skilful. **Gewandtheit** *f* dexterity, skill.

Gewässer [gəˈvɛsər] *neut* (*pl* -) water(s).

Gewebe [gəˈveːbə] *neut* (*pl* -) material, textile; (*Biol*) tissue; (*Lügen, usw.*) web, network.

geweckt [gəˈvɛkt] *adj* bright, lively.

Gewehr [gəˈveːr] *neut* (*pl* -e) rifle, gun.

–kugel *f* (rifle) bullet.

Geweih [gəˈvaɪ] *neut* (*pl* -e) antlers *pl.*

Gewerbe [gəˈvɛrbə] *neut* (*pl* -) trade. **–schule** *f* technical school. **gewerblllich** *adj* industrial. **–smäßig** *adj* professional.

Gewerkschaft [gəˈvɛrkʃaft] *f* (*pl* -en) (trade) union. **–ler** *m* (trade) unionist. **gewerkschaftlich** *adj* trade-union.

Gewicht [gəˈvɪçt] *neut* (*pl* -e) weight; (*fig*) importance. **–heben** *neut* weight-lifting. **gewichtig** *adj* heavy; (*fig*) important.

Gewimmel [gəˈvɪm əl] *neut* (*pl* -) crowd, swarm.

Gewinde [gəˈvɪndə] *neut* (*pl* -) (*Schraube*) thread.

Gewinn [gəˈvɪn] *m* (*pl* -e) profit; (*Ertrag*) yield, returns; (*Preis*) prize; (*Erwerben*) gaining. **–beteiligung** *f* profit-sharing. **gewinnllbringend** *adj* profitable. **–en** *v* (*Preis*) win; (*erwerben*) gain, acquire; (*siegen*) win. **–süchtig** *adj* acquisitive.

Gewirr [gəˈvɪr] *neut* (*pl* -e) confusion, tangle.

gewiß [gəˈvɪs] *adj* certain, sure. *adv* certainly. *ein gewisser Herr Schmidt* a certain Mr Schmidt. *ein gewisses Etwas* a certain something.

Gewissen [gəˈvɪsən] *neut* (*unz.*) conscience. **gewissenllhaft** *adj* conscientious. **–los** *adj* unscrupulous. **Gewissensllbisse** *pl* pangs of conscience. **–konflikt** *m* conflict of conscience.

gewissermaßen [gəˈvɪsəm aːsən] *adv* to some extent.

Gewißheit [gəˈvɪshaɪt] *f* (*unz.*) certainty.

Gewitter [gəˈvɪtər] *neut* (*pl* -) thunderstorm. **gewitterhaft** *adj* stormy.

gewogen [gəˈvoːgən] *adj* well disposed, favourably inclined.

gewöhnen [gəˈvøː nən] *v* accustom. **sich gewöhnen an** become accustomed to, get used to. **Gewohnheit** *f* (*pl* -en) habit; (*Brauch*) custom. **gewohnheitsmäßig** *adj* customary. **gewöhnlich** *adj* usual, ordinary; (*unfein*) vulgar. *adv* usually. **gewohnt** *adj* used (to).

Gewölbe [gəˈvœ bə] *neut* (*pl* -) vault. **gewölbt** *adj* arched, vaulted.

Gewühl [gəˈvyːl] *neut* (*unz.*) crowd, tumult.

Gewürz [gəˈvyrts] *neut* (*pl* -e) spice, seasoning. **gewürzig** *adj* spicy. **gewürzt** *adj* spiced, seasoned.

gezackt [gəˈtsakt] *adj* serrated; (*Fels*) jagged.

geziemend [gəˈtsiːmənt] *or* **geziemlich** *adj* seemly.

geziert [gəˈtsiːrt] *adj* affected.

gezwungen [gəˈtsvʊŋən] *adj* forced; (*steif*) formal, stiff.

Gicht [gɪçt] *f* (*unz.*) gout.

Giebel [ˈgiːbəl] *m* (*pl -*) gable. **–dach** *neut* gabled roof.

Gier [giːr] *f* greed; (*nach etwas*) craving, burning desire (for). **gierig** *adj* greedy.

*****gießen** [ˈgiːsən] *v* pour; (*Pflanzen*) water; (*schmelzen*) cast. **Gießllerei** *f* (*pl -en*) foundry. **–kanne** *f* watering can.

Gift [gɪft] *neut* (*pl -e*) poison. **–gas** *neut* poison gas. **giftig** *adj* poisonous. **Giftschlange** *f* poisonous snake.

Ginster [ˈgɪnstər] *m* (*pl -*) (*Bot*) broom.

Gipfel [ˈgɪpfəl] *m* (*pl -*) peak, summit. **–gespräche** *pl* summit talks. **–leistung** *f* record.

Gips [gɪps] *m* (*pl -e*) gypsum; (*erhitzt*) plaster (of Paris). **–verband** *m* plaster cast.

Giraffe [giˈrafə] *f* (*pl -n*) giraffe.

Giro [ˈdʒiːroː] *neut* (*pl -s*) giro. **–konto** *neut* current account.

Gitarre [giˈtarə] *f* (*pl -n*) guitar.

Gitter [ˈgɪtər] *neut* (*pl -*) grille, grating; (*Fenster*) bars; (*Spalier*) trellis.

Glanz [glants] *m* (*unz.*) shine, brilliance, brightness; (*fig*) splendour.

glänzen [ˈglɛntsən] *v* gleam, shine; (*fig*) excel, shine. **–d** *adj* brilliant.

Glas [glaːs] *neut* (*pl* Gläser) glass. **–haus** *neut* greenhouse, hothouse. **–perle** *f* bead. **–scheibe** *f* (window) pane. **glasieren** *v* glaze; (*Kuchen*) ice. **Glasur** *f* glaze; (*Kuchen*) icing.

glatt [glat] *adj* smooth; (*glitschig*) slippery. **Glatteis** *neut* (*Mot*) black ice. **glattrasiert** *adj* clean-shaven.

Glaube [ˈglaubə] *m* (*unz.*) belief; (*Rel*) faith. **glauben** *v* believe; (*vermuten*) think, suppose; (*vertrauen*) trust. **glaubhaft** *adj* credible.

gläubig [ˈglɔybɪç] *adj* believing; (*fromm*) pious. **Gläubige(r)** *m* believer; (*Komm*) creditor.

glaublich [ˈglauplɪç] *adj* credible. **glaubwürdig** *adj* (*Person*) trustworthy; (*Sache*) credible.

gleich [glaiç] *adj* (the) same, equal; (*eben*) level. *adv* equally; (*sofort*) at once; (*schon*) just. **von gleichem Alter** of the same age. **das ist mir gleich** it makes no difference to me. **das gleiche gilt für Dich** the same goes for you. **Ich komme gleich** I'm just coming. **gleich viel** just as much. **gleichllartig** *adj* similar. **–bedeutend** *adj* synonymous. **–berechtigt** *adj* having equal rights.

*****gleichen** [ˈglaiçən] *v* equal; (*ähnlich sein*) resemble.

gleichermaßen [ˈglaiçərˌmaːsən] *or* **gleicherweise** *adv* likewise.

gleichllfalls *adv* also, likewise. **–gesinnt** *adj* like-minded.

Gleichgewicht [ˈglaiçgəˌviçt] *neut* equilibrium, balance.

gleichgültig [ˈglaiçgʏltiç] *adj* unconcerned, indifferent. **Gleichgültigkeit** *f* indifference.

Gleichllheit *f* equality. **–maß** *neut* proportion, symmetry. **–mut** *m* equanimity. **–nis** *neut* (*pl -se*) simile; (*Erzählung*) parable.

gleichschalten [ˈglaiçˌʃaltən] *v* coordinate; (*Tech*) synchronize.

Gleichschritt [ˈglaiçˌʃrɪt] *m* **Gleichschritt halten** keep step.

Gleichllstrom *m* direct current. **–ung** *f* (*pl -en*) equation.

gleichllviel *adv* no matter. **–wertig** *adj* equivalent, of the same value. **–wohl** *adv* nonetheless. **–zeitig** *adj* simultaneous.

Gleis [glais] *neut* (*pl -e*) track, platform.

*****gleiten** [ˈglaitən] *v* slide, slip. **Gleitflugzeug** *neut* glider, sailplane.

Gletscher [ˈglɛtʃər] *m* (*pl -*) glacier. **Gletscherspalte** *f* crevasse.

Glied [gliːt] *neut* (*pl -er*) limb; (*Kette*) link. **gliedern** *v* organize, arrange; divide into. **Gliederung** *f* (*pl -en*) organization, arrangement.

Glocke [ˈglɔkə] *f* (*pl -n*) bell. **Glockenllblume** *f* bluebell. **–turm** *m* belltower.

glorreich [ˈglɔrraiç] *adj* glorious.

Glossar [glɔˈsaːr] *neut* (*pl -e, -ien*) glossary. **Glosse** *f* (*pl -n*) comment.

glotzen [ˈglɔtsən] *v* stare.

Glück [glʏk] *neut* luck; (*Geschick*) fortune; (*Freude*) happiness. **glückllich** *adj* happy, fortunate. **–licherweise** *adv* fortunately, luckily. **–selig** *adj* blissful. **Glücksllfall** *m* lucky chance. **–spiel** *neut* game of chance.

glühen ['ɡlyːən] v glow. **Glüh∥hitze** f white heat. **–wein** m mulled wine.

Glut [ɡluːt] f (pl -en) glow. **–asche** f embers pl.

Gnade ['ɡnaːdə] f (pl -n) grace, mercy. **Gnaden∥frist** f reprieve, period of grace. **–stoß** m coup de grâce.

gnädig ['ɡnɛːdɪç] adj gracious; kind. **gnädige Frau** Madam.

Gold [ɡɔlt] neut (unz.) gold. **–barren** m gold bar or ingot. **gold∥en** adj golden. **–ig** adj sweet, lovely.

Golf[1] [ɡɔlf] m (pl -e) gulf.

Golf[2] neut (unz.) (Sport) golf.

gönnen ['ɡœnən] v not begrudge; grant, allow.

Gönner m (pl -) patron, sponsor. **gönnerhaft** adj patronizing; condescending.

Gosse ['ɡɔsə] f (pl -n) gutter.

Gott [ɡɔt] m God; (pl Götter) god. **grüß Gott!** greetings! God be with you! **Gott sei dank!** thank God! **um Gottes willen!** for God's sake! **Gottes∥dienst** m (church) service. **–lästerung** f blasphemy. **Gottheit** f godhead, divinity.

Göttin ['ɡœtɪn] f (pl -nen) goddess. **göttlich** adj divine.

Götze ['ɡœtsə] m (pl -n) idol, false god.

Grab [ɡraːp] neut (pl Gräber) grave. **graben** v dig. **Graben** m ditch, trench. **Grab∥schrift** f epitaph. **–stätte** f grave. **–stein** m tombstone.

Grad [ɡraːt] m (pl -e) degree; (Rang) rank, grade. **–messer** m (fig) indication, sign.

graduieren [ɡraduˈiːrən] v graduate. **Graduierte(r)** m graduate.

Graf [ɡraːf] m (pl -en) countess.

Gräfin ['ɡrɛːfɪn] f (pl -en) countess.

Grafschaft ['ɡraːfʃaft] f (pl -en) county.

Gram [ɡraːm] m (unz.) grief.

Gramm [ɡram] neut (pl -e) gram(me).

Grammatik [ɡraˈmatɪk] f (pl -en) grammar.

Granatapfel [ɡraˈnaːtapfəl] m (pl Granatäpfel) pomegranate.

Granate [ɡraˈnaːtə] f (pl -n) shell, grenade.

Granit [ɡraˈniːt] m (pl -e) granite.

Graphik ['ɡraːfɪk] f (unz.) graphics. **-er** m (pl -) designer, commercial artist. **graphisch** adj graphic. **graphische Darstellung** graph.

Gras [ɡraːs] neut (pl Gräser) grass.

grasen v graze.

gräßlich ['ɡrɛːslɪç] adj horrible, ghastly.

Grat [ɡraːt] m (pl -e) ridge, edge.

Gräte ['ɡrɛːtə] f (pl -n) fishbone. **–nmuster** neut herringbone pattern.

gratulieren [ɡratuˈliːrən] v congratulate.

grau [ɡrau] adj grey. **Graubrot** neut rye bread.

grauen ['ɡrauən] v be horrible. **es graut mir vor** I have a horror of. **–haft** adj dreadful, horrible.

Graupe ['ɡraupə] f (pl -n) groats pl, pearl barley.

graupeln ['ɡraupəln] pl sleet sing.

grausam ['ɡrauzaːm] adj cruel. **Grausamkeit** f cruelty. **grausig** adj fearful, dreadful.

gravieren [ɡraˈviːrən] v engrave.

greif∥en ['ɡraifən] v seize, grasp. **–bar** adj (Waren) available, at hand; (fig) tangible. **greifen an** touch. **greifen in** dip into.

Greis [ɡrais] m (pl -e) old man.

grell [ɡrɛl] adj (Ton) shrill, harsh; (Farbe) glaring, garish.

Grenze ['ɡrɛntsə] f (pl -n) (eines Staates) border, frontier; (einer Stadt, Zone) boundary; (fig) limit. **grenzen** border (on). **Grenz∥fall** m borderline case. **–übergang** m crossing (of a frontier).

Greuel ['ɡrɔyəl] m (pl -) (Abscheu) horror; (Scheußlichkeit) atrocity, abomination.

Grieche ['ɡriːçə] m (pl -n) Greek (man). **Griechenland** neut Greece. **Griechin** f (pl -nen) Greek (woman). **griechisch** adj Greek.

Grieß [ɡriːs] m (unz.) (Essen) semolina; (Kies) gravel. **–pudding** m semolina pudding.

Griff [ɡrɪf] m (pl -e) (Henkel, Knopf, usw.) handle; (Greifen) hold, grip.

Grille ['ɡrɪlə] f (pl -n) (Insekt) cricket; (Laune) whim.

Grimasse [ɡrɪmˈasə] f (pl -n) grimace.

grimmig ['ɡrɪmɪç] adj furious.

grinsen ['ɡrɪnzən] v grin.

Grippe ['ɡrɪpə] f (pl -n) influenza.

grob [ɡroːp] adj coarse; (Benehmen) coarse, rude; (Scherz) crude, coarse; (Fehler) gross, serious. **Grobheit** f coarseness, rudeness.

Groll [ɡrɔl] m animosity, rancour. **grollen** v be resentful, be angry.

gros [groː] en gros wholesale.

Gros¹ [groː] neut (pl -) (Armee) main body.

Gros² [grɔs] neut (pl -e) gross, twelve dozen.

Groschen ['grɔʃən] m (pl -) (Österreich) Groschen; (BRD) ten-pfennig piece; (fig) penny.

groß [groːs] adj big, large; (wichtig) great, grand; (hoch) tall. im großen und ganzen on the whole. –artig adj splendid, grand.

Großbritannien [groːsbrɪtaniən] neut Great Britain.

Großbuchstabe ['groːsbuːxʃtaːbə] m capital (letter).

Großeltern ['groːsɛltərn] pl grandparents.

großenteils ['groːsəntails] adv mostly, for the most part.

Groß||handel m wholesale trade. –händler m wholesaler.

großherzig ['groːshɛrtsɪç] adj magnanimous.

Groß||industrie f large-scale industry. –macht f great power. –markt m (pl –märkte) hypermarket. –maul neut braggart, big-mouth. –mutter f grandmother. –stadt f large town, city.

größtenteils ['grœːstəntails] adv mostly, largely.

Groß||teil m bulk. –tuer m show-off, bighead. –vater m grandfather.

großzügig ['groːstsyːgɪç] adj generous; (weittragend) large-scale. Großzügigkeit f generosity; largeness.

grotesk [groˈtɛsk] adj grotesque.

Grübchen ['gryːpçən] neut (pl -) dimple.

Grube ['gruːbə] f (pl -n) pit, hole; (Bergbau) mine, pit; (Höhle, Bau) hole, burrow; (Falle) snare.

grübeln ['gryːbəln] v brood, ponder.

grün [gryːn] adj green. Grün neut green. –anlage f public park, open space.

Grund [grunt] m (pl Gründe) (Erdboden) ground, soil; (Veranlassung) reason, grounds pl; (Grundlage) basis, base; (Grundbesitz) land; (eines Meeres) bottom. –bau m foundation. –besitz m landed property, real estate. im Grunde (genommen) basically.

gründen ['gryndən] v found, establish. sich gründen auf be based on. Gründer m (pl -) founder.

Grund||gesetz neut basic law; (Verfassung) constitution. –lage f basis,

foundation.

gründlich ['gryntlɪç] adj thorough.

grundlos ['gruntloːs] adj unfounded, baseless.

Grund||maß neut standard of measurement. –riß m outline, design. –satz m principle, axiom. grundsätzlich adj fundamental.

Grund||schule f primary school. –stoff m raw material; (Chem) element. –stück neut lot of land.

Gründung ['grynduŋ] f (pl -en) establishment, foundation.

Grund||unterschied m basic difference. –zahl f cardinal number. –zug m characteristic, feature.

Grünkohl ['gryːnkoːl] m kale.

grunzen ['gruntsən] v grunt.

Grünzeug ['gryːntsɔyk] neut greens pl, green vegetables pl.

Gruppe ['grupə] f (pl -n) group. –nführer m section leader. gruppieren v group.

gruselig ['gruːzəlɪç] adj gruesome; (umg.) creepy.

Gruß [gruːs] m (pl Grüße) greeting; (Mil) salute. herzliche Grüße kind regards, best wishes. Grüß Dich! (interj) Hi!

grüßen ['gryːsən] v greet; (Mil) salute.

gucken ['gukən] v (take a) look, peep.

Gulasch ['guːlaʃ] neut, m (pl -e) goulash.

gültig ['gyltɪç] adj valid; (Gesetz) in force. Gültigkeit f validity, currency. –sdauer f (period of) validity.

Gummi ['gumi] neut (pl -s) rubber; (Klebstoff) gum; (Kau-) (chewing) gum. –band neut rubber band. gummiert adj (Briefmarke, usw.) gummed.

Gunst [gunst] f (unz.) favour.

günstig ['gynstɪç] adj favourable, advantageous.

gurgeln ['gurgəln] v gargle. Gurgelwasser neut gargle.

Gurke ['gurkə] f (pl -n) cucumber; (saure) gherkin.

Gurt [gurt] m (pl -e) belt; (Pferd) girth.

Gürtel ['gyrtəl] m (pl -) belt; (Geog) zone. –reifen m radial-ply tyre, (umg.) radial.

Guß [gus] m (pl Güsse) (Regen) downpour, gush; (Metall) casting, founding.

gut [guːt] adj good. adv well. gut sein mit be on good terms with. es wird schon alles gut werden everything will be all right. das *tut mir gut* that does me good. *schon gut!* that's all right. **gut aussehen** look good; (*gesund*) look well. **Gut** *neut* (*pl* **Güter**) possession; (*Land*) landed estate; (*Ware*) commodity. **gutartig** *adj* good-natured.

Gutdünken *neut* discretion. **nach (Ihrem) Gutdünken** at your discretion.

Güte ['gyːtə] *f* (*unz.*) kindness, goodness; (*Qualität*) quality.

Güter||flugzeug *neut* cargo plane. **–zug** *m* freight train.

gut||gelaun *adj* good-humoured. **–gesinnt** *adj* friendly, well-disposed. **–gläubig** *adj* acting in good faith, bona-fide; *adv* in good faith.

Guthaben ['guːthaːbən] *neut* credit (balance).

***gut||heißen** *v* approve. **–herzig** *adj* kind-hearted.

gütig ['yːtɪç] *adj* kind.

gutmachen ['guːtmaxən] *v* **wieder gutmachen** make amends for, make good.

gutmütig ['guːtmyːtɪç] *adj* good-natured.

Gutschein ['guːtʃain] *m* (*pl* **-e**) voucher. credit-note.

Gymnasium [gym'naːzium] *neut* (*pl* **Gymnasien**) grammar school.

Gymnastik [gym'nastɪk] *f* gymnastics. **gymnastisch** *adj* gymnastic.

H

Haag, Den [deːnˈhaːk] *m* The Hague.

Haar [haːr] *neut* (*pl* **-e**) hair. **sich die Haare schneiden lassen** have a haircut. **haarig** *adj* hairy. **Haar||nadelkurve** *f* hairpin bend. **–schnitt** *m* haircut. **haarsträubend** *adj* hair-raising.

Habe ['haːbə] *f* (*unz.*) property, possessions *pl*. **haben** *v* have. **habsüchtig** *adj* greedy, (*umg.*) grasping.

Hackbrett ['hakbrɛt] *neut* chopping board. **hacken** *v* chop, hack; (*Fleisch*) mince. **Hackfleisch** *neut* mince, minced meat.

Hafen ['haːfən] *m* (*pl* **Häfen**) port, harbour. **–arbeiter** *m* docker. **–damm** *m* pier, mole. **–sperre** *f* embargo. **–stadt** *f* port.

Hafer ['haːfər] *m* (*pl* **-**) oats *pl*. **–flocken** *f pl* rolled oats, oat-flakes.

Haft [haft] *f* arrest, detention, custody. **haften** *v* adhere, cling. **haften für** be liable for, answer for. **Haftpflichtversicherung** *f* (compulsory) third-party insurance.

Hagel ['haːgəl] *m* (*pl* **-**) hail. **–korn** *neut* hailstone. **hageln** *v* **es hagelt** it is hailing.

hager ['aːgər] *adj* lean, haggard.

Hahn [haːn] *m* (*pl* **Hähne**) cock; (*Wasser-, usw.*) tap. **Hahnenkamm** *m* cockscomb.

Hähnchen ['hɛːnçən] *neut* (*pl* **-**) cock; (*Wasser-, usw.*) tap.

Hai [hai] *m* (*pl* **-e**) or **Haifisch** *m* shark.

Hain [hain] *m* (*pl* **-e**) grove.

Häkelarbeit ['hɛːkəlaːrbait] *f* crochet work. **häkeln** *v* crochet.

haken ['haːkən] *v* hook. **sich haken an** catch on, get caught on. **Haken** *m* (*pl* **-**) hook; (*fig*) snag. **–kreuz** *neut* swastika.

halb [halp] *adj* half. **um halb drei** at half past two. **eine halbe Stunde** half an hour. **–entrahmt** *adj* semi-skimmed. **–jährlich** *adj* half-yearly. **Halb||kreis** *m* semicircle. **–kugel** *f* hemisphere. **–messer** *m* radius. **–starke(r)** *m* hooligan. **halbwegs** *adv* halfway. **Halbzeit** *f* halftime.

Hälfte ['hɛlftə] *f* (*pl* **-n**) half.

Halfter ['halftər] *f* or *neut* (*pl* **-n**) halter.

Hall [hal] *m* (*pl* **-e**) sound, peal.

Halle ['halə] *f* (*pl* **-n**) hall; (*Hotel*) lobby; (*Flugzeug-*) hangar.

hallen ['halən] *v* sound, resound.

Hallenbad ['halənbaːt] *neut* indoor swimming pool *or* baths.

Hallo! ['halo] (*interj*) Hello!, Hi!; (*Warnruf*) Excuse me!

Halm [halm] *m* (*pl* **-e**) stalk; (*Gras*) blade.

Hals [hals] *m* (*pl* **Hälse**) neck; (*innerer Hals, Kehle*) throat. **–band** *neut* (*Hund*) collar; (*Frauen*) necklace, choker. **–binde** *f* tie. **–kette** *f* necklace. **–weh** *neut* sore throat.

Halt [halt] *m* (*pl* **-e**) (*Anhalten*) stop, halt; (*Stütze*) hold, support; (*Standhaftigkeit*) steadiness, firmness. **haltbar** *adj* durable, lasting. **haltbar bis ...** (*Speisen*) use by .... **halten** *v* hold; (*bewahren*) keep; (*dauern*) last, keep; (*Gebot, usw.*) observe; (*anhalten*) stop. **viel halten von** think highly of. **halten für** consider (to be), think of as. **Halte||stelle** *f* (*Bus*) busstop. **–tau** *neut* guy-rope. **haltmachen** *v* stop. **Haltung** *f* (*pl* **-en**) attitude; (*Körper-*) bearing, posture.

hämisch ['hɛːmɪʃ] *adj* spiteful, sardonic.

Hammelfleisch ['ham əlflaʃ] *neut* mutton.

Hammer ['ham ər] *m* (*pl* **Hämmer**) hammer.

hämmern ['hɛm əm] *v* hammer.

Hämorrhoiden [hɛm ɔːˈɪdən] *pl* piles, haemorrhoids *pl*.

Hamster ['ham stər] *m* (*pl* -) hamster. **hamstern** *v* hoard.

Hand [hant] *f* (*pl* **Hände**) hand. **an Hand von** with the aid of. **bei der Hand** ready, at hand. **mit der Hand** by hand. **von Hand gemacht** hand-made. **zur linken/rechten Hand** on the left/right hand side. **Hand||arbeit** *f* handiwork; (*Nadelarbeit*) needlework. **–becken** *neut* hand basin. **–bremse** *f* handbrake. **–buch** *neut* manual, handbook.

Händedruck ['hɛndədɪŋk] *m* handshake.

Handel ['handəl] *m* trade, commerce; (*Geschäft*) transaction, deal. **handeln** *v* act. **handeln mit** (*Person*) trade *or* deal with; (*Waren*) trade *or* deal in. **handeln von** treat, deal with. **Handels||beziehungen** *pl* trade relations. **–bilanz** *f* balance of trade. **–schule** *f* business *or* commercial school. **–sperre** *f* (*trade*) embargo.

handfest ['hantfɛst] *adj* sturdy, strong.

Hand||fläche *f* palm. **–gebrauch** *m* everyday use. **–gelenk** *neut* wrist. **–gepäck** *neut* hand luggage.

handhaben ['hanthaːbən] *v* (*gebrauchen*) use, employ; (*fig*) handle.

Händler ['hɛntlər] *m* (*pl* -) trader, dealer.

handlich [hantlɪç] *adj* handy.

Handlung ['hantlʊŋ] *f* (*pl* -en) deed, act; (*Roman, usw.*) plot; (*Geschäft*) business, firm; (*Laden*) shop.

Hand||schellen *pl* handcuffs *pl*. **–schuh** *m* glove. **–tasche** *f* handbag. **–tuch** *neut* towel. **–werk** *neut* craft, trade. **–werker** *m* craftsman, workman.

Handy ['hɛntɪ] *neut* (*pl* -s or **Handies**) mobile phone, cellphone.

Hang [haŋ] *m* (*pl* **Hänge**) slope; (*Neigung*) tendency.

Hängematte ['hɛŋəm atə] *f* hammock.

***hängen**[1] [hɛŋən] *v* be suspended, hang; (*sich neigen*) slope; (*unentschieden*) be pending, remain undecided; (*abhängen*) depend.

hängen[2] *v* hang, suspend; (*hinrichten*) hang.

Hannover [haˈnoːər] *neut* Hanover.

hantieren [hanˈtiːən] *v* busy oneself, potter around.

Happen ['hapən] *m* (*pl* -) mouthful, bite.

Harfe ['harfə] *f* (*pl* -n) harp.

harmlos ['harm boːs] *adj* harmless.

Harmonie [harm ɔˈniː] *f* (*pl* -n) harmony. **harmonisch** *adj* harmonic. **harmonisieren** *v* harmonize.

Harn [harn] *m* urine. **–blase** *f* (*Anat*) bladder.

Harnisch ['harnɪʃ] *m* (*pl* -e) armour; harness.

Harpune [harˈpuːnə] *f* (*pl* -n) harpoon.

harren ['harən] *v* wait for, await.

hart [hart] *adj* hard; (*fig*) harsh, rough.

Härte ['hɛːrtə] *f* (*pl* -n) hardness; (*Strenge*) severity; (*Grausamkeit*) cruelty. **härten** *v* harden; (*Metall*) temper.

hart||gekocht *adj* hard-boiled. **–näckig** *adj* stubborn.

Harz [harts] *neut* (*pl* -e) resin.

Haschisch ['haʃɪʃ] *neut* hashish.

Hase ['haːzə] *m* (*pl* -n) hare. **Häsin** *f* doe.

Haselnuß ['haːzəlnus] *f* hazelnut.

Haspe ['haspə] *f* (*pl* -n) hinge.

Haß [has] *m* hate.

hassen ['hasən] *v* hate. **–swert** *adj* hateful, odious.

häßlich ['hɛslɪç] *adj* ugly; (*fig*) wicked, nasty. **Häßlichkeit** *f* ugliness; (*fig*) wickedness.

Hast [hast] *f* haste. **hasten** *v* hasten. **hastig** *adj* hasty.

hätscheln ['hɛːtʃəln] *v* (*liebkosen*) caress, fondle; (*verwöhnen*) pamper.

Haube ['haubə] *f* (*pl* -n) bonnet, cap; (*Mot*) bonnet, (*US*) hood.

Hauch [haux] *m* (*pl* -e) breath; (*fig*) touch, trace.

Haue ['hauə] *f* (*pl* -n) pick; (*umg.*) beating, spanking. **hauen** *v* hew; (*zerhacken*) chop up; (*umg.*) beat, belt.

Haufen ['haufən] *m* (*pl* -) heap, pile; (*umg.*) heaps of, lots of.

häufen ['hɔyfən] *v* heap (up), accumulate.

häufig ['hɔyfɪç] *adj* frequent, numerous. *adv* frequently.

Haupt [haupt] *neut* (*pl* **Häupter**) head; (*Führer*) leader, chief. **–bahnhof** *m* main railway station, central station. **–buch** *neut* ledger. **–film** *m* feature film, main film. **–leitung** *f* (*Gas, Strom*) mains *pl.* **–mann** *m* (*Mil*) captain. **–rolle** *f* (*Theater*) leading part *or* role.

Hauptsache ['hauptzaxə] *f* main thing *or* point. **hauptsächlich** *adj* essential *adv* principally, mainly.

Haupt||sitz *m* head office. **–stadt** *f* capital (city). **–straße** *f* main street. **–verwaltung** *f* head office. **–wort** *neut* noun.

Haus [haus] *neut* (*pl* **Häuser**) house; (*Heim*) home. **zu Hause** at home. **–arbeit** *f* housework; (*Schule*) homework *sing*.

Häuschen ['hɔsçən] *neut* (*pl* -) cottage, small house.

Haus||frau *f* housewife. **–halt** *m* household; (*Budget*) budget. **–hälterin** *f* housekeeper. **–haltsplan** *m* budget.

hausieren [hau'ziːrən] *v* peddle, hawk.

häuslich ['hɔyslɪç] *adj* domestic.

Haus||mädchen *neut* housemaid. **–meister** *m* caretaker. **–tür** *f* front door. **–wart** *m* caretaker. **–wirt** *m* landlord. **–wirtin** *f* landlady. **–wirtschaft** *f* housekeeping.

Haut [haut] *f* (*pl* **Häute**) skin; (*Tier*) hide, pelt. **–auschlag** *m* rash. **–krem** *m* skin cream.

Hebamme ['heːpam ə] *f* (*pl* -n) midwife.

Hebel ['heːbəl] *m* (*pl* -) lever.

***heben** ['heːbən] *v* lift, raise; (*Steuer*) raise, levy. **sich heben** rise. **Hebung** *f* raising; (*Beseitigung*) removal.

Hecht [hɛçt] *m* (*pl* -e) pike.

Heck [hɛk] *neut* (*pl* -e) stern; (*eines Autos*) rear. **–klappe** *f* (*Mot*) hatchback, tailgate.

Hecke ['hɛkə] *f* (*pl* -n) hedge; (*Brut*) brood, hatch. **–nschütze** *m* sniper.

Heer [heːr] *neut* (*pl* -e) army.

Hefe ['heːfə] *f* yeast.

Heft [hɛft] *neut* (*pl* -e) notebook, exercise book; (*Zeitschrift*) issue; (*Griff*) handle, haft.

heftig ['hɛftɪç] *adj* violent; (*leidenschaftlich*) passionate, vehement.

hegen ['heːgən] *v* (*hätscheln*) cherish; (*schützen*) protect; (*Gedanken*) nurture.

Heide¹ ['haidə] *m* (*pl* -n) heathen, pagan.

Heide² *f* (*pl* -n) heath, moor. **–kraut** *neut* heather.

Heidelbeere ['haidəbɛːrə] *f* bilberry.

heidnisch ['haidnɪʃ] *adj* heathen, pagan.

heikel ['haikəl] *adj* delicate, awkward.

heil [hail] *adj* safe, uninjured; (*geheilt*) healed; (*ganz*) whole. **Heil** *neut* welfare; (*Kirche*) salvation. **–and** *m* saviour. **heil|||bringend** *adj* salutary. **–en** *v* heal, cure.

heilig ['hailɪç] *adj* holy, sacred. **Heiliger Abend** Christmas Eve. **Heilige(r)** *m* saint. **Heiligenschein** *m* halo.

Heil||kunde *f* medicine, medical science. **–mittel** *neut* remedy, cure.

heim [haim] *adv* home(ward). **Heim** *neut* (*pl* -e) home.

Heimat ['haim aːt] *f* (*unz.*) home(land), native place. **–land** *neut* homeland. **heimatlos** *adj* homeless. **Heimatstadt** *f* home town.

Heimfahrt ['haim faːrt] *f* return journey. **heimisch** *adj* domestic; (*heimatlich*) native. **Heimkehr** *f* return (home).

heim||lich *adj* secret. **–suchen** *v* plague, afflict. **–tückisch** *adj* malicious, insidious.

Heimweh ['haim veː] *neut* homesickness. **Heimweh haben** be homesick.

Heirat ['hairat] *f* (*pl* -en) marriage. **heiraten** *v* marry.

heiser ['haizər] *adj* hoarse.

heiß [hais] *adj* hot.

***heißen** ['haisən] *v* be called *or* named; (*bedeuten*) mean. **wie heißt Du?** what's your name? **das heißt** (**d.h.**) that is (i.e.).

heiter ['haitər] *adj* (*Person*) serene; (*Erählung*) happy; (*Wetter*) bright, clear. **Heiterkeit** *f* serenity.

Heiz||apparat ['haitsaparaːt] *m* (*pl* -e) heater. **–decke** *f* electric blanket. **heizen** *v* heat. **Heiz||ung** *f* heating. **–material** *neut* fuel.

Hektar [hɛk'taːr] *neut* (*pl* -e) hectare.

Held [hɛlt] *m* (*pl* -en) hero. **Helden||mut** *m* heroism. **–tat** *f* heroic deed, exploit. **Heldin** *f* (*pl* -nen) heroine.

helfen ['hɛlfən] *v* help, assist; (*nützen*) help, do good. **Helfer** *m* (*pl* -), **Helferin** *f* (*pl* -nen) helper, assistant.

hell [hɛl] *adj* (*Licht*) bright; (*Farbe*) light; (*Klang*) clear. **hellblau** *adj* light blue. **Hellseher** *m* (*pl* -), **Hellseherin** *f* (*pl* -nen) clairvoyant.

Helm [hɛlm] *m* (*pl* -e) helmet; (*Naut*) rudder; (*Kuppel*) dome.

Hemd [hɛm t] *neut* (*pl* -en) shirt. **–särmel** *m* shirtsleeve.

hemmen [ˈhɛm ən] v restrain, hinder, inhibit; (*Psychol*) inhibit. **Hemmung** f (pl -en) hindrance, stoppage; (*Psychol*) inhibition. **hemmungslos** adj unrestrained.

Hengst [hɛŋst] m (pl -e) stallion.

Henkel [ˈhɛŋkəl] m (pl -) handle.

Henker [ˈhɛŋkər] m (pl -) hangman.

her [heːr] adv (to) here; (*zeitlich*) ago, since; (*von*) from. **hin und her** to and fro, back and forth. **komm her!** come here! **wo kommen Sie her?** where do you come from? **schon lange her** a long time ago. **von weit her** from afar.

herab [hɛˈrap] adv down(wards). **–hängen** v hang down. **–lassen** v lower. **sich herablassen** condescend, deign. **herab‖lassend** adj patronizing. **–setzen** v reduce; (*Person*) degrade. **–setzend** adj contemptuous. **–würdigen** v debase, degrade.

heran [hɛˈran] adv near, up to; (*hierher*) (to) here. **–gehen** v go up to, approach. **–kommen** v approach, draw near.

herauf [hɛˈrauf] adv (up) here; (*hinauf*) upwards. **–beschwören** v conjure up. **–ziehen** v pull up.

heraus [hɛˈraus] adv out; (*draußen, aus dem Hause*) outside. **–fordern** v challenge. **Herausforderung** f challenge. **herausgeben** v give out; (*Buch, usw.*) publish. **Herausgeber** m publisher. **herauswachsen aus** v grow out of.

herb [hɛrp] adj sharp, tart; (*Wein*) dry; (*fig*) harsh.

herbei [hɛrˈbai] adv (to) here, this way. **–führen** v cause.

Herberge [ˈhɛrbɛrgə] f (pl -n) hostel.

Herbst [hɛrpst] m (pl -e) autumn, (*US*) fall. **herbstlich** adj autumnal.

Herd [heːrt] m (pl -e) cooker, stove.

Herde [ˈheːrdə] f (pl -n) herd.

herein [hɛˈrain] adv in, inside, in here. **–führen** v usher in. **–treten** v enter.

*hergeben [ˈheːrgeːbən] v hand over.

hergebracht [ˈheːrgəbraxt] adj traditional, customary.

Hering [ˈheːrɪŋ] m (pl -e) herring.

*herkommen [ˈheːrkɔm ən] v come here; (*abstammen*) come from. **herkommen von** be caused by, be due to. **herkömmlich** adj customary, traditional.

Herkunft [ˈhɛrkunft] f (*unz*) origin; (*Person*) birth, descent.

herleiten [ˈheːrlaitən] v lead here; (*fig*) derive, deduce. **Herleitung** f derivation.

Hermelin [hɛrməˈliːn] neut (pl -e) ermine.

hernach [hɛrˈnaːx] adv afterwards, after this.

Heroin [heroˈiːn] neut heroin.

Herr [hɛr] m (pl -en) (*Anrede*) Mr; (*Herrscher*) master, lord. **der Herr Gott** Lord God. **dieser Herr** this gentleman. **Herren‖artikel** pl men's clothing. **–haus** neut manor house. **–toilette** f men's lavatory.

herrichten [ˈhɛrɪçtən] v prepare, arrange.

Herrin [ˈhɛrɪn] f (pl -nen) lady, mistress.

herr‖isch adj overbearing, domineering. **–lich** adj splendid, magnificent. **Herr‖lichkeit** f splendour, magnificence. **–schaft** f power, rule; (*fig*) mastery. **herrschen** v rule, govern; (*vorhanden sein*) prevail. **Herrscher** m (pl -) ruler.

her‖rühren v originate (from). **–stammen** v descend (from). **–stellen** v manufacture, make; (*reparieren*) repair. **Hersteller** m manufacture, maker. **Herstellung** f manufacture.

herüber [hɛˈryːbər] adv across, over here.

herum [hɛˈrum] adv (a)round, about. **–fahren** v drive around. **–pfuschen** v tinker, mess around (with). **–streichen** v roam about, wander around.

herunter [hɛˈruntər] adv downwards, down (here). **–kommen** v come down; (*sinken*) decline. **–laden** (*comp*) v download.

hervor [hɛrˈfoːr] adv forth, out. **–bringen** v produce; (*Worte*) utter. **–heben** v make prominent, bring out. **–ragen** v stand out, jut out. **–ragend** adj outstanding. **–rufen** v arouse; (*verursachen*) cause. **–treten** v come forward.

Herz [hɛrts] neut (pl -en) heart. **–anfall** m heart attack. **herz‖erfreuend** adj heartening, cheering. **–erschütternd** adj appalling. **–haft** adj stout-hearted. **–ig** adj lovely. **–lich** adj hearty. **–los** adj heartless.

Herzog [ˈhɛrtsoːk] m (pl Herzöge) duke. **–in** f (pl -nen) duchess. **Herzogtum** neut duchy, dukedom.

herzu [hɛrˈtsuː] adv (to) here, towards.

Hessen [ˈhɛsən] neut Hesse.

Hetze [ˈhɛtsə] f (pl -n) hounding, baiting; (*Eile*) mad rush, dash; (*Jagd*) hunt. **hetzen** v hound; rush, dash; hunt.

Heu [hɔy] neut hay. **Heu‖fieber** neut hay

fever. **–gabel** f pitchfork. **–schober** m haystack. **–schrecke** f grasshopper, locust.

Heuchelei [hɔyçə'lai] f (pl -en) hypocrisy. **heucheln** v be hypocritical. **Heuchler** m (pl -), **Heuchlerin** f (pl -nen) hypocrite. **heuchlerisch** adj hypocritical.

heulen ['hɔylən] v cry, howl.

heute ['hɔytə] adv today. **heutig** adj today's; (gegenwärtig) present, current. **heutzutage** adv nowadays, these days.

Hexe ['hɛksə] f (pl -n) witch.

Hieb [hip] m (pl -e) blow, stroke; (Schnitt) cut, slash.

hier [hiːr] adv here. **hier und da** now and then. **hier und dort** here and there. **hier‖auf** adv then, upon this. **–aus** adv from this. **–bei** adv hereby, herewith; (Brief) enclosed. **–für** adv for this.

hi-fi ['haifai] adj hi-fi.

Hilfe ['hilfə] f (pl -n) help, assistance. **–ruf** m cry for help. **hilf‖los** adj helpless. **–reich** adj helpful. **–sbereit** adj eager to help. **Hilfs‖lehrer** m assistant teacher. **–mittel** neut remedy, aid.

Himbeere ['himbeːrə] f raspberry.

Himmel ['himəl] m (pl -) sky; (Paradies) heaven. **–fahrt** f Ascension. **–reich** neut heaven. **–skörper** m celestial body.

himmlisch ['himlif] adj celestial, heavenly.

hin [hin] adv (to) there, from here, towards. **hin und her** to and fro, back and forth. **hin und wieder** now and again. **hin und zurück** there and back. **vor sich hin** to oneself. **es ist noch lange hin** there's a long time to go.

hinab [hinap] adv down(wards). **–lassen** v lower, let down. **–steigen** v descend.

hinan [hinan] adv up (to), upwards.

hinauf [hinauf] adv up (there), upwards. **die Treppe hinauf** up the stairs. **–setzen** v put up. **–ziehen** v pull up, (umziehen) move up.

hinaus [hinaus] adv out, forth. **–gehen** v go out. **hinausgehen über** surpass, exceed. **hinaus‖kommen** v come out. **–werfen** v throw out.

Hinblick ['hinblik] m **im Hinblick auf** with regard to.

hinderlich ['hindərliç] adj restrictive, hindering. **hindern** v hinder; (verhindern) prevent. **Hindernis** neut (pl -se) obstacle, hindrance.

hindeuten ['hindɔytən] v point (at); (fig) hint (at).

hindurch [hin'durç] adv through, across; (zeitlich) throughout.

hinein [hinain] adv in(to). **sich hineindrängen** v force one's way in. **hineinziehen** v draw in; (fig: verwickeln) involve; (umziehen) move to.

hinfahren ['hinfaːrən] v drive there; (hinbringen) take there. **Hinfahrt** f outward journey, way there.

*hinfallen ['hinfalən] v fall down. **hinfällig** adj feeble, frail; (Meinung) untenable, invalid.

Hingabe ['hingaːbə] f devotion.

*hingeben ['hingeːbən] v give up. **sich hingeben** devote oneself (to).

hingegen ['hingeːgən] conj on the other hand, whereas.

*hingehen ['hingeːən] v go there; (Zeit) pass, elapse. **etwas hingehen lassen** let something pass.

hinken ['hinkən] v limp.

hin‖kommen v arrive, get there; (umg.) manage. **–langen** v reach. **–länglich** adj sufficient. **–legen** v put down. **sich hinlegen** lie down. **hin‖nehmen** v put up with, bear. **–reichend** adj sufficient.

Hinreise ['hinraizə] f outward journey, way there.

hinreißen ['hinraisən] v carry along; (entzücken) charm, transport. **–d** adj charming, enchanting.

hinrichten ['hinriçtən] v (Person) execute. **Hinrichtung** f execution.

*hinschreiben ['hinʃraibən] v write down.

Hinsicht ['hinziçt] f **in Hinsicht auf** with regard to. **in dieser Hinsicht** in this regard. **hinsichtlich** adv with regard to.

hinten ['hintən] adv behind, at the back. **nach hinten** to the back, backwards. **von hinten** from behind.

hinter ['hintər] prep behind, after. adj rear, back. **Hinter‖achse** f rear axle. **–bein** neut hind leg. **Hintere(r)** m back part; (Körper) bottom, backside. **hintergehen** v deceive, fool.

Hinter‖grund m background. **–halt** m ambush. **aus dem Hinterhalt überfallen** ambush. **Hinterhof** m rear court, back yard.

hinter‖lassen v leave (behind).

–legen v deposit.

Hintern ['hɪntɐn] m (pl -) bottom, backside.

Hinter||schiff neut stern. **–teil** m back part. **–tür** f back door.

hinterziehen [hɪntɐˈtsiːən] v (Steuern) evade. **Hinterziehung** f (tax) evasion.

hinüber [hɪnyːbɐ] adv over, across, to the other side. **–gehen** v cross (over).

hinunter [hɪnʊntɐ] adv downwards, down (there). **die Treppe hinunter** downstairs.

hinweg [hɪnˈvɛk] adv away (from here), off. **Hinweg** m outward journey. **hinwegkommen über** get over.

Hinweis ['hɪnvais] m (pl -e) indication, hint. **hinweisen** v point out, show; (Person) direct; (anspielen) refer, allude.

*hinziehen ['hɪntsiːən] v draw, attract; (verzögern) drag out.

hinzu [hɪnˈtsuː] adv in addition, as well. **–fügen** v add. **–kommen** v be added. **–kommend** adj additional. **–ziehen** v draw or bring in; (Fachmann) consult.

Hirn [hɪrn] neut (pl -e) brain.

Hirsch [hɪrʃ] m (pl -e) stag. **–fleisch** neut venison. **–kalb** neut fawn. **–kuh** f doe, hind.

Hirt [hɪrt] m (pl -en) shepherd, herdsman. **–in** f (pl -nen) shepherdess.

hissen ['hɪsən] v hoist.

Historiker [hɪstoːrɪkɐ] m (pl -) historian. **historisch** adj historical; (bedeutend) historic.

Hi-tech- ['haitɛk] adj hi-tech, high-tech.

Hitze ['hɪtsə] f (unz.) heat; (Leidenschaft) passion. **hitzebeständig** adj heat-resistant. **hitzig** adj hot; (fig) fiery, passionate. **Hitz||kopf** m hothead. **–schlag** m heat-stroke.

HIV m (med) HIV. **HIV-positiv** adj HIV-positive.

hoch [hoːx] (**hoher, hohe, hohes, höher, höchst**) adj high; (Baum) tall; (Alter) old, advanced. adv highly, greatly. **hohe Blüte** full bloom. **hohe See** high or open sea. **10 hoch 4** 10 to the power of 4. **Hoch** neut (pl -s) cheer; (Hochdruckgebiet) high-pressure area. **Dreimal hoch** three cheers.

Hochachtung ['hoːxaxtʊŋ] f respect, esteem. **hochachtungsvoll** respectfully, yours faithfully.

hochdeutsch ['hoːxdɔytʃ] adj high German, standard German.

Hoch||druck m high pressure. **–ebene** f plateau. **–flut** f high tide. **–frequenz** f high frequency.

*hochhalten ['hoːxhaltən] v think highly of, esteem.

Hoch||haus neut tall building, high-rise block. **–konjunktur** f boom. **–land** neut highland(s). **–leistung–**adj heavy-duty. **–mut** m pride, arrogance. **hochmütig** adj proud, arrogant. **hochnäsig** adj hoity-toity, supercilious

Hoch||ruf m cheer. **–schätzung** f (high) esteem. **–schule** f college, university; (technische) polytechnic. **–spannung** f high tension, high voltage. **–sprung** m high jump. **–verrat** m high treason. **–wasser** neut high tide, high water; (Überschwemmung) flooding. **Hochzeit** f wedding. **hochzeitlich** adj nuptial, bridal. **Hochzeitskleid** neut wedding dress.

höchst [høːxst] adj highest, greatest. adv very (much), greatly, highly.

hochstehend ['hoːxʃtɛːənt] adj high-ranking, eminent.

höchstens ['høːxstəns] adv at most, at best.

Höchst||geschwindigkeit f maximum speed. **–preis** m maximum price.

hocken ['hɔkən] v squat, crouch. **Hocker** m (pl -) stool.

Hode ['hoːdə] f (pl -n) or **Hoden** m (pl -) testicle.

Hof [hoːf] m (pl Höfe) (court)yard; (Landwirtschaft) farm; (fürstlich) court.

hoffen ['hɔfən] v hope. **hoffentlich** adv hopefully, I hope (so), let us hope (that). **Hoffnung** f (pl -en) hope. **hoffnungs||los** adj hopeless. **–voll** adj hopeful.

höflich ['høːflɪç] adj polite, courteous. **Höflichkeit** f courtesy, politeness.

hohe(r) ['hoːə (r)] V hoch.

Höhe ['høːə] f (pl -n) height; (Gipfel) top; (Geog) latitude; (Hügel) hill.

Hoheit ['hoːhait] f (unz.) grandeur, greatness; (Titel) Highness. **–sgewässer** pl territorial waters.

Höhepunkt ['høːəpʊŋkt] m climax.

höher ['høːə (r)] V hoch.

hohl [hoːl] adj hollow, (Linse) concave.

Höhle ['høːə ːə] f (pl -n) cave; (Loch) hole; (eines Tiers) burrow, hole. **höhlen** v hollow (out).

höhnen ['hœ :nən] v mock, taunt. **höhnisch** adj mocking, scornful.

hold [hɔlɫ] adj charming, gracious. **-selig** adj most charming, most gracious.

holen ['ho:lən] v fetch. **Atem holen** draw breath. **sich Rat holen bei** ask for advice.

holistisch [ho:lɪstʃ] adj holistic.

Holländer ['hɔlɛndər] m (pl -) Dutchman. **-in** f (pl -nen) Dutchwoman. **holländisch** adj Dutch.

Hölle ['hœ ɫə] f (pl -n) hell.

Holunder [ho'lundər] m (pl -) elder (tree). **-beere** f elderberry.

Holz [hɔlɫs] neut (pl **Hölzer**) wood. **-blasinstrument** neut woodwind instrument.

hölzern ['hœ ɫsɛrn] adj wooden; (fig) stiff, awkward, clumsy.

holzig ['hɔlɫsɪç] adj woody.

Holz||klotz m wooden block. **-kohle** f charcoal. **-schnitt** m woodcut. **-weg** m **auf dem Holzwege sein** be on the wrong track. **Holzwurm** m woodworm.

Homepage ['houm peiʤ] f (pl -s) (Internet) home page.

homöopathisch [hom œ o:'pa:tiʃ] adj homeopathic.

Homosexualität [hom o:zɛksualɛ:t] f homosexuality. **homosexuell** adj homosexual. **Homosexuelle(r)** m homosexual.

Honig ['ho:nɪç] m honey. **-biene** f honeybee.

Honorar [hono'ra:r] neut (pl -e) fee, honorarium; (eines Autors) royalties pl.

Hopfen ['hɔpfən] m (pl -) hops pl.

hörbar ['hœ :ba:r] adj audible.

horchen ['hɔrçən] v listen (to); (heimlich) eavesdrop.

Horde ['hɔrdə] f (pl -n) horde.

hören ['hœ :rən] v hear; (Radio) listen to. **Hören** neut (sense of) hearing. **-sagen** neut hearsay. **Hörer** m hearer; (Radio) listener; (Telef) receiver; (pl) audience; **-schaft** f audience. **Hörgerät** neut hearing aid.

Horizont [hɔritsɔnt] m (pl -e) horizon. **horizontal** adj horizontal.

Hormon [hɔrˈmo:n] neut (pl -e) hormone.

Horn [hɔrn] neut (pl **Hörner**) horn. **-brille** f horn-rimmed spectacles. **-haut** f (Anat) cornea.

Horoskop [horo'sko:p] neut (pl -e) horoscope.

Hör||probe f audition. **-saal** m lecture hall. **-spiel** neut radio play.

Hose ['ho:zə] f (pl -n) trousers. **Hosen||schlitz** m flies, (US) fly. **-träger** pl braces, (US) suspenders.

Höschen ['hœ :sçən] neut (pl -) knickers pl; panties pl.

Hotel [ho'tɛl] neut (pl -s) hotel.

Hub [hu:p] m (pl **Hübe**) lift; (Mot) stroke. **-raum** m cylinder capacity.

hübsch [hypʃ] adj pretty, nice; (Mann) good-looking.

Hubschrauber ['hupʃrraubər] m (pl -) helicopter.

Huf [hu:f] m (pl -e) hoof. **-eisen** neut horseshoe.

Hüftbein ['hyftbain] neut hipbone. **Hüfte** f hip.

Hügel ['hy:gəl] m (pl -) hill. **hügelig** adj hilly.

Huhn [hu:n] neut (pl **Hühner**) hen; (Küche) chicken.

Hühner||auge neut (Med) corn. **-braten** m roast chicken. **-brühe** f chicken broth. **-ei** neut hen's egg. **-stall** m henhouse.

huldigen ['huldigən] v pay homage to; (Ansicht) hold, subscribe to. **Huldigung** f homage.

Hülle ['hylə] f covering, wrapping; (Umschlag) envelope; (Buch) jacket, cover. **in Hülle und Fülle** in abundance. **hüllen** v wrap, cover.

Hülse ['hylzə] f (pl -n) husk, shell; (Erbse) pod; (aus Papier, usw.) case, casing.

human [hu'm a:n] adj humane. **Humanist** m (pl -en) humanist. **humanitär** adj humanitarian.

Hummel ['hum əl] f (pl -n) bumblebee.

Hummer ['hum ər] m (pl -) lobster.

Humor [hu'm o:r] m (sense of) humour. **humorvoll** adj humorous.

humpeln ['hum pəln] v hobble, limp.

Hund [hunt] m (pl -e) dog. **Hunde||hütte** f kennel. **-leine** f leash.

hundert ['hundərt] adj, pron hundred. **Hundert||füßler** m centipede. **-jahrfeier** f centenary. **hundert||mal** adv a hundred times. **-prozentig** adj one-hundred-percent, complete.

Hündin ['hyndin] f (pl -nen) bitch.

Hunger ['hunər] m hunger. **Hunger haben** be hungry. **-lohn** m starvation wages pl;

pittance. **hungern** v starve; be hungry. **Hungersnot** f famine. **Hungerstreik** m hungerstrike. **hungrig** adj hungry.

Hupe ['huːpə] f (pl -n) (Mot) horn. **hupen** v sound the horn, beep.

hüpfen ['hypfən] v hop, skip.

Hürde ['hyrdə] f (pl -n) hurdle; (Schafe) fold, pen.

Hure ['huːrə] f (pl -n) whore.

hurra [hu'raː] interj hurrah!

husten ['huːstən] v cough. **Husten** m (pl -) cough.

Hut¹ [huːt] m (pl Hüte) hat.

Hut² f (unz.) (Schutz) protection; (Vorsicht) care; (Aufsicht) guard. **auf der Hut sein (vor)** be on one's guard (against).

hüten ['hyːtən] v guard. **sich hüten (vor)** be careful or wary (of).

Hütte ['hytə] f (pl -n) hut, cabin; (Metall) foundry, ironworks. **–nkäse** m cottage cheese.

Hyäne [hy'ɛːnə] f (pl -n) hyena.

Hydraulik [hy'draulik] f hydraulics. **hydraulisch** adj hydraulic.

Hygiene [hy'giːnə] f hygiene. **hygienisch** adj hygienic.

Hymne ['hym nə] f (pl -n) hymn.

hyperaktiv [hypər'aktiːf] adj hyperactive.

Hypnose [hyp'noːzə] f (pl -n) hypnosis. **hypnotisch** adj hypnotic. **–tisieren** v hypnotize.

Hypothek [hypo'teːk] f (pl -en) mortgage.

Hypothese [hypo'teːzə] f (pl -n) hypothesis. **hypothetisch** adj hypothetical.

Hysterie [hyste'riː] f hysteria. **hysterisch** adj hysterical. **hysterische Anfälle** pl hysterics.

I

ich [iç] pron I. **Ich** neut self, ego. **ichbezogen** adj egocentric.

ideal [ide'aːl] adj ideal. **Ideal** neut (pl -e) ideal. **Idealismus** m idealism.

Idee [i'deː] f (pl -n) idea.

identifizieren [identifiˈtsiːrən] v identify. **identisch** adj identical. **Identität** f identity.

Idiot [idi'oːt] m (pl -en) idiot. **idiotisch** adj idiotic.

Igel ['iːgəl] m (pl -) hedgehog.

ignorieren [igno'riːrən] v ignore.

ihm [iːm] pron (Person) (to) him; (Sache) (to) it.

ihn [iːn] pron (Person) him; (Sache) it.

ihnen ['iːnən] pron (to) them. **Ihnen** pron (to) you.

ihr [iːr] pron you; (Dat) (to) pron, adj (Person) her; its; their. **Ihr** pron, adj your. **ihrer, ihre, ihres** pron hers; its; theirs. **Ihrer, Ihre, Ihres** yours. **ihrerseits** adv for your part. **ihr||esgleichen** adv like her (it, them). **–etwegen** or **–etwillen** on her (its, their) account. **der, die, das ihrige** pron hers; its; theirs.

Illusion [iluˈzioːn] f (pl -en) illusion. **illusorisch** adj illusory.

illustrieren [iluˈstriːrən] v illustrate. **Illustrierte** f (illustrated) magazine.

im [im] prep + art in dem.

Imbiß ['imbis] m (pl Imbisse) snack. **–stube** f snack bar.

Immatrikulation [imatrikulaˈtsioːn] f (pl -en) matriculation, registration.

immer ['imər] adv always. **immer mehr** more and more. **immer noch** still. **immer wieder** again and again. **wenn auch immer** although. **auf immer** forever. **–fort** adv constantly. **–grün** adj evergreen. **–hin** adv nevertheless. **–zu** adv all the time.

Immigrant [imiˈgrant] m (pl -en) immigrant.

Immobilien [imoˈbiːlən] pl real estate sing.

Imperialismus [imperiaˈlismus] m imperialism. **Imperialist** m (pl -en) imperialist.

impfen ['impfən] v inoculate, vaccinate. **Impfung** f (pl -en) inoculation, vaccination.

imponieren [impo'niːrən] v impress. **–d** adj impressive.

Import [im'pɔrt] m (pl -e) import(ation); (Ware) import. **–eur** m (pl -e) importer. **–handel** m import trade. **importieren** v import.

impotent ['impotent] adj impotent.

imprägnieren [impregˈniːrən] v impregnate, saturate.

improvisieren [improˈviːzərən] v improvise. **improvisiert** adj improvized, ad-lib.

imstande [in 'ʃtandə] *adv* **imstande sein** be able *or* capable.

in [in] *prep* (+*Dat*) in; (+*Acc*) into, in; (*Zeit*) (with)in.

Inanspruchnahme [in'anʃprʊxnaːmə] *f* demands *pl*.

Inbegriff ['inbəgrif] *m* essence, epitome. **mit Inbegriff von** inclusive of. **inbegriffen** *adj, adv* (*Steuer*) included, inclusive(ly).

Inbrunst ['inbrʊnst] *f* ardour, fervour.

indem [in'deːm] *conj* (*dadurch daß*) in that, by; (*während*) while.

Inder ['indər] *m* (*pl* -) (Asian) Indian.

indessen [in'dɛsən] *conj* (*inzwischen*) meanwhile, in the meantime; (*immerhin*) however, nevertheless.

Indianer [indi'aːnər] *m* (*pl* -) (American) Indian. **indianisch** *adj* (American) Indian.

Indien ['indiən] *neut* India.

indirekt ['indirɛkt] *adj* indirect.

indisch ['indʃ] *adj* (Asian) Indian.

indiskret ['indiskreːt] *adj* indiscreet, tactless.

Individualist [individua'list] *m* (*pl* -en) individualist. **individualistisch** *adj* individualist(ic). **individuell** *adj* individual. **Individuum** *neut* (*pl* -duen) individual.

industrialisieren [industriːalizɪːrən] *v* industrialize. **Industrie** *f* (*pl* -n) industry. **-gebiet** *neut* industrial region. **industriell** *adj* industrial. **Industrielle(r)** *m* industrialist.

ineinander [inain'andər] *adv* in(to) each other. **-greifen** *v* (*Tech*) engage; (*fig*) overlap.

Infanterie [infantə'riː] *f* infantry. **Infanterist** *m* (*pl* -en) infantryman.

infiltrieren [infiltrɪːrən] *v* infiltrate.

infizieren [infitsɪːrən] *v* infect. **sich infizieren** become infected, catch a disease.

Inflation [inflatsloːn] *f* (*Komm*) inflation. **inflationär, inflationistisch** *adj* inflationary.

infolge [in'folgə] *prep* on account of, owing to. **-dessen** *adv* consequently.

Information [informatsloːn] *f* (*pl* -en) information. **eine Information** a piece of information. **Informationstechnologie** *f* information technology (IT).

informell ['informɛl] *adj* informal.

informieren [informɪːrən] *v* inform,

instruct. **sich informieren über** find out about, gather information about.

Ingenieur [inʒeˈnjøːr] *m* (*pl* -e) engineer. **-schule** *f* engineering college. **-wesen** *neut* engineering.

Ingwer ['iŋvɛːr] *m* ginger.

Inhaber ['inhaːbər] *m* (*pl* -) owner; (*Titel, Paß, Patent*) holder.

inhalieren [inhaˈliːrən] *v* inhale.

Inhalt ['inhalt] *m* (*pl* -e) contents *pl*; (*Bedeutung*) meaning, content. **-sverzeichnis** *neut* table of contents.

Initiative [initsiaˈtiːvə] *f* (*unz.*) initiative. **die Initiative ergreifen** take the initiative.

inklusive [inkluˈziːvə] *prep* including, inclusive of.

inkonsequent ['inkonzekvɛnt] *adj* inconsistent.

Inkontinenz ['inkontinɛnts] *f* incontinence.

inkorporieren [inkorpoˈriːrən] *v* incorporate.

Inkrafttreten [in'kraftreːtən] *neut* coming into effect.

Inland ['inlant] *neut* inland, interior.

inmitten [in'm itən] *prep* in the midst of, among.

inne ['inə] *adv* within.

innen ['inən] *adv* within, inside. **nach innen** inwards. **Innen‖ausstattung** *f* interior decoration, decor. **-minister** *m* Home Secretary, Minister of the Interior. **-politik** *f* domestic policy. **innenpolitisch** *adj* (relating to) internal affairs. **Innenraum** *m* interior.

inner ['inər] *adj* internal, inner. **Innereien** *pl* offal. **Innere(s)** *neut* (*pl* -(e)n) interior. **inner‖halb** *prep* within. **-lich** *adj* inward, internal. **innerst** *adj* innermost.

innewohnen ['inəvoːnən] *v* be inherent (in).

innig ['iniç] *adj* (*Gefühle*) sincere; (*Freunde*) intimate.

ins [ins] *prep*+*art* **in das.**

Insasse ['inzasə] *m* (*pl* -n) inmate.

insbesondere [insbəˈzondərə] *adv* particularly.

Inschrift ['inʃrift] *f* inscription.

Insekt [in'zɛkt] *neut* (*pl* -en) insect. **-enpulver** *neut* insect powder. **-izid** *neut* insecticide.

Insel ['inzəl] *f* (*pl* -n) island.

Inserat [inze'raːt] *neut* (*pl* -e) (newspaper) advertisement.

insgesamt [insgə'zamt] *adv* altogether.

insofern [inzo'fɛrn] *conj* so far as; [in'zofɛrn] (*bis zu diesem Punkt*) to that extent. **insofern als** inasmuch as.

insoweit [inzo'vait] *adv* to that extent.

Inspektor [inspɛk'tor] *m* (*pl* -en) inspector.

instand halten [in'ʃtanthaltən] *v* maintain (in good order). **instand setzen** *v* repair, overhaul; (*Person*) enable. **Instandhaltung** *f* unkeep, maintenance.

Instanz [in'stants] *f* (*pl* -en) authority. **durch die Instanzen** through official channels.

instinktiv [instiŋk'tiːf] *adj* instinctive.

Institut [insti'tuːt] *neut* (*pl* -e) institute.

Instrument [instru'mɛnt] *neut* (*pl* -e) instrument.

inszenieren [instse'niːrən] *v* (*Film, Schauspiel*) produce; (*fig*) create, engineer.

integrieren [inte'griːrən] *v* integrate. **Integration** *f* integration.

intellektuell [intɛlektu'ɛl] *adj* intellectual.

intelligent [intɛli'gɛnt] *adj* intelligent, clever.

interaktiv [intər'aktiːf] *adj* interactive.

interessant [intər'sant] *adj* interesting. **Interesse** *neut* interest. **interessieren** *v* interest. **sich interessieren für** take an interest in, be interested in.

intern [in'tɛrn] *adj* internal.

Internat [intər'naːt] *neut* (*pl* -e) boarding school.

international [intrnatsio'naːl] *adj* international.

Internet [intər'net] *neut* Internet. **–dienstanbieter** *m* Internet service provider (ISP).

Interview [intər'vjuː] *neut* (*pl* -s) interview. **interviewen** *v* interview. **Interviewer** *m* interviewer. **Interviewte(r)** interviewee.

intim [in'tiːm] *adj* intimate.

Intrige [in'triːgə] *f* (*pl* -n) intrigue. **intrigieren** *v* plot, scheme.

Invalide(r) [inva'liːdə (r)] *m* invalid. **Invaliden‖heim** *neut* home for the disabled. **–rente** *f* disability pension. **invalid** *adj* invalid.

Inventar [invɛn'taːr] *neut* (*pl* -e) inventory.

Inventur [invɛn'tuːr] *f* (*pl* -en) stock-taking.

inwendig ['invɛndiç] *adj* inner.

inwiefern [invi'fɛrn] *conj* to what extent, how far.

inzwischen [in'tsviʃən] *adv* meanwhile.

IQ *m* IQ (intelligence quotient).

irdisch ['irdiʃ] *adj* earthly, worldly.

Ire ['iːrə] *m* (*pl* -n) Irishman. **Irin** *f* (*pl* -nen) Irishwoman.

irgend ['irgənt] *adv* perhaps, ever. *pron* some, any. **irgend etwas** something, anything. **irgend jemand** someone, anyone. **irgend‖ein** *adj* some, any. **–wann** *adv* (at) sometime (or other). **–was** *pron* something, anything. **–wie** *adv* somehow, anyhow. **–wo** *adv* somewhere, anywhere.

Iris ['iris] *f* (*pl* -) (*Anat*) iris.

irisch ['iriʃ] *adj* Irish.

Irland ['irlant] *neut* Ireland. **Irländer** *m* (*pl* -) Irishman. **Irländerin** *f* (*pl* -nen) Irishwoman. **irländisch** *adj* Irish.

Ironie [iro'niː] *f* (*pl* -n) irony. **ironisch** *adj* ironic; (*spöttisch*) ironical.

irre ['irə] *adj* (*geistesgestört*) insane, mad; (*verwirrt*) confused. *adv* (*von Ziel weg*) astray. **irr werden** go insane. **irren** *v* err.

Irre(r) madman/-woman. **irreführen** *v* lead astray; (*täuschen*) mislead. **Irrenanstalt** *f* mental home. **Irrglaube** *m* heresy. **irrig** *adj* erroneous. **Irrsinn** *m* insanity, madness. **irrsinnig** *adj* insane. **Irrtum** *m* (*pl* Irrtümer) error. **irrtümlich** *adj* erroneous, wrong.

Isolierband [izo'liːrbant] *neut* insulating tape; **isolieren** *v* isolate; (*Elek*) insulate. **Isolierung** *f* isolation; insulation.

Italien [i'taːliən] *neut* Italy. **Italiener** *m* (*pl* -). **Italienerin** *f* (*pl* -nen) Italian. **italienisch** *adj* Italian.

J

ja [jaː] *adv* yes. **ja doch** to be sure, but yes. **ja freilich** yes indeed. **wenn ja** if so.

Jacht [jaxt] *f* (*pl* -en) yacht.

Jacke ['jakə] *f* (*pl* -n) jacket.

Jagd [jaːkt] *f* (*pl* -en) hunt; (*Jagen*) hunting. **–flugzeug** *neut* fighter plane. **–hund** *m* hound. **–schloß** *neut* hunting lodge.

jagen ['jɑːgən] v hunt; (*treiben*) drive (away); (*verfolgen*) pursue; (*eilen*) rush, race.

Jäger ['jɛːgə] m (pl -) hunter; (*Flugzeug*) fighter.

jäh [jɛː] adj steep; (*plötzlich*) sudden.

Jahr [jɑːɹ] neut (pl -e) year. **–buch** neut yearbook. **jahrelang** adv for years. **Jahres||einkommen** neut annual income. **–ende** neut end of the year. **–tag** m anniversary. **–viertel** neut quarter. **–wende** f New Year, turn of the year. **–zeit** f season. **jahreszeitlich** adj seasonal. **Jahrhundert** neut century.

jährig ['jɛːriç] adj lasting a year. **dreijährig** adj three-year-old.

jährlich ['jɛːriç] adj yearly, annual.

Jahr||markt m fair. **–zehnt** neut decade.

Jalousie [ʒaluˈziː] f (pl -n) venetian blind.

Jammer ['jam ər] m (unz.) wailing; (*Elend*) misery; (*Verzweiflung*) despair.

jämmerlich ['jɛm əriç] adj pitiable.

jammern ['jam əm] v wail; (*klagen*) complain.

Januar ['januːaːɹ] m (pl -e) January.

Japan ['jɑːpan] neut Japan. **–er** m (pl -), **Japanerin** f (pl -nen) Japanese. **japanisch** adj Japanese.

jauchzen ['jauxtsən] v shout joyfully, rejoice.

jawohl [jaˈvoː] adv, interj yes indeed, certainly.

Jazz [dʒɛs] m jazz.

je [jɛː] adv ever. **je und je** always. **je zwei** two each. conj **je mehr, desto besser** the more, the better. **je nachdem** that depends.

jedenfalls ['jeːdənfals] adv in any case.

jeder ['jeːdə] **jede, jedes** pron, adj each, every, **jedermann** pron everybody. **jederzeit** adv always, (at) any time.

jedesmal ['jeːdəsmaːl] adv each time.

jedoch [jɛˈdɔx] adv however, yet.

jemals ['jeːm aːs] adv ever, at any time.

jemand ['jeːm ant] pron someone; (*Fragen*) anyone.

jener ['jeːnə] **jene, jenes** pron, adj that, pl those; (*zuerst erwähnt*) the former. **jenseits** adv on the other side. prep on the other side of, across.

jetzig ['jɛtsiç] adj current, present. **jetzt** adv now, at present.

jeweilig ['jeːvailiç] adj at the time; (*Vergangenheit*) at that time, then. **jeweils** adv at a(ny) given time.

Jiddisch ['jidɪʃ] neut Yiddish (language).

Joch [jɔx] neut (pl -e) yoke.

Jockei ['dʒɔki] m (pl -s) jockey.

Jod [joːt] neut iodine.

jodeln ['joːdəln] v yodel.

Joghurt ['joːgurt] neut (pl -s) yoghurt.

Johannisbeere [joˈhanisbeːrə] f redcurrant. **schwarze Johannisbeere** blackcurrant.

Journalismus [ʒurnaˈlismus] m journalism. **Journalist** m (pl -en) journalist. **journalistisch** adj journalistic.

Jubel ['juːbəl] m rejoicing, jubilation. **jubeln** v rejoice. **Jubiläum** neut (pl -äen) anniversary, jubilee.

jucken ['jukən] v itch. **Jucken** neut itch.

Jude ['juːdə] m (pl -n), **Jüdin** f (pl -nen) Jew. **jüdisch** adj Jewish.

Judo ['juːdo] neut judo.

Jugend ['juːgənt] f (unz.) youth. **–gericht** neut juvenile court. **–herberge** f youth hostel. **–kriminalität** f juvenile delinquency. **jugendlich** adj youthful, young, juvenile. **jugendlicher Verbrecher** m juvenile delinquent. **Jugendliche(r)** m youth, juvenile.

Jugoslawe [jugoˈslaːvə] m, **Jugoslawin** f Yugoslav. **Jugoslawien** neut Yugoslavia. **jugoslawisch** adj Yugoslav.

Juli ['juːli] m (pl -s) July.

jung [juŋ] adj young. **Junge** m (pl -n) boy; (*Lehrling*) apprentice; (*Karten*) jack. **jungenhaft** adj boyish.

jünger ['jyŋə] adj younger, junior. **Jünger** m (pl -) disciple.

Junges ['juŋəs] neut (pl **Jungen**) young (animal), offspring.

Jung||fer f (pl -n) virgin; (*Mädchen*) girl. **alte Jungfer** old maid, spinster. **–frau** f virgin. **jungfräulich** adj maidenly, chaste. **Junggeselle** m bachelor.

Jüngling ['jyŋliŋ] m (pl -e) youth, young man. **–salter** neut youth, adolescence.

jüngst [jyŋst] adj youngest; (*letzt*) latest. **das jüngste Gericht** the Last Judgment.

Juni ['juːni] m (pl -s) June.

Junker ['juŋkə] m (pl -) squire; (*jung*) young aristocrat.

Jura¹ ['juːra] f law sing. **Jura studieren** study law.

Jura² [m (pl -s)] the Jura, Jura Mountains.

Jurist [juˈrɪst] m (pl -en) lawyer.

just [jʊst] adv just, exactly.

Justiz [jʊsˈtiːts] f (unz.) justice, administration of the law. **–irrtum** m miscarriage of justice. **–wesen** neut legal affairs, the law.

Juwel [juˈveːl] neut (pl -en) jewel. **–ier** m (pl -e) jeweller.

Jux [jʊks] m (pl -e) joke, prank. **aus Jux** as a joke, for fun.

K

Kabarett [kabaˈrɛt] neut (pl -e) cabaret.

Kabel [ˈkaːbəl] neut (pl -) cable.

Kabeljau [ˈkaːbəljau] m (pl -e) cod.

kabeln [ˈkaːbəln] v cable, wire.

Kabine [kaˈbiːnə] f (pl -n) (Schiff) cabin; (Umkleide-) cubicle; (Seilbahn) cable-car.

Kabinett [kabiˈnɛt] neut (pl -e) (Pol) cabinet; (Zimmer) closet.

Kadaver [kaˈdaːvər] m (pl -) carcass.

Kadett [kaˈdɛt] m (pl -en) cadet.

Käfer [ˈkɛːfər] m (pl -) beetle.

Kaffee [kaˈfeː] m (pl -s) coffee. **–bohne** f coffee bean. **–kanne** f coffee-pot. **–mühle** f coffee-grinder. **–satz** m coffee grounds pl.

Käfig [ˈkɛːfiç] m (pl -e) cage.

kahl [kaːl] adj bald; (Landschaft) bare, barren. **Kahlheit** f baldness. **kahlköpfig** adj bald-headed.

Kahn [kaːn] m (pl Kähne) small boat, punt; (Last-) barge.

Kai [kai] m (pl -e) quay, wharf.

Kaiser [ˈkaizər] m (pl -) emperor. **–in** f empress. **kaiserlich** adj imperial. **Kaiserreich** neut empire.

Kaiserschnitt [ˈkaizərʃnit] m (pl -e) Caesarean (section). **durch Kaiserschnitt geboren werden** be born by Caesarean.

Kakao [kaˈkao] m cocoa.

Kaktee [kakˈteː] f, **Kaktus** m (pl Kakteen) cactus.

Kalb [kalp] neut (pl Kälber) calf. **–fleisch** neut veal. **–sbraten** m roast veal.

Kalender [kaˈlɛndər] m (pl -) calendar.

Kaliber [kaˈliːbər] neut (pl -) calibre.

Kalk [kalk] m (pl -e) lime. **–stein** m limestone.

Kalorie [kaloˈriː] f (pl -n) calorie.

Kalt [kalt] adj cold. **–blütig** adj cold-blooded.

Kälte [ˈkɛltə] f (unz.) cold(ness).

Kamel [kaˈmeːl] neut (pl -e) camel.

Kamera [ˈkamˌeraː] f (pl -s) camera. **–mann** m cameraman.

Kamerad [kamˈeˈraːt] m (pl -en) companion, comrade. **–schaft** f companionship, comradeship.

Kamin [kaˈmin] m (pl -e) (Feuerstelle) hearth, fireplace; (Schornstein) chimney. **–feger** m chimneysweep. **–gesims** neut mantelpiece. **–vorsatz** m fireguard, fender.

Kamm [kam] m (pl Kämme) comb; (Vogel) crest; (Berg) ridge, crest.

kämmen [ˈkɛmən] v comb. **sich kämmen** comb one's hair.

Kammer [ˈkamər] f (pl -n) small room, chamber; (Mil, Pol) chamber. **–frau** f chambermaid. **–herr** m chamberlain. **–musik** f chamber music.

Kampf [kampf] m (pl Kämpfe) fight, struggle; (Schlacht) battle.

kämpfen [ˈkɛmpfən] v fight, struggle. **Kämpfer** m (pl -) fighter. **Kampflhandlung** f (Mil) engagement; action. **–platz** m battlefield. **–wagen** m (Mil) tank.

Kanada [ˈkanadaː] neut Canada. **Kanadier** m (pl -), **Kanadierin** f (pl -nen) Canadian. **kanadisch** adj Canadian.

Kanal [kaˈnaːl] m (pl Kanäle) canal; (natürlicher, auch Radio, fig) channel; (Abwasser) drain, sewer. **–inseln** pl Channel Islands.

Kanarienvogel [kaˈnaːriˌənfoːgəl] m canary.

Kandidat [kandiˈdaːt] m (pl -en) candidate. **kandidieren** v (Wahl) stand (for election); (Posten) apply (for).

Känguruh [kɛŋguˈruː] neut (pl -s) kangaroo.

Kaninchen [kaˈninçən] neut (pl -) rabbit. **–stall** m rabbit hutch.

Kanne [ˈkanə] n (pl -n) can; (Kaffee, Tee) pot; (Krug) jug, pitcher.

Kannibale [kaniˈbaːlə] m (pl -n) cannibal. **kannibalisch** adj cannibal.

Kanon [ˈkanɔn] m (pl -s) canon.

Kanone [kaˈnoːnə] f (pl -n) cannon, gun. **Kanonenllfeuer** neut bombardment. **–kugel** f cannonball.

Kante [ˈkantə] f (pl -n) edge.

Kantine [kan'ti:nə] f (pl -n) canteen.

Kanton [kan'to:n] m (pl -e) canton.

Kanzel ['kantsəl] f (pl -n) pulpit. **-rede** f sermon.

Kanzlei [kants'laɪ] f (pl -en) (Büro) office; (Behörde) chancellery. **-papier** neut foolscap.

Kanzler ['kantslər] m (pl -) chancellor.

Kap [kap] neut (pl -s) cape, headland.

Kapazität [kapatsi'tɛ:t] 1 f (unz.) capacity. 2 f (pl -en) (Können) authority, expert.

Kapelle [ka'pɛlə] f (pl -n) chapel; (Musik) band.

Kaper ['ka:pər] f (pl -n) (Gewürz) caper.

kapieren [ka'pi:rən] v (umg.) understand, catch on, (umg.) get.

Kapital [kapi'ta:l] neut (Komm) capital. **-ismus** m capitalism. **-ist** m capitalist. **kapitalistisch** adj capitalist.

Kapitän [kapi'tɛ:n] m (pl -e) (ship's) captain.

Kapitel [ka'pi:təl] neut (pl -) chapter.

kapitulieren [kapitu'li:rən] v capitulate, surrender. **Kapitulation** f (pl -en) capitulation, surrender.

Kaplan [ka'pla:n] m (pl Kapläne) chaplain.

Kappe ['kapə] f (pl -n) cap; (Deckel) top; (Arch) dome; (Schuh) toecap.

Kapriole [kapri'o:lə] f (pl -n) caper, cartwheel.

kaputt [ka'put] adj broken, (umg.) bust; (erschöpft) exhausted, (umg.) shattered. **-machen** v break, ruin.

Kapuze [ka'pu:tsə] f (pl -n) hood.

Karaffe [ka'rafə] f (pl -n) carafe.

Karamelle [kara'mɛlə] f (pl -n) toffee.

Karat [ka'ra:t] neut (pl -e) carat.

Karate [ka'ra:tə] neut karate.

Karawane [kara'va:nə] f (pl -n) caravan.

Kardinal [kardi'na:l] m (pl Kardinäle) cardinal.

Karfreitag [ka:r'fraɪtak] m Good Friday.

karg [kark] adj meagre, poor; (geizig) miserly.

kärglich ['kɛrklɪç] adj scanty, poor.

Karibik [ka'ri:bik] f (the) Caribbean. **karibisch** adj Caribbean.

kariert [ka'ri:rt] adj chequered, checked.

Karies ['ka:riɛs] f (Med) caries.

Karikatur [karika'tu:r] f (pl -en) caricature.

karmesin [karmɛ'zi:n] adj crimson.

Karneval ['karnɛval] m (pl -s) (Shrovetide) carnival.

Karo ['ka:ro] neut (pl -s) square; (Karten) diamonds.

Karosserie [karosə'ri:] f (pl -n) body, coachwork.

Karotte [ka'rɔtə] f (pl -n) carrot.

Karpfen ['karpfən] m (pl -) carp.

Karre ['karə] f (pl -n), **Karren** m (pl -) cart.

Karriere [kari'ɛ:rə] f (pl -n) rise, (successful) career; (Pferd) full gallop.

Karte ['kartə] f (pl -n) (Blatt) card; (Land-) map; (Eintritt, Reise) ticket.

Kartei [kar'taɪ] f (pl -en) card file, card index.

Kartell [kar'tɛl] neut (pl -e) cartel, combine.

Karten||ausgabe f ticket office. **-schwarzhändler** m ticket tout. **-spiel** neut card game.

Kartoffel [kar'tɔfəl] f (pl -n) potato. **-chips** pl potato crisps (US chips). **-püree** neut mashed potatoes pl. **-puffer** m potato pancake. **-salat** m potato salad.

Karton [kar'tɔ:] m (pl -s) cardboard; (Schachtel) cardboard box, carton; (Skizze) cartoon.

Kartusche [kar'tuʃə] f (pl -n) cartridge.

Karussell [karu'sɛl] neut (pl -s) roundabout, merry-go-round.

Kaschmir [kaʃ'mi:r] neut cashmere.

Käse [kɛ:zə] m (pl -) cheese.

Kaserne [ka'zɛrnə] f (pl -n) barracks pl.

Kasino [ka'zi:no] neut (pl -s) casino; (Mil) (officers') mess; (Gesellschaftshaus) club.

Kasse ['kasə] f (pl -n) cash box, till; (Laden, Supermarkt) cash-desk; (Kino, Theater) box office; (Bank) cashier's window, counter. **gut/schlecht bei Kasse sein** be flush/hard up. **Kassen||buch** neut cash book. **-wart** m treasurer.

Kassette [ka'sɛtə] f (pl -n) small box, casket; (Geld) strong-box; (Tonband) cassette. **-nrecorder** m cassette recorder.

kassieren [ka'si:rən] v (Geld) receive; (Scheck) cash; (Urteil) annul, reverse; (Mil) cashier, dismiss. **Kassierer** m cashier.

Kastanie [ka'sta:niə] f (pl -n) chestnut. **kastanienbraun** adj chestnut, auburn.

Kasten ['kastən] m (pl Kästen) box, chest; (Schrank) cupboard.

kastrieren [kaˈstriːən] castrate.

Kasus [ˈkaːzus] m (pl -n) (Gramm) case.

Katalog [kataˈloːg] m (pl -e) catalogue.

Katarakt¹ [kataˈrakt] m (pl -e) rapids, waterfall.

Katarakt² f (pl -e) (Med) cataract.

Katarrh [kaˈtar] m (pl -e) catarrh.

katastrophal [katastroˈfaːl] adj catastrophic. **Katastrophe** f (pl -n) catastrophe.

Kategorie [kategoˈriː] f (pl -n) category. **kategorisch** adj categorical.

Kater [ˈkaːtər] m (pl -) tom cat; (Katzenjammer) hangover.

Kathedrale [kateˈdraːlə] f (pl -n) cathedral.

Katholik(in) [katoˈliːk(ɪn)] Catholic. **katholisch** adj Catholic. **Katholizismus** m Catholicism.

Kätzchen [ˈkɛtsçən] neut kitten.

Katze [ˈkatsə] f (pl -n) cat. **katzenartig** adj feline, cat-like. **Katzen||auge** neut (Rückstrahler) rear reflector. **–jammer** m hangover.

Kauderwelsch [ˈkaudərvɛlʃ] neut gibberish, double Dutch.

kauen [ˈkauən] v chew.

kauern [ˈkauərn] v cower.

Kauf [kauf] m (pl **Käufe**) purchase. **einen guten Kauf machen** make a good buy, get a bargain. **kaufen** v buy, purchase.

Käufer [ˈkɔyfər] m (pl -) buyer.

Kauf||haus neut department store. **–kraft** f purchasing power.

käuflich [ˈkɔyflɪç] adj saleable, purchasable; (bestechlich) corrupt, venal.

Kaufmann m businessman; (Kleinhandel) shopkeeper; (Großhandel) merchant. **kaufmännisch** adj commercial, mercantile. **Kaufpreis** m purchase price.

kaum [kaum] adv hardly, scarcely.

Kaution [kauˈtsioːn] f (pl -en) security, deposit. **gegen Kaution freilassen** release on bail.

Kauz [kauts] m (pl **Käuze**) screech owl; (fig) odd fellow.

Kavaller||ie [kavaləˈriː] f (pl -n) cavalry. **–ist** m cavalryman.

Kaviar [ˈkaːviar] m (pl -e) caviar.

keck [kɛk] adj pert, cheeky.

Kegel [ˈkeːgəl] m (pl -) cone; (Spiel) skittle. **–bahn** f bowling alley. **kegel||förmig** adj conical. **–n** v play skittles, go bowling.

Kegelspiel neut skittles, bowling.

Kehle [ˈkeːlə] f (pl -n) throat. **Kehlkopf** m larynx. **–entzündung** f laryngitis.

kehren¹ [ˈkeːrən] v sweep, brush.

kehren² v turn. **sich kehren** turn (round). **sich kehren an** pay attention to.

Kehricht [ˈkeːrɪçt] m (unz.) sweepings pl.

Kehr||reim m refrain. **–seite** f reverse, other side.

Keil [kail] m (pl -e) wedge; (Arch) keystone. **keilen** v wedge; (werben) win over. **sich keilen** scuffle.

Keiler [ˈkailər] m (pl -) (wild) boar.

Keilriemen [ˈkailriːmən] m (Mot) fanbelt.

Keim [kaim] m (pl -e) germ; (Med) bud; embryo; (Anfang) origin. **keimen** v germinate; bud. **Keim||träger** m carrier. **–ung** f germination.

kein [kain] **keine, kein** pron, m, f no one, nobody; neut nothing, none. adj no, not any. **kein anderer als** none other than. **keine Ahnung!** (I've) no idea! **keiner von beiden** neither (of the two). **keinerlei** adj of no sort. **keines||falls** adv on no account. **–wegs** adv not at all.

Keks [keːks] m (pl -e) biscuit.

Keller [ˈkɛlər] m (pl -) cellar. **–ei** f wine cellar. **–geschoß** neut basement.

Kellner [ˈkɛlnər] m (pl -) waiter. **–in** waitress.

*kennen [ˈkɛnən] v know. **–lernen** v get to know, become acquainted with. **Kenner** m (Wein, Kunst) connoisseur; (Fachmann) expert. **kenntlich** adj distinguishable, distinct. **Kenntnis** f knowledge. **kenntnisreich** adj experienced. **Kennwort** neut password. **kennzeichnen** v (fig) characterize, distinguish. **-d** adj characteristic. **Kennziffer** f reference or code number; (Math) index.

kentern [ˈkɛntərn] v capsize.

Kerbe [ˈkɛrbə] f (pl -n) notch.

Kerker [ˈkɛrkər] m (pl -) dungeon.

Kerl [kɛrl] m (pl -e) fellow.

Kern [kɛrn] m (pl -e) kernel; (Obst) stone, pit; (Atom) nucleus; (fig) core, essence. **kerngesund** adj thoroughly healthy. **Kern||haus** neut core. **–reaktion** f nuclear reaction. **–waffe** f nuclear weapon. **–kraftwerk** neut nuclear power station.

Kerze [ˈkɛrtsə] f (pl -n) candle. **Kerzen||leuchter** neut candlestick. **–licht**

neut candlelight.

Kessel ['kɛsəl] *m* (*pl* -) kettle; (*Tech*) boiler; (*Geog*) depression, hollow.

Kette ['kɛtə] *f* (*pl* -n) chain. **ketten** *v* chain, link. **Ketten‖gebirge** *neut* mountain range. **-geschäft** *neut* chain store. **-raucher** *m* chain smoker. **-reaktion** *f* chain reaction.

Ketzer ['kɛtsər] *m* (*pl* -) heretic. **-ei** *f* (*pl* -en) heresy. **ketzerisch** *adj* heretical.

keuchen ['kɔyçən] *v* gasp, pant. **keuchhusten** *m* whooping cough.

Keule ['kɔylə] *f* (*pl* -n) club, bludgeon; (*Fleisch*) leg.

keusch [kɔyʃ] *adj* chaste, modest. **Keuschheit** *f* chastity.

kichern ['kiçərn] *v* giggle.

Kiefer¹ ['ki:fər] *m* (*pl* -) (*Anat*) jaw.

Kiefer² *f* (*pl* -n) (*Bot*) pine.

Kieferknochen ['ki:fərknoxən] *m* jawbone.

Kiefern‖holz *neut* pinewood. **-wald** *m* pine forest.

Kiel [ki:l] *m* (*pl* -e) keel.

Kieme [ki:mə] *f* (*pl* -n) gill.

Kies [ki:s] *m* (*pl* -e) gravel. **Kiesel** *m* (*pl* -) pebble, flint. **-stein** *m* pebble. **Kiesgrube** *f* gravelpit.

Kilo ['ki:lo] *neut* (*pl* -) kilo, kilogram(me). **-byte** *neut* (*pl* - *or* -s) (*comp*) kilobyte. **-gramm** *neut* (*pl* -) kilogram(me). **Kilometer** *neut* kilometre. **-zähler** *m* milometer, odometer.

Kind [kint] *neut* (*pl* -er) child. **ein Kind bekommen/erwarten** have/expect a baby.

Kinder‖arzt *m* paediatrician. **-bett** *neut* cot, crib. **-buch** *neut* children's book. **-heilkunde** *f* paediatrics. **-hort** *m* crèche. **-jahre** *pl* childhood *sing*. **-lähmung** *f* polio. **-spiel** *neut* children's game; (*fig*) child's play. **-wagen** *m* pram, buggy, (*US*) baby carriage.

Kindheit *f* childhood. **kindisch** *adj* childish. **kindlich** *adj* childlike.

Kinn [kin] *neut* (*pl* -e) chin.

Kino ['ki:no] *neut* (*pl* -s) cinema.

Kiosk ['ki:ɔsk] *m* (*pl* -e) kiosk.

kippen ['kipən] *v* tip, tilt. **Kippwagen** *m* tipper, tip cart.

Kirche ['kirçə] *f* (*pl* -n) church. **Kirchen‖gemeinde** *f* parish. **-lied** *neut* hymn. **-schändung** *f* desecration, profanation. **Kirch‖gänger** *m* church-goer. **-hof** *m* churchyard. **kirchlich** *adj* ecclesiastical, church.

Kirsch [kirʃ] *m* kirsch, cherry brandy. **-e** *f* (*pl* -n) cherry.

Kissen ['kisən] *neut* (*pl* -) cushion; (*Kopf-*) pillow; (*pl*) bedding.

Kiste ['kistə] *f* (*pl* -n) chest, case, box.

Kitsch [kitʃ] *m* (tasteless) trash, kitsch. **kitschig** *adj* trashy.

Kittel ['kitəl] *m* (*pl* -) smock.

Kitzel ['kitsəl] *m* (*pl* -) tickle. **kitzeln** *v* tickle. **kitzlig** *adj* ticklish.

klaffen ['klafən] *v* gape, yawn. **-d** *adj* gaping.

Klage ['kla:gə] *f* (*pl* -n) complaint, grievance; (*Jur*) action, lawsuit. **klagen** *v* complain, (*Jur*) bring an action. **Klagende(r)** plaintiff.

kläglich ['klɛ:kliç] *adj* miserable, pitiful.

Klammer ['klamər] *f* (*pl* -n) clamp; (*kleine*) clip; (*Wäsche*) peg. **klammern** *v* clamp; (*befestigen*) fasten. **sich klammern an** cling to.

Klamotten [kla'mɔtən] *pl* (*umg.*) gear *sing*, clothes *pl*.

Klang [klaŋ] *m* (*pl* **Klänge**) sound.

klapp‖en ['klapən] flap, clap; (*umg.*) work out, be all right. **-bar** *adj* collapsible, folding. **Klappe** *f* flap; (*umg.*) mouth, trap. **halt die Klappe!** (*vulg*) shut up!

Klapper ['klapər] *f* (*pl* -n) rattle. **klapperig** *adj* clattering, rattling. **klappern** *v* rattle, clatter.

Klapp‖messer *neut* jack-knife. **-stuhl** *m* folding chair. **-tür** *f* trapdoor.

klar [kla:r] *adj* clear.

klären ['klɛ:rən] *v* clarify.

Klarheit ['kla:rhait] *f* clarity, clearness.

Klarinette [klari'nɛtə] *f* (*pl* -n) clarinet. **Klarinettist** *m* clarinettist.

klarlegen ['kla:rle:gən] *v* clear up.

Klärung ['klɛ:ruŋ] *f* clarification.

klarwerden ['kla:rve:rdən] *v* become clear.

klasse ['klasə] *adj* (*umg.*) marvellous, splendid. **Klasse** *f* class. *ein Musiker von Klasse* an excellent musician. *ein Restaurant erster Klasse* a first-class restaurant. **klassenbewußt** *adj* class-conscious. **Klassenzimmer** *neut* classroom.

Klassik ['klasik] *f* classical era; (*Literatur, Musik*) classicism. **-er** *m* classicist. **klasisch**

adj classical.

Klatsch [klatʃ] *m* (*pl* -e) slap, smack; (*Gerede*) gossip, chatter. **–base** *f* gossip, chatterbox. **klatschen** *v* clap; (*reden*) gossip, chatter.

Klaue ['klaʊə] *f* (*pl* -n) claw; (*Raubvogel*) talon. **klauen** *v* (*umg.*) steal, pinch.

Klausel ['klaʊzəl] *f* (*pl* -n) clause.

Klavier [klaˈviːr] *neut* (*pl* -e) piano. **–spieler(in)** pianist.

Klebeband ['kleːbəbant] *neut* (adhesive) tape. **kleben** *v* glue, paste; (*anhaften*) stick. **klebrig** *adj* sticky. **Klebstoff** *m* glue.

Klecks [klɛks] *m* (*pl* -e) blot, spot.

Klee [kleː] *m* clover. **–blatt** *neut* cloverleaf.

Kleid [klaɪt] *neut* (*pl* -er) garment; (*Frau*) dress; (*pl*) clothes. **kleiden** *v* clothe. **Kleider‖bügel** *m* coat-hanger. **–bürste** *f* clothes brush. **–schrank** *m* wardrobe. **Kleidung** *f* clothing, clothes. **–sstück** *neut* article of clothing, garment.

Kleie ['klaɪə] *f* bran.

klein [klaɪn] *adj* small, little. **der kleine Mann** the ordinary man. **klein stellen** turn down, put on low. **im kleinen** in miniature; (*Komm*) retail.

Klein‖anzeige *f* classified advertisement, small ad. **–asien** *neut* Asia Minor. **–bürger** *m* petty bourgeois. **–bus** *m* minibus. **–geld** *neut* (small) change. **–handel** *m* retail trade. **Kleinigkeit** *f* (*pl* -en) trifle, trivial matter. **Klein‖kind** *neut* infant. **–lebewesen** *neut* microorganism. **klein‖lich** *adj* petty. **–mütig** *adj* faint-hearted, cowardly.

Kleinod ['klaɪnoːt] *neut* (*pl* -ien) jewel, gem.

Kleister ['klaɪstər] *m* (*pl* -) paste, gum.

Klemme ['klɛmə] *f* (*pl* -n) clamp; (*Haar*) grip; (*Klammer*) clip. **in der Klemme sitzen** be in a dilemma *or* tight corner. **klemmen** *v* squeeze, pinch.

Klempner ['klɛmpnər] *m* (*pl* -) plumber; (*Metall*) metalworker. **–ei** *f* plumbing. **klempnern** *v* do plumbing.

Kleriker ['kleːrikər] *m* (*pl* -) cleric, clergyman. **Klerus** *m* (*unz.*) clergy.

Kletterer ['klɛtərər] *m* (*pl* -) climber. **klettern** *v* climb. **Kletterpflanze** *f* climbing plant, creeper.

Klima ['kliːma] *f* (*pl* -te) climate. **–anlage** *f* air-conditioning (equipment). **klimatisch** *adj* climatic.

Klinge ['klɪŋə] *f* (*pl* -n) blade.

Klingel ['klɪŋəl] *f* (*pl* -n) (door)bell. **klingeln** *v* ring the bell, ring.

klingen ['klɪŋən] *v* sound; ring.

Klinik ['kliːnik] *f* (*pl* -en) clinic, hospital. **klinisch** *adj* clinical.

Klinke ['klɪŋkə] *f* (*pl* -n) doorhandle, latch.

Klippe ['klɪpə] *f* (*pl* -n) cliff; (*im Meer*) rocks *pl*, reef.

klirren ['klɪrən] *v* tinkle, jangle.

Klischee [klɪˈʃeː] *neut* (*pl* -s) (*fig*) cliché.

Klo [kloː] *neut* (*pl* -s) (*umg.*) toilet, loo.

Kloake [kloˈaːkə] *f* (*pl* -n) sewer.

Klon [kloːn] *m* (*pl* -e) clone *m*. **klonen** *v* clone.

klopfen ['klɔpfən] *v* (*Tür*) knock; (*Herz*) beat; (*Schulter*) tap, pat. **Klopfen** *neut* knocking; beating.

Klosett [kloˈzɛt] *neut* (*pl* -s) toilet. **–papier** *neut* toilet paper.

Kloß [kloːs] *m* (*pl* **Klöße**) dumpling; (*Fleisch*) meatball.

Kloster ['kloːstər] *neut* (*pl* **Klöster**) monastery, abbey, convent. **–gang** *m* cloister.

Klotz [klɔts] *m* (*pl* **Klötze**) block, log.

Klub [klup] *m* (*pl* -s) club, association.

Kluft [kluft] *m* (*pl* **Klüfte**) cleft; (*Abgrund*) chasm, abyss; (*fig*) rift.

klug [kluːk] *adj* clever; (*Ansicht, Rat*) sensible, prudent. **Klugheit** *f* cleverness, intelligence.

Klumpen ['klumpən] *m* (*pl* -) lump; (*Gold*) nugget.

knabbern ['knabərn] *v* nibble.

Knabe ['knaːbə] *m* (*pl* -n) boy. **–nalter** *neut* boyhood, youth. **knabenhaft** *adj* boyish.

Knäckebrot ['knɛkəbroːt] *neut* crispbread.

knacken ['knakən] *v* crack.

Knall [knal] *m* (*pl* -e) bang; explosion. **–bonbon** *m* cracker. **knallen** *v* crack, bang; explode. **Knallfrosch** *m* banger, jumping jack.

knapp [knap] *adj* scant, insufficient; (*Kleidung*) tight. **knapp sein** be in short supply. **knapp werden** be running short *or* out. **knapp bei Kasse sein** be hard up. *knapp drei Meter* just under (*or* barely) three metres.

knarren ['knarən] *v* creak.

knattern ['knatərn] *v* crackle, rattle.

Knebel [ˈkneːbəl] *m (pl* -) gag. **knebeln** *v* gag.

Knecht [knɛçt] *m (pl* -e) (farm) worker; (*Diener*) servant.

***kneifen** [ˈknaifən] *v* pinch, nip. **Kneifzange** *f* pincers.

Kneipe [ˈknaipə] *f (pl* -n) pub, bar. **kneipen** *v* go boozing.

kneten [ˈkneːtən] *v* knead; (*Körper*) massage.

Knick [ˈknik] *m (pl* -e) crack; (*Kniff*) crease; (*Kurve*) sharp bend. **knicken** *v* break, crack; fold, crease.

Knicks [kniks] *m (pl* -e) curtsey.

Knie [kniː] *neut (pl* -) knee. **knien** *v* kneel. **-d** *adj* kneeling, on one's knees. **Kniescheibe** *f* kneecap.

Kniff [knif] *m (pl* -e) pinch; (*Falte*) crease; trick. **den Kniff beraushaben** get the hang of it.

knipsen [ˈknipsən] *v* punch, clip; (*Foto*) snap.

knirschen [ˈkniɾʃən] *v* gnash.

Knitter [ˈkniːtəɾ] *m (pl* -) crease. **knitter- frei** *adj* crease-resistant. **-n** *v* crease.

Knoblauch [ˈknoːplaux] *m* garlic.

Knöchel [ˈknœçəl] *m (pl* -) (*Finger*) knuckle; (*Bein*) ankle.

Knochen [ˈknɔxən] *m (pl* -) bone. **-bruch** *m* fracture. **-gerüst** *neut* skeleton. **-mark** *neut* (bone) marrow. **knochig** *adj* bony.

Knödel [ˈknøːdəl] *m (pl* -) dumpling.

Knolle [ˈknɔlə] *f (pl* -n) tuber; (*Zwiebel, Tulpe*) bulb.

Knopf [knɔpf] *m (pl* **Knöpfe**) button.

knöpfen [ˈknœpfən] *v* button.

Knorpel [ˈknɔɾpəl] *m (pl* -) cartilage; (*bei gekochtem Fleisch*) gristle.

Knospe [ˈknɔspə] *f (pl* -n) bud. **knospen** *v* bud.

Knoten [ˈknoːtən] *m (pl* -) knot; (*Tech*) node. **knoten** *v* knot. **Knotenpunkt** *m* junction.

knüpfen [ˈknypfən] *v* join, tie.

knusprig [ˈknusprik] *adj* crisp.

Koalition [koalitsioːn] *f (pl* -en) coalition.

Kobold [ˈkoːbɔlt] *m (pl* -e) goblin.

Koch [lɔx] *m (pl* **Köche**) cook. **-buch** *neut* cookery book. **kochen** *v* cook; (*sieden*) boil. **-d** boiling. **Kocher** *m* cooker. **Kochherd** *m* kitchen range.

Köchin [ˈkœçin] *f (pl* -nen) (female) cook.

Koch||platte *f* hotplate, ring. **-topf** *m* saucepan, pot.

Köder [ˈkøːdəɾ] *m (pl* -) bait. **ködern** *v* lure, entice.

Koexistenz [koːɛksistɛnts] *f* coexistence. **koexistieren** *v* coexist.

koffeinfrei [ˈlɔfainfrai] *adj* decaffeinated, decaf.

Koffer [ˈlɔfəɾ] *m (pl* -) suitcase; (*Schrank-koffer*) trunk. **-kuli** *m* (*luggage*) trolley. **-raum** *m* (*Mot*) boot.

Kohl [koːl] *m (pl* -e) cabbage.

Kohle [ˈkoːlə] *f (pl* -n) coal; (*Holzkohle*) charcoal. **Kohlen||bergwerk** *neut* coal mine, pit. **-säure** *f* carbonic acid; (*in Getränken*) carbon dioxide. **-hydrat** *neut* carbohydrate. **-stoff** *m* carbon. **Kohle||papier** *neut* carbon paper. **-stift** *m* charcoal crayon.

Kohl||rabi [koːlɾabi] *m (pl* -s) kohlrabi. **-rübe** *f* swede.

Koje [ˈkoːjə] *f (pl* -n) bunk, berth; (*Zimmer*) cabin.

kokett [koˈkɛt] *adj* coquettish. **-ieren** *v* flirt.

Kokosnuß [ˈkoːkosnus] *f* coconut.

Koks [koːks] *m (pl* -e) coke.

Kolben [ˈlɔlbən] *m (pl* -) club; (*Gewehr*) butt; (*Zylinder*) piston.

Kollege [lɔˈleːgə] *m (pl* -n) **Kollegin** *f (pl* -nen) colleague.

kollektiv [lɔlɛkˈtiːf] *adj* collective.

Köln [kœln] *neut* Cologne. **-ischwasser** *neut* eau de Cologne.

Kolon [ˈkoːlɔn] *neut (pl* -s) colon.

kolonial [lɔloˈniaːl] *adj* colonial. **Kolonialwaren** *pl* groceries. **-händler** *m* grocer.

Kolonne [lɔˈlɔnə] *f (pl* -n) column.

Kombi [ˈlɔm bi] *m (pl* -s) estate car.

Kombination [lɔm binaˈtsioːn] *f (pl* -en) combination; (*Sport*) teamwork; (*Unterkleidung*) combinations *pl*; (*Schützkleidung*) one-piece suit; (*Ideen*) conjecture. **kombinieren** *v* combine.

Komet [koˈmeːt] *m (pl* -en) comet.

Komfort [lɔm ˈfoːɾ] *m (unz.)* comfort. **komfortabel** *adj* comfortable.

Komiker [ˈkoːm iɾəɾ] *m (pl* -) comedian. comic. **komisch** *adj* funny; (*seltsam*) strange.

Komitee [kɔm iːteː] *neut (pl -s)* committee.

Komma ['kɔm a] *neut (pl -s)* comma.

Kommandant [kɔm an'dant] *m (pl -en)* commander. **kommandieren** *v* command.

Kommanditgesellschaft (KG) [kɔm an-'diːtgəzɛlʃaft (kaˈgeː)] *f* limited-liability company.

Kommando [kɔ'm andoː] *neut (pl -s)* order, command; (*Abteilung*) squad, detachment, detail. **-truppe** *f* commando (unit).

***kommen** ['kɔm ən] *v* come. **kommen lassen** send for. **um etwas kommen** lose something. **hinter etwas kommen** get to the bottom of something. **Kommen** *neut* arrival, coming. **kommend** *adj* coming.

Kommentar [kɔm ɛn'taːr] *m (pl -e)* commentary. **kommentieren** *v* comment on.

Kommerz [kɔ'm ɛrts] *m* commerce. **komerziell** *adj* commercial.

Kommisar [kɔm isaːr] *m (pl -e)* commissioner; (*Polizei*) inspector. **Kommission** *f* commission.

kommun [kɔ'm uːn] *adj* common. **-al** *adj* municipal. **Kommune** *f (pl -n)* commune; (*Gemeinde*) municipality.

Kommunikation [kɔm unika'tsioːn] *f (pl -en)* communication.

Kommuniqué [kɔm yniːkeː] *neut (pl -s)* communiqué.

Kommunismus [kɔm u'nizm us] *m* communism. **Kommunist(in)** communist. **kommunistisch** *adj* communist.

Komödie [kɔ'm œ :diə] *f (pl -n)* comedy; (*Ereignis*) farce.

Kompaß [kɔm pas] *m (pl Kompasse)* compass. **-strich** *m* point of the compass.

kompetent [kɔm pɛ'tɛnt] *adj* competent.

Komplex [kɔm 'plɛks] *m (pl -e)* complex.

Kompliment [kɔm plɪm ɛnt] *neut (pl -e)* compliment.

komplizieren [kɔm plitsiːrən] *v* complicate. **kompliziert** *adj* complicated, complex.

Komplott [kɔm 'plɔt] *neut (pl -e)* plot, conspiracy.

komponieren [kɔm po'niːrən] *v* compose. **Komponist** *m (pl -en)* composer.

Kompott [kɔm 'pɔt] *neut (pl -n)* stewed fruit, compote.

Kompresse [kɔm 'prɛsə] *f (pl -n)* compress.

Kompromiß [kɔm pro'm is] *m (pl Kompromisse)* compromise. **kompromittieren** *v* compromise.

kondensieren [kɔndɛn'siːən] *v* condense. **Kondensmilch** *f* condensed milk.

Konditorei [kɔndiːto'rai] (*pl -en*) patisserie, cake shop. **-waren** *pl* pastries, cakes.

Kondom [kɔn'doːm] *m (pl -e)* condom.

Konferenz [kɔnfˈɛrɛnts] *f (pl -en)* conference.

Konfession [kɔnfˈsioːn] *f (pl -en)* confession, creed, faith.

Konflikt [kɔn'flikt] *m (pl -e)* conflict.

konform [kɔn'fɔm] *adj* in agreement, in accordance.

Konfrontation [kɔnfronta'tsioːn] *f (pl -en)* confrontation. **konfrontieren** *v* confront.

konfus [kɔn'fuːs] *adj* confused, muddled. **Konfusion** *f* confusion.

Kongreß [kɔŋ'grɛs] *m (pl Kongresse)* congress.

König ['køː :niː] *m (pl -e)* king. **-in** *f (pl -nen)* queen. **-inmutter** *m* queen mother. **königlich** *adj* royal, regal. **Königreich** *neut* kingdom, realm.

Konjunktur [kɔnjuŋktuːr] *f (pl -en)* (state of the) economy, economic trends *pl*; (*Aufschwung*) boom.

Konkurrent [kɔnku'rɛnt] *m (pl -en)* competitor. **Konkurrenz** *f (unz.)* competition. **konkurrenzfähig** *adj* competitive. **konkurrieren** *v* compete.

Konkurs [kɔn'kurs] *m (pl -e)* bankruptcy, insolvency. **in Konkurs gehen** become bankrupt.

***können** ['kœ nən] *v* can, be able (to); (*dürfen*) may, be allowed (to); (*gelernt haben*) know. **tun können** know how to do. **eine Sprache können** speak a language. *Ich kann nicht mehr!* I can't go on. **das kann sein** it may be so. *er kann nichts dafür* it's not his fault, he can't help it. **Können** *neut* ability.

konsequent [kɔnzˈkvɛnt] *adj* consistent. **Konsequenz** *f* consistency; (*Folge*) consequence. **die Konsequenzen tragen** bear the consequences. **Konsequenzen ziehen** draw conclusions.

konservativ [kɔnzɛrva'tiːf] *adj* conservative. **Konservative(r)** conservative.

Konserve [kɔn'zɛrvə] *f (pl -n)* preserve, tinned *or* bottled food. **Konservenbüchse** *f* tin (of preserves). **konservieren** *v* preserve.

konsolidieren [kɔnzɔlidiːrən] *v* consolidate.

Konsonant [kɔnzo'nant] *m* (*pl* **-en**) consonant.

Konstant [kɔn'stant] *adj* constant.

konstruieren [kɔnstru'iːrən] *v* construct. **Konstruktion** *f* (*pl* **-en**) construction; (*Entwurf*) design.

Konsul [kɔn'zuːl] *m* (*pl* **-n**) consul. **-at** *neut* (*pl* **-e**) consulate.

Konsum [kɔn'zuːm] *m* consumption. **-gesellschaft** *f* consumer society. **konsumieren** *v* consume. **Konsumverein** *m* co-operative society.

Kontakt [kɔn'takt] *m* (*pl* **-e**) contact.

Kontinent [kɔntinɛnt] *m* (*pl* **-e**) continent.

Konto ['kɔnto] *neut* (*pl* **Konten**) account. **-auszug** *m* (bank) statement. **-buch** *neut* passbook. **-inhaber** *m* accountholder.

Kontrabaß ['kɔntrabas] *m* double bass.

Konträr [kɔn'trɛː] *adj* adverse.

Kontrast [kɔn'trast] *m* (*pl* **-e**) contrast. **kontrastieren** *v* contrast.

Kontrolle [kɔn'trɔlə] *f* (*pl* **-n**) control, supervision. **-abschnitt** *m* counterfoil. **-eur** *m* controller. **kontrollieren** *v* control, supervise. **Kontrollpunkt** *m* checkpoint. **unter Kontrolle** under control.

konventionell [kɔnvɛntsio'nɛl] *adj* conventional.

Konversation [kɔnvɛrza'tsioːn] *f* (*pl* **-en**) conversation. **-slexikon** *neut* encyclopedia.

konvertieren [kɔnvɛr'tiːrən] *v* convert.

konvex [kɔn'vɛks] *adj* convex.

Konzentrat [kɔntsən'traːt] *neut* (*pl* **-e**) concentrate. **-ion** *f* (*pl* **-en**) concentration. **-ionslager** *neut* concentration camp. **konzentrieren** *v* concentrate.

Konzept [kɔn'tsɛpt] *neut* (*pl* **-e**) rough draft.

Konzert [kɔn'tsɛrt] *neut* (*pl* **-e**) concert; (*Stück*) concerto.

Kopf [kɔpf] *m* (*pl* **Köpfe**) head. **auf den Kopf stellen** turn upside down. **pro Kopf** per capita, each. **im Kopf haben** be preoccupied with. **-ball** *m* (*Sport*) header.

köpfen ['kœpfən] *v* behead, decapitate.

Kopf‖haut *f* scalp. **-hörer** *m* headphone. **-kissen** *neut* pillow. **-putz** *m* headdress. **-salat** *m* lettuce. **-schmerzen** *pl* headache *sing.* **-sprung** *m* header. **-stand** *m* headstand. **kopfüber** *adv* headlong, head first.

Kopie [ko'piː] *f* (*pl* **-n**) copy. **kopieren** *v* copy.

Kopulation [kopula'tsioːn] *f* (*pl* **-en**) copulation. **kopulieren** *v* copulate; (*Bäume*) graft.

Koralle [ko'ralə] *f* (*pl* **-n**) coral. **-nriff** *neut* coral reef.

Korb [kɔrp] *m* (*pl* **Körbe**) basket. **-ball** *m* basketball. **-geflecht** *neut* basketwork.

Kord [kɔrt] *or* **Kordsamt** *m* cord(uroy). **Kordhose** *f* corduroy trousers; (*umg.*) cords.

Korinthe [ko'rintə] *f* (*pl* **-n**) currant.

Kork [kɔrk] *m* (*pl* **-e**) cork. **-enzieher** *m* corkscrew.

Korn [kɔrn] *neut* (*pl* **Körner**) grain, corn.

Körnchen ['kœrnçən] *neut* (*pl* **-**) granule.

Koronarthrombose [koro'nartrɔmboːzə] *f* (*pl* **-n**) coronary thrombosis.

Körper [kœrpər] *m* (*pl* **-**) body. **-bau** *m* physique, build. **körperbehindert** *adj* physically handicapped. **Körper‖bildung** *f* body-building. **-geruch** *m* body odour. **-gewicht** *neut* weight. **-haltung** *f* posture.

körperlich ['kœrpərliç] *adj* bodily, physical; (*Strafe*) corporal.

Körper‖maß *neut* cubic measure. **-pflege** *f* hygiene. **-schaft** *f* (*pl* **-en**) corporation.

Korporal [kɔrpo'raːl] *m* (*pl* **-e**) corporal.

korporativ [kɔrpora'tiːf] *adj* corporate.

korrekt [ko'rɛkt] *adj* correct. **Korrektur** *f* (*pl* **-en**) correction; (*Druck*) proof.

Korrespondent [kɔrɛspɔn'dɛnt] *m* (*pl* **-en**) correspondent. **Korrespondenz** *f* correspondence.

korrigieren [kɔrig'iːrən] *v* correct; (*gedrucktes*) proofread.

Kosename ['koːzənaːmə] *m* pet name.

Kosmetik [kɔz'meːtik] *f* (*unz.*) cosmetics *pl.* **kosmetisch** *adj* cosmetic.

Kosmos ['kɔsmɔs] *m* (*pl* **Kosmen**) cosmos, universe. **kosmisch** *adj* cosmic.

Kost [kɔst] *f* (*unz.*) food, fare. **Kost und Wohnung** board and lodging. **kräftige Kost** rich diet.

kostbar ['kɔstbaːr] *adj* expensive; (*sehr wertvoll*) precious.

kosten¹ ['kɔstən] *v* (*probieren*) taste, try, sample.

kosten² *v* cost. **Kosten** *pl* costs. **auf meine Kosten** at my expense. **kostenlos** *adj* free (of charge).

köstlich ['kœstliç] *adj* delicious; (*reizend*) charming; (*wertvoll*) precious.

kostspielig ['kɔstʃpiːliç] *adj* expensive.

Kostüm [kɔsˈtyːm] neut (pl -e) costume; (Damen-) suit. **-ball** m fancy-dress ball. **-probe** f dress rehearsal.

Kot [koːt] m dung, droppings pl; (Schmutz) dirt, mud.

Kotelett [kɔtəˈlɛt] neut (pl -e) chop, cutlet. **-en** pl sideburns, mutton-chop whiskers.

Kotflügel [ˈkoːtflyːɡəl] m mudguard; wing.

kotzen [ˈkɔtsən] v (vulg) puke, be sick. **zum Kotzen** enough to make you sick.

Krabbe [ˈkrabə] f (pl -n) shrimp.

krabbeln [ˈkrabəln] v scuttle, scurry.

Krach [krax] m (pl -e) noise; (Streit) quarrel, row; (Knall) crash.

krächzen [ˈkrɛçtsən] v croak.

kraft [kraft] prep on the strength of, by virtue of. **Kraft** f (pl Kräfte) strength; (Macht) power. **-fahrer** m driver. **-fahrzeug** neut motor vehicle.

kräftig [ˈkrɛftiç] adj strong; (mächtig) powerful; (Essen) substantial. **-en** v strengthen. **-end** adj invigorating.

kraftlos adj powerless. **Kraft||probe** f trial of strength. **-rad** neut motorcycle. **-stoff** m fuel. **-wagen** m motor vehicle. **-werk** neut power station.

Kragen [ˈkraːɡən] m (pl -) collar.

Krähe [ˈkrɛːə] f (pl -n) crow. **krähen** v crow.

Kralle [ˈkralə] f (pl -n) claw. **krallen** v claw. **sich krallen an** clutch.

Kram [kraːm] m stuff, trash; (umg.) things, stuff. **lästiger Kram** hassle.

Krampf [krampf] m (pl Krämpfe) cramp, spasm. **krampfhaft** adj convulsive; (heftig) frenzied, frantic.

Kran [kraːn] m (pl Kräne) (Mech) crane.

Kranich [ˈkraːniç] m (pl -e) (Zool) crane.

krank [krank] adj sick, ill, unwell. **Kranke(r)** patient.

kränken [ˈkrɛŋkən] v vex, annoy.

Kranken||haus neut hospital. **-kasse** f health insurance (company). **-schein** m medical certificate. **-schwester** f nurse. **-versicherung** f health insurance. **-wagen** m ambulance. **krankhaft** adj diseased, unhealthy. **Krankheit** f (pl -en) disease, illness.

Kranz [krants] m (pl Kränze) wreath, garland.

Krapfen [ˈkrapfən] m (pl -) fritter; doughnut.

kraß [kras] adj crass, gross.

kratzen [ˈkratsən] v scratch. **Kratzwunde** f scratch.

kraulen [ˈkraulən] or **kraulschwimmen** v swim the crawl. **Kraulstil** m crawl.

kraus [kraus] adj curly, crinkled.

Kraut [kraut] neut (pl Kräuter) herb; (Kohl) cabbage; (grüne Pflanzen) vegetation.

Kräuter||buch [ˈkrɔytərbuːx] neut herbal. **-tee** m herb tea.

Krawall [kraˈval] m (pl -e) brawl.

Krawatte [kraˈvatə] f (pl -n) (neck)tie.

Krebs [kreːps] m (pl -e) crab; (Med) cancer; (Astrol) Cancer.

Kredit [kreˈdiːt] m (pl -e) (Komm) credit. **-brief** m letter of credit. **kreditieren** v credit.

Kreide [ˈkraidə] f (pl -n) chalk. **-fels** m chalk cliff.

Kreis [krais] m (pl -e) circle; (Gebiet) district, area. **-bahn** f orbit. **-bewegung** f rotation, revolution. **-bogen** m arc (of a circle).

kreischen [ˈkraiʃən] v screech, shriek.

Kreisel [ˈkraizəl] m (pl -) (spinning) top. **kreiseln** v spin (like a top).

kreis||en v revolve, rotate. **-förmig** adj circular. **Kreis||lauf** m circulation. **-säge** f circular saw. **-umfang** m circumference.

Krem [kreːm] f (pl -s) cream.

Krematorium [kremaˈtoːriʊm] neut (pl Krematorien) crematorium.

Kreml [ˈkreml] m Kremlin.

Krempel [ˈkrempəl] m junk, rubbish.

krepieren [kreˈpiːrən] v burst; (umg.) die.

Kresse [ˈkrɛsə] f (pl -n) cress.

Kreuz [krɔyts] neut (pl -e) cross; (Karten) club(s); (Anat) small of the back. **kreuz und quer** in all directions. **kreuzen** v cross; (Schiff) cruise. **sich kreuzen** intersect. **Kreuzer** m (pl -) cruiser. **Kreuz||fahrer** m crusader. **-fahrt** f (Schiff) cruise; (Kreuzzug) crusade.

kreuzigen [ˈkrɔytsiɡən] v crucify. **Kreuzigung** f (pl -en) crucifixion.

Kreuzkümmel [ˈkrɔytskyməl] m cumin (seed).

Kreuzung [ˈkrɔytsʊŋ] f (pl -en) crossing.

Kreuz||verhör neut cross-examination. **-verweis** m cross-reference. **-weg** m crossroads. **-worträtsel** neut crossword puzzle. **-zug** m crusade.

*kriechen [ˈkriːçən] v creep, crawl; (fig)

cringe, grovel. **kriecherisch** *adj* cringing, servile.

Krieg [kriːk] *m* (*pl* -e) war. **den Krieg erklären/führen** declare/wage war. **Krieger** *m* (*pl* -) warrior. **kriegführend** *adj* belligerent. **Kriegs||dienstverweigerer** *m* conscientious objector. **–gefangene(r)** prisoner of war. **–gericht** *neut* courtmartial. **–hetzer** *m* warmonger. **–verbrecher** *m* war criminal. **–zeit** *f* wartime.

Krimi [ˈkriːmi] *neut* (*pl* -s) detective novel, thriller.

kriminal [krimiˈnaːl] *adj* criminal. **Kriminal||polizei** *f* detective force, CID. **–roman** *m* detective novel, thriller.

Krippe [ˈkripə] *f* (*pl* -n) crib; (*Kinder*-) crèche.

Krise [ˈkriːzə] *f* (*pl* -n) crisis.

Kristall [krisˈtal] *m* (*pl* -e) crystal. **kristallisieren** *v* crystallize.

Kritik [kriˈtiːk] *f* (*pl* -en) criticism. **-er** *m* critic. **kritisch** *adj* critical. **kritisieren** *v* criticize; (*Buch, Film*) review.

kritzeln [ˈkritsəln] *v* doodle, scribble.

Kroatien [kroˈaːtiən] *neut* Croatia. **Kroate** *m*, **Kroatin** *f* Croatian. **kroatisch** *adj* Croatian.

Krokodil [krokoˈdiːl] *neut* (*pl* -e) crocodile.

Krone [ˈkroːnə] *f* (*pl* -n) crown.

krönen [ˈkrøːnən] *v* crown. **Krönung** *f* coronation.

Kröte [ˈkrøːtə] *f* (*pl* -n) toad.

Krücke [ˈkrykə] *f* (*pl* -n) crutch.

Krug [kruːk] *m* (*pl* Krüge) jug; (*Becher*) mug.

Krume [ˈkruːmə] *f* (*pl* -n) crumb.

Krümel [ˈkryːməl] *m* (*pl* -) crumb.

krümelig [ˈkryːməliç] *adj* crumbly.

krumm [krum] *adj* crooked. **–beinig** *adj* bow-legged.

Krumme [ˈkrumə] *f* (*pl* -n) sickle.

Krümmung [ˈkrymuŋ] *f* curve, bend.

Krüppel [ˈkrypəl] *m* (*pl* -) cripple.

Kruste [ˈkrustə] *f* (*pl* -n) crust. **–ntier** *neut* crustacean.

Kruzifix [kruːtsiˈfiks] *neut* (*pl* -e) crucifix.

Kubikinhalt [kuˈbiːkinhalt] *m* volume.

Küche [ˈkyçə] *f* (*pl* -n) kitchen; cookery, cuisine.

Kuchen [ˈkuːxən] *m* (*pl* -) cake.

Küchen||schabe *f* cockroach. **–schrank**

m kitchen cupboard.

Kuckuck [ˈkukuk] *m* (*pl* -e) cuckoo.

Kugel [ˈkuːgəl] *f* (*pl* -n) ball; (*Gewehr*) bullet; (*Math*) sphere. **kugel||fest** *adj* bulletproof. **–förmig** *adj* spherical. **Kugel||lager** *neut* ball-bearing. **–schreiber** *m* ball(point) pen.

Kuh [kuː] *f* (*pl* Kühe) cow.

kühl [kyːl] *adj* cool. **Kühle** *f* coolness. **kühlen** *v* cool. **Kühl||schrank** *m* refrigerator. **–ung** *f* cooling.

kühn [kyːn] *adj* daring, bold, audacious. **Kühnheit** *f* daring, boldness, audacity.

Kuhstall [ˈkuːʃtal] *m* cowshed.

Kulissen [kuˈlisən] *pl* (*Theater*) scenery *sing*. **hinter den Kulissen** (*fig*) behind the scenes.

Kult [kult] *m* (*pl* -e) cult; (*Verehrung*) worship.

kultivieren [kultiˈviːrən] *v* cultivate.

Kultur [kulˈtuːr] *f* (*pl* -en) culture; (*Boden*) cultivation; (*Bakterien*) culture. **kulturell** *adj* cultural.

Kümmel [ˈkyməl] *m* caraway (seed).

Kummer [ˈkumər] *m* (*unz.*) sorrow, distress.

kümmerlich [ˈkymərliç] *adj* miserable, poor. **kümmern** *v* grieve; (*angehen*) concern. **sich kümmern um** take care of, look after.

Kumpel [ˈkumpəl] *m* (*pl* -s) (*umg.*) mate, buddy; (*Bergmann*) miner.

kund [kunt] *adj* (generally) known.

Kunde[1] [ˈkundə] *f* information, (*Nachrichten*) news.

Kunde[2] *m*, **Kundin** *f* customer, client. **Kunden anreißen** *v* tout for custom(ers).

Kundendienst [ˈkundəndiːnst] *m* aftersales service.

*kundgeben [ˈkuntgeːbən] *v* make known, declare. **Kundgebung** *f* demonstration; (*Kundgeben*) declaration.

kündigen [ˈkyndigən] *v* give notice. **Kündigung** *f* notice.

Kundschaft [ˈkuntʃaft] *f* (*unz.*) customers *pl*, clientele.

künftig [ˈkynftiç] *adj* future.

Kunst [kunst] *f* (*pl* Künste) art; (*Fertigkeit*) skill. **–akademie** *f* art college. **kunstfertig** *adj* skilled. **Kunst||gegenstand** *m* objet d'art. **–griff** *m* trick, dodge. **–handwerker** *m* craftsman.

Künstler [ˈkynstlər] *m* **Künstlerin** *f* artist.

künstlerisch adj artistic.
künstlich ['kynstlɪç] adj artificial. **künstliche Atmung** f artificial respiration.
Kunst||stück [neut stunt, trick. **–werk** neut work of art.
Kupfer ['kupfər] neut (pl -) copper. **kupfer||farben** adj copper(-coloured). **–n** adj copper.
Kuppel ['kupəl] f (pl -n) dome, cupola.
Kuppelei [kupə'lai] f (unz.) procuring, pimping. **kuppeln** v unite, couple; (Mot) declutch. **Kuppler** m procurer. **Kupplerin** f procuress. **Kupplung** f coupling; (Mot) clutch.
Kur [kuːr] f (pl -en) (course of) treatment. **–anstalt** f sanatorium.
Kurbel ['kurbəl] f (pl -n) crank, handle. **–welle** f crankshaft.
Kürbis ['kyrbɪs] m (pl -se) pumpkin.
Kurfürst ['kuːrfyrst] m elector, electoral prince.
Kurort m spa.
Kurs [kurs] m (pl -e) course; (Komm) rate. **–buch** neut railway timetable.
kursiv [kur'ziːf] adv in italics.
Kursor ['kurzoːr] m (pl -e) (comp) cursor.
Kurve ['kurvə] f (pl -n) curve; (Straße) bend.
kurz [kurts] adj short. **kurze Hose** shorts pl. **kurz und gut** in a word, in short. **sich kurz fassen** be brief, make it short. **Kurz||arbeit** f short time (work). **–ausgabe** f abridged edition.
Kürze ['kyrtsə] f shortness; (Zeit) brevity. **kürzen** v shorten. **kürzlich** adv recently, lately.
Kurz||meldung f news flash. **–schluß** m short circuit. **–schrift** f shorthand. **kurzsichtig** adj nearsighted, shortsighted.
Kürzung ['kyrtsun] f (pl -en) shortening, reduction.
Kurz||waren f pl haberdashery. **–welle** f shortwave.
Kusine [ku'ziːnə] f (pl -n) (female) cousin.
Kuß [kus] m (pl Küsse) kiss.
küssen ['kysən] v kiss.
Küste ['kystə] f (pl -n) coast, shore. **–nwache** f coastguard.
Kutsche ['kutʃə] f (pl -n) carriage, coach. **–r** m (pl -) coachman.

L

labil [la'biːl] adj unstable; (oft krank) delicate, sickly.
Labor [la'boːr] neut (pl -s) (umg.) lab.
Laboratorium [labora'toːrium] neut (pl **Laboratorien**) laboratory, (umg.) lab.
lächeln ['lɛçəln] v smile. **Lächeln** neut smile.
lachen ['laxən] v laugh. **Lachen** neut laughter, laugh. **zum Lachen bringen** make laugh. **das ist zum Lachen** that's ridiculous.
lächerlich ['lɛçərlɪç] adj ridiculous.
Lachs [laks] m (pl -e) salmon.
Lack [lak] m (pl -e) lacquer; (mit Farbstoff) (enamel) paint. **–farbe** f (enamel) paint. **–leder** neut patent leather.
*laden[1] ['laːdən] v load.
*laden[2] v invite; (Jur) summon.
Laden ['laːdən] m (pl Läden) shop; (Fenster) shutter. **–diebstahl** m shoplifting. **–schluß** m closing time. **–tisch** m counter.
Lade||platz m loading place; (Schiff) wharf. **–raum** m hold. **Ladung** (pl -en) f load; (Schiffe) cargo.
Lage ['laːgə] f (pl -n) situation, position. **in der Lage sein zu** be in a position to.
Lager ['laːgər] neut (pl -) camp; (Speicher) store(s); (Tier) lair; (Geol) stratum, layer; (Tech) bearing. **–feuer** neut campfire. **–haus** neut warehouse. **lagern** v (im Freien rasten) camp; (aufbewahren) store; (einlegen) lay down, place; (aufbewahrt werden) be stored.
Lagune [la'guːnə] f (pl -n) lagoon.
lahm [laːm] adj crippled; (müde) exhausted; (schwach) lame, feeble.
lähmen ['lɛːmən] v cripple, paralyse; (fig) obstruct. **Lähmung** f (pl -en) paralysis.
Laib [laip] m (pl -e) loaf.
Laie ['laiə] m (pl -n) layman. **Laien||priester** m lay preacher. **–stand** m laity.
Lakritze [la'krɪtsə] f (pl -n) liquorice.
Lamm [lam] neut (pl Lämmer) lamb. **–fleisch** neut lamb. **–wolle** f lambswool.
Lampe ['lam pə] f (pl -n) lamp.
Land [lant] 1 neut (unz.) (Erdboden, Grundstück, Festland) land; (Landschaft) country(side). 2 neut (pl Länder) land, country; (Provinz) state, province. **an Land gehen** go ashore, disembark. **Hügeliges**

Land hilly country *or* terrain. **auf dem Lande** in the country. **Land||arbeiter** *m* farmworker. **–besitz** *m* land, property. **landen** *v* land; (*umg.*) land up, end up. **Landenge** *f* isthmus.

Land||bank *f* national bank; regional bank. **–flagge** *f* national flag. **–verrat** *m* high treason.

Land||gut *neut* (landed) estate. **–haus** *neut* country house. **–karte** *f* map. **–leute** *pl* country folk.

ländlich ['ɛntlɪç] *adj* rural.

Land||mann *m* countryman; (*Bauer*) farmer. **–messer** *m* surveyor. **–mine** *f* landmine. **–schaft** *f* countryside; (*Malerei*) landscape; (*Gebiet*) area, region. **–schule** *f* village school. **–smann** *m* fellow countryman. **–spitze** *f* cape, headland. **–straße** *f* highway, main road. **–streicher** *m* tramp, vagrant.

Landung ['landʊŋ] *f* (*pl* -en) landing. **–ssteg** *m* gangway, landing ramp.

Landweg ['antvɛːk] *m* land route. **auf dem Landwege** by land.

Landwirt ['antvɪrt] *m* farmer. **landwirtschaftlich** *adj* agricultural.

lang [laŋ] *adj* long; (*Mensch*) tall. **viele Jahre lang** for many years. **lange** *adv* (for) a long time.

Länge ['lɛŋə] *f* (*pl* -n) length; (*Mensch*) height; (*Größe*) size; (*Geog*) longitude.

langen ['laŋən] *v* suffice. **langen nach** reach for.

länger ['lɛŋər] *adj* longer; taller. **länger machen** lengthen, extend. **auf längere Zeit** for a considerable period.

Langeweile ['laŋəvaɪlə] *f* boredom.

lang||jährig *adj* of long standing. **–lebig** *adj* long-lived.

länglich ['lɛŋlɪç] *adj* oblong, longish. **–rund** *adj* oval, elliptical.

längs [lɛŋs] *prep* along.

langsam ['laŋzaːm] *adj* slow. **Langsamkeit** *f* slowness.

Langspielplatte ['laŋʃpiːlplatə] *f* long-playing record, LP.

längst [lɛŋst] *adj* longest. *adv* long ago. **–ens** *adv* (*höchstens*) at the most; (*spätestens*) at the latest.

langweilen ['laŋvaɪlən] *v* bore. **sich langweilen** be bored. **langweilig** *adj* boring, tedious.

Lanze ['lantsə] *f* (*pl* -n) lance.

Lappen ['lapən] *m* (*pl* -) rag, (cleaning) cloth; (*Anat, Bot*) lobe. **lappig** *adj* (*umg.*) flabby; (*Anat, Bot*) lobed.

Lärche ['lɛrçə] *f* (*pl* -n) larch.

Lärm [lɛrm] *m* (*unz.*) noise, din. **lärmen** *v* make a noise. **–d** *adj* noisy.

Laser ['leːzər] *m* (*pl* -) laser.

*lassen ['lasən] *v* (*erlauben*) let, allow; (*unterlassen*) leave, stop; (*überlassen*) leave. **außer Acht lassen** disregard. **bleiben lassen** leave alone. **fallen lassen** (let) drop. **kommen lassen** send for. **sich machen lassen** have done *or* made. **lassen von** renounce. **sich nicht beschreiben lassen** be indescribable *or* beyond words. **laß mich gehen!** let me go! **laß mich in Ruhe!** leave me alone. **es läßt sich nicht machen** it can't be done.

lässig ['lɛsɪç] *adj* careless, negligent.

Last [last] *f* (*pl* -en) load; (*Bürde*) burden; (*Gewicht*) weight; (*Fracht*) cargo.

Laster[1] ['lastər] *m* (*pl* -) (*umg.*) lorry, truck.

Laster[2] *neut* (*pl* -) vice. **lasterhaft** *adj* immoral.

lästern ['lɛstərn] *v* slander. **Lästerung** *f* slander.

lästig ['lɛstɪç] *adj* irksome, bothersome.

Last||kahn *m* barge, lighter. **–kraftwagen** (**Lkw**) *m* lorry, truck. **–pferd** *neut* packhorse.

Latein [la'taɪn] *neut* Latin (language). **–amerika** *neut* Latin America. **lateinisch** *adj* Latin.

Laterne [la'tɛrnə] *f* (*pl* -n) lantern. **–npfahl** *m* lamppost.

Latte ['latə] *f* (*pl* -n) lath.

lau [lau] *adj* lukewarm, tepid; (*Wetter*) mild.

Laub [laup] *neut* (*pl* -e) foliage. **–baum** *m* deciduous tree. **–säge** *f* fretsaw. **–wald** *m* deciduous forest. **–werk** *neut* foliage.

Lauch [laux] *m* (*pl* -e) leek.

lauern ['lauərn] *v* lurk, lie in ambush; (*umg.*) hang around, wait impatiently.

Lauf [lauf] *m* (*pl* Läufe) run; (*Sport*) race; (*Fluß*) course; (*Gewehr*) barrel; (*Maschine*) running, operation. **–bahn** *f* career. **laufen** *v* (*Maschine, Wasser, Weg, usw.*) run; (*zu Fuß gehen*) walk. **laufend** *adj* current, running; (*Zahl*) consecutive. **auf dem laufenden** up to date.

Läufer ['lɔyfər] *m* (*pl* -) (*Sport*) runner;

(*Schach*) bishop.
läufig ['lyfɪç] *adj* (*Hündin*) in heat.
Lauf||planke *f* gangway. **–werk** *neut* mechanism, drive.
Lauge ['lauɡə] *f* (*pl* -n) lye; (*Seifen-*) suds. **laugenartig** *adj* alkaline, (*Chem*) basic.
Laune ['launə] *f* (*pl* -n) mood, temper; (*Grille*) whim. **launenhaft** *adj* capricious, whimsical. **launig** *adj* humorous, funny. **launisch** *adj* moody, capricious.
Laus [laus] *f* (*pl* Läuse) louse.
lauschen ['lauʃən] *v* listen (to); (*heimlich*) listen in, eavesdrop.
lausig ['lauzɪç] *adj* lousy.
laut¹ [laut] *adj* loud. *adv* aloud.
laut² *prep* according to.
Laut [laut] *m* (*pl* -n) sound.
Laute ['lautə] *f* (*pl* -n) lute.
lauten ['lautən] *v* read, say; (*klingen*) sound.
läuten ['lɔytən] *v* ring, sound.
lauter ['lautər] *adj* pure; (*echt*) genuine; (*nichts als*) nothing but, sheer.
Laut||sprecher *m* loudspeaker. **–stärke** *f* volume, loudness.
lauwarm ['lauvarm] *adj* lukewarm.
Lawine [a'viːnə] *f* (*pl* -n) avalanche.
lax [laks] *adj* lax.
leben ['leːbən] *v* live. **von ... leben** live on ... **Es lebe die Königin!** Long live the Queen! **Leben** *neut* (*pl* -) life; (*Geschäftigkeit*) activity, bustle. **am Leben** alive. **ums Leben kommen** lose one's life, die. **lebend** *adj* living, alive. **–ig** *adj* alive, living; (*munter*) lively.
Lebens||art *f* lifestyle. **–freude** *f* joy of life. **–funktion** *f* vital function. **–gefahr** *f* danger to life. **–haltungskosten** *pl* cost of living *sing*. **–jahr** *neut* year of one's life. **im 16. Lebensjahr** during the sixteenth year of his/her life.
lebenslänglich ['leːbənslɛŋlɪç] *adj* lifelong; (*Jur*) for life.
Lebens||lauf *m* curriculum vitae, c.v. **–mittel** *pl* food *sing*. **–standard** *m* standard of living. **–stil** *m* lifestyle. **–unterhalt** *m* livelihood. **–versicherung** *f* life insurance. **–weise** *f* way of life.
Leber ['leːbər] *f* (*pl* -n) liver. **–fleck** *m* birthmark. **–wurst** *f* liver sausage.
Lebe||wesen *neut* living creature, organism. **–wohl** *neut* farewell.
lebhaft ['leːphaft] *adj* lively. **Lebhaftig-**

keit *f* liveliness.
leblos ['leːploːs] *adj* lifeless.
leck [lɛk] *adj* leaky. **Leck** *neut* (*pl* -e) leak.
lecken ['lɛkən] *v* lick.
lecker ['lɛkər] *adj* delicious. **–bissen** *m* delicacy, titbit.
Leder ['leːdər] *neut* (*pl* -) leather. **–hose** *f* leather shorts *pl*. **ledern** *adj* leather; (*fig*) dry, boring. **Leder||riemen** *m* leather strap. **–waren** *pl* leather goods.
ledig ['leːdɪç] *adj* single, unmarried; (*frei*) free (of). **lediger Stand** *m* celibacy. **lediglich** *adv* solely.
Lee [leː] *f* lee.
leer [leːr] *adj* empty; (*unbesetzt*) unoccupied; (*Stellung*) open; (*Seite*) blank. **Leere** *f* emptiness; (*Physik*) vacuum. **leeren** *v* empty. **Leer||lauf** *m* (*Mot*) idling, tick-over. **–ung** *f* (*pl* -en) emptying; (*Post*) collection.
legal [leˈɡaːl] *adj* legal.
legen ['leːɡən] *v* lay, place, put (down); (*Eier*) lay; (*installieren*) install, fit. **sich legen** lie down; (*wind*) abate.
Legende [leˈɡɛndə] *f* (*pl* -n) legend.
legieren [leˈɡiːrən] *v* (*Metalle*) alloy; (*Suppe*) thicken.
legitim [leɡiˈtiːm] *adj* legitimate.
Lehm [leːm] *m* (*pl* -e) loam.
Lehne ['leːnə] *f* (*pl* -n) support, prop; (*Stuhl*) back. **lehnen** *v* lean, rest. **sich lehnen** lean, rest. **Lehn||sessel** *or* **–stuhl** *m* armchair, easy chair.
Lehrbuch ['leːrbuːx] *neut* textbook. **Lehre** *f* (*pl* -n) teaching; (*Lehrzeit*) training. **lehren** *v* teach. **Lehrer** *m* (*pl* -) teacher, schoolmaster. **–in** *f* (*pl* -nen) teacher, schoolmistress. **Lehr||film** *m* educational film. **–gang** *m* curriculum, course of instruction. **–ling** *m* (*pl* -e) apprentice. **lehrreich** *adj* instructive. **Lehr||plan** *m* curriculum. **–satz** *m* rule, proposition. **–zeit** *f* training, apprenticeship.
Leib [laip] *m* (*pl* -er) body. **Leibes||frucht** *f* foetus. **–übung** *f* physical exercise.
Leiche ['laiçə] *f* (*pl* -n) corpse. **Leichen||halle** *f* mortuary. **–schau** *f* postmortem, autopsy. **Leichnam** *m* (*pl* -e) corpse.
leicht [laiçt] *adj* light; (*einfach*) easy. **leicht zugänglich** easily accessible. **es sich leicht machen** take it easy. **Leichtathletik** *f* athletics. **leichtfertig** *adj* super-

ficial; (*Antwort*) glib. **Leichtgewichtler** *m* lightweight. **leichtgläubig** *adj* credulous. **Leichtigkeit** *f* lightness; (*Mühelosigkeit*) ease. **leichtlebig** *adj* easy-going. **–sinnig** *adj* thoughtless.

leid [laɪt] *adj* disagreeable, painful. **es ist** (*or* **es tut**) **mir leid** I am sorry. **Leid** *neut* (*unz.*) sorrow, grief; (*Schaden*) harm. **leiden** *v* suffer; (*erlauben*) tolerate, allow. **leiden an** suffer from. *ich kann ihn nicht leiden* I can't stand him. **leidend** *adj* suffering; (*kränklich*) sickly.

Leidenschaft [ˈlaɪdənʃaft] *f* (*pl* **-en**) passion. **leidenschaftlich** *adj* passionate. **–slos** *adj* dispassionate.

leider [ˈlaɪdər] *adv* unfortunately. **leider muß ich** ... I am afraid I have to ....

leidig [laɪɪç] *adj* tiresome, disagreeable.

leidlich [ˈlaɪtlɪç] *adj* tolerable.

Leier [ˈlaɪər] *f* (*pl* **-n**) lyre. **die alte Leier** the same old story. **leiern** *v* (*sprechen*) drawl.

leihen [ˈlaɪən] *v* lend; (*borgen*) borrow. **Leihbibliothek** *f* lending library.

Leim [laɪm] *m* (*pl* **-e**) glue.

Lein [laɪn] *m* (*pl* **-e**) flax.

Leine [ˈlaɪnə] *f* (*pl* **-n**) line, cord; (*Hund*) leash.

leinen [ˈlaɪnən] *adj* linen. **Leinen** *neut* linen.

leise [ˈlaɪzə] *adj* quiet; (*sanft*) gentle, soft.

Leiste [ˈlaɪstə] *f* (*pl* **-n**) (*Anat*) groin.

leisten [ˈlaɪstən] *v* do; (*schaffen*) accomplish, achieve; (*ausführen*) carry out. **Hilfe leisten** help, assist. **sich leisten** allow oneself. *ich kann mir einen neuen Wagen nicht leisten* I cannot afford a new car. **Leistung** *f* (*pl* **-en**) achievement, accomplishment; (*Tat*) deed; (*Arbeit*) output. **leistungsfähig** *adj* capable; productive. **Leistungsfähigkeit** *f* ability (to work); productivity.

leiten [ˈlaɪtən] *v* (*führen*) (*Elek, Musik*) conduct. **–d** *adj* guiding, leading; (*Person*) prominent, senior.

Leiter[1] [ˈlaɪtər] *m* (*pl* **-**) leader; manager.

Leiter[2] *f* (*pl* **-n**) ladder.

Leitfaden *m* clue; (*Lehrbuch*) guide, textbook. **–satz** *m* guiding principle. **–ung** *f* (*pl* **-en**) (*Führung*) leadership; (*Verwaltung*) management; (*Elek*) circuit; (*Draht*) wire; (*Wasser*) pipes *pl*, mains *pl*. **mit neuen Leitungen versehen** *v* rewire.

Lektüre [lɛkˈtyːrə] *f* (*pl* **-n**) reading;

(*Lesestoff*) reading material, literature.

Lende [ˈlɛndə] *f* (*pl* **-n**) (*Anat*) lumbar region; (*Fleisch*) loin.

lenken [ˈlɛŋkən] *v* steer; (*führen*) direct. **Lenker** *m* guide; (*Flugzeug*) pilot; (*Leiter*) manager. **–rad** *neut* steering wheel. **–ung** *f* (*pl* **-en**) (*Mot*) steering; (*Leitung*) direction.

Leopard [leoˈpart] *m* (*pl* **-en**) leopard.

lepra [ˈlɛpra] *f* leprosy. **–kranke(r)** leper.

Lerche [ˈlɛrçə] *f* (*pl* **-n**) lark.

lernen [ˈlɛrnən] *v* learn. **Lernen** *neut* (*unz.*) learning.

lesbar [ˈlɛsbaːr] *adj* readable. **Lese** *f* (*pl* **-n**) vintage. **Lesebuch** *neut* reading book. **lesen** *v* read; lecture; (*sammeln, ernten*) gather, harvest. **Leser** *m* (*pl* **-**), **Leserin** *f* (*pl* **-en**) reader. **leserlich** *adj* legible. **Leserschaft** *f* readership, readers. **Lessaal** *m* reading room.

Lettland [ˈlɛtlant] *neut* Latvia. **Lette** *m*, **Lettin** *f* Latvian. **lettisch** *adj* Latvian.

letzt [lɛtst] *adj* last; (*spätest*) latest, final. **letzte Nummer** current issue. **letztens** *adv* lately; (*zum Schluß*) lastly.

Leuchte [ˈlɔʏçtə] *f* (*pl* **-n**) light, lamp. **leuchten** *v* emit light, shine. **–d** *adj* shining, luminous. **Leuchter** *m* (*pl* **-**) candlestick. **Leuchtturm** *m* lighthouse.

leugnen [ˈlɔʏgnən] *v* deny.

Leukämie [lɔʏkɛˈmiː] *f* leukaemia.

Leute [ˈlɔʏtə] *pl* people.

Leutnant [ˈlɔʏtnant] *m* (*pl* **-e**) lieutenant.

leutselig [ˈlɔʏtzeːlɪç] *adj* affable, sociable.

Lexikon [ˈlɛksikon] *neut* (*pl* **Lexika**) dictionary.

Libelle [liˈbɛlə] *f* (*pl* **-n**) (*Insekt*) dragonfly; (*Tech*) (spirit) level.

liberal [libeˈraːl] *adj* liberal.

licht [lɪçt] *adj* bright; (*Farbe*) light; (*Wald*) sparse, thin. **Licht** *neut* (*pl* **-er**) light; (*Kerze*) candle. **–bild** *neut* photograph. **lichtdurchlässig** *adj* translucent.

lichten [ˈlɪçtən] *v* (*Wald*) clear; (*Anker*) weigh.

Lichtjahr *neut* lightyear. **–pause** *f* blueprint. **–signal** *neut* light signal. **lichtundurchlässig** *adj* opaque.

Lichtung [ˈlɪçtʊŋ] *f* (*pl* **-en**) glade, clearing.

Lid [liːt] *neut* (*pl* **-er**) eyelid.

lieb [liːp] *adj* dear; (*nett*) nice; (*angenehm*) agreeable. *ein liebes Kind* a good child. *es wäre ihm lieb* he would appreciate it. *das ist* *lieb von Ihnen* that is most kind of you.

Liebchen ['lɪpçən] *neut* (*pl* -) darling.

Liebe ['liːbə] *f* (*pl* -en) love. **Liebelei** *f* (*pl* -en) firtation. **lieben** *v* love. **liebens||wert** *adj* lovable, endearing. **-würdig** *adj* amiable, helpful, kind.

lieber ['liːbər] *adj* dearer, *adv* rather; (*besser*) better. **lieber haben** prefer. **lieber also** rather than. **Ich gehe lieber zu Fuß** I prefer to walk. *das hättest Du lieber nicht sagen sollen* you had better not say that.

Liebes||affäre *f* (love) affair. **-brief** *m* love letter. **-paar** *neut* lovers *pl*, couple.

liebevoll ['liːbəfɔl] *adj* affectionate, loving.

***liebhaben** ['liːphaːbən] *v* love, like. **Liebhaber** *m* (*pl* -), **Liebhaberin** *f* (*pl* -nen) lover.

lieb||kosen *v* caress, fondle. **-lich** *adj* lovely. **Lieb||ling** *m* darling; (*Günstling*) favourite. **-reiz** *m* charm, attraction.

liebst [liːpst] *adj* favourite, best-loved. *adv* **am liebsten haben** like best of all. **am liebsten machen** like doing best.

Lied [liːt] *neut* (*pl* -er) song. **-erbuch** *neut* songbook; (*Rel*) hymnbook.

liederlich *adj* slovenly; (*sittenlos*) debauched, dissipated.

Lieferant [liːfəˈrant] *m* (*pl* -en) supplier. **liefern** *v* deliver, supply; (*Ertrag*) yield. **Lieferung** *f* (*pl* -en) delivery, supply.

Liege ['liːgə] *f* (*pl* -n) couch. **liegen** *v* lie. **-bleiben** *v* remain; (*Waren*) be unsold; (*Arbeit*) remain unfinished; (*Panne haben*) break down. **-lassen** *v* leave (behind). **Liege||platz** *m* berth. **-stuhl** *m* deckchair.

Liga ['liːga] *f* (*pl* Ligen) league.

Likör *m* (*pl* -e) liqueur.

lila ['liːla] *adj* lilac, purple. **Lila** *neut* lilac, purple.

Lilie ['liːliə] *f* (*pl* -n) lily.

Limonade [limoˈnaːdə] *f* (*pl* -n) lemonade, soda-pop.

Linde ['lɪndə] *f* (*pl* -n) lime tree.

lindern ['lɪndərn] *v* alleviate, mitigate.

Lineal [lineˈaːl] *neut* (*pl* -e) ruler, rule.

Linie ['liːniə] *f* (*pl* -n) line.

Linke ['lɪŋkə] *f* (*pl* -n) left, left(-hand) side; (*Pol*) the Left. **linkisch** *adj* clumsy. **links** *adv* (on *or* to) the left. **Linkshänder** *m* left-hander. **linkshändig** *adj* left-handed. **Links||radikale(r)** *m* (radical) left-winger. **-steuerung** *f* left-hand drive.

Linse ['lɪnzə] *f* (*pl* -n) (*Foto*, *Anat*) lens; (*Küche*) lentil.

Lippe ['lɪpə] *f* (*pl* -n) lip. **-nstift** *m* lipstick.

lispeln ['lɪspəln] *v* lisp.

Lissabon ['lɪsabɔn] *neut* Lisbon.

List [lɪst] *f* (*pl* -en) (*Schlauheit*) cunning, trick, ruse, ploy.

Liste ['lɪstə] *f* (*pl* -n) list.

listig ['lɪstɪç] *adj* cunning.

Litanei [litaˈnai] *f* (*pl* -en) litany.

Litauen ['lɪtauən] *neut* Lithuania. **Litauer(in)** Lithuanian. **litauisch** *adj* Lithuanian.

Liter ['liːtər] *neut or m* (*pl* -) litre.

literarisch [liteˈraːrɪʃ] *adj* literary. **Literatur** *f* literature.

Live-Sendung ['laifzɛnduŋ] *f* live *or* direct broadcast.

Lizenz [liˈtsɛnts] *f* (*pl* -en) licence. **-inhaber** *m* licensee.

Lob [loːp] *neut* (*pl* -e) praise. **loben** *v* praise. **Lob||gesang** *m* song of praise. **-hudelei** *f* adulation.

Loch [lɔx] *neut* (*pl* Löcher) hole; (*Reifen*) puncture. **lochen** *v* pierce, punch; (*perforieren*) perforate.

löcherig ['lœçərɪç] *adj* full of holes.

Lochung ['lɔxuŋ] *f* (*pl* -en) perforation.

Locke ['lɔkə] *f* (*pl* -n) curl, lock.

locken ['lɔkən] *v* lure, entice.

locker ['lɔkər] *adj* loose; (*Lebensart*) lax, slack. **lockern** *v* loosen (up). **sich lockern** *v* become loose; (*entspannen*) relax.

lockig ['lɔkɪç] *adj* curly.

Lock||speise *f* bait. **-vogel** *m* decoy.

lodern ['loːdərn] *v* blaze (up); (*fig*) glow, smoulder.

Löffel ['lœfəl] *m* (*pl* -) spoon.

Loge ['loːʒə] *f* (*pl* -n) (*Theater*) box; (*Freimauren*) lodge.

logieren [loˈʒiːrən] *v* lodge.

Logik ['loːgɪk] *f* logic. **logisch** *adj* logical.

Lohn [loːn] *m* (*pl* Löhne) (*Gehalt*, *Bezahlung*) wages *pl*, pay; (*Belohnung*) reward; (*verdiente Strafe*) deserts *pl*. **-arbeiter** *m* wage-earner, (weekly-paid) worker. **lohnen** *v* reward. **es lohnt sich (nicht)** it's (not) worth it. **Lohn||forderung** *f* wage claim. **-schreiber** *m* hack (writer). **-stopp** *m* wage freeze. **-tag** *m* payday.

lokal [loˈkaːl] *adj* local. **Lokal** *neut* (*pl* -e)

pub, tavern.

Lokomotive [bkom o'tːvə] f (pl -n) loco-motive.

Lorbeer ['bɔbeːr] m (pl -en) laurel. **–blatt** neut bay leaf. **–kranz** m laurel wreath.

los [bːs] adj free; (nicht fest) loose. adv away, off. **los!** go on! off you go! **was ist los?** what's going on? **was ist mit dir los?** what's the matter (with you)? **etwas/ jemanden los sein/werden** be/get rid of something/someone.

Los neut (pl -e) (Schicksal) fate, lot; (Lotterie) lottery ticket. **das Los ziehen** draw lots.

lösbar ['lɛ ːsbaːr] adj soluble.

*los||binden v untie. **–brechen** v break loose.

löschen ['lɛ ʃən] v (Feuer) put out, extin-guish; (Licht) turn off, switch off; (Schuld) cancel, write off; (Tinte) blot; (Firma) liqui-date; (Durst) quench. **Löscher** m (Feuer) extinguisher; (Tinte) blotter.

lose ['bːzə] adj loose.

Lösegeld ['lɛ ːzəgɛlt] neut ransom.

lösen ['lɛ ːzən] v loosen; (Knoten) unravel (a plot); (Verschluß) unfasten; (Rätsel, Problem) solve; (abtrennen) detach; (Chem) dissolve.

*los||fahren v drive off. **–gehen** v set out, get going. **–knüpfen** v untie. **–kommen** v get away or free. **–lassen** v let go.

löslich ['lɛ ːzlɪç] adj soluble.

los||lösen v free, detach. **–machen** v unfasten, release. **–reißen** v tear away. **–sagen** v **sich lossagen von** renounce. **los||schießen** v fire away/off. **–schrauben** v unscrew. **–sprechen** v acquit, release.

Losung ['bːzuŋ] f (pl -en) password.

Lösung ['lɛ ːzuŋ] f (pl -en) solution; (Lösen) loosening. **–smittel** neut solvent.

los||werden v get rid of. **–ziehen** v set out.

Lot [bːt] neut (pl -e) plumbline; (zum Löten) solder. **loten** v take soundings.

löten v solder.

lotrecht ['bːtrɛçt] adj perpendicular, verti-cal.

Lotse ['bːtsə] f (pl -n) (Schiff) pilot.

Lotterie [btɛ'riː] f (pl -n) lottery.

Löwe ['lɛ ːvə] m (pl -n) lion. **–nzahn** m dandelion. **Löwin** f lioness.

Luchs [lʊks] m (pl -e) lynx.

Lücke ['lyːkə] f (pl -n) gap; (Auslassung) omission; (eines Gesetzes) loophole.

–nbüßer m stopgap. **luckenhaft** adj defec-tive; (fig) patchy, full of gaps.

Luft [lʊft] f (pl Lüfte) air. **–ansicht** f aerial view. **–bild** neut aerial photograph. **–bremse** f air brake. **–brücke** f airlift. **luft-dicht** adj airtight.

lüften ['lyftən] v ventilate, air.

Luftfahrt ['lʊftfaːrt] f aviation. **luft-gekühlt** adj air-cooled. **Lufthafen** m air-port. **luftig** adj airy, breezy. **Luft|| krankheit** f airsickness. **–krieg** m aerial warfare. **–post** f airmail. **–reifen** m pneu-matic tyre, (US tire). **–röhre** f windpipe. **–schiff** neut airship.

Lüftung ['lyftuŋ] f (pl -en) ventilation.

Luftverkehr ['lʊftvɛːrkɛːr] m air traffic. **–sgesellschaft** f airline.

Lüge ['lyːgə] f (pl -n) lie. **lügen** v (tell a) lie. **–haft** adj lying. **Lügner** m liar.

Lump [lʊmp] m (pl -) rag. **–händler** m rag-and-bone man.

Lunge ['lʊŋə] f (pl -n) lung. **Lungen|| entzündung** f pneumonia. **–krebs** m lung cancer.

Lupe ['luːpə] f (pl -n) magnifying glass. **unter die Lupe nehmen** scrutinize, exam-ine closely.

Lust [lʊst] f (pl Lüste) delight, pleasure; (Verlangen) desire; (Wollust) lust. **Lust haben an** take pleasure in. **Lust haben (zu tun)** feel like (doing). **keine Lust haben (zu tun)** not be in the mood (to do), not feel like (doing).

lüstern ['lystərn] adj (geil) lascivious, lech-erous.

Lustfahrt ['lʊstfaːrt] f pleasure trip. **lustig** adj merry, joyful; (unterhaltend) amusing, funny. **sich lustig machen über** make fun of. **Lustigkeit** f gaiety, merriment. **lustlos** adj dull, inactive. **Lust||mord** m sex mur-der. **–spiel** neut comedy.

lutschen ['lʊtʃən] v suck. **Lutscher** m (baby's) dummy, (US) pacifier.

Luxus ['lʊksus] m luxury. **–artikel** m luxury item; pl luxuries.

Luzern ['lʊtsɛrn] neut Lucerne.

lyrisch ['lyːrɪʃ] adj lyrical.

M

Maat [m a:t] *m* (*pl* -e) mate; (*Kriegsmarine*) petty officer.

machen ['m axən] *v* make; do; (*Rechnung*) come to. **eine Prüfung machen** sit an exam **fertig machen** get ready. **Licht machen** switch on a light. (**das**) **macht nichts**, it doesn't matter, never mind. **mach's gut!** good luck! all the best!

Macht [m axt] *f* (*pl* **Mächte**) power.

mächtig ['m ɛçtiː] *adj* powerful; mighty; (*riesig*) immense.

Machtkampf *m* power struggle. **machtlos** *adj* powerless. **Machtprobe** *f* trial of strength.

Mädchen ['m ɛːtçən] *neut* (*pl* -) girl. **mädchenhaft** *adj* girlish. **Mädchenname** *m* maiden name.

Made ['m a:də] *f* (*pl* -n) maggot.

Mädel ['m ɛːdə] *neut* (*pl* -) girl.

Magazin [m aga'tsiːn] *neut* (*pl* -e) store(house); (*Zeitschrift, auch Gewehr-*) magazine.

Magd [m a:kt] *f* (*pl* **Mägde**) maid(servant).

Magen ['m a:gən] *m* (*pl* -**Mägen**) stomach. -**brennen** *neut* heartburn. -**schmerzen** *pl* stomach-ache *sing*.

mager ['m a:gər] *adj* thin, lean.

Magie [m a'giː] *f* magic. **magisch** *adj* magic(al).

Magnet [m ag'neːt] *m* (*pl* -en) magnet. **magnetisch** *adj* magnetic.

Mahagoni [m aha'goːniː] *neut* (*pl* -s) mahogany.

Mähdrescher ['m ɛːdrɛʃər] *m* combine harvester. **mähen** *v* mow.

Mahl [m a:l] *neut* (*pl* -e) meal.

***mahlen** ['m a:lən] *v* mill, grind.

Mahl||zahn *m* molar. -**zeit** *f* meal; *interj* good appetite!

Mähne ['m ɛːnə] *f* (*pl* -n) mane.

mahnen ['m a:nən] *v* remind, admonish; warn. **Mahnung** *f* reminder, warning.

Mai [m a] *m* (*pl* -e) May. -**blume** *f* lily of the valley.

Mais [m ais] *m* maize, (*US*) corn. -**kolben** *m* cob of corn. -**mehl** *neut* cornflour.

Majestät [m aɟstɛːt] *f* (*pl* -en) majesty. **majestätisch** *adj* majestic.

Majoran [m aɟoˈraːn] *m* marjoram.

Makel ['m aːkəl] *m* (*pl* -) stain, spot; (*Fehler*) defect, fault. **makellos** *adj* spotless; faultless.

Makler ['m aːklər] *m* (*pl* -) broker.

Makrele [m aˈkreːlə] *f* (*pl* -n) mackerel.

mal [m a:] *adv* (*Math*) times; (*einmal*) once, just. **drei mal fünf** three times five. **hör' mal!** just listen!

Mal¹ [m a:l] *neut* (*pl* -e) time. **zum ersten Mal** for the first time.

Mal² *neut* (*pl* -e *or* **Mäler**) mark, sign; (*Denkmal*) monument; (*Grenzstein*) boundary stone.

Malaria [m aˈlaːriə] *f* malaria.

malen ['m a:lən] *v* paint; (*zeichnen*) draw. **Maler** *m* (*pl* -) painter. **Malerei** *f* (*pl* -en) painting. **malerisch** *adj* picturesque.

Malz [m alts] *neut* (*pl* -e) malt. -**bier** *neut* malt beer, stout.

Mama [m aˈma] *f* (*pl* -s) mamma.

man [m an] *pron* one, you; (*die Leute*) people. **man sagt** people say, it is said. *man tut das nicht* that is not done, you shouldn't do that.

Manager ['m ɛniɟər] *m* (*pl* -) manager.

manch [m anç] *pron, adj* many a, some. **manche** *pl* several, many. -**mal** *adv* sometimes.

Mandat [m an'da:t] *neut* (*pl* -e) mandate.

Mandel ['m andəl] *f* (*pl* -n) almond; (*Anat*) tonsil. -**entfernung** *f* tonsillectomy. -**entzüdung** *f* tonsillitis.

Mangel¹ ['m aŋəl] *f* (*pl* -n) mangle.

Mangel² [*m* (*pl* **Mängel**) lack, want; (*Knappheit*) shortage; (*Fehler*) fault.

mangeln ['m aŋəl] *v* lack, want. *es mangelt mir an* I lack.

Manie [m a'niː] *f* (*pl* -n) mania.

Manier [m a'niːr] *f* (*pl* -en) manner, way; (*Stil*) style. **Manieren** *pl* manners. **maniert** *adj* affected, mannered. **manierlich** *adj* well-mannered, civil.

Manifest [m anˈfɛst] *neut* (*pl* -e) manifesto.

manisch ['m a:nʃ] *adj* manic.

Mann [m an] *m* (*pl* **Männer**) man; (**Ehemann**) husband.

Männchen ['m ɛnçən] *neut* (*pl* -) little man; (*Tier*) male.

Mannesalter ['m anəsaltər] *neut* (age of) manhood. **mannhaft** *adj* manly.

Mannequin [m anə'kɛ̃] *neut* (*pl* -s) mannequin, fashion model.

mannigfaltig ['m anɪçfaltɪç] *adj* varied, manifold.

männlich ['m ɛnlɪç] *adj* male; (*fig, Gramm*) masculine. **Männlichkeit** *f* manhood; masculinity.

Mannschaft ['m anʃaft] *f* (*pl* -en) crew; (*Sport*) team; (*Belegschaft*) personnel. **-führer** *m* (*Sport*) captain.

Manöver [m a'nø ːvər] *neut* (*pl* -) manoeuvre. **manövrieren** *v* manoeuvre.

Manschette [m an'ʃɛtə] *f* (*pl* -n) cuff.

Mantel [m antəl] *m* (*pl* -Mäntel) coat; (*Umhang*) cloak.

Manuskript [m anu'skrɪpt] *neut* (*pl* -e) manuscript.

Mappe ['m apə] *f* (*pl* -n) briefcase; (*Aktenmappe*) folder, portfolio.

Märchen ['m ɛːrçən] *neut* (*pl* -) fairytale. **märchenhaft** *adj* fairytale, magical.

Margarine [m arga'riːnə] *f* (*pl* -n) margarine.

Marien||bild *neut* (picture of the) Madonna. **-käfer** *m* ladybird.

Marine [m a'riːnə] *f* (*pl* -n) (*Kriegsmarine*) navy; (*Handelsmarine*) merchant navy. **-soldat** *m* marine.

marinieren [m arɪniːən] *v* marinate.

Marionette [m arɪo'nɛtə] *f* (*pl* -n) marionette.

Mark¹ [m ark] *neut* (*unz.*) (bone) marrow. **bis ins Mark** (*fig*) to the core.

Mark² *f* (*pl* -) (*Geld*) mark.

Mark³ *f* (*pl* -en) boundary; (*Grenzgebiet*) marches *pl*, border-country.

Marke ['m arkə] *f* (*pl* -n) (*Zeichen*) mark, stamp; (*Fabrikat, Sorte*) brand; (*Handelszeichen*) trademark; (*Briefmarke*) (postage) stamp; (*Wertschein*) token. **-nname** *m* tradename, brand-name.

Markt [m arkt] *m* (*pl* Märkte) market. **-halle** *f* covered market, market hall. **-platz** *m* marketplace. **-tag** *m* market day. **-wirtschaft** *f* (free) market economy.

Marmelade [m am ə'laːdə] *f* (*pl* -n) jam.

Marmor ['m am ɔr] *m* (*pl* -e) marble.

Mars [m aːrs] *m* Mars. **-bewohner** *m* Martian.

Marsch¹ [m arʃ] *m* (*pl* Märsche) march.

Marsch² [m arʃ] *f* (*pl* -en) marsh.

Marschall ['m arʃal] *m* (*pl* Marschälle) marshal.

marschieren [m aːrʃiːən] *v* march.

Märtyrer ['m ɛrtyrər] *m* (*pl* -) martyr. **-tum** *neut* martyrdom.

Märtyrin [m ɛːrtyrɪn] *f* (*pl* -nen) martyr.

Marxismus [m arksɪsm us] *m* (*unz.*) Marxism.

März [m ɛrts] *m* (*pl* -e) March.

Masche ['m aʃə] *f* (*pl* -n) mesh; (*Stricken*) stitch; (*Trick*) trick.

Maschine [m a'ʃiːnə] *f* (*pl* -en) machine; (*Mot*) engine. **Maschinen||bau** *m* mechanical engineering. **-fabrik** *f* engineering works. **-gewehr** *neut* machinegun. **-schreiben** *neut* typewriting, typing. **-schreiber(in)** *m* typist.

Maske ['m askə] *f* (*pl* -n) mask. **Masken|| ball** *m* fancy-dress ball. **-kostüm** *neut* fancy dress (costume).

Maß [m aːs] *neut* (*pl* -e) measure; (*Mäßigung*) moderation; (*Grenze*) limit; (*Umfang*) extent. **in hohem Maße** to a great extent. **Maß halten** be moderate.

Masse ['m asə] *f* (*pl* -n) mass; (*Jur*) estate, assets. **die Massen** the masses. **Massen||erzeugung** *f* mass production. **-karambolage** *f* multiple collision, (*umg.*) pile-up. **-versammlung** *f* mass meeting. **-vernichtungswaffen (MVW)** *f pl* weapons of mass destruction (WMD). **massenweise** *adv* wholesale, in large numbers.

Maßgabe ['m aːsgaːbə] *f* standard. **maßgeblich** *adj* authoritative.

mäßig ['m ɛːsɪç] *adj* moderate. **mäßigen** *v* moderate. **Mäßigung** *f* modulation.

massiv [m a'siːf] *adj* massive.

maßlos ['m aːsloːs] *adj* immoderate. **Maßnahme** *f* (*pl* -n) measure, step. **Maßnahmen treffen** take steps. **Maßstab** *m* measure; (*Tech*) scale; (*fig*) yardstick.

Mast [m ast] *m* (*pl* -e *or* -en) mast.

mästen ['m ɛstən] *v* fatten.

Material [m aterɪaːl] *neut* (*pl* -ien) material. **-ismus** *m* materialism. **materialistisch** *adj* materialist(ic).

Materie [m a'teːrɪə] *f* (*pl* -n) matter, stuff, substance.

Mathematik [m atem a'tiːk] *f* (*unz.*) mathematics. **-er** *m* (*pl* -) mathematician. **mathematisch** *adj* mathematical.

Matratze [m a'tratsə] f (pl -n) mattress.
Mätresse [m ɛ'trɛsə] f (pl -n) mistress.
Matrize [m a'trɪtsə] f (pl -n) (Druck) stencil; (Math) matrix.
Matrose [m a'tro:zə] m (pl -n) sailor.
Matsch [m atʃ] m mud; (Schnee-) slush; **matschig** adj muddy; (breiig) squashy.
matt [m at] adj faint, weary; (glanzlos) dull, matt; (Licht) dim; (Schach) mate.
Matte ['m atə] f (pl -n) mat.
Mattheit ['m athait] f weariness; dullness. **mattherzig** adj fainthearted.
Mauer ['m auər] f (pl -n) wall. **mauern** v build (a wall). **Mauerwerk** neut masonry.
Maul [m aul] neut (pl **Mäuler**) (animals) mouth, snout, muzzle; (vulg) (person's) mouth.
Maurer ['m aurər] m (pl -) bricklayer. building worker.
Maus [m aus] f (pl **Mäuse**) mouse. **Mausefalle** f mousetrap. **-loch** neut mousehole.
maximal [m aksim a:l] adj maximum. **Maximum** neut maximum.
Mechanik [m e'ca:nik] 1 f (unz.) mechanics. 2 (pl -en) (Mechanismus) mechanism. **-er** m mechanic. **mechanisch** adj mechanical.
meckern ['m ɛkərn] v bleat; (nörgeln) grumble, moan.
Medaille [m e'dailə] f (pl -n) medal.
Medikament [m edika'm ɛnt] neut (pl -e) medicine.
Medizin [m editsi:n] f (pl -en) medicine. **-er** m doctor, physician; (student) medical student. **medizinisch** adj medical.
Meer [m e:r] neut (pl -e) sea. **-enge** f straits pl. **Meeresboden** m sea bed. **-spiegel** m sea level.
Megabyte ['m ɛgəbait] neut (comp) megabyte.
Mehl [m e:l] neut (pl -e) flour. **mehlig** adj floury, mealy.
mehr [m e:r] adv, adj more. **mehr als** more than. **nicht mehr** no longer. **immer mehr** more and more. **noch mehr** still more. **Mehrbetrag** m surplus. **mehrdeutig** adj ambiguous.
mehrere ['m ɛ:rərə] pl pron, adj several. **mehrfach** adj multiple.
Mehr||gepäck neut excess baggage. **-gewicht** neut excess weight. **-heit** f majority.

mehr||mals adv repeatedly, several times. **-seitig** adj many-sided; (Math) polygonal. **-sprachig** adj multilingual. **-stöckig** adj multistoreyed.
Mehr||wertsteuer (MwSt) f value added tax (VAT). **-zahl** f majority; (Gramm) plural.
meiden ['m aidən] v avoid.
Meierei ['m aiərai] f (pl -en) farm; (Milchwirtschaft) dairy farm.
Meile ['m ailə] f (pl -n) mile.
mein [m ain] adj, pron my; mine. **meinerseits** adv for my part. **meinesgleichen** pron people like me, the likes of me. **meinethalben, meinetwegen, meinetwillen** adv for my sake. **meinige** pron (der, die, das meinige) mine.
Meineid ['m ainait] m (pl -e) perjury.
meinen ['m ainən] v mean; (denken) think; (äußern) say; (beabsichtigen) intend. **Meinung** f opinion. **Ich bin der Meinung, daß** I am of the opinion that. **meiner Meinung nach** in my opinion. **Meinungs||forschung** f opinion research. **-umfrage,** f opinion poll. **-verschiedenheit** f difference of opinion.
Meißel ['m aisəl] m (pl -) chisel. **meißeln** v chisel.
meist [m aist] adj most. **die meisten(Leute)** most people. **am meisten** for the most part. **Meistbietende(r)** m highest bidder. **meistens** adv mostly.
Meister ['m aistər] m (pl -) master; (Sport) champion. **meisterhaft** adj masterly. **Meisterin** f (Sport) champion. **meistern** v master. **Meister||schaft** f mastery; (Sport) championship. **-schaftsspiel** neut championship match. **-stück** or **-werk** neut masterpiece.
meistgekauft ['m aistgəkauft] adj best-selling.
Meldeamt ['m ɛldəam t] neut registration office. **melden** v inform; (ankündigen) announce. **sich melden** report, present oneself; (Stelle) apply. **Meldung** f report; (ankündigung) announcement; (bei der Polizei, usw.) registration.
***melken** ['m ɛlkən] v milk. **Melkmaschine** f milking machine.
Melodie [m eb'di] f (pl -n) melody. **melodisch** adj melodious.
Melone [m e'b:nə] f (pl -n) melon.
Membran(e) [m em 'bra:n] f (pl

Membranen) membrane.

Menge ['m ɛŋə] f (pl -n) quantity; (Menschen) crowd. **eine (ganze) Menge** a lot (of), lots (of). **mengen** v mix. **sich mengen in** meddle.

Mensa ['m ɛnsa] f (pl **Mensen**) student refectory.

Mensch [m ɛnʃ] m (pl -en) human (being), man, person. **Menschenfeind** m misanthrope. **menschenfeindlich** adj misanthropic. **Menschenfreund** m philanthropist. **menschenfreundlich** adj philanthropic; (gütig) affable. **Menschen‖kunde** f anthropology. **-leben** neut human life; (Lebenszeit) lifetime. **-liebe** f human kindness. **-rechte** pl human rights. **-würde** f human dignity.

Menschheit ['m ɛnʃhait] f mankind, human race. **menschlich** adj human; (human) humane. **Menschlichkeit** f humanity.

menstrual [m ɛnstruˈaːl] adj menstrual. **Menstruation** f (pl -nen) menstruation. **menstruieren** v menstruate.

Mentalität [m ɛntalitɛːt] f (pl -en) mentality.

merkbar ['m ɛɪkbaːr] adj noticeable. **merken** v notice, note. **sich etwas merken** make a mental note of something. **merklich** adj evident. **Merkmal** (pl -e) neut characteristic, attribute. **merkwürdig** adj remarkable, peculiar.

Meßband ['m ɛsbant] neut tape measure. **meßbar** adj measurable.

Messe ['m ɛsə] f (pl -n) (Rel) mass; (Ausstellung) (trade) fair.

*****messen** ['m ɛsən] v measure. **sich messen mit** compete with.

Messer¹ ['m ɛsər] m (pl -) (Gerät) gauge, meter.

Messer² neut (pl -) knife.

Messing ['m ɛsɪŋ] neut (pl -) brass.

Messung ['m ɛsuŋ] f (pl -en) measurement; (Messen) measuring.

Metall [m eˈtal] neut (pl -e) metal. **metallisch** adj metallic.

Meteor [m eteˈoːr] neut (pl -e) meteor. **-ologe** m meteorologist. **-ologie** f meteorology. **meteorologisch** adj meteorologist.

Meter ['m eːtər] neut (pl -) metre.

Methode [m eˈtoːdə] f (pl -n) method. **methodisch** adj methodical.

metrisch ['m eːtrɪʃ] adj metric.

Mettwurst ['m ɛtvurst] f a type of German sausage.

metzen ['m ɛtsən] v massacre, slaughter.

Metzger m (pl -) butcher. **-ei** f (pl -en) butcher's shop.

Meuchelmord ['m ɔyçəlmɔrt] m assassination.

Meuterei [m ɔytəˈrai] f (pl -en) mutiny. **meutern** v mutiny.

Mexiko ['m ɛksikoː] neut Mexico. **Mexikaner(in)** Mexican. **mexikanisch** adj Mexican.

mich [m ɪç] pron me.

Mieder ['m iːdər] neut (pl -) bodice.

miefen ['m iːfən] v pong.

Miene ['m iːnə] f (pl -n) expression, look.

mies [m iːs] adj (umg.) nasty, wretched.

Miete ['m iːtə] f (pl -n) hire; (für Wohnung) rent. **mieten** v (Haus, Wohnung) rent; (Wagen, usw.) hire. **Mieter** m (pl -), **Mieterin** f (pl -nen) tenant, lessee. **Miet‖shaus** neut block of flats, tenement. **-wagen** m hired car. **-wohnung** f rented flat.

Mikrochip [m iːkroˈtʃip] m (pl -s) (comp) microchip.

Mikrophon [m iːkroˈfoːn] neut (pl -e) microphone.

Mikroskop [m iːkroˈskoːp] neut microscope. **mikroskopisch** adj microscopic.

Milbe ['m iːbə] f (pl -n) mite.

Milch [m ɪlç] f milk. **milchig** adj milky. **Milchstraße** f Milky Way.

mild [m ɪlt] adj mild; (sanft) soft, gentle. **Milde** f mildness; gentleness. **mildern** v alleviate, moderate. **Milderung** f (pl -en) alleviation. **mildtätig** adj charitable.

Militär [m ilitɛːr] **1** neut (unz.) army, military. **2** m (pl -s) military man, soldier.

Milliarde [m iˈljardə] f (pl -n) thousand million, (US) billion.

Million [m iˈljoːn] f (pl -en) million. **-är** m (pl -e) millionaire.

Mimik ['m ɪm ɪk] f (pl -en) mimicry, miming. **-er** m (pl -) mimic.

minder ['m ɪndər] adj lesser, smaller. adv less.

Minderheit f minority. **Minderjährige(r)** minor. **minderjährig** adj under age. **minderwertig** adj inferior. **Minderwertigkeit** f inferiority.

mindest ['m ɪndəst] adj least; (kleinst) smallest. **–ens** *adv* at least. **Mindestzahl** *f* minimum number; (*Pol*) quorum.

Mine ['mi:nə] *f* (*pl* -n) mine.

Mineral [mine'ra:l] *neut* (*pl* -ien) mineral. **–wasser** *neut* mineral water.

Miniatur [minia'tu:r] *f* (*pl* -en) miniature.

minimal [mini'ma:l] *adj* minimum. **Minimum** *neut* minimum.

Minister [mi'nistər] *m* (*pl* -) minister. **–ium** *neut* ministry. **–präsident** *m* prime minister.

minus ['mi:nus] *adv* minus, less.

Minute [mi'nu:tə] *f* (*pl* -n) minute.

mir [mi:r] *pron* (to) me.

mischen ['miʃən] *v* mix, blend. **sich mischen in** meddle *or* interfere in. **Misch|ling** *m* (*Pflanze*) hybrid; (*Tier*) mongrel; (*Mensch*) half-breed. **–sprache** *f* pidgin. **–ung** *f* (*pl* -en) mixture.

mißach||ten [mis'axtən] *v* disregard. **Mißachtung** *f* disregard.

Mißbildung [mis'bilduŋ] *f* deformity.

mißbilligen ['mis'biligən] *v* disapprove (of), object (to). **Mißbilligung** *f* disapproval.

Mißrauch ['mis'braux] *m* misuse, abuse. **mißbrauchen** *v* misuse, abuse.

mißdeuten [mis'dɔytən] *v* misinterpret, misunderstand. **Mißdeutung** *f* misinterpretation.

Mißerfolg ['mis'ɛrfɔlk] *m* failure.

Missetat ['misətat] *f* misdeed. **Missetäter** *m* wrong-doer; (*Verbrecher*) criminal.

*mißfallen [mis'falən] *v* displease. **Mißfallen** *neut* displeasure.

Mißgeschick ['mis'gəʃik] *neut* misfortune.

mißgestaltet ['mis'gəʃtaltət] *adj* misshapen.

mißhandeln [mis'handəln] *v* maltreat. **Mißhandlung** *f* maltreatment.

Mission [mi'sio:n] *f* (*pl* -en) mission. **–ar** *m* (*pl* -e) missionary.

Mißklang ['mis'klaŋ] *m* discord.

mißlich ['mis'liç] *adj* awkward, embarrassing.

*mißlingen *v* fail. **mißlungen** *adj* failed, unsuccessful.

mißtrauen [mis'trauən] *v* distrust. **Mißtrauen** *neut* distrust. **–svotum** *neut* vote of no confidence.

Mißverständnis ['mis'fɛrʃtɛntnis] *neut* misunderstanding. **mißverstehen** *v* misunderstand.

Mist [mist] *m* (*pl* -e) dung, manure.

Mistel ['mistəl] *f* (*pl* -n) mistletoe.

mit [mit] *prep* with; (*mittels*) by; (*Zeit*) at. *adv* along with; (*außerdem*) also, as well. *kommst du mit?* are you coming (with us)? *mit 10 Jahren* at the age of ten. **mit einemmal** suddenly. **mit dabei sein** be concerned *or* involved.

Mitarbeiter ['mit'arbaitər] *m* colleague, fellow worker; (*Zeitschrift*) contributor.

Mitbestimmung ['mit'bəʃtimuŋ] *f* worker participation, co-determination.

mitbeteiligt ['mit'bətailiçt] *adj* participating, taking part.

*mitbringen ['mit'briŋən] *v* bring along.

miteinander [mit'ain'andər] *adv* together, with each other.

miteinbegriffen [mit'ainbəgrifən] *adj* included.

Mitgefühl ['mit'gəfy:l] *neut* sympathy.

Mitglied ['mit'gli:t] *neut* member. **–schaft** *f* membership.

mithin [mit'hin] *adv* consequently, therefore.

*mitkommen ['mit'kɔmən] *v* come along (with); keep up.

Mitlaut ['mit'laut] *m* consonant.

Mitleid ['mit'lait] *neut* pity, sympathy. **mitleid haben mit** have pity on, be sorry for.

mitmachen ['mit'maxən] *v* take part in, join in; (*erleben*) go *or* live through.

Mitmensch ['mit'mɛnʃ] *m* fellow man.

*mitnehmen ['mit'ne:mən] *v* take (along); (*im Auto*) give a lift to; (*erschöpfen*) exhaust. **Essen zum Mitnehmen** food to take away.

mitnichten [mit'niçtən] *adv* by no means.

*mitreißen ['mit'raisən] *v* drag along; (*fig*) sweep along, transport.

Mittag ['mita:k] *m* noon, midday. **–essen** *neut* lunch, midday meal. **mittags** *adv* at noon. **Mittagspause** *f* lunch hour.

Mitte ['mitə] *f* (*pl* -n) middle, centre; (*Math*) mean.

mitteilen ['mit'tailən] *v* communicate, inform of, tell. **jemandem etwas mitteilen** inform *or* notify someone of something. **Mitteilung** *f* communication, report.

Mittel ['mit'əl] *neut* (*pl* -) means, way; (*Ausweg*) remedy; (*Durchschnitt*) average, mean. **–alter** *neut* Middle Ages. **mitte-**

laterlich *adj* medieval.

Mittel||amerika *f* Central America. **–gewichtler** *m* middleweight.

mittelgroß ['m ɪtəlɡroːs] *adj* of medium size.

Mittelläufer ['m ɪəlɔyfər] *m* (*Fußball*) centre-half.

mittel||los *adj* destitute. **–mäßig** *adj* mediocre.

Mittel||meer *neut* Mediterranean (Sea). **–punkt** *m* centre.

mittels ['m ɪəls] *prep* by (means of).

Mittel||stand *m* middle classes *pl*. **–stürmer** *m* (*Fußball*) centre-forward.

mitten ['m ɪtən] *adv* in the middle, midway. **mitten in/auf/unter** in the middle of. **mitten drin** in the middle.

Mitternacht ['m ɪtənaxt] *f* midnight.

mittler ['m ɪtlər] *adj* in mittlerem Alter middle-aged. **mittlerweile** *adv* in the meantime.

Mittwoch ['m ɪtvɔx] *m* (*pl* -e) Wednesday.

mitwirken ['m ɪtvɪrkən] *v* cooperate, take part, participate. **–d** *adj* participating, contributing.

Möbel ['m œːbəl] *neut* (*pl* -) piece of furniture; (*pl*) furniture *sing*.

mobil [m oˈbiːl] *adj* movable, mobile; (*flink*) active, lively.

möblieren [m œ ˈbliːrən] *v* furnish. **möbliert** *adj* furnished.

Mode ['m oːdə] *f* (*pl* -n) fashion, vogue. **in Mode sein** be in fashion. **aus der Mode kommen** become unfashionable. **Modeartikel** *pl* fancy goods, fashions.

Modell [m oˈdɛl] *neut* (*pl* -e) model; (*Muster*) pattern. **Modellierbogen** *m* cutting-out pattern. **modellieren** *v* model.

Modem ['m oːdɛm] *neut* (*comp*) modem.

Modenschau ['m oːdənʃau] *f* fashion show. **Modezeichner** *m* dress *or* fashion designer.

Moder ['m oːdər] *m* decay, mould. **moderig** *adj* mouldy, putrid. **modern** *v* rot, decay.

modern [m oˈdɛrn] *adj* modern. **modernisieren** *v* modernize.

modifizieren [m odifitsiːrən] *v* modify.

modisch ['m oːdɪʃ] *adj* fashionable.

mogeln ['m oːɡəln] *v* cheat.

***mögen** ['m œ ːɡən] *v* like; (*wünschen*) wish; (*können*) may, might. *nicht mögen* dislike. *Ich mag ihn* I like him. *das mag sein* that may be so. *Wer mag das sein?* who might

that be? *Ich möchte* I would like. *Ich möchte lieber* I would prefer. *Er mag ruhig warten!* let him wait!

möglich ['m æ ːɡlɪç] *adj* possible. **–erweise** *adv* possibly. **Möglichkeit** *f* possibility. **möglichst** *adv* as … as possible.

Mohammedaner [m oham eˈdaːnər] *m* (*pl* -) Muslim, Mohammedan. **mohammedanisch** *adj* Muslim, Mohammedan.

Mohn [m oːn] *m* (*pl* -e) poppy; (*Samen*) poppy seed.

Mohr [m oːr] *m* (*pl* -en) moor, black(man).

Möhre ['m œ ːrə] *f* (*pl* -n) carrot.

Mohrrübe ['m oːryːbə] *f* (*pl* -n) carrot.

Moldau ['m ɔldau] *f* Moldova. **Moldauer(in)** Moldovan. **moldauisch** *adj* Moldovan.

Molekül [m oleˈkyːl] *neut* (*pl* -e) molecule. **molekular** *adj* molecular.

Molkerei [m ɔlkəˈrai] *f* (*pl* -en) dairy.

Moll [m ɔl] *neut* (*unz.*) (*Musik*) minor.

Moment¹ [m oˈm ɛnt] *m* (*pl* -e) moment, instant. **Moment mal!** Just a moment!

Moment² *neut* (*unz.*) (*Physik*) moment; (*Anlaß*) motive; (*Umstand*) factor.

Monarch [m oˈnarç] *m* (*pl* -en) monarch. **–ie** *f* (*pl* -n) monarchy. **–ist** *m* (*pl* -en) monarchist.

Monat ['m oːnat] *m* (*pl* -e) month. **monatelang** *adv* for months. **monatlich** *adj* monthly. **Monats||blutung** *f* menstruation. **–karte** *f* (monthly) season ticket.

Mönch [m œ nç] *m* (*pl* -e) monk.

Mond [m oːnt] *m* (*pl* -e) moon. **–finsternis** *f* lunar eclipse. **–schein** *m* moonlight. **–strahl** *m* moonbeam.

Monogramm [m onoˈɡram] *neut* (*pl* -e) monogram, initials.

Monopol [m onoˈpoːl] *neut* (*pl* -e) monopoly. **monopolisieren** *v* monopolize.

Montag ['m oːntaːk] *m* Monday. **montags** *adv* (on) Mondays.

Montage [m ɔnˈtaːʒə] *f* (*pl* -n) assembly; installation. **–band** *neut* assembly line.

Monteur ['m ɔntøː ːr] *m* (*pl* -e) mechanic, fitter. **montieren** *v* install, assemble.

Moor [m oːr] *neut* (*pl* -e) marsh, moor.

Moos [m oːs] *neut* (*pl* -e) moss.

Moped ['m opɛt] *neut* (*pl* -s) moped.

Moral [m oˈraːl] *f* (*pl* -en) moral; (*Sittlichkeit*) morality; (*Zuversicht*) morale. **moralisieren** *v* moralize.

Mord [mɔrt] *m (pl -e)* murder.
Mörder ['mœːrdər] *m (pl -)* murderer.
mörderisch *adj* murderous.
morgen ['mɔrgən] *adv* tomorrow. **morgen früh** tomorrow morning. **Morgen** *m (pl -)* morning. **–dämmerung** *f* dawn. **–land** *neut* Orient. **–stern** *m* morning star, Venus.
Morphium ['mɔrfium] *neut* morphine.
morsch [mɔrʃ] *adj* rotten.
Morseschrift ['mɔrzəʃrift] *f* Morse code.
Mörtel ['mœːrtəl] *m (pl -)* mortar, cement.
Mosaik [mozaˈiːk] *neut (pl -e)* mosaic.
Moschee [mɔˈʃeː] *f (pl -n)* mosque.
Mosel ['moːzəl] *f* Moselle.
Moskau ['mɔskau] *neut* Moscow.
Most [mɔst] *m (pl -e)* new wine, must.
Motiv [moˈtiːf] *neut (pl -e) (Antrieb)* motive; *(Kunst, Dichtung)* theme, motif. **motivieren** *v* motivate.
Motor ['moːtɔr] *m (pl -en)* motor, engine. **–ausfall** *m* engine failure. **–boot** *neut* motorboat. **–haube** *f* bonnet, *(US)* hood. **–rad** *neut* motorcycle. **–roller** *m* (motor) scooter.
Motte ['mɔtə] *f (pl -n)* moth.
Möwe ['mœːvə] *f (pl -n)* seagull.
Mücke ['mykə] *f (pl -n)* midge, gnat. **Mücken‖netz** *neut* mosquito net. **–stich** *m* midge *or* gnat bite.
müde ['myːdə] *adj* tired. **Müdigkeit** *f* tiredness fatigue.
Muff[1] [muf] *m (unz.)* musty smell.
Muff[2] *m (pl -e) (Pelz)* muff.
Muffel ['mufəl] *m (pl -)* grumpy person. **muffelig** *adj* grumpy, sullen.
muffig ['mufic] *adj (moderig)* musty.
Mühe ['myːə] *f (pl -n)* trouble, pains *pl.* **sich Mühe geben** take pains. **nicht der Mühe wert** not worth the trouble. **mühelos** *adj* effortless. **sich mühen** trouble oneself, take pains. **mühevoll** *adj* laborious, troublesome.
Mühle ['myːlə] *m (pl -n)* mill.
mühsam ['myːzam] *adj also* **mühselig** troublesome; *(schwierig)* difficult.
Mulde ['muldə] *f (pl -n)* trough; *(Landschaft)* depression, hollow.
Mull [mul] *m (pl -e)* muslin.
Müll [myl] *m* refuse, rubbish, *(US)* garbage. **–abfuhr** *f* refuse disposal. **–eimer** *m* dustbin.

Müller ['mylər] *m (pl -)* miller.
Multiplikation [multiplikatsloːn] *f (pl -en)* multiplication. **multiplizieren** *v* multiply.
Mumie ['muːmiə] *f (pl -n)* mummy.
Mummenschanz ['mumənʃants] *m (pl -e)* masquerade.
München ['mynçən] *neut* Munich. **Münchner** *adj* (of) Munich.
Mund [munt] *m (pl* **Münder***)* mouth. **–art** *f* dialect.
münden ['myndən] *v* **münden in** *(Fluß)* flow into; *(Straße)* run into, join.
mund‖faul *adj* taciturn. **–fertig** *adj* glib. **–gerecht** *adj* appetizing. **Mund‖geruch** *m* bad breath, halitosis. **–harmonika** *f* mouth organ, harmonica.
mündig ['myndic] *adj* of age. **mündig werden** come of age. **Mündigkeit** *f* majority, full legal age.
mündlich ['myntlic] *adj* oral.
Mundstück ['muntʃtyk] *neut* mouthpiece.
Mündung ['myndun] *f (pl -en) (Fluß)* estuary.
Munition [munitsloːn] *f (pl -en)* ammunition.
munter ['muntər] *adj* lively, cheerful, merry. **Munterkeit** *f* liveliness, cheer.
Münze ['myntsə] *f (pl -n)* coin; *(Anstalt)* mint. **für bare Münze nehmen** take at face value. **Münz‖einwurf** *m* coin-slot. **–fernsprecher** *m* pay phone, call box.
mürbe ['myrbə] *adj (Fleisch)* tender; *(morsch)* rotten, soft; *(brüchig)* brittle; *(Gebäck)* crumbly. **Mürbeteig** *m* short pastry.
murmeln ['murməln] *v* murmur.
murren ['murən] *v* grumble.
mürrisch ['myrʃ] *adj* morose, grumpy.
Mus [muːs] *neut* purée.
Muschel ['muʃəl] *f (pl -n)* mussel; *(Telef)* (telephone) receiver. **–tier** *neut* mollusc.
Museum [muˈzeːum] *neut (pl* **Museen***)* museum.
Musical [ˈjuːzikəl] *neut (pl -s)* musical.
Musik [muˈziːk] *f* music; *(Kapelle)* band. **musikalisch** *adj* musical. **Musik‖antenknochen** *m (umg.)* funnybone. **–er** *m (pl -)* musician. **–freund** *m* music-lover. **–instrument** *m* musical instrument.
Muskat [muskaːt] *m (pl -e)* nutmeg. **–blüte** *f* mace. **–nuß** *f* nutmeg.

Muskel ['m usɘl] *m* (*pl* -n) muscle. **–kraft** *f* muscular strength. **–krampf** *m* muscle spasm. **–zerrung** *f* pulled muscle.

Muße ['m u:sɘ] *f* leisure. **müßig** *adj* idle.

*müssen ['m ysən] *v* must, have to. *ich mußgehen* I must go. *ich muß nicht gehen* I don't have to go. *ich muß fort* I must leave. *ich müßte* I ought to.

Muster ['m ustər] *net* (*pl* -) model, pattern, exemplar; (*Stoffverzierung*) pattern, design; (*warenprobe*) sample. **–stück** *neut* sample, specimen. **–zeichnung** *f* design.

Mut [m u:t] *m* courage. **mutig** *adj* brave, courageous. **mutlos** *adj* discouraged, despondent.

mutmaßen ['m utm a:sən] *v* suppose, surmise. **Mutmaßung** *f* (*pl* -en) conjecture.

Mutter¹ ['m utər] *f* (*pl* Mütter) mother.

Mutter² *f* (*pl* -n) (*Tech*) nut.

mütterlich ['m ytərlic] *adj* motherly. **–erseits** *adv* on one's mother's side, maternal.

Mutter||liebe *f* mother-love. **–mal** *neut* birthmark. **–schaft** *f* motherhood. **–sprache** *f* mother tongue, native language.

Mütze ['m ytsə] *f* (*pl* -n) cap.

MwSt *neut* VAT (value-added tax).

mysteriös [m ysterɪɘ :s] *adj* mysterious.

Mystik ['m ystik] *f* (*unz.*) mysticism. **–er** *m* mystic. **mystisch** *adj* mystical.

Mythe ['m ytə] *f* (*pl* -n) myth. **mythisch** *adj* mythical.

N

na [na] *interj* well! (come) now!

Nabe ['na:bə] *f* (*pl* -n) hub.

Nabel ['na:bəl] *m* (*pl* -) navel. **–schnur** *f* umbilical cord.

nach [na:x] *prep* after; (*örtlich*) to, towards; (*gemäß*) according to, by. *adv* after. **nach und nach** gradually. **der Größe nach** by size. **nach außen** externally.

nachahmen ['na:xa:m ən] *v* imitate. **Nachahmung** *f* imitation.

Nachbar ['na:xba:r] *m* (*pl* -n) neighbour. **–land** *neut* neighbouring country. **–schaft**

f neighbourhood.

Nachbildung ['na:xbiɫduŋ] *f* copy, replica.

nachdem [na:xde:m] *adv* afterwards. *conj* after. **je nachdem** according as.

*nachdenken ['na:xdɛŋkən] *v* think (over), reflect. **Nachdenken** *neut* reflection, thinking over. **nachdenklich** *adj* reflective, thoughtful.

Nachdruck ['na:xdruk] *m* (*Betonung*) emphasis, stress; (*Festigkeit*) vigour. **nachdrücklich** *adj* emphatic; forceful.

nacheifern ['na:xaifəm] *v* emulate.

nacheinander ['na:xainandər] *adv* one after another.

Nachfolge ['na:xɔlɡə] *f* succession. **nachfolgen** *v* succeed, follow. **Nachfolger** *m* successor.

Nachfrage ['na:xfɑ:ɡə] *f* (*Erkundigung*) inquiry; (*Komm*) demand.

*nachgeben ['na:xɡe:bən] *v* give way *or* in.

Nachgeburt ['na:xɡəburt] *f* afterbirth.

*nachgehen ['na:xɡe:ən] *v* follow; (*untersuchen*) investigate; (*Uhr*) be slow.

nachgemacht ['na:xɡəm axt] *adj* imitated, false.

Nachgeschmack ['na:xɡəʃm ak] *m* aftertaste.

nachgiebig ['na:xɡibi:] *adj* pliable, flexible; (*Person*) compliant, yielding.

nachher [na:xhe:r] *adv* afterwards.

Nachhilfe ['na:xhiɫə] *f* help, assistance. **–stunden** *pl* coaching *sing*, private tuition *sing*.

nachholen ['na:xho:lən] *v* fetch later; (*fig*) make up for, catch up on.

Nach||hut ['na:xhu:t] *f* rearguard. **–klang** *m* echo, resonance.

Nachkomme ['na:xɔm ə] *m* (*pl* -n) descendant. **nachkommen** *v* follow, come after; (*Verpflichtung*) fulfil. **Nachkommenschaft** *f* posterity, descendants *pl*.

Nachkriegszeit ['na:xkri:kstsait] *f* postwar era.

Nachlaß ['na:xlas] *m* (*pl* Nachlässe) (*Preis*) reduction, discount; (*Erbschaft*) inheritance, estate. **nachlassen** *v* slacken, abate; (*aufhören*) cease; (*Strafe*) remit; (*Preis*) reduce. **nachlässig** *adj* careless, negligent.

nachmachen ['na:xm axən] *v* copy, imitate, clone (*fig*).

Nachmittag ['na:xm ɪa:k] *m* afternoon. **nachmittags** *adv* in the afternoon(s).

Nachnahme ['naːxnaːm ə] f **gegen** or **per Nachnahme** cash on delivery (COD).

Nachname ['naːxnaːm ə] m (pl -n) surname.

nachprüfen ['naːxpryː fən] v verify, check again.

Nachricht ['naːxrɪçt] f (pl -en) report, (item of) news. **Nachrichten** pl news sing. **Nachrichten‖büro** neut news agency. **–dienst** m (Radio) news service; (Mil) intelligence service.

Nachruf ['naːxuː f] m (Zeitung) obituary; (Rede) memorial address.

*****nachschlagen** ['naːxʃlaː gən] v (Buch) look up, consult. **Nachschlagebuch** neut reference book.

Nach‖schrift ['naːxʃrɪft] f (Brief) postscript; (eines Vortrages) transcript. **–schub** m (Mil) reinforcement(s); (Material) supplies pl.

*****nach‖sehen** ['naːxzeː ən] v (nachblicken) watch, follow with one's eyes; (prüfen) examine, check; (nachschlagen) consult; (verzeihen) overlook. **–senden** v send on; (Post) forward.

Nach‖sicht ['naːxzɪçt] f leniency. **–sorge** f (medical) aftercare. **–spiel** neut epilogue, sequel. **–speise** f dessert.

nächst [nɛːçst] adj next; (Entfernung) nearest; (Verwandte) close, closest; (umg: kürzest) shortest. adv next. prep next to. **am nächsten** next. **nächste Woche** next week. das nächste Dorf liegt 10 km von hier entfernt the nearest village is 10 km away. **Nächste(r)** fellowman, neighbour.

*****nach‖stehen** ['naːxʃteː ən] v be inferior to. **–stellen** re-adjust; (Uhr) put back; (Frau) molest, bother.

Nächstenliebe ['nɛːçstənliːbə] f charity, love of one's fellow men. **nächstens** adv shortly.

Nacht [naxt] f (pl Nächte) night. **heute Nacht** tonight. **über Nacht** overnight.

Nachteil ['naːxtaɪl] m disadvantage; (Schaden) damage, detriment. **nachteilig** adj disadvantageous, unfavourable.

Nachthemd ['naxthɛm t] neut nightshirt, nightgown.

Nachtigall ['naxtigal] f (pl -en) nightingale.

Nach‖tisch ['naːxtɪʃ] m dessert. **–trag** m supplement. **nachträglich** adj subsequent, later.

nachts [naxts] adv at or by night. **Nachtwächter** m nightwatchman. **nacht-**

wandeln v sleepwalk.

Nach‖untersuchung ['naːxuntərzuː xuŋ] f check-up. **–wahl** f by-election. **–weis** m proof, evidence. **nachweisen** v prove, demonstrate.

Nach‖wirkung ['naːxvɪrkuŋ] f after-effect. **–wort** neut epilogue. **–wuchs** m new or young generation.

*****nachziehen** ['naːxtsiː ən] v drag, draw along; (nachzeichnen) trace; (folgen) follow.

Nachzügler ['naːxtsyː klər] m (pl -) straggler, late-comer.

Nacken [nakən] m (pl -) (nape of the) neck.

nackt [nakt] adj naked, bare. **Nacktheit** f nakedness.

Nadel ['naːdə] f (pl -n) needle; (Stecknadel) pin. **–baum** m conifer. **–öhr** neut eye (of a needle). **–wald** m coniferous forest.

Nagel ['naːgə] m (pl Nägel) nail. **–feile** f nail-file. **–haut** f cuticle. **–lack** m nail varnish. **nageln** v nail. **nagelneu** adj brand-new. **Nagelschere** f nail scissors pl.

nagen ['naːgən] v gnaw.

Nagetier ['naːgətiːr] neut rodent.

nah(e) ['naː (ə)] adj, adv near, close. prep near to. **einer Person zu nahe treten** offend a person. **nahe dabei** or **gelegen** nearby. **nahe Freundschaft** close friendship.

Nahaufnahme ['naːaufnaːm ə] f (Foto) close-up.

Nähe ['nɛː ə] f nearness; (Sicht-, Hörweite) vicinity, **in der Nähe** close by, in the vicinity.

*****nahe‖kommen** v approach. **–liegend** adj obvious; (örtlich) close, nearby.

nähen ['nɛː ən] v sew, stitch.

näher ['nɛːər] adj nearer, closer; (ausführlicher) more detailed. **nähere Angaben** further details. **nähere Umstände** exact circumstances. **Nähere(s)** neut particulars pl, details pl. **nähern** v bring near. **sich nähern** approach, draw near.

nahe‖stehend adj close, friendly. **–zu** adv nearly, almost.

Näh‖kasten m sewing box. **–machine** f sewing machine. **–nadel** f sewing needle.

nähren ['nɛː ən] v nourish; (unterhalten) support. **sich nähren von** live on.

nahrhaft ['naːrhaft] adj nutritious.

Nährmittel ['nɛː m itə] pl foodstuffs, food sing.

Nahrung ['naːʊ̯ŋ] *f* (*unz.*) food; (*Unterhalt*) support. **–smittel** *pl* foodstuffs.

Naht ['naːt] *f* (*pl* **Nähte**) seam; (*Med*) suture.

naiv [na'iːf] *adj* naive.

Name ['naːmə] *or* **Namen** *m* (*pl* **Namen**) name. **namens** *adv* named, by the name of.

nämlich ['nɛːm lɪç] *adv* that is (to say), namely.

Napf [napf] *m* (*pl* **Näpfe**) basin, bowl.

Narbe ['narbə] *f* (*pl* **-n**) scar.

Narkose [nar'koːzə] *f* (*pl* **-n**) (*Betäubung*) anaesthesia. **Narkotikum** *neut* (*pl* **Narkotika**) narcotic. **narkotisch** *adj* narcotic.

Narr [nar] *m* (*pl* **-en**) fool. **zum Narren haben** make a fool of. **Narrheit** *f* folly, foolishness.

närrisch ['nɛrʃ] *adj* foolish, crazy, silly.

Nase ['naːzə] *f* (*pl* **-n**) nose. **die Nase voll haben von** be fed up with. **Nasen||loch** *neut* nostril. **–höhle** *f* (*anat*) sinus. **–spitze** *f* tip of the nose. **naseweis** *adj* cheeky.

naß [nas] *adj* wet; (*feucht*) moist, damp.

Nässe ['nɛsə] *f* wet, wetness.

Nation [natsloːn] *f* (*pl* **-en**) nation. **national** *adj* national. **National||flagge** *f* national flag. **–hymne** *f* national anthem.

nationalisieren [natsionaːliːzɪrən] *v* nationalize. **Nationalisierung** *f* nationalization. **Nationalismus** *m* nationalism. **nationalistisch** *adj* nationalist(ic).

National||mannschaft *f* national team. **–sozialismus** *m* national socialism, Nazism. **–tracht** *f* national costume.

Natter ['natər] *f* (*pl* **-n**) adder.

Natur [na'tuːr] *f* (*pl* **-en**) nature. **–anlage** *f* temperament, disposition. **–forscher** *m* scientist, naturalist. **naturgetreu** *adj* lifelike. **Naturkunde** *f* natural history. **natürlich** *adj* natural. **Natur||schutz** *m* preservation (of nature). **–trieb** *m* instinct. **–wissenschaft** *f* natural science.

Nazi ['naːtsi] *m* (*pl* **-s**) Nazi.

Nebel ['neːbəl] *m* (*pl* **-**) fog; (*dünner*) mist. **–horn** *neut* foghorn. **nebelig** *adj* foggy; misty.

neben ['neːbən] *prep* near (to), beside; (*im Vergleich zu*) compared with, next to. **–an** *adv* next door. **–bei** *adv* by the way; (*außerdem*) besides. **Neben||beschäftigung** *f* second job, sideline. **–buhler** *m* rival.

nebeneinander ['neːbənaɪnandər] *adv* side by side. **–stellen** *v* juxtapose.

Neben||fach *neut* subsidiary subject. **–fluß** *m* tributary. **–gebäude** *neut* annexe. **–kosten** *pl* extras, additional expenses.

nebensächlich ['neːbənsɛçlɪç] *adj* incidental.

necken ['nɛkən] *v* tease.

Neffe ['nɛfə] *m* (*pl* **-n**) nephew.

negativ ['neːgatɪf] *adj* negative.

Neger ['neːgər] *m* (*pl* **-**) Negro, Black. **–in** *f* (*pl* **-nen**) Black (woman).

***nehmen** ['neːmən] *v* take.

Neid [naɪt] *m* envy, jealousy. **neid||en** *v* envy. **–isch** *adj* envious, jealous.

Neige ['naɪɡə] *f* (*pl* **-n**) slope, incline. **neigen** *v* incline. **neigen zu** tend (to), be inclined (to). **sich neigen** incline, slope. **Neigung** *f* slope; (*fig*) inclination.

nein [naɪn] *adv* no.

Nektarine [nɛktaˈriːnə] *f* (*pl* **-n**) nectarine.

Nelke ['nɛlkə] *f* (*pl* **-n**) carnation; (*Gewürz*) clove.

***nennen** ['nɛnən] *v* call, name. **Nenn||er** *m* denominator. **–ung** *f* naming; (*Sport*) entry. **–wert** *m* nominal value.

Nerv [nɛrf] *m* (*pl* **-en**) nerve. **Nerven||kitzel** *m* thrill. **–krankheit** *f* nervous disease. **nervös** *adj* nervous.

Nessel ['nɛsəl] *f* (*pl* **-n**) nettle.

Nest [nɛst] *neut* (*pl* **-er**) nest.

nett [nɛt] *adj* nice; (*gepflegt*) neat.

netto ['nɛto] *adv* net. **Netto||gewinn** *m* net profit. **–preis** *m* net price.

Netz [nɛts] *neut* (*pl* **-e**) net; (*System*) grid, network. **–haut** *f* retina. **–werk** *neut* network.

neu [nɔy] *adj* new; (*modern*) modern. **–artig** *adj* novel.

Neu||ausgabe *f* new edition. **–bau** *n* new building.

neuerdings ['nɔyərdɪŋs] *adv* recently, lately.

Neuerer ['nɔyərər] *m* (*pl* **-**) innovator.

Neuerscheinung ['nɔyɛːɾʃaɪnuŋ] *f* (*pl* **-en**) new book.

Neu||erung ['nɔyərʊŋ] *f* (*pl* **-en**) innovation.

neuestens ['nɔyəstəns] *adv* of late.

neu||geboren *adj* new-born. **–gestalten** *v* reorganize.

Neugier(de) [ˈnɔygɪr(də)] f (unz.) curiosity.
neugierig adj curious.

Neu||heit f (pl -en) novelty. **–igkeit** f (pl -en) (item of) news. **–jahr** neut New Year. **–jahrstag** m New Year's Day.

neulich [ˈnɔylɪç] adv recently, lately.

neun [nɔyn] pron, adj nine. **neunte** adj ninth. **neunzehn** pron, adj nineteen. **neunzig** pron, adj ninety.

Neu||ordnung f reorganization. **–reiche(r)** nouveau riche, wealthy parvenu.

Neurologe [nɔyroˈloːgə] m (pl -n) neurologist. **Neurologie** f neurology. **neurologisch** adj neurological.

Neurose [nɔyˈroːzə] f (pl -n) neurosis. **neurotisch** adj neurotic.

Neuseeland [nɔyˈzeːlant] neut New Zealand.

neutral [nɔyˈtraːl] adj neutral. **neutralisieren** v neutralize. **Neutralität** f neutrality.

neuzeitlich [ˈnɔytsaitlɪç] adj modern.

nicht [nɪçt] adv not. **durchaus nicht** not at all. **nicht einmal** not even. **bitte nicht** please don't. **nicht mehr** no longer. **nicht wahr?** isn't it? don't you agree?

Nicht||achtung f disregard. **–annahme** f nonacceptance. **–beachtung** f nonobservance.

Nichte [ˈnɪçtə] f (pl -n) niece.

Nicht||einmischung f nonintervention. **–erscheinen** neut nonappearance.

nichtig [ˈnɪçtɪç] adj futile, empty; (ungültig) null, void. **Nichtigkeit** f futility; invalidity.

Nicht||mitglied neut non-member. **–raucher** m non-smoker. **–raucherabteil** neut no-smoking compartment.

nichts [nɪçts] pron nothing. **nichts daraus machen** not take seriously. **(es) macht nichts** it doesn't matter. **nichts dergleichen** nothing of the kind. **Nichts** neut nothing(ness).

nichts||sagend adj meaningless. **–würdig** adj worthless, base.

Nicht||vorhandensein neut lack, absence. **–zutreffende(s)** neut (that which is) non-applicable.

Nickel [ˈnɪkəl] neut nickel.

nicken [ˈnɪkən] v nod, bow; doze, nod off. **Nickerchen** neut nap.

nie [niː] adv never.

nieder [ˈniːdər] adj low; (fig) inferior. adv down.

***nieder||brennen** v burn down. **–drücken** v depress. **–fallen** v fall down.

Nieder||frequenz f low frequency. **–gang** m decline, downfall; (Sonne) setting.

***nieder||gehen** v go down; (Aero) land. **–geschlagen** adj depressed.

Niederlage [ˈniːdərlaːgə] f defeat.

Niederlande [ˈniːdərlandə] pl Netherlands. **Niederländer** m Dutchman. **–in** f Dutchwoman. **niederländisch** adj Dutch.

***niederlassen** [ˈniːdərlasən] v lower. **sich niederlassen** settle down; (Vogel) land, settle. **Niederlassung** f (pl -en) settlement; (Komm) branch.

niederlegen [ˈniːdərleːgən] v lay down.

Niedersachsen [ˈniːdəzaksən] neut Lower Saxony.

Niederschlag [ˈniːdərʃlaːk] m (Regen, usw.) precipitation; (auf Fensterscheiben) condensation; (Chem) sediment, precipitation; (Boxen) knock-down.

***niederschlagen** v knock down; (Augen) lower; (Aufstand) suppress.

nieder||schmettern v strike down. **–schreiben** v write down. **–setzen** v put down. **–werfen** v throw down. **sich niederwerfen** prostrate oneself.

niedlich [ˈniːdlɪç] adj nice, (umg.) cute, dainty.

niedrig [ˈniːdrɪç] adj low. **Niedrigkeit** f lowness. **Niedrigwasser** neut low water, low tide.

niemals [ˈniːmaːls] adv never.

niemand [ˈniːmant] pron no one, nobody. **Niemandsland** neut no-man's-land.

Niere [ˈniːrə] f (pl -n) kidney.

nieseln [ˈniːzəln] v drizzle.

niesen [ˈniːzən] v sneeze. **Niesen** neut sneeze.

Niet [niːt] neut (pl -e) rivet.

Niete [ˈniːtə] f (pl -n) (Lotterie) blank (ticket); (Person) nonentity, failure; (Theater) flop.

Nikotin [nikoˈtiːn] neut nicotine.

Nilpferd [ˈniːlpfɛːrt] neut hippopotamus.

nimmer [ˈnɪmər] adv never. **–mehr** adv never again.

nippen [ˈnɪpən] v sip.

nirgends [ˈnɪrgənts] or **nirgendwo**

adv nowhere.

Nische [ˈnɪʃə] *f (pl -n)* niche, alcove.

nisten [ˈnɪstən] *v* (build a) nest.

Niveau [niˈvoː] *neut (pl -s)* level; (*fig*) standard; (*geistig*) culture, good education. **Niveau haben** be cultured *or* sophisticated.

noch [nɔx] *adv* (*außerdem*) in addition. *conj* nor. **noch nicht** not yet. **noch einmal** once again. **noch etwas?** anything else? **noch dazu** in addition. **weder ... noch ...** neither ... nor ... **nochmals** *adv* once again.

Nockenwelle [ˈnɔkənvɛlə] *f* camshaft.

Nomade [noˈmaːdə] *m (pl -n)* nomad.

Nominativ [ˈnoːminatiːf] *m (pl -e)* nominative.

nominell [nomiˈnɛl] *adj* nominal.

Nonne [ˈnɔnə] *f (pl -n)* nun. **-nkloster** *neut* convent, nunnery.

Nord [nɔrt] *m* north. **-amerika** *f* North America. **-en** *m* north. **nordisch** *adj* northern; (*Skandinavisch*) nordic. **Nordländer** **1** *m (pl -)* Northerner. **2** *pl* northern countries.

nördlich [ˈnœrtlɪç] *adj* northern. *adv* northwards. *prep* to the north of.

Nordost(en) [ˈnɔrdɔstən)] *m* northeast. **nordöstlich** *adj* northeast(ern).

Nord||pol *m* North Pole. **-rhein-Westfalen** *neut* North Rhine-Westphalia. **-see** *f* North Sea. **nordwärts** *adv* northwards.

Nordwest(en) [ˈnɔrtvɛstən)] *m* northwest. **nordwestlich** *adj* northwest(ern).

nörgeln [ˈnœːrgəln] *v* grumble, grouse.

Norm [nɔrm] *f (pl -en)* standard, norm. **normal** *adj* normal. **-erweise** *adv* normally. **normalisieren** *v* normalize. **-maß** *neut* standard measure. **normgerecht** *adj* conforming to a standard.

Norwegen [ˈnɔrveːgən] *neut* Norway. **Norweger** *m (pl -)*, **Norwegerin** *f (pl -nen)* Norwegian. **norwegisch** *adj* Norwegian.

Not [noːt] *f (pl Nöte)* (*Armut*) need, want; (*Gefahr*) danger; (*Bedrängnis*) distress; (*Knappheit*) lack, shortage.

Notar [noˈtaːr] *m (pl -e)* notary.

Not||ausgang *m* emergency exit. **-bremse** *f* emergency brake. **-durft** *f* call of nature. **-dürftig** *adj* scanty; hard up.

Note [ˈnoːtə] *f (pl -n)* note; (*Schul-*) mark,

grade; banknote, (*US*) bill; (*Musik*) note. **-nständer** *m* music stand.

Not||fall *m* emergency. **-hilfe** *f* emergency service.

notieren [noˈtiːrən] *v* note.

nötig [ˈnœːtɪç] *adj* necessary. **-en** *v* compel, force.

Notiz [noˈtiːts] *f (pl -en)* notice; (*Vermerk*) note. **-buch** *neut* notebook.

Not||lage *f* distress, predicament. **-landung** *f* emergency landing. **-lüge** *f* white lie. **notleidend** *adj* distressed; (*arm*) needy, destitute.

notorisch [noˈtoːrɪʃ] *adj* notorious.

Not||ruf *m* distress call; (*Telef*) emergency call. **-stand** *m* emergency.

notwendig [ˈnoːtvɛndɪç] *adj* necessary. **Notwendigkeit** *f* necessity.

Notzucht [ˈnoːttsuxt] *f* rape.

Novelle [noˈvɛlə] *f (pl -n)* short story, short novel.

November [noˈvɛmbər] *m (pl -)* November.

Novize [noˈviːtsə] *m (pl -n)* novice.

Nuance [nyˈãsə] *f (pl -n)* nuance.

Nüchternheit [ˈnyçtərnhaɪt] *f* sobriety; (*fig*) realism, clear-headedness.

Nudeln [ˈnuːdəln] *pl* noodles.

null [nul] *adj* nil, zero; (*ungültig*) null. **null und nichtig** null and void. **Null** *f (pl -en)* nought, zero.

numerieren [numeˈriːrən] *v* number. **numerisch** *adj* numerical.

Nummer [ˈnum ər] *f (pl -n)* number. **Nummern||scheibe** *f* (telephone) dial. **-schild** *neut* number plate.

nun [nuːn] *adv* now. *interj* well! **was nun?** what now? **nun also** why then. **-mehr** *adv* (by) now.

nur [nuːr] *adv* only, merely; (*eben*) just. *conj* nevertheless, but. **nur noch** only, still. **nicht nur ... sondern auch ...** not only ... but also ....

Nürnberg [ˈnyrnbɛrk] *neut* Nuremberg.

Nuß [nus] *f (pl Nüsse)* nut. **-baum** *m* walnut tree. **Nuß||knacker** *m* nutcracker. **-schale** *f* nutshell.

nutz [nuts] *adj* useful. **-bar** *adj* useful. **-bringend** *adj* profitable.

nutzen [ˈnutsən] *or* **nützen** *v* be of use, be useful; (*gebrauchen*) make use of, use. **Nutzen** *m (pl -)* use; (*Vorteil*) profit, advantage. **Nutzen ziehen aus** derive advantage from, benefit from. **zum Nutzen von** for the benefit of. **Nutzfahrzeug** neut commercial vehicle.

nützlich ['nytslɪç] adj useful. **Nützlichkeit** f usefulness.

nutzlos ['nutsloːs] adj useless. **Nutzllosigkeit** f uselessness. **-nießer** m beneficiary. **-ung** f use, utilization.

Nylon ['naɪlɔn] neut (pl -s) nylon.

O

Oase [o'aːzə] f (pl -n) oasis.

ob [ɔp] conj whether. **als ob** as if, as though.

Obdach ['ɔpdax] neut (unz.) shelter. **obdachlos** adj homeless.

oben ['oːbən] adv above, at the top; (Haus) upstairs. **oben auf** on top of. **von oben** from above.

ober ['oːbər] adj upper, higher; (fig) superior; (Dienstgrad) senior, principal. **Ober** m (pl -) (head) waiter. **die Oberen** those in authority.

Oberllarm m upper arm. **-befehlshaber** m commander-in-chief. **-bürgermeister** m (lord) mayor. **-fläche** f surface (area). **oberflächlich** adj superficial.

oberhalb ['oːbərhalp] adv, prep above.

Oberllhand f upper hand, ascendancy. **-haupt** m chief, head. **-hemd** neut shirt. **-in** f (pl -nen) (Rel) mother superior; (Krankenschwester) matron.

oberirdisch [oːbərˈɪrdɪʃ] adj above ground; (Leitung) overhead.

Oberllkellner m head waiter. **-klasse** f upper class. **-schicht** f ruling class, upper classes pl. **-schule** f secondary school. **-schwester** f (Med) sister. **-seite** f upper side.

oberst ['oːbərst] adj highest, uppermost; (fig) supreme. **Oberst** m (pl -en) colonel.

obgleich [ɔpˈglaɪç] conj although.

Obhut ['ɔphuːt] f (unz.) care, protection. **in seine Objut nehmen** take care of, take under one's wing.

obig ['oːbɪç] adj above-mentioned, foregoing.

Objekt [ɔpˈjɛkt] neut (pl -e) object. **objektiv** adj objective.

*obliegen ['ɔplɪgən] v (einer Aufgabe) perform, carry out. **es liegt ihm ob, zu** it is his job or duty to. **Obliegenheit** f duty.

obligatorisch [obligaˈtoːrɪʃ] adj obligatory, compulsory.

Obmann ['ɔpman] m foreman; (Vorsitzender) chairman; (Sprecher) spokesman.

Oboe [o'boːə] f (pl -n) oboe. **Oboist** m oboist.

Obrigkeit ['oːbrɪçkaɪt] f (pl -en) authorities pl, government.

obschon [ɔpˈʃoːn] conj although.

Observatorium [ɔpzɛrvaˈtoːrɪum] neut (pl **Observatorien**) observatory.

obskur [ɔpskuːr] adj obscure.

Obst [oːpst] neut (unz.) fruit. **-baum** m fruit tree. **-garten** m orchard. **-händler** m fruiterer.

obszön [ɔpstsøːn] adj obscene.

obwohl [ɔpˈvoːl] conj although.

Ochse ['ɔksə] m (pl -n) ox. **Ochsenllfleisch** neut beef. **-schwanz** m oxtail.

Ode ['oːdə] f (pl -n) ode.

öde ['øː.də] adj desolate, bleak; (fig) dull, bleak. **Öde** f (unz.) desert, wasteland; (fig) dullness, tedium.

oder ['oːdər] conj or.

Ofen ['oːfən] m (pl **Öfen**) stove; (Back-Tech) oven.

offen ['ɔfən] adj open; (freimütig) open, frank; (Stellung) vacant. **-baren** v reveal, disclose. **Offenheit** f openness, frankness. **offenllherzig** adj open-hearted. **-kundig** adj evident. **-sichtlich** adj obvious, evident.

offensiv [ɔfɛnˈziːf] adj offensive. **Offensive** f (pl -n) offensive.

offenstehend ['ɔfənʃtɛːənt] adj open; (Schuld) outstanding.

öffentlich ['œfəntlɪç] adj public. **Öffentlichkeit** f publicity; (das Volk) public. **Öffentlichkeitsllarbeit** f public relations (PR).

offiziell [ɔfɪtsɪˈɛl] adj official.

Offizier [ɔfɪtsiːr] m (pl -e) officer. **Offiziersllmesse** f officers' mess. **-patent** neut (officer's) commission.

offiziös [ɔfɪtsiːøːs] adj semi-official.

offline ['ɔːflaɪn] adj, adv (Internet) off-line.

öffnen ['œfnən] v open. **Öffnung** f opening. **-szeiten** pl opening hours.

oft [ɔft] *adv* often; frequently. **wie oft?** how many times?

öfter [ˈœftər] *adj* frequent. *adv* more often *or* frequently. **öfters** *adv* often.

Oheim [ˈoːhaim] *m* (*pl* -e) uncle.

ohne [ˈoːnə] *prep, conj* without. **ohne daßich es wußte** without my knowledge. **ohne‖dies** *or* **-hin** *adv* all the same, besides.

Ohnmacht [ˈoːnmaxt] *f* unconsciousness, faint. **ohnmächtig** *adj* unconscious. **ohnmächtig werden** *v* faint.

Ohr [oːɐ] *neut* (*pl* -en) ear. **die Ohren spitzen** prick up one's ears. **ganz Ohr sein** be all ears.

Öhr [œːɐ] *neut* (*pl* -e) eye (of a needle).

Ohren‖schmalz *neut* ear wax. **–schmerz** *m* earache. **Ohrfeige** *f* slap across the face. **ohrfeigen** *v* slap (across the face). **Ohr‖läppchen** *neut* ear lobe. **–muschel** *f* (external) ear. **–ring** *m* earring.

Ökonom [œkoˈnoːm] *m* (*pl* -en) (*Hausverwalter*) caretaker, steward; (*Wirtschaftswissenschaftler*) economist. **–ie** *f* housekeeping; economics. **ökonomisch** *adj* economic; (*sparsam*) economical.

Oktave [ɔkˈtaːvə] *f* octave.

Oktober [ɔkˈtoːbər] *m* (*pl* -) October.

Okzident [ˈɔktsiːdɛnt] *m* occident.

Öl [œːl] *neut* (*pl* -e) oil. **–baum** *m* olive tree. **ölen** *v* oil, lubricate. **Ölfarbe** *f* oil paint.

Olive [oˈliːvə] *f* (*pl* -n) olive. **olivengrün** *adj* olive-green. **olivenöl** *neut* olive oil.

Öl‖leitung *f* (oil) pipeline. **–meßstab** *m* dipstick.

Olympiade [olympiˈaːdə] *f* (*pl* -n) Olympiad, Olympic games. **olympisch** *adj* Olympic.

Ölzweig [ˈœːltsvaik] *m* olive branch.

Oma [ˈoːma] *f* (*pl* -s) granny, grandma.

Omelett [ɔməˈlɛt] *neut* (*pl* -e) *or* **Omelette** *f* (*pl* -n) omelette.

Ondulieren [ɔnduˈliːrən] *v* wave.

Onkel [ˈɔŋkəl] *m* (*pl* -) uncle.

online [ˈɔnlain], **Online-** *adj, adv* (*Internet*) online.

Opa [ˈoːpa] *m* (*pl* -s) grandad, grandpa.

Opal [oˈpaːl] *m* (*pl* -e) opal.

Oper [ˈoːpər] *f* (*pl* -n) opera; (*Opernhaus*) opera house.

Operation [operaˈtsioːn] *f* (*pl* -en) operation. **–ssaal** *m* operating theatre. **operieren** *v* operate.

Opfer [ˈɔpfər] *neut* (*pl* -) (*Verzicht, Gabe*) sacrifice; (*Geopfertes*) victim. **opfern** *v* sacrifice, offer. **Opferung** *f* sacrifice.

Opium [ˈoːpium] *neut* opium.

opportum [ɔpɔrˈtuːm] *adj* opportune.

Opposition [ɔpoziˈtsioːn] *f* (*pl* -n) opposition. **–sführer** *m* leader of the opposition.

Optik [ˈɔptik] *f* optics. **-er** *m* optician.

optimal [ɔptiˈmaːl] *adj* optimum. **Optimismus** *m* optimism. **Optimist** *m* optimist, **optimistisch** *adj* optimistic.

optisch [ˈɔptʃ] *adj* optic(al).

Orange [oˈrãːʒə] *f* (*pl* -n) orange. **orange** *adj* orange. **Orangensaft** *m* orange juice.

Orchester [ɔrˈkɛstər] *neut* (*pl* -) orchestra.

Orchidee [ɔrçiˈdeːə] *f* (*pl* -n) orchid.

Orden [ˈɔrdən] *m* (*pl* -) (*Gesellschaft*) order; (*Ehrenzeichen*) decoration, order. **Ordens‖bruder** *m* member of an order; (*Rel*) monk, friar. **–schwester** *f* nun.

ordentlich [ˈɔrdəntliç] *adj* (*ordnungsgemäß*) orderly; (*ordnungsliebend, geordnet*) tidy; (*anständig, auch umg.*) proper, decent. **Ordentlichkeit** *f* orderliness; decency, respectability.

ordinär [ɔrdiˈnɛːr] *adj* common, vulgar.

Ordinarius [ɔrdiˈnaːrius] *m* (*pl* **Ordinarien**) professor.

Ordination [ɔrdinaˈtsioːn] *f* (*pl* -en) ordination. **ordinieren** *v* ordain.

ordnen [ˈɔrdnən] *v* put in order, arrange, classify. **Ordner** *m* (*pl* -) organizer; (*Versammlungen*) steward; (*Mappe*) file. **Ordnung** *f* (*pl* -en) order; (*Regel*) regulation. **ordnungs‖gemäß** *or* **–mäßig** *adj* orderly, lawful. *adv* properly, duly. **–widrig** *adj* irregular, illegal.

Organ [ɔrˈgaːn] *neut* (*pl* -e) organ. **–isation** *f* organization. **organ‖isch** *adj* organic. **–isieren** *v* organize. **Organismus** *m* (*pl* **Organismen**) organism.

Orgasmus [ɔrˈgasmus] *m* (*pl* **Orgasmen**) orgasm.

Orgel [ˈɔrgəl] *f* (*pl* -n) organ. **–spieler** *m* (*pl* -), **–spielerin** *f* (*pl* -nen) organist.

Orgie [ˈɔrgiə] *f* (*pl* -n) orgy.

Orient [ˈoːriɛnt] *m* Orient. **Orientale** *m* (*pl* -n), **Orientalin** (*pl* -nen) Oriental. **orientalisch** *adj* oriental.

Orientieren [oriɛnˈtiːrən] *v* locate. **sich ori-**

entieren orientate oneself. **Orientierung** f orientation. **Orientierungs||punkt** m reference point. **–vermögen** neut sense of direction.

original [orɡiˈnaːl] adj original. **Original** neut (pl -e) original.

originell [orɡiˈnɛl] adj original, novel; (eigenartig) peculiar.

Orkan [ɔrˈkaːn] m (pl -e) hurricane.

Ornat [ɔrˈnaːt] m (pl -e) (official) robes.

Ort [ɔrt] m (pl -e) place; (Ortschaft) town; (Dorf) village; (Punkt) point.

orthodox [ɔrtoˈdɔks] adj orthodox.

Orthopädie [ɔrtopɛˈdiː] f orthopaedics.

örtlich [ˈœrtlɪç] adj local.

Orts||gespräch neut local call. **–verkehr** m local traffic. **–zeit** f local time.

Öse [ˈœːzə] f (pl -n) eye(let). **Haken und Ösen** hooks and eyes.

Ost(en) [ˈɔst(ən)] m east. **der Nahe/Ferne Osten** the Middle/Far East. **Ostblock** m Eastern bloc, Eastern Europe.

Oster||ei neut Easter egg. **–hase** m Easter bunny.

Ostern [ˈoːstərn] neut pl Easter.

Österreich [ˈœːstəraiç] neut Austria. **Österreicher** m (pl -), f **Österreicherin** (pl -nen) Austrian. **Österreichisch** adj Austrian.

Osteuropa [ˈɔstɔyropa] f Eastern Europe.

östlich [ˈœstlɪç] adj east(ern).

Ost||politik f East policy, policy towards the Eastern bloc. **–see** f Baltic Sea.

Otter [ˈɔtər] m (pl -) or f (pl -n) otter.

Ouvertüre [uvɛrˈtyːrə] f (pl -n) overture.

Ovarium [oˈvaːrium] neut (pl **Ovarien**) ovary.

oval [oˈvaːl] adj oval.

Oxyd [ɔˈksyːt] neut (pl -e) oxide. **oxydieren** v oxidize.

Ozean [ˈoːtseaːn] m (pl -e) ocean. **ozeanisch** adj oceanic.

Ozon [oˈtsoːn] neut ozone. **Ozongürtel** m ozone layer.

P

paar [paːr] adj **ein paar** a few. **Paar** neut

(pl -e) pair, couple. **paaren** v (Tiere) pair, couple; (vereinigen) join. **sich paaren** couple, mate. **Paarung** f (pl -en) mating. **paarweise** adv in couples.

Pacht [paxt] f (pl -en) lease; (Entgelt) rent. **–brief** m lease. **pachten** v lease.

Pächter [ˈpɛçtər] m (pl -) leaseholder; (Bauer) tenant farmer.

Pack [pak] m (pl **Päcke**) pack; packet; bundle.

Päckchen [ˈpɛkçən] neut (pl -) packet, small parcel.

packen [ˈpakən] v grasp, seize; (einpacken) pack. **–d** adj thrilling, fascinating. **Pack||kasten** m packing case. **–pferd** neut pack-horse. **–esel** m (fig) drudge. **–stoff** m packing (material). **Packung** f (pl -en)package.

Pädagogik [pɛdaˈgoːgik] f pedagogy, education. **pädagogisch** adj pedagogic. **pädagogische Hochschule** teacher-training college.

Paddel [ˈpadəl] neut (pl -) paddle. **paddeln** v paddle.

Page [ˈpaːʒə] m (pl -n) page(boy).

Paket [paˈkeːt] neut (pl -e) packet, parcel.

Pakistan [ˈpakistaːn] neut Pakistan. **Pakistaner(in)** Pakistani. **pakistanisch** adj Pakistani.

Pakt [pakt] m (pl -e) pact, agreement.

Palast [paˈlast] m (pl **Paläste**) palace.

Palästina [paˈlɛstina] neut Palestine.

Palette [paˈlɛtə] f (pl -n) palette.

Palme [ˈpalmə] f (pl -n) palm. **Palmsonntag** m Palm Sunday.

Pampelmuse [ˈpampəlmuːzə] f (pl -n) grapefruit.

Panda [ˈpanda] m (pl -) panda.

Paneel [paˈneːl] neut (pl -e) panel, panelling.

paniert [paˈniːrt] adj coated with breadcrumbs.

Panik [ˈpaːnik] f (pl -en) panic. **panisch** adj panic-stricken, panicky.

Panne [ˈpanə] f (pl -n) breakdown.

Pantoffel [panˈtɔfəl] m (pl -n) slipper.

Pantomime [pantoˈmiːmə] f (pl -n) pantomime.

Panzer [ˈpantsər] m (pl -) armour; (Panzerwagen) tank; (Tiere) shell. **–hemd** neut coat of mail. **panzern** v armour. **Panzer||ung** f (pl -en) armour plating.

–wagen *m* tank, armoured car. **–weste** *f* bullet-proof vest.

Papa [pa'paː, 'papa] *m* (*pl* -s) daddy, papa.

Papagei [papa'gaɪ] *m* (*pl* -en) parrot.

Papier [pa'piːɐ] *neut* (*pl* -e) paper. **–bogen** *m* sheet of paper. **–korb** *m* wastepaper basket. **–tüte** *f* paper bag. **–waren** *pl* stationery *sing*.

Pappe ['papə] *f* (*pl* -n) cardboard.

Pappel ['papəl] *f* (*pl* -n) poplar.

pappen ['papən] *v* paste (together).

Pappschachtel ['papʃaxtəl] *f* cardboard box.

Paprika ['paprɪka] *m* (*pl* -s) paprika. **–schote** *f* green *or* red pepper, capsicum.

Papst [paːpst] *m* (*pl* **Päpste**) pope.

päpstlich ['pɛːpstlɪç] *adj* papal.

Parabel [pa'raːbəl] *f* (*pl* -n) parable; (*Math*) parabola.

Parade [pa'raːdə] *f* (*pl* -n) parade. **paradieren** *v* parade; (*fig*) make a show, show off.

Paradies [para'diːs] *neut* (*pl* -e) paradise.

paradox [para'dɔks] *adj* paradoxical. **Paradoxie** *f* paradox.

Paragraph [para'graːf] *m* (*pl* -en) paragraph, section.

parallel [para'leː] *adj* parallel. **Parallele** *f* parallel.

Paralyse [para'lyːzə] *f* (*pl* -n) paralysis. **paralysieren** *v* paralyse. **Paralytiker** *m* paralytic. **paralytisch** *adj* paralytic.

Paranuß ['paranus] *f* Brazil nut.

Parasit [para'ziːt] *m* (*pl* -en) parasite.

Pärchen ['pɛːrçən] *neut* (*pl* -) couple, lovers.

Parenthese [parɛn'teːzə] *f* (*pl* -n) parenthesis.

Parfüm [par'fyːm] *neut* (*pl* -e) perfume. **parfümieren** *v* perfume, scent.

parieren [pa'riːrən] *v* (*Angriff*) parry; (*Pferd*) rein (in); (*gehorchen*) obey, toe the line.

Parität [pari'tɛːt] *f* (*pl* -en) parity.

Park [park] *m* (*pl* -s) park. **–anlagen** *pl* park, public gardens. **parken** *v* park.

Parkett [par'kɛt] *neut* (*pl* -e) (*Fußboden*) parquet; (*Theater*) stalls.

Park||platz *m* car park, (*US*) parking lot. **–uhr** *f* parking meter.

Parlament [parla'mɛnt] *neut* (*pl* -e) parliament. **–arier** *m* (*pl* -) parliamentarian. **parliamentarisch** *adj* parliamentary.

Parodie [paro'diː] *f* (*pl* -n) parody. **parodieren** *v* parody.

Partei [par'taɪ] *f* (*pl* -en) (*Pol, Jur*) party. **–führer** *m* party leader. **parteiisch** *or* **–lich** *adj* biased, partial. **–los** *adj* impartial. **Parteipolitik** *f* party politics. **–tag** *m* party conference.

Parterre [par'tɛr] *neut* (*pl* -s) ground floor; (*Theater*) pit. **–wohnung** *f* ground floor; flat.

Partie [par'tiː] *f* (*pl* -n) (*Teil, Musik*) part; (*Spiel, Heirat*) match; (*Jagd-*) party.

Partikel [par'tɪkəl] *f* (*pl* -n) particle.

Partisan [partiza'n] *m* (*pl* -en) partisan.

Partitur [parti'tuːr] *f* (*pl* -en) (*Musik*) score.

Partizip [parti'tsɪp] *neut* (*pl* -ien) participle.

Partizipation [partitsipa'tsɪoːn] *f* participation. **partizipieren** *v* participate.

Partner ['partnər] *m* (*pl* -) partner. **Partnerschaft** *f* partnership.

Party ['paːrti] *f* (*pl* -s) party.

Parzelle [par'tsɛlə] *f* (*pl* -n) plot (of land).

Paß [pas] *m* (*pl* **Pässe**) (*Reisepaß*) passport; (*Durchgang*) pass.

passabel [pa'saːbəl] *adj* tolerable, passable.

Passage [pa'saːʒə] *f* (*pl* -n) passage. **Passagier** *m* (*pl* -e) passenger.

Passant [pa'sant] *m* (*pl* -en) passer-by.

Paßbild ['pasbɪlt] *neut* passport photograph.

passen ['pasən] *v* fit, suit; (*Kartenspiel*) pass. **gut zueinander passen** go well together. **das paßt mir nicht** that doesn't suit me. **passend** *adj* fitting, suitable.

passieren [pa'siːrən] *v* (*geschehen*) happen; (*vorübergehen*) pass; (*überqueren*) cross. **Passierschein** *m* permit, pass.

Passion [pasi'oːn] *f* (*pl* -en) passion. **sich passionieren für** be enthusiastic about. **passioniert** enthusiastic, dedicated. **Passionsspiel** *neut* Passion Play. **–woche** *f* Holy Week.

passiv ['pasiːf] *adj* passive. **Passiv** *neut* passive.

Paßkontrolle ['paskɔntrɔlə] *f* passport inspection.

Pastellfarbe [pa'stɛlfarbə] *f* pastel colour.

Pastete [pa'steːtə] *f* (*pl* -n) (savoury) pie, pasty.

pasteurisieren [pastøri'ziːrən] *v* pasteurize.

Pastille [pa'stiə] f (pl -n) lozenge.

Pastor ['pastɔr] m (pl -en) pastor, priest.

Pate ['pa:tə] m (pl -n) godfather. **-nkind** neut godchild.

Patent [pa'tɛnt] neut (pl -e) patent; (Erlaubnis) licence; (Mil) commission. **patentieren** v patent. **Patentinhaber** m patentee.

pathetisch [pa'te:tʃ] adj (feierlich) solemn, lofty; (übertrieben) rhetorical, flowery.

Pathologe [pato'lo:gə] m (pl -n) pathologist. **Pathologie** f pathology. **pathologisch** adj pathological.

Patient [patsiɛnt] m (pl -en) patient.

Patin ['pa:tin] f (pl -nen) godmother.

Patriot [patrio:t] m (pl -en) patriot. **patriotisch** adj patriotic. **Patriotismus** m patriotism.

Patron [pa'tro:n] m (pl -e) patron; (umg.) fellow, customer.

Patrone [pa'tro:nə] f (pl -n) cartridge.

Patrouille [pa'tuljə] f (pl -n) patrol.

Patt [pat] neut (pl -s) stalemate.

Pauke ['paukə] f (pl -n) kettledrum. **pauken** v (umg.) cram, swot. **Pauker** m drummer; (umg.) crammer.

pausbackig ['pausbakiç] adj chubby (-faced).

pauschal [pau'ʃa:l] adj all-inclusive. **Pauschalsumme** f lump sum.

Pause ['pauzə] f (pl -n) pause, break; (Theater) interval. **Pause machen** take a break. **pausenlos** adj uninterrupted, continuous.

Pavian ['pa:viən] m (pl -e) baboon.

Pazifik [pa'tsi:fik] m Pacific Ocean. **pazifisch** adj Pacific.

Pazifismus [patsi'fismus] m pacifism. **Pazifist** m (pl -en) pacifist.

Pech [pɛç] neut (pl -e) pitch; (fig) bad luck. **Pech haben** be unlucky. **pechdunkel** adj pitch dark.

Pedal [pe'da:l] neut (pl -e) pedal.

Pedant [pe'dant] m (pl -en) pedant. **pedantisch** adj pedantic.

peilen ['pailən] v take (one's) bearings; (loten) sound; (umg.) sound out.

Pein [pain] f (unz.) pain, torment, agony. **peinigen** v torment. **-lich** adj awkward, embarrassing; (genau) (over-)careful, fussy.

Peitsche ['paitʃə] f (pl -n) whip, lash.

Pelikan ['pe:lika:n] m (pl -e) pelican.

Pelle ['pɛlə] f (pl -n) peel, skin. **Pellkartoffel** pl potatoes (boiled) in their jackets.

Pelz [pɛls] m (pl -e) fur, pelt. **pelzig** adj furry. **Pelzmantel** m fur coat.

Pendel ['pɛndəl] neut (pl -) pendulum. **pendeln** v swing, oscillate; (fig) commute. **Pendler** m commuter.

penibel [pe'ni:bəl] adj meticulous.

pennen ['pɛnən] v (umg.) doss, kip down. **Penne** f (umg.) school. **Penner** m dosser, down-and-out.

Pension [pã'sjo:n] f (pl -en) guest house, boarding house; (Ruhegehalt) pension. **pensionieren** v pension off. **Pensionierte(r)** pensioner.

per [pɛr] prep by, per. **per Adresse** care of, c/o.

perfekt [pɛr'fɛkt] adj perfect. **einen Vertrag perfekt machen** clinch a deal.

perforieren [pɛrfo'ri:rən] v perforate. **Perforation** f perforation.

Pergament [pɛrga'mɛnt] neut (pl -e) parchment. **-papier** neut greaseproof paper.

Periode [perio:də] f (pl -n) period. **periodisch** adj periodic.

Perle ['pɛrlə] f (pl -n) pearl; (Glas-) bead. **perlen** v sparkle. **Perllenkette** f string of pearls. **-mutter** f mother-of-pearl.

permanent [pɛrma'nɛnt] adj permanent.

perplex [pɛr'plɛks] adj perplexed, confused.

Person [pɛr'zo:n] f (pl -en) person.

Personal [pɛrzo'na:l] neut staff, personnel. **-abteilung** f personnel department. **-ausweis** m pass, ID card. **-chef** m personnel manager.

Personen||kraftwagen (Pkw) m (passenger) car. **-verzeichnis** neut (Theater) dramatis personae. **-zug** m (local) passenger train.

persönlich [pɛr'zø:nliç] adj personal. **persönliche Geheimnummer** f PIN (personal identification number). **Persönlichkeit** f personality.

Perspektive [pɛrspɛk'ti:və] f (pl -n) perspective.

Perücke [pe'rykə] f (pl -n) wig.

pervers [pɛr'vɛrs] adj perverse. **Perversion** f perversion.

Pessimismus [pɛsi'mismus] m pessimism. **Pessimist** m (pl -en) pessimist. **pessimistisch** adj pessimistic.

Pest [pɛst] f (pl -en) plague.

Petersilie [petər'ziːliə] f (pl -n) parsley.

Petroleum [pe'troːləum] neut petroleum; (*Kerosin*) paraffin, (US) kerosene.

petzen ['pɛtsən] v (*umg.*) tell tales, sneak.

Pfad [pfaːt] m (pl -e) path. **–finder** m Boy Scout. **–finderin** f Girl Guide, Brownie.

Pfahl [pfaːl] m (pl **Pfähle**) post, stake; (*Stange*) pole. **–werk** neut paling, palisade.

Pfalz [pfals] f Palatinate.

Pfand [pfant] neut (**Pfänder**) pledge, security; (*Flaschen, usw.*) deposit. **–brief** m mortgage (deed). **–leiher** m pawnbroker.

Pfanne ['pfanə] f (pl -n) pan. **Pfannkuchen** m pancake.

Pfarrbezirk ['pfaːrbətsirk] m parish. **Pfarrer** m parson. **Pfarrhaus** neut parsonage.

Pfau [pfau] m (pl -en) peacock.

Pfeffer ['pfɛfər] m (pl -) pepper. **–kuchen** m gingerbread. **–minz** neut (pl -e) peppermint (sweet). **–minze** f (*Bot*) peppermint.

Pfeife ['pfaifə] f (pl -n) pipe. **pfeifen** v whistle. **Pfeifer** m whistler; (*Pfeife*) piper.

Pfeil [pfail] m (pl -e) arrow.

Pfeiler ['pfailər] m (pl -) pillar.

pfeilschnell ['pfailʃnɛl] adj swift as an arrow. **Pfeilschütze** m archer.

Pfennig ['pfɛnik] m (pl -e) pfennig; (*fig*) penny.

Pferch [pfɛrc] m (pl -e) fold, pen. **pferchen** v pen.

Pferd [pfeːrt] neut (pl -e) horse. **Pferdebremse** f horsefly. **–knecht** m groom. **–rennbahn** f race course. **–rennen** neut horseracing. **–stall** m stable. **–stärke** (**Ps**) f horsepower (hp).

Pfiff [pfif] m (pl -e) (*Ton*) whistle; (*Kniff*) trick.

Pfifferling ['pfifərliŋ] m (pl -e) (*Bot*) chanterelle (edible mushroom). **das ist keinen Pfifferling wert** that's (worth) nothing.

Pfingsten ['pfiŋstən] neut (pl -) Whitsun(tide).

Pfirsich ['pfirziç] m (pl -e) peach.

Pflanze ['pflantsə] f (pl -n) plant. **pflanzen** v plant. **–fressend** adj herbivorous. **Pflanzenfresser** m herbivore. **–öl** neut vegetable oil. **–reich** neut vegetable kingdom.

Pflaster ['pflastər] neut (pl -) (*Straße*) pavement; (*Wunden*) plaster. **–stein** m paving stone.

Pflaume ['pflaumə] f (pl -n) plum.

Pflege ['pfleːgə] f (pl -n) care. **–dienst** m service. **–eltern** pl foster parents. **–kind** neut foster child. **–mutter** f foster mother. **pflegeleicht** adj easy-care.

pflegen ['pfleːgən] v care for; (*Kranken*) nurse; (*Pflanzen*) cultivate; (*gewohntsein*) be accustomed to. **er pflegte zu sagen** he used to say. **Pfleger** m male nurse; (*vormund*) guardian. **Pflegerin** f nurse, sister.

Pflege||sohn m foster son. **–tochter** f foster daughter. **–vater** m foster father.

pfleglich ['pfleːkliç] adj careful. **pfleglich behandeln** handle with care.

Pflicht [pfliçt] f (pl -en) duty. **pflicht||bewußt** adj conscientious. **–gemäß** adj dutiful; (*in*), in accordance with duty. **–getreu** adj dutiful, conscientious.

Pflock [pflɔk] m (pl **Pflöcke**) peg, pin.

pflücken ['pflykən] v pluck; gather.

Pflug [pfluːk] m (pl **Pflüge**) plough.

pflügen ['pflyːgən] v plough.

Pflüger ['pflyːgər] m ploughman.

Pforte ['pfɔrtə] f (pl -n) door, gate.

Pförtner ['pfœ rtnər] m (pl -) doorkeeper, porter.

Pfosten ['pfɔstən] m (pl -) post, stake.

Pfote ['pfoːtə] f (pl -n) paw.

Pfropf [pfrɔpf] m (pl -e *oder* **Pfröpfe**) (*Blutgerinsel*) blood clot; (*Watte*) wad (of cotton wool). **pfropfen** v (*Flasche*) cork, stopper; (*Bäume*) graft; (*stopfen*) pack, stuff. **Pfropfen** m (pl -) cork, stopper. **–reis** neut graft.

pfui [pfuː] interj pooh, ugh.

Pfund [pfunt] neut (pl -e) pound.

pfuschen ['pfuʃən] v botch, bungle, make a mess. **Pfuscher** m botcher, bungler. **–ei** f bungling; (*Arbeit*) botch-job, botch-up.

Pfütze ['pfytsə] f (pl -n) puddle.

Phänomen [fɛno'mɛn] neut (pl -e) phenomenon.

Phantasie [fanta'ziː] f (pl -n) (*Einbildungskraft*) imagination; (*Trugbild*) fantasy. **phantasie||los** adj unimaginative. **–reich** adj imaginative. **–ren** v fantasize, daydream; (*Med*) be delirious. **phantastisch** adj fantastic.

Phantom [fan'toːm] neut (pl -e) phantom.

Phase ['faːzə] f (pl -n) phase.

Philister [fɪlistər] m (pl -) philistine. **philisterhaft** adj philistine, narrow-minded.

Philosoph [filo'zo:f] *m* (*pl* -en) philosopher. **-ie** *f* philosophy. **philosophisch** *adj* philosophical.

Phonetik [fo'ne:tik] *f* (*unz.*) phonetics. **phonetisch** *adj* phonetic.

Phosphor ['fɔsfɔr] *m* (*unz.*) phosphorus.

Photo ['fo:to] *neut* (*pl* -s) photo, photograph. **-album** *neut* photograph album. **-apparat** *m* camera. **photogen** *adj* photogenic. **Photograph** *m* (*pl* -en) photographer. **-ie** *f* photography. **photograph||ieren** *v* photograph. **-isch** *adj* photographic.

Phrase ['fra:zə] *f* (*pl* -n) phrase; (*fig*) empty talk, fine phrases.

Physik [fy'zi:k] *f* physics. **-er** *m* physicist.

Physiologie [fyziolo'gi:] *f* physiology. **physiologisch** *adj* physiological.

physisch ['fy:zɪʃ] *adj* physical.

Pianist [pia'nist] *m* (*pl* -en), **Pianistin** *f* (*pl* -nen) pianist.

Pickel¹ ['pɪkəl] *m* (*pl* -), **Picke** *f* (*pl* -n) pick-axe.

Pickel² ['pɪkəl] *m* (*pl* -) (*Med*) pimple, spot.

piep [pi:p] *interj* cheep. **nicht piep sagen** not say a word. **Piep** *m* (*pl* -se) peep, chirp. **piep||en** *v* chirp. **-sen** *v* (*Maus*) squeak.

Pietät [pie'tɛ:t] *f* piety; (*Ehrfurcht*) reverence.

Pik [pi:k] *neut* (*pl* -s) spades *pl*.

pikant [pi'kant] *adj* spicy; (*fig*) suggestive, racy.

Pikkoloflöte ['pɪkolofflø:tə] *f* piccolo.

Pilger ['pɪlgər] *m* (*pl* -), **Pilgerin** *f* (*pl* -nen) pilgrim. **Pilgerfahrt** *f* pilgrimage.

Pille ['pɪlə] *f* (*pl* -n) pill. **die Pille** (*umg.*) the (contraceptive) pill.

Pilot [pi'lo:t] *m* (*pl* -en) pilot.

Pilz [pɪlts] *m* (*pl* -e) mushroom.

Pinguin [pɪŋgu'i:n] *m* (*pl* -e) penguin.

Pinie ['pi:niə] *f* (*pl* -n) stone pine. **-nnuß** *f* pine kernel.

Pinne ['pɪnə] *f* (*pl* -n) pin, peg; (*Ruder-*) tiller.

Pinsel ['pɪnzəl] *m* (*pl* -) brush; (*Farbe*) paint-brush. **pinseln** *v* paint, daub.

Pionier [pio'ni:r] *m* (*pl* -e) pioneer.

Pirat [pi'ra:t] *m* (*pl* -en) pirate.

Piste ['pɪstə] *f* (*pl* -n) track; (*Ski*) ski-run; (*Flugzeug*) runway.

Pistole [pɪsto:lə] *f* (*pl* -n) pistol.

pissen ['pɪsən] *v* (*vulg*) piss.

Plackerei [plakə'rai] *f* (*pl* -en) drudgery, toil.

plädieren [plɛ'di:rən] *v* plead. **Plädoyer** neut (*pl* -s) (*Jur*) plea.

Plage ['pla:gə] *f* (*pl* -n) nuisance, bother, vexation. **plagen** *v* torment, annoy.

Plagiat [pla'gia:t] *neut* (*pl* -e) plagiarism. **plagiieren** *v* plagiarize.

Plakat [pla'ka:t] *neut* (*pl* -e) poster, placard.

Plan [pla:n] *m* (*pl* **Pläne**) (*Absicht*) plan, intention; (*Zeichnung*) plan, diagram; (*Stadt*) map; (*Skizze*) design, scheme.

Plane ['pla:nə] *f* (*pl* -n) awning.

planen ['pla:nən] *v* plan.

Planet [pla'ne:t] *m* (*pl* -en) planet. **-arium** *neut* (*pl* -**arien**) planetarium.

planieren [pla'ni:rən] *v* plane, level, smooth. **Planierraupe** *f* grader, bulldozer.

Planke ['plaŋkə] *f* (*pl* -n) plank.

Plänkelei [plɛŋkə'lai] *f* (*pl* -en) (*Gefecht*) skirmish; (*Wortstreit*) bantering.

planmäßig ['pla:nmɛ:sɪç] *adj* systematic; (*nach einem Plan*) according to plan. *der Zug fährt planmäßig um drei Uhr ab* the train is scheduled to leave at 3 o'clock.

Plantage [plan'ta:gə] *f* (*pl* -n) plantation.

Planung ['pla:nuŋ] *f* planning. **Planwirtschaft** *f* planned economy.

plappern ['plapərn] *v* chatter.

plärren ['plɛrən] *v* blubber, cry, sob.

Plastik ['plastɪk] *f* (*pl* -en) (*Kunst*) sculpture; (*Med*) plastic surgery; (*Kunststoff*) plastic. **plastisch** *adj* plastic.

Platin [pla'ti:n] *neut* platinum.

plätschern ['plɛtʃərn] *v* (*Bach*) babble; (*Regen*) splash, patter; (*planschen*) paddle.

platt [plat] *adj* flat, level; (*Redensart*) silly, trite; (*erstaunt*) tongue-tied, flabbergasted. **Plattdeutsch** *neut* Low German.

Platte ['platə] *f* (*pl* -n) plate, dish; (*Stein*) flag; (*Metall, Holz*) sheet, slab; (*Tisch*) leaf; (*Schallplatte*) record, disc. **-nspieler** *m* record-player.

Platz [plats] *m* (*pl* **Plätze**) place; (*Sitz.*) seat; (*Raum*) space, room; (*Stadt*) square. **-anweiser** *m* usher. **-anweiserin** *f* usherette.

platzen ['platsən] *v* burst, split; (*explodieren*) explode; (*Scheck*) bounce.

Platz||karte *f* seat-reservation ticket.

–patrone *f* blank cartridge. **–regen** *m*
downpour, heavy shower.

plaudern ['plaudən] *v* chat.

plausibel [plau'ziːbəl] *adj* plausible.

Plazenta [pla'sɛnta] *f (pl* **-s** *or* **Plazenten)**
placenta.

pleite ['plaɪtə] *adj* bankrupt; *(umg.)* broke.
Pleite *f* bankruptcy; *(fig)* flop, wash-out.

Plinthe ['plɪntə] *f (pl* **-n)** plinth.

plombieren [plɔm'biːən] *v* seal; *(Zahn)* fill.

plötzlich ['plœtslɪç] *adj* sudden.

plump [plʊmp] *adj (grob)* coarse;
(ungeschickt) clumsy. **plumps** *Interj* bump,
thud. **plumpsen** *v* fall down (with a thud),
plump down.

plündern ['plyndən] *v* plunder.

Plural ['pluːraːl] *m (pl* **-e)** plural.

pneumatisch [pnɔy'maːtʃ] *adj* pneumatic.

Pöbel ['pøːbəl] *m* mob, rabble.

pochen ['pɔxən] *v* knock, tap; *(Herz)* beat.

Pocken ['pɔkən] *pl* smallpox *sing.*

Podcast ['pɔdkaːst] *m (pl* **-s)** podcast.

Pokal [po'kaːl] *m (pl* **-e)** *(Sport)* cup. **–endspiel** *neut (Sport)* cup final. **–spiel** *neut* cup
tie.

Pökel ['pøːkəl] *m (pl* **-)** brine (for pickling).
pökeln *v* pickle, salt.

Pol [poːl] *m (pl* **-e)** pole. **polar** *adj* polar.
Polarmeer *neut* Arctic Ocean. **südliches
Polarmeer** Antarctic Ocean.

Polemik [po'lɛmɪk] *f (pl* **-en)** polemic, controversy. **polemisch** *adj* polemic(al).

Polen ['poːlən] *neut* Poland. **Pole** *m (pl* **-n)**,
Polin *f (pl* **-nen)** Pole. **polnisch** *adj* Polish.

Police [po'liːs, po'liːsə] *f (pl* **-n)** (insurance)
policy.

polieren [po'liːən] *v* polish. **Poliermittel**
neut polish.

Politik [poli'tiːk] *f (unz.) (Staatskunst)* politics; *(Verfahren, Programm)* policy. **–er** *m
(pl* **-)** politician. **politisch** *adj* political.

Politur [poli'tuːr] *f (pl* **-en)** polish.

Polizei [poli'tsaɪ] *f (pl* **-en)** police. **–hund** *m*
police dog. **–kommisar** *or* **–kommissär** *m*
police inspector. **polizeilich** *adj* police.
Polizei||präsident *m* chief constable,
commissioner. **–stunde** *f* closing time.
–wache *f* police station. **Polizist** *m (pl* **-en)**
policeman. **–in** *f (pl* **-nen)** policewoman.

Poller ['pɔlər] *m (pl* **-)** bollard.

Polster ['pɔlstər] *neut (pl* **-)** cushion;
(Polsterung) upholstery. **polstern** *v* upholster. **Polsterung** *f* upholstery.

Poltergeist ['pɔltərgaɪst] *m* poltergeist,
hobgoblin.

Polyp [po'lyːp] *m (pl* **-en)** *(umg.)* copper.

Polytechnikum [poly'tɛçnikum] *neut (pl*
Polytechniken) technical college.

Pommern ['pɔmərn] *neut (unz.)*
Pomerania.

Pommes frites [pɔm'friːt] *pl* (potato) chips,
(US) French fries.

Pomp [pɔmp] *m* pomp. **pomphaft** *adj*
stately, with pomp.

Pony ['pɔniː] *neut (pl* **-s)** pony; *(Frisur)*
fringe.

Pop-Musik ['pɔp muːziːk] *f* pop (music).

populär [popu'lɛːr] *adj* popular. **popular-
isieren** *v* popularize.

Pore ['poːrə] *f (pl* **-n)** pore.

Pornographie [pɔrnogra'fiː] *f* pornography. **pornographisch** *adj* pornographic.

porös [po'røːs] *adj* porous.

Porree ['pɔre] *m (pl* **-s)** leek.

Portion [pɔrtsioːn] *f (pl* **-en)** portion, helping.

Porto ['pɔrto] *neut (pl* **-s)** postage,
portofrei *adv* post-free.

Porträt [pɔrtrɛː, pɔrtrɛːt] *neut (pl* **-s)** portrait.

Portugal ['pɔrtugal] *neut* Portugal.
Portugiese *m (pl* **-n)**, **Portugiesin** *f (pl*
-nen) Portuguese. **portugiesisch** *adj*
Portuguese.

Porzellan [pɔrtsɛ'laːn] *neut (pl* **-e)** porcelain, china.

Posaune [po'zaunə] *f (pl* **-n)** trombone.

Pose ['poːzə] *f (pl* **-n)** pose, attitude. **Poseur**
m poseur. **posieren** *v* (strike a) pose.

Position [pozitsioːn] *f (pl* **-en)** position.

positiv ['poːzitiːf] *adj* positive.

Posse ['pɔsə] *f (pl* **-n)** *(Theater)* farce.
Possen *m (pl* **-)** prank, practical joke, trick.
possenhaft *adj* farcical.

possessiv ['pɔsɛstiːf] *adj* possessive.

Post [pɔst] *f (pl* **-en)** post (office), postal service; *(Briefe)* post, mail. **–amt** *neut* post
office. **–anweisung)** *f* postal order.
–beamte(r) *m* post office official. **–bote** *m*
postman.

Posten ['pɔstən] *m (pl* **-)** place, post;
(Stellung) position, post; *(Mil)* sentry;

(*Ware*) item; (*Streik-*) picket.

Post||fach ['pɔstfax] *neut* post-office box, PO box. **–gebühr** *f* postage. **–karte** *f* postcard.

postlagernd ['pɔstlaːgɛrnt] *adj* poste restante, (*US*) general delivery.

Post||leitzahl *f* postal code. **–sparkasse** *f* post-office savings bank. **–stempel** *m* postmark.

Postulat [pɔstuˈlaːt] *neut* (*pl* -e) postulate. **postulieren** *v* postulate.

postwendend ['pɔstvɛndənt] *adj* by return (of) post. **Postwertzeichen** *neut* postage stamp.

potent [poˈtɛnt] *adj* capable; (*Med*) potent.

potential [potɛntsiaːl] *adj* potential. **Potential** *neut* potential. **potentiell** *adj* potential, possible.

Potenz [poˈtɛnts] *f* (*pl* -en) power.

Pottasche ['pɔtaʃə] *f* potash.

Pracht [praxt] *f* splendour, magnificence.

prächtig ['prɛçtiç] *adj* splendid, magnificent.

Prag [praːk] *neut* Prague.

Präge ['prɛːgə] *f* (*pl* -n) mint. **prägen** *v* stamp; (*Münze*) mint, coin.

pragmatisch [pragˈmaːtʃ] *adj* pragmatic. **Pragmatiker** *m* (*pl* -) pragmatist.

prägnant [prɛgˈnant] *adj* precise, terse.

prahlen ['praːlən] *v* brag, boast. **Prahler** *m* (*pl* -) braggart. **prahlerisch** *adj* boastful.

Praktikant [praktiˈkant] *m* (*pl* -en), **Praktikantin** *f* (*pl* -nen) trainee, probationer. **Praktik||er** *m* experienced person, expert. **–um** *neut* (*pl* -a) training course, field course. **praktisch** *adj* practical; (*zweckmäßig*) useful; (*Person*) handy.

prall [pral] *adj* (*rund*) plump, chubby; (*straff*) tight; (*sonne*) blazing. **Prall** *m* (*pl* -e) collision, impact. **prallen** *v* (*Ball*) bounce, rebound. **prallen gegen** collide with, bump into.

Prämie ['prɛːm ə] *f* (*pl* -n) bonus; (*Versicherungs-*) premium.

Prämisse [prɛˈmɪsə] *f* (*pl* -n) premise.

pränatal ['prɛːnataːl] *adj* antenatal.

Präparat [prɛpaˈraːt] *neut* (*pl* -e) preparation; (*Med*) medicament.

präsentieren [prɛzɛnˈtiːrən] *v* present. **Präsenz** *f* (*pl* -en) presence.

Präsident [prɛziˈdɛnt] *m* (*pl* -en) president. **–enwahl** *f* presidential election. **–schaft** *f*

presidency. **präsidieren** *v* preside, act as chairman.

prasseln ['prasəln] *v* clatter; (*Regen*) patter, drum; (*Feuer*) crackle.

präventiv [prɛvɛnˈtiːf] *adj* preventive. **Präventiv||maßnahme** *f* preventive measure. **–mittel** *neut* contraceptive.

Praxis ['praksis] *f* (*pl* **Praxen**) practice.

Präzedenzfall [prɛtseˈdɛntsfal] *m* precedent.

präzis [prɛˈtsiːs] *adj* precise.

predigen ['preːdigən] *v* preach. **Prediger** *m* (*pl* -) preacher. **Predigt** *f* (*pl* -en) sermon.

Preis [prais] *m* (*pl* -e) price; (*Belohnung*) prize; (*Lob*) praise.

Preißelbeere ['praisəbeːrə] *f* cranberry.

preisgeben ['praisgeːbən] *v* give up, abandon; (*opfern*) sacrifice. **Preisgebung** *f* surrender; sacrifice.

Preis||lage *f* (*pl* -n) price range, price level. **in der unteren Preislage/ gehobenen Preislage** downmarket/ upmarket. **–liste** *f* price list. **–senkung** *f* price reduction. **–steigerung** *f* price rise. **–stopp** *m* price freeze. **–sturz** *m* slump or fall in prices. **–zettel** *m* price tag. **preiswert** *adj* cheap.

prellen ['prɛlən] *v* (*betrügen*) swindle, cheat; (*Ball*) bounce.

Premiere [prəmˈjiːrə] *f* (*pl* -n) première, first night.

Premierminister [prəmˈjeːrm inistər] prime minister, premier.

Presse ['prɛsə] *f* (*pl* -n) (*Zeitungen*) the press; (*Druckmaschine*) press; (*Saft*) squeezer. **–agentur** *f* press agency. **–freiheit** *f* freedom of the press. **pressen** *v* press.

Preß||holz *neut* chipboard. **–kohle** *f* briquette. **–luftbohrer** *m* pneumatic drill.

Preuße ['prɔysə] *m* (*pl* -n), **Preußin** *f* (*pl* -nen) Prussian. **Preußen** *neut* Prussia. **preußisch** *adj* Prussian.

prickeln ['prɪkəln] *v* prickle, tingle. **–d** *adj* tingling.

Priester ['priːstər] *m* (*pl* -) priest. **–in** *f* priestess. **priesterlich** *adj* priestly.

prima ['priːma] *adj* (*umg.*) first-rate, excellent. **Prima** *f* sixth form.

primär [priˈmɛːr] *adj* primary.

Primarschule [priˈmaːrʃuːlə] *f* primary school (in Switzerland).

Primel ['priːməl] *f* (*pl* -n) primrose.

primitiv [prɪmˈiːtɪf] *adj* primitive.

Prinz [prɪnts] *m* (*pl* **-en**) prince. **-essin** *f* (*pl* **-nen**) princess.

Prinzip [prɪnˈtsiːp] *f* (*pl* **-ien**) principle. **aus Prinzip** on principle. **im Prinzip** in principle, theoretically. **Prinzipal** *m* principal.

Priorität [prɪɔrɪˈtɛːt] *f* (*pl* **-en**) priority.

Prise [ˈpriːzə] *f* (*pl* **-n**) pinch.

Prisma [ˈprɪsma] *neut* (*pl* **Prismen**) prism.

privat [prɪˈvaːt] *adj* private. **Privat|| adresse** *f* home address. **–angelegenheit** *f* personal matter.

Privileg [prɪvɪˈleːk] *neut* (*pl* **-ien**) privilege. **privilegiert** *adj* privileged.

Probe [ˈproːbə] *f* (*pl* **-n**) (*Versuch*) test, trial; (*Theater*) rehearsal; (*Muster*) sample, specimen. **auf Probe** on approval. **auf die Probe stellen** put to the test. **Probe|| abzug** *m* (*Druck*) proof. **–zeit** *f* probationary period. **probieren** *v* (*versuchen*) try, attempt; (*Speise*) taste, sample.

Problem [proˈbleːm] *neut* (*pl* **-e**) problem. **problematisch** *adj* problematic.

Produkt [proˈdukt] *neut* (*pl* **-e**) product; (*Landwirtschaft*) produce. **–ion** *f* production. **produktiv** *adj* productive. **Produzent** *m* producer; (*Landwirtschaft*) grower. **produzieren** *v* produce.

Professor [proˈfɛsor] *m* (*pl* **-en**) professor. **professorisch** *adj* professorial. **Professur** *f* (*pl* **-en**) professorship.

Profil [proˈfiːl] *f* (*pl* **-e**) profile; (*Reifen*) tread. **profilieren** *v* outline, sketch.

Profit [proˈfiːt] *m* (*pl* **-e**) profit. **profit|| abel** *adj* profitable. **–ieren** *v* profit, gain. **Profitmacher** *m* profiteer.

Prognose [proˈgnoːzə] *f* (*pl* **-n**) (*Med*) prognosis; (*Wetter*) outlook, forecast.

Programm [proˈgram] *neut* (*pl* **-e**) programme; (*comp*) program. **programmgemäß** *adj* according to plan. **programmieren** *v* (*Computer*) program. **Programm|| geber** *m* (*pl* **-**), **–geberin** *f* (*pl* **-nen**) (computer) programmer. **–ierung** *f* programming.

Projekt [proˈjɛkt] *neut* (*pl* **-e**) (*Plan*) plan; (*Entwurf*) scheme. **projektieren** *v* plan; scheme. **Projektionsapparat** *m* projector.

projizieren [projɪˈtsiːrən] *v* project.

proklamieren [proklaˈmiːrən] *v* proclaim.

Proletariat [proletaˈriaːt] *neut* (*pl* **-e**) proletariat. **Proletarier** *m* proletarian. **pro-** **letarisch** *adj* proletarian.

Proll [ˈprɔl] *m* (*pl* **-s**) (*derog*) chav, scally, oik.

Prolog [proˈloːk] *m* (*pl* **-e**) prologue.

Promenade [proməˈnaːdə] *f* (*pl* **-n**) promenade.

Promotion [promoˈtsioːn] *f* (*pl* **-en**) (awarding of a) doctorate; (*Komm*) (sales) promotion. **promovieren** *v* be awarded a doctorate.

prompt [prɔmpt] *adj* prompt.

Propaganda [propaˈganda] *f* propaganda. **Propagandist** *m* (*pl* **-en**) propagandist.

Propeller [proˈpɛlər] *m* (*pl* **-**) propeller.

Prophet [proˈfeːt] *m* (*pl* **-en**) prophet. **-ie** *f* prophecy. **prophe||tisch** *adj* prophetic. **–zeien** *v* prophesy. **Prophezeiung** *f* (*pl* **-en**) prophecy.

Proportion [proporˈtsioːn] *f* (*pl* **-en**) proportion. **proportional** *adj* proportional.

Prosa [ˈproːza] *f* prose.

prosit [ˈproːzɪt] *interj* cheers! your health! **prosit Neujahr!** a Happy New Year!

Prospekt [proˈspɛkt] *m* (*pl* **-e**) prospectus, leaflet; (*Ansicht*) prospect.

prostituieren [prostɪtuˈiːrən] *v* prostitute. **Prostituierte** *f* (*pl* **-n**) prostitute. **Prostitution** *f* prostitution.

Protest [proˈtɛst] *m* (*pl* **-e**) protest.

Protestant [protɛsˈtant] *m* (*pl* **-en**) Protestant. **protest||antisch** *adj* protestant. **–ieren** *v* protest.

Prothese [proˈteːzə] *f* (*pl* **-n**) prosthesis; (*Arm-, Bein-*) artificial limb; (*Zahn-*) denture.

Protokoll [protoˈkɔl] *neut* (*pl* **-e**) (*Jur*) record; (*einer Versammlung*) minutes *pl*; (*Diplomatie*) protocol.

Protz [prɔts] *m* (*pl* **-en**) snob. **protzen** *v* put on airs, swagger. **–haft** *adj* snobbish.

Proviant [proˈviant] *m* provisions *pl*, victuals *pl*.

Provinz [proˈvɪnts] *f* (*pl* **-en**) province. **provinzial** *adj* provincial, regional. **provinziell** *adj* provincial, narrow-minded.

Provision [proˈviːzioːn] *f* (*pl* **-en**) (*Komm*) commission.

provisorisch [proviˈzoːrɪʃ] *adj* provisional.

provozieren [provoˈtsiːrən] *v* provoke.

Prozedur [protseˈduːr] *f* (*pl* **-en**) procedure.

Prozent [proˈtsɛnt] *neut* (*pl* **-e**) percent. **–satz** *m* percentage.

Prozeß [prɔ'tsɛs] *m* (*pl* **Prozesse**) (*Jur*) lawsuit, trial; (*Vorgang*) process.

Prozession [prɔtsɛsio:n] *f* (*pl* -**en**) procession.

prüde ['pry:də] *adj* prudish.

prüfen ['pry:fən] *v* (*Kenntnisse*) examine, test; (*erproben*) try, test; (*untersuchen*) inspect, check. **Prüf‖ling** *m* (*pl* -**e**) (examination) candidate. -**stein** *m* touchstone. -**ung** *f* (*pl* -**en**) examination, test.

Prügel ['pry:gəl] *m* (*pl* -) cudgel, club; *pl* beating. **prügeln** *v* beat, thrash. **Prügelstrafe** *f* corporal punishment.

Prunk [prʊŋk] *m* pomp, show, splendour. **prunken** *v* show off. **Prunkstück** *neut* showpiece. **prunk‖süchtig** *adj* ostentatious. -**voll** *adj* magnificent, gorgeous.

Psalm [psalm] *m* (*pl* -**en**) psalm.

Pseudonym [psɔydo'ny:m] *neut* (*pl* -**e**) pseudonym.

Psychiater [psykia:tər] *m* (*pl* -) psychiatrist. **Psychiatrie** *f* psychiatry. **psychiatrisch** *adj* psychiatric. **psychisch** *adj* psychic.

Psycho‖analyse [psyçoanaˈly:zə] *f* psychoanalysis. -**loge** *m* (*pl* -**n**) psychologist. **psychologisch** *adj* psychological.

Psycho‖path *m* (*pl* -**en**) psychopath. -**therapeut** *m* (*pl* -**en**) psychotherapist. -**therapie** *f* psychotherapy.

Pubertät [pubɛrtɛ:t] *f* puberty.

Publikum ['pu:blikum] *neut* public; (*Zuhörer*) audience.

publizieren [publiˈtsi:rən] *v* publish. **Publizist** *m* journalist.

Pudding ['pudiŋ] *m* (*pl* -**s**) pudding.

Pudel ['pu:dəl] *m* (*pl* -) poodle.

Puder ['pu:dər] *m* (*pl* -) powder.

Puff[1] [puf] 1 *m* (*pl* **Püffe**) push, thump. 2 *m* (*pl* -**e**) pouffe.

Puff[2] *neut* (*Spiel*) backgammon.

puffen ['pufən] *v* shove, thump; (*knallen*) pop. **Puffer** *m* buffer; (*Kartoffel*-) pancake, fritter. **Puff‖mais** *m* popcorn. -**spiel** *neut* backgammon.

Pulli ['puli] *m* (*pl* -**s**) pullover. **Pullover** *m* (*pl* -) pullover.

Puls [puls] *m* (*pl* -) pulse. **pulsieren** *v* pulsate, throb. **Puls‖schlag** *m* pulse; -**zahl** *f* pulse rate.

Pult [pult] *neut* (*pl* -**e**) desk. -**dach** *neut* lean- to roof.

Pulver ['pulvər] *neut* (*pl* -) powder. **pul-**ver‖artig *adj* powdery. -**isieren** *v* pulverize.

Pumpe ['pumpə] *f* (*pl* -**n**) pump. **pumpen** *v* pump.

Pumpernickel ['pumpərnikəl] *m* black (rye) bread.

Punk [puŋk] *m* (*pl* -**s**) (*mus*) punk.

Punkt [puŋkt] *m* (*pl* -**e**) point; (*Ort*) place, spot; (*Gramm*) full stop. **punktieren** *v* punctuate; (*Med*) puncture; (*tüpfeln*) dot. **punktiert** *adj* dotted.

pünktlich ['pyŋktliç] *adj* punctual, on time. **Pünktlichkeit** *f* punctuality.

Pupille [pu'pilə] *f* (*pl* -**n**) (*Anat*) pupil.

Puppe ['pupə] *f* (*pl* -**n**) doll; (*Theater*) puppet; (*Insekten*) pupa, chrysalis. **Puppen‖haus** *neut* doll's house. -**theater** *neut* puppet show.

pur [pu:r] *adj* pure, unadulterated; (*Getränk*) neat.

Puritaner [puri'ta:nər] *m* (*pl* -) Puritan. **puritanisch** *adj* puritan.

Purpur ['purpur] *m* purple. **purpurn** *adj* purple.

Purzelbaum *m* somersault. **purzeln** *v* (*Kind*) stumble and fall.

Pustel ['pustəl] *f* (*pl* -**n**) pustule.

Pute ['pu:tə] *f* (*pl* -**n**) turkey(hen). **Puter** *m* (*pl* -) turkey (cock).

Putsch [putʃ] *m* (*pl* -**e**) putsch, uprising. **putschen** *v* revolt, rise.

Putz ['puts] *m* (*pl* -**e**) (*Kleidung*) finery, fine dress; (*Zierat*) ornaments *pl*, trimmings *pl*; (*Bewurf*) plaster. **putzen** *v* clean; (*Schuhe*) polish. **sich putzen** dress up. **sich die Nase putzen** wipe one's nose. **Putzer** *m* (*pl* -), **Putzerin** *f* (*pl* -**nen**) cleaner. **Putz‖frau** *f* charwoman, cleaner. -**tuch** *f* polishing cloth.

Pyjama [piˈdʒa:ma] *m* (*pl* -**s**) pyjamas *pl*.

Pyramide [pyraˈmi:də] *f* (*pl* -**n**) pyramid.

Q

quabbelig ['kvabəliç] *adj* flabby, wobbly. **quabbeln** *v* wobble, quiver.

Quacksalber ['kvakzalbər] *m* (*pl* -) quack, charlatan.

Quadrat [kva'dʀaːt] *neut* (*pl* -e) square.
–meter *neut* square metre. **–wurzel** *f*
square root. **–zahl** *f* (*Math*) square. **qua-
drieren** *v* (*Math*) square.

quäken ['kvɛːkən] *v* squeak.

Qual [kvaːl] *f* (*pl* -en) torment, pain.

quälen ['kvɛːlən] *v* torment; (*foltern*) torture. **sich quälen** toil. **quälerisch** *adj* tor-
menting.

Qualifikation [kvaliḟɪkatsioːn] *f* (*pl* -en)
qualification; (*Fähigkeit*) ability, fitness.
qualifizieren *v* qualify. **sich qualifizieren** be fit (for).

Qualität [kvalitɛːt] *f* (*pl* -en) quality.

Qualle ['kvalə] *f* (*pl* -n) jellyfish.

Qualm [kvalm] *m* dense smoke; (*Wasser*)
vapour, steam. **qualmen** *v* smoke; (*Wasser*)
steam.

qualvoll ['kvaːlḟɔl] *adj* painful; agonizing.

Quantität [kvantɪtɛːt] *f* (*pl* -en) quantity.

Quarantäne [kvaran'tɛːnə] *f* (*pl* -n) quarantine.

Quark [kvaʀk] *m* curds *pl*, curd cheese; (*fig*)
tripe, rubbish. **–käse** *m* curd cheese.

Quartal [kvaʀ'taːl] *neut* (*pl* -e) quarter (of a
year).

Quartett [kvaʀˈtɛt] *neut* (*pl* -e) quartet.

Quartier [kvaʀˈtiːr] *neut* (*pl* -e) accommodation; (*Mil*) quarters *pl*; (*Stadt*) quarter, district.

Quarz [kvaʀts] *m* (*pl* -e) quartz.

quasi ['kvaːzi] *adv* as it were, in a way.

Quatsch [kvatʃ] *m* (*umg.*) rubbish, nonsense. **quatschen** *v* babble, talk nonsense.

Quecksilber ['kvɛkzilbər] *neut* quicksilver,
mercury.

Quelle ['kvɛlə] *f* (*pl* -n) (*Wasser*) spring;
(*Herkunft*) source, origin; (*Öl*) well. **aus
guter Quelle** on good authority. **quellen** *v*
spring, gush; arise.

quer [kveːr] *adj* cross, transverse; (*seitlich*)
lateral. *adv* across, crosswise. **kreuz und
quer** hither and thither. **Quer‖balken** *m*
crossbeam. **–baum** *m* crossbar. **querdurch**
adv (right) across.

quetschen ['kvɛtʃən] *v* squeeze, squash.
Quetschung *f* (*pl* -en) bruise.

quietschen ['kviːtʃən] *v* (*Person, Bremsen*)
squeal; (*Tür*) squeak.

Quintett [kvin'tɛt] *neut* (*pl* -e) quintet.

Quirl [kviʀl] *m* (*pl* -e) whisk, beater. **quirlen**
v whisk, beat.

quitt [kvɪt] *adj* quits, even.

Quitte [kvɪtə] *f* (*pl* -n) quince.

quittieren [kvɪtiːən] *v* (*aufgeben*) abandon;
(*Rechnung*) give a receipt for. **Quittung** *f* (*pl*
-en) receipt.

R

Rabatt [ʀa'bat] *m* (*pl* -e) discount, rebate.

Rabbiner [ʀa'biːnər] *m* (*pl* -) rabbi.

Rabe ['ʀaːbə] *m* (*pl* -n) raven. **rabenschwarz** *adj* jet-black.

rabiat [ʀabi'aːt] *adj* furious, raging.

Rache ['ʀaxə] *f* revenge, vengeance. **Rache
nehmen an** revenge oneself on.

Rachen ['ʀaxən] *m* (*pl* -) throat; (*Maul*) jaws
pl, mouth.

rächen ['ʀɛçən] *v* avenge. **sich rächen an**
take revenge on.

Rad [ʀaːt] *neut* (*pl* Räder) wheel.

Radar ['ʀaːdaʀ] *neut or m* radar.

Rädchen ['ʀɛːtçən] *neut* (*pl* -) caster.

Rädelsführer ['ʀɛːdəlsfyːrər] *m* ringleader.

*radfahren ['ʀaːtfaːrən] *v* cycle. **Radfahrer**
m (*pl* -), **Radfahrerin** *f* (*pl* -nen) cyclist.

radieren [ʀa'diːrən] *v* erase, rub out;
(*Kupfer*) etch. **Radiergummi** *m* rubber,
eraser.

Radieschen [ʀa'diːsçən] *neut* (*pl* -) radish.

radikal [ʀadiˈkaːl] *adj* radical. **Raki-
kal‖le(r)** radical. **–ismus** *m* radicalism.

Radio ['ʀaːdio] *neut* (*pl* -s) radio. **radioaktiv** *adj* radioactive. **Radioaktivität** *f*
radioactivity.

Radium ['ʀaːdium] *neut* radium. **–therapie**
f radiotherapy.

raffen ['ʀafən] *v* snatch (up); (*Stoff*) gather;
(*langes Kleid*) take up.

raffinier‖en [ʀafiˈniːrən] *v* refine. **-t** *adj*
refined; (*fig*) clever, crafty.

ragen ['ʀaːgən] *v* project, tower up.

Rahm [ʀaːm] *m* cream.

rahmen ['ʀaːmən] *v* frame. **Rahmen** *m*
(*pl* -) frame; (*fig*) framework, limit;
(*Umgebung*) surroundings *pl*, setting. **im
Rahmen von** in the context of.

Rakete [ʀaˈkeːtə] *f* (*pl* -n) rocket.

Rakett [ra'kɛt] *neut* (*pl* -s) (*Sport*) racket.

Ramme ['ram ə] *f* (*pl* -n) pile-driver.

Rampe ['ram pə] *f* (*pl* -n) ramp; (*Bühne*) apron. **–nlicht** *neut* footlight.

'ran [ran] *V* **heran**.

Rand [rant] *m* (*pl* **Ränder**) edge; (*Seite*) margin; (*Gefäß, Hut*) brim; (*Grenze*) border, boundary. **–bemerkung** *f* marginal note.

Rang [raŋ] *m* (*pl* **Ränge**) rank, class; (*Theater*) circle.

rangieren [rã'ʒiːrən] *v* rank; (*Eisenbahnwagen*) shunt.

Ranke ['raŋkə] *f* (*pl* -n) tendril, shoot.

Ränke ['rɛŋkə] *pl* intrigues *pl*, machinations *pl*.

Ranzen ['rantsən] *m* (*pl* -) knapsack; (*Schule*) satchel.

ranzig ['rantsiç] *adj* rancid.

rar [raːr] *adj* rare, scarce. **Rarität** *f* (*pl* -en) rarity.

rasch [raʃ] *adj* rapid, swift.

rascheln ['raʃəln] *v* rustle.

Raschheit ['raʃhait] *f* swiftness.

rasen ['raːzən] *v* rage, storm; (*eilen*) race.

Rasen ['raːzən] *m* (*pl* -) lawn, grass.

rasend ['raːzənt] *adj* furious, raving. **rasend werden** go mad, (*umg.*) blow one's top.

rasieren [ra'ziːrən] *v* shave. **Rasierapparat** *f* safety razor. **elektrischer Rasierapparat** electric razor. **sich rasieren** shave (oneself). **Rasier||klinge** *f* razor blade. **–krem** *f* shaving cream. **–messer** *neut* razor. **–pinsel** *m* shaving brush. **–wasser** *neut* aftershave.

Raspel ['raspəl] *f* (*pl* -n) rasp; (*Küche*) grater.

Rasse ['rasə] *f* (*pl* -n) race; (*Tiere*) breed. **Rassehund** *m* pedigree dog.

Rassel ['rasə] *f* (*pl* -n) rattle. **rasseln** *v* rattle, clatter.

Rassen||diskriminierung *f* racial discrimination. **–haß** *m* racial hatred. **–integration** *f* racial integration. **–kreuzung** *f* cross-breeding. **–trennung** *f* racial segregation.

rassig ['rasiç] *adj* purebred; (*schwungvoll*) racy.

rassisch ['rasiʃ] *adj* racial. **Rassismus** *m* racialism, (*US*) racism. **rassistisch** *adj* racialist, (*US*) racist.

Rast [rast] *f* (*pl* -en) rest; (*Pause*) halt, break. **rasten** *v* rest. **rastlos** *adj* restless; (*uner-*

müdlich) unwearying. **Raststätte** *f* (motorway) service area.

Rasur [razuːr] *f* (*pl* -en) (*Radieren*) erasure; (*Rasieren*) shave.

Rat [raːt] **1** *m* (*unz.*) advice. **2** (*pl* **Räte**) (*Versammlung*) council; (*Beamter*) councillor. **um Rat fragen** ask for advice. **sich Rat holen bei** consult. **Rat wissen** know what has to be done.

Rate ['raːtə] *f* (*pl* -n) instalment, payment.

*raten ['raːtən] *v* advise; (*mutmaßen*) guess.

Ratenkauf ['raːtənkauf] *m* hire purchase. **ratenweise** *adv* by instalments.

Rat||geber(in) adviser, counsellor. **–haus** *neut* town hall.

ratifizieren [ratifitstrən] *v* ratify. **Ratifizierung** *f* ratification.

Ration [ra'tsioːn] *f* (*pl* -en) ration.

rationalisieren [ratsionalizrən] *v* rationalize. **Rationalisierung** *f* rationalization. **rationell** *adj* rational.

rationieren [ratsio'niːrən] *v* ration.

rat||los ['raːtloːs] *adj* helpless, perplexed. **–sam** *adj* advisable; (*nützlich*) useful; (*förderlich*) expedient. **Ratschlag** *m* (piece of) advice. **ratschlagen** *v* deliberate, consult together.

Rätsel ['rɛːtsəl] *neut* (*pl* -) puzzle, riddle; (*Geheimnis*) mystery. **rätselhaft** *adj* puzzling; mysterious.

Rats||herr ['raːtshɛːr] *m* (town) councillor. **–keller** *m* town-hall restaurant. **–versammlung** *f* council meeting.

Ratte ['ratə] *f* (*pl* -n) rat.

Raub [raup] *m* robbery; (*Beute*) loot. **–anfall** *m* (armed) raid. **rauben** *v* rob; (*Person*) abduct; (*plündern*) plunder.

Räuber ['rɔybər] *m* (*pl* -) robber.

raubgierig ['raupgiriç] *adj* rapacious. **Raub||tier** *m* beast of prey. **–vogel** *m* bird of prey.

Rauch [raux] *m* smoke. **–rauchen** *v* smoke. **Rauchen** *neut* smoking. **Raucher** *m* (*pl* -) smoker.

räuchern ['rɔyçərn] *v* cure, smoke.

Rauch||fang *m* chimney. **–fleisch** *neut* smoked meat. **rauch||frei** smokeless. **–ig** *adj* smokey.

'rauf [rauf] *V* **herauf**.

Raufbold ['raufbɔlt] *f* (*pl* -e) ruffian, rowdy. **raufen** *v* (*Haare*) tear out. **sich raufen mit** brawl with. **Rauferei** *f* (*pl* -en) fight, brawl.

rauflustig *adj* quarrelsome.

rauh [rau] *adj* rough; (*grob*) coarse; (*Klima*) inclement. **Rauheit** *f* roughness; coarseness; harshness.

Raum [raum] **1** *m* (*unz.*) room, space. **2** *m* (*pl* **Räume**) room; (*Gebiet*) area.

räumen ['rɔym ən] *v* evacuate, remove; (*Zimmer*) vacate.

Raum||fähre *f* space shuttle. **–fahrt** *f* space travel. **–inhalt** *m* volume, capacity.

räumlich ['rɔym lɪç] *adj* spatial, of space.

Raumschiff ['raum ʃɪf] *neut* space ship.

Räumung ['rɔym uŋ] *f* (*pl* **-en**) evacuation, removal; (*Gebiet*) cleaning.

Raupe [raupə] *f* (*pl* **-n**) caterpillar. **–nkette** *f* caterpillar track.

'raus [raus] *V* **heraus.**

Rausch [rauʃ] *m* (*pl* **Räusche**) intoxication.

rauschen ['rauʃən] *v* (*Blätter*) rustle; (*Bach*) babble, murmur.

Rauschgift ['rauʃgɪft] *neut* drug, narcotic. **–sucht** *f* drug addiction. **–süchtige(r)** (drug) addict.

Rautentaste ['rautəntastə] *f* (*Telefon*) (*pl* **-n**) hash key.

Reagenzglas [rea'gɛntsglaːs] *neut* test tube.

reagieren [rea'giːrən] *v* react.

Reaktion [reaktsioːn] *f* (*pl* **-en**) reaction. **reaktionär** *adj* reactionary.

real [re'aːl] *adj* real. **-isieren** *v* realize. **Real||ismus** *m* realism. **-ist** *m* (*pl* **-en**) realist. **realistisch** *adj* realistic.

Rebe ['reːbə] *f* (*pl* **-n**) vine.

Rebell [re'bɛl] *m* (*pl* **-en**) rebel. **rebellieren** *v* rebel. **Rebellion** *f* (*pl* **-en**) rebellion. **rebellisch** *adj* rebellious.

Rebhuhn ['rɛphuːn] *neut* partridge.

Rebstock ['rɛpʃtɔk] *m* vine.

rechen ['rɛçən] *v* rake. **Rechen** *m* (*pl* **-**) rake.

Rechen||fehler *m* miscalculation. **-kunst** *f* arithmetic. **-maschine** *f* calculating machine. **-schaft** *f* (*unz.*) account.

rechnen ['rɛçnən] *v* calculate. **rechnen auf** count on. **rechnen mit** reckon with. **Rechnen** *neut* arithmetic. **Rechner** *m* calculator. **Rechnung** *f* calculation; (*Waren*) invoice; (*Gaststätte*) bill. **Rechnungs|| abschluß** *m* balancing of accounts. **-führer** *m* accountant, bookkeeper. **-prüfer** *m* auditor. **-wesen** *neut* accountancy, accounting.

recht [rɛçt] *adj* right. *adv* (*sehr*) quite, very. *mir ist das recht* that suits me. **recht haben** be (in the) right. **ganz recht!** just so! **Recht** *neut* (*pl* **-e**) right; (*Gesetze*) law. **-e** *f* right (side), right-hand side; (*Pol*) the Right. **-eck** *neut* rectangle. **Rechtfertigung** *f* justification. **recht||fertigen** *v* justify. **-gläubig** *adj* orthodox. **Rechthaber** *m* (*pl* **-**) dogmatic person, (*umg.*) know-all. **recht||haberisch** *adj* dogmatic, obstinate. **-lich** *adj* legal, of law; (*ehrlich*) honest, just. **-mäßig** *adj* legal, lawful.

rechts [rɛçts] *adv* on *or* to(wards) the right.

Rechtsanwalt *m* lawyer.

Rechtschreibung *f* spelling.

Rechts||fall *m* law suit, case. **-gleichheit** *f* equality before the law. **-händer** *m* right-handed person, right-hander. **rechts|| händig** *adj* right-handed. **-kräftig** *adj* legally binding, legal.

Rechtsprechung *f* (*pl* **-en**) judicial decision, verdict; (*Gerichtsbarkeit*) jurisdiction.

rechtsradikal *adj* extreme right-wing **Rechts||radikale(r)** *m* right-wing radical. **-spruch** *m* (*Urteil*) verdict, judgment; (*Strafe*) sentence. **-steuerung** *f* right-hand drive. **-streit** *m* law suit. **rechtswidrig** *adj* illegal.

recht||winklig *adj* right-angled. **-zeitig** *adj* timely, opportune; *adv* in (good) time.

recken ['rɛkən] *v* stretch.

Redakt||eur [redak'tøːr] *m* (*pl* **-**) editor. **-ion** *f* editing; (*Arbeitskräfte*) editorial staff.

Rede ['reːdə] *f* (*pl* **-n**) speech, talk. **redefertig** *adj* fluent, eloquent. **Rede||freiheit** *f* freedom of speech. **-kunst** *f* rhetoric.

reden ['reːdən] *v* speak, talk. **offen reden** speak out. **mit sich reden lassen** be open to persuasion, listen to reason. **Reden** *neut* speech, talking. **-sart** *f* expression, idiom. **Redewendung** *f* turn of speech, idiom.

redigieren [redi'giːrən] *v* edit.

redlich ['reːdlɪç] *adj* honest, upright, just. **Redlichkeit** *f* honesty.

Redner ['reːdnər] *m* (*pl* **-**) speaker, orator.

reduzieren [redu'tsiːrən] *v* reduce, decrease. **sich reduzieren** diminish, be reduced.

Reeder ['reːdər] *m* (*pl* **-**) shipowner.

reell [re'ɛl] *adj* respectable, honest, reliable.

Referat [refe'raːt] *neut* (*pl* **-e**) lecture, talk; (*Gutachten*) report, review. **Referent** *m* lecturer, speaker; (*Fachmann*) expert adviser, reviewer.

reflektieren [ʀeflɛkˈtiːʀən] *v* reflect.

Reflex [ʀeˈflɛks] *m* (*pl* -e) reflex. **-bewegung** *f* reflex action.

Reform [ʀeˈfɔrm] *f* (*pl* -en) reform. **-ation** *f* reformation. **-er** *m* (*pl* -) reformer. **-haus** *neut* health-food shop. **reformieren** *v* reform.

Regal [ʀeˈgaːl] *neut* (*pl* -e) (book)shelf.

rege [ˈʀeːgə] *adj* active, lively.

Regel [ˈʀeːgəl] *f* (*pl* -n) rule. **regelllos** *adj* irregular (*unordentlich*) chaotic. **-mäßig** *adj* regular. **Regelmäßigkeit** *f* regularity. **regeln** *v* regulate, arrange. **Regelung** *f* regulation, arrangement. **regelwidrig** *adj* against the rule(s). **Regelwidrigkeit** *f* irregularity; (*Sport*) foul.

Regen [ˈʀeːgən] *m* rain. **-bogen** *m* rainbow. **-fall** *m* rainfall. **-mantel** *m* raincoat. **-tropfen** *m* raindrop. **-wetter** *neut* rainy weather. **-wurm** *m* earthworm. **-zeit** *f* rainy season, rains *pl*. **saurer Regen** acid rain.

Regie [ʀeˈʒiː] *f* (*pl* -n) (*Theater, Film*) direction; (*Verwaltung*) administration, management.

regieren [ʀeˈgiːʀən] *v* rule, govern. **Regierung** *f* government.

Regiment [ʀegiˈmɛnt] *neut* (*pl* -er) regiment.

Regisseur [ʀeʒiˈsøːʀ] *m* (*pl* -e) (theatre *or* film) director.

Register [ʀeˈgistər] *neut* (*pl* -) register; (*Buch*) index. **registrieren** *v* register. **Registrierkasse** *f* cash register.

Regler [ˈʀeːglər] *m* (*pl* -) regulator.

regnen [ˈʀeːgnən] *v* rain. **regnerisch** *adj* rainy.

regulieren [ʀeguˈliːʀən] *v* regulate.

Regung [ˈʀeːguŋ] *f* (*pl* -en) motion; (*Gefühle*) stirring, emotion; (*Antrieb*) impulse.

Reh [ʀeː] *neut* (*pl* -e) roe deer. **-bock** *m* roebuck. **rehfarben** *adj* fawn. **Rehllfleisch** *neut* venison. **-kalb** *neut* fawn. **-ziege** *f* doe.

*reiben [ˈʀaɪbən] *v* rub; (*Käse, usw.*) grate. **Reibung** *f* rubbing; (*fig, Tech*) friction; (*Käse*) grating.

reich [ʀaɪç] *adj* rich.

Reich [ʀaɪç] *neut* (*pl* -e) empire; (*fig*) realm;

(*Tier-, Pflanzen*) kingdom.

reichen [ˈʀaɪçən] *v* reach; (*überreichen*) pass, hand; (*anbieten*) offer; (*genügen*) be enough.

reichllhaltig *adj* copious; (*Programm*) full. **-lich** *adj* plentiful, ample.

Reichslladler *m* (German) imperial eagle. **-tag** *m* (German) Imperial Parliament (1871–1934).

Reichtum [ˈʀaɪçtuːm] *m* (*pl* **Reichtümer**) wealth, riches *pl*; (*Fülle*) abundance.

Reichweite [ˈʀaɪçvaɪtə] *f* range.

reif [ʀaɪf] *adj* (*Frucht*) ripe; (*Person*) mature.

Reif [ʀaɪf] *m* hoarfrost.

Reife [ˈʀaɪfə] *f* (*Frucht*) ripeness; (*Person*) maturity. **reifen** *v* mature.

Reifen [ˈʀaɪfən] *m* (*pl* -) ring, hoop; (*Mot*) tyre. **-druck** *m* tyre pressure.

Reihe [ˈʀaɪə] *f* (*pl* -n) row; (*Satz*) series, set. **ich bin an der Reihe** it is my turn. **eine ganze Reihe (von)** a lot (of), a whole series (of). **reihen** *v* line up, put in a row; (*Perlen*) string; (*Stoff*) gather; (*heften*) tack. **Reihenfolge** *f* order, sequence.

Reiher [ˈʀaɪər] *m* (*pl* -) heron.

Reim [ʀaɪm] *m* (*pl* -e) rhyme. **reimen** *v* rhyme. **sich reimen** make sense.

rein [ʀaɪn] *adj* pure; (*sauber*) clean; (*vollkommen*) perfect; (*Komm*) net. **ins Reine bringen** clear up, settle. **adv** completely. **die reine Wahrheit** the plain truth.

'rein [ʀaɪn] *V* herein.

Reinemachen [ˈʀaɪnəmaxən] *neut* cleaning. **Reinheit** *f* purity; cleanness, cleanliness. **reinigen** *v* clean; (*fig*) purify, cleanse. **Reinigung** *f* cleaning; purification. **chemische Reinigung** *f* dry cleaning. **reinllich** *adj* clean, neat, tidy. **-rassig** *adj* purebred; (*Pferd*) thoroughbred.

Reis [ʀaɪs] *m* rice.

Reise [ˈʀaɪzə] *f* (*pl* -n) trip, journey; (*See*) voyage. **-büro** *neut* travel agency. **-leiter(in)** courier. **reisen** *v* travel. **-d** *adj* itinerant, travelling. **Reisende(r)** traveller. **Reisellpaß** *m* passport. **-tasche** *f* travelling bag. **-scheck** *m* traveller's cheque.

Reißbrett [ˈʀaɪsbʀɛt] *neut* drawing board. **reißen** *v* tear, rip; (*zerren*) pull. **sich reißen um** fight for. **reißend** *adj* rapid; (*Schmerz*) sharp, shooting. **Reißllkohle** *f* charcoal. **-verschluß** *m* zip, zipper.

*reiten [ˈʀaɪtən] *v* ride. **Reitllen** *neut* riding. **-er** *m* rider, horseman. **-erin** *f* rider, horsewoman. **–kunst** f horsemanship, equitation.

Reiz [raits] m (pl -e) charm, attractiveness; (Erregung) stimulation. **reiz||bar** adj irritable. **–en** v excite, stimulate; (anziehen) attract, charm; (zornig machen) irritate. **–end** adj charming, enchanting.

Reklame [re'kla:mə] f (pl -n) advertising, publicity; (einzelne) advertisement. **–schwindel** m (umg.) hype. **Reklame machen für** promote, advertise.

Rekord [re'kort] m (pl -e) record.

Rekrut [re'kru:t] m (pl -en) recruit. **rekrutieren** v recruit.

Rektor ['rɛktor] m (pl -en) (Universität) vice-chancellor; (andere Schulen) principal, head.

relativ [rela'ti:f] adj relative. **Relativität** f relativity.

Relief [rə'ljɛf] neut (pl -s) (Kunst) relief.

Religion [religio:n] f (pl -en) religion. **–sbekenntnis** neut confession of faith. **religiös** adj religious.

Ren [rɛn] neut (pl -e) reindeer.

Rennbahn ['rɛnba:n] f racecourse. **rennen** v run; (Sport) race. **Renn||en** neut running; race. **–pferd** neut racehorse. **–wagen** m racing car.

renovieren [reno'vi:rən] v renovate.

rentabel [rɛn'ta:bəl] adj profitable. **Rentabilität** f profitability. **Rente** f (Alters-) pension; (Versicherung) annuity. **rentieren** v **sich rentieren** be profitable. **Rentner** m (pl -) **Rentnerin** f (pl -nen) pensioner.

Reparatur [repara'tu:r] f (pl -en) repair. **–werkstatt** f repair shop. **reparieren** v repair.

Report [re'port] m (pl -e) report. **–age** f (pl -n) (eye-witness) report. **–er** m (pl -) reporter.

Repressalien [repre'sa:lən] pl reprisals.

Reproduktion [reproduk'tsio:n] f (pl -en) reproduction. **reproduzieren** v reproduce.

Reptil [rep'ti:l] neut (pl -ien) reptile.

Republik [re'publik] f (pl -en) republic. **–aner** m (pl -) republican. **republikanisch** adj republican.

Reserve [re'zɛrvə] f (pl -n) reserve. **–rad** neut spare wheel. **reservier||en** v reserve, book. **–t** adj reserved.

Residenz [rezi'dɛnts] f (pl -en) residence.

Resonanz [rezo'nants] f (pl -en) resonance.

Respekt [re'spɛkt] m respect. **respekt||abel** adj respectable. **–ieren** v respect. **–los** adj disrespectful. **–voll** adj respectful.

Rest [rɛst] m (pl -e) remainder, rest.

Restaurant [resto'rã] neut (pl -s) restaurant.

Restbetrag m balance, remainder. **restlich** adj remaining.

Resultat [rezul'ta:t] neut (pl -e) result.

retablieren [reta'bli:rən] v re-establish.

Retorte [re'tortə] f (pl -n) retort.

retten ['rɛtən] v save. **Retter** m (pl -) rescuer; (Rel) Saviour. **Rettung** f (pl -en) rescue, deliverance. **Rettungs||assistent(in)** paramedic. **–boot** neut lifeboat. **–gürtel** m lifebelt.

Reue ['rɔyə] f remorse, regret. **reuen** v regret. es reut mich, daß ich es getan habe I regret doing that, I am sorry I did that.

Revanche [re'vã:ʃə] f (pl -n) revenge, vengeance. **sich revanchieren** v take one's revenge.

Revers[1] [re'vɛrs] m (pl -e) (Rückseite) reverse, back.

Revers[2] [re'vɛ:r] m or neut (pl -) (Jacke) lapel.

Revers[3] [re'vɛrs] m (pl -e) written undertaking, bond.

reversibel [revɛr'si:bəl] adj (Med, Chem) reversible.

revidieren [revi'di:rən] v revise.

Revier [re'vi:ər] neut (pl -e) district; (Polizei) beat; (Wache) station.

Revis||ion [revi'zio:n] f (pl -en) revision, (Jur) appeal; (Komm) auditing. **–or** m auditor.

Revolte [re'voltə] f (pl -n) revolt, insurrection.

Revolution [revolu'tsio:n] f (pl -en) revolution. **revolutionär** adj revolutionary. **Revolutionär** m (pl -e) revolutionary. **revolutionieren** v revolutionize.

Revolver [re'volvər] m (pl -) revolver.

rezensieren [retsɛn'zi:rən] v review.

Rezept [re'tsɛpt] neut (pl -e) recipe; (Med) prescription.

Rhabarber [ra'barbər] m rhubarb.

Rhapsodie [rapso'di:] f (pl -n) rhapsody.

Rhein [rain] m Rhine. **–hessen** neut Rhenish Hesse. **rheinisch** adj Rhine, Rhenish. **Rheinland** neut Rhineland. **–Pfalz** f Rhineland-Palatinate. **Rheinwein** m hock, Rhine wine.

rhetorisch [re'toːɾɪʃ] *adj* rhetorical.

Rheumatismus [ɾɔymaˈtɪzm ʊs] *m* (*pl* **Rheumatismen**) rheumatism.

Rhinozeros [ɾɪnoːtsɛɾɔs] *neut* (*pl* -**se**) rhinoceros.

rhythmisch [ˈɾytmɪʃ] *adj* rhythmic(al). **Rhythmus** *m* (*pl* **Rhythmen**) rhythm.

richten [ˈɾɪçtən] *v* (*zurechtmachen*) arrange, prepare; (*einstellen*) adjust, set; (*reparieren*) repair; (*Frage, Brief*) address; (*Gewehr*) aim; (*Jur*) judge. **sich richten an** address oneself to. **sich richten nach** follow. **Richter** *m* (*pl* -) judge.

richtig [ˈɾɪçtɪç] *adj* correct, right. *ein richtiger Berliner* a real Berliner. **Richtigkeit** *f* correctness, rightness. **richtigstellen** *v* correct, set right.

Richt||linie *f* guideline. –**preis** *m* recommended price.

Richtung [ˈɾɪçtʊŋ] *f* (*pl* -**en**) direction; (*Neigung*) trend, tendency.

Richtweg [ˈɾɪçtveːk] *m* short cut.

Ricke [ˈɾɪkə] *f* (*pl* -**n**) doe (deer).

*****riechen** [ˈɾɪçən] *v* smell. **riechen nach** smell of. **gut/übel riechen** smell good/bad.

Riegel [ˈɾiːɡəl] *m* (*pl* -) bolt, bar; (*Seife, Schokolade*) bar. **riegeln** *v* bolt, bar.

Riemen [ˈɾiːm ən] *m* (*pl* -) strap, belt; (*Gürtel*) belt.

Riese [ˈɾiːzə] *m* (*pl* -**n**) giant. **Riesen-** *adj* colossal, huge. **Riesenerfolg haben** be a great success, (*umg.*) be a smash hit. **riesengroß** *or* **riesig** *adj* gigantic, huge. **Riesin** *f* (*pl* -**nen**) giantess.

Riff [ɾɪf] *neut* (*pl* -**e**) reef.

Rille [ˈɾɪlə] *f* (*pl* -**n**) groove; (*Furche*) furrow.

Rind [ɾɪnt] *neut* (*pl* -**er**) (*Ochse*) ox; (*Kuh*) cow.

Rinde [ˈɾɪndə] *f* (*pl* -**n**) (*Baum*) bark; (*Käse*) rind; (*Brot*) crust.

Rind||erbraten *m* roast beef. –**fleisch** *neut* beef. –**vieh** *neut* cattle.

Ring [ɾɪŋ] *m* (*pl* -**e**) ring; (*Straße*) ring road; (*Komm*) combine, cartel; (*Kettenglied*) link. –**elchen** *neut* (*pl* -) ringlet.

*****ringen** [ˈɾɪŋən] *v* wrestle; (*Hände*) wring. **ringen um** struggle for. **Ringen** *neut* struggle, battle.

Ringfinger *m* ring finger. **ringförmig** *adj* ring-shaped.

Ringkampf *m* wrestling (match).

rings [ɾɪŋs] *adv* around. –**herum** *adv* all around.

Ringstraße *f* ring road.

Rinne [ˈɾɪnə] *f* (*pl* -**n**) channel, groove; (*Dach-*) gutter.

Rippchen [ˈɾɪpçən] *neut* (*pl* -) cutlet, chop. **Rippe** *f* (*pl* -**n**) rib.

Risiko [ˈɾiːziko] *neut* (*pl* -**s** *or* **Risiken**) risk. **risk||ant** *adj* risky. –**ieren** *v* risk.

Riß [ɾɪs] *m* (*pl* **Risse**) (*Stoff, Haut*) tear; (*Mauer*) crack; (*fig*) breach, rift; (*Zeichnung*) technical drawing, plan.

rissig [ˈɾɪsɪç] *adj* cracked; (*Haut*) chapped.

Ritt [ɾɪt] *m* (*pl* -**e**) ride.

Ritter [ˈɾɪtəɾ] *m* (*pl* -) knight. **ritterlich** *adj* chivalrous. **Ritterlichkeit** *f* chivalry.

rittlings [ˈɾɪtlɪŋs] *adv* astride.

rituell [ɾɪtuˈɛl] *adj* ritual. **Ritus** *m* (*pl* **Riten**) rite.

Ritz [ɾɪts] *m* (*pl* -**e**) *or* **Ritze** *f* (*pl* -**n**) crack; (*Schramme*) scratch.

Robbe [ˈɾɔbə] *f* (*pl* -**n**) seal.

Roboter [ˈɾɔbɔtəɾ] *m* (*pl* -) robot.

Rock [ɾɔk] *m* (*pl* **Röcke**) (*Frauen*) skirt; (*Obergewand*) cloak; (*Jacke*) jacket, coat.

Rodel [ˈɾoːdəl] *m* (*pl* -) toboggan. **rodeln** *v* toboggan.

roden [ˈɾoːdən] *v* clear (land). **Rodung** *f* (*pl* -**en**) cleared land.

Rogen [ˈɾoːɡən] *m* (*pl* -) (fish) roe.

Roggen [ˈɾɔɡən] *m* rye. –**brot** *neut* rye bread.

roh [ɾoː] *adj* raw; (*grausam*) cruel, brutal; (*Stein, Person*) rough. **rohe Gewalt** brute force. **Roheit** *f* rawness; brutality; roughness. **Roh||gewicht** *neut* gross weight. –**öl** *neut* crude oil.

Rohr [ɾoːɾ] *neut* (*pl* -**e**) tube, pipe; (*Gewehr*) barrel; (*Bot*) seed.

Röhre [ˈɾøː ːɾə] *f* (*pl* -**n**) tube, pipe; (*Radio*) valve; (*Leitung*) conduit, duct.

Rohr||leitung *f* pipeline. –**leitungen** *pl* pipes, plumbing *sing*. –**stock** *m* cane, bamboo. –**stuhl** *m* cane chair. –**zucker** *m* cane sugar.

Rohstoff *m* raw material.

Rolladen [ˈɾɔlaːdən] *m* (*pl* -*or* **Rolläden**) rolling shutter.

Rollbahn *f* runway.

Rolle [ˈɾɔlə] *f* (*pl* -**n**) roll; (*Theater, Film*) role; (*Tech*) pulley. **eine Rolle spielen** play a part. **keine Rolle spielen** make no difference, not matter.

rollen ['rɔlən] v roll; (*Flugzeug*) taxi.

Roll||mops m pickled herring. **-schuh** m roller skate. **-schuhlaufen** neut rollerskating. **-stuhl** m wheelchair. **-treppe** f escalator. **-tür** f sliding door.

Rom [roːm] neut Rome.

Roman [ro'mɑːn] m (pl -e) novel.

Romantik [ro'mantik] f Romanticism. **-er** m (pl -) romantic. **romantisch** adj romantic.

Römer ['rœːmər] m (pl -) Roman. **römisch** adj Roman. **römisch-katholisch** adj Roman Catholic.

röntgen [rœntɡən] v x-ray. **Röntgen||behandlung** f radiation therapy. **-bild** neut x-ray (photograph). **-strahlen** pl x-rays.

rosa ['roːza] adj pink, rose.

Rose ['roːzə] f (pl -n) rose. **Rosen||busch** m rose bush. **-kohl** m Brussels sprouts pl. **-kranz** m rose garland; (*Rel*) rosary.

Rosine [ro'ziːnə] f (pl -n) raisin.

Rosmarin [rɔsma'riːn] m rosemary.

Roß [rɔs] neut (pl Rosse) steed, horse. **-kastanie** f horse chestnut.

Rost¹ [rɔst] m (pl -e) grate; (*Kochen*) grill.

Rost² m rust.

rost||beständig adj rustproof. **-braun** adj rust(-brown).

Röstbrot ['rœːstbroːt] neut toast.

rosten ['rɔstən] v rust.

rösten ['rœːstən] v roast; (*Brot*) toast.

rot [roːt] adj red. **Rot** neut red.

Röte ['rœːtə] f red(ness).

Röteln ['rœːtəln] pl German measles, rubella.

rot||glühend adj red-hot. **-haarig** adj redhaired. **Rot||käppchen** neut Little Red Riding Hood. **-kehlchen** neut robin.

rötlich ['rœːtliç] adj reddish.

Rotte ['rɔtə] f (pl -n) gang, band; (*Tiere*) pack. **sich rotten** v band together, gang up.

Roulade [ruˈlɑːdə] f (pl -n) rolled meat; (*Musik*) trill.

Rowdy ['raudi] m (pl -s) hooligan, thug; (*umg*) yob.

Rübe ['ryːbə] f (pl -n) (*Bot*) rape. **weiße/gelbe/rote Rübe** turnip/carrot/beetroot.

Rubin [ru'biːn] m (pl -e) ruby.

Rubrik ['ruːbrik] f (pl -en) (*Titel*) title, heading; (*Spalte*) column; (*fig*) category.

ruchbar ['ruːxbaːr] adj notorious.

Ruck [ruk] m (pl -e) jolt, jerk, start.

Rück||ansicht f rear view. **-blende** f flashback. **-blick** m glance back; (*fig*) retrospect.

rücken ['rykən] v move, shift; (*Platz machen*) move up, shift up.

Rücken ['rykən] m (pl -) back. **-lehne** f back (of a chair). **-mark** neut spinal cord. **-schmerzen** pl backache sing. **-schwimmen** neut backstroke.

Rück||erstattung f return; (*Geld*) repayment. **-fahrkarte** f return ticket. **-fahrt** f return journey. **-gabe** f return, restoration. **-gang** m decline, retrogression. **rückgängig** adj retrograde. **rückgängig machen** cancel, annul. **Rück||grat** neut backbone. **-griff** m recourse. **-halt** m support. **-handschlag** m (*Tennis*) backhand (stroke). **-kehr** f return. **-licht** neut rear light.

Rucksack ['rukzak] m rucksack, pack.

Rück||schlag m set-back, reverse. **-schritt** m retrogression, relapse. **-seite** f reverse (side), back.

Rücksicht f consideration, regard. **Rücksicht nehmen auf** take into consideration; (*Person*) show consideration to **mit Rücksicht auf** with respect to. **Rücksichtnahme** f consideration, regard. **rücksichtslos** adj inconsiderate, (*hart*) ruthless. **Rücksichtslosigkeit** f lack of consideration; ruthlessness.

Rück||sitz m back seat. **-spiegel** m rearview mirror. **-spiel** neut return match.

Rückstand m rest, remainder. **im Rückstand** in arrears. **rückständig** adj in arrears; (*altmodisch*) old-fashioned, backward.

Rücktritt m resignation; (*in den Ruhestand*) retirement.

rückwärts adv back(wards). **-gehen** v decline, retrogress.

Rück||wirkung f reaction, repercussion. **-zug** m retreat. **-zahlung** f repayment, reimbursement.

Rudel ['ruːdəl] neut (pl -) (*Schar*) troop; (*Hunde*) pack; (*Rehe, Schafe*) herd.

Ruder ['ruːdər] neut (pl -) oar; (*Steuer*) rudder. **-boot** neut rowing boat. **rudern** v row. **Rudersport** m rowing.

Ruf [ruːf] *m* (*pl* -e) call, shout; (*Tier*) cry; (*Vogel*) call; (*Ruhm*) reputation, good name; (*Aufforderung*) summons. **rufen** *v* call, shout, cry. **Rufnummer** *f* telephone number.

Rüge ['ryːgə] *f* (*pl* -n) rebuke, reprimand. **rügen** *v* rebuke, reprimand.

Ruhe ['ruːə] *f* quiet, stillness; (*Erholung*) rest; (*Gefaßtsein*) composure, calm. **in Ruhe lassen** leave alone. **zur Ruhe gehen** go to bed. **ruhelos** *adj* restless. **Ruhelosigheit** *f* restlessness. **ruhen** *v* rest; (*schlafen*) sleep; (*begründet sein*) be based. **-d** *adj* resting; (*Tech*) latent.

Ruhe||pause *f* break, rest period. **-platz** *m* resting place. **-stand** *m* retirement. **-stätte** *f* resting place. **-störung** *f* breach of the peace. **-tag** *m* day of rest.

ruhig ['ruːiç] *adj* still, quiet; (*gefaßt*) calm, composed.

Ruhm [ruːm] *m* fame, glory.

rühmen ['ryːmən] *v* praise. **sich rühmen** boast. **rühmlich** *adj* glorious.

Ruhr [ruːr] *f* dysentery.

Rührei ['ryːrai] *neut* scrambled egg(s). **rühren** *v* (*bewegen*) move; (*vermischen*) stir; (*innerlich*) move, affect. **sich rühren** stir, move. **rühr||end** *adj* (*fig*) touching, moving. **-selig** *adj* sentimental. **Rührung** *f* (*unz.*) feeling, emotion.

Ruine [ru'iːnə] *f* (*pl* -n) ruin. **ruinieren** *v* ruin.

Rülps [rybs] *m* (*pl* -e) belch, burp. **rülpsen** *v* belch.

Rum [rum] *m* (*pl* -s) rum.

Rumäne [ru'm ɛːnə] *m* (*pl* -n) Rumanian. **Rumänien** *n* Rumania. **Rumänin** *f* (*pl* -nen) Rumanian (woman). **rumänisch** *adj* Rumanian.

Rummel ['rum əl] *m* (*unz.*) (*umg.*) bustle, activity; (*Lärm*) hubbub, racket. **-platz** *m* fairground.

Rumpf [rum pf] *m* (*pl* **Rümpfe**) trunk, torso; (*Tier*) carcass; (*Schiff*) hull; (*Flugzeug*) fuselage.

rümpfen [rym pfən] *v* turn up (one's nose).

rund [runt] *adj* round. *adv* about. **Rundblick** *m* panorama. **Runde** *f* (*pl* -n) circle; (*Boxen*) round; (*Rennen*) lap; (*Sport*) heat; (*Polizist*) beat. **runden** *v* round (off).

Rund||fahrt *f* (circular) tour. **-frage** *f* questionnaire. **-funk** *m* radio; (*Übertragung*) broadcasting. **-funksendung**

f radio programme. **-gang** *m* tour (of inspection); (*Spaziergang*) stroll. **-heit** *f* roundness.

rund||heraus *adv* frankly, flatly. **-lich** *adj* rotund, plump.

Rund||schau *f* panorama; (*Zeitschrift*) review. **-schreiben** *neut* circular. **-ung** *f* curve.

'runter ['runtər] *V* **herunter**.

Runzel ['runtsəl] *f* (*pl* -n) wrinkle. **runzelig** *adj* wrinkled. **runzeln** *v* wrinkle. **die Stirn runzeln** frown.

rupfen ['rupfən] *v* pluck.

Ruß [ruːs] *m* soot.

Russe ['ruːsə] *m* (*pl* -n) Russian.

rußig ['ruːsiç] *adj* sooty.

Russin ['rusin] *f* (*pl* -nen) Russian (woman). **russisch** *adj* Russian.

Rußland ['ruslant] *neut* Russia.

rüsten ['rystən] *v* prepare; (*Mil*) arm, prepare for war. **sich rüsten (auf)** get ready (for). **Rüstung** *f* armament; (*Kriegsvorbereitung*) arming; **Rüstungs||fabrik** *f* armaments factory. **-wettbewerb** *m* arms race.

Rute ['ruːtə] *f* (*pl* -n) rod; (*Gerte*) switch; (*Anat*) penis.

Rutsch [rutʃ] *m* (*pl* -e) slide; (*Erde*) landslip. **rutsch||en** *v* slip; (*gleiten*) slide. **-ig** *adj* slippery.

rütteln ['rytəln] *v* shake (up); (*beim Fahren*) jolt.

S

Saal [zaːl] *m* (*pl* **Säle**) hall, large room.

Saat [zaːt] *f* (*pl* -en) (*Samen*) seed; (*Säen*) sowing; (*grün*) green corn. **-korn** *neut* seed corn.

Sabbat ['zabat] *m* (*pl* -e) Sabbath.

Säbel ['zɛːbəl] *m* (*pl* -) sabre.

Sabotage [zabo'taːʒə] *f* sabotage. **sabotieren** *v* sabotage.

Saccharin [zaxa'riːn] *neut* saccharine.

Sachbearbeiter ['zaxbəarbaitər] *m* executive, official in charge. **Sache** *f* thing; (*Angelegenheit*) affair, matter; (*Tat*) fact. **Sachen** *pl* things, belongings; (*Kleider*) things, clothes. **Sach||kundige(r)** expert.

–**lage** f situation, state of affairs. **sachlich** adj businesslike, matter-of-fact; (objektiv) objective.

Sachse ['zaksə] m (pl -n) Saxon. **Sachsen** neut Saxony.

Sächsin ['zɛksɪn] f (pl -nen) Saxon (woman). **sächsisch** adj Saxon.

sacht(e) [zaxt(ə)] adv softly, gently.

Sack [zak] m (pl Säcke) sack, bag. –**gasse** f cul-de-sac, (US) dead end.

Sadismus [za'dɪzmus] m sadism. **Sadist** m (pl -en) sadist. **sadistisch** adj sadistic.

säen ['zɛːən] v sow.

Safari [za'faːrɪ] f (pl -s) safari.

Safe [sɛːf] m (pl -s) safe.

Saft [zaft] m (pl Säfte) juice; (Baum) sap; (umg.: Strom, Benzin) juice. **saftig** adj juicy; (Witz) spicy.

Sage ['zaːgə] f (pl -n) legend, fable.

Säge ['zɛːgə] f (pl -n) saw. –**maschine** f mechanical saw. –**mehl** neut sawdust.

*****sagen** ['zaːgən] v say; (mitteilen) tell. was Sie nicht sagen! you don't say! sagen wir let's say, suppose. wie gesagt as I said. das sagt mir etwas that means something to me.

sägen ['zɛːgən] v saw.

sagenhaft ['zaːgənhaft] adj legendary; (umg.) splendid, great.

Sahne ['zaːnə] f cream. –**kuchen** m cream cake. **sahnig** adj creamy.

Saison [zɛ'zɔ̃] f (pl -s) season. **stille Saison** off-season.

Saite ['zaitə] f (pl -n) string. –**ninstrument** neut stringed instrument.

Sakrament [zakra'm ɛnt] neut (pl -e) sacrament.

Salat [za'laːt] m (pl -e) salad; (Kopfsalat) lettuce. –**kopf** m head of lettuce.

Salbe ['zalbə] f (pl -n) ointment, salve.

Salbei [zalbai] f or m (Bot) sage.

salben ['zalbən] v anoint.

Saldo ['zaldo] m (pl Salden) (Komm) balance.

Salon [za'lɔ̃] m (pl -e) drawing room. **salonfähig** adj presentable (in society).

Salut [za'luːt] m (pl -e) salute. **salutieren** v salute.

Salve ['zalvə] f (pl -n) volley.

Salz [zalts] neut (pl -e) salt. **salzen** v salt. **Salzfaß** neut salt cellar. **salzig** adj salty. **Salz||kartoffeln** pl boiled potatoes.

–**wasser** neut salt water.

Samen ['zaːmən] m (pl -) seed; (Tiere) sperm. –**erguß** m ejaculation. –**händler** m seed merchant. –**pflanze** f seedling. –**staub** m pollen.

Sämischleder ['zɛːm ʃleːdər] neut chamois (leather).

sammeln ['zaməln] v gather; (Hobby) collect. **Samm||elplatz** m assembly point. –**ler** m collector. –**lung** f collection.

Samstag ['zamstaːk] m Saturday. **samstags** adv on Saturdays.

samt [zamt] prep (together) with, including.

Samt [zamt] m (pl -e) velvet.

sämtlich ['zɛmtlɪç] adj complete, entire; (alle) all; (Werke) complete.

Sand [zant] m (pl -e) sand.

Sandale [zan'daːlə] f (pl -n) sandal.

Sandbank f sandbank. **sandfarben** adj sandy(-coloured). **Sand||papier** neut sandpaper. –**stein** m sandstone.

sanft [zanft] adj gentle, soft. **Sanftheit** f gentleness, softness. **sanftmütig** adj gentle, mild.

Sänger ['zɛŋər] m (pl -), **Sängerin** f (pl -nen) singer.

sanieren [za'niːrən] v heal; (Betrieb) rationalize, make viable; (Stadt, Viertel) redevelop. **Sanierung** f (Komm) reorganization; (Gebäude) renovation.

sanitär [zani'tɛːr] adj sanitary, hygienic. **sanitäre Anlagen** pl sanitation sing.

Sankt [zaŋkt] adj Saint.

Sanktion [zaŋk'tsioːn] f (pl -en) sanction. **sanktionieren** v sanction.

Saphir ['zafiːr] m (pl -e) sapphire.

Sardelle [zar'dɛlə] f (pl -n) anchovy.

Sardine [zar'diːnə] f (pl -n) sardine.

Sarg [zark] m (pl Särge) coffin.

sarkastisch [zar'kastʃ] adj sarcastic.

Satan ['zaːtan] m (pl -e) Satan; (böser Mensch) devil, demon. **satanisch** adj satanic.

Satellit [zate'liːt] m (pl -en) satellite.

Satin [za'tɛ̃] m (pl -s) satin.

Satire [za'tiːrə] f (pl -n) satire. **Satiriker** m (pl -) satirist. **satirisch** adj satirical.

satt [zat] adj satisfied, satiated; (Farbe) deep, rich. **satt sein** have had enough; (nach dem Essen) be full. **satt haben** have had enough of, be tired of.

Sattel ['zatəl] *m* (*pl* **Sättel**) saddle. **satteln** *v* saddle. **Sattel‖schlepper** *m* (tractor for an) articulated truck. **–tasche** *f* saddlebag.

Satz [zats] *m* (*pl* **Sätze**) (*Sprung*) leap, jump; (*Gramm*) sentence; (*Sammlung, Math*) set; (*Musik*) movement; (*Bodensatz*) sediment; (*Wein*) dregs *pl*; (*Grundsatz*) principle; (*Geld*) price, rate; (*Druck*) composition, setting. **–lehre** *f* syntax.

Satzung ['zatsuŋ] *f* (*pl* **-en**) statute; (*Vorschrift*) rule. **satzungs‖gemäß** *or* **–mäßig** *adj* statutory.

Sau [zau] *f* (*pl* **Säue**) sow.

sauber ['zaubər] *adj* clean; (*hübsch*) pretty, nice; (*ordentlich*) tidy. **Sauberkeit** *f* cleanliness; niceness; tidiness.

säuberlich ['zɔybərlɪç] *adj* clean; (*ordentlich*) tidy; (*anständig*) proper. **saubermachen** *v* clean (up).

sauer ['zauər] *adj* (*Geschmack*) sour; (*säurehältig*) acid. **Sauerbraten** *m* roast marinated beef.

Sauerei *f* (*pl* **-en**) (*Unanständigkeit*) smuttiness; (*Pfuscherei*) mess.

Sauerkraut ['zauərkraut] *neut* pickled cabbage, sauerkraut.

Sauerstoff *m* oxygen. **sauersüß** *adj* bittersweet; (*Speise*) sweet-and-sour.

*saufen ['zaufən] *v* drink; (*umg.*) drink, booze.

Säufer ['zɔyfər] *m* (*pl* -) heavy drinker, boozer.

*saugen ['zaugən] *v* suck; (*einziehen*) absorb. **Saugen** *neut* suction, sucking.

säugen ['zɔygən] *v* suckle, nurse. **Säug‖en** *neut* suckling, nursing. **–etier** *neut* mammal. **–ling** *m* baby.

Säule ['zɔylə] *f* (*pl* **-n**) column, pillar.

Saum [zaum] *m* (*pl* **Säume**) seam, hem; (*Rand*) border, margin.

säumen¹ ['zɔymən] *v* (*Kleid*) hem; (*allgemein*) edge; (*fig*) skirt, fringe.

säumen² *v* (*zögern*) delay, hesitate.

Säumnis ['zɔymnɪs] *f* (*pl* **-se**) *or neut* (*pl* **-e**) delay.

Saumpferd ['zaumpfɛrt] *neut* packhorse.

Sauna ['zauna] *f* (*pl* **-s**) sauna.

Säure ['zɔyrə] *f* (*pl* **-n**) acid; sourness.

Sauregurkenzeit [zaurə'gurkəntsait] *f* silly season.

sausen ['zauzən] *v* (*eilen*) rush, dash, zoom;

(*Wind*) howl, whistle.

Saxophon [zakso'foːn] *neut* (*pl* **-e**) saxophone.

schaben ['ʃaːbən] *v* scrape; (*Fleisch*) cut into strips.

schäbig ['ʃɛːbɪç] *adj* shabby, sleazy.

Schablone [ʃaˈbloːnə] *f* (*pl* **-n**) stencil, pattern, model.

Schach [ʃax] *neut* (*Spiel*) chess; (*Warnruf*) check. **in Schach halten** keep in check. **Schachbrett** *neut* chessboard.

Schacherei [ʃaxə'rai] *f* haggling, bargaining.

Schachfigur *f* chessman.

Schacht [ʃaxt] *m* (*pl* **-e**) shaft.

Schachtel ['ʃaxtəl] *f* (*pl* **-n**) box.

schade ['ʃaːdə] *adv* a pity. **es ist schade** it's a pity, it's a shame. *schade, daß Sie…*what a pity that you…. *wie schade!* what a pity!

Schädel ['ʃɛːdəl] *m* (*pl* -) skull.

schaden ['ʃaːdən] *v* harm, injure, hurt. **Schaden** *m* damage; (*Verlust*) loss; (*körperlich*) injury, harm. **–ersatz** *m* compensation. **–freude** *f* malicious joy, gloating. **schadenfroh** *adj* malicious, gloating. **schadhaft** *adj* damaged.

schädigen ['ʃɛːdɪɡən] *v* harm, damage; (*körperlich*) injure. **Schädigung** *f* damage; injury. **schädlich** *adj* dangerous, injurious.

Schaf [ʃaːf] *neut* (*pl* **-e**) sheep.

Schäfer ['ʃɛːər] *m* (*pl* -) shepherd. **–hund** *m* sheepdog; (*deutscher*) Alsatian (dog). **–in** *f* (*pl* **-nen**) shepherdess.

Schaffell *neut* sheepskin, fleece.

*schaffen¹ ['ʃafən] *v* (*hervorbringen, gestalten*) create.

schaffen² *v* (*bringen*) bring, convey; (*fertigbringen*) manage, accomplish; (*arbeiten*) work.

Schaffner ['ʃafnər] *m* (*pl* -) (*Zug*) guard; (*Bus*) conductor. **–in** *f* (*pl* **-nen**) guard; conductress.

Schaf‖pelz *m* sheepskin. **–stall** *m* sheepfold.

Schaft [ʃaft] *m* (*pl* **Schäfte**) shaft; (*Griff*) handle; (*Gewehr*) stock; (*Baum*) trunk.

Schale ['ʃaːlə] *f* (*pl* **-n**) (*Schüssel*) bowl, basin; (*Ei, Nuß*) shell; (*Frucht, Gemüse*) peel, skin; (*fig*) cover(ing).

schälen ['ʃɛːlən] *v* shell; peel.

Schalk [ʃalk] *m* (*pl* **-e**) rogue, knave. **schalkhaft** *adj* roguish.

Schall [ʃal] *m* (*pl* -e) sound. –**dämpfer** *m* silencer. **schallen** *v* sound, resound; (*Glocke*) ring, peal. **Schall‖platte** *f* (gramophone) record. –**welle** *f* soundwave.

schalten [ʃaltən] *v* switch; (*Mot*) change (gear). **Schalt‖ler** *m* (*Bank*, *usw.*) counter, window; (*Elek*) switch. –**hebel** *m* control lever, switch; (*Mot*) gear lever. –**jahr** *neut* leap year. –**plan** *m* circuit diagram. –**ung** *f* wiring; (*Mot*) gear-change.

Scham [ʃaːm] *f* shame; (*Scheu*) modesty.

schämen [ʃɛːm ən] *v* **sich schämen** *v* be ashamed.

scham‖haft *adj* bashful, modest. –**los** *adj* shameless, immodest.

Schampoo [ʃam'puː] *neut* shampoo. **schampoonieren** *v* shampoo.

Schande [ʃandə] *f* (*pl* -n) disgrace, shame.

schänden [ʃɛndən] *v* disgrace; (*verderben*) spoil; (*entheiligen*) desecrate; (*Frau*) rape, violate.

Schandfleck [ʃantflɛk] *m* blemish, stain.

schändlich [ʃɛntliç] *adj* shameful, disgraceful.

Schandtat [ʃanttaːt] *f* misdeed, crime.

Schank [ʃaŋk] *m* (*pl* **Schänke**) bar.

Schanze [ʃantsə] *f* (*pl* -n) fortification; (*Erdwall*) earthworks *pl*; (*Skilauf*) skijump.

Schar [ʃaːr] *f* (*pl* -en) troop, band; (*Gänse*) flock; (*Hunde*) pack. **sich scharen** *v* gather, congregate.

scharf [ʃarf] *adj* sharp; (*Gewürze*) spicy, hot.

Schärfe [ʃɛrfə] *f* (*pl* -n) sharpness, edge; (*Ätzkraft*) acidity; (*Klarheit*) clarity. **schärfen** *v* sharpen.

Scharfschütze *m* marksman, sharpshooter. **scharfsichtig** *adj* sharp-sighted. **Scharfsinn** *m* shrewdness. **scharfsinnig** *adj* shrewd.

Scharlachfieber [ʃarlaxfiːbər] *neut* scarlet fever. **scharlachrot** *adj* scarlet.

Scharm [ʃarm] *m* charm. **scharmant** *adj* charming, delightful.

Scharnier [ʃar'niːr] *neut* (*pl* -e) hinge.

scharren [ʃarən] *v* scrape, scratch.

Schatten [ʃatən] *m* (*pl* -) shadow; (*Dunkel*) shade. **in den Schatten stellen** overshadow. **Schattenbild** *neut* silhouette. **schatten‖haft** *adj* shadowy. –**ig** *adj* shaded.

Schatz [ʃats] *m* (*pl* **Schätze**) treasure; (*fig*) darling. –**amt** *neut* treasury.

schätzen [ʃɛtsən] *v* value; (*ungefähr*) estimate. –**swert** *adj* valuable, estimable.

Schatz‖kammer *f* treasury. –**meister** *m* treasurer.

Schätzung [ʃɛtsuŋ] *f* (*pl* -en) estimate; (*Hochschätzung*) esteem. **schätzungsweise** *adv* approximately; at a guess.

Schau [ʃau] *f* (*pl* -en) show; (*Ausstellung*) exhibition; (*Überblick*) survey, review. **zur Schau stellen** exhibit.

schaudern [ʃaudərn] *v* shudder, shiver. –**haft** *adj* horrible.

schauen [ʃauən] *v* look (at), observe.

Schauer [ʃauər] *m* (*pl* -) (*Regen*) shower; (*Schrecken*) horror; (*Zittern*) thrill.

Schaufel [ʃaufəl] *f* (*pl* -n) shovel; (*Tech*) blade.

Schaufenster *neut* shop window.

Schaukel [ʃaukəl] *f* (*pl* -n) (child's) swing. –**pferd** *neut* rocking horse. –**stuhl** *m* rocking chair.

Schaum [ʃaum] *m* (*pl* **Schäume**) foam; (*Seife*) lather.

schäumen [ʃɔym ən] *v* foam; (*Wein*) sparkle.

schaumig [ʃaum iç] *adj* foamy.

Schauspiel *neut* play; drama; (*fig*) spectacle. –**er** *m* (*pl* -) actor. –**erin** *f* (*pl* -nen) actress. –**haus** *neut* theatre.

Scheck [ʃɛk] *m* (*pl* -s) cheque, (*US*) check. –**buch** *neut* cheque book.

Scheibe [ʃaibə] *f* (*pl* -n) disc; (*Brot, Wurst*) slice; (*Glas*) pane. **Scheiben‖bremse** *f* disc brake. –**wischer** *m* windscreen wiper.

Scheide [ʃaidə] *f* (*pl* -n) sheath; (*Anat*) vagina; (*Grenze*) limit. **scheiden** *v* separate; (*Ehepartner*) divorce. **sich scheiden** part, separate. **sich scheiden lassen** get a divorce. **Scheideweg** *m* crossroads. **Scheidung** *f* separation; (*Ehe*) divorce.

Schein [ʃain] *m* (*pl* -e) (*Aussehen*) appearance; (*Licht*) light; (*Glanz*) shine; (*Geld*) bill (*US*); banknote; (*Bescheinigung*) certificate. **schein‖bar** *adj* apparent, ostensible. –**en** *v* (*aussehen*) appear, seem; (*leuchten*) shine. –**heilig** *adj* sanctimonious. **Schein‖heilige(r)** hypocrite. –**krankheit** *f* feigned sickness. –**werfer** *m* (*pl* -) searchlight; (*Reflektor*) reflector; (*Theater*) spotlight; (*Mot*) headlight.

Scheiße [ʃaisə] *f* (*vulg*) shit. **scheißen** *v* shit.

Scheitel [ʃaitəl] *m* (*pl* -) top; (*Kopf*) crown,

top of the head; (*Haar*) parting.

scheitern ['ʃaɪtərn] *v* fail, come to nought; (*Schiff*) be wrecked.

Schelle ['ʃɛlə] *f* (*pl* -n) small bell; (*Hand*-) handcuff.

Schellfisch ['ʃɛlfɪʃ] *m* haddock.

Schelm [ʃɛlm] *m* (*pl* -e) rogue.

Schema ['ʃeːma] *neut* (*pl* -ta *or* **Schemen**) scheme; (*Muster*) pattern; (*Darstellung*) diagram.

Schenkel ['ʃɛŋkəl] *m* (*pl* -) thigh. **-knochen** *m* thigh bone, femur.

schenken ['ʃɛŋkən] *v* give, present; (*Getränk*) pour (out). **Schenk||er** *m* (*pl* -) donor, giver. **-ung** *f* donation.

Scherbe ['ʃɛrbə] *f* (*pl* -n) fragment.

Schere ['ʃeːrə] *f* (*pl* -n) scissors *pl*; (*große*) shears *pl*; (*Krebs*) claw. **scheren** *v* (*Wolle*) shear; (*Haare*) cut; (*Hecke*) cut, trim; (*Rasen*) mow.

Scherz [ʃɛrts] *m* (*pl* -e) joke; (*Unterhaltung*) fun. **scherz||en** *v* joke, have fun. **-haft** *adj* joking.

scheu [ʃɔy] *adj* shy.

Scheuche ['ʃɔyçə] *f* (*pl* -n) scarecrow.

scheuen ['ʃɔyən] *v* shy away from, avoid; (*Pferd*) shy; (*Mühe, usw.*) spare. **sich scheuen vor** be afraid of.

Scheuerbürste ['ʃɔyərbyrstə] *f* scrubbing brush. **scheuern** *v* scrub, scour.

Scheune ['ʃɔynə] *f* (*pl* -n) barn.

Scheusal ['ʃɔyzaːl] *neut* (*pl* -e) monster.

scheußlich ['ʃɔyslɪç] *adj* horrible, hideous. **Scheußlichkeit** *f* hideousness.

Schicht [ʃɪçt] *f* (*pl* -en) layer; (*Arbeit*) shift; (*Gesellschaft*) class. **-arbeit** *f* shift work. **-holz** *neut* plywood. **-ung** *f* stratification; (*fig*) classification.

schick [ʃɪk] *adj* elegant, chic, smart.

schicken ['ʃɪkən] *v* send. **sich schicken** (*sich gehören*) suit, be becoming; (*sich entwickeln*) happen.

schicklich ['ʃɪklɪç] *adj* becoming, fit, proper. **Schicklichkeit** *f* fitness, propriety.

Schicksal ['ʃɪkzaːl] *neut* (*pl* -e) fate, destiny. **-sschlag** *m* stroke of fate, blow.

Schiebedach ['ʃiːbədax] *neut* sliding roof; (*Mot*) sun-roof. **schieben** *v* push; (*Schuld*) pass on; (*Arbeit*) put off. **Schiebetür** *f* sliding door.

Schieds||gericht ['ʃiːtsgərɪçt] *neut* arbitration court, tribunal. **-richter** *m* arbitrator;

(*Sport*) referee, umpire. **-spruch** *m* arbitration, award.

schief [ʃiːf] *adj* slanting, sloping; (*fig*) wrong, amiss.

Schiefer ['ʃiːfər] *m* (*pl* -) slate.

*****schiefgehen** *v* go wrong *or* amiss.

schielen ['ʃiːlən] *v* squint. **Schielen** *neut* (*Med*) strabismus, squint.

Schienbein ['ʃiːnbaɪn] *neut* shin(bone).

Schiene ['ʃiːnə] *f* (*pl* -n) rail; (*Med*) splint.

*****schießen** ['ʃiːsən] *v* shoot. **Schieß||en** *neut* shooting. **-erei** *f* gunfight.

Schiff [ʃɪf] *neut* (*pl* -e) ship; (*Kirche*) nave. **-ahrt** *f* navigation; (*Verkehr*) shipping. **-bau** *m* shipbuilding. **-bruch** *m* shipwreck. **-brüchig** *adj* shipwrecked. **Schiffs||küche** *f* galley. **-raum** *m* hold; (*Inhalt*) tonnage. **-verkehr** *m* shipping. **-werft** *f* shipyard.

Schikane [ʃiˈkaːnə] *f* (*pl* -n) chicanery. **schikanieren** *v* make trouble for, (*umg.*) hassle.

Schild[1] [ʃɪlt] *m* (*pl* -e) shield.

Schild[2] *neut* (*pl* -er) sign; (*Namen*-) nameplate; (*Flasche*) label; (*Mütze*) peak.

schildern ['ʃɪldərn] *v* depict, describe. **Schilderung** *f* depiction, description.

Schildkröte *f* turtle; (*Land*) tortoise.

Schilf [ʃɪlf] *neut* (*pl* -e) reed.

Schilling ['ʃɪlɪŋ] *m* (*pl* -e) (Austrian) Schilling.

Schimmel ['ʃɪməl] *m* (*pl* -) mildew, mould. **schimmel||ig** *adj* mouldy. **-n** *v* become mouldy.

Schimmer ['ʃɪmər] *m* (*pl* -) glimmer, gleam. **schimmern** *v* gleam, shine.

Schimpanse [ʃɪmˈpanzə] *m* (*pl* -n) chimpanzee.

Schimpf [ʃɪmpf] *m* (*pl* -e) abuse, insult. **schimpfen** *v* swear, curse; (*umg.: tadeln*) curse, scold. **Schimpfwort** *neut* swearword.

*****schinden** ['ʃɪndən] *v* (*ausnützen*) exploit. **sich schinden** work hard, slave.

Schinken ['ʃɪŋkən] *m* (*pl* -) ham.

Schippe ['ʃɪpə] *f* (*pl* -n) shovel; (*Karten*) spade(s).

Schirm [ʃɪrm] *m* (*pl* -e) (*Regen*-) umbrella; (*Lampen*-) shade; (*Bild*-) screen; (*Mütze*) peak; (*fig: Schutz*) protection. **schirmen** *v* protect, screen.

schizophren [ʃitsoˈfreːn] *adj* schizophrenic. **Schizophrenie** *f* schizophrenia.

Schlacht [ʃaxt] f (pl -en) battle.
schlachten v slaughter.

Schlächter [ʃɛçtər] m (pl -) butcher.

Schlacht||feld neut battlefield. **–hof** m
slaughterhouse. **–schiff** neut battleship.

Schlaf [ʃaːf] m sleep. **–anzug** m pyjamas pl.
schlafen v sleep. **–d** adj sleeping; (fig) dormant. **Schlafenszeit** f bedtime.

Schläfer [ʃlɛːfər] m (pl -) sleeper.

schlaff [ʃlaf] adj slack; (fig) lax; (welk)
limp.

Schlaf||losigkeit f sleeplessness, insom-
nia. **–mittel** neut sleeping pill.

schläfrig [ʃlɛːfriç] adj sleepy.

Schlaf||wagen m sleeping car. **–zimmer**
neut bedroom.

Schlag [ʃlaːk] m (pl **Schläge**) blow, stroke;
(Elek) shock; (Med) stroke; (Art) sort, kind.
schlagen v hit, strike; (besiegen) beat,
defeat; (mit der Faust) punch; (Vögel) warble, sing; (Wurzel) take root. **kurz und
klein schlagen** smash to pieces. **Alarm
schlagen** sound the alarm. **nach jemandem schlagen** take after someone.
Schlagen neut striking, hitting. **schlagend**
adj striking; (fig) impressive; (entscheidend)
decisive. **Schlager** m (pl -) (great) success,
hit; (Musik) hit (song).

Schläger [ʃlɛːgər] m (pl -) (Tennis) racket;
(Golf) club; (Kochen) beater; (Raufbold)
rowdy.

schlagfertig [ʃlaːkfɛrtiç] adj quick-witted.
Schlag||instrument neut percussion
instrument. **–sahne** f whipped cream.
–wort neut slogan. **–zeile** f headline. **–zeug**
neut percussion (instruments) pl.

Schlamm [ʃlam] m (pl -e) mud. **schlammig** adj muddy.

Schlampe [ʃlampə] f (pl -n) slut. **schlampig** adj slovenly.

Schlange [ʃlaŋə] f (pl -n) snake; (Reihe
Menschen) queue, (US) line. **Schlange
stehen** v queue, (US) line up.
Schlangen||gift neut snake venom. **–leder**
neut snakeskin.

schlank [ʃlaŋk] adj slender, slim.
Schlank||heit f slenderness, slimness.
–skur f (reducing) diet.

schlapp [ʃlap] adj slack, limp.

schlau [ʃlau] adj cunning, sly, clever.
Schlauheit f cunning, slyness.

Schlauch [ʃlaux] m (pl **Schläuche**) hose;

(Reifen) inner tube.

schlecht [ʃlɛçt] adj bad; (unwohl) ill;
(Qualität) poor, inferior; (Luft) stale, foul.
mir ist schlecht I feel ill. **–gelannt** adj
bad-tempered. **Schlechtigkeit** f wickedness. **Schlechtheit** f badness. **schlechthin**
adv simply, plainly.

Schlegel [ʃlɛːgəl] m (pl -) (wooden) mallet;
(Trommel) drumstick.

***schleichen** [ʃlaiən] v creep; (heimlich)
slink, sneak.

Schleier [ʃlaiər] m (pl -) veil.

Schleife [ʃlaifə] f (pl -n) loop, slip-knot;
(Band) bow.

***schleifen**¹ [ʃlaifən] v slide, glide, slip.

schleifen² v (schleppen) drag; (Messer)
sharpen, grind; (Edelstein) cut.

Schleim [ʃlaim] m (pl -e) slime; (Med)
mucus. **schleimig** adj slimy; mucous.

***schleißen** [ʃlaisən] v slit; (spalten) split;
(reißen) rip, tear.

schlendern [ʃlɛndərn] v saunter.
Schlendrian m (pl -) (umg.) old routine.

Schleppboot [ʃlɛpboːt] neut tug(boat).
schleppen v drag, pull; (tragen) carry, lug.
sich schleppen v drag oneself along.

Schlesien [ʃleːziən] neut Silesia.

Schleuder [ʃlɔydər] f (pl -n) sling, catapult;
(Wäsche) spin-drier, spinner; (Zentrifuge)
centrifuge. **–preis** m cut-price, give-away
price. **schleudern** v sling, hurl; (Mot) skid;
(Wäsche) spin-dry; (Komm) dump, sell off
cheap.

schleunig [ʃlɔyniç] adj prompt, speedy.

Schleuse [ʃlɔyzə] f (pl -n) sluice; (Kanal)
lock.

schlicht [ʃliçt] adj simple, plain;
(bescheiden) modest. **–en** v (glätten) smooth;
(ebnen) level; (Streit) settle. **Schlichtung** f
(pl -en) settlement.

***schließen** [ʃliːsən] v close, shut; (mit dem
Schlüssel) lock; (zum Schluß bringen) close,
end, conclude; (folgern) conclude, infer.
Schließfach neut (Bank) safe-deposit box.
schließlich adv finally, (at) last.

schlimm [ʃlim] adj bad. **schlimmstenfalls**
adv at worst.

Schlinge [ʃliŋə] f (pl -n) noose, loop; (Jagd,
fig) snare, trap.

***schlingen**¹ [ʃliŋən] v wind; (flechten) twist;
(verknüpfen) tie, knot.

***schlingen**² v (schlucken) swallow; (gierig

essen) devour, wolf.

Schlitten ['∫lɪtən] *m* (*pl* -) sledge. **Schlittschuh** *m* stake. **Schlittschuh laufen** skate.

Schlitz [∫lɪts] *m* (*pl* -e) slit; (*Münzeinwurf*) slot; (*Hosen-*) fly.

Schloß [∫bs] *neut* (*pl* **Schlösser**) lock; (*Burg*) castle.

Schlosser ['∫bsər] *m* (*pl* -) fitter, mechanic, locksmith.

Schlot [∫bːt] *m* (*pl* -e) chimney.

schlott(e)rig ['∫btə)rɪç] *adj* (*wackelig*) wobbly, shaky; (*schlaff*) loose; (*kleider*) baggy.

Schluck [∫lʊk] *m* (*pl* -e) sip, gulp, mouthful. **-auf** *m* hiccup. **schlucken** *v* swallow.

Schlund [∫lʊnt] *m* (*pl* **Schlünde**) throat; (*geog*) abyss, gorge; (*fig*) gulf.

schlüpfen ['∫lʏpfən] *v* slip, slide. **Schlüpfer** *m* knickers *pl*. **schlüpfrig** *adj* slippery; (*fig*) lewd.

Schlupfwinkel ['∫lʊpfvɪŋkəl] *m* hiding place.

Schluß [∫lʊs] *m* (*pl* **Schlüsse**) end, close; (*Folgerung*) inference, conclusion. **zum Schluß** finally. **Schluß machen** stop, finish.

Schlüssel ['∫lʏsəl] *m* (*pl* -) key; (*Musik*) clef; (*Tech*) spanner, (*US*) wrench. **-bein** *neut* collarbone. **-bund** *m* bunch of keys. **-loch** *neut* keyhole. **-ring** *m* keyring.

Schluß‖prüfung *f* final examination, finals *pl*. **-runde** *f* (*Sport*) final. **-verkauf** *m* end-of-season sale.

Schmach [∫max] *f* disgrace, dishonour.

schmächtig ['∫mɛçtɪç] *adj* slim, slender.

schmackhaft ['∫makhaft] *adj* appetizing, delicious.

schmal [∫maːl] *adj* narrow, thin, slender; (*fig*) scanty, poor.

Schmalz [∫mals] *neut* (*pl* -e) fat, grease, dripping; (*fig*) sentimentality.

schmarotzen [∫maˈrɔtsən] *v* (*umg.*) sponge, scrounge. **Schmarotzer** *m* (*Tier, Pflanze*) parasite; (*Person*) scrounger, parasite.

schmatzen ['∫matsən] *v* smack one's lips, eat noisily; (*küssen*) give a smacking kiss.

schmecken ['∫mɛkən] *v* taste; (*gut*) taste good. **schmecken nach** taste of. **(wie) schmeckt es?** do you like it? **es schmeckt (mir)** I like it, it's good.

Schmeichelei [∫maɪçəˈlaɪ] *f* (*pl* -en) flattery. **schmeicheln** *v* flatter. **Schmeichler** *m*

(*pl* -) flatterer. **schmeichlerisch** *adj* flattering.

*****schmeißen** ['∫maɪsən] *v* throw, cast; (*umg.*) chuck; (*Schlagen*) strike, smash.

Schmelz [∫mɛls] *m* (*pl* -e) (*Email*) enamel; (*Glasur*) glaze; (*Stimme, Töne*) mellowness, sweetness. **schmelzen** *v* melt; (*Erz*) smelt.

Schmerz [∫mɛrts] *m* (*pl* -en) pain; (*seelisch*) grief, pain. **Schmerzen haben** be in pain. **Schmerzen** *v* hurt; (*seelisch*) grieve, pain. **schmerz‖haft** *adj* painful. **-lich** *adj* painful, hurtful. **-los** *adj* painless.

Schmetterling ['∫mɛtərlɪŋ] *m* (*pl* -e) butterfly. **-sschwimmen** *neut* butterfly (stroke).

Schmied [∫miːt] *m* (*pl* -e) (black)smith. **Schmiede** *f* (*pl* -n) forge, smithy. **-eisen** *neut* wrought iron. **schmieden** *v* forge; (*Pläne*) devise.

Schmiere ['∫miːrə] *f* (*pl* -n) grease; (*Theater, umg.*) small (touring) company. **schmieren** *v* (*fetten*) grease; (*ölen*) oil, lubricate; (*streichen*) spread. **Schmierung** *f* (*pl* -en) lubrication.

Schminke ['∫mɪŋkə] *f* (*pl* -n) make-up. **schminken** *v* make up. **sich schminken** put on make-up; make oneself up.

Schmorbraten ['∫moːrbraːtən] *m* stewed steak, pot roast. **schmoren** *v* stew, braise.

Schmuck [∫mʊk] *m* (*pl* -e) ornament, decoration; (*Juwelen*) jewellery.

schmücken ['∫mʏkən] *v* adorn, decorate; (*Kleider*) trim.

schmuggeln ['∫mʊgəln] *v* smuggle. **Schmuggelware** *f* contraband. **Schmuggler** *m* (*pl* -) smuggler.

Schmus [∫muːs] *m* (*umg.*) (empty) chatter, soft soap; **schmusen** *v* chatter, soft-soap.

Schmutz [∫mʊts] *m* dirt, filth. **schmutzig** *adj* dirty, filthy. **Schmutzpresse** *f* gutter press.

Schnabel ['∫naːbəl] *m* (*pl* **Schnäbel**) bill, beak.

Schnalle ['∫nalə] *f* (*pl* -n) clasp; (*Schuh, Gürtel*) buckle; (*Tür*) latch. **schnallen** *v* buckle.

schnappen ['∫napən] *v* snap; (*erwischen*) grab, catch. **nach Luft schnappen** gasp for air.

Schnaps [∫naps] *m* (*pl* **Schnäpse**) liqueur, schnaps, brandy.

schnarchen ['∫narçən] *v* snore.

schnattern ['∫natərn] *v* (*Geflügel*) cackle; (*Menschen*) prattle.

schnaufen [ˈʃnaufən] *v* pant, puff.

Schnauze [ˈʃnautsə] *f (pl -n)* snout, muzzle; (*Kanne*) spout. **halt die Schnauze!** (*vulg*) shut up! belt up!

Schnecke [ˈʃnɛkə] *f (pl -n)* snail; (*nackte*) slug.

Schnee [ʃneː] *m* snow. **–glöckchen** *neut* snowdrop. **–lawne** *f* avalanche. **–mann** *m* snowman. **–schläger** *m* egg whisk. **–schuh** *m* ski. **–sturm** *m* blizzard. **–wehe** *f* snowdrift.

Schneide [ˈʃnaidə] *f (pl -n)* (cutting) edge. **schneiden** *v* cut; (*Braten*) carve. **Schneider** *m (pl -)* tailor. **–ei** *f (pl -en)* tailor's shop. **–in** *f (pl -nen)* dressmaker, seamstress.

schneien [ˈʃnaiən] *v* snow.

schnell [ʃnɛl] *adj* fast, quick. **mach schnell!** hurry up! get a move on! **Schnellboot** *neut* speedboat. **schnellen** *v* jerk, spring. **Schnell‖gaststätte** *f* fast-food restaurant, cafeteria. **–igkeit** *f* speed. **–imbiß** *m* snack. **–imbißstube** *f* snack bar, takeaway. **–zug** *m* express train.

schnippisch [ˈʃnɪpɪʃ] *adj* pert, saucy.

Schnitt [ʃnɪt] *m (pl -e)* cut; (*Scheibe*) slice; (*Art*) style; (*Math*) intersection; (*Zeichnung*) (cross-)section. **–lauch** *m* chive(s). **–ling** *m* (*Bot*) cutting.

Schnitzel [ˈʃnɪtsəl] *neut (pl -)* chip, shaving; (*Fleisch*) cutlet, escalope.

schnitzen [ˈʃnɪtsən] *v* carve (wood). **Schnitzer** *m* carver; (*Fehler*) blunder, bloomer.

Schnörkel [ˈʃnœrkəl] *m (pl -)* flourish; (*Kunst, Architektur*) scroll.

schnüffeln [ˈʃnyfəln] *v* snuffle, sniff; (*fig*) snoop, nose around.

Schnuller [ˈʃnulər] *m (pl -)* (baby's) dummy, (*US*) pacifier.

schnupfen [ˈʃnupfən] *v* take snuff. **Schnupfen** *m (pl -)* catarrh, (head) cold. **einen Schnupfen bekommen/haben** catch/have a cold. **Schnupftabak** *m* snuff.

Schnur [ʃnuːr] *f (pl Schnüre)* string, cord; (*Elek*) flex, wire.

schnüren [ˈʃnyːrən] *v* tie (up), fasten.

schnurgerade [ˈʃnuːrɡəraːdə] *adj, adv* (as) straight (as a die).

Schnurrbart [ˈʃnurbaːrt] *m* moustache.

schnurren [ˈʃnurən] *v* hum, buzz; (*Katze*) purr.

Schock [ʃɔk] *m (pl -s or -e)* shock. **schok-**

–ieren *v* shock, scandalize.

Schokolade [ʃokoˈlaːdə] *f (pl -n)* chocolate.

Scholle [ˈʃɔlə] *f (pl -n)* (*Erde*) clod, clump; (*Eis*) floe; (*Fisch*) plaice; (*fig*) native soil, home.

schon [ʃoːn] *adv* already; (*bestimmt*) certainly; (*zwar*) indeed. **schon lange** for a long time. **schon lange her** a long time ago. **ich komme schon!** I'm coming! **schon wieder** yet again. **schon der Name** the mere name, the name alone.

schön [ʃøːn] *adj* beautiful, pretty; (*Wetter*) fine, fair. **danke schön** thank you. **bitte schön** (if you) please. **schön machen** beautify.

schonen [ˈʃoːnən] *v* spare; treat carefully, go carefully with. **–d** *adj* considerate, careful.

Schönheit [ˈʃøːnhait] *f (pl -en)* beauty. **Schönheits‖fehler** *m* blemish, flaw. **–königin** *f* beauty queen. **–pflege** *f* beauty treatment.

Schonkost [ˈʃoːnkɔst] *f* (bland) diet.

Schopf [ʃɔpf] *m (pl Schöpfe)* shock, tuft.

schöpfen [ˈʃœpfən] *v* scoop, ladle; (*Atem*) take, draw; (*Mut*) take.

Schöpfer¹ [ˈʃœpfər] *m (pl -)* creator.

Schöpfer² *m (pl -)* (*zum Schöpfen*) scoop.

schöpferisch [ˈʃœpfərɪʃ] *adj* creative.

Schöpflöffel [ˈʃœpflœfəl] *m* ladle.

Schöpfung [ˈʃœpfuŋ] *f* creation.

Schornstein [ˈʃɔrnʃtain] *m* chimney. **–feger** *m* chimney-sweep. **–kappe** *f* chimney-pot.

Schoß¹ [ʃoːs] *m (pl Schöße)* lap; (*fig*) bosom. **–hund** *m* lap-dog.

Schoß² [ʃɔs] *m (pl Schosse)* (*Bot*) shoot, sprout.

Schote [ˈʃoːtə] *f (pl -n)* pod. **Schoten** *pl* (green) peas.

Schotte [ˈʃɔtə] *m (pl -n)* Scot, Scotsman. **Schottin** *f (pl -nen)* Scot, Scotswoman. **schottisch** *adj* Scottish, Scots. **Schottland** *neut* Scotland.

schräg [ʃrɛːk] *adj* sloping, slanting, oblique.

Schrank [ʃraŋk] *m (pl Schränke)* cupboard; (*Kleider*) wardrobe.

Schranke [ˈʃraŋkə] *f (pl -n)* barrier, bar. **schrankenlos** *adj* limitless, boundless.

Schraube [ˈʃraubə] *f (pl -n)* screw. **Schraubdeckel** *m* screw-cap. **Schrauben‖schlüssel** *m* spanner, (*US*) wrench. **–zieher** *m* screwdriver.

Schrebergarten [ˈʃreːbərɡartən] *m* allotment (garden).

Schreck [ʃrɛk] *m* (*pl* **-e**) *or* **Schrecken** *m* (*pl* **-**) fright, terror. **einen Schreck bekommen/kriegen** receive/get a fright. **schrecken** *v* terrify, frighten. **schrecklich** *adj* terrible, frightful.

Schrei [ʃrai] *m* (*pl* **-e**) cry, shout, scream. **schreien** *v* cry, shout; (*kreischen*) shriek, screech; (*weinen*) cry, weep.

*schreiben [ˈʃraibən] *v* write; (*buchstabieren*) spell. **schreibfaul** *adj* lazy about writing (letters). **Schreib||fehler** *m* spelling error. **–krampf** *m* writer's cramp. **–maschine** *f* typewriter. **–tisch** *m* desk. **–ung** *f* (*pl* **-en**) spelling. **–waren** *pl* stationery *sing*.

Schrein [ʃrain] *m* (*pl* **-e**) (*Kasten*) chest, box; (*Reliquien*) shrine. **–er** *m* (*pl* **-**) joiner, carpenter.

*schreiten [ˈʃraitən] *v* stride, step.

Schrift [ʃrift] *f* (*pl* **-en**) writing; (*Handschrift*) handwriting; (*Geschriebenes*) pamphlet, paper; (*Art*) script, type. **Schriftart** *f* (*pl* **-en**) (*Typografie*) font, typeface. **schriftlich** *adj* in writing, written. **Schrift||steller** *m* (*pl* **-**), **–stellerin** *f* (*pl* **-nen**) writer, author. **–stück** *neut* document, paper.

Schritt [ʃrit] *m* (*pl* **-e**) step, stride; (*Gangart*) gait; (*Tempo*) pace. **Schritt halten mit** keep pace with. **Schrittmacher** *m* (*fig*, *Med*) pacemaker. **schrittweise** *adv* step-by-step.

schroff [ʃrɔf] *adj* steep, precipitous; (*fig*) gruff, surly.

Schrot [ʃroːt] *m or neut* (*pl* **-e**) (*Getreide*) groats *pl*; (*Bleikügelchen*) (buck)shot. **–brot** *neut* wholemeal bread.

Schrott [ʃrɔt] *m* (*pl* **-e**) scrap (metal).

schrubben [ˈʃrubən] *v* scrub.

schrumpfen [ˈʃrumpfən] *v* shrink. **Schrumpfung** *f* shrinking, contraction.

Schub [ʃuːp] *m* (*pl* **Schübe**) shove, push; (*Tech*) thrust. **–fach** *neut* drawer. **–karren** *m* wheelbarrow. **–lade** *f* drawer.

schüchtern [ˈʃʏçtərn] *adj* shy. **Schüchternheit** *f* shyness.

Schuft [ʃuft] *m* (*pl* **-e**) rascal, rogue.

schuften *v* (*umg*.) toil, sweat, graft.

Schuh [ʃuː] *m* (*pl* **-e**) shoe. **–krem** *f* shoe polish. **–macher** *m* shoemaker. **–werk** *neut* footwear.

Schul||arbeit *f* homework, task. **–buch** *neut* school book.

schuld [ʃult] *adj* guilty. **schuld haben** be guilty. **Schuld** *f* (*pl* **-en**) (*Geld, fig*) debt; (*Rel, Jur*) guilt. **schuld sein an** be to blame for. **Schulden haben** be in debt. **die Schuld schieben auf** push the blame onto. **schulden** *v* owe. **Schuldgefühl** *neut* sense of guilt. **schuldig** *adj* guilty; (*Geld*) indebted. **Schuldig||e(r)** guilty person, culprit. **–keit** *f* (*unz*.) obligation; (*Pflicht*) duty. **–schein** *m* (*pl* **-e**) IOU. **–sprechung** *f* conviction, verdict of guilty.

Schuldirektor *m* headmaster. **–in** *f* headmistress.

schuldlos [ˈʃultloːs] *adj* innocent. **Schuld||ner** *m* (*pl* **-**), **–nerin** *f* (*pl* **-nen**) debtor.

Schule [ˈʃuːlə] *f* (*pl* **-n**) school. **schulen** *v* school, train.

Schüler [ˈʃyːlər] *m* (*pl* **-**) schoolboy; (*beieinem Meister*) pupil; (*Rel*) disciple. **–in** *f* (*pl* **-nen**) schoolgirl; pupil; disciple.

Schul||fach *neut* (school) subject. **–ferien** *pl* school holidays. **schulfrei haben** have a holiday. **Schul||freund** *m* school friend. **–geld** *neut* school fees. **–hof** *m* (school) playground. **–junge** *m* schoolboy. **–lehrer** *m* (*pl* **-**), **–lehrerin** *f* (*pl* **-nen**) schoolteacher. **–mädchen** *neut* schoolgirl. **–schluß** *m* end of term, breaking-up.

Schulter [ˈʃultər] *f* (*pl* **-en**) shoulder. **–blatt** *neut* shoulder blade.

Schulung [ˈʃuːluŋ] *f* (*pl* **-en**) schooling, training. **Schul||wesen** *neut* educational system. **–zimmer** *neut* classroom, schoolroom.

Schund [ʃunt] *m* trash, rubbish.

Schuppe [ˈʃupə] *f* (*pl* **-n**) scale. **Schuppen** *pl* dandruff. **schuppig** *adj* scaly.

schüren [ˈʃyːrən] *v* stir up, incite; (*Feuer*) poke, stoke.

schürfen [ˈʃʏrfən] *v* (*Haut*) scratch, graze; (*Metall*) prospect. **Schürfung** *f* (*pl* **-en**) graze, abrasion; prospecting.

Schurke [ˈʃurkə] *m* (*pl* **-n**) villain, scoundrel.

Schürze [ˈʃʏrtsə] *f* (*pl* **-n**) apron.

Schuß [ʃus] *m* (*pl* **Schüsse**) shot. **–loch** *neut* bullet-hole. **–waffe** *f* firearm. **–weite** *f* range. **–wunde** *f* gunshot wound.

Schüssel [ˈʃʏsəl] *f* (*pl* **-n**) bowl, dish.

Schuster [ˈʃuːstər] *m* (*pl* **-**) cobbler, shoemaker.

Schutt [ʃut] *m* (*Trümmer*) debris; (*Abfall*) refuse.

schütteln [ˈʃytəln] *v* shake.

schütten [ˈʃytən] *v* pour (out). **es schüttet** it's pouring (with rain).

schüttern [ˈʃytərn] *v* tremble, shake.

Schutz [ʃuts] *m* (*pl* -e) protection; (*Obdach*) shelter; (*Schirm*) screen. **-anzug** *m* protective clothing. **-brille** *f* goggles *pl*.

Schütze [ˈʃytsə] *m* (*pl* -n) marksman, sharpshooter; (*Bogen*) archer. **schützen** *v* protect, defend; (*behüten*) guard.

Schutz||farbe *f* camouflage. **-heilige(r)** *m* patron saint.

Schützling [ˈʃytsliŋ] *m* (*pl* -e) protégé(e), charge.

schutzlos [ˈʃutsloːs] *adj* defenceless. **Schutz||mann** *m* policeman. **-maßnahme** *f* precaution, preventive measure. **-mittel** *neut* preservative. **-umschlag** *m* (Book) jacket, dust cover.

Schwabe [ˈʃvaːbə] *m* (*pl* -n) Swabian (man). **-n** *neut* Swabia.

Schwäbin [ˈʃvɛːbin] *f* (*pl* -nen) Swabian woman. **schwäbisch** *adj* Swabian.

schwach [ʃvax] *adj* weak; (*kränklich*) delicate, sickly; (*klein*) small; (*gering*) scanty, poor.

Schwäche [ˈʃvɛçə] *f* (*pl* -n) weakness. **schwächen** *v* weaken.

Schwachheit [ˈʃvaxhait] *f* (*pl* -en) weakness.

schwächlich [ˈʃvɛçliç] *adj* feeble, sickly, delicate.

Schwachsinn [ˈʃvaxzin] *m* feeblemindedness. **schwachsinnig** *adj* feebleminded.

Schwager [ˈʃvaːgər] *m* (*pl* **Schwäger**) brother-in-law.

Schwägerin [ˈʃvɛːgərin] *f* (*pl* -nen) sister-in-law.

Schwalbe [ˈʃvalbə] *f* (*pl* -n) (*Vogel*) swallow.

Schwall [ʃval] *m* (*pl* -e) flood, torrent.

Schwamm [ʃvam] *m* (*pl* **Schwämme**) sponge.

Schwan [ʃvaːn] *m* (*pl* **Schwäne**) swan.

schwanger [ˈʃvaŋər] *adj* pregnant. **Schwangere** *f* (*pl* -n) pregnant woman. **Schwangerschaft** *f* pregnancy. **-vorsorge** *f* ante-natal care.

schwanken [ˈʃvaŋkən] *v* sway, swing; (*taumeln*) stagger, reel; (*zögern*) waver; (*Preise*) fluctuate. **-d** *adj* (*Person*) wavering.

Schwankung *f* (*pl* en) swaying, wavering, fluctuation.

Schwanz [ʃvants] *m* (*pl* **Schwänze**) tail.

Schwarm [ʃvarm] *m* (*pl* **Schwärme**) swarm; (*Vogel*) flock; (*Fische*) shoal; (*Rind, Schaf*) herd; (*Menschen*) crowd; (*fig*) craze.

schwärmen [ˈʃvɛrmən] *v* swarm; (*Mil*) deploy. **schwärmen für** rave about, gush over. **schwärmerisch** *adj* wildly enthusiastic.

schwarz [ʃvarts] *adj* black. **Schwarz** *neut* black (colour). **-brot** *neut* black bread. **-e(r)** Black, Negro. **-fahren** *v* travel without a valid ticket.

Schwärze [ˈʃvɛːrtsə] *f* (*pl* -n) blackness; (*Druck*) printer's ink. **schwärz||en** *v* blacken. **-lich** *adj* blackish, darkish.

Schwarz||markt *m* black market. **-wald** *m* Black Forest. **schwarzweiß** *adj* black-and-white.

schwatzen [ˈʃvatsən] *v also* **schwätzen** chatter, prattle; (*Geheimnisse*) gossip.

Schwebe [ˈʃveːbə] *f* suspense. **in der Schwebe** undecided, pending. **schweben** *v* float, hover; (*hängen*) hang, be suspended; (*fig*) remain undecided.

Schwede [ˈʃveːdə] *m* (*pl* -n), **Schwedin** *f* (*pl* -nen) Swede. **Schweden** *neut* Sweden. **schwedisch** *adj* Swedish.

Schwefel [ˈʃveːfəl] *m* sulphur.

schweifen [ˈʃvaifən] *v* roam, wander.

***schweigen** [ˈʃvaigən] *v* be silent. **ganz zu schweigen von** to say nothing of. **Schweigen** *neut* silence. **schweigsam** *adj* silent; (*fig*) secretive.

Schwein [ʃvain] *neut* (*pl* -e) pig; (*fig*) (good) luck. **Schweine||braten** *m* roast pork. **-fett** *neut* lard. **-fleisch** *neut* pork. **-hund** *m* (*vulg*) bastard, swine. **-rei** *f* filthy mess; (*fig*) dirty trick. **-stall** *m* pigsty. **Schweinsrippchen** *neut* pork chop.

Schweiß [ʃvais] *m* (*pl* -e) sweat, perspiration. **schweißen** *v* weld; (*Wild*) bleed.

Schweiz [ʃvaits] *f* **die Schweiz** Switzerland. **Schweizer** *m* (*pl* -), **Schweizerin** *f* (*pl* -nen) Swiss. **schweizerisch** *adj* Swiss.

Schwelle [ˈʃvɛlə] *f* (*pl* -n) threshold; (*Eisenbahn*) sleeper.

***schwellen** [ˈʃvɛlən] *v* swell.

schwemmen [ˈʃvɛmən] *v* wash down; (*Vieh*) water.

Schwengel [ˈʃvɛŋəl] *m* (*pl* -) (*Glocke*) clapper; (*Pumpe*) pump handle.

schwenken [ˈʃvɛŋkən] *v* turn; (*Fahne, Hut*) wave, flourish.

schwer [ʃveːr] *adj* heavy; (*schwierig*) difficult; (*ernst*) serious. **es ist 2 Kilo schwer** it weighs two kilos. **schwere Arbeit** hard work. **–beschädigt** *adj* seriously disabled. **Schwere** *f* weight. **schwerfällig** *adj* clumsy, awkward. **Schwergewichtler** *m* heavyweight. **schwerhörig** *adj* hard of hearing. **Schwer||industrie** *f* heavy industry. **–kraft** *f* gravity. **schwer||lich** *adj* with difficulty, hardly. **–mütig** *adj* melancholy, sad.

Schwert [ʃveːrt] *neut* (*pl* -er) sword.

Schwester [ˈʃvɛstər] *f* (*pl* -n) sister. **schwesterlich** *adj* sisterly. **Schwesternschaft** *f* sisterhood.

Schwieger||eltern *pl* parents-in-law; (*umg.*) in-laws. **–mutter** *m* mother-in-law. **–sohn** *m* son-in-law. **–tochter** *f* daughter-in-law. **–vater** *m* father-in-law.

schwierig [ˈʃviːrɪç] *adj* difficult, hard. **Schwierigkeit** *f* (*pl* -en) difficulty.

Schwimmbad [ˈʃvɪm baːt] *neut* swimming pool. **Schwimmbecken** *neut* swimming pool. **schwimmen** *v* swim; (*Gegenstand*) float. **Schwimmen** *neut* swimming, **schwimmend** *adj* swimming; floating. **Schwimmer** *m* (*pl* -) swimmer; float.

Schwindel [ˈʃvɪndəl] *m* (*pl* -) giddiness; (*Täuschung*) swindle, fraud. **schwindel||haft** *adj* giddy; fraudulent. **–ig** *adj* giddy, dizzy. **schwindeln** *v* cheat, swindle. **mir schwindelt** I feel giddy. **Schwindler** *m* (*pl* -) swindler, cheat.

***schwingen** [ˈʃvɪŋən] *v* swing; (*Fahne, Waffe*) wave, flourish. **Schwingung** *f* (*pl* -en) oscillation, vibration.

schwitzen [ˈʃvɪtsən] *v* sweat.

***schwören** [ˈʃvøː ːən] *v* swear.

schwul [ʃvuːl] *adj* (*vulg*) queer, homosexual. **schwül** [ʃvyːl] *adj* sultry, hot and humid.

Schwulst [ʃvʊlst] *m* (*pl* Schwülste) bombast, pomposity. **schwülstig** *adj* bombastic, pompous.

Schwund [ʃvʊnt] *m* contraction, shrinkage; (*Med*) atrophy.

Schwung [ʃvʊŋ] *m* (*pl* Schwünge) impetus, momentum; (*fig*) drive, vitality, verve. **–kraft** *f* centrifugal force; (*fig*) verve. **–rad** *neut* flywheel.

Schwur [ʃvuːr] *m* (*pl* Schwüre) oath. **–gericht** *neut* court with jury.

sechs [zɛks] *pron, adj* six. **sechst** *adj* sixth. **Sechstel** *neut* sixth (part).

sechzehn [ˈzɛçtseːn] *pron, adj* sixteen. **sechzehntel** *adj* sixteenth.

sechzig [ˈzɛçtsɪç] *pron, adj* sixty. **die sechziger Jahre** the '60s. **sechzigst** *adj* sixtieth.

See [zeː] **1** *m* (*pl* -n) lake. **2** *f* (*pl* -n) sea. **–fahrt** *f* voyage. **–jungfer** *f* mermaid. **seekrank** *adj* seasick.

Seele [ˈzeːlə] *f* (*pl* -n) soul, spirit. **seelisch** *adj* spiritual.

See||löwe *m* sealion. **–räuber** *m* pirate. **–wasser** *neut* sea water.

Segel [ˈzeːɡəl] *neut* (*pl* -) sail. **–boot** *neut* sailing boat. **–flugzeug** *neut* glider, sailplane. **segeln** *v* sail. **Segeltuch** *neut* canvas.

Segen [ˈzeːɡən] *m* (*pl* -) blessing; (*Tischgebet*) grace. **segnen** *v* bless. **Segnung** *f* (*pl* -en) blessing.

***sehen** [ˈzeːən] *v* see; (*anblicken*) look; (*beobachten*) watch, observe. **sehen lassen** display, show. **Sehen** *neut* (eye)sight, vision. **–swürdigkeit** *f* (tourist) sight. **Seh||feld** *neut* field of vision. **–kraft** *f* eyesight, vision.

Sehne [ˈzeːnə] *f* (*pl* -n) sinew, tendon; (*Bogen*) string.

sehnen [ˈzeːnən] *v* **sich sehnen nach** long for.

sehr [zeːr] *adv* very.

Sehweite [ˈzeːvaɪtə] *f* range of vision.

seicht [zaɪçt] *adj* shallow.

Seide [ˈzaɪdə] *f* (*pl* -n) silk.

Seife [ˈzaɪfə] *f* (*pl* -n) soap. **Seifen||schaum** *m* lather. **–wasser** *neut* suds *pl*, soapy water.

Seil [zaɪl] *neut* (*pl* -e) rope; (*Kabel*) cable. **–bahn** *f* funicular.

sein¹ [zaɪn] *adj, pron* his, its. **seinerseits** *adv* on *or* for his part. **seinesgleichen** *pron* the likes of him *pl*, people like him *pl*. **seinethalben, seinetwegen,** *or* **seinetwillen** *adv* for his sake. **seinige** *pron* **der, die, das seinige** his.

***sein²** *v* be. **es sei denn, daß** unless. **kann sein** perhaps. **sein lassen** leave alone. **mir ist kalt/warm** I feel cold/warm.

seit [zaɪt] *prep* since. **–dem** *conj* since; *adv* since then. **seit damals** since then. **seit**

wann? since when? **seit zwei Jahren** for two years.

Seite ['zaɪtə] f (pl -n) side; (Buch) page. **auf die Seite bringen** put aside. **von seiten** on the part (of). **Seiten||lampe** f side lamp. **-schiff** neut aisle. **-straße** f side street. **-wagen** m sidecar.

seither [zaɪˈheːr] adv since then.

seitlich ['zaɪtliç] adj lateral, side. **seitwärts** adv sideways.

Sekretär [zekreˈtɛːr] m (pl -e) secretary; (Schreibschrank) bureau, locking desk. **-in** f (pl -nen) secretary.

Sekt [zɛkt] m (pl -e) sparkling wine.

Sekte ['zɛktə] f (pl -n) sect. **sektiererisch** adj sectarian.

sekundär [zekunˈdɛːr] adj secondary.

Sekunde [zeˈkundə] f (pl -n) second.

selber ['zɛlbər] V selbst.

selbst [zɛlpst] pron self. adv even. **ich selbst** I myself. **von selbst** on one's own accord; (Sache) by itself. **sie kann es selbst machen** she can do it by herself. **selbst wenn** even though. **Selbst** neut self. **-achtung** f self-respect.

selbständig ['zɛlpstɛndiç] adj independent. **Selbständigkeit** f independence.

Selbst||bedienung f self-service. **-beherrschung** f self-control. **-mitleid** f self-pity. **-bestimmung** f self-determination.

selbstbewußt adj self-confident; (eingebildet) conceited. **Selbstbewußtsein** neut self-confidence; conceit.

Selbsterkenntnis f self-knowledge.

selbst||gebacken adj home-made. **-gefällig** adj self-satisfied. **-gerecht** adj self-righteous.

Selbsthilfe f self-help; (Jur) self-defence.

selbst||klebend adj adhesive, gummed. **-los** adj selfless.

Selbst||mord m suicide. **-mörder** m suicide. **-schutz** m self-defence.

selbstsicher adj self-confident. **Selbstsicherheit** f self-confidence.

Selbstsucht f selfishness. **selbstsüchtig** adj selfish.

Selbst||täuschung f self-deception. **-versorgung** f self-sufficiency.

selbstverständlich adj self-evident. adv obviously, naturally.

Selbstvertrauen neut self-confidence.

selig ['zeːliç] adj blessed; (verstorben) late, deceased; (überglücklich) blissful, delighted.

Sellerie ['zɛləri] f (pl -n) or m (pl -s) celeriac. **-stangen** pl celery sing.

selten ['zɛltən] adj rare. adv rarely, seldom.

seltsam ['zɛltzam] adj strange, odd, curious.

Semester [zeˈmɛstər] neut (pl -) semester, (half-yearly) session.

Seminar [zemiˈnaːr] neut (pl -e) training college; tutorial group.

Semit [zeˈmiːt] m (pl -en) Semite. **semitisch** adj Semitic.

Semmel ['zɛməl] f (pl -n) bread roll.

Senat [zeˈnaːt] m (pl -e) senate. **-or** m (pl -en) senator.

*senden ['zɛndən] v send; (Funk) transmit, broadcast. **Sender** m (pl -) transmitter; (Anstalt) station. **Sendung** f (pl -en) package; (Waren) consignment; (Funk) broadcast.

Senf [zɛnf] m (pl -e) mustard.

sengen ['zɛŋən] V singe.

Senkblei ['zɛŋkblaɪ] neut plumb-line.

Senkel ['zɛŋkəl] m (pl -) (shoe)lace.

senken ['zɛŋkən] v lower; (Kopf) bow; (Preise) reduce. **sich senken** sink. **senkrecht** adj vertical, perpendicular. **Senkung** f (pl -en) sinking; (Preise) reduction; (Vertiefung) depression.

Sensation [zɛnzatsioːn] f (pl -en) sensation. **sensationell** adj sensational.

Sense ['zɛnzə] f (pl -n) scythe.

sensibel [zɛnˈziːbəl] adj sensitive.

sentimental [zɛntimɛnˈtaːl] adj sentimental.

separieren [zepaˈriːrən] v separate.

September [zɛpˈtɛmbər] m (pl -) September.

septisch ['zɛptiʃ] adj septic.

Serbien ['zɛrbiən] neut Serbia. **Serbe** m, **Serbin** f Serbian. **serbisch** adj Serbian.

Serie ['zeːriə] f (pl -n) series. **-nherstellung** f mass production.

seriös [zeriˈøːs] adj serious, earnest; (Firma) reliable, honourable.

Serum ['zeːrum] neut (pl Seren) serum.

Service¹ ['zɛrvis] neut (pl -) (dinner) service.

Service² neut or m (pl -s) (customer) service.

servieren [zɛrˈviːrən] v serve. **Servierwagen** m trolley. **Serviette** f (pl -n) (table) napkin.

Sesam ['zɛzaːm] *m* sesame.

Sessel ['zɛsəl] *m* (*pl* -) armchair. **–lift** *m* chairlift.

seßhaft ['zɛshaft] *adj* settled, established; (*ansässig*) resident.

setzen ['zɛtsən] *v* set, put, place; (*einpflanzen*) plant; (*Druck*) compose, set; (*Spiel*) wager, bet. **in Bewegung setzen** set in motion. **außer Kraft setzen** invalidate. **in die Welt setzen** give birth to. **sich setzen** sit down. **sich in Verbindung setzen mit** get in contact with.

Seuche ['zɔyçə] *f* (*pl* -n) epidemic.

seufzen ['zɔyftsən] *v* sigh. **Seufzer** *m* (*pl* -) sigh.

Sex [zɛks] *m* (*pl* -) sex. **Sexual‖ität** *f* sexuality. **–aufklärung** *f* sex education. **sexuell** *adj* sexual. **sexy** *adj* sexy.

sezieren [ze'tsiːrən] *v* dissect.

sich [ziç] *pron* himself, herself, itself, yourself, oneself, yourselves; themselves; (*miteinander*) (with) one another, each other. **an (und für) sich** in itself. **bei sich haben** have with one. **sich die Hände waschen** wash one's hands. **sie lieben sich** they love each other.

Sichel ['ziçəl] *f* (*pl* -n) sickle; (*Mond*-) crescent.

sicher ['ziçər] *adj* safe, secure; (*gewiß*) sure, certain. *adv* surely, certainly. **Sicherheit** *f* safety; certainty; trust-worthiness; (*Pol, Psychol*) security. **Sicherheits‖bestimmungen** *pl* safety regulations. **–gurt** *m* safety belt. **–nadel** *f* safety pin.

sicher‖lich *adv* surely, certainly. **-n** *v* secure; (*schützen*) protect. **–stellen** *v* secure, guarantee, (*comp*) back up. **Sicherung** *f* (*pl* -en) protection; (*Elek*) fuse; (*Tech*) safety device.

Sicht [ziçt] *f* (*unz.*) sight; (*Aussicht*) view; (*Sichtbarkeit*) visibility. **sichtbar** *adj* visible. **Sichtbarkeit** *f* visibility.

sickern ['zikərn] *v* trickle, seep.

sie [ziː] *pron* she, it; her; they; them. **Sie** *pron* you.

Sieb [ziːp] *neut* (*pl* -e) sieve; (*Tee*) strainer.

sieben¹ ['ziːbən] *v* sift, sieve.

sieben² *pron, adj* seven. **siebent** *or* **siebt** *adj* seventh.

siebzehn ['ziːptseːn] *pron, adj* seventeen. **siebzehnt** *adj* seventeenth.

siebzig ['ziːptsiç] *pron, adj* seventy. **siebzigt** *adj* seventieth.

siedeln ['ziːdəln] *v* settle, colonize.

***sieden** ['ziːdən] *v* boil. **Siedepunkt** *m* boiling point.

Siedler ['ziːdlər] *m* (*pl* -) settler. **Siedlung** *f* (*pl* -en) settlement (place); (*am Stadtrand*) housing estate.

Sieg [ziːk] *m* (*pl* -e) victory.

Siegel ['ziːgəl] *neut* (*pl* -) seal, signet.

siegen ['ziːgən] *v* win, triumph, be victorious. **Sieger** *m* (*Mil*) conqueror, victor; (*Sport*) winner. **siegreich** *adj* victorious.

Signal [zi'naːl] *neut* (*pl* -e) signal. **–feuer** *neut* beacon. **–rakete** *f* rocket-flare.

Signatur [zigna'tuːr] *f* (*pl* -en) mark, symbol; (*Unterschrift*) signature.

Silbe ['zilbə] *f* (*pl* -n) syllable.

Silber ['zilbər] *neut* silver. **silbern** *adj* silver.

Silicium/Silizium [zilitsium] *neut* silicon. **–chip** *m* (*pl* -s) silicon chip.

Silvesterabend [zilvɛstəraːbənt] *m* New Year's Eve.

simpel ['zimpəl] *adj* simple.

Sims [zims] *neut* (*pl* -e) (*Fenster*) window-sill.

simulieren [zimu'liːrən] *v* pretend; (*Krankheit*) malinger; (*Tech*) simulate.

Sinfonie [zinfo'niː] *f* (*pl* -n) symphony.

***singen** ['ziŋən] *v* sing. **Singvogel** *m* songbird.

***sinken** ['ziŋkən] *v* sink; (*fig*) diminish; (*Preise*) fall. **Sinken** *neut* fall, drop; (*Werte*) depreciation; (*fig*) decline.

Sinn [zin] *m* (*pl* -e) sense; (*Gedanken*) mind, thoughts *pl*. **es hat keinen Sinn** it makes no sense, *es kam mir in den Sinn, daß* ... it crossed my mind that ... **Sinn für Humor** sense of humour. **Sinnfür Literatur** interest in literature. **Sinnbild** *neut* symbol. **sinn‖bildlich** *adj* symbolic. **–en** *v* reflect, think (over). **–lich** *adj* sensual. **–los** *adj* senseless. **Sinnspruch** *m* epigram, maxim.

Sippe ['zipə] *f* (*pl* -n) tribe; (*Verwandte*) kin.

Sirup ['ziːrup] *m* (*pl* -e) syrup.

Sitte ['zitə] *f* (*pl* -n) custom; (*Gewohnheit*) habit. **Sitten** *pl* morals. **Sittenlehre** *f* ethics. **sittenlos** *adj* immoral. **sittlich** *adj* moral. **Sittlichkeit** *f* morality. **–sverbrechen** *neut* indecent assault.

Situation [zituatsioːn] *f* (*pl* -en) situation.

Sitz [zits] *m* (*pl* -e) seat; (*Kleidung*) fit.

–bank f bench. **sitzen** v sit; (*Kleidung*) fit.
–bleiben v remain seated. **Sitzung** f (*pl
-en*) sitting; (*Versammlung*) session.

Skala ['ska:la] f (*pl* **Skalen**) scale. **Skalen-
scheibe** f dial.

Skandal [skan'da:l] m (*pl -e*) scandal. **skandalös** adj scandalous.

Skandinavien [skandina:vən] neut
Scandinavia. **Skandinavier** m (*pl -*),
Skandinavierin f (*pl -nen*) Scandinavian.
skandinavisch adj Scandinavian.

Skelett [ske'lɛt] neut (*pl -e*) skeleton.

Skeptiker ['skɛptikər] m (*pl -*) sceptic. **skeptisch** adj sceptical.

Ski [ʃi] m (*pl -er*) ski. **–fahrer(in)** skier.

Skizze ['skitsə] f (*pl -n*) sketch. **skizzieren** v
sketch.

Sklave ['skla:və] m (*pl -n*) slave. **Sklaverei** f
slavery. **Sklavin** f (*pl -nen*) (female) slave,
slave girl.

Skorpion ['skɔrpiɔn] m (*pl -e*) (*Tier*) scorpion; (*Astrol*) Scorpio.

Skrupel ['skru:pəl] m (*pl -*) scruple. **skru-
pellos** adj unscrupulous. **skrupulös** adj
scrupulous.

Skulptur [skulp'tu:r] f (*pl -en*) sculpture.

Slowakei [slo:vak'ai] f Slovakia. **Slowake**
m, **Slowakin** f Slovakian. **–slowakisch** adj
Slovakian.

Slowenien [slo:'veini:ən] neut Slovenia.
Slowene m, **Slowenin** f Slovenian.
slowenisch adj Slovenian.

Smaragd [sma'rakt] m (*pl -e*) emerald.
smaragdgrün adj emerald(-green).

Smoking ['smo:kiŋ] m (*pl -s*) dinner jacket,
(US) tuxedo.

so [zo:] adv so, in this way. conj consequently, therefore. **so daß** so that. **so ein**
such a. **so sehr** so much. **so ... wie** ... as ...
as ... **um so besser** all the better. **–bald**
conj as soon as.

Socke ['zɔkə] f (*pl -n*) sock.

Sockel ['zɔkəl] m (*pl -*) pedestal, base,
plinth.

sodann [zo'dan] adv, conj then, in that
case.

Sodawasser ['zo:davasər] neut soda water.

Sodbrennen ['zo:tbrɛnən] neut heartburn.

soeben [zo'e:bən] adv just (now).

Sofa ['zo:fa] neut (*pl -s*) sofa.

sofern [zo'fɛrn] conj as or so far as.

sofort [zo'fɔrt] adv at once, immediately.

–ig adj immediate.

Software ['sɔftwɛə] f (*comp*) software.

Sog [zo:k] m (*pl -e*) suction; (*Boot*) wake.

sogar [zo'ga:r] adv even.

sogenannt ['zo:gənant] adj so-called.

Sohle ['zo:lə] f (*pl -n*) (*Fuß, usw.*) sole.
sohlen v sole.

Sohn [zo:n] m (*pl* **Söhne**) son.

solang(e) [zo'laŋ ə)] conj as long as;
(*während*) while.

solch [zɔlç] pron, adj such. **solcher||art**
adv of this sort, along these lines. **–lei** adj
of such a kind. **–weise** adv in such a way.

Soldat [zɔlda:t] m (*pl -en*) soldier. **Soldat
werden** enlist, join up.

Söldner ['zœldnər] m (*pl -*) mercenary.

solid [zo'li:t] adj also **solide** (*Person*) reliable, decent; (*Leben*) decent, respectable;
(*Gegenstand*) solid, robust. **–arisch** adj
united, unanimous. **Solidarität** f solidarity.

Solist [zo'list] m (*pl -en*), **Solistin** f (*pl -nen*)
soloist.

Soll [zɔl] neut (*pl -s*) (*Komm*) debit;
(*Produktion*) target. **sollen** v ought to, have
to, should; (*angeblich*) be supposed to be.
ich sollte I should. *was soll das?* what is this
supposed to be or mean? *sie soll reich sein*
she is said to be rich. *Kinder sollen gehorchen*
children should be obedient. *du sollst nicht
töten* thou shalt not kill.

Solo ['zo:lo] neut (*pl -s or* **Soli**) solo.
–sänger m soloist, solo singer.

Sommer ['zɔmər] m (*pl -*) summer. **–ferien**
pl summer holidays. **–sprosse** f freckle.

Sonate [zo'na:tə] f (*pl -n*) sonata.

Sonde ['zɔndə] f (*pl -n*) (*Tech*) probe.

Sonder||angebot neut special offer. **–aus-
gabe** f special edition. **sonder||bar** adj
strange, peculiar. **–lich** adj remarkable, special.

sondern¹ ['zɔndərn] v separate.

sondern² conj but. **nicht nur ... sondern
auch** ... not only ... but also ....

Sonder||preis m special price. **–ung** f (*pl
-en*) separation.

Sonnabend ['zɔna:bənt] m Saturday.
sonnabends adv on Saturdays.

Sonne ['zɔnə] f (*pl -n*) sun. **sonnen** v air,
put out in the sun. **sich sonnen** sun oneself, lie in the sun.

Sonnen||aufgang m sunrise. **–blume** f

sunflower. **–brand** *m* sunburn. **–bräune** *f* suntan. **–finsternis** *f* solar eclipse. **–schein** *m* sunshine. **–stich** *m* sunstroke. **–system** *neut* solar system. **–untergang** *m* sunset.

sonnig ['zɔnɪç] *adj* sunny.

Sonntag ['zɔntaːk] *m* Sunday. **sonntags** *adv* on Sundays.

sonst [zɔnst] *adv* otherwise, else. **sonstetwas?** anything else? **sonst nichts** nothing else. **wer sonst?** who else? **wie sonst** as usual. **–ig** *adj* other, miscellaneous. **–wie** *adv* some other way. **–wo** *adv* elsewhere.

Sopran [zo'praːn] *m* (*pl* **-e**) soprano. **–istin** *f* (*pl* **-nen**) soprano (singer).

Sorge ['zɔrgə] *f* (*pl* **-n**) (*Kummer*) care, worry; (*Pflege*) care. **sich Sorgen machen (um)** worry (about). **sorgen für** take care of. **dafür sorgen, daß** make sure that, see to it that. **sich sorgen** be anxious, worry. **sorgen‖frei** or **–los** *adj* carefree. **–voll** *adj* careworn. **sorg‖lich** *adj* careful, caring. **–los** *adj* careless. **–sam** *adj* careful, cautious.

Sorte ['zɔrtə] *f* (*pl* **-n**) sort, kind; (*Ware*) brand. **sortieren** *v* sort (out). **Sortiment** *neut* (*pl* **-e**) assortment.

Soße ['zoːsə] *f* (*pl* **-n**) sauce; (*für Fleisch*) gravy.

Souveränität [suvɛrɛniːtɛːt] *f* sovereignty.

soviel ['zoːfiːl] *conj* as far as. *adv* as or so much. **soviel wie** as much as. **soweit** *conj* as *or* so far as; *adv* so far. **sowenig(wie)** *conj* as little (as). **sowie** *conj* as soon as; (*außerdem*) as well as, and also. **sowieso** *adv* in any case.

Sowjet [zɔ'vjɛt] *m* (*pl* **-e**) Soviet. **sowjetisch** *adj* Soviet. **Sowjetunion** *f* Soviet Union.

sowohl [zɔ'voːl] *conj* as well as. **sowohl ... als auch ...** both ... and ....

sozial [zotsiaːl] *adj* social. **Sozial‖abgaben** *pl* national insurance contributions. **–demokrat** *m* social democrat. **–einrichtungen** *pl* social services. **–fürsorge** *f* (social) welfare.

Sozialismus [zotsia'lizmus] *m* socialism. **Sozialist** *m* socialist. **sozialistisch** *adj* socialist.

Sozial‖politik *f* social policies *pl*. **–produkt** *neut* (gross) national product. **–unterstützung** *f* social security.

Soziologe [zotsio'loːgə] *m* (*pl* **-n**) sociologist. **Soziologie** *f* sociology. **soziologisch** *adj* sociological.

sozusagen [zotsu'zaːgən] *adv* so to speak.

spähen ['ʃpɛːən] *v* look out, watch; (*Mil*) scout.

Spalt [ʃpalt] *m* (*pl* **-e**) crack, slit. **-e** *f* (*Druck*) column; crack, crevice. **spalten** *v* split.

Spam [spam] *m* (*Internet*) spam.

Span [ʃpaːn] *m* (*pl* **Späne**) chip, shaving; (*Splitter*) splinter.

Spange ['ʃpaŋə] *f* (*pl* **-n**) clasp; (*Schnalle*) buckle.

Spanien ['ʃpaːniən] *new* Spain. **Spanier** *m* (*pl* **-**), **Spanierin** *f* (*pl* **-nen**) Spaniard. **spanisch** *adj* Spanish.

Spann [ʃpan] *m* (*pl* **-e**) instep.

Spanne ['ʃpanə] *f* (*pl* **-n**) span.

spannen ['ʃpanən] *v* stretch; (*straffziehen*) tighten. **-d** *adj* thrilling, exciting. **Spann‖seil** *neut* guy(-rope). **–ung** *f* (*pl* **-en**) tension.

sparen ['ʃpaːrən] *v* save; (*sparsam sein*) economize. **Sparer** *m* (*pl* **-**) saver.

Spargel ['ʃpargəl] *m* (*pl* **-**) asparagus. **–kohl** *m* broccoli.

Sparkasse ['ʃpaːrkasə] *f* savings bank **–nbuch** *neut* deposit book.

spärlich ['ʃpɛːlɪç] *adj* scanty, meagre. **Spärlichkeit** *f* scarcity.

Sparmaßnahme ['ʃpaːrmaːsnaːmə] *f* economy measure.

Spaß [ʃpaːs] *m* (*pl* **Späße**) fun; (*Scherz*) joke. **Spaß haben an** enjoy. *es macht uns Spaß* it amuses us, it is fun. **spaß‖en** *v* make fun, joke. **–haft** or **–ig** *adj* comical. **Spaßvogel** *m* joker, clown.

spät [ʃpɛːt] *adj* late. *wie spät ist es?* what is the time?

Spaten ['ʃpaːtən] *m* (*pl* **-**) spade.

später ['ʃpɛːtər] *adj* later. **spätestens** *adv* at the latest.

Spatz [ʃpats] *m* (*pl* **-en**) sparrow.

spazieren [ʃpa'tsiːrən] *v* go for a walk, stroll. **–fahren** *v* go for a drive. **–gehen** *v* go for a walk, walk. **Spazier‖fahrt** *f* drive. **–gang** *m* walk, stroll.

Specht [ʃpɛçt] *m* (*pl* **-e**) woodpecker.

Speck [ʃpɛk] *m* (*pl* **-e**) bacon; (*Schmalz*) lard, fat. **speckig** *adj* greasy.

spedieren [ʃpe'diːrən] *v* forward, transport, ship. **Spediteur** *m* (*pl* **-e**) shipping agent, haulier, carrier. **Spedition** *f* (*pl* **-en**) shipping (agency).

Speer [ʃpeːr] *m* (*pl* **-e**) spear.

Speichel [ˈʃpaɪçəl] *m* spittle, saliva.

Speicher [ˈʃpaɪçər] *m* (*pl* -) warehouse, storehouse; (*Getreide*) granary; (*Computer*) memory. **speichern** *v* store.

Speise [ˈʃpaɪzə] *f* (*pl* -n) food; (*Gericht*) dish. **-eis** *neut* ice cream. **-karte** *f* menu. **speisen** *v* dine, eat. **Speise‖röhre** *f* gullet. **-saal** *m* dining room. **-wagen** *m* dining car.

Spektakel [ʃpɛkˈtaːkəl] *m* (*pl* -) spectacle; (*Aufregung*) uproar.

Spekulation [ʃpekuˈlatsioːn] *f* (*pl* -en) speculation. **spekulieren** *v* speculate.

Spende [ˈʃpɛndə] *f* (*pl* -n) donation. **spenden** *v* contribute, donate. **Spender** *m* (*pl* -), **Spenderin** *f* (*pl* -nen) donor.

Sperre [ˈʃpɛrə] *f* (*pl* -n) barrier; (*Verbot*) ban, blockade. **sperren** *v* close, bar; (*untersagen*) ban; (*Strom*) cut off. **Sperr‖riegel** *m* (door) bolt. **-kette** *f* door chain. **-klinke** *f* safety catch. **-ung** *f* blocking, barring. **-zeit** *f* closing time.

Spesen [ˈʃpeːzən] *pl* expenses.

Spezialfach [ʃpetsiaːlfax] *neut* speciality. **spezialisieren** *v* specialize. **Spezialist** *m* specialist. **speziell** *adj* special.

spezifisch [ʃpeˈtsiːfiʃ] *adj* specific.

Sphäre [ˈsfɛːrə] *f* (*pl* -n) sphere.

Spiegel [ˈʃpiːgəl] *m* (*pl* -) mirror; (*Schiff*) stern. **-ei** *neut* fried egg. **-glas** *neut* plate glass. **spiegeln** *v* reflect; (*glänzen*) shine. **Spiegelung** *f* (*pl* -en) reflection.

Spiel [ʃpiːl] *neut* (*pl* -e) game; (*Theater*) play; (*Glücksspiel*) gambling. **aufs Spiel setzen** put at stake. **-automat** *m* slot machine. **-bank** *f* casino. **-brett** *neut* board.

spielen [ˈʃpiːlən] *v* play; (*Geld*) gamble.

Spieler [ˈʃpiːlər] *m* (*pl* -), **Spielerin** *f* (*pl* -nen) player; (*Schauspiel*) actor *m*, actress *f*; (*Geld*) gambler. **Spielergebnis** *neut* result, (final) score. **spielerisch** *adj* playful. **Spiel‖feld** *neut* playing field. **-karte** *f* playing card. **-platz** *m* playground. **-zeug** *neut* toy.

Spieß [ʃpiːs] *m* (*pl* -e) spear; (*Bratspieß*) spit. **-bürger** *m* philistine.

Spinat [ʃpiˈnaːt] *m* (*pl* -e) spinach.

Spindel [ˈʃpindəl] *f* (*pl* -n) spindle, axle.

Spinne [ˈʃpinə] *f* (*pl* -n) spider. **spinnen** *v* spin; (*umg.*) talk nonsense. **du spinnst ja!** you're crazy!

Spion [ʃpioːn] *m* (*pl* -e) spy. **-age** *f* espionage. **spionieren** *v* spy.

Spirale [ʃpiˈraːlə] *f* (*pl* -n) spiral.

Spirituosen [ʃpirituˈoːzən] *pl* spirits, liquor *sing*.

spitz [ʃpits] *adj* sharp, pointed. **Spitze** *f* (*pl* -n) point, tip. **Spitzen** *pl* (*Gewebe*) lace *sing*. **spitzen** *v* sharpen. **Spitzen‖ geschwindigkeit** *f* top speed. **-leistung** *f* maximum performance, record. **Spitzer** *m* (*pl* -) pencil-sharpener. **spitzfindig** *adj* shrewd, ingenious; (*haarspalterisch*) over-critical, hair-splitting. **Spitzname** *m* nickname.

Splitter [ˈʃplitər] *m* (*pl* -) splinter. **-gruppe** *f* splinter group.

spontan [ʃpɔnˈtaːn] *adj* spontaneous.

Spore [ˈʃpoːrə] *f* (*pl* -n) spore.

Sporn [ʃpɔrn] *m* (*pl* **Sporen**) spur. **spornen** *v* spur.

Sport [ʃpɔrt] *m* (*pl* -e) sport. **Sport treiben** go in for sport(s). **Sport‖feld** *neut* sports ground. **-ler** *m* (*pl* -) sportsman. **-lerin** *f* (*pl* -nen) sportswoman. **sportlich** *adj* sporting.

Spott [ʃpɔt] *m* ridicule. **spottbillig** *adj* dirt cheap. **spotten über** ridicule, deride.

spöttisch [ˈʃpœtiʃ] *adj* mocking, scornful.

Sprache [ˈʃpraːxə] *f* (*pl* -n) language, speech. **Sprachfehler** *m* speech defect; (*Gramm*) grammatical error. **sprach‖lich** *adj* linguistic. **-los** *adj* speechless.

*sprechen [ˈʃprɛçən] *v* speak. **sprechen mit** talk to, speak with. **Sprecher** *m* (*pl* -), **Sprecherin** *f* (*pl* -nen) speaker; (*offiziell*) spokesman.

sprengen [ˈʃprɛŋən] *v* explode, blow up; (*aufbrechen*) burst open; (*bespritzen*) sprinkle. **Spreng‖kopf** *m* warhead. **-stoff** *m* explosive.

Sprichwort [ˈʃpriçvɔrt] *neut* (*pl* **Sprichwörter**) proverb.

*sprießen [ˈʃpriːsən] *v* sprout.

Spring [ʃpriŋ] *m* (*pl* -e) spring. **-brunnen** *m* fountain. **Springen** *v* jump, spring; (*Ball*) bounce; (*platzen*) burst, break; (*Schwimmen*) dive. **Springen** *neut* jumping; (*Schwimmen*) diving. **Springer** *m* (*pl* -) jumper; (*Schach*) knight. **Spring‖feder** *f* spring. **-seil** *neut* skipping rope.

Sprit [ʃprit] *m* (*pl* -e) (*umg.*) gas, juice.

Spritze [ˈʃpritsə] *f* (*pl* -n) syringe; (*Einspritzung*) injection; (*Tech*) spray. **spritzen** *v* squirt; (*besprengen*) sprinkle;

(Med) inject.

spröde [ˈʃprɛːdə] *adj* brittle; *(Person)* reserved, cool.

Sproß [ʃprɔs] *m (pl* **Sprosse)** shoot, sprout.

Spruch [ʃprʊx] *m (pl* **Sprüche)** saying, aphorism; *(Jur)* sentence.

Sprudel [ˈʃpruːdəl] *m (pl* -**)** spring, source (of water); mineral water. **sprudeln** *v* bubble up; *(Mineralwasser, usw.)* sparkle. –**d** *adj* bubbling; sparkling. **Sprudelwasser** *neut* mineral water.

Sprühdose [ˈʃpryːdoːzə] *f* spray can, aerosol pack. **sprühen** *v* spray; *(Regen)* drizzle. **Sprühregen** *m* drizzle.

Sprung [ʃprʊŋ] *m (pl* **Sprünge)** leap, jump; *(Schwimmen)* dive; *(Riß)* crack, split. –**brett** *neut* diving board.

spucken [ˈʃpʊkən] *v* spit.

Spuk [ʃpuːk] *m (pl* -**e)** ghost.

Spülbecken [ˈʃpyːlbɛkən] *neut* sink.

Spule [ˈʃpuːlə] *f (pl* -**n)** spool; *(Elek)* coil. **spulen** *v* wind.

spülen [ˈʃpyːlən] *v* rinse, wash; *(Geschirr)* wash up; *(WC)* flush. **Spül|lung** *f* rinsing, washing; flushing. –**wasser** *neut* dishwater.

Spur [ʃpuːr] *f (pl* -**en)** track, trail; *(fig)* trace.

spürbar [ˈʃpyːrbaːr] *adj* perceptible, noticeable. **spüren** *v* trace; *(folgen)* track; *(fühlen)* feel. **Spürsinn** *m* shrewdness.

Staat [ʃtaːt] *m (pl* -**en)** state. **staatlich** *adj* state. **Staats||angehörige(r)** *m* citizen, national. –**angehörigkeit** *f* nationality. –**anwalt** *m* public prosecutor. –**bürger** *m* citizen. –**mann** *m* statesman. –**streich** *m* coup d'état.

Stab [ʃtaːp] *m (pl* **Stäbe)** staff; *(Metall)* bar; *(Holz)* stick, pole.

stabil [ʃtaˈbiːl] *adj* stable. –**isieren** *v* stabilize. **Stabilität** *f* stability.

Stachel [ˈʃtaxəl] *m (pl* -**n)** spike, prickle; *(Biene)* sting. –**beere** *f* gooseberry. –**draht** *m* barbed wire. **stachel||ig** *adj* prickly; stinging. –**n** *v* prick; sting. **Stachelschwein** *neut* porcupine.

Stadion [ˈʃtaːdiɔn] *neut (pl* **Stadien)** stadium.

Stadt [ʃtat] *f (pl* **Städte)** town, city.

städtisch [ˈʃtɛtʃ] *adj* urban; *(Verwaltung)* municipal.

Stadt||mitte *f* town centre. –**plan** *m* town map. –**rat** *m* town council; *(Person)* councillor.

Staffel [ˈʃtafəl] *f (pl* -**n)** rung, step; *(Mil)* detachment; *(Lauf)* relay. –**ei** *f (pl* -**en)** easel.

Stahl [ʃtaːl] *m (pl* -**e)** steel.

Stall [ʃtal] *m (pl* **Ställe)** *(Pferde)* stable; *(Hunde)* kennel; *(Schweine)* sty; *(Kuhe)* cowshed.

Stamm [ʃtam] *m (pl* **Stämme)** *(Volk)* tribe; *(Baum)* trunk; *(Stengel)* stalk, stem. –**baum** *m* family tree, genealogy; *(Hund)* pedigree. **stammen (von)** *v (Ort)* come (from); *(Familie)* be descended (from); *(fig, Gramm)* be derived (from).

stampfen [ˈʃtam pfən] *v* stamp; *(zerstampfen)* mash, crush.

Stand [ʃtant] *m (pl* **Stände)** stand; *(Markt)* stall; *(Höhe)* level, height; *(Stellung)* position, situation.

Standard [ˈʃtandart] *m (pl* -**s)** standard.

Standbild [ˈʃtantbilt] *neut* statue.

Ständer [ˈʃtɛndər] *m (pl* -**)** stand.

Standesamt [ˈʃtandəzamt] *neut* registry office.

standhaft [ˈʃtanthaft] *adj* steadfast. **Standhaftigkeit** *f* steadfastness. **standhalten** *v* stand firm.

ständig [ˈʃtɛndiç] *adj* permanent; *(laufend)* constant.

Stand||ort *m* position, station. –**punkt** *m* standpoint.

Stange [ˈʃtaŋə] *f (pl* -**n)** pole, bar.

Stanniol [ʃtanˈioːl] *neut (pl* -**e)** tinfoil.

Stapel [ˈʃtaːpəl] *m (pl* -**)** pile, heap, stack. **stapeln** *v* pile up.

Star¹ [ʃtaːr] *m (pl* -**e)** *(Vogel)* starling.

Star² *m (pl* -**s)** *(Film)* star.

Star³ *m (pl* -**e)** *(Med)* cataract.

stark [ʃtark] *adj* strong; *(Zahl)* numerous; *(dick)* thick(set). **starke Erkältung** severe cold. **stark gesucht** in great demand.

Stärke [ˈʃtɛrkə] *f (pl* -**n)** strength; *(Dicke)* stoutness; *(Gewalt)* violence; *(Wäsche-, Chem)* starch. **stärken** *v* strengthen.

starr [ʃtar] *adj* rigid; *(Blick)* fixed, staring. **starren** *v* stare. **Starrheit** *f* rigidity; *(Charakter)* obstinacy.

Start [ʃtart] *m (pl* -**e)** start; *(Flugzeug)* takeoff. **starten** *v* start; take off. **Starter** *m (pl* -**)** *(Mot, Sport)* starter. –**klappe** *f (Mot)* choke. –**seite** *f (comp)* home page.

Station [ʃtatsˈioːn] *f (pl* -**en)** station; *(Krankenhaus)* ward.

Statistik [ʃtaˈtɪstɪk] f (pl -en) statistics. **statistisch** adj statistical.

statt [ʃtat] prep instead of. **Statt** f place, stead.

Stätte [ˈʃtɛtə] f (pl -n) place, spot.

*statt||finden v take place. **–haft** adj allowed, permissible. **–lich** adj stately; (Summe) considerable.

Statut [ʃtaˈtuːt] neut (pl -en) statute.

Staub [ʃtaup] m dust. **staubig** adj dusty. **Staub||sauger** m (pl -) vacuum cleaner. **–tuch** neut duster.

stauen [ˈʃtauən] v dam (up); (Ladung) stow (away). **sich stauen** accumulate, pile up.

staunen [ˈʃtaunən] v be astonished. **Staunen** neut (pl -) astonishment.

Steak [steːk] neut (pl -s) steak.

*stechen [ˈʃtɛçən] v (Insekt) sting; (Dorn) prick; (mit einer Waffe) stab, jab. **–d** adj stinging; (fig) piercing. **Stechpalme** f holly.

Steck||brief m warrant (for arrest). **–dose** f (Elek) socket.

stecken [ˈʃtɛkən] v put, place, insert; (sich befinden) be, lie. etwas in die Tasche stecken put something in one's pocket. **in Brand stecken** set fire to. da steckt er! there he is! that's where he's hiding! es steckt etwas dahinter there's more to it than meets the eye. **steckenbleiben** v be or get stuck. **Steck||enpferd** neut hobby-horse; (fig) hoby. **–er** m (pl -) (Elek) plug. **–nadel** f pin.

Steg [ʃteːk] m (pl -e) (foot)path; (Brücke) (foot)bridge; (Geige) bridge.

*stehen [ˈʃteːən] v stand; (sein) be (situated). **in Verdacht stehen** be suspected. **offen stehen** be open. das Kleid steht dir (gut) the dress suits you. **stehen||bleiben** v (nicht weitergehen) come to a standstill, stop; (nicht umfallen) remain standing. **–d** adj standing; (ständig) permanent.

*stehlen [ˈʃteːlən] v steal. **Stehlen** neut (unz.) stealing, theft.

steif [ʃtaif] adj stiff. **Steifheit** f stiffness.

Steig [ʃtaik] m (pl -e) path. **–bügel** m stirrup. **steigen** v rise; (klettern) climb. **–d** adj rising; (wachsend) growing.

steigern [ˈʃtaigərn] v raise, increase. **Steigerung** f (pl -en) rise, increase.

Steigung [ˈʃtaigun] f (pl -en) rise, incline.

steil [ʃtail] adj steep.

Stein [ʃtain] m (pl -e) stone. **–bock** m (Tier) ibex; (Astrol) Capricorn. **–bruch** m quarry.

steinern adj stone. **Steingut** neut stoneware, pottery. **steinigen** v stone (to death). **Stein||platte** f (pl -n) stone slab, flagstone. **–zeit** f Stone Age.

Stelle [ˈʃtɛlə] f (pl -n) place; (Arbeit) job, position; (in einem Buch) passage. **an Ort und Stelle** on the spot. **an Stelle von** in place of. **eine Stelle bekleiden** hold a position.

stellen [ˈʃtɛlən] v put, place; (Frage) ask; (Forderung) make. **zufriedenstellen** satisfy. eine Falle stellen set a trap. sich stellen present oneself; (vortäuschen) pretend, feign.

Stellen||angebot neut vacancy, vacant position. **–nachweis** m employment agency.

Stellung [ˈʃtɛlun] f (pl -en) position; (Arbeit) post, position; (Ansicht) attitude, opinion; (Körperhaltung) posture. **–nahme** f comment, opinion.

stellvertretend adj deputy, delegated. **Stellvertret||er** m deputy, representative. **–ung** f representation.

Stelze [ˈʃtɛltsə] f (pl -n) stilt.

Stempel [ˈʃtɛmpəl] m (pl -) stamp. **–geld** neut (umg.) dole money. **stempeln** v stamp. **stempeln gehen** (umg.) go on the dole.

Stengel [ˈʃtɛnəl] m (pl -) stalk.

Stenograph [ʃtenoˈgraːf] m (pl -en) stenographer. **–ie** f shorthand. **Stenotypist(in)** shorthand typist.

Steppe [ˈʃtɛpə] f (pl -n) steppe, prairie.

Sterbe||bett neut deathbed. **–fall** m a death.

*sterben [ˈʃtɛrbən] v die. **Sterben** neut death. **sterblich** adj mortal. **Sterblichkeit** f mortality.

Stereoanlage [ˈʃtereoanlaːgə] f stereo (system).

steril [ʃteˈriːl] adj sterile. **–isieren** v sterilize.

Stern [ʃtɛrn] m (pl -e) star. **–bild** neut constellation. **–chen** neut asterisk. **–kunde** f astronomy.

stet [ʃteːt] or **stetig** adj constant, continual. **stets** adv always, constantly.

Steuer [ˈʃtɔyər] f (pl -n) tax.

Steuer||behörde f inland revenue, (US) internal revenue. **–berater** m tax consultant. **–erklärung** f tax return. **–hinterziehung** f tax evasion.

steuern [ˈʃtɔyərn] v steer.

steuerpflichtig [ˈʃtɔyərpflɪçtɪç] adj taxable,

subject to taxation.
Steuer||rad *neut* steering wheel. **–säule** *f*
steering column.
Steuerung [ˈʃtɔyərʊŋ] *f* (*pl* **-en**) steering.
Steuerzahler [ˈʃtɔyɐtsaːlɐ] *m* tax-payer.
Stich [ʃtɪç] *m* (*pl* **-e**) prick; (*Insekt*) sting;
(*Messer*) stab; (*Nähen*) stitch; (*Kartenspiel*)
trick. **im Stich lassen** abandon, leave in
the lurch.
sticken [ˈʃtɪkən] *v* embroider. **Stickerei** *f*
embroidery.
Stickstoff [ˈʃtɪkʃtɔf] *m* nitrogen.
Stiefbruder [ˈʃtiːfbruːdɐ] *m* stepbrother.
Stiefel [ˈʃtiːfəl] *m* (*pl* -) boot.
Stief||eltern *pl* step-parents. **–kind** *neut*
stepchild. **–mutter** *f* stepmother. **–müt-
terchen** *neut* pansy. **–schwester** *f* stepsister. **–sohn** *m* stepson. **–tochter** *f*
stepdaughter. **–vater** *m* stepfather.
Stiel [ʃtiːl] *m* (*pl* **-e**) handle; (*Bot*) stalk.
Stier [ʃtiːɐ] *m* (*pl* **-e**) bull. **–kampf** *m* bullfight.
Stift[1] [ʃtɪft] *m* (*pl* **-e**) peg; (*Bleistift*) pencil;
(*Pflocke*) pin.
Stift[2] *neut* (*pl* **-e** *or* **-er**) (charitable) foundation; (*Kloster*) monastery.
stiften [ˈʃtɪftən] *v* donate; (*gründen*) found,
establish; (*Frieden*) make. **Stifter** *m*
founder. **Stiftung** *f* (*pl* **-en**) (charitable)
foundation, institution; (*geschenktes
Vermögen*) endowment, bequest.
Stil [ʃtiːl] *m* (*pl* **-e**) style.
still [ʃtɪl] *adj* quiet, still; (*schweigend*) silent.
Stille *f* quiet, stillness, silence. **stillen** *v*
allay, stop; (*Schmerz*) soothe; (*Durst*)
quench; (*Säugling*) nurse. **stillschweigen** *v*
be silent. **–d** *adj* silent; (*fig*) implicit, tacit.
Stillstand *m* standstill. **stillstehen** *v* stand
still; (*aufhören*) stop.
Stimme [ˈʃtɪmə] *f* (*pl* **-n**) voice; (*Wahl*) vote;
(*Musik*) part. **seine Stimme abgeben** cast one's
vote. **sich der Stimme enthalten** abstain
(from voting). **Stimmen** *v* (*richtig sein*) be
right *or* true, tally; (*Wahl*) vote; (*Instrument*)
tune. **hier stimmt etwas nicht!** something's wrong here! **stimmt schon!** that's
all right. **Stimm||enthaltung** *f* absten-
tion. **–recht** *neut* franchise. **–ung** *f* (*pl* **-en**)
mood, atmosphere; (*Musik*) tuning.
*stinken [ˈʃtɪŋkən] *v* stink.
Stipendium [ʃtɪpɛndiʊm] *neut* (*pl*
Stipendien) scholarship, (student) grant.

Stirn [ʃtɪrn] *f* (*pl* **-en**) forehead. **die Stirn
runzeln** frown.
stöbern [ˈʃtøːbərn] *v* rummage (about).
Stock [ʃtɔk] *m* (*pl* **Stöcke**) stick, rod;
(*Musik*) baton; (*Etage*) storey. **stockdunkel**
adj pitch dark.
stocken [ˈʃtɔkən] *v* stoop, come to a standstill; (*Milch*) curdle. **Stockung** *f* (*pl* **-en**)
standstill, stop; (*Verkehr*) congestion, jam.
Stockwerk [ˈʃtɔkvɛːrk] *neut* floor, storey.
Stoff [ʃtɔf] *m* (*pl* **-e**) matter; (*Gewebe, fig*)
material.
stöhnen [ˈʃtøːnən] *v* groan.
Stolle [ˈʃtɔlə] *f* (*pl* **-n**) *or* **Stollen** *m* (*pl* -)
(German) Christmas cake.
stolpern [ˈʃtɔlpərn] *v* stumble.
stolz [ʃtɔlts] *adj* proud. **Stolz** *m* pride.
stopfen [ˈʃtɔpfən] *v* stuff, fill; (*Strümpfe*)
darn; (*sättigen*) fill up; (*Med*) constipate.
Stopp [ʃtɔp] *m* (*unz.*) hitchhiking.
Stoppel [ˈʃtɔpəl] *f* (*pl* **-n**) stubble.
stoppen [ˈʃtɔpən] *v* stop. **Stopplicht** *neut*
brake light.
Stöpsel [ˈʃtøːpsəl] *m* (*pl* -) stopper; (*Elek*)
plug.
Storch [ʃtɔrç] *m* (*pl* **Störche**) stork.
stören [ˈʃtøːrən] *v* disturb; (*belästigen*)
bother, trouble; (*Radio*) interfere. **–d** *adj*
disturbing, troublesome. **Störenfried** *m*
troublemaker. **Störung** *f* (*pl* **-en**) disturbance; trouble; (*Radio*) interference.
Stoß [ʃtoːs] *m* (*pl* **Stöße**) push, shove;
(*Schlag*) blow; (*Tritt*) kick; (*Haufen*) heap.
–dämpfer *m* shock-absorber. **stoßen** *v*
push, shove; knock; (*fig*) take offence.
stoßen an bump into *or* against. **stoßen
auf** run across. **Stoß||stange** *f* bumper.
–zahn *m* tusk.
stottern [ˈʃtɔtərn] *v* stutter, stammer.
Straf||anstalt *f* prison, penal institution.
–arbeit *f* (*Schule*) punishment, lines *pl.*
strafbar *adj* punishable.
Strafe [ˈʃtraːfə] *f* (*pl* **-n**) punishment; (*fig*)
penalty; (*Jur*) sentence. **strafen** *v* punish.
Straferlaß *m* pardon; (*allgemeiner*)
amnesty.
straff [ʃtraf] *adj* tight, taught; (*fig*) strict,
stern.
Straf||geld *neut* fine. **–gericht** *neut* crimi-
nal court.
sträflich [ˈʃtrɛːflɪç] *adj* punishable.
Sträffing *m* prisoner.

Straf||recht *neut* criminal law. **-tat** *f* offence.

Strahl [ʃtrɑːl] *m* (*pl* -en) ray, beam; (*Blitz*) flash; (*Wasser*) jet. **strahlen** *v* radiate; (*fig*) beam. **-d** *adj* beaming. **Strahlmotor** *m* jet engine. **Strahlung** *f* radiation.

Strand [ʃtrant] *m* (*pl* -e) beach, shore. **stranden** *v* run aground; (*fig*) founder.

strapazieren [ʃtrapaʦiːən] *v* fatigue, tire; (*abnutzen*) wear out.

Straße [ʃtrɑːsə] *f* (*pl* -n) street. **Straßen||bahn** *f* tram, (*US*) street car. **-kreuzung** *f* crossing. **-laterne** *f* street lamp. **-sperre** *f* roadblock. **-überführung** *f* overpass. **-unterführung** *f* underpass.

sträuben [ʃtrɔybən] *v* ruffle (up). **sich sträuben** (*Haare*) stand up on end; (*fig*) struggle (against), resist.

Strauch [ʃtraux] *m* (*pl* Sträucher) bush.

Strauß[1] [ʃtraus] *m* (*pl* -e) (*Vogel*) ostrich.

Strauß[2] *m* (*pl* Sträuße) bouquet, bunch (of flowers).

streben [ʃtreːbən] *v* strive. **Streber** *m* (*pl* -) careerist, swot, nerd.

Strecke [ʃtrɛkə] *f* (*pl* -n) stretch, distance; (*Math*, *Sport*) distance; (*Teilschnitt*) section. **strecken** *v* stretch (out), extend.

Streich [ʃtraiç] *m* (*pl* -e) stroke, blow; (*Peitsche*) lash; (*Possen*) trick, prank.

streicheln [ʃtraiçəln] *v* stroke, pet.

*streichen [ʃtraiçən] *v* stroke, rub; (*Farbe*) paint; (*gehen*) wander, ramble. **Streich||instrument** *neut* string instrument. **-musik** *f* string music. **-quartett** *neut* string quartet.

Streife [ʃtraifə] *f* (*pl* -n) patrol; (*Streifzug*) stroll, look around.

Streifen [ʃtraifən] *m* (*pl* -) stripe; (*Land*) strip.

streifen [ʃtraifən] *v* streak, stripe; (*berühren*) brush (against), touch; (*wandern*) wander, roam.

Streik [ʃtraik] *m* (*pl* -s) strike. **-brecher** *m* strike-breaker; (*umg.*) scab. **streiken** *v* (go on) strike.

Streit [ʃtrait] *m* (*pl* -e) dispute, quarrel; (*Kampf*) conflict; (*Schlägerei*) fight, brawl. **streiten** *v* dispute, quarrel. **sich streiten um** quarrel about, fight over. **Streitfrage** *f* matter in dispute. **streit||ig** *adj* contested; (*fraglich*) controversial. **-lustig** *adj* quarrelsome, aggressive.

streng [ʃtrɛŋ] *adj* stern, severe, strict. **Strenge** *f* severity, strictness.

Streß [ʃtrɛs] *m* stress. **streßfrei** *adj* stress-free, hassle-free.

streuen [ʃtrɔyən] *v* scatter, spread.

Strich [ʃtriç] *m* (*pl* -e) stroke, line; (*Vogel*) flight; (*Gebiet*) district; (*Kompaß*) compass point. **-punkt** *m* semicolon.

Strick [ʃtrik] *m* (*pl* -e) cord, string, (thin) rope; (*Kind*) rascal. **-arbeit** *f* knitting; (*Artikel*) knitwear. **stricken** *v* knit. **Strick||maschine** *f* knitting machine. **-nadel** *f* knitting needle. **-zeug** *neut* knitting.

strittig [ʃtritiç] *adj* questionable, debatable; (*Angelegenheit*) disputed.

Stroh [ʃtroː] *neut* straw. **-dach** *neut* thatched roof.

Strolch [ʃtrɔlç] *m* (*pl* -e) tramp, vagabond. **strolchen** *v* roam, stroll about.

Strom [ʃtroːm] *m* (*pl* Ströme) (*Fluß*) (large) river; (*Strömung, Elek*) current; (*fig*) stream. **strom||abwärts** *adv* downstream. **-aufwärts** *adv* upstream.

strömen [ʃtrœ mən] *v* stream, flow; (*Regen*) pour.

Strom||erzeuger *m* generator. **-sperre** *f* power cut.

Strömung [ʃtrœ mun] *f* (*pl* -en) current.

Struktur [ʃtruktuːr] *f* (*pl* -en) structure.

Strumpf [ʃtrumpf] *m* (*pl* Strümpfe) stocking; (*Socke*) sock. **-hose** *f* tights, (*US*) pantyhose.

Stube [ʃtuːbə] *f* (*pl* -n) room, chamber. **Stubengelehrte(r)** (*pl* (die) -n) geek. **stubenrein** *adj* house-trained.

Stück [ʃtyk] *neut* (*pl* -e) piece; (*Theater*) play; (*Vieh*) head. **in Stücke gehen** fall to pieces. **Stückchen** *neut* bit, little piece; (*Papier*) scrap. **stückeln** *v* cut *or* chop into pieces.

Student [ʃtuˈdɛnt] *m* (*pl* -en) student. **-enheim** *neut* hall of residence, (*US*) dorm(itory). **Studentin** *f* (*pl* -nen) (woman) student.

Studien||direktor *m* headmaster, (*US*) principal. **-plan** *m* syllabus, curriculum.

studieren [ʃtuˈdiːən] *v* study. **Studio** *neut* studio. **Studium** *neut* studies *pl*; (*Untersuchung*) study.

Stufe [ʃtuːfə] *f* (*pl* -n) step; (*Leiter*) rung; (*fig*) stage. **stufen||los** *adj* infinitely variable. **–weise** *adv* gradually.

Stuhl [ʃtuːl] *m (pl* **Stühle**) chair; *(ohne Lehne)* stool. **–gang** *m* bowel movement.

stumm [ʃtʊm] *adj* mute, dumb; *(schweigend)* silent. **Stumme(r)** *m* mute, dumb person.

Stummel [ʃtʊm əl] *m (pl* -) stump. **Stumm‖film** *m* silent film. **–heit** *f* dumbness.

stumpf [ʃtʊm pf] *adj* blunt; *(Mensch)* dull. **Stumpf‖heit** *f* bluntness; dullness. **–sinn** *m* stupidity. **stumpfsinnig** *adj* stupid, dull-witted.

Stunde [ʃtʊndə] *f (pl* -n) hour; *(Unterricht)* lesson. **Stunden‖plan** *m* timetable. **–satz** *m* hourly rate.

stupid [ʃtuˈpiːt] *adj* half-witted, idiotic.

stur [ʃtuːr] *adj* stubborn.

Sturm [ʃtʊrm] *m (pl* **Stürme**) storm; *(Angriff)* attack.

stürmen [ʃtʏrm ən] *v* storm; *(Wind)* blow. **Stürmer** *m (pl* -) assailant; *(Fußball)* forward. **stürmisch** *adj* stormy.

Sturz [ʃtʊrts] *m (pl* **Stürze**) fall; *(Zusammenbruch)* collapse.

stürzen [ʃtʏrtsən] *v (fallen)* fall (down); *(umkippen)* overturn; *(Regierung)* overthrow; *(eilen)* dash, rush. **sich stürzen auf** rush at.

Sturzhelm [ʃtʊrtshelm] *m* crash-helmet.

Stute [ʃtuːtə] *f (pl* -n) mare. **–nfüllen** *neut* foal, filly.

Stütze [ʃtʏtsə] *f (pl* -n) prop, support.

stutzen¹ [ʃtʊtsən] *v* stop short, be startled.

stutzen² *v (schneiden)* clip, trim; *(Schwanz)* dock.

stützen [ʃtʏtsən] *v* prop, support. **Stützpunkt** *m* fulcrum; *(Mil)* stronghold.

subjektiv [sʊbjɛkˈtiːf] *adj* subjective.

subtil [zʊpˈtiːl] *adj* subtle.

Subvention [zʊpvɛntsloːn] *f (pl* -en) subsidy.

Suche [ˈzuːxə] *f (pl* -n) search. **suchen** *v* look for, search for. **Sucher** *m (pl* -) searcher. **Sucht** *(pl* **Süchte**) addiction; *(fig)* craving, passion.

süchtig [ˈzʏçtiç] *adj* addicted. **Süchtige(r)** *m* addict.

Süd(en) [zyːt (zyːdən)] *m* south. **Süd‖afrika** *neut* South Africa. **–amerika** *neut* South America. **–länder(in)** southerner.

südlich [ˈzyːtliç] *adj* southern.

Südost(en) [zyːdˈɔstən)] *m* southeast. **südöstlich** *adj* southeast(ern); *(Wind, Richtung)* southeasterly.

Südpol [ˈzyːtpoːl] *m* South Pole.

südwärts [ˈzyːtvɛrts] *adv* southwards.

Südwest(en) [zyːdˈvɛstən)] *m* southwest. **südwestlich** *adj* southwest(ern); *(Wind, Richtung)* southwesterly.

Sühne [zyːnə] *f (pl* -n) atonement. **sühnen** *v* atone for.

Sultanine [zʊltaˈniːnə] *f (pl* -n) sultana.

Sülze [ˈzʏlzə] *f (pl* -n) brawn.

Summe [ˈzʊm ə] *f (pl* -n) sum total; *(Geld)* sum, amount.

summen [ˈzʊm ən] *v* buzz, hum.

summieren [zʊˈm iːrən] *v* add up. **Summierung** *f* summation.

Sumpf [zʊm pf] *m (pl* **Sümpfe**) swamp, marsh.

Sund [zʊnt] *m (pl* -e) sound, channel.

Sünde [ˈzʏndə] *f (pl* -n) sin. **–nbock** *m* scapegoat. **Sünder(in)** sinner. **sündhaft** *adj* sinful.

Suppe [ˈzʊpə] *f (pl* -n) soup.

süß [zyːs] *adj* sweet. **Süße** *f* sweetness. **süßen** *v* sweeten. **Süßigkeit** *f* sweetness. **Süßigkeiten** *pl* sweets, *(US)* candy *sing*. **süßlich** *adj* sweetish; *(fig)* slushy, sentimental. **Süß‖waren** *pl* sweets, *(US)* candy *sing*. **–wasser** *neut* fresh water.

Symbol [zym ˈboːl] *neut (pl* -e) symbol. **symbol‖isch** *adj* symbolic. **–isieren** *v* symbolize.

sympathisch [zym ˈpaːtʃ] *adj* likeable, congenial.

Symptom [zym pˈtoːm] *neut (pl* -e) symptom.

Synagoge [zynaˈgoːgə] *f (pl* -n) synagogue.

synchron [ˈzynkron] *adj* synchronous. **–isieren** *v* synchronize.

Synthese [zynˈteːzə] *f (pl* -n) synthesis.

Syphilis [ˈzyːfilis] *f* syphilis.

System [zysˈteːm] *neut (pl* -e) system. **systematisch** *adj* systematic.

Szene [ˈstseːnə] *f (pl* -n) scene.

T

Tabak ['taːbak] *m (pl -e)* tobacco.
Tabelle [taˈbɛlə] *f (pl -n)* table, list. **tabellenförmig** *adj* tabular.
Tablette [taˈblɛtə] *f (pl -n)* pill, tablet.
Tadel ['taːdəl] *m* blame; reproach, reprimand; *(Schule)* bad mark. **tadellos** *adj* faultless. **tadeln** *v* reproach, scold, criticize.
Tafel ['taːfəl] *f (pl -n)* board; *(Schule)* blackboard; *(Schokolade)* bar; *(Tabelle)* table, chart. **die Tafel decken** lay the table.
Tag [taːk] *m (pl -e)* day. **am Tag** by day. **Tagesllanbruch** *m* dawn, daybreak. **–licht** *neut* daylight. **–zeitung** *f* daily (newspaper). **täglich** *adj* daily.
Taille ['taljə] *f* waist.
Takelwerk ['taːkəlvɛrk] *neut* rigging.
Takt [takt] *m (Musik)* time, beat; *(Tech)* stroke; *(Höflichkeit)* tact. **Zweitaktmotor** *m* two-stroke engine.
Taktik ['taktik] *f (pl -en)* tactics *pl.* **taktisch** *adj* tactical.
taktlos ['taktloːs] *adj* tactless.
Tal [taːl] *neut (pl Täler)* valley, vale.
Talent [taˈlɛnt] *neut (pl -e)* talent, gift. **talentiert** *adj* talented, gifted.
Talk [talk] *m* talcum.
Tampon [tãˈpõ] *m (pl -s) (Med)* swab; *(für Frauen)* tampon.
tändeln ['tɛndəln] *v* flirt; *(langsam gehen, usw.)* dawdle, dally. **Tändelei** *f (pl -en)* flirtation.
Tang [taŋ] *m (pl -e)* seaweed.
Tanga ['taŋə] *m (pl -s) (Unterwäsche)* thong.
Tank [taŋk] *m (pl -e)* tank. **tanken** *v (Mot)* refuel, fill up. **Tankllschiff** *neut* tanker. **–stelle** *f* petrol station.
Tanne ['tanə] *f* fir. **Tannenllbaum** *m* firtree. **–zapfen** *m* fir-cone.
Tante ['tantə] *f (pl -n)* aunt.
Tanz [tants] *m (pl Tänze)* dance; *(Tanzen)* dancing. **tanzen** *v* dance. **Tänzer** *m (pl -),* **Tänzerin** *f (pl -nen)* dancer. **Tanzlllokal** *neut* dancehall. **–platz** *m* dance-floor.
Tapete [taˈpeːtə] *f (pl -n)* wallpaper. **tapezieren** *v* paper, decorate.
tapfer ['tapfər] *adj* brave, courageous. **Tapferkeit** *f* bravery, courage.

tappen ['tapən] *v* grope, fumble about.
Tarif [taˈriːf] *m (pl -e)* price list. **–verhandlungen** *pl* collective bargaining *sing.*
tarnen ['tarnən] *v* camouflage. **Tarnung** *f* camouflage.
Tasche ['taʃə] *f (pl -n)* pocket; suitcase; handbag; *(Schule)* satchel; *(Aktentasche)* briefcase. **Taschenlldieb** *m* pickpocket. **–geld** *neut* pocket money. **–lampe** *f* torch. **–messer** *neut* penknife.
Tasse ['tasə] *f (pl -n)* cup. **eine Tasse Kaffee** a cup of coffee.
Taste ['tastə] *f (pl -n) (Klavier, Schreibmaschine)* key; (push)button. **tasten** *v* feel, touch. **Tastenbrett** *(Musik) neut also* **Tastatur** keyboard.
Tat [taːt] *f (pl -en)* deed, act. **in der Tat** in reality, really.
tätig ['tɛːtiç] *adj* active, busy, employed. **tätig sein als** be employed as, practise. **tätig sein bei** work for. **Tätigkeit** *f (pl -en)* activity; *(Beruf)* work, occupation.
tätowieren [tɛtoˈviːrən] *v* tattoo. **Tätowierung** *f (pl -en)* tattoo.
Tatsache ['taːtzaxə] *f (pl -n)* fact. **tatsächlich** *adj* real, actual. *adv* really, actually. *interj* really? is that so?
Tatze ['tatsə] *f (pl -n)* paw.
Tau¹ [tau] *neut (pl -e) (Seil)* rope, cable.
Tau² *m (unz.)* dew. **Tauwetter** *neut* thaw.
taub [taup] *adj* deaf.
Taube ['taubə] *f (pl -n)* pigeon, dove.
taubstumm ['taupʃtum] *adj* deaf and dumb. **Taubstumme(r)** *m/f* deaf mute.
tauchen ['tauxən] *v* dive, plunge; immerse, dip. **Tauchen** *neut* diving. **Taucher** *m (pl -)* diver.
tauen ['tauən] *v* thaw, melt.
Taufe ['taufə] *f (pl -n)* baptism, christening. **taufen** *v* baptize, christen. **Taufname** *m* Christian name.
taugen ['taugən] *v* **taugen zu** be good *or* fit for. **zu nichts taugen** be useless *or* worthless. **Taugenichts** *m (pl -e)* good-for-nothing.
taumeln ['taum əln] *v* stagger, reel.
Tausch [tauʃ] *m (pl -e)* exchange. **tauschllbar** *adj* exchangeable. **–en** *v* exchange, swap.
täuschen ['tɔyʃən] *v* deceive, delude. **–d** *adj* deceptive.
Tauschhandel ['tauʃhandəl] *m* barter.

Täuschung ['tɔyʃuŋ] f (pl -en) delusion, illusion; (Schwindel) deception, fraud.

tausend ['tauzənt] adj thousand.

Taxe ['taksə] f (pl -n) charge, fee; (Schätzung) valuation. **taxieren** v value, assess.

Taxi ['taksi] neut or m (pl -s) taxi. **-fahrer** m taxi-driver.

Technik ['tɛçnik] f (pl -n) technique; engineering, technology. **-er** m (pl -) technician. **Technologie** f technology. **technologisch** technological.

Tee [te:] m tea. **-kanne** f teapot. **-löffel** m teaspoon. **-service** neut tea-set.

Teer [te:r] m (pl -e) tar, pitch.

Teich [taiç] m (pl -e) pond.

Teig [taik] m (pl -e) dough; (flüssig) batter. **-waren** pl noodles pl.

Teil [tail] m or neut (pl -e) part; share, portion. **teilbar** adj divisible. **Teil‖beschäftigung** f part-time work. **-chen** neut particle. **teil‖en** v divide; share out. **-haben** take part (in). **Teilnahme** f participation; interest; (Mitleid) sympathy. **teil‖nehmen** v take part in. **-s** adv partly. **Teilung** f (pl -en) division, partition; sharing out, distribution. **teilweise** adj partial. adv partly.

Telefon [tele'fo:n] neut (pl -e) telephone. **-buch** neut telephone directory. **telefonieren** v telephone, ring up. **Telefon‖zelle** f call box. **-zentrale** f telephone exchange.

Telegramm [tele'gram] neut (pl -e) telegram.

Teleskop [tele'sko:p] neut (pl -e) telescope.

Teller ['tɛlər] m (pl -) plate; (Tech) disc.

Tempel ['tɛmpəl] m (pl -) temple.

Temperament [tɛm pera'mɛnt] neut (pl -e) temperament, disposition. **temperamentvoll** adj high-spirited, lively.

Temperatur [tɛm pera'tu:r] f temperature.

Tempo ['tɛm po] neut (pl -s or -pi) pace, tempo.

temporär [tɛm po'rɛ:r] adj temporary.

Tendenz [tɛn'dɛnts] f (pl -en) tendency, propensity.

Tennis ['tɛnis] neut tennis. **-platz** m tennis court. **-schläger** m tennis racket.

Tenor [te'no:r] m (pl -e) tenor.

Teppich ['tɛpiç] m (pl -e) carpet, rug; (Wand) tapestry.

Termin [tɛr'mi:n] m (pl -e) fixed date; closing date, deadline. **-geschäft** neut (Komm) futures pl.

Terpentinöl [tɛrpɛn'ti:nœ :l] neut turpentine.

Terrasse [tɛ'rasə] f (pl -n) terrace.

Terror ['tɛrɔr] m terror. **-ismus** m terrorism. **-ist(in)** terrorist. **terroristisch** adj terrorist.

Testament [tɛsta'mɛnt] neut (pl -e) will; (Bibel) testament. **Testaments‖bestätigung** f probate. **-vollstrecker** m executor.

testieren [tɛs'ti:rən] v make one's will; bequeath.

teuer ['tɔyər] adj expensive, dear; (lieb) dear, cherished. adv dearly. **Teuerung** f (pl -en) rising prices pl, increase in the cost of living. **Teuerungszulage** f cost-of-living bonus.

Teufel ['tɔyfəl] m devil, Satan. **Teufels‖beschwörung** f exorcism. **-skreis** m vicious circle. **teuflisch** adj devilish, diabolical.

Text [tɛkst] m (pl -e) text; (Lied) lyrics pl; (Oper) libretto. **-buch** neut libretto.

Textilien [tɛks'ti:liən] or **Textilwaren** pl textiles.

Theater [te'a:tər] neut (pl -) theatre; (umg.) fuss, to-do. **theatralisch** adj theatrical.

Thema ['te:m ə] neut (pl **Themen**) theme, subject.

Theologe [teo'lo:gə] m (pl -n) theologian. **Theologie** f theology. **theologisch** adj theological.

Theoretiker [teo're:tikər] m (pl -) theorist. **theoretisch** adj theoretical. **Theorie** f (pl -n) theory.

Therapie [tera'pi:] f (pl -n) therapy.

thermisch ['tɛrm ʃ] adj thermal.

Thermometer [tɛrm o'm e:tər] neut (pl -) thermometer.

Thermosflasche ['tɛrm ɔsflaʃə] f vacuum flask, thermos.

Thermostat [tɛrm o'ʃtat] m (pl -en) thermostat.

Thesaurus [te'zaurus] m (pl **Thesauren**) thesaurus.

These [te:zə] f (pl -n) thesis.

Thrombose [trɔm 'bo:zə] f (pl -n) thrombosis.

Thron [tro:n] m (pl -e) throne. **-erbe** m heir to the throne.

Thunfisch ['tu:nfʃ] m tuna.

Thüringen ['tyrɨŋən] neut Thuringia.

Thymian ['tyːmiːan] *m* thyme.

ticken ['tɪkən] *v* tick.

tief [tiːf] *adj* deep; (*Musik*) low(-pitched), bass; (*Stimme*) deep; (*Sinn*) profound; extreme. *adv* deep; (*Atmen*) deeply. **aus tiefstem Herzen** from the bottom of one's heart. **tief in der Nacht** at dead of night. **tiefbewegt** *adj* deeply moved. **Tief‖druckgebiet** *neut* low-pressure area. **-e** *f* depth. **-ebene** *f* lowlands *pl.* **tief‖gekühlt** *adj* deep-frozen. **-greifend** *adj* far-reaching. **Tief‖kühltruhe** *f* freezer, deep freeze. **-punkt** *m* low(est) point.

Tiegel ['tiːɡəl] *m* (*pl* -) saucepan.

Tier [tiːr] *neut* (*pl* -e) animal, beast. **hohes Tier** (*umg.*) big shot. **Tier‖arzt** *m* veterinary surgeon, (*US*) vet. **-garten** *m* zoological gardens *pl.* **tierisch** *adj* animal; (*brutal*) bestial, brutal. **Tier‖kreis** *m* zodiac. **-welt** *f* animal kingdom, fauna. **-zucht** *f* livestock breeding.

Tiger ['tiːɡər] *m* (*pl* -) tiger.

tilgen ['tɪlɡən] *v* (*streichen*) delete, erase; (*ausrotten*) exterminate; (*Schuld*) pay off. **Tilgung** *f* (*pl* -en) deletion; extermination; discharge, repayment.

Tinte ['tɪntə] *f* ink. **-nklecks** *m* ink-stain.

Tip [tɪp] *m* (*pl* -s) hint; (*Sport*) tip.

tippen ['tɪpən] *v* tap; (*mit der Schreibmaschine*) type. **Tippfehler** *m* typing error.

Tisch [tɪʃ] *m* (*pl* -e) table. **den Tisch decken/abdecken** lay/clear the table. **Tich‖gast** *m* diner, guest (at table). **-gesellschaft** *f* dinner party.

Tischler ['tɪʃlər] *m* carpenter, cabinetmaker. **-arbeit** *f* carpentry.

Titel ['tiːtəl] *m* (*pl* -) title. **-bild** *neut* frontispiece. **-kopf** *m* heading.

Toast [toːst] *m* (*pl* -e) toast. **toasten** *v* toast. **Toaster** *m* (*pl* -) toaster.

toben ['toːbən] *v* rage, rave. **tobsüchtig** *adj* raving, frantic.

Tochter ['tɔxtər] *f* (*pl* Töchter) daughter.

Tod [toːt] *m* (*pl* -e) death. **Todes‖anzeige** *f* obituary. **-fall** *m* (a case of) death. **-kampf** *m* death throes *pl.* **-strafe** *f* death penalty. **-wunde** *f* mortal wound. **Todfeind** *m* deadly enemy. **tödlich** *adj* deadly, fatal, lethal. **todmüde** *adj* dead tired.

Toilette [toaˈlɛtə] *f* (*pl* -n) toilet, lavatory; toilette; dressing-table. **-artikel** *m pl* toiletries. **-papier** *neut* toilet paper.

tolerant [toleˈrant] *adj* tolerant. **Toleranz** *f* toleration. **tolerieren** *v* tolerate.

toll [tɔl] *adj* raving mad, crazy, wild; (*umg.*) fantastic. **Toll‖heit** *f* (*pl* -en) madness; fury. **-wut** *f* rabies.

Tölpel ['tœlpəl] *m* (*pl* -e) awkward person; oaf, boor.

Tomate [toˈmaːtə] *f* (*pl* -n) tomato.

Ton¹ [toːn] *m* (*pl* -e) clay.

Ton² *m* (*pl* Töne) sound; (*Musik*) tone, note; accent, stress; tone, fashion. **-art** *f* (*Musik*) key, pitch. **-band** *neut* magnetic tape. **-bandgerät** *neut* tape-recorder. **-blende** *f* tone control.

tönen ['tøːnən] *v* ring, resound; (*Foto*) shade, tint.

Ton‖fall *m* intonation; (*Musik*) cadence. **-fülle** *f* volume (of sound). **-leiter** *f* (musical) scale. **-spur** *f* soundtrack.

Tonne ['tɔnə] *f* (*pl* -n) ton; cask, barrel.

Topf [tɔpf] *m* (*pl* Töpfe) pot.

Töpfchen ['tœpfçən] *neut* (*pl* -) (child's) potty. **Töpfer** *m* (*pl* -) potter. **-waren** *pl* pottery *sing.*

Tor¹ [toːr] *m* (*pl* -en) fool.

Tor² *neut* (*pl* -e) gate; (*Sport*) goal. **-schütze** *m* (football) scorer.

Torf [tɔrf] *m* peat.

Torheit ['toːrhait] *f* (*pl* -en) folly.

töricht ['tøːrɪçt] *adj* foolish. **Törin** *f* (*pl* -nen) fool, foolish woman.

torkeln ['tɔrkəln] *v* stagger, reel.

Torpedo [tɔrˈpeːdo] *m* (*pl* -s) torpedo. **-boot** *neut* torpedo boat.

Torte ['tɔrtə] *f* (*pl* -n) (fruit) flan, tart, gâteau.

Tor‖wächter *m* (*pl* -) gatekeeper. **-wart** *m* goalkeeper.

tot [toːt] *adj* dead.

total [toˈtaːl] *adj* total, complete.

Tote(r) ['toːtə(r)] dead person.

töten ['tøːtən] *v* kill.

Toten‖bett *neut* deathbed. **-gräber** *m* gravedigger. **-hemd** *neut* shroud. **-wagen** *m* hearse.

totgeboren ['toːtɡəboːrən] *adj* stillborn. **sich totlachen** *v* split one's sides laughing. **totschießen** *v* shoot dead.

Totschlag ['toːtʃlaːk] *m* manslaughter. **tot‖schlagen** *v* slay, kill; (*Zeit*) waste (time). **-schweigen** *v* hush up. **-sicher** *adj* absolutely *or* dead certain.

Tötung ['tœ :tʊŋ] *f* (*pl* -en) killing.

Tour [tuːr] *f* (*pl* -en) tour, trip. **-ismus** *m* tourism. **-ist** *m* (*pl* -en) tourist.

Trab [traːp] *m* trot. **traben** *v* trot.

Tracht [traxt] *f* (*pl* -en) costume, dress.

Tradition [tradiʦɪoːn] *f* (*pl* -en) tradition. **traditionell** *adj* traditional.

träge ['trɛ:gə] *adj* (*faul*) lazy; (*langsam*) ponderous, slow; (*schläfrig*) sleepy.

***tragen** ['traːgən] *v* carry; (*Kleider*) wear; (*stützen*) support; (*ertragen*) endure, bear.

Träger ['trɛ:gər] *m* (*pl* -) carrier; (*Mensch*) porter; (*Balken*) girder.

Trägheit ['trɛ:khait] *f* laziness; (*Langsamkeit*) slowness.

tragisch ['traːgɪʃ] *adj* tragic. **Tragödie** *f* (*pl* -n) tragedy.

Trainer ['trɛːnər] *m* (*pl* -) (*Sport*) coach, trainer. **trainieren** *v* train. **Training** *neut* training. **-sanzug** *m* track suit.

Traktor ['traktɔr] *m* (*pl* -en) tractor.

trampeln ['tram pəln] *v* trample, stamp.

trampen ['trɛm pən] *v* hitchhike.

Tran [traːn] *m* (*pl* -e) whale oil.

tranchieren [trã:'ʃi:rən] *v* carve. **Tranchiermesser** *neut* carving knife.

Träne ['trɛ:nə] *f* (*pl* -n) tear.

Trank [traŋk] *m* (*pl* **Tränke**) drink.

tränken ['trɛŋkən] *v* water; (*durchtränken*) soak.

transatlantisch [transat'lantʃ] *adj* transatlantic.

Transmission [transm ɪsɪoːn] *f* (*pl* -en) transmission.

Transport [transpɔrt] *m* (*pl* -e) transportation. **transportieren** *v* transport. **Transportunternehmen** *neut* haulage *or* shipping company.

Tratte ['tratə] *f* (*pl* -n) bill of exchange, draft.

Traube ['traubə] *f* (*pl* -n) grape; bunch of grapes. **Traubenllese** *f* vintage. **-saft** *m* grape juice. **-zucker** *m* glucose.

trauen ['trauən] *v* trust; (*Ehepaar*) marry, join in wedlock. **sich trauen** dare.

Trauer ['trauər] *f* sorrow, grief; (*für Tote*) mourning. **-anzeige** *f* death notice. **-gottesdienst** *m* funeral service. **trauern** *v* grieve, mourn. **Trauerllspiel** *neut* tragedy. **-weide** *f* weeping willow. **traurig** *adj* sad.

Traufe ['traufə] *f* (*pl* -n) eaves *pl*. **aus dem Regen in die Traufe** out of the frying pan into the fire. **Traufrinne** *f* gutter.

traulich ['traulɪç] *adj* snug, cosy, comfortable.

Traum [traum] *m* (*pl* **Träume**) dream. **-bild** *neut* vision.

träumen ['trɔym ən] *v* dream. **Träumer** *m* (*pl* -) dreamer. **-ei** *f* (*pl* -en) daydream, reverie. **träumerisch** *adj* dreamy.

Trau||ring *m* wedding ring.

***treffen** ['trɛ fən] *v* (*begegnen*) meet; (*erreichen*) hit; (*betreffen*) concern; (*Vorkehrungen*) make; (*Maßnahmen*) take. **sich treffen** meet; (*zufällig geschehen*) happen. **Treffen** *neut* meeting. **treffend** *adj* striking; (*Antwort*) pertinent. **Treffpunkt** *m* meeting place.

***treiben** ['traibən] *v* drive, move; (*drängen*) urge, impel; (*Metall*) work; (*Pflanzen*) force; (*tun*) do, occupy oneself with; (*Blüte*) blossom; (*im Wasser*) float. **treibend** *adj* driving; (*im Wasser*) floating. **Treibller** *m* driver; (*Vieh*) drover. **-haus** *neut* hothouse. **-kraft** *f* moving force. **-stoff** *m* fuel.

trennbar ['trɛnbaːr] *adj* separable. **trennen** *v* separate; (*abtrennen*) sever, cut; (*Telef*) cut off. **sich trennen** part, separate. **Trennung** *f* (*pl* -en) separation.

Treppe ['trɛpə] *f* (*pl* -n) staircase, stairs *pl*. **-ngeländer** *neut* handrail, banister.

Tresse ['trɛsə] *f* (*pl* -n) tress, braid.

***treten** ['trɛ:tən] *v* tread, step; (*betreten*) step on; (*stoßen*) kick. **Trethebel** *m* treadle.

treu [trɔy] *adj* loyal, faithful, true; (*redlich*) honest, sincere. **Treubruch** *m* disloyalty, breach of faith. **Treue** *f* loyalty, faithfulness. **treu||lich** *adj* loyal, faithful. **-los** *adj* disloyal, faithless.

Tribüne [tribyːnə] *f* (*pl* -n) platform; (*für Zuschauer*) gallery.

Trichter ['trɪçtər] *m* (*pl* -) funnel; (*Bombe*) crater.

Trick [trɪk] *m* (*pl* -s) trick. **-film** *m* animated cartoon.

Trieb [triːp] *m* (*pl* -e) force, drive; (*Antrieb*) impulse; (*Bot*) shoot; (*Instinkt*) instinct.

***triefen** ['triːfən] *v* trickle, drip. **triefnaß** *adj* dripping wet.

triftig ['trɪftɪç] *adj* convincing, plausible.

Triller ['trɪlər] *m* (*pl* -) trill. **trillern** *v* trill.

trinkbar ['trɪŋkbaːr] *adj* drinkable, potable.

trinken *v* drink. **Trinkller** *m* (*pl* -) drinker.
-geld *neut* tip. **-halm** *m* (drinking) straw.
-spruch *m* toast.

Tripper ['trɪpər] *m* (*pl* -) gonorrhoea.

Tritt [trɪt] *m* (*pl* -e) step, tread; (*Stoß*) kick;
(*Fußspur*) footprint. **-leiter** *f* stepladder.

Triumph [triˈʊmf] *m* (*pl* -e) triumph.

trocken ['trɔkən] *adj* dry. **Trockenheit** *f*
dryness. **trocknen** *v* dry. **Trockner** *m* (*pl* -)
drier.

Trödel ['trøː:dəl] *m* junk, rubbish. **trödeln**
v dawdle; (*handeln*) trade in old junk.

Trommel ['trɔm əl] *f* (*pl* -n) drum. **-fell** *neut*
drumskin; (*Anat*) eardrum. **trommeln** *v*
drum. **Trommler** *m* (*pl* -) drummer.

Trompete [trɔm'peːtə] *f* (*pl* -n) trumpet.

Tropen ['troː:pən] *pl* tropics.

tröpfeln ['trœ pəln] *v* trickle, drip.

Tropfen ['trɔpfən] *m* (*pl* -) drop.

tropisch ['troː:pɪʃ] *adj* tropical.

Trost [troːst] *m* consolation, solace, comfort.

trösten ['trœ stən] *v* console, solace, comfort, **sich trösten mit** take comfort in.

trostlos ['trɔstloːs] *adj* disconsolate.

Tröstung ['trœ stʊŋ] *f* (*pl* -en) consolation, comfort.

Trott [trɔt] *m* (*pl* -e) trot.

Trottel ['trɔtəl] *m* (*pl* -) idiot, fool.

trotz [trɔts] *prep* despite, in spite of. **Trotz**
m defiance; (*Eigensinn*) obstinacy. **trotzdem** *conj*, *adv* nevertheless. **trotzen** *v* defy;
(*widersetzlich sein*) be obstinate. **trotzig** *adj*
defiant, obstinate.

trüb(e) ['tryː:b ə)] *adj* cloudy, opaque;
(*glanzlos*) dull; (*fig*) gloomy. **trüben** *v*
cloud, dim, darken. **Trübsinn** *m* gloom,
depression. **trübsinnig** *adj* gloomy, miserable.

Trug [truː:k] *m* (*Täuschung*) fraud, deceit;
(*Sinnes*) delusion.

*trügen ['tryːgən] *v* be deceptive; (*betrügen*)
deceive. **trügerisch** *adj* treacherous,
deceitful.

Truhe ['truː:ə] *f* (*pl* -n) chest, trunk.

Trümmer *pl* ruins, debris *sing*.

Trumpf [trʊm pf] *m* (*pl* **Trümpfe**) trump.
-karte *f* trump (card).

Trunk [trʊŋk] *m* (*pl* **Trünke**) drink.
-enheit *f* drunkenness, intoxication.
-sucht *f* alcoholism.

Trupp [trʊp] *m* (*pl* -s) troop, gang, band.
Truppe *f* (*pl* -n) (*Theater*) company; (*Mil*)
(combat) troops *pl*. **Truppen** *pl* troops.

Truthahn ['truː:thaːn] *m* turkey-cock.

Tscheche ['tʃɛçə] *m* (*pl* -n), **Tschechin** *f* (*pl*
-nen) Czech. **tschechisch** *adj* Czech.
Tschechische Republik *f* Czech Republic.

Tuberkulose [tubɛrkuˈloː:zə] *f* tuberculosis,
TB.

Tuch [tuː:x] **1** *neut* (*pl* -e) cloth, fabric.
2 *neut* (*pl* **Tücher**) (piece of) cloth; (*zum
Trocknen*) towel. **-händler** *m* draper.

tüchtig ['tyçtɪç] *adj* capable, able; (*leistungsfähig*) efficient; (*fleißig*) hard-working;
(*klug*) clever. **Tüchtigkeit** *f* ability; efficiency; cleverness.

Tücke ['tykə] *f* (*pl* -n) spite, malice. **tück-
isch** *adj* spiteful.

Tugend ['tuː:gənt] *f* (*pl* -en) virtue. **tugendhaft** *adj* virtuous.

Tulpe ['tʊlpə] *f* (*pl* -n) tulip.

*tun [tuː:n] *v* do; (*machen*) make. **tun als
ob** pretend to. **nur so tun** pretend. **zu tun
haben** be busy, have things to do. **groß-
tun** boast. **etwas in etwas tun** put something into something.

Tünche ['tʏnçə] *f* (*pl* -n) whitewash, distemper.

Tunke ['tʊŋkə] *f* (*pl* -n) sauce. **tunken** *v*
dip, dunk.

Tunnel ['tʊnəl] *m* (*pl* -) tunnel.

Tupfen ['tʊpfən] *m* (*pl* -) dot, spot. **tupfen**
v dot.

Tür [tyː:r] *f* (*pl* -en) door.

Türkis [tʏrˈkɪs] *m* (*pl* -e) turquoise.

Türke [tʏrkə] *m* (*pl* -n) **Türkin** *f* (*pl* -nen)
Turk. **Turkei** *f* Turkey. **turkisch** *adj*
Turkish.

Türklinke ['tyː:rklɪŋkə] *f* doorhandle.

Turm [tʊrm] *m* (*pl* **Türme**) tower; (*Schach*)
rook, castle; (*Elek*) pylon. **-spitze** *f* spire,
steeple.

turnen ['tʊrnən] *v* do gymnastics. **Turnen**
neut gymnastics. **Turnhalle** *f* gymnasium.

Turnier [tʊrˈniːr] *neut* (*pl* -e) tournament.

Türschwelle ['tyː:ʃvɛlə] *f* threshold.

Tusche ['tʊʃə] *f* (*pl* -n) Indian ink, drawing
ink.

tuscheln ['tʊʃəln] *v* whisper.

Tüte ['tyː:tə] *f* (*pl* -n) bag.

tuten ['tuː:tən] *v* hoot, honk.

Typ [ty:p] *m* (*pl* -en) type. **-e** *f* (*Druck*) type.
Typhus ['ty:fus] *m* typhoid (fever).
typisch ['ty:pɪʃ] *adj* typical.
Tyrann [ty'ran] *m* (*pl* -en) tyrant. **-ei** *f*
tyranny. **tyrann‖isch** *adj* tyrannical.
-isieren *v* tyrannize.

U

U-Bahn ['u:ba:n] *f* underground (railway),
(*US*) subway.
übel ['y:bə] *adj* evil, wicked; (*schlecht*) bad;
(*unwohl*) sick, ill. *mir wird übel* I feel sick.
übel daran sein be in a bad way. **Übel** *neut*
(*pl* -) evil; (*Mißgeschick*) misfortune;
(*Krankheit*) sickness. **übel‖gelaunt** *adj*
bad-tempered. **-gesinnt** *adj* evil-minded.
-nehmen *v* be offended by, take amiss.
-riechen *v* smell bad.
üben ['y:bən] *v* practise.
über ['y:bər] *prep* over, above; (*quer über*)
across; (*während*) during. (*betreffend*) about;
(*mehrmals*) over; (*weg*) via.
überall [y:bər'al] *adv* everywhere.
überanstrengen [y:bər'anʃtrɛŋən] *v* overwork. **sich überanstrengen** overexert
oneself. **Überanstrengung** *f* overexertion.
überarbeiten [y:bər'a:rbaitən] *v* revise. **sich
überarbeiten** *v* overwork, work too hard.
überbelichten ['y:bərbəlɪçtən] *v* (*Foto*)
overexpose.
***überbieten** ['y:bərbi:tən] *v* outbid; (*fig*)
surpass, beat.
Überbleibsel ['y:bərblaipsəl] *neut* (*pl* -)
remainder.
Überblick ['y:bərblɪk] *m* survey, overall
view.
***überbringen** [y:bər'brɪŋən] *v* deliver.
überbrücken [y:bər'brykən] *v* bridge.
überdies [y:bər'di:s] *adv* besides.
überdrüssig ['y:bərdrʏsɪç] *adj* sick (of), disgusted (with).
übereifrig ['y:bəraifrɪç] *adj* too eager, over-
zealous.
übereilen [y:bər'ailən] *v* rush, hurry too
much. **übereilt** *adj* hasty; (*Benehmen*)
inconsiderate.

übereinander [y:bərain'andər] *adv* one
upon another. **-greifen** *v* overlap. **-legen** *v*
lay one upon another.
***übereinkommen** [y:bər'ainkom ən] *v*
agree. **Überein‖kommen** *neut* (*pl* -) *or*
kunft *f* agreement.
übereinstimmen [y:bər'ainʃtɪm ən] *v* concur, agree; (*zueinander passen*) correspond,
tally. **Übereinstimmung** *f* agreement, con-
cord.
überempfindlich ['y:bərɛm pfɪntlɪç] *adj*
hypersensitive.
***überfahren** ['y:bərfa:rən] take *or* drive
across. (*Mot*) run over. **Überfahrt** *f* crossing.
Überfall ['y:bərfal] *m* (sudden) attack,
assault. **überfallen** *v* attack (suddenly).
Überfallkommando *neut* flying squad.
Überfluß ['y:bərflus] *m* excess, overabun-
dance. **überflüssig** *adj* superfluous.
überführen ['y:bərfy:rən] *v* transport, convey. [-'fy:rən] (*Jur*) convict. **Überführung** *f*
transport; (*Brücke*) viaduct, overpass.
Übergabe ['y:bərga:bə] *f* surrender, hand-
ing-over.
Übergang ['y:bərgaŋ] *m* crossing, passage;
(*fig*) transition.
***übergeben** ['y:bərge:bən] *v* deliver, hand
over; (*Mil*) surrender. **sich übergeben** be
sick, vomit.
übergehen ['y:bərge:ən] *v* cross (over);
(*werden*) pass into, become. [-'ge:ən] omit,
overlook.
Übergewicht ['y:bərgəvɪçt] *neut* overweight.
***übergreifen** ['y:bərgraifən] *v* overlap.
übergreifen auf encroach on.
übergroß ['y:bərgro:s] *adj* outsize, king-
sized. **übergroße Portion** *f* (*Fastfood*)
supersize.
***überhandnehmen** [y:bər'hantne:m ən] *v*
increase (rapidly).
überhaupt [y:bər'haupt] *adv* in general.
wenn überhaupt if at all. **überhaupt
nicht** not at all. **überhaupt kein...** no ...
whatever.
***überheben** [y:bər'he:bən] *v* exempt,
spare. **einer Mühe überheben** spare the
trouble. **überheblich** *adj* presumptuous,
arrogant.
überholen [y:bər'ho:lən] *v* overtake; (*Tech*)
overhaul. **überholt** *adj* outmoded.

überhören [yːbɐˈhøːɐn] v not hear; (*ignorieren*) ignore, let pass.
überirdisch [ˈyːbɐʔɪrdɪʃ] adj celestial; (*übernatürlich*) supernatural.
überkochen [ˈyːbɐkɔxən] v boil over.
***überlassen** [yːbɐˈlasən] v leave.
überlaufen [ˈyːbɐlaufən] v overflow; (*Mil*) defect.
überleben [yːbɐˈleːbən] v survive.
überlegen [yːbɐˈleːgən] v consider, reflect. adj superior. **Überlegenheit** f superiority. **überlegt** adj considered, deliberate. **Überlegung** f consideration, reflection.
überleiten [ˈyːbɐlaitən] v lead on to; (*fig*) convert.
überliefern [yːbɐˈliːfɐn] v deliver; (*der Nachwelt*) pass on, hand down.
Übermacht [ˈyːbɐmaxt] f superiority. **übermächtig** adj overwhelming, too powerful.
Übermaß [ˈyːbɐmaːs] neut excess. **übermäßig** adj excessive.
Übermensch [ˈyːbɐmɛnʃ] m superman. **übermenschlich** adj superhuman.
übermitteln [yːbɐˈmɪtəln] v convey.
übermorgen [ˈyːbɐmɔrgən] adv the day after tomorrow.
übermüdet [yːbɐˈmyːdət] adj overtired.
Übermut [ˈyːbɐmuːt] m arrogance; (*Ausgelassenheit*) high spirits pl. **übermütig** adj arrogant; high-spirited.
übernächst [yːbɐˈnɛːçst] adj the next but one, the one after.
übernachten [yːbɐˈnaxtən] v spend the night, stay overnight.
übernatürlich [yːbɐnaˈtuːrlɪç] adj supernatural.
***übernehmen** [yːbɐˈneːmən] v take over; (*Pflicht*) undertake.
überprüfen [yːbɐˈpryːfən] v verify, check, examine. **Überprüfung** f verification, check.
überqueren [yːbɐˈkvɛːrən] v cross.
überragen [yːbɐˈraːgən] v rise above, tower above; (*fig*) surpass, outdo. **-d** adj excellent.
übersinnlich [ˈyːbɐzɪnlɪç] adj spiritual, transcendental.
überspannen [yːbɐˈʃpanən] v overstretch, overtighten; (*fig*) go too far, exaggerate; (*bedecken*) stretch over. **überspannt** adj eccentric.

***überspringen** [yːbɐˈʃprɪŋən] v jump over; (*auslassen*) omit, skip.
***überstehen** [yːbɐˈʃteːən] v survive.
***übersteigen** [yːbɐˈʃtaigən] v climb over, surmount; (*fig*) exceed.
Überstunden [ˈyːbɐʃtundən] pl overtime sing. **Überstunden machen** v work overtime. **überstürzen** [yːbɐˈʃtyrtsən] v rush, hurry. **sich überstürzen** rush, act too hastily. **überstürzt** adj hasty.
Übertrag [ˈyːbɐtraːk] m (pl **Überträge**) balance brought forward. **übertragen** v carry over; (*Komm*) bring forward; (*befördern*) transport; (*übersetzen*) translate; (*Radio, Med*) transmit. **Übertragung** f transfer; (*Radio, med*) transmission; (*Übersetzung*) translation.
***übertreffen** [yːbɐˈtrɛfən] v excel, surpass.
***übertreiben** [yːbɐˈtraibən] v exaggerate. **Übertreibung** f exaggeration.
***übertreten** [yːbɐˈtreːtən] v overstep. [ˈyːbɐ-] (*Fluß*) overflow; (*Sport*) step over.
übertrieben [yːbɐˈtriːbən] adj exaggerated.
Übervölkerung [yːbɐˈfœlkəruŋ] f overpopulation.
überwachen [yːbɐˈvaxən] v supervise. **Überwachung** f supervision, surveillance.
überwältigen [yːbɐˈvɛltigən] v overpower, overwhelm. **-d** adj overwhelming. **Überwältigung** f overpowering, conquest.
***überweisen** [yːbɐˈvaizən] v transfer. **Überweisung** f transfer; (*Post-*) money order.
überwiegend [yːbɐˈviːgənt] adj preponderant. adv primarily, mainly.
***überwinden** [yːbɐˈvɪndən] v overcome. **sich überwinden (zu)** bring oneself (to). **Überwindung** f overcoming, conquest.
überwuchern [yːbɐˈvuːxɐn] v overrun, overgrow.
überzeugen [yːbɐˈtsɔygən] v convince. **-d** adj convincing. **überzeugt** adj convinced, sure. **Überzeugung** f conviction.
***überziehen** [ˈyːbɐtsiːən] v pull over, put on. [-ˈtsiːən] cover; (*Konto*) overdraw; (*Bett*) change (the sheets of). **Überziehung** f overdraft.
Überzug [ˈyːbɐtsuːk] m cover(ing).
üblich [ˈyːplɪç] adj usual.
U-Boot [ˈuːboːt] neut submarine.
übrig [ˈyːbrɪç] adj remaining, left(-over).

die Übrigen the rest, the others. **übrig haben** have left (over). **-bleiben** v remain, be left (over). **-ens** adv by the way, incidentally.

Übung ['y:bʊŋ] f (pl -en) exercise; (Üben) practice.

Ufer ['u:fər] neut (pl -) bank, shore. **-damm** m embankment.

Uhr [u:r] f (pl -en) clock; (Armbanduhr) watch; (Gas, usw.) meter; (Kraftstoff) gauge. **-armband** neut watch strap. **-werk** neut clockwork. **-zeiger** m (clock) hand. **-zeigersinn** m clockwise direction. **im Uhrzeigersinn** adv clockwise. **entgegen dem Uhrzeigersinn** adv anticlockwise (US) counterclockwise.

Ukraine [u:'kraɪnə] f Ukraine. **Ukrainer** m, **Ukrainerin** f Ukrainian. **ukrainisch** adj Ukrainian.

Ulk [ʊlk] m (pl -e) fun, lark. **ulkig** adj funny.

Ulme ['ʊlmə] f (pl -n) elm.

Ultraschall ['ʊltraʃal] m ultrasound. **-untersuchung** f ultrasound scan.

um [ʊm] prep (zeitlich, örtlich) around, about; (wegen) for; (Maßangaben) by; (ungefähr) about. adv about. conj in order to. **um zu** (in order) to. **um diese Zeit** around this time. **um so besser** so much the better. **bitten um** ask for. **um 2 cm länger** longer by 2 cm.

umändern ['ʊm ɛndərn] v change, alter. **Umänderung** f change, alteration.

umarmen [ʊm'arm ən] v embrace. **Umarmung** f embrace.

Umbau ['ʊm bau] m alteration, rebuilding, conversion. **umbauen** v rebuild, alter, convert.

umbilden ['ʊm bɪldən] v transform, remodel. **Umbildung** f transformation.

*umbinden ['ʊm bɪndən] v tie (up), tie around (oneself), put on.

Umblick ['ʊm blɪk] m panorama, survey. **umblicken** v (sich umblicken) look around.

*umbringen ['ʊm brɪŋən] v kill. (sich umbringen) commit suicide.

umdrehen ['ʊm dreːən] v turn over or around. **sich umdrehen** rotate, spin; (Person) turn around. **Umdrehung** f turn, rotation.

*umfahren ['ʊm faːrən] v run over, knock down; ['faːrən] drive around.

*umfallen ['ʊm faln] v fall over.

Umfang ['ʊm faŋ] m (pl Umfänge) (Kreis) circumference; (Ausdehnung) extent; (Größe) size. **umfangreich** adj extensive.

umfassen [ʊm 'fasən] v put one's arm around, hold, clasp; (fig) embrace, cover, encompass; (Mil) encircle. **-d** adj comprehensive.

Umfrage ['ʊm fraːgə] f poll, inquiry.

Umgang ['ʊm gaŋ] m circuit, turn; (Verkehr) intercourse, (social) contact. **umgänglich** adj sociable.

*umgeben [ʊm 'geːbən] v surround.

Umgebung f surroundings pl, environment.

*umgehen v ['ʊm geːən] go around; (behandeln) handle, deal with; (mit Menschen) associate (with). ['geːən] go around; (vermeiden) avoid.

umgekehrt ['ʊm gəkeːrt] adv the other way round. adj inverted, reverse(d).

umgestalten ['ʊm gəʃtaltən] v alter, transform; (umorganisieren) reorganize. **Umgestaltung** f alteration, transformation; reorganization.

Umhang ['ʊm haŋ] m wrap, cape.

umher [ʊm 'heːr] adv about, (a)round. **-blicken** v look around. **-laufen** run around.

umhüllen [ʊm 'hylən] v wrap up.

Umkehr ['ʊm keːr] f turning back, return; (fig) change, conversion. **umkehren** v turn back, return; (umdrehen) turn over; (fig) reform.

umkippen ['ʊm kɪpən] v tip over.

umklammern [ʊm 'klam ərn] v clasp.

umkleiden ['ʊm klaɪdən] v **sich umkleiden** change (one's clothes). **Umkleideraum** m changing room.

*umkommen ['ʊm kɔm ən] v die, perish, be killed; (verderben) go bad.

Umkreis ['ʊm kraɪs] m neighbourhood, vicinity, **umkreisen** v (en)circle.

Umlauf ['ʊm lauf] m circulation. **im Umlauf** in circulation.

Umlaut ['ʊm laut] m vowel modification.

umleiten ['ʊm laɪtən] v divert. **Umleitung** f diversion.

umlernen ['ʊm lɛrnən] v learn anew, relearn.

umliegend ['ʊm liːgənt] adj surrounding.

umordnen ['ʊm ɔrdnən] v rearrange.

umpflanzen ['ʊm pflantsən] v transplant.

umrahmen [um 'raːm ən] *v* frame.

umrechnen ['um ʀɛçnən] *v* convert, (ex)change. **Umrechnung** *f* conversion. **–skurs** *m* rate of exchange.

***umreißen** ['um ʀaɪsən] *v* pull down, demolish. [-'ʀaɪsən] sketch, outline.

umringen [um 'ʀɪŋən] *v* surround.

Umriß ['um ʀɪs] *m* sketch, outline. **umrissen** *adj* defined.

umrühren ['um ʀyːʀən] *v* stir.

ums [um s] *prep* + *art* **um das**.

Umsatz ['um zats] *m* turnover, sales.

umsäumen ['um zɔym ən] *v* hem. [-'zɔym ən] enclose, surround.

umschalten ['um ʃaltən] *v* (*fig*) switch *or* change over. **Umschaltung** *f* (*fig*) changeover, switch.

umschauen ['um ʃauən] *v* **sich umschauen** look around.

umschiffen [um 'ʃɪfən] *v* circumnavigate; transship. **Umschiffung** *f* circumnavigation.

Umschlag ['um ʃlaːk] *m* cover; (*Brief*) envelope; (*Buch*) wrapper, jacket; (*Hose*) turn-up; (*Kleid*) hem; (*Veränderung*) change; (*Komm*) turnover. **umschlagen** *v* change (*Boot*) capsize; (*Wind*) veer; (*umwenden*) turn over; (*umwerfen*) knock down.

***umschließen** [um 'ʃliːsən] *v* surround, enclose.

***umschreiben** ['um ʃʀaɪbən] *v* rewrite; transcribe. [-'ʃʀaɪbən] paraphrase.

umschulen ['um ʃuːlən] *v* retrain; (*neue Schule*) send to a new school. **Umschulung** *f* retraining.

Umschwung ['um ʃvuŋ] *m* turn; (*fig*) sudden change, reversal.

***umsehen** ['um zeːən] *v* **sich umsehen** look around; (*rückwärts*) look round.

umsetzen ['um zɛtsən] *v* transpose; (*Pflanze*) transplant; (*verkaufen*) sell.

Umsicht ['um zɪçt] *f* prudence, circumspection. **umsichtig** *adj* prudent, circumspect.

umsiedeln ['um zɪdəln] *v* resettle. **Umsiedlung** *f* resettlement.

umsonst [um 'zɔnst] *adv* free (of charge); (*vergebens*) in vain.

Umstand ['um ʃtant] *m* circumstance. **in anderen Umständen** (*umg.*) expecting, in the family way. **keine Umstände!** no problem!, it's no hassle. **ohne Umstände** without fuss. **nähere Umstände** further

particulars. **unter diesen Umständen** in these circumstances.

***umsteigen** ['um ʃtaɪgən] *v* change (trains, buses, etc.). **Umsteiger** *m* through-ticket.

***umstoßen** ['um ʃtoːsən] *v* overturn, knock over; (*ungültig machen*) revoke; (*Pläne*) upset.

Umsturz ['um ʃtuʀts] *m* overthrow; (*Pol*) revolution. **umstürzen** *v* overturn; (*Regierung*) overthrow; (*umfallen*) fall over.

Umtausch ['um tauʃ] *m* exchange. **umtauschen** *v* exchange, (*umg.*) swap.

umwälzen ['um vɛlsən] *v* roll over; (*gründlich ändern*) revolutionize.

umwandeln ['um w andəln] *v* change, transform; (*Elek*) transform, (*Komm*) convert.

Umweg ['um veːk] *m* detour, long way round.

Umwelt ['um vɛlt] *f* environment. **umweltfreundlich** *adj* environment-friendly, non-polluting, conservationist. **Umweltverschmutzung** *f* (environmental) pollution.

***umwenden** ['um vɛndən] *v* turn over; (*Wagen*) turn round.

***umwerben** [um 'vɛʀbən] *v* court.

***umwerfen** ['um vɛʀfən] *v* upset, overturn; (*Kleider*) wrap round oneself.

umwickeln [um 'vɪkəln] *v* wrap round.

umzäunen [um 'tsɔynən] *v* fence in.

***umziehen** ['um tsiːən] *v* move (house); (*Kind*) change (clothes). **sich umziehen** change (clothes).

Umzug ['um tsuːk] *m* move, removal; procession.

unabänderlich [unap'ɛndəʀlɪç] *adj* unalterable.

unabhängig ['unaphɛŋɪç] *adj* independent. **Unabhängigke(r)** (*Pol*) independent. **–keit** *f* independence.

unabkömmlich ['unapkœm lɪç] *adj* indispensable.

unablässig ['unapˈlɛsɪç] *adj* incessant.

unabsichtlich ['unapzɪçtlɪç] *adj* unintentional.

unachtsam ['unaxtzaːm] *adj* careless.

unähnlich ['unɛːnlɪç] *adj* unlike, dissimilar (to).

unangemessen ['unangəm ɛsən] *adj* unsuitable; (*Forderung*) unreasonable.

unangenehm ['unangəneːm] *adj* unpleasant; (*peinlich*) awkward.

Unannehmlichkeit ['unanneːm lɪçkaɪt] f
unpleasantness; (*lästige Mühe*) inconvenience.

unansehnlich ['unanzeːnlɪç] *adj* unsightly.

unanständig ['unanʃtɛndɪç] *adj* indecent,
improper. **Unanständigkeit** f indecency.

unartig ['unaːrtɪç] *adj* badly-behaved, rude.

unauffällig ['unaufɛlɪç] *adj* inconspicuous.

unaufgefordert ['unaufɡəfɔrdət] *adj*
unbidden, unasked.

unaufhörlich ['unaufhøː rlɪç] *adj* incessant.

unaufmerksam ['unaufm ɛrkzaːm] *adj* inattentive.

unaufrichtig ['unaufrɪçtɪç] *adj* insincere.

unausgeglichen ['unausɡəɡlɪçən] *adj*
uneven, unbalanced.

unbändig ['unbɛndɪç] *adj* tremendous.

unbeabsichtigt ['unbəapzɪçtɪçt] *adj* unintentional.

unbeachtet ['unbəaxtət] *adj* unnoticed,
unheeded.

unbedacht ['unbədaxt] *adj* inconsiderate,
thoughtless, rash.

unbedeutend ['unbədɔytənt] *adj* unimportant, insignificant.

unbedingt ['unbədɪŋt] *adj* absolute,
unconditional. *adv* by all means.

unbefahrbar ['unbəfaːrbaːr] *adj* impassable.

unbefriedigend ['unbəfriːdɪɡənt] *adj*
unsatisfactory.

unbefugt ['unbəfuːkt] *adj* unauthorized.

unbegreiflich ['unbəɡraɪflɪç] *adj* incomprehensible, inconceivable.

Unbehagen ['unbəhaːɡən] *neut* uneasiness,
discomfort. **unbehaglich** *adj* uneasy,
uncomfortable.

unbeholfen ['unbəhɔlfən] *adj* clumsy, awkward.

unbekannt ['unbəkant] *adj* unknown.

unbekümmert [unbəˈkym ərt] *adj* unconcerned.

unbemerkt ['unbəm ɛrkt] *adj* unnoticed,
unobserved.

unbemittelt ['unbəm ɪtəlt] *adj* poor, without means.

unbequem ['unbəkveːm] *adj* uncomfortable.

umberechenbar ['unbərɛçənbaːr] *adj*
incalculable.

unberechtigt ['unbərɛçtɪçt] *adj* (*ungerecht-*

fertigt) unjustified; (*unbefugt*) unauthorized.
adv without authority.

unberührt ['unbəryːrt] *adj* untouched,
intact, pristine.

unbeschränkt ['unbəʃrɛnkt] *adj* unlimited,
unrestricted.

unbeschreiblich ['unbəʃraɪplɪç] *adj* indescribable.

unbesonnen ['unbəzɔnən] *adj* imprudent;
(*unüberlegt*) rash, hasty.

unbeständig ['unbəʃtɛndɪç] *adj* unsettled,
unstable; (*nicht dauernd*) inconstant.

unbestimmt ['unbəʃtɪm t] *adj* indefinite.

unbestreitbar [unbəʃˈtraɪbaːr] *adj* indisputable.

unbestritten ['unbəʃtrɪtən] *adj* undisputed,
uncontested.

unbeteiligt ['unbətaɪlɪçt] *adj* unconcerned;
(*nicht beteiligt*) uninvolved.

unbeweglich ['unbəveːklɪç] *adj* immovable; (*bewegungslos*) motionless.

unbewußt ['unbəvust] *adj* unconscious.

unbiegsam ['unbiːkzaːm] *adj* unbending.

unbrauchbar ['unbrauxbaːr] *adj* useless.

und [unt] *conj* and.

undankbar ['undaŋkbaːr] *adj* ungrateful;
(*Arbeit*) thankless. **Undankbarkeit** f
ingratitude.

undenkbar [un'dɛŋkbaːr] *adj* unthinkable.

undeutlich ['undɔytlɪç] *adj* unclear, indistinct.

undurchdringlich ['undurçdrɪŋ lɪç] *adj*
impenetrable.

undurchlässig ['undurçlɛsɪç] *adj* impermeable; (*Wasser-*) water-proof.

undurchsichtig ['undurçzɪçtɪç] *adj* opaque;
(*Person*) inscrutable.

uneben ['uneːbən] *adj* uneven, rough.

unecht ['unɛçt] *adj* not genuine, false;
(*künstlich*) artifical.

unehelich ['uneːəlɪç] *adj* illegitimate.

unehrlich ['uneːrlɪç] *adj* dishonest.
Unehrlichkeit f dishonesty.

unendlich ['unɛntlɪç] *adj* endless, infinite.

unentbehrlich [unɛntˈbeːrlɪç] *adj* indispensable.

unentschieden ['unɛntʃiːdən] *adj* undecided; (*Fussball*) drawn. **Unentschiedenheit** f indecision.

unentschlossen ['unɛntʃlɔsən] *adj* undecided, irresolute. **Unentschlossenheit** f indecision, irresolution.

unentwickelt ['unɛntvɪkəlt] *adj* undeveloped.

unentzündbar ['unɛntzyntbaːɐ] *adj* nonflammable.

unerbittlich [unɛrˈbɪtlɪç] *adj* relentless.

unerfahren ['unɛrfaːrən] *adj* inexperienced.

unerhört [unɛrˈhøː rt] *adj* unheard-of, outrageous.

unerklärbar [unɛrkˈlɛːrbaːɐ] *adj* inexplicable.

unerläßlich [unɛrˈlɛslɪç] *adj* indispensable.

unerlaubt ['unɛrˈlaupt] *adj* not permitted; (*ungesetzlich*) forbidden, illegal.

unermeßlich [unɛrˈmɛslɪç] *adj* immense, immeasurable.

unermüdlich [unɛrˈmyːtlɪç] *adj* indefatigable, untiring.

unerreichbar ['unɛraiçbaːɐ] *adj* unattainable. **unerreicht** *adj* unequalled, unrivalled.

unersättlich ['unɛrzɛtlɪç] *adj* insatiable.

unerschrocken ['unɛrʃrɔkən] *adj* fearless, undaunted.

unerschütterlich ['unɛrʃytərlɪç] *adj* imperturbable, unshakeable.

unersetzlich ['unɛrzɛtslɪç] *adj* irreplaceable.

unerträglich ['unɛrtrɛːklɪç] *adj* unbearable, intolerable.

unerwartet ['unɛrvaːrtət] *adj* unexpected.

unfähig ['unfɛːiç] *adj* incapable; (*nicht instande*) unable. **unfähig machen** incapacitate. **Unfähigkeit** *f* incapacity; inability.

unfair ['unfɛːr] *adj* unfair.

Unfall ['unfal] *m* accident. **–station** *f* first-aid post. **–verhütung** *f* accident prevention.

unfaßbar ['unfasbaːɐ] *adj* inconceivable.

unfehlbar [un'feːlbaːɐ] *adj* infallible.

unflätig ['unflɛːtɪç] *adj* filthy, coarse.

unfreundlich ['unfrɔyntlɪç] *adj* unfriendly; (*barsch*) rude; (*Wetter*) disagreeable, inclement. **Unfreundlichkeit** *f* unfriendliness, unkindness.

unfruchtbar ['unfruxtbaːɐ] *adj* infertile.

Unfug ['unfuːk] *m* misconduct; (*Dummheiten*) mischief.

unfühlbar ['unfyːlbaːɐ] *adj* intangible, impalpable.

Ungar ['uŋɡaɐ] *m* (*pl* **-n**), **Ungarin** *f* (*pl* **-nen**) Hungarian. **ungarisch** *adj* Hungarian. **Ungarn** *neut* Hungary.

ungastlich ['ungastlɪç] *adj* inhospitable.

ungeachtet ['ungəaxtət] *adj* overlooked, disregarded. *prep* notwithstanding.

ungebeten ['ungəbeːtən] *adj* uninvited.

ungebildet ['ungəbɪldət] *adj* uneducated; (*Benehmen*) ill-mannered.

ungeboren ['ungəboːrən] *adj* unborn.

ungebührend ['ungəbyːrənt] *or* **ungebührlich** *adj* improper, unbecoming.

ungebunden ['ungəbundən] *adj* unbound; (*fig*) unrestrained, free.

Ungeduld ['ungədult] *f* impatience. **ungeduldig** *adj* impatient.

ungeeignet ['ungəaiknət] *adj* unsuitable.

ungefähr ['ungəfɛːr] *adv* approximately, about, roughly. *adj* approximate.

ungefährlich ['ungəfɛːrlɪç] *adj* not dangerous.

ungeheuer ['ungəhɔyər] *adj* enormous. **Ungeheuer** *neut* (*pl* -) monster.

ungehorsam ['ungəhoːrzaːm] *adj* disobedient. **Ungehorsam** *m* disobedience.

ungekünstelt ['ungəkyːnstəlt] *adj* unaffected, natural.

ungelegen ['ungəleːgən] *adj* inconvenient.

ungelernt ['ungəlɛːrnt] *adj* unskilled.

ungemächlich ['ɪngəm ɛçlɪç] *adj* uncomfortable, unpleasant.

ungemein ['ungəm ain] *adj* uncommon, extraordinary.

ungemütlich ['ungəm yːtlɪç] *adj* uncomfortable; (*grob*) unpleasant, nasty.

ungenannt ['ungənant] *adj* unnamed.

ungeniert ['unʒənɪrt] *adj* free and easy, relaxed and informal.

ungenießbar ['ungənɪsbaːɐ] *adj* inedible, unenjoyable.

ungenügend ['ungənyːgənt] *adj* insufficient; (*Qualität*) inadequate.

ungeraten ['ungəraːtən] *adj* (*Kind*) spoiled.

ungerecht ['ungərɛçt] *adj* unjust.

ungereimt ['ungəraim t] *adj* (*fig*) nonsensical, absurd.

ungern ['ungərn] *adv* unwillingly, reluctantly.

Ungeschick ['ungəʃɪk] *neut* ineptitude, clumsiness. **ungeschickt** *adj* clumsy, awkward.

ungesellig ['ʊngəzɛlɪç] *adj* unsociable.

ungesetzlich ['ʊngəzɛtslɪç] *adj* illegal, unlawful.

ungestüm ['ʊngəʃtyːm] *adj* impetuous.

ungesund ['ʊngəzʊnt] *adj* unhealthy, unwell.

ungewiß ['ʊngəvɪs] *adj* uncertain. **Ungewißheit** *f* uncertainty.

ungewöhnlich ['ʊngəvøːnlɪç] *adj* unusual, uncommon. **ungewohnt** *adj* unaccustomed.

Ungeziefer ['ʊngətsiːfər] *neut* vermin.

ungezogen ['ʊngətsoːgən] *adj* rude; (*Kind*) naughty.

ungezwungen ['ʊngətsvʊŋən] *adj* free, natural, uninhibited.

ungläubig ['ʊngɔybɪç] *adj* incredulous, disbelieving; (*Rel*) unbelieving. **Ungläubige(r)** *m* sceptic; (*Rel*) unbeliever.

unglaublich ['ʊngɬaʊplɪç] *adj* incredible, unbelievable. **unglaubwürdig** *adj* (*Person*) untrustworthy, unreliable; (*Sache*) incredible.

ungleich ['ʊngɬaɪç] *adj* unequal, uneven; (*verschieden*) different; (*unähnlich*) unlike; (*Zahl*) odd. **Ungleichheit** *f* inequality; difference.

Unglück ['ʊngɬʏk] *neut* misfortune; (*Katastrophe*) disaster, catastrophe; (*Pech*) bad luck. **unglücklich** *adj* unlucky; (*traurig*) unhappy. **–erweise** *adv* unfortunately. **Unglücksfall** *m* accident.

Ungnade ['ʊngnaːdə] *f* disgrace, displeasure. **ungnädig** *adj* ungracious, churlish.

ungünstig ['ʊngʏnstɪç] *adj* unfavourable.

unhaltbar ['ʊnhaltbaːr] *adj* untenable.

Unheil ['ʊnhaɪl] *neut* mischief, harm. **unheillbar** *adj* incurable. **–bringend** *adj* unlucky, fateful.

unheimlich ['ʊnhaɪmlɪç] *adj* weird, sinister, uncanny. *adv* (*umg.*) tremendously.

unhöflich ['ʊnhøːflɪç] *adj* impolite, rude. **Unhöflichkeit** *f* rudeness, incivility.

unhörbar ['ʊnhøːrbaːr] *adj* inaudible.

uniform [unɪfɔrm] *adj* uniform. **Uniform** *f* (*pl* -en) uniform.

uninteressant ['ʊnɪntərɛsant] *adj* uninteresting. **uninteressiert** *adj* disinterested.

universal [univɛrzaːl] *or* **universell** *adj* universal.

Universität [univɛrzɪtɛːt] *f* (*pl* -en) university.

Universum [univɛrzʊm] *neut* universe.

unkenntlich ['ʊnkɛntlɪç] *adj* unrecognizable. **Unkenntnis** *f* ignorance.

unklar ['ʊnklaːr] *adj* unclear, obscure; (*trübe*) muddy, cloudy.

unklug ['ʊnkluːk] *adj* unwise, unintelligent.

Unkosten ['ʊnkɔstən] *pl* expenses, costs; (*Komm*) overheads.

Unkraut ['ʊnkraʊt] *neut* weed.

unlängst ['ʊnlɛŋst] *adv* recently, lately.

unlauter ['ʊnlaʊtər] *adj* impure; (*nicht ehrlich*) unfair, dishonest. **unlauterer Wettbewerb** unfair competition.

unlesbar ['ʊnleːzbaːr] *adj* illegible, unreadable.

unlogisch ['ʊnloːgɪʃ] *adj* illogical.

unlösbar ['ʊnløːsbaːr] *adj* insoluble.

unmäßig ['ʊnmɛːsɪç] *adj* immoderate.

Unmenge ['ʊnmɛŋə] *f* huge quantity.

Unmensch ['ʊnmɛn] *m* brute, monster, barbarian. **unmenschlich** *adj* inhuman, brutal. **Unmenschlichkeit** *f* inhumanity.

unmittelbar ['ʊnmɪtəlbaːr] *adj* immediate, direct.

unmodisch ['ʊnmoːdɪʃ] *adj* unfashionable.

unmöglich ['ʊnmøːklɪç] *adj* impossible. **Unmöglichkeit** *f* impossibility.

unmoralisch ['ʊnmoraːlɪʃ] *adj* immoral.

unmündig ['ʊnmʏndɪç] *adj* under age.

unnachgiebig ['ʊnnaːxgiːbɪç] *adj* unyielding, uncompromising.

unnatürlich ['ʊnnatyːrlɪç] *adj* unnatural.

unnötig ['ʊnnøːtɪç] *adj* unnecessary.

unnütz ['ʊnnʏts] *adj* useless, unprofitable.

unordentlich ['ʊnɔrdəntlɪç] *adj* disorderly, untidy. **Unordllentlichkeit** *f* untidiness, disorderliness. **–nung** *f* disorder.

unorganisch ['ʊnɔrgaːnɪʃ] *adj* inorganic.

unpaar ['ʊnpaːr] *adj* odd.

unparteiisch ['ʊnpartaɪʃ] *or* **unparteilich** *adj* impartial, unbiased. **Unparteilichkeit** *f* impartiality.

unpassend ['ʊnpasənt] *adj* unsuitable, inappropriate; (*unschicklich*) improper.

unpersönlich ['ʊnpɛrzøːnlɪç] *adj* impersonal.

unpolitisch ['ʊnpoliːtɪʃ] *adj* nonpolitical.

unpraktisch ['ʊnpraktɪʃ] *adj* impractical.

Unrat ['ʊnraːt] *m* refuse, dirt.

unratsam ['ʊnraːtzaːm] *adj* inadvisable.

unrecht ['unrɛçt] *adj* wrong; (*ungerecht*) unjust. **Unrecht** *neut* wrong; (*Ungerechtigkeit*) injustice. **unrechtmäßig** *adj* illegal, unlawful, illegitimate.

unregelmäßig ['unregəln ɛ:ʃiç] *adj* irregular. **Unregelmäßigkeit** *f* irregularity.

unreif ['unraif] *adj* unripe; (*Mensch*) immature.

unrein ['unrain] *adj* dirty, unclean; (*fig*) impure.

unrentabel ['unrenta:bəl] *adj* unprofitable.

unrichtig ['unriçtiç] *adj* incorrect.

Unruhe ['unru:ə] *f* restlessness; (*Aufruhr*) unrest. (*Uhr*) balance(-wheel). **unruhig** *adj* restless.

uns [uns] *pron* (to) us; (*Reflexiv*) (to) ourselves.

unsauber ['unzaubər] *adj* unclean, dirty; (*unfair*) unfair.

unschätzbar ['unʃɛtsba:r] *adj* inestimable.

unscheinbar ['unʃainba:r] *adj* inconspicuous.

unschicklich ['unʃiklic] *adj* improper, unseemly.

unschlüssig ['unʃlysiç] *adj* irresolute.

unschön ['unʃø:n] *adj* unlovely, unpleasant.

Unschuld ['unʃult] *f* innocence. **unschuldig** *adj* innocent.

unselbständig ['unzɛlbʃtɛndiç] *adj* dependent.

unselig ['unze:liç] *adj* unfortunate, fatal.

unser ['unzər] *adj* our. *pron* ours. **unser(er) seits** *adv* for our part, as for us. **unser(es)gleichen** *pron* people like us. *pron* **der, die, das uns(e)rige** ours. **unserthalben, unsertwegen, unsertwillen** for our sakes.

unsicher ['unziçər] *adj* unsafe, insecure; (*zweifelhaft*) uncertain. **Unsicherheit** *f* insecurity, uncertainty.

unsichtbar ['unziçtba:r] *adj* invisible.

Unsinn ['unzin] *adj* nonsense. **unsinnig** *adj* nonsensical.

unsittlich ['unzitliç] *adj* indecent, immoral. **Unsittlichkeit** *f* immorality.

unsre ['unzrə] *V* **unser**.

unsrige ['unzrigə] *V* **unser**.

unsterblich ['unʃtɛrpliç] *adj* immortal. **Unsterblichkeit** *f* immortality.

unstet ['unʃtɛt] *adj* unsteady, inconstant.

Unstimmigkeit ['unʃtimiçkait] *f* (*pl* **-en**) inconsistency; (*Meinungsverschiedenheit*) disagreement.

unsympathisch ['unzympa:tʃ] *adj* disagreeable, unpleasant.

Untat ['unta:t] *f* outrage, crime.

untätig ['untɛ:tiç] *adj* inactive, idle. **Untätigkeit** *f* inactivity, idleness.

untauglich ['untaukliç] *adj* unfit; (*Sache*) unusable.

unten ['untən] *adv* below, at the bottom; (*im Hause*) downstairs. **nach unten** downwards. **von oben bis unten** from top to bottom. **von unten an** from the bottom (up).

unter ['untər] *prep* below, under; (*zwischen*) between, among. *adj* lower. **unter allen Umständen** under any circumstances. **unter uns** between you and me. **unter vier Augen** in private. **unter der Hand** secretly.

Unterarm ['untərarm] *m* forearm.

Unterbau ['untərbau] *m* foundations *pl*.

unterbelichten ['untərbəliçtən] *v* (*Foto*) underexpose.

unterbevölkert ['untərbəfœlkərt] *adj* underpopulated.

unterbewußt ['untərbəvust] *adj* subconscious. **Unterbewusstsein** *neut* subconsciousness.

***unterbleiben** [untərblaibən] *v* not occur.

***unterbrechen** [untərbrɛçən] *v* interrupt; (*Telef*) cut off, disconnect. **Unterbrechung** *f* interruption.

***unterbringen** ['untərbriŋən] *v* accommodate, lodge, shelter; (*lagern*) store.

unterdrücken ['untərdrykən] *v* suppress. **Unterdrückung** *f* suppression.

untereinander [untərain'andər] *adv* with each other, with one another.

unterentwickelt ['untərɛntvikəlt] *adj* underdeveloped.

Unterführung [untər'fy:ruŋ] *f* underpass.

Untergang ['untərgaŋ] *m* (*Sonne*) setting; (*Schiff*) sinking, wreck; (*fig*) decline, fall.

Untergebene(r) [untər'ge:bənə (r)] *m* subordinate.

***untergehen** ['untərge:ən] *v* sink; (*Sonne*) set; (*fig*) perish, be lost.

untergeordnet ['untərgəɔrdnət] *adj* subordinate.

Untergestell [ˈʊntɐɡəʃtɛl] *neut* under-
carriage.

Untergewicht [ˈʊntɐɡəvɪçt] *neut* short
weight. **Untergewicht haben** be underweight.

*****untergraben** [ˈʊntɐɡraːbən] *v* under-
mine.

Untergrund [ˈʊntɐɡrʊnt] *m* subsoil.
–bahn *f* underground (railway), (*US*) subway.

unterhalb [ˈʊntɐhalp] *prep* below,
under(neath).

Unterhalt [ˈʊntɐhalt] *m* support, keep;
(*Instandhaltung*) maintenance. **unterhalten** *v* (*Person*) keep, support; (*Instand
halten*) maintain; (*zerstreuen*) entertain.
sich unterhalten enjoy oneself; (*reden
(mit)*) converse (with), talk (to). **unterhaltsam** *adj* entertaining, amusing. **Unterhaltung** *f* entertainment, amusement;
(*Instandhaltung*) maintenance. **–skosten** *pl*
maintenance costs.

unterhandeln [ˈʊntɐhandəln] *v* negotiate.

Unterhaus [ˈʊntɐhaus] *neut* lower chamber (of parliament).

Unterhemd [ˈʊntɐhɛmt] *neut* vest, (*US*)
undershirt.

Unterholz [ˈʊntɐhɔlts] *neut* undergrowth.

Unterhose [ˈʊntɐhoːzən] *f* underplants *pl*.

unterirdisch [ˈʊntɐɪrdɪʃ] *adj* underground.

*****unterkommen** [ˈʊntɐkɔmən] *v* find
accommodation *or* shelter; (*Arbeit*) find
work.

Unterkunft [ˈʊntɐkʊnft] *f* accommodation, lodgings *pl*.

Unterlage [ˈʊntɐlaːɡə] *f* base, basis, foundation; (*Beweisstück*) (documentary) evidence.

Unterlaß [ˈʊntɐlas] *m* **ohne Unterlaß**
incessantly, unceasingly.

*****unterlassen** [ˈʊntɐlasən] *v* neglect, fail
(to do), omit. **Unterlassung** *f* omission.

unterlegen [ˈʊntɐleːɡən] *adj* inferior.

Unterleib [ˈʊntɐlaip] *m* abdomen.

*****unterliegen** [ˈʊntɐliːɡən] *v* be defeated.
es unterliegt keinem Zweifel it is not
open to doubt.

Untermieter [ˈʊntɐmiːtɐ] *m* lodger.

*****unternehmen** [ˈʊntɐneːmən] *v* under-
take, attempt. **Unternehmen** *neut* undertaking, enterprise; (*Firma*) firm.
Unternehmer *m* entrepreneur, contractor.

unternehmungslustig *adj* enterprising.

Unteroffizier [ˈʊntɐɔfitsiːr] *m* noncom-
missioned officer, NCO.

Unterredung [ˈʊntɐreːdʊŋ] *f* (*pl* -en) conversation, discussion.

Unterricht [ˈʊntɐrɪçt] *m* (*pl* -e) instruction,
lessons *pl*, teaching. **Unterricht geben**
teach, give lessons. **unterrichten** *v*
instruct, teach; (*benachrichtigen*) inform.

Unterrock [ˈʊntɐrɔk] *m* slip, petticoat.

unters [ˈʊntɐs] *prep* + *art* unter das.

untersagen [ˈʊntɐzaːɡən] *v* forbid, prohibit.

*****unterscheiden** [ˈʊntɐʃaidən] *v* distin-
guish. **sich unterscheiden** differ.

*****unterschieben** [ˈʊntɐʃiːbən] *v* attribute
(to); substitute.

Unterschied [ˈʊntɐʃiːt] *m* (*pl* -e) difference.
unterschiedlich *adj* different.

*****unterschlagen** [ˈʊntɐʃlaːɡən] *v* (*Geld*)
embezzle; (*Nachricht*) suppress. **Unterschlagung** *f* embezzlement; suppression.

Unterschlupf [ˈʊntɐʃlʊpf] *m* (*pl* **Unter-
schlüpfe**) refuge, hiding place.

*****unterschreiben** [ˈʊntɐʃraibən] *v* sign.

Unterschrift [ˈʊntɐʃrɪft] *f* signature.

Unterseeboot [ˈʊntɐzeːboːt] *neut* submarine. **unterseeisch** *adj* submarine.

unterst [ˈʊntɐst] *adj* lowest, bottom,
undermost.

*****unterstehen** [ˈʊntɐʃteːən] *v* be subordi-
nate (to). **sich unterstehen** dare.

*****unterstreichen** [ˈʊntɐʃtraiçən] *v* under-
line.

unterstützen [ˈʊntɐʃtytsən] *v* support,
assist. **Unterstützung** *f* (*pl* -en) support,
assistance.

untersuchen [ˈʊntɐzuːxən] *v* examine.
Untersuchung *f* examination. **–shaft** *f*
imprisonment on remand.

Untertan [ˈʊntɐtaːn] *m* (*pl* -en) subject.

Untertasse [ˈʊntɐtasə] *f* saucer.

untertauchen [ˈʊntɐtauxən] *v* dive; (*verschwinden*) disappear.

Unterteil [ˈʊntɐtail] *m* bottom (part).

Untertitel [ˈʊntɐtiːtəl] *m* (*Film*) subtitle.

unterwärts [ˈʊntɐvɛrts] *adv* downwards.

Unterwäsche [ˈʊntɐvɛʃə] *f* underwater.

unterwegs [ˈʊntɐveːks] *adv* on the way,
en route.

*****unterweisen** [ˈʊntɐvaizən] *v* instruct,

teach. **Unterweisung** f instructions pl.

Unterwelt ['ʊntɐvɛlt] f underworld.

*unterwerfen [ʊntɐˈvɛrfən] v subject (to); (besiegen) subjugate. **sich unterwerfen** submit, surrender. **unterworfen** adj subject (to).

unterwürfig [ʊntɐˈvʏrfɪç] adj obsequious.

unterzeichnen [ʊntɐˈtsaɪçnən] v sign. **Unterzeichnung** f signature.

*unterziehen [ʊntɐˈtsiːən] v subject. **sich unterziehen** undergo, submit (to).

untief ['ʊntiːf] adj shallow.

untreu ['ʊntrɔy] adj unfaithful.

untrüglich [ʊnˈtryːklɪç] adj infallible, certain.

untüchtig ['ʊntʏçtɪç] adj incompetent, incapable.

Untugend ['ʊntuːɡənt] f vice.

unüberlegt [ʊnyːbɐˈleːkt] adj ill-considered, hasty.

unüberwindlich ['ʊnyːbɐvɪntlɪç] adj impregnable; insurmountable, insuperable.

ununterbrochen ['ʊnʊntɐbrɔxən] adj uninterrupted.

unveränderlich ['ʊnfɛrɛndɐlɪç] adj unchangeable.

unverantwortlich [ʊnfɛrˈantvɔrtlɪç] adj irresponsible. **Unverantwortlichkeit** f irresponsibility.

unverbesserlich [ʊnfɛrˈbɛsɐlɪç] adj incorrigible.

unverbindlich ['ʊnfɛrbɪntlɪç] adj not binding; (Komm) without obligation.

unverdaulich ['ʊnfɛrdaʊlɪç] adj indigestible.

unverderblich ['ʊnfɛrdɛrplɪç] adj incorruptible.

unverdient ['ʊnfɛrdiːnt] adj unearned, undeserved.

unverdorben ['ʊnfɛrdɔrbən] adj unspoilt, pristine.

unvereinbar [ʊnfɛrˈaɪnbaːr] adj incompatible.

unverfroren ['ʊnfɛrfroːrən] adj impudent, brazen. **Unverfrorenheit** f impudence.

unvergänglich ['ʊnfɛrɡɛslɪç] adj imperishable; immortal.

unvergeßlich [ʊnfɛrˈɡɛslɪç] adj unforgettable.

unverhältnismäßig ['ʊnfɛrhɛltnɪsmɛːsɪç] adj disproportionate.

unverheiratet [ʊnfɛrˈhaɪraːtət] adj unmarried.

unvermeidlich [ʊnfɛrˈmaɪtlɪç] adj unavoidable.

unvermittelt ['ʊnfɛrmɪtəlt] adj sudden, unexpected.

Unvermögen ['ʊnfɛrmøːɡən] neut inability, powerlessness.

unvermutet ['ʊnfɛrmuːtət] adj unexpected.

unvernünftig ['ʊnfɛrnʏnftɪç] adj unreasonable.

unverschämt ['ʊnfɛrʃɛːmt] adj impudent, impertinent. **Unverschämtheit** f impudence, impertinence.

unversehens ['ʊnfɛrzeːəns] adv suddenly, unexpectedly.

unversöhnlich ['ʊnfɛrzøːnlɪç] adj irreconcilable.

unverstädlich ['ʊnfɛrʃtɛntlɪç] adj unintelligible.

unverträglich ['ʊnfɛrtrɛːklɪç] adj incompatible; unsociable.

unverzagt ['ʊnfɛrtsaːkt] adj undaunted, fearless.

unverzüglich ['ʊnfɛrtsyːklɪç] adj immediate, instant.

unvollkommen ['ʊnfɔlkɔmən] adj imperfect.

unvoreingenommen ['ʊnfoːraɪnɡənɔmən] adj unprejudiced.

unvorsichtig ['ʊnfoːrzɪçtɪç] adj careless, incautious; (unklug) imprudent.

unvorstellbar ['ʊnfoːrʃtɛlbaːr] adj unimaginable.

unvorteilhaft ['ʊnfoːrtaɪlhaft] adj unfavourable.

unwahr ['ʊnvaːr] adj untrue. **–haftig** adj untruthful. **Unwahrheit** f untruth, falsehood. **unwahrscheinlich** adj unlikely, improbably; (umg.) fantastic, incredible. adv (umg.) incredibly.

unweit ['ʊnvaɪt] prep, adv near, not far (from).

Unwetter ['ʊnvɛtɐ] neut storm.

unwichtig ['ʊnvɪçtɪç] adj unimportant. **Unwichtigkeit** f unimportance; (Sache) trifle.

unwiderruflich [ʊnvɪdɐˈruːflɪç] adj irrevocable.

unwiderstehlich [ʊnvɪdɐˈʃteːlɪç] adj irresistible.

unwillig ['ʊnvɪlɪç] adj indignant; (wider-

willig) unwilling, reluctant.

unwillkürlich ['ʊnvɪlkyːrlɪç] *adj* involuntary; instinctive.

unwirksam ['ʊnvɪrkzaːm] *adj* ineffective.

unwissend ['ʊnvɪsənt] *adj* ignorant.
Unwissenheit *f* ignorance. **unwissentlich** *adv* unconsciously, unwittingly.

unwürdig ['ʊnvyrdɪç] *adj* unworthy.

Unzahl ['ʊntsaːl] *f* endless number.

unzählbar ['ʊntsɛːlbaːr] *or* **unzählig** *adj* innumerable.

unzeitgemäß ['ʊntsaɪtɡəm ɛːs] *adj* inopportune; *(unmodisch)* outdated. **unzeitig** *adj* premature; *(Obst)* unripe.

unzerbrechlich [ʊntsɛrbrɛçlɪç] *adj* unbreakable.

unzertrennlich [ʊntsɛrtrɛnlɪç] *adj* inseparable.

unziemlich [ʊntsɪm liç] *adj* unseemly.

Unzucht ['ʊntsʊxt] *f* lechery, fornication; *(Jur)* sexual offence. **unzüchtig** *adj* lewd, lecherous.

unzufrieden ['ʊntsufriːdən] *adj* dissatisfied.

unzugänglich ['ʊntsuːɡɛnlɪç] *adj* inaccessible.

unzulänglich ['ʊntsuːlɛŋlɪç] *adj* inadequate, insufficient.

unzulässig ['ʊntsuːlɛsɪç] *adj* inadmissible.

unzureichend ['ʊntsuːraɪçənt] *adj* insufficient, inadequate.

unzuverlässig ['ʊntsufɛrlɛsɪç] *adj* inadmissible.

unzweifelhaft ['ʊntsfaɪfəlhaft] *adj* undoubted.

Upgrade ['ʌpɡreɪd] *neut (pl -s) (comp)* upgrade.

üppig ['ʏpɪç] *adj* abundant, luxuriant; *(blühend)* exuberant; *(wollüstig)* voluptuous.

uralt ['uːralt] *adj* very old, ancient.

Uran [u'raːn] *neut* uranium.

uranfänglich ['uranfɛŋlɪç] *adj* original, primordial.

Uraufführung ['uːrauffyːruŋ] *f* first performance, première.

urban [ʊrˈbaːn] *adj* urbane.

urbar ['uːrbaːr] *adj* arable.

Ureinwohner ['uːraɪnvoːnər] *m* aboriginal.

Ureltern ['uːrɛltərn] *pl* ancestors.

Urenkel ['uːrɛŋkəl] *m (Kind)* great-grandchild, *(Junge)* great-grandson. **-in** *f* great-granddaughter.

Urgeschichte ['uːrɡəʃiçtə] *f* prehistory.

Urgroß||eltern ['uːrɡroːsɛltərn] *pl* great-grandparents. **-mutter** *f* great-grandmother. **-vater** *m* great-grandfather.

Urheber ['uːrheːbər] *m (pl -)* author, creator. **-recht** *neut* copyright.

Urin [u'riːn] *m* urine. **urinieren** *v* urinate.

Urkunde ['uːrkʊndə] *f* document, deed; *(Zeugnis)* certificate. **urkundlich** *adj* documentary.

Urlaub ['uːrlaup] *m (pl -e)* leave (of absence); *(Ferien)* holiday, vacation. **im** *or* **auf Urlaub** on holiday, on vacation.

Urmensch ['uːrm ɛnʃ] *m* primitive man.

Urne ['ʊrnə] *f (pl -n)* urn.

Ursache ['uːrzaxə] *f* cause. **keine Ursache!** don't mention it!

Ursprung ['uːrʃprʊŋ] *m* source, origin. **ursprünglich** *adj* original. **Ursprungsland** *neut* country of origin.

Urteil ['ʊrtaɪl] *neut* judgment, verdict; *(Strafmaß)* sentence; *(Urteilskraft)* judgment. **urteilen** *v* judge. **Urteils||kraft** *f* (power of) judgment, discernment. **-spruch** *m* verdict, sentence.

Urvater ['uːrfaːtər] *m* forefather.

Urwelt ['uːrvɛlt] *f* primeval world.

Urzeit ['uːrtsaɪt] *f* prehistory, earliest times *pl.* **urzeitlich** *adj* primordial, primeval.

Utopie [utoˈpiː] *f (pl -n)* Utopia. **utopisch** *adj* utopian.

V

vag [vaːk] *adj* vague.

Vagabund [vagaˈbʊnt] *m (pl -en)* vagabond, tramp.

vakant [vaˈkant] *adj* vacant.

Vakuum ['vaːkuum] *neut (pl Vakua)* vacuum.

validieren [validiːən] *v* make valid, validate.

Valuta [vaˈluːta] *f (pl Valuten) (Wert)* value; *(Währung)* currency.

Vampir ['vam piːr] *m (pl -e)* vampire.

Vandale [vanˈdaːlə] *m (pl -n)* vandal. **Vandalismus** *m* vandalism.

Vanille [vaˈnɪljə] *f* vanilla.

Varietät [varieˈtɛːt] f (pl -en) variety.
Variation [variatsˈioːn] f (pl -en) variation.
Vase [ˈvaːzə] f (pl -en) vase.
Vater [ˈfaːtər] m (pl **Väter**) father. **–land**
neut native land, fatherland. **vater-
ländisch** *adj* national; patriotic.
väterlich [ˈfɛːtərlɪç] *adj* paternal, fatherly.
väterlicherseits *adv* on the father's side.
Vaterschaft [ˈfaːtərʃaft] f (pl -en) paternity.
Veganer(in) [veˈɡeːnər] vegan. **vegan** *adj*
vegan.
Vegetarier [veɡeˈtaːriər] m (pl -) vegetarian.
vegetarisch *adj* vegetarian.
Veilchen [ˈfaɪlçən] *neut* (pl -) violet.
veilchenblau *adj* violet.
Vene [ˈveːnə] f (pl -n) vein. **Venenent-
zündung** f (*Med*) phlebitis.
Venedig [veˈneːdɪç] *neut* Venice. **venezi-
aner** m (pl -), **Venezianerin** f (pl -nen)
Venetian. **venezianisch** *adj* Venetian.
Ventil [vɛnˈtiːl] *neut* (pl -e) valve. **–ator** m
(pl -en) ventilator; (*Mot*) fan; (*Elek*) electric
fan.
verabreden [fɛrˈapreːdən] v agree (upon);
(*Ort, Zeitpunkt*) fix, appoint. **Verabredung**
f agreement; appointment.
verabscheuen [fɛrˈapʃɔyən] v abhor, detest.
verabschieden [fɛrˈapʃiːdən] v dismiss;
(*Gesetze*) pass. **sich verabschieden von**
take one's leave of, say goodbye to.
verachten [fɛrˈaxtən] v despise. **verächtlich** *adj* contemptible. **Verachtung** f contempt.
verallgemeinern [fɛralɡəˈmaɪnərn] v gen-
eralize. **Verallgemeinerung** f generaliza-
tion.
veralten [fɛrˈaltən] v become outmoded, go
out of use. **veraltet** *adj* out-of-date.
veränderlich [fɛrˈɛndərlɪç] *adj* changeable.
verändern v change, alter. **sich verändern** change, alter. **Veränderung** f
change, alteration.
verängstigt [fɛrˈɛŋstɪçt] *adj* jittery.
Verankern [fɛrˈaŋkərn] v moor, anchor.
veranlagt [fɛrˈanlaːkt] *adj* talented, gifted.
veranlassen [fɛrˈanlasən] v cause, bring
about. **Veranlassung** f cause; (*Beweggrund*)
motive.
veranschaulichen [fɛrˈanʃaʊlɪçən] v make
clear.
veranstalten [fɛrˈanʃtaltən] v organize,
arrange. **Veranstaltller** m (pl -) organizer.

–ung f (pl -en) event, function;
(*Veranstalten*) organization.
verantworten [fɛrˈantvɔrtən] v take
responsibility for, answer for. **verantwortlich** *adj* responsible. **Verantwortll
lichkeit** f responsibility. **–ung** f (pl -en)
responsibility; (*Rechtfertigung*) justification.
verarbeiten [fɛrˈarbaɪtən] v manufacture,
make; (*bearbeiten*) work, process; (*durch-
denken*) assimilate. **Verarbeitung** f manufacture; working; assimilation.
verargen [fɛrˈarɡən] v blame.
verärgern [fɛrˈɛrɡərn] v annoy, vex.
verarmen [fɛrˈarmən] v become poor. **verarmt** *adj* impoverished.
Verb [vɛrp] *neut* (pl -en) verb.
Verband [fɛrˈbant] m (pl **Verbände**) (*Med*)
bandage, dressing; (*Verein*) association,
society.
verbannen [fɛrˈbanən] v banish. **Ver-
bannllte(r)** exile. **–ung** f banishment,
exile.
*****verbergen** [fɛrˈbɛrɡən] v hide.
verbessern [fɛrˈbɛsərn] v improve; (*berichtigen*) correct. **Verbesserung** f (pl -en) improvement; correction.
verbeugen [fɛrˈbɔyɡən] v **sich verbeugen**
bow.
*****verbieten** [fɛrˈbiːtən] v forbid, prohibit.
*****verbinden** [fɛrˈbɪndən] v connect, join;
(*Med*) bandage, dress; (*Telef*) connect, put
through. **sich verbinden mit** join up
with, combine with. **verbindlich** *adj* binding, obligatory; (*zuvorkommend*) obliging.
Verbindung f connection; (*Med*) bandage,
dressing; (*Telef*) connection. **in Verbindung mit** in association with. **im Verbindung treten mit** get in touch with. **im
Verbindung stehen mit** be in contact
with. **in Verbindung setzen mit** put in
contact with.
verbissen [fɛrˈbɪsən] *adj* grim, dogged.
verbittern [fɛrˈbɪtərn] v embitter.
Verbitterung f bitterness.
verblassen [fɛrˈblasən] v turn or grow pale;
(*Farbe, Erinnerung*) fade.
Verbleib [fɛrˈblaɪp] m whereabouts. **verbleiben** v remain.
verblenden [fɛrˈblɛndən] v blind, dazzle,
delude; (*Mauerwerk*) face. **Verblendung** f
blindness, delusion.
verblüffen [fɛrˈblʏfən] v dumbfound, non-

plus. **verblüfft** *adj* dumbfounded, non-plussed. **Verblüffung** *f* amazement, stupefaction.

verbluten [fɛrˈbluːtən] *v* bleed to death.

verbohrt [fɛrˈboːrt] *adj* stubborn.

verborgen [fɛrˈbɔrgən] *adj* hidden. **Verborgenheit** *f* concealment, secrecy.

Verbot [fɛrˈboːt] *neut* (*pl* -e) prohibition, ban. **verboten** *adj* prohibited, forbidden.

Verbrauch [fɛrˈbraux] *m* consumption, use. **verbrauchen** *v* consume, use up. **Verbraucher** *m* (*pl* -) consumer. **Verbrauchsgüter** *pl* consumer goods *pl*.

Verbrechen [fɛrˈbrɛçən] *neut* crime. **–er** *m* criminal. **verbrechen** *v* commit a crime. **verbrecherisch** *adj* criminal.

verbreiten [fɛrˈbraitən] *v* spread. **weit verbreitet** *adj* widespread.

*****verbrennen** [fɛrˈbrɛnən] *v* burn; (*Leichen*) cremate. **Verbrennung** *f* burning; cremation. **–smotor** *m* internal combustion engine.

*****verbringen** [fɛrˈbrɪŋən] *v* spend (time).

verbrühen [fɛrˈbryːən] *v* scald.

Verbum [ˈvɛrbum] *neut* (*pl* **Verben**) verb.

verbünden [fɛrˈbyndən] *v* **sich verbünden mit** ally oneself with. **Verbündete(r)** *m* ally.

verchromt [fɛrˈkroːmt] *adj* chromium-plated. **Verchromung** *f* chromium plating.

Verdacht [fɛrˈdaxt] *m* (*pl* -e) suspicion. **in Verdacht kommen** arouse suspicion, be suspected. **verdächtig** *adj* suspicious. **–en** *v* suspect.

verdammen [fɛrˈdamən] *v* condemn, damn. **verdammt** *adj* damned. *interj* damn! **Verdammung** *f* damnation.

verdampfen [fɛrˈdampfən] *v* evaporate, vaporize. **Verdampfung** *f* evaporation, vaporization.

verdanken [fɛrˈdaŋkən] *v* owe.

verdauen [fɛrˈdauən] *v* digest. **verdaulich** *adj* digestible. **Verdauung** *f* digestion.

Verdeck [fɛrˈdɛk] *neut* (*pl* -e) canopy, covering; (*Mot*) roof; (*Schiff*) deck. **verdecken** *v* cover, conceal. **verdeckt** *adj* masked, concealed.

Verderb [fɛrˈdɛrp] *m* ruin, destruction. **verderben** *v* spoil, ruin; (*verführen*) corrupt; (*Speisen*) spoil, go bad; (*Menschen*) come to grief, perish. **Verderben** *neut* ruin, destruction. **verderblich** *adj* destructive,

pernicious; (*Waren*) perishable. **verderbt** *adj* corrupt(ed).

verdeutlichen [fɛrˈdɔytliçən] *v* make clear, elucidate.

verdichten [fɛrˈdɪçtən] *v* compress. **Verdichtung** *f* compression.

verdicken [fɛrˈdɪkən] *v* thicken.

verdienen [fɛrˈdiːnən] *v* (*Geld*) earn; (*Beachtung, Lob*) deserve. *er hat es verdient* he deserves it; (*negativ*) it serves him right. **Verdienst 1** *m* (*pl* -e) earnings *pl*, gains *pl*. **2** *neut* (*pl* -e) deserts *pl*. **–spanne** *f* margin (of profit).

verdingen [fɛrˈdɪŋən] *v* hire out.

verdoppeln [fɛrˈdɔpəln] *v* double. **Verdoppelung** *f* doubling.

verdorben [fɛrˈdɔrbən] *adj* spoilt; (*fig*) corrupted.

verdrängen [fɛrˈdrɛŋən] *v* displace, push out; (*vertreiben*) drive away; (*Psychol*) repress.

verdrehen [fɛrˈdreːən] *v* distort, twist.

*****verdrießen** [fɛrˈdriːsən] *v* vex, annoy. **verdrießlich** *adj* sullen, disgruntled; tiresome irksome.

verdrossen [fɛrˈdrɔsən] *adj* sullen.

Verdruß [fɛrˈdrus] *m* annoyance.

verdummen [fɛrˈdumən] *v* stupefy; (*dumm werden*) grow stupid.

verdunkeln [fɛrˈduŋkəln] *v* darken.

verdünnen [fɛrˈdynən] *v* dilute, thin.

veredeln [fɛrˈeːdəln] *v* ennoble; (*fig*) improve, refine.

verehren [fɛrˈeːrən] *v* (*Rel*) worship; (*lieben*) adore; (*hochschätzen*) venerate, respect. **Verehr||er** *m* worshipper; adorer; admirer. **–ung** *f* worship; adoration; veneration.

Verein [fɛrˈain] *m* (*pl* -e) society, association; (*Klub*) club. **vereinbar** *adj* reconcilable, compatible. **vereinbar||en** *v* agree upon. **–t** *adj* agreed (upon). **Vereinbarung** *f* (*pl* -en) agreement.

vereinfachen [fɛrˈainfaxən] *v* simplify.

vereinheitlichen [fɛrˈainhaitliçən] *v* unify, standardize.

vereinigen [fɛrˈainɪgən] *v* unite, join. **sich vereinigen** unite. **vereinigt** *adj* united. **die Vereinigten Staaten** *pl* the United States. **Vereinigung** *f* (*pl* -en) union; association, society; (*Zusammenschluß*) combination. **–spunkt** *m* meeting point.

vereint [fɛrˈaint] *adj* united.

vereiteln [ɛɾˈaitəln] v frustrate, (fig) blight.
Vereitelung f frustration.

vererben [ɛɾˈɛɾbən] v leave, bequeath;
(Krankheit, Eigenschaft) transmit.
vererblich adj hereditary. **Vererbung** f
heredity.

verewigen [ɛɾˈeːvigən] v immortalize.

verfahren [ɛɾˈfaːɾən] v act, proceed. **sich
verfahren** lose one's way. **Verfahren** neut
procedure; (Methode) method; (Tech)
process.

Verfall [ɛɾˈfal] m ruin; (allmählich) decline,
decay. **verfallen** v decline, decay.

verfälschen [ɛɾˈfɛlʃən] v falsify. **Verfälschung** f falsification.

verfassen [ɛɾˈfasən] v compose, write;
(Urkunde) draw up. **Verfasser** m (pl -),
Verfasserin f (pl -nen) author, writer.

*verfechten [ɛɾˈfɛçtən] v fight for, defend.

verfehlen [ɛɾˈfeːlən] v miss, not reach; (versäumen) fail. **Verfehlung** f mistake, lapse.

verfeinern [ɛɾˈfainəɾn] v refine.

verflechten [ɛɾˈflɛçtən] v interweave; (fig)
involve.

verfluchen [ɛɾˈfluːxən] v curse. **verflucht**
adj cursed, damned. interj damn (it)!

verfolgen [ɛɾˈfɔlgən] v pursue; (beobachten)
follow; (gerichtlich) prosecute; (plagen) persecute. **Verfolger** m pursuer; persecutor.
Verfolgung f pursuit; prosecution; persecution.

Verformung [ɛɾˈfɔɾmuŋ] f distortion,
warping.

verfügbar [ɛɾˈfyːkbaːɾ] adj available. **verfügen** v order, decree. **verfügen über** have
at one's disposal, dispose of. **Verfügung** f
disposal; (Anordnung) order. **zur Verfügung stehen/stellen** be/put at the disposal
(of).

verführen [ɛɾˈfyːɾən] v seduce; (verleiten)
lead astray. **Verführ∥er** m seducer;
tempter. **–ung** f seduction; temptation.

vergangen [ɛɾˈgaŋən] adj past.
Vergangenheit f past. **vergänglich** adj
transitory, impermanent.

Vergaser [ɛɾˈgaːzəɾ] m (pl -) carburettor.

*vergeben [ɛɾˈgeːbən] v (verzeihen) forgive;
(verschenken) give away; (verteilen) distribute. **vergeb∥lens** adv in vain. **–lich** adj
vain. adv in vain. **Vergebung** f forgiveness.
interj pardon me!

vergegenwärtigen [ɛɾgeːgənˈvɛɾtigən]
v represent.

*vergehen [ɛɾˈgeːən] v pass. **vergehen vor**
die of. **sich vergehen** v commit an
offence, err. **Vergehen** neut misdeed.

*vergelten [ɛɾˈgɛltən] v pay back. **Vergeltung** f reward; retaliation.

*vergessen [ɛɾˈgɛsən] v forget.
Vergessenheit f oblivion. **vergeßlich** adj
forgetful.

vergeuden [ɛɾˈgɔydən] v waste, squander,
dissipate. **Vergeudung** f waste, dissipation.

vergewaltigen [ɛɾgəˈvaltigən] v rape. **Vergewaltiger** m rapist. **Vergewaltigung** f
rape.

*vergießen [ɛɾˈgiːsən] v shed, spill.

vergiften [ɛɾˈgiftən] v poison. **Vergiftung**
f poisoning.

Vergißmeinnicht [ɛɾˈgismainiçt] neut (pl
-e) forget-me-not.

verglasen [ɛɾˈglaːzən] v glaze.

Vergleich [ɛɾˈglaiç] m (pl -e) comparison;
(Redewendung) simile; (Abkommen) agreement, settlement. **einen Vergleich
schließen** come to an agreement. **im
Vergleich mit/zu** in comparison with/to.
vergleichbar adj comparable. **vergleichen** v compare; settle, agree.

Vergnügen [ɛɾˈgnyːgən] neut enjoyment.
vergnügen v amuse. **sich vergnügen**
amuse oneself. **vergnügt** adj merry, happy.
Vergnügung f pleasure, enjoyment.
–spark m amusement park.

vergoldet [ɛɾˈgɔldət] adj (Metall) gold-
plated; (Holz) gilt.

vergöttern [ɛɾˈgœtəɾn] v deify; (fig) idolize.

vergraben [ɛɾˈgraːbən] v bury.

vergriffen [ɛɾˈgrifən] adj sold out; (Buch)
out of print.

vergrößern [ɛɾˈgrøːsəɾn] v enlarge, magnify. **Vergrößerung** f (pl -en) enlargement.

Vergünstigung [ɛɾˈgynstiguŋ] f (pl -en)
privilege, perk; (Rabatt) discount.

vergüten [ɛɾˈgyːtən] v compensate (for);
(Unkosten) reimburse. **Vergütung** f (pl -en)
compensation; reimbursement.

verhaften [ɛɾˈhaftən] v arrest. **verhaftet**
adj arrested; (fig) bound, connected.
Verhaftung f (pl -en) arrest.

*verhalten [ɛɾˈhaltən] v hold back. **sich
verhalten** behave, act; (Sache) be. **Verhalten** neut behaviour.

Verhältnis [fɛɐ̯'hɛltnɪs] *neut* (*pl* -**se**) relation, proportion; (*Beziehungen*) relation; (*Liebesaffäre*) relationship; liaison. **im Verhältnis zu** in comparison with. **Verhältnisse** *pl* circumstances. **Verhältnismäßig** *adj* proportional. *adv* relatively, comparatively.

verhandeln [fɛɐ̯'handəln] *v* negotiate. **Verhandlung** *f* negotiation.

Verhängnis [fɛɐ̯'hɛŋnɪs] *neut* (*pl* -**se**) fate, destiny. **verhängnisvoll** *adj* fateful.

verhaßt [fɛɐ̯'hast] *adj* odious, hated.

verheeren [fɛɐ̯'heːrən] *v* devastate, lay waste.

verheimlichen [fɛɐ̯'haɪmlɪçən] *v* conceal, keep secret.

verheiraten [fɛɐ̯'haɪraːtən] *v* marry. **sich verheiraten** get married, marry.

*verheißen [fɛɐ̯'haɪsən] *v* promise.

*verhelfen [fɛɐ̯'hɛlfən] *v* assist, help.

verherrlichen [fɛɐ̯'hɛrlɪçən] *v* glorify. **Verherrlichung** *f* glorification.

verhindern [fɛɐ̯'hɪndərn] *v* prevent. **Verhinderung** *f* prevention.

verhöhnen [gɛɐ̯'høːnən] *v* ridicule, mock.

Verhör [fɛɐ̯'høːr] *neut* (*pl* -**e**) interrogation, examination. **verhören** *v* interrogate, examine. **sich verhören** hear wrongly, misunderstand.

verhungern [fɛɐ̯'huŋərn] *v* starve (to death).

verhüten [fɛɐ̯'hyːtən] *v* prevent, ward off. **-d** *adj* preventive. **Verhütung** *f* prevention. **-smittel** *neut* contraceptive.

verirren [fɛɐ̯'ɪrən] *v* **sich verirren** go astray, get lost.

verjüngen [fɛɐ̯'jʏŋən] *v* rejuvenate; (*erneuern*) renew. **Verjüngung** *f* rejuvenation; renewal.

Verkauf [fɛɐ̯'kauf] *m* sale. **verkaufen** *v* sell. **Verkäufer** *m* seller; (*Angestellter*) salesman; (*im Laden*) sales assistant. **-in** *f* saleswoman, sales assistant. **verkäuflich** *adj* for sale. **Verkaufs||abteilung** *f* sales department. **-automat** *m* vending machine. **-bedingungen** (*pl*) terms of sale. **-förderung** *f* sales promotion. **-preis** *m* selling price.

Verkehr [fɛɐ̯'keːr] *m* traffic; (*Umgang*) intercourse; (*Handel*) trade. **verkehren** *v* (*Bus*) run; (*verdrehen*) distort; (*besuchen*) frequent; (*Menschen*) associate (with). **Verkehrs|| ampeln** *f pl* traffic lights. **-ordnung** *f* traffic regulation. **-spitze** *f* rush hour. **-stockung** *f* traffic jam. **-unfall** *m* road accident. **verkehrt** *adj* inverted, wrong way round; (*falsch*) wrong.

*verkennen [fɛɐ̯'kɛnən] *v* mistake, misjudge; (*Person*) not recognize.

verklagen [fɛɐ̯'klaːgən] *v* (*Jur*) sue (for); (*umg.*) inform against.

verklären [fɛɐ̯'klɛːrən] *v* transfigure; (*fig*) illumine. **Verklärung** *f* transfiguration; illumination.

verkleiden [fɛɐ̯'klaɪdən] *v* cover, mask; (*Wand*) face. **sich verkleiden** disguise oneself. **Verkleidung** *f* (*pl* -**en**) disguise; facing, lining.

verkleinern [fɛɐ̯'klaɪnərn] *v* reduce, diminish. **Verkleinerung** *f* (*pl* -**en**) reduction, diminution.

verknüpfen [fɛɐ̯'knʏpfən] *v* knot (together), join; (*fig*) connect. **verknüpft** *adj* connected.

*verkommen [fɛɐ̯'kɔmən] *v* (*Person*) degenerate, (*umg.*) go to the dogs; (*speisen*) go bad; (*Gebäude*) decay, be neglected.

verkörpern [fɛɐ̯'kœrpərn] *v* embody. **Verkörperung** *f* embodiment, incarnation.

verkrümmen [fɛɐ̯'krʏmən] *v* bend, make crooked. **Verkrümmung** *f* (*pl* -**en**) crookedness, distortion; (*Rückgrat*) curvature.

verkrüppeln [fɛɐ̯'krʏpəln] *v* cripple.

verkünden [fɛɐ̯'kʏndən] *v* announce, proclaim; (*Urteil*) pronounce. **verkündigen** *v* proclaim. **Mariä Verkündigung** Annunciation, Lady Day.

verkürzen [fɛɐ̯'kʏrtsən] *v* shorten, abbreviate; (*Buch*) abridge. **sich verkürzen** shrink, diminish. **Verkürzung** *f* shortening; (*Buch*) abridgment.

*verladen [fɛɐ̯'laːdən] *v* load; (*verschicken*) dispatch. **Verladung** *f* loading.

Verlag [fɛɐ̯'laːk] *m* (*pl* -**e**) publishing house, publisher.

verlagern [fɛɐ̯'laːgərn] *v* relocate (*Produktion*).

verlangen [fɛɐ̯'laŋən] *v* demand; (*benötigen*) require. **verlangen nach** long for. **Verlangen** *neut* demand; (*Wunsch*) desire. **auf Verlangen** on demand.

verlängern [fɛɐ̯'lɛŋərn] *v* extend, lengthen; (*Gültigkeit, usw.*) extend. **Verlängerung** *f* (*pl* -**en**) extension.

verlangsamen [fɛɐˈlaŋzaːm ən] v slow down.

Verlaß [fɛɐˈlas] m trustworthiness, reliability. **verlassen** v leave; (im Stich lassen) desert, abandon. adj abandoned, forsaken. **sich verlassen auf** rely on. **verläßlich** adj reliable.

Verlauf [fɛɐˈlauf] m course. **verlaufen** v (Zeit) pass; (Angelegenheit) go, turn out; (Weg) run, to. es ist alles gut verlaufen everything went very well. **sich verlaufen** lose one's way.

verlautbaren [fɛɐˈlautbaːrən] v notify.

verlegen [fɛɐˈleːgən] v misplace; (Platzändern) transfer, remove, relocate; (Buch) publish; (Termin) postpone. adj embarrassed. **Verlegllenheit** f embarrassment; (Schwierigkeit) difficulty. **–er** m (pl -) publisher.

***verleihen** [fɛɐˈlaɪən] v lend; (Preise) confer, bestow.

verleiten [fɛɐˈlaɪtən] v lead astray, mislead.

verlernen [fɛɐˈlɛrnən] v forget.

***verlesen** [fɛɐˈleːzən] v read out; (auslesen) pick. **sich verlesen** misread.

verletzen [fɛɐˈlɛtsən] v injure, wound; (kränken) hurt, offend; (Gesetze) infringe. **verletzlich** adj vulnerable; (fig) sensitive, touchy. **Verletzung** f (pl -en) injury; (Vergehen) offence.

verleugnen [fɛɐˈbygnən] v deny; (Kind, Freunde) disown.

verleumden [fɛɐˈbʏm dən] v slander. **Verleumder** m (pl -) slanderer. **verleumderisch** adj slanderous. **Verleumdung** f (pl -en) slander.

verlieben [fɛɐˈliːbən] v **sich verlieben in** fall in love with.

***verlieren** [fɛɐˈliːrən] v lose. **sich verlieren** get lost.

verloben [fɛɐˈloːbən] v **sich verloben mit** get engaged to. **Verlobte** f (pl -n) fiancée. **Verlobter** m (pl -en) fiancé. **Verlobung** f (pl -en) engagement.

verlocken [fɛɐˈlɔkən] v tempt, entice. **–d** adj tempting. **Verlockung** f (pl -en) enticement, temptation.

verlogen [fɛɐˈloːgən] adj untruthful, lying.

verloren [fɛɐˈloːrən] adj lost. **–gehen** v be lost.

Verlust [fɛɐˈlʊst] m (pl -e) loss. **verlustbringend** adj detrimental.

vermachen [fɛɐˈmaxən] v bequeath, leave. **Vermächtnis** neut (pl -se) (Testament) will; (Vermachtes) legacy, bequest.

vermehren [fɛɐˈmeːrən] v also **sich vermehren** increase. **Vermehrung** f (pl -en) increase.

***vermeiden** [fɛɐˈmaɪdən] v avoid. **vermeidlich** adj avoidable. **Vermeidung** f avoidance.

vermeintlich [fɛɐˈmaɪntlɪç] adj supposed, presumed.

Vermerk [fɛɐˈmɛrk] m (pl -e) note, remark. **vermerken** v note, remark.

***vermessen** [fɛɐˈmɛsən] v measure; (Land) survey. adj presumptuous. **Vermessller** m surveyor. **–ung** f measurement; (Land) survey.

vermieten [fɛɐˈmiːtən] v let, rent (out). **Vermietller** m landlord. **–ung** f letting.

vermindern [fɛɐˈmɪndɛrn] v reduce, decrease. **Verminderung** f reduction, decrease.

vermischen [fɛɐˈmɪʃən] v mix, blend.

vermissen [fɛɐˈmɪsən] v miss. **vermißt** adj missing.

vermitteln [fɛɐˈmɪtəln] v mediate, negotiate; (verschaffen) procure, obtain. **Vermittller** m mediator, go-between; (Komm) agent. **–ung** f (pl -en) mediation, negotiation; (Telef) exchange.

***vermögen** [fɛɐˈmœ ːgən] v be able (to). **–d** adj well-to-do. **Vermögen** neut fortune, wealth, property; (Fähigkeit) ability. **–sverwalter** m trustee (of an estate).

vermuten [fɛɐˈmuːtən] v suppose, suspect. **vermutlich** adj supposed. adv probably, presumably. **Vermutung** f (pl -en) supposition, suspicion.

vernachlässigen [fɛɐˈnaːxlɛsɪgən] v neglect.

vernarren [fɛɐˈnarən] v **sich vernarren in** become infatuated with; (Kind) dote on.

***vernehmen** [fɛɐˈneːm ən] v perceive; (Gefangene) interrogate. **vernehmlich** adj perceptible.

verneinen [fɛɐˈnaɪnən] v deny; (Frage) say no, answer in the negative. **Verneinung** f denial; negation.

vernichten [fɛɐˈnɪçtən] v destroy, annihilate. **–d** adj annihilating, crushing. **Vernichtung** f destruction, annihilation.

vernieten [fɛɐˈniːtən] v rivet.

Vernunft [fɛɐˈnʊnft] f reason; (Besonnenheit)

sense, commonsense. **zur Vernunft kommen** come to one's senses. **vernünftig** *adj* sensible, reasonable.

veröden [fɛːʁə ˈdøːn] *v* become desolate.

veröffentlichen [fɛːʁə ˈœntlɪçən] *v* publish. **Veröffentlichung** *f* publication.

verordnen [fɛːʁ ˈɔdnən] *v* order; (*Med*) prescribe. **Verordnung** *f* order; prescription.

verpachten [fɛːʁ ˈpaxtən] *v* lease, let.

verpacken [fɛːʁ ˈpakən] *v* pack.

verpassen [fɛːʁ ˈpasən] *v* miss.

verpfänden [fɛːʁ ˈpfɛndən] *v* pawn, pledge.

verpflegen [fɛːʁ ˈpfleːgən] *v* feed, cater for. **Verpflegung** *f* food, board.

verpflichten [fɛːʁ ˈplɪçtən] *v* oblige, commit. **sich verpflichten** bind *or* commit oneself. **Verpflichtung** *f* obligation, commitment, duty.

verpfuschen [fɛːʁ ˈpfuʃən] *v* bungle, botch, make a mess of.

verprügeln [fɛːʁ ˈpryːgəln] *v* thrash, beat.

verputzen [fɛːʁ ˈputsən] *v* plaster; (*umg.*) scoff, put away.

Verrat [fɛːʁˈaːt] *m* (*unz.*) treachery; (*Pol*) treason; (*eines Geheimnisses*) betrayal. **verraten** *v* betray. **Verräter** *m* (*pl* -) traitor. **verräterisch** *adj* treacherous.

verrechnen [fɛːʁˈɛçnən] *v* reckon up. **sich verrechnen** miscalculate. **Verrechnung** *f* miscalculation.

verreisen [fɛːʁˈaɪzən] *v* go away (on a journey).

verrenken [fɛːʁˈɛŋkən] *v* dislocate, sprain. **Verrenkung** *f* (*pl* -en) dislocation, sprain.

verrichten [fɛːʁˈɪçtən] *v* perform, do, execute.

verriegeln [fɛːʁˈiːgəln] *v* bolt, bar.

verringern [fɛːʁˈɪŋəm] *v* reduce, lessen.

verrotten [fɛːʁˈɔtən] *v* rot. **verrottet** *adj* rotten.

verrücken [fɛːʁˈʏkən] *v* shift, displace. **verrückt** *adj* crazy.

Verruf [fɛːʁˈuːf] *m* ill repute, disrepute. **in Verruf bringen/kommen** bring/fall into disrepute.

Vers [fɛːʁs] *m* (*pl* -e) line; (*Strophe*) verse.

versagen [fɛːʁˈzaːgən] *v* fail; (*verweigern*) refuse. **Versager** *m* (*pl* -) failure.

versammeln [fɛːʁˈzam əln] *v* assemble, gather. **sich versammeln** meet. **Versammlung** *f* (*pl* -en) meeting, assembly, convention.

Versand [fɛːʁˈzant] *m* dispatch, shipment, forwarding. **–handel** *m* mail-order (trading).

versäumen [fɛːʁˈzɔym ən] *v* neglect, fail; (*verpassen*) miss. **versäumnis** *f* neglect, omission.

verschaffen [fɛːʁˈʃafən] *v* obtain, procure.

verschämt [fɛːʁˈʃɛːmt] *adj* bashful, ashamed.

Verschandelung [fɛːʁˈʃandəluŋ] *f* (*pl* -en) blight.

Verschanzung [fɛːʁˈʃantsuŋ] *f* (*pl* -en) fortification, entrenchment.

verschärfen [fɛːʁˈʃɛʁfən] *v* sharpen, intensify.

*verscheiden *v* die. **verschieden** *adj* dead.

verschicken [fɛːʁˈʃɪkən] *v* send off, dispatch.

*verschieben [fɛːʁˈʃiːbən] *v* move, shift; (*Termin*) postpone. **Verschiebung** *f* displacement; postponement.

verschieden [fɛːʁˈʃiːdən] *adj* different. **–artig** *adj* various. **Verschiedenheit** *f* difference.

verschiffen [fɛːʁˈʃɪfən] *v* ship.

verschimmeln [fɛːʁˈʃɪm əln] *v* moulder, grow mouldy.

*verschlafen [fɛːʁˈʃlaːfən] *v* oversleep; (*Sorgen*) sleep off. *adj* sleepy.

Verschlag [fɛːʁˈʃlaːk] *m* shed.

verschlechtern [fɛːʁˈʃlɛçtəm] *v* make worse, aggravate. **sich verschlechtern** deteriorate, get worse. **Verschlechterung** *f* deterioration.

verschleiern [fɛːʁˈʃlaɪəm] *v* veil; (*fig*) camouflage, conceal.

Verschleiß [fɛːʁˈʃlaɪs] *m* (*pl* -e) wear and tear. **verschließen** *v* wear out.

verschleudern [fɛːʁˈʃlɔydəm] *v* waste, squander.

verschließbar [fɛːʁˈʃliːsbaːʁ] *adj* lockable. **verschließen** *v* lock; (*Sachen*) lock up *or* away.

verschlimmern [fɛːʁˈʃlɪm əm] *v* make worse, aggravate. **sich verschlimmern** become worse, deteriorate. **Verschlimmerung** *f* deterioration.

*verschlingen [fɛːʁˈʃlɪŋən] *v* devour, gorge; (*verflechten*) twist, intertwine.

verschlossen [fɛːʁˈʃlɔsən] *adj* locked; (*Person*) reserved, withdrawn.

verschlucken [fɛːʁˈʃlukən] *v* swallow.

Verschluß [ɛrʃlus] *m* fastening; (*Propfen*) stopper, plug; (*Phot*) shutter.

verschmähen [ɛrʃmɛ:ən] *v* disdain, scorn.

***verschmelzen** [ɛrʃmɛlzən] *v* melt, fuse; (*ineinander*) merge.

***verschneiden** [ɛrʃnaidən] *v* trim, prune; (*Wein*) mix, adulterate; (*kastrieren*) castrate.

verschollen [ɛrʃɔlən] *adj* missing.

verschonen [ɛrʃo:nən] *v* spare.

verschönern [ɛrʃøːnərn] *v* beautify.

verschränken [ɛrʃrɛŋkən] *v* fold, cross.

verschulden [ɛrʃuldən] *v* fall into *or* be in debt; (*Übel*) be to blame for. **Verschulden** *neut* guilt, fault. **verschuldet** *adj* in debt.

***verschweigen** [ɛrʃvaigən] *v* keep secret, hide. **Verschweigung** *f* concealment.

verschwenden [ɛrʃvɛndən] *v* waste, squander. **verschwenderisch** *adj* wasteful. **Verschwendung** *f* waste.

verschwiegen [ɛrʃviːgən] *adj* discreet; (*Platz*) secluded, quitet. **Verschwiegenheit** *f* discretion.

***verschwinden** [ɛrʃvindən] *v* disappear.

verschwommen [ɛrʃvɔmən] *adj* blurred, hazy.

verschwören [ɛrʃvøː:rən] *v* renounce, abjure. **sich verschwören** conspire, plot. **Verschwörer** *m* conspirator, plotter. **–ung** *f* conspiracy.

***versehen** [ɛrze:ən] *v* (*versorgan*) provide, supply; (*Dienst*) discharge; (*Haus, usw.*) look after. **sich versehen** make a mistake. **Versehen** *neut* mistake; (*Übersehen*) oversight. **versehentlich** *adv* by mistake.

***versenden** [ɛrzɛndən] *v* send, dispatch.

versengen [ɛrzɛŋən] *v* singe, scorch.

versenken [ɛrzɛŋkən] *v* lower; (*unter Wasser*) submerge; (*Schiff*) sink. **sich versenken in** become absorbed in.

versessen [ɛrzɛsən] *adj* **versessen auf** mad about *or* on.

versetzen [ɛrzɛtsən] *v* move, transfer; (*verpfänden*) pawn; (*umg.*) leave in the lurch, jilt. **Versetzung** *f* removal, transfer.

verseuchen [ɛrzɔyçən] *v* contaminate.

versichern [ɛrziçərn] *v* insure; (*überzeugen*) assure. **sich versichern** make certain. **Seien Sie versichert, daß** you may rest assured that. **Versicherung** *f* insurance. **–spolice** *f* insurance policy.

versiegeln [ɛrziːgəl] *v* seal.

versöhnen [ɛrzøː:nən] *v* reconcile. **sich**

versöhnen mit become reconciled with. **versöhnlich** *adj* conciliatory. **Versöhnung** *f* reconciliation.

versorgen [ɛrzɔrgən] *v* (*Kind, usw.*) provide for. **versorgen mit** provide *or* supply with. **Versorgung** *f* care, provision; (*staatlich*) maintenance, (public) assistance.

verspäten [ɛrʃpɛː:tən] *v* delay. **verspätet** *adj* late, delayed. **Verspätung** *f* (*pl* -en) delay. **10 Minuten Verspätung haben** be running 10 minutes late.

versperren [ɛrʃpɛrən] *v* bar; obstruct.

verspielen [ɛrʃpiːlən] *v* gamble away, lose.

verspotten [ɛrʃpɔtən] *v* scoff at, ridicule. **Verspottung** *f* ridicule.

***versprechen** [ɛrʃprɛçən] *v* promise. **sich versprechen** make a (verbal) mistake. **Versprechen** *neut* (*pl* -) promise.

versprengen [ɛrʃprɛŋən] *v* (*Mil*) scatter, disperse.

versprochen [ɛrʃprɔxən] *adj* promised.

verstaatlichen [ɛrʃtaː:tliçən] *v* nationalize. **Verstaatlichung** *f* nationalization.

Verstand [ɛrʃtant] *m* understanding; (*Geist*) mind, intelligence. **den Verstand verlieren** lose one's reason, go out of one's mind. **verständig** *adj* intelligent; sensible. **verständigen** *v* inform. **sich verständigen mit (über)** come to an understanding with (about). **Verständigung** *f* understanding, arrangement. **verständlich** *adj* intelligible. **Verständnis** *neut* understanding, comprehension. **verständnislos** *adj* uncomprehending, unappreciative. **–voll** *adj* understanding, sympathetic.

verstärken [ɛrʃtɛrkən] *v* strengthen; (*Ton*) amplify; (*Farbe, Spannung*) intensify. **Verstärker** *m* amplifier. **–ung** *f* strengthening; (*Ton*) amplification; (*Mil*) reinforcements *pl.*

Versteck [ɛrʃtɛk] *neut* (*pl* -e) hiding place. **verstecken** *v* hide. **sich verstecken** hide. **versteckt** *adj* hidden; (*Anspielung*) veiled, implied.

***verstehen** [ɛrʃte:ən] *v* understand. **zu verstehen geben** give to understand. **sich verstehen mit** come to an understanding with.

Versteigerer [ɛrʃtaigərər] *m* (*pl* -) auctioneer. **versteigern** *v* (sell by) auction. **Versteigerung** *f* (*pl* -en) auction.

versteinern [ɛrʃtainərn] *v* petrify. **versteinert** *adj* petrified.

verstellbar [ɛɐ̯ˈʃtɛlbaːɐ̯] *adj* adjustable, movable. **verstellen** *v* adjust; (*versperren*) block, bar; (*unkenntlich machen*) disguise. **sich verstellen** feign, dissemble. **Verstellung** *f* (*pl* -en) adjustment; (*fig*) pretence.

verstimmt [ɛɐ̯ˈʃtɪmt] *adj* (*Musik*) out of tune; (*Person*) bad-tempered; (*Magen*) upset.

verstockt [ɛɐ̯ˈʃtɔkt] *adj* stubborn.

verstohlen [ɛɐ̯ˈʃtoːlən] *adj* furtive, stealthy.

verstopfen [ɛɐ̯ˈʃtɔpfən] *v* plug, stop up; (*Med*) constipate. **Verstopfung** *f* obstruction; (*Med*) constipation.

verstorben [ɛɐ̯ˈʃtɔrbən] *adj* deceased, late. **Verstorbene(r)** the deceased.

Verstoß [ɛɐ̯ˈʃtoːs] *m* offence. **verstoßen** *v* offend; (*von sich stoßen*) reject.

verstricken [ɛɐ̯ˈʃtrɪkən] *v* entangle, ensnare.

verstümmeln [ɛɐ̯ˈʃtʏməln] *v* mutilate, maim.

Versuch [ɛɐ̯ˈzuːx] *m* (*pl* -e) attempt; (*Probe*) test, trial; (*Experiment*) experiment. **versuchen** *v* attempt, try; (*kosten*) taste, try. **Versuchs||fahrt** *f* trial run. **–kaninchen** *neut* (*fig*) guinea pig.

vertagen [ɛɐ̯ˈtaːgən] *v* adjourn.

vertauschen [ɛɐ̯ˈtaʊʃən] *v* exchange.

verteidigen [ɛɐ̯ˈtaɪdɪgən] *v* defend. **Verteidig||er** *m* (*pl* -) defender; (*Jur*) defence counsel. **–ung** *f* (*pl* -en) defence.

verteilen [ɛɐ̯ˈtaɪlən] *v* distribute; (*zerteilen*) divide. **Verteil||er** *m* (*pl* -) distributor. **–ung** *f* (*pl* -en) distribution.

vertiefen [ɛɐ̯ˈtiːfən] *v* deepen. **sich vertiefen in** be absorbed in. **vertieft** *adj* sunk; (*fig*) absorbed. **Vertiefung** *f* depression, hollow; (*fig*) absorption.

vertikal [vɛrtiˈkaːl] *adj* vertical.

vertilgen [ɛɐ̯ˈtɪlgən] *v* exterminate; (*vernichten*) destroy. **Vertilgung** *f* extermination; destruction.

Vertrag [ɛɐ̯ˈtraːk] *m* (*pl* Verträge) contract; (*Pol*) treaty. **vertragen** *v* bear, endure. **sich vertragen mit** get on well with. **verträglich** *adj* stipulated, agreed.

verträglich [ɛɐ̯ˈtrɛːklɪç] *adj* (*Person*) good-natured, obliging; (*Speise*) light, digestible.

Vertrags||bruch *m* breach of contract. **–nehmer** *m* contractor.

vertrauen [ɛɐ̯ˈtraʊən] *v* trust. **vertrauen auf** trust in, have confidence in. **Ver-**trauen *neut* trust, confidence. **Vertrauens||sache** *f* confidential affair. **–votum** *neut* vote of confidence. **vertrauens||voll** *adj* trustful, trusting. **–würdig** *adj* trustworthy. **vertraulich** *adj* confidential. **vertraut** *adj* familiar.

*vertreiben [ɛɐ̯ˈtraɪbən] *v* expel, drive away; (*verkaufen*) sell. **Vertreibung** *f* (*pl* -en) expulsion.

*vertreten [ɛɐ̯ˈtreːtən] *v* represent; (*vorübergehend*) replace, stand in for; (*eintreten für*) advocate. **Vertret||er** *m* (*pl* -) representative; (*Komm*) sales representative; **–ung** *f* (*pl* -en) representation.

Vertrieb [ɛɐ̯ˈtriːp] *m* (retail) sale.

*vertun [ɛɐ̯ˈtuːn] *v* squander, spend.

vertuschen [ɛɐ̯ˈtʊʃən] *v* hush up.

verunglimpfen [ɛɐ̯ˈʊnglɪmpfən] *v* defame, revile.

verunglücken [ɛɐ̯ˈʊnglʏkən] *v* be involved in an accident; (*Angelegenheit*) fail.

verunreinigen [ɛɐ̯ˈʊnraɪnɪgən] *v* pollute, soil.

verunstalten [ɛɐ̯ˈʊnʃtaltən] *v* disfigure.

veruntreuen [ɛɐ̯ˈʊntrɔʏən] *v* embezzle.

verursachen [ɛɐ̯ˈʊrzaxən] *v* cause, bring about.

verurteilen [ɛɐ̯ˈʊrtaɪlən] *v* condemn; (*Jur*) sentence. **Verurteilung** *f* condemnation; conviction.

vervielfältigen [ɛɐ̯fiːlˈfɛltɪgən] *v* duplicate, copy. **Vervielfältigung** *f* reproduction, duplication.

vervollkommnen [ɛɐ̯fɔlˈkɔmnən] *v* perfect.

vervollständigen [ɛɐ̯fɔlˈʃtɛndɪgən] *v* complete.

*verwachsen [ɛɐ̯ˈvaksən] *v* grow together; (*Wunde*) heal up; (*bucklig werden*) become deformed; (*sich verbinden*) be tied to. *adj* deformed.

verwahren [ɛɐ̯ˈvaːrən] *v* keep; (*schützen*) protect, preserve.

verwahrlosen [ɛɐ̯ˈvaːrloːzən] *v* neglect. **verwahrlost** *adj* neglected; (*Kind*) scruffy, unkempt.

verwalten [ɛɐ̯ˈvaltən] *v* administer, manage. **Verwalter** *m* administrator; (*Fabrik, Büro*) manager; (*Gut, Haus*) steward. **Verwaltung** *f* administration; management.

verwandeln [ɛɐ̯ˈvandəln] *v* transform; (*ändern*) change. **Verwandlung** *f* transformation; change.

verwandt [ɛr̩vant] *adj* related. **Verwandtlle(r)** relative, relation. **-schaft** *f* relationship; (*Verwandte*) relatives *pl*.

verwechseln [ɛr̩vɛksəln] *v* confuse. **verwechseln mit** mistake for, confuse with. **Verwechslung** *f* confusion.

verwegen [ɛr̩ve:gən] *adj* bold, audacious.

verweichlicht [ɛr̩vaiçlıçt] *adj* effeminate.

verweigern [ɛr̩vaigərn] *v* refuse. **Verweigerung** *f* refusal.

verweilen [ɛr̩vailən] *v* linger, stay.

Verweis [ɛr̩vais] *m* (*pl* -e) reprimand, rebuke; (*Hinweis*) reference. **verweisen** *v* reprimand, rebuke; (*verbannen*) exile, banish. **verweisen auf** refer to.

*****verwenden** [ɛr̩vɛndən] *v* use, employ; apply; (*Zeit*) spend. **Verwendung** *f* use; application.

*****verwerfen** [ɛr̩vɛrfən] *v* throw away; (*zurückweisen*) reject.

verwesen¹ [ɛr̩ve:sən] *v* (*verwalten*) administer.

verwesen² *v* (*verfaulen*) decay.

verwickeln [ɛr̩vikəln] *n* entangle. **sich verwickeln in** become involved in. **verwickelt** *adj* complicated. **Verwicklung** *f* (*pl* -en) entanglement, complication.

verwirken [ɛr̩virkən] *v* forfeit.

verwirklichen [ɛr̩virkliçən] *v* realize. **sich verwirklichen** come true, materialize. **Verwirklichung** *f* realization.

*****verwirren** [ɛr̩virən] *v* confuse, bewilder. **verwirrt** *adj* confused. **Verwirrung** *f* confusion.

verwischen [ɛr̩vıʃən] *v* blur, smear; (*fig*) cover up, wipe out.

verwitwet [ɛr̩vıtvət] *adj* widowed.

verwöhnen [ɛr̩vø:nən] *v* spoil. **verwöhnt** *adj* pampered, spoiled.

verworfen [ɛr̩vorfən] *adj* depraved.

verworren [ɛr̩vorən] *adj* confused.

verwundbar [ɛr̩vuntbar] *adj* vulnerable. **verwunden** *v* wound, hurt. **verwundet** *adj* wounded. **Verwundete(r)** injured person; (*Mil*) casualty. **Verwundung** *f* wound, injury.

verwunderlich [ɛr̩vundəarlıç] *adj* surprising. **verwundern** *v* surprise, astonish. **sich verwundern über** be astonished by, wonder about. **Verwunderung** *f* astonishment.

verwünschen [ɛr̩vynʃən] *v* curse. **ver-**

wünscht *adj* cursed, bewitched.

verwüsten [ɛr̩vy:stən] *v* devastate. **Verwüstung** *f* devastation.

verzagt [ɛr̩tsa:kt] *adj* downcast, despondent.

verzaubern [ɛr̩tsaubərn] *v* enchant, charm. **verzaubert** *adj* enchanted, magic.

Verzehr [ɛr̩tse:r] *m* consumption (of food and drink). **verzehren** *v* consume, take, eat.

verzeichnen [ɛr̩tsaiçnən] *v* note, enter, write down. **Verzeichnis** *neut* (*pl* -se) list, catalogue; (*Buch*) index; (*Register*) register.

*****verzeihen** [ɛr̩tsaiən] *v* pardon, forgive. **verzeihen Sie!** pardon (me)! I'm sorry! **Verzeihung** *f* pardon, forgiveness. *interj* I beg your pardon! excuse me!

verzerren [ɛr̩tsɛrən] *v* distort.

verzetteln [ɛr̩tsɛtəln] *v* (*Zeit*) dissipate.

Verzicht [ɛr̩tsıçt] *m* (*pl* -e) renunciation. **verzichten auf** renounce, do without.

verziehen [ɛr̩tsi:ən] *v* distort; (*Kinder*) spoil.

verzieren [ɛr̩tsi:rən] *v* decorate, adorn.

verzögern [ɛr̩tsœ:gərn] *v* delay. **Verzögerung** *f* (*pl* -en) delay.

verzollen [ɛr̩tsolən] *v* pay duty on.

verzücken [ɛr̩tsukən] *v* enrapture. **verzückt** *adj* enraptured, ecstatic. **Verzückung** *f* (*pl* -en) rapture, ecstasy.

verzuckern [ɛr̩tsukərn] *v* sugar.

Verzug [ɛr̩tsuk] *m* (*unz.*) delay.

verzweifeln [ɛr̩tsvaifəln] *v* despair. **verzweifelt** *adj* desperate. **Verzweiflung** *f* despair.

verzwickt [ɛr̩tsvıkt] *adj* complicated, difficult.

veterinär [veterinɛ:r] *adj* veterinary. **Veterinär** *m* (*pl* -e) veterinary surgeon.

Vetter ['fɛtər] *m* (*pl* -n) (male) cousin.

Vibration [vibratsio:n] *f* (*pl* -en) vibration. **vibrieren** *v* vibrate.

Video- ['vi:deo:] *adj* video-. **auf Videoband aufnehmen** videotape. **Videollkassette** *f* (*pl* -n) videocassette. **-konferenz** *f* (*pl* -en) videoconference. **-recorder** *m* (*pl* -) videorecorder.

Vieh [fi:] **1** *neut* (*unz.*) cattle *pl*. **2** *neut* (*Viecher*) beast. **viehisch** *adj* bestial, brutal. **Viehllstall** *m* cowshed. **-treiber** *m* drover. **-zucht** *f* cattle-breeding.

viel [fi:l] *adj* much. **viele** *pl adj* many. **so**

viel so much. **viel besser** much better. **viel mehr als** far more than. **recht viel** a great deal. **viel halten von** think much or highly of. **viel||fach** adj multiple. adv frequently, many times. **–fältig** adj various, manifold.

vielleicht [fɪˈlaɪçt] adv perhaps.

viel||mal(s) adv often, many times. **–mehr** adv, conj rather. **–seitig** adj many-sided. **–versprechend** adj (very) promising.

vier [fiːr] pron, adj four. **Viereck** neut square, rectangle. **viereckig** adj square, rectangular. **viermal(s)** adv four times. **viert** adj fourth. **Viertaktmotor** m fourstroke engine. **Viertel** neut quarter. **–stunde** f quarter (of an) hour. **viertens** adv fourthly.

vierzehn [ˈfɪrtseɪn] pron, adj fourteen. **vierzehn Tage** fortnight. **vierzehnt** adj fourteenth.

vierzig [ˈfɪrtsɪç] pron, adj forty. **vierzigst** adj fortieth.

Villa [ˈvɪla] f (pl **Villen**) villa.

Viola [viˈoːla] f (pl **Violen**) viola. **Viol||ine** f violin. **–inist** m (pl -), **–inistin** f (pl -nen) violinist. **–oncello** neut violoncello, cello.

virtuell [vɪrtuˈel] adj (comp) virtual. **virtueller Raum** m cyberspace. **virtuelle Realität** f virtual reality.

Virtuose [vɪrtuˈoːzə] m (pl -n) virtuoso.

Visite [vɪˈziːtə] f (pl -n) visit. **–nkarte** f visiting card.

Visum [ˈviːzum] neut (pl **Visa**) visa.

Vitamin [vitaˈmiːn] neut (pl -e) vitamin.

Vlies [fliːs] neut (pl -e) fleece.

Vogel [ˈfoːgəl] m (pl **Vögel**) bird. **–gesang** m birdsong. **–haus** neut aviary. **–kunde** f ornithology. **–perpektive** f or **–schau** f bird's-eye view.

vokal [voˈkaːl] adj vocal. **Vokal** m vowel.

Volk [fɔlk] neut (pl **Völker**) people, folk; nation.

Völker||kunde f ethnology. **–schaft** people, tribe. **völkisch** adj national.

Volks||eigentum neut public property. **–entscheid** m plebiscite, referendum. **–gruppe** f ethnic group. **–lied** neut (traditional) folksong. **–menge** f crowd. **–schule** f primary school. **–staat** m republic. **–tanz** m folk dance. **–tracht** f national costume.

volkstümlich [ˈfɔlkstyːmlɪç] adj popular.

Volkswirt [ˈfɔlksvɪrt] m economist. **–schaft** f (political) economy. **volkswirtschaftlich** adj economic.

voll [fɔl] adj full. adv fully. der Topf ist voll Wasser the pot is full of water. ein Glas voll Milch a glassful of milk. in voller Blüte in full bloom. volles Gesicht round face. **voll||auf** adv in abundance. **–automatisch** adj fully automatic. **–berechtigt** adj fully authorized. **–beschäftigt** adj fully authorized. **–beschäftigt** adj fully employed. **–blütig** adj full-blooded.

*****vollbringen** [fɔlˈbrɪŋən] v accomplish. **Vollbringung** f accomplishment.

vollenden [fɔlˈɛndən] v finish, end, complete. **vollendet** adj completed; (vervollkomnet) perfect. **Vollendung** f completion; perfection.

voller [ˈfɔlər] adj or **voll von** full (of).

völlig [ˈfɛlɪç] adj complete, entire, whole.

vollkommen [ˈfɔlkɔmən] adj perfect, finished. **Vollkommenheit** f perfection.

Voll||kornbrot neut wholemeal bread. **–macht** f power of attorney, authority. **–milch** f whole milk.

voll||ständig adj complete. **–stopfen** v stuff.

vollstrecken [fɔlˈʃtrɛkən] v execute, carry out. **Vollstreck||er** m (pl -), **–erin** f (pl -nen) executor. **–ung** f (pl -en) execution.

*****vollziehen** [fɔlˈtsiːən] v carry out, execute.

Volontär [volɔnˈtɛːr] m (pl -e) volunteer (worker), unpaid helper.

vom [fɔm] prep + art von dem.

von [fɔn] prep from; (einer Person gehörig) of; (einer Person stammend) by. das Buch von Peter Peter's book. ein Buch von Greene a book by Greene. ein Freund von ihm a friend of his. **von ... an** starting, from. **von nun an** from now on. von mir aus as far as I am concerned. **von selbst** by itself, automatically.

vor [foːr] prep in front of; (zeitlich) before. vor acht Tagen a week ago. vor allem above all. nach wie vor as ever. nicht vor not until. Viertel vor 12 (a) quarter to twelve. **vor Zeiten** formerly.

Vorabend [ˈfoːraːbənt] m eve.

Vorahnung [ˈfoːraːnuŋ] f presentiment.

voran [foˈran] adv at the head, in front, first. **–gehen** v go ahead, precede. **–kommen** v make progress.

Voranschlag [ˈfoːrˌanʃlaːk] *m* rough estimate.

Vorarbeiter [ˈfoːrˌarbaɪtər] *m* foreman, supervisor.

voraus [fɔˈraʊs] *adv* ahead, in front. **im voraus** in advance. **vorausbestimmen** *v* predetermine. **vorausgesetzt daß** provided that. **Voraussage** *f* prediction. **voraus‖sagen** *v* predict, forecast. **–sehen** *v* foresee. **Voraus‖setzung** *f* assumption; (*Vorbedingung*) prerequisite. **–sicht** *f* foresight. **voraussichtlich** *adv* probably. **Vorauszahlung** *f* advance payment.

vorbedacht [ˈfoːrbədaxt] *adj* premeditated. **Vorbedacht** *m* forethought. **mit Vorbedacht** on purpose, advisedly.

Vorbedingung [ˈfoːrbədɪŋuŋ] *f* precondition, prerequisite.

Vorbehalt [ˈfoːrbəhalt] *m* (*pl* -e) reservation, proviso. **vorbehalten** *v* hold in reserve, withhold.

vorbei [fɔrˈbaɪ] *adv* (*örtlich*) past, by; (*zeitlich*) past, over. **vorbei sein** be all over. **vorbei‖gehen** *v* go past, pass. **–kommen** *v* pass by. **–marschieren** *v* march past.

vorbereiten [ˈfoːrbəraɪtən] *v* prepare. **Vorbereitungen** *pl* preparations.

vorbestellen [ˈfoːrbəʃtɛlən] *v* book in advance.

Vorbestrafte(r) [ˈfoːrbəʃtraːftə (r)] *m* person with previous conviction.

vorbeugen [ˈfoːrbɔygən] *v* prevent. **Vorbeugung** *f* prevention.

Vorbild [ˈfoːrbɪlt] *neut* model, example, paragon. **vorbildlich** *adj* model, exemplary.

***vorbringen** [ˈfoːrbrɪŋən] *v* bring up, put forward.

vorder [ˈfɔrdər] *adj* fore(most) front. **Vorder‖bein** *neut* foreleg. **–grund** *m* foreground. **–radantrieb** *m* front-wheel drive. **–seite** *f* façade; obverse; face (of coin). **–teil** *m* front (part). **–tür** *f* front door.

***vordringen** [ˈfoːrdrɪŋən] *v* advance, press forward. **vordringlich** *adj* urgent, pressing.

voreilig [ˈfoːraɪlɪç] *adj* premature, hasty, precipitate.

voreingenommen [ˈfoːraɪngənɔmən] *adj* prejudiced. **voreingenommen gegen** prejudiced against. **voreingenommen für** biased in favour of. **Voreingenommenheit** *f* prejudice.

***vorenthalten** [ˈfoːrɛnthaltən] *v* hold back, withhold.

vorerst [ˈfoːrˈeːrst] *adv* for the time being.

vorerwähnt [ˈfoːrɛrvɛːnt] *adj* above-mentioned, already mentioned, aforesaid.

Vorfahr [ˈfoːrfaːr] *m* (*pl* -en) ancestor.

Vorfahrt [ˈfoːrfaːrt] *f* right-of-way.

Vorfall [ˈfoːrfal] *m* incident.

vorführen [ˈfoːrfyːrən] *v* bring forward, present; (*zeigen*) show; (*Film*) project. **Vorführung** *f* presentation, demonstration; (*Film*) showing.

Vorgang [ˈfoːrgaŋ] *m* event, incident; (*Tech*) process; (*Komm*) file, record. **Vorgänger** *m* predecessor.

***vorgeben** [ˈfoːrgeːbən] *v* pretend.

Vorgebirge [ˈfoːrgəbɪrgə] *neut* foothills *pl*; (*Kap*) promontory.

vorgeblich [ˈfoːrgeːplɪç] *adj* alleged, ostensible.

vorgefaßt [ˈfoːrgəfast] *adj* preconceived.

Vorgefühl [ˈfoːrgəfyːl] *neut* presentiment.

***vorgehen** [ˈfoːrgeːən] *v* go forward; (*handeln*) act, proceed; (*geschehen*) occur; (*Uhr*) be fast; (*wichtiger sein*) take precedence; (*führen*) lead (on). **Vorgehen** *neut* advance; proceedings *pl*.

vorgenannt [ˈfoːrgənant] *adj* above-mentioned.

Vorgeschichte [ˈfoːrgəʃɪçtə] *f* previous history; (*Urgeschichte*) prehistory.

Vorgeschmack [ˈfoːrgəʃmak] *m* foretaste.

Vorgesetzte(r) [ˈfoːrgəzɛtstə] *neut* superior.

vorgestern [ˈfoːrgɛstərn] *adv* the day before yesterday.

***vorhaben** [ˈfoːrhaːbən] *v* intend, plan. *haben Sie heute etwas vor?* have you anything arranged for today?

Vorhalle [ˈfoːrhalə] *f* vestibule, entrance (hall).

vorhanden [foːrˈhandən] *adj* existing, available. **Vorhandensein** *neut* existence, availability.

Vorhang [ˈfoːrhaŋ] *m* (*pl* **Vorhänge**) curtain.

vorher [foːrˈheːr] *adv* before(hand), previously. **Vorhersage** *f* predict. **vorher‖sagen** *v* predict. **–sehen** *v* foresee.

vorherrschend [ˈfoːrhɛrʃənt] *adj* predominant.

vorhin [ˈfoːrhɪn] *adv* a short while ago,

just now.

Vorhut ['foːrhuːt] *f* (*pl* -en) vanguard.

vorig ['foːrɪç] *adj* previous.

Vorjahr ['foːrjaːr] *neut* last year. **vorjährig** *adj* last year's.

vorjammern ['foːrjam ərn] *v* lament, complain.

Vorkämpfer ['foːrkɛm pfər] *m* (*pl* -) advocate, champion.

Vorkehrung ['foːrkeːruŋ] *f* (*pl* -en) precaution.

Vorkenntnis ['foːrkɛntnɪs] *f* previous knowledge. **Vorkenntnisse** *pl* rudiments, basic knowledge *sing*.

*vorkommen ['foːrkɔm ən] *v* (*geschehen*) happen, take place; (*sich finden*) occur, be found; (*nach vorn kommen*) come forward; (*scheinen*) seem, appear.

*vorladen ['foːrlaːdən] *v* summon. **Vorladung** *f* summons.

Vorlage ['foːrlaːgə] *f* submission, presentation; (*Muster*) model; (*Gesetz*) bill.

Vorläufer ['foːrbɔyfər] *m* forerunner. **vorläufig** *adv* provisional, temporary.

vorlaut ['foːrlaut] *adj* forward, nosy.

vorlegen ['foːrleːgən] *v* present; (*Essen*) serve.

*vorlesen ['foːrleːzən] *v* read out, read aloud. **Vorlesung** *f* (*pl* -en) lecture.

vorletzt ['foːrlɛtst] *adj* last but one, penultimate.

Vorliebe ['foːrliːbə] *f* preference, liking.

*vorliegen ['foːrliːgən] *v* be, exist; (*Arbeit*) be in hand. **der vorliegende Fall** the case in point, the case in question.

Vormachtstellung ['foːrm axtʃtɛluŋ] *f* hegemony.

vormals ['foːrm aːls] *adv* formerly.

Vormittag ['foːrm ɪtaːk] *m* morning. **vormittags** *adv* in the morning.

Vormund ['foːrm unt] *m* guardian.

vorn [fɔrn] *adv* in front, ahead. **nach vorn** forward. **von vorn** from the start.

Vorname ['foːrnaːm ə] *m* first name, Christian name.

vornehm ['foːrneːm] *adj* (*von höherem Stand*) distinguished; (*edel*) noble; elegant, (*umg.*) posh.

vornherein ['fɔrnhɛrain] *adv* **von vornherein** from the start.

Vorort ['foːrɔrt] *m* suburb.

Vorrang ['foːrraŋ] *m* precedence, priority.

Vorrat ['foːrraːt] *m* supply, stock. **vorrätig** *adj* in stock.

Vorrecht ['foːrrɛçt] *neut* privilege.

Vorrede ['foːrreːdə] *f* introduction; (*Buch*) preface.

Vorrichtung ['foːrrɪçtuŋ] *f* (*pl* -en) device.

vorrücken ['foːrrykən] *v* move forward, advance.

Vorsatz ['foːrzats] *m* intention, purpose. **vorsätzlich** *adj* intentional.

Vorschau ['foːrʃau] *f* preview; (*Film*) trailer.

*vorschieben ['foːrʃiːbən] *v* push forward; (*Entschuldigung*) plead (as an excuse).

vorschiessen ['foːrʃiːsən] *v* advance (money).

Vorschlag ['foːrʃlaːk] *m* suggestion, proposal. **vorschlagen** *v* suggest, propose.

Vorschlußrunde ['foːrʃlusrundə] *f* semifinal.

vorschneiden ['foːrʃnaidən] *v* carve.

vorschreiben ['foːrʃraibən] *v* prescribe, order.

Vorschrift ['foːrʃrɪft] *f* rule, regulation; (*Befehl*) order; (*Med*) prescription. **vorschrifts||gemäß** *adj*, *adv* in accordance with regulations. **–widrig** *adj*, *adv* contrary to regulations.

Vorschub ['foːrʃuːp] *m* assistance, support. **Vorschub leisten** assist, support.

Vorschule ['foːrʃuː ə] *f* prep school.

Vorschuß ['foːrʃus] *m* (cash) advance.

vorschützen ['foːrʃytsən] *v* pretend. **Unwissenheit vorschützen** plead ignorance.

vorsehen ['foːrzeːən] *v* assign, earmark. **sich vorsehen** take care, mind. **Vorsehung** *f* providence.

vorsetzen ['foːrzɛtsən] *v* put (forward); (*anbieten*) offer, put before.

Vorsicht ['foːrzɪçt] *f* caution, care. *interj* be careful! take care! **vorsichtig** *adj* careful, cautious. **Vorsichtsmaßnahme** *f* precaution.

Vorsitz ['foːrzɪts] *m* chair(manship). **den Vorsitz führen** be in the chair, preside. **Vorsitzende(r)** chairman, chairperson.

Vorsorge ['foːrzɔrgə] *f* (*unz.*) provision, precaution, advance measure. **vorsorglich** *adj* provident. *adv* as a precaution.

Vorspeise ['foːrʃpaizə] *f* hors d'oeuvre, starter.

vorspiegeln ['fɔːʃpiːgəln] v **jemandem etwas vorsiegeln** delude someone with something. **Vorspiegelung** f misrepresentation.

Vorspiel ['fɔːʃpiːl] neut prelude.

***vorspringen** ['fɔːʃprɪŋən] v leap forward; (hervorragen) project.

Vorsprung ['fɔːʃprʊŋ] m (Vorteil) lead, advantage; (Arch) projection.

Vorstadt ['fɔːʃtat] f suburb.

Vorstand ['fɔːʃtant] m board of directors, management.

***vorstehen** ['fɔːʃteːən] v protrude; (leiten) manage, be head of. **-d** adj protruding; (vorangehend) preceding. **Vorsteher** m chief, superintendant, manager. **-in** f manageress.

vorstellbar ['fɔːʃtɛlbaːr] adj imaginable. **vorstellen** v put forward; (Person) introduce; (bedeuten) mean. **sich vorstellen** introduce oneself. **sich etwas vorstellen** imagine something. **Vorstellung** f introduction; (Begriff) idea; (Theater) performance. **-skraft** f (power of) imagination.

vorstrecken ['fɔːʃtrɛkən] v stretch out.

Vorstufe ['fɔːʃtuːfə] f first stage.

Vorteil ['fɔːrtail] m advantage. **vorteilhaft** adj advantageous, favourable. **die Vorteile und Nachteile** the pros and cons.

Vortrag ['fɔːrtraːk] m (pl **Vorträge**) (Vorlesung) talk, lecture; (Komm) balance carried forward. **vortragen** v lecture; (Gedicht) recite; (Meinung) express; (Rede) deliver. **Vortragssaal** m lecture hall.

vortrefflich ['fɔːrtrɛflɪç] adj excellent.

***vortreten** ['fɔːrtreːtən] v step forward; (hervorragen) protrude.

Vortritt ['fɔːrtrɪt] m precedence.

vorüber ['fɔːrыːbər] adv past; (Zeit) over, past. **-gehen** v pass. **-gehend** adj passing, temporary.

Vorurteil ['fɔːrʊrtail] neut prejudice. **vorurteilsfrei** adj unprejudiced.

Vorverkauf ['fɔːrfɛrkauf] m advance sale; (Theater) advance booking.

Vorwahl ['fɔːrvaːl] f preliminary election, (US) primary. **Vorwahlnummer** f (Telef) area code.

Vorwand ['fɔːrvant] f pretence, pretext, excuse.

vorwärts ['fɔːrvɛrts] adv forward(s), onward(s). **-bringen** v promote, further.

-gehen v go ahead. **-kommen** v make progress.

vorweg ['fɔːrvɛk] adv in advance. **-nehmen** v anticipate, forestall.

***vorwerfen** ['fɔːrvɛrfən] v reproach with.

vorwiegend ['fɔːrviːɡən] adj preponderant. adv chiefly, mostly.

Vorwissen ['fɔːrvɪsən] neut foreknowledge, prescience.

Vorwort ['fɔːrvɔrt] neut (pl -e) preface, foreword.

Vorwurf ['fɔːrvʊrf] m reproach.

Vorzeichen ['fɔːrtsaiçən] neut omen; (Math) sign.

***vorzeigen** ['fɔːrtsaiɡən] v produce, display.

Vorzeit ['fɔːrtsait] f antiquity. **vorzeitig** adj premature, too early.

***vorziehen** ['fɔːrtsiːən] v (bevorzugen) prefer; (hervorziehen) pull forward.

Vorzug ['fɔːrtsuːk] m preference; (Vorteil) advantage; (Eigenschaft) merit, good quality. **vorzüglich** adj excellent, superb. **Vorzugsrecht** neut priority.

vulgär [vʊlɡɛːr] adj vulgar.

Vulkan [vʊlkaːn] m (pl -e) volcano. **vulkanisch** adj volcanic.

W

Waage ['vaːɡə] f (pl -n) scales pl. **waagerecht** adj horizontal.

wabbelig ['vabəlɪç] adj wobbly, flabby.

Wabe ['vaːbə] f (pl -n) honeycomb.

wach [vax] adj awake. **Wache** f (pl -n) watch, guard; (Polizei) station. **wachen** v be awake; (Wache halten) keep watch. **wachen über** watch over.

Wachs [vaks] neut (pl -e) wax.

wachsam ['vaxzaːm] adj watchful, alert. **Wachsamkeit** f watchfulness, vigilance.

***wachsen** ['vaksən] v grow. **-d** adj increasing, growing. **Wachstum** neut growth.

Wacht [vaxt] f (pl -en) watch, guard.

Wachtel ['vaxtəl] f (pl -n) quail.

Wächter [vɛçtər] m (pl -) watchman, guard. **Wacht‖meister** m sergeant-major; (Polizist) constable. **-turm** m watchtower.

wackelig ['vakəlɪç] *adj* wobbly, shaky. **wackeln** *v* wobble, shake.

wacker ['vakər] *adj* brave, stout; (*anständig*) worthy.

Wade ['vaːdə] *f* (*pl* -n) (*Anat*) calf.

Waffe ['vafə] *f* (*pl* -n) weapon.

Waffel ['vafəl] *f* (*pl* -n) waffle; (*Eis*) wafer.

waffenlos ['vafənloːs] *adj* unarmed. **Waffenlager** *neut* arms dump, arms cache. **Waffenstillstand** *m* armistice. **waffnen** *v* arm.

wagehalsig ['vaːgəhalzɪç] *adj* reckless, daring. **Wagemut** *m* daring. **wagen** *v* dare, risk, venture. **sich wagen** venture.

Wagen ['vaːgən] *m* (*pl* -) (*Mot*) car; (*Kutsche*) coach; (*Karren*) wagon, cart; (*Eisenbahn*) carriage.

*wägen ['vɛːgən] *v* weigh.

Wagen||führer *m* driver. **–heber** *m* (*Mot*) jack.

Waggon [va'gɔ̃] *m* (*pl* -s) (railway) wagon.

Wagnis ['vaːknɪs] *neut* (*pl* -se) (*Mut*) daring; (*Unternehmen*) venture; (*Risiko*) risk.

wahl [vaːl] *f* (*pl* -en) choice; (*Pol*) election. **wahlberechtigt** *adj* enfranchised, entitled to vote. **Wahl||bezirk** *m* constituency, electoral district. **–bude** *f* polling booth.

wählen ['vɛːlən] *v* choose; (*Pol*) elect; (*Telef*) dial.

wählerisch ['vɛːlərɪʃ] *adj* particular, fussy, choosy. **Wählerschaft** *f* electorate, voters *pl*.

Wahl||gang *m* ballot. **–kampf** *m* (*election*) campaign. **wahllos** *adj* indiscriminate. **Wahlrecht** *neut* franchise, suffrage.

Wählscheibe ['vɛːʃaɪbə] *f* (telephone) dial.

Wahl||tag *m* election day. **–zettel** *m* ballot (paper).

Wahn [vaːn] *m* (*unz.*) delusion; madness. **–sinn** *m* insanity, madness. **wahnsinnig** *adj* insane, mad. **Wahnsinnige(r)** madman, madwoman.

wahr [vaːr] *adj* true; (*wirklich*) real; (*echt*) genuine.

wahren ['vaːrən] *v* take care of; (*schützen*) protect; (*erhalten*) maintain.

währen ['vɛːrən] *v* last.

während ['vɛːrənt] *prep* during. *conj* while.

wahrhaft ['vaːrhaft] *adj* true, genuine. *adv* really, truly. **–ig** *adj* sincere, truthful. *adv* really, indeed. **Wahr||haftigkeit** *f* truthfulness. **–heit** *f* (*pl* -en) truth. **wahr||**

nehmen *v* perceive; (*Interessen*) protect; (*Gelegenheit*) seize, take. **–sagen** *v* foretell (the future). **–scheinlich** *adj* likely, probable. **Wahrscheinlichkeit** *f* probability.

Wahrung ['vaːrʊŋ] *f* preservation, maintenance.

Währung ['vɛːrʊŋ] *f* (*pl* -en) currency.

Waise ['vaɪzə] (*pl* -n) orphan. **–nknabe** *m* orphan boy.

Wal [vaːl] *m* (*pl* -e) whale.

Wald [valt] *m* (*pl* Wälder) wood, forest. **–beere** *f* cranberry. **–brand** *m* forest fire. **waldig** *adj* wooded. **Wald||ung** *f* (*pl* -en) woodland. **–wirtschaft** *f* forestry.

Walfang ['vaːlfaŋ] *m* whaling.

Wall [val] *m* (*pl* Wälle) earthworks *pl*. embankment.

wallen ['valən] *v* boil.

*wallfahren ['valfaːrən] *v* go on a pilgrimage. **Wall|||fahrer** *m* pilgrim. **–fahrt** *f* pilgrimage.

Walnuß ['valnuːs] *f* walnut.

Wal||öl *neut* whale-oil. **–roß** *neut* walrus.

Walze ['valtsə] *f* (*pl* -n) roller. **walzen** *v* roll; (*tanzen*) waltz.

wälzen ['vɛltsən] *v* roll.

Walzer ['valtsər] *m* (*pl* -) waltz.

Wand [vant] *f* (*pl* Wände) wall.

Wandel ['vandəl] *m* change. **wandelbar** *adj* variable; (*Person*) changeable, fickle. **wandeln** *v* change. **sich wandeln in** change *or* turn into.

Wanderer ['vandərər] *m* (*pl* -) wanderer; (*auf dem Lande*) hiker, rambler. **Wanderlust** *f* wanderlust. **wandern** *v* wander; ramble, hike. **–d** *adj* wandering; (*Volk, Tiere*) migratory. **Wanderung** *f* (*pl* -en) (*zu Fuß*) walking-tour, hike; (*Volk, Tiere*) migration.

Wandgemälde ['vantgəmɛːldə] *neut* mural.

Wandlung ['vandlʊŋ] *f* (*pl* -en) change; (*total*) transformation; (*Rel*) transubstantiation.

Wange ['vaŋə] *f* (*pl* -n) cheek.

Wankelmut ['vaŋkəlmuːt] *m* fickleness, inconstancy. **wankelmütig** *adj* fickle, inconstant.

wanken ['vaŋkən] *v* rock, sway; (*Person*) totter, reel; (*fig*) waver, vacillate. **–d** *adj* wavering.

wann [van] *adv* when.

Wanne ['vanə] *f* (*pl* -n) tub; (*Badewanne*)

bath(tub). **-nbad** *neut* bath.

Wanze ['vantsə] *f (pl* -n) bug.

Wappen ['vapən] *neut (pl* -) (coat of) arms. **-kunde** *f* heraldry.

Ware ['vaːrə] *f (pl* -n) article, commodity. **Waren** *pl* goods, wares, merchandise *sing*. **Waren‖haus** *neut* department store. **-markt** *m* commodity market.

warm [varm] *adj* warm; (*Getränk, Essen*) hot. **warmer Bruder** (*umg*.) homosexual.

Wärme ['vɛrmə] *f* warmth; temperature; (*Physik*) heat. **wärmen** *v* warm (up), heat. **Wärmflasche** *f* hot-water bottle.

Warndreieck ['varndraik] *neut* (*Mot*) warning triangle.

warnen ['varnən] *v* warn. **Warnung** *f (pl* -en) warning.

Warschau ['varʃau] *neut* Warsaw.

warten ['vartən] *v* wait; (*pflegen*) care for; (*Maschine*) service, maintain. **warten auf** wait for.

Wärter ['vɛrtər] *m (pl* -) , **Wärterin** *f (pl* -nen) attendant; (*Kranken*) nurse; (*Gefängnis*) warder.

Warte‖saal *m* waiting room. **-zimmer** *neut* waiting room. **Wartung** *f* maintenance, upkeep.

warum [va'rum] *adv* why.

Warze ['vartsə] *f (pl* -n) wart; (*Brust*) nipple.

was [vas] *pron* what; (*umg*.) something. **ach was!** nonsense! **was ist mit** ... how about .... **was für** ... what sort of .... *alles was ich sehe* everything that I see.

Waschbecken ['vaʃbekən] *neut* wash basin.

Wäsche ['vɛʃə] *f (pl* -n) washing, laundry.

waschecht [vaʃɛçt] *adj* (*Farbe*) (colour-) fast; (*fig*) thorough, dyed-in-the-wool.

Wäsche‖klammer *f* clothes peg, (*US*) clothes pin. **-korb** *m* laundry basket. **-leine** *f* clothes line.

*waschen [vaʃən] *v* wash.

Wäscherei ['vɛʃa'rai] *f (pl* -en) laundry.

Wasch‖lappen *m* facecloth. **-maschine** *f* washing machine. **-mittel** *neut* detergent, washing powder. **-tag** *m* wash(ing) day.

Wasser ['vasər] *neut (pl* -) water. **-abfluß** *m* drain. **-abfuhr** *f* drainage. **-behälter** *m* tank, reservoir. **-dampf** *m* steam, water vapour.

wasser‖dicht *adj* waterproof; (*Gefäß*) watertight. **-fest** *adj* waterproof.

wässerig ['vɛsəriç] *adj* watery.

Wasser‖kraftwerk *neut* hydroelectric plant. **-leitung** *f* water mains *pl*. **-mann** *m* (*Astrol*) Aquarius.

wässern ['vɛsərn] *v* water; (*bewässern*) irrigate; (*Erbsen, usw*.) soak.

Wasser‖flanze *f* aquatic plant. **-rad** *neut* water wheel. **-stoff** *m* hydrogen. **-tier** *neut* aquatic animal.

Wässerung ['vɛsəruŋ] *f* watering; (*Bewässern*) irrigation.

Wasser‖versorgung *f* water supply. **-weg** *m* waterway. **-werk** *neut* waterworks *pl*.

Watte ['vatə] *f (pl* -n) wadding, cotton wool. **-bausch** *m* swab.

weben ['veːbən] *v* weave. **Web‖ler** *m* (*Ḷ* -), **Weberin** *f (pl* -nen) weaver. **-stoff** *m* textile. **-stuhl** *m* loom.

Wechsel ['vɛksəl] *m (pl* -) change; (*Austausch*) exchange; (*Komm*) bill (of exchange). **-folge** *f* alternation. **-geld** *neut* change. **-jahre** *pl* menopause *sing*, change of life *sing*. **wechseln** *v* (ex)change; (*variieren*) vary. **wechselseitig** *adj* alternating; (*gegenseitig*) mutual, reciprocal. **Wechsel‖strom** *m* alternating current. **-zahn** *f* milk tooth.

wecken ['vɛkən] *v* awaken, wake up. **Wecker** *m (pl* -) alarm clock.

wedeln ['veːdəln] *v* (*Schwanz*) wag.

weder ['veːdər] *conj* neither. **weder ... noch** ... neither ... nor ....

weg [vɛk] *adv* away, off, gone. *Hände weg!* hands off! *er ist schon weg* he has already left. *meine Uhr ist weg* my watch has gone. **weit weg** far off. **Weg** *m (pl* -e) way; (*Straße*) road; (*Pfad*) path. **weg‖bleiben** *v* stay away. **-blicken** *v* look away. **-bringen** *v* take away, remove.

wegen ['veːgən] *prep* because of, on account of.

weg‖fahren *v* drive away; (*abfahren*) leave. **-fallen** *v* fall away; (*aufhören*) stop; (*ausgelassen werden*) be omitted. **-führen** *v* lead away. **-gehen** *v* go away. **-kommen** *v* get away. **-lassen** *v* omit. **-müssen** *v* must go, have to leave.

Wegnahme [vɛknaːmə] *f (pl* -n) confiscation, seizure. **wegnehmen** *v* take away; (*beschlagnahmen*) confiscate, seize; (*Zeit, Raum*) occupy.

weg‖räumen *v* clear away. **-schaffen**

v get rid of. **–schikken** *v* send away. **–schließen** *v* lock away. **–treiben** *v* drive off.

Wegweiser [veːkvaɪzər] *m* (*pl* -) signpost; (*Buch, Mensch*) guide.

weg||wenden *v* turn aside. **–werfen** *v* throw away, discard. **–werfend** *adj* disdainful. **–ziehen** *v* pull aside; (*Wohnsitz wechseln*) move away.

weh [veː] *adj* sore, painful; (*seelisch*) sad. *interj* alas. *mein Hals tut mir weh* my throat hurts. **sich weh tun** hurt oneself. **jemandem weh tun** hurt someone, cause someone pain. **Weh** *neut* (*pl* -e) pain; sorrow.

Wehe [veːə] *f* (*pl* -n) drift (of snow or sand). **wehen** *v* blow; (*Fahne*) flutter.

Wehr[1] [veːr] *f* (*pl* -en) (*Waffe*) weapon; (*Schutz*) defence; (*Rüstung*) armament; (*Widerstand*) resistance.

Wehr[2] *neut* (*pl* -e) weir, dam.

Wehrdienst [veːrdɪnst] *m* military service. **–verweigerer** *m* conscientious objector. **wehren** *v* restrain. **sich wehren gegen** defend oneself against. **wehrlos** *adj* (*waffenlos*) unarmed; (*schutzlos*) defenceless. **Wehr||macht** *f* armed forces *pl*. **–pflicht** *f* compulsory military service. **–pflichtige(r)** person liable for military service.

Weib [vaɪp] *neut* (*pl* -er) woman; (*Gattin*) wife. **–chen** *neut* (*Tier*) female. **weiblich** *adj* female; (*Gramm*) feminine.

weich [vaɪç] *adj* soft; (*sanft*) gentle.

Weiche [vaɪçə] *f* (*pl* -n) (*Anat*) side, flank.

weichen[1] [vaɪçən] *v* soften; (*einweichen*) soak.

weichen[2] *v* give way; (*nachgeben*) yield; (*Preise*) fall.

Weichheit [vaɪçhaɪt] *f* softness. **weichherzig** *adj* tender-hearted, gentle. **Weichkäse** *m* soft cheese. **weichlich** *adj* soft, weak, effeminate.

Weide[1] [vaɪdə] *f* (*pl* -n) (*Baum*) willow.

Weide[2] *f* (*pl* -n) (*Wiese*) pasture.

*****weiden** [vaɪdən] *v* graze. **sich weiden an** feast one's eyes on.

weigern [vaɪɡərn] *v* **sich weigern** refuse. **Weigerung** *f* (*pl* -en) refusal.

Weihe [vaɪə] *f* (*pl* -n) consecration; (*Einweihung*) initiation. **weihen** *v* consecrate.

Weihnachten [vaɪnaxtən] *neut* (*pl* -) Christmas. **Weihnachts||abend** *m*

Christmas Eve. **–baum** *m* Christmas tree. **–geschenk** *neut* Christmas present. **–lied** *neut* Christmas carol. **–mann** *m* Father Christmas, (*US*) Santa Claus.

weil [vaɪl] *conj* because, since.

Weile [vaɪlə] *f* while, short time.

Wein [vaɪn] *m* (*pl* -e) wine; (*Pflanze*) vine. **–berg** *m* vineyard. **–brand** *m* brandy.

weinen [vaɪnən] *v* cry, weep. **Weinen** *neut* crying, weeping, tears *pl*.

Wein||lese *f* (*pl* -n) vintage. **–stock** *m* vine. **–stube** *f* wine bar. **–traube** *f* bunch of grapes.

weise [vaɪzə] *adj* wise.

Weise [vaɪzə] *f* (*pl* -n) manner, way; (*Melodie*) melody. **Art und Weise** manner, way. **auf diese/jede/kleine Weise** in this way/in any case/by no means.

weisen [vaɪzən] *v* show; (*Finger, Zeiger*) point. **weisen auf** point to. **weisen nach** direct to.

Weisheit [vaɪshaɪt] *f* (*pl* -en) wisdom. **–szahn** *m* wisdom tooth.

weiß [vaɪs] *adj* white. **Weißbrot** *neut* white bread. **Weiße** *f* whiteness. **Weiße(r)** White (man/woman). **weiß||en** *v* whitewash. **–glühend** *adj* white-hot. **Weiß||kohl** *m* (white) cabbage. **–waren** *pl* linens. **–wein** *m* white wine.

weit [vaɪt] *adj* wide; (*breit*) broad; (*geräumig*) vast, spacious; (*lang*) long; (*entfernt*) far (off). **bei weitem** by far. **von weitem** from a distance. **weit entfernt (von)** far away (from). **weit||lab** *adv* far away. **–aus** *adv* by far. **Weite** *f* (*pl* -n) width; (*Ausdehnung*) extent; (*Größe*) size. **weiten** *v* widen; (*vergrößern*) enlarge.

weiter [vaɪtər] *adj* wider; (*Entfernung*) farther; (*zusätzlich*) further. *adv* (*Entfernung*) farther; (*fig*) further; (*sonst*) else; (*weiterhin*) furthermore. **ohne weiteres** directly, immediately. **bis auf weiteres** for the present. **weiter nichts?** nothing else? **und so weiter** and so forth. **es geht weiter** it goes on. **weiter||bringen** *v* harp on. **–geben** *v* pass (to). **–gehen** *v* move on. **–hin** *adv* moreover, furthermore. **–kommen** *v* make progress, get on. **–machen** *v* carry on.

weit||gehend *adj* far-reaching. **–her** *adv* from afar. **–hergeholt** *adj* far-fetched. **–herzig** *adj* broad-minded. **–reichend** *adj* far-reaching. **–sichtig** *adj* far-sighted. **–ver-**

breitet *adj* widespread.

Weizen ['vaɪtsən] *m* wheat. **-brot** *neut* white bread. **-kleie** *f* bran.

welch [vɛlç] *adj, pron* which, what, who. **welche** *pl* some, any. *welch ein Glück!* what luck! *welches Kind?* which child? *welche schöne Blumen* what beautiful flowers. *möchtest du welche?* would you like some?

welk [vɛlk] *adj* withered. **welken** *v* wither.

Welle ['vɛlə] *f* (*pl* **-n**) wave; (*Tech*) shaft, axle. **wellen** *v* wave; (*rollen*) roll. **Wellen∣länge** *f* wavelength. **-sittich** *m* budgerigar.

Welt [vɛlt] *f* (*pl* **-en**) world. **-all** *neut* universe. **-anschauung** *f* (*pl* **-en**) philosophical outlook. **welt∣berühmt** *adj* world-famous. **-bürglich** *adj* cosmopolitan. **-erschütternd** *adj* world-shaking. **-lich** *adj* worldly, mundane. **Welt∣macht** *f* world power. **-raum** *m* (outer) space. **-rekord** *m* world record.

wem [veːm] *pron* to whom.

wen [veːn] *pron* whom.

Wende ['vɛndə] *f* (*pl* **-n**) turn; (*Änderung*) change. **-l** *f* (*pl* **-n**) coil, spiral. **wenden** *v* turn. **Wendepunkt** *m* turning point. **wendig** *adj* manoeuvrable; (*Person*) agile. **Wendung** *f* (*pl* **-en**) turn; (*Änderung*) change.

wenig ['veːnɪç] *adj* little. *adv* not much, slightly. **ein wenig** a little. **wenige** *pl* a few. **-er** *adj* less, fewer. **wenigst** *adj* least. **am wenigsten** *adv* least (of all). **wenigstens** *adv* at least.

wenn [vɛn] *conj* (*falls*) if; (*sobald*) when. **auch wenn** even if. **wenn nicht** unless. **wenn nur** if only.

wer [veːr] *pron* who; (*derjenige, der*) whoever.

Werbe∣büro *neut* advertising agency. **-feldzug** *m* advertising campaign.

werben ['vɛrbən] *v* advertise, publicize; (*Rekruten*) enlist. **Werb∣esendung** *f* commercial. **-ung** *f* advertising.

*werden ['veːrdən] *v* become; (*allmählich*) grow; (*Futurum*) will, shall; (*Passiv*) be. *es wird dunkel* it is growing *or* getting dark. *er wird kommen* he will come. *er will Arzt werden* he wants to be a doctor. *der Baum wurde gefällt* the tree was felled. *würden Sie so freundlich sein?* would you be so kind? **Werden** *neut* development, growth. **werdend** *adj* developing, growing;

(*Mutter*) expectant.

*werfen ['vɛrfən] *v* throw.

Werft [vɛrft] *f* (*pl* **-en**) shipyard, dockyard.

Werk [vɛrk] *neut* (*pl* **-e**) work; (*Fabrik*) factory, works *pl*; (*Getriebe*) mechanism. **-statt** *or* **statte** *f* workshop. **-tag** *m* working day. **-zeug** *neut* tool.

Wermut ['veːrmuːt] *m* wormwood; (*Wein*) vermouth.

wert [vɛrt] *adj* worth; (*würdig*) worthy; (*lieb*) dear. **für wert halten** consider worthwhile. **nicht der Mühe wert** not worth the bother. **fünf Mark wert** worth five Marks. **Wert** *m* value, worth. **wert∣en** *v* value. **-los** *adj* worthless. **Wert∣sachen** *pl* valuables. **-ung** *f* (*pl* **-en**) (e)valuation.

Wesen ['veːzən] *neut* (*pl* -) being; (*Kern*) essence; (*Natur*) nature; (*Benehmen*) conduct. **-sart** *f* nature, character. **wesentlich** *adj* essential.

weshalb [vɛshalp] *adv, conj* why.

Wespe ['vɛspə] *f* (*pl* **-n**) wasp.

wessen ['vɛsən] *pron* (*Person*) whose; (*Sache*) of which.

West [vɛst] *m* west.

Weste ['vɛstə] *f* (*pl* **-n**) waistcoat.

Westen ['vɛstən] *m* west. **West∣europa** *f* western Europe. **-falen** *neut* Westphalia. **-indien** *neut* West Indies *pl*. **westlich** *adj* western; (*Wind, Richtung*) westerly.

wett [vɛt] *adj* equal, even.

Wettbewerb ['vɛtbəvɛrp] *m* competition. **-er** *m* competition **wettbewerbsfähig** *adj* competitive.

Wette ['vɛtə] *f* (*pl* **-n**) bet. **Wetteifer** *m* rivalry. **wetteifern mit** vie with, compete with, **wetten** *v* bet.

Wetter ['vɛtər] *neut* (*pl* -) weather. **-bericht** *m* weather report. **-kunde** *f* meteorology. **-vorhersage** *f* weather forecast.

Wett∣kampf *m* contest, match. **-kämpfer** *m* contestant. **-lauf** *m* race. **-streit** *m* contest.

wichtig ['vɪçtɪç] *adj* important. **Wichtig∣keit** *f* importance. **-tuer** *m* busybody; pompous person.

Widder ['vɪdər] *m* (*pl* -) ram; (*Astrol*) Aries.

wider ['vɪdər] *prep* against, contrary to. **-fahren** *v* happen to, befall.

Wider∣haken *m* barbed hook. **-hall** *m* response; (*Echo*) echo. **widerhallen** *v* echo.

wider||legen v refute. **–lich** adj repulsive; (ekelhaft) disgusting. **–natürlich** adj unnatural. **–rechtlich** adj unlawful, illegal.

Widerruf ['vɪdərʊːf] m (Befehl) revocation, countermand; (Nachricht) denial. **widerrufen** v revoke, countermand; deny.

widersetzen [vɪdərˈzɛtsən] v **sich widersetzen** oppose. **widersetzlich** adj obstructive.

wider||spenstig adj contrary, difficult, stubborn. **–spiegeln** v reflect. **–sprechen** v contradict. **Widerspruch** m contradiction.

Widerstand ['vɪdərʃtant] m resistance, opposition.

*widerstehen [vɪdərˈʃteːən] v resist.

Widerstreit ['vɪdərʃtraɪt] m (Kampf) conflict; (Widersprüche) opposition.

widerwärtig ['vɪdərvɛrtɪç] adj disgusting, repulsive.

Widerwille ['vɪdərvɪlə] m aversion, intense dislike. **widerwillig** adj reluctant, unwilling.

widmen ['vɪmən] v devote, dedicate; (Buch) dedicate. **Widmung** f (pl -en) dedication.

widrig ['vɪdrɪç] adj adverse, unfavourable.

wie [viː] adv how. conj as.

wieder ['vɪdər] adv again; (zurück) back. **immer wieder** again and again.

Wiederaufbau ['vɪdərˈaʊfbaʊ] m reconstruction, rebuilding. **wiederaufbauen** v reconstruct, rebuild. **Wiederauf||erstehung** f resurrection. **–nahme** f resumption. **wiederauf||nehmen** v resume. **–tauchen** v come to light again, resurface.

*wieder||bringen v bring back, return. **–erkennen** v recognize.

Wiedergabe ['vɪdərgaːbə] f reproduction. **wiedergeben** v give back, return; (darbieten) render.

wiedergeboren ['vɪdərgəboːrən] adj reborn, regenerated. **Wiedergeburt** f rebirth, regeneration.

*wieder||gewinnen v recover, retrieve. **–gutmachen** v make up for, compensate for.

wiederholen [vɪdərˈhoːlən] v repeat. **wiederholt** adj repeated. **Wiederholung** f (pl -en) repetition.

Wiederhören ['vɪdərhøːrən] n **auf Wiederhören!** (Telef) goodbye!

wieder||kehren v return. **–kommen** v come back, return.

*wiedersehen ['vɪdərzeːən] v see or meet again. **Wiedersehen** neut reunion. **auf Wiedersehen!** goodbye!

wiederum ['vɪdərʊm] adv (nochmals) again, afresh; (andererseits) on the other hand.

wieder||vereinigen v reunite; (versöhnen) reconcile. **–verheiraten** v remarry. **–verwerten** v recycle.

Wiege ['viːgə] f (pl -n) cradle.

wiegen[1] ['viːgən] v (Gewicht) weigh.

wiegen[2] v (sanft schaukeln) rock.

Wiegenlied ['viːgənliːt] neut lullaby.

wiehern ['viːəm] v neigh; (Mensch) guffaw.

Wien [viːn] neut Vienna.

Wiese ['viːzə] f (pl -n) meadow.

Wiesel ['viːzəl] neut (pl -) weasel.

wieso [viːˈzoː] adv why.

wieviel [viːˈfiːl] adj, adv how much. **wieviele** pl how many.

wild [vɪlt] adj wild; (unzivilisiert, ungestüm) savage. **Wild** neut game. **–dieb** m poacher. **–heit** f wildness; savageness. **–leder** neut deerskin. **–nis** f wilderness.

Wille ['vɪlə] m (pl -n) or **Willen** m (pl -) will. **um...willen** for the sake of. **willens||schwach** adj weak-willed. **–stark** adj strong-willed. **willig** adj willing.

willkommen ['vɪlkɔmən] adj welcome. **willkommen heißen** v welcome, greet. **Willkommen** neut welcome.

Willkür ['vɪlkyːr] f arbitrariness, whim. **willkürlich** adj arbitrary.

wimmeln ['vɪməln] v **wimmeln von** swarm or teem with.

Wimper ['vɪmpər] f (pl -n) eyelash. **ohne mit der Wimper zu zucken** without batting an eyelid.

Wind [vɪnt] m (pl -e) wind.

Winde ['vɪndə] f (pl -n) windlass; (Bot) bindweed.

Windel ['vɪndəl] f (pl -n) nappy, (US) diaper.

*winden ['vɪndən] v wind, twist. **sich winden** wind.

Wind||hund m greyhound. **–mühle** f windmill. **–park** m (elec) wind farm. **–pocken** pl chickenpox sing. **–schutzscheibe** f windscreen, (US) windshield. **–stoß** m gust, blast of wind. **–surfen** neut windsurfing.

Windung ['vɪndʊŋ] f (pl -en) winding, turn.

Wink [vɪŋk] m (pl -e) sign; (Hand) wave; (Kopf) nod; (Augen) wink; (fig) hint.

Winkel [vɪŋkəl] m (pl -) (Ecke) corner; (Math) angle. **winkelig** adj angular. **winkelrecht** adj rectangular.

Winter [vɪntər] m (pl -) winter. **winterlich** adj wintry. **Winter∥schlaf** m hibernation. **–sport** m winter sports pl.

winzig [vɪntsɪç] adj tiny.

Wipfel [vɪpfəl] m (pl -) treetop.

Wippe [vɪpə] f (pl -n) seesaw, balance.

wir [viːr] pron we.

Wirbel [vɪrbəl] m (pl -) whirl; (Wasser) whirlpool; (Luft) whirlwind; (Trommeln) roll; (Rücken) vertebra; (Scheitel) crown (of head). **wirbel∥los** adj spineless; (Tiere) invertebrate. **–n** v whirl, swirl; (Trommeln) roll. **Wirbel∥säule** f spine. **–tier** neut vertebrate. **–wind** m whirlwind.

wirken [vɪrkən] v work (on), act (on). **–d** adj active; (erfolgreich) effective. **wirklich** adj real, actual; (echt) genuine. **Wirklichkeit** f reality. **wirksam** adj effective. **Wirkung** f (pl -en) effect.

wirr [viːr] adj tangled, disorderly; (Haare) dishevelled. **Wirrwarr** m chaos, jumble, disorder.

Wirt [vɪrt] m (pl -e) innkeeper, landlord; (Gastgeber) host; (Zimmervermieter) landlord. **–in** f (pl -nen) innkeeper, landlady; hostess; landlady. **wirtlich** adj hospitable.

Wirtschaft [vɪrtʃaft] f (pl -en) economy; (Haushaltung) housekeeping; (Gaststätte) inn, public house. **wirtschaft∥en** v manage; (Haushalt) keep house. **–lich** adj economic; (sparsam) economical. **Wirtschafts∥krise** f economic crisis. **–politik** f economic policy. **–wunder** neut economic miracle.

Wirtshaus [vɪrtshaus] neut inn, public house.

wischen [vɪʃən] v wipe. **Wischlappen** m cloth, duster.

wispeln [vɪspəln] or **wispern** v whisper.

Wißbegier(de) [vɪsbəgiːr(də)] f intellectual curiosity, thirst for learning. **wißbegierig** adj inquisitive, eager to learn.

***wissen** [vɪsən] v know. **etwas tun wissen** know how to do something. **Wissen** neut knowledge.

Wissenschaft [vɪsənʃaft] f (pl -en) science, knowledge. **–ler** m (pl -), **–lerin** f (pl -nen) scientist. **wissenschaftlich** adj scientific.

wissentlich [vɪsəntlɪç] adj conscious, deliberate. adv knowingly, wittingly.

Witterung [vɪtərʊŋ] f (pl -en) weather (conditions).

Witwe [vɪtvə] f (pl -n) widow. **Witwer** m (pl -) widower.

Witz [vɪts] m (pl -e) (Gabe) wit; (Spaß) joke. **–bold** m witty fellow, clown. **–blatt** neut comic (paper). **witzig** adj witty; (spaßhaft) humorous, funny. **witzeln über** joke about.

wo [voː] adv where. conj when. **ach wo!** what nonsense! **wo∥anders** adv elsewhere. **–bei** adv whereby, by which.

Woche [vɔxə] f (pl -n) week. **Wochen∥blatt** neut weekly (paper). **–ende** neut weekend.

wöchentlich [vœçtlɪç] adj weekly.

Wodka [vɔdka] m (pl -s) vodka.

wo∥durch adv whereby, by which; (Frage) how? by what means? **–für** adv for which; (Frage) for what? what ... for? **–gegen** adv against which. conj whereas. **–her** adv from where, whence. **–hin** adv (to) where, whither.

wohl [voːl] adv well; (vermutend) probably, I suppose. **Wohl** neut well-being, welfare.

wohlauf [voːlauf] adv well. interj come on! cheer up!

Wohl∥befinden neut well-being, (good) health. **–behagen** neut comfort.

wohl∥bekannt adj well-known. **–erzogen** adj well brought up.

Wohlfahrt [voːlfaːrt] f welfare. **–sstaat** m welfare state.

wohl∥gemeint adj well-intentioned. **–geraten** adj well done; (Kind) well-behaved.

Wohl∥geruch m perfume, fragrance. **–geschmack** m pleasant or agreeable taste.

wohlhabend [voːlhaːbənt] adj well-to-do, well-off.

Wohlklang [voːlklaŋ] m harmony.

Wohlstand [voːlʃtant] m prosperity, affluence. **–sgesellschaft** f affluent society.

Wohl∥tat f kindness, kind deed; (Annehmlichkeit) boon, benefit. **–täter** m benefactor. **–täterin** f benefactress. **wohltätig** adj charitable. **Wohltätigkeit** f charity. **–sverein** m charitable association.

***wohltun** [voːltuːn] v do good.

Wohlwollen [voːlvɔlən] neut good will,

benevolence. **wohlwollend** adj benevolent.

wohnen ['vo:nən] v live, dwell, reside. **wohnhaft** adj resident. **Wohn‖mobil** neut camper van. **–ort** m place of residence. **–Schlafzimmer** neut bedsitting room, (umg.) bedsit. **–ung** f (pl -en) flat, (US) apartment. **–wagen** m caravan, (US) trailer. **–zimmer** neut living-room, sitting-room.

Wölbung ['vœlbuŋ] f (pl -en) vault, arch, dome.

Wolf [vɔlf] m (pl **Wölfe**) wolf.

Wölfin ['vœlfin] f (pl -nen) she-wolf.

Wolke ['vɔlkə] f (pl -n) cloud. **–nkratzer** m skyscraper.

Wolle ['vɔlə] f (pl -n) wool.

*wollen¹ ['vɔlən] v want, wish. ich will gehen I want to go, I intend to go. ich will nicht gehen I don't want to go, I will not go. wollen Sie bitte … would you please. … tun Sie, was Sie wollen do as you please.

wollen² adj woollen, (US) woolen.

wollig ['vɔliç] adj woolly.

Wollust ['vɔlust] f lust, voluptuousness. **wollüstig** adj lustful, voluptuous, sensual.

wo‖mit adv with which; (Frage) with what? **–nach** adv after which, whereupon.

Wonne ['vɔnə] f (pl -n) bliss; (Freude) joy; (Entzücken) rapture.

woran [vo'ran] adv on which. **woran denkst du?** what are you thinking about? **woran liegt es, daß…?** how is it that …? **wo‖rauf** adv upon which, whereupon. **–raus** adv from which, whence. **–rin** adv in(to) which.

Wort [vɔrt] 1 neut (pl **Wörter**) word. 2 neut (pl **Worte**) (spoken) word.

Wörterbuch ['vœrtərbux] neut dictionary. **wörtlich** adj literal.

Wort‖schatz m vocabulary. **–spiel** neut pun.

wovon [vo'fɔn] of or from which; (Frage) from what? **wovon lebt er?** what does he live on? **wovon spricht er?** what is he talking about? **wozu** adv to which; (warum) what … for, why.

Wrack [vrak] neut (pl -s) wreck.

*wringen ['vriŋən] v wring.

Wucher ['vu:xər] m profiteering. **wuchern** v profiteer; (Pflanze) proliferate, be rampant. **Wucherpreis** m exorbitant price.

Wuchs [m (pl **Wüchse**) growth; (Körper-

bau) physique, build.

Wucht [vuxt] f (pl -en) weight, impetus, force. **wuchtig** adj heavy, weighty.

wülen ['vy:lən] v root, dig; (durchstöbern) rummage; (Gefühle) well up. **sich wühlen in** burrow into. **wühlerisch** adj subversive.

Wulst [vulst] m (pl **Wülste**) swelling, bulge. **wulstig** adj swollen.

wund [vunt] adj sore. **Wunde** f (pl -n) wound.

Wunder ['vundər] neut (pl -) miracle, wonder. **wunderbar** adj wonderful, marvellous. **Wunder‖kind** neut child prodigy. **–land** neut fairy-land. **wunder‖lich** adj odd, strange, peculiar. **–n** v surprise, astonish. **sich wundern über** be astonished by, wonder at. **wunderschön** adj (very) beautiful. **Wundertat** f miracle, miraculous feat.

Wunsch [vunʃ] m (pl **Wünsche**) wish, desire.

wünschen ['vynʃən] wish, desire. **–swert** adj desirable.

Würde ['vyrdə] f (pl -n) dignity; (Ehre) honour. **würde‖los** adj undignified. **–voll** adj dignified. **würdig** adj worthy. **–en** v appreciate. **Würdigung** f (pl -en) appreciation.

Wurf [vurf] m (pl **Würfe**) throw, cast; (Tiere) litter, brood.

Würfel ['vyrfəl] m (pl -) cube; (Spielstein) die.

würgen ['vyrgən] v choke, retch; (erwürgen) strangle, throttle.

Wurm [vurm] m (pl **Würmer**) worm. **wurmig** adj worm-eaten.

Wurst [vurst] f (pl **Würste**) sausage.

Würstchen ['vyrstçən] neut (pl -) (small) sausage; (Mensch) little man, insignificant person.

Würze ['vyrtsə] (pl -n) seasoning, spice.

Wurzel ['vyrtsəl] f (pl -n) root. **wurzeln** v take root; (fig) be rooted in.

würzen ['vyrtsən] v season, spice. **würzig** adj seasoned, spiced.

wüst [vy:st] adj desert, desolate; (wirr) disorderly; (Person) coarse, vile. **Würste** f (pl -n) desert, waste.

wut [vu:t] f rage, fury.

wüten ['vy:tən] v rage, be furious. **–d** adj furious.

X

X-Beine ['iksbainə] *pl* knock-knees.
X-beinig *adj* knock-kneed.
x-mal ['iksm aːl] *adj* (*umg.*) many times, *n* times.
X-Strahlen ['iksʃtraːlən] *pl* x-rays.

Z

Zacke ['tsakə] *f* (*pl* -n) *or* **Zacken** *m* (*pl* -) point, jag; (*Gabel*) prong; (*Kamm*) tooth. **zackig** *adj* pointed, jagged; pronged; toothed.
zaghaft ['tsaːkhaft] *adj* timid.
zäh [tsɛː] *adj* tough; (*Flüssigkeit*) thick; (*Person*) stubborn.
Zahl [tsaːl] *f* (*pl* -en) number; (*Ziffer*) figure, numeral. **zahlbar** *adj* payable. **zahlen** *v* pay.
zählbar ['tsɛːlbaːr] *adj* countable. **zählen** *v* count; (*Sport*) keep the score. **zählen auf** count or rely on.
Zahler ['tsaːlər] *m* (*pl* -) payer.
Zähler ['tsɛːlər] *m* (*pl* -) counter; (*Bank*) teller; (*Gerät*) meter, recorder.
zahl‖los *adj* countless. **–reich** *adj* numerous. **Zahl‖tag** *m* payday. **–ung** *f* (*pl* -en) payment.
Zählung ['tsɛːluŋ] *f* (*pl* -en) counting; (*Volkszählung*) census.
zahlungs‖fähig [*adj* (*Komm*) solvent. **–unfähig** *adj* insolvent.
zahm [tsaːm] *adj* tame.
zähmen ['tsɛːmən] *v* tame.
Zahn [tsaːn] *m* (*pl* Zähne) tooth. **–arzt** *m* dentist. **–bürste** *f* toothbrush. **–fleisch** *neut* gum, gums *pl*. **–paste** *f* toothpaste. **–rad** *neut* cogwheel, gearwheel. **–schmerz** *m* toothache.
Zange ['tsaŋə] *f* (*pl* -n) pliers *pl*, tongs *pl*; (*Pinzette*) tweezers *pl*.
Zank [tsaŋk] *m* (*pl* Zänke) quarrel. **zanken** *v* scold. **sich zanken** quarrel.
Zapfen ['tsapfən] *m* (*pl* -) plug, bung; (*Bot*) cone.

zappelig ['tsapəlɪç] *adj* fidgety. **zappeln** *v* fidget.
zappen ['tsapən] *v* (*umg; Fernsehprogramme umschalten*) zap, channel-hop.
Zar [tsaːr] *m* (*pl* -en) tsar, czar. **–in** *f* (*pl* -nen*) tsarina.
zart [tsaːrt] *adj* (*Fleisch, Gemüt*) tender; (*sanft*) gentle, soft; (*zerbrechlich*) delicate. **–heit** *f* tenderness; gentleness.
zärtlich ['tsɛːrtlɪç] *adj* tender, loving, affectionate. **Zärtlichkeit** *f* tenderness, affection.
Zauber ['tsaubər] *m* (*pl* -) magic. **–bann** *m* spell, charm. **–ei** *f* magic, sorcery. **–er** *m* (*pl* -) magician, sorcerer. **–erin** *f* (*pl* -nen) magician, sorceress. **zauberhaft** *adj* magical. **Zauber‖kunst** *f* sorcery; (*Sinnestäuschung*) conjuring. **–künstler** *m* conjurer. **–kunststück** *neut* conjuring tricks *pl*. **zaubern** *v* practise magic; (*Zauberkunst*) conjure. **Zauberspruch** *m* magic spell.
zaudern ['tsaudərn] *v* hesitate, waver, dither.
Zaum [tsaum] *m* (*pl* Zäume) rein, bridle.
zäumen ['tsɔymən] *v* (*Pferd*) bridle; (*fig*) curb, restrain.
Zaun [tsaun] *m* (*pl* Zäune) fence; (*Hecke*) hedge.
Zebra ['tseːbra] *neut* (*pl* -s) zebra.
Zeche ['tsɛçə] *f* (*pl* -n) (*Gasthaus*) bill; (*Bergwerk*) mine, pit.
Zechgelage ['tsɛçgəlaːgə] *neut* (*pl* -) binge (*Alkohol*).
Zehe ['tseːə] *f* (*pl* -n) toe. **–nspitze** *f* tip of the toe.
zehn [tseːn] *pron, adj* ten. **zehnte** *adj* tenth. **Zehntel** *neut* tenth (part).
zehren ['tseːrən] *v* **zehren an** (*fig*) gnaw at. **zehren von** live *or* feed on.
Zeichen ['tsaiçən] *neut* (*pl* -) sign; (*Merkmal*) mark; (*Signal*) signal; (*Hinweis*) indication. **–brett** *neut* drawing board. **–(trick)film** *m* animated cartoon. **zeichnen** *v* draw; (*kennzeichnen*) mark; (*unterschreiben*) sign; (*Muster*). design. **Zeichnung** *f* drawing; marking; (*Muster*) design.
Zeigefinger ['tsaigəfɪŋər] *m* forefinger, index finger. **zeigen** *v* point out, show; (*zur Schau stellen*) show, display; (*beweisen*) demonstrate, show. **Zeiger** *m* pointer, indicator; (*Uhr*) hand.
Zeile ['tsailə] *f* (*pl* -n) line.

Zeit [tsaɪt] f (pl -en) time. **auf Zeit** on credit. **freie Zeit** spare or free time. **für alle Zeiten** for all time. **in kurzer Zeit** shortly, soon. **Zeit||alter** neut age, era. **–folge** f chronological order. **–geist** m spirit of the age.

Zeitgenosse ['tsaɪtgənɔsə] m (pl -n), **Zeitgenossin** f (pl -nen) contemporary. **zeitgenössisch** adj contemporary.

zeitig ['tsaɪtɪç] adj early.

Zeit||karte f season ticket. **–lang** f while. **ein Zeitlang** for some time, for a while. **Zeitlauf** m course of time.

zeitlich ['tsaɪtlɪç] adj temporal.

Zeit||punkt m (point in) time, moment. **–raum** m period. **–schrift** f magazine, periodical.

Zeitung ['tsaɪtuŋ] f (pl -en) newspaper. **Zeitungs||anzeigt** f newspaper advertisement. **–ausschnitt** m press cutting. **–händler** m newsagent. **–stand** m newsstand, kiosk. **–wesen** neut the press, journalism.

Zeit||verschwendung f waste of time. **–vertreib** m pastime, diversion. **zeitweilig** adj temporary.

Zeitwort ['tsaɪtvɔrt] neut verb.

Zelle ['tsɛlə] f (pl -n) cell.

Zelt [tsɛlt] neut (pl -e) tent. **–decke** f awning, canopy. **zelten** v camp. **Zeltplatz** m camp.

Zement [tsɛ'mɛnt] m (pl -e) cement.

Zensur [tsɛn'zuːr] f (pl -en) censorship; (Schule) mark.

Zentimeter [tsɛntɪ'meːtər] m or neut centimetre.

Zentner ['tsɛntnər] m (pl -) hundredweight, 50 kilos.

zentral [tsɛn'traːl] adj central. **Zentrale** f (pl -n) central office; (Telef) telephone exchange. **Zentral||heizung** f central heating. **–isierung** f centralization. **Zentrum** neut (pl Zentren) centre.

zerbrechen [tsɛr'brɛçən] v break (in pieces), shatter. **zerbrechlich** adj fragile, breakable.

zerdrücken [tsɛr'drykən] v crush; (Kleider) crumple, crease.

Zeremonie [tseʀemo'niː] f (pl -n) ceremony. **zeremoniell** adj ceremonial.

Zerfall [tsɛr'fal] m decay, disintegration; (Chem) decomposition. **zerfallen** v disintegrate, fall to pieces; (auflösen) dissolve. **zer fallen mit** fall out with.

zerfetzen [tsɛr'fɛtsən] v shred, tear up.

*zerfressen [tsɛr'frɛsən] v gnaw; (Chem) corrode.

*zergehen [tsɛr'geːən] v melt.

zergliedern [tsɛr'gliːdərn] v dismember; (fig) analyse.

zerhacken [tsɛr'hakən] v chop up, chop into pieces.

zerkleinern [tsɛr'klaɪnərn] v cut up, chop up.

zerlegen [tsɛr'leːgən] v take apart, separate; (Fleisch) carve; (fig) analyse. **Zerlegung** f (pl -en) taking apart; carving; analysis.

zerlumpt [tsɛr'lumpt] adj ragged.

zermahlen [tsɛr'maːlən] v grind.

zermürben [tsɛr'myrbən] v wear down. **Zermürbung** f attrition. **–skrieg** m war of attrition.

zerplatzen [tsɛr'platsən] v explode, burst.

zerquetschen [tsɛr'kvɛtʃən] v squash, crush.

Zerrbild ['tsɛrbɪlt] neut distortion, caricature.

*zerreißen [tsɛr'raɪsən] v tear up/to pieces; (entzweigehen) rip, tear, break.

zerren ['tsɛrən] v tug, pull; (Med) strain, pull. **Zerrung** f (pl -en) (Med) strain.

zerschellen [tsɛr'ʃɛlən] v be dashed to pieces.

*zerschlagen [tsɛr'ʃlaːgən] v knock or smash to pieces.

zerschlissen [tsɛr'ʃlɪsən] adj tattered, shredded.

*zerschneiden [tsɛr'ʃnaɪdən] v cut up.

zersetzen [tsɛr'zɛtsən] v disintegrate; (untergraben) undermine, demoralize. **sich zersetzen** disintegrate; (Chem) decompose. **Zersetzung** f disintegration.

zersplittern [tsɛr'ʃplɪtərn] v splinter, shatter; (fig) split up. **Zersplitterung** f splintering; splitting-up.

zersprengen [tsɛr'ʃprɛŋən] v blow up, burst (open).

zerstäuben v pulverize; (Flüssigkeit) spray, atomize. **Zerstäuber** m spray atomizer.

zerstören [tsɛr'ʃtøːrən] v destroy. **–d** adj destructive. **Zerstör||er** m destroyer. **–ung** f destruction.

zerstreuen [tsɛr'ʃtrɔyən] v disperse, scatter; (unterhalten) amuse, entertain. **zerstreut**

adj scattered; (*geistig*) distracted, absent-minded. **Zerstreuung** *f* dispersion; distraction; (*Unterhaltung*) amusement.

zerteilen [tsɛr'tailən] *v* divide, separate; (*zerstückeln*) cut up.

*zertreten [tsɛr'treːtən] *v* tread on, trample on.

zertrümmern [tsɛr'trymərn] *v* smash, wreck; (*vernichten*) destroy.

zerzausen [tsɛr'tsauzən] *v* rumple, tousle. **zerzaust** *adj* tousled, dishevelled.

zetern ['tseːtərn] *v* cry out, shout (for help).

Zettel ['tsɛtəl] *m* (*pl* -) slip (of paper); (*Merkzettel*) note; (*Preis*) ticket.

Zeug [tsɔyk] *neut* (*pl* -e) material, stuff; (*Arbeitsgeräte*) tools *pl*; (*allerlei Dinge*) stuff, things *pl*.

Zeuge ['tsɔygə] *m* (*pl* -n) witness.

zeugen[1] ['tsɔygən] *v* testify, give evidence. **von etwas zeugen** be evidence of something.

zeugen[2] *v* (*Kind*) procreate, beget; (*fig*) generate, produce.

Zeugen||bank *f* witness box. **–beweis** *m* evidence. **Zeugin** (*pl* -nen) *f* (female) witness. **Zeugnis** *neut* evidence, testimony; (*Bescheinigung*) certificate; (*Schule*) report.

Zeugung ['tsɔygun] *f* (*pl* -en) generation, procreation.

Zickzack ['tsɪktsak] *m* (*pl* -e) zigzag.

Ziege ['tsiːgə] *f* (*pl* -n) goat.

Ziegel ['tsiːgəl] *m* (*pl* -) (*Backstein*) brick; (*Dachziegel*) (roof-)tile. **–stein** *m* brick.

Ziegen||bock *m* billy goat. **–leder** *neut* kid (leather), goatskin. **–milch** *f* goat's milk.

*ziehen ['tsiːən] *v* pull, draw; (*Zeichnen*) draw; (*strecken*) stretch; (*wandern*) wander; (*marschieren*) march; (*Tee*) infuse; (*Zigarre*) draw *or* pull (on); (*umziehen*) move. **es zieht** (*Luft*) there is a draught. **sich in die Länge ziehen** drag on.

Ziel [tsiːl] *neut* (*pl* -e) aim, goal; (*Geschoß*) target; (*Wettlauf*) finish. **ziel||en** *v* aim (at). **–los** *adj* aimless. **Zielscheibe** *f* target.

ziemlich ['tsiːm lɪç] *adj* considerable. *adv* rather, moderately.

Zier [tsiːr] *f* (*pl* -en) decoration. **zier||en** *v* decorate. **sich zieren** be affected, behave with affectation. **–lich** *adj* dainty; (*elegant*) elegant.

Ziffer ['tsɪfər] *f* (*pl* -n) cipher, numeral.

–blatt *neut* clock-face.

Zigarette [tsiga'rɛtə] *f* (*pl* -n) cigarette. **Zigaretten||etui** *neut* cigarette case. **–stümmel** *m* cigarette end. **Zigarre** *f* (*pl* -n) cigar.

Zigeuner [tsigɔynər] *m* (*pl* -), **Zigeunerin** *f* (*pl* -nen) Gipsy.

Zimmer ['tsɪm ər] *neut* (*pl* -) room. **–arbeit** *f* carpentry. **–mann** *m* carpenter. **–spiel** *neut* (parlour) game.

zimperlich ['tsɪm pərlɪç] *adj* prim.

Zimt [tsɪm t] *m* (*pl* -e) cinnamon.

Zink [tsɪŋk] *neut* zinc.

Zinke ['tsɪŋkə] *f* (*pl* -n) prong; (*Kamm*) tooth.

Zinn [tsɪn] *neut* tin. **zinnern** *adj* tin. **Zinnfolie** *f* tinfoil.

Zins [tsɪns] *m* (*pl* -en) (*Miete*) rent; (*Abgabe*) tax, duty. **Zinsen** *pl* interest. **Zinsfuß** *m* rate of interest.

Zipfel ['tsɪpfəl] *m* (*pl* -) tip; (*Ecke*) corner.

Zirkel ['tsɪrkəl] *m* (*pl* -) (*Kreis*) circle; (*Gerät*) (pair of) compasses *pl*.

Zirkus ['tsɪrkus] *m* (*pl* -se) circus.

zirpen ['tsɪrpən] *v* chirp.

zischen [tsɪʃən] *v* kiss.

Zitat [tsiˈtaːt] *neut* (*pl* -e) quotation, quote. **zitieren** *v* quote, cite; (*vorladen*) summon.

Zitrone [tsiˈtroːnə] *f* (*pl* -n) lemon.

zittern ['tsɪtərn] *v* tremble, shake.

Zitze ['tsɪtsə] *f* (*pl* -n) nipple, teat.

zivil [tsiˈviːl] *adj* civil. **Zivilisation** *f* (*unz.*) civilization. **zivil||isieren** *v* civilize. **–isiert** *adj* civilized, cultured. **Zivil||ist** *m* (*pl* -en) civilian. **–kleidung** *f* civilian clothes *pl*.

zögern ['tsø:gərn] *v* hesitate.

Zoll[1] [tsɔl] *m* (*pl* -e) (*Längenmaß*) inch.

Zoll[2] *m* (*pl* Zölle) (customs) duty; (*umg.: Zollabfertigungsstelle*) customs *pl*.

Zoll||abfertigung *f* customs clearance. **–beamte(r)** *m* customs official.

Zone ['tso:nə] *f* (*pl* -n) zone.

Zoo [tso:] *m* (*pl* -s) zoo. **–loge** *m* (*pl* -n) zoologist. **–logie** *f* zoology. **zoologisch** *adj* zoological.

Zopf [tsɔpf] *m* (*pl* Zöpfe) plait, pigtail.

Zorn [tsɔrn] *m* anger. **zornig** *adj* angry.

zu [tsu:] *prep* (*Richtung*) to, toward(s); (*Ziel*, *Ort*) at, in; (*neben*) beside. *adv* too; (*geschlossen*) closed, shut. **zu Hause** at home. **zu verkaufen** for sale. **zu Mittag** at noon. **zu Fuß** on foot. **ab und zu** now and then. **um zu** in order to.

Zubehör ['tsuːbəhøːɐ ːɐ] *neut* (*pl* **-e**) fittings *pl*; (*Tech*) accessories *pl*. **–teil** *neut* attachment, accessory.

zubereiten ['tsuːbəraɪtən] *v* prepare.

***zubringen** ['tsuːbrɪŋən] *v* bring *or* take (to); (*Zeit*) spend.

Zucht [tsuxt] **1** *f* (*unz.*) discipline; (*Pflanzen*) cultivation, breeding; (*Vieh*) rearing, breeding. **2** *f* (*pl* **-en**) breed.

züchten ['tsʏçtən] *v* breed. **Züchter** *m* breeder; (*Bienen*) beekeeper; (*Pflanzen*) grower.

züchtigen ['tsʏçtɪgən] *v* punish, discipline. **Züchtigung** *f* (*pl* **-en**) punishment.

zuchtlos ['tsuxtloːs] *adj* undisciplined.

Zuck [tsuk] *m* (*pl* **-e**) jerk. **zucken** *v* start, jerk.

Zucker ['tsukər] *m* sugar. **zuckerkrank** *adj* diabetic. **Zucker‖kranke(r)** *m* diabetic. **–krankheit** *f* diabetes. **–rohr** *m* sugarcane.

zudecken ['tsuːdɛkən] *v* cover (up).

zudem [tsuˈdeːm] *adv* moreover, besides.

zudrehen ['tsuːdreːən] *v* turn off.

zudringlich ['tsuːdrɪŋlɪç] *adj* importunate, pushing.

zueinander [tsuaɪˈnandər] *adv* to each other.

zuerst [tsuˈeːrst] *adv* (at) first.

Zufahrt ['tsuːfaːrt] *f* approach, driving in. **–straße** *f* access road; (*Haus*) driveway.

Zufall ['tsuːfal] *m* chance, accident. **glücklicher Zufall** happy coincidence. **zufällig** *adj* accidental, chance; *adv* by chance, accidentally.

Zuflucht ['tsuːfluxt] *f* refuge, shelter.

Zufluß ['tsuːflus] *m* influx; (*Fluß*) tributary; (*Waren*) supply.

zufolge [tsuˈfɔlgə] *prep* owing to, in consequence of.

zufrieden [tsuˈfriːdən] *adj* contented. **Zufriedenheit** *f* contented. **zufriedenstellen** *v* satisfy.

zufügen ['tsuːfyːgən] *v* add (to); (*Böses*) inflict (on).

Zufuhr ['tsuːfuːr] *f* (*pl* **-en**) supply. **zuführen** *v* supply; (*zuleiten*) lead to.

Zug [tsuːk] *m* (*pl* **Züge**) pull; (*Eisenbahn*) train; (*Charakter*) trait; (*Gesicht*) feature; (*Luft*) draught; (*Schub*) thrust; (*Brettspiel*) move; (*Einatmen*) inhalation; (*Rauchen*)

puff, pull; (*Festzug*) procession; (*Zeichnen*) stroke, dash; (*Umriß*) outline; (*Vögel*) migration.

Zugabe ['tsuːgaːbə] *f* addition; (*Zuschlag*) extra.

Zugang ['tsuːgaŋ] *m* entry, access; (*Eingang*) entrance; accession. **zugänglich** *adj* accessible; (*Mensch*) approachable.

Zugbrücke ['tsuːgbrʏkə] *f* drawbridge.

***zugeben** ['tsuːgeːbən] *v* add; (*einräumen*) admit; (*gestatten*) permit.

zugegen [tsuˈgeːgən] *adj* present.

***zugehen** ['tsuːgeːən] *v* close, be closed; (*weitergehen*) go on; (*geschehen*) happen.

zugehören ['tsuːgəhøːrən] *v* belong (to).

Zügel ['tsyːgəl] *m* (*pl* **-**) rein(s); (*fig*) curb, **zügel‖los** *adj* unrestrained, unbridled. **–n** *v* rein; (*beherrschen*) control, curb.

Zugeständnis ['tsuːgəʃtɛntnis] *neut* concession.

***zugestehen** ['tsuːgəʃteːən] *v* admit, concede.

Zugführer ['tsuːkfyːrər] *m* (*Eisenbahn*) guard, (*US*) conductor.

***zugießen** ['tsuːgiːsən] *v* pour (in).

zugig ['tsuːgiç] *adj* draughty.

Zugluft ['tsuːgluft] *f* draught.

***zugreifen** ['tsuːgraɪfən] *v* grasp, grab; (*helfen*) lend a hand; (*bei Tisch*) help oneself.

zugrunde [tsuˈgrundə] *adv* **zugrunde gehen** *v* perish, be ruined.

zugunsten [tsuˈgunstən] *prep* in favour of.

zugute [tsuˈguːtə] *adv* to one's advantage. **zugute halten** *v* take into consideration, allow for.

Zugvogel ['tsuːgfoːgəl] *m* (*pl* **Zugvögel**) migratory bird.

***zuhalten** ['tsuːhaltən] *v* keep shut. **zuhalten auf** head for. **Zuhälter** *m* pimp.

zuhanden [tsuˈhandən] *adj* (ready) at hand, ready.

Zuhause ['tsuːhauzə] *f* (*unz.*) home.

zuhören ['tsuːhøːrən] *v* listen. **Zuhörer** *m* (*pl* **-**), **Zuhörerin** *f* (*pl* **-nen**) listener. **Zuhörer** *pl* audience *sing*; (*Radio*) listeners.

zuklappen ['tsuːklapən] *v* slam, clap shut.

zuknöpfen ['tsuːknœpfən] *v* button up.

***zukommen** ['tsuːkɔm ən] *v* (*gebühren*) befit. **zukommen lassen** send, supply. **zukommen auf** come up to.

Zukunft ['tsuːkʊnft] f future. **zukünftig** adj future; adv in (the) future.

Zulage ['tsuːlaːgə] f extra pay, bonus.

zulänglich ['tsuːlɛŋlɪç] adj sufficient.

***zulassen** ['tsuːlasən] v permit, admit; (hereinlassen) let in, admit. **zulässig** adj permissible. **Zulassung** f permission; admission; (Mot) registration. **–sschein** m permit, licence.

zuleiten ['tsuːlaɪtən] v lead to.

zuletzt [tsuːˈlɛtst] adv finally, last.

zuliebe [tsuːˈliːbə] adv **jemandem zuliebe** to please someone.

Zulieferer ['tsuːliːfəːrər] m (pl -) subcontractor.

zum [tsʊm] prep + art **zu dem**.

zumachen ['tsuːm axən] v shut, close.

zumeist [tsuːmˈaɪst] adv mostly.

zumindest [tsuːmˈɪndəst] adv at least.

zumute [tsuːmˈuːtə] adv **gut/schlecht zumute sein** be in high/low spirits.

zumuten ['tsuːm uːtən] v expect, demand. **Zumutung** f presumption, unreasonable expectation.

zunächst [tsuːˈnɛːçst] adv first (of all). prep near, close to.

Zunahme ['tsuːnaːm ə] f (pl -n) increase.

Zuname ['tsuːnaːm ə] m surname.

zünden ['tsyndən] v catch fire, light; (Mot, Tech) ignite.

Zunder ['tsʊndər] m (pl -) tinder.

Zünder ['tsyndər] m (pl -) fuse, detonator. **Zünd||kerze** f sparking plug. **–schlüssel** m ignition key. **–ung** f ignition; (Sprengladung) detonation.

***zunehmen** ['tsuːneːm ən] v increase; (wachsen) grow; (dicker werden) put on weight. **–d** adj increasing, accelerating.

zuneigen ['tsuːnaɪgən] v incline, lean; (fig) incline, tend. **Zuneigung** f inclination; (Sympathie) affection.

Zunft [tsʊnft] f (pl **Zünfte**) guild.

Zunge ['tsʊŋə] f (pl -n) tongue. **zungenfertig** adj glib, fluent.

zunichte [tsuːˈnɪçtə] adv **zunichte machen** (Hoffnungen) destroy, shatter; (Pläne) frustrate.

zunicken ['tsuːnɪkən] v nod to.

zunutze [tsuːˈnʊtsə] adv **sich etwas zunutze machen** utilize something, put something to use.

zuoberst [tsuːˈoːbərst] adv at the top.

zupfen ['tsʊpfən] v pluck; (Fasern) pick.

zur [tsuːr] prep + art **zu der**.

zurechnen ['tsuːrɛçnən] v (zuschreiben) ascribe, attribute. **Zurechnung** f attribution.

zurecht [tsuːˈrɛçt] adv right, correctly, in order. **sich zurechtfinden** v find one's way. **zurechtkommen** v arrive in time. **zurechtkommen mit** get along with. **zurecht||machen** v prepare. **–weisen** v reprimand.

zureden ['tsuːreːdən] v urge, coax.

zureichen ['tsuːraɪçən] v (ausreichen) do, be enough; (hinreichen) hand, pass. **–d** adj sufficient.

zurichten ['tsuːrɪçtən] v prepare, get ready; (umg.) mess up, make a mess of.

zürnen ['tsyrnən] v be angry.

zurück [tsuːˈrʏk] adv back(wards); (hinten) behind. **–behalten** v keep back, detain. **–bekommen** v get back, recover. **–bezahlen** v refund, pay back. **–bleiben** v remain behind. **–blicken** v look back. **–bringen** v bring back. **–datieren** v backdate; (stammen aus) date back; **–erstatten** v return, restore; (ausgelegtes Geld) reimburse. **–fahren** v drive back; (vor Schreck) recoil, start.

Zurückgabe [tsuːˈrʏkgaːbə] f restitution, restoration. **zurückgeben** v give back, restore.

zurück||gehen v go back, return; (nachlassen) decrease, fall off. **zurückgehen auf** originate in, go back to. **–gezogen** adj retiring, withdrawn.

zurückhalten [tsuːˈrʏkhaltən] v (Person) keep, detain; (Sache) retain, withhold. **–d** adj reserved; (vorsichtig) cautious. **Zurückhaltung** f reserve.

zurück||kehren v return. **–kommen** v come back; (wieder aufgreifen) revert (to), **–legen** v put aside; (Geld) put by. **–melden** v report back.

Zurücknahme [tsuːˈrʏknaːm ə] f (pl -n) withdrawal, taking back. **zurücknehmen** v take back; (Worte) withdraw; (Anordnung, Auftrag) cancel.

zurück||scheuen v shrink back (from), shy (at). **–schicken** v send back. **–setzen** v put or place back; (herabsetzen) reduce; (Person) neglect, slight. **–strahlen** v reflect. **–stufen** v demote, downgrade. **–treten** v step back; (*vom Posten*) resign, retire. **–weisen** *v* refuse, reject. **–zahlen** *v* pay back, repay. **–ziehen** *v* draw back, withdraw. **sich zurückziehen** withdraw, retire.

Zuruf ['tsuːruːf] *m* shout. **zurufen** *v* shout, call.

Zusage ['tsuːzaːgə] *f* promise; (*Bejahung*) assent, consent. **zusagen** *v* (*versprechen*) promise; (*Einladung*) accept, agree to come; (*gefallen*) suit, please.

zusammen [tsuˈzamən] *adv* together; (*insgesamt*) all told, all together.

Zusammenarbeit *f* cooperation. **zusammenarbeiten** *v* cooperate.

zusammenballen *v* roll up; (*Faust*) clench. **sich zusammenballen** gather.

*zusammenbrechen *v* collapse, break down. **Zusammenbruch** *m* collapse.

zusammendrängen *v* **sich zusammendrängen** crowd together.

*zusammen‖fahren *v* travel together; (*aufeinanderstoßen*) collide; (*zusammenschrecken*) wince, start. **–fallen** *v* fall down, collapse; coincide.

zusammenfassen *v* summarize. **–d** *adj* comprehensive. **Zusammenfassung** *f* summary.

zusammengesetzt *adj* composed, compounded.

Zusammenhang *m* (*verbindung*) connection; (*Text*) context. **zusammenhängen** *v* (*verbunden sein*) be connected. **–d** *adj* coherent.

zusammenklappen *v* fold up.

Zusammenkunft *f* (*pl* **Zusammenkünfte**) meeting.

zusammen‖legen *v* put together; (*falten*) fold (up); (*vereinigen*) combine; (*Geld*) pool. **–passen** *v* go (well) together, match; (*Menschen*) get on well.

Zusammenprall *m* collision. **zusammenprallen** *v* collide.

*zusammenschließen *v* join together. **sich zusammenschließen** unite. **Zusammenschluß** *m* union, merger.

zusammensetzen *v* put together, construct. **sich zusammensetzen** sit down with one another; (*bestehen*) consist (of). **Zusammensetz‖spiel** *neut* jigsaw puzzle. **–ung** *f* composition.

zusammenstellen *v* (*vereinigen*) join; (*vergleichen*) compare.

Zusammenstoß *m* collision; (*Streit*) clash, conflict. **zusammenstoßen** *v* collide; clash, conflict.

Zusammentreffen *neut* coincidence; (*Begegnung*) encounter, meeting.

*zusammenziehen *v* close, draw together; (*verkürzen*) shorten, contract; (*verbinden*) join together; (*sammeln*) gather. **sich zusammenziehen** (*Stoff*) shrink. **Zusammenziehung** *f* shrinking; contraction.

Zusatz ['tsuːzats] *m* addition; (*Ergänzung*) supplement; (*Anhang*) appendix. **–mittel** *neut* (*pl* -) additive. **zusätzlich** *adj* additional, extra.

zuschauen ['tsuːʃauən] *v* watch, look on, observe. **Zuschauer** *m* (*pl* -), **Zuschauerin** *f* (*pl* **-nen**) spectator, onlooker.

Zuschlag ['tsuːʃlaːk] *m* surcharge, extra charge. **zuschlagen** *v* hit (out); (*Tür*) slam (shut).

*zuschließen ['tsuːʃliːsən] *v* lock (up).

*zuschneiden ['tsuːʃnaidən] *v* cut out. **Zuschnitt** *m* cut, style.

*zuschreiben ['tsuːʃraibən] *v* attribute, ascribe; (*übertragen*) transfer to. *das hast du dir selbst zuzuschreiben* you have yourself to blame for that.

Zuschuß ['tsuːʃus] *m* subsidy, allowance.

*zusehen ['tsuːzeːən] *v* look on, watch. **zusehen, daß** see to it that.

*zusenden ['tsuːzɛndən] *v* send on, forward.

zusetzen ['tsuːzɛtsən] *v* (*hinzufügen*) add; (*verlieren*) lose; (*bedrängen*) press, importune.

Zuspruch ['tsuːʃprux] *m* encouragement, approval.

Zustand ['tsuːʃtant] *m* condition, state.

zustande [tsuˈʃtandə] *adv* **zustande bringen** achieve, bring about. **zustande kommen** come about, materialize.

zuständig ['tsuːʃtɛndiç] *adj* appropriate; competent; responsible.

zustellen ['tsuːʃtɛlən] *v* deliver; (*Klage*) serve on. **Zustellung** *f* (*pl* **-en**) delivery.

zustimmen ['tsuːʃtimən] *v* consent, agree. **Zustimmung** *f* consent, agreement.

zustopfen ['tsuːʃtɔpfən] *v* plug (up), stop (up); (*flicken*) darn.

*zustoßen ['tsuːʃtoːsən] *v* (*Tür*) push to; (*geschehen*) happen (to), befall.

zutage [ˈtsuːˈtaːgə] *adv* **zutage bringen** bring to light.

Zutaten [ˈtsuːˈtaːtən] *f pl* ingredients; (*Beiwerk*) trimmings.

zuteilen [ˈtsuːtaɪlən] *v* assign, allocate, issue. **Zuteilung** *f* allocation.

zutiefst [tsuˈtiːfst] *adv* deeply.

*zutragen [ˈtsuːtraːgən] *v* carry to. **sich zutragen** happen, take place. **zuträglich** *adj* beneficial.

zutrauen [ˈtsuːtraʊən] *v* credit (with), believe (of). **Zutrauen** *neut* confidence, trust, faith.

*zutreffen [ˈtsuːtrɛfən] *v* be right, be *or* hold true. **-d** *adj* right, accurate.

Zutritt [ˈtsuːtrɪt] *m* access. **Zutritt verboten!** keep out! no admission!

*zutun [ˈtsuːtuːn] *v* (*hinzutun*) add; (*schließen*) shut.

zuverlässig [ˈtsuːfɛrlɛsɪç] *adj* reliable. **Zuverlässigkeit** *f* reliability.

Zuversicht [ˈtsuːfɛrzɪçt] *f* confidence, trust. **zuversichtlich** *adj* confident.

zuviel [tsuˈfiːl] *adv* too much.

zuvor [tsuˈfoːr] *adv* before, previously. **-kommen** *v* anticipate, preempt.

Zuwachs [ˈtsuːvaks] *m* growth; (*Vermehrung*) increase.

zuwege [tsuˈveːgə] *adv* **zuwege bringen** bring about, cause.

zuweilen [tsuˈvaɪlən] *adv* sometimes, at times.

*zuweisen [ˈtsuːvaɪzən] *v* assign, allot.

*zuwenden [ˈtsuːvɛndən] *v* turn (towards); (*geben*) present, let have. **sich zuwenden** apply oneself (to).

zuwider [tsuˈviːdər] *prep* (*entgegen*) contrary to. *adj* (*widerwärtig*) repugnant.

zuwinken [ˈtsuːvɪŋkən] *v* wave (to).

*zuziehen [ˈtsuːtsiːən] *v* draw together; (*Vorhänge*) draw; (*Wohnung*) move in. **sich zuziehen** incur; (*Med*) contract, catch.

Zwang [tsvaŋ] *m* (*pl* **Zwänge**) compulsion; (*Gewalt*) force; (*Hemmung*) restraint.

zwängen [ˈtsvɛŋən] *v* force, press.

zwanglos [ˈtsvaŋloːs] *adj* unconstrained; (*ohne Förmlichkeit*) informal. **Zwangs‖arbeit** *f* hard labour. **-kauf** *m* compulsory purchase. **zwangsläufig** *adj* inevitable.

zwanzig [ˈtsvantsɪç] *pron, adj* twenty. **zwanzigst** *adj* twentieth.

zwar [tsvaːr] *adv* indeed, certainly. **und zwar** namely, in fact.

Zweck [tsvɛk] *m* (*pl* -e) purpose, object; (*Ziel*) goal. *es hat keinen Zweck* it's pointless, it is of no use.

Zwecke [ˈtsvɛkə] *f* (*pl* -n) tack; (*Reißnagel*) drawing pin, (US) thumbtack.

zweck‖los *adj* pointless. **-mäßig** *adj* expedient, appropriate. **-s** *prep* for the purpose of.

zwei [tsvaɪ] *pron, adj* two. **zwei‖deutig** *adj* ambiguous. **-erlei** *adj* of two kinds *or* sorts.

Zweifel [ˈtsvaɪfəl] *m* (*pl* -) doubt. **zweifel‖haft** *adj* doubtful. **-los** *adj* doubtless. **-n** *v* doubt.

Zweig [tsvaɪk] *m* (*pl* -e) branch, twig; (*fig*) branch. **-stelle** *f* branch (office).

zwei‖jährig *adj* two-year-old; (*Bot*) biennial. **-jährlich** *adj* biennial. **-mal** *adv* twice. **-seitig** *adj* two-sided; (*fig*) bilateral. **-sprachig** *adj* bilingual.

zweit [tsvaɪt] *adj* second. **-ens** *adv* secondly. **-klassig** *adj* second-rate.

zweiwöchentlich [ˈtsvaɪvœçəntlɪç] *adj* fortnightly.

Zwerchfell [ˈtsvɛrçfɛl] *neut* diaphragm.

Zwerg [tsvɛrk] *m* (*pl* -e) dwarf. **zwergenhaft** *adj* dwarf.

Zwetsche [ˈtsvɛtʃə] *or* **Zwetschge** *f* (*pl* -n) plum.

Zwick [tsvɪk] *m* (*pl* -e) pinch. **zwicken** *v* pinch; (*Fahrschein*) punch, clip.

Zwieback [ˈtsviːbak] *m* (*pl* -e) rusk, biscuit.

Zwiebel [ˈtsviːbəl] *f* (*pl* -n) onion; (*Blumen*) bulb.

Zwiegespräch [ˈtsviːgəʃprɛç] *neut* dialogue.

Zwielicht [ˈtsviːlɪçt] *neut* twilight.

Zwiespalt [ˈtsviːʃpalt] *m* (inner) conflict; (*Uneinigkeit*) dissension, discord.

Zwietracht [ˈtsviːtraxt] *f* conflict, dissension.

Zwilling [ˈtsvɪlɪŋ] *m* (*pl* -e) twin. **Zwillinge** *pl* (*Astrol*) Gemini. **Zwillings‖bruder** *m* twin brother. **-schwester** *f* twin sister.

Zwinge [ˈtsvɪŋə] *f* (*pl* -n) vice.

*zwingen [ˈtsvɪŋən] *v* force, compel; (*leisten können*) manage, cope with.

zwischen [ˈtsvɪʃən] *prep* between; (*mitten unter*) among. **Zwischen‖bemerkung** *f* remark, aside. **-händler** *m* middleman.

–raum *m* (intervening) space, interval.
–satz *m* insertion. **–stunde** *f* free period,
break, interval. **–zeit** *f* interim, interval. **in
der Zwischenzeit** (in the) meantime.
zwitschern ['tsvɪtʃəm] *v* chirp, twitter.
zwo [tsvoː] *V* **zwei.**
zwölf [tsvœlf] *pron, adj* twelve. **zwölft** *adj*
twelfth.
zyklisch ['tsyːklɪʃ] *adj* cyclic.
Zyklone [tsy'kloːnə] *f* (*pl* **-n**) low-pressure

area, depression.
Zyklus ['tsyːklus] *m* (*pl* **Zyklen**) cycle.
Zylinder [tsɪ'lɪndər] *m* (*pl* -) cylinder; (*Hut*)
top hat. **–kopf** *m* cylinder head.
Zyniker ['tsyːnɪkər] *m* (*pl* -) cynic. **zynisch**
adj cynical.
Zypern ['tsyːpərn] *neut* Cyprus. **Zyprer** *m*
(*pl* -), **Zyprerin** *f* (*pl* **-nen**) Cypriot.
zyprisch *adj* Cypriot.

Penguin Pocket Reference

THE PENGUIN POCKET FRENCH DICTIONARY
ROSALIND FERGUSSON

The Penguin Pocket French Dictionary is an invaluable and handy wordfinder for students and travellers alike. Covering both English–French and French–English, it offers clear definitions in an easy-to-use format, ensuring that you find the word you need quickly and efficiently.

- Includes over 35,000 entries

- Gives entry-by-entry guidance on pronunciation

- Lists irregular verbs in both languages

PENGUIN POCKET REFERENCE

THE PENGUIN POCKET SPANISH DICTIONARY
JOSEPHINE RIQUELME-BENEYTO

The Penguin Pocket Spanish Dictionary is an invaluable and handy wordfinder for students and travellers alike. Covering both English–Spanish and Spanish–English, it offers clear definitions in an easy-to-use format, ensuring that you find the word you need quickly and efficiently.

- Includes over 36,000 entries

- Gives entry-by-entry guidance on pronunciation

- Lists irregular verbs in both languages

PENGUIN POCKET REFERENCE

THE PENGUIN POCKET ENGLISH DICTIONARY

This pocket edition of the bestselling *Penguin English Dictionary* is the perfect reference book for everyday use. Compiled by Britain's foremost lexicographers, up to date and easy to use, it is the ideal portable companion for quick reference.

- Includes a wealth of words, phrases and clear definitions, with more information than other comparable dictionaries

- Covers standard and formal English, as well as specialist terms, slang and jargon

- Provides invaluable guidance on correct usage, commonly confused words and grammar and spelling

www.penguin.com

PENGUIN POCKET REFERENCE

POCKET ROGET'S® THESAURUS
GEORGE DAVIDSON

Roget's Thesaurus is the world's most trusted wordfinder and a writer's best friend, and this Pocket edition is ideal for helping you to find the exact words you need for all your written work. It will help improve your knowledge and use of the English language, build up your vocabulary and provide the key to stimulating and creative writing.

- Contains over 880 sections, covering objects, activities and abstract words and phrases

- Includes formal English, technical language, slang and jargon

- Provides full cross-referencing

'The indispensable guide to the English language' *Daily Express*

PENGUIN POCKET REFERENCE

THE PENGUIN POCKET SPELLING DICTIONARY
EDITED BY DAVID CRYSTAL

The Penguin Pocket Spelling Dictionary is indispensable for anyone
who wishes to check a spelling quickly and easily. It shows how to
spell virtually all the words you are likely to encounter on a daily basis
and highlights areas where mistakes are commonly made.

– Includes over 70,000 entries

– Gives capsule definitions for unusual and frequently confused words,
  and panels discussing points of interest

– Provides British and American spellings

PENGUIN POCKET REFERENCE

THE PENGUIN POCKET DICTIONARY OF BABIES' NAMES
DAVID PICKERING

The Penguin Pocket Dictionary of Babies' Names is essential reading for all expectant parents wishing to choose the perfect name for their child. It gives the meanings and stories behind thousands of names from all parts of the world – ranging from the most well-known choices to more unusual names.

- Gives variations and shortened forms for each name

- Highlights names popularized by books, films and celebrities

- Lists the most popular girls' and boys' names from 1700 to the present

- Shows how tastes for names have changed in the twenty-first century

PENGUIN POCKET REFERENCE

THE PENGUIN POCKET DICTIONARY OF QUOTATIONS
EDITED BY DAVID CRYSTAL

The Penguin Pocket Dictionary of Quotations is essential reading for
anyone searching for the perfect quotation – whether you need a
snappy one-liner for a speech or a remark of brilliant insight for your
written work. With this pithy and provocative selection of wit and
wisdom, you will never be lost for words again.

- Includes quotations from a vast range of people, from film stars to
  politicians
- Arranged alphabetically by name of person quoted, with the original
  source for each quotation given
- Provides a full index of key words to help you find each quotation
  quickly and easily

He just wanted a decent book to read ...

Not too much to ask, is it? It was in 1935 when Allen Lane, Managing Director of Bodley Head Publishers, stood on a platform at Exeter railway station looking for something good to read on his journey back to London. His choice was limited to popular magazines and poor-quality paperbacks – the same choice faced every day by the vast majority of readers, few of whom could afford hardbacks. Lane's disappointment and subsequent anger at the range of books generally available led him to found a company – and change the world.

'We believed in the existence in this country of a vast reading public for intelligent books at a low price, and staked everything on it'
Sir Allen Lane, 1902–1970, founder of Penguin Books

The quality paperback had arrived – and not just in bookshops. Lane was adamant that his Penguins should appear in chain stores and tobacconists, and should cost no more than a packet of cigarettes.

Reading habits (and cigarette prices) have changed since 1935, but Penguin still believes in publishing the best books for everybody to enjoy. We still believe that good design costs no more than bad design, and we still believe that quality books published passionately and responsibly make the world a better place.

So wherever you see the little bird – whether it's on a piece of prize-winning literary fiction or a celebrity autobiography, political tour de force or historical masterpiece, a serial-killer thriller, reference book, world classic or a piece of pure escapism – you can bet that it represents the very best that the genre has to offer.

Whatever you like to read – trust Penguin.